# Strangers & Neighbors

# Strangers *&* Neighbors

## Relations between **Blacks** *&* **Jews** in the United States

Edited by **Maurianne Adams** *&* **John Bracey**

University of Massachusetts Press  Amherst

Copyright © 1999 by
The University of Massachusetts Press
Introduction copyright © 1999 by Julian Bond
All rights reserved
Printed in the United States of America
LC 99-30346
ISBN 1-55849-235-6 (cloth); 236-4 (pbk.)
Set in Adobe Minion by Keystone Typesetting, Inc.
Printed and bound by Sheridan Books

Library of Congress
Cataloging-in-Publication Data
Strangers and neighbors : relations between Blacks
and Jews in the United States /
edited by Maurianne Adams and John Bracey.
    p.   cm.
Includes bibliographical references and index.
ISBN 1-55849-235-6 (cl. : alk. paper). —
ISBN 1-55849-236-4 (pa. : alk. paper)
1. Afro-Americans—Relations with Jews.
I. Adams, Maurianne. II. Bracey, John H.
E184.36.A34S77    1999
305.8'00973—dc21        99-30346
                        CIP

British Library Cataloguing in Publication data
are available.

# CONTENTS

## Part 3: The Atlantic Slave Trade and Slavery in the New World

## Part 4: From Emancipation to the Great Depression

## Part 5: The Era of the Depression and World War II

## Part 6: World War II through 1967

## Part 7: 1968 to the Present

## Part 8: Where Do We Go from Here?

## PREFACE

The idea for this volume of essays, documents, and narratives on the history of black and Jewish relations in the United States emerged from our ongoing concerns with the rather contentious interactions of segments of the black and Jewish communities on our campus. Our university has addressed this situation with symposia, dialogues, and joint religious services, and in 1996 we directed a faculty seminar on the history of black-Jewish relations sponsored by the university's Institute for Advanced Studies in the Humanities. We hoped to educate ourselves and others about this history and to create a reading list for undergraduate and graduate courses. We found at that time that materials for a course on black-Jewish relations were not readily available.

The need for such a course had become painfully obvious during a discussion with a very bright and concerned Jewish student who responded to John Bracey's question as to why Ralph Bunche had been so overlooked in recent discussions of the history of blacks and Jews with the counterquestion: "Who is Ralph Bunche and why would a black man help the Jews?"*

As we worked to gather historical documents, contemporary reflections, and systematic analyses that would express the long and complex relations of blacks and Jews in the United States over the past three hundred years, we became even more aware of the enormous scope of our subject. The relative success of the seminar and the numerous requests for our reading list led us to conclude that the material we had gathered would be useful to a larger audience, and we began to prepare a publication that would make them more widely accessible.

One of the assumptions behind broadening our focus was to minimize the tendency toward comparing degrees of suffering, or of posing an "Us and Them" framework that ignored the nuanced and multifaceted interactions that have historically characterized black-Jewish relations. In our efforts to broaden the framework for discussion, we located essays and documents that illustrate the range and complexity of black-Jewish relations from the period of slavery and the slave trade up to the present day. We wanted to know more about the relations of these two groups in cities and rural areas of the South and Midwest; we wanted to understand topics such as black anti-Semitism and

*Ralph J. Bunche (1903–1971) drafted the Partition Plan for Palestine and negotiated the armistice that ended the Arab-Israeli war in 1949 while he was serving in the office of the secretariat of the United Nations. His work was regarded as crucial in establishing the peace that allowed the fledgling state of Israel to survive and to enjoy eighteen years of peace. In recognition of his achievements, Bunche was awarded the Nobel Peace Prize in 1950, the first African American so honored. (The most recent biographies are Brian Urquhart, *Ralph Bunche: An American Life* [1993], and Charles P. Henry, *Ralph J. Bunche: Model Negro or American Other?* [1999].)

Jewish racism, black claims to a Jewish religious heritage, itinerant Jewish peddlers and black customers in the Jim Crow South, black teachers of Jewish schoolchildren in the Lower East Side, black domestics in Jewish households in the Bronx, and the consequences of riots in Detroit and of black-Jewish business competition in Chicago and Harlem; we wanted to explore the convergent or conflicting black-Jewish interests in the civil rights movement and Ocean Hill-Brownsville; and we hoped to cover contemporary debates in greater depth than has been given in popular accounts of the speeches or writings of Minister Farrakhan, Leonard Jeffries, Ed Koch, or the *New York Times*. Rather than proposing a thesis concerning black-Jewish relations over the centuries and across spheres of power and influence, we have attempted to build up a suggestive, composite portrait as in a jigsaw puzzle, piece by piece.

The biographical identification of authors for these materials is taken, whenever possible, from the original citation, but we have also tried to provide information, when we could, for authors who are not identified in the books or journals in which their essays appear.

The introduction by Julian Bond and the essays in part 1 frame black-Jewish relations. Part 2 documents the ways that both groups have seen themselves and their histories as those of a Chosen People. Parts 3 through 7 are organized in a chronological fashion. The concluding part 8 offers several proposals for ways out of the black-Jewish impasse.

Part 3, on the Atlantic slave trade and slavery in the New World presents scholarly articles and historical documents, and results in what we consider to be a balanced overview of issues more often treated polemically than with nuanced historical perspective. Part 4 begins with Emancipation and proceeds through the rise of Jim Crow, the urban migrations, and the onset of the Great Depression. The documents and articles of part 5 plunge us into the events of the Depression, World War II, and the emerging shock of the Jewish Holocaust in Europe.

"World War II through 1967," part 6, covers the period that has subsequently been categorized as the Golden Age of the black-Jewish alliance, although the roots of this relationship clearly go back to the mid-1930s. We have selected documents that not only describe this high point, but also call into question the extent to which this alliance—primarily among the elite advancement organizations of both groups—can be made to stand for all relations between the two populations. Even at the height of the civil rights movement, some Jewish organizations, primarily in the South, were reluctant to support desegregation.

Part 7 opens with several contemporary perspectives on Ocean Hill-Brownsville, a controversy that at the time represented the convergence of several issues of bitter contention: namely, community control versus union rights, and open admissions and affirmative action versus individual merit. A crucial development in this period is the rise of Black Power and Black Nationalism, with their emphases on black control of black communities and accusations of white (including Jewish) paternalism. Within this same period, the Six-Day War stimulated a tremendous resurgence of Jewish identity and pride and support for the survival of Israel. Thus, the second group of essays in this section reflects the tensions and crosscurrents of differing ethnic identities and group interests. These articles document the often acrimonious debate of the mid-1970s on the role of Andrew Young in negotiating with the PLO and on Jesse Jackson's bid for the presidency. We also include evidence of the substantial and continuing political areas of cooperation between black and Jewish leaders and of the range of ongoing efforts to understand what is in the best interests of both communities in building new coalitions.

Part 8, "Where Do We Go from Here?" considers specific ways to rebuild the coalition and it closes with a description of a promising effort at black-Jewish dialogue on a college campus.

The history and nature of black-Jewish relations in the United States have already generated a large body of published material, some of which is especially helpful in addressing the issues that we consider here. The one that we think of as outstanding is the recent volume by Jack Salzman and Cornel West. *Struggles in the Promised Land: Toward a History of Black-Jewish Relations in the United States* was published while we were preparing this book, and its coverage of affirmative action, Black Nationalism, and the debates about the Middle East allowed us to set aside several topics that Salzman and West have treated quite thoroughly and enabled us to include instead a number of more personal voices and contemporary documents, as well as a range of more traditional scholarly pieces.

It is impossible, of course, even in a book of this length, to represent fully the extraordinary and unpredictable range of the interactions of these large and complex groups of people who exist together in this large and complex country. We hope that other scholars will be stimulated to fill in gaps we have left and to deepen the analyses of subjects that we have been able to only touch on. This volume is not intended to serve as the last word on the topic, but instead to continue an ongoing dialogue in the quest for better understanding.

Maurianne Adams
John Bracey
Amherst, Massachusetts 1999

## ACKNOWLEDGMENTS

This book started out in early 1996 as a set of readings for a seven-week faculty seminar sponsored by the Institute for Advanced Studies in the Humanities and funded by the Chancellor's Office on our campus. We want to acknowledge warmly the continuing support we've received for this ongoing work from David K. Scott, chancellor, and Marcellette G. Williams, deputy chancellor of the University of Massachusetts, Amherst campus, whose generosity made possible the faculty seminar and this volume.

We thank Esther M. Terry and Robert P. Wolff, codirectors of the Institute for Advanced Studies in the Humanities, for the hospitality of IASH and for the tremendous staff support we received for a large faculty seminar and even more cumbersome mailing list. We learned a great deal from the intense discussions among our faculty colleagues in the spring 1996 IASH seminar and appreciate their contribution. Grant M. Ingle, director of the Office of Human Relations, kept the idea of a faculty seminar on everyone's front burner, and Larry H. Goldbaum, director of the Office of Jewish Relations, did everything in his power to make this volume—as well as the related undergraduate course on blacks and Jews—actually happen.

For the idea that we really must sit down and prepare a book, rather than continue to circulate a hefty set of readings, we are grateful to Jules Chametzky. The offices of the Chancellor and the Vice Chancellor for Research helped to subsidize publication. Bruce Wilcox, director of the University Press, understood and warmly endorsed the idea of this volume from its inception, and Pamela Wilkinson proved a superb, interested, and eagle-eyed editor. We stand in her debt for the care and attention with which she read our text and raised difficult questions about complex bibliographical issues. Mary McClintock, true to her motto, "Better Me Than You," once again proved her genius with computers, libraries, data bases, and endless negotiations over permissions. Tricia Loveland was a patient, cheerful, and reliable telephone and message bridge during our three-year collaboration.

We thank Jules Chametzky, Cheryl Greenberg, August Meier, and Robert Weisbord for careful readings and useful suggestions about revising our manuscript at critical junctures in our own decision-making. They helped us resist our impulse to add rather than to balance. Many of the authors whose works are included in this volume were generous in answering our many questions. We especially thank Joel Dreyfuss, Karen Brodkin, Nat Hentoff, Herbert Hill, Julius Lester, and Morris Schappes.

# Strangers & Neighbors

# Introduction

I want to talk about the historic relationship between American blacks and Jews. It is, of course, much in the news today.

The civil rights movement whose history I teach represents the highest and best collaboration between blacks and Jews toward a common goal. Today that cooperation is threatened by a variety of forces, including increased conservatism from some American Jews and increasingly vocal anti-Semites in black America.

Most prominent is the controversy engendered by Nation of Islam minister Louis Farrakhan and his lieutenant Khalid Muhammad in their attacks on Jews as slavemasters and exploiters of black America, and in their repetition of the old and long-discredited libel about the Protocols of Zion, an alleged Jewish master plan for domination of the world.

The facts are that Jews were a small, small percentage of slave-holders and a small percentage of merchants in the slave trade, but the libel persists nonetheless.

Of course, the locus of most anti-Semitism in the United States isn't fringe groups in black America; it is most pronounced and most widely distributed in the extremes of the overwhelmingly white Christian right, whose attacks on Jews and non-Christians in America do much to fuel hatred and division. For example, Rev. Donald Wildmon of the American Family Association, which claims 700 chapters and 600,000 members, recently published a report charging that 59 percent of all media professionals are Jewish; this figure, he charges, accounts for "anti-Christian bias" in the media.[1] Anti-abortion groups like Operation Rescue list "Jewish doctors" as the leading performers of abortion. Thousands of private Christian schools and Christian home schools use anti-Semitic textbooks, including the "original" *McGuffey's Reader* and books published by Bob Jones University Press for use in such education.

"A few of you don't like Jews and I know why," Rev. Jerry Falwell said. "He can make more money accidentally than you can make on purpose." Rev. Bailey Smith wonders, "I don't know why God chose the Jew. They have such funny noses. God," Smith said, "does not hear the prayers of a Jew."[2]

A recent national public opinion survey recently revealed that a majority of Americans believe minorities are the majority. According to a Gallup Poll, the average Ameri-

Julian Bond is a distinguished visiting professor at American University, a professor of history at the University of Virginia, and Chairman of the Board of Directors of the NAACP.

Originally presented as the keynote speech for the Conference on Black-Jewish Relations on the College Campus, cosponsored by the Religious Action Center of Reform Judaism, the United Negro College Fund, Hillel, and NAACP, on October 13, 1996, Washington, D.C. Printed with permission of Julian Bond.

can thinks that 18 percent of all Americans are Jewish; the real figure is 3 percent. Average Americans think that 21 percent of all Americans are Hispanic; the real figure is 8 percent. Most Americans think that 32 percent of all Americans are black; the exact number is 12 percent. These imagined percentages of minorities add up to 71 percent of the total population.

The FBI reported in March 1994 that six out of every ten hate crimes were motivated by racial bias, and that blacks remain the likeliest victims. Most of these crimes—39 percent—were against blacks; attacks against Jews accounted for 12 percent.[3]

This common status as victims and objects of disdain has not prevented the relationship between blacks and Jews from fragmenting. More than three decades after the coalition of blacks and Jews helped to pass the Civil Rights Act of 1964, that important portion of the national coalition of conscience threatens to come undone.

If there was ever a time when the relationship between blacks and Jews ought to be examined and strengthened with honest admissions on both sides, that time is now.

The rift between blacks and Jews is real. That division is tragic. It threatens a progressive coalition as old as the twentieth century, a tradition that has humanized American politics, a relationship of intersecting agendas based on religious faith. Black and Jewish agendas intersect because these groups sadly share a history of attack.

We all recall the outrageous comments by Jimmy "The Greek" Snyder about black athletes. Snyder said blacks were bred for strength during slavery and thus were superior athletes today.

Few of us recall similar comments made, fifty years ago, about Jews. "Jewish players seem to take naturally to the game of basketball," Ed Sullivan wrote in 1933. "Perhaps," he said, "that is because the Jew is a natural gambler and will take chances."

Few noticed—and fewer denounced—a statement from another sports figure, Hall of Fame baseball player Steve Carlton. Carlton said "the Elders of Zion, 12 Jewish bankers meeting in Switzerland, a committee of 300 meeting in Rome, the National Education Association, Yale's Skull and Bones Society and the World Health Organization" are "plotting against us."[4]

Racial and ethnic turmoil and conflict seem to be constants, in every corner of the nation. A national survey finds that white Americans believe that blacks and Hispanics are lazier and less patriotic than whites, Jews a little less lazy and a little more patriotic; neither blacks nor Jews can find much comfort in these results.

These findings and repeated events of bigotry send a clear signal that race and ethnicity are too much with us, that we remain a nation divided.

Let me begin with some history, and conclude, if you will, with an agenda we both ought to share.

The first blacks came to the American colonies in 1619; the first Jews, thirty-five years later. Those first blacks were indentured servants and slaves; the first Jews were merchants and professionals.

The difference between blacks, arriving in chains before the *Mayflower* sailed from England, and Jews, who arrived in relative comfort, remains a measurable difference between blacks and Jews today; no matter how many steps upward blacks have taken in the three centuries since we both arrived, Jews, having started upward first, still stand today on a higher rung. Even the impoverished Jewish immigrants arriving here at the end of the nineteenth century, refugees from Czarist terror and economic hardship, were better off than those blacks who had already called America home for more than two hundred years.

Jews had never been slaves in America. Nor had the entire weight of public policy conspired to keep them politically and economically impotent for nearly all of their history in this land. For more than two-thirds of their history in America, blacks were denied the chance to form families, to learn to read, add, or write. Slavery gave way to state-sponsored racial subjugation; lynch law and Jim Crow ensured a permanent position at the bottom for blacks.

Until the middle of the nineteenth century, Jews were passive observers, not aggressive participants, in American society. "The Jews who first came to America in the seventeenth, eighteenth, and early nineteenth centuries were heirs to a conservative political tradition that tended to embrace the status quo and sought not to rock the boat."[5]

"Unlike the Quakers," Jonathan Kaufman writes, "or even the blue-blooded Protestant Brahmins of Boston, American Jews did not have a history of becoming involved in liberal causes, even during the Civil War. . . . It was a paradox," Kaufman says, "that America's Jews—who would come to be seen in the twentieth century as defenders of the poor and the weak, eager to vote for social programs and back civil rights protests—largely sat out the epic battles of reform and emancipation that coursed through America in the nineteenth century."[6]

Before the Civil War, some Jews were involved on both sides of the growing and passionate debate over slavery. If some Jews, like Rabbi David Einhorn of Baltimore, joined with the opponents of slavery, others, like the Confederacy's secretary of state Judah P. Benjamin, endorsed and defended it. But Gen. Ulysses S. Grant issued an order in 1862 expelling Jews from doing business in the portion of the South occupied by federal troops, and this blatant anti-Semitism from the man who would be president, the growing instances of social and economic segregation visited upon Jews, and then the lynching of Leo Frank in Atlanta in 1913 quickened a growing consciousness that the United States might not be as secure a haven from Europe's terrors as many Jews had hoped.

A new wave of Jewish immigrants, two million strong, poor and working class, from Russia and Eastern Europe, steeped in socialism and trade union activism, had poured into the United States after 1880, overwhelming the largely German Jewish population of 250,000 already here. These new arrivals, Kaufman writes, "hurled themselves into politics, union organizing, and public life."[7]

As immigration changed the population and politics of American Jews, population shifts produced changes in black America as well. Before the dawn of the twentieth century, 90 percent of all blacks lived in the American South. Between 1910 and 1920, the first large wave of modern migration by southern blacks had begun. Those ten years saw Detroit's black population increase 600 percent, Cleveland's blacks grow by 300 percent, Chicago's, by 150 percent, and the black populations of New York, Philadelphia, and Cincinnati double.

The Jewish press began to bring Jews a picture of the suffering of blacks. The shared experiences of the descendants of Egyptian and American slaves, of the victims of Cossacks and the victims of the Ku Klux Klan, were real and exact. Pogroms in Russia and lynch mob action in America were the same—"the same soil, the same people," the Yiddish *Forward* wrote in 1917.

Populist anti-Semitism and the terrifying rhetoric of growing American nativism made black-Jewish alliance inevitable and necessary, and Jewish support for black causes—for democracy's causes—absolute. Blacks and Jews helped form the NAACP in 1909, and the Urban League a year later.

Grant's infamous General Order 11, the growing wave of anti-Semitism that erupted in Leo Frank's murder, and the institutionalization of anti-Semitism in American life pushed blacks and Jews closer together—fellow sufferers at the hands of a hostile white and Gentile majority—in an alliance that would continue for more than half a century.

Despite continuing and deep-seated prejudices, by the 1940s American Jews were moving upward in society, and by the 1950s, must have been rated the most successful of ethnic groups in the United States by any measure—economic attainment, academic achievement, and professional status.

It was in this period that black Americans began to make advances and quickened their demands as well. In 1954 and 1955, the United States Supreme Court declared segregated schools illegal and ordered steps be taken to destroy unequal education. The Court's ruling destroyed segregation's legality, and an army of nonviolent protestors quickly arose to challenge its morality as well.

In 1955 the Montgomery bus boycott began and the modern civil rights movement followed. The Civil Rights acts of 1957 and 1960 made a modest national commitment to equal rights. The next several years saw real progress made, and the coalition of conscience continued on. Legal segregation in the United States was ended. In 1965 the Voting Rights Act became law, and slowly but surely black Americans began to take their proper place in public life.

Blacks and Jews died in a common grave in Mississippi in 1964, and again in Greensboro in 1979. Sadly today, much of the common history of blacks and Jews rests in popular memory on the lonely shoulders of the civil rights movement's 1964 martyrs, James Cheney, Andrew Goodman, and Mickey Schwerner.

There is a largely unknown story with anonymous heroes, which predates this sad sacrifice. Many of the Jewish partners in the earlier struggle for civil rights were junior partners voluntarily; in consequence, their names are little known today.

In the civil rights movement, Martin Luther King often spoke words written for him by his closest white friend, Stanley Levison, a Jew. Clarence Mitchell, a black man, stalked votes in Congress's halls arm in arm with Joseph Rauh, a Jew.

Jack Greenberg joined the Legal Defense Fund of the NAACP in 1949 and became its director in 1961. Arnold Aaronson was founder—with Roy Wilkins and A. Philip Randolph—of the Leadership Conference on Civil Rights in 1950. Kivie Kaplan was a longtime president of the NAACP, and two Jewish brothers, Arthur and Joel Spingarn, were among its first officers. New York's Rep. Emmanuel Cellar was prime sponsor of the 1964 Civil Rights and 1965 Voting Rights acts. There are other names—Will Maslow,

Hyman Bookbinder, Rabbi Jack Rothschild, Henry Scwarzschild, and so many others that are all too often forgotten today.

Jewish philanthropy did more than support civil rights; it helped support black education and a host of other causes. Julius Rosenwald's gifts alone had helped build more than 5,000 schools in the South by 1932. Before the Depression, as many as 40 percent of southern black school children were educated in Rosenwald schools.

Rosenwald spent $22 million between 1917 and 1948—when a million was a million. The recipients included Morehouse College, my alma mater, where two of my sons were enrolled; Spelman College, where two daughters studied; Fisk University, from which my mother graduated; Meharry Medical College, where I was born; Lincoln University, from which my father graduated and became its first black president; Fort Valley State College, where my father was its first president, and Atlanta and Dillard universities, where my father served as dean. Rosenwald gave money to help create the Southern Regional Council, where I was once employed; he helped support the NAACP, upon whose board I serve today with Rabbi David Saperstein.

The Rosenwald Fellowships are a Who's Who of black America in the 1930s and 1940s; they include five of my college teachers, and W.E.B. DuBois and James Baldwin and Kenneth Clark and Ralph Ellison and Aaron Douglas and John Hope Franklin and Langston Hughes and Carl Holman and Percy Julian and Claude McKay and Gordon Parks and Margaret Walker and Augusta Savage and Ralph Bunche and Grace Towns Hamilton and Adelaide Cromwell Hill and my uncle J. Max Bond, and my father, Horace Mann Bond.

My father told me that while working for the Rosenwald Fund, he found himself stuck in mud up to his axles on a deserted Alabama farm road. Two black men—who had apparently set the trap—and a mule appeared as if by magic and rescued him. Before he dared to ask them what their fee would be for helping his escape from a mudhole they surely had created, they asked him why he found himself so far from civilization in such a nice suit and car. He told them he worked for the Rosenwald Fund, and asked how expensive his salvation would be.

"You work for Cap'n Julius?" they exclaimed! There would be no charge for sending one of Julius Rosenwald's employees safely on his way.

If Jewish liberalism was not a given in the nineteenth century, by the twentieth it was a foregone conclusion. From passive bystanders, Jews had become active participants, and by the 1930s, they had found a political home.

Blacks shifted allegiance too in the 1940s from the Republican to the Democratic Party; today both blacks and Jews remain more loyal to Franklin Roosevelt's party than any other group of voters.

In 1945, newly elected congressman Adam Clayton Powell made his first speech on the House floor on anti-Semitism: "I will always oppose anyone who tries to besmirch any group because of race creed or color," he said.[8]

Blacks and Jews still vote together today, at least in most national elections. Black candidates Harold Washington in Chicago, Wilson Goode in Philadelphia, Mel King in Boston, and David Dinkins in New York received more votes from Jews than from non-Jewish white voters; black voters overwhelmingly supported Elizabeth Holtzman when she ran for Congress in Brooklyn and Elliott Levitas when he became Georgia's first Jewish Congressman in 1974. In 1992, among white voters, only Jewish voters came close to casting as high a percentage of their votes for Bill Clinton as did blacks.

It would be wrong to suppose that ruptures in the relationship began only when Rev. Jesse Jackson used offensive language, or when Minister Louis Farrakhan said Judaism was a gutter religion. As they began to occupy the same cities, blacks and Jews began to edge apart. In northern cities, blacks and Jews weren't always soldiers marching for civil rights; they were sometimes "landlord and tenant, housewife and servant, employer and employee, merchant and customer, professional and client."[9]

Blacks in the ghetto, Bayard Rustin wrote, "see four kinds of white people: the policeman, the businessmen, the teacher and the welfare worker. . . . Three of these four are Jewish."[10] If three-quarters of the representatives to the poor from the power that controls their community from afar share a religion, it is an easy if incorrect step toward believing that they and all their coreligionists are a common enemy.

Writing in 1948, James Baldwin said blacks and Jews "do not dare to trust each other—the Jew because he feels he must climb higher on the American social order and has, so far as he is concerned, nothing to gain from identification with any minority even more unloved than he; while the Negro is in the even less tenable position of not really daring to trust anyone."[11]

These divisions gained credence in 1963 when *Commentary* editor Norman Podhoretz wrote in "My Negro Problem—and Ours" that his childhood hatred, fear, and envy of blacks continued into his mature thinking years. Jews, he wrote, were "tied to a memory of past glory and a dream of imminent redemption. What does the American Negro have," he asked, "that might correspond to this? His past is a stigma, his color is a stigma, and his vision of the future is the hope of erasing the stigma by making the color irrelevant, by making it disappear as a fact of consciousness."[12]

Two years later, in 1965, Rabbi Arthur Hertzberg declared that Jews were no longer "have-nots" but had joined the "haves" and consequently needed to reassess their relationship with American society, and with the then-active civil rights movement. Within the next decade, the reassessment was complete.

The focus of the civil rights movement had shifted north, toward communities where conflict between blacks and Jews was deep-seated, rooted in tension between landlord and tenant, merchant and customer.

A Jew in Harlem, James Baldwin wrote, "is singled out by Negroes not because he acts different from other white men, but because he doesn't."[13] And in 1967, the struggle in tribal New York City over school decentralization, which pitted black parents and students against largely Jewish teachers and administrators, transcended the political struggle it was; instead, it became a national object lesson in anti-Semitism for Jews and in Jewish intransigence for blacks. For blacks, Jews who controlled New York's school system were unwilling to share power with blacks; for Jews, blacks wanted Jews removed from power only because they were Jews. This conflict could only erupt in New York, and only in New York-centric America would New York's narrow example become a national lesson.

Then with *DeFunis v. Odegaard* in 1974 and *Bakke v. Regents* in 1977, the lines of black forward progress were sharply drawn. Major Jewish organizations—the Anti-Defamation League, the American Jewish Committee, and the American Jewish Congress—took an active role in opposing programs designed to include qualified minorities; to succeed, they claimed, these programs would have to exclude some qualified members of the majority.

Black organizations took the opposite view: these programs placed no arbitrary ceilings on the already limitless aspirations of whites; instead, they placed a firm foundation beneath the aspirations of blacks, denying race as a future rationale for permanent placement at life's bottom, insuring competition that is fair in fact as well as in promise.

The language of the briefs supporting Alan Bakke and others like him would later find its way into the legal arguments of the Reagan and Bush Justice departments, an oxymoron if ever one existed.

The resignation of Andrew Young from his United Nations post in 1979 hastened the split; only two officials of Jewish organizations had asked President Jimmy Carter to fire Young, but many blacks felt as if the entire weight of Jewish America had landed on a popular black hero.

But blacks and Jews, then and now, expressed similar longings—to become a part of American society. Blacks wanted what Jews wanted, but these two groups saw themselves in different lights. For Jews, the promise of this new land was to be treated equally while remaining different, to enjoy the pluralism of the New World. For blacks, assimilation was a requirement to achieving integration. As James Farmer put it, "[America] would become color blind when we gave up our color. The white man . . . would presumably only give up his prejudices. We would have to give up our identification."[14]

Rejecting this process—as American Jews quite properly reject abandoning their Jewishness—began to tear further at the web connecting blacks and Jews. The paradox of the relationship was revealed. Blacks and Jews, in the North, at least, were strangers and neighbors, living in proximity without equality. They were allies on the civil rights battlefield who parted company over the direction the war might take and the choice of weapons that might be used.

Blacks wanted strong measures that would do the job, that would right the wrong. Some Jews resisted using tools that had once been used to vanquish them. The new black pride awakened in the early 1960s seemed offensive to many liberals, including many Jews. It was ironic, Peter Rose wrote, that blacks now wanted "what Jews already possessed, a chauvinistic sense of their own collective worth, a pride in the uniqueness of their past."[15] For blacks, as Podhoretz had told us, there was no pride of past—only stigma.

It must be our imperfect collective memories that suggest the Civil Rights Act of 1964 and the Voting Rights Act of 1965 were the last great results of the strained alliance between blacks and Jews. The coalition has quietly continued its record of success into the 1980s and 1990s, throughout the Reagan, Bush, and Clinton years. It helped to defeat the nomination of Robert Bork to the Supreme Court and to pass the 1988 Fair Housing amendments, the Civil Rights Restoration Act, the Martin Luther King Holiday Bill, the Japanese-American Redress Act, and the 1990 and 1991 Civil Rights acts.

Together, blacks and Jews successfully urged Congress to fund the Legal Services Corporation and to repudiate the discredited Civil Rights Commission. Together, they tried to defeat Clarence Thomas's nomination to the Supreme Court. Major Jewish organizations do support race-conscious remedies for discrimination, including goals and time tables; a few support quotas when a court has made a finding of pervasive discrimination.

Despite Louis Farrakhan and Steve Coakley, despite Meir Kahane and Ed Koch, blacks and Jews voted in near lockstep for Michael Dukakis in 1988 and for Bill Clinton in 1992, and black and Jewish members of Congress vote together today—on aid to Israel and on civil rights.

If our more recent common history seems depressing, and if it seems as though past achievements won in common struggle are insufficient to bind black and Jew together now, reflect where we each might have been had we faced our common enemies alone.

The more than half century of solid, productive cooperation between us produced real progress. It did then, and it can now. It put civil rights—for black and brown and other Americans—on the national agenda. It created a progressive infrastructure in America that, however weakened, stands today. And it built this creative, caring coalition on a heritage of shared religious belief and ancient and present suffering, on shared values, on common ground.

Through all its differences, the political coalition remains intact. But the alliance is strained, over differences both real and perceived.[16]

We ought never forget that there are Jews who do not like blacks and blacks who do not like Jews. Ignoring this reality, and refusing to fight against it, allows its eventual development into terrifying final solutions.

The victims of racial and religious bigotry, on power's edge, should try in ordinary self-interest to hold their disagreements to a minimum. Disagree as they will, but there is still much on which they should agree.

In a historic speech at Howard University almost three decades ago, Lyndon Johnson said: "To be black in white society is not to stand on level ground. Until we overcome unequal history, we cannot overcome unequal opportunity. . . . Negroes," he continued, "have been another nation, deprived of freedom, crippled by hatred, the doors of opportunity closed to hope."

"The task," he said then, "is to give twenty million American Negroes the same chance as every American to learn and grow—to work and share in society—to develop their abilities, physical, mental and spiritual, and to pursue their individual happiness. To this end equal opportunity is essential, but equal opportunity is not enough."[17]

Johnson, as you know, was an unlikely source for such a sentiment. To come to that realization, he had to overcome his heritage and environment. He was a Texan and a Christian, born of that generation of white Americans who demanded, enforced, and accepted their superiority as the natural order, God ordained.

Another nation's past leadership might be quoted here too. It was the late Israeli prime minister Itzhak Rabin who said in March 1977: "[Twenty-nine years ago] we thought that equal opportunity would solve the problem of the gap between the Ashkenazi and Sephardic communities. If we have learned anything [in the last twenty-nine years] it is that equal opportunity is not sufficient. Preferential treatment is necessary if we are to bridge the gap and catch up that 50 percent of our population who came out of the Arab and Moslem countries and who, through no fault of their own, but because of centuries of cultural and education discrimination could not compete with the European Jews."

For us Americans, are the three decades since 1964 sufficient time to end the effort aimed at eradicating three centuries of white skin privilege? May honest efforts, adopted when moral suasion and the force of law had failed, be permitted to prove their worth, or must the few forward steps black Americans have taken be reversed because the victimizers now claim they are victims, and the old victims have received too much?

I think not, and I cannot help believing that other victims of discrimination on these shores will agree.

There is much else upon which we all agree. The past two administrations were more hostile to civil rights than any in recent memory; we agreed on their defeat.

Some of us believe that racial justice cannot be achieved without economic justice at its side. Some of us believe that working people are being starved to death and asked to survive on a diet of hate. Some of us believe there is something criminally wrong in America when the richest two-fifths have the largest share of the national income and the poorest two-fifths, the smallest share since 1947. Some of us believe much of the political leadership in both parties is bankrupt, corrupted by greed, lapping reelection funds from the same trough.

We agree that bigotry in a presidential or gubernatorial campaign—or anywhere else in public or private life—is real cause for fear and concern. Its practitioners must be rebuffed and rejected, as must those anywhere who preach the doctrines of division and hate.

Strains between blacks and Jews at the fringes of our society or at the center cannot become reasons why yesterday's cooperation cannot continue.

There was a special magic—not in blacks and Jews alone—that made the alliance grow and prosper for more than fifty years. That magic was found elsewhere in America in the promise that all could be free, that all were equal. Blacks and Jews and other Americans believed the magic then, and because they believed it, they worked to make it so.

It may be that only some of us—some blacks and some Jews—believe it now. But if we believe alone, our charge is to make others believe again.

As we do, let us remind ourselves that we cannot build a common future on common graves alone. Yesterday's sacrifices by Cheney, Goodman, and Schwerner are not sufficient foundation to carry us through the challenges of today. They are the hard rocks upon which we must build, but in our common struggle for political and social justice, credentials must be renewed every day.

Despite the rise in the publicized incidents of racism and anti-Semitism, the devils we must face don't always loudly shout out Hitler's praise or wear white robes. They sometimes say softly that America faces decline because too many of the wrong people have gotten in. They write books that argue liberalism died because too many blacks or women made unreasonable demands for fair play. They explain away racism at the ballot box as the proper response of alienated Americans threatened by intrusions from outsiders with darker skin or foreign accents or larger families.

Some years ago, the right wing blamed progressives because, they said, we always blamed America. They were wrong then as they are wrong now—we only wanted America to be what it had promised that it would be.

Today, they blame minorities first. Blacks, women, and Hispanics, they say, have destroyed the meritocracy that was America, a land where jobs went only to the skilled, a land full of successful suburbs, where every child waved an American flag, where every day was the Fourth of July.

At least several times each year for most of my adult life I have stood before audiences of blacks and Jews and talked about our common history and struggle. More recently, I've begun to have second thoughts about the wisdom of these appearances.

I value the importance of the alliance, however strained, between blacks and Jews. I believe it is vital that the cooperation between us continues and gets stronger. But the recent American obsession with anti-Semitism from blacks seems more and more to be a deliberate attempt to avoid and obscure the nightmare of white supremacy in this country.

Public condemnation of hateful talk, especially if that talk comes from within one's own community, is the principled thing to do. All people of good will should condemn speech that offends humane values and promotes evil. Denunciations by black leaders of the recent psychotic ravings we've heard were both imperative and welcome.

But where, I wonder, is the vigorous debate and argument over anti-Semitism in white America and racism among the American majority?

If you've been reading the newspapers for much of the last few years, you'd have to conclude that black anti-Semitism is a major social ill afflicting America. If black anti-Semitism statements draw blood and create fear and anger, what about Richard Nixon's words? James Baker's? Pat Buchanan's? Pat Robertson's? Ernest Hollins's? Dollie Parton's? Jackie Mason's? Howard Stern's? Steve Carlton's? Roald Dahl's? Donald Wildmon's? In two races for president, Jesse Jackson never came close to exercising the power over or influencing as many people as these people do every day.

Sister Souljah? Steve Coakley? A rap singer and a low-level figure in Chicago? How do these two possibly compare with the power and influence of the anti-Semites and racists who have sat in the White House's Oval Office, in the House and Senate, and who sit today in the board rooms of multinational corporations all over the world?

During a recent mayoral campaign in New York City, a radio talk-show host routinely referred to David Dinkins as "that washroom attendant," and he routinely called black women "black bitches." While interviewing New York's new mayor, he called Congressman Charles Rangel "one of those pygmies." The mayor did not object.

What's lacking today isn't critical examination by blacks of any of the currents, good and evil, that flow through black America. What's missing is critical examination of the ugly virus of racism and ethnic hatred that is running rampant in majority America, endorsed by members of the majority.

In years past, whenever some black figure, however marginal, uttered anti-Semitic sentiments, I was sure to get a call, which demanded I quickly denounce the speaker and the words that had been spoken. Denunciation of figures like Louis Farrakhan, for some, has become a litmus test imposed on black American leaders, through which blacks legitimize their right to participate in mainstream politics. Many understandably perceive this test as a humiliating power play.

Today, I want someone to denounce the powerful figures of evil who threaten my existence daily, and I want an end to defining anti-Semitism as if only black people practiced it; as if race problems are only black problems, all along.

The black scholar Julius Lester, a Jew, argues that black anti-Semitism, however serious, is different here from the European variety. In Europe Jews were a distinct minority; here they are part of the white majority, and have been able to become white in America only because there are people here who are called black and who are treated differently—worse—because they are.

In a speech before the executive committee of the Anti-Defamation League, Lester said:

> Regardless of the extent to which an individual may regard her or himself as a Jew, when he and she walk down the street, they blend in with the majority. White skinned Jews look white in a crowd. . . . Because Jews partake of and share in the majority identity as whites, Jews have benefitted economically. In Europe, Jews were victims; in America, Jews are a success story. . . . Blacks are aware, in ways many Jews are not, that within the American context, blacks and Jews do not share common experiences of oppression and suffering.
>
> Thus, on college campuses, what often comes out as anti-Semitic expression is an attempt to express resentment toward Jews for assuming a relationship of shared suffering. As far as many young blacks are concerned, none exists. Blacks resent the Jewish assumption of shared oppression and use the language of anti-Semitism to make that resentment clear. This is not to excuse the use of anti-Semitism. . . . Using the language of anti-Semitism is a grievous moral error at any time.[18]

Listing other examples of differences in social and economic status between blacks and Jews, Lester asked an important question: "In focusing attention on black-Jewish relations, have we been reacting to a symptom?"

"I wonder," he asks, "if it is in our self interest as Jews any longer to speak of black-Jewish tensions. Yes, they exist, but are they the problem?"[19]

His solution is to begin an attack on racism among whites. I believe he is right.

In today's climate, the ravings of black anti-Semites are likely to increase. They serve, for these bigots, several purposes.

The first is an attack, not on Jews, but on mainstream civil rights leaders who are accused of being appendages of Jewish interests, unable to act independently, uninterested in solving the problems that afflict black America.

Destabilizing mainstream leadership is an old goal among a sector of black nationalist thought, and tying that leadership to Jews—or to other interests outside black communities—is part of that tradition. Tying their failures to Jews helps to weaken them and increases the strength of their critics.

A second purpose is much older. Scapegoating others as responsible for problems that seem insoluble is an ancient dodge; it serves to solidify the oppressed community against a powerful outside "other." There are powerful historical precedents for this tactic, both in the history of European anti-Semitism and in the development of racist thought over centuries.

There is something comfortable in discovering a cause for your problems in a class that is already suspect. Sadly, for some, there is great appeal in attacking a vulnerable people, especially if you are even more vulnerable yourself.

There is also some comfort found in comparing and contrasting victimhood—whose tragedy was the greatest, the European Holocaust during the Second World War or the holocaust of slavery and the Middle Passage, followed by the continuing degradation of slavery, segregation, and today's racism.

Here the truth is that these events are beyond comparison—there is no way to place the suffering of Jews on one side of a scale and the suffering of blacks on the other and to judge which group suffered more. Even if there were, what would the side that wins gain? Is there a prize for the most people killed? If there is, what is it? Can Burundi and Rwanda compete? Are there regional contests?

There is also power found in attacking people who respond angrily to your provocations. When blacks mouth anti-Semitic slogans, they gather much more attention than anti-Semitic whites, and attention is what many of these figures badly want. The irony of members of a despised class attacking members of another despised class is news today and will be news tomorrow.

Finally, one ought not forget the powerful influence of religion—not Islam, but Christianity—in creating the image of the greedy Jew, the Christ-killer. That image competes in black America with the historic self-identification among blacks and Jews as former slaves. It should be no surprise when black Americans adopt the evil attitudes of the people who taught them Christianity years ago. I mentioned the religious Right when I began—they represent more than a conservative force in our society. They are central to the contention that things "Christian" are American and right; things non-Christian—including Jews—are less American and wrong.

Thirty years ago, my father spoke to a gathering like this one, a 1965 conference on Negro-Jewish relations in the United States. To prepare, he read the then-current literature on anti-Semitism, he interviewed the Atlanta minister of the Nation of Islam, and he recalled his youthful clash, forty-eight years earlier, with a Jewish boy who had called him "nigger." In his anger, he called the boy "Christ-killer."

In his closing remarks, he talked about the gratitude southern blacks of his generation felt toward Julius Rosenwald's generosity. It was, he said, "enough to make one weep; especially if you realized this enormous philanthropy was only a drop in the bottomless bucket of needs that these people had in the brutalizing, dehumanizing, deculturative society in which they and their children—and their grandchildren, now living (here) in New York and Brooklyn—had to grow up. If anything, I felt the edge of their gratitude was sharpened by the sense of Rosenwald's generosity coming as an appropriate gesture of help from an elder brother in the family of oppression. Their old familiar friend, the people of Israel who had once suffered in Egypt land, as they were now doing, had not forgotten them or forgotten the history of their own people."[20]

Anti-Semitism, like racism, may always be with us. It ought to be our responsibility to recognize it when we see it, to oppose it, and to dedicate ourselves to ending it.

When the idea of racial justice seemed a widely accepted idea three decades ago, we never imagined achieving it would be painless and cost free. It hasn't been, of course; change never is. And when it began to cost and pinch, its popularity began to fade.

In the long run, however, the cost of achieving justice is never so great as the cost of justice denied; that cost is measured in social disruption and human decay.

The coalition between blacks and Jews helped make the American promise real. Strengthened, that coalition can finish what it helped begin, and in the process, revive the spirit that brought black and white, Jew and Gentile together in common cause.

We can, and shall, overcome.

NOTES

1. "Christian Right Anti-Semitism," *Activist Update* [Center for Democratic Renewal, Atlanta, Ga.], March 1994.

2. *Freedom Writer* [Institute for the First Amendment Studies, Great Barrington, Mass.], May 1994.

3. "Christian Right Anti-Semitism."

4. "Carlton Controversy," *Washington Post*, April 12, 1994.

5. Jonathan Kaufman, *Broken Alliance, The Turbulent Times between Blacks and Jews in America* (New York: Charles Scribner's Sons, 1988), 20.

6. Ibid., 19, 20, 22, 23.

7. Ibid., 25.

8. Wil Haygood, *King of the Cats* (New York: Houghton Mifflin, 1933), 118.

9. Sigmund Diamond, "Summation" in Papers and Proceedings of a Conference on Negro-Jewish Relations in the United States, *Jewish Social Studies* 27, no. 1 (January 1965).

10. Bayard Rustin, "The Anatomy of Frustration," in *Down the Line: The Collected Writings of Bayard Rustin* (Chicago: Quadrangle Books, 1971), 223.

11. James Baldwin, "The Harlem Ghetto," *Commentary* (1948).

12. Norman Podhoretz, "My Negro Problem—And Ours," *Commentary* 35(2) (February 1963), 93–101.

13. James Baldwin, "Negroes Are Anti-Semitic Because They're Anti-White," *New York Times Magazine*, April 9, 1967.

14. James Farmer, *Freedom When?* (New York: Random House, 1965), 87.

15. Peter Rose, "Blacks and Jews: The Strained Alliance," *Annals of the American Academy of Political Science*.

16. See "Topic: Anatomy of an Error," *USA Today*, January 29, 1986, an account of the spread of the false rumor that Southern Christian Leadership Conference president Joseph Lowery, NAACP Executive director Benjamin Hooks, and the author had visited Libya and presented Libyan president Muammar Khadafy the "decoration of Martin Luther King."

17. President Lyndon B. Johnson, Commencement Address, Howard University, Washington, D.C., June 1965.

18. Julius Lester, "A Report on Black Anti-Semitism, 1992," *Jewish Currents* 46(5) (1992): 5–9; quotation from p. 6.

19. Ibid.

20. Horace Mann Bond, "Negro Attitudes toward Jews," *Jewish Social Studies* 27, no. 1 (January 1965).

# Part 1 **Themes and Issues**

This first section both introduces the resurgence of the controversy over the historical and contemporary nature of black-Jewish relations in the United States and takes a step back from the immediate or local concerns in an attempt to determine how best to characterize this long and complicated history. This controversy calls into question fundamental relationships between blacks and Jews. When one talks about a Golden Age and its decline, one is making certain assumptions about the historical character of black-Jewish relations, and these assumptions—that there was once a halcyon time that has now passed—are borne out in the titles of book-length studies such as Jonathan Kaufman's *Broken Alliance*, Murray Friedman's *What Went Wrong?* and Jack Salzman and Cornel West's collection, *Struggles in the Promised Land.*

The first essay in this section, by Andrew Hacker, accepts as a given the realities of Jewish racism and black anti-Semitism, both seen as almost inevitable consequences of the social realities of American life. While Hacker assumes the existence of the phenomenon called Jewish racism or black anti-Semitism, Adolph Reed's essay strongly challenges the notion that black anti-Semitism is any different from other forms of American anti-Semitism. These claims and counterclaims will be dealt with at length in later sections of this book.

John Bracey and August Meier point out how little we actually know of the historical interactions of these two very different groups. They speak of the limitations of the popular analogies made between the two experiences (slavery, diaspora, suffering, a sense of themselves as chosen people, and being forced into ghettoes, etc.) and the paucity of detailed research. Their view is that much more needs to be done before sound conclusions can be drawn. In one regard, this book can be read as a partial response to some of the questions raised in that essay.

We close with the rather pointed exchange between a black scholar and a Jewish scholar over the historical record itself. The dispute between Oscar Williams and Morris Schappes is notable not only for the extent of the disagreement over the basic facts of the record, but also for the level of animosity generated by differences in perspective and interpretation. This dispute over the "ownership" of the interpretation, or who gets to define the relationship, will be repeated several times throughout this volume.

**FURTHER REFERENCES**

To our knowledge, the only book-length study that considers the full United States history of black-Jewish relations is the edited collection of Jack Salzman and Cornel West, *Struggles in the Promised Land: Toward a History of Black-Jewish Relations in the United States* (1997). Norman H. Finkelstein's *Heeding the Call: Jewish Voices in Amer-*

*ica's Civil Rights Struggle* (1992) presents a less-detailed overview of the history, with an emphasis on the Jewish side of the relationship. A dissertation by Harold Brackman, "The Ebb and Flow of Conflict: A History of Black-Jewish Relations through 1900" (1977), deals with that period. A thoughtful if brief piece by Hasia R. Diner, "Black-Jewish Relations" in Jack Fischel and Sanford Pinsker, eds., *Jewish-American History and Culture: An Encyclopedia* (1992), opens with this provocative sentence, "Few issues in American Jewish culture and history have engendered as heated a discussion and as sparse an objective and analytic literature as black-Jewish relations" (63) and concludes, "and scholars have tended to read back into the history of that relationship their contemporary views of the current conflict" (65).

Two other essays also offer suggestive historical surveys: Eugene I. Bender's "Reflections on Negro-Jewish Relationships: The Historical Dimension" (1969), and William Toll's "Pluralism and Moral Force in the Black-Jewish Dialogue" (1987). Salzman's introduction to *Struggles in the Promised Land* provides an informative and helpful overview. A bibliography compiled by Lenwood G. Davis, *Black-Jewish Relations in the United States, 1752–1984* (1984), covers a similar period. Abraham Peck's *Blacks and Jews: The American Experience, 1654–1987* is the publication of an exhibit sponsored by the American Jewish Archives on the campus of the Hebrew Union College–Jewish Institute of Religion.

Although Robert G. Weisbord and Arthur Stein's *Bittersweet Encounter: The Afro-American and the American Jew* (1970) emphasizes late-nineteenth-century and twentieth-century themes, its first two chapters deal with the earlier history, as do the beginning chapters of Murray Friedman's *What Went Wrong? The Creation and Collapse of the Black-Jewish Alliance* (1995), and Jonathan Kaufman's *Broken Alliance: The Turbulent Times between Blacks and Jews in America* (1988, 1995).

Personal reflections on the meaning of the relations between blacks and Jews, written by both African Americans and American Jews from a wide range of political and religious perspectives, can be found in Paul Berman, ed., *Blacks and Jews: Alliances and Arguments* (1994); James Baldwin et al., *Black Anti-Semitism and Jewish Racism* (1969); Shlomo Katz, ed., *Negro and Jew: An Encounter in America* (1967); Michael Lerner and Cornel West, *Jews and Blacks: A Dialogue on Race, Religion, and Culture in America* (1995); Jack Salzman, ed., *Bridges and Boundaries: African Americans and American Jews* (1992); and in Salzman and West, *Struggles in the Promised Land.* See also Melanie Kaye/Kantrowitz's "Class, Feminism, and 'The Black-Jewish Question'" (1992) and Cornel West's "On Black-Jewish Relations" (1994). In January 1965, a full issue of *Jewish Social Studies* published the proceedings of a 1964 Conference on Negro-Jewish Relations in the United States, with papers and responses by Horace Mann Bond, Howard Brodtz, Bayard Rustin, and Ben Halpern, among others.

To place the history of African Americans and American Jews in the larger context of United States history, we recommend starting with Lerone Bennett Jr., *Before the Mayflower: A History of Black America* (1988); Lucy S. Dawidowicz, *On Equal Terms: Jews in America 1881–1981* (1982); Leonard Dinnerstein, *Anti-Semitism in America* (1994); John Hope Franklin and Alfred A. Moss Jr., *From Slavery to Freedom: A History of African Americans* (1994); August Meier and Elliot Rudwick, *From Plantation to Ghetto* (1976);

Benjamin Quarles, *The Negro in the Making of America* (1986); and Howard M. Sachar, *A History of the Jews in America* (1993). For the most recent scholarly history of the Jews in America, consult the five-volume *Jewish People in America:* volume 1, Eli Faber, *A Time for Planting: The First Migration, 1654–1820;* volume 2, Hasia R. Diner, *A Time for Gathering: The Second Migration, 1820–1880;* volume 3, Gerald Sorin, *A Time for Building: The Third Migration, 1880–1920;* volume 4, Henry L. Feingold, *A Time for Searching: Entering the Mainstream, 1920–1945;* and volume 5, Edward S. Shapiro, *A Time for Healing: American Jewry since World War II.*

Further references dealing with other specific periods of American history will be cited in subsequent headnotes. For an analysis of how blacks have portrayed Jews in black literature, and Jews, blacks in Jewish literature, see Emily Miller Budick, *Blacks and Jews in Literary Conversation* (1998).

# Jewish Racism, Black Anti-Semitism

If some black Americans show less than friendly feelings towards Jews, they are in excellent company. After all, similar sentiments are common in all-white country clubs. As it happens, no one really knows if blacks and whites differ strongly on this topic. (Pollsters avoid it altogether nowadays.) What can be said, though, is that if any black public figure makes a statement that could be construed as anti-semitic, it is seen as symptomatic of a deep and disturbing trend.

But, first, what is meant by anti-semitism, at least in the context we are considering? At one level, the phrase simply suggests a distaste for some attributes deemed to be "Jewish." This was probably behind Jesse Jackson's description of New York City as "Hymietown," as well as the way Spike Lee depicted two nightclub owners in *Mo' Better Blues*. It can also have a theological resonance, as when Louis Farrakhan chose to call Judaism a "gutter religion." Or when Imamu Amiri Bakara (then LeRoi Jones) wrote, "the empty Jew betrays us, as he does hanging stupidly from a cross." Strong opposition to Israel, whether to its existence or its policies, may—or may not—carry anti-semitic overtones. And then, of course, there is the wish to rid the world of all Jewish people. The fact that Adolph Hitler gassed infants in his Holocaust made that objective clear. However, this extreme view has never gained much of a following within the United States.

There are other, less invidious, factors at work. Talking about "The Jews" is a common American pastime. Bringing them up in a conversation gives people a certain lift. Since Jews are regarded as outsiders, being able to make remarks about "them" gives you an insider status. This helps to explain why at least some black Americans talk as much as they do about Jews. It is a way of locating one's self within the national mainstream, since anti-semitism is almost as American as cherry pie.

These tendencies are not new; they go back a long way. In *The Souls of Black Folk*, published in 1903, W.E.B. Du Bois took his readers on a tour of the Black Belt region of Georgia. "The Jew is heir to the slavebaron," he wrote. As a matter of fact, Jews owned only a small share of the land; yet Du Bois felt some need to specify their presence. Later, speaking of hard times, he added that "only a Yankee or a Jew could squeeze more blood from debt-cursed tenants." So the attitude that led to Jesse Jackson's remark about New York has common features with black America's most distinguished scholar.

However, the past is long ago. Even so, it can persist as a force if its patterns are

Andrew Hacker is a professor of political science at Queens College.

Originally published in *Reconstruction* 1, no. 3 (1992): 14–17. Copyright © 1992, *Reconstruction*. Reprinted with permission of Andrew Hacker.

perpetuated in the present. So it must be said that as black Americans moved to northern cities, roughly from the 1920s through to the 1960s, they found themselves in contact with Jews. Until about twenty years ago, Jews were often the most visible merchants and landlords in black neighborhoods. Here is how James Baldwin remembered it:

> When we were growing up in Harlem, our demoralizing series of landlords were Jews, and we hated them. We hated them because they were terrible landlords and did not take care of the buildings.
>
> The grocer was a Jew, and being in debt to him was very much like being in debt to the company store. The butcher was a Jew and, yes, we certainly paid more for bad cuts of meat than other New York citizens.

In addition, many middle-class Jewish families employed black women as domestic servants. The sad reality was that black servants and tenants and shoppers had few choices and little bargaining power. They saw themselves as exploited, and that was an accurate assessment: they were being overcharged and underpaid. Needless to say, they would have been treated in exactly the same way by Christian employers and merchants and landlords. (After all, from slavery onward, most of the suffering experienced by black people in the south was at the hands of white Christians.) If they were less likely to have that direct experience in the north, it was because Christian women there preferred to hire white servants, while Christian-owned stores and apartment houses tended to be in areas where blacks knew they would not be welcome.

Moreover, the reason why Jews bought real estate and opened businesses in black neighborhoods was that, at that time, they themselves faced barriers in the more established sectors of the city. If many Jewish families appeared to prefer employing black women as their cooks and maids and laundresses, it may simply be that black help was cheaper, although a curious kind of symbiosis may also have been involved. Still, it may be noted that as Jews grew wealthier, they tended to shift to white servants.

During the generation extending from the 1930s through the 1960s, Jews began to play a prominent role in the civil service, where they often administered rules affecting black citizens. In many cities, they were also becoming public school teachers and administrators, which gave them a crucial authority over children and parents. In these settings, Jews often had more direct relationships with blacks than did other white Americans. (The most visible exception has been the police.)

As has been suggested, most Jews did not place themselves in proximity to blacks as a matter of choice. Indeed, fewer would do so when better business and professional opportunities opened up to them. Still, there was a lag, since some were tied to civil service careers. The issue came to a head in New York City some twenty years ago, in a section of Brooklyn then called Ocean Hill–Brownsville. A group of black parents charged that their children were falling behind educationally because of the lack of concern on the part of Jewish teachers and principals, who at that time still held most of the positions. As a result, there came a call for complete community control, one aim of which was to replace existing personnel. A bitter strike followed, and its fallout is still being felt. While fewer teachers today are Jewish, black disaffection from the schools persists.

Another cause for focusing on Jews is that they make a vivid target, while the alternatives are often vague. For example, the lending policies of commercial banks have played a central role in maintaining residential segregation and discouraging the development of black businesses. Moreover, few of the nation's major corporations have made more than a token effort to promote blacks to executive positions. Yet most of the banks and firms are owned and managed by Christians. Indeed, by any proportionate measure, Christian Americans have done far more than Jews to keep blacks down and back. So insofar as anti-semitism has a political purpose—a way of intimidating the people who are harming you—it is a rather pathetic response. Even if no Jews at all lived in the United States, blacks would face the very same conditions they confront today. The same thing can be said of campaigns directed against Korean merchants in New York and Middle Eastern store-owners in Detroit.

Finally, there is a more recent source of anti-semitism. The last decade or so has seen among American blacks a resurgence of fellow feeling, not only for African nations and movements, but for Islamic aspirations as well. Needless to say, the presence of Israel in the Middle East is perceived as thwarting the rightful status of people of color. Some blacks view Israel as essentially a white and European power, supported from the outside, and occupying space that rightfully belongs to the original inhabitants of Palestine. Nor can it be denied that Israel is a military power, engaged in hostilities with darker people. That it is also a Jewish state allows anti-Israeli sentiment to meld into anti-semitism. (The fact that Arabs are also members of the Semitic group is irrelevant here; in current parlance, anti-semitism refers only to Jews.)

In the eyes of many people, not all of them black, many Jews living in the United States seem to style themselves as honorary citizens of Israel. Some even seem reflexively to defend all its activities, on the ground that anything less than full support could bring about the homeland's destruction. In response, some American blacks have begun to show sympathy for the feelings many Moslems have about Israel and its supporters.*

By way of transition, it should be said that a further reason for anti-semitic tendencies is that blacks may feel that Jews are especially vulnerable to charges of racism. This issue would not arise if whatever prejudices Jews may have were as blatant and bigoted as those held by many white Christians. But Jews have usually asked to be judged by separate, and higher, standards.

Many Jews will claim that they have—or once had—a special relationship with black Americans. If some Jews simply took their profits from ghetto shops and tenements, others devoted themselves to improving social conditions and relations between the races. Julius Rosenwald gave millions to Negro education, as it was then called, while

---

*This is not the place to consider the attraction of Islam for some black Americans. Much of black Africa has been Islamic for many centuries, so it is a legitimate legacy. At the same time, we know that hardly any blacks who were brought to the Americas came from Islamic communities. Moreover, Islamic religion and culture arose not in Africa, but in the Middle East. Embracing this identity may be a way of distancing at least part of one's self from a purely tribal past.

Joel and Arthur Spingarn helped to found and sustain the NAACP. In the 1960s, Northern Jews were prominent among those taking part in voter registration drives. Andrew Goodman and Michael Schwerner, about whom more will be said, sacrificed their lives for that cause.

Many of these Jews will also say that they have had a special devotion to liberty and justice, and the poor and deprived. In part, they may add, this stems from their own people's experience. But much of it is a matter of moral principle, and not simply sympathy. How, then, can such individuals be called racists?

Like anti-Semitism, racism can take several forms. At its simplest, it involves stereotyping. In this form, racism begins with the presumption that certain traits are common among black people, and after that ascribes those attributes to every black individual. Examples are hardly necessary; but one will suffice. When a taxicab driver refuses to stop for a black rider, it is because he presumes that the odds are high that that passenger may turn out to be a robber. This racism could be called personal; it is a stereotype within the head of the driver.

There is also institutional racism. The XYZ Corporation, for example, says it promotes individuals simply on the basis of their qualifications. Moreover, its executives will be quick to tell you what kinds of qualities they look for: maturity, vision, judgment, and so forth. Yet one "qualification" they never mention is that a candidate should look and act "white." Needless to say, it is not easy for black people to satisfy that institutional standard.

But the most serious form of racism goes further and deeper. It posits that people of African origin belong to an inferior sub-species of humanity, and no matter how hard they work or how much help they get, they can never perform on a par with members of other races. Whether they admit it or not, virtually all white people believe that, in terms of both genetic and evolutionary development, theirs is the highest racial stratum among the human species.

Given that this form of racism is common to whites, can it be said that with Jews it takes on a special flavor? It isn't easy to address this question with precision. Much of what will be said on this subject refers to liberalism generally, so the attitudes and reactions are not uniquely Jewish. At the same time, Jews are more likely than Christians, on average, to veer in a leftward direction. As will be seen, there can be some peculiarly Jewish responses to racial issues.

What can be said, first, is that more Jews are apt to insist that they do not harbor racist sentiments. Unlike many white Christians, for example, they will never be caught saying that they believe blacks to be genetically inferior. Or, if they are willing to admit that they sometimes react in racist ways, they will add that they hope they can exorcise whatever it is that gives rise to those actions and feelings. Hence one hears of a willingness to be taught, indeed to atone. If this would seem to mix a measure of self-righteousness with some guilt and humility, that is hardly a surprising combination.

Three black writers have provided some thoughtful comments on the racism they see as inherent in many Jewish well-wishers. It should be noted at the outset that these writers are not saying that Jews are the most racist of white Americans. On the contrary, for real racism, one has to go to those Christians who feel free to proclaim that "niggers" are not only thugs and scum, but apes hardly out of the trees. Far fewer Jews talk this way. (Even the term "shvartze," seldom heard now compared with immigrant days, never carried such scabrous connotations.)

Harold Cruse once remarked that what really roused his "enmity toward Jews" was hearing people who are Jewish say, "I know how you feel because I, too, am discriminated against." What concerned him, clearly, was an attempt to proclaim not only fellow-feeling, but a bond of experience. To Cruse and many others, this equating of racial and religious discrimination insults the ordeals black Americans have undergone since they were first loaded on slave ships. About the only Jews who have such a claim are those who were consigned to Germany's death camps. Those who died, and they were the vast majority, suffered in the same hideous way as did the percentage of blacks who were expected to perish while crossing the Atlantic. Yet the Jews who survived the camps were, on their release, again accepted as members of the white—and privileged—race. In the years since 1945, none of them has known what it is like to be black.

It is more than a little revealing that whites who travelled south in 1964, referred to that sojourn as their "Mississippi Summer." It is as if all the efforts of local blacks for voter registration and the desegregation of public facilities had not even existed until white help arrived. Moreover, many of those who came were Jewish. And, as Nathan Wright observed at the time, at least some seemed to feel that their organizational experience and skills entitled them to leadership. Of course, this was done with benign intentions, as if to say: 'we have come in answer to your calls for assistance.' The problem was not a lack of fellow-feeling, but the condescending tone. One only had to look in on meetings to hear the new arrivals doing most of the talking. As Wright noted, they seemed to style themselves "patrons" or "parents," with black adults consigned to the role of "children." Needless to say, this has been a common expression of racism: the belief that black people need white "help" because they lack the capacity to organize activities on their own.

For Jewish liberals, the great memory of that summer has been the deaths of Andrew Goodman and Michael Schwerner and—almost as an afterthought—James Chaney. Indeed, Chaney's name tends to be listed last, as if the life he lost was worth only three-fifths of the others'. Of course, the fact that two whites were murdered generated both media attention and FBI intervention. We might speculate whether this would have happened had the doomed group consisted of two black persons and only one white.

Some even sharper comments have come from Julius Lester. A radio statement he once made deserves to be quoted at some length.

> Jews tend to be a little self-righteous about their liberal record, always jumping to point out that they have been in the forefront of the fight for racial equality. . . .
>
> When they remind us continually of this role, then we realize that they were pitying us and wanted our gratitude, not the realization of the principles of justice and humanity. . . . Jews consider themselves liberals. Blacks consider them paternalistic.
>
> Black people have destroyed the previous relationship which they had with the Jewish community, in which we were the victims of a kind of paternalism, which is only a benevolent racism.

This is a serious indictment, for it suggests that Jewish involvement in racial matters has been essentially an ego trip, almost as if it were selected as an agreeable area for a few charitable works. It could be argued that help is help, and one shouldn't worry about the motives that impel it. Still, as Lester suggests, Jews gave their support on their own terms. At best, blacks were junior partners, who were expected to accept not only the pace and goals decided by whites, but also to maintain a demeanor which allowed whites to feel comfortable. Thus, there was the presumption that black recipients would murmur "thank you" frequently, passively, and politely. And once those responses were no longer forthcoming, a lot of Jews and other white liberals began looking for other causes. Indeed, more than a few felt that blacks had betrayed the interracial compact. So Lester's association of "benevolent racism" with Jews is truly important. It raises the question whether well-intended motives should cast a "Jewish racism" in a different light from other expressions that are more overtly insulting.

A further fact warrants at least passing comment. Over the past generation, a large share of the nation's research on race has been conducted by social scientists who are Jewish. Indeed, given their numbers, it is likely that they have received more funds and recognition for their work than have black scholars. One difficulty is that at least some of those who devote themselves to research on human beings cease looking on their "subjects" as actual people but regard them rather as "data." This is especially so with research on race, which thrives on typologies like "the black family," "black crime," and "black learning styles." A lot of Jewish academics have made good careers by passing black people through mathematical models and churning them into columns of statistics. This has given rise to whispers that social science research involving black Americans displays hints of a Jewish racism. Such claims are, of course, problematic. Few dispute researchers' good intentions. And many insist that research on race provides knowledge that will bring improvements in real life. Perhaps. As the social scientists themselves might say, however, these are all hypotheses which need to be tested.

# What Color Is Anti-Semitism?

I long ago stopped reading Nat Hentoff, even though we've been columnists simultaneously for the *Voice* and the *Progressive*. . . .

But Hentoff's recent tirade about Sharod Baker, the anti-Semitic black Columbia student, has given me a prod to make a point I've wanted to make for some time: There's no such thing as *black* anti-Semitism.

Obviously, I don't mean that there are no black people who are anti-Semites. Young Sharod Baker quite plainly appears to qualify as one. Khallid Muhammad certainly deserves the label, though perhaps as a subset of the classification "dangerous psychopath." Louis Farrakhan, Steve Cokely, and Len Jeffries also have earned it, as have many other, anonymous black Americans. Nor do I mean to suggest that anti-Semitism among black people doesn't count because: (a) they got it from white Christians or (b) they don't have the power to enforce it. Those arguments are just immoral sophistry. Is Dinesh D'Souza not really a racist because his views come via his Anglo-American tutors? Did David Duke only become one officially when he won a seat in the Louisiana legislature? Anti-Semitism is a form of racism, and it is indefensible and dangerous wherever it occurs.

What doesn't exist is Blackantisemitism, the equivalent of a German compound word, a particular—and particularly virulent—strain of anti-Semitism. Black anti-Semites are no better or worse than white or other anti-Semites, and they are neither more nor less representative of the "black community" or "black America" than Pat Buchanan, Pat Robertson, Tom Metzger—or your coworker or roommate who whispers about "their" pushiness and clannishness—are of white American gentiles.

Blackantisemitism is a species of the same genus as "Africanized" killer bees, crack babies, and now the rising generation of hardened 10-year-olds soon to be career criminals. It is a racialized fantasy, a projection of white anxieties about dark horrors lurking just beyond the horizon.

Yet there's more at work here than arbitrary, irrational scapegoating, which doesn't explain how black people become the repositories of those anxieties. As Stephen Steinberg argues forcefully in *Turning Back: The Retreat From Racial Justice in American Thought and Policy*, reducing racism to its generically psychological dimension obscures its roots in structured inequality. American racism, as is the nature of ideologies, is a complex dialectic of attitudes and material relations, but psychological scapegoating is

Adolph L. Reed Jr. was a professor of political science at the University of Illinois, Chicago.
Originally published in *Village Voice*, December 26, 1995, 26. Copyright © 1995, *The Village Voice*. Reprinted with permission of Adolph L. Reed Jr.

ultimately more its effect than its cause (I'm reminded here of a quip, attributed to Bob Fitch, that 90 per cent of what goes on in the world can be explained adequately with vulgar Marxism). The social categories "white," "black," and "race" itself, after all, only arise historically from a concern to formalize a system of hierarchy and define its boundaries. These boundaries—expressed as law, enforced custom, and structures of feeling—create the populations that enact them, so that for example, in W. E. B. Du Bois's wonderful definition, "the black man is a person who must ride 'Jim Crow' in Georgia." Racial stereotypes are a feature of oppression, not its source.

Blackantisemitism's specific resonance stems from its man-bites-dog quality. Black Americans are associated in the public realm with opposition to racial prejudice, so the appearance of bigotry among them seems newsworthy. But that newsworthiness also depends on a particular kind of racial stereotyping, the notion that, on some level, all black people think with one mind. Ralph Ellison complained most eloquently about white Americans' general refusal to recognize black individuality. Charles Rangel put the problem succinctly: When approached to declare himself on Khallid Muhammad, he complained that he was tired of being called on to denounce people he'd never even heard of. Any black anti-Semite is seen not as an individual but as a barometer of the black collective mind; belief in Blackantisemitism, therefore, is itself a form of racialist thinking.

In an overheated moment a couple of years ago, during Khallid's elevation to cause célèbre and the concurrent wave of ritual demands on black political leaders to denounce him and Farrakhan, *The New York Times* exposed this notion's repugnant face. In response to protests like Rangel's, the *Times* editorialized that indeed all black leaders (whoever that group includes) must "renounce root and branch Mr. Farrakhan's . . . message" and that "*in return,* black organizations and leaders have a right to ask for heightened white sensitivity to the commonplace discrimination of everyday life and to the increasing tolerance for parlor—and campus—prejudice against blacks" [my italics]. So black people must prove, by passing a litmus test for moral and ideological responsibility, that they deserve basic protections accorded automatically to all other citizens; unlike everyone else (at least at the moment), black Americans' claims to equal rights depend on their demonstration of moral rectitude. If this isn't racism, the term has no meaning.

But Blackantisemitism appeals to more actively sinister, malicious sentiments as well. The patient-suffering, slow-to-anger, morally superior imagery on which the civil rights movement traded was always at bottom a homegrown representation of the Noble Savage. As such, it's a setup for the Nasty Savage response. And that's what Blackantisemitism is. Here's how it works. First, posit the single racial mind, so that whatever any black person does speaks for—and reflects on—all others. Then comes the syllogism: Blacks deserve equal rights to the extent that they are morally exemplary. Blackantisemitism shows that blacks aren't morally exemplary. Therefore, black demands for equal citizenship are tainted, and need not be taken seriously.

That partly explains why black anti-Semites ruffle public feathers—even among Jewish interest group elites—in a way that more powerfully connected, and therefore more potentially dangerous, white anti-Semites don't. Sure, a kind of biting-the-hand-that-feeds-you, after-all-we've-done-for-you, you-always-hurt-the-one-you-love pater- nalistic thing is going on, based on the peculiar tensions of the "special relationship" between blacks and Jews. But, generally speaking, Blackantisemitism is a rationale, an excuse for whites who either want to demand that blacks be uniformly decent and admirably fair in ways that apply to no other group of Americans, or are simply looking to justify their dissent from a racially egalitarian social and political agenda. That's the beauty of the one-mind view: What any lone black person does can be a pretext for joining the racist opposition. Remember all those outraged white people who an- nounced that the O. J. Simpson verdict ended their support for affirmative action, social spending, and the Reconstruction Amendments?

# Towards a Research Agenda on Blacks and Jews in United States History

The comparison and interaction of blacks and Jews in the history of the United States together form a significant and interesting field that has yet to be explored in a systematic way. What we propose are a series of questions that we hope will stimulate thinking among historians, and provide a useful agenda for future research. We do not claim to have covered all possible topics, but the lines of inquiry we suggest could lead to fruitful results.

We intend to raise questions in the two broad areas of (1) the comparative study of the Jewish and African-American experiences, and (2) the interaction between Jews and blacks throughout American history.

## NOTES TOWARD A COMPARISON

The obvious problems involved in comparing a European immigrant group with a racial minority are further complicated by (1) the differences in appropriate periodization; (2) the disparate size of the two groups; (3) the differing degree of prejudice and discrimination that each group faced; and (4) differing cultural traditions.

Concerning periodization, for purposes of our analysis we are limiting ourselves to developments in the United States. In African-American history there have been two great watersheds: (1) the Civil War and Emancipation, and (2) the Great Migration that began with World War I. In Jewish-American history there have also been two watersheds: (1) the migration of many German Jews to the United States beginning in the 1840s, and (2) the large influx of Eastern European migrants during the late nineteenth and early twentieth centuries. A third watershed that both groups share is World War II and its consequences. For Jewish Americans the Holocaust and the establishment of the state of Israel, and for black Americans the demise of the more explicit ideologies of white supremacy and the rise of independent African states, were important in promoting profound changes in group consciousness. It is also important to note that throughout American history the Jewish population has been distinctly smaller than the black population (for example, at the opening of the Civil War there were one hundred fifty thousand Jews; four hundred thousand Free People of Color, and four million black slaves). Finally, while varying in intensity, the prejudice and discrimination experienced by blacks has been of a far greater magnitude than that experienced by American Jews.

John Bracey is a professor in the W.E.B. Du Bois Department of Afro-American Studies at the University of Massachusetts Amherst. August Meier is Emeritus Professor of History at Kent State University.
Originally published in *Journal of American Ethnic History* 12, no. 3 (1993): 60–67. Copyright © 1993 by the Immigration History Society. Reprinted with permission of John Bracey.

Looking at the first two-thirds of the nineteenth century there is a fruitful comparison that can be made between Jews and free blacks. How does one explain the differences and similarities that were evident? How was it that the two groups came to have such disparate political rights and economic circumstances? Is it true, as the present state of our knowledge indicates, that both groups were disproportionately urbanized, and if so, were the reasons for this the same? The available scholarly literature suggests that while not yet living in large ghettos, African Americans were concentrated in undesirable areas while Jews were more dispersed residentially; if this is so, how is it to be explained? On the other hand, what were the factors responsible for similar developments in African-American and Jewish communities in regard to religious and educational institutions, and fraternal and mutual aid societies? Though both had religious institutions dating back to the eighteenth century, what needs explanation is the fact that blacks began their extensive institutional development of fraternal orders and mutual aid societies by the turn of the nineteenth century, while Jews did not undertake theirs until about the middle of the century. The most important part played in each community by religious leadership is notable. Also, why was there no American Jewish counterpart to such a figure of national and international importance as Frederick Douglass?

For the half-century and more between the 1880s and the New Deal, a different set of patterns emerges. This, of course, was the era of the apogee of "scientific racism" in both Europe and the United States, and also of the enormous influx into Northern cities of first, the Eastern European Jews, and then the Southern blacks. To what extent did these two groups share experiences, and to what extent were their experiences different? To what extent was the anti-Semitism that led the Jewish experience to converge in many ways with the African-American experience at this time a product of the same forces that produced the rampant Negrophobia of the period? And to what extent did anti-Semitism and anti-black racism develop as discrete phenomena? Were the forces that led to the rise of the Jewish ghettos, and the larger black ghettos that followed, the same or different? To what extent were the nature and sequence of ghettoization and dispersal similar or different? If different, what were the reasons? What was common and what was distinctive in the ways that the "old settlers" among Northern blacks, and the well established German Jews responded to the newcomers to their respective communities?

Given certain parallels in the Jewish and black experiences during this period we think that a careful and systematic examination should be made of the differential rates of economic development and social mobility. We need to get beyond the impressionistic explanations such as a Jewish alleged proclivity for entrepreneurial activity and the professions, and respect for education. Upwardly mobile African Americans had for generations displayed a similar affinity for these bourgeois values, and the faith of blacks in education as a means of advancement has become an historical truism. What does need explaining is the different route taken by each group. For example, why is it that Jews devoted enormous efforts in securing their education at mainstream colleges and universities, while blacks during the Jim Crow era developed an extensive network of institutions? (In addition, why is it that historically more black women than men have had access to education, while the opposite appears to have been true for Jews?) There is a substantial literature on the role of both groups in the areas of politics, sports, entertainment, and even organized crime. But a systematic comparative evaluation of those routes to upward mobility would be helpful. For example, in the realm of politics, what can we learn from an examination of the factors that produced a Jewish member of the United States Supreme Court prior to the United States entry into World War I, a full half-century before the seating of Thurgood Marshall?

The period since World War II witnessed momentous changes for both Jews and for African Americans. What needs to be examined is the degree of change for each group, and the degree to which such alterations have been the result of similar strategies for social change on the part of the two minorities.

This concern leads to the question of the nature of leadership and advancement organizations in both communities. Are there Jewish counterparts to Booker T. Washington and W.E.B. Du Bois? Were Jewish leaders and organizations lined up as radicals and conservatives? Did they become increasingly militant over the years? What accounts for the fact that many black advancement organizations had interracial leadership for much of their histories, while a comparable phenomenon did not exist among Jewish organizations? The role of women in many African-American organizations and as leaders has been extremely important. To what extent have there been parallels among Jewish leaders and organizations, and assuming that there were differences, why so?

Finally, one would welcome a dispassionate inquiry comparing the ideologies of the two groups especially of the various aspects of Jewish and black nationalism including Zionism and African-American emigrationism. Moreover, why did the white gentile majority respond differently to these two phenomena?

### INTERACTIONS

In regard to the history of the interaction between Jews and African Americans one should begin with the slave trade, both transatlantic and domestic. The role of Africans in the slave trade has been the subject of considerable literature. There is a small body of literature on Jews and slavery and the slave trade in the Caribbean. But to our knowledge the role of Jews in the slave trade of Holland, France, England and even Newport, Rhode Island has not been fully investigated. In regard to Jewish owners of slaves there has been some work done on the South, but a systematic study of both North and South remains to be done. Moreover, the role of Jews in all areas of plantation life needs to be researched. To what extent, if any, were there Jewish overseers or cotton factors? Also what role might Jewish peddlers have played in the internal economy of slavery and in the development of the crop-lien system after the Civil War?

While some scholarship has been done on attitudes of Jews toward abolition and the Civil War, the most authoritative work on the topic does not even involve the use of the major antislavery publications. On the other side there is a need for a systematic study of the antebellum blacks to see what attitudes, if any, are expressed about American Jews. Of particular value here would be studies of opinions expressed in the black press, speeches and sermons—published and unpublished—and in the collected correspondence of the black abolitionists.

The mass migration of Jews from Eastern Europe that began a century ago transformed the American Jewish population and paved the way for the more extensive contacts between the two groups that came in the twentieth century, particularly after Southern blacks began to move to the cities in large numbers. The result was an incredibly complex situation with many forms of interaction both friendly and antagonistic. In fact there is a need for a comprehensive treatment of the seemingly contradictory and often paradoxical attitudes that the two groups have held toward each other. Of course, beginning in the 1930s there has been a body of literature on anti-Semitic attitudes among blacks. But we are lacking comparable analyses of the racial attitudes of American Jews. In what follows we have selected certain other themes for discussion.

In regard to residential patterns at least two questions are deserving of additional research. First, it is notable that in contrast to other groups in American society Jews exhibited a relative lack of overt and violent resistance as blacks moved into predominantly Jewish neighborhoods. Apparently Jews opted for the policies of selling and moving, or renting to black tenants. Secondly, the Jewish landlord/black tenant antagonism which was especially salient in the 1930s needs reassessment. For both of these issues cities such as New York, Baltimore, Chicago, and Philadelphia with large black and Jewish populations would seem to be prime targets for study.

In the realm of economic interactions there are several possible areas of contact: employer-employee, i.e., blacks working for Jews and Jews working for blacks; employee-employee relations, Jews and blacks working together, e.g., at a job site or in a trade union; patronage of black businesses by Jews and Jewish businesses by blacks; the utilization of professional services of Jews by blacks and of blacks by Jews. The main focus of past research has been on the merchant-customer relationship with blacks always in the subordinate role. More systematic work needs to be done on a city-by-city basis to ascertain what exactly was happening. What particularly begs for explanation are the areas in which Jews have worked for blacks, e.g., as physicians, lawyers, teachers at black colleges, staff members of black advancement organizations, business agents, accountants, etc. Have blacks been more likely to hire Jews in preference to other whites in these professional categories? Have Jews been more likely to accept such employment? And have Jews been more likely than other whites to hire blacks in a variety of positions? And for all of these possible situations were there any differences to be found between cities where Jews were numerous and cities where Jews were quite few in numbers? Particularly in this connection one should study black-Jewish business relations in Southern cities.

Another avenue of inquiry is the role of Jewish entrepreneurs in the entertainment industry. This research would involve looking at the role of Jews in promoting black entertainers, i.e., singers, musicians, and actors and as agents, producers, club and theater owners. One should look at whether these efforts tended to help or to hinder the independent efforts of black entrepreneurs in these areas? Jewish producers like others in Hollywood, apparently did little in the way of aiding blacks in the development of the varying skills necessary to function at all levels of the movie industry. Moreover, what was the role of Jews in the entertainment industry in general in perpetuating the stereotypes of blacks that were prevalent in popular culture? To what extent did Jewish radicals working in the film industry attempt to counteract the negative image of blacks and provide a wider range of employment opportunities?

An area that is virtually unexplored is the interaction between Jews and African Americans in the urban political arenas in those cities where there have been significant numbers of both groups. How often did a situation arise such as that in Cleveland in the 1920s when the Jewish Republican boss Maurice Maschke controlled the vote in the black wards and doled out patronage jobs to blacks? Or how often was there a situation like that in post–World War II Baltimore where there was a powerful Democratic organization headed by a Jew, and dependent on both Black and Jewish votes? Was the kind of Republican coalition that Fiorello LaGuardia, himself of Italian and Jewish descent, fashioned consisting of Jewish, Italian and black voters unique? To what extent were black votes critical to the election of Jewish politicians and vice versa? Are we correct in hypothesizing that it is unlikely that Jews have contributed substantially to the election of such black candidates as those from Chicago in the 1930s and the 1940s? Has this situation changed at all in the last twenty years with the rise in the number of black elected officials? It would be especially interesting to ascertain the role of Jewish votes and financial support for those blacks who have run for statewide or national office.

On the other hand, in New York, liberal Democratic Jews such as Governor Herbert Lehman and Representative Emanuel Celler seemed to have cornered the black vote and were highly regarded by many black leaders. Even Republican Jewish senators Irving M. Ives and Jacob Javits seem to have enjoyed substantial black support at the ballot box. We would hypothesize that this kind of coalition was related to the rise and coalescence of a liberal Jewish political bloc in the 1930s whose agenda included support of the NAACP's program for the attainment of equal rights for blacks in all areas of American society. To what extent did these politicians represent concerns of their Jewish constituencies on these issues? A final area of interest would be the extent of cooperation among black and Jewish elected officials.

The role of Jews in the establishment of an American radical or socialist tradition has been much studied. What needs to be looked at is the extent to which these secular Jewish radicals exhibited a particular concern for or insight into the conditions of blacks. What also needs to be examined with more precision is the interaction between Jews and African Americans within the Socialist party, the Communist party, and between the radical Jews and blacks within the trade union movement. In regard to the trade unions, there needs to be an examination of the relations between blacks and Jews, from the racist policies of Samuel Gompers to the role of Ralph Helstein in developing the egalitarian policies of the United Packinghouse Workers. Illustrative of the complexity of the topic is the long history of blacks and Jews in the garment industry, where both the ILGWU and the ACWU were led by Jews, but developed rather different ways of relating to their black members. In this connection we would like to note that the ILGWU led by David Dubinsky was of enormous help to the work of A. Philip Randolph and the Brotherhood of Sleeping Car Porters, but in the last generation has come under severe criticism for its racial policies.

There has been much speculation about the nature and extent of Jewish support for black causes, and involvement in black advancement organizations, but precious little careful empirical research exists. For example, take the case of Julius Rosenwald, the leading Jewish contributor in American history to virtually all aspects of black activity. Little is known of the personal and/or ideological beliefs that underlay this activity. Exactly what motivated Rosenwald to give money in support of black education, the building of black YMCA's and the establishment of the Rosenwald Fund? One needs to examine the possible mixture of a concern for eliminating prejudice against Jews with a broader humanitarian idealism.

A most important question is what exactly has been the role of Jews in the civil rights movement in the twentieth century, beginning with the NAACP, and later including CORE, SCLC, and SNCC. It is our impression that substantial Jewish involvement came only with the New Deal and the Second World War. We would not deny the importance of Jews like Joel and Arthur Springarn in the early days of the NAACP, or the valuable legal assistance rendered in the 1920s by Louis Marshall, the distinguished constitutional lawyer and founder of the American Jewish Committee. But at that period the interaction was between black organizations and a small group of Jews acting as individuals. The American Jewish Committee was not involved with the question of racial equality during Marshall's lifetime, and we tentatively have concluded that active cooperation between black and Jewish *organizations* such as the American Jewish Congress and the Anti-Defamation League came only in the aftermath of the Roosevelt era. How much of this was due to black sympathy for the plight of Jews in Nazi Germany? How much of this was due to the rise of Jewish liberalism and radicalism? How much was due to the mutual interest in fair employment practices that had crystallized as a result of the black-led March on Washington Movement in 1941, and how much was due to the mutual benefits to be gained from the enactment of fair housing and fair employment legislation during the postwar era? Certainly in the case of CORE the heavy representation of Jews as activists and contributors came only with the 1960s.

Of interest is the nature of the role played by liberals and radicals on the national staffs of civil rights organizations such as the NAACP and CORE. The advice rendered by Stanley Levison to Martin Luther King, Jr. is now well known. But, if it could be done, it would be very valuable to have an analysis of the magnitude of the role of Jews both as activists and as financial contributors in the work of SCLC, SNCC, and the NAACP Legal Defense Fund. Similarly, did Jews have a disproportionate role in the ranks of lawyers who assisted in the local struggles? From where in the religious-secular spectrum did these participants come? (In regard to religious orientation our surmise is that the activists were more secular than religious.) And from where in the political spectrum were they coming? In this regard local studies of protest movements should (in the future) address themselves to these questions. We anticipate that patterns will vary due to demographic, regional, time and other factors.

Much of the current misunderstanding about the nature of a "Black-Jewish Alliance" is based on a lack of understanding about what took place during the period between the end of World War II and the 1960s when black-Jewish cooperation was at its height. What needs to be explored is precisely the nature of an alliance which has been romanticized and considerably exaggerated. This research of course will pave the way for a serious and careful study of the increased tensions of the past two decades. Keeping in mind the pervasiveness of both racism in a society based on white supremacy and of the anti-Semitism that is largely rooted in some aspects of Christianity, we also should not ignore the particulars of the interactions in recent years.

A final topic of interest is the role of Jewish scholars in the fields of race relations and the African-American experience. From the early years of the twentieth century, and especially after Jews entered academia in large numbers after World War II, Jewish scholars played a significant role in anthropology, and later sociology and history. One can think of anthropologists such as Franz Boas and Melville Herskovits, and the liberal and radical historians who began to contribute to the field of African-American history in the late 1930s. Basically the story of the Jewish anthropologists has to be fleshed out. An inquiry should also be made as to why Jews were not more prominent among sociologists working on race relations and the African-American experience before the 1960s.

Conversely, what is the explanation for the lack of scholarship by blacks on the Jewish experience (or that of other white ethnic groups)? The contours of the histories and interactions of the two groups likely would have looked a bit different if the pattern of research had not been mainly a one-way street.

NOTES
We wish to thank Jules Chametzky, David Katzman, David Gerber and Meyer Weinberg for their critiques of an earlier version of this essay.

SOURCES CONSULTED (SELECTED LIST)

1. Davis, Lenwood G. *Black-Jewish Relations in the United States, 1752–1984: A Selected Bibliography.* Westport, Conn., 1984.

2. Diner, Hasia. *In The Almost Promised Land: American Jews and Blacks, 1915–35.* Westport, Conn., 1977.

3. Dinnerstein, Leonard, and Palsson, Mary Dale, eds. *Jews In the South.* Baton Rouge, La., 1973.

4. Evans, Eli N. *The Provincials: A Personal History of Jews in the South.* New York, 1976.

5. Gerber, David A., ed. *Anti-Semitism in American History.* Urbana, Ill., 1987.

6. Higham, John. *Send These To Me: Jews and Other Immigrants in Urban America.* New York, 1975.

7. Korn, Bertram W. *American Jewry and the Civil War.* New York, 1970.

8. Lewis, David Levering. "Parallels and Divergences: Assimilation Strategies of Afro-American and Jewish Elites from 1910 to the Early 1930's" *Journal of American History,* vol. 71 no. 3 (December, 1984): 543–564.

9. Weinberg, Meyer. *Because They Were Jews: A History of Anti-Semitism.* Westport, Conn., 1986.

10. Weisbord, Robert G., and Stein, Arthur. *Bittersweet Encounter: The Afro-American and the American Jew.* Westport, Conn., 1970.

# Historical Impressions of Black-Jewish Relations prior to World War II

In an attempt to understand the historical relationship between Jews and Blacks, it should be understood that both are minorities in America.[1] One was a Black minority and one was a White minority. Blacks obviously felt the discrimination of color from the oppressor while Jews suffered slightly from the discrimination of religion but not color. Essentially, Black and Jewish relationships prior to the 1920s were limited basically to contact between the Southern Jews and Southern Blacks. When examining the southern Jewish and Black relations it is essential to realize that the Southern Jew was assimilated into the mainstream of American culture, much more than the northern Jew or the Jews in other regions of America. Black and Jewish relations prior to 1920 were basically a southern race problem. Jews invariably reacted to Black people just as other southern white people reacted to Black people.[2] During slavery, Jews were slave masters, slave traders, merchants, peddlers, and statemen. In general, Jews were everything in the Old South except abolitionists.[3] Little in the annals of southern history would allow Blacks to apply the internal stratification of Black and Jewish relations in the North to a broader race picture of Whites versus Blacks in the South.[4]

Only after World War I and the resulting migration of Blacks to the urban North can a meaningful discussion of Black and Jewish relations begin. Increased contact of northern Blacks and Whites, chiefly Jews, resulted in Black "anti-Semitism." Black anti-Semitism was only a reaction to white racism and it was nonreligious in nature. Most, if not all, of the Black outcry against Jews was anti-oppressor, not anti-Judaism.

Black and Jewish race relations within America were a microcosm of the greater Black-White race problem beginning in the Colonial Period. The initial Jewish contact with Blacks was an extension of the Dutch Slave Trade in which the Dutch tried desperately to eliminate "Jews and Jobbers" from the Slave Trade. Jewish history in America shows that Jews played an active role in the institution of slavery. Almost from the beginning there were Jewish slaveholders in New Amsterdam. Rhode Island history shows that Aaron Lopez and Jacob Rivera, refugees from the Spanish Inquisition, were well known slave traders of colonial Newport.[5] For the most part Jews in the North adopted the prevailing patterns of the people in the North. When slavery died out in the North so did Jewish participation in the institution.

In 1977 Oscar R. Williams Jr. was professor of history at Virginia State College in Petersburg.
Originally published in *Negro History Bulletin* 40, no. 4 (1977): 728–31. Copyright © 1977 by the Association for the Study of Negro Life and History. Reprinted with permission of Associated Publishers, Inc.

As a group, Jews did not adopt a position toward slavery in the manner which Quakers made their position clear. When the abolition movement surfaced the Jewish Community remained aloof and took no concerted stand on the issue.

The majority of Black and Jewish contacts in Colonial America was in the southern Colonies, especially South Carolina and Georgia. Historian Carl Bridenbaugh indicated that the South Carolina Planter class was America's only aristocratic society. This group became the early American "Jet Set" in their attempt to avoid heat and the fever season of South Carolina. Subsequently, they failed to establish stable government because they were on the move from March to October. Jews, as a result, were quite prominent in this colony as well as Georgia. This fact did not cause Jews to treat Blacks any better than other colonial Whites.[6] As historians Bertram Korn and Jacob R. Marcus indicated, the Jewish treatment toward Blacks did not differ from their fellow white Gentiles.

The presence of the southern Jews complimented the system of slavery; their mercantilistic interest made slavery a more effective labor system. While most Jews were not to be found on plantations, their activities made the plantation a self-sufficient unit. What was not produced on the plantation was delivered by Jewish merchants. The southern Jew had as much, if not more, to gain by maintaining the system of slavery as any other white segment within the South. During the Civil War Jews defended the system which insured them acceptance and success in the South. Neither the Civil War nor Reconstruction changed the southern Jews' perception of Blacks as an animal to be used and exploited.[7]

The belief that Jews were superior to Blacks was not alien to Jewish circles. An article in a Jewish newspaper in 1863 illustrated that some Jews had a strong leaning in the direction of white supremacy:

> We know not how to speak in the same breath of the Negro and the Israelite. The very names have startling opposite sounds—one representing all that is debased and inferior in the hopeless barbarity and heathenism of six thousand years; the other, the days when Jehovah conferred on our fathers the glorious equality which led the Eternal to converse with them and allow them to enjoy the communion of angels. Thus the abandoned fanatics insult the choice of God himself in endeavoring to reverse the inferiority which He stamped on the African to make him compeer even in bondage of His chosen people. There is no parallel between such races . . . The judicious in all the earth agree that to proclaim the African equal to the surrounding races would be a farce which would lead the civilized conservatives of the world to denounce this outrage.

The above blunt opinion reflected Jewish sentiment about Blacks after slavery ended. In the New South Jews were deeply ingrained in the southern system. Historian John S. Ezell stated:

> Probably in no other region of the United States have Jews been so integrated with the general population or subject to less discrimination. Most came into the South after a period of assimilation in the North. They were welcomed because of their

business connection which fitted in well with the philosophy of the New South as they quickly occupied an impartial position in the retail dry-good business.[8]

Often in the New South, success of Jewish merchants depended upon winning Black trade. Jewish merchants appeared more courteous and obviously spent more time with black customers than fellow white merchants. Blacks were often the victims of sales pressure when Jews refused to accept no-sale for an answer. *No* became the signal for the ritual to begin. Merchants would insist that the potential buyer try-on the item. After this came what Blacks call "Jewing Down," in which naive Blacks were led to believe that Jewish merchant had allowed himself to be beaten on the price. The marked up and then down concession scheme left both parties happy. The Jewish merchant received his desired price and the naive Black went away with the over priced goods.[9]

The 1903 edition of *Souls of Black Folks* contains examples of Jews victimization of Blacks. DuBois wrote:

> I have seen, in the Black Belt of Georgia, an ignorant, honest Negro buy and pay for a farm in installments three separate times, and then in the face of law and decency the enterprising Russian Jew who sold it to him pocketed the money and deed and left the black man landless, to labor on his own farm at thirty cents a day.[10]

DuBois further illustrated that Jews became an enterprising force in the New South, replacing the planter class but maintaining the policy of exploitation of Blacks and poor Whites:

> The rod of empire that passed from the hands of Southern gentlemen in 1865, partly by force, partly by their own petulance, has never returned to them. Rather it has passed to those men who have come to take charge of the industrial exploitation of the New South—the sons of poor whites fired with a new thirst for wealth and power, thrifty and avaricious Yankees, shrewd and unscrupulous Jews. Into the hands of these men the Southern laborers, white and black, have fallen; and this to their sorrow. For the laborers as such there is in these few captains of industry neither love nor hate, sympathy nor romance; it is a cold question of dollars and dividends. Under such a system all labor is bound to suffer.[11]

With respect to white Protestants, their deeply entrenched prejudice against Blacks and Catholics left little time to hate Jews. Religiously, Jews did not compete with Southern Protestantism for "Lost Souls." Economically, they, likewise, offered no competition to the Southerner in his major economic activities. Jewish acceptance by the Ku Klux Klan and later Jewish participation in the White Citizens Council provide concrete evidence of total acceptance in the southern racial scheme of Black versus White.[12]

Black migration during World War I, brought Blacks and Jews into wholesale contact for the first time in American History. The proximity of the Black newcomer and Jews created for the first time in Blacks an awareness of Jews or the notion that Jews were different from other Whites. The prosperity of the 1920s produced harmonious relationships between these groups, that would be partly shattered by the depression of the 1930s.

During the depression, the urban cities of the North brought a new dimension to the Black Experience in America, starvation. When Blacks migrated North during and after World War I, they often moved into Jewish neighborhoods or areas controlled by Jews. The depression forcefully instilled in Blacks the lesson that Jews held an economic stranglehold on the Black neighborhood. As a result the new, easily identifiable Jews became oppressors in the eyes of many Blacks. The effects of Adolph Hitler's propaganda in Germany coupled with the fear that the influx of Jewish refugees would affect the job market took its toll. Rumors circulated that Black workers were to be summarily replaced by Jewish refugees.[13]

The juxtaposition of these circumstances ignited what has been called "Black Anti-Semitism." But what has been labeled as "Black anti-Semitism" of the 1930s and 1940s was merely anti-white or anti-oppressors outcries. The deep seated hostility to Jews based on religious and cultural difference that existed among White Gentiles did not exist in Black communities. As Roi Ottley stated:

> Actually, the whole business of anti-Jewish sentiment among Negroes is largely an urban manifestation, and stems directly from the Negro's own depressed condition socially and economically, and is essentially an anti-white manifestation. To begin with, the Northern Negro comes into contact with the white race, and thus white discrimination and white antipathy, at four vital points: fellow worker, landlord, merchant, and employer. It is within these areas that the friction between Whites and Blacks exists. By some unique accident, it is the Jew who is today the Negro's main point of contact with the white race—landlord, merchant, employer, and to a small degree the professional people. Thus the treatment which the Negro experiences from the white group is mainly at the hands of Jews.[14]

A description of the so-called "Bronx-Slave Market" of New York City provided further insight to Jewish exploitation of Black females:

> Rain or shine, cold or hot, you will find them there—Negro women, old and young— sometimes bedraggled, sometimes neatly dressed—but with the invariable paper bundle, waiting expectantly for Bronx housewives to buy their strength and energy for an hour, two hours, or even for a day at the magnificent rate of fifteen, twenty, twenty-five or, if luck be with them, thirty cents an hour . . . Fortunate indeed, is she who gets the full hourly rate promised. Often her day's slavery is rewarded with a single dollar bill or whatever her unscrupulous employer pleases to pay. More often, the clock is set back for an hour or more. Too often she is sent away without any pay at all.[15]

Novelist James Baldwin in his own autobiography describes the feeling of most urban Blacks toward Jews in the 1930s and 1940s.

> When we were growing up in Harlem our demoralizing series of landlords were Jewish, and we hated them. We hated them because they were terrible landlords, and did not take care of the buildings. . . . Our parents were lashed down to futureless jobs, in order to pay the outrageous rent. We knew that the landlord treated us this way only because we were colored, and he knew we could not move out.

The grocer was a Jew, and being in debt to him was very much like being in debt to the company store. The butcher was a Jew and, yes, we certainly paid more for bad cuts of meat than other New York citizens and we very often carried insults home, along with the meat. We bought our clothes from a Jew and sometimes, our secondhand shoes, and the pawnbroker was a Jew—perhaps we hated him most of all. The merchants along 125th street were Jewish—at least many of them were. . . .

Not all of these white people were cruel—on the contrary I remember some who were certainly as thoughtful as the bleak circumstances allowed—but all of them were exploiting us, and that was why we hated them all.[16]

This Black resentment of Jewish exploitation cannot be interpreted as resentment of Judaism or the "Christ Killer" issue long associated with Jews.

Ironically, while Jews have persistently exploited, Black have consciously and unconsciously held Jews as a success model in America. Black admiration of Jews began almost as early as Black's introduction to Christianity. Black religion has always been obsessed with Blacks being compared with Jews in Egyptland. Historian Miles Mark Fisher noted that Blacks were singing, "Let My People Go," as early as the 1790s.[17] Paradoxically, their admiration of Jews continued long after slavery ended. In the minds of Black slaves the Union victory was living proof that Blacks were the "Modern Day Children of Israel." "The Promise Land," became the major theme of Black history in the Nineteenth Century. Likewise, slave narratives often compared the plight of Blacks with that of the children of Israel, in Pharaoh's land.

Black leaders from Frederick Douglass to Martin Luther King have continued to use Jews as models for Black people. Frederick Douglass predicted:

The Jew was once despised and hated in Europe, and is so still in some parts of that continent; but he has risen, and is rising to higher consideration, and no man is now degraded by association with him anywhere. In like manner the Negro will rise in social scale.[18]

Just as Frederick Douglass predicted Blacks would rise on the racial scale, Booker T. Washington further implied that unless Blacks have unity, pride, love of race and become more influential in this country, like Jews, they could not expect to obtain any degree of success in America. Washington's message implied that Black failure to imitate Jews would insure failure in America.[19]

While W.E.B. DuBois wrote sympathetically about Jews, his statements were not as prophetic as Booker T. Washington's. DuBois suggested that economic progress would come to Blacks if they followed the example of Jewish unionization. He roundly condemned Anti-Semitism, specifically Hitler's racial nonsense of the 1930s and 1940s. In retrospect, however, it should be remembered that he condemned Jews in general for being totally silent on the question of lynching and violence directed toward Blacks in the South. DuBois implied that Blacks would be more sympathetic toward Jews and their plight in America and Europe, if Jews would speak out against the discrimination and violence perpetrated against Blacks.[20]

Marcus Garvey attacked Black urban problems of the 1920s indicating that Jews were a major portion of those problems. But an analysis of Garvey's comments will reveal that they were anti-oppressor and anti-White, not anti-Semitic. Many of his statements were complimentary to Jews.[21]

Carter G. Woodson, father of Afro-American History, used Jews and their tradition as a model for Blacks:

If a race has no history, if it has no worthwhile tradition, it becomes a negligible factor in the thought of the world, and it stands in danger of being exterminated. The American Indian left no continuous record. He did not appreciate the value of tradition; and where is he today? The Hebrew keenly appreciated the value of tradition, as it attested by the Bible itself. In spite of worldwide persecution, therefore, he is still a great factor in civilization.[22]

Martin Luther King's praise of Jews was but a culmination of admiration:

The limited degree of Negro anti-Semitism is substantially a Northern ghetto phenomenon; it virtually does not exist in the South. The urban Negro has a special relationship to Jews. He meets them in two dissimilar roles. On the one hand, he is associated with Jews as some of his most committed and generous partners in the civil rights struggle. On the other hand, he meets them daily as some of his most direct exploiters in the ghetto as slum landlords and gouging shopkeepers. Jews had identified with Negroes voluntarily in the freedom movement, motivated by the religious and cultural commitment to justice. The other Jews who are engaged in commerce in the ghettos are remnants of older communities. A great number of Negro ghettos were formerly Jewish neighborhoods; some storekeepers and landlords remained as population changes occurred. They operate with the ethics of marginal business entrepreneurs, not Jewish ethics, but the distinction is lost on some Negroes who are maltreated by them. Such Negroes, caught in frustration and irrational anger, parrot racial epithets. They foolishly add to the social poison that injures themselves and their own people.

It would be a great tragic and immoral mistake to identify the mass of Negroes with the very small number that succomb to cheap and dishonest slogans, just as it would be a serious error to identify all Jews with the few who exploit Negroes under their economic sway.

Negroes cannot rationally expect honorable Jews to curb the few who are rapacious; they have no means of disciplining or suppressing them. We can only expect them to share our disgust and disdain. Negroes cannot be expected to curb and eliminate the few who are anti-Semitic, because they are subject to no controls we can exercise. We can, however, oppose them and have, in concrete ways. There has never been an instance of articulated Negro anti-Semitism that was not swiftly condemned by virtually all Negro leaders with the support of the overwhelming majority. I have myself directly attacked it within the Negro community, because it is wrong. I will continue to oppose it, because it is immoral and self-destructive.[23]

Even though Martin Luther King is recognized as a Black leader of the 1950s and 1960s, his thoughts expressed above symbolized the future spirit of detente which was to emerge among Black and Jewish liberals during the Civil Rights Movement.

On the eve of World War II the rigid social and physical distance between Blacks and Jews of the nineteenth century had begun to disappear. By 1940 certain historical conclusions could be reached in regard to Blacks and Jewish relations:

1. While both Blacks and Jews were minorities, and shared somewhat parallel patterns of oppression, their experiences were not comparable.
2. In early America, Jews maintained firm social distance from free Blacks. Jews enjoyed prominent places in life at the expense of Blacks both slave and free.
3. After the Civil War, Jews' prosperity depended more than ever upon the victimization of Blacks since Jewish merchants were often relegated to Black customers and Black neighborhoods.
4. Black admiration of Jews had a dual focus: First, the admiration and identification of Blacks and their plight of Biblical Jews was noted. Secondly, the constant reminder of Black leaders such as Frederick Douglass and Booker T. Washington that their only hope for prosperity in America was to imitate Jews.
5. Migration from the rural South to southern cities and migration northward brought Blacks and Jews into wholesale contact for the first time. This confrontation brought into sharp focus the pending crisis of economic domination of Jews over Blacks.
6. Anti-Black attitude of Jews served as identification with and protection from the dominant group.
7. The Depression accelerated the Americanization of Black attitudes toward Jews in the form of Black Anti-Semitism. Possibly the reason for Black Anti-Semitism extended from the humiliating status of Blacks and to their desire to identify with a dominant white culture.
8. Never has Anti-Semitism served as an organizing factor among Black social organizations. The "Christ killer" issue Whites link to Jews has found little support in Black communities.

On the eve of World War II, Black and Jewish relations had witnessed a shift from southern race relations to a national race relations. With the migration of rural black to southern cities, came a realization that Jews were different from other Whites. In the North, the same lesson was forged with a greater force. Thus by 1940, Black and Jewish Relations had entered a new era of awareness, from which there developed communication along the lines of basic civil rights, and a marked degree of mutual interests and understandings.

NOTES

*These notes have been reproduced exactly as they appeared in the original publication. Morris Schappes, in his response to this article (herein, p. 43), questions the factual accuracy of some of them.*

1. This paper was read at The Black-Jewish Relations: A National Consultation Co-sponsored by The Department of Religious and Philosophical Studies at Fisk University and The Interreligious Affairs Department of The American Jewish Committee June 9–12, 1974. Fisk University, Nashville, Tennessee.

2. The following books include data and information bearing on reactions of Jews to southern Blacks: George J. Becker, *Anti-Semite and Jews* (New York: Schocken Books, Inc., 1948); Pierie Butler, *Judah P. Benjamin* (Philadelphia: George W. Jacobs and Company, 1906); Leonard Dinnerstein and Mary Dale Palsson, *Jews in the South* (Baton Rouge: Louisiana State University Press, 1973); Barnett A. Elzas, *Jews of South Carolina* (Charleston, South Carolina: The Daggett Printing Company, 1903); Herbert T. Ezekiel and Gastor Lichtenstein, *The History of Jews of Richmond from 1769 to 1917* (Richmond, Virginia: Herbert T. Ezekiel, 1917); Miriam Freud, *Jewish Merchants in Colonial America* (New York: Behram's Jewish Book House, 1939); Lewis Ginsberg, *History of the Jews of Petersburg* (Petersburg, Virginia: The Williams Printing Company, 1954); Lewis Ginsberg, *Chapters on the Jews in Virginia: 1657–1900*, Richmond, Virginia: Cavelier Press, 1969); ——, *Jews in American Agriculture: The History of Farming by Jews in the United States* (New York: Jewish Agriculture Society, Inc., 1959); Ben Halpern, *Jews and Black* (New York: Herder and Herder, Inc., 1917); Leo Herschkowitz, *The Lee Max Friedman Collection of American Jewish Colonial Correspondence* (Waltham, Massachusetts: American Jewish Historical Society, 1968); Leon Huhner, *Jews in America in Colonial and Revolutionary Times* (New York: Gertz Bros., 1959); A Memorial Volume—Bertram Wallace Korn, *The Early Jews of New Orleans* (Waltham, Massachusetts: American Jewish Historical Society, 1969); Bertram Wallace Korn, *American Jewry and the Civil War* (Philadelphia: Jewish Publication Society of America, 1951); Jacob Rader Marcus, *Early American Jewry* (New York: American Book–Stratford Press, Inc., Vols. I and II, 1951–1953); Jacob Rader Marcus, *Jews of Pennsylvania and the South* (New York: American Book–Stratford Press, Inc., 1970); Jacob Rader Marcus, *The Jewish Background and Influence in the Confederacy* (Charleston, South Carolina: Charleston Printing Company, 1965); Leon L. Watters, *The Pioneer Jews of Utah* (Waltham, Massachusetts: American Jewish Historical Society, 1952); James Yaffe, *The American Jews* (New York: Random House, 1968).

3. With the one exception of Rabbi David Einhorn's *Latter Day* 1861 entry into the Abolition Movement, there is no appreciable involvement of Jews in the Abolition Movement in the Old South. As a result of his April 1861 position on slavery he was driven from his Baltimore pulpit and fled the Slave-holding city.

4. Virginia Bever Platt, *And Don't Forget the Guinea Voyage: The Slave Trade of Aaron Lopez on Newport* (Williamsburg, Virginia: The William & Mary Quarterly, 1975).

5. See Carl Bridenbaugh, *Myths and Realities: Societies of the Colonial South* (Baton Rouge: Louisiana State University Press, 1952).

6. Bertram Korn, *American Jewry and the Civil War* (Philadelphia: Jewish Publication Society, 1951), pp. 15–31. For a shorter version of Bertram Wallace Korn's book, *Jews and Negro Slavery in the Old South 1789–1865*); Leonard Dinnerstein and Mary Dale Palsson, *Jews and the South* (Baton Rouge: Louisiana State University Press, 1973), pp. 88–134; Jacob Rader Marcus, *Early American Jewry* (Philadelphia: Jewish Publication Society, Vol. I, 1961), p. 419.

7. Hugh H. Smythe and Martin S. Price, "The American Jew and Negro Slavery," *The Midwest Journal: A Magazine of Research and Creative Writing* (Vol. 7, No. 4, Winter 1955–56), p. 318.

8. John S. Ezell, *The South Since 1865* (New York: The Macmillan Company, 1963), p. 227; an example of southern Jewish behavior toward Blacks and the institution of slavery can be illustrated by examining the history of Petersburg, Virginia. Jews sold and traded slaves freely in Petersburg. The Davis Family was one of the largest slave trading firms in the Old South. Jewish vested interest in maintaining the system of slavery was clearly illustrated by recent arrivals in Petersburg volunteering to defend the system of slavery during the Civil War.

> While Blacks and Jewish relations may have differed in other places, Petersburg does not vary too much from the historical pattern found in Black and Jewish behavior in the South prior to the Civil War:

9. See Lewis Ginsberg, *History of Jews in Petersburg, 1657–1900* (Richmond, Virginia: Cavilier Press, 1969), p. 43.

10. W.E.B. DuBois, *Souls of Black Folks: Essays and Sketches* (Chicago: A.G. McClug and Company, 1907), p. 170. For other comments about Jewish exploitation of Blacks see Herbert Aptheker's *Souls of Black Folks: A Comparison*, 1903 and 1952 edition from the Negro History Bulletin, January 1971, pp. 15–18.

11. Ibid., 169.

12. For a broad discussion, see Joshua A. Fishman, *Jews and Desegregation*, pp. 307–333. Albert Vorspan, "The Dilemma of the Southern Jew," pp. 334–340. Krause, "The Rabbis and Negro Rights 1954–1957," pp. 360–385. Dinnerstein and Palsson.

13. Roi Ottley, *New World Acoming: Inside Black America* (Boston: Houghton Mifflin Company, 1943), pp. 122–123.

14. Ibid.

15. Ella Baker and Marvell Cook, "The Bronx Slave Market," *The Crisis*, Vol. XXXXII November 1935, p. 330.

16. Quoted from Robert G. Weisbord and Arthur Weisbord, *Bittersweet Encounters: The Afro-American and the American Jew* (Westport: Negro University Press), p. 76.

17. Miles Mark Fisher, *Negro Slave Songs in the United States* (New York: Citadel Press, 1963), pp. 39–40, 44–45.

18. Quoted in Richard C. Wade, Ed., *The Negro in American Life: Selected Readings* (Boston: Houghton-Mifflin Company, 1965), p. 97.

19. Booker T. Washington, *The Future of the American Negro* (Boston: Small Marnord and Company, 1900), pp. 182–183.

20. W.E.B. DuBois, *Dusk of Dawn: An Essay Toward an Autobiography of Race Concept* (New York: Schocken Books), pp. 207–215. See Weisbord and Stein.

21. W.E.B. DuBois, "The Jews," *The Crisis*, Vol. XXXX, No. 5 (May 1933), p. 117. W.E. Burghardt DuBois, *Annals of the American Academy of Political and Social Sciences*, Vol. 233, Book Department (September 1942), pp. 199–200.

22. [The original article provided no note for the Woodson quote.—Eds.]

23. Martin Luther King, *Where Do We Go from Here: Chaos or Community?* (Boston: Beacon Press, pp. 92–93.

# Historical Impressions of Black-Jewish Relations prior to World War II
## Another Comment and Response

In your July-August, 1977 issue, I was especially interested in the paper by Oscar R. Williams Jr., "Historical Impressions of Black-Jewish Relations Prior to World War II," for two reasons: I have been studying the matter for some 40 years both as historian and activist, and Mr. Williams' essay was originally presented to a "National Consultation" sponsored in 1974 both by Fisk University and the American Jewish Committee, an act in itself an example of Black-Jewish cooperation. Examining Mr. Williams' article, I of course found many observations and quotations of value, but there also seemed to me to be *mis*impressions which I ask your indulgence and space to record.

First, much more has been published about Jews and abolitionism even in the Old South than Mr. Williams reports when he says (p. 726), ". . . Jews were everything in the Old South except abolitionists" and then in his Reference Note 3 records what he considers "the one exception of Rabbi David Einhorn's *latter day* 1861 entry into the Abolition Movement." As for Rabbi Einhorn, his abolitionism did not begin in 1861. As soon as he arrived in this country and assumed his pulpit in 1855 in Baltimore, he began to denounce slavery. When he founded his German language monthly magazine, *Sinai*, in Feb., 1856, he began to write frequently against slavery. Rabbi Einhorn's pamphlet exposing the fallacies in New York Rabbi Morris J. Raphall's sermon of Jan. 4, 1861 that argued that the Bible supported slavery was translated into English and published in New York. Einhorn's views were quoted in the New York anti-slavery press. (See my *A Documentary History of the Jews in the United States, 1654–1875*, 3rd ed., rev., New York, 1971, pp. 444f, 405f.)

But there were other Jews in the South who should be known. In 1856, Mrs. Kate E. R. Pickard, in *The Kidnapped and the Ransomed*, told the amazing story of how Peter Still was helped to buy himself out of slavery by two German Jews, Joseph and Isaac Friedman in Tuscumbia, Ala. (See the facsimile reprint of this book by the Jewish Publication Society of America, Philadelphia, 1970, with an 103-page introductory essay on Jews in the anti-slavery movement by Maxwell Whiteman—and a critical review of the introduction, adding to the anti-slavery record, by Louis Ruchames in the *American Jewish History Quarterly*, Dec., 1971.)

Then there is the abolitionist orator, Ernestine L. Rose, who in 1847 came to Colum-

Morris U. Schappes is the editor of *Jewish Currents*. In 1977, Oscar R. Williams Jr. was professor of history at Virginia State College in Petersburg.

Originally published in *Negro History Bulletin* 41, no. 5 (1978): 890–91, 892. Copyright © 1978 by the Association for the Study of Negro Life and History. Reprinted with permission of Associated Publishers, Inc.

bia, S. C. and made an anti-slavery speech there (see *The Journal of Negro History*, July, 1949, p 351, "Ernestine L. Rose: Her Address on the Anniversary of West Indian Emancipation" (1853), ed. by Morris U. Schappes).

Or consider the case of August Bondi, who arrived in New Orleans in 1848 as a refugee from the counterrevolution that crushed the German revolution, was repelled, as he tells us in his *Autobiography*, by what he saw of slavery in Louisiana and Texas, rejected a proposed marriage to a southern "woman with slaves" because he "felt that my father's son was not born to be a slave-driver," went up the Mississippi to St. Louis, there enlisted in John Brown's company to fight in Kansas (there were two other Jews in that company), and finally enlisted in the Union Army and fought all through the war (for his Kansas experience, see Schappes, *A Documentary History*, pp. 352f).

Or take Julius J. Hirshheimer, who in New Orleans was imprisoned several times for expressing Union sentiments, and then, when the Union army occupied the city, enlisted in the 92nd U.S. Colored Infantry and served until 1865 (See Schappes, *A Pictorial History of the Jews in the United States*, New York, 1965, rev. ed., p. 94).

And then there was Abram J. Dittenhoefer, "born in Charleston, S.C., of Democratic proslavery parents," as he wrote in his reminiscences, *How We Elected Lincoln*. A graduate of Columbia College and advised to join the Democratic party in New York to make a political career, he read the account of Judah P. Benjamin's pro-slavery speech in the U.S. Senate in 1858 and of an anti-slavery senator's taunt that Benjamin was "an Israelite with Egyptian principles." Dittenhoefer switched to the Republican party (persuaded his father to do so too), and became so well known as an abolitionist that, in the 1863 draft riots in New York, his home was besieged by a crowd shouting "Down with the abolitionist" and "Death to Dittenhoefer!" (see my *A Documentary History*, pp. 394f).

Finally, for this purpose, I would call attention to Isidor Bush of the border state of Missouri. Mr. Williams, citing a vicious anti-Black statement in a New York Jewish newspaper (*The Jewish Record*, Jan. 28, 1863), adds this comment (p. 728): "The above blunt opinion reflected Jewish sentiment about Blacks after slavery ended." His is much too simple and sweeping a generalization. I offer as another Jewish sentiment that which was delivered by Isidor Bush on June 29, 1863, in the Missouri State Convention in Jefferson City. It will be remembered that Lincoln's Proclamation of Emancipation did not apply to the border states. Bush, as an outstanding abolitionist, had been elected to the convention Committee on Emancipation. When the majority of eight agreed on a report proposing that emancipation be delayed to 1876, Bush presented a minority report of one, proposing emancipation to take effect Jan. 1, 1864. In support of his minority view he made a magnificent address, in which he goes far beyond abolition to defend the Black people against charges of rape and murder. Citing census data in rebuttal, Bush concluded: "It is not enough that you hold them in bondage, toys of your whim and your lust, but you must charge them with crimes they never committed and never dreamt of. I pray you have pity for yourselves, *not* for the Negro. Slavery demoralizes, slavery fanaticism blinds you; it has arrayed brother against brother, son against father; it has destroyed God's noblest work—a free and happy people. . . ." (For full text, see my *A Documentary History*, pp. 476f.) Perhaps evidence such as is found in this sampling of citations might persuade Mr. Williams to revise such a harsh and extreme generalization as (p. 728): "Neither the Civil War nor Reconstruction changed the southern Jews' perception of Blacks as an animal to be used and exploited." I wonder where in anything said or written by a Jew Mr. Williams found the word *animal* used.

There is another concept of Mr. Williams that seems to me to need scrutiny. He expresses it in such statements as these: "Black anti-Semitism was only a reaction to white racism and it was non-religious in nature. Most, if not all, of the Black outcry against Jews was anti-oppressor, not anti-Judaism" (p. 728). Again, Mr. Williams writes: "The depression forcefully instilled in Blacks the lesson that Jews held an economic stranglehold on the Black neighborhood" (p. 729). Further on, Mr. Williams states, "This Black resentment of Jewish exploitation cannot be interpreted as resentment of Judaism or the 'Christ Killer' issue long associated with Jews" (p. 729).

To begin with, can one ignore the "Christ-killer" myth that Black Christians share with white Christians? In a paper, "Negro Attitudes toward Jews," Horace Mann Bond remembered that in 1916, at the age of 12, under provocation, he cried out to a Jewish boy, "You Christ-killer!"—and he has "felt badly about it ever since." ("Papers and Proceedings of a Conference on Negro-Jewish Relations in the United States," *Jewish Social Studies,* Jan., 1965, pp. 3–4; see also "Remarks by Discussant Morris U. Schappes," pp. 57–65.) Dr. Bond was hard put to it to explain how that epithet came to him; obviously it came to him from the Christian culture of family and Sunday School and church.

More important, however, is the need to distinguish between the economic exploitation that is inherent in the system of capitalism and the ethnic or religious or racial identity of the landlords, employers or merchants who practice that exploitation. There is no such thing as "Jewish exploitation." There is capitalist exploitation as practiced by Jews or Christians or whites or even Blacks, as the latter become landlords, employers or merchants. W. E. B. DuBois' *The Souls of Black Folks,* in which DuBois refers to "thrifty and avaricious Yankees, shrewd and unscrupulous Jews . . ." In his Note 10, Mr. Williams adds, "For other comments about Jewish exploitation of Blacks see Herbert Aptheker's "Souls of Black Folks: A Comparison, 1903 and 1952 edition," *Negro History Bulletin,* Jan., 1971. But in this article Aptheker does not discuss "Jewish exploitation of Blacks." Instead he shows that Dr. DuBois, eager to avoid the possible anti-Semitic effect of the phrase, "shrewd and unscrupulous Jews," changed the text in 1952 so that it read "unscrupulous foreigners."

Take the second quotation given above from Mr. Williams, ". . . Jews held an economic stranglehold on the Black neighborhood." In his reference Note 13, Mr. Williams cites Roi Ottley's *New World A-Coming,* pp. 122–123. Now Ottley's chapter, "Jews in Negro Life," is a fine, perceptive description of this complex matter. In it, he makes other statements that Mr. Williams might well have quoted to round out his view: "Obviously, sharp business practices are common to all merchants, gentiles as well as Jews. . . . This situation is not of the Jew's making, nor is it of his inspiration, but he receives much of the abuse intended for all whites. . . . Housing authorities regard the number of properties owned by Jews as extremely small" (pp. 125–126). Then Ottley adds a factor that Mr. Williams ignores altogether: "Actually, a good deal of the anti-Jewish feeling is stimulated by unscrupulous Negroes, and Axis agents—both white and

Negro—who seek to exploit the Negro community's legitimate grievances" (p. 129—the book was published in 1943, when we were at war with the Axis). The unscrupulous, "both white and Negro," are still with us, inciting Blacks to anti-Semitism—and Jews to white-supremacist, anti-Black ideas. Therefore it seems to me that instead of arguing that "This Black resentment of Jewish exploitation cannot be interpreted" as anti-Semitic, Mr. Williams would have rendered a service by explaining that the exploitation is not Jewish but systemic, capitalist.

Jewish leaders, on their part, have to help Jews understand the evil of white-supremacist, anti-Black prejudices and practices.

Mr. Williams makes another point that I want to examine. He declares, speaking about southern Jews in contemporary times, "Jewish acceptance by the Ku Klux Klan and later Jewish participation in the White Citizens Council provide concrete evidence of total acceptance in the southern racial scheme of Black versus White" (p. 729). Acceptance by the Ku Klux Klan!? When? Where? The fact is that the first Jew to be lynched in the USA was not Leo Frank on Aug. 17, 1915 in Marietta, Ga. but S. A. Bierfeld in 1868 in Franklin, Tenn. In my *A Documentary History,* pp. 515f, I tell the story of this "Double Lynching of a Jew and a Negro" by the Ku Klux Klan: Bierfeld was a Russian Jew operating a dry-goods store, known as a Radical Republican and employing a Negro clerk. On Aug. 15, 1868, while Bierfeld, his Negro clerk Lawrence Bowman, and a second Negro, Henry Morton, were eating watermelon in the back of the store, the KKK rode into the store on horses, lynched Bierfeld and Bowman, with Morton escaping—and telling the tale to a Federal investigation committee into KKK terrorism.

But as documentation for his statement Mr. Williams, in his reference Note 12, refers to three papers in *Jews in the South,* edited by Leonard Dinnerstein and Mary Dale Palsson. The first, by Joshua Fishman, entitled "Southern City" (Montgomery, Ala.), referring to the KKK writes: "In addition to the anti-Negro bias which it shares with the WCC, the Klan has voiced anti-Catholic and anti-Jewish views" (p. 315) and "the Klan, which often singles out Jews as targets" (p. 319). About the White Citizens Council, Fishman reports, "As the 'decent citizenry' [Christian] tumbled over each other to join the WCC, a number of prominent Jewish businessmen . . . also joined" (p. 315). Mr. Williams' second cited source is Albert Vorspan's "The Dilemma of the Southern Jew." He writes: "Some Jews have joined White Citizens Councils; in some cases for sheer economic survival, in a few cases out of conviction. A few Jews in Mississippi actually toyed with the idea of forming a Jewish White Citizens Council until the rabbis of the state angrily threatened to publicly repudiate them from their pulpits. But, it is significant that the few Jews who are members of White Citizens Councils are held in universal contempt by their fellow Jews" (p. 335). As for Mr. Williams' third citation, Allen Krause, "Rabbis and Negro Rights in the South, 1954–1967, "Rabbi Krause concludes his survey with the following judgment: "the southern rabbi has done a good deal, but he could do so much more" (p. 385). In other words, his three sources do not bear out the statement by Mr. Williams quoted above. I may add another judgment, in the same book, by a non-Jewish scholar, Alfred O. Hero Jr., who in "Southern Jews" writes: "The majority of the small number of Jews on the rolls of Citizens Council and other racist groups were by and large rather inactive and probably joined primarily to appease their segregationist neighbors, clients, and customers, to help keep these organizations 're-spectable,' and to *prevent development of anti-Semitism which many feared might be latent in such groups*" (p. 222, italics added).

Finally, I wish to point to certain problems that arise from Mr. Williams' carelessness, to say the least, in his reference notes. I shall take them in order. Note 2 begins: "The following books include data and information bearing on reactions of Jews to southern Blacks: George J. Becker, *Anti-Semite and Jews,* New York, Schocken Books, Inc., 1948." There is no such book by Becker. After wasting time checking university libraries and the Library of Congress catalogue, I turned to Schocken, from whom I learned the following: in 1948 they published *Anti-Semite and Jew* by Jean-Paul Sartre, *translated* by George J. Becker; another translation of the same French book appeared in England in 1948 as *Portrait of an Anti-Semite.* The French title is *Reflexion su le Question Juif.* The book has nothing to do with "Jews and southern Blacks."

Further on in Note 2, Mr. Williams cites Jacob Rader Marcus, *The Jewish Background and Influence in the Confederacy,* Charleston, 1965. Knowing Dr. Marcus' work well and having never heard of this one, I wrote to him at the American Jewish Archives in Cincinnati to inquire how I might obtain a copy. He replied that he knows nothing of this work, "There must be a mistake."

In Note 6, Mr. Williams cites Marcus, *Early American Jewry,* Philadelphia: Jewish Publication Society, Vol. 1, 1961, p. 419. But Vol. 1 was published in 1951 and there is no p. 419; and p. 419 in Vol. 2 has no connection with what Mr. Williams is discussing when he cited this reference.

In Note 9, Mr. Williams writes: "See Lewis Ginsberg, *History of Jews in Petersburg, 1657–1900,* Richmond, Va. . . . 1969, p. 43. Again, there is no such book. *Louis* Ginsberg has published two books: *History of the Jews of Petersburg, 1789–1950,* Petersburg, Va., 1954, and *Chapters on the Jews of Virginia, 1658–1900,* Petersburg, Va., 1969. I consulted p. 43 in each volume and found nothing to bear out the point Mr. Williams was making on page 729. In fact, p. 43 of the first book seems to contradict statements made by Mr. Williams in Note 8, "Jews sold and traded slaves freely in Petersburg. The Davis Family was one of the largest slave trading firms in the Old South." But Mr. Ginsberg wrote: "The statement has been made by the historian, Mr. Herman Schuricht [*History of the German Element in Virginia,* Baltimore, 1898, Vol. 2, p. 93], that the Jews advocated the secession movement because of their interest in the 'Negro trade.' Ownership of the largest auction-house in Richmond for the sale of slaves by a Jew is also cited in this source. The background of the Jewish Confederate soldiers from Petersburg listed above does not substantiate any such conclusion. Without exception, every one of these men were recent arrivals in America and in the South and were small merchants trying to make a living. It also appears that the Jews flocked to the colors primarily from patriotic motivations rather than from any vested interests which might have impelled others to join the southern cause." In neither of his two books does Mr. Ginsberg mention such a Davis Family as Mr. Williams cites.

Note 16 cites Robert G. Weisbord and Arthur *Stein* (not Arthur Weisbord, as Mr. Williams has it), *Bittersweet Encounter: The Afro-American and the American Jew,* p. 76, as the source for a quotation from what Mr. Williams calls James Baldwin's *autobiogra-*

*phy.* In fact, the quotation is from an article by Baldwin in the *New York Times Magazine,* April 9, 1967, which was widely discussed at the time. I too had a radio broadcast on Baldwin's views (printed in *Jewish Currents,* June, 1967).

I would also call the editor's attention to the fact that in the first four quotations by Mr. Williams (p. 728, col. 3 and p. 729, col. 1), there are many errors in transcription, including the changing of five words in the original texts.

In concluding, I applaud Mr. Williams' quotation from Martin Luther King Jr. (p. 730) and his own comment, "Even though Martin Luther King is recognized as a Black leader of the 1950s and 1960s, his thoughts expressed above symbolized the future spirit of detente which was to emerge among Black and Jewish liberals during the Civil Rights Movement." That spirit is now strained, as is well known. That was the reason that Fisk University and the American Jewish Committee sponsored the National Consultation in 1974 at which Mr. Williams first presented his paper. It will take understanding, wisdom and statesmanship on the part of both Blacks and Jews to ease the strains and restore the coalition that we all need in this period of what Mr. Jesse Jackson has pointedly called the "callous neglect" with which the Black people and all the poor are currently being treated.

### RESPONSE

I view Mr. Schappes' comments as a warning to the Association [The Association for the Study of Afro-American Life and History] not to publish articles concerning Jews unless they are first approved by him or persons of his persuasion. I refuse to enter a debate over my interpretation of the sources used in my article: "Historical Impression of Black and Jewish Relations," *Negro History Bulletin* (August 1977). The entire tone of his criticisms is to deny me the right of interpretation unless it meets with his unique approval. In preparing this article I cited forty-one sources, and at no point can he prove "misimpression."

Mr. Schappes failed to realize that I wrote an article rather than a book. Neither time nor space would allow me to cover every minor Jewish abolitionist. As indicated in the article Jews had no appreciative impact upon the abolitionist movement.

I feel compelled to answer his response concerning my alleged "carelessness."

*Comments Footnote 2*

I cite Anti-Semite and Jews to serve as an introductory source to persons desiring to gain familiarity with the concept of anti-semitism. Traces of anti-semitism Jews experienced in Europe could be found in the South. The only inconsistance with the source is that I cited the translator as the author which he points out.

*Comments Footnote 6*

The comment concerning Marcus' *Early American Jewry* Volume I and Volume II is totally incorrect. Volume one was published in 1951 and Volume two was published in 1953 as earlier indicated in footnote 2. See *The National Union Catalog* 1975 Volume X page 382 to support this point. In 1975 Volume I and Volume II combined.

*Comment Footnote 9*

He challenged the statement that the Davis Family was not Jewish. My statement is supported by Frederick Bancroft, *Slave Trading in the Old South,* J. H. Furst Co. Baltimore, MD 1931, pp. 93–94, 100, 117; Harriet Beecher Stowe, *The Key to Uncle Tom's Cabin* John P. Jewett and Company Cleveland, Ohio 1854, pp. 296–297 (Arno Press and the New York Times Reprint 1968).

"The Davis' in Petersburg are the great slave-dealers. They are Jews, who came to that place many years ago as poor peddlers; and, I have been informed are members of a Family which has its representatives in Philadelphia, New York, and etc. The men are always in the market giving the highest prices for slaves. During the summer and fall they buy them up at low prices, trim, shave, wash, and fatten them so that they may look sleek and sell them for great profit." Mr. Schappes is incorrect when he attributes the originality of the statement to Mr. Herman Schuricht's *History at the German Element in Virginia and Baltimore* in 1898.

*Comment Footnote 16*

The statement by James Baldwin is cited accurately. There is no need for comment!

In closing I view Mr. Schappes' comments as thinly veiled attempts to discredit my eight historical conclusions because they are not complimentary according to his standards. Reality is never pleasant.

# Part 2 **African Americans as the Chosen People**

A little known and often misunderstood aspect of the relationship of blacks and Jews in the United States stems from the claims of both groups to be God's Chosen People. All Jews define themselves as God's Chosen People, based on their genealogical descent from the Old Testament Covenant with Abraham. This lineal heritage is claimed by Ashkenazi and Sephardic Jews, but also by Falashas and the Black Jews discussed below.

A metaphorical set of claims has been made by blacks who were struck by the parallels between the ancient Hebrews held in bondage in Egypt and their own situation under slavery and post-Emancipation discrimination in the New World. This view is reflected in the use of Old Testament allusions and metaphors that refer to blacks as the Chosen People and to black leaders, such as Marcus Garvey and Harriet Tubman, as the Moses of their people. This view does not conceptualize African Americans as literal descendants of the ancient Hebrews, but, to quote the Paul Laurence Dunbar poem included here, looks at the parallel situations "In a Bibleistic way." The first few selections, from the spiritual "Go Down, Moses" through the account of the Exodusters in the postbellum South, illustrate the force of this religious and secular tradition. Recent examples occur in Martin Luther King Jr.'s final speech: "I have been to the mountain top and I have seen the promised land" and in the titles of the first two volumes of Taylor Branch's history of America during the King years, *Parting the Waters* (1988) and *Pillar of Fire* (1998).

More literal claims are made by members of small groups who call themselves Black Jews, Black Hebrews, or Black Israelites and who hold that all blacks are directly descended from the House of David. These groups believe that the entire African American population are the lost tribes of Israel. Whereas Sephardic and Ashkenazi Jews recognize that the Falashas of Ethiopia share a common religious and genealogical heritage with them, the Black Jews claim that peoples of African descent are the only true Jews and that Jews of European descent have usurped the claim to Israel. This view is represented by the followers of Ben-Ami Carter, described in this section by Bill Kurtis and in a pamphlet from one of their temples. These groups see their Zion as located in Liberia, or Kansas (see Nell Irvin Painter's essay), or Israel (see Kurtis). This brand of Zionism constitutes an important strand of black nationalist thought, dating from the early nineteenth century and therefore predating the modern Zionist movement among European Jews that began with Theodor Herzl.

These different strains of Black Judaism, often extremely complex in their genealogical and theological formulations, and in the historical crosscurrents and interrelations among them, are described in some detail by Albert Raboteau, Roi Ottley, and Kurtis.

## FURTHER REFERENCES

For background on the various metaphorical as well as literal claims concerning Black Jews, one can consult a large and growing literature, which includes the following (listed alphabetically): Julian Baldick, *Black God: The Afroasiatic Roots of the Jewish, Christian, and Muslim Religions* (1997); Graenum Berger, *Black Jews in America: A Documentary with Commentary* (1978) and "Black Jews in America," in Jack Fischel and Sanford Pinsker, eds., *Jewish-American History and Culture: An Encyclopedia* (1992); Lenora E. Berson, "Zionism and Black Nationalism" in *The Negroes and the Jews* (1971); Howard Brotz, *The Black Jews of Harlem: Negro Nationalism and the Dilemmas of Negro Leadership* (1964); J. G. St. Clair Drake, "African Diaspora and Jewish Diaspora: Convergence and Divergence" in Joseph R. Washington Jr., ed., *Jews in Black Perspectives: A Dialogue* (1984); Arthur Huff Fauset, *Black Gods of the Metropolis: Negro Religious Cults of the Urban North* (1944); Israel Gerber, *The Heritage Seekers: American Blacks in Search of Jewish Identity* (1977); Jose Malcioln, *The African Origin of Modern Judaism: From Hebrews to Jews* (1996); Nell Irvin Painter, *Exodusters: Black Migration to Kansas after Reconstruction* (1977), an extract from which is included here; and Robert G. Weisbord, "Israel and the Black Hebrew Israelites" (1975).

Gerald Early, in "Who Is the Jew? A Question of African-American Identity" (1996), discusses recent books that refer to slavery and the slave trade as "The Black Holocaust" in the context of the "larger Afrocentric claim to Jewish cultural and historical terms" (43). For an extended history that traces the origin of Black Jews to Abraham, a black Shemite, and claims that the original Israelites were black, see Rudolph Windsor's *From Babylon to Timbuktu: A History of the Ancient Black Races Including the Black Hebrews* (1969).

An interesting treatment of the role of civil rights lawyer Charles Hamilton Houston as a Moses leading to the Promised Land appears in Jack Greenberg, "Prologue: The Moses of the Journey" in *Crusaders in the Courts: How a Dedicated Band of Lawyers Fought for the Civil Rights Revolution* (1994). For Marcus Garvey, see E. David Cronon, *Black Moses: The Story of Marcus Garvey and the Universal Negro Improvement Association* (1955), and Robert A. Hill, "Black Zionism: Marcus Garvey and the Jewish Question" (1998).

# Go Down, Moses

## Hymns of Deliverance

### Go Down, Moses

Transcribed by the editor from
the singing of the Hampton students
led by Paige I. Lancaster

Reprinted from *Religious Folk-Songs of the Negro as Sung at the Hampton Institute*, ed. R. Nathaniel Dett (Hampton, Va.: Hampton Institute Press, 1927).

Tell__ ole Pha - raoh__ Let my peo - ple go.

2

Thus saith the Lord, bold Moses said,
   Let my people go;
If not I'll smite your first-born dead,
   Let my people go.

3

No more shall they in bondage toil,
   Let my people go;
Let them come out with Egypt's spoil,
   Let my people go.

4

The Lord told Moses what to do,
   Let my people go;
To lead the children of Israel thro',
   Let my people go.

5

When they had reached the other shore,
   Let my people go;
They sang a song of triumph o'er.
   Let my people go.

At Hampton Institute the first two measures of the last score are sung as here indicated, and while this is undoubtedly a colloquialism it, nevertheless, is highly effective.—Editor

Tell__ ole Pha - raoh

## An Ante-Bellum Sermon

We is gathahed hyeah, my brothahs,
   In dis howlin' wildaness,
Fu' to speak some words of comfo't
   To each othah in distress.
An' we chooses fu' ouah subjic'
   Dis—we 'll 'splain it by an' by;
   "An' de Lawd said, 'Moses, Moses,'
   An' de man said, 'Hyeah am I.' "

Now ole Pher'oh, down in Egypt,
   Was de wuss man evah bo'n,
An' he had de Hebrew chillun
   Down dah wukin' in his co'n;
'T well de Lawd got tiahed o' his foolin',
   An' sez he: "I'll let him know—
Look hyeah, Moses, go tell Pher'oh
   Fu' to let dem chillun go."

"An' ef he refuse to do it,
   I will make him rue de houah,
Fu' I 'll empty down on Egypt
   All de vials of my powah."
Yes, he did—an' Pher'oh's ahmy
   Was n't wuth a ha'f a dime;
Fu' de Lawd will he'p his chillun,
   You kin trust him evah time.

An' yo' enemies may 'sail you
   In de back an' in de front;
But de Lawd is all aroun' you,
   Fu' to ba' de battle's brunt.

Dey kin fo'ge yo' chains an' shackles
   F'om de mountains to de sea;
But de Lawd will sen' some Moses
   Fu' to set his chillun free.

An' de lan' shall hyeah his thundah,
   Lak a blas' f'om Gab'el's ho'n,
Fu' de Lawd of hosts is mighty
   When he girds his ahmor on.
But fu' feah some one mistakes me,
   I will pause right hyeah to say,
Dat I 'm still a-preachin' ancient,
   I ain't talkin' 'bout to-day.

But I tell you, fellah christuns,
   Things 'll happen mighty strange;
Now, de Lawd done dis fu' Isrul,
   An' his ways don't nevah change,
An' de love he showed to Isrul
   Was n't all on Isrul spent;
Now don't run an' tell yo' mastahs
   Dat I 's preachin' discontent.

'Cause I is n't; I 'se a-judgin'
   Bible people by deir ac's;
I 'se a-givin' you de Scriptuah,
   I 'se a-handin' you de fac's.
Cose ole Pher'oh b'lieved in slav'ry,
   But de Lawd he let him see,
Dat de people he put bref in,—
   Evah mothah's son was free.

Paul Laurence Dunbar was the leading black poet at the turn of the century.
Reprinted from *The Complete Poems of Paul Laurence Dunbar* (New York: Dodd, Mead & Co., 1913), 13–15.

An' dahs othahs thinks lak Pher'oh,
　　But dey calls de Scriptuah liar,
Fu' de Bible says "a servant
　　Is a-worthy of his hire."
An' you cain't git roun' nor thoo dat,
　　An' you cain't git ovah it,
Fu' whatevah place you git in,
　　Dis hyeah Bible too 'll fit.

So you see de Lawd's intention,
　　Evah sence de worl' began,
Was dat His almighty freedom
　　Should belong to evah man,
But I think it would be bettah,
　　Ef I 'd pause agin to say,
Dat I 'm talkin' 'bout ouah freedom
　　In a Bibleistic way.

But de Moses is a-comin',
　　An' he 's comin', suah and fas'
We kin hyeah his feet a-trompin',
　　We kin hyeah his trumpit blas'.
But I want to wa'n you people,
　　Don't you git too brigity;
An' don't you git to braggin'
　　'Bout dese things, you wait an' see.

But when Moses wif his powah
　　Comes an' sets us chillun free,
We will praise de gracious Mastah
　　Dat has gin us liberty;
An' we'll shout ouah halleluyahs,
　　On dat mighty reck'nin' day,
When we 'se reco'nised ez citiz'—
　　Huh uh! Chillun, let us pray!

# African-Americans, Exodus, and the American Israel

*Canaan land is the land for me,*
*And let God's saints come in.*
*There was a wicked man,*
*He kept them children in Egypt land.*
*Canaan land is the land for me,*
*And let God's saints come in.*
*God did say to Moses one day,*
*Say, Moses, go to Egypt land,*
*And tell him to let my people go.*
*Canaan land is the land for me,*
*And let God's saints come in.*
—Slave Spiritual

In the encounter with European Christianity in its Protestant form in North America, enslaved Africans and their descendants encountered something new: a fully articulated ritual relationship with the Supreme Being, who was pictured in the book that the Christians called the Bible not just as the Creator and Ruler of the Cosmos, but also as the God of History, a God who lifted up and cast down nations and peoples, a God whose sovereign will was directing all things toward an ultimate end, drawing good out of evil. As the transplanted Africans reflected upon the evil that had befallen them and their parents, they increasingly turned to the language, symbols, and worldview of the Christian holy book. There they found a theology of history that helped them to make sense of their enslavement. One story in particular caught their attention and fascinated them with its implications and potential applications to their own situation: the story of Exodus. What they did with that ancient story of the Near East is the topic of this essay. . . .

## EXODUS

No single symbol captures more clearly the distinctiveness of Afro-American Christianity than the symbol of Exodus. From the earliest days of colonization, white Chris-

Albert J. Raboteau is Henry W. Putnam Professor of Religion, chair of the religion department and dean of the graduate school at Princeton University.

Excerpted from *African-American Christianity: Essays in History,* ed. Paul E. Johnson (Berkeley: University of California Press, 1994), 1, 9–17. Copyright © 1994 the Regents of the University of California. Reprinted with permission of the Regents of the University of California and the University of California Press.

tians had represented their journey across the Atlantic to America as the exodus of a New Israel from the bondage of Egypt into the Promised Land of milk and honey. For black Christians, the imagery was reversed: the Middle Passage had brought them to Egypt land, where they suffered bondage under a new Pharaoh. White Christians saw themselves as the New Israel; slaves identified themselves as the Old. This is, as Vincent Harding remarked, one of the abiding and tragic ironies of our history: the nation's claim to be the New Israel was contradicted by the Old Israel still enslaved in her midst.[1]

American preachers, politicians, and other orators found in the story of Exodus a rich source of metaphors to explicate the unfolding history of the nation. Each section of the narrative—the bondage in Egypt, the rescue at the Red Sea, the wandering in the wilderness, and the entrance into the Promised Land—provided a typological map to reconnoiter the moral terrain of American society. John Winthrop, the leader of the great Puritan expedition to Massachusetts Bay, set the pattern in his famous "A Modell of Christian Charity" sermon composed on his ship in 1630. Having elaborated the covenantal obligations that the settlers had contracted with God, echoing the Sinai covenant of Israel with Yahweh, Winthrop concluded his discourse with a close paraphrase of Moses' farewell instruction to Israel (Deuteronomy 30):

> Beloved there is now sett before us life, and good, deathe and evill in that wee are Commaunded this day to love the Lord our God, and to love one another, to walke in his wayes and to keepe his Commaundements and his Ordinance, and his lawes, and the Articles of our Covenant with him that wee may live and be multiplied, and that the Lord our God may blesse us in the land whither we goe to posess it: But if our heartes shall turne away soe that wee will not obey, but shall be seduced and worship . . . other Gods, our pleasures, and proffitts, and serve them; it is propounded unto this day, wee shall surely perishe out of the good Land whither wee passe over this vast Sea to possesse it. . . .[2]

Notice the particular application that Winthrop draws from the Exodus story: possession of the land is contingent upon observing the moral obligations of the covenant with God. It is a mark of the greatness of Winthrop's address that the obligations he emphasizes are justice, mercy, affection, meekness, gentleness, patience, generosity, and unity—not the qualities usually associated with taking or keeping possession of a land. Later and lesser sermons would extol much more active and aggressive virtues for the nation to observe.

Already in Winthrop's address there is an explicit notion of reciprocity between God's Will and America's Destiny: God has made a contract with us; if we live up to our part of the bargain, so will He. This pattern of reciprocity between Divine Providence and American Destiny had tremendous hortative power, which Puritan preachers exploited to the full over the next century and more in the jeremiad. In sermon after sermon, a succession of New England divines deciphered droughts, epidemics, Indian attacks, and other misfortunes as tokens of God's displeasure over the sins of the nation. Unless listeners took the opportunity to humble themselves, repent, and reform, they might expect much more of the same.

Implicit in this relationship of reciprocity there lay a danger: the danger of converting God's Will into America's Destiny. Winthrop was too good a Puritan to succumb to this temptation. Protected by his belief in the total sovereignty of God, he knew that the relationship between God's Will and human action was one-sided and that the proper human attitude was trust in God, not confidence in man. God's Will was the measure of America's deeds, not vice versa. Of course, no American preacher or politician would have disagreed, but as time went on the salient features of the American Exodus story changed. As the actual experience of migration with all its fear and tenuousness receded, Americans tended to lose sight of their radical dependence upon God and to celebrate their own achievements as a nation.

We can catch sight of the change by comparing the tone of Winthrop's "A Modell of Christian Charity" with the mood of an election sermon entitled "The United States Elevated to Glory and Honor," preached by Ezra Stiles in 1783. Flushed with excitement over the success of the Revolution, Stiles dwelled at length on the unfolding destiny of the new nation. Quoting, like Winthrop, from the book of Deuteronomy, Stiles struck a celebratory rather a hortatory note:

"And to make thee high above all nations which he hath made, in praise, and in name, and in honour; and that thou mayest be an holy people unto the Lord thy God. . . ." I have assumed [this] text as introductory to a discourse upon the political welfare of God's American Israel, and as allusively prophetic of the future prosperity and splendour of the United States. Already does the new constellation of the United States begin to realize this glory. It has already risen to an acknowledged sovereignty among the republicks and kingdoms of the world. And we have reason to hope, and I believe to expect, that God has still greater blessings in store for this vine which his own right hand hath planted, to make us "high among the nations in praise, and in name, and in honour."[3]

Stiles went on at great length to identify the reasons for his optimism about America's present and future preeminence, including the fact that "in our civil constitutions, those impediments are removed which obstruct the progress of society towards perfection."[4] It's a long way from Winthrop's caution to Stiles' confidence, from an "Errand in the Wilderness" to "progress towards perfection." In Stiles' election sermon we can perceive God's New Israel becoming the Redeemer Nation. The destiny of the New Israel was to reach the pinnacle of perfection and to carry liberty and the gospel around the globe.

In tandem with this exaggerated vision of America's Destiny went an exaggerated vision of human capacity. In an increasingly confident and prosperous nation, it was difficult to avoid shifting the emphasis from divine sovereignty to human ability. Historian Conrad Cherry has succinctly summarized the change in perception of America's destiny: "Believing that she had escaped the wickedness of the Old World and the guilt of the past, God's New Israel would find it all too easy to ignore her vices and all too difficult to admit a loss of innocence."[5]

Among the realities this optimistic vision ignored was the presence of another, darker Israel:

America, America, foul and indelible is thy stain! Dark and dismal is the cloud that hangs over thee, for thy cruel wrongs and injuries to the fallen sons of Africa. The blood of her murdered ones cries to heaven for vengeance against Thee. . . . You may kill, tyrannize, and oppress as much as you choose, until our cry shall come up before the throne of God; for I am firmly persuaded, that he will not suffer you to quell the proud, fearless and undaunted spirits of the Africans forever; for in his own time, he is able to plead our cause against you, and to pour out upon you the ten plagues of Egypt.[6]

So wrote Maria Stewart, a free black reform activist in Boston, in 1831. Her words were addressed to an America that projected itself as the probable site of the coming Millennium, Christ's thousand-year reign of peace and justice. From the perspective of slaves, and of free blacks like Maria Stewart, America was Egypt, and as long as she continued to enslave and oppress Black Israel, her destiny was in jeopardy. America stood under the judgment of God, and unless she repented, the death and destruction visited upon Biblical Egypt would be repeated here. The retribution envisaged was quite literal, as Mary Livermore, a white governess, discovered when she overheard a prayer uttered by Aggy, the slave housekeeper, whose daughter had just been brutally whipped by her master:

Thar's a day a comin'! Thar's a day a comin'. . . . I hear de rumblin' ob de chariots! I see de flashin' ob de guns! White folks' blood is a-runnin' on de ground like a riber, an' de dead's heaped up dat high! . . . Oh, Lor'! hasten de day when de blows, an' de bruises, an' de aches, an' de pains, shall come to de white folks, an' de buzzards shall eat 'em as dey's dead in de streets. Oh, Lor'! roll on de chariots, an' gib de black people rest an' peace.[7]

Nor did slaves share the exaggerated optimism of white Americans about human ability. Trapped in a system from which there seemed little, if any, possibility of deliverance by human actions, they emphasized trusting in the Lord instead of trusting in man. Sermon after sermon and prayer after prayer echoed the words that Moses spoke on the banks of the Red Sea: "Stand still and see the salvation of the Lord." Although the leaders of the three principal slave revolts—Gabriel Prosser in 1800, Denmark Vesey in 1822, and Nat Turner in 1831—all depended upon the Bible to justify and motivate rebellion, the Exodus story was used mainly to nurture internal resistance, not external revolution among the slaves.

The story of Exodus contradicted the claim made by white Christians that God intended Africans to be slaves. It seemed to prove that slavery was against God's will and that slavery would inevitably end, although the when and the how remained hidden in Divine Providence. Christian slaves thus applied the Exodus story, whose end they knew, to their own experience of slavery, which had not yet ended, and so gave meaning and purpose to lives threatened by senseless and demeaning brutality. Exodus functioned as an archetypal myth for the slaves. The sacred history of God's liberation of his people would be or was being reenacted in the American South. A white Union Army chaplain working among freedmen in Decatur, Alabama, commented disapprovingly on the slaves' fascination with Exodus: "There is no part of the Bible with which they are so familiar as the story of the deliverance of Israel. Moses is their *ideal* of all that is high, and noble, and perfect, in man. I think they have been accustomed to regard Christ not so much in the light of a *spiritual* Deliverer, as that of a second Moses who would eventually lead *them* out of their prison-house of bondage."[8]

Thus, in the story of Israel's exodus from Egypt, the slaves envisioned a future radically different from their present. In times of despair, they remembered Exodus and found hope enough to endure the enormity of their suffering. As a slave named Polly eloquently explained to her mistress, "We poor creatures have need to believe in God, for if God Almighty will not be good to us some day, why were we born? When I heard of his delivering his people from bondage, I know it means the poor Africans."[9]

By appropriating the story of Exodus as their own story, black Christians articulated their own sense of peoplehood. Exodus symbolized their common history and common destiny. It would be hard to exaggerate the intensity of their identification with the children of Israel. A.M.E. pastor William Paul Quinn demonstrated how literal the metaphor of Exodus could become when he exhorted black Christians, "Let us comfort and encourage one another, and keep singing and shouting, great is the Holy One of Israel in the midst of us. Come thou Great Deliverer, once more awake thine almighty arm, and set thy African captives free."[10] As Quinn's exhortation reveals, it was prayer and worship that made the identification seem so real. Sermons, prayers, and songs recreated in the imagination of successive generations the travail and triumph of Israel. Exodus became dramatically real, especially in the songs and prayer meetings of the slaves, who reenacted the story as they shuffled in the ring dance they called "the shout." In the ecstasy of worship, time and distance collapsed, and the slaves literally became the children of Israel. With the Hebrews, they traveled dry-shod through the Red Sea; they, too, saw Pharaoh's army "get drownded"; they stood beside Moses on Mount Pisgah and gazed out over the Promised Land; they crossed Jordan under Joshua and marched with him around the walls of Jericho. Their prayers for deliverance resonated with the experiential power of these liturgical dramas.

Identification with Israel, then, gave the slaves a communal identity as a special, divinely favored people. This identity stood in stark contrast with racist propaganda, which depicted them as inferior to whites, as destined by nature and providence to the status of slaves. Exodus, the Promised Land, and Canaan were inextricably linked in the slaves' minds with the idea of freedom. Canaan referred not only to the condition of freedom but also to the territory of freedom—the North or Canada. As Frederick Douglass recalled, "A keen observer might have detected in our repeated singing of 'O Canaan, sweet Canaan, / I am bound for the land of Canaan,' something more than a hope of reaching heaven. We meant to reach the *North,* and the North was our Canaan."[11] Slave owners, too, were well aware that the Exodus story could be a source of unflattering and even subversive analogies. It took no genius to identify Pharaoh's army in the slave song "My army cross ober, My army cross ober / O Pharaoh's army drownded."

The slaves' faith that God would free them just as he had freed Israel of old was validated by Emancipation. "Shout the glad tidings o'er Egypt's dark sea / Jehovah has triumphed, his people are free!" the ex-slaves sang in celebration of freedom. But it did not take long for the freedmen to realize that Canaan Land still lay somewhere in the distance. "There must be no looking back to Egypt," a band of refugee slaves behind Union lines were instructed by a slave preacher in 1862. "Israel passed forty years in the wilderness, because of their unbelief. What if we cannot see right off the green fields of Canaan, Moses could not. He could not even see how to cross the Red Sea. If we would have greater freedom of body, we must free ourselves from the shackles of sin. . . . We must snap the chain of Satan, and educate ourselves and our children."[12]

But as time went on and slavery was succeeded by other forms of racial oppression, black Americans seemed trapped in the wilderness no matter how hard they tried to escape. Former slave Charles Davenport voiced the despair of many when he recalled, "De preachers would exhort us dat us was de chillen o' Israel in de wilderness an' de Lord done sent us to take dis land o' milk and honey. But how us gwine-a take land what's already been took?"[13] When race relations reached a new low in the 1880s and 1890s, several black leaders turned to Africa as the black Promised Land. Proponents of emigration, such as Henry McNeal Turner, urged Afro-Americans to abandon the American wilderness for an African Zion. Few black Americans, however, heeded the call to emigrate to Africa; most continued to search for their Promised Land here. And as decade succeeded decade they repeated the story of Exodus, which for so many years had kept their hopes alive. It was, then, a very old and evocative tradition that Martin Luther King, Jr., echoed in his last sermon:

> We've got some difficult days ahead. But it really doesn't matter with me now. Because I've been to the mountaintop. Like anybody I would like to live a long life. Longevity has its place. But I'm not concerned about that now. I just want to do God's will. And He's allowed me to go up to the mountain. And I've seen the Promised Land. And I may not get there with you. But I want you to know tonight that we as a people will get to the Promised land.[14]

A period of over three hundred years stretches between John Winthrop's vision of an American Promised Land and that of Martin Luther King. The people whom Winthrop addressed long ago took possession of their Promised Land; the people whom King addressed still wait to enter theirs. For three centuries, white and black Americans have dwelt in the same land. For at least two of those centuries, they have shared the same religion. And yet, during all those years, their national and religious identities have been radically opposed. It need not have been so. After all, Winthrop's version of Exodus and King's were not so far apart. Both men understood that charity is the charter that gives title to the Promised Land. Both taught that mercy, gentleness, and justice are the terms for occupancy. Both believed that the conditions of the contract had been set by God, not by man. At times in our history, the two visions have nearly coincided, as they did in the antislavery stance of the early evangelicals, or in the abolitionist movement, or in Lincoln's profound realization that Americans were an "almost chosen people," or in the civil rights movement of our own era. Yet, despite these moments of coherence, the meaning of the Exodus story for America has remained fundamentally ambiguous. Is America Israel, or is she Egypt?

NOTES

[The original notes have been renumbered in this excerpted text.—Eds.]

1. Vincent Harding, "The Uses of the Afro-American Past," in *The Religious Situation, 1969,* ed. Donald R. Cutter (Boston: Beacon, 1969), 829–40.

2. John Winthrop, "A Modell of Christian Charity," in *Winthrop Papers* (Boston: Massachusetts Historical Society, 1931), 2: 282–84, 292–95. Reprinted in Conrad Cherry, *God's New Israel: Religious Interpretations of American Destiny* (Englewood Cliffs, N.J.: Prentice-Hall, 1971), 43.

3. Ezra Stiles, "The United States Elevated to Glory and Honor," in *A Sermon Preached before Gov. Jonathan Trumbull and the General Assembly . . . May 8th, 1783,* 2d. ed. (Worcester, Mass.: Isaiah Thomas, 1785), 5–9, 58–75, 88–92, 95–98. Reprinted in Cherry, *God's New Israel,* 82–84.

4. Ibid., in Cherry, *God's New Israel,* 84.

5. Cherry, *God's New Israel,* 66.

6. Marilyn Richardson, ed., *Maria W. Stewart, America's First Black Woman Political Writer: Essays and Speeches* (Bloomington: Indiana University Press, 1987), 39–40.

7. Mary A. Livermore, *My Story of the War: A Woman's Narrative of Four Years Personal Experience . . .* (Hartford, Conn.: A. D. Worthington, 1889), 260–61.

8. William G. Kephart to L. Tappan, May 9, 1864, American Missionary Association Archives, Decatur, Ala., Reel 2; also in *American Missionary* 8, no. 7 (July 1864), 179.

9. As cited in diary entry of 12 December 1857 by her mistress: Barbara Leigh Smith Bodichon, *An American Diary, 1857–1858,* ed. Joseph W. Reed, Jr. (London: Routledge & Kegan Paul, 1972), 65.

10. W. Paul Quinn, *The Sword of Truth Going "Forth Conquering and to Conquer"; The Origin, Horrors, and Results of Slavery Faithfully and Minutely Described . . .* (1834); reprinted in *Early Negro Writing, 1760– 1837,* ed. Dorothy Porter (Boston: Beacon, 1971), 635.

11. Frederick Douglass, *Life and Times of Frederick Douglass: Written by Himself* (1892; reprint, New York: Crowell-Collier, 1969), 159–60.

12. *American Missionary* 6, no. 2 (February 1862): 33.

13. Norman R. Yetman, ed., *Voices from Slavery* (New York: Holt, Rinehart and Winston, 1970), 75.

14. Martin Luther King, Jr., sermon of April 3, 1968, delivered at Mason Temple, Memphis, Tenn., reprinted in *A Testament of Hope: The Essential Writings of Martin Luther King, Jr.,* ed. James Melvin Washington (San Francisco: Harper & Row, 1986), 286.

# Thomas Wentworth Higginson to Louise Storrow Higginson

WORCESTER, June 17, 1859

Dearest Mother:

. . . . . . . . . . . . . . . . . . . . . . . . . . . . . .

We have had the greatest heroine of the age here, Harriet Tubman, a black woman, and a fugitive slave, who has been back *eight times* secretly and brought out in all sixty slaves with her, including all her own family, besides aiding many more in other ways to escape. Her tales of adventure are beyond anything in fiction and her ingenuity and generalship are extraordinary. I have known her for some time and mentioned her in speeches once or twice—the slaves call her Moses. She has had a reward of twelve thousand dollars offered for her in Maryland and will probably be burned alive whenever she is caught, which she probably will be, first or last, as she is going again. She has been in the habit of working in hotels all summer and laying up money for this crusade in the winter. She is jet black and cannot read or write, only *talk,* besides acting.

Thomas Wentworth Higginson was a colonel in a black regiment during the Civil War.
Originally published in *Letters and Journals of Thomas Wentworth Higginson: 1846–1906,* ed. Mary Thacher Higginson (Boston: Houghton Mifflin, 1921), 81.

# Preface to *Harriet: The Moses of Her People*

The title I have given my black heroine, in this second edition of her story, viz.: THE MOSES OF HER PEOPLE, may seem a little ambitious, considering that this Moses was a woman, and that she succeeded in piloting only three or four hundred slaves from the land of bondage to the land of freedom.

But I only give her here the name by which she was familiarly known, both at the North and the South, during the years of terror of the Fugitive Slave Law, and during our last Civil War, in both of which she took so prominent a part.

And though the results of her unexampled heroism were not to free a whole nation of bond-men and bond-women, yet this object was as much the desire of her heart, as it was of that of the great leader of Israel. Her cry to the slave-holders, was ever like his to Pharaoh, "Let my people go!"

Sarah H. Bradford was a school teacher in Auburn, New York, and supporter of Harriet Tubman. She also wrote *Scenes in the Life of Harriet Tubman* (1868).
From *Harriet: The Moses of Her People*, expanded 2nd. ed. of *Scenes in the Life of Harriet Tubman* (New York: G. R. Lockwood & Son, 1886).

# The Kansas Fever Exodus of 1879

Liberia Fever followed fast on the heels of Reconstruction in the Carolinas, Mississippi, and Louisiana, as Blacks perceived clearly and cheerlessly that they stood alone. In the aftermath of the violence surrounding the campaign of 1876, many Afro-Americans admitted that they would never be first-class citizens in this country; they might as well relinquish their American identity and emphasize their African descent. Turning to the most American part of Africa—Liberia—they envisioned building a perfected America, free from racial hatred and color disabilities. Unfortunately, in their quest for safe harbor from injustices suffered on Southern soil, Afro-Americans gave little thought to the native Liberians.

For all too many emigrants, their own American troubles obliterated their ideals of fairness toward African Liberians. Like Harrison Bouey of South Carolina, prospective emigrants looked to Liberia convinced "that the colored man has no home in America" and certain that whites "believe that my race have no more right to any of the profits of their labor than one of their mules. . . ."[2] But unlike Bouey, few of them served as teachers and missionaries in Liberia. (Americo-Liberians tyrannized native Liberians for years. During the nineteenth century, Liberians of American Negro descent formed a social and economic elite which rigorously excluded any but the most assimilated Africans.)

. . . .

A significant body of Afro-American opinion opposed any emigration whatever. This point of view was most prevalent among "representative colored men" who were well off financially, and their position received widespread publicity. Opponents of the Liberia and Kansas movements were articulate, and they enjoyed far greater access to newspapers edited by other anti-migrationists and whites. Since the Liberia idea circulated longer and seemed unthinkably radical, it stirred up considerable opposition. The editor of the Philadelphia *Christian Recorder,* the Reverend B. T. Tanner, condemned the Liberia idea "in so far as it partakes of anything like a wholesale egress from the country."[13] But Tanner bravely attempted to straddle the issue, as did Senator Blanche K. Bruce of Mississippi. While the *Christian Recorder* published articles and letters from

In 1977, Nell Irvin Painter was assistant professor of American and Afro-Am history at the University of Pennsylvania, Philadelphia.

Excerpted from Nell Irvin Painter, *The Exodusters: Black Migration to Kansas after Reconstruction* (New York: Alfred A. Knopf, 1977) 138, 141–42, 145, 184–201, 256–61. Reprinted with permission of Nell Irvin Painter.

pro-Liberia writers, it counseled caution and stressed the formidable obstacles that massive emigration entailed.

. . . .

It is difficult to determine whether interest in Kansas migration grew out of the ground already prepared by Liberia Fever or it was the fruit of the same desire of Southern Blacks to escape oppression. Certainly in the late 1870s in Mississippi and Louisiana (and, to a certain extent, Texas), Liberia Fever and Kansas Fever flourished in the same fields. Many of the organizational characteristics of planned migration to Kansas were common to the Liberia emigrationists.

. . . .

The Kansas Fever Exodus—the most remarkable migration in the United States after the Civil War—took some six thousand Blacks from Louisiana, Mississippi, and Texas to Kansas in the space of a few months.[1] Rooted in faith and in fear, the movement in Louisiana fixed upon a particular object, the constitutional convention. The motivating fear in Mississippi and Texas were no less real, although it was not focused on any concrete event. In mid-1879 a Black Texan groped toward a description of this mood of alarm among the freedpeople:

> There are no words which can fully express or explain the real condition of my people throughout the south, nor how deeply and keenly they feel the necessity of fleeing from the wrath and long pent-up hatred of their old masters which they feel assured will ere long burst loose like the pent-up fires of a volcano and crush them if they remain here many years longer.[2]

Pushed by fears of damnation and pulled by belief in the Kansas Fever idea, thousands left Mississippi and Louisiana between March and May 1879, and Texas in the latter part of the year.

Although the first large groups of Exodusters arrived in St. Louis in March, the movement had been building up since the end of 1878 in Madison, Tensas, and Concordia parishes in Louisiana, and in Hinds, Warren, and Madison counties in Mississippi. In late November and early December, the *Hinds County Gazette* drew attention to the local Blacks' vivid interest in migration. In late December a Columbus, Mississippi, newspaper reported that "one thousand negroes will emigrate this season from Hinds and Madison Counties to Kansas."[3]

By February the Exodus was under way, and the characteristics that marked the millenarian movement attracted comment: the Exodusters' unshakable faith in the Kansas Fever idea and their conviction that this faith was sufficient to assure their future. Early on, for instance, a white Mississippian tried to disabuse an Exoduster of his faith in the Kansas Fever idea:

> We questioned him and discovered that he knew not to what particular point he was going, knew not the value or kind of land he was to occupy, knew not the conditions on which he was to take it, and in fact knew absolutely nothing. . . . [He was] most

thoroughly in the dark as to hopes for the future. All that we said did not in the least waver his belief in that a fortune awaited him in Kansas, to be gotten by his making his home there.[4]

At the same time, Exodusters showed the tenacity of their faith, even as they discovered that free transportation to Kansas fell short of their expectations. Kansas Fever had already affected many Blacks in the Delta and Vicksburg area when this report appeared in February:

> The African hegira continues. . . . We learn that quite a number of negroes left Madison parish yesterday [February 27], and others are expected to follow. A few days ago a number of would-be emigrants, about sixty of them, took passage on a passing steamer for St. Louis, intending to go thence by train to Kansas. When the clerk passed around among them he found they had just enough money to pay their way to the next landing, and at the next landing they were put off, less than twenty-five miles from their starting place. This little incident is a sufficient illustration of the improvidence and want of sagacity of the negro.[5]

The "little incident" did not in the least slow the Exodus or diminish its allure. The idea of free transportation neatly accommodated hard fact, shifting to a promise of free transportation from St. Louis, after Exodusters paid their way there (about four dollars from the Vicksburg-Delta area).

When these Exodusters arrived in St. Louis about a week later, the peculiar nature of the movement, as well as its great numbers, began to provoke comment. During the first week of March, seventy-five migrants arrived in St. Louis on the packet boats *City of Vicksburg* and *Gold Dust*, and in the South thousands more anticipated a speedy departure. Planters estimated, with some hyperbole, that fifteen hundred Exodusters had already left for Kansas. At Delta, Louisiana, P. B. S. Pinchback was astonished by the fervor of the massive crowds on the river. Arriving on March 8, he found the banks of the Mississippi "literally covered with colored people and their little store of worldly goods." Within two days, the crowd increased from about three hundred to about five hundred people. Pinchback reported "every road leading to the river . . . filled with wagons loaded with plunder and families who seem to think anywhere is better than here."[6] At the same time, a rumor spread in Mississippi that on or about March 15 "a through train, or steamboat, (the best informed do not seem to know which,) will leave Vicksburg for Kansas City, conveying all colored people who wish to go to Kansas."[7] The Exodus had begun in earnest, and poor Black families flocked to the landings on both sides of the river around Vicksburg.

Between March 12 and 16 approximately eight hundred migrants arrived in St. Louis on the *Colorado,* the *Grand Tower* (the "government boat," as the Exodusters called this Anchor Line packet boat), and the *Joe Kinney.* They continued to arrive, almost without pause, until the middle of May. The overwhelming number of people of all ages in the Exodus astonished observers, but the Exodusters' apparent credulity surprised them most. Exodusters had set out knowing nothing of Kansas, trusting entirely in the Kansas

Fever idea. Although eyewitness descriptions often cruelly ridiculed the Exodusters' faith, they caught the special character of the movement.

One observer found the second large group of Exodusters arriving in mid-March "as needy and ignorant as their predecessors. Most of them have not sufficient means to take them to their Mecca [Kansas]. . . . They have no recognized leader and no definite plans. They say they 'want to git dar, an' dat's all.' "[8] Another witness likened the Exodusters to livestock:

[The Exodus] started among the black people themselves, how or when nobody knows, and the negroes keep their own counsel about it. Persons of limited intelligence are often not unlike unreasoning animals in the way of following blindly on a given direction in which they have been started, like a flock of sheep jumping over a fence. The migration of the blacks having begun, it is not easy to tell where it will end. Something much like a panic seems to have set in.[9]

Other observers enjoyed little more success in discovering credible motivations for the Exodus. "As to the causes of the simultaneous stampede," wrote one witness, "no definite account can be obtained. It is one of those cases where the whole thing seemed to be in the air, a kind of migratory epidemic."[10] A Northern white noted that "the timid learned that they could escape what they have come to regard as a second bondage, and they flocked together to gain the moral support which comes from numbers."[11] For another witness, the Exodus seemed "a sort of religious exaltation, during which they had regarded Kansas as a modern Canaan and the God-appointed home of the negro race."[12]

As hundreds of millenarians arrived in St. Louis on nearly every boat from the South, reporters first sought the cause in some kind of trickery. Indeed, early headlines cried, "Duped Darkies!"[13] At first it seemed that a circular had fooled the Blacks into believing the Kansas Fever idea, and the Exodusters' illiteracy aggravated the confusion around the elusive flier. Only one handbill actually turned up; it was issued by a Black labor contractor in Vicksburg, warning them not to be taken in by rumors of free transportation, land, and so forth. The circular only proved that it responded to an already pervasive Kansas Fever idea.

As the Exodus surged on, observers discovered and discarded a whole panoply of so-called causes, ranging from supposed railroad promotional fliers to an obvious burlesque of a Kansas handbill by "Lycurgius P. Jones."[14] When the first apparent causes of the Exodus, "lying circulars," led to a dead end, Exodus-watchers turned to "rascally colored politicians," and "emigration agents" who supposedly misled the colored people with false promises about Kansas. According to these arguments, the Blacks naively believed them all, as they had a "childlike confidence in their chosen leaders, founded partly on their primitive character."[15] But false leaders were not the answer, and there was only one real emigration agent.

The Exodus had no anointed leader. Rather than being deluded by false leaders, the Exodusters rejected leadership altogether. "We have found no leader to trust but the God overhead of us," said a typical group of Exodusters.[16] In New Orleans, a prospective migrant summed up their position: "Every black man is his own Moses now."[17] Exodusters refused to hear out prominent Blacks who contradicted their beliefs. William Murrell, a popular political figure in Madison Parish, Louisiana, found that he could not reason with millenarians about their belief in the Kansas Fever myth, even though he had visited Kansas and could offer firsthand information. He opposed the movement, and the Exodusters ignored him.[18]

In Texas, millenarians regarded a "representative colored man," C. P. Hicks, with extreme skepticism as he tried to disprove the Kansas Fever idea. A white friend of Hicks wrote Governor John P. St. John of Kansas:

> When Mr. Hicks read your Excellency's letter—written some ten days ago—to a large meeting of the freedmen telling them Kansas had no free land, etc., it fell like a wet blanket upon the hopes of a large class of freedmen. Many declare the letter a forgery, while others think that Hicks' misrepresentations to you, induced you to write it. . . . Now there are not any of the leading colored men here who has more influence over the masses of their people than Mr. Hicks really has, but the very moment he or other colored leaders, throw themselves against the popular wishes and tide of sentiment of their people—right then their influence begins to ebb.[19]

Once the Kansas Fever idea gained a considerable following, ministers dared not express their own misgivings or convey the reservations of Exodusters who had gone to Kansas and now counseled others at home to wait. The Reverend Mr. Middleton of the Mount Hebron Baptist Church in Vicksburg would not read letters counseling patience from the pulpit, because "the members of his congregation would not like it. They were impatient and angry at everybody who tried to interfere with them."[20] And in New Orleans, an observer learned of a fruitless attempt to dampen Kansas Fever: "An influential colored man had tried at the last emigration meeting to temper the excitement of the people, and a motion to give him a vote of thanks for attending and addressing the meeting was denied . . . had the speaker been a less popular man, he would have been mobbed."[21] "When one tries to reason with and warn them against Kansas," wrote a Northern white who had tried to correct Exodusters' unreasonable expectations, "if they fail to excuse their act of leaving home in a matter-of-fact speech, they resort to religion and the laws of destiny. If you tell them they will die, they answer as a soldier who goes into battle, that they know some must die."[22] Millenarians still clung to their faith, despite well-intentioned advice and attempts at dissuasion.

Unscrupulous leadership was not at the heart of the Exodus, nor were "emigration agents," the favorite explanation of the Southern white press. Most often the "emigration agents" were merely local Blacks asking themselves why, indeed, they should stay in the South. But various Black men, and a Madame Walker in Texas, traveled about, lecturing on the Exodus.[23] James Caldwell even wrote to President Hayes for validation of his work:

> I am well received by the Colored people. They have been hoping for such terms as I offer them to move to Kansas, for they are, many of them, in distress notwith-standing they have made the wealth of the South for which they now receive no

thanks. They are treated by the white people as though they were under obligations to the whites.

I left the State of Louisiana the 1st of May where we were badly treated by the white people. Four of us, the writer one of them, was taken out of the Church and beaten until the blood ran down our backs. We did more good work in Mississippi. I ask you for authority over your own signature (if you deem such necessary) to continue to address the Colored people and advise them to go to Kansas.[24]

Caldwell's is a unique case, however, for he was an admitted emigration agent, offering "terms" for prospective migrants. Later on, in the summer and fall, when the Kansas Fever Exodus was widely known, swindlers and con men moved through areas where the fever prevailed, taking advantage of the interest and confusion surrounding the subject. Then, ill-informed Blacks were susceptible to hoaxes.

As an original stimulus to the Exodus, the role of drummers was negligible; at most, they may have helped keep the Exodus going. Terrorism and poverty lay at the root of the Exodus, and a Black Mississippian identified them as the reputed emigration agents: "The National government has stood idly by and refused to protect us against lawlessness, and to-day the blood of 5000 innocent colored martyrs calls from the ground and arouses us to action. These are the 'agents' and 'free homes.'"[25]

White observers of the Exodus finally came to realize what Blacks had known all along: no frivolous motives propelled the phenomenon. The Exodusters' implacable determination not to return to the South, despite the cold and hunger, despite their discovery that there was no free transportation to Kansas and no free land, and despite offers of free transportation back to the South, etched a deep impression on witnesses. A St. Louis reporter, for instance, asked a woman with a child at her breast if she would consent to going back to the South. "What, go back!" she exclaimed. "Oh, no; I'd sooner starve here!"[26] The same firm refusal to return home marked a dialogue between an old man and the people who had come up with him, as they learned the empty reality of the Kansas Fever idea:

"Childer," addressed an aged darky to the rest of the company, "this genneman 'forms us what we have 'ready larned—that we've been fooled about that raillerd and land and mewl biz. And then this yar genneman asks us whether we'd not go back to Egypt. Childer, I've been gibben him de 'wing of old Missippi. I knows what you thinks, and I told him you'd rader jine hands and walk into Jordan's tide. And was I not right, childer?"

And the "childer" all said "yes."[27]

They had, after all, escaped the South.

From the very beginning of the Exodus, Black onlookers pointed to political terrorism as the immediate cause, and they cast about very little for additional motives. In fact, bulldozing offered an entirely sufficient explanation. Most of the Exodusters interviewed by reporters and refugee-relief workers could provide firsthand accounts of blood-chilling violence within the last few years. At a mass meeting held on March 17 by

St. Louis Blacks to collect money, food, and clothing for the Exodusters stranded there, the very first addresses were given by migrants from the South. A former state senator from Louisiana, Andrew Pollard, stressed that Exodusters were not migrants, but refugees "fleeing from oppression and bondage."[28] The Reverend J. D. Daniels, also from Louisiana, explained that Exodusters "were not emigrating because of inducements held out to them by parties in Kansas, but because they were terrorized, robbed, and murdered by the bulldozing desperadoes of Louisiana and Mississippi."[29] And Blacks persistently stressed this theme throughout the life of the movement.

Once they understood that Exodusters were not duped into leaving their homes by unprincipled leaders or emigration agents, some whites began listening to their stories of terrorism. But Exodusters' testimonies concerning bulldozing showed that the violence which had occurred in the immediate past—such as the hanging of two Black men in Vicksburg at the beginning of the movement—was a white response to the Exodus, not its cause; planters attempting to stop the Exodus assassinated men whom they suspected of encouraging the movement.[30] An Exoduster from Warren County, Mississippi, told of an incident in Grand Gulf in which a mob of thirty-five whites tried to stop Blacks from going to Kansas by seizing them at night and beating them.[31] Such Exodus-inspired crimes recurred as whites sought to halt the migration, but, as one might expect, the result was just the opposite of the perpetrators' intentions.

In addition to violence directly related to the Exodus, millenarians told of bulldozing incidents stretching back over several years. Of particular import was the violence that had occurred in the northern parishes of Louisiana and adjacent areas in Mississippi in 1878. Frederick Marshall, from Natchez, Mississippi (right across the river from Vidalia in Concordia Parish), told of being taken out of his house by nightriders:

> Just before Christmas, 1878, three or four men came to my house to kill me, and I run out of the way; just before daylight they came there and wanted matches; after they came in the house I ran out doors and staid out the rest of the night; they went away; didn't know the men; they said they would kill me, and had a rope around my neck, and said they were going to kill all the smart men, and I told them I didn't know anything.[32]

Marshall arrived in St. Louis in mid-March 1879, and his fairly representative testimony merits closer scrutiny.

Marshall's immediate reaction to violence was very much like that of other rural Blacks—he left home to hide in the woods. When the trouble passed, he returned home. He did not immediately take his family to the riverbanks and flee to Kansas. He left months later, citing terrorism as one of his main reasons for going. For Frederick Marshall, as for most Exodusters, bulldozing was a basic, but not immediate, cause for leaving Mississippi. The immediate cause was a vivid fear of future violence, stemming from remembrance of past terrorism. The memory of bulldozing combined with the memory of slavery to produce the threat of evils to come. That threat goaded the Exodusters forward with urgency.

Their fear of future evil and their dread of renewed slavery were intertwined. The Reverend W. D. Lynch, who worked extensively with Exodusters in Kansas, believed that "the mainspring of all this exodus movement" lay in the conviction of Blacks in the South that "slavery is not dead, but sleeping in disguise, as [if] it were a wolf in sheep's clothing."[33] Other freedpeople felt that the Democrats would reinstitute slavery, making it impossible for Blacks ever to leave the South. Henry Adams voiced this common fear that "the Democrats, as the Slave Holders, of the South will fix it so that we can not get from the South to the North unless we run away, for we Believed that not any colored man will be allowed to Leave the South without a Pass."[34] One migrant saw the resurgence of the Democratic party as motivating the Exodusters' urgent flight:

Dere wan't no time to lose. A little while back de Democrats got hold o' one end o' Congress, an' now dey's got de odder end. The Democrat party was de party dat kep' us in slavery, an' de Republican party was de party dat sot us free. When de party dat set us free goes out, an' de party dat kep' us in slavery comes in, it's time for de nigger to look out for himself. Constitutional Amendments an' all dem things us very nice for de white man to talk about, but it's mighty risky business for us.[35]

Bulldozing, slavery, Democratic government, Blacks knew all three from hard experience, and that knowledge propelled the Exodus.

The Kansas Fever idea offered a helping hand to the very poor, who would otherwise languish in the South, condemned to damnation; for no matter how urgently Blacks sought to leave the South, without money they were doomed to stay. An itinerant Black preacher described their frustrations: "We colored people have heard from that country [Kansas], and we are very anxious to go there." Even though they had labored since the end of the war, he explained, "we never realize a nickle from our cotton. The white folks take all."[36] Blacks had been saying this for years. A young Black woman in Mississippi summarized their predicament: "The way we are paid for labor in Miss. there will be very few of us that will be able to come without aid."[37] The Kansas Fever idea provided the promise of that aid.

The various rumored permutations of the Kansas Fever idea puzzled observers who were often at a loss to understand the causes of the Exodus.[38] They went wrong in examining the content of the rumors and the idea, and in trying to match them to the movement that seemed to follow. But the import of the Kansas Fever idea was not to be found in the exact nature of its promises, but in their function. The existence of the idea provided a means for leaving the South that impoverished Exodusters otherwise would have lacked entirely. It served as an enabling factor, supplying the missing link between renewed slavery and assured freedom, and closing the yawning chasm between what some Exodusters deemed the "young hell" of Mississippi and Louisiana and the "promised land," Kansas. This explains why when Exodusters learned on the Mississippi River banks or in St. Louis that there was no free transportation, no free land, no General Sherman, and no Negro state, it made no difference whatsoever. They still meant to leave the South, and once disembarked in St. Louis, they would not go back.

St. Louis occupied a pivotal position in the mythology of the Exodus. It linked the two parts of the idea, negative and positive, slavery and freedom. The first step, and the most decisive, took Exodusters out of the South, beyond the grasp of re-enslavement. Arriving in Kansas, where there had never been any slavery and where salvation awaited, represented the final step. If they only got out of the South, Exodusters would automatically reach Kansas on the strength of their belief in the idea. The crucial point was St. Louis. When Exodusters reached that city they were out of danger: they had done their part. St. Louis was like the Red Sea, explained an Exoduster, drawing a parallel between Southern Black people and the Israelites:

> . . . we's like de chilun ob Israel when dey was led from out o' bondage by Moses. De chilun ob Israel was a promised to be sot free by Pharoah, but wen Pharoah got over his skear he sot 'em back agin to makin' bricks out o' straw. Den Moses he said dat shouldn't be de case, an' he took 'em out o' bondage, and wen dey was all awaverin' an' mighty feared he took 'em 'cross de Red Sea an' den dey was safe. Now chile, jes' listen to me. Dis is our Red Sea, right hyah in St. Louis, atween home an' Kansas, an' if we sticks togeder an' keeps up our faith we'll git to Kansas and be out o' bondage for shuah. We's been sot free by Massa Linkum, but it war jes' sich another sot free as Pharoah gib de chilen of Israel. You heah me, chile, dem as is awaverin' an' is a'feared is goin' to sink in dis hyah Red Sea. . . .[39]

To reach safety, they needed only to stick together and keep up their faith.

The Old Testament analogy has long held special significance for American Black people, and the identification of Afro-Americans with the Children of Israel transcends the Kansas Fever Exodus. The themes of "Black Moses," "Go Down Moses," "Let My People Go," "The Land of Bondage," and so forth are still familiar and evocative. In the Kansas Fever Exodus, Kansas was often termed the "Negro Canaan," or the "Promised Land." Beyond providing colorful terminology for the Exodus, the identification between Blacks and the biblical Chosen People enhanced many Blacks' conviction that the time had come for them to be taken out of the South. Many anticipated that day's arrival as simply a matter of time. A white Texan termed this conviction "religious fanaticism" and said many hard-working Black men he knew refused to buy real property in the South "because they have believed since their emancipation some general movement would eventually be made to take them out of the South. . . . all freedmen seemed to be embued with the idea that God has foreordained that they shall be made a great people whereby he will manifest to all nations His great power, etc."[40] These beliefs and expectations reinforced Kansas Fever, for they laid the groundwork for the time when the move would be possible. The Kansas Fever Exodus was the fruit of faith in an idea, but the Exodusters' belief was functional, selective, and strong. Yet it was no match for the determination of white Southerners and St. Louis merchants to stem the tide of migration before the region was emptied of its traditional work force and its agricultural economy ruined.

From the first moment Exodusters appeared on the banks of the Mississippi River on their way to Kansas, Southern whites tried to halt the movement. Newspapers ran letters from railroad companies insisting that they offered free transportation to the purchasers of their land but to no others. Later, letters from migrants unhappy in Kansas filled column after column. But this propaganda effort was no more effective than face-to-face conversations with Exodusters.

To keep Exodusters at home, white Southerners resorted to several techniques, most of which were not as gentle as verbal persuasion. Yet the planters' two favorite methods, imprisonment for debt and brute force, did not significantly impede the Exodus. In the end, only the refusal of riverboats to stop for Exodusters and their slow starvation on the banks of the Mississippi broke the movement's momentum.

For the entire duration of the Exodus, Blacks arriving in St. Louis and Kansas described coercive measures used to frustrate their departure. In March, for instance, an Exoduster testified that early in the month two Black men were waiting near Greenville, Mississippi, to take a steamboat to St. Louis. They were accosted by a number of whites who talked to them about their going away. "The leading man among the whites was one Charlie Smith," said the Exoduster, "and they killed one of the colored men and the other ran off; they killed him because he wanted to go to Kansas."[41] Exodusters repeatedly reported incidents of this nature, but while they lamented the misfortunes of their comrades, they were not deterred from leaving. Similarly, Exodusters whose property was attached for trumped-up debts came away propertyless rather than remain in the South. One Exoduster said that his mules had been taken by a deputy sheriff and twenty-five armed men, but he nevertheless boarded the boat—ten miles below his original point of departure.[42]

Arresting a would-be Exoduster for breach of contract was another procedure commonly used to disrupt the Exodus, according to a north Louisiana Black man, J. H. Cox. (Contracts ran from January to January, and the Exodusters were leaving in March, April, and May.) When an Exoduster was taken to jail, the jailer stripped him of his money and did not return it on his release. Since he would have been carrying all his money in anticipation of paying his family's passage to St. Louis, this method was unquestionably effective in keeping individual families at home, at least for the time being. Two of Cox's personal acquaintances suffered this fate, and he reckoned that about a dozen other men were in the same straits in the Tensas Parish jail.[43]

While this piecemeal obstruction could not bar thousands from going to Kansas, their utter inability to get passage to St. Louis did. In late April and May, steamboats simply refused to pick up Exodusters. This policy lasted no more than about a month, but it disturbed the impetus of the salvationist movement. Prospective Exodusters were stranded for weeks on end on the river; local white merchants refused to sell them food, and health authorities harassed and dispersed them. In late April an observer counted twenty-four different camps of Blacks "with their poor, battered and tattered household goods stacked up, waiting for a boat to give them the transportation they were capable of paying for." Many of them evidently had come long distances to reach the Mississippi; "with barely enough money to pay their steamboat passage, and the white people along the shore refusing them the ordinary necessaries of life, and they having no provisions of their own capable of lasting them a day or two, they are scattered along the banks of the broad Mississippi, famishing." The Exodusters' efforts to hail riverboats were futile:

The encampments all had hailing-signals up for the north-bound steamboats, and when these wildly, frantically waved signals were cruelly ignored while the boat proceeded complacently on its way, I saw colored men and women cast themselves to the ground in despair, and heard them groan and shout their lamentations.

What is to become of these wretched people God only knows. Here were nearly half a thousand, refused, scattered along the banks of the mighty Mississippi, without shelter, without food, with no hope of escaping from their present surrounding, and hardly a chance of returning whence they came.[44]

Despite the difficulty of stopping the St. Louis packets, the Exodusters waited and hoped. On April 23, a group of about ten families from the area of Lake Concordia, just inland from the Mississippi River, camped at the landing at Vidalia. Their numbers increased as other families joined them, but three weeks later they still had not succeeded in stopping a boat to St. Louis. Across the river at Natchez-under-the-hill, a camp of about 150 people suffered similar frustrations.[45] On the Mississippi side of the river, camps of 100 to 150 Exodusters each waited at Skipwith's Landing and Bullit's Bayou; on the Louisiana side, equally large camps waited at Delta, Waterproof, and Good Hope.[46] Up and down both sides of the Mississippi, from Greenville to Natchez, "the number of would-be Kansas emigrants increase," reported a witness. "Almost every landing has its camps of devoted colored people looking longingly down the river for the approach of a steamer that will carry them to the promised land."[47]

In mid-May, Thomas W. Conway estimated that the largest numbers of Exodusters camped at five landings: 200 at Vidalia, 300 at Buttonwood Bayou, 500 at Bass Bayou, 250 at Bonant, and 300 at New Carthage. Many others still waited in smaller camps.[48] From Concordia Parish, Louisiana, an Exoduster wrote to the postmaster of Topeka that members of his camp had "hailed boats but they wont stop. The Democrats have monopolized the thing."[49] At the Leota and Carolina landings in Washington County, Mississippi, about one hundred miles above Vicksburg, 150 Exodusters armed themselves to seize a northbound steamer to take them to Kansas.[50] And at Natchez, Exodusters had the Republican collector of customs write the United States attorney general on their behalf.[51]

Exodusters stranded on the riverbanks for long periods suffered terribly from exposure, and J. H. Cox noted that "some who have had a right smart of money have disposed of a good deal of it in taking care of themselves."[52] Conway's scheme of chartering boats to go up the river aimed to correct this pitiable situation. Then the boats finally relented, threatened with the Conway plan and lawsuits against their discriminatory actions (the steamboats were common carriers regulated by provisions of the Civil Rights Act of 1875). Nevertheless, the burdens imposed by weeks of waiting forced many hundreds to seek subsistence near the banks of the river and postpone migration to Kansas. The millenarian Exodus subsided, its momentum interrupted, and nearby planters wasted no time in tapping the pools of needy working-class Blacks. They sent recruiters and labor agents, whom Cox considered unprincipled hypocrites, to lure or force the disappointed Exodusters to work:

These people [the Exodusters] are visited every day by people of their own race, who are employed by planters and merchants to persuade them to stay and go back on the plantation. The refugees have put up rails and ropes to keep these agents out of their camps. I know of one or two instances where, after refugees had started, their wagon and clothes were taken away, but were returned to them on condition that they would remain South. These very agents would leave themselves, if they did not expect to make money from the planters and merchants by keeping the emigrants back.[53]

What stopped the Kansas Fever Exodus was not the discovery that there was no free transportation or land in Kansas, nor the fulminations and proclamations printed in Southern newspapers, nor the advice of "representative colored men," nor the suffering that Exodusters experienced on the banks of the Mississippi River, in St. Louis or in Kansas. Trickery and murder could not stay the Exodusters. Only the physical impossibility of keeping body and soul together during the long wait broke the back of the Kansas Fever Exodus. Once the boats began picking up migrants again later in the summer, the movement revived. But the urgent, millenarian Kansas Fever Exodus had closed. Migration steadily continued well into 1881, but never again was it as massive or sudden as it had been in the spring of 1879.

After the intensive spring migration, Exodusters trickled out of Mississippi and Louisiana by the tens, instead of by the hundreds. Except for a spasm of Kansas Fever activity in late July and early August in Louisiana, Mississippi, and Texas (and in Texas in the winter of 1879–80), the millenarian aspect of the migration ended in May 1879. Migrants flowed from the three states into Kansas and the Midwest for over a year, but they planned their moves. In August 1879 there was a reflux of Exodusters from Mississippi and Louisiana to Texas, via Kansas.[54]

Migration from Texas exhibited the same characteristics as the earlier migration from Mississippi and Louisiana, in both its millennial and nonmillennial phases. Exodusters left the heavily Black ("Senegambian") counties of east-central Texas: Washington, Burleson, Grimes, Nacogdoches, Walker, and Waller. From Texas, Exodusters either went by railroad from Denison and Sherman to Parsons, Kansas, or by wagon across Arkansas and part of the Indian Territory. Since the distance was only about three hundred miles from northern Texas to Kansas, Texas Exodusters suffered rather less than did their predecessors who had passed through St. Louis. Between November 1879 and March 1880, an estimated three to four thousand Texas Exodusters arrived in Kansas.[55]

The Kansas Fever Exodus very possibly represents the first massive millenarian movement in this country.[56] The extraordinary magnitude of the Exodus, its lack of central leadership, and the nationwide charity efforts it called into play all combined to bring it tremendous publicity. The nation's public figures and newspapers were forced to take positions on the Exodus if they had any connection with partisan politics or with Blacks at all. A Senate select committee investigated the causes of the move. The Exodus also spurred nonmillenarian Blacks to consider seriously migrating to Kansas to better their condition. In sharp contrast to the Kansas Fever Exodusters, they proceeded deliberately and cautiously.

．．．．

No more than a hazy picture emerges of the Exodusters in Kansas after 1879.[1] But letters, oral testimony, newspaper articles, census data, and two reports support tentative conclusions about the Exodusters' fate. In early 1880 roughly fifteen thousand migrants still remained in Kansas. Of that number, one estimate counted between four and five thousand who had come during the spring 1879 Kansas Fever Exodus. Most of the fifteen thousand migrants worked as laborers, on farms, in industry (especially on the railroads or in the mines), or as domestics and washerwomen. Another reporter estimated that about one third were on farms, one third in towns, working and saving to purchase land, and one third employed on a daily or weekly basis. Exodusters had bought or entered approximately twenty thousand acres of land, of which about three thousand acres were broken. Discounting the unusually severe weather over the Christmas holidays, the mild winter of 1879–80 proved a great boon for the Exodusters, for they were ill-clad and had few teams. "God seed dat de darkeys had thin clothes," remarked an Exoduster preacher, "an' He done kep' de cole off." It was possible to plow most of the time, and in Graham County, Black settlers plowed virgin prairie with ordinary spades.

About one fourth of the migrants arriving between the summer and winter of 1879 came with some money, and they took up land immediately. The minority of migrants able to put in crops before the 1879 growing season closed fared reasonably well the following year, purchasing land and sometimes even putting aside small savings. During the first year, the Exodusters accumulated property and money worth roughly $40,000, or, had it been evenly spread, some $2.25 per person. While this was an encouraging figure, it was little enough. Additionally, that sum was unevenly divided, with those migrants who arrived penniless (and such migrants continued to arrive through the winter of 1879–80) likely to continue in precarious financial straits.[2]

Economically, the Exodusters remained relatively poor, but many of them thought themselves better off than they had been in the South. And as early as January 1880 a correspondent surveying the Exodusters' fortunes discovered that they found in Kansas "the first real prosperity which has ever come to their race in America."[3] By 1886, according to a Kansas Bureau of Labor and Industrial Statistics report, a small sample of Exoduster heads of household in Wyandotte (Kansas City, Kansas) were earning an average of $262.75 annually, while comparable white laborers were averaging $333.09 per year. Nearly all the Exoduster wives worked, usually as washerwomen, and the combined incomes of husband and wife brought the yearly average to $363.28. About three quarters of the families owned their own homes. Yet, several of the Exodusters reported difficulties in finding steady work, and this may explain the tremendous mobility of the Exodusters in the years immediately following 1879.[4]

George H. Hardy experienced the mobility and frustrations common to Exodusters in Kansas. In 1879 Hardy arrived in Kansas from Texas with $250. He settled first in Emporia, about fifty miles southwest of Topeka, then three months later he moved west and took up farmland. He left the farm in May 1880 ("I was not able to stane the famine,") and then went to Parsons, in the extreme southeast. In Parsons his children, like other Black Texan children, were consigned to a separate school. By 1882 Hardy wearied of the color line and wanted to "com home" to Liberia. He and another Exoduster from Texas started out for Africa, via New York, but they ran out of money in Chicago. Hardy went to work, his wife sickened and died, and he too grew ill. When finally he got on his feet again, he decided to stay in Chicago.[5] Hardy did not discover an interest in Liberia in Parsons by accident, for that city witnessed considerable emigration activity in the early 1880s. In fact, George Charles, a migration activist in Mississippi from 1876, corresponded with the American Colonization Society in 1881–82 and sustained interest in Liberia well into the 1880s.[6]

Former Exodusters in Parson, Topeka, and Wyandotte encountered difficulty in obtaining steady work although they were fairly well paid when they found it. Some families were never able to save enough money to take up homesteads or buy land, for lack of long-range, remunerative employment. Others floundered in both attempts, and the agricultural depression that afflicted the New West in the late 1880s only aggravated their problems. The Nicodemus Colony in Graham County, for instance, knew its greatest business-flush times in the mid-1880s, with good rainfall and high expectations that the railroad would pass through the town. But the rain dried up, the railroad stopped short of Nicodemus, and the boom burst. Yet, the population of Nicodemus continued to grow slowly until 1910.[7] Nicodemus's growth, like that of the Black population in Kansas after the early 1880s, depended on natural increase rather than on new migration from the South.

After the very early 1880s there seems to have been a limited, secondary migration out of Kansas, especially to Nebraska and Oklahoma. A brief movement of Blacks from St. Louis and Kansas into Nebraska increased by nearly 2,000 the number of Southern-born Blacks in the state, according to the 1890 census, and this trend was followed in the succeeding decade by a decrease of some 1,100 of the Black Southern-born population. In the meantime, the same decade witnessed a sizable jump in Black Southern-born population in Oklahoma territory, about 3,350, some of whom came from Kansas.

In the 1890s the Indian Territory was opened for settlement, and E. P. McCabe, one of the leading Black figures of Nicodemus and Kansas, went to what would become Oklahoma in hopes of creating a Black, politically autonomous area—perhaps a state. He had been elected state auditor of Kansas but was eased out of office in the mid-1880s. McCabe and other migrants noticed that the rising tide of racism in the United States in the late nineteenth century affected Kansas, too.[8]

Racism in Kansas was not entirely novel in the 1880s and 1890s, for the massive influx of Blacks in 1879 had inspired some limited resentment among white Kansans. They feared that large numbers of Blacks would turn the tide of white migration from Kansas to Nebraska and Minnesota. (It did not have that effect at all.) Whites also thought Blacks were "immoral" and that the association of Black and white children in schools would somehow harm white children.[9] In the cities, but not in the rural areas, segregated schools had long been the rule, even before the Kansas Fever Exodus vastly increased the state's Black population.

By 1900 Blacks in Kansas were generally, if not overwhelmingly, more prosperous than their counterparts in the South; politically they were enormously better off. Although they might not enjoy their civil rights to the extent that white Kansans did, they were far freer and less discriminated against than were their peers in the South. Kansas was no Canaan, but it was a far cry from Mississippi and Louisiana. Relative to those states, Kansas was better in the 1880s and still better in the 1890s and early twentieth century. The sad fact was that first-class citizenship existed nowhere in this country for Afro-Americans. Any Black movement seeking real freedom within America was destined to realize no more than a relative measure of success. To the degree that the Exodusters aimed to escape the South and the specter of reenslavement, they succeeded. All in all, the Exodus to Kansas was a qualified but real success.

Although the Exodus of 1879 shared the effect of removing significant numbers of Blacks from the South with the Great Migration of the First World War years, the resemblance ends there. The Exodus was a rural-to-rural migration, at least in intent, whereas the later movement was rural-to-urban. After the turn of the century, the Afro-American quest for land subsided, or turned into a hunt for jobs. In a sense, then, the Exodus was atavistic, for the fundamental drift of American population in the late nineteenth and the twentieth century was toward the cities. Although the Exodus may have had limited demographic impact, politically it spoke volumes.

The Exodus presented proof that Afro-Americans did not quietly resign themselves to the political or economic order of the Redeemed South. They cared that their civil rights were extinguished; they missed public school education for their children; they minded that they were victimized economically unless they bargained away some of their rights. But lacking the classic tool for public redress—the reasonably independent exercise of the vote—their best alternative was flight. Exodusters on their way to Free Kansas said no, we do not acquiesce in Redemption; we do not believe that this is the way of American democracy. Yet, of the more than six million Blacks subjected to Southern rule, only a few thousand acted on their faith that a Promised Land of freedom and equality might exist for them somewhere in this country.

NOTES

*Chapter 11. Liberia Fever*

2. Harrison N. Bouey to the Reverend Henry N. Turner, Edgefield, South Carolina, May 23, 1877. *Am. Col. Soc. Papers,* Ser. IA, 227: 142.

13. Philadelphia *Christian Recorder,* April 18, 1878. The *Christian Recorder* was the organ of the African Methodist Episcopal Church and the most respected Black newspaper of the time.

*Chapter 15. The Kansas Fever Exodus of 1879*

1. The actual number of Exodusters who passed through St. Louis and reached Kansas, however briefly, is exceedingly difficult to figure. Charleton H. Tandy of the Colored Relief Board in St. Louis estimated that 20,000 Exodusters reached the city in 1879–80. (*Senate Report 693,* III: 68.) According to the St. Louis *Globe-Democrat's* figures, approximately 6,206 Exodusters arrived in St. Louis between mid-March and mid-April 1879. Not all the migrants to St. Louis made it from there to Kansas, and many reaching Kansas soon moved on, sometimes to Kansas City, Missouri.

2. C. P. Hicks to Governor St. John, Brenham, Texas, July 30, 1879, CRSF [Correspondence Received, Subject File], St. John, box 10, KSHS [Kansas State Historical Society].

3. *Hinds County Gazette,* November 27 and December 11, 1878; Columbus (Miss.) *Democrat* in the New Orleans Daily *Picayune,* December 20, 1878.

4. *Hinds County Gazette,* February 26, 1879.

5. Vicksburg *Herald,* February 28, 1879, quoted in St. Joseph *North Louisiana Journal,* March 8, 1879.

6. St. Louis *Globe-Democrat,* March 7, 13, 14, 16, 1879; New Orleans Weekly *Louisianian,* March 15, 1879; St. Joseph *North Louisiana Journal,* March 8, 1879. New Orleans *Louisianian,* March 15, 1879.

7. *Hinds County Gazette,* March 5, 1879.

8. St. Louis *Globe-Democrat,* March 18, 1879.

9. Cincinnati *Commercial,* quoted in ibid., March 26, 1879.

10. Chicago Daily *Tribune,* March 28, 1879.

11. James B. Runnion, "The Negro Exodus," *Atlantic Monthly* XLIV, no. 262 (August 1879): 223. Runnion was also an Exodus correspondent in Louisiana and Mississippi for the Chicago Daily *Tribune.*

12. F. R. Guernsey, "The Negro Exodus," *International Review* VII, no. 4 (October 1879): 375.

13. St. Louis *Globe-Democrat,* March 12, 1879.

14. Natchez Daily *Democrat,* April 19, 1879.

15. James B. Runnion, "The Negro Exodus," p. 228.

16. Chicago Daily *Tribune,* March 27, 1879. Each little group had someone who organized the actions of the group, but there was no one leader of the whole Exodus.

17. Ibid., March 23, 1879.

18. *Senate Report 693,* II: 258; St. Joseph *North Louisiana Journal,* March 8, 1879.

19. S. A. Hackworth to Governor St. John, Brenham, Texas, August 4, 1879, CRSF, St. John, box 10, KSHS. Hackworth pointed out the "suspicious ideas and character" of the millenarians.

20. Chicago Daily *Tribune,* May 2, 1879.

21. Ibid., May 23, 1879.

22. Ibid.

23. Denison Daily *News,* September 27, 1879.

24. James Caldwell to President Hayes, Bowling Green, Kentucky, June 26, 1879, Record Group 60, Department of Justice Source–Chronological Files, President, box 7. Caldwell was probably a combination labor contractor and migration conductor.

25. Samuel W. Winn, Enterprise, Mississippi, New Orleans *Southwestern Christian Advocate,* May 29, 1879.

26. St. Louis *Globe-Democrat,* March 14, 1879.

27. Ibid.

28. Ibid., March 18, 1879. Pollard was helping Exodusters bring their household effects to the river landings when a group of whites blamed the Exodus on him and forced him to board the boat with the Exodusters.

29. Ibid.

30. Ibid., March 31, 1879.

31. C. H. Tandy, *Senate Report 693,* III: 43.

32. Ibid., p. 53.

33. The Reverend W. D. Lynch, Topeka, Kansas, New Orleans *Southwestern Christian Advocate,* July 22, 1880.

34. Henry Adams to William Coppinger, New Orleans, Louisiana, April 28, 1879, *Am. Col. Soc. Papers,* Ser. IA, 234: 78. Apropos of having to steal away out of the South, a letter from Topeka, Kansas, printed in the Chicago Daily *Inter-Ocean* of December 30, 1879, reported the following: "The negroes who arrive here daily now almost all report that they did not dare make their intentions known before leaving the South, and in many cases that they have traveled by night on foot until the limits of their State were reached, fearing to travel by public conveyance."

35. New York Daily *Herald,* April 17, 1879.

36. The Reverend Henry Smith to Governor St. John, Marshall, Texas, May 7, 1879, CRSF, St. John, box 10, KSHS.

37. Roseline Cunningham to Governor St. John, West Point, Mississippi, June 1, 1879, ibid.

38. A rumor reported from Vicksburg, Mississippi, in March 1879 said that "the negroes in this part of the country have the 'Kansas Fever.' They have, in a manner, quit work, and are preparing to go to Kansas with Gen. Sherman, who is now in New Orleans with his troops, so they say. The report is that the United States Government has set Kansas apart as a negro State, and will give every family free land and $500 in money, build houses, etc., and all that are here after the 15th of March will be killed by order of President Hayes, who has turned Democrat." (New York *Tribune*, quoted in St. Louis *Globe-Democrat*, March 21, 1879.)

39. St. Louis *Globe-Democrat*, March 19, 1879.

40. S. A. Hackworth to Governor St. John, Brenham, Texas, August 11, 1879, CRSF, St. John, box 10, KSHS.

41. Thomas Carroll, *Senate Report 693*, III: 57.

42. George Halliday, quoted in Frank H. Fletcher, *Negro Exodus*, n.p., n.d. [Topeka, Kansas, April 1879], p. 20.

43. J. H. Cox, quoted in ibid., p. 15.

44. Cincinnati *Commercial*, quoted in Chicago Daily *Inter-Ocean*, April 25, 1879.

45. Natchez Daily *Democrat*, April 24, 27, and May 10, 14, 1879.

46. Chicago Daily *Tribune*, May 4, 10, 23, 1879.

47. Ibid., May 23, 1879.

48. Daily Memphis *Avalanche*, May 13, 1879.

49. Ellis Jones to postmaster of Topeka, Kansas, Point Pleasant, Louisiana, May 18, 1879, CRSF, St. John, box 10, KSHS.

50. New Orleans *Times*, May 6, 1879; Nashville Weekly *American*, May 8, 1879; Marshall (Texas) Tri-Weekly *Herald*, May 10, 1879.

51. E. J. Castello, Collector of Customs, Natchez, to U.S. Attorney General Charles Devens, Natchez, Mississippi, May 14, 1879, Record Group 60, Department of Justice Source–Chronological Files, Southern Mississippi, box 497.

52. J. H. Cox, quoted in Fletcher, *Negro Exodus*, p. 15.

53. Ibid.

54. Dallas *Herald-Commercial*, quoted in Brenham Weekly *Banner*, August 15, 1879; St. Joseph *North Louisiana Journal*, August 30, 1879.

55. New Orleans *Southwestern Christian Advocate*, December 4, 1879; Henry King, "A Year of the Exodus in Kansas," *Scribner's Monthly* XX, no. 2 (June 1880): 216.

56. The movement of slaves to Union lines during the Civil War possibly had some of the same millenarian overtones; certainly it was massive and looked to a millennial era of freedom that would totally change the lives of the followers.

*Epilogue*

1. Thomas C. Cox's Princeton dissertation, "Blacks in Topeka, Kansas, 1865–1900," analyzes one of Kansas's largest Black communities in considerable detail and includes coverage of the post-Exodus period.

2. Chicago Daily *Inter-Ocean*, October 10, 24, and December 31, 1879; January 2, 22, and February 7, 10, 1880. Manuscript census of 1880, passim. Henry King, "A Year of the Exodus in Kansas," *Scribner's Monthly* XX, no. 2 (June 1880): 213–15. This figure does not include what was given the Exodusters through charity, which touched approximately 8,000 migrants.

3. Chicago Daily *Inter-Ocean*, January 2, 1880.

4. Kansas, *First Annual Report of the Bureau of Labor and Industrial Statistics* (Topeka 1886), p. 255. I am grateful to Thomas C. Cox for bringing this report to my attention.

Material cited in Stephan Thernstrom's *The Other Bostonians, Poverty and Progress in the American Metropolis, 1880–1970* (Cambridge, 1973), pp. 225–27, sheds some additional light on horizontal mobility: "The only marked deviation from this pattern [persistence rates in the 40 to 60 percent range] appeared in the earliest years of settlement on the frontier, in which population turnover was exceptionally rapid. No more than a third of the adult male residents of newly opened farm areas remained there as long as a decade—whether it was Wapello County, Iowa, in the 1850s, Trempealeau County, Wisconsin, and various townships in eastern and east-central Kansas in the 1860s, Roseburg, Oregon, in the 1870s, Grant County, Wisconsin, between 1885 and 1895, or West Kansas from 1895 to 1905. After an initial period of extraordinary rapid reshuffling of the population, however, a distinct settling-in took place, and rural persistence rates tended to rise to the general level of those in cities."

5. George H. Hardy to William Coppinger, Parsons, Kansas, April 26, July 4, and September 28, 1882; November 1, 10, 1882, Chicago, Illinois, *Am. Col. Soc. Papers,* Ser. IA, 247: 54; 248: 10, 223; 249; 92, 108.

6. Chicago Daily *Inter-Ocean,* January 1, 1880; George Charles to William Coppinger, December 4, 11, 1881; January 6, March 10, and April 17, 1882, *Am. Col. Soc. Papers,* Ser. IA, 245: 195, 208; 246: 24, 206; 247: 41.

7. Glen Schwendemann, "Nicodemus: Negro Haven on the Solomon," *Kansas Historical Quarterly* XXXIV, no. 1 (Spring 1968): 29–31.

8. United States Bureau of the Census, *Negro Population, 1790–1915* (Washington, 1918), p. 68; Bittle and Geis, *The Longest Way Home: Chief Sam's Back-to-Africa Movement,* pp. 18–39; Rayford W. Logan, *The Betrayal of the Negro,* 2d ed. (London, 1965), p. 143; Mozel C. Hill, "The All-Negro Communities of Oklahoma," *Journal of Negro History* XXXI, no. 3 (July 1946): 260–62.

9. F. R. Guernsey, "The Negro Exodus," p. 377.

In his comprehensive study of the *Brown v. Board of Education* decision of 1954, Richard Kluger notes that the state of Kansas provided for the separation of the races in schools at the first meeting of its legislature. Later sections limited segregated schools to the larger cities, then extended them to smaller ones in 1867. Between 1876 and 1879, Kansas schools were desegregated, but in 1879, after the Exodus, they were resegregated on the elementary level in cities of more than 15,000. On the secondary level, however, integrated education remained the rule until 1905, when Kansas City was allowed to put Negro students in a separate high school. William Reynolds of Topeka brought the first (unsuccessful) suit against segregated schools in 1903. (Richard Kluger, *Simple Justice* [New York, 1976], pp. 371–72.)

# Found: The Lost Tribe of Black Jews

*In keeping with the sacred custom and rites of centuries, Harlem's Black Jews joined with their [white] co-religionists throughout the world in celebrating the 5702d anniversary of Jewish liberation from Egyptian bondage. Their observances started with the sounding of the Ram's Horn at sunset....*

—*NEWS ITEM*, AMSTERDAM-STAR NEWS

Some twenty years ago, when a slight, black, almost effeminate African Jew, who spoke Hebrew, Arabic, and German as well as English, gathered together eleven of his black *landsmen* to worship in a Harlem basement, the first Negro synagogue came into being in the Black Metropolis—and, more important, people suddenly became aware of the existence of thousands of Negro Jews scattered throughout the country.

In those days, I remember distinctly, sections of Harlem were essentially Jewish in character, abounding in kosher butcher shops, Yiddish theaters, Hebrew schools, and Jewish delicatessen stores. Lilly Daché was operating a popular hat shop on Lenox Avenue; Nettie Rosenstein was turning out dress creations off on a side street; and crowds gathered nightly for tasty snacks at The Pomerantz Delicatessen. Along the sidewalks, people stumbled over fat housewives who sat on chairs in an almost endless row, their amiable chatting punctuated occasionally by the shrill cry of a neglected baby. In the background hovered Stars of Zion, standing squat and sturdy above countless temples.

Yet the Black Jews were without adequate quarters for worship; nor were they lucky enough to inherit one of the deserted houses of prayer when the white Jews made a pell-mell exodus to the Bronx and Brooklyn as Negroes by the thousand surged into Harlem. Unable to raise the necessary sum to purchase one of the vacant temples, the Black Jews were forced to remain in their makeshift place of worship and watch the black Baptists take over the temples.

These were indeed the 'Jews without money!'

Today that hardy little band of Black Jews has expanded to a determined congregation of more than five thousand souls, known as the Commandment Keepers, and is living a rigid, self-sufficient communal life according to the solemn dictates of the Talmud. Independent of white Jews, they maintain a second-floor *schul*, Beth Hatphala Number 1, in the loft of a red-brick tenement on Lenox Avenue. Here a Talmud Torah,

In 1943, Roi Ottley was director of public relations for the National C.I.O. War Relief Committee.
Originally published as chapter 11 in Roi Ottley, *"New World A-Coming": Inside Black America* (New York: New World Publishing, 1943), 137–50.

or Hebrew school for Jewish children, is conducted in conjunction with the synagogue; and here, too, there is a Yeshiva, or college for adults and advanced students. The group supports a Beth Zekanim, a home for Jewish aged; maintains its own burial grounds, and controls a number of small businesses. From Friday sundown to Saturday sunset, men, women, and children abstain from all manner of work and assemble in their synagogue, passing the time in prayer.

Truckloads of nonsense have been written about Harlem cults. At first glance the congregation of Black Jews is often dismissed as yet another religious freak. Even Negroes ask, 'Why does a black man want to be a Jew, and pile more trouble on his head?' It may indeed seem a strange phenomenon to white people, if not downright fraud. But white Jewish circles acknowledge the existence of Black Jews and their kinship to the Jewish community. Rabbi Levinger, in his authoritative *The Story of the Jew,* describes them as a tribe 'who have almost forgotten their Judaism, and in every way but a few religious rites resemble the dark-skinned, thick-lipped [African] natives among whom they have lived so long.' Harlem's Black Jews, in the view of Jewish scholars, are the descendants of the Falashas, whose form of worship is distinct from white Jewry, influenced as it is by African culture. As far as I can learn, white and black Jews are branches of the same tree, with striking similarities as well as curious dissimilarities.

As to be expected, the history of the Black Jews goes back a long way. The legend—according to Jewish authorities—is that about twenty-six hundred years ago a band of Jews, fleeing from Palestine, which was then under the oppressive rule of the Babylonians, sought refuge in Egypt and along the cataracts of the Nile. They pushed on into the deserts of Africa and ultimately penetrated the highlands of Ethiopia, where they became known as Falashas, or outsiders. They designated themselves as Beth-Israel—the House of Israel.

The wanderings of this tribe are still clouded in obscurity. But it appears that from time to time the group was augmented by refugees whose lands had been conquered by the Romans, and toward the end of the fifth century, by others escaping the wars of the Ethiopians. These people gathered in the same province, almost the same centers, and fused finally into a single community. Protected by the mountains and supported by natives converted to Judaism (and assimilated), they evolved a small independent state, and this independence they maintained for hundreds of years. The Falashas played a prominent rôle in raising the material and intellectual standards of their adopted country by strict adherence to the faith of their forefathers. A self-reliant and self-supporting people, they earned their livelihood as farmers, blacksmiths, masons, potters, weavers, tanners, saddlers, and basket-makers; and others, curiously enough, as mercenaries. Until modern times, the Falashas were virtually the only skilled workers in Ethiopia.

When Christianity was adopted by Ethiopia in 333 A.D., the lot of the Black Jews changed radically. Thousands of them were ruthlessly slaughtered and many compelled to embrace the new religion. Others were driven from their lands and scattered in search of new abodes in more hospitable—and indeed more inaccessible—sections of Ethiopia. Century after century they persevered as Jews. Eventually the number of

Falashas, estimated originally at several hundred thousand, dwindled to a mere remnant. Many Jewish centers were completely dissolved, imperiling the continued existence of the entire Falasha community. Today only sixty thousand live in Ethiopia—a country in which every fourth person belongs to the priesthood. Traits that these long-isolated people have exhibited are those that their white co-religionists have come to accept as inherent characteristics of Judaism: cohesion, unity, industry, thirst for knowledge, long-suffering fortitude under persecution.

For centuries the Black Jews regarded themselves as the only surviving Jews, living in entire ignorance of the existence of any other Jews—white or black. Nor had world Jewry at large any inkling of the Falashas' existence in the hills of Ethiopia. They were first discovered by James Bruce, a Scotch traveler who brought the story back to London in 1790. Not until the early part of this century, when Doctor Jacques Faitlovitch, a European Jew, organized an expedition and penetrated the interior of that country, was the first actual contact made with them by European Jews. He reported to white Jewry when he returned that though their skins were 'black,' they 'possessed the characteristics of our [Jewish] race.' Family life, he said, was patriarchal; great respect for parents was shown by children; there were no bachelors, nor was concubinage or polygamy tolerated; and all professed the same faith, practiced the same customs, and everyone lived on a basis of equality. Soon after this journey, Faitlovitch founded a movement, according to his own words 'to further the efforts for the spiritual redemption of the Abyssinian Jews.' The movement was transferred to the United States in 1922, and the American Pro-Falasha Committee was organized and sponsored by prominent white Jews.

Besides the Falashas, there are three distinct tribes of Black Jews in existence—the Sudanese Jews, the Black Jews of Cochin, and the Beni Israel of India, apparently descendants of the Jews who migrated to Asia and Africa after the final destruction of Jerusalem. The Jews of Soudan are mainly a scattering of small tribes who resemble the Arabs. Moslems once called them Yahoodee, meaning Jews. A unique group are the Beni Israel—the Black Jews of India, who know very little of their own history. They are said to be the descendants of the Jews who were sent to India by King Solomon to capture elephants and to work in the gold mines. Today they are indistinguishable from the natives. Perhaps the most famous are the Black Jews of Cochin, with a strong Chinese strain, who live in Bombay, maintain a thriving temple and number about eight thousand. Unmistakable traces of Hebraic influence among the various African tribes are found to survive even to this day—evidence by the groups called 'Judaized tribes' and 'Judeo-Negroes,' whose existence helps to document certain survivals of Hebrewism among African Negroes.

Arrival of the first Black Jews in America probably coincides with the early days of colonization, when they might have been shipped here among other African captives to work the plantations. Only a rare handful was ever seen in this country. Yet as early as the turn of the last century, according to the records of the Common Council, Black Abyssinian Jews immigrated to the United States as free men to escape anti-Semitism abroad and opened a synagogue in lower Manhattan, where they observed freely all the traditions and customs of Judaism. There is no record of their ever having disbanded, nor is there any trace of their descendants. Whether they left this city to join a Zionist movement then active that sought to establish a Promised Land outside of Buffalo, or eventually were absorbed by the black population (or the white), is a moot question. But considerable speculation surrounds the fact that in 1808, in a wooden shack on Waverly Place, eighteen black men from Abyssinia started the Abyssinian Baptist Church, a Negro institution that is in lusty existence today.

It is obviously impossible to check the numbers of Black Jews that have entered the country. But a census taken in 1938 quoted by the *Jewish Family Journal,* and so far as I know the only one ever taken, estimates the Black Jewish population in New York City at ten thousand, and another hundred thousand scattered throughout the United States, in such principal centers as Salt Lake City, Cincinnati, Youngstown, Philadelphia, Newark, and St. Louis. There are perhaps a quarter-million living in the Western Hemisphere. Some authorities say that there are more than three million black adherents of the Jewish faith living in Africa today.

Until Hitler began to persecute the Jews in Germany, and American newspapers dramatized the atrocities, Harlem's Black Jews were denounced as imposters, fakers, and fools; their bearded rabbi was excluded from *Who's Who in Colored America,* and local wits irreverently called him Rasputin. The majority of white Jews hardly knew of their existence, nor was there any manifest concern when the fact was mentioned. The one Jewish organization aware of Black Jews had its eyes turned toward Addis Ababa, Ethiopia, where it was supporting a Hebrew school. Today, however, the Black Jews have gained status, a status born of the persecution of their white co-religionists. Their dignified rabbi, Wentworth Arthur Matthew, is frequently invited to conduct services in the white synagogues about the city, and he has been a candidate at the yearly elections for delegates to the American Jewish Congress. A few Negro Jews have been admitted to the Cantors' Association of America. The United Yeshivos Foundation, when raising funds for white Jewish colleges in recent years, has shown sympathetic interest in the educational work of the Harlem tribe. They also receive favorable attention from the Negro newspapers, which devote considerable space to reporting the events of the holy days. The Jewish press is no less interested nowadays. Before the holy days in 1941, one publication carried a full-page picture of the black rabbi on its Yiddish title page.

The organizer and spiritual head of Harlem's congregation, Rabbi Matthew, is a picturesque and attractive character. He is a grave, intelligent black man who appears to be about fifty years of age with the vigor of a man of thirty. He dresses in severe black— definitely unusual in Harlem—and wears the traditional yarmelke, or skullcap. He looks like one of the Negro figures in Rubens's *Bacchanale.*

His origins are humble. He was born of poor laboring parents in Lagos, British West Africa, center of a large colony of Black Jews, and was given the Hebrew name, Yoseh Ben Moshea Benyehuda. His father was a Falasha, or African Negro Jew, and his mother a Christian whose father had been a slave in Nevis, B.W.I., and had returned to Africa with his family when the British Emancipation Act freed him. The mother of Harlem's rabbi met and married the cobbler Benyehuda in Lagos. How Harlem's rabbi comes to have the name 'Wentworth Arthur Matthew' is plausible: English traders, finding the elder Benyehuda's name difficult to pronounce, called him simply 'Matthew's man,' after his white employer. His mother adopted the name after the death of her husband and her return to the West Indies with her son. Later, young Matthew tacked on the 'Wentworth Arthur' to give it an 'English sound.'

He is eminently prepared to lead his flock. Shortly after going to the West Indies, he left and came to New York, where he entered the Hayden Theological Seminary and later the Bishop Ecclesiastical School, both Christian institutions. But when he suddenly heard the 'call' to Judaism—a period he recalls as the most thrilling of his life—he enrolled at the Rose of Sharon Theological Seminary in Cincinnati, an institution once conducted by Falashas. He returned to Harlem in 1919 and organized the congregation of Commandment Keepers, of which he is now chief rabbi. Five years later he went abroad to study theology at the University of Berlin, on a scholarship obtained for him by an influential white rabbi. In his absence, Rabbi Arnold Josiah Ford, a Negro immigrant from Barbadoes, a Garvey follower who later migrated to Ethiopia to join his African co-religionists, carried on his work until 1927, when Rabbi Matthew returned to his flock and his rabbinical chores.

Harlem's Black Jews do not practice conversion, and in this they follow strictly the dictates of their faith—yet many of the followers are former 'Garveyites.' The chief factor in swelling the congregation—though Rabbi Matthew did not mention it—was the phenomenal growth in Harlem's Negro population. The law of averages alone would have brought a few Black Jews to the community, but hundreds seemed to have arrived to make their fortunes in the Black Metropolis. They came largely from the West Indies, where it is said more than a hundred thousand live, and from faraway Africa. To build the Commandment Keepers, I was told, only 'enlightening' was necessary, a fine distinction that Rabbi Matthew explained in an interview with the Pittsburgh *Courier*.

'The black man is a Jew,' he said, 'because he is a direct lineal descendant of Abraham. Isaac, son of Abraham, was father of Esau (whose skin was hairy, like the white man's) and of Jacob (whose skin was smooth, like the black man's).

'Jacob, also known as Israel, was the father of the Twelve Tribes, and King Solomon, son of David, was a great-grandson in the Tribe of Judah. King Solomon mated with the Queen of Sheba, who returned to Africa, where she bore him a son, known in Biblical history as Menelik I.

'When Menelik was thirteen years of age,' Rabbi Matthew continued, 'he was sent to Palestine to be confirmed. And at the age of twenty-four his father sent him to Ethiopia to colonize that country as part of the great King Solomon empire. That household has ruled continuously in Ethiopia for three-thousand-odd years. There has been an unbroken succession of six hundred and thirteen kings from Menelik I to the present Haile Selassie ("King of the Tribe of Judah"). Hence, all genuine Jews are black men.'

That the kings of Ethiopia have sworn allegiance to the Coptic Christian Church is a fact that Rabbi Matthew dismisses as the result of a diplomatic appeasement policy. This interpretation of their history settles the ancestry and racial loyalties of the Black Jews, and conditions their outlook upon the contemporary scene. For example, the Black Jews do not acknowledge themselves to be 'Negroes.'

'Don't submit meekly to being called a Negro,' Rabbi Matthew has been heard to admonish his flock. 'The Negro, so-called, has no history prior to the fourteenth century. And when that history began, it began in bondage, poverty, humiliation, and degradation. Insist on being called an *Ethiopian,* an *African,* or even an *Afro-American.* As such, yours is the most glorious history in the world. You are descended from kings, and the white man knows it. It is his purpose to keep you ignorant of your past so that he can exploit you. That is why he has falsified the history of the world.'

In practices of Judaism, however, there is little difference from white Jews. The rite of B'rith or circumcision is performed on the eighth day after the birth of a child. The ritual is done by white rabbis or mohelim only. It is in this one respect that Harlem's rabbi confesses to a lack of recognition. This rite, however, is the only one delegated to a white rabbi. Otherwise, Rabbi Matthew officiates at all religious services, appoints functionaries, and has the power of ordaining new rabbis. Besides himself, there are nine ordained Negro rabbis and two elders who assist in ministering to the Commandment Keepers.

At their *schul,* during the holy days, strict orthodox services are conducted by Rabbi Matthew, who recites much of the Hebrew Holy Scriptures from memory. He is assisted by a seventeen-year-old Negro cantor who sings the litany. To accommodate the entire membership of 5702, it is necessary to hold services from six o'clock in the morning until nine at night. Those who live in New Jersey, Brooklyn, Bronx, Long Island, or other outlying sections, and would have to travel to Harlem in violation of certain Jewish tenets, are provided with rooms above the synagogue so that they may stay overnight. A sprinkling of white Jewish merchants, who live in the neighborhood, often join their colored co-religionists in worship. (The white Rabbi Philip Goodman, of the Harlem Institutional Synagogue, at 37 West 116th Street—which serves white Jews primarily—reports that a number of unaffiliated Negro Jews attend his services, Hebrew school, and institutional activities.)

During the observance of Yom Kippur, the Day of Atonement and most sacred day in the Jewish religious calendar, the women attend services wearing white trailing veils; the men dress in ordinary business suits and wear their hats. When I attended the services, a soft light flickered from the ornamental Menorah, or seven-candle candelabra, and gave the low-ceilinged synagogue a quiet, subdued air—decidedly rare for Negro worship. But this loftiness was quickly dispelled when the whole congregation lifted its voice in the plaintive chant of the hallowed hymn, *Kol Nidre.* Suddenly, they flung their hands up in supplication—throwing startling shadows against the isinglass-covered windows. If you have seen the Reuben Mamoulian-directed 'Wake Scene' from *Porgy and Bess,* then you have a fair idea of what that temple was like.

Harlem's Black Jews, like their more successful white brethren, seek to be self-sufficient. They have built up fifty-odd business establishments that include cigar and stationery stores, tailor shops, laundries, a gas-range repair shop, and restaurants serving kosher dishes. They patronize almost exclusively stores owned by Jews, whether white or Negro; and wherever possible, Black Jewish merchants employ Jews. There is also a similarity of employments: the Negro Jews are garment workers, painters, plumbers, and carpenters; Rabbi Matthew himself once earned his living as a carpenter. A few are Yiddish-speaking dairy salesmen.

But from here sharply vivid differences enter: not one Black Jew is a night-club entertainer, musician, or actor—traditional occupations of the Negro that attract many white Jews. The bulk of them, unlike white Jews but like most Negroes, are employed as domestics—not as ordinary domestics, however; they are 'certified kosher cooks'(!) and carefully observe all the Jewish dietary laws, even to the use of separate dishes, towels, and soaps. But they work for orthodox Jews only. Few will accept employment with Reformed Jews because they do not maintain 'kosher homes.' Although the killing and preparation of meats is an all-important rite of Jewish life, there are no butchers in the congregation of the Commandment Keepers, so they must depend on the white kosher markets, which of course is little hardship.

'Not more than three or four Black Jews have ever received public relief,' Rabbi Matthew says in his proud comment on his congregation's self-sufficiency. 'And,' he adds, 'no member of our connection has ever been arrested for a felony or misdemeanor.'

These people are rational and law-abiding. They do not drink, fight, or quarrel among themselves. Nor will they quarrel with anyone else, particularly about their faith—in this respect, they follow their rabbi's solemn admonition not to argue religion. Nowadays there is, of course, general recognition and respect for their beliefs in the community. Negro Jewish children who attend the public schools of Harlem are excused from classes during the holy days like other children of the Jewish faith—the Board of Education makes no distinction between Black and white Jews. The Jewish youth move normally in the stream of community life, even to stomping at the Savoy Ballroom.

Negro characteristics curiously enough thread through their practice of Judaism (as witness 'certified kosher cooks'). During the Jewish holidays, bearded rabbis attired in orthodox ceremonial robes proudly lead the faithful in processions through the community, on their way to the Lenox Avenue temple. Through membership in Masonic lodges, affiliated with the Royal Order of Ethiopian Hebrews, they also march in colorful parades that provide the community with highlights during its marching season (from April to October). Through these lodges also they are in constant touch with other Black Jews throughout the country.

White and Black Jews draw their culture, religion, and philosophy from the same sources, yet they have little contact with each other, beyond perfunctory business and employer-employee relationships. There is of course an occasional social meeting. When the Educational Alliance staged a Yiddish show, *A Night in Harlem*, the Black Jews were invited. Certainly, no antagonism exists between the groups. Rabbi Matthew is frank to say, 'The white Jews regard us very, very sympathetically.' However, sheer principle makes the Black Jews prefer not to have social relationships with white Jews, an attitude that once caused their rabbi to be roundly criticized by the *Daily Forward*, a Jewish newspaper.

The Black Jews are particularly against 'crossing tribal traits.' This was the case when a white Jew approached Rabbi Matthew about his plans to marry a Negro woman of the Jewish faith. The marriage was opposed, as the amiable little rabbi put it, on the ground that 'Each of the Twelve Tribes of Israel should strive to preserve its own traits.' But when a Black Jewish woman sought to marry a white Jew, after assuring her rabbi that the prospective bridegroom earned sufficient money to support her in style, he sagely gave his approval and indeed performed the ceremony. 'Since she was outside the breeding age, I could give my consent without violating the unwritten law,' he explained blandly.

The Black Jews oppose intermarriage for a deeper and more significant reason, a reason they share in common with other Negroes of whatever faith. The exigencies of American life, they believe, make the conditions of such a relationship prohibitive. Yet, to be sure, they feel a genuine kinship to the white Jews—especially in the broad question of anti-Semitism, although they themselves have felt its lash in a minor way only. They are alarmed, too, by the anti-Jewish disclosures in recent years, because they feel that if anti-Semitism takes solid root in the United States, they will suffer doubly— 'Not only as Jews,' Rabbi Matthew says candidly, 'but even as so-called Negroes.'

In their efforts to stamp out anti-Semitism, the Black Jews have actively taken up the cudgels of white Jewry by holding anti-Nazi meetings in Harlem to bring the menace of Naziism and Fascism before the Negro public, and many have contributed to and participated in anti-Fascist organizations. Rabbi Matthew is quick to defend white Jews against the charge that they are exploiters of the Negro, and attributes the appearance of anti-Jewish feeling in Harlem to the careless expressions of street speakers, both white and Negro, who seek to capitalize upon the desperate condition of the Negro people.

'We are determined,' he says, 'to put our shoulders to the wheel and cooperate with white Jews in driving out anti-Semitism wherever it may be found in America; for in doing so we shall be protecting ourselves.'

Yet—to illustrate further the complex character of anti-Semitism in Negro life—the Black Jews have aligned themselves with organizations like the U.N.I.A., a principal source of anti-Semitic propaganda. They have participated in demonstrations held by this group, and seem not to be feazed by its anti-Semitic character nor by the frequent anti-Jewish utterances of its leaders. The reason for this apparent contradiction is that the Black Jews—like many of their co-religionists—seek a homeland. They await the Messiah who will re-establish a Negro nation—not a Jewish nation—through the re-demption of Africa. The U.N.I.A. still dangles before the Negro, Marcus Garvey's dream of an African utopia as a homeland for the black man; many Black Jews were formerly members of the Back-to-Africa Movement, and to them Africa, not Palestine, is the homeland of the Jew. So, captivated by the 'Black Zionist' character of the U.N.I.A., they regard its anti-Semitic features as merely incident to the larger, more compelling dream of Africa's redemption. And since the anti-Semitism of the U.N.I.A. does not by any means include *black* Jews, the Black Jews are apathetic to the broader implications of the movement's anti-Jewish propaganda.

The Black Jews, it appears, are more intensely Negro than Jew. Actually, the movement of the Black Jews in the United States largely has the form of the Jewish *Landsmann-shaften* organizations in its spirit of self-help and concern for the weak, needy, and oppressed. Whatever its true character and ultimate aims, the future of the Black Jews— inescapably identified as they are with the Negro people—is bound to the future of the black man. They apparently know this well!

# Strangers in the Holy Land

Dimona rises out of the Negev desert in dusty-brown apartment complexes. Old men sit in a small park near the central shopping mall, exactly as they sat in the sun of Poland or Russia, trading stories in the language of Europeans, their faces wrinkled with the indelible furrows of a difficult life lived elsewhere. The old men have much to talk about—but their conversation does not concern Israel's pressing economic problems or the controversial settlements in the West Bank. The old men talk about the blacks from the United States who live in the "slums" at the western edge of the city, who brought their American "ghetto" to Dimona. They talk about the Black Hebrews.

What began as a small black sect in Chicago has grown into a "nation" of nearly 2,000 members, following a charismatic leader as their "savior" and residing illegally in three Israeli towns on the edge of the Negev desert. The Black Hebrews have alarmed the Israeli Government by declaring themselves the "true" Jews, by denouncing the Israelis as mere "trustees" of the land and by vowing to replace them with thousands of blacks returning to the Promised Land.

By any definition, the Black Hebrews are not ordinary Jews but, rather, a strange cult. The rule of their 41-year-old leader, Ben-Ami Carter, is absolute. He has created a closed society that the Israelis have found difficult to penetrate, much less fully understand. Defectors have told Israeli authorities that some followers are held against their will within the sect, even mistreated. The United States Federal Bureau of Investigation believes that fugitives from the United States have taken refuge in the Dimona community after carrying out fraudulent schemes to raise money for the group.

The Black Hebrews' way of life has antagonized their Israeli neighbors and touched off open comparison with the People's Temple, the religious sect in Jonestown, Guyana, that was led to mass suicide in November 1978. Their presence has posed a dilemma for the Israelis, creating a fear of world criticism and protests by American blacks if the Government expels the cult from Israel. Today the issue seems no closer to a resolution than when the Black Hebrews first arrived, a decade ago.

If the early Hebrews wandered for 40 years in the desert, the Black Hebrews spent almost a decade in the wasteland of America's ghettos and Liberian encampments before reaching the Promised Land. They were inspired by Ben Carter, a young dropout from Chicago's tough Marshall High School, who in 1960 had attended a meeting of the

In 1981, Bill Kurtis was a reporter-anchorman for WBBM/TV in Chicago.

Original Hebrew Israelite Nation on the city's South Side. Carter's search for identity—at a time when a revolution in black consciousness was about to sweep the country—found answers among the teachings of the Torah, as interpreted for him by two black "rabbis." His teachers explained that the Black Hebrews were the direct descendants of the patriarchs Abraham, Isaac and Jacob and the 10 lost tribes, who had been exiled from Israel for their sins and condemned to wander throughout Africa until they were kidnapped and sold into slavery in America.

Two years later, at the age of 22, Ben Carter was ordained a "rabbi" in the Original Hebrew Israelite Nation and given a Hebrew name, Ben-Ami Carter. His preaching attracted a small following on Chicago's impoverished South Side, where he filled his sermons with quotations that established the "blackness" of the original Hebrews—for instance, Numbers 12: 1: "And Miriam and Aaron spake against Moses because of the Ethiopian woman whom he had married, for he had married an Ethiopian woman." Carter and his followers carried their message into the streets, gathering donations from merchants and sympathetic listeners.

In 1966, Carter announced that a vision from God instructed him to lead his people back to the Promised Land. Riots were sweeping the nation's cities, which Carter interpreted as evidence that Armageddon would soon destroy the United States. Blacks, however, would be saved by returning to the land of their birthright—Israel—led by their messiah, Ben-Ami Carter.

It was not a new dream. Bible stories of an exodus into freedom have excited the imagination of America's black population since slavery. Upward of 15,000 American blacks are believed to have embraced aspects of Judaism in an effort to discard the "white man's established Christian church." Some blacks in Harlem and other ghettos of the United States celebrate Jewish customs, including Passover. Others combine their Christian belief in Jesus with Old Testament laws. Ben-Ami Carter's sect, however, represents a distinct break with those American blacks who have adopted parts of Judaism.

Mixing black history with his reading of the Old Testament, Carter adopted the ideas of Marcus Garvey, who led the Back-to-Africa movement in the 1920's, and decided to settle in Liberia as a "purifying" stop before moving into the Promised Land itself. In July 1967, his followers sold their clothes and furniture to raise money and turned their savings over to Carter, who made arrangements for the trip. One woman remembers selling everything, including her home, then giving the money to Carter, only to sit with neighbors waiting for a call that it was time for her to leave. The call never came. The woman, who has kept her Hebrew name, Youlananda, is still in Chicago, living with the bitter memories of having lost her possessions to the Liberian sojourners.

By November 1967, 160 Black Hebrews had camped in a settlement near Monrovia, Liberia, trying to learn enough farming to grow crops. "One hundred sixty-six inches of rain fell there a year," remembers Asiel Ben-Israel, international ambassador for the Black Hebrews. "We were living in tents. We had to train midwives to deliver the babies. We were Chicago bus drivers and carpenters, teachers and businessmen who knew nothing about life in the bush. It was a real hardship." The colony lived under severe strain, near starvation at times. By 1969, only 125 had survived the experiment. The

Liberian Government issued an expulsion order against the sect, then withdrew it, but Ben-Ami Carter had already decided it was time to leave.

Carter has visited Israel as a tourist in 1968, along with one of the group's leaders, Charles Blackwell, who stayed for a full year, working in Kibbutz Mabarot. Blackwell's enthusiastic reports led Ben-Ami Carter to send five Black Hebrew families into Israel in August 1969. The families were admitted under Israel's Law of Return, which encourages Jews from all over the world to return to their homeland. Under the law, Jews are given immediate citizenship, directed to special housing and issued work permits, and they become eligible for all the Government benefits that any other citizen receives.

But when a second group of 39 Black Hebrews arrived in December 1969, the immigration authorities questioned their eligibility for citizenship by challenging their claim to being Jews. They issued them only tourist visas. When a third group of 49 arrived in March 1970, the Israelis realized what was happening: The Black Hebrews were immigrating to Israel under the questionable claim of being Jews. Although the third group was finally admitted on humanitarian grounds—to visit their relatives—Israel's immigration authorities were ordered not to allow any more Black Hebrews into the country.

The Black Hebrews' claim to Jewishness delayed any official action while Israel's high court adjudicated the issue. Carter attempted to prove that his sect fit the definition by submitting the same scriptural references he had preached in Chicago. There was not a single historic link with the Jewish people, however, that went beyond the passages plucked from the Old Testament.

Nor did the group's religious duties conform to Jewish tradition and practice. The Black Hebrews did not recognize the Oral Law, which sets detailed guidelines for implementing the Hebrew commandments contained in the Written Law. They adhered to a strictly vegetarian diet. Their religious observances contained elements of American black fundamentalism. (They fasted from Sabbath eve until the end of Sabbath, and during their service they sang black gospels.) Carter's revelations also allowed polygamy, which Jews have not practiced for centuries. Each male could take up to seven wives, who were given inferior roles within the group, serving the men at home.

All of the arguments put forward by Ben-Ami Carter failed to fulfill the definition required under the Law of Return. An individual must show a mother who was Jewish, or some evidence of conversion to Judaism, along with evidence that he does not belong to any other religion. The Black Hebrews fell short on all points. But in a moment of charity before the final hearing on the matter, Israeli Government authorities suggested that the issue could easily be settled if the Black Hebrews converted. Carter vehemently refused, insisting that such a conversion would imply that the Black Hebrews were not the "real" Jews. The Israeli Supreme Court subsequently rejected the Black Hebrews' claim, ruling: "In effect, this community is a separate sect, distinct from Judaism and remote from the Jewish world, its traditions and its culture and its heritage down the generations."

The Israelis had the legal right to expel the cult but they quickly realized that it was no longer a matter of deporting a small band of black Americans. The sect's numbers had swelled to 2,000, primarily as new members had infiltrated the country as tourists. They occupied sections of three Israeli cities—Dimona, Arad and Mizpe Ramon. No Government official seemed anxious to take action against them, fearing a charge of racism from the world press, and it was soon clear that Ben-Ami Carter would bring the issue to the news media's attention.

Carter declared war on the Israeli Government, unleashing a propaganda campaign that took on a viciously anti-Semitic and racist tone. The Baltimore Sun carried an interview with Carter on Nov. 6, 1971, quoting him as warning that two million blacks would come from the United States to wrest the Land of Israel from its Jewish inhabitants, because "the Lord personally ordered me to take possession of Israel."

In the Black Hebrews' own journal on Sept. 25, 1977, Jewish residents of Chicago were accused of money-grabbing and exploiting the Christian population. Under a picture of the Israeli Prime Minister was the caption: "Menachem Begin—the spirit of Hitler." Another quotation from the same publication said, "Money is the God of the sinful, white Jewish dogs."

Reports filtered back to Israel of the extreme statements that appeared in an underground black paper in San Francisco in September 1977, quoting an Associated Press account in which the Black Hebrews declared: "The Jews carry out the very same kind of abominable deeds which they claim Hitler perpetrated. They are the same Jews who stole the Palestinians' homeland and drove them out like animals into refugee camps where they are living in inhuman conditions. . . . Let us tear away the veil from these Israeli criminals."

A Black Hebrew brochure was cited by Israeli authorities as an example of anti-Semitic incitement against American Jews: "We should remind our Black Hebrew brethren that $500 million of the American taxpayers' money has been given to the racialist regime in Israel without any protest forthcoming from the black community. In addition, $800 million collected by the United Jewish Appeal was in most part stolen from the blacks by money-grabbing Jewish merchants. . . . We call upon our black brethren to rise up against the Jewish subjection of our community. These same racialist Jews have got control of all the arteries of our economic life. . . ."

In the storm of unceasing propaganda, the Black Hebrews petitioned black members of the United States Congress to boycott all Jewish businesses in the United States. In October 1977, International Ambassador Asiel Ben-Israel called upon supporters in the United States to seek a halt to all United States aid in money, arms and food to Israel, to boycott all Jewish-owned businesses and Jewish political candidates, to sever all black church contacts with Israel and to end tourism to Israel. One of the leaders of the Black Hebrews, Shalik Ben Yehuda, even appealed for help in a letter to Idi Amin of Uganda on July 31, 1978.

Carter's vitriolic attacks turned Israeli public sentiment against the Black Hebrews. Many Israelis were shocked, having mistaken the Black Hebrews for Falasha Jews (black Jews from Ethiopia) or North Africans. Their bright African dress and rich music had been welcomed in the bland atmosphere of the desert towns. The Black Hebrew singing groups had even performed with acclaim from Israeli military forces during the 1973 Yom Kippur War.

At the same time, there surfaced some explicit complaints from the Israeli citizens who lived next to the Black Hebrew families that had received the illegal infiltrators into their homes. The overcrowding was intolerable, they said, with sometimes 30 people in a single apartment. The high density clogged sewers and sanitary facilities, making conditions worse than in slum areas in the United States. The residents spoke of a general lowering of the quality of life. Apartment prices slumped. Those Israelis who wanted to sell their homes found there were no buyers. When the Government failed to address these complaints, the residents formed citizen committees to take matters into their own hands.

For years, Hanoch Platner and his wife, Fruma, lived in Dimona and watched their friends and neighbors move away as the Black Hebrews moved closer. When the Platners learned that the newcomers had purchased an apartment adjacent to their stairwell, they took action. It was not without agonizing personal examination. "When the war started," Platner said, "I was in Poland and then I was in concentration camps like Auschwitz. Maybe that's why it took us so much time to come to this decision, but after all we've been through, to come to Israel and be told by these people that we're not good enough Jews, that's it."

Hanoch and Fruma erected an iron gate across the entrance to their stairwell to keep their black neighbors out. "To our surprise, the tactic worked," Fruma said. "It was an aggressive attitude and it spread. Other Dimonans put up gates as well. We should have done this years ago. Instead, we let the Government and blacks push us around. Never again!"

Platner insists that his action was not racially motivated. "It was their life style—how would you describe it?—strange and bizarre, something I could not dream of."

Dr. Bernard Resnikoff of the American Jewish Committee in Jerusalem agrees that the racial issue is not a factor. "The Israeli is colorblind. We have interracial marriages here with no vestiges of concern on the part of either side of the family. The Black Hebrew problem is, rather ethnicity, cultural and economic problems, and a great deal of uncertainty about what their aspirations are."

In response to growing citizen complaints, the Minister of the Interior, Joseph Burg, appointed a committee headed by David Glass, a member of the Israeli Parliament, to study the Black Hebrew problem. Glass took 23 months to conduct his investigation. His final report, submitted last June, included some surprising conclusions.

According to Glass, many of the complaints were nothing more than unfounded rumor. He agreed that housing was badly overcrowded, but added, "The cleanliness ought to be mentioned with praise as compared with the yards of other houses in the town." Regarding the status of the Black Hebrews, he said, "It is inconceivable that thousands of people should reside in the State of Israel without any legal status, beyond the law, and violating legal norms in various areas every day."

As for the option of expelling the sect from Israel—recommended by the Israeli police out of a concern for security—the report said: "To expel the cult from Israel would create hostile public opinion against Israel throughout the world, of an intensity which cannot be accurately foreseen." The Glass report predicted severe repercussions for the delicate relationship between blacks and Jews in the United States and, worse, it said of the sect: "Their high motivation, iron discipline and blind obedience to the instructions of their leader are likely to lead to a tragedy which would scar the conscience of those responsible for the expulsion. Such a possibility cannot be ignored."

The Glass report concluded that the Black Hebrews should be allowed to remain in Israel, if a number of conditions were met. Since the Black Hebrews did not meet the criteria of the Law of Return, the report said, they should be allowed to qualify for citizenship under the Law of Entry, which allows non-Jews to become citizens through various stages, beginning with the granting of a tourist visa.

The report proposed taking the Black Hebrews through a transition period to test their willingness to become members of Israeli society, without endangering security and disrupting life, until full citizenship was attained, making each cult member subject to all the benefits and obligations of an Israeli citizen—including population registration, education, employment and national insurance.

The report further recommended that the cult be removed from the crowded conditions of Dimona and the other towns and given a special village community of its own. This would separate the Black Hebrews from their Jewish neighbors, which the sect apparently wanted, and bring the group under the control of the Israeli authorities.

There was one final condition: In order to qualify for the offer of an independent village, the Black Hebrew leadership would have to agree not to add immigrants from abroad to their community.

Ben-Ami Carter embraced the Glass committee report with enthusiasm, agreeing that, "if we are requested, we shall not add illegally a single person to our community, and we will continue to try to convince the State of Israel to accept other Black Hebrews only through official channels."

At last, it seemed, the crisis was near an end. The anti-Semitic propaganda had ceased during the Glass committee's investigation, largely because of the efforts of Jewish organizations in the United States—the American Jewish Congress, the American Jewish Committee and the Anti-Defamation League—which negotiated a period of "calm" through American black organizations, which in turn communicated with Ben-Ami Carter.

So far, however, no action has been taken on the Glass committee's politically unpopular recommendations. The report was criticized, primarily by those officials and citizens much closer to the problem, as "too liberal" and "unrealistic." When it appeared that the report would quietly sink into oblivion, the Dimona officials allowed some of Carter's group to move into a section of 23 deteriorating duplex apartments in an old absorption center at the edge of the city.

During a visit to the new Black Hebrew residences early this year, it was clear that they had taken to their new quarters with enthusiasm. They had painted, decorated and repaired the small houses, which had been vandalized and were wasting in the Israeli sun. The dirt lawns were raked neatly into herringbone patterns, with melon-sized rocks, placed in the outline of Africa, interrupting the small furrows. The "official" tour was carefully planned to show Black Hebrew children performing gymnastics in a public park, as evidence of their strength and health in response to charges of malnutrition.

The Black Hebrews gave the appearance of having created a new world in which they spoke Hebrew, with an American accent, conversed about the politics of Israel and rejected everything from their past, devoting themselves totally to the teachings of their messiah—Ben-Ami Carter—who had designed the dress, the diet and, of course, the worship. Karen Williams of Detroit, Ahaviella by her Hebrew name, said, "I think he is the savior of the world. Who have you seen move black people across a continent and give them a better life?" Eleanor Heims, from Bermuda, said, "He's given me a freedom I've never known before."

Just how "free" it is depends on how one defines freedom—and on how closely one lives by the difficult rules laid down by Ben-Ami Carter and enforced by his 12 "princes." Some former members accuse these community "leaders" of carrying out Carter's orders too zealously, even beating members for minor violations of his directives.

At noon, the tour led to a dining hall where nearly 75 children, wearing their soft skullcaps, were awaiting their midday meal. Diet is perhaps the most difficult test for the Black Hebrews, and Ben-Ami Carter admits some early problems: "We're strict vegetarians. All vegetarians in the world have problems with infants in the first year. We had this problem. Some of our children had vitamin deficiencies, and we've lost a few of the infants, but it's not a shortage of food that caused it."

It was clear that there is rarely an opportunity for competent medical personnel to judge whether anyone is suffering from malnutrition. Health problems are handled by "divine healers" and "preventive medicine." The followers are discouraged from seeing Israeli doctors even though the Israelis have offered their medical services since the arrival of the first Black Hebrews.

Moreover, some members of the sect have defected and returned to the United States. Thomas Whitfield and his wife, Hazel, broke away in 1978, after two of their children died from malnutrition. Both were dedicated followers of Ben-Ami Carter. But Hazel Whitfield could not adjust to the practice of multiple wives. The group pressured her to accept her role and, when she refused, her children were taken away from her and placed with other families as punishment. In the course of the separation, one child developed symptoms of malnutrition that were ignored by the "divine healers" of the sect. Hazel Whitfield writes in a book about their experiences, "From Night to Sunlight," "I religiously followed all of Ben-Ami's directives. I bathed the baby's skin with beet juice, for instance, and tried to make him drink vegetable juices. . . . But the child died. . . . Ben Carter worked with him for two days after he died, trying to resurrect him." A second child was taken to an Israeli hospital after developing similar symptoms but it, too, died. Carter has replied to the Hazel Whitfield resurrection account: "I am concerned about the children, but we have no rituals trying to raise the dead."

In the book, Thomas Whitfield describes a fellow Black Hebrew named Amran. "His 12-year-old daughter died under symptoms similar to [those of] our daughter. Amran came to pieces. He couldn't take it any longer. I watched him going out of his mind. Other men in the settlement would beat him. They thought he was jiving them, that he was putting on. . . . Discontent was widespread, but the people were scared stiff. Any oppressive system feeds on distrust and fear. Call the system what you will—it was foul, inhuman, repressive."

Although relatives in the United States have sought State Department help in locating family members who have joined the Black Hebrews in Israel, they have received little assistance. The United States Government regards the problem as an issue strictly within the jurisdiction of the Israelis.

Fifteen Federal warrants have been issued, however, for crimes allegedly committed in the United States by members of the cult for the purpose of sending money to the Black Hebrew community in Dimona. There are also 40 state violations outstanding in Chicago, Atlanta and Washington. Among the schemes investigated by the F.B.I. in connection with the "fund-raising" activities of the Black Hebrews are embezzlement, airline-ticket thefts, burglary and credit-card fraud.

The Black Hebrew sect has been praised by black Americans like Alexander Allen, vice president of the National Urban League, who commented after a recent visit: "I believe, based on what I saw, that there is a potential for a very constructive contribution to any society in which they are located, provided some of what I consider extreme and irrational theological arguments can be modified or eliminated."

But Bayard Rustin, director of BASIC (Black Americans to Support Israel Committee), after a recent visit to the Black Hebrew community, called Ben-Ami Carter a "dictator" and said, "Dictators don't have the same moral standards as democratic leaders." Rustin and five other leaders of black American organizations, including Allen, traveled to Israel in response to charges of Government harassment against black Americans entering the country. Rustin said that "Israel risks being perceived as racist if it persists in harassing black American tourists it fears may be Black Hebrews arriving to join the ranks of the sect."

Israel, of course, has no history of racial discrimination—quite the contrary: It deplores it. The Government recoils at the thought of being called racist. This is undoubtedly the main reason that it has not deported the Black Hebrews—a solution that would be not only within the country's legal rights but also understandable, given Ben-Ami Carter's avowed goals.

One possible answer to Israel's dilemma is to allow the sect's members to convert their "temporary" quarters in the absorption center into permanent quarters. The move to the center has alleviated much of the overcrowding that inspired the neighbors' complaints. In exchange, the authorities might reach some agreement on citizenship, obligating the sect to pay taxes, restrict its membership, support the national defense and subject its members to Government regulation. The Government might gain the benefits of the Glass committee's recommendations without officially implementing the report, which would certainly bring criticism from Israeli citizens.

Some observers believe that Ben-Ami Carter has entered what is called the "second phase of charismatic leadership"—a realization that "compromise" is necessary to exist in any society. But he has also made it clear that, as far as the Black Hebrews are concerned, "we don't have any intentions of leaving Israel."

# A-Beta Israel Hebrew Center Leaflet

THIS INFORMATION IS AN UNCOVERING OF THE
GREATEST MYSTERY, THE BEST KEPT SECRET
IN THE WORLD TODAY.
THE TRUE IDENTITY OF THE PEOPLE CALLED NEGROES

## THE DIVINE TRUTH

Q. WHO ARE THE PEOPLE CALLED NEGROES?

A. They are the Children of Israel, descendants of the people whose history is recorded in the Old Testament of your Bible. The same people as were Moses, Jesus, Joshua and all the prophets.

Q. ARE THE ISRAELITES GOD'S CHOSEN PEOPLE?

A. Yes, they were chosen and given the law, by the God of Abraham, Isaac and Jacob.

Q. THEN WHY DO WE SUFFER?

A. For disobedience to God, by breaking the law and profaning His Name. We were then cast off to serve the Gentiles (Pagans) until the time of the Gentile is fulfilled.

Q. WERE JESUS AND THE JEWS WHITE?

A. NO! Jesus and the Jews were of the same people as the (so called) Negro. They looked just as your brethren. They were and still are a black nation of people. (Jews, Hebrews, Israelites all pertain to the same people.)

Q. WHO ARE THE PEOPLE WHO CALL THEMSELVES JEWS IN AMERICA AND HAVE CONTROL OF ISRAEL TODAY?

A. They are Europeans, that came into the East during the reign of Alexander the Great, and the Roman Empire, adopted your culture, way of life, and carried it back into Europe.

Q. ARE THERE ANY WHITE JEWS? (HEBREWS, ISRAELITES)

A. There are no White Jews (Hebrews, Israelites). The whites that call themselves Jewish are not the Descendants of the Biblical Jews (Hebrew, Israelites). They are only following the culture.

Q. WERE THE PEOPLE CALLED NEGRO PICKED UP FROM THE GOLD COAST OF AFRICA?

A. Yes. Our people fled into Africa during their many troublous times. Last from the persecution of the Romans (Titus) in 70 A.D. This was foretold by the prophets years ago.

Q. WILL THE EUROPEAN ORIGINATED (JEW-ISH) WHITES WHO CALL THEMSELVES JEWS, GIVE UP OR BE DRIVEN OUT OF THE NOW STATE OF ISRAEL?

A. Yes, according to prophesies in the Bible, God will restore the land to the rightful owners, the true Children of Israel. (The people called Negro in America).

Q. CAN WE PROVE THAT THE (SO CALLED) NEGROES ARE THE HOUSE OF ISRAEL?

A. Yes. We can prove beyond a shadow of a doubt, that the people called Negro are the House of Israel.

Q. WHERE CAN I LEARN MORE ABOUT THE JEWS, (HEBREWS, ISRAELITES)?

A. For Biblical and historical proof of these questions, phone, write or come to

A-BETA ISRAEL HEBREW CENTER

4654 Cottage grove::Chicago, Illinois

Phone 285-9339—DR 3-9404

# Part 3 **The Atlantic Slave Trade and Slavery in the New World**

One of the more contentious issues in the contemporary debate between African Americans and Jewish Americans has concerned the involvement of Jews in the African slave trade and in slavery in the New World. Both sides have clouded this debate with rhetorical excesses and factual distortions and inaccuracies. Some argue that Jews played a dominant role; others deny that Jews were involved at all. The most obvious example of these extremes can be found in the controversy surrounding the 1991 publication by the Nation of Islam's historical research department, of *The Secret Relationships between Blacks and Jews.* This section presents some of the best scholarship on the nature, locale, and extent of the involvement of Jews in these regrettable chapters of American history.

The piece by Seymour Drescher is an effective and balanced discussion of the role of Jews as traders and financiers in the Atlantic slave trade and slavery. Ralph Austen's essay considers the excesses from both sides of the debate initiated by the publication of *The Secret Relationship,* and, as a Jew, he tries to acknowledge and better understand "even the most uncomfortable elements in our common past." Virginia Platt examines the activities of specific Jewish slave traders in Newport, Rhode Island, and the documents quoted in the Morris Schappes collection include early-nineteenth-century accounts of manumission of slaves by Jewish owners.

For three decades, scholars who have had an interest in the role of southern Jews in slavery have depended upon the work of Bertram Korn. Korn's work is characterized by his careful, systematic presentation of the multiple but limited roles Jews played in the slave economy. He also points out those few instances of cooperation and empathy between blacks and Jews. The obvious conclusion is that as morally repugnant as the Jews' actions might be, they pale when compared with the role of other groups in establishing and maintaining slavery.

We conclude this section with Jayme Sokolow's discussion of the role of German Jews in the abolition movement and Korn's analysis of the complex response of leading Jewish rabbis to abolition and the onset of the Civil War.

**FURTHER REFERENCES**

For further analysis of the role of Jews in the Atlantic slave trade see David Brion Davis, "The Slave Trade and the Jews" (1994) and "A Big Business" (1998), and Seymour Drescher, "Jews and New Christians in the Atlantic Slave Trade," in Paolo Bernadini, ed., *The Jews and the Expansion of Europe to the West, 1450–1825* (forthcoming). There are two recent book-length studies: Eli Faber, *Jews, Slaves, and the Slave Trade* (1998) and Saul S. Friedman, *Jews and the American Slave Trade* (1998). Jack Salzman and Cornel

West have several essays on Jews and slavery in their collection of essays, *Struggles in the Promised Land* (1997). In his review of Lenwood Davis's selected bibliography, *Black-Jewish Relations in the United States, 1752–1984*, Morris Schappes notes that the first sale of a slave was earlier than 1752, placing it at 1683, when Abraham Franckfoort of Flatbush, Brooklyn, sold "a negro man" to Pieter Strijker.

The major overviews of black-Jewish interaction in the South during the period of slavery are Bertram Korn, *American Jewry and the Civil War* (1970) and *Jews and Negro Slavery in the Old South, 1789–1865* (1961).

The most damning claims for the Jewish role in the Atlantic slave trade are made in the Nation of Islam, *The Secret Relationship between Blacks and Jews* (1991), and answered in a point-by-point fashion by Harold Brackman in *Farrakhan's Reign of Historical Error: The Truth behind the Secret Relationship between Blacks and Jews* (1992) and in *Ministry of Lies: The Truth behind the Nation of Islam's "The Secret Relationship between Blacks and Jews"* (1994).

SEYMOUR DRESCHER

# The Role of Jews in the Transatlantic Slave Trade

*The recent controversy instigated by Leonard Jeffries has prompted discussion of the relationship between the development of the transatlantic slave trade and European Jewish communities. Closer attention to the role played by Jews in the development of the trade, and its associated enterprises, suggests that little direct involvement can be identified. In the Dutch slave trade Jews can be said to have had tangible significance, but even here their involvement was relatively marginal. Through detailed analysis of the historiography of slavery, the 'conspiracy theory' approach to the issue is substantially challenged and disproved.*

**I**

Hostility to Jews has a long history in the West. They have been used to signify the antithetical, unassimilable, threatening, other, the malevolent outsider responsible as a people for killing the God/Saviour, for undermining the belief in one true faith and for exercising enormous and mysterious power over rulers, peoples and economic activity.

A peculiar internal coherence is often ascribed to them, whether in religious, cultural or racial terms, depending upon the dominant conceptual metaphors of the time. As vast uncontrolled historical processes or world-shaking events unfolded, Jews were assigned a principal role as instigators or disseminators of the process, especially by those who condemned or feared the phenomenon in question.[1] Over the past two centuries, Jews have been designated as the architects of the French and Russian Revolutions, as initiators of the two world wars, as the generators of democracy, of capitalism and of communism. Responsibility for worldwide epidemics and for the disintegration of the Soviet Union has been added to this long and open-ended series of manipulations of the course of history.

Developers of these conspiracy or dominance theories usually cite in support of their arguments a small number of highly-prominent individuals or brief moments of collective Jewish success contemporary with the time period or location of the event. They correspondingly ignore or trivialize the counter-evidence of Jewish helplessness, impoverishment, persecution, expulsion and mass murder which are prominent elements of the record for so much of the last millennium of Western and world history.

Attaching principal responsibility to Jews for the initiation and organization of the

Seymour Drescher is professor of history at the University of Pittsburgh and is most recently the editor with Stanley Engerman of *A Historical Guide to World Slavery* (New York: Oxford University Press, 1998). Originally published in *Immigrants and Minorities* 12, no. 2 (July 1993): 113–25. Copyright © 1993 by Frank Cass & Co. Ltd. Reprinted by permission of *Immigrants & Minorities*, published by Frank Cass and Company, Ilford, Essex, England.

African slave trade therefore fits into a clear historical tradition. Until recently a dominant role in the African slave trade had not been among the primary responsibilities assigned to the Jews. In July 1991, however, the Chairman of the Black Studies department of the City College of the City University of New York identified Jews as foremost among the principal financiers, planners, organizers and sustainers of the Atlantic slave trade and the transatlantic slave system.[2] It is no accident that this perspective bypasses the general historical patterns of Jewish history as well as the specific way in which two major diasporas, Jewish and African, partially coincided during the first two and a half centuries after the European encounter with sub-Saharan Africa and the settlement of the Americas.

The story of the black African diaspora has been the focus of major reinvestigations during the past generation. The general outlines of the story are now clearer and more widely disseminated in the curricula of American secondary and higher education and research publications than ever before.[3] For half a century before the voyages of Columbus, thousands of Africans were forcibly transported northward across the Atlantic to serve as coerced labour in Europe and, for more than three centuries after Columbus, at least four out of every five transatlantic migrants were black Africans rather than white Europeans. Ironically, only in that part of the Americas which became the United States did the European migration stream (often also coming in various forms of coerced labour) outnumber African slaves. In terms of pre-1850 migration patterns, the transatlantic movement was far more African than European.[4]

Less familiar is the diaspora which was occurring among the Jews of Europe after 1450. The Holocaust of the twentieth century was not the first near-elimination of Jewry from Western and Central Europe. That situation first occurred in the later fifteenth century, almost simultaneous with the beginning of the transoceanic African slave diaspora. After a century of increasing persecution of the Spanish Jews, their general expulsion or forced conversion was implemented in 1492, only a few months before the launching of Columbus's first expedition. The mass expulsion from Spain was followed by the coerced mass baptism of the 70,000 or so Jews (mostly Spanish refugees) who resided in Portugal in 1497. These events paralleled the expulsion of Jews from most of Northern and Southern Italy between 1491 and 1510, and from most of the Swiss and German lands between 1490 and 1520.

The final denouement of these successive expulsions came between 1520 and 1550. This last phase was the result of princely and ecclesiastical authorities as much as of popular mobilization. Except for areas directly under the authority of the Holy Roman Emperors (the Habsburgs), the collapse of Jewish life in both Catholic and Protestant Europe was virtually complete by 1570. Open allegiance to Judaism was entirely extinguished in Spain, Portugal, Italy south of Rome, the Netherlands, England, France, the Germanies and northern Italy. In isolated areas where Jews were not physically expelled, the Jewish role in Western and Central Europe had become altogether marginal. The age of European exploration was therefore also initially the age of 'the most fundamental restructuring of Jewish life in Europe' between the Roman destruction of the Jewish nation and the later German annihilation of the twentieth century.[5]

By 1570 the major centres of Jewish life had shifted definitively eastward to the

Ottoman dominions in the Balkans and the Levant and to Poland–Lithuania in north-eastern Europe. In 1492 Polish Jewry amounted to only around 30,000 less than the Jewish population of Italy and one-fifth of Spanish Jewry. By the end of the sixteenth century, Polish Jewry had increased by up to five times, or only slightly less than Spanish Jewry on the eve of expulsion. The overwhelming mass of European Jewry in the four centuries of the Atlantic slave trade therefore lived outside of the area of Europe which was most directly involved in the Atlantic economy. The role of the Jews in the Atlantic slave trade becomes clearer in the light of the framework of these two diaspora movements at the dawn of the early modern era—one moving north and west from Africa, the other moving north and east within Europe and the Levant.

That there was a Jewish involvement with the slave trade is not a new discovery. The nature of the involvement, however, requires further elaboration. A small fragment of the Jewish diaspora fled northward in Europe and westward into the Americas, there becoming entwined with the African slave trade. So often and so long barred by Western European societies from securing high political positions, large landholdings, high military rank, the right to participate in established crafts, professions, commercial and educational institutions, and even denied full rights to residence in most of the West, a small minority of European Jewry succeeded in re-entering the areas of Western domination. Since they remained at the social margin of society, they could prosper only by moving into high risk and new areas of economic development. In the expanding Western European economy after the Columbian voyages, this meant getting footholds within the new markets at the fringes of Europe, primarily in its overseas enclaves. One of these new 'products' was human beings. It was here that Jews, or descendants of Jews, appeared on the roster of Europe's slave trade.

## II

With this as background, we may address the specific issue of Jewish involvement in the African slave trade. Were Jews, as claimed, the principal mediators of slavery's transference from the medieval Mediterranean world to the islands of the Atlantic and to the Americas in the wake of European expansion? Regarding the initiation of the various European slave trades, the answer is unequivocal. In none of the major transatlantic slaving zones within or outside of Europe was the slave traffic initiated by Jews, individually or collectively. Even in the earlier medieval systems of Spain and of Central and Eastern Europe, Jewish slaving was an extension of non-Jewish conquest and raiding armies.[6] The slave trades within Europe were initiated by non-Jews, Christians, pagans or Muslims. On the eve of the Muslim conquest of Spain, for example, the last Visigothic Christian king was hunting down and flogging Jews at the same time as he was pursuing fugitive slaves. Only when the Moorish conquest had settled down into cross-border raiding between Christians and Moslems did Jews play a significant mercantile role in the Iberian slave trade. At that point, the position of Jews as intermediaries on both sides of the political/religious border offered advantages to both sides in slaving activities.

By the late medieval period, however, when the prototype of the slave plantation system began its diffusion from the Eastern to the Western Christian Mediterranean,

Jews played no role in the process. In the period of the Latin–Byzantine supremacy, Jews were forbidden from acquiring non-Jewish slaves. They are absent from the list of the area's slave traders. The mercantile city-states of Italy dominated and sponsored the transfer of sugar plantation and slave systems across the Mediterranean and into the Atlantic islands.[7]

A similar observation may be made concerning the origins of the Atlantic slave trade itself. The Portuguese who opened up the Euro-African Atlantic slave trade in the mid-fifteenth century were Christians, funded and dispatched under the exclusive authority of a Portuguese prince seeking to outflank Moslem-controlled trade routes. Once Europeans reached the Americas, the Spaniards who undertook wholesale enslavements of native populations were Catholic Conquistadors. Far more rigorously than in Latin Byzantium, Jews were officially barred by the Iberian monarchs of both Portugal and Spain from settling in their overseas transatlantic empires.

All of the great trading companies which dominated the Atlantic slave trade in the seventeenth century—those of Portugal, Brazil, Holland, France and England—began as exclusive monopolies, organized and headed by Christian rulers. In the foundation of all of these major Atlantic slave trade systems, the role of Jews was at best a subordinate one. Only in the ephemeral schemes and ventures of some Baltic rulers, such as those of the Great Elector of Brandenburg (the Brandenburg Africa Company of 1682), and of Duke James of Courland, did wealthy Jews of Amsterdam and Hamburg play an entrepreneurial role. In these instances, too, however, the slaving ventures were state-sponsored and state-dominated enterprises. The ultimate decision-makers were always the political rulers, who more often than not were religiously intolerant sovereigns as well.[8]

### III

If Jews did not found any of the major European transatlantic slave trades, what role did they play in organizing or financing them once established? Two of the largest slaving powers, England and France, were responsible for shipping at least 40 per cent of the total number of African slaves to the New World.[9] In these two cases, Jewish participation was so insignificant that historians of the slave trade no more than occasionally cite a few Jewish individuals or families in French or English seaports who engaged in slaving activities. These were rare instances among the hundreds of Catholic and Protestant investors who dominated all of the trades of England and France, including the African. Were one to include in such an accounting additional thousands of Europeans and Africans who commanded or manned the slave ships, or the Afro-Europeans and Africans who participated in the trade on the African supply side, the relative significance of the Jewish role in these enterprises would diminish even further.

This leaves us with the Spanish, Portuguese and Dutch slave trades as the remaining potential sources of a major Jewish role in the transatlantic slave trade. Spain relied upon the fleets, mercantile networks and capital of other European powers to monopoly contracts or *asientos*. Before the third decade of the seventeenth century, that is, for more than a century and a quarter after the mass expulsions of the 1490s, the Spanish *asiento* was entirely in the hands of the Genoese and Flemish capitalists. During the first century after 1492 when memories of or affiliations with Jewish traditions might have been most intense, Spanish *New Christians,* whether 'grandees' or otherwise, simply had no opportunity to take the lead in organizing, financing or otherwise directing the Atlantic slave trade to Spanish America. The Portuguese in the late sixteenth and early seventeenth centuries, succeeded by the Dutch in the mid-seventeenth century, were the principal early carriers to the Spanish possessions. The French and the British moved in as major competitors for the Spanish slaving *asientos* at the end of the seventeenth century.

The Portuguese slave trade creates a knotty problem for any historian who undertakes to apportion shares of participation in the slave trade by confessional affiliation. Descendants of Jews did play a significant role in the sixteenth and early seventeenth century transatlantic slave trades as they did in all of the European and transoceanic trades of Portugal's seaborne empire from Asia to Angola, and from Mexico to Cartagena. Until the mid-seventeenth century their linkages with overseas Jews helped to sustain their mercantile position in Portugal. However, the Portuguese case amply demonstrates the difficulty of apportioning the slave trade by religious categories, especially as applied to Iberians.

Portugal's Jews, as indicated above, were forcibly Christianized through mass baptism in 1497. The resultant population was designated as a separate legal category of *Conversos* or *New Christians,* just as the previously-converted Spanish Jews had been. After one generation, the term *New Christians* therefore became an oxymoron, a hereditary legal category designating a suspect and underprivileged social class. For centuries after 1497 'New' Christians lived under the same kinds of legal, occupational and social restrictions previously applied by European rulers against openly-professing Jews.[10] As early as the late sixteenth century, when Portuguese *New Christians* were allowed to re-enter Spain, a large number were sincere Catholics, neither adhering to Jewish traditions nor desiring to maintain cultural ties with the Iberian Jewish diaspora outside the Iberian peninsula. The most definitive evidence of prominent Jewish connections in the Portuguese New Christian slave trade lies in the activities of Duarte Dias Henriques, who farmed the Crown monopoly for exporting slaves from Angola in 1607–14. He also helped to maintain Jewish institutions in Palestine.[11]

Of course, if one accepts the Inquisition's legal definition, all descendants of those converted at the end of the fifteenth century may be classified as secret or 'occult' Jews, or *Marranos.* In Iberian legal terms *New Christians* lacked the 'purity of blood' of 'Old Christians'. In this perspective, descendants of Jews took any opportunity to escape the Inquisition's jurisdiction, to subvert the faith and to revenge themselves for the humiliation of coerced ancestral conversion. From the Inquisition's perspective, any *New Christians* involved in the slave system would be classified as potential 'Jews'.[12]

Modern scholars, overwhelmingly rejecting this racist and biologizing definition, treat the problem of Iberian Jewish identity as a historical process, with each generation of *New Christians* probably having fewer members who regarded themselves as Jews, or having any desire to revert or convert to Judaism. Even at the outset, at the end of the fifteenth century, the majority of converted Portuguese Jews did not consist of *forced* converts. It was the Inquisition which, within the jurisdiction of the Spanish and

Portuguese empires, froze the identity of the descendants of *New Christians* and prevented their complete assimilation into the 'old' Catholic fold.[13]

Finally, the bulk of the Luso-Brazilian (Portuguese) slave trade occurred in the eighteenth and nineteenth centuries, eight to twelve generations after the initial mass conversion. Scholars have not assigned a 'Jewish' role of any kind to that period of the slave trade which accounts for five-sixths of the Africans landed in Brazil. When the Portuguese monarchy later removed all disabling impositions from the *New Christians* and invited the return of descendants of Jews who had fled Portugal centuries before, there was no large-scale reversion or conversion to Jewish practice among the old *New Christians* of Portugal nor any other collective manifestation of crypto-Jewish identity.

It therefore becomes crucial whether one uses cultural or racial criteria in considering the role of Jews in organizing and financing the forced transfer of African slaves to the Portuguese Americas. By 1650, there is overwhelming evidence that the Jewish diaspora outside Iberia and the *New Christians* who remained within the peninsula had also taken divergent paths regarding the slave trade. During the Dutch–Portuguese struggle for Brazil in the 1640s, it was Portuguese *New Christians* who financed the successful Portuguese expedition to recapture Brazil from the Dutch, who tolerated open Jewish practice in that colony. The ritual public burning in Lisbon of one of the captured Brazilian Jews marked a definitive cultural and commercial alienation between the main Jewish refugee community in Holland and the *New Christians* in Portugal.[14]

Hardest to disentangle is the Jewish role in the Portuguese African slave trade of the sixteenth century. As indicated above, Jews had no part in the founding or the initial financing of Portugal's slave trade. It was only after the mass conversion of 1497 that *New Christians* could have entered the slave trade. Here, too, attempts to identify even second-generation *New Christians* as 'Jews' leads in to a conceptual morass. How should one categorize the children of forcibly-baptized Jews who were deported to the island of São Tome in the Atlantic soon after the forced conversion of the parents? Since many deportees were allotted African slaves as wives, how does one proceed to disentangle the hereditary identity of subsequent generations of Afro-Europeans in the manner of the Inquisition?

It was the persecution, not the religious affinities of the *New Christians* driven or fleeing to the peripheral zones of Africa and America, which helped to determine their role in the expansion of the transatlantic slave trade. One of the frontier trades to which *New Christians* had easy access was the slave trade. They could quickly move into this 'new' trade and then out into other branches of economic activity once they had established themselves. There is ample evidence that the sixteenth-century *New Christians* were linked with diaspora Judaism. These early Iberian *New Christians* played a subordinate role as intermediaries in the transatlantic slave trade.[15]

## IV

The Dutch slave trade is one instance about which we can be certain of unambiguous Jewish participation in the Afro-Caribbean slave trade. Unlike the Portuguese or Spanish *Conversos,* the Jews of Holland possessed a recognized corporate religious status. Even in Holland, of course, Jews were restricted from entering certain occupations and were excluded from political office. In the Dutch American colonies, Jews were likewise prohibited from engaging in the direct purchase of slaves on the African coast. But in the colonies they could settle as Jews and acquire and sell slaves once imported from Africa.

In the Netherlands itself, they could invest freely in the Dutch West India Company, which had the monopoly of Dutch African purchases until well into the eighteenth century. Since the mid-seventeenth century was the period in which the Dutch controlled a substantial portion of the Atlantic slave trade, the Jewish role in the Atlantic trade could, therefore, have been both substantial and important for a generation after 1640, via the Dutch trade. It turns out, however, that Jews played a limited and subordinate role, both managerially and financially, among the major Dutch slavers. They did not serve on the *Heren X*, the directorate of the Dutch West India Company. Their investment share amounted to only 0.5 per cent (or one two-hundredths) of the company's capital.[16]

Elsewhere in Northern Europe, the last third of the seventeenth century marked the high point of Jewish involvement in the scramble for the Afro-Caribbean trades. Whether as occasional agents for negotiating Spanish *asiento* contracts, or as go-betweens for the founding of new West Indian trading companies, a handful of wealthy Jews negotiated with European rulers and merchants who were anxious to get into the expanding Afro-Caribbean economic systems of the late seventeenth century. But this flurry of Jewish entrepreneurial activity in Northern Europe signified almost nothing for Africa. Jews were most important in organizing the most insignificant slave trades. All of the Baltic states together accounted for less than 0.7 per cent of Africans transported to the New World.

The *indirect* significance of Jews in the Atlantic system was more important than was their role in organizing the forced migration of Africans to the Americas. They were active in the transportation and processing of certain tropical commodities—sugar, diamonds and tropical wood. In the generation after 1640 Jews were also among the transmitters of tropical plantation technology and know-how throughout the Caribbean. As artisans, as managerial experts on plantations and as mercantile pioneers, they helped to expand the production and transportation networks of new tropical products which their co-religionists often then processed in Europe. Here, and not in the slave trade, the forced diaspora of the Jews did contribute, at least briefly, to the mid-seventeenth century expansion of sugar and slavery. Fleeing from Brazil with the defeat of the Dutch, they scattered through the Caribbean, becoming plantation owners and merchants in the Dutch, English and French colonies.

Jewish participation in the slave system was greatest under Dutch sovereignty. On the island of Curaçao, Jews became re-export agents of the Dutch West India Company, selling slaves, manufactures and commodities to the Spanish mainland, and to the British and French colonies. Jews also became a significant mainland settler group among the white colonists of Dutch Guiana in the second half of the seventeenth century. At one point the Dutch colonies contained the largest Jewish community in the Americas. They had their own self-governing community, 'Joden Savanne' (Jewish Savanah), in Surinam. In this medium-sized colony, they became a substantial segment of the propertied classes, including the possession of slave plantations. They were extractors of coerced labour and the owners of human bodies for three full centuries before Dutch slave emancipation (1863).[17]

## V

What then was the overall role of the Jews in organizing and financing the transatlantic slave trade? The four most substantial trades—the British and French trades of the late seventeenth and eighteenth centuries and the Brazilian and Cuban slave trades of the eighteenth and nineteenth centuries—accounted for almost 90 per cent of the forced African migration to the Americas. In those four great trades, the Jewish role ranged from marginal to virtually nil.

Only by conflating *New Christians* with Jews can the latter be said to have been major participants in the sixteenth and seventeenth-century Iberian slave trades. Jews played their largest role in the Dutch slave trade, but even here, they lacked the organizational and financial significance of their more powerful Christian neighbours. Finally, in the minor Danish and the miniscule Brandenburg, Swedish and Courland slave trades, Jews did play significant entrepreneurial or organizational roles. But even were we absurdly to assign *all* Africans transported under the flags of Denmark, Sweden, Brandenburg, etc. to a 'Jewish' account, all of these 'Baltic' trades combined did not account for as much as 0.7 per cent of Europe's transatlantic slave trade.

In any global analysis of the transatlantic slave trade, including Islamic and other Old World participants, Jews could not qualify as major players compared to other social groups, whether categorized by religion, race, class or ethnicity. Moreover, the futility of assigning responsibility for the Atlantic slave trade by religious or cultural groups should already be apparent. The transatlantic slave trade entailed a vast number of interlocking economic ventures and divided along political lines. It engaged the interest of warriors, sailors, merchants, and artisans, people of both sexes and all races from Scandinavia to Southern Africa. Ironically, the only major state in Europe whose people or rulers evinced no interest whatever in getting into the Afro-Caribbean system during the four centuries after Columbus's voyages was the kingdom of Poland, proportionally the most 'Jewish' area of Europe until its final partition in the 1790s. This irony is of recent vintage because, for five centuries, no one imagined European Jewry to be dominant in the transatlantic slave trade.

The scholarship of modern slavery confirms the conventional assessment. Historians of the slave trade have devoted little attention to Jews as a distinct social group in the long and terrible story of its operation as revealed by the texts and indexes of scholarly histories of the slave trade. They rate attention only in detailed monographs of the individual European slave trades, works which focus on mid-seventeenth century Brazil, and on the seventeenth-century Caribbean.

To find extended attention devoted to Jews in the Atlantic slave trade, one therefore has to go to the scholarship of modern Jewry, rather than of slavery. That is precisely why proponents of a Judeo-centric slave trade ironically depend upon historians and biographers of Jews for their information. The paradox is easily explained. The Atlantic slave system was more important to certain segments of early modern Jewry than early modern Jewry was to the Atlantic slave system.

In evaluating the role of Jews in New World slavery, no serious scholar would mitigate the basic fact that Jews bought, used, sold, and otherwise coerced human beings in whom they held rights as chattels. One does not, however, have to grossly exaggerate the significance of a religious group which neither initiated the transatlantic slave trade, nor controlled any of its major components in Europe, Africa, or the Americas. This was the function of groups and rulers belonging to other faiths—Christian, Muslim and pagan. They dominated the world which generated both the African and the Jewish diasporas after 1450.

In terms of the relationship between these two groups, the most important underlying fact remains that they constituted two contemporary cohorts of people driven from their habitations at about the same moment in world history. In the Old World, the two diasporas rarely overlapped. In the Americas, it was a tragic irony that Jews, like other oppressed groups in Europe, could conceive of the New World as a land of promise while sustaining and enriching themselves through the enslavement of others. Prosperity and liberty for Jews, as for other Western migrants, entailed participation in systems of coercion, degradation, and indifference to the fate of non-Europeans. In the tropical Americas, liberation for Jews was eased by the enslavement of Africans. Only centuries after millions of Africans had contributed so tragically to the establishment of freer Jewish diasporas in the New World, did they achieve their own liberation from enslavement.[18]

NOTES

1. See Norman Cohn, *Warrant for Genocide: The Myth of the Jewish World-Conspiracy and the Protocols of the elders of Zion* (London, 1967) and Henry Gates, Jr., 'Black Demagogues and Psuedo-Scholars', *The New York Times,* 20 July 1992, p.11.

2. See text of a speech by Leonard Jeffries, 20 July 1991 at the Empire State Black Arts and Cultural Festival in Albany, New York, reprinted in *New York Newsday,* Monday, 18 Aug. 1991, pp.3, 25–9:

> So I said, 'Where do you want us to start? What period of history? You want us to start in the Spanish-Portuguese period of the starting of the slave trade in the 1400's and 1500's? Do you want us to move it from Seville and Lisbon on to Amsterdam and Hamburg, where the new Jewish community continued the slave trade for the Dutch, the Germans, and the English? Or do you want us to move it to Brazil and the Caribbean and Curaçao, which became a new Amsterdam, the new center of the slave trade in the western world centered around the Jewish immigrants that moved into Curaçao? Or do you want us to move it to New York and Rhode Island? Where do you want us to start?'
>
> When do you want us to start? Do you want to go to Amsterdam? Then get a book by Jonathan Israel on 'European Jewry in the Age of Mercantilism, 1550–1750'.
>
> And there's a picture of the Amsterdam synagogue, which was the center of slave trading for the Dutch. Amsterdam became a leading port in this period of time for slaving. And it was around this synagogue that the slaving system was established. . . .
>
> . . . We'll have the ten major books relating to the Jewish community (the wealthy Jewish community) and enslavement.
>
> In Spain there were the grandees, managing the money of the Spanish throne. In Germany in the

16- and 1700's there were the court Jews, managing the political and economic apparatus of Europe, the Hapsburg Empire, the German states, etcetera. We have the names. We know who they were, what they were, what they controlled. We know when they set up the Dutch East Indian (sic) Co., Dutch West Indian (sic) Co., the Portuguese Company, the Brazilian Company. We know who and what documents. We know that even when they converted to Christianity, they maintained links with their Jewish community brothers who had not converted; and that's why they had a network around the world.

. . . they became the lifeline of the fallen Roman Empire in the 15- and 1600's, and they began to institutionalize a trade link with the Middle East.

3. See, *inter alia*, Phillip Curtin, *The Atlantic Slave Trade: A Census* (Madison, 1969); David Eltis, *Economic Growth and the Ending of the Transatlantic Slave Trade* (New York, 1987); Robert William Fogel, *Without Consent or Contract: The Rise and Fall of American Slavery* (New York, 1989).

4. David Eltis, 'Free and Coerced Transatlantic Migration: Some Comparisons', *American Historical Review*, 88 (1983), pp.251–80.

5. Jonathan I. Israel, *European Jewry in the Age of Mercantilism, 1550–1750* (Oxford, 1985). Long before the Iberian rulers, the kings of England and France had expelled the Jews of their realms.

6. See Charles Verlinden, *L'esclavage dans l'Europe medievale*, 2 vols. (Brugge and Ghent, 1955–77) and Pierre Bonnassie (trans. Jean Birrell), *From Slavery to Feudalism in South-Western Europe* (Cambridge, 1991), pp.96–9.

7. It is important to emphasize that there was no general inhibition against slave-holding or slave-dealing in any of the major religious communities of the early medieval period. Jews apparently participated in the slave trades of Southwestern and East Central Europe as fully as circumstances permitted. Nor did Jews merely designate slavery as a necessary evil in a mundane present. The large-scale enslavement of gentiles was often part of their messianic future, as well. In terms of Europe's historical slave trades, however, the role of the Jews waxed and waned in the ninth and tenth centuries CE, almost half a millennium before the burgeoning of the transatlantic slave trade. See Charles Verlinden, *L'Esclavage dans l'Europe Medievale*, 2 vols. (Brugge and Ghent, 1955–77), Vol. I, pp.216–19, 245, 672, 707–16. Note that Verlindenden's second volume covering the late medieval Italian Mediterranean colonies, the Latin Levant and the Byzantine Empire, contains no index reference to Jews as 'merchants of slaves'. See also Charles Verlinden (trans. Yvonne Freccero), *The Beginnings of Modern Colonization: Eleven Essays with an Introduction* (Ithaca, NY, 1970), Parts II and III; Steven B. Bowman, *The Jews of Byzantium 1204–1453* (Alabama, 1985), pp.118–9.

8. Israel, *European Jewry*, p. 139.

9. Based upon Curtin, *Census*, p. 88. Revisions of estimates since Curtin do not substantially alter his percentages. See Paul E. Lovejoy, 'Volume of the Atlantic Slave Trade: A Synthesis', *Journal of African History*, 23 (1982), pp.473–501.

10. Israel, *European Jewry*, pp. 24–5, 58–9, and Salo Baron, *A Social and Religious History of Jews*, Vol. XIII, pp.141–55, 264, 275–7. On the complexity of the 'New Christian' identity over three centuries see Anita Novinsky, 'Sephardim in Brazil: The New Christians', in R.D. Barnett and W.M. Schwab (eds.), *The Sephardi Heritage* 2 vols. (Grendon Northants, 1989), Vol.II, pp.431–44.

11. Israel, *European Jewry*, pp.58, 111; C.R. Boxer, *The Portuguese Seaborne Empire, 1415–1825* (Newark, NJ, 1965), pp.266–7, 331, and Daniel M. Sweschinski, 'Conflict and Opportunity in Europe's Other Sea', *American Jewish History* (Dec. 1982), pp.218–38. On the complexity of the cultural identity of the early settlers of Sao Tome, see David Birmingham, *Trade and Conflict in Angola* (Oxford, 1966), p.25; Jews and criminals were sent to the island. Each settler was given a slave wife from the Kongo, and their offspring became planters. See also Pierre Chaunu, *Seville et l'Atlantique 1504–1650*, 8 vols. (Paris, 1959), Vol. VII, pp.60–85, 277–86; Frederic Mauru, *Portugal et l'Atlantique* (Paris, 1960), p.162 and Edgar R. Samuel, 'The Trade of the "New Christians" of Portugal in the Seventeenth Century', in *The Sephardi Heritage*, Vol.II, pp.100–14.

12. See Leon Poliakov, *Histoire de l'antisemitisme* 3 vols. (Paris, 1961), Vol.II, *De Mahomet aux Marranes,* Ch.10, 11. See also Jeffries' speech, p.27.

13. There is a long and complex debate about the religious and cultural status of the Conversos and their descendants in Iberia even before the establishment of the Spanish Inquisition. B. Netanyahu shows that the Jewish leadership outside Iberia assumed the erosion of Jewish identity to be the norm and concludes that as early as the early sixteenth century, the majority of converted Portuguese Jewry did not consist of *forced* converts. Exceptions to this normative position were made to first generation Portuguese converts, but not to those who were children of converts and certainly not to descendants for generations. *The marranos of Spain From the Late XIVth to the Early XVIth Century According to Contemporary Hebrew Sources,* 2nd edn. (New York, 1973), pp.211–15. It was the Inquisition which froze the identity of the New Christians in assuming the propensity to crypto-Judaism.

14. Israel, 'Dutch Sephardi Jewry, Millenarian Politics, and the struggle for Brazil (1640–1654)', in David S. Katz and Jonathan I. Israel (eds.), *Skeptics, Millenarians and Jews* (Leiden/New York, 1990), pp.76–97. On Brazilian Jewry, see Arnold Wiznitzer, *Jews in Colonial Brazil* (New York, 1960).

15. See Edgar R. Samuel, 'The Trade of the "New Christians" of Portugal in the Seventeenth Century', in R.D. Barnett and W.M. Schwab (eds.), *The Shepardi Heritage,* 2 vols. (Grendon Northants, 1989), Vol.II, pp.100–14. In the first century of the transatlantic slave trade, 'the distribution and marketing of sugar were in the hands of the Italians, who also predominated as slave traders', and the same capitalists who financed the latter trade reaped the main profits from it. See Kenneth Maxwell, '¡Adios Columbus!', *New York Review of Books,* 28 Jan. 1983, pp.38–45; and Ruth Pike, *Enterprise and Adventure: The Genoese in Seville and the Opening of the New World* (Ithaca, NY, 1966).

16. Private correspondence with Professor Pieter C. Emmer, of the *Institute for the History of European Expansion,* 8 Oct. 1991. See also Johannes Menne Postma, *The Dutch in the Atlantic Slave Trade* (Cambridge, 1990), for the most recent estimate of the Dutch slave trade. In the British West Indies, 'Jewish activity in the slave trade was neither as great as rumored nor as negligible as claimed'. Stephen Alexander Fortune, *Merchants and Jews: The Struggle for British West Indian Commerce, 1650–1750* (Gainesville, FL, 1984), pp.162–3.

17. See, *inter alia,* the two volumes by Cornelius Ch. Goslinga, *The Dutch in the Caribbean and in Surinam 1791–1942* (Assen/Maastricht, 1990) and Isaac S. and Suzanne A. Emmanuel, *History of the Jews of the Netherlands Antilles,* 2 vols. (Cincinnati, 1970), pp.41–8, 78–80; 226.

18. See, above all, David Brion Davis, *Slavery and Human Progress* (New York, 1984), Part I, Ch.6, 'Jews and the Children of Strangers', for an excellent overview of Jews and New World slavery by a historian of slavery.

# "And Don't Forget the Guinea Voyage"
## The Slave Trade of Aaron Lopez of Newport

Recent studies of the transatlantic economy in the third quarter of the eighteenth century have indicated that New England merchants played only a minor role in the slave trade to the English colonies. It has even been contended that the so-called triangular trade, of which the commerce in slaves was an important part, is in fact a myth invented by such nineteenth-century historians as George H. Moore and William B. Weeden.[1] While it is surely true that the notion of the triangular trade was exaggerated by these scholars, the current tendency to regard the trade as mythical overlooks the activities of a prominent Newport, Rhode Island, merchant, Aaron Lopez, who sent fourteen vessels to the slave coast between 1761 and 1774. These voyages are documented in detail in the Lopez commercial papers. They enable us to begin a more accurate appraisal of the extent and significance of New England's participation in the slave trade.[2]

Lopez, a Sephardic Jew, emigrated in 1752 from Lisbon to Newport, where he joined his brother Moses and his cousin Jacob Rodriguez Rivera. There he set up shop as a candlemaker, in association with Rivera, and engaged in various brokerage operations involving cocoa, lime, and molasses. During the 1750s he expanded rather tentatively into overseas commerce, combining a little tea smuggling[3] with the legal importing of goods from England. Candlemaking led him to invest in whaling ventures to obtain spermaceti, and need for funds for the purchase of English commodities spurred him in the 1760s to send ships to many ports, including those of the West Indies and the African slave coast.[4]

The family connection with Rivera, soon to become his father-in-law, made it easy for Lopez to add a close association in shipping to the joint operation of the chandlery. The account books indicate that the active prosecution of such business as Rivera shared came to be directed almost entirely by the younger man. Lopez owned the wharf, arranged for building, chartering, and outfitting the vessels, hired captains and crews, and kept detailed accounts. Rivera invested in the enterprises but usually left even the insuring of his share of the ventures to Lopez. His most consistent involvement in overseas enterprises was in the series of slaving voyages, in each of which he held a third to a half interest and part ownership of the vessel.[5] Perhaps Rivera instigated the first of these voyages: he had sent out a slaver, the *Sherbro*, in 1754, in partnership with the prominent slave trader, William Vernon.[6]

In 1975, Virginia Bever Platt was a member of the Department of History, Bowling Green State University. Originally published in *William and Mary Quarterly*, 3d. ser., 32, no. 4 (1975): 601–18. Reprinted with permission of the Omohundro Institute of Early American History and Culture.

Lopez entered into shipping despite the provision of the Navigation Acts that all vessels engaged in trade with the English colonies must be owned by British subjects. In 1760, two years before he became a naturalized subject of the king, he had acquired a half interest in Rivera's brig *Grayhound,* which made a trading voyage to Jamaica in that year. On November 2, 1761, the two owners began to prepare the vessel for a second voyage, this time to Africa, obtaining flour from Philadelphia, beef from New York, and the indispensible rum, amounting to 15,281 gallons, from local distilleries. Additional cargo included four hogsheads (1,750 pounds) of tobacco, in violation of the law that required that tobacco be shipped only to Britain or another British colony. The captain was William Pinneger, a man who had carried out at least two slaving voyages before this one, in 1752 and 1756. A slaving captain was not hard to find in Newport, for slavers had been sent from that port for more than a half-century by such owners as Abraham Redwood, John Bannister, Samuel and William Vernon, and even the Quaker Wantons.[7] Pinneger was at Anomabu on the Gold Coast in the spring and by May 1, 1762, had loaded 50 slaves. On January 7, 1763, he reached Charleston, South Carolina, where he delivered a cargo of 134 slaves to Lopez's agents, DaCosta and Farr.[8]

Lopez presumably realized a profit from the venture, for it was followed by a series of six slaving voyages in the years 1764 through 1768:[9]

Sloop *Spry,* Capt. William Pinneger, July 16, 1764–May 22, 1766, stopping at
Barbados, Jamaica, and New York on the return voyage, slaves sold     57
Brig *Africa,* Capt. Abraham All, May 3, 1765–July 11, 1766, slaves sold at
Kingston     45
Sloop *Betsey,* Capt. Nathaniel Briggs, July 22, 1765–August 21, 1766, slaves
sold at Kingston     40
Brig *Sally* (the old *Spry* rerigged), Capt. Nathaniel Briggs, August 21, 1766–
July 1767, slaves sold at St. Kitts     ca. 33
Brig *Africa,* Capt. Abraham All, October 20, 1766–January 9, 1768, slaves
sold at Kingston     69
Brig *Hannah,* Capt. Nathaniel Briggs, May 3, 1768–May 4, 1769, slaves sold
in South Carolina and Barbados     63

Rum composed the bulk of the outward-bound cargoes, varying from 52 percent of the value of the cargo on *Africa*'s second voyage to 79 percent of that of *Hannah.* No dry goods are listed in the invoices of the first three voyages, but English and India dry goods and ready-made ruffled shirts appear in the last three, making up 21 percent of the value of *Sally*'s cargo.[10] The vessels were small by Liverpool standards, but one must take with a grain of salt the registered tonnage of 25 for *Africa* and *Spry* and 15 for *Betsey* recorded in the Jamaica Naval Office lists.[11] A brig bought by Lopez in 1768 that can be identified with some assurance as *Hannah* had an estimated carrying capacity of 125 or 130 tons.[12]

Records of slaves sold in America survive for five of these voyages. The number ranges from forty to sixty-nine per vessel and averages fifty-five. The total for *Sally*'s voyage was probably considerably lower than the average. Captain Briggs had taken aboard twenty-one slaves at the Windward Coast south of Cape Verde, ten at Cape

Mount on the Grain Coast, and sixty-seven along the Gold Coast—a total of ninety-eight. However, as Lopez informed his London correspondent, William Stead, there was severe loss of life at sea, and much sickness among the survivors forced a hurried sale at St. Kitts. *Sally*'s log records the burial of six slaves at sea, dead "with the feaver and flox"; the loss was doubtless much heavier, as the log does not cover a four-month period of coasting southward and eastward from the Windward Coast to Cape Coast Castle, an additional ten days during which the ship was buffeted between the latter port and the island of St. Thomas in the Gulf of Guinea, or the more than six weeks spent at St. Kitts. The figure, given above, of thirty-three slaves sold is calculated from the sum realized on the sale of the survivors, who may have been more numerous than this but of low value because of their debilitated condition.[13]

The evidence suggests that each of these voyages incurred a loss. Lopez recorded the deficit on *Spry* as £495.16.2 on an outlay of £1,586.9.2½ Lawful Money of Rhode Island, or about £326.6 stg. lost on his two-thirds of the investment. None of the other voyages was balanced by Lopez in his ledger; outlays were shown but income was not. Accounts of *Hannah* in Lopez's shipping book would set the loss for that voyage at £209 on an investment of £1,903.0.4½ Lawful Money of Rhode Island, or about £137.10 stg.[14] Bad luck dogged the whole series, beginning with the death of Captain Pinneger six hours before *Spry* made a landfall at Barbados after a prolonged voyage of five months on the Middle Passage, and including difficulties in collecting the proceeds from the sale of the slaves. The agent who sold three of the cargoes at Kingston, Philip Livingston, Jr., had to be threatened with a lawsuit before he would settle the debt he owed to Lopez. It is therefore not surprising that the repeated request of Captain Briggs after *Hannah*'s voyage of 1768–1769 that he be sent on another Guinea enterprise fell for a time on deaf ears.[15]

Neither is it surprising that Briggs wanted to go once more to Africa. Although the Lopez captains accepted lower wages when serving on slaving voyages—£60 Old Tenor of Rhode Island or about £1.13.9 stg. instead of the usual £80 per month or about £2.4.9 stg.—certain perquisites made such voyages lucrative for the captain. He was entitled to a "Coast Commission" of 4 out of every 104 slaves taken on board in Africa in return for his efforts in making the purchases. His "privilege"—the private cargo that he could carry free of charge—amounted by custom to four and one-half slaves, and Lopez's captains may have purchased these slaves in Africa at the expense of Lopez and Rivera. Payment of the privilege and the coast commission by the commission agent who sold the cargo in the West Indies was made at the rate of the average price for which the slaves were sold. A captain who acted as agent in collecting a homeward cargo of molasses and other goods in the West Indies would receive another commission, usually set at 2.5 percent in value of the purchases made, although it was sometimes as high as 5 percent. Briggs collected an additional sum for the wages of his black "servant," Quam, who served as a seaman at the rate of £50 Old Tenor per month.[16] On the voyage of *Sally*, on whose cargo of nonprivilege slaves Lopez realized £820.8.8 stg., Briggs received at least £200 stg. for his privilege and commissions in addition to his wages and those of Quam. In fact, Lopez had to give him a note of hand for five hundred Spanish dollars on May 5, 1768, for sums owed him in connection with the voyage. The captain's enthusiasm for the trade, and the profits it brought him, caused him to end each of two letters addressed to Lopez from Mole St. Nicholas on Hispaniola, dated March 11 and 17, 1770, "And don't forget the Guinea voyage."[17]

Between May 3, 1768, and June 4, 1770, no slaver left Newport in the Lopez-Rivera interest. It was not disgust with slavery or the slave traffic that accounted for this temporary cessation. Both Lopez and Rivera owned slaves—Lopez held five, Rivera twelve in 1774—and employed them, with those of other owners, in the unpleasant work of "trying" or rendering the whale head-matter for the making of candles. The ill success of the early slave voyages no doubt made slaving less attractive. The available investment capital could be spread only so far, and for a time it was largely absorbed in expanding the firm's direct trade with Jamaica and other West Indian islands, in procuring logwood in Honduras, and in the London trade. Sometime during this period Lopez declined an offer to become involved in a joint venture in the Guinea trade made to him by Abraham Lopez (no relation) of Savanna La Mar, Jamaica, pleading "the immense distance of [their] situations, which rendered it not only difficult to close such accounts but occasioned much writing."[18]

In May 1770 a large cargo of English goods coming from London on *Diana*, a Lopez vessel, was sequestered by the Newport Committee of Safety for infringing the nonimportation agreement. This incident caused Lopez to alter drastically his plan of trade. Briggs was now to get his Guinea voyage, which would not be interdicted by the nonimporters. Ship *Cleopatra* was diverted from its projected fourth voyage to London and prepared instead for Africa. With *Cleopatra* went sloop *Mary*, William English captain, which was to serve as tender to the larger vessel.[19] These were the first two of seven voyages that complete the history of the Lopez-Rivera slaving concern:[20]

Sloop *Mary*, Capt. William English, June 4, 1770–spring 1771, slaves sold in
    Barbados                                                       ca. 57

Ship *Cleopatra*, Capt. Nathaniel Briggs, July 1770–1771, slaves sold in
    Barbados                                                         96

Ship *Cleopatra*, Capt. Nathaniel Briggs, June 16, 1771–May 27, 1772, slaves
    sold in Barbados                                              230

Brig *Ann*, Capt. William English, November 27, 1772–winter 1773–1774
    (arrived in Jamaica October 8, 1773), slaves sold at Kingston        104

Ship *Africa*, Capt. Nathaniel Briggs, April 22, 1773–July 24, 1774, slaves sold
    in Jamaica                                                ca. 49

Ship *Cleopatra*, Capt. James Bourk, June 30, 1773–August 1774, Cargo
    consigned to Briggs, slaves sold in Jamaica                    ca. 77

Brig *Ann*, Capt. William English, spring 1774–March 1775, slaves sold in
    Jamaica                                                     112

Captain English had served as mate under Briggs on both *Betsey* and *Sally* on their Guinea voyages, and the two men carried out their voyages of 1770–1771 with uncommon dispatch. *Cleopatra*, "quite unexpected so early," arrived at Barbados on January 11, 1771, with a cargo of 96 slaves, and *Mary* came in about the same time, although the trade on the coast of Africa had been reported extremely dull and the price of slaves high.

Nevertheless, something went sour: Hayley and Hopkins, Lopez's chief London correspondents, in a letter of June 8, 1771, to Lopez, acknowledged "with concern the disappointment you experience in the remittance intended us from the *Cleopatra's* Voyage" and they were also in communication with Rivera about the insurance on the cargo. Probably *Cleopatra* had experienced very heavy mortality, for she brought the much higher number of 230 blacks to Barbados on her next voyage.[21] Briggs had followed orders in applying to the firm of Daniel and Lytcott to conduct the sale of *Cleopatra's* cargo, but their terms did not satisfy him. They wrote to Lopez and Rivera that

> we went off and viewed his slaves, which appear'd healthy, but rather a great proportion of privelege and male slaves; we however made Capt Briggs the offer of taking him up, to make the most we cou'd of his Cargo, and to sell his privelege free of Commission, but for such to take the Bills we might receive in payment without our guaranteeing them, this he objected to . . . after which we recommended to him to try what Messrs. Jones and Moe wou'd do, and we make no doubt their terms were more agreeable, so he struck with them.[22]

The merchants pointed out that they never had known so many bills to be protested in any year as in the last, and they complained that Briggs "bore rather hard on them, wanting them to guarantee the bills in payment for his privilege, which they would not do as they got neither profit nor loss by selling them."[23] Briggs had dealt with the firm of Jones and Moe when he brought *Hannah* into Barbados in 1769, and they were a highly respected house; he later had reason to regret that he went back to them.

After *Mary's* voyage English was withdrawn from the Africa trade for nearly two years, during which time he carried out two voyages to Lisbon for the purpose of smuggling wine into Newport. Briggs sailed again for Africa in *Cleopatra* in June 1771, carrying a large cargo of 192 hogsheads of rum. In due course he brought 230 slaves into Barbados and sold 210 of them at an average of £33 stg. through Jones and Moe. Indeed, it seemed that he would "make a good voyage."[24] But 1772 was a bad year in the international money market; many mercantile and banking houses were failing in London and Amsterdam, and the firm of Jones and Moe was seriously affected. When the bills they drew on Allen Marlar and Company of London to pay for the slaves were noted for nonacceptance, Lopez and Rivera were unable to collect on them.[25]

Once more Briggs was taken off the Guinea run and dispatched to Barbados in *Cleopatra*, laden with flour, lumber for cooperage, and livestock, and carrying 183 doubloons. His sailing orders instructed him to sell the commodities for specie, to be used in buying molasses at the Spanish port of Mole St. Nicholas on Hispaniola; nevertheless, the "chief motive" for sending him to Barbados was to determine whether Jones and Moe "are making sufficient disposition for payment of all bills they sent to London for the net proceeds of *Cleopatra's* last cargo of Slaves—all noted for nonacceptance." Briggs could continue on to Hispaniola if he were satisfied that the firm was taking care of its indebtedness, but if not, he must demand securities of them and stay at Barbados while dispatching his mate to the Mole for the molasses.[26] Whether the Barbadians were able to make full restitution is not known, but they did remit some cargo in place of bills of exchange: 10,980 gallons of West India rum and about 160 hundredweight of refined sugar reached Newport in August 1773.[27] In the meantime, the two Newport merchants had determined on a different pattern for their slaving voyage—their vessels would bring no more slaves to Barbados.

Lopez was considering a resumption of his earlier shipment of slaves to Jamaica at least as early as November 1771, when he resurrected the proposal for a joint undertaking, a "Guinea Concern," that had been made to him in 1769 by Abraham Lopez. He broached the matter in three letters to the Jamaican, and instructed his resident agent, Capt. Benjamin Wright, to extend the same proposition to Abraham orally. Doubtless news of the higher prices being paid for slaves in Jamaica had reached Newport, the increase being traceable to the fact that Jamaica's sugar economy was still on the rise whereas that of Barbados was not.[28] At the same time, most of the Lopez cargoes of New England goods were now being sent to the Jamaica market, where Wright had been established as factor for part of each year since the autumn of 1767. Wright acted as salesman of the New England cargoes and as collector of molasses, sugar, and rum to be returned to Newport by both provision ships and slaving vessels. In several instances he also transmitted cargo and freight to London by the provision ships although not by the slavers. Should the Lopez-Rivera slavers be diverted from Barbados to Jamaica, Wright would be the logical person to serve as agent to sell the blacks and to provide the homeward cargo for the vessels. Unfortunately, such a system was made impractical by his insistence on spending part of each year with his family in Newport, and since the dates of future landfalls of the vessels from Africa were always uncertain, Wright might well be off the island when vessels arrived. The collaboration of some permanent resident was essential to the successful handling of slave cargoes; hence Aaron's approach to Abraham Lopez.[29]

Neither Abraham Lopez nor Captain Wright took to the idea of a Lopez and Lopez "Guinea Concern." Abraham believed that the scheme could answer "extreemly well," but could not at the moment raise the money for his part of the venture since he was paying a large sum in dowry for his eldest daughter. He would be quite happy, however, to accept all slave cargoes on consignment for the usual commission of 5 percent on sales.[30] Wright was so distressed at the thought that Aaron would consider consigning slave cargoes "over my Back," as he said, and thus deprive him of the available commission, that he threatened to quit the Jamaica operation entirely. In a series of bitterly sarcastic letters he complained about the quality of the lumber, flour, and fish cargoes dispatched from Newport—consignments that often arrived out of season or in leaky vessels to which he had to give time and attention. Flour billed as "Philadelphia Superfine" too often was of low grade; staves and hoops for the making of molasses hogsheads were often worm-eaten and frequently arrived without the necessary lumber to head them up; and fish was putrid from being packed in insufficient brine. He found it difficult to dispose of such cargoes and implied that slave cargoes were easier to handle and more profitable. "Whenever," he wrote, "you consign a Cargo of Slaves address to the same Person 7 or 800 Barrels of Shads, that the Bitter and the sweet may go together."[31]

The "Guinea Concern" was dropped from consideration, partly no doubt because of the unwillingness of Abraham Lopez to invest money in the project but chiefly because of the need to keep Captain Wright as agent for the provision-molasses trade. Another agent was still needed to handle slave cargoes that might reach the island when Wright was not there. In the event, the scheme devised for what proved to be the last four African voyages was spelled out in sailing orders for Captain English in *Ann*, dated November 27, 1772, sending him to Africa. Should he arrive at Jamaica before the end of June, the slaves he carried were to be delivered to Wright at Savanna La Mar on the southwest coast of the island; should the landfall occur between July 1 and December 1, he was to carry his cargo to Thomas Dolbeare, a merchant at Kingston, on the southeast shore.[32]

It is difficult to make an informed estimate of the value of these last four "adventures." No journal or ledger for the post-1770 period has survived; neither is there an extant invoice book giving the prices of the goods exported from Newport or the sums of the returning cargoes. The invaluable shipping book peters out after 1771. Still, there is much to be learned from the existing Lopez papers about how the trade was carried on—about the cargoes shipped from and to Newport, the conditions on the coast of Africa, and the methods of sale in the West Indies.

Brig *Ann*, the smallest of the three vessels that made the last four voyages, came into the trade rather by accident. Captain English's first attempt to smuggle wine from Portugal into Newport on board the brig in 1771 had been a great success; the second effort resulted in the seizure and condemnation of the vessel and its cargo, and *Ann* had to be bought back at auction, albeit for a nominal sum.[33] Two months later, on November 27, 1772, her captain signed a bill of lading for a voyage to Africa that enumerated ninety-eight hogsheads and fourteen tierces of New England rum, and included some sheep and poultry that were to be delivered to Gov. David Mill of Cape Coast Castle. Upon his arrival on the coast, English found the price of rum low and the price of slaves high. Although he had reached Sierra Leone in mid-January and had written to his owners from Cape Coast Castle on March 10, he did not leave Anomabu for Jamaica until mid-July. His instructions required him to include in his cargo twenty-seven male and thirteen female slaves who had been left by Briggs in the hands of Governor Mill, there having been no room for them in *Cleopatra* when she sailed for the West Indies the previous year. After waiting a month, English had received thirty slaves toward the settlement of the account but could not wait longer for the other ten "as my provisions expends fast and am afraid of sickness getting among the slaves I have on board." His final cargo included sixty-five slaves on account of *Ann*, thirty on account of *Cleopatra*, and fourteen privilege slaves for himself and his mates.[34]

Captain Wright, at Savanna La Mar, hoped that *Ann* would arrive at Jamaica before July 1, when he expected to leave for Newport, and consulted by letter with the experienced slaver from Newport, Capt. Peleg Clarke, who had reached Jamaica from Cape Coast Castle in mid-February, as to whether this was possible. Clarke's answer of February 27, 1773, from Kingston punctured his hopes. The brig, said Clarke, if bound to the leeward African coast adjacent to Cape Coast Castle, would not make Anomabu until March: "Rum is there in plenty and slaves there are scarce so she won't leave the Coast under 5 or 6 months. . . . Another thing, in May the rains setts in, and lasts 'til the latter end of July, at which time there is but little trade, and from June till November, it is difficult to make a passage under three months, to this place, Oweing to small winds and strong lee Currents, acomeing off the Coast, which I have expereced [sic] in my last Voyage, therefore I do not believe she will be with you in June." In the same letter Clarke rejoiced that he had sold all his slaves, averaging £42 stg., and all for cash: "So high sales and so Emeditt pay, never before was known in Kingston." Jamaica in his view provided a better market than Barbados, where his friend Capt. William Barden had currently been able to dispose of only part of his cargo at the lower rate of £34 stg.[35]

Resigning himself to the delay and instructed to avoid another spate of questionable bills of exchange such as those previously given by Jones and Moe, Wright began negotiations with Dolbeare at Kingston for the handling of *Ann*'s cargo. A letter from Wright to Lopez, dated Savanna La Mar, May 12, 1773, specified the terms of agreement:

> Mr. Dolbear is prepareing security to take up Capt. Inglis [English] when he arrives, he agrees to take him up on the [sic] these Conditions viz, to sell the slaves to the best advantage he posibly can to stand to all bad debts, to Close the voyage on your Brigs saleing for Rhode Island to ship you some produce in said Brig should you order it, the remainder he is to transmit you in good bills of Exchang at four Eight and twelve months sight the bills are to be Indorsed by Christopher Main [?], which Gentleman he offers as a security I think him as good a Man as any in the Island, the Sooner you dispatch your Instructions for Capt Inglis the better, you will please to Order Inglis to see this Security given before he delivers his Cargo into their hands.[36]

English reached Kingston on October 7, having lost five slaves on the voyage but with his people apparently healthy. By the time the sale could be made, two more had died and the prevalence of "the Swelling" among the remainder caused a drastic reduction in their value; instead of £42 stg., the price averaged only £33.15. The gross sales in sterling came to £3,501, of which sum about £540 went to the captain and mates in payment of their privilege and £116 to the captain for his cost commission. Duties amounted to £112, Dolbeare's commission to £175, and there were incidental expenditures of £35 that may have represented port dues or commissions on the purchase of £1,983.5.11 in sterling bills of exchange that were to be transmitted to England. The brig carried £540 of the proceeds to the Mole for the purchase of molasses. Whether this all added up to a profit is unknown; it must be remembered that thirty of the slaves had been bought out of the cargo of *Cleopatra*'s second voyage. Dolbeare reported to Lopez that he had made every effort to assure a profit; he was disturbed, however, by the large sums that had to be paid to English. "There are generous priveliges allowed out of your port," he told the Rhode Islander.[37]

There is little information about the voyage of *Africa* and the final voyage of *Cleopatra* to the slave coast. The two were paired, even to the consignment of both cargoes to Briggs, a precautionary measure probably owing to the inexperience in the African trade of Capt. James Bourk of *Cleopatra*. The investment was considerably lower than on *Cleopatra*'s second voyage, which had been insured for £2,150, whereas now she carried only £1,350 coverage while £1,400 was placed on *Africa*. The rum cargoes were very large, including 217 hogsheads in *Africa* and 234 in *Cleopatra*. The remaining goods were almost entirely provisions, but they also included such novelties as a barrel of venison hams, four hounds, several cases of window frames and shutters, and a keg of vegetable seeds. *Africa* left Newport about April 23, 1773; *Cleopatra* followed on June 30.[38]

We know little of how the vessels fared at Anomabu, although the records indicate that Briggs was unable to obtain delivery of the ten slaves still owed from *Cleopatra*'s second voyage. The price of slaves was high, amounting to 210 to 220 gallons of rum per slave. Since *Africa* and *Cleopatra* carried only enough rum to purchase at that rate fewer than one hundred slaves apiece, and since neither had much else in merchantable cargo, they could not have reached Jamaica with many more than two hundred slaves between them. *Cleopatra* was in Jamaica by the end of February, and *Africa* must have come in very soon thereafter. The cargoes were consigned to Wright, and on July 20, 1774, Hayley and Hopkins in London were already writing to Lopez to congratulate him on Wright's satisfactory sale of *Cleopatra*'s slaves and to express their hope for equal success in selling those brought by *Africa*.[39]

Captain Bourk of *Cleopatra* was not quite so happy. Prices of slaves continued high in Jamaica, probably increased by a trade agreement between England and Spain described by both Captain English and Dolbeare in letters to Lopez and Rivera, and the Guinea cargoes could be sold rapidly. But Jamaica cargoes of molasses, sugar, and rum were hard come by, and as early as June 18, 1773, Wright had expressed his concern at the great number of vessels reaching Jamaica from the continental colonies and competing for island produce. On June 24, 1774, Bourk reported to his owners that he had been at the island for more than four months, had been to Green Island and back to Savanna La Mar, and still had only 160 casks of molasses and 19 puncheons of rum on board. "It seems," he wrote, "that Capt. Wright is so busy of Dispatching Capt. Briggs that I can't even find out what I came round here for. . . . Capts. Briggs and Sessions know no more than I. A great deal of expense. My brother in your Brigg [*Charlotte*] Lays in the same manner nor cant Set any time about his Sailing."[40] It is apparent that Wright was overextending himself as a Jamaica factor.

The aggressive Briggs sailed into Newport a good month ahead of Bourk, and his small cargo of Jamaica rum, molasses, and sugar was divided on July 24, 1774, between *Africa*'s two owners. Bourk entered his ship at the customhouse on August 29 with a fuller but probably less valuable cargo of 15,590 gallons of molasses; his 19 puncheons of rum had somehow been transferred to Briggs. The voyages must have turned a profit, as sterling bills to the value of £2,047.4.7 from the slave cargo of *Cleopatra* and £871.19.9½ from the slave cargo of *Africa* were sent to Hayley and Hopkins in London on September 1 by Wright. In addition, the cargoes home to Newport were probably bought out of the proceeds of the Guinea voyages. Still, the London agents found that remittances from Jamaica fell far short of expectations, and a year later Hayley complained to Lopez that "the delay of remittances [from Wright] to such an unreasonable length in his hands greatly hurts me. I must hope you will be able to fall upon some method of quickening him in the future."[41]

In the spring of 1774 brig *Ann*, with English in command, sailed once more for Africa. Hayley and Hopkins reported on April 29 that they had been able to insure her for the required £1,700 from Newport to Africa and thence to the port of unlading in

America at the rate of seven guineas per cent rather than at the longstanding eight-guinea rate, the reduction being occasioned by "the great success which the African Vessels have had." Once more English attempted to collect the ten slaves still due from *Cleopatra*'s second cargo, and once more he failed. Mill assured Rivera and Lopez in a letter of September 30 that he would deliver the slaves to Briggs when the captain came in on his next voyage, a voyage that never occurred; Mill also referred to a projected second voyage by Bourk, which also did not take place. *Ann* wrote finis to the Lopez-Rivera Guinea voyages as she traced a fifty-five-day journey from Cape Coast Castle to Barbados, arriving there on November 27, 1774, with a cargo of 112 blacks: 72 men and boys and 40 women and girls—"as good a rum Cargoe as I ever saw." English died at sea a few days before the brig reached Barbados, and his mate, Charles Davis, took the vessel to Wright in Jamaica, where the cargo was sold. Once more George Hayley in London rejoiced, somewhat prematurely, that he was to receive remittances from Jamaica, this time out of *Ann*'s profits.[42]

Aaron Lopez dispatched well over two hundred voyages during his active shipping career in Newport, which lasted from 1760 to 1776. Fourteen of these voyages were directed to Africa for the purpose of slaving. Although all fourteen of the slavers reached their ports of discharge in safety and proceeded back to Newport, there is strong evidence that less than half of them, and possibly only a total of four, turned a profit. The number of slaves actually landed in America by the ten vessels whose cargoes are specifically stated came to 950. The other four cargoes can be estimated on the basis of the size of the vessel, the value of the outgoing cargo and its purchasing power on the coast of Africa, and the sum received in the islands for the slaves. When this estimated total of 216 is added to the above figure, one discovers that the probable total of slaves brought to America by this so-called "most successful slaving business" of Rhode Island amounted to 1,166 for its whole career.[43] The smallness of this involvement in the slave trade becomes apparent when one notes that in the same week in December 1773 when *Cleopatra* brought about 77 slaves into Kingston, two other vessels entered the same port from Anomabu carrying a total of 700 slaves.[44]

Although by 1773, despite vicissitudes, the slave trade was beginning to prove remunerative for Lopez and Rivera, it was not on the whole a profitable part of their business. The failure of the earlier voyages in particular can be traced to the usual problems facing the New England rum shippers in the Guinea trade: markets on the slave coast glutted with rum; frequent shortages of slaves for sale; mortality both on the coast and during the Middle Passage; the need to sell rapidly in the West Indies because of the debilitated condition of the blacks; and the difficulty in obtaining prompt pay—and sometimes any pay at all—from the planters and factors who purchased the slaves. Quite apart from these difficulties, moreover, it is doubtful that the Newport traders of the 1760s and 1770s could have competed effectively with the Liverpool slavers. The American vessels were smaller, as they needed to be for coasting in the West Indies in search of cargo; this small size was also advantageous in the run up the coast from the West Indies to their home port. Capital resources were limited even had the merchants wished to construct larger vessels, and such vessels would have required larger crews, not readily available in labor-short America. Lack of "connections" on the African coast equal to those of Englishmen—connections that would produce quick cargoes at the various "castles" and forts—would make the stay on the coast too prolonged and too precarious to support a large ship. Lack of established financial relations with the English planters in the West Indies resulted in slow pay for slave cargoes and protracted negotiations for the return cargoes of molasses and other products. Here, too, larger vessels would have proved uneconomical.

Despite these handicaps, the Newporters would probably have continued in the slave trade had there been no break with England. The specie and bills of exchange procured from the sale of the slaves made up a good part of the remittances sent to London in an effort to cope with the perennially unfavorable sterling balance owed to suppliers of English goods. Those goods were essential in the whole Lopez-Rivera operation; they served in lieu of cash in the complicated exchanges of goods and services that are recorded in the account books. They financed the purchase of cargoes to be sent to the West Indies and the Mediterranean, to the Newfoundland fisheries, and to England itself, and they paid the men who built the ships to carry those cargoes. A slaving voyage that operated at an apparent loss might provide enough good bills and specie to keep an English creditor sufficiently happy to fill another invoice to be sent to Newport. The advance charged on the dry goods, hardware, and glass that he sent might provide enough barter power to cover the loss on a slaving voyage. Aaron Lopez, supposedly an "oppulent" merchant, operated on a precarious credit base and could not neglect any source of remittances for London; the Newport-slave coast-Jamaica-Newport triangle must have continued to look promising as such a source.

Aaron Lopez was not the only Newport merchant who engaged in trading for slaves. The seven Rhode Island vessels seen at Anomabu on May 1, 1762, by John Harwood and the fifteen slaves that cleared for Africa from Newport during 1763, taken together with Lopez's fourteen voyages, demonstrate that the triangular trade was by no means mythical.[45] Yet slaving was never the dominant interest of Lopez nor was it necessarily crucial to New England's economy. In comparison with the Liverpool traders, Lopez brought few slaves to America and made no fortune by them. His slaving ventures constituted only a small part of his commercial activities. If Lopez and Rivera did indeed own "the most successful slaving business" in Rhode Island before the Revolution, one must conclude—pending studies of other New Englanders who participated in the slave trade—that the triangular trade, while not mythical, was not a major factor in the commerce of colonial New England.

NOTES

1. Gilman M. Ostrander, "The Making of the Triangular Trade Myth," *William and Mary Quarterly*, 3d Ser., XXX (1973), 635–644. Ostrander cites (n. 1) the writings of several revisionist historians, but see Virginia Bever Platt, "Triangles and Tramping: Captain Zebediah Story of Newport, 1769–1776," *American Neptune*, XXXIII (1973), 294–303, for a presentation of another triangle involving the trade with the Iberian peninsula, the existence of which is questioned by the same set of scholars.

2. The Lopez papers are deposited at the Newport Historical Society, Newport, R. I.; the American

Jewish Historical Society, Waltham, Mass.; the Massachusetts Historical Society, Boston; the Baker Library of Harvard University, Cambridge, Mass.; the Essex Institute, Salem, Mass.; Yale University, New Haven, Conn.; the John Carter Brown Library, Providence, R. I.; the Rhode Island Historical Society, Providence; Mystic Seaport, Mystic, Conn.; and the New York State Library, Albany. Numerous lacunae in the accounts and haphazard accounting methods combine with the chaotic currency situation of the time to make the use of the papers frustrating, especially to determine profit and loss. Nevertheless, it is valid to conclude that all of the Lopez slaving voyages between 1761 and 1775 have been identified.

3. Smuggling of Dutch tea to the colonies began to assume substantial proportions after 1745, when Parliament (18 Geo. II c. 26) terminated the drawback of customs and excise duties allowed on tea that was reexported, amounting to 52% ad valorem. See Virginia Margaret Bever, "The Trade in East India Commodities to the American Colonies, 1690–1775" (Ph.D. diss., State University of Iowa, 1940), Chap. 6.

4. The Lopez and Rivera families can be well followed in the magnificent study by Jacob R. Marcus, *The Colonial American Jew, 1492–1776* (Detroit, Mich., 1970), and in the more informal study by Stanley F. Chyet, *Lopez of Newport: Colonial American Merchant Prince* (Detroit, Mich., 1970), Chap. 2.

5. Lopez Account Books, Lopez Papers, Newport Hist. Soc., *passim.* All subsequent citations of the Lopez Papers refer to the collection at the Newport Hist. Soc. The existence of only one volume—81—of Rivera's commercial records, a letterbook incorrectly attributed to Lopez, severely restricts knowledge of his business career. *Ibid.* The expansion of the Lopez-Rivera connection into overseas commerce may have been established in part as a dowry to Aaron at the time of his marriage to Sarah, Jacob's daughter, in 1762.

6. Elizabeth Donnan, ed., *Documents Illustrative of the History of the Slave Trade to America* (Washington, D. C., 1930–1935), III, 147.

7. Account of Oct. 29, 1760, Vol. 740, Lopez Papers; Pinneger accounts of Nov. 2, 1761, Mar. 29, 1762, Rosenbach Collection, folders for 1760, 1761, and 1762, Am. Jewish Hist. Soc. (The captain's name is sometimes spelled Pinnegar; he should not be confused with his son of the same name who carried out several slaving voyages for merchants other than Lopez.) For Pinneger's earlier voyages see Donnan, ed., *Documents,* III, 139, 173; names of owners of slave vessels, *ibid.,* 109, 131–138, 142–150, 157–159.

8. *Newport Mercury,* Sept. 7, 1762; Isaac DaCosta to Aaron Lopez, Jan. 11, 1763, Vol. 622, nos. 59, 77, Lopez Papers; entry of Jan. 7, 1763, C.O. 5/510, Public Record Office. The African port is spelled Annamaboe in the Lopez Papers.

9. *Spry: Newport Merc.,* July 16, 1764, Feb. 10, June 2, 1766; invoice of July 18, 1764, Vol. 479, Vol. 480, 49, Vol. 577, fols. 64, 72, Vol. 622, nos. 26, 29, Lopez Papers; folder for 1766, Rosenbach Coll.; C.O. 142/17, fols. 8, 25; Donnan, ed., *Documents,* III, 214.

*Africa,* first voyage: invoice of May 3, 1765, Vol. 479, Vol. 555, fols. 42, 111, Vol. 629, no. 8, Lopez Papers; folder for 1765, Rosenbach Coll.; C.O. 142/17, fol. 2.

*Betsey:* invoice of July 22, 1765, Vol. 479, Vol. 480, fol. 131, Vol. 557, fol. 65, Vol. 559, fol. 160, Vol. 597, 28, 29, 31, Vol. 622, no. 68, Lopez Papers; C.O. 142/17, fols. 8, 29 (incorrectly listed as *Betty*); Donnan, ed., *Documents,* III, 208–209, 211–212, 213, 215; *Commerce of Rhode Island, 1726–1800* (Massachusetts Historical Society, *Collections,* 7th Ser., IX–X [Boston, 1914–1915]), I, 117, hereafter cited as *Commerce of Rhode Island.*

*Sally:* invoice of Aug. 21, 1766, Vol. 479, Vol. 480, 173, Vol. 557, fols. 72, 163, Vol. 558, 565, 647, 649, 660, Vol. 629, no. 26, Lopez Papers.

*Africa,* second voyage: *Newport Merc.,* Oct. 20, 1766; Vol. 554, fol. 210, Vol. 555, fols. 42, 111, 152, Vol. 557, fols. 76, 97, 213, Vols. 558, 556, 716, 744, Vol. 629, nos. 27, 32, letters of Nov. 2, 10, Dec. 10, 14, 1767, Vol. 72, Lopez Papers; C.O. 142/17 fols. 50, 67; *Commerce of Rhode Island,* I, 203, 205.

*Hannah:* invoice of May 3, 1768, Vol. 479, Vol. 557, fols. 65, 215, 264, 285, 316, 317, Vol. 558, 566, 729, 768, 941, Vol. 560, fol. 118, Vol. 630, no. 56, Lopez Papers.

10. Invoices of July 18, 1764, May 3, July 22, 1765, Aug. 21, Oct. 20, 1766, Vol. 479, Vol. 480, fols. 13, 49, *ibid.*

11. C.O. 142/17, fols. 8, 25, 29, 50, 67. The Naval Office lists record registered tonnage, construed by two

recent students of colonial commerce to amount to about ⅔ of a vessel's "real tonnage." John J. McCusker, "Colonial Tonnage Measurement: Five Philadelphia Merchant Ships as a Sample," *Journal of Economic History*, XXVII (1967), 82–91; Gary M. Walton, "Colonial Tonnage Measurements: A Comment," *ibid.*, 392–397. Actually, "real tonnage" might be any one of a number of measures. Frederic C. Lane, "Tonnages, Medieval and Modern," *Economic History Review*, 2d Ser., XVII (1964–1965), 213–223. Eighteenth-century officials were aware that the tonnage put on a registry varied as its owners tried to reduce payments required by current tonnage duties levied in their ports of call. For example, John Williams, a New York customs official, reported in 1768 that judging by the bulk of entering cargoes recorded in the New York Customhouse, the vessels carrying these cargoes were of four times the burden of their registry. T. 1/505, fol. 292, P.R.O. There are no extant Naval Office lists for Rhode Island; tonnage can be estimated from other sources, such as advertisements of vessels for sale or contracts for ship construction. A sloop built for the Guinea trade was advertised at 50 tons in the *Newport Merc.*, Dec. 3, 1764; brigs, not specifically for Guineamen, were offered at 112 tons on Mar. 19, 1764, and at 160 tons on Feb. 22, 1773, *ibid.* A vessel with a brigantine rig might conceivably be as small as 25 tons—plus the ⅓ assumed by McCusker and Walton—but this is not likely. Philip D. Curtin estimates that in the last third of the 18th century a carriage rate of two slaves per ton was considered to be normal in the British vessels. *The Atlantic Slave Trade: A Census* (Madison, Wis., 1969), 134. This would put *Spry* at 30 tons, *Betsey* at 20, and *Africa* at 35 had they lost no slaves on the voyages. They may not have had stowage capacity equal to that of the Bristol and Liverpool vessels.

12. *Commerce of Rhode Island*, I, 219.

13. Purchases from *Sally*'s cargo on coast of Africa, 1766, Misc. Papers, Rosenbach Coll.; letter of Aug. 7, 1767, Vol. 72, Lopez Papers; log of brig *Sally*, MS 980, microfilm 136, International Marine Manuscripts Archives, Nantucket, Mass.; price of slaves at St. Kitts as of Feb. 10, 1768, estimated at "Near £30 St'g per head," Donnan, ed., *Documents*, III, 242. Heavy mortality on the Windward coast was suffered in the previous year aboard another brig *Sally*. Darold D. Wax, "The Browns of Providence and the Slaving Voyage of the Brig *Sally*, 1764–1765," *Am. Neptune*, XXXII (1972), 176.

14. *Spry*'s loss, Vol. 480, fol. 49, Lopez Papers; apparent loss on *Hannah*, Vol. 557, fol. 316, Vol. 560, fol. 118, *ibid.*

15. *Newport Merc.*, Feb. 10, 1776; Vol. 629, no. 2, Lopez Papers; Livingston's account as of Aug. 21, 1767, folder for 1767, Rosenbach Coll.; *Commerce of Rhode Island*, I, 209, 213. The nature of Livingston's settlement is not specified.

16. The captain's wage is shown in Donnan, ed., *Documents*, III, 208. An invoice of Dec. 24, 1767, shows a ratio of 35.5 to 1 between Old Tenor and sterling. Vol. 479, Lopez Papers. Information about coast commissions and privilege slaves may be found in letters of Samuel and William Vernon to Brewton and Smith, Apr. 15, 1773, and Wilkinson and Ayrault to Capt. David Lindsay, June 19, 1754, in Donnan, ed., *Documents*, III, 269, 149. The coast commission of £4 in £104 seems to have been fairly standard, and Donnan finds that the captain's privilege was usually set at the same figure. *Ibid.*, 149, 150, 162, 246, 247. The commission and privilege allowances for sloop *Betsey*'s voyage are given in Capt. Briggs's sailing orders dated July 22, 1765, Box for 1760–1769, Shipping Papers, Newport Hist. Soc.

17. Lopez to William Stead, Aug. 7, 1767, Lopez to Nathaniel Briggs, Aug. 27, 1767, Vol. 72, Vol. 480, fol. 173, entries for Nov. 16, 1767, May 5, 1768, Vol. 554, Vol. 560, fol. 52, Lopez Papers; Briggs to Lopez, Mar. 17, 1770, *Commerce of Rhode Island*, I, 318. Instead of his desired Guinea voyage, Briggs was assigned a voyage to Dominica, St. Kitts, St. Croix, and the Mole for 1770. Vol. 631, no. 62, Lopez Papers; folder 1–50, 1771, Rosenbach Coll.

18. For Lopez and Rivera's ownership of slaves see *Census of the Inhabitants of the Colony of Rhode Island and Providence Plantations, Taken by Order of the General Assembly, in the Year 1774* . . . (Providence, R. I., 1858), 21. For Abraham Lopez's proposal see Benjamin Wright to Aaron Lopez, Feb. 21, 1772, Box 78, folder 14, Shipping Papers. Sloop *Betsey Ann*, Capt. English, carried some slaves into Newbern, N. C., on Mar. 16, 1770; but she brought them *out* of Newport on Feb. 26, 1770. There is no indication whence they came or how many there were. Naval Office Clearances, 1770, folder 51–100, Rosenbach Coll.; *Commerce of Rhode Island*, I, 318.

19. *Diana's* sequestration, Vol. 631, no. 26, Lopez Papers; *Cleopatra* and *Mary*, Vol. 557, 425–430, *ibid.*

20. Citations for the specific voyages are given in succeeding footnotes. Dates of the voyages come from the *Newport Merc.* and from invoices given in Vol. 166, Lopez Papers, where they are entered in chronological sequence. It should be noted that four of the Lopez-Rivera vessels reported in Donnan, ed., *Documents*, III, 265, n. 3, as "apparently" loaded for Africa in 1772 and 1773 did not in fact go there, as the bills of lading cited make clear. *Royal Charlotte*, went to Jamaica, *George* to North Carolina, and *Charlotte* and *Active* both to Hispaniola. Bills of lading dated Apr. 23, Dec. [?] 1772, Jan. 19, June 14, 1773, Vol. 166, Lopez Papers.

21. Vol. 631, nos. 28, 62, Vol. 632, no. 28, Lopez Papers; *Newport Merc.*, Mar. 11, 1771; Donnan, ed., *Documents*, III, 246–247 and nn.; *Commerce of Rhode Island*, I, 398–399.

22. Vol. 631, no. 62, Lopez Papers.

23. *Ibid.*, no. 67.

24. For the rum cargo see Box 78, folder 14, Shipping Papers; for the slave cargo see *Commerce of Rhode Island*, I, 398–399.

25. Vol. 634, nos. 31, 58, Vol. 636, no. 36, entry for Dec. 14, 1772, Vol. 672, Lopez Papers; protested bills registered, Public Notary Records, VIII, 158, Rhode Island Statehouse, Providence.

26. Sailing orders for *Cleopatra*, Dec. 14, 1772, folder 351–400, Rosenbach Coll.; invoice dated Dec. 14, 1772, Vol. 166, Lopez Papers.

27. Entry of Aug. 21, 1773, Vol. 464, Lopez Papers.

28. Abraham Lopez to Aaron Lopez, June 21, 1772, Vol. 633, no. 49, *ibid.;* R. B. Sheridan, "The Wealth of Jamaica in the Eighteenth Century," *Econ. Hist. Rev.*, 2d Ser., XVIII (1965–1966), 292–311; Donnan, ed., *Documents*, II, xliv–xlvi, III, 255. John Fletcher wrote from London to Capt. Peleg Clarke, Feb. 24, 1772, that good slaves were then averaging £40 stg. at Jamaica. *Ibid.*, III, 255.

29. Wright had been recommended to Aaron Lopez by Abraham Lopez as an able sea captain and had carried out two trading voyages for Aaron to Jamaica before assuming the periodic residency. Aaron Lopez to Abraham Lopez, Aug. 20, 1767, Vol. 72, invoice of Oct. 11, 1768, Vol. 479, Lopez Papers; letters from Wright to Aaron Lopez, 1769–1776, Box 78, folder 14, Shipping Papers; Lopez Papers, *passim; Commerce of Rhode Island*, I, 216, 255–256, 260–263, 268–273, 279, 362–364, 366–367, 379, 392, 400, 415, 431, 442, 495, 496, 503, II, 10, 25, 27, 53, 66, 77, 79; Marcus, *Colonial American Jew*, II, 589–590.

30. Vol. 633, no. 49, Lopez Papers.

31. Letters from Wright to Aaron Lopez, Feb. 21, 29, Mar. 22, 1772, Box 78, folder 14, Shipping Papers.

32. Donnan, ed., *Documents*, III, 264–265.

33. For *Ann's* smuggling activities see Virginia Bever Platt, "Tar, Staves, and New England Rum: The Trade of Aaron Lopez of Newport, Rhode Island, with Colonial North Carolina," *North Carolina Historical Review*, XLVIII (1971), 16–18.

34. Invoice dated Nov. 27, 1772, Vol. 166, Lopez Papers; William English to Aaron Lopez, July 15, 1773, Box 52, no. 222, Shipping Papers; Donnan, ed., *Documents*, III, 264–266, 271–272, 272n.

35. Peleg Clarke to Wright, Feb. 27, 1773, Box 78, folder 14, Shipping Papers. Donnan uses Clarke's letterbook extensively. She refers to Capt. William Barden as Capt. Charles Bardine, another active Newport slaver. *Documents*, III, 130n, 209, 254, 259–262, 307.

36. Vol. 634, no. 49, Lopez Papers.

37. Donnan, ed., *Documents*, III, 272–277, quotation on p. 274. Jamaica currency has been converted to sterling.

38. Invoices dated Apr. 23, June 30, 1773, Vol. 166, Lopez Papers; insurance account, May 31, 1773, Misc. Papers, Rosenbach Coll.; Donnan, ed., *Documents*, III, 250. A European gardener was employed at Anomabu in 1764. Philip D. Curtin, ed., *Africa Remembered: Narratives by West Africans from the Era of the Slave Trade* (Madison, Wis., 1967), 120, n. 49.

39. Vol. 638, no. 25, Lopez Papers; Donnan, ed., *Documents*, III, 286, 291; *Commerce of Rhode Island*, I, 500–501.

40. James Bourk to Aaron Lopez, June 24, 1774, Box 78, folder 14, Shipping Papers; Vol. 634, no. 70, Lopez Papers; Donnan, ed., *Documents*, III, 273–275.

41. Entry of Sept. 8, 1774, and last page, Vol. 656, Lopez Papers; George Hayley to Aaron Lopez, Aug. 31, 1775, *Commerce of Rhode Island*, II, 28.

42. Vol. 638, nos. 25, 50, 51, Lopez Papers; Hayley and Hopkins to Aaron Lopez, Apr. 29, 1774, *Commerce of Rhode Island*, I, 494; George Hayley to Lopez, Apr. 30, 1775, *ibid.*, II, 17; William Moore, Jr., to Lopez, Nov. 27, 1774, Vol. 638, no. 51, Lopez Papers. American captains other than Capt. English found it difficult to obtain promised cargoes from Gov. Mill, who was deeply involved in private trading, contrary to the rules of his organization, the Company of Merchants Trading to Africa. Donnan, ed., *Documents*, II, 402, 538n, 539, 548, III, 314, 325.

43. This figure has been reached by using the import figures from the Naval Office lists where they exist; estimates based on the sums realized on the cargoes of *Sally* (in 1767), *Africa*, and *Cleopatra* (1774), information from private letters (*Grayhound*, 1763, and *Cleopatra*, 1772), and finally a figure for *Mary* in 1771 giving her the largest number listed for any vessel of equivalent build. See also James Pope-Hennessy, *Sins of the Fathers: A Study of the Atlantic Slave Traders, 1441–1807* (New York, 1968), 226, 240–241.

44. Donnan, ed., *Documents*, III, 277.

45. *Newport Merc.*, Jan. 3, 31, Feb. 14, 28, May 2, 23, July 18, Aug. 1, 22, Sept. 5, 26, Oct. 24, Dec. 5, 12, 19, 1763. See also report of John Harwood of schooner *Success, ibid.*, Sept. 7, 1762.

RALPH A. AUSTEN

# The Uncomfortable Relationship
## African Enslavement in the Common History of Blacks and Jews

In 1978, I attended a faculty luncheon at the University of Chicago Hillel House, where the distinguished African-American historian, John Hope Franklin, was giving a talk on the Jewish community in the nineteenth-century Southern United States. After the formal presentation, a member of the audience asked a question about Southern Jewish participation in the debate on slavery. As I remember it, Franklin replied that he did not know too much about the subject. I recall very clearly one of the Hillel regulars remarking that since many of the early Southern Jews were Sephardim who had fled Spanish and Portuguese persecution, they must have been sympathetic to the plight of Black slaves.

I remember this statement because it was allowed to pass without comment, although John Hope Franklin and I (we discussed it afterwards) were both aware that Sephardi Jews in the New World had been heavily involved in the African slave trade. Why did two professional historians in a university setting hesitate to provide our colleagues with such an important piece of information? I cannot answer for Franklin but I, as a Jew sitting in a Jewish institution that was entertaining an African-American guest, felt that pointing out the role of Jews in the history of Black slavery would, in this context, have constituted something of a betrayal. I did not want to undermine the sense of solidarity between the two communities which had been reinforced by Franklin's very presence, as well as through his references to our common confrontation with white Gentile Southern bigots.

Franklin and I, in effect, were condoning a benign historical myth: that the shared liberal agenda of twentieth-century Blacks and Jews has a pedigree going back through the entire remembered past. *Avodim hayinu!* We, the Jews, had also experienced history on the side of the enslaved and always cried out in anguish against the oppression of the enslavers.

For better or worse, it is no longer possible to maintain that this myth has any but the most abstract bearing on the facts of our pre-emancipation relationship with Africans and their New World descendants. Jewish students of Jewish history have known it was untrue and, over several decades, have produced a significant body of scholarship detailing the involvement of our ancestors in the Atlantic slave trade and Pan-American slavery. Until recently, this work remained buried in scholarly journals, read only by

Ralph A. Austen is professor of African history and co-chair of the Committee on African and African-American Studies at the University of Chicago.

Reprinted from TIKKUN MAGAZINE, A BI-MONTHLY JEWISH CRITIQUE OF POLITICS, CULTURE AND SOCIETY 9, no. 2 (1994): 65–68, 86.

other specialists. It had never been synthesized in a publication for a non-scholarly audience. A book of this sort has now appeared, however, written not by Jews but by an anonymous group of African Americans associated with the Reverend Louis Farrakhan's Nation of Islam.

Since its publication in 1991, *The Secret Relationship between Blacks and Jews* has become the subject of considerable furor, although little serious analysis. It was cited by Professor Leonard Jeffries in his infamous speech in July 1991 at the Empire State Black Arts and Cultural Festival that led to his removal from the chairmanship of the Black Studies Department at the City University of New York. (He was subsequently reinstated as chairman and awarded damages in a suit he brought against the university.) The book was also the topic of an even more publicized and virulently anti-Semitic speech by Farrakhan's representative, Khalid Abdul Muhammad, at Kean College in New Jersey in November 1993.

Early in 1993, a furor arose at Wellesley College when Tony Martin, a Black Studies professor, assigned the book in one of his African-American history courses, causing vociferous protest from Jewish groups. During a long, stormy discussion in Wellesley's Academic Council about the ethics of teaching such a text, Selwyn Cudjoe, the chair of the college's Africana Studies Department, denounced *The Secret Relationship* as anti-Semitic and deplored Martin's uncritical presentation of the text. Martin has subsequently chronicled and defended his and Jeffries's position in two broadside publications, *Blacks and Jews at Wellesley News* (a play on the name of the campus newspaper) and *Blacks and Jews News* (published by the Nation of Islam). Martin has now published a book of his own, *The Jewish Onslaught: Despatches from the Wellesley Battlefront*, which elicited a public denunciation by Wellesley's president. Martin has also announced the imminent publication of Volumes II and III of *The Secret Relationship*.

Among Martin's arguments in support of *The Secret Relationship*, there is at least one which Jewish intellectuals need to take seriously: that few of the Jewish leaders who have attacked the book have actually read it. Martin is apparently unaware (as, it appears, are many Jewish critics) of a carefully researched, if somewhat polemical, report on the book by Harold Brackman published in 1992 under the auspices of the Simon Wiesenthal Center, titled *Farrakhan's Reign of Historical Error: the Truth Behind the Secret Relationship between Blacks and Jews*. Indeed, the fact that the present article is appearing more than two years after the publication of *The Secret Relationship* in a journal very much concerned with Black-Jewish relations itself requires some explanation.

One can understand the hesitation of Jews to buy *The Secret Relationship* and thus put $19.95 (plus $3 for shipping and handling) into the coffers of an organization notorious for its anti-Semitic pronouncements (I bought my copy in a Black bookstore in Chicago which also sells such classic anti-Semitic tracts as *The Protocols of the Elders of Zion* and Henry Ford's *The International Jew*). *The Secret Relationship*'s association with the rantings of Leonard Jeffries, and its denunciation in a *New York Times* op-ed piece on Black anti-Semitism by the very prominent and widely respected African-American scholar Henry Louis Gates, Jr., have made it easier for Jewish critics to dispense with examining the book themselves.

But none of these facts really excuses Jews from the obligation of opening up this notorious tome and seeing what is actually inside it. We might even be somewhat comforted if we never go past the prefatory "Editor's Note":

> This study is structured as a presentation of historical evidence regarding the relationship of one people with another. The facts, *as established by highly respected scholars of the Jewish community* [emphasis added] are here established and linked by as sparse a narrative as is journalistically permitted for review by those interested in the subject . . . Those who would use this material as a basis for the violation of the human rights of another are abusing the knowledge herein. The wise will benefit to see this as an opportunity to develop a more equitable relationship between the families of man.

The text which follows remains faithful to at least one of the goals set out here. It relies for its information almost entirely upon Jewish scholarship most, but not all, of it quite respectable and extremely little falling into the category which a "Note on Sources" proscribes as "anti-Semitic and/or anti-Jewish." (Brackman, in his study of *The Secret Relationship*, notes a number of references to three authors hostile to Jews— Frederick Law Olmsted, Werner Sombart, and Fyodor Dostoyevsky—but these play a very minor role in a book with 1,275 footnotes.) The easy accessibility of such material of course contradicts the assertion of the book's title, that Jewish participation in the slave trade was hitherto a *secret*. Nonetheless the contents of this book will come as a surprise to many—perhaps most—readers for reasons already discussed.

The anti-Semitic character of *The Secret Relationship* emerges not from its substantive content—which seems fairly accurate—or even the aura of conspiracy conveyed by its title. It comes out rather in the tone of the narrative, which binds together the sources and fosters, without any evidence, a stereotype of Jews as a uniquely greedy and untrustworthy population. Brackman treats the content of the book as a series of "Big Lies" but, as the details of his well-documented critique indicate, distortions are produced almost entirely by selective citation rather than explicit falsehood. Sometimes the attack is simply appended to the story of the slave trade by the authors/editors, as in the opening paragraph, which links "the blanket expulsion of Jews from so many places around the world" to charges of "economic exploitation of Gentile communities."

More frequently, there are innuendos imbedded in the accounts of Jewish involvement in the slave trade which "incited the moral indignation of Europe's Gentile population." Jews in the slave-trading Dutch West India Company "remained internationalists without the patriotic fervor of their Gentile countrymen." In the British West Indies, Jews who owned no plantations and relatively few slaves and were excluded from public office are presented (through local government pleas to place a special tax upon them) as enjoying "civic advantages." Here as elsewhere the text revels in citations of anti-Jewish charges from historical documents but then, when discussing the failure of Jews to play a significant role in the United States abolitionist movement (a truth which very directly undermines the "benign myth"), insists that fear of persecution could have nothing to do with this reticence since Jews were, even before 1860, better off in America than they had ever been in any Diaspora situation.

Along with African enslavement, Jews are given special blame here (again with little evidence or logic) for many other crimes of European expansion, beginning with the voyages of Columbus (the authors manage to cover their insinuations with some acknowledgement of scholarly doubts by heading a sub-chapter "Columbus the Slave-dealing Jew?"), the selling of poisoned blankets to North American Indians by a British general, loyalist opposition to the American Revolution, the opium trade to China, the operations of the New Orleans pirate Jean Lafitte, and even the conversion of slaves in colonial Georgia to Christianity "to pacify and subdue the Black African."

Unpleasant as this book is to read (although occasionally long quotes from the Jewish sources are used to offset the authors' own voices) it does raise a serious historical question: How significant were the Jews in the slave trade? The authors' primary method, for which they have been attacked by Gates and Brackman, is the crude use of statistics. Thus Jews are said to have "used kidnapped Black Africans disproportionately more than any other ethnic or religious group in New World history." This may possibly be true, since there were not very many Jews in the Americas between 1492 and the 1860s, and quite a few had been involved in the slave trade. The authors do not undertake any systematic count or comparison with other groups (e.g., Portuguese, Scots, Huguenots), however, and in any case such a statistic does not have much meaning. The vast majority of New World slaves were captured, bought, traded, and forced into labor by non-Jews. Nor is there much analytic (as opposed to polemical) sense in the book's various counts of slaves owned by Jews and the alphabetical list, occupying the last 100 pages, of various Jews or Jewish families known to have been associated with slavery.

None of this data is placed in any context which would indicate its statistical, not to say broader historical, significance. As the authors correctly note, the role in the slave trade of Gentile Europeans, Muslims, and even African "tribal traitors" has been studied more extensively than that of the Jews. But the team responsible for *The Secret Relationship* does not seem to have examined much of this vast literature and misreads some of that which they do use (on pp. 177–78, they inaccurately cite historian Philip Curtin's statistics on the trade and ignore entirely the debate on this issue among various American, European, and African scholars).

In fact, because of their poor grasp of the historical economy of slavery, the authors *underestimate* the structural, as opposed to statistical, importance of the Jews in the early stages of the New World slave trade. Rather than toying with the rumors of Columbus's "secret" identity, the book might better have focused on the coincidence of the Jewish expulsion from Spain with the establishment of triangular links between Europe, Africa, and the Americas. As a result of this situation, the Sephardim found themselves dispersed over the critical nodes of the new system, especially Amsterdam and Brazil. It was not the material wealth of the Jews that made them so crucial to this emerging South Atlantic economy but rather (as with other ethnic-commercial diasporas such as the Huguenots, the Quakers, the overseas Chinese, Muslims in Africa) their ability to transfer assets and information among themselves across the entire economic network.

As even this book notes, Jews owned a small minority of shares in the Dutch West India Company (an unsuccessful commercial enterprise in any case). Their value to the Dutch lay instead in the fact that many of them, seeking to escape the Iberian Inquisition, had migrated to Brazil where they helped found the first major New World sugar plantations. When the Dutch first conquered northern Brazil from Portugal and were in turn driven out by a Portuguese reconquest, most local Jews left with them to disseminate the sugar production system to the Dutch and later British Islands. The only places where Jews really came close to dominating a New World plantation system were the Dutch colonies of Curaçao and Surinam (the language of the escaped slave communities in the Surinam interior still refers to prohibited foods as "*mi trefu*").

But the Dutch territories were small, and their importance was shortlived. By the time the slave trade and European sugar-growing reached its peak in the 1700s, Jewish participation was dwarfed by the enterprise of British and French planters who did not allow Jews among their number. During the nineteenth century, Jews owned some cotton plantations in the southern United States but not in any meaningful numbers. (*The Secret Relationship*, to its credit, is not the basis for Farrakhan's recent statement that three-quarters of all southern slaves belonged to Jews.) Jews of Portuguese Brazilian origin did play a significant (but by no means dominant) role in the eighteenth-century slave trade of Rhode Island, but this sector accounted for only a very tiny portion of the total human exports from Africa.

For all its shortcomings, *The Secret Relationship* does force us to confront the history which John Hope Franklin and I avoided discussing publicly in 1978. The fact that our forefathers were generally, and at times quite significantly, on the side of the slavers in the cruel world of the Atlantic economy may also help call into question the whole image of Diaspora Jews as "victims" in medieval-to-modern world history. Indeed, some of the very terms associated with this status, such as "Diaspora," "ghetto," and, in several chapter headings of *The Secret Relationship*, "Holocaust," have been appropriated by African Americans to define a trajectory of suffering which ultimately has placed them in a far more disadvantaged position than that of Jews.

One response to such a new understanding of our history is to take the path of neoconservatism, identifying with the white Gentile establishment and perceiving all proponents of "Third Worldism" (including militant African Americans) as our enemies. The rhetoric of *The Secret Relationship* along with the use made of it by Professors Jeffries and Martin certainly encourages such a move on the part of Jews. The book—to say nothing of Khalid Abdul Muhammad and Louis Farrakhan's gratuitous fantasies about Jewish crimes against Blacks—may indeed have been intended, despite its opening disclaimers, to push African Americans into the same kind of polarization. Looking at the examples of the former Yugoslavia and extremist groups on both sides of the Arab-Israeli conflict, one might easily conclude that the memorialization of past sufferings must inevitably stoke the fires of contemporary hate. Even a historian is thus tempted to prefer forgetfulness or the comfort of benign myths.

We Jews, however, even liberal ones, who justifiably insist that the history of the Nazi Holocaust not be denied, can hardly urge African Americans to suppress the record of the slave trade and the involvement of our own ancestors in it. It also does not help to accompany all discussions of Jewish slave trading with indictments of Christians and Arab Muslims as the true villains of the African slave trade. (Brackman, for example, provides a somewhat lurid catalogue of "Arab slave raids" using, among other sources, my own research. In fact, the Muslim or Oriental slave trade out of Africa involved mainly Berber, Swahili, and other Black African raiders and merchants rather than Arabs.) Thus while we should not ignore the anti-Semitism of *The Secret Relationship* (limited at least to accusations of avarice rather than blood libels or plots to rule the world), we must recognize the legitimacy of the stated aim of examining fully and directly even the most uncomfortable elements in our common past. There are certainly better ways than those of this book, from both a scholarly and moral perspective, to carry out such an examination. But carried out it must be, not to apportion or remove guilt but rather to learn who we are through what we were and to incorporate this knowledge into the struggle to become something better.

# Four Documents concerning Jews and Slavery

### NEWPORT SLAVE TRADE

*Instructions to a Ship Captain, October 29, 1762[1]*

[Shocking as it may seem today, some of the "best people," including pious Christians and Jews, participated in the slave trade in the eighteenth and nineteenth centuries. This fact is additional evidence that the level of morality both of individuals and groups is determined not so much by any abstract religious or moral code as by the relations of production that govern the conduct of men in any given time and place. In the mid-eighteenth century, only a tiny minority in America was beginning to question the morality of the slave trade. In fact, Newport's pre-eminence then as an American port depended largely on two factors: the spermaceti (candle) industry and the African slave trade. When the latter declined, Newport lost its economic position. Noteworthy in this document is the matter-of-fact, business-like manner in which these two Jewish merchants give their instructions to the captain of their slave ship.]

Captain John Peck,

As you are at present master of the sloop *Prince George* with her Cargo on board and ready to sale you are to observe the following orders:

That you Imbrace the first fair wind and proceed to sea and make the best of your way to the windward part of the Coast of Affrica, and at your arrival there dispose of your Cargo for the most possible can be gotten, and Invest the neat proceeds into as many good merchantable young slaves as you can, and make all the Dispatch you possibly can. As soon as your Business there is Compleated make the best of your way from thence to the Island of New Providence and there dispose of your Slaves for Cash, if the Markets are not too dull: but if they should [be], make the Best of your way home to this port, take pilates and make proper protest where ever you find it necessary. You are further to observe that all the Rum on board your Sloop shall come upon an average in case of any Misfortune, and also all the slaves in general shall come upon an Average

Morris U. Schappes is editor of *Jewish Currents*.

Reprinted from *A Documentary History of the Jews in the United States, 1654–1875*, ed. Morris U. Schappes, preface by Joshua Bloch, Director, Jewish Division, New York Public Library, New York (New York: Citadel Press, 1950), 37–38; 118–21; 134; 394–98. Copyright © 1950, 1971 by Morris U. Schappes. Reprinted by permission of Morris U. Schappes.

in case any Casualty or Misfortune happens, and that no Slaves shall be brought upon freight for any person, neither Direct nor Indirect.

And also we allow you for your Commission four Slaves upon the purchase of one hundred and four, and the priviledge of bringing home three slaves and your mate one.

Observe not neglect writing us by all opportunitys of every Transaction of your Voyage. Lastly be particular Carefull of your Vessell and Slaves, and be as frugal as possible in every expense relating to the voyage. So wish you a Good Voyage and are your Owners and humble Servants.

[No firm signature]

But further observe if you dispose of your Slaves in Providence lay out as much of your neat proceeds as will Load your Vessel in any Commodity of that Island that will be best for our advantage and the remainder of your Effects bring home in money.

Isaac Elizer
Samuel Moses[2]

## MANUMISSION OF SLAVES

*The Will of Isaiah Isaacs of Virginia, August 30, 1803 and January 8, 1806*[1]

[It is not uncommon for slave owners to provide for the freeing of their slaves in their wills, and at times even during their lifetime. In 1790, there were 59,527 free Negroes in the United States, most of whom had at one time been slaves. By 1860, the number of free Negroes, owing to natural increases and to manumissions, had grown to 488,070; from 1790 to 1860 the number of slaves, however, had increased from 697,897 to 3,950,531. The records show that Jews, like others, sometimes freed their slaves. In 1692, Arthur Levy's slave, Cresie, was thus freed in New York, and in 1761 Jacob Franks manumitted his slave, Cato.[2] Of special interest in the following Will of Isaiah Isaacs[3] is the declaration of his opinion that "all men are by nature equally free." This theory, however, did not impel him to the immediate freeing of his slaves; instead he sets a schedule covering some thirty years, which he modified in a codicil two years later.]

I, Isaiah Isaacs, of the town of Charlottesville and county of Albemarle, do make the following testamentary disposition of all my estate real and personal. It is my will that all my debts be paid and to enable my executors herein named to do the same. It is hereby directed that all the perishable part of my estate be sold as soon after my death as my executors can, with convenience and out of the money arriving therefrom, discharge such debts as I may owe at the time of my death, and the remaining surplus is to remain as an assisting fund in the hands of my executors for the maintenance of my children. It is my will that strict justice be done my children in the division of my estate. It is therefore my will, and I do hereby devise to Fanny Isaiah Isaacs, David Isaiah Isaacs, Patsy Isaiah Isaacs and Hayes Isaiah Isaacs, my four children by my dec'd wife Hetty Isaacs, formerly Hetty Hayes, all my estate both real and personal to them and their heirs forever. But as all my said children are in a state of infancy and incapable of acting for themselves, all the property aforesaid devised to them is hereby committed to the care of my executors until the youngest of my sd children shall *arrive* to the full age of twenty-one years. It is my will, and my executors are earnestly entreated so to manage my real estate, consisting partly in houses and Lots, as that it may at the period before prescribed for a division be delivered to my children unimpaired in its value; no part of my real estate is to be sold, but when my youngest child comes of age my executors are to exercise (cause) a just and fair valuation thereof to be made by disinterested commissioners to be appointed by the Court of that County where this will shall be recorded and divide the same into four parts, and allot one-fourth thereof to each of my said children, and as equality of division cannot be obtained in this manner those haveing [sic] the most valuable lots assigned to them are to make them of less value equal to the most valuable by paying the deficiency in money. It is my will that my tract of land in the County of Powhatan shall not be divided, but remain to my children and their heirs in common. It is my will that if any of my said children should die before he, she or they arrive at the age of twenty-one years, in that case the survivors or survivor shall enjoy the proportion of him, her or they who may die. But this clause of my will is to be so construed as only to take effect in case of such death or deaths without Issue; and the term of issue is meant to entitle any child or children that my daughters may have legitimate or illegitimate to their mother's proportion. It is my will that my children may be so educated as to make them useful citizens, they are therefore to be educated in such a manner as my executors may think their talents and capacities may justify, and to enable my executors to maintain and educate them the rents of my real estate are added to the surplus money arising from the sale of my Chattel Estate, and my executors are to place my children in the families of respectable *Jews* to the end that they may be brought up in the religion of their forefathers. Being of opinion that all men are by nature equally free and being possessed of some of those beings who are unfortunate doomed to slavery, as to them I must enjoin upon my executors a strict observance of the following clause in my will. My slaves hereafter named are to be and they are hereby manumitted and made free so that after the different periods hereafter mentioned they shall enjoy all the privileges and immunities of freed people. My slave Rachel is to go free and quit all manner of claim of servitude from and after the first day of January, which shall be in the year one thousand eight hundred and sixteen, James from and after the first day of January which shall be in the year one thousand eight hundred and twenty, Polly on the first day of January eighteen hundred and twenty-two, Henry on the first day of January which shall be in the year one thousand eight hundred and thirty, and William on the first day of January which shall be in the year one thousand eight hundred and thirty-four, and should either of my female slaves Rachel or Polly have a child or children before the time they become free such issue is to serve to the age of thirty-one and then to be discharged from servitude; the said slaves are not to be sold, but to remain the property of my children and to be divided in the same manner as directed as to the division of my real estate; each one of my slaves are to receive the value of twenty dollars in clothing on the day of their manumission. I constitute and appoint my friends Jacob I Cohen Adam Craig and Robert Mitchell and my brother David Isaacs[4] executors of this my last will and testament. In testimony whereof I have hereunto subscribed my name and affixed my seal this thirtieth day of August in the year one thousand eight hundred and three.

Signed sealed and published as and for the last will and testament of Isaiah Isaacs in presence of us the said Isaac's [sic] signature being in the Hebrew language. John Carr, Thos. C. Fletcher, W. Wardlaw.

[*Hebrew Signature*]    [Seal]


*A Codicil to be annexed to this my last will*

In as much as I have not been sufficiently explicit in that clause of my will which directs the course to be observed with respect the education of my children I have thought fit to add the following clause which is to be taken and considered as a part of this my will. It is my meaning and I do hereby request my executors before named to educate my sons for such professions as their talents may lead them to pursue and at proper ages to bind them to upright and discreet persons engaged in the professions their capacities may enable them to follow.

Signed sealed and published as and for the last will and testament of Isaiah Isaac's [sic] in presence of us the signature of the said Isaacs being in Hebrew, John Carr, Thos. C. Fletcher, W. Wardlaw.

[*Hebrew Signature*]    [*Seal*]

I Isaiah *Isaaks* being of sound mind have thought proper to make the following codicil to the within will to wit It is my will and desire that Joseph Marks[5] of the City of Richmond be added to the number of my executors heretofore appointed to the within will. It is my desire that my Negro woman Polly be free from and after the first day of January 1818 and whereas it is directed in my will that in case my female slaves Polly and Rachel should have children during their servitude the said children shall serve till their age of thirty-one—It is further my will that if the said children of my female slaves should have children during their servitude the said last mentioned Issue shall be free from their birth. It is also my will that if Mary the child of my Negro woman Rachel should have a child or children during her time of service that the sd child or children shall be free from the birth. It is also my will that Clement Washington the youngest child of Rachel shall be free from and after the first day of January 1836 and shall at his being free have same clothing given to him as in my will directed to be given to the others as witness my hand and seal this 8th day of January 1806.

[*Hebrew Signature*]    [*Seal*]

Teste Jas. Lewis, Thos. C. Fletcher, D. Carr.

An Instrument of writing purporting to be the last will and testament of Isaiah Isaacs deceased with a codicil thereto annexed were produced into Court and proved the will by the oaths of John Carr and Thos. C. Fletcher two of the witnesses thereto and the codicil by the oaths of Thos. C. Fletcher and Dabney Carr two of the witnesses thereto and by the Court ordered to be recorded.

Teste Jno. Carr, C. C.

A Copy Teste Alex'r. Garrett, C. C.

A Copy Teste Wm. G. Pendleton, C. C.

## A SLAVE PROMISED HIS FREEDOM

*Legal paper promising freedom to George Roper from Jacob Levy, Jr., April 8, 1814*[1]

[An interesting relationship is here revealed between Jacob Levy, Jr. and his slave. Roper asked for his liberation, and was promised it in three years, depending upon his good behavior. Levy was obviously influenced by the New York Society for Promoting the Manumission of Slaves, in whose records this manuscript was found.]

Whereas my Slave George Roper has solicited me to give him his freedom at the expiration of three years from the thirteenth day of June next;[2] and in consideration thereof, he hath promised to serve me faithfully for the said term; Now I hereby agree to manumit & make free the said George Roper, at the expiration of the said term, of three years from the thirteenth day of June next; provided & upon the express condition that the said George Roper shall during that term well & faithfully serve me & my family as a Slave, & dutifully obey all my lawful commands.

[Signed] Jacob Levy Junr[3]

New York April 8th. 1814
Witnessed by Geo Brinckerhoff
Recorded 12th of 4 mo. 1814 by Nathan Comstock

## HELPING ELECT LINCOLN

*Excerpts from Abram J. Dittenhoefer,* How We Elected Lincoln—Personal Recollections of Lincoln and Men of His Time,[1]*—1860*

[In the first of these selections, Dittenhoefer explains intimately how difficult it was, in the overwhelmingly Democratic pro-slavery atmosphere of New York City, for a young Jewish college graduate with political ambitions to become an opponent of slavery and an active Republican. His account of what motivated his decision that a Jew particularly should be anti-slavery is notable.[2] In the second selection, we have a vivid recollection of the horrors of the Draft Riots of 1863. Abram Jesse Dittenhoefer, son of Isaac and Babetta Dittenhoefer, was born in Charleston, S. C. on March 17, 1836, and was brought to New York at the age of four. He served one term as the Magistrate of a City Court, but distinguished himself especially as a lawyer and political figure. In 1864, he was one of the New York Electors on the Lincoln ticket, and he acted as chairman of the General Republican Central Committee for twelve terms. In his legal practise, he was counsel to large corporations and several important banks, but he made his most important contribution as a specialist in the copyright law of the theater. He died in New York, February 23, 1919.[3]]

Circumstances brought to me personal knowledge of Mr. Lincoln for nearly four years. I had frequent interviews with him, and so was able to form a well-considered estimate of the great Emancipator's character and personality.

Born in Charleston, South Carolina, of Democratic pro-slavery parents, I was brought in early youth to New York; and although imbued with the sentiments and antipathies of my Southern environment, I soon became known as a Southerner with Northern principles. At that time there were many Northern men with Southern principles.

The city of New York, as I discovered upon reaching the age of observation, was virtually an annex of the South, the New York merchants having extensive and very profitable business relations with the merchants south of the Mason and Dixon line.[4]

The South was the best customer of New York. I often said in those days, "our merchants have for sale on their shelves their principles, together with their merchandise."

An amusing incident occurred to my knowledge which aptly illustrates the condition of things in this pro-slavery city. A Southerner came to a New York merchant, who was a dealer in brushes and toilet articles, and offered him a larger order for combs. The New York merchant, as it happened, was a Quaker, but this was not known to the Southerner. The latter made it a condition, in giving this large order, that the Quaker merchant should exert all his influence in favor of the South. The Southerner wished to do something to offset the great agitation headed by the abolitionists which had been going on for years in the North for the extinction of slavery in the South. The Quaker merchant coolly replied that the South would have to go lousy for a long time before he would sell his combs to them under any such conditions.

Another occurrence that took place at an earlier period still further illuminates this intense pro-slavery feeling. When Wendell Phillips, to my mind one of the greatest orators of America, delivered a radical and brilliant anti-slavery speech at the old Tabernacle, situated in Broadway below Canal Street, the hall was filled with pro-slavery shouters; they rotten-egged Phillips in the course of his address. With some friends I was present and witnessed this performance.

At nineteen I was wavering in my fidelity to the principles of the Democratic party, which, in the city of New York, was largely in favor of slavery.

I had just graduated from Columbia College,[5] which was then situated in what is now known as College Place, between Chambers and Murray streets. At that time many of our prominent and wealthy families lived in Chambers, Murray, and Warren streets, and I frequently attended festivities held by the parents of the college boys in the old-fashioned mansions which lined those thoroughfares.

Soon after leaving college I became a student in the law office of Benedict & Boardman, occupying offices in Dey Street, near Broadway. At that time the late John E. Parsons, a distinguished member of the New York bar, was the managing clerk; and Charles O'Conor,[6] the head of the New York bar in that generation, and who, in later years, ran as an Independent candidate for the Presidency, was connected with that firm as counsel.

Sitting one day at my desk, I took up a newspaper, and the debate between Judah P. Benjamin, the rabid but eloquent pro-slavery Senator from Louisiana, and Benjamin F. Wade, the free-soil Senator from Ohio, attracted my attention.

Benjamin had made a strong address in defense of slavery when Wade arose and replied. He began his reply with some bitter and memorable words, words which completely changed my political views.

"I have listened with intense interest," said he, "as I always do to the eloquent speech of my friend, the Senator from Louisiana—an Israelite with Egyptian principles."[7]

My father, who was a prominent merchant of New York in those days, and very influential with the German population,[8] had urged me to become a Democrat, warning me that a public career, if I joined the Republican party, would be impossible in the city of New York. I felt that he was right in that view, as the party was in a hopeless minority, without apparent prospect of ever being able to elect its candidates.

This was absolutely plain from the fact that Tammany Hall controlled the entire election machinery in this city, there being no law at that time which required the registration of voters before Election Day. Moreover, the inspectors of election were Tammany heelers, without any Republican representation on the election boards. In consequence, fraudulent voting prevailed to a large extent.

And yet my convictions were irrevocably changed by the reading of Wade's speech in answer to Benjamin. It struck me with great force that the Israelite Benjamin, whose ancestors were enslaved in Egypt, ought not to uphold slavery in free America, and could not do so without bringing disgrace upon himself.

Having convinced my father that slavery should no longer be tolerated, he abandoned his old political associations, cast his vote for Lincoln and Hamlin, and remained a Republican until his death.[9]

Several years later, if I may anticipate, William M. Tweed,[10] who had not yet become "Boss," but who had great and powerful influence in Tammany Hall, besought me to join Tammany, calling my attention to the fact that the power of the Democratic party was supreme in the city of New York, and that the organization needed some one to influence the German element.

He gave me his assurance that if I came into Tammany Hall I should receive prompt recognition, and in a few years undoubtedly would become judge of the Supreme Court; later on I might go still higher up. I thanked Mr. Tweed for his friendly interest in me, but told him that no political preferment could induce me to abandon my convictions and lead me to support slavery.

When Tweed became the absolute "Boss" of Tammany, some years later, he renewed his request that I should join Tammany Hall. Recurring to his previous promise, he again urged me to become a member of his organization; again I refused.

One can hardly appreciate to-day what it meant to me, a young man beginning his career in New York, to ally myself with the Republican party. By doing so, not only did I cast aside all apparent hope of public preferment, but I also subjected myself to obloquy from and ostracism by my acquaintances, my clients, and even members of my own family.

I was about twenty years of age when the first Republican convention met at Pittsburg.

· · · ·

The relief experienced through General Lee's defeat at Gettysburg and his retreat across Maryland into Virginia was followed,[11] ten days later (July, 1863), by the draft riots in New York.

The horrors of those three days have never been fully described.[12]

Led and encouraged by Southern sympathizers, who had retained the feelings they held before the war, the rabble of the city surged through the streets, destroying property, burning a Negro orphan-asylum, and killing black men. Nominally a protest against enforced enlistment, the riots were really an uprising of the dangerous element that existed in the city at the time.

I lived in Thirty-fourth Street, near Eighth Avenue, and had been a persistent speaker against the extension of slavery and in favor of the Federal cause. The day before the riots began, an anonymous note was received by my family, stating that our home would be attacked and that we had best leave the city. We did not heed the warning.

On the first day of the riots, July 13, 1863, a crowd gathered in front of my house, shouting: "Down with the abolitionists!" "Death to Dittenhoefer!" I sent a messenger for the police, and a squad arrived as the leaders of the mob were preparing to break in my door. Active club work dispersed the crowd, and by order of the captain of the precinct several policemen were kept on guard until the end of the riots.

It was at this time that I met Mrs. Carson, the daughter of the only Union man in South Carolina, who, with her father, was compelled, after the firing on Fort Sumter, to leave South Carolina, while his property was confiscated.[13] I had been anxious to sell my house in Thirty-fourth Street. Noticing a "For Sale" sign on the property, Mrs. Carson called on me and expressed a willingness to buy the house at the price named, asking me to see Samuel Blatchford, who in later years became a Supreme Court Judge of the United States, and who, she said, was the head of an association raising funds for her support in New York. I saw Judge Blatchford,[14] and a contract was signed for the sale. Later, in consequence of the serious illness of my wife, I was obliged to ask Judge Blatchford to cancel the contract, saying that, by way of making up for the disappointment, I would gladly contribute a sum of money to the fund for Mrs. Carson. The contract was accordingly canceled. I never saw Mrs. Carson afterward. About a year before the close of the rebellion, Mr. Lincoln offered to appoint me judge of the district court of South Carolina, my native State, but my increasing business in the city of New York and the disinclination of my wife[15] to move to South Carolina compelled me to decline the honor.

A little while before the offer of the Carolina judgeship was made me by the President I received a letter signed by Mrs. Carson, in which the writer said that the President had asked her to recommend a man for the position, and, remembering what I had done years before, she had suggested my name to him. . . .

NOTES

*Newport Slave Trade*

1. *Massachusetts Historical Society Collections,* 7 Ser., IX, *Commerce of Rhode Island, 1726–1774,* I, 96–97.

2. Isaac Elizer was a merchant and an active figure in the Newport Congregation. On March 11, 1762, shortly before this document was written, Aaron Lopez and he had been denied the right of naturaliza-

tion by the Superior Court of Newport on the equivocal grounds that the colony was already full and that only Christians could be naturalized. (Max J. Kohler, "The Jews in Newport." *AJHSP*, VI, 1897, p. 71; Goodman, *op. cit.*, 53–59; *AJHSP*, XXVII, 1920, *passim.*)

Very little is known about Samuel Moses. For a letter by Moses and Elizer connected with this voyage, sent to Christopher Champlin, merchant in New Providence, Bahamas, asking him to send the slave cargo on the *Prince George* to Charlestown, S. C., if the prices of slaves are too low in the Bahamas, see Elizabeth Donnan, ed., *Documents Illustrative of the History of the Slave Trade to America,* Washington, 1930–1935, III, 189–190.

*Manumission of Slaves*

1. *Will Book 13,* p. 486, Chancery Court of Richmond, Va. Ezekiel and Lichtenstein, *The History of the Jews of Richmond,* Richmond, 1917, pp. 327–330, garbles a passage.

2. Samuel McKee, Jr., *Labor in Colonial New York, 1664–1776,* New York, 1935, pp. 133–134.

3. Isaiah Isaacs (1747–1806) was the first Jew in Richmond, Va., where he settled before the revolution. On June 11, 1783, he was one of those signing a petition calling upon the State Legislature to deprive of the rights of citizenship those who had sided with the British during the war. He was a tax assessor, twice elected to the Common Hall of Richmond, and a founder of the Congregation Beth Shalome (Ezekiel and Lichtenstein, *op. cit.*, 14–16, 32, 63–64, 240, 326–327). In 1799, he freed one of his female slaves, Lucy.

4. Jacob I. Cohen (c.1744–1823) was the partner of Isaacs from 1781 to 1792; in his own will, January 10, 1816, Cohen provides for the freeing of his own slaves immediately on his death (*ibid.,* 18, 19, 330–335).

5. Joseph Marx, a Richmond Jew, died in 1840 in his 69th year (*ibid.,* 303).

Isaiah's younger brother, David Isaacs, had been born in Frankfort on the Main, 1760; he died in Richmond, 1837 (*ibid.,* 297).

*A Slave Promised His Freedom*

1. *Manumission Society, New York City, Indentures, 1809–1829,* III, 75 (New-York Historical Society).

2. On June 30, 1817, in accordance with this agreement, Roper was set free. The legal document manumitting him is in *ibid., Register of Manumission of Slaves, New York City, 1816–1818,* II, 81. On March 5, 1817, Jacob Levy, Jr. had also liberated his slave Mary Mundy; on March 6, 1817, he freed John Jackson, Samuel Spures, Edwin Jackson, Elizabeth Jackson, and James Jackson, (*ibid.,* 51, 50, 52). Ephraim Hart (1747–1825) liberated his slave Silvia on January 30, 1818 (*ibid.,* 110); Haym M. Solomon liberated his slave Anna, "now aged ten years & two months or thereabouts," (*ibid., Indentures, 1809–1829,* p. 64). The quantity of manumissions in 1817 may have been influenced by the fact that early that year the New York State Legislature passed a complete abolition act to take effect on July 4, 1827, on which day 10,000 slaves were freed. The Manumission Society was instrumental in achieving these results (Alice Dana Adams, *The Neglected Period of Anti-Slavery in America, 1808–1831,* Boston and London, 1908, pp. 89–90).

3. Jacob Levy, Jr. (died 1837) was active in the Congregation Shearith Israel, and was connected with prominent Jewish families: his daughter Judith married Moses B. Seixas; another daughter, Abby, was the wife of Moses I. (or J.) Hays; a third daughter married Joseph L. Joseph. George Brinckerhoff, who is the witness for the promise of freedom to George Roper, was also a witness when Jacob Levy, Jr., "Gentleman," wrote his will on March 25, 1837 (*New York City Hall of Records, Record of Wills, Surrogate's Court,* Lib. 76, pp. 299–304).

*Helping Elect Lincoln*

1. New York and London, 1916, pp. 1–5, 62–64. For other material on the same subject, see Markens, *AJHSP*, XVII, 1909, pp. 109–166.

2. For a sketch of the relationship of the Jews to the new party, see Schappes, *Jewish Life,* New York, October, 1948, pp. 13–16.

3. *Who's Who in America,* I, 1899–1900, p. 192; obituary, *The New York Times,* February 24, 1919, p. 13, col. 2, where the date of his birth, however, is incorrectly given.

4. For a penetrating scholarly description of this relationship between New York and the South, see Philip Foner, *Business and Slavery,* Chapel Hill, N. C., 1941, *passim.*

5. He graduated at the head of his class in 1856 (*The New York Times, loc. cit.*).

6. The firm consisted of Jesse W. Benedict and Andrew Boardman (1813–1881) and had its offices at 2 Dey Street (*Trow's New York City Directory,* 1856–57, pp. 66, 83; David McAdam et al., eds., *History of the Bench and Bar of New York,* New York, 1897, I, 264).

John Edward Parsons (1829–1915) had been admitted to the bar in 1852; later he was counsel for the City Bar Association when it moved against the Tweed Ring; still later he used his talents as a lawyer, as Dittenhoefer also did, to defend the sugar trust against federal action. (*DAB,* XIV, 267, by Edward Conrad Smith.)

O'Conor (1804–1884) had already been the unsuccessful Democratic candidate for Lieutenant-Governor of New York in 1848; a supporter of slavery, he was very popular with southern Democrats; in 1872 he was the candidate for president on the "Straight-out" Democratic ticket.

7. Benjamin's speech on the Kansas question was delivered on March 11, 1858. On March 13, Wade (1800–1878), toward the end of a long and powerful address, made the following observation about the Northern men with Southern principles: "Your allies, the doughfaces of the North, in my judgment, are the most despicable of men. The modern doughface is not a character peculiar to the age in which we live, but you find traces of him at every period of the world's history. . . . Why, sir, when old Moses, under the immediate inspiration of God Almighty, enticed a whole nation of slaves, and ran away, not to Canada, but to old Canaan, I suppose that Pharoah and all the chivalry of old Egypt denounced him as a most furious Abolitionist . . . there were not wanting those who loved Egypt better than they loved liberty; . . . They were not exactly northern men with southern principles; but they were Israelites with Egyptian principles." (*Congresstional Globe,* 35 Cong., 1 Sess., p. 1115.) Although this was originally only an oblique reference to Benjamin, the press promptly applied it pointedly to him and made it stick (*New-York Tribune,* March 20, 1858, "Judah Benjamin.")

8. Isaac Dittenhoefer (c. 1812–1860) had arrived in Baltimore from Germany in 1834, and had moved to Charleston and then New York, where he prospered as a drygoods merchant. He was one of the founders of B'nai Brith and active in the German Hebrew Benevolent Society. (Obituary, *The Israelite,* December 7, 1860, p. 181, cols. 1–2; Grinstein, *op. cit.,* 109, 552.)

9. Hannibal Hamlin (1809–1891), a strong abolitionist, was elected Vice-President on the Lincoln ticket. Isaac Dittenhoefer died on November 21, 1860, only a few weeks after the election.

10. William Marcy Tweed (1823–1878) was already a Tammany power in 1859 and practically dominated the State by 1868.

11. Lee began his retreat to the Potomac on July 4, 1863.

12. The best and most accessible description of the riots is in Carl Sandburg, *Abraham Lincoln, The War Years,* New York, 1939, II, 360–364. Thirty Negroes were killed, 400 other persons killed or wounded, and about $5,000,000 worth of property destroyed. The Colored Orphan Asylum that was burned down was at Lexington Avenue and 43 Street. "So definite were the slogans and purposes of some of the mobs that they would be more correctly termed crowds, or units of mass action, operating an insurrection." It was not until August 19th that the draft was able to proceed peacefully.

13. Writing a half century after the events, Dittenhoefer here errs in several respects. Mrs. Carson was Caroline Petigru Carson (1820–1892), daughter of James Louis Petigru (1789–1863). Not compelled to leave Charleston, she did come to New York in June 1861 because her health was very bad and her Union views had made her women friends malevolent. Her father, however, refused to follow his daughter, and stayed on in Charleston until his death, serving incidentally all the time as a Commissioner elected by the legislature to codify the Statutes of South Carolina at $5,000 a year. As a Union man in South Carolina, furthermore, Petigru was not alone: Benjamin F. Perry was more prominent and vigorous. (James Petigru Carson, *Life, Letters and Speeches of James Louis Petigru, The Union Man of South Carolina,* Washington, D. C., 1920, pp. 381–82, 425, 429, 442, 488. I am indebted to A. S. Salley, State Historian of South Carolina, for identifying Mrs. Carson for me.)

14. Samuel Blatchford (1820–1893), an expert in international and maritime law, after serving as federal judge from 1867, was appointed to the United States Supreme Court in 1882.

15. In 1858, Dittenhoefer had married Miss Sophie Englehart of Cleveland (*AJYB,* 5665, p. 82, McAdam, *op. cit.,* II, 137–38).

# Jews and Negro Slavery in the Old South, 1789–1865

Slavery was the dominant social and economic fact of life in the Southern states. It was also the focus of the increasing strife between the North and South which culminated in the secession of the Southern states, the formation of the Confederate States of America, and the effort of the North and West to reform the Union which, in its military phase, is known as the Civil War. While it is true that there were many other factors which contributed to the outbreak of the Civil War, it is equally true that there would have been no armed conflict if slavery had not been the integral aspect of the economic and social life of the South. Slavery was the single indigestible element in the life of the American people which fostered disunion, strife, and carnage, just as the concomitant race problem has continued to an important degree to be a divisive force in American life to this very day.

This chapter is an effort to assess the experiences of Jews with slavery, to evaluate their participation in and acceptance of the system, and to establish the relationship of Jewish status in the Southern states to the existence of the institution of slavery, during the period from the adoption of the Constitution to the end of the Civil War.[1] The following themes are treated in detail: Jews as planters, and as owners of slaves; the treatment of slaves by Jews; the emancipation of slaves by Jews; Jews as harsh taskmasters; business dealings of Jews with slaves and free Negroes; Jews as slave dealers; cases of miscegenation involving Jews and Negroes; and opinions of Jews about the slave system.

## I. JEWS AS PLANTERS AND AS OWNERS OF SLAVES

Only a small number of Jews in the Old South were planters. Sociological and economic factors explain why so few Jews achieved this characteristic Southern status of ownership and occupation. History had ordained that European Jews could not own land; the selection of occupations in which Jews could train their sons was severely delimited. Most Jews, out of natural inclination and the pressure of circumstances, felt safer in urban areas, where they could share each other's fellowship and find support in each other's presence. If Jews desired to be loyal to their ancestral faith, they could fulfill this need only where other Jews resided, not in the rural areas. An additional pressure was the poverty which accompanied most immigrant Jews when they came to America.

In 1973, Bertram Wallace Korn was senior rabbi at Reform Congregation Kneseth Israel in Elkins Park, Pennsylvania.

Originally published in *Publications of the American Jewish Historical Society* 50, no. 3 (1961): 151–201, and reprinted in Bertram Wallace Korn, *American Jewry and the Civil War* (New York: Atheneum, 1970), xxiii–lxiii. Used by permission of the Jewish Publication Society.

The average Southern Jew was, therefore, a peddler or store-keeper, with comparatively slim resources, who tended to live in a town or city, and would not even think of aspiring to the ownership of a plantation.

Some Jews found their way to the highest rung of the economic and social ladder through prosperous careers as merchants or professional men. Among this small number of men, probably the best-known was Judah P. Benjamin, the brilliant New Orleans attorney, who purchased an extensive plantation twenty miles below the city in 1844, in partnership with Theodore Packwood, who served as the resident manager. Not content with the rather smallish mansion house, Benjamin rebuilt Bellechasse into a magnificent house which finally fell victim to a housing development in 1960. Benjamin's home, in which he installed his sisters after his wife and daughter moved to Paris, was an elegant example of ante-bellum grace, with "great, double-leveled porches, almost fifteen feet across, a parade of massive, rectangular pillars and everything else in proportion; curving stairways of mahogany, massive carved decorations, silver-plated doorknobs, extensive rose gardens between the house and the levee, and an enormous bell into which Benjamin was said to have dropped five hundred silver dollars during the melting, to 'sweeten the tone.'" Though Benjamin continued to practice his legal profession, he devoted great interest to his plantation, unlike the typical absentee landlord, and wrote articles and delivered speeches on the problems of sugar-planting. Bellechasse was staffed with one hundred and forty slaves, of whom about eighty were field-hands. Benjamin sold the plantation after his election to the Senate.[2]

Several other prosperous New Orleans Jews owned shares of plantations, but none of them took Benjamin's personal interest in their management. Among these investors were Jacob Hart and Hart Moses Shiff. Hart, at the time of his bankruptcy in 1823, owned a half-interest in a plantation in St. Tammany Parish, and in the fourteen slaves who worked the farm.[3] In Ascension Parish J. Levy had forty-one slaves working on his plantation.

Another working Jewish planter was Major Raphael J. Moses who owned land at Esquiline Hill, near Columbus, Georgia. Moses, who became Chief Commissary Officer of Longstreet's Corps during the war, wrote in his memoirs that

> when the war broke out, I had forty-seven slaves, and when it ended I had forty-seven freedmen—all left me except one, old London, who staid with me until he died.[4]

Among the Jewish planters in other states were: Nathan Nathans, who was a President of Beth Elohim Congregation of Charleston, South Carolina, with a plantation on the Cooper River; Isaiah Moses, who worked thirty-five slaves on his farm at St. James, Goose Creek, South Carolina; Mordecai Cohen, who had twenty-seven slaves on his plantation at St. Andrews, South Carolina, and his two sons Marx and David, both of whom owned nearby farms; Isaac Lyons, of Columbia, South Carolina; Barnet A. Cohen of King's Creek, South Carolina; and Chapman Levy, who turned from the law to planting when he moved to the Mississippi Territory. Various members of the Mordecai family had plantations in North Carolina and Virginia. Among other large plantation holdings, Moses Levy owned a magnificent home, "Parthenope," on a plantation at the juncture of the Matamzas River and Moses Creek, in Florida, which he sold to Achille

Murat, the French refugee. One of the few lady planters was Abigail Minis, who had a small plantation near Savannah on which she employed seventeen slaves.[5]

There were undoubtedly a number of other Jewish owners of plantations, but altogether they constituted only a tiny proportion of the Southerners whose habits, opinions, and status were to become decisive for the entire section, and eventually, for the entire country. In contradistinction, it is astonishing to discover even one Jew who tried his hand as a plantation overseer even if only for a brief time. He was the much-traveled, restless and adventurous Solomon Polock, a member of the well-known Philadelphia family, who worked on a plantation near Mobile in the late 1830's.[6]

But the typical Jew had no thought of working on a plantation, much less of owning one. He was likely to be a petty trader, trying to eke out a marginal living in an occupation which ranked quite low on the social scale of the Old South. He considered himself fortunate if he could pay his bills on time; and rated it a high accomplishment to own his shop with a few rooms on the floor above where his family could live. If he were as yet unmarried, he and a brother or uncle or nephew would live in a room behind the store, and the men would try to save up enough money to make their future more secure. Such men as these had no reason to invest their small capital in a slave, nor had they any need for a slave's services. Take, for example, young Samuel Adler and his brother who had a store in Talladega, Alabama. These two men, both unmarried, slept in the room behind their store, while two or three young clerks lived upstairs. They sent their laundry out, and ate their meals at a local hotel, except on Sunday, when their food was sent over to the store. What would the Adlers have done with a slave even if they could have afforded one?[7] Or consider the fourteen Jewish men who lived in a Mobile, Alabama, boarding house. They were all between the ages of nineteen and thirty-nine, and earned their living as shopkeepers or clerks, with one tailor added for good measure. These men might be served at table by a slave, but this was the extent of their need. Furthermore, a slave would only be in the way in their little stores.[8]

On the other hand, Jews who were more firmly established in a business or professional career, as well as in their family relationships, had every reason to become slave-owners, although of course, some socially prominent families took pride in employing white servants in their homes.[9] Precise statistics concerning the ownership of slaves by Jews are hard to locate. Census records must be used with caution, because certain Jews known from other sources to be resident in a specific area at a given time were not listed at all; peddlers and traveling merchants, for example, were apt to be on the road when the census was taken; some of the manuscript census returns are quite illegible; and, in addition to frequent misspelling, the identification of Jewish names will always constitute a problem.

It is possible, nevertheless, to gain some information of value from the 1790 manuscript census returns. Unfortunately, the returns for Georgia and Virginia were destroyed, but the South Carolina data provide valuable insight. Seventy-three heads of households have been identified as Jewish; of these, at least thirty-four owned one or more slaves to a total of 151 slaves. The only large holdings of slaves were possessed by Jacob Jacobs of Charleston (11), and Abraham Cohen (21), Solomon Cohen (9), and Esther Myers (11), all of the Georgetown District.[10]

The proportion of slave-owners was much higher by 1820. More than three-fourths of the Jewish households in the major communities of Richmond, Charleston, and Savannah contained slaves. Twenty-five of the thirty-two heads of households in Richmond owned a total of eighty-eight slaves; ninety-six slaveholders among the 109 heads of household in Charleston and Charleston Neck held 488 Negroes in bondage; seventeen of the twenty-one Jewish heads of household in Savannah owned a total of 116 slaves. The largest Jewish holdings of slaves recorded in the 1820 census were those of Jacob Mordecai of Henrico County, Va. (20); Mordecai Cohen (15), Jacob Henry (15), Samuel Hyams (21), Jacob Lazarus, Jr. (20), Lyon Levy, Jr., (15), and M. C. Levy (26), all of Charleston; Solomon Cohen of Georgetown, S.C. (20); Chapman Levy of Columbia, S.C. (31); B. A. Cohen of Barnwell, S.C. (20); and Abraham D. Lyon, Sr. (18), Isaac Minis (16), and Benjamin Sheftall (17) of Savannah.[11]

The returns for other censuses have not yet been subjected to intensive investigation for Jewish data. But some guidance may be obtained from the results of a study of the returns for New Orleans over a period of twenty years. In the 1820 manuscript census records for New Orleans, it has been possible to identify only eleven of the eighteen Jews known to be in town at that time. Nine of the eleven recorded as owning slaves, one of whom, Samuel Jacobs, held twenty, and the others a total of forty-six. By 1830, thirty-seven Jews can be identified in the census returns—a very low number, since there were about sixty-six Jews in the area when the newly established congregation published its list of contributors in 1828, although some of the donors were not permanent residents. Only eight of the thirty-seven did not own slaves; the twenty-nine held a total of 178 Negroes, ten owning seventy-five slaves. By 1840, when sixty-two Jews can be identified in the census returns—again a very small number, since there must have been at least several hundred Jewish families in the community by that time—the newcomers had prospered to so great a degree that only seven reported that they owned no slaves. The fifty-five identifiable Jewish slave-owners of New Orleans in 1840 held a total of three hundred and forty-eight Negroes in bondage, an index to growing prosperity.[12]

A large proportion of the early Jewish settlers in New Orleans were migrants not from foreign countries, but from well-established communities like Charleston. This was not true of Mobile, where only a small number of Jews were other than German and Polish immigrants, who were likely to be less prosperous and less assimilated than the New Orleans residents. Yet, according to the Mobile 1850 census, which lists seventy-two identifiable Jewish heads of family, thirty-one Jews were owners of slaves, to a total of ninety slaves. The proportion is even higher in view of the fact that we include in the figure for heads of families, nineteen young clerks and peddlers who lived in the homes of relatives, and fourteen Jewish bachelors who lived in a single boarding house.[13]

Another statistical indication of Jewish ownership of slaves, probably more accurate in terms of proportions than the census returns, are references to slaves in Jewish wills. Over the years, Professor Jacob R. Marcus has assembled at the American Jewish Archives, one hundred and twenty-nine wills of identifiable Southern Jews who died during the period of our interest. Of these, thirty-three refer to the ownership and disposition of slaves. This would mean, if it is a reliable index, that perhaps one-fourth of Southern Jewish adults were slave-owners. It is instructive that this matches the Federal figures for the 1860 census, namely, that three-fourths of the white population of the South were not slave-owners. Equally important, however, is the fact that only one-seventh of Southern Negroes were domiciled in towns or cities. The proportion of Jewish slave-owners, then, was possibly even larger than that of non-Jews, since the overwhelming majority of Southern Jews lived in the towns and cities.[14]

It would seem to be realistic to conclude that any Jew who could afford to own slaves and had need for their services would do so. Jewish owners of slaves were not exceptional figures. Slavery was an axiomatic foundation of the social pattern of the Old South. Jews acclimated themselves in every way to their environment; in both a social and psychological sense, they followed most of the life patterns of their fellow-citizens. It was, therefore, only a matter of financial circumstance and familial status whether they were to become slave-owners.

## II. THE TREATMENT OF SLAVES BY JEWS

How did these Jewish slave-owners treat their Negroes? What did they feel towards them as human beings? Were they inclined to be lenient masters, motivated by tender sympathy, or were they, like other Southerners, sometimes kindly, sometimes harsh—but always masters?

It is obviously hard to secure answers to these questions. But some indication of the feelings of Jews towards their slaves may be derived from a detailed study of the wills to which we have alluded.

Apologists for the slave system have often contended that the cruel master was an exception, and that most slave-owners were considerate, kindly, and thoughtful. Much depends on the definition of a word like consideration. However kindly a man might be as a master, what of the future of his slaves after his death? In nineteen of these thirty-three wills, more than half, slaves were merely bequeathed to relatives or friends without specific instructions; in five, the executors were instructed to sell them. In the majority of these wills, then, slaves were treated like other property, to be retained if convenient and expedient, to be sold if that seemed the judicious course. The word kindness surely cannot encompass any relationship where a faithful servant could be torn away from familiar moorings and sold to a stranger who might or might not be a "good" master. It was probably typical that the executor of the estate of Emanuel Stern, who died in New Orleans in 1828, sold off his twelve-year old slave, Mathilda, at auction, for $400. This was a profitable transaction, for in the inventory, Mathilda was valued at $250.[15]

On the other hand, although the kindly feelings of some slave-owners cannot possibly be regarded as justification for the slave system, it is important to realize that some masters went far beyond a commercial attitude in their relationships with slaves. The proof of this is to be found in numerous cases of loyalty even after the emancipation which was produced by the Civil War. One example of this reciprocated regard is to be found in old London's decision to stay with his former master, Major Moses. Another is revealed in a letter which Emma Mordecai received in 1867 from a former slave, Sarah P. Norris. The letter itself, beautifully composed and written, is evidence of Emma's opinion of the law which forbade whites to teach reading and writing to slaves. Sarah sends Emma news of the family and acquaintances in Richmond. But more, she assures her erstwhile mistress that she and her husband are looking after the family graves in the Richmond cemetery, and that all is well. "I never could forget my people," she writes, "I loved them then, I love them now."[16] It would be pure prejudice to gainsay the humane motivations of slave-owners like Miss Mordecai.

Nine of the Archives' wills contain specific provisions relating to Negroes which reflect feelings of warm generosity. In his last testament, proved on February 18, 1796, Philip Hart of Charleston bequeathed freedom to his slave Flora. Jacob Cohen of Charleston emancipated his slave Tom, in his will proved on June 6, 1800. Samuel Jones of Charleston, in his will proved on January 20, 1809, instructed his executors to emancipate his slave Jenny and her son Emanuel, if he had not already done so in his lifetime, and bequeathed to Jenny his "Bed, Sheets, Bedstead, Blankets, Tables, Pots, Plates, Chairs, Looking Glass," allowing two other slaves such part of these possessions as they might desire. Jones also bequeathed the income from certain properties to Jenny and her son, and to six slaves who were not to be emancipated. A further provision stipulated that

> it is my further desire not to drive Jenny and her children out of my House in King Street, until they have time to Procure a Place for their abode.

Jones gave no indication of his reason for failing to emancipate his other slaves.

Col. Chapman Levy's mother, Sarah Levy of Kershaw District, South Carolina, who died in 1839, revealed a special affection for two old slaves in her will. "It is my directions, desire and earnest request," she wrote, "that old Kennedy shall be kept with his wife and each treated with kindness and all reasonable indulgence and if my son Chapman Levy shall desire to purchase him to add to his happiness it is my directions that he shall have him at the price of three hundred dollars." Rachel D'Azevedo of Charleston, whose will was proved on February 23, 1843, did her best to assure the contentment of her slaves, Maria, Rose, Dinah, and Flora, despite the adamant provisions of state law. She bequeathed these slaves and their issue to her daughter, Mrs. Sarah A. Motta,

> with the express, and particular Conditions, that immediately after the death of the said Mrs. Sarah A. Motta, the Servants aforesaid with their issue or increase Shall work for their own use and time or services, being the same to all intents and purposes as if they were entirely free.

She also asked that her executor, Abraham Moïse, act as "a kind protector to my Servants Should they require his Valuable Services."

Dr. Jacob De La Motta of Charleston, whose will was proved on February 22, 1845, directed that his sister Rachel treat his slaves, Ann Maria Simmons, and her son Augustus, "with lenity," that she allow them to work at their own option, that they pay her only "moderate" wages, "and on no account to be sold on account of their being family servants born and bred in the same."

Benjamin Levy, the New Orleans printer and publisher, directed in his will, probated just after his death on January 10, 1860, that his slave Richard White, a barber, be given the opportunity to purchase his freedom for $500. If this were not possible during his son, Alexander Levy's lifetime, White was to be set free after the son's death. Levy furthermore stipulated that the slave was

> never to be sold, Mortgaged, or hired out for a longer term than one Year at a time, and never to be hired out of the State of Louisiana.

Another provision in Levy's will expressed his hope that a token of esteem be given by his family to each of the eight slaves who had been his property, and now belonged to other members of the family, as a "Small Memorial of their old Master."

Two of the wills refer to free Negroes. Benjamin Davis of Charleston, in his last testament which was proved on September 26, 1831, bequeathed one hundred and fifty dollars "for her faithful Services" to "a free colod woman named Elsey." Far more unusual was a provision in the will of David Perayra Brandon of Charleston, proved on April 24, 1838:

> I recommend my faithful Servant and friend Juellit or Julien free Negro, to my dear Rachel [his stepdaughter] and W. C. Lambert [her husband] my friend and request them to take him under their protection to treat him as well as they would do me and to give him Such portion of my Cloths as they will think useful to him and never forsake him being the best friend I ever had.

How many white men in the Old South would have wanted to describe a Negro as their "best friend" in the most permanent document of their lives, and how many would have dared do so?

These wills are ample evidence that some Jewish Southerners were deeply sensitive to the human character of their Negroes, and thought of them as fellow men rather than as cattle or merchandise.

### III. EMANCIPATION OF SLAVES BY JEWS

No matter what kindnesses were bestowed upon slaves by their masters, only one gift was permanently meaningful, the gift of freedom. Fortunately, Samuel Jones, Jacob Cohen, Philip Hart, and Benjamin Levy were not the only folk who wanted to emancipate their slaves. Isaiah Isaacs of Charlottesville, Virginia, whose firm had once been compelled to take a Negro slave as security for a debt, outlined an elaborate program for the freeing of his slaves in his will which was proved in April, 1806:

> Being of opinion that all men are by nature equally free and being possessed of some of those beings who are unfortunate[ly] doomed to slavery, as to them I must enjoin upon my executors a strict observance of the following clause in my will. My slaves hereafter named are to be and they are hereby manumitted and made free so that after the different periods hereafter mentioned they shall enjoy all the privileges and immunities of freed people. My slave Rachel is to go free and quit all manner of claim

of servitude from and after the first day of January, which shall be in the year [1816], James from and after the first day of January [1820], Polly on the first day of January [1822], Henry on the first day of January [1830], and William on the first day of January [1834], and should either of my female slaves Rachel or Polly have a child or children before the time they become free such issue is to serve to the age of thirty-one, and then to be discharged from servitude; the said slaves are not to be sold, but to remain the property of my children and to be divided in the same manner as directed as to the division of my real estate; each one of my slaves are to receive the value of twenty dollars in clothing on the day of their manumission.[17]

No comparable Jewish will exists, with so complete a plan of emancipation, but in 1796, Samuel Myers of Petersburg, Virginia, purchased a mulatto woman, Alice, from the trustees of the estate of a neighbor, with the obvious intention of emancipating her, which purpose he fulfilled a little over a year later.[18] A similar case of purchasing a slave for rapid emancipation was that of Joseph Tobias of Charleston who, on July 23, 1798, bought a slave named Jenny for $500 from Dr. James Cletherall, and promptly freed her "for former services rendered me." Perhaps she had nursed him during an illness while she was still the physician's property.[19] In the same year, Solomon Raphael of Richmond, and his partner, freed their slave Sylvia and her child; and six years later Raphael emancipated another slave, Priscilla.[20] In 1812, Solomon Jacobs, also of Richmond, freed his slave Esther.[21]

A Northern owner of Southern slaves,[22] Jacob I. Cohen, formerly of Richmond, and now of Philadelphia, provided for the emancipation of his slaves in his will which was probated in Philadelphia on October 31, 1823. Cohen directed that his slaves

Dick, Spencer, Meshack, Fanny and Eliza together with their children be manumitted from slavery immediately after my decease; and I do give and bequeathe to the said Dick, Spencer, Meshack, Fanny and Eliza twenty-five dollars each. But if any of my said Negroes will not accept their freedom I do then will and direct that they have the choice of their own master.

Cohen also directed that the children of Mary Andrew, a slave who was to be freed at a later time, be regarded as "free from their birth."[23]

It will be noticed, of course, that these examples of emancipation were all quite early. This is no coincidence, since most of the Southern states gradually tightened their restrictions until it was virtually impossible to free a slave except through stratagem or deceit. Those who believe that the Civil War could have been avoided through a general realization of the coming collapse of the slave economy ought to be compelled to read the enactments of the various states which were contrived to make the slave system a one-way street with no escape. It is quite possibly true that the expansion of slavery was economically unfeasible, but there is no indication that Southern leaders and framers of law were prepared to make emancipation easy. To the contrary, they bent every effort to keep the slaves in chains, and gradually encroached on the lives and activities of free Negroes, as well.

## IV. JEWS AS HARSH TASKMASTERS

Acts of kindness towards Negroes were the only relief in the reality of a system which placed white masters in a position of absolute and total control over their slaves. Jews participated in every aspect and process of the exploitation of the defenseless blacks. The most extreme case on record was the murder of a slave by Joseph Cohen of Lynchburg, Virginia, in 1819, a crime for which he was indicted, tried and convicted— although of course the penalty for the murder of a Negro by a white was much less severe than the penalty for a trivial misdemeanor committed by a Negro.[24]

Crimes of violence against slaves by Jews were probably quite rare, since most of these occurred in rural areas where there were few Jews. But Jews in the towns and cities appear to have been quite content to abide by the excessively cruel punishments meted out to blacks who were caught by the law. These are a few examples of the testimony of Jews against Negroes taken from the Richmond court records. In 1798, Polly, a mulatto slave, was tried for taking a loaf of white sugar worth two dollars from Benjamin Solomon's home, and was sentenced to five lashes on her bare back and ordered to be branded on her left hand.[25] Two years later, Joseph Darmstadt had "a bag and lot of beeswax," valued at fifty shillings, stolen from his store by Daniel Clayton, a free Negro, and heard Clayton sentenced to thirty-nine lashes on the bare back.[26] Another free Negro was accused of stealing two silver watches valued at $32 from Myer Angel in 1832, and the culprit was sentenced to five years imprisonment, six months of which was to be spent in solitary confinement.[27] Benjamin Wolfe's store was broken into in 1797, and $500 in merchandise was stolen. Three slaves were tried for the crime, but only one was convicted. He was sentenced to be hung. One of Hart Shiff's slaves in New Orleans was tried for the murder of another of Shiff's slaves, and was executed for the crime.[28]

Jews were among the many Southern citizens who appealed for the apprehension and return of runaway slaves. Characteristic was this advertisement by Reuben D. Rochelle and Hart Moses Shiff of New Orleans in the *Louisiana Gazette* of January 18, 1812:

20 DOLLARS REWARD

Absconded from the house of the subscribers, on the night of the 16th inst. a mulatto boy, named Ovid, (the property of Judge A. Trouard, of the German Coast,) about 17 years of age, about five feet high, he had on a grey coloured coatee, with a black velvet collar and plated buttons, a grey waistcoat, white nankeen pantaloons, and short boots. Whoever will deliver him to the subscribers, or to his owner, or secure him in any Jail, shall receive a reward of twenty dollars, besides all reasonable charges. Masters of vessels are forewarned from harboring or carrying off said boy at their peril.

Ovid may have been at Rochelle and Shiff's place awaiting sale, or merely there on an errand. Jews also advertised rewards for the apprehension of their own slaves. In 1832, Maurice Barnett appealed for help in securing the return of his slave Henry, who was described as having "a scar on his cheek, in consequence of a blow from a whip."[29]

Not only did Jews bring slaves to court as private citizens, but they also participated as public officials in legal action against slaves. In 1792, for instance, Mordecai Sheftall of Georgia was responsible for issuing warrants for the arrest of runaway slaves in his district.[30] A large number of Charleston Jews held public positions which required their constant involvement in the apprehension and punishment of Negroes: Lewis Gomez was Turnkey of the Jail in 1802; Moses Solomon (1802), Nathan Hart (1821), and Solomon Moses (1822) were Constables; Samuel Hyams was Keeper of the Jail in 1822; Elisha Elizer (1802), Mark Marks (1822), and Solomon Moses, Jr. (1822) were City Deputy Sheriffs.[31] Moses Levy, also of Charleston, achieved a state-wide reputation as the most successful detective on the city's police force.[32] Moses N. Cardozo, who had a plantation near Richmond, was also the Jailer of Powhatan Courthouse. One of his responsibilities was the incarceration and disposition of runaway slaves.[33] J. S. Cohen was City Marshal of Mobile in 1841 and 1842. In connection with ordinary bankruptcies, Cohen was required to supervise the sale of Negro slaves for the account of the creditors. In the *Mobile Daily Advertiser and Chronicle* of November 4, 1841, he offered ten Negroes for sale for immediate cash, including "a first rate mantua maker, and several good cooks, washers and ironers."[34]

From testifying against Negroes in court, to apprehending a runaway slave, to inflicting punishment upon a convicted Negro, these Jews were thoroughly a part of their society.

### V. BUSINESS DEALINGS OF JEWS WITH SLAVES AND FREE NEGROES

Jewish merchants were probably more likely than others to have dealings with slaves and free Negroes, because large numbers of immigrant German Jews in the Southern states were marginal traders. Frederick Law Olmsted commented on the large numbers of Negroes who paraded the streets of Richmond on Sunday, wearing "the cast-off clothes of the white people . . . purchased of the Jews, whose shops show that there must be considerable importation of such articles, probably from the North." Olmsted was not, of course, an unbiased observer; he manifested a constant antipathy to Jews in all of his books. But there was probably some truth to his assertion that Jews in many Southern towns engaged in "an unlawful trade with the simple Negroes, which is found very profitable."[35]

Not all business dealings with Negroes were illegal. Slaves were frequently authorized to make purchases with their own small savings; sometimes they were sent on errands for their masters. Free Negroes, and even slaves who were permitted to hire themselves out for work, could transact business in stores where they were well-known. The difference between Jewish and non-Jewish merchants was probably this: that the Jewish traders displayed somewhat less reluctance to do business with Negroes. Such, at any rate, was the impression of those who wrote of the post-bellum transactions of Jewish merchants with former slaves.[36] There is no question that this observation applied to Lewis B. Levy of Richmond, a manufacturer and vendor of "Servants' Clothing," who publicly solicited the patronage of slave traders, and masters who were selling or hiring out their slaves. A number of New Orleans merchants also advertised their stock of cloth especially suited for use for Negro clothing; among these were Andrews and Brothers, and the firm of Aaron Daniels and Daniel Goodman.[37]

A number of law cases record difficulties which some Jews encountered in their business dealings with slaves. In 1836, Daniel Becker was convicted of illegal liquor sales to Negroes in South Carolina.[38] In 1843, Samuel F. Isaacs was convicted of selling a horse to a slave without permission, in the same state. But this case was based on a technicality which reveals the rigidity of laws relating to slaves: the overseer had given verbal consent to the slave and to Isaacs, but the law required written permission.[39] In 1859, Charlotte Levy of New Orleans leased a house to a slave, and was hauled into court over the illegal transaction.[40]

All merchants had perennial troubles with the law over the question of Sunday sales, both to whites and to Negroes, but slaves were particularly involved because Sunday was generally their only shopping day. In 1806, when the Richmond officials conducted a special campaign against merchants who did business on Sunday, two of the thirty-one merchants who were prosecuted were Jews, Marcus Levi and Reuben Cantor.[41] Among many other subsequent cases, Walter Thalheimer was fined $20, in 1847, for selling goods to slaves on Sunday without the consent of their owners.[42]

But these business dealings with Negroes pale into insignificance compared to the major business involvement with slaves, namely slave-trading itself.

## VI. JEWS AS SLAVE-TRADERS

Everyone who owned slaves participated in the barter of human beings. There were three classes of people so involved. The first group were those who purchased and sold slaves only in connection with their own personal needs. There was hardly a slave-owner who had never bought or sold a slave; only as an heir to a sizeable workforce could he fail to do so. But there were few who did not see fit at some time or other to dispose of a few superfluous slaves, or to increase their holdings through additional purchases. And even if one treated his slaves with the utmost of kindness, short of outright emancipation which was forbidden in most Southern states in the last two decades before the Civil War, no one could predict the fate of his slaves after his death. A particularly tragic case was that of "A Negro named Sam, about Eighty Years of age, diseased, and a Negro Woman named Sylvie about Seventy five years of Age," who were sold for ninety dollars in 1852 by Benjamin D. Lazarus, as Executor of the estate of Dr. Jacob De La Motta.[43] This was the same Dr. De La Motta who gave directions in his will for kindly treatment to other slaves. Perhaps the estate required cash, and un-doubtedly the slaves were too old for any useful purpose, but what future could they have at the hands of a purchaser who would be compelled somehow to regain his investment?

After Solomon Jacobs, Acting Mayor of Richmond in 1818–1819, died in 1827, his family composed a tombstone epitaph which described him in most sentimental fashion:

> Fond as a Husband.
> Indulgent as a Father.
> Kind as a Master . . .

If these were more than words, what would Jacobs have thought of his widow, Hetty, who in 1829 succeeded in having a special law passed by the Virginia House and Senate, allowing the sale of a number of female slaves and children because the "conduct of said slaves towards their mistress . . . was so very malevolent and very objectionable?"[44]

Thin though it may have been, there was still a line of demarcation between persons who bought or sold slaves as individuals, and those who dealt in slaves as part of their occupational pursuit. The second group of those who participated in the sale of Negroes were those merchants who dealt in many commodities, including slaves. Philip Sartorius of Louisiana and Mississippi, for instance, recalled the time in 1850 that his partner Sam Rothschild

> gambled all our money off and sold [our trading] boat and stock to another flat boat man for a Negro girl, took her to New Orleans and traded her off for tobacco.[45]

To Sam Rothschild, there was little difference between buying and selling a slave girl and any other kind of merchandise.

Sometimes Jewish store-keepers would take a flier at an investment in slaves for purely speculative purposes. An example of this activity was the purchase of three Negro slaves "named Joe William and Friendly" for $4,500, in July, 1863, by Jacob Adler and Herman Cone of Jonesboro, Tennessee. Adler and Cone lost their investment, however; the Union victories deprived them of both capital and property.[46]

An outstanding example of this kind of speculator was Jacob Barrett, an early merchant in Columbia, South Carolina, and later a resident of Charleston. Barrett was a characteristic store-keeper of the time, who carried a stock which included dry-goods, groceries, provisions, liquor, hardware, crockery, shoes, hats, saddles, horses, real estate, and when the opportunity presented itself, slaves as well. One of his clerks recalled the time when a gang of twenty Negroes was sent to him from Charleston; he promptly disposed of the slaves

> at very large profits, keeping for his own use Armistead Booker, a good-looking, active carriage driver and barber, who attended to his horses and in the store, and Aunt Nanny, a first rate cook.

Barrett later married the daughter of his cousin, Jacob Ottolengui of Charleston, another speculator in Negroes, and claimed before the Civil War to have around a thousand slaves working his rice plantations near the Savannah River.[47]

Among this group of merchants were numerous Jewish auctioneers, commission merchants, and brokers. This was an avenue of commerce in which many Jews found their niche, because no stock of merchandise or investment of capital was required, at least at the beginning. As a merchant achieved a record in the community for sagacious advice, clever salesmanship, and financial reliability, he prospered, and then could build his own warehouses and auction rooms, and buy and sell for his own account as well as for his clients. Auctioneers were licensed by law in most communities; they were, in a sense, public officials. Even if they disliked the traffic in human flesh, therefore, they could not avoid it; they were expected by the public to deal in slaves as readily as in any other sort of merchandise. To all intents and purposes, they were slave-traders, but not exclusively. This is a list of Jewish auctioneers and commission merchants in various communities:

| ATLANTA, GA., | D. Mayer, Jacobs & Co.[48] |
| CHARLESTON, S. C., | Jacob Cohen[49] |
| | H. H. DeLeon[50] |
| | Jacob Jacobs[51] |
| | Meyer Moses[52] |
| | Jacob Ottolengui[53] |
| | Ralph de Pass[54] |
| | Abraham Mendes Seixas[55] |
| COLUMBIA, S. C., | J. and L. T. Levin[56] |
| GEORGETOWN, S. C., | Abraham Cohen[57] |
| KNOXVILLE, TENN., | Isaac Joseph[58] |
| MOBILE, ALA., | George Davis[59] |
| | S. I. and I. I. Jones[60] |
| NATCHEZ, MISS., | Jacob Soria[61] |
| NEW ORLEANS, LA., | S. S. DeJonge[62] |
| | Edward Gottschalk[63] |
| | Jacob Hart[64] |
| | E. J. Hart & Co. |
| | Hemingway, Friedlander & Co. |
| | Joseph Lasalle[65] |
| | Jacob Levy and Lewis Florance[66] |
| | Levy & Summers[67] |
| RICHMOND, VA., | Benjamin Davis |
| | David Judah[68] |
| | Ash Levy |
| | Samuel Reese[69] |

Special attention is directed to two of these firms, J. and L. T. Levin of Columbia, and S. I. and I. I. Jones of Mobile, in order to underscore the fact that these members of Jewish communities who were dealers in slaves were not scorned by their fellow Jews. Both Jacob Levin and Israel I. Jones occupied particularly prominent positions in the Jewish life of their towns.

Levin was the acting rabbi and recognized leader of the Jews of Columbia. For many years he gave the main address at the annual public meetings and examinations of the Columbia Hebrew Sunday School, of which his wife was directress. His speeches, which were deemed important enough to be reported and even quoted at length in Rabbi Isaac Leeser's Philadelphia monthly journal, *The Occident and American Jewish Advocate*, were high-minded appeals to Jewish adults as well as children to devote themselves to the traditional ideals of Judaism. Levin was also an early Secretary and Treasurer of the Hebrew Benevolent Society of Columbia. His non-Jewish neighbors held him in equally high esteem: he was elected Illustrious Grand Master of the Masonic Council.[70]

Israel Jones was an even more distinguished leader. One of the first of Mobile Jewish residents to cleave loyally to his faith, he was the President of the first congregation in Alabama, Congregation Shaarai Shomayim, from its founding in 1844 until 1873. During the few brief years of activity of the pioneering Board of Delegates of

American Israelites, the first national Jewish organization for the purpose of national and international representation, Israel Jones was honored with the office of Vice-President. Jones took great pride in the fact that his daughter Emily married the talented Rabbi James K. Gutheim of New Orleans. Occupying a similar position of high repute in the general community, he was at various times a member of the City Council of Mobile, President of the Mobile Musical Association, and founder of Mobile's street car line.[71]

Slave-dealing obviously did not disqualify Jews from receiving the friendship and esteem of their co-religionists any more than it disqualified Christians; engaging in business transactions in Negro flesh was not regarded as incompatible with being a good Jew.[72]

Abraham Mendes Seixas was not a Jewish leader, but his brother was the famous rabbi of Colonial and early Federal New York and Philadelphia, Gershom Mendes Seixas. Abraham, like other auctioneers of slaves was neither ashamed of nor apologetic about his offerings of Negroes. He even burst into doggerel about his slave merchandise:

> ABRAHAM SEIXAS,
> All so gracious,
> Once again does offer
> His service pure
> For to secure
> Money in the coffer.
>
> He has for sale
> Some Negroes, male,
> Will suit full well grooms,
> He has likewise
> Some of their wives
> Can make clean, dirty rooms.
>
> For planting, too,
> He has a few
> To sell, all for the cash,
> Of various price,
> To work the rice
> Or bring them to the lash.
>
> The young ones true,
> If that will do,
> May some be had of him
> To learn your trade
> They may be made,
> Or bring them to your trim.
>
> The boatmen great,
> Will you elate

They are so brisk and free;
What e'er you say,
They will obey,
If you buy them of me.[73]

The third group of those who dealt in Negroes were, of course, the full-time slave-traders, whose sole income was derived from purchasing, transporting and selling slaves. None of the major slave-traders was Jewish, nor did Jews constitute a large proportion of traders in any particular community. Frederic Bancroft, who has made an exhaustive study of the business, attempted to classify all traders and auctioneers in the major Southern markets. In Richmond, according to his list, only three of seventy were Jews; in Charleston, four out of forty-four; in Memphis, only one of more than a dozen.[74] Other standard works limited to the investigation of the slave-trade in Kentucky and Mississippi list many dozens of slave-traders among whom not a single Jewish name appears.[75] Probably all of the Jewish slave-traders in all of the Southern cities and towns combined did not buy and sell as many slaves as did the firm of Franklin and Armfield, the largest Negro traders in the South.

These are the Jewish slave-traders whose identity we can establish:

| | |
|---|---|
| ATLANTA and AUGUSTA, GA., | Solomon Cohen[76] |
| CHARLESTON, S. C., | B. Mordecai[77] |
| LUMPKIN, GA., | J. F. Moses[78] |
| MOBILE, ALA., | Philip Goldsmith[79] |
| NEW ORLEANS, LA., | Maurice Barnett;[80] |
| | Levy Jacobs[81] |
| PETERSBURG AND RICHMOND, VA., | Ansley, Benjamin, George, and Solomon Davis[82] |
| RICHMOND, VA., | Abraham Smith[83] |

Slave-dealing was an extremely profitable business. Through natural increase, the upper South produced more slaves than its over-worked soil required, while the lower South needed constant recruits for an ever-increasing labor force on its newly developed plantations. When the price of cotton was high, slave-traders could double their investment by leading long coffles of slaves from one section of the South to the other, despite the expenses of fattening up their wares and giving them medical attention.[84]

A simple example of the profit to be made in a slave sale is given in two bills of sale relating to transactions of B. Mordecai's firm in Charleston. Mordecai purchased a slave named Abram or Abraham, about fifty years old, for $180, from an estate, on December 3, 1851. The slave was sold about six weeks later for $250. The slave must have been fairly undesirable to bring such a small sum of money, but thirty-nine percent profit was a good return on a six weeks' investment.[85]

The largest Jewish slave-trading firm in the South seems to have been the Davis family of Petersburg and Richmond, including Ansley, Benjamin, George and Solomon.[86] They were the only Jews mentioned by Harriett Beecher Stowe in her little-known commentary, *A Key to Uncle Tom's Cabin*.[87] Mrs. Stowe quotes a letter by Dr. Gamaliel Bailey, referring to them:

The Davises, in Petersburg, are the great slave-traders. They are Jews, came to that place many years ago as poor peddlers . . . These men are always in the market, giving the highest price for slaves. During the summer and fall they buy them up at low prices, trim, shave, wash them, fatten them so that they may look sleek, and sell them to great profit.

The Davis family traveled far and wide with their slave merchandise. A bill of sale imprinted with Ansley Davis' name, produced for use in South Carolina, attests to the receipt of $475 for "a female slave named Savry about 15 years of age warranted Sound and Healthy," from the purchaser, Abraham Tobias of Charleston, signed as witness by another Jew, M. Lopez, on Dec. 14, 1854.[88] The Davises were obviously well-prepared to do business in various Southern states, with legal forms already printed for their use. The family was also known in Georgia. Benjamin Davis advertised in the Columbus *Enquirer* of April 12, 1838, that he had for sale

> Sixty Likely Virginia Negroes—House Servants, Field Hands, Blow boys, Cooks, Washers, Ironers, and three first-rate Seamstresses.

Davis was remaining in Columbus, and assured the local folk that he would continue to receive shipments of additional bargains "by every arrival" for almost two more months.[89]

In these ways did Jews participate in the commercial components of the slave system.

## VII. CASES OF MISCEGENATION INVOLVING JEWS

Inter-racial cohabitation was quite common in the South, but there is little available documentary evidence which can be utilized to establish statistical indices, either for the general white population, or for any minor division thereof.

A search in the available records for Jewish names borne by Negroes encounters the inevitable difficulty of distinguishing Jewish from non-Jewish names. Many, like Aaron, Abrahams, Benjamin, David, Davis, Emanuel, Hart, Isaacs, Lyons, Marks, Moses, Myers, Noah, Samuels, Salomons, and Stein, can be Jewish or Gentile, as the case may be. Nor have we any notion of whether Northern Negroes with names like Hannah Adler, Perry Cohen, Isaac Farber, Richard Levy, Peter Levy, Benjamin Levy, Isaac Nathans, Abraham Stern, and thirteen Negro Tobias', went North before or after receiving their names. But it is likely that some of these Negroes did receive their names either from Jewish owners or Jewish fathers. This is probably also true of Sheldon Cohen of St. Peters Parish, South Carolina, Constance Herschell of New Orleans, Levy Jacobs of Fayetteville, North Carolina, George and Samuel Kauffman of King and Queen County, Virginia, Affey Levy of Charleston, Justine Moïse of New Orleans, Harry Mordecai of Frankfort, Kentucky, Betty Rosenberg of Charleston Neck, and Catherine Sasportes of Charleston.[90] Lists of Negroes active in Reconstruction days in South Carolina provide a few additional Jewish-sounding names: H. B. Da Costa, a well-regarded teacher; Philip E. Ezekiel, who was nominated for the positions of inspector general and adjutant on the Reform Republican ticket in 1872; Richard Moses, who was a leader in the South Carolina Conference of the Methodist Episcopal Church in 1870; Julius Mayer, a

Representative from Barnwell District; T. K. Sasportas, a delegate and secretary of the 1867 organizational convention of the South Carolina Republican Party; Charles C. Levy and J. R. Levy, who were South Carolina delegates to National Republican Party Conventions in later days.[91]

There is no available data to help us to ascertain whether these Negroes took their names from Jewish masters, or fathers, or neighbors, or benefactors, or, in certain cases, from the Bible. But there are situations where a relationship of friendship if not of parentage seems quite likely, as for instance, George Darmstadt, a free Negro of Richmond, who, with his wife Patty, was given permission in September, 1816, to live in the city in recognition of his "faithful services, honesty, and good demeanor."[92]

We do not even have the help of religious affiliation in our investigation of this question, since Jewish congregations would not accept Negro members. The Richmond congregation required that its members be free; and the Charleston Beth Elohim constitution of 1820 accepted proselytes only if "he, she, or they are not people of colour."[93] There is only one reference to a Jewish Negro in all of Southern Jewish records, "a free man of color" who was converted to Judaism by his master, and was accustomed to attending services at the Charleston synagogue in 1857, during the tenure of Rabbi Maurice Mayer.[94] The fact that Jewish masters, with this exception, did not educate their slaves in the Jewish faith, and that synagogues did not welcome Negro worshippers, would seem to negate the contention that present-day Negroes who regard themselves as Jews are descended from slave-converts of Jewish masters.

There are actually only six instances in which documentary evidence indicates cohabitation of Jews with Negro women, and in all but one they were free Negro women. In the first, the only one to be brought to court, David Isaacs, an immigrant from Germany who conducted a dry goods store, and Nancy West, a free mulatto woman, were indicted in 1826 by the grand jury of Albermarle County, Va., "for outraging the decency of society . . . by cohabiting together . . . as man and wife, without being lawfully married." A higher court reduced the serious charge of the indictment to the lesser charge of fornication. Yet the seven children of this illicit marriage seem to have found a place for themselves. They are reported to have attended school in Charlottesville with white children. One son, Frederick, was a well-educated man who became a printer and who published a local paper, *The Chronicle;* another son, Tucker, became a painter, and later moved to Chillicothe, Ohio. Several other children became property owners in the area.[95]

In our second case, the evidence is less positive. Samuel Simons, whose will was proved in Charleston on February 13, 1824, left his entire estate to relatives and Jewish institutions in London, with the exception of an extensive bequest to his "House Keeper Maria Chapman a free woman of Colour." Simons left Maria

the Sum of fourteen hundred Dollars, two Negroes named Pompey and Peggy with the issue and increase of the females and also two Bedsteads bedding and six chairs.

Negro concubines were frequently called "housekeepers," and Simons' bequest to Maria was extraordinarily large. The supposition would be that her employer had a much more personal relationship with Maria than would be mentioned in polite society.[96]

This may also be true of other men whose generous bequests have already been noted, especially when the names of children are also mentioned.

The third instance is far more definite. The will of Moses Nunes of Savannah, who died on September 6, 1797, acknowledges "Mulatta Rose" as his concubine, and recognizes her children, Robert, James, Alexander, and Frances (married to George Galphin), as his own progeny. He bequeathed certain tracts of land, his home, furniture and clothing, and thirteen Negro slaves, to Rose and his four children, in addition to

> a full and perfect freedom from all Slavery and servitude in reward and as an acknowledgement of the faithful conduct and behaviour of the said Mulatta Rose towards me and my Children.[97]

Moses Nunes' will became an important document in 1853 when it was exhumed in connection with a lawsuit which was carried through the courts during the next eleven years. The case concerned the legality of Moses' grandson, Joseph's, sale of five slave children, his own, by his Negro concubine, Patience. What was at stake was the question of Joseph's race, since his father, James Nunes, had passed for white, and had been married to a white woman. Many witnesses testified to their belief that both James and Joseph were of pure white ancestry. Unfortunately, however, the grandfather's will was strong evidence of mixed blood. But Sherman's march through Georgia made the entire question an academic one before the final appeal was adjudicated.[98]

A less complicated example, in certain ways, was that of the Negro branch of the Cardozo family, which produced two leading figures in Reconstruction governments. It is a moot question whether their father was Jacob N. Cardozo, the famous Southern journalist and economist, or his lesser-known brother Isaac, who for twenty-four years was a weigher in the Charleston Custom House. Historical writers seem to have favored Jacob's name, while present-day members of the family believe that Isaac was their ancestor.[99]

Be that as it may, Francis Lewis Cardozo, Sr., was probably the most distinguished member of the Cardozo family between his father or uncle Jacob, and Supreme Court Justice Benjamin Nathan Cardozo. Francis was born in Charleston on Jan. 1, 1837, the son of Lydia Williams, a free mulatto of mixed Negro and Indian blood. He went to school from the ages of five to twelve, and probably received some private tutoring from Jacob Cardozo; he was apprenticed to a carpenter for five years, and then pursued the trade independently for a few more. At the age of twenty-one, with money which he had saved over the years, and possibly with some help from the family and from the American Missionary Association, he went to Scotland. He matriculated first at the University of Glasgow, where he won prizes in Latin and in Greek, and then at the theological seminary in Edinburgh. He later studied at the London School of Theology, was ordained, and then returned to the United States to become the minister of the Temple Street Congregational Church in New Haven, Conn. A year later, immediately after the conclusion of the Civil War, he was sent by the American Missionary Association to Charleston, where he founded the Avery Institute, a normal school. In the following years, he was president of the South Carolina State Council of Union Leagues, a member of the South Carolina Constitutional Convention of 1868, a member of the Board of

Trustees of the University of South Carolina in 1869, Secretary of State in the Scott administration of 1868–72, and State Treasurer in the Moses and Chamberlain administration, 1872–76. During the latter years he studied at the South Carolina College and received his LL.B. degree in 1876. Cardozo was described by those who knew him as a "handsome, well-groomed man, with cultivated manners," as "almost white in color," with a "tall, portly . . . figure and elaborate, urbane manners." He was removed from office during the upheavals of 1877, although there was virtually no evidence of corruption on his part. To the contrary, he had fought hard to keep the state's financial condition free of peculation. In this regard, he stands in strong contrast to Franklin Moses, Jr., the notorious Reconstruction Governor, also of Jewish parentage, though never a practicing Jew. Even the most vigorously pro-Bourbon historians have been hardpressed to uncover any excuses for criticism of Cardozo's leadership and record.

This is, of course, not the proper place for an extensive evaluation of Cardozo's services to his people and to the state of South Carolina, or of his later career as an educator in the nation's capital, but it is vital to underscore his reputation both among whites and Negroes as one of the most brilliant and highly educated public servants in South Carolina. Governor Daniel H. Chamberlain, in the midst of great corruption and mismanagement, said of Cardozo,

> I have never heard one word or seen one act of Mr. Cardozo's which did not confirm my confidence in his personal integrity and his political honor and zeal for the honest administration of the State Government. On every occasion and under all circumstances he has been against fraud and jobbery and in favor of good measures and good men.

I would not want to conclude this brief sketch of Cardozo without quoting an excerpt from the comments on school desegregation which he made during the debates of the Constitutional Convention of 1868: "The most natural method of removing race distinctions," he said, "would be to allow children, when five or six years of age, to mingle in school together . . . Under such training prejudices will eventually die out." How far we would have been in the solution of all of the problems of race relations, if Francis Lewis Cardozo, Sr., and other honorable Reconstruction leaders, had been given a genuine opportunity to erase the vestiges of slavery.[100]

The other member of the Cardozo family to occupy an important position in the Reconstruction period was Francis' brother, Thomas Y. Cardozo, who had a far less distinguished career in Mississippi political life. He came out of an obscure background which has not been recorded to any significant degree, to become a circuit court clerk in Warren County, Mississippi, following which he was elected Mississippi State Superintendent of Education, which office he held from 1874 to 1876. In the latter year he resigned under threat of impeachment. He seems to have been quite intelligent and well educated, for during 1875 he was editor of the Vicksburg *Plain Dealer,* and a man of natural capacity for leadership, in view of his founding the same year, the Vicksburg branch of the Grand United Order of Odd Fellows of America. He was, however, accused of participation in certain corrupt bargains of the time, and there was seeming proof of his embezzlement of two thousand dollars from the funds of Tougaloo University. It has not been possible to learn any further details of his training, career, or activities after 1876.[101]

It is instructive to note that some historians of the Reconstruction are far more eager to dwell upon those political figures who were guilty of corruption than those who had an honorable and useful career. Both Claude G. Bowers and E. Merton Coulter take occasion to mention Thomas Y. Cardozo as an example of a corrupt, politically-oriented Negro office-holder, without even a bare mention of his more important, more talented, and more honorable brother Francis.[102]

Our fifth example of miscegenation concerns the family of Barnet A. Cohen, who was born in 1770 in Bristol, England, had plantations in King's Creek, South Carolina, and died there on March 23, 1839. The fortunate preservation of a batch of family papers enables us to comprehend, in a uniquely personal way, the difficult social and psychological problems which faced a free mulatto.[103]

By 1810, when the first of these papers was drawn up, Barnet A. Cohen had fathered two children, Barnet Owens Cohen and Benjamin Phillip Owens Cohen, by a "free woman of Colour," Catherine Owens. A number of neighbors, including four Jews, signed a document attesting to the family relationship and the free status of the woman and her children. According to the second document, in March, 1822, Barnet A. Cohen, the father, as legal guardian for his son Benjamin, and on his behalf, purchased "a Negro wench named Sarah and her child Lina," the mother probably being bought as a concubine for Benjamin. The lot of a free Negro was far from simple; his choice of mates was extremely limited. Most frequently he had to buy his own women, and unless he could emancipate them, which was next to impossible, he was compelled also to own title to his own children.

In 1832, with the approval of his father-guardian, Benjamin Cohen purchased a nine-month old Negro, "Alonzo," for $100. It would seem obvious that Alonzo must have been his own child by a slave woman whose owner refused to part with her; why else should he, or for that matter, anyone, buy a Negro infant?

In 1837, two years before his father's death, Benjamin purchased some land in Barnwell District, adjoining farms which belonged to his father and his mulatto brother, Barnet. By now, his white half-brother, Moses A. Cohen, was signing as his guardian. It is significant that the Negro and white members of this family lived in such close proximity and, apparently, harmony, as well. The father's white wife, Bella, died in 1836; and when the father died in 1839, there was no sign of strain in the family's feelings, at least on Barnet's tombstone, which commemorated "the virtues of a beloved parent . . . as a memorial of [his childrens'] love and veneration . . ." What a shame that we have no way of telling whether Benjamin and Barnet had a hand in composing this epitaph!

From 1840 to 1850, Benjamin was worrying about the future of his slave family. He wanted to set them free, and thus assure their status after his own death, but he could not find the way. In 1840, he consulted an attorney who informed him that

> no Slave can be Set free in this State except by Act of the Legislature on a Petition. But it is *almost impossible* to have such a Petition granted—The Legislature almost always refuses them.

If it was "*almost impossible*" in 1840, it became altogether so, on December 17, 1841, when the South Carolina legislature passed "An Act to Prevent the Emancipation of Slaves," a copy of which Benjamin secured and kept among his papers. According to this law, any effort through "bequest, deed or trust, or conveyance," to send slaves out of the state for the purpose of emancipation, was declared null and void. The act also prohibited any stratagem whereby "slaves shall be held in nominal servitude." In 1844, Benjamin Cohen consulted another lawyer, and, after paying a fee of ten dollars, received the categorical advice that

> a free coloured man can purchase a Slave, but he cannot give her her freedom—the Slave and her children will always remain Slaves.

In 1850, Benjamin Cohen, free man of color, but without the freedom to do very much, by then about fifty years of age or perhaps older, was altogether anxious to do something for his family. So he drew up a draft of a will—one of the most pathetic wills I have ever been privileged to read. After the usual formalities, including a request for "Christian burial," he bequeathes all his property to his "esteemed patron and benefactor, Samuel Cohen," who must have been another white half-brother. Then, in an effort to forestall the effects of the law of 1841, he offers this declaration of loyalty and disclaimer of intention:

> SECONDLY. I give and devise unto the aforesaid Samuel Cohen, the following Slaves, viz—Jane, John, Susan, Benjamin, Alonzo, Moses, Dani[e]l, Emma, Sarah, and Frances, and as most of them are my offspring, and Jane my wife, it may be thought that this devise is intended to avoid and defeat, the laws of this commonwealth, which affords me protection, and to which I defferentially bow, in gratitude. I therefore declare and Solemnly asseverate that I intend no such unlawful act. I know that by the law, they are slaves, and must remain so. Wherefore through the means of this my will I choose their Master, preferring him, for my heir at Law to any one else. Neither is there any understanding secret, or otherwise, that the above named Slaves are to be held in nominal servitude only.

Benjamin makes only one bequest—he provides for a gift of $100 to his niece Emily, the daughter of his deceased mulatto brother Barnet (or "Barney" as he calls him in this document). All other property is left to Samuel Cohen, "in consideration of my friendship and his many kindnesses to me." It was apparently no longer proper for a will to mention the familial relationship of Negroes and whites.

This is the final document which concerns Benjamin Philip Owens Cohen. A probated will cannot be discovered in the records of the Barnwell Court House. Only this rough draft has been preserved, together with his other papers, among the records of his half-brother Samuel, who lived into the 1870's and had a store in a town with one of the most remarkable names in the United States, Cohen's Bluff, South Carolina. But the fact that these papers relating to Benjamin were preserved by Samuel, without the inventories and other documents an executor would have needed to prepare, would seem to be convincing proof that the will was never executed in its present form. Perhaps Benjamin

Philip Owens Cohen outlived the institution of slavery and was able to spend his last days with a family freed from involuntary servitude by the bloodshed which began in 1861.

One final example of miscegenation involved Daniel Warburg, the first member of the distinguished German-Jewish family of bankers, scientists, and philanthropists to establish residence in the United States. Born in Hamburg on October 10, 1789, Warburg was established in the commission business in New Orleans by 1821. An eccentric who believed that he was a mathematical genius and who had some political aspirations, Warburg was very successful in real estate and other investments, but appears to have gone broke in the panic of 1839. Warburg's first mulatto child, Eugène, was born a slave, and had to be freed in a public act which was announced in March, 1830; the mother, a Cuban Negro named Marie Rose, must also have been freed, although I can find no trace of the documents. Their other children, four in number, appear to have been born free. Eugène and a younger son, Daniel, Jr., have some significance in the history of artistic endeavor among American Negroes. Daniel was active as a stonecutter, tomb designer, and engraver, and spent his entire life in New Orleans. Eugène, apparently more ambitious, temperamental, and talented, studied with a French artist named Garbeille and left the city about 1853 to study and work in England, France, and Italy. In England he is said to have been commissioned by the Duchess of Sutherland to design bas-reliefs illustrating the story of *Uncle Tom's Cabin*. In 1855 he did a bust of John Y. Mason, the United States Minister to France; this sole surviving example of Eugène's work is now in the Virginia Historical Society in Richmond. Two further pieces, *Le Pêcheur* and *Le Premier Baiser,* are mentioned by a biographer, but are not known other than by title. Another piece is known only from an extensive description in the *Bee,* December 13, 1850:

> A CREOLE SCULPTOR—We paid a visit to Hall's gilding establishment in Canal street yesterday, and examined with some attention a marble statue chiseled by a young Creole of our city, EUGENE WARBURG, a pupil of GARBEILLE. It represents, we presume, GANYMEDE, Jove's cupbearer kneeling and presenting a flowing beaker of Nectar to the King of Gods and Men. The design is beautiful, and the execution reflects infinite credit upon the taste and talent of our townsman. The statue is offered for raffle, and is estimated to be worth $500. Every patron of art, and admirer of native talent should gladly take a chance on this exquisite specimen of sculpture. If MR. WARBURG will bestow proper study on his models and labor assiduously at his profession, he will doubtless attain deserved excellence.

Eugène Warburg died in Rome on January 12, 1859, when he was about thirty-three years old.[104]

### VIII. OPINIONS OF JEWS ABOUT SLAVERY

This study has thus far traced a pattern of almost complete conformity to the slave society of the Old South on the part of its Jewish citizens. They participated in the buying, owning, and selling of slaves, and the exploitation of their labor, along with their neighbors. The behavior of Jews towards slaves seems to have been indistinguishable from that of their non-Jewish friends. This description also characterizes the opinions of Jews about slavery.

No Jewish political figure of the Old South ever expressed any reservations about the justice of slavery or the rightness of the Southern position. Men like David Levy Yulee of Florida and David S. Kaufman of Texas were typical exponents of Southern views on states' rights and the spread of slavery.[105] Judah P. Benjamin of Louisiana was regarded as one of the most eloquent defenders of the Southern way of life. Though far from a fanatic, he stood squarely with his Senatorial colleagues every inch of the way that led from Washington to Montgomery and then to Richmond. Benjamin did question the wisdom of entrusting Negro slaves with complicated agricultural machinery, and advised sugar planters to employ trained white mechanics, but he never admitted that this deterrent to progressive agriculture was an inevitable consequence of the slave economy. Despite his conservative views, however, he was the only notable Confederate leader who advocated the arming of slaves during the Civil War, and who urged that they be emancipated as reward for this effort. He seems to have been far ahead of most Southerners in his willingness to use any weapon for the deliverance of the Confederacy. "The true issue," he said, is, "is it better for the Negro to fight for us or against us?" He urged the adoption of his policy as an answer to the ever-present manpower shortage, but he also believed that "the action of our people on this point will be of more value to us abroad than any diplomacy or treaty-making." But most Southerners would rather have lost the war, as they did, than weaken the slave system in any way.[106]

Benjamin's proposal was certainly not a repudiation of slavery. Neither was the program which Judge Solomon Heydenfeldt of Alabama advocated in 1849 as an antidote to the problems created by the concentration of Alabama capital in slave property. Heydenfeldt first published his *Communication on the Subject of Slave Immigration, Addressed to Hon. Reuben Chapman, Governor of Alabama,* in the Huntsville *Democrat* on Jan. 31, 1849, and subsequently in pamphlet form. The jurist questioned the economic wisdom of unlimited slave immigration and protested that the state would become impoverished through the uncontrolled "dumping" of slaves in Alabama. But his arguments were denounced by fellow-Alabamians. One critic said, in the Wetumpka *Daily Stateguard* of February 12, 1849, that if Heydenfeldt's proposal were to be adopted, an artificial scarcity of slaves would be created, the prices of slaves would soar, and the rich would become richer, while the poor who hoped sometime to become slaveowners would be deprived of any expectation of economic advancement. Heydenfeldt was far from being the abolitionist some have imagined him to be.[107]

Long after the Civil War had been fought and lost by the South, Philip Phillips of Alabama, who for a time served in the House of Representatives and was perhaps the outstanding Jewish attorney of the ante-bellum South, said that he regarded emancipation as a new opportunity for the South. "So far as the loss of property in slaves was involved," he said, "I regard it as the greatest blessing . . . A new generation with self-reliant spirit will create a new South, and crown it by their energy and industry, with all that enriches and enobles a land . . ." But he never criticized slavery as an enemy of self-reliance and creativity while it was the accepted economic and social foundation of his state and section.[108]

Nor was there anyone among the many Jewish journalists, writers, and publicists of the Old South who questioned the moral, political, or economic justice of slavery. Jacob De Cordova, the Texas real-estate promoter, newspaper editor, and geographer, emphatically denied charges that he had given voice to "free-soil doctrines" during his lecture tour in the North in 1858, and "wish[ed] it distinctly understood that our feelings and education have always been pro-slavery."[109] Isaac Harby, the Charleston dramatist and political essayist, was writing in Charleston in opposition to "the abolitionist society and its secret branches," as early as 1824. A number of Louisiana Jews were leaders in the public outcry in 1835–36, when the abolitionists were believed to be bent on securing a following among both whites and slaves. Samuel Hermann, Jr. and Benjamin Levy were members of a special grand jury in New Orleans which demanded a standing military force to guard the city from abolitionist attacks. Jacob Luria, a newcomer at the bar, was a speaker at anti-abolitionist meetings in New Orleans, as was Henry M. Hyams, a future lieutenant-governor of the state, at similar meetings in Donaldsonville, La.[110] Jacob N. Cardozo, the editor and political economist, asserted that slavery was defensible both economically and morally. In the former respect, he maintained that

> Slavery brought not only great wealth to the South, but to the slaves a greater share of its enjoyment than in many regions where the relation between employer and employee was based on wages.

In regard to the ethical question, he placed the responsibility squarely on the Deity: "The reason the Almighty made the colored black is to prove their inferiority." After the Civil War, in his well-known *Reminiscences of Charleston,* Cardozo expressed his sympathy with the planters who were now suffering great privation:

> The owner of two hundred to five hundred slaves, with a princely income, has not only to submit to the most degraded employments, but he frequently cannot obtain them. In some instances, he has to drive a cart, or attend a retail grocery, while he may have to obey the orders of an ignorant and course menial. There is something unnatural in this reverse of position—something revolting to my sense of propriety in this social degradation.[111]

Edwin De Leon, the journalist and Confederate diplomat, devoted many pages of his reminiscences to an extended apologia for slavery.[112] His brother, Thomas Cooper De Leon, one of the most prolific Southern literateurs of the second half of the nineteenth century, wrote many novels and other works in the Southern romantic style of which he was a major practitioner. In one of his most famous works, *Belles, Beaux and Brains of the Confederacy,* De Leon described all talk of cruelty in the slave system as propaganda and mythology; he underlined the fact that Harriett Beecher Stowe was compelled to ascribe a Yankee origin to her famous character, Simon Legree.[113] Samuel Mordecai, the bachelor journalist of Richmond, derived part of his income from his articles in Edmund Ruffin's *The Farmer's Register,* a journal devoted primarily to the interests of

Southern employers of slave labor forces. Mordecai loved everything about old Virginia, and wrote tenderly of the old colored aristocracy, in his *Richmond in By-Gone Days*. He too regarded slavery as a natural and desirable condition of society.[114]

Even in the days of the secession crisis, and the subsequent prolongated war and eventual defeat, many Southern Jews believed slavery to be indispensable to their happiness and security. George W. Mordecai, born a Jew but later an Episcopalian banker, railroad executive, and plantation owner in North Carolina, wrote to a Northern Republican in Dec., 1860:

> I would much sooner trust myself alone on my plantation surrounded by my slaves, than in one of your large manufacturing towns when your labourers are discharged from employment and crying aloud for bread for themselves and their little ones.[115]

In 1864, Private Eugene Henry Levy of the Confederate Army objected to the radical suggestion that Negroes be utilized in the war effort and be freed for this assistance. "The slaves," he said, "are in their proper sphere as they are at present situated within the boundaries of the Confederacy."[116]

After the war was over, some Southern Jews still believed that slavery had been a necessary foundation of human society. Eleanor H. Cohen, the daughter of Dr. Philip Melvin Cohen of Charleston, said in the innocent selfishness of young maidenhood:

> I, who believe in the institution of slavery, regret deeply its being abolished. I am accustomed to have them wait on me, and I dislike white servants very much.[117]

Perhaps no more concise and self-deceptive rationalization of slavery was ever written than the observations which were recorded by Solomon Cohen, the distinguished civic leader and merchant of Savannah, who had lost a son in the war, in a letter which he wrote to his sister-in-law, Emma Mordecai, shortly after the end of the war:

> I believe that the institution of slavery was refining and civilizing to the whites— giving them an elevation of sentiment and ease and dignity of manners only attainable in societies under the restraining influence of a privileged class—and at the same time the only human institution that could elevate the Negro from barbarism and develop the small amount of intellect with which he is endowed.[118]

Such sentiments might well be expected of members of families long resident in the South and thoroughly acclimated to its habits and assumptions. The De Leons, Mordecais, and Cardozos had lived with their neighbors long enough to share their ideas and attitudes. But what of the newly immigrant German Jews who came to the South in increasing numbers beginning in the 1840's? There is no evidence that they found it very difficult to adjust to the slave society of which they became a part. Julius Weis, of New Orleans, who came to the United States in 1845, recorded his shock at his first sight of a Negro

> being whipped upon his bare back by an overseer. The sight of a human being punished in this manner was very repugnant to me, though living in the midst of a country where slavery existed. I afterwards got somewhat accustomed to it, but I always felt a pity for the poor slaves.

But Weis' compassion seemed to be limited to this matter of punishment, for he owned several slaves during the period from 1853 to 1857, and bought a Negro barber in 1862. He notes that "I never found it necessary to punish them in such a manner," but his feeling of pity never led him to adopt a critical attitude toward the entire system of slavery.[119]

Louis Stix of Cincinnati wrote of a German Jewish immigrant to the South who became violent in his pro-slavery opinions. They met at a Jewish boarding house in New York City; at dinner one night this unidentified Southern Jew said that "Southerners could not live without slavery." "I replied to this," wrote Stix, "by a very uncalled-for remark not at all flattering to our race who were living in the South . . . The Souther-ner . . . drew his pistol to compel me to take back my words . . . I hope [he] has since learned to do without slaves, or has returned to the place from which he came, where he was almost a slave himself."[120] But such a direct application of logic from Jewish experi-ence in Europe to the situation of the Negroes in the South could only stem from the mind of a Northern Jew; it was never, to my knowledge, expressed in such blunt terms by a Southern Jew. To the contrary, the average Southern Jew would probably have agreed with Aaron Hirsch, who came to the United States in 1847 and worked through Mississippi and Arkansas, and who said that

> the institution of Slavery as it existed in the South was not so great a wrong as people believe. The Negroes were brought here in a savage state; they captured and ate each other in their African home. Here they were instructed to work, were civilized and got religion, and were perfectly happy.[121]

Some Southern Jews, however, did not deceive themselves into thinking that the Negro slaves were "perfectly happy." These sensitive spirits were appalled at human exploitation of the life and labor of other human beings. Most of them reacted in a purely personal way, by avoiding the owning of slaves or by helping slaves. Major Alfred Mordecai of the United States Army, reared in the South and brother to planters and defenders of slavery, purchased only one slave in his life, simply to emancipate her. He believed that slavery was "the greatest misfortune and curse that could have befallen us." Yet he would do nothing to oppose slavery, and when the lines were drawn, he resigned his commission rather than fight for the North, without being willing to take up arms for the South.[122] Judah Touro, the New Orleans merchant, is reported to have emanci-pated many slaves whom he purchased solely for that purpose, and is even said to have established some of them in business at his own expense. There is no evidence to justify these reports, but it is extremely significant that Touro designated a mulatto as one of the executors of his famous, magnanimous will. This executor was Pierre Andre Destrac Cazenae, who in 1853 was described as a "pet" and former confidential clerk of Touro. Cazenae was bequeathed $10,000 in his former employer's will.[123] Another such spirit was Lazarus Straus, immigrant store-keeper of Talbotton, Ga., who used to argue with local Protestant ministers about the Biblical grounds for the defense of slavery. Accord-ing to his son, Oscar, hired slaves who worked for the Straus family would beg to be purchased by them. "As the result of such pleadings," Oscar said, "my father purchased household slaves one by one from their masters, although neither he nor my mother believed in slavery.[124] Probably many Jews as well as non-Jews were caught in the dilemma of purchasing slaves just because they did not believe in slavery; since emancipation was virtually impossible, all they could do was to become the most generous masters possible under the circumstances. But there is, of course, no way of telling what proportion of people who could not conscientiously condone slavery was included in the statistics of slave-owners.

The literature has preserved only one instance of Jewish participation in the dangerous game of taking a Negro slave to the North for clandestine emancipation. This was the risk taken by the Friedman brothers of Cincinnati, Ohio, and Tuscumbia, Alabama, who purchased Peter Still and conspired to take him North after he had earned enough money to refund his purchase price. This exciting story is told in Kate E. R. Packard's *The Kidnapped and the Ransomed*.[125] Joseph Friedman and his brother Isaac had been regarded by the townsmen with suspicion and dislike when they first came to Tuscumbia, but their behavior gradually overcame the local prejudices. Six or seven years later, Peter Still, beloved by his owners and by the community in general, prevailed on the Friedmans to hire him. After he felt certain that he could trust them, he confided to their ears his hope of obtaining freedom, so they purchased him from his owner. There was much criticism of the transaction in the town. People knew that the Friedmans had no use for a slave in their business, and that they maintained no home. The townsfolk therefore suspected that Joseph Friedman would ultimately sell Peter away from the community to some stranger who would mistreat him. Kate Packard quotes a child as saying, "Ma says he's a Jew, and she says *Jews will sell their own children for money.*" The authoress highlights the contrast between the behavior of "the slandered Jew" who is Peter's friend, and "the gaudy hypocrisy of his traducers" who "had bought and sold, and beaten and oppressed the poor until their cry had gone up to heaven." The plot succeeds: Peter saves up enough money to repay Joseph Friedman; the brothers close up their store and return to Cincinnati, taking Peter with them so that he can be freed. But the brothers never return to Alabama, for eventually their duplicity is revealed. Peter's well-wishers are indignant that the slave has been emancipated: that was carrying friendship too far! Joseph and Isaac Friedman are worthy of remembrance as anti-slavery activists: though other Southern Jews may well have risked fortune and reputation to evade state laws which restricted the emancipation of slaves, theirs are the only names recorded as having taken part in this risky venture.

We should not be surprised to discover that there was not a single abolitionist among the Jews of the South, but at least one did stem from this background. He was Marx E. Lazarus, eccentric scion of two distinguished Southern Jewish families, who was attracted to various radical social movements, including Fourierism, the North American Phalanx, Socialism, phrenology, spiritualism and homeopathy. In 1860, Lazarus contributed a number of articles and translations to Moncure D. Conway's radical journal, *The Dial*, which was published in Cincinnati. One of these was entitled "True Principles of Emancipation," and was signed, "A Native of North Carolina and a Citizen of the World." In this article, Lazarus reminded his readers that Negro slavery was only one aspect of "the manifold cruelties that labor elsewhere suffers at the hands of capital, classes or castes, from their social superiors . . ." He warned idealists against the "conversion of chattel slavery into that of labor for wages, changing the form, but not the facts, of slavery and oppression." "This prolonged crucifixion of a martyr race," he said, "demands a resurrection more humane than the liberty of selling oneself by the day, the cut-throat competitions of labor for wages, the outrages sanctioned by prejudice against color, careworn indigence or paralyzed pauperism." Despite these advanced views, Lazarus, in contrast to Major Mordecai, would not abandon the land of his birth-place; with the outbreak of war he returned home to enlist in the Confederate army as a private.[126]

But men like Marx Lazarus were outright anomalies. The Southern intellectual scene, in the main, was a drab, monochromatic landscape of unquestioning adherence to the dominant Southern doctrine about slavery during the two decades before the Civil War. Jews not only accepted this doctrine; some of them helped to formulate and circulate it, although their role was by no means a significant one.

### IX. AN EVALUATION

This investigation has traced Jewish participation in various aspects of the "peculiar institution" of the Old South. Jewish opinions about and relationships to the system of slavery were in no appreciable degree different from those of their non-Jewish neighbors. If more Jews owned slaves in terms of their numerical proportion of the population, it was because larger percentages of Jews lived in the towns and cities; if more Jews were auctioneers of slaves, it was because they were also auctioneers of every kind of merchandise; if fewer Jews were large-scale planters, it was for understandable social and economic reasons.

The significant thing is that being Jewish did not play any discernible role in the determination of the relationship of Jews to slavery. Except for the teachings of a very few rabbis like David Einhorn of Baltimore, Judaism in America had not yet adopted a "social justice" view of the responsibility of Jews towards society. Ante-bellum Southern Jews were more likely to quote the Talmudic maxim that "the law of the land is the law [for Jews]," and to regard the institution of slavery as part of the law which they were bound to uphold and follow, than they were to evaluate the failings of slavery in the light of the prophetic ethic.

Their acceptance of slavery as a natural aspect of the life of their section should not be regarded as a deliberately contrived "protective coloration," in order that they might remain inconspicuous. There is no iota of evidence, no line in a letter, no stray remark, which would lead us to believe that these Jews gave conscious support to the slave system out of fear of arousing anti-Jewish prejudice. Any such motivation for their behavior and attitudes, if it existed at all, was well hidden in the unconscious psyche.

It is true, however, that their small numbers militated against the creation of a distinctively Jewish approach to any political or social question other than anti-Semitism. Jews were only a fragment of the Southern population, thinly distributed throughout the area. Even in the largest cities, New Orleans, Charleston, Richmond, they were a tiny group. They would be entirely likely, therefore, to derive their opinions from discussions with non-Jewish neighbors, rather than with Jewish friends. This was especially true of the more prominent Jews, planters, attorneys, physicians, newspaper editors, merchants, whose associations with non-Jews were quite intimate.

Whatever prejudice there was in the South, before the Civil War aggravated every possible source of tension, was directed largely against the alien Jew, the immigrant peddler and petty store-keeper, the insecure newcomer, whose very survival was in the hands of his customers. He would, therefore, be inclined to adopt their opinions and attitudes, not because he was afraid to disagree with them, but because he wanted to succeed in his new home.

Slavery played an unacknowledged role in this question of Jewish status in the Old South, too. Although Southern society fostered a caste system which also applied to various classes of whites, and which distinguished the store-keeper from the wealthier merchant, the merchant in turn from the professional man, and the attorney and physician from the planter, the all-pervasive division was between the races. The Jews were white, and this very fact goes a long way towards accounting for the measurably higher social and political status achieved by Jews in the South than in the North. Foreign observers like Salomon de Rothschild and I. J. Benjamin were acutely aware of the sharp contrast between the South, where so many Jews were elected to high office, and the North, where Jews constituted a larger percentage of the population, yet had achieved fewer honors.[127] The Negroes acted as an escape-valve in Southern society. The Jews gained in status and security from the very presence of this large mass of defenseless victims who were compelled to absorb all of the prejudices which might otherwise have been expressed more frequently in anti-Jewish sentiment. As I. J. Benjamin said,

> The white inhabitants felt themselves united with, and closer to, other whites—as opposed to the Negroes. Since the Israelites there did not do the humbler kinds of work which the Negro did, he was quickly received among the upper classes, and early rose to high political rank.

Although this was too broad a generalization, and not all Jews were treated so generously, the road to social and economic advancement and acceptance for many Jews was smoothed by the ever-present race distinction which imputed superiority to all whites. And even the path of the poor, foreign Jew was made easier by the institution of slavery. Oscar Straus remembered that when his father was peddling through the rural areas of Georgia, he

> was treated by the owners of the plantations with a spirit of equality that is hard to appreciate today. Then, too, the existence of slavery drew a distinct line of demarcation between the white and black races. This gave to the white [peddler] a status of equality that probably otherwise he would not have enjoyed to such a degree.[128]

Slavery, therefore, played a more significant role in the development of Jewish life in the Old South, than Jews themselves played in the establishment and maintenance of the institution. The history of slavery would not have differed one whit from historic reality if no single Jew had been resident in the South. Other whites would have owned slaves; other traders and auctioneers would have bought and sold slaves; other political and intellectual leaders would have propagandized in behalf of slavery; a few slaves might have fared better or worse at the hands of other masters, but their feelings were immaterial details in the total story of the institution itself. But whether so many Jews would have achieved so high a level of social, political, economic and intellectual status and recognition, without the presence of the lowly and degraded slave, is indeed dubious. How ironic that the distinctions bestowed upon men like Judah P. Benjamin, Major Raphael J. Moses, and the Honorable Solomon Cohen were in some measure dependent upon the sufferings of the very Negro slaves they bought and sold with such equanimity.

NOTES

Delivered as the Presidential Address at the Fifty-Ninth Annual Meeting of the American Jewish Historical Society, February 18, 1961, printed first in *Publication of the American Jewish Historical Society,* vol. L (1961), pp. 151–201, reprinted as a separate monograph, and included here with the kind permission of the American Jewish Historical Society.

1. I begin with 1789 for the following reasons: firstly, before discussing Jewish ownership of slaves in the Colonies, it would be necessary to consider the question of Jewish legal status in the Colonies in order to investigate the problems of all property ownership by Jews; secondly, the Colonial period was the heyday of slave importation from Africa, and Northern Jews were far more active in this aspect of the slave-trade than Southern Jews; and thirdly, Jewish settlers in the West Indian Colonies were at least as influential as those on the North American mainland, and a study of slavery during that time would therefore require extensive reference to those non-Southern Jewish communities. Only in a few instances has material prior to 1789 or subsequent to 1865 been utilized, and these data are clearly germane. An additionally complicating factor has been avoided through the elimination of reference to the Jews of the border states, Maryland, Kentucky, and Missouri, which were at least as much a part of the North as they were of the South, as the Confederate leaders eventually discovered.

2. Meade, *Judah P. Benjamin,* pp. 57, 63, and 90; J. Carlyle Sitterson, *Sugar Country, The Cane Sugar Industry in the South, 1753–1950* (Lexington, Ky., 1953), pp. 131, 154; *The Life of Judah Philip Benjamin,* A Publication of the Louisiana State Museum (New Orleans, 1937); Harnett T. Kane, *Deep Delta Country* (New York, 1944), pp. 68–69; Baton Rouge *Advocate,* Mar. 27, 1960, magazine section, p. 1.

3. Bertram W. Korn, *The Early Jews of New Orleans* (Waltham, 1969), pp. 101–102, 133, hereafter *KEJNO;* 1840 Mss. Census Returns for New Orleans and Vicinity, National Archives.

4. Jacob Rader Marcus, *Memoirs of American Jews, 1775–1865,* 3 vols. (Philadelphia, 1955–1956), vol. I, p. 184, hereafter *MM.*

5. Addendum on "Absentee Ownership of Slaves in the United States in 1830," in Carter G. Woodson, *Free Negro Owners of Slaves in the United States in 1830* (Washington, D.C., 1924), p. 61; Charles Reznikoff with Uriah Z. Engelman, *The Jews of Charleston* (Philadelphia, 1950), p. 92, hereafter *RE;* Elzas, *Jews of South Carolina,* pp. 51 and 143, hereafter *E;* Joseph R. Rosenbloom, A *Biographical Dictionary of Early American Jews* (Lexington, Ky., 1960), pp. 25 and 89, hereafter *R;* Jacob Rader Marcus, *Early American Jewry,* vol. II (Philadelphia, 1953), p. 385, hereafter *ME;* A. J. Hanna, *A Prince in Their Midst: The Adventurous Life of Achille Murat on the American Frontier* (Norman, 1946), p. 86; Leon Hühner, "David L. Yulee, Florida's First Senator," *PAJHS,* no. 25 (1917), pp. 4–7. Hühner, however, reports that Moses Levy favored the abolition of slavery, despite his extensive ownership of slaves.

6. Letter, Barnett Polock to Sarah Polock, Sept. 6, 1836, in collection of Edwin Wolf, 2nd.

7. We know about the Adler brothers' laundry and meals from 26 Ala. 145, quoted in Helen Tunnicliff Catterall, *Judicial Cases Concerning American Slavery and the Negro,* 4 vols. (Washington, 1926–1936), vol. III, p. 201, hereafter *HTC.* On Dec. 2, 1854, a slave, Vincent, broke into their store and stole some goods; the trial revolved around the question of whether the slave had actually rifled a store or a residence. If the latter, the penalty would, of course, be much more severe.

8. 1850 Mss. Census Returns for Mobile County, National Archives.

9. This is an aspect of Southern social life about which little has been written. Among the Jews of Mobile, according to the 1850 Mss. Census Returns, some of the most prosperous Jews reported white servants—Solomon I. Jones (the brother of Israel Jones) kept two white servants, and Philip Phillips had "four female Irish"—undoubtedly needed to take care of his large brood of children.

10. Malcolm H. Stern, "Some Additions and Corrections to Rosenwaike's 'An Estimate and Analysis of the Jewish Population of the United States in 1790.'" *AJHQ*, vol. LIII (1964), pp. 285–288. There is an interesting contrast between ownership of slaves in South Carolina and other states. These statistics are as follows: of twenty-three Jewish heads of household in the New England states, five owned a total of twenty-one slaves; of sixty Jewish heads of household in New York, twenty owned a total of forty-three slaves; of thirty-one Jewish heads of household in Pennsylvania, only three owned a total of six slaves; and of eight Jewish heads of household in Maryland, three owned a total of three slaves.

11. Ira Rosenswaike, "The Jewish Population of the United States as Estimated from the Census of 1820," *AJHQ*, vol. LIII (1963), pp. 131–178.

12. 1820, 1830, and 1840 Mss. Census Returns for New Orleans and Vicinity, National Archives. The statistics for 1830 are somewhat deceptive: of the ten slaveowners, one, L. Jacobs, owned thirty slaves, and another, Samuel Hermann, owned seventeen. More accurate approximations of the Jewish population of New Orleans are obtainable from city directories, congregational records, and newspaper advertisements, but these, of course, give no data on the ownership of slaves. See *KEJNO*, pp. 157–159. Samuel Jacobs may have been a brother of the slave-trader Levy Jacobs.

13. 1850 Mss. Census Returns for Mobile, National Archives.

14. The thirty-three wills refer specifically to one hundred and thirty-two slaves; in two cases slave children are not enumerated or named; in a number of others, only a few slaves are referred to by name, while unspecified numbers are grouped together in general categories. It is quite likely that some of the ninety-seven remaining decedents owned slaves and lumped them together with all other types of property, but this can neither be proved nor disproved without extensive reference to the estate inventories. The Federal statistics are derived from John Hope Franklin, *From Slavery to Freedom*, 2nd ed. (New York, 1956), pp. 185 and 189.

15. Not in the Marcus collection at the American Jewish Archives, hereafter *AJA*. Data from Inventory of Estate of Emanuel Stern, Record Room, Civil District Court, New Orleans. Stern did not own Mathilda's parents. See *KEJNO*, esp. pp. 329–330.

16. Letter, dated Nov. 23, 1867, Mordecai Collection, Duke University Library.

17. *EL*, pp. 15, 327–329.

18. Photostat of deed of emancipation, *AJA*. But Myers did not free all his slaves. Louis Ginsburg, *The Jews of Petersburg* (Petersburg, 1954), p. 7, offers data on a number of his slaves, and in 1830, Myers' firm in Richmond was listed as owning eighty-two slaves: Woodson, "Absentee Ownership of Slaves in the United States in 1830," p. 73. Professor Jacob R. Marcus suggests to me that Myers may have purchased Alice as a concubine in view of his first wife's death just four months before. The relevant dates are as follows: Sarah Judah Myers died on Oct. 12, 1795; Myers bought Alice on Jan. 4, 1796; Myers married Judith Hays on Sept. 27, 1796; he sold Alice on Oct. 2, 1797. There is, of course, no documentary evidence of Myers' purpose, nor of the relationship.

19. Deeds from vol. 3-L, p. 174, Miscellaneous Records, South Carolina Archives Department, Columbia, in Thomas J. Tobias' collection of photostats of family papers.

20. Ezekiel and Lichtenstein, *Jews of Richmond*, pp. 78 and 80, hereafter *EL*.

21. *EL*, p. 85.

22. Historians have failed to express much interest in Northern owners of property in the South, property which frequently included Negro slaves. Michael Hart of New York City, for instance, who died in September, 1861, owned a plantation in Virginia. His son, Henry, went South, and "fearing that Richmond would be taken . . . left the city and went to North Carolina, taking with him most of the slaves belonging to the estate"; 25 Grattan 795 ff., cited in *HTC*, vol. I, p. 265. The well-known naval officer, Commodore Uriah P. Levy, who was so proud of his part in the agitation for the abolition of flogging in

the American Navy, was apparently not an abolitionist when slavery was under discussion. He held title not only to Jefferson's Monticello, a fact which has been well publicized, but also to a Virginia plantation known as Washington Farm, on which Negro slaves were worked; 3 A. K. Marsh 480, cited in *HTC*, vol. I, p. 296.

23. *EL* pp. 330–332.

24. 2 Va 158–159, cited in *HTC*, vol. I. p. 131. The records of the Lynchburg courts are so incomplete that it has not been possible to discover any details of Cohen's crime.

25. *EL*, p. 78.

26. *EL*, p. 79.

27. *EL*, p. 91.

28. *EL*, pp. 77–78; *Louisiana Gazette*, Sept. 23, 1824.

29. *New Orleans Bee*, Feb. 7, 1832.

30. Jacob R. Marcus, *American Jewry, Documents, Eighteenth Century* (Cincinnati, 1959), p. 63.

31. *E*, p. 142.

32. Jack Kenny Williams, *Vogues in Villainy, Crime and Retribution in Ante-Bellum South Carolina* (Columbia, 1939), p. 73.

33. Richmond *Enquirer*, May 21, 1805.

34. B. W. Korn, "The Jews of Mobile, Alabama, Prior to the Organization of the First Congregation, in 1841," *Hebrew Union College Annual*, vol. XLI (1970), p. 27 of the article.

35. Frederick Law Olmsted, *The Cotton Kingdom*, ed. by Arthur M. Schlesinger (N. Y., 1953), pp. 37 and 196.

36. E. Merton Coulter, *The South During Reconstruction, 1865–1877* (Baton Rouge, 1947), pp. 202–203. See also *Seventy Fifth Anniversary Brochure, Temple Beth Tefilloh, Brunswick, Ga.*, (Brunswick, 1961), p. 2 of "History," for reference to the confidence which the Negroes of St. Simons, Ga., felt in Bob Levison, whose store and grounds they dubbed "Jewtown."

37. Richmond *City Directory* for 1852, p. 27 of the advertising section; *New Orleans Bee*, Apr. 23, Nov. 9, 1835; Mar. 12, 26, 1836.

38. Riley 155, cited in *HTC*, vol. II, p. 361.

39. 1 Spears 223, cited in *HTC*, vol. II, p. 385.

40. 15 La. An. 38, cited in *HTC*, vol. III, p. 676.

41. *EL*, p. 82.

42. *EL*, p. 98.

43. Bill of sale, dated May 11, 1852, in the writer's collection.

44. *EL*, pp. 43 and 298.

45. *MM*, vol. II, p. 28.

46. Photostats of slave bills loaned to me by Ben Cone of Greensboro, N. C., Herman's grandson.

47. Edwin J. Scott, *Random Recollections of a Long Life* (Columbia, S. C., 1884), pp. 82–85.

48. Advertisement in Knoxville, Tenn., *Daily Register*, Apr. 30, 1863.

49. Advertisement in Charleston *Daily Courier*, Apr. 28, 1857. Though he auctioned other commodities, slaves were a very substantial part of his business. Frederic Bancroft, in his *Slave Trading in the Old South* (Baltimore, 1931), p. 190, states that Cohen was the tenth largest Charleston dealer in slaves, earning $2,500 in commissions on slave sales in 1860.

50. Bancroft, *op. cit.*, p. 175.

51. Reference in his will in *AJA*, dated Nov. 20, 1797.

52. Advertisement in Charleston *Southern Patriot*, Aug. 14, 1815, cited in Morris U. Schappes, *Documentary History of the Jews in the United States* (New York, 1950), p. 612.

53. Advertisement in Charleston *Daily Courier*, Jan. 1, 1857.

54. *R*, p. 139.

55. *RE*, p. 76.

56. Advertisements in Columbia *Daily South Carolinian*, Nov. 15, Dec. 2, Dec. 9, Dec. 17, and Dec. 29, 1852.

57. Arthur Hecht, "Abraham Cohen: Deputy Postmaster at Georgetown, South Carolina (1789–1800)," *PAJHS*, Vol. XLVIII (1959), p. 178.

58. Advertisement in Knoxville *Daily Register,* Apr. 30, 1863.

59. Mobile *City Directories* for 1839 and 1842; article on Mobile Jewish History by Alfred G. Moses, Mobile *Register,* June 19, 1932; Korn, "Jews of Mobile," pp. 10–14.

60. Advertisement in Mobile *Daily Advertiser and Chronicle,* Feb. 6, 1841; Korn, "Jews of Mobile," pp. 16–18.

61. *Mississippi Free-Trader and Natchez Tri-Weekly Gazette,* Sept. 29, 1836; *Natchez Daily Courier,* Dec. 18, 1837; Edwin Adams Davis and William Ransom Hogan (eds.), *William Johnson's Natchez: The Ante-Bellum Diary of a Free Negro* (Baton Rouge, 1951), pp. 66, 175, 224, 366, *passim.* The Johnson diary contains frequent references to sales of various kinds of merchandise, including slaves, at the Soria auctions. Davis and Hogan, *The Barber of Natchez* (Baton Rouge, 1954), pp. 31, 173.

62. *Louisiana Courier,* July 13, 1808.

63. *Louisiana Gazette,* July 8, 1808.

64. *Louisiana Gazette,* July 8, 1808.

65. *New Orleans Bee,* Feb. 11, 1833.

66. New Orleans *City Directory* for 1832; *Historical Epitome of the State of Louisiana . . .* (New Orleans, 1840), p. 252.

67. New Orleans *City Directory* for 1855.

68. *EL,* pp. 44–54 and 143.

69. Bancroft, *op. cit.,* pp. 97–98.

70. *OCC,* vol. II (1844), pp. 83–87, 147–150; vol. IV (1846), pp. 387–389; vol. V (1847), p. 164; vol. VI (1848), p. 153; vol. VIII (1850), pp. 145–158; vol. IX (1851), pp. 268–269; vol. XII (1854), p. 326; Helen Kohn Hennig, *The Tree of Life . . .* (Columbia, S. C., 1945), pp. 3–4. Melvin S. Harris, *The Columbia Hebrew Benevolent Society* (Columbia, 1947), p. 12, quotes the listing of the Levin business in the Columbia city directory of 1850 as "auctioneer and commission merchant for the sale of Real Estate, stocks and bonds, Negroes, cotton, flour and corn."

71. Bertram W. Korn, "An Historical Excursus," in *1844–1944, Congregation Shaarai Shomayim, Mobile, Alabama* (Mobile, 1944); Mobile *City Directories* for 1839, pp. iii, 24a; 1842, p. 64; 1850, p. 48; 1856, p. 57; Korn mss. files on Jones; letter, Myer S. Isaacs to Jones, Aug. 14, 1860, Board of Delegates Mss. Files, Library of the American Jewish Historical Society. Korn, "Jews of Mobile," pp. 16–18.

72. A. J. Marks, acting rabbi of New Orleans in the 1830's, listed eleven slaves in his household in the 1840 Census for New Orleans. See *KEJNO,* pp. 240–245.

73. Quoted from the Charleston *South Carolina State Gazette,* Sept. 6, 1784, in *E.* pp. 129–130.

74. Bancroft, *op. cit.,* pp. 97–98, 175–177, 251–252.

75. J. Winston Coleman, *Slavery Times in Kentucky* (Chapel Hill, 1940), and Charles Sackett Sydnor, *Slavery in Mississippi* (New York, 1933).

76. Receipt for sale of slave "Warren," dated Augusta, Feb. 20, 1864, signed by Jacob Reese, for "S. Cohen, Dealer in Slaves, Ellis Street, Augusta, Ga." in the writer's collection; this Reese may have been related to Samuel Reese, a slave auctioneer of Richmond. *AJA* has a similar receipt, dated July 3, 1863, with an imprinted address in Atlanta which has been crossed out, with "Augusta" superimposed in handwriting. Cohen probably had offices in both cities. *AJA* also has receipts for three slaves purchased by Levi Cohen in various Georgia towns in 1862–1864; there is no indication whether these Cohen's were related.

77. Mordecai, an important mercantile power in Charleston is listed here, in spite of the fact that this was not his only source of income, because his slave-dealings were so extensive; his traffic in Negroes was so constant that he had his own slave-pens alongside his warehouses. In 1859, Mordecai purchased $12,000 worth of slaves in a single sale. 12 Richardson 547, cited in *HTC,* vol. II, p. 325; Charleston *Mercury,* Jan. 10, 1859, cited in Bancroft, *op. cit.,* p. 183; Charleston *Courier,* Jan. 1, 1857.

78. Broadside dated Nov. 14, 1859, reproduced in Charles F. Heartman, *Americana Catalogue No. 120* (1947), p. 145.

79. Mobile *City Directories,* for 1850 and 1856.

80. Barnett was an auctioneer who began business in 1835. His first sale included a slave. Most of his other sales also included slaves. His business was so concentrated on slaves that he was remembered as the auctioneer of slaves *par excellence*. In the post-bellum period, his auction stand at the St. Louis Hotel was pointed out to visitors, and picture post-cards of Barnett's "Old Slave Block," with his sign above it, were sold to tourists in the French quarter of New Orleans. *New Orleans Bee*, May 21, 1835; *KEJNO* pp. 104–110, with the picture of the slave block reproduced as illustration 11.

81. New Orleans *City Directories*, for 1823, 1824, 1827, and 1835; *KEJNO*, pp. 163–165; Jacobs' slave-selling activity also extended to Mobile, where he used George Davis as agent, see Korn, "Jews of Mobile," pp. 10–11.

82. Bancroft, *op. cit.*, pp. 93–94.

83. Interview with his grand-daughter, Mrs Hattie E. Genbrun, recorded by Louis Ginsburg, Petersburg, Aug. 29, 1958.

84. Every once in a while an unconscionable dealer would foist a sickly slave on an unwary customer. *HTC* gives instances of such occurrences which were brought to court: In June, 1821, a man named Samuel sold a slave woman ill of a venereal disease to a client named Minter; the woman died soon afterwards, and Minter went to court to regain the purchase price. 3 A. K. Marsh 480, cited in I, p. 296. In Nov., 1860, B. Cahn of New Orleans sued a slave-trader who had sold him a consumptive slave; the vendor had to repay Cahn the money involved in the transaction. 15 La. An. 612, cited in III, p. 685.

85. Bills of sale in the writer's collection.

86. Data about these men is given in Ginsburg, *op. cit.*, pp. 25, 31, 35–36, and *EL*, p. 143.

87. Boston, 1853, p. 151.

88. Photostat from the family papers of Thomas J. Tobias, Charleston.

89. Cited in Ralph Betts Flanders, *Plantation Slavery in Georgia* (Chapel Hill, 1933), p. 185. The Cloutier Collection in the Library of Northwestern State College of Louisiana, Natchitoches, has the notarized bill of sale of two slaves by Benjamin Davis to Jean Baptiste Cloutier for $2050, on Mar. 22, 1837, in New Orleans.

90. Carter G. Woodson, *Free Negro Heads of Families in the United States in 1830* (Washington, 1925). Eight of these Negroes, incidentally, owned a total of thirty-nine slaves: Woodson, *Free Negro Owners of Slaves . . .* pp. 4ff.

91. John S. Reynolds, *Reconstruction in South Carolina 1865–1877* (Columbia, 1905) pp. 60–61; Alrutheus Ambush Taylor, *The Negro in South Carolina During the Reconstruction* (Washington, 1929), pp. 98, 116, 127 and 207; "South Carolina Negro Delegates to Republican National Conventions," *JNH*, vol. XII (1922).

92. A Louisiana Negro named Walter L. Cohen was Register of the Orleans Parish Land Office late in the nineteenth century; Henry C. Dethloff and Robert R. Jones, "Race Relations in Louisiana, 1877–1898," *Louisiana History*, vol. IX (1968), p. 310.

93. *ME*, vol. II, p. 224; *E*, p. 153; *Constitution of the Hebrew Congregation Kaal Kodesh Beth-Elohim, or House of God. Charleston, 1820* (reprinted Charleston, 1904), p. 16. The first New Orleans congregation, incorporated in 1828, also restricted its membership to "white Israelits [*sic*]": Schappes, *op. cit.*, p. 180; *KEJNO*, p. 196.

94. *RE*, p. 78. Thomas J. Tobias of Charleston has directed my attention to two further references to the same person, "Old Billy," "a Jewish Negro, then about 70 years of age . . . gained his living carrying newspapers" (*Weekly Gleaner*, San Francisco, Jan. 16, 1857); the man died in 1860, as reported in the *Jewish Chronicle* (London), May 11, 1860, which stated that "for years he has been a faithful attendant at the Jewish Synagogue on the Day of Atonement, making his appearance on these occasions in a ruffled shirt."

95. *HTC*, vol. I, p. 145, citing 5 Randolph 634. The 1820 census lists Isaacs as forty-five years or over, with ten free Negroes and two slaves. Personal data about the family and the children are included in *Early Charlottesville: Recollections of James Alexander, 1828–1874* (Charlottesville, 1942), pp. 72–4, 79, 81, 86. Malcolm H. Stern, *Americans of Jewish Descent* (Cincinnati, 1960), p. 192, has the names and a few of the dates of the children.

96. Will in *AJA*.

97. Will in *AJA*.

98. 14 Ga. 185–207; 20 Ga. 480–512; 33 Ga. 11–29, as cited in *HTC*, vol. III, pp. 33, 50–51, 87–88.

99. For Jacob N. Cardozo, see Alexander Brody, "Jacob Newton Cardozo, American Economist," *Historia Judaica*, vol. XV (1955), pp. 135–166, and Melvin M. Leiman, *Jacob N. Cardozo: Economic Thought in the Antebellum South* (New York, 1966), p. 6; for Isaac, see *E*, pp. 161, 163–164, and 204; and Barnett A. Elzas, *The Old Jewish Cemeteries of Charleston, S. C.* (Charleston, 1903), p. 12.

100. The literature on Cardozo and his participation in South Carolina political affairs is extensive. Works consulted include: William J. Simmons, *Men of Mark* (Cleveland, 1887); W. E. B. Du Bois, *Black Reconstruction* (N. Y., 1935); John E. Farley, "Francis L Cardozo," ms. senior thesis, Princeton University, Apr. 13, 1949; Franklin, *op. cit.;* William Francis Guest, *South Carolina, Annals of Pride and Protest* (New York, 1960); Ralph Selph Henry, *The Story of Reconstruction* (New York, 1938); Daniel Walker Hollis, *University of South Carolina* (Columbia, 1956), vol. II; L. P. Jackson, "The Educational Efforts of the Freedmen's Bureau and the Freedmen's Aid Society in South Carolina, 1862–1872," *JNH*, vol. VIII (1922); James S. Pike, *The Prostrate State: South Carolina Under Negro Government* (New York, 1874); Reynolds, *op. cit.;* Francis Butler Simpkins and Robert Hilliard Woody, *South Carolina During Reconstruction* (Chapel Hill, 1932); Taylor, *op. cit.;* Mary Church Terrell, "History of the High School for Negroes in Washington," *JNH*, vol. II (1917). Additional data has been provided by Cardozo's grandson, W. Warrick Cardozo, M.D., of Washington, D.C.

101. Data about Thomas Cardozo is difficult to locate. The first appearance of his name, according to the records of the Mississippi State Department of Archives, is in the Warren County tax rolls for 1871. The following works supply the few available facts: James Wilford Garner, *Reconstruction in Mississippi* (New York, 1901); John R. Lynch, *The Facts of Reconstruction* (New York, 1913); *Journal of the State of Mississippi—Sitting as a Court of Impeachment, in the Trials of Adalbert Ames, Governor; Alexander K. Davis, Lieutenant-Governor; Thomas Y. Cardozo, Superintendent of Instruction* (Jackson, 1876); Vernon Lane Wharton, *The Negro in Mississippi, 1865–1890* (Chapel Hill, 1947). Dr. W. W. Cardozo supplies these dates for his great-uncle's birth and death: Dec. 19, 1838, and Apr. 13, 1881. There was a third brother, Rev. Henry W. Cardozo, born in 1831, who died on Feb. 21, 1886.

102. Claude G. Bowers, *The Tragic Era* (Cambridge, 1929), p. 414; Coulter, *op. cit.*, pp. 322–323.

103. These papers, in the writer's collection, are dated Apr. 4, 1810; Mar. 30, 1822; Jan. 23, 1833; Nov. 13, 1837; May 2, 1840; Apr. 8, 1844; no date, 1850. Data about Barnet A. Cohen from *E*, pp. 133 and 144; Cecil Roth, *The Rise of Provincial Jewry* (London, 1950), p. 41; *R.*, p. 24; Barnett A. Elzas, *The Old Jewish Cemeteries of Charleston* (Charleston, 1903), pp. 5–6.

104. *KEJNO*, pp. 181–182; some data on Daniel and Eugène are in R.-L. Desdunes, *Nos Hommes et Notre Histoire* (Montreal, 1911), pp. 95–98; James A. Porter, *Modern Negro Art* (New York, 1943), pp. 46–47; Cedric Dover, *American Negro Art* (New York, 1960), p. 26. The Frick Art Reference Library has been helpful in assembling information about the sons. Desdunes reports that Eugene did some statuary for the St. Louis Cathedral, and that some of Daniel's cemetery monuments were impressive, but no precise evidence has identified any of these works. *KEJNO*, p. 142, gives the data on the possible fathering of two mulatto children by Asher Moses Nathan, but the evidence is flimsy.

105. *Speech of Hon. David S. Kaufman, of Texas, on The Slavery Question. Delivered in the House of Representatives, February 10, 1847* (Washington, 1847); *Speech of Hon. D. S. Kaufman, of Texas, on The Slavery Question and Its Adjustment. Delivered in the House of Representatives, Monday, June 10, 1850* (Washington, 1850); Hühner, *op. cit.*, pp. 14, 20–22. Although Kaufman has generally been regarded as stemming from Jewish parents, there is no contemporary evidence for the assumption; all such testimony is of comparatively late date, as for instance, Henry Cohen *et al.*, *One Hundred Years of Jewry in Texas* (Dallas, 1936), p. 8.

106. Sitterson, *op. cit.*, pp. 131, 154; Meade, *op. cit.*, pp. 92, 100 ff; Bell Irvin Wiley, *Southern Negroes 1861–1865* (New Haven, 1938), pp. 152, 154, and 157; *Speech of Hon. J. P. Benjamin, of Louisiana. Delivered in the Senate of the United States, May 22, 1860* (Washington, 1860).

107. Schappes, *op. cit.*, pp. 293–301 and 643–644; James Benson Sellars, *Slavery in Alabama* (University, 1950), pp. 188–190.

108. *MM*, vol. III, p. 149; Korn, "Jews of Mobile," pp. 22–24.

109. *Lecture on Texas Delivered by Mr. J. De Cordova, at Philadelphia, New York, Mount Holly, Brooklyn and Newark. Also a paper read by him before the New York Geographical Society, April 15th, 1858.* (Philadelphia, 1858), pp. 2 and 24–25. For De Cordova's personal and familial background, see Korn, "The Haham De Cordova of Jamaica," *American Jewish Archives*, XVIII (1966), pp. 141–154.

110. "Essays by Junius," I, pp. 95 and 135, in Henry L. Pinckney and Abraham Moïse, *A Section from the Miscellaneous Writings of the Late Isaac Harby, Esq.* (Charleston, 1829); *New Orleans Bee*, Aug. 12, 17, 1835; May 30, 1836.

111. *Reminiscences of Charleston* (Charleston, 1866), p. 10; Brody, *op. cit.*, pp. 150–151; Leiman, *Cardozo*, pp. 173–203.

112. *Thirty Years of My Life on Three Continents* (London, 1890), vol. I, pp. 13–36.

113. (New York, 1909), pp. 15–16; see also his *Four Years in Rebel Capitals* (Mobile, 1890), p. 370.

114. "Writers of Anonymous Articles in *The Farmer's Register* by Edmund Ruffin," *Journal of Southern History*, vol. XXIII (1957), pp. 90–102; *Richmond in By-Gone Days* (Richmond, 1946), pp. 354–355; letter, Samuel Mordecai to G. W. Mordecai, Dec. 17, 1860, Mordecai Mss., Duke University Library.

115. Quoted in Clement Eaton, *Freedom of Thought in the Old South* (Durham, 1940), p. 232.

116. *MM*, vol. III, pp. 308–309.

117. *MM*, vol. III, p. 368.

118. Letter, dated Jan. 8, 1866, Mordecai Mss., Duke University Library. A more extensive apology for slavery, embodied in a letter from Cohen to his aunt, Rebecca Gratz, has been published by Joseph R. Rosenbloom in his article, "Rebecca Gratz, Example of Conflicting Sectional Loyalties during the Civil War," in *The Filson Club History Quarterly*, vol. XXXV (1961), pp. 8–10.

119. *MM*, vol. I, pp. 51 and 56.

120. *MM*, vol. I, p. 338.

121. *MM*, vol. II, p. 138.

122. Stanley L. Falk, "Divided Loyalties in 1861: The Decision of Major Alfred Mordecai," *PAJHS*, vol. XLVIII (1959), pp. 149–150.

123. Leon Hühner, *The Life of Judah Touro* (Philadelphia, 1946), p. 69; *KEJNO*, pp. 89–90.

124. *MM*, vol. II, pp. 295–296.

125. First published in 1856, and reprinted in part in *AJAM*, vol. IX (1957), pp. 3–31, with notes and introduction by Maxwell Whiteman.

126. Caroline Cohen, *Records of the Myers, Hays and Mordecai Families from 1707 to 1913* (Washington, 1913), p. 56; Moncure Daniel Conway, *Autobiography, Memories and Experiences* (Boston, 1904), vol. I, pp. 313–314; Eaton, *op. cit.*, p. 322; Frank Luther Mott, *A History of American Magazines 1850–1865* (Cambridge, 1938), p. 535; letter, Marx E. Lazarus to George W. Mordecai, New York, March 24, 1846, Mordecai Mss., Southern Historical Collection, University of North Carolina Library; *The Dial*, vol. I (1860), pp. 219–228.

127. *MM*, vol. III, p. 104; I. J. Benjamin, *Three Years in America* (Philadelphia, 1956), p. 76.

128. *MM*, vol. II, p. 291.

JAYME A. SOKOLOW

# Revolution and Reform
## The Antebellum Jewish Abolitionists

Many antebellum abolitionists condemned discrimination throughout the world and tried to enlist the aid of traditionally oppressed ethnic groups in the antislavery crusade. They were spectacularly unsuccessful, however, in soliciting Irish support.[1] The antebellum Jews' apparent unwillingness to participate in the emancipation struggle also puzzled and hurt the abolitionists. In the 1853 report of the American & Foreign Antislavery society, they wondered why the

> ... Jews of the United States have never taken any steps whatever with regard to the Slavery question. As citizens, they deem it their policy 'to have every one choose which ever side he may deem best to promote his own interests and the welfare of his country' ... It cannot be said that the Jews have formed any denominational opinion on the subject of American slavery. ...
>
> The objects of so much mean prejudice and unrighteous oppression as the Jews have been for ages, surely they, it would seem, more than any other denomination, ought to be the enemies of CASTE, and the friends of UNIVERSAL FREEDOM.[2]

The abolitionists' evaluation was essentially correct. Before the 1850s, there were only a few scattered examples of Jewish antislavery activities. While some Jews emancipated their slaves, most Southern Jews accepted and defended slavery until the Civil War ended. They supported the peculiar institution because Southern Jews lived in a proslavery environment, profited economically and psychologically from slavery, and lacked Reform Jewish Temples which might have challenged slavery. Most antebellum northern and midwestern Jews also maintained a discreet silence on the subject.

Their European experiences and religious traditions, their lowly economic and educational backgrounds, and the fear of antisemitic backlash made them politically conservative and detached from controversial causes outside the scope of Judaism.[3]

Previous scholars have examined the abolitionists' attitude toward antebellum Jews but they have ignored any significant abolitionist activities by pre-Civil War Jews.[4] Bertram W. Korn, a prominent historian of nineteenth century American Judaism, has contended that most abolitionist leaders were uninterested in defending the civil rights of Jews and sometimes uttered antisemitic statements because their obsessive concern for Blacks blinded them to the plight of the Jews.[5] Although the abolitionists could have been more vocal during the Mortara case and Grant's infamous 1862 Order No. 11

In 1984, Jayme A. Sokolow was in the Department of History at Texas Tech University.
Originally published in *Journal of Ethnic Studies* 9, no. 1 (1984): 27–43. Reprinted with the permission of Jayme A. Sokolow.

barring Jews from trading in Tennessee, Ruchames' contentions appear valid: the anti-slavery crusade's attempts to help Blacks involved a considerable effort to understand and defend Judaism.[6]

In the 1850s, however, Jewish abolitionists emerged who publicly criticized slavery and participated in antebellum America's most controversial reform. By examining the social backgrounds, careers, and ideology of the Jewish abolitionists (see Table 1), we can better understand the origins and complexity of antebellum abolitionism and the momentous changes taking place in American Judaism, for with one exception all the Jewish abolitionists were Reform Jewish émigrés. While most native abolitionists were motivated by evangelical Protestantism and American democratic ideals, the Jewish abolitionists' decision to participate in antislavery activities was primarily a function of their European political and religious experiences.

Until the 1840s, Jewish immigration to America usually involved individuals and isolated families. After this period there was a mass migration of German and Eastern European Jews (Austria, Hungary, Poland, Bohemia) which raised America's Jewish population from 50,000 in 1850 to 150,000 by the Civil War. During this decade the number of congregations increased from 37 to 77; seating capacity almost doubled from 19,588 to 34,412, and there was a threefold increase in the value of religious property. In 1850 there were eleven states with congregations; by 1860, nineteen states, led by New York and Pennsylvania, registered congregations according to the second American Census of Social Statistics. Crop failures, the disruption of internal trade, the failures of the 1848 revolutions, and continuous outbreaks of antisemitic violence propelled Jews to America.[7] From these immigrant ranks came all the Jewish abolitionists.

The revolutions of 1848 encouraged two groups of Jews to enter America. The largest group migrated because they were determined to find the personal opportunity, economic freedom, and civic equality denied them in Europe. For these immigrants, the revolutions accelerated a process which had begun in the early nineteenth century. Earlier Jewish immigrants were Sephardim who often had mercantile connections in Europe and the Caribbean. The German and Eastern European Ashkenazic Jews, in contrast, arrived without significant business interests, were generally quite poor, and usually started their American careers as peddlers.[8]

The second, smaller group fled to America because they had participated in the 1848 revolutions or were opposed to the restoration of the conservative regimes. These revolutions, which occurred in areas inhabited by one-third of world Jewry, had a strong effect on the process of Jewish emancipation. Jews played prominent roles in the European revolutions. In Vienna they were among the leaders of the National Guard and the Students Legion. The Jewish delegates in the Austrian Diet campaigned for the annulment of the special taxes on Jews and argued for complete civic equality. And at the Frankfurt parliament and the Prussian Assembly the Jewish representatives pleaded for equal rights. Throughout these struggles, the general principle of equality, rather than the peculiar situation of the Jews, was consistently invoked by protagonists of emancipation.[9] This was the attitude that the émigrés who became abolitionists would take in America.

Many of the Jewish political radicals never became involved in abolitionist activities.

## TABLE 1. ANTEBELLUM JEWISH ABOLITIONISTS*

| Name | Occupation | Reform or Orthodox | Location of Abolitionist Activities | Abolitionist Activities |
|---|---|---|---|---|
| Leibman Adler | rabbi | Reform | Detroit | speaker, writer |
| Jacob Benjamin | merchant | ? | Lawrence, Kansas | free soil guerilla fighter |
| Leopold Blumenberg | merchant | Reform | Baltimore | financier |
| August Bondi | clerk, farmer | Reform | St. Louis Pottawatomie Creek, Kansas | speaker, writer, free soil guerilla fighter |
| Isidor Busch | merchant politician | Reform | St. Louis | politician |
| David Einhorn | rabbi | Reform | Baltimore, Philadelphia | speaker, writer |
| Bernard Felsenthal | rabbi | Reform | Madison, Indiana, Chicago | speaker, writer |
| Michael Greenbaum | lawyer | ? | Chicago | speaker, writer, assisted fugitive slaves |
| Michael Hellprin | writer | Reform | New York City | writer |
| Abraham Jacobi | doctor | ? | New York City | speaker, writer |
| Philip J. Joachimsen | lawyer, judge | ? | New York City | speaker, writer |
| Ernest Krackowitzer | doctor | ? | New York City | speaker, writer |
| Leopold Mayer | lawyer | Reform | Chicago | speaker, writer |
| Sabato Morais | rabbi | Orthodox | Philadelphia | speaker, writer |
| Moritz Pinner | writer, newspaper editor | ? ? | St. Louis, Kansas City, Kan. | politician, newspaper editor |
| Wilhelm Rapp | writer newspaper ed. | ? | Baltimore | newspaper editor |
| Ernestine L. Rose | reformer | atheist | New York City | speaker, writer |
| Theodore Weiner | merchant | ? | Lawrence, Kansas | free soil guerilla fighter |

*The list includes Jews who began working publicly to end slavery before 1861.

Jayme A. Sokolow    185

Sigismund Kaufman actively participated in the September 1848 Frankfurt uprising and then fled to England and later Brooklyn, where he practiced law after 1852. Although he became a dedicated member of the Republican Party, there is no evidence that abolitionism ever claimed his attention.[10] Isaac Hartman, who was imprisoned in Wurzburg after the revolutionaries were defeated, taught European languages in New York schools and shunned politics until he died of tuberculosis in 1855.[11] Some of the Jewish political refugees settled in the South and became proslavery advocates. Louis Schlessinger, a veteran of the Kossuth campaigns, joined the William Walker filibuster in Nicaragua and became the baron of a coffee plantation there. And Adolphus Adler defended slavery and was commissioned a Confederate colonel at the outbreak of the Civil War.[12]

Because there is little biographical information on the forty active Jewish 48'ers that migrated to America, it is unclear exactly why certain Jewish émigrés became abolitionists while others remained indifferent or defended slavery. I would suggest that the answer lies in their political-religious ideologies and social backgrounds, for all the refugee abolitionists came from emancipated, cosmopolitan homes where parents vigorously defended liberalism (in the mid-nineteenth century sense liberalism included a belief in individualism, civic equality, and representative government).

Probably the most dramatic and adventurous abolitionist was August Bondi. As a child in Vienna, he was tutored in an urbane, scholarly environment in Hebrew, German, French, Hungarian, and Latin. When the March 1848 Vienna revolution occurred, August had been in the Academic Gymnasium for five years and was accepted into the Students Legion at the age of fourteen. After the revolution his family prudently left Austria and moved to St. Louis, where August quickly became involved in antislavery rallies and activities. He tried a variety of trades but found them all boring and so August migrated to frontier Kansas to start a farm: "I was most anxious for a strenuous life. I was tired of the hum-drum life of a clerk. Any struggle, any hard work would be welcome to me. I thirsted for it, for adventure."[13] Soon afterwards he fought with John Brown in Kansas and participated in the battles of Black Jack and Osawatomie with two other Jewish immigrants, Theodore Weiner and Jacob Benjamin. When the Civil War began, Bondi enlisted in the Union Army and served with distinction until wounded in 1864.[14]

Michael Heilprin similarly moved from European revolutionary activities to American abolitionism. His father was a merchant scholar and an avid student of Jewish literature and the German romantics. Michael developed into a literary genius whose linguistic ability attracted the attention of distinguished Hebraists. When the 1848 Hungarian Revolution began, Heilprin's friendship with Louis Kossuth and other revolutionaries led to a literary post in the new government. After barely escaping capture by the Austrians, he migrated to Paris, London and eventually settled in Philadelphia, where he immediately became involved in the abolitionist movement. When an antislavery Democratic Party rally in Philadelphia's Carpenter's Hall was disrupted by proslavery forces in 1858, Heilprin arose from the front row, serenely mounted the stage, and in clear, vigorous German lambasted the pro-slavery Democrats! Fortunately he was quickly ushered out of the hall before any harm befell him. Heilprin later worked with William Lloyd Garrison, William H. Seward, and Charles Sumner, and criticized slaveholders in *The Nation* and the New York *Tribune*.[15]

Isidor Busch, like Bondi and Heilprin, emigrated to America as a result of his revolutionary activities. As a young man in Vienna, he was active in the field of Jewish letters. From 1842 to 1847 he edited the first popular German-Jewish periodical in Austria, the *Kalender und Jahrbuch fur Israeliten*, which tried to publicize the scientific and literary accomplishments of leading Jewish scholars. During the Vienna revolution he published another journal that fiercely advocated revolution and the need for political and religious freedom. After the revolution failed, the young Busch family migrated to St. Louis where Isidor distinguished himself in business, banking agronomy, and politics.[16] An avowed abolitionist, Busch's greatest contribution to the antislavery cause came at the Missouri state conventions held between 1861 and 1863 to decide whether the state should remain in the Union or join the Confederacy. He led the abolitionist forces at the convention and consistently argued that the "position of our national affairs, the preservation of the Union . . . the interest of the slave-owner, as well as humanity to the slaves, imperatively demand *speedy* emancipation."[17] His oratory and leadership were instrumental in keeping the state within the Union and he helped develop the plan which freed Missouri slaves without compensating their masters.

Bondi, Heilprin, Busch, and the other émigré abolitionists had similar European backgrounds. They were raised in comfortable, stimulating homes and their fathers were often involved in manufacturing, commerce, or publishing. In Europe these radicals were certainly not economically or socially oppressed. Recently emancipated, they were gaining status in mid-nineteenth century Europe and America, tended to be occupationally versatile, and pursued careers which required broadly applicable skills (see the list of occupations in Table 1). Their home environments and urban experiences propelled them into political activities that challenged the conservative order.

Abraham Jacobi neatly summarized these political beliefs when he characterized his friend and fellow abolitionist Ernst Krackowitzer. Jacobi had been active in the 1848 German revolution and was imprisoned for his role in the Bonn uprising. After escaping to America in 1853, Jacobi became an abolitionist and a pioneering pediatrics physician.[18] According to him, the former Viennese student council revolutionary Krackowitzer

> . . . did not *drift* into politics; he was a born politician. . . . No oppression or injustice found grace before his eyes. Thus he was a free soiler, thus he was an abolitionist; no matter whether the chains to be broken were those of color, or religion, or sex. . . . He supported Fremont, supported Lincoln, supported energetically the war for the Union. . . .[19]

Recent historians have developed a similar social portrait of the native American abolitionists that substantially modifies David Donald's theory about the abolitionists as a displaced social elite trying to reassert traditional values. According to Leonard L. Richards, Gerald Sorin, and James Brewer Stewart, the abolitionists were a broad and diverse group of farmers, urban manufacturers, tradesmen, and artisans who were gaining status during the Jacksonian era.[20] Although the Jewish abolitionists' backgrounds support Richards, Sorin, and Stewart, Donald's findings remain very suggestive as to the role of parental guidance. As numerous biographers have shown, the families of abolitionists placed a stern emphasis on moral righteousness and social responsibility. Wendell Phillips, the Tappen brothers, and William Lloyd Garrison internalized the religious dictates of dominating mothers. James G. Birney, Elijah P. Lovejoy, and Elizabeth Cady Stanton modeled their early lives to please their demanding fathers.

The Jewish abolitionists were also heavily influenced by strong father figures. Isidor Busch's father taught him scholarship, printing, and the need for political and religious freedom.[21] Samuel Morais was a devoted Italian republican ("even the boards of my bed are Republican") who transmitted a flaming liberalism to his son Sabato.[22] And Bondi claimed that he "became imbued with a hatred of spiritual and governmental tyranny. . . . We boys were fairly fanaticized with sympathy for the downtrodden of the globe." He did not marry a Southerner because Bondi "felt that my father's son was not to be a slave-driver."[23] The fathers of Jewish abolitionists inculcated a lasting liberal religious and social conscience in their sons. A strong sense of individuality and an earnestness about moral issues characterized the abolitionists in their youths. In their reminiscences, Jewish abolitionists often paid homage to strong fathers whose moral fervor dominated their households.

Aside from their familial and political experiences, religion was the other crucial factor which impelled emigré Jews to become abolitionists. Except for the Orthodox rabbi Sabato Morais of Philadelphia, who had a similar background to the other Jewish abolitionists aside for his religion,[24] there were no Orthodox Jews in the antislavery movement. Only German Reform rabbis and Reform Jews became avowed abolitionists. It makes no sense to isolate Jewish radicals as William O. McCragg, Jr. has done, and ignore their religious experiences by merely portraying them as urban modernizers in revolt against a traditional agrarian society.[25] The conspicuous role played by Jews in nineteenth and twentieth century social movements can be partially explained by analyzing their social backgrounds, but historians who neglect religion by portraying Jewish rebels as liberal secularists miss the impact of religion on social reform. The abolitionists were Reform Jews because the issues surrounding abolitionism seemed related to the problems Reform Judaism faced in the mid-nineteenth century.

Until the late eighteenth century, European Jews in central and Eastern Europe lived in self-governing Jewish communities and were regarded as part of one dispersed Jewish nation. But during the next hundred years Jewish communities were transformed in ways that changed their legal status, occupational distribution, cultural habits, and their religious perspective and behavior as Talmudic or Rabbinic laws were dissolved and Jews were allowed to become citizens. This dramatic revolution, variously called the period of Enlightenment, Haskalah, early reform, or emancipation, occurred when European states, with various degrees of success, gradually eliminated the special and separate status of Jews and their communities. Concurrently, high social status German Jews began a religious movement called Reform that tried to modify traditional Jewish religious practices and values in the direction of a more decorous, rationalistic faith freed from ancient Talmudic learning and rites. Its supporters accentuated those elements of Biblical and even Talmudic Judaism that had universalistic elements and neglected or omitted conflicting notions that were no less a part of that tradition. Finally, Reform Jews discarded Judaism as a set of revealed laws and instead perceived their religion as a body of dogma and moral teachings. For the Reformers, Judaism was now a confession of faith and the Reform Jewish community was united by its adherence to an abstract body of teachings.[26]

In America, Reform Judaism rapidly captured the majority of American congregations for two reasons. First, in Europe Reformers had to contend with Orthodox Jews who still controlled many Jewish communities; in America the Reformers were leaders of independent congregations entirely free to translate their principles into action. And second, insofar as Reform implied the negation of ritual observances, the movement was aided by the tendency of the immigrants to drop cultural impediments to material success and to Americanization. By the Civil War, most American Jews believed that their religion was a form of ethical monotheism capable of indefinite development and expansion, were mildly antinomian and antiritualistic, and believed that Reform Judaism was in the vanguard of mankind's progress toward a universal religion of humanity.[27] David Einhorn, an abolitionist and one of the founders of German and American Judaism summed up the new creed when he said that Reform Judaism believed "in one humanity, all of whose members, being of the same heavenly and earthly origin, possess a like nobility of birth and a claim to equal rights, equal laws, and in an equal share of happiness."[28] For many American Jews, the Haskalah, Jewish emancipation, and new conditions in America made Reform appear more appropriate than Orthodoxy.

Importantly, a similar religious development took place among the Garrisonian abolitionists, who also jettisoned revealed law and instead emphasized the progressive ethical nature of Christianity. Both the Garrisonians and the Reformers began as Biblical literalists. But changing social conditions and new ideologies encouraged both groups to modify their theologies. In the case of the Garrisonians, establishment Protestantism's unwillingness to embrace antislavery and the proslavery use of the Bible turned the New England abolitionists away from Calvinist orthodoxy toward a belief in the social gospel. They gradually downplayed Biblical literalism and began stressing natural law and conscience. For the Garrisonians, theological Christianity had to be judged pragmatically by its effects. Original sin and predestination were deemphasized as a vague ethical Christianity which was a rationale for social concern evolved. God became a name which was applied to the Garrisonians' perceptions of correct conduct: "*Humanity before all things*—before all books and before all institutions; and God in the soul is the only authority."[29]

As Richards, Sorin, and Steward have explained, the abolitionists' northern opponents held leadership positions in traditional Protestant denominations such as the Episcopal Church and the old school Presbyterian Church. The Protestant and Jewish abolitionists came from less distinguished religious stock; their religious beliefs stood in sharp contrast to their foes' sacramental elitism. For the Protestant abolitionists, evangelicalism often provided a break with tradition and a sense of immediatism and moral fervor. The Jewish abolitionists used reform to reject the dogmas of Orthodoxy; this dissenting attitude led to a crusading moral assertiveness and a searching reexamination of accepted Jewish, European, and American institutions. Reform Judaism's belief in the "approach of the realization of Israel's great Messianic hope for the establishment of the kingdom of truth, justice, and peace among all men" also encouraged Jews to solve on the basis of justice and righteousness the problems presented by the contrasts and evils of the present organization of society."[30] This zealousness and dedication to a world mission, and not just the social position of mid-nineteenth century Jewry, explains why fighting Reform Jews in Europe became abolitionists in America.

They used their liberal European beliefs and Reform Judaism to defend antebellum Blacks. One of the most formidable obstacles to abolitionism was the widespread popular and scientific belief in the innate inferiority of Blacks. Those abolitionists who believed that Blacks were not inherently inferior attacked the concept of racial inequality on two fronts: they attempted to demonstrate, from the Bible, science, history, and observed facts the essential equality of the races, and they also tried to show that the unfavorable environmental conditions of slavery and segregation, rather than natural inferiority, had caused the disabilities of American Blacks.

The Jewish abolitionists were quite sensitive to these arguments. One reason was the proslavery use of the Bible, which relied on Mosaic law and ancient slavery to defend the peculiar institution. Since Reform Jews only accepted those Mosaic laws which would "elevate and sanctify,"[31] their lives, they rejected any suggestions that the Bible could be used to defend modern slavery. The second reason was related to the position of nineteenth century European Jews. During the emancipation struggle, the "Jewish question"[32] was whether Jews were innately inferior to Gentiles or whether the ghetto environment explained the Jews' "backward" social customs and traditions. Because Reform Jews believed that emancipation would elevate the position of European Jewry and expose the Gentiles to a superior religion purged of its excrescenses and anachronisms, the Jewish abolitionists felt threatened by proslavery arguments. They ominously resembled antisemitic doctrines and could be used against American Jews. Therefore for religious and social reasons, Jewish abolitionists tried to weaken antebellum racial myths.

They did not deny that ancient slavery was sanctioned by the Bible. But the Jewish abolitionists did argue, using a Reform perspective, that Biblical bondage had to be interpreted in a historical context and could not be used to justify modern slavery. This approach was exemplified best in the famous debate over Rabbi Morris Jacob Raphall's 1861 proslavery sermon.

President Buchanan had proclaimed January 4, 1861 a National Fast Day in an effort to mobilize national sentiment against secession. On this day, Raphall, a famous and distinguished New York City Orthodox rabbi, delivered a sermon accepted by many as the Jewish position on the slavery question. Accusing the abolitionists of being "impulsive declaimers, gifted with great zeal, but little knowledge; more eloquent than learned; better able to excite our passions than to satisfy our reason,"[33] he proceeded to investigate three related questions. How far back could the influence of slavery be traced? Was slavery condemned as a sin in the Bible? And what were the condition of slaves in Biblical times? His answer to all three questions gave no succor to the abolitionists. Raphael believed that slavery existed before the flood and was nowhere contradicted by the Mosaic code or the New Testament. Thus he accused abolitionist preachers like Henry Ward Beecher of perverting the meaning of the Bible. Abraham, Isaac, Jacob, and Job all were slaveholders and so the Bible was opposed to abolitionism. Although Raphell made a minor distinction between ancient and southern slavery—Hebrews could only be enslaved for theft or poverty—he triumphantly concluded that "slavery has existed since the earliest time," and thus "slaveholding is no sin" because "slave property is expressly placed under the protection of the Ten Commandments."[34]

Raphall's sermon contributed nothing novel to the slavery debate; since the colonial period proslavery apologists had used the Bible to sanction bondage while the abolitionists continued to argue that slavery was a moral sin condemned in the scriptures. But Raphall was a prominent Orthodox rabbi and so the sermon was used in the South to prove the Biblical sanction of slavery and the American Jews' sympathy with the secession movement.[35] Pro-Southern New York Democrats and the American Society for Promotion of National Unity had Raphall repeat his speech on January 17 and printed it in newspapers, pamphlets, and book form.[36] But even Raphall's mild distinction between ancient and modern slavery was too corrosive for the defenders of slavery. On the second occasion some people in the audience "required him to withdraw his remarks on the character of Southern slavery."[37]

Although Einhorn first attacked Raphall in his monthly magazine *Sinai*, the rebuttal probably reached a small audience because it was written in German.[38] Michael Heilprin's slashing criticism of Raphall attracted the most publicity because it was printed in the influential *New York Daily Tribune*, where Horace Greeley described Heilprin as a "learned Jew" who had few living equals in "historical, philogical, and biblical knowledge."[39] The noted Jewish scholar used his linguistic and rhetorical skills to attack Raphall's interpretation of the Bible. First he argued that the proslavery rabbi had mistranslated the word "slave," which should have been rendered "servant" or "bondsman." Heilprin believed Raphall's Biblical quotations were inaccurate, for there was a "rigorously limited allowance" for the purchase of a freeman's life services.

Heilprin's second major point concerned the interpretation of Scriptures. In standard Reform fashion he argued there was much "contradictory, unjust, and even barbarous" material in the Bible that rabbis wisely rejected or ignored. It was nonsense to believe everything in the Bible retained a divine sanction. Heilprin challenged Raphall to "make your Bible, by some process of reasoning, to be pure, just, and humane," or else reject it as full of human frailty. It was shocking to Heilprin that any Jew would support slavery, for the "reproach of Egypt" was a stigma that had haunted Jews throughout history.[40]

Heilprin's argument was repeated by other abolitionists and even by rabbis indifferent to the antislavery cause. A telling poem entitled "Rabbi Raphall" asked, "He that unto thy fathers freedom gave— / Hath he not taught thee pity for the slave?"[41] Einhorn agreed with Heilprin and argued that since ancient slavery could not be eradicated immediately, regulations were introduced to limit its most serious abuses and eventually abolish it.[42] Protestant abolitionists supported Heilprin and Einhorn by translating and publishing the doctoral dissertation of Moses Mielziner, a German rabbi who had recently migrated to New York. Applying the contemporary methods of German

Biblical criticism to the scriptural laws regarding slavery, Mielziner concluded that Hebrew slavery was definitely circumscribed and ceased with the destruction of the First Temple.[43] And even Isaac Mayer Wise, the pragmatic leader of American Reform who believed that Jewish abolitionists were schismatics threatening to disunify American Judaism, argued that the Scriptures did not sanction slavery.[44] Like most Orthodox and Reform rabbis of the period, though, Wise avoided controversial causes which might lead to increased antisemitism or weaken the congregational structure. Perhaps the most prudent and typical Jewish response to the Raphall-Heilprin debate was that of *The Jewish Messenger,* which refused to print Heilprin's remarks because they had "no desire to take part in a controversy of this nature."[45]

This debate transcended the slavery controversy; it was a major conflict between Orthodoxy and Reform Judaism. Raphall defended the traditional, literal interpretation of the Bible while Heilprin wanted Biblical slavery passages analyzed historically in a critical, liberal spirit. Jewish abolitionism and Garrisonian theology, however, had already triumphed before the debate. The Republican Party, which condemned slavery in the territories but promised not to attack it in the Southern states, endorsed the abolitionist Biblical interpretation in its 1860 campaign when it stated that the Mosaic code tried to soften slavery "among the rude tribes, among a people so ignorant, being just delivered from Egyptian bondage. . . . It is therefore, the opposite of the American system [which] is without a peer for its cruelty."[46] Although this statement might appear condescending or even antisemitic, it was substantially similar to the position of contemporary Reform rabbis who believed the Bible "reflected the primitive ideas of its own age" and thus had to be reinterpreted according to the "spirit of broad humanity of our age."[47]

The Jewish abolitionists not only denied the proslavery interpretation of the Bible but they also rejected racialist thinking with its emphasis on contrasting stereotypes. The heightened consciousness about "white" racial characteristics, abetted by romanticism and national expansion, helped make it easier for many people on both sides of the sectional debate over slavery to accept a stereotype of Blacks that made them anti-Caucasians. During the 1830s racialist arguments led to change in the character of the debate over Black personality and prospects. Until the 1840s, discussions about slavery occurred between environmentalist defenders of a single human species and proponents of inherent racial differences. In the two decades before the Civil War, the dialogue tended increasingly to start from the common assumption that the races differed fundamentally. Although many abolitionists argued that Blacks were different from Whites, they projected a flattering image of the slave; like Harriet Beecher Stowe's Uncle Tom, the slave seemed to be a childlike, innocent creature free of the lust for power and wealth.[48]

Other abolitionists believed that the adverse environmental effects of slavery and discrimination, rather than innate deficiencies, were responsible for the seeming inferiority of American Blacks. The Jewish abolitionists supported the environmentalist argument and rejected racialist thinking because they realized that even a flattering racialism could be transmuted into an overt doctrine of Black inferiority, distinguished from harsher forms of racism only by a certain flavor of humanitarian paternalism.

They perceived a strong similarity between European tyranny, discrimination against Jews, and slavery. Emphasizing that the question was not one of race, but of human rights, the Jewish abolitionists made frequent pleas for racial and political equality based on Jewish history and tried to counteract the growing popularity of racialist thinking among abolitionists and their opponents.

Bondi, for example, enlisted in the Union army because he believed that "as a Jehudi, I had a duty to perform, to defend the institutions which gave equal rights to all beliefs."[49] Busch described abolitionism as "part of that everlasting war between Ormuzd and Ariman, between light and darkness, between right and wrong."[50] And Ernestine L. Rose, the only female Jewish abolitionist, became a popular platform speaker partly because she dramatically linked women, Blacks, and Jews in the struggle against discrimination and oppression. At an 1852 women's rights convention, she delivered her standard argument:

> I am an example of the universality of our claims; for not American women only, but a daughter of poor crushed Poland, and the downtrodden and persecuted people called the Jews . . . I go for emancipation of all kinds—white and black, man and woman. Humanity's children are, in my estimation, all one and the same family.[51]

Perhaps the two most effective critics of racialist thinking were Rabbis David Einhorn and Bernard Felsenthal. Einhorn, who was forced to flee both Hungary and Baltimore because of his liberal political beliefs, was one of the most prominent antebellum Jewish abolitionists. He believed there was a fundamental relationship between the rights of Jews and the rights of Blacks because there could be no freedom for minorities in an atmosphere of enslavement. Therefore he criticized the Know-Nothings and the proslavery forces because both groups were trying to exclude and degrade ethnic groups. Einhorn wanted democratic rights extended to Blacks not only because it was right but also to safeguard the status of other traditionally outcast groups like the Jews. Innate inferiority arguments were dangerous because they could be against any oppressed minorities as a reason for further oppression.[52]

Felsenthal, a midwestern abolitionist who had delivered many antislavery sermons and speeches before the Civil War,[53] explicitly made the same parallels between Jewish oppression and slavery. He had called slavery the "most shameful institution on earth."[54] Now he was angry about an 1862 bill declaring Blacks incompetent to act as witnesses in the District of Columbia. Felsenthal traced similar restrictions in the case of the Jews from Justinian to Russia and in the modern Germanic states. Again a minority group was being degraded, and their degradation then was used as an excuse to deny them equal rights: "What can justify such barbarism? Russia does not lie only between Kalisz and Kamchatka, but also on the shores on the Potomac and Lake Michigan."[55] The Jewish abolitionists made telling parallels between Poland, Russia, the Germanic states, and America; between women and Blacks, and Jews and Blacks. The Jewish antislavery crusade was extraordinarily sensitive to charges of innate inferiority and civic inequality. They believed that slavery was not only wrong but dangerous. Its defenders could use their arguments against other groups and thus all minorities had a stake in showing that the Blacks' shortcomings had environmental, not racial causes.

Jewish abolitionism was a conditioned response to the existence of American slavery. But many strains of western and Jewish thought converged in the mid-nineteenth century to produce the particular emotional and intellectual intensity of the Jewish antislavery movement. The Haskalah, emancipation, and the liberal ideas of the 1848 revolutions were all synthesized in an American environment. Reform Judaism absorbed elements from all these movements and added to them a moral, crusading fervor. Its adherents were particularly attracted to two prophetic ideas: the belief that Judaism had a special mission in the world, and the concept of social justice. As a result, European Jews who were emancipated, supported the Haskalah movement, and participated in European revolutionary activities continued their prostelytizing in America on behalf of a race that resembled them in its social and political disabilities.

The Jewish abolitionists were involved in a wide variety of antislavery activities throughout the free states, Kansas, and Maryland. Bondi, Benjamin, and Weiner fought with John Brown in Kansas. Michael Greenbaum assisted fugitive slaves in Chicago.[56] Moritz Pinner and Wilhelm Rapp courageously edited abolitionist newspapers in Kansas City and Baltimore.[57] And abolitionist rabbis and their supporters publicly criticized slavery in St. Louis, New York City, Baltimore, Chicago, Philadelphia, Detroit, and Madison, Indiana. Although the Jewish abolitionists had a unique perspective on American slavery, they could not form separate organizations because of their small numbers. Instead, they worked with local and national abolitionists and reform organizations to destroy the peculiar institution.

These freedom fighters were an unusual group of individuals who came from urban cosmopolitan families and were active in European and American civic life; they also socialized with Gentiles and experimented in leading lives in the contemporary world while remaining Jews. An upwardly mobile immigrant group, the Jewish abolitionists used European liberalism and reform Judaism to challenge established American institutions and ideas related to slavery because they were autocratic, discriminatory, and had antisemitic implications.

NOTES

1. Gilbert Osofsky, "Abolitionists, Irish Immigrants, and the Dilemmas of Romantic Nationalism," *American Historical Review*, 80 (1975), 889–912.

2. *The Thirteenth Annual Report of the American & Foreign Anti-Slavery Society, Presented at New York, May 11, 1853 (New York, 1953)*, pp. 114–115.

3. Robert G. Weisbord and Arthur Stein, *Bittersweet Encounter: The Afro-American and the American Jew* (Westport, Conn., 1970), pp. 19–26; Bertram W. Korn, "Jews and Negro Slavery in the Old South, 1789–1865," *Publications of the American Jewish Historical Society*, L (1961), 151–201; Hugh H. Smythe and Martin S. Price, "The American Jew and Negro Slavery," *Midwest Journal*, VII (1956), 315–319.

4. The only exceptions to this statement are Morris U. Schappes, ed., *A Documentary History of the Jews in the United States, 1654–1875* (New York, 3rd edition, 1971), which contains good primary material on the slavery controversy and the Jews, and the pioneering article by Max J. Kohler, "The Jews and the Anti-Slavery Movement," *Publications of the American Jewish Historical Society*, V, (1897), 137–155.

5. Bertram W. Korn, "Isaac Mayer Wise on the Civil War," *Hebrew Union College Annual*, XX (1947), 635–658; *American Jewry and the Civil War* (Philadelphia, 1951).

6. Louis Ruchames, "The Abolitionists and the Jews," *Publications of the American Jewish Historical Society*, XLL (1952), 131–156. In his preface to the 1961 paperback edition of *American Jewry*, Korn

admitted that Ruchames' article was a useful corrective to Wise's prejudices against the abolitionists, but Korn continued to insist that the abolitionists' humanitarian concerns were very limited. See Korn, *American Jewry* (1961), xviii–xix.

7. Marcus Lee Hansen, *The Atlantic Migration, 1607–1860* (Cambridge, Mass., 1940), p. 280; Nathan Glazer, *American Judaism* (Chicago, 1957), p. 23; Guido Kisch, "The Jewish 'On to America Movement,'" *Publications of the American Jewish Historical Society*, XXVIII (1949), 185–234; Mack Walker, *Germany and the Emigration, 1816–1885* (Cambridge, Mass., 1964), pp. 42–133; Uriah Zwi Engelman, "Jewish Statistics in the U.S. Census of Religious Bodies (1850–1936)," *Jewish Social Studies*, IX (1947), 129–131; Max J. Kohler, "The German Jewish Migration to America," *Publications of the American Jewish Historical Society*, IX (1901), 87–105.

8. Nathan Glazer, "Social Characteristics of American Jews, 1654–1954," *American Jewish Year Book*, LVI (1955), 3–20; Rudolph Glanz, "The Immigration of German Jews up to 1880," *Yivo Annual of Jewish Social Science*, II–III (1947–1948), 81–99.

9. Salo W. Baron, "The Impact of the Revolution of 1848 on Jewish Emancipation," *Jewish Social Studies*, XI (1949), 195–248; Adolph Kober, "Jews in the Revolution of 1848 in Germany," *Jewish Social Studies*, X (1948), 135–164.

10. *The Sun*, September 17, 1870.

11. *The Asmonean*, August 24, 1855.

12. Bertram W. Korn, "Jewish 'Forty-Eighters' in America," *American Jewish Archives*, II (1949), 12–14.

13. August Bondi, *Autobiography of August Bondi* (Galesburg, Ill., 1910), p. 33.

14. Bondi, *Autobiography*, pp. 5–132; "With John Brown in Kansas," *Transactions of the Kansas State Historical Society*, VIII (1903–1940), 275–289; Leon Huhner, "Some Jewish Associates of John Brown," *Publications of the American Jewish Historical Society*, XXIII (1915), 55–78.

15. Gustav Pollack, *Michael Heilprin and His Sons* (New York, 1912), pp. 3–12; *Jewish Exponent*, October 17, 1899.

16. Leon Ruzicka, "Isidor Busch," *Judisches Archiv*, I (1928), 16–21; James Wax, "Isidor Busch, American Patriot and Abolitionist," *Historia Judaica*, V (1943), 183–203.

17. *Proceedings of the Missouri State Convention held in Jefferson City, June, 1863* (St. Louis, 1863), p. 135.

18. *Medical Life*, XXXV (1928), 214–258.

19. *American Medicine*, IX (1905), 243.

20. Leonard L. Richards, *"Gentlemen of Property and Standing": Anti-Abolition Mobs in Jacksonian America* (New York, 1970); Gerald Sorin, *The New York Abolitionists: A Case Study of Political Radicalism* (Westport, Conn., 1971), James Brewer Stewart, *Holy Warriors: The Abolitionists and American Slavery* (New York, 1976); David Donald, "Toward a Reconsideration of Abolitionists," *Lincoln Reconsidered* (New York, 1956), pp. 19–36.

21. *The Jewish Tribune*, December 21, 1883; *The Menorah*, June, 1889, October, 1890, September, 1898.

22. Henry S. Morais, "Sabato Morais," *Proceedings of the Sixth Biennial Convention of the Jewish Theological Seminary Association* (New York, 1892), pp. 63–84. The quotation is from page 67.

23. Bondi, *Autobiography*, pp. 27, 24.

24. Although Morais was the only Orthodox rabbi to embrace abolitionism, his European history was similar to the other Jewish abolitionists. Samuel Morais was a liberal, scholarly, individual who belonged to the Masonic order in Italy. Sabato became an ardent republican; Mazzini used Morais' passport when he was forced to travel throughout Europe in disguise. After his arrival in 1851, Morais became a bold, fearless advocate of abolitionism in Philadelphia. By the early 1870's, Morais, as chazan of Sephardic Mikveh Israel, had modified the religious services along Reform lines to achieve an "American Judaism more comfortable to our changed circumstances." Thus Morais' social background, political ideology, and religious beliefs were much closer to the Jewish abolitionists than to Orthodoxy. See Morais, "Sabato Morais," *Proceedings of the Sixth Biennial Convention of the Jewish Theological Seminary Association*, pp. 63–84; *The Jewish Messenger*, XXXVIII, November 12, 1875.

25. William O. McCragg, Jr., "Jews in Revolutions: The Hungarian Experience," *Journal of Social History*, 6 (1972), 78–105.

26. Jacob Katz, *Out of the Ghetto: The Social Background of Jewish Emancipation, 1770–1870* (Cambridge, Mass., 1973); "The Term 'Jewish Emancipation': Its Origin and Historical Impact," in *Studies in Nineteenth Century Jewish Intellectual History,* ed. Alexander Altman (Cambridge, Mass., 1964), pp. 1–25; Michael A. Meyer, *The Origins of the Modern Jew: Jewish Identity and European Culture in Germany, 1749–1824* (Detroit, 1967); Isaac Eisenstein-Barzilay, "The Ideology of the Berlin Haskalah," *Proceedings of the American Academy for Jewish Research,* XXV (1956), 1–37.

27. David Philipson, *The Reform Movement in Judaism* (New York, 1931); Martin B. Ryback, "The East-West Conflict in American Reform, 1854–1879," *American Jewish Archives,* II (1950), 3–14; Stephen Steinberg, "Reform Judaism: The Origins and Evolution of a 'Church Movement,' " *Journal for the Scientific Study of Religion,* V (1965), 117–129; Leon A. Jick, *The Americanization of the Synagogue, 1820–1870* (Hanover, N.H., 1976), pp. 79–97, 133–194.

28. David Einhorn, *Antirittspredight Gehalten in Tempel des Har Sinai Vereins* (Baltimore, 1855), p. 10.

29. *The Liberator,* March 30, 1855.

30. "Declaration of Principles Adopted by a Group of Reform Rabbis at Pittsburgh, 1885," *Yearbook of the Central Conference of American Rabbis,* XLV (1935), p. 200. Although the platform was drawn up after the Civil War, it is a rather moderate statement and thus would have been acceptable to the antebellum Jewish abolitionists.

31. "Declaration of Principles," *Yearbook of the Central Conference of American Rabbis,* p. 199.

32. For an excellent discussion of the "Jewish question" during the early struggle for emancipation, see Katz, *Out of the Ghetto,* pp. 8–103.

33. *The New York Herald,* January 5, 1861.

34. *The New York Herald,* January 5, 1861.

35. *Memphis Daily Appeal,* January 23, 1861; *Richmond Daily Dispatch,* January 7, 29, 1861.

36. *The New York Herald,* January 17, 19, 1861; *The Evening Post,* January 17, 1861.

37. *The New York Herald,* January 19, 1861.

38. *Sinai,* VI, February, March, April, 1861.

39. *New York Daily Tribune,* January 9, 1861.

40. *New York Daily Tribune,* January 15, 1861.

41. *The Independent,* February 21, 1861.

42. *Sinai,* VI, March, April, 1861; David Einhorn, *War with Amalek* (Philadelphia, 1864), pp. 4, 5.

43. E. M. F. Mielziner, *Moses Mielziner, 1823–1903* (New York, 1931), pp. 21–23, 64–103.

44. *The Israelite,* II, January 23, 1856, VI, January 18, 1861. Wise considered Whites superior to Blacks but he never defended slavery. After the Civil War, he admitted that emancipation was desirable and progressive. See Jacob Rader Marcus, *The Americanization of Isaac Mayer Wise* (Cincinnati, 1931), pp. 10–18.

45. *The Jewish Messenger,* January 18, 1861.

46. William Henry Fry, *Republican "Campaign" Textbook* (New York, 1860), pp. 10–11.

47. "Declaration of Principles," *Yearbook of the Central Conference of American Rabbis,* pp. 199–200.

48. George M. Fredrickson, *The Black Image in the White Mind: The Debate on Afro-American Character and Destiny, 1817–1914* (New York, 1971), pp. 97–129; William R. Stanton, *The Leopard's Spots: Scientific Attitudes Toward Race in America, 1815–1859* (Chicago, 1960); William R. Taylor, *Cavalier and Yankee; The Old South and American National Character* (New York, 1961), pp. 123–155, 279–294.

49. Bondi, *Autobiography,* p. 72.

50. *Journal of Missouri State Convention,* p. 326.

51. *The Proceedings of the Women's Rights Convention Held in Syracuse, September 8th, 9th and 10th, 1852* (Syracuse, 1952), p. 63. For a similar argument, see her speech on the anniversary of West Indian emancipation in *The Liberator,* August 19, 1853.

52. *Sinai,* I, October, 1856, VII, June, July, August, 1861; Einhorn, *War with Amalek,* pp. 4, 5; David Einhorn to Samuel Adler, January 21, 1864, American Jewish Archives, Cincinnati, Ohio; Kaufman Kohler, ed., *David Einhorn Memorial Volume* (New York, 1911), pp. 403–455.

53. Emma Felsenthal, *Bernard Felsenthal, Teacher in Israel* (New York, 1924), p. 23; Bernard Falsenthal to Max J. Kohler, October 25, 1901, American Jewish Archives, Cincinnati, Ohio.

54. Bernard Felsenthal, "Die Juden und die Sclaveri," *Illinois Staatzeitung,* June 6, 1862.

55. Bernard Felsenthal, "Legislatoriche Barbarei, Nagerrecht und 'Juden-Recht,'" *Illinois Staatszeitung,* July 9, 1862.

56. Simon Wolf, *The American Jew as Patriot, Soldier and Citizen* (Philadelphia, 1895), pp. 425–426.

57. *St. Louis Republican,* February 13, 1860; George William Brown, *Baltimore and the 19th of April, 1861: A Study of the War* (Baltimore, 1887), p. 53; Dieter Cunz, *The Maryland Germans: A History* (Princeton, N.J., 1948), pp. 304–306.

# The Rabbis and the Slavery Question

The Jews of the United States have never taken any steps whatever with regard to the Slavery question. As citizens, they deem it their policy "to have every one choose which ever side he may deem best to promote his own interests and the welfare of his country." They have no organization of an ecclesiastical body to represent their general views; no General Assembly or its equivalent. The American Jews have two newspapers, but they do not interfere in any discussion which is not material to their religion. It cannot be said that the Jews have formed any denominational opinion on the subject of American slavery. Some of the Jews who reside in slave States, have refused to have any property in man, or even to have any slaves about them. They do not believe that anything analogous to slavery, as it exists in this country, ever prevailed among the ancient Israelites ... The objects of so much mean prejudice and unrighteous oppression as the Jews have been for ages, surely they, it would seem, more than any other denomination, ought to be the enemies of *caste* and the friends of *universal freedom*.[1]

This report by a non-Jew on the relationship of the synagogue to the slavery issue, presented to the 1853 meeting of the American and Foreign Anti-Slavery Society, was substantially correct, and in that regard rather unusual for an age in which so much misinformation about the Jews was broadcast far and wide. The autonomy of the individual congregation, and the freedom of individual rabbis from hierarchical control, precluded any official Jewish pronouncements on the most important single religio-cultural question of the day.

Individual Jews, of course, had participated in the development of the institution of slavery, as well as in the discussion of its merits, from the very first. Jewish merchants of Newport, Rhode Island, had been active, before the Revolution, in the well-known "triangle trade" which brought African slaves to the colonies.[2] Jewish residents of the slave states had bought Negroes for use on their plantations and in their homes, and had even made their living from slave marketing.[3] As the report to the Anti-Slavery Society stated, there were other Jews, in the South as well as in the North, who had, out of

In 1973, Bertram Wallace Korn was senior rabbi at Reform Congregation Kneseth Israel in Elkins Park, Pennsylvania.

Reprinted in Bertram Wallace Korn, *American Jewry and the Civil War* (New York: Atheneum, 1970), p. 15–31. Copyright © 1951, 1961, The Jewish Publication Society. Used by permission of the Jewish Publication Society.

personal kindness or in keeping with their general convictions, freed their slaves. The records of the Manumission Society of New York City preserve the names of many Jews who emancipated their Negroes.[4] In the political arena, Jews were to be found on both sides of the question: Mordecai M. Noah's New York newspapers took a strong pro-slavery position,[5] while Moritz Pinner's *Kansas Post* was vehemently pledged to the opposite course.[6] Judah P. Benjamin[7] and David Yulee,[8] the two Jewish senators, were both champions of the slave system, while other Jews who were active in politics, like Isidor Bush[9] of St. Louis and Philip J. Joachimsen[10] of New York, were enlisted in the anti-slavery ranks.

If it were possible to uncover and catalogue the opinions of all the Jews who lived in the United States during the years leading up to the Civil War—slave dealers like J. F. Moses of Lumpkin, Ga., who, "being a regular trader to this market," said that he would "warrant every Negro sold to come up to the bill, squarely and completely";[11] immigrants like Seligman Kakeles of New York who, in the perennial manner of hero-worshippers, named his first-born American child after the abolitionist leader Gerrit Smith,[12] philanthropists like Judah Touro who, living in a slavery environment, disagreed with the system enough to free his own slaves;[13] abolitionists like Michael Heilprin of Philadelphia, who was mobbed by a pro-slavery crowd at a Democratic Party meeting in 1858.[14]—we should have to conclude that Jews were represented in all the various shadings of opinion from fanatic abolitionists to fire-eating slavery proponents. The Jews were as thoroughly divided as the American population itself. It is possible, however, that we should discover that there were fewer Jews than other Americans, proportionately, at the extreme wings of the controversy, and more in the middle ground, because, as immigrants, the great majority of them would naturally have taken less interest in theoretical and sectional political questions than in the more personal problems of economic and social adjustment.

Since there was no unified expression of Jewish opinion on the subject, Judaism, unlike the various Christian denominations, played no role in the moulding of public sentiment in the crucial years when the battle lines were being drawn. This is not to say, however, that Jewish leaders were silent. The rabbis and publishers spoke *for* no official group of Jews, certainly not for their congregations and readers—but, speaking *to* American Jewry they could hardly avoid exerting the influence of their religious and intellectual leadership. An examination of the opinions voiced by the rabbis during the turmoil over slavery will be interesting for a number of reasons. It will, firstly, demonstrate the extent to which the rabbis participated in the various political currents which eddied through American life, and, secondly, it will indicate how far they were from unanimity.

I

The most highly publicized rabbinical pronouncement on the merits of slavery was made at the very peak of the secession crisis by Dr. Morris J. Raphall of New York City, one of the most celebrated orators in the American rabbinate of his time. President Buchanan had proclaimed January 4, 1861, as a National Fast Day, in an effort to mobilize national sentiment against the impending break-up of the Union. Jews as well as non-Jews all over the nation gathered for worship and prayer; Rabbi Raphall believed that this was the logical occasion for a discourse on "The Bible View of Slavery."[15]

What he did was to place Judaism squarely in opposition to the philosophy of abolitionism. He denied that any statement or law in the Bible could be interpreted to prohibit slavery, and insisted that, to the contrary, biblical tradition and law guaranteed the right to own slaves. Translating the Hebrew word for servant ('ebed) as "slave," he claimed that "the very highest authority" in the Bible, the Ten Commandments, sanctioned human slavery.[16] He accused Henry Ward Beecher and the other abolitionist preachers of rationalistic attempts to pervert the meaning of the biblical text and challenged them to produce factual evidence to back up their contention that biblical law was designed to abolish slavery:

> I would therefore ask the reverend gentleman from Brooklyn and his compeers How dare you . . . denounce slaveholding as a sin? When you remember that Abraham, Isaac, Jacob, Job—the men with whom the Almighty conversed, with whose names he emphatically connects his own most holy name . . .—that all these men were slaveholders, does it not strike you that you are guilty of something very little short of blasphemy? And if you answer me, "Oh, in their time slaveholding was lawful, but now it has become a sin," I in my turn ask you, "When and by what authority you draw the line? Tell us the precise time when slaveholding ceased to be permitted, and became sinful?"[17]

Raphall made a half-hearted attempt to appear objective by distinguishing biblical slavery from the evils of the Southern system. The Bible, he said, had regarded the slave as "a *person* in whom the dignity of human nature is to be respected," while the Southerners treated the slave as "a *thing*" without rights and privileges. The Bible had safeguarded the slaves against cruelty, mutilation, and abuse; the Bible was humanitarian, and the South would do well to adopt its merciful attitude.[18] But he directed his major attack against the abolitionists for their misrepresentation of the Bible and for their agitation against the legitimate rights of the Southerners who, to his mind, had done no wrong. He claimed that he himself was not an adherent of slavery, but that an objective consideration of the text of the Bible forced him to assume this position.[19]

This sermon aroused more comment and attention than any other sermon ever delivered by an American rabbi. The pro- and anti-slavery forces had for years been arguing about the attitude of the Old Testament to slavery. For Fundamentalist ministers, at least, the testimony of the Bible on slavery was preeminently important. Now, at the very time when propagandists, both North and South, were delivering their final appeals for support, a learned rabbi had finally settled the argument in favor of the proponents of slavery. Printed in its entirety in the daily press,[20] as a separate pamphlet, and in a compilation of similar sermons, "The Bible View of Slavery" was given wide circulation. The *Richmond Daily Dispatch* said that it "receives the praise of the press as the most powerful argument delivered" in the entire religious controversy about slavery.[21] It was used frequently, throughout the Southland, as proof of the sympathy of the Jews for the seceding states. In the Virginia House of Delegates, for instance, when ex-Governor

Wyndham Robertson[22] was urging support for his resolution to invite the Richmond rabbis to open the daily sessions of the House with prayer (only Christian clergymen had previously been permitted to do so), the Raphall sermon served as a fine argument:

.... It is fit, at a time when we are standing on our rights of equality in other respects, we should be careful not to refuse lightly the benefit of that principle to others. Nor perhaps is it inappropriate to remember here a late powerful and eloquent voice that has been raised by a learned Israelite in New York in vindication of that social institution in which our peace and welfare are vitally involved, and in defense of which we are now engaged in a struggle before (I might almost say against) the world.[23]

In Memphis, when the Rev. Simon Tuska wrote a letter to the *Memphis Daily Appeal* defending Jews as loyal citizens, he pointed to the fact that it was not a Christian clergyman, but a rabbi who had delivered "the most forceful arguments in justification of the slavery of the African race, and the most thorough refutation of the rabid, abolition views of Henry Ward Beecher."[24] The *Charleston Mercury* praised Raphall for "defend[ing] us in one of the most powerful arguments put forth north or south."[25]

Abolitionist Jews and non-Jews could not, therefore, permit Raphall's theses to go unanswered, or it would be assumed that he spoke for all Jews, and that his summary of the biblical attitude was the final, definitive one.

The first Jewish answer to Raphall's presentation, published in *The New York Tribune*,[26] was written by Michael Heilprin, a Polish-Jewish intellectual who had taken an active part in the 1848 Revolution in Hungary and was now a member of the editorial staff of Appleton's *New American Cyclopaedia*.[27] He was shocked that a Jewish voice should be raised in support of slavery:

I had read similar nonsense hundreds of times before; I knew that the Father of Truth and Mercy was daily invoked in hundreds of pulpits in this country for a Divine sanction of falsehood and barbarism; still, being a Jew myself, I felt exceedingly humbled, I may say outraged, by the sacrilegious words of the Rabbi. Have we not had enough of the "reproach of Egypt?" Must the stigma of Egyptian principles be fastened on the people of Israel by Israelitish lips themselves? . . .[28]

A learned Jew himself, Heilprin proceeded to examine and refute each of Raphall's contentions and interpretations. His invective and scorn of Raphall's scholarship and ideas were unbounded. He did not even try to disguise his feeling that Raphall was either a fool or a knave; he could discover no excuse for the rabbi's misinterpretation of Judaism. Beyond all the details of translation and interpretation, he could not understand how Raphall could ignore the fact that Jewish law is fluid, flexible and organic. The rabbis of the Talmud had "explained away" many "contradictory, unjust, and even barbarous" laws and statements in the Bible, he said—it was nonsense to pretend that everything preserved in the Bible retained a divine sanction.

Several months later, Christian abolitionists began the serial publication of another Jewish analysis of the biblical attitude towards slavery, a treatise on "Slavery Among the Ancient Hebrews" by Dr. Moses Mielziner, then principal of the Jewish school at Copenhagen, later to become the rabbi of Anshi Chesed Congregation of New York

City. Written as Mielziner's doctoral dissertation at the University of Giessen, without any reference to the contemporary American agitation, Mielziner's work was a dispassionate, rationalistic study of the scriptural law governing slavery. The Danish rabbi was convinced that the Mosaic law had so thoroughly delimited the practice of slavery as to all but abolish it, and that the enslavement of Hebrews had actually ceased with the destruction of the First Temple. Of course, he had not intended to write a textbook for abolitionist clergymen, but his work so impressed its first American reader, Professor Francis Lieber of Columbia University, as an antidote to Raphall's supposedly authoritative presentation, that its translation and publication were arranged for immediately, first in the *American Theological Review* of New York in April 1861, and again in the *Evangelical Review* of Gettysburg, Pa., in January 1862."[29]

Raphall's sermon was answered even in England. Rabbi Gustav Gottheil, later to become rabbi of Temple Emanu-El of New York City, preached two sermons to his Manchester congregation on the subject:[30]

> We have had to learn, by reports in the public journals, that a Teacher in Israel, a man to whom people would look as having a right to speak with authority; and at a time when any utterance on the Slave Question could not fail to be eagerly listened to, did from his pulpit maintain that *slave-holding is no sin according to the Scriptures* . . . How can we be silent when we find him using [this] . . . as an argument to show that the people of the Republic are wrong in condemning and denouncing the slavery of the south . . .[31]

He, like Heilprin, examined and refuted Raphall's points, one by one, and discussed the relevance of Negro rights to Jewish rights, of Negro freedom to human freedom. For him, slavery found justification neither in the Bible nor in Jewish history.

## II

The leading abolitionist propagandist among the rabbis was David Einhorn of Baltimore, who had been writing and preaching against slavery since 1856.[32] He devoted four separate articles in his monthly, *Sinai*, to the Raphall sermon and its arguments.[33] The question, he said, was not whether slavery was mentioned in the Bible, but

> whether Scripture merely *tolerates* this institution as an evil not to be disregarded, and therefore infuses in its legislation a mild spirit gradually to lead to its dissolution, or whether it *favors, approves of* and *justifies* and *sanctions* it in its moral aspect.[34]

*Christian* clergymen were apologizing for slavery, even in the South, he said; could a *rabbi* sanction it? If a Christian, he continued, had said Judaism was pro-slavery, all Jews, from the extremest Orthodox wing to the most radical Reformers, would have "call[ed] the wrath of heaven and earth upon such falsehoods."[35]

Einhorn had never had any patience with literalists like Raphall. Jews should be concerned with the spirit of the Bible, he felt, not with its letter. Of course, slavery was acknowledged in the Bible: it had been established long before biblical times. Since it could not be eradicated all at once, certain regulations were ordained to prohibit its most serious abuses. But it was always intended that the system would be abolished in its entirety. It was blasphemy, he believed, for the proponents of slavery to identify God and the Bible with the cruelty and heartlessness of slavery:

> . . . Is it anything else but a deed of Amalek, rebellion against God, to enslave human beings created in His image, and to degrade them to a state of beasts having no will of their own? Is it anything else but an act of ruthless and wicked violence, to reduce defenseless human beings to a condition of merchandise, and relentlessly to tear them away from the hearts of husbands, wives, parents, and children . . . ?
>
> It has ever been a strategy of the advocate of a bad cause to take refuge from the spirit of the Bible to its letter, as criminals among the ancient heathen nations would seek protection near the altars of their gods. Can *that* Book hallow the enslavement of any race, which sets out with the principles, that Adam was created in the image of God, and that all men have descended from *one* human pair? Can *that* Book mean to raise the whip and forge chains, which proclaims, with flaming words, in the name of God: "break the bonds of oppression, let the oppressed go free and tear every yoke!" Can *that* Book justify the violent separation of a child from its human mother, which, when speaking of birds' nests, with admirable humanity commands charitable regard for the feelings even of an animal mother? . . .[36]

Arguing religious sanctions for human bondage on the basis of ancient practice made as much sense to Einhorn as urging the reestablishment of polygamy, blood vengeance, or royalty, because they were conventional in biblical times. As to the historic right to enslave others, could custom ever justify evil? "Does a disease, perchance, cease to be an evil on account of its long duration?" Would mankind ever progress if improvements were thwarted out of consideration for the past? Would the United States ever have been created if the national founders had been moved by regard for "historic right?" "If such principles were true, could it ever have been possible to cease burning heretics and witches, aye! even to sacrifice the blood of one's own children?" Did God himself show any regard for "historic right" when he emancipated the Hebrew slaves from Egyptian slavery? Religious principles of freedom and righteousness, Einhorn maintained, must ultimately triumph over "ancient prejudices, over usurped titles and privileges, over hallowed atrocities."[37]

Like Heilprin and Dr. Gottheil, Einhorn perceived a fundamental relationship between the rights of the Jew and the rights of the Negro. He saw no possibility of freedom for minorities in an atmosphere which condoned the enslavement of any people. The philosophy of exclusionism would inevitably set more and more people outside the bounds of equality, unless it were repudiated completely. For him, slavery and the Know-Nothing agitation against aliens were of a piece; as it was intended to enslave the Negro forever, so foreigners were to be degraded into second class citizens. The extension of democratic rights to the Negro would safeguard the status of all other groups. Even more important, it would also enable America to forge to the forefront of leadership in the movement for world-wide democracy.[38]

The Rabbi of Har Sinai Temple in Baltimore was not merely preaching. Maryland was a festering sore of sectional strife; it would in all probability have joined the Confederacy after the outbreak of hostilities, had it not been for the prompt action of the government in arresting secessionist ring-leaders and declaring martial law in order to safeguard the passage of Northern troops through to the national capital. Anti-slavery declarations were not idle talk in such an atmosphere. Einhorn had been warned many times before, by both friends and enemies, to discontinue his public crusade. His articles against Raphall, printed in New York papers and in separate pamphlet form, were the last straw; open threats were made against him, and Baltimore Jews who belonged to other congregations were forced to state in the public press that they did not accept his leadership.

Open rioting between Baltimore Unionists and Confederate sympathizers broke out on April 19, 1861. Abolitionists and many innocent persons who were merely suspected of sharing their ideas were molested; some were beaten and killed. Printing presses, including those which printed Einhorn's *Sinai*, were destroyed; homes were set afire. His friends urged the rabbi to flee north, but he refused to show the white feather. Soldiers came to him with proof that his name was listed among those proscribed by the secessionist instigators of the riots. Still he refused to leave. A group of young men of his congregation, armed for guard duty, set up a cordon around his home to protect him and his family. Finally, on the fourth day of the rioting, he consented to leave, for his family's sake, proposing to return as soon as law and order were restored in Baltimore.[39]

He never did return. His congregation was itself so riddled by political differences, and many members were so thoroughly frightened by the violence of the rioters, that the only condition on which they would consent to their rabbi's return was that he promise to refrain from political controversy. On May 13, the Board of Trustees directed that he be written to as follows: "it would be very desirable—for your own safety, as well as out of consideration for the members of your congregation—if in the future there would be no comment in the pulpit on the excitable issues of the time."[40]

Such a condition was utterly unacceptable to David Einhorn. If he had been interested in conciliating the secessionists he would never have undertaken to write and preach against slavery in the first place. He could not and would not compromise one of his most fundamental principles for the sake of expediency.

It was painful to part with his first American congregation without a word of personal farewell; Baltimore had been the scene of his initiation into America and American-Jewish life. There he had first flexed his muscles against American Orthodox and Conservative Judaism in the battle for Reform. He had made many enemies, with his ruthless logic, and his outspoken criticism of reaction in religion and politics; but he had found close friends and supporters in Baltimore, men and women who upheld his hands in controversy, and with whom he still longed to sit and talk.[41]

But a warm welcome had been given him in Philadelphia. Keneseth Israel Congregation promptly invited him to occupy its pulpit; there he could speak his mind and his heart without hindrance. The problems of the war continued to be a major subject of his preaching and writing, but the *Sinai* lasted only another year and a half. Its transfer to Philadelphia was healthier for its editor, but completely unprofitable. Even in the

North, Jews were not prepared to identify their religious thinking with the anti-slavery movement. Einhorn wrote in the final number of the journal that "Sinai ... dies in the battle against slavery."[42]

The only other abolitionist among the rabbis was the Rev. Bernhard Felsenthal of Chicago, who had, while occupying the pulpit in Madison, Ind., taken an active role in the Fremont presidential campaign in 1856,[43] and later refused to apply for the rabbinical position in Mobile, Ala., because he felt that he could not live at peace with himself in a slave environment.[44] As the rabbi of Sinai Temple in Chicago, and then of the newly organized Zion Congregation, he is said to have delivered many anti-slavery sermons and speeches during the war.[45] In his only sermon to be preserved in print, a Thanksgiving Day message of 1865,[46] he rejoiced over the successful termination of the war and the final death-blow to slavery. God had freed America from the bondage of Egypt, he said; the nation was now rid of "an ugly and hateful institution" which had shamed her before the entire world:

Four millions of men, children of the same heavenly Father, descendants of the same Adam, were held in—slavery! And now they were freed, and now they will be free ... And should the nation not rejoice? Still many more millions of white people languished in slavery. They were fettered by the shackles of prejudices. Were not those who spoke for universal freedom and acted for universal justice in a small, small minority? And was not the name *Abolitionist* a name of disgrace? And now this name has become a name of honor, and three-fourths or seven-eighths of the nation glory in this name. The fetters of prejudices are broken. The white people have become emancipated just as well as the black people. The Abolitionists were the true statesmen of the nation. . . .

Unlike Einhorn, who believed that "any Jew who lifts his hand against the Union, is as a Jew to be considered equal to a parricide,"[47] Felsenthal apologized for but did not condemn Jews who approved of slavery and supported the Confederacy.[48] They were in the small minority, he said; American Jews by and large were "heart and soul, dedicated to the antislavery movement." He agreed that "if anyone, it is the Jew above all others who should have the most burning and irreconcilable hatred for the 'peculiar institution of the South,'" but he was still unwilling to disown them for their mistaken ideas.

### III

Indicative of the mood of large segments of the Jewish population of the North were the comments of Isaacs' *Jewish Messenger* on Einhorn's flight from Baltimore:

It seems that he has been mistaking his vocation, and making the pulpit the vehicle for political invective. The citizens of Baltimore, not regarding this as part of the Dr's duty, politely informed him, that 12 hours' safe residence was about all that they could guarantee him, in *that* place. Accordingly, taking the hint, the political Rabbi left, and at last accounts, was in the neighborhood of Philadelphia. We wonder whether our Baltimore co-religionists grieve over his departure? At the same time, we commend his fate to others, who feel inclined to take a similar course. A Minister has enough to do, if he devotes himself to the welfare of his flock; he can afford to leave politics to others. Let Dr. E's fate be a warning.[49]

Samuel M. Isaacs nursed his own private grudge against the Baltimore rabbi for his refusal to co-operate in the establishment of the Board of Delegates of American Israelites. This accounted in part for his gloating over the Baltimore experience. But Isaacs did honestly seek to avoid controversy over national politics unless a Jewish issue was involved. When letters about the Raphall sermon poured into the *Messenger's* office, he refused to print any of them. "We are determined not to engage in a controversy, and have made up our mind to admit in our columns *no* articles on the subject, either for or against slavery."[50]

Later, when inflammatory discussions of slavery were no longer so common, the *Messenger* was willing to commit itself by reprinting parts of a learned German treatise which maintained that slavery did not have divine sanction.[51] Still later, it gave its support to the passage of the Thirteenth Amendment, but cautioned that equality would have to be earned by the Negro, rather than legislated for him.[52]

Although his Virginia background undoubtedly gave a pro-slavery bent to his thinking, Isaac Leeser never published his personal views in *The Occident*. Like the *Messenger's* editors, he said he was profoundly opposed to any Jewish discussion of general political questions. Judaism, so far as he was concerned, had nothing specific to say about slavery and abolitionism, about the North and the South. So he chose not to preach on the National Fast Day on January 4, 1861, because "we could not have avoided political allusions had we spoken"; instead he gave a brief prayer for peace and harmony. He regretted that Dr. Raphall had decided to speak on slavery, although he admitted that he agreed with most of the New York rabbi's conclusions.[53]

The closest that Leeser ever came to discussing slavery was an editorial in which he cautioned Jewish merchants in the South against disobeying local regulations concerning commerce with Negro slaves. In late 1860 he wrote, "we have been shown a notice from a committee of vigilance addressed to a Hebrew in a town of Georgia, ordering him 'and his brethren' to quit the place by the 15th of November, alleging as a reason, that they had offended the public sense of propriety by their traffic . . ." If Jews disagreed with regulations against commercial intercourse with Negroes, said Leeser, let them move North rather than stir up trouble.[54]

**IV**

Isaac Mayer Wise[55] was another rabbi-editor who objected to political discussions from a Jewish viewpoint, from any religious viewpoint, in fact. He carried his attack against the Protestant abolitionists so far, however, that he actually did take a political position without admitting that he did so. He considered the abolitionists to be "fanatics," "demagogues," "red republicans and habitual revolutionaries, who feed on excitement and delight in civil wars, German athei[sts] coupled with American puritan[s] who know of no limits to their fanaticism, visionary philanthropists and wicked preachers who have that religion which is most suitable to their congregations," and "demons of hatred and destruction." It was the Protestant preachers, in the final analysis, who were responsible for the outbreak of the civil war, Wise was convinced:

Who in the world could act worse, more extravagant and reckless in this crisis than Protestant priests did? From the very start of the unfortunate difficulties the consequences of which we now suffer so severely, the Protestant priests threw the firebrand of abolitionism into the very heart of this country . . . There was not a Protestant paper in existence that had not weekly an abolitionist tirade. There was scarcely a sermon preached without a touch at least of the "existing evil." You know who made Jefferson Davis and the rebellion? The priests did, and their whiners and howlers in the press. The whole host of priests would rather see this country crushed and crippled than discard their fanaticism or give up their political influence.[56]

Never did the editor of *The Israelite* write on an issue connected with the war without pausing to attack abolitionism. But he was not a proponent of slavery, although he would have been quite willing to see the perpetuation of slavery guaranteed forever, in order to avoid civil bloodshed.[57] From a moral and ethical viewpoint he was moderately anti-slavery. Far from approving Raphall's stand, as has been charged, Wise was one of those who found many flaws in Raphall's analysis of the biblical text.[58] When the controversial discussions of slavery in the Bible died down, he published a series of articles in which he concluded that Moses had attempted to abolish slavery "by indirect-direct laws which rendered its existence impossible."[59] Agreeing with Einhorn to a surprising extent, he said:

It is evident that Moses was opposed to slavery from the facts: 1. He prohibited to enslave a Hebrew, male or female, adult or child. 2. He legislated to a people just emerging from bondage and slavery. 3. He legislated for an agricultural community with whom labor was honorable. 4. He legislated not only to humanize the condition of the alien laborers, but to render the acquisition and retention of bondmen contrary to their will a matter of impossibility.[60]

Taking a totally unrealistic view of the situation in the South, however, he said that:

We are not prepared, nobody is, to maintain it is absolutely unjust to purchase savages, or rather their labor, place them under the protection of the law, and secure them the benefit of civilized society and their sustenance for their labor. Man in a savage state is not free; the alien servant under the Mosaic law was a free man, excepting only the fruits of his labor. The abstract idea of liberty is more applicable to the alien laborer of the Mosaic system than to the savage, and savages only will sell themselves or their offspring.[61]

For all his theoretical objections to the inhumanity of slavery he was more hostile to the war-mongers in the North than to the evils of slavery, and became, in effect, a defender of the South.[62]

In thorough agreement with Wise on the question of abolitionism was the Rev. Judah Wechsler of Portsmouth, Ohio. He, too, believed that the abolitionist preachers were responsible for the war.

> Under the pretext of philanthropy [he said], the everlasting slavery question has been made the text point of almost every sermon. This more than anything else has been instrumental in [bringing on] this war . . . Had the clergymen excluded politics entirely from the pulpit . . . I for one believe we should not have experienced this war.[63]

Wechsler's ideas on the subject were well known to the Indianapolis Hebrew Congregation, whose rabbi he had been in 1858–1860; when he applied for the position again in 1863, the Board of the congregation resolved that he be not permitted even to conduct services on trial because of his "disloyal" political ideas.[64]

Another rabbi who agreed with Wise was Einhorn's Orthodox colleague in Baltimore, the Rev. Bernard Illowy, who denounced the abolitionists as "ambitious aspirants and selfish politicians, who, under the color of religion and in the disguise of philanthropy, have thrown the country into a general state of confusion." Illowy preached the same kind of message as Raphall on the National Fast Day on January 4, 1861, but it did not attract the same amount of attention from the public as Raphall's; it must have been partially responsible, however, for Einhorn's violent outbursts against pro-slavery rabbis. Illowy asked:

> Why did not Moses, who, as it is to be seen from his code, was not in favor of slavery, command the judges in Israel to . . . take forcibly away a slave from a master? . . . Why did Abraham, Ezra, etc., not free slaves? . . . All these are irrefutable proofs that we have no right to exercise violence against . . . institutions even if religious feelings and philanthropic sentiments bid us disapprove of them. It proves, furthermore, that the authors of the many dangers, which threaten our country with ruin and devastation, are not what they pretend to be, the agents of Religion and Philanthropy . . .[65]

One of Wise's major objections to the abolitionists was his suspicion that they were not actually humanitarians who were interested in the progress of mankind, but politicians bent on securing power. He believed that their religious fanaticism would fasten upon the Jews as their next victims, after the conquest of the South. As evidence of this he cited the 1859 Massachusetts law which denied the right to vote and hold office to the foreign-born until they could certify a residence of seven years in the United States. "Do you think," he asked, "the Israelites of the South must be your white slaves, as you in your naturalization laws treat the foreigner, placing him below the Negro?" The preachers who were so incensed about the treatment of the Negro, Wise claimed, turned a deaf ear to the Jew's claim for equality.[68]

*The Jewish Record* of New York seconded Wise's opposition to the abolitionist forces on the grounds of their attitude towards the Jews. They were only scheming fanatics who were determined to seize hold of the government and then destroy every free institution, smother every group, with which they disagreed. After the Confederacy was quelled, said the *Record,* the New England radicals would set themselves to the task of disfranchising the Jews.[67]

It is interesting to compare the diametrically opposed views of the *Record* with Einhorn's *Sinai* in reference to the Negroes. For Einhorn, Jewish rights would not be safe until Negro rights were secure. His humanitarianism made him the friend of the oppressed Negro. The *Record,* however, became a vicious spokesman of anti-Negro prejudice:

> We know not how to speak in the same breath of the Negro and the Israelite. The very names have startlingly opposite sounds—one representing all that is debased and inferior in the hopeless barbarity and heathenism of six thousand years; the other, the days when Jehovah conferred on our fathers the glorious equality which led the Eternal to converse with them, and allow them to enjoy the communion of angels. Thus the abandoned fanatics insult the choice of God himself, in endeavoring to reverse the inferiority which he stamped on the African, to make him the compeer, even in bondage, of His chosen people.
>
> There is no parallel between such races. Humanity from pole to pole would scout such a comparison. The Hebrew was *originally* free; and the charter of his liberty was inspired by his Creator. The Negro was never free; and his bondage in Africa was simply duplicated in a milder form when he was imported here . . . The judicious in all the earth agree that to proclaim the African equal to the surrounding races, would be a farce which would lead the civilized conservatism of the world to denounce the outrage . . .
>
> Alas, that the holy name and fame of the Prophet Moses should be desecrated by a comparison with the quixotic achievements of President Lincoln![68]

The *Record,* in typical Democratic fashion, revealed no sympathy with the Administration's program of emancipation or with its hopes for the Negro. Lincoln might just as well have abolished the institution of monarchy throughout Europe, it said, as proclaim the emancipation of slaves in the very parts of the South which were not under Union control.[69] It objected to every step taken for the welfare of the Negro with sarcastic comments to the effect that whites would soon have to disguise themselves as colored men to obtain favors from the government.[70] The *Record* had no faith in the ability of the Negro to take his place in the ranks of the civilized. Those who said that he would do as well as the Jew were blind to the facts. Compare the achievements of Jews in the arts and sciences even under the most oppressive regimes of Europe with the failure of freed Negroes in the North to demonstrate any potentialities whatever, said the *Record,* and it would be clear that the Negro did not deserve freedom.[71]

At the very beginning of the slavery agitation, one of the most respected rabbis in America, Max Lilienthal of Cincinnati, had agreed with most of his colleagues that the abolitionists were incendiary radicals who were bringing the nation to the brink of disaster. However much he believed that slavery was an immoral institution, he was willing to defend the right of the Southern states to determine their own economic system. But once the war broke out, he threw all his strength on the side of Lincoln and the Union cause, confident that it was right and just to drive back "the surging waves of the ocean of rebellion" for the sake of the Union.[72]

Lithographs of Lilienthal, a very popular rabbi, had been sold all over the country. One of these was returned to him, shortly after his declaration of allegiance to the Union, with a message scrawled across its face:

Sir:

Since you have discarded the Lord and taken up the Sword in defense of a Negro government, your picture that has occupied a place in our Southern home, we return herewith, that you may present it to your *Black Friends,* as it will not be permitted in our dwelling. Your veneration for the Star Spangled Banner is, I presume, in your pocket, like all other demagogues who left their country for their country's good. I shall be engaged actively in the field and should be happy to rid Israel of the disgrace of your life. Be assured that we have memories; our friends we shall not forget. Should you ever desire to cultivate any acquaintance with me, I affix my name and residence, and you may find someone in your place who can inform you who I am.

Jacob A. Cohen,
New Orleans, La., C.S.A.[73]

How wrong Jacob Cohen was to regard Lilienthal as an abolitionist was demonstrated in his Victory Sermon, delivered on April 14, 1865, in which he publicly apologized for not having been anti-slavery until Lincoln issued the Emancipation Proclamation! He confessed his shame that he had been willing to defend the slave property of the Southern states, and that he had been wanting in the moral courage to denounce "the scourge of slavery." He realized now, he said, that the abolitionists were the heroes of the age: "Right must be right, whatever may be the consequences." All the credit for having "freed [the country] from the ever-lasting blemish of slavery" was due to the abolitionists who had risked reputation, honor, and security, for a moral principle.

**v**

If the rabbis of the North were in such thorough disagreement about the Jewish approach to slavery and abolitionism, it is not surprising to find that their Southern colleagues gave complete support to the slave system. At least one of them, George Jacobs of Richmond, employed slaves in his own home without feeling that he was acting contrary to the dictates of Judaism. He was no Simon Legree, of course; in fact, long after the Negroes had been freed, a former slave woman continued to cling to his family, following them to Philadelphia where the Rev. Jacobs accepted a pulpit. She continued to serve them until old age forced her retirement.[74]

The Rev. J. M. Michelbacher of Richmond appears to have been completely convinced of the justice of Negro slavery, judging from his only war-time sermon to be preserved. In a lengthy prayer summoning God to the assistance of the Confederacy in an hour of danger, he revealed his belief that slavery was ordained of God:

The man servants and maid servants Thou has given unto us, that we may be merciful to them in righteousness and bear rule over them, the enemy are attempting to seduce, that they, too, may turn against us, whom Thou has appointed over them as instructors in Thy wise dispensation . . . Behold, O God, [our enemies] invite our man-servants to insurrection, and they place weapons of death and the fire of desolation in their hands that we may become an easy prey unto them; they beguile them from the path of duty that they may waylay their masters, to assassinate and to slay the men, women and children of the people that trust only in Thee. In this wicked thought, let them be frustrated, and cause them to fall into the pit of destruction, which in the abomination of their evil intents they digged out for us, our brothers and sisters, our wives and our children.[75]

Michelbacher was voicing the fears of most Southerners in this prayer, unjustified fears that the Union would inspire the slaves to savage destruction.

## VI

It is important to note that, with the exception of the activities of the two abolitionist rabbis, David Einhorn and Bernard Felsenthal, and of a few isolated editorials on abolitionism and the Fugitive Slave Law in *The Asmonean*[76] in 1850–51, the discussion of slavery among the rabbis did not begin until late 1860, when the fate of the nation had already been fixed, and public opinion, by and large, already formulated.[77] This would indicate that the rabbis, with the exceptions already noted, were followers, rather than leaders, in political thought, and that they were not prepared to discuss the most burning issue of the day until it was already tearing the Union apart. As immigrants new to the nation's problems and as spiritual leaders of a minority faith, then, they were, for the most part, wary of political activity.

Once they felt it essential to commit themselves, however, they adopted no single political formula, but, to the contrary, all the varieties of political thought then current on the national scene. Personal background and environment, rather than Jewish teachings, determined their views; their version of Judaism was cut to fit the pattern of the conclusions which they reached independently. As with the Christian denominations, so with Judaism; religious ideals and principles were interpreted in widely disparate ways when a crucial issue faced the entire nation.

Yet another observation is necessary. The division of the United States into two warring fragments had been foreshadowed long before 1861 by the violent sectional strife in Christian denominational conventions, conferences and assemblies. As early as 1845, the Southern Baptists had seceded from their national convention over the issue of slavery. In 1854, after eleven days of heated debate, the Annual Methodist General Conference ordered a slave-holding Methodist bishop to dispose of his slaves; the Southerners left the Methodist fold the following year. Schism along sectional lines took another form in the Presbyterian ranks when the New School group, including most of the abolitionists, withdrew from the national synod in 1857. The inability of Southerners and Northerners to adjust their differences within a religious framework concretized and perhaps even deepened the nation's dilemma.[78]

Such a split did not occur among the Jews. There *were* national Jewish bodies, although they were not in the least comparable to the Protestant denominational organizations. The Independent Order of B'nai B'rith and other fraternal groups appear to have ignored the South-North turmoil in the pre-war years, tolerated the enforced separation of the war years, and continued as before once the war had been ended; indeed, in 1866, the Memphis Lodge of B'nai B'rith urged that the annual district convention be held in that Southern city because "it would tend greatly to the extension of our beloved Order in the South."[79] The Board of Delegates of American Israelites discussed only Jewish subjects during its few pre-war years, and hardly even met during the period of the war. It was a weak, incomplete organization, altogether, but its leaders were moderates who would not for an instant have injected politics into its proceedings. Einhorn and Felsenthal might have attempted to do so, but they were among its more forceful opponents. There was actually, then, no attempt to divide the few nation-wide organizations along sectional lines on the basis of the slave question, nor on the issue of war either, although, as we shall see, certain rabbis did take an active political role when the military phase of the Civil War followed hard upon the heels of the propaganda phase.

NOTES

1. *Annual Report of the American and Foreign Anti-Slavery Society*, pp. 114–5.

2. E. Donnan, *Documents Illustrative of the History of the Slave Trade to America*, III, 21 ff., cited by A. V. Goodman, *American Overture*, p. 50.

3. For the statement that the largest house for the sale of slaves in Richmond was owned by Jews, see Hermann Schuricht, *History of the German Element in Virginia*, II, pp. 92–3.

4. See M. Vaxer, "Haym M. Solomon Frees His Slave," pp. 447–8, for the text of one indenture. Schappes, *A Documentary History of the Jews in the United States*, pp. 118 *passim*, lists a sizable number of Jews who freed their slaves under the auspices of this Society.

5. Isaac Goldberg, *Major Noah*, pp. 251–2, 265–8.

6. M. J. Kohler, "The Jews and the American Anti-Slavery Movement," pp. 152–3, gives the details of Pinner's abolitionist activities, as well as much interesting data about other Jews who participated in the abolitionist movement.

7. See R. D. Meade, *Judah P. Benjamin, Confederate Statesman*, pp. 100–3.

8. Yulee letter to *East Floridian* reprinted in *St. Augustine Examiner*, Nov. 17, 1860.

9. J. A. Wax, "Isidor Bush, American Patriot and Abolitionist."

10. Kohler, *op. cit.*, p. 152.

11. A facsimile of a broadside of a sale of slaves by Moses, dated Nov. 14, 1859, was printed in Charles F. Heartman, *Americana Catalogue* (1947), p. 145. The word "Negro" has been capitalized here and in subsequent citations, in keeping with current practice.

12. Letters, Kakeles to Smith, Nov. 13, 1850, and Jan. 26, 1851, Numbers 447 and 481 of the Gerrit Smith Papers.

13. Leon Hühner, *Judah Touro*, p. 69.

14. Gustav Pollak, *Michael Heilprin and His Sons*, pp. 169–70.

15. Morris J. Raphall, *The Bible View of Slavery*, reprinted in E. M. F. Mielziner, *Moses Mielziner 1823–1903*, pp. 212–24. Mrs. Mielziner performed a genuine service by reprinting this controversial sermon together with three other items bearing upon the subject, to be referred to below, in her volume on her father-in-law.

16. Raphall, *op. cit.*, pp. 27–8; Mielziner, *op. cit.*, p. 219.

17. *Ibid.*

18. Raphall, *op. cit.*, pp. 37–8; Mielziner, *op. cit.*, p. 223.

19. Raphall, *op. cit.*, p. 30; Mielziner, *op. cit.*, p. 220. See Schappes, *op. cit.*, p. 683, for the intriguing discovery that Raphall was made an honorary member of the American Society for Promoting National Unity, a group of pro-slavery Northerners and Southerners, including in their number the Reverends George Jacobs, James Gutheim and J. Blumenthal.

20. For text and comment, see *New York Tribune,* Jan. 5, 14, 18, 22, 1861; *New York Daily News,* Jan. 5; *New York Herald,* Jan. 5, 1861.

21. *Richmond Daily Dispatch,* Jan. 7, 1861.

22. L. G. Tyler (ed.), *Encyclopedia of Virginia Biography,* II, p. 52.

23. *Richmond Daily Dispatch,* Jan. 29, 1861.

24. *Memphis Daily Appeal,* Jan. 23, 1861.

25. Quoted *ibid.,* May 12, 1861.

26. *New York Tribune,* Jan. 15, 1861, reprinted in Mielziner, *op. cit.*, pp. 224–34. For various answers to Raphall by non-Jews, see Schappes, *op. cit.*, pp. 685–7. Most effective of all, perhaps, were the lines of a poem written by R. S. H. for *The Independent* and entitled "Rabbi Raphall":

He that unto thy fathers freedom gave—
Hath he not taught thee pity for the slave?

Reprinted in Schappes, *ibid.*

27. Pollack, *op. cit.*, pp. 3–9.

28. Mielziner, *op. cit.*, pp. 224–5.

29. *Ibid.*, pp. 21–23; treatise reprinted pp. 64–103.

30. G. Gottheil, *Moses Versus Slavery: Being Two Discourses on the Slave Question.*

31. *Ibid.*, p. 4.

32. *Sinai,* I, No. 9, pp. 258–9, Oct. 1856; No. 11, pp. 353–9, Dec., 1856; II, No. 6, pp. 599–601, July, 1857; see also VII, No. 7, pp. 183–92, Aug. 1862.

33. *Sinai,* VI, No. 1, pp. 2–20, Feb., 1861; No. 2, pp. 45–50, 60–1, Mar., 1861; No. 3, pp. 99–100, Apr., 1861. The first article is reprinted in Mielziner, *op. cit.*, pp. 234–50.

34. Mielziner, *op. cit.*, p. 241.

35. *Ibid.*, p. 250.

36. David Einhorn, *War With Amalek,* pp. 4–5.

37. *Ibid.*, p. 4.

38. *Sinai,* I, No. 9, pp. 258–9, Oct. 1856; VII, No. 7, pp. 207–9, Aug. 1861.

39. *Sinai,* VII, No. 5, pp. 135–42, June, 1861; *Isr,* VII, No. 48, p. 382, May 31, 1861.

40. *Sinai,* VII, No. 5, p. 140, June, 1861.

41. Letter, Einhorn to R. Oppenheimer, Aug. 13, 1861, Marcus Collection.

42. *Sinai,* VII, No. 10, p. 319, Dec., 1862; letter, Einhorn to Felsenthal, Sept. 3, 1862, in AJHS Library.

43. Letter, Felsenthal to M. J. Kohler, Oct. 25, 1901, American Jewish Archives.

44. Emma Felsenthal, *Bernhard Felsenthal, Teacher in Israel,* p. 23.

45. *Ibid.*, pp. 33–4.

46. Reprinted from the *Chicago Republican* in *HL,* VII, No. 11, p. 1, Dec. 22, 1865.

47. *Sinai,* VI, No. 7, p. 208, Aug. 1861.

48. Felsenthal, "The Jews and Slavery," letter to *Illinois Staatszeitung,* June 6, 1862, reprinted in *Sinai,* VII, No. 6, pp. 158–63, July, 1862; also *HL,* VI, No. 25, p. 1, Sept. 8, 1865. The German-language abolitionist press made frequent anti-Jewish comments about Jews who supported the Confederacy. Felsenthal sought to defend his people, recognizing that the attacks were not realistic discussions of the issue, but were motivated by hostility to the Jews brought from Germany. Isaac M. Wise understood this thoroughly, and delivered himself of some blistering rebuttals to Felsenthal's defense as well as the German attacks, in *Isr.,* IX, No. 4, pp. 3–4, July 25, 1862. The specialist in immigrant adjustment to life in the United States will be interested in comparing the political affiliation and activities of German non-Jews and Jews during this period. The Germans were much more a compact, unified body, than were the Jews.

See Ella Lonn's excellent study, *Foreigners in the Confederacy,* for material on German refusal to support the Confederacy, and on the strong prejudice against Germans which existed in the South.

49. *Mess.*, IX, No. 17, p. 133, May 3, 1861. Julius Eckman's San Francisco *Weekly Gleaner* disagreed with the *Messenger's* "ungenerous" attitude towards Einhorn and told its readers that Einhorn was "a martyr." *Mess.*, X, No. 1, p. 5, July 12, 1861.

50. *Mess.*, IX, No. 3, p. 21, Jan. 18, 1861; No. 4, p. 28, Jan. 25; No. 5, p. 37, Feb. 1. The editors were not entirely consistent. On the same day that Raphall had delivered his sermon, *Mess.* published an article by one of its regular contributors, "Judaeus," completely siding with the South:

> . . . No matter how patriotic and unpartisan Mr. Lincoln may be, the mass of the Southern people, relying on the statements of their political leaders, believe him to be an uncompromising abolitionist . . . Northern men must leave their Southern brethren to regulate their own internal concerns . . . It was designed [in the Constitution] that wherever slavery existed, it should be protected and not disturbed . . . [Abolitionism] is the primary cause of the present dissatisfaction at the South. The interference of abolitionists was entirely uncalled for . . . That the country will pass safely through the present ordeal, I am confident . . . (*Mess.*, IX, No. 1, p. 2, Jan. 4, 1861).

51. *Mess.*, XIV, No. 13, pp. 108–9, Oct. 9, 1863.

52. *Mess.*, XVII, No. 5, p. 36, Feb. 3, 1865; XIX, No. 4, p. 1, Jan. 26, 1866; No. 5, p. 1, Feb. 2. The editors of the paper had changed their tune by the end of the war, and printed, every week, a digest of national news in which the editorial policy was consistently conservative and anti-vindictive. One cannot help feeling that S. M. and Myer Isaacs were afraid to take an editorial stand in the pre-war months, rather than convinced that they should not.

53. *Occ.*, XVII, No. 43, p. 259, Jan. 17, 1861; No. 44, p. 268, Jan. 24; No. 45, p. 274, Jan. 31. It was somewhat typical of Leeser's cast of mind that, in one breath, he should say he will not take a public stand, and in the next reveal his substantial agreement with Raphall by differing with him on minor points.

54. *Occ.*, XVIII, No. 33, p. 197, Nov. 8, 1860. For Frederick Law Olmsted's comments on this problem, see Chapter 7, Note 132, of the present work.

55. See the writer's essay on "Isaac Mayer Wise On the Civil War," for a fuller discussion of the subject.

56. *Isr.*, VII, No. 22, p. 173, Nov. 30, 1860; No. 24, p. 188, Dec. 14; No. 26, p. 205, Dec. 23; No. 31, p. 244, Feb. 1, 1861; No. 37, p. 292, Mar. 15; No. 48, p. 381, May 31; VIII, No. 16, p. 124, Oct. 18; No. 30, p. 236, Jan. 24, 1862. Lincoln agreed, at least in part, with Wise's judgement of the role of the clergymen. He said, to a visitor in 1863, "Sir . . . the parsons and the women made this war," D. Barbee, "President Lincoln and Doctor Gurley," p. 11.

The degree to which misinformation about the Jews found its way into print was indicated by an editorial in the *Memphis Argus,* in March, 1861, accusing Wise of being an abolitionist! "This paper," said the *Argus,* "ostensibly devoted to the religious needs of the editor's Israelitish brethren is, in truth, little more than a Jewified repeater of the doctrines of Beecher & Co. The editor . . . has . . . deduced two prominent facts: First, that the nigger is superior to the white race, even 'the chosen race' of God, which He once held in bondage, and secondly, that the abolition of slavery is as much enjoined by Moses as by Theodore Parker." Wise was as likely to be anti-slavery as the *Argus* itself. How it came to print such nonsense must remain a mystery. *Isr.*, VII, No. 40, p. 318, Apr. 5, 1861.

57. *Isr.*, VII, No. 26, p. 205, Dec. 28, 1860.

58. *Isr.*, VII, No. 29, p. 230, Jan. 18, 1861; XIV, No. 52, p. 4, July 3, 1868. M.J. Kohler in his essay on "Jews and the American Anti-Slavery Movement," p. 150, and Philip S. Foner in *The Jews in American History, 1654–1865,* p. 60, both state erroneously that Wise endorsed Raphall's sermon. As late as 1897, Wise himself, still alive, felt impelled to print a formal denial that he "shared the opinion of Dr. Raphall . . . that slavery was a divine institution, sanctioned by the Old Testament Scriptures, or that there is on record one paragraph to show that the said Isaac M. Wise ever was a pro-slavery man or favored the institution of slavery at any time." *Isr.*, LXVIII, No. 52, p. 4, June 24, 1897, in answer to charges by the *London Jewish Chronicle.*

59. *Isr.,* XI, No. 20, p. 156, Nov. 11, 1864, to No. 26, p. 204, Dec. 23. The series is entitled "On the Provisional Portion of the Mosaic Code, with Special Reference to Polygamy and Slavery." Around the same time, Lewis N. Dembitz, one of Wise's Louisville friends and supporters, published an article "On Slavery and Polygamy Tolerated by the Bible," in one of the Louisville newspapers. Its conclusions were similar to Wise's. *Isr.,* XI, No. 19, pp. 148–9, Nov. 4, 1864.

60. *Isr.,* XI, No. 26, p. 204, Dec. 23, 1864.

61. *Isr.,* XI, No. 25, p. 196, Dec. 16, 1864.

62. See Korn, *op. cit.,* pp. 639–40.

63. *Isr.,* X, No. 5, p. 36, July 31, 1863.

64. *Indianapolis Hebrew Congregation Trustees Minute Book,* May 3, 1863, called to the writer's attention by Rabbi Morris M. Feuerlicht of Indianapolis.

65. *Occ.,* XVIII, No. 44, pp. 267–8, Jan. 24, 1861.

66. *Isr.,* VII, No. 38, p. 301, Mar. 22, 1861; VIII, No. 35, p. 278, Feb. 28, 1862. The Rev. A. Gunzberg of Rochester was another rabbi who was convinced that the Jews were a peculiar blind spot in the liberal thinking of the abolitionists and so he wrote in a letter to G. F. Train, referring to "high standing politicians who are very zealous for the half-civilized Negro, [but] so illiberal against our nation." *Isr.,* XI, No. 46, p. 364, May 12, 1865; No. 48, p. 381, May 26; No. 49, p. 388, June 2, 1865.

67. *JR,* I, No. 18, p. 2, Jan. 9, 1863.

68. *JR,* I, No. 20, p. 2, Jan. 23, 1863.

69. *Ibid.*

70. *JR,* No. 21, p. 2, Jan. 30, 1863; No. 22, p. 2, Feb. 6.

71. *JR,* VI, No. 2, p. 2, Mar. 24, 1865. Benjamin Szold was one rabbi who disagreed with the *Record.* After Maryland freed her slaves, H. L. Bond and others organized "The Baltimore Association for the Educational and Moral Improvement of the Colored People." A letter was sent to the ministers asking for their support, because the sponsors felt it was a project which should appeal to "every Christian man's charity." It did not; many ministers did not answer; others wrote bitter attacks against the society. Rabbi Szold mailed fifty dollars to the Association, noting that it appealed to his "*Jewish* charity." His note made so forceful an impression on the officers that they elected him to their Board. H. L. Bond, "Dr. Szold and Timbuctoo."

72. Lilienthal's Victory Sermon, printed in *Isr.,* XI, No. 44, pp. 349–350, Apr. 28, 1865, a profoundly revealing expression of Lilienthal's personal opinions.

73. Sophie Lilienthal, *The Lilienthal Family Record,* pp. 56–7.

74. Receipts for payment of slave rental fees in George Jacobs Scrapbook; information supplied by Miss Rebecca Jacobs.

75. Sermon printed in *JR,* II, No. 13, p. 1, June 5, 1863. The *Record's* editor found it difficult to understand how Michelbacher could be so loyal to the Confederacy. Isaac M. Wise had little to say about the sermon except that it was "a partisan rigamarole dictated by some partisan stump speaker," but criticised the *Record* for saying Michelbacher was a rabbi:

> . . . "The Rev. Rabbi Michelbacher" never was and is not now a rabbi, never made any studies to this end, never received any such title of any authorized person or persons, and to the best of our knowledge never claimed any such title . . . Mr. Michelbacher could as easy write a work on astronomy as he writes a sermon. He can do neither. He can sing and chant . . . (*Isr.,* IX, No. 50, p. 394, June 19, 1863).

76. There had been one pardonable error in the 1853 report of the Anti-Slavery Society. Its officers could hardly have been expected to read every issue of the Jewish periodicals. Robert Lyon's *Asmonean* had already committed itself to a pro-slavery position in 1850–1, by defending the wisdom of the Fugitive Slave Law, (*Asm.,* III, No. 1, p. 6, Jan. 10, 1851; IV, No. 12, p. 92, Oct. 12, 1851) and by registering itself against the abolitionist crusade. Lyon felt that England was responsible for fostering the anti-slavery movement in order to weaken the young republic. He was fearful of the results of the agitation for emancipation,

warning his readers that events in Jamaica and Haiti foreshadowed what would occur in the United States, if the Negroes were to be given their freedom. Lyon adopted that line of reasoning which regarded the slaves as property, and therefore inviolate:

> Let our citizens, one and all, resolve this day, to put down Abolitionism, in whatever shape or form it may present itself, to discountenance it, by whomsoever its principles may be advocated, and to crush out at once and forever this attempt to plunder our Southern citizens of their property . . . Once more, Down with Abolitionism! Let us stand by the Union, and nothing but the Union. (*Asm.,* IV, No. 11, p. 88, July 4, 1851.)

Although Lyon had said nothing about Judaism, the very fact that he had printed such sentiments in a professedly Jewish newspaper subjected him to abolitionist rebuttal. The *Christian Freeman,* edited by the Rev. Sylvanus Cobb of Boston, thought it ill became Jews to favor slavery:

> Well done, Mr. Israelite . . . Had not our government better make slaves of you and all your people we can catch? For this we might plead some sanction from the word of God, which declares that you shall be trodden underfoot of all nations! Jehovah never said this of Africans. (*Asm.,* IV, No. 13, p. 104, July 18, 1851.)

Not in the least disconcerted, Lyon turned tables and accused Cobb of being a poor Christian, thus to threaten the Jews with slavery. The Bible, said he, did not teach abolition, but respect for property!

77. The only congregational action on record was the adoption by the Beth Elohim Congregation of Charleston, S. C., of a provision in its 1820 constitution that all duly converted proselytes be accepted as members of the Congregation "provided he, she, or they are not people of color." B. Elzas, *The Jews of South Carolina,* p. 153.

78. W. W. Sweet, *The Story of Religions in America,* pp. 412–47. See also C. B. Staiger, "Abolitionism and the Presbyterian Schism of 1837–1838."

79. *Report of the Proceedings of the Thirteenth Annual Meeting of District Grand Lodge No. 2, Independent Order of B'nai B'rith, Held in Cincinnati Ohio, on July 9, 1865, and Following Days,* pp. 6, 20.

# Part 4 **From Emancipation to the Great Depression**

Eastern Europeans immigrated to the United States in large numbers beginning in the 1870s and 1880s and for the first time there were occasions for significant contacts between Jews and African Americans, as large numbers of both groups migrated to the cities of the Midwest and East with the hope of making a better life. Most discussions of this period focus on the urban relations of the two groups, but those are not the whole story, and we begin this section in the South.

We open with an account of the lynching of a Russian Jew and his black clerk in Franklin, Tennessee, in the years shortly after the Civil War and follow with Louis Schmier's family reminiscence of a Russian Jewish peddler and his black customers. Philip S. Foner's essay then examines black-Jewish relations in view of the federal government's attention to anti-Semitism in Europe and its indifference to lynchings in the South. Three pieces on Atlanta follow Foner's chapter. The first, by Steven Hertzberg, focuses on urban interactions. Chapters by Eugene Levy and Leonard Dinnerstein consider the complex responses of both communities to the trial and lynching of Leo Frank, which made headlines between 1913 and 1915. Herbert Aptheker's chapter comparing two editions of W.E.B. Du Bois's *Souls of Black Folks* throws an interesting light on Du Bois's response to criticisms that some passages could be read as anti-Semitic. The last of the southern pieces in this section, "Booker T. Washington's Discovery of Jews" by Louis R. Harlan, discusses Washington's attitude toward Jews.

With the accounts by Jessie Fortune and David Hellwig, we turn our attention to the North and to blacks' perspectives on their Jewish neighbors. Illustrations of popular sheet music and a brief account of vaudeville by Irving Howe offer a sampling of the stereotypic views some Jews held of blacks and demonstrate a willingness to draw upon these stereotypes in the emerging economy of show business.

This section closes with David Lewis's analysis of African American and Jewish political elites at a time when both groups were developing strategies for assimilation that would take into account the Eastern European Jewish immigrants and the black migrants from the rural South.

### FURTHER REFERENCES

For further accounts of blacks and Jews in the South during this period, see Mark K. Bauman and Berkley Kalin, *The Quiet Voices: Southern Rabbis and Black Civil Rights, 1880s to 1990s* (1997) and Leonard Dinnerstein and Mary Dale Palsson, *Jews in the South* (1973), which includes a bibliographical essay. For three overviews of the relationship between blacks and immigrant Jews beginning in the 1870s, see David J. Hellwig's dissertation, "The Afro-American and the Immigrant, 1880–1930: A Study in Black

Social Thought" (1973); Stanley Lieberson's *A Piece of the Pie: Blacks and White Immigrants since 1880* (1980); and Arnold Shankman's *Ambivalent Friends: Afro-Americans View the Immigrant* (1982). Shankman has also written "Brothers across the Sea: Afro-Americans on the Persecution of Russian Jews, 1881–1917" (1975).

Nancy Maclean, in "The Leo Frank Case Reconsidered: Gender and Sexual Politics in the Making of Reactionary Populism" (1991), presents a careful reinterpretation of the factors at play in that case and places the black-Jewish tensions embedded in it within the context of class, gender, and politics.

Hasia Diner, *In the Almost Promised Land: American Jews and Blacks, 1915–1935* (1977), and V. P. Franklin et al., *African Americans and Jews in the Twentieth Century: Studies in Convergence and Conflict* (1998), both deal with early-twentieth-century issues, which Joseph R. Washington Jr., *Jews in Black Perspectives: A Dialogue* (1984), continues. Other general accounts of interaction in the cities of the North from the turn of the century to the 1930s can be found in Lenora E. Berson, *The Negroes and the Jews* (1971); in chapters on early black-Jewish relations and in the 1920s in Murray Friedman, *What Went Wrong? The Creation and Collapse of the Black-Jewish Alliance* (1995); in William M. Phillips Jr., "The Nadir of Injustice and Inequality: 1890–1919," in *An Unillustrious Alliance: The African American and Jewish American Communities* (1991); and in chapters by Jason H. Silverman, Hasia R. Diner, Jonathan Kaufman, and Nancy J. Weiss, all available in Jack Salzman and Cornel West's collection, *Struggles in the Promised Land* (1997).

# Document concerning Lynching

## DOUBLE-LYNCHING OF A JEW AND A NEGRO

*News-story, "The Franklin, Tenn., Double Murder,"* The Israelite, *Cincinnati, Ohio, August 28, 1868*[1]

[It was in Tennessee that the Ku Klux Klan was first organized in 1866, to become an instrument for the terrorizing of Negro and white supporters of the Radical Reconstruction government in the state, to keep the enfranchised Negroes away from the polls, and to restore economic and political power to the class that had led Tennessee into the Confederacy.[2] Disfranchised former Confederate Army generals were its state-wide leaders.

In the town of Franklin, the seat of Williamson county in Central Tennessee, S. A. Bierfield,[3] a young Russian Jew operating a dry-goods store, was known as a Radical Republican. He was friendly with the Negro population, employed a Negro as a clerk, and attracted a good number of Negroes as customers.[4] With the presidential elections approaching, the Klan terror intensified in the spring and summer of 1868, and a special session of the State Legislature convened on July 27 to cope with the problem by reconstituting an armed militia of Negro and white volunteers. On the night of August 15th, while Bierfield and his clerk, Lawrence Bowman, and a second Negro named Henry Morton were eating watermelon in the store, a masked lynch-mob broke in, and only Henry Morton escaped alive, to tell his story later to an official investigator.

Reports of the outrage appeared not only in the Tennessee press, but in the New York *Times* (front-page) as well as in newspapers in Philadelphia, Cincinnati, and elsewhere. After carrying the account printed below, *The Israelite* took no further notice of the event. In a few years, the Klan and the elements it represented succeeded in re-establishing the oppression of the Negro through minority rule.]

The deliberate and fiendish murder of Mr. Bierfeld, an Israelite, and a gentleman of

Morris U. Schappes is editor of *Jewish Currents.*
Reprinted from *A Documentary History of the Jews in the United States, 1654–1875,* ed. Morris U. Schappes, preface by Joshua Bloch, Director, Jewish Division, New York Public Library, New York (New York: Citadel Press, 1950), 515–17. Copyright © 1950, 1971 by Morris U. Schappes. Reprinted by permission of Morris U. Schappes.

good standing and character, as also the murder at about the same time a Negro in Bierfeld's [sic] employ, has been reported a week ago by telegraph, but so vaguely, that we refrained from mentioning the dark affair until the receipt of a more reliable account. This we find in the Nashville *Republican* of the 19th inst., sent us by a friend, and we reproduce the same below. The hands of the Ku Klux are, doubtless, red with guilt in the sad premises, and their real grounds consisted of but the fact, that Bierfeld was an intelligent advocate of the present reconstruction policy of Congress,[5] and a friend to the freedmen of his neighborhood, among whom—he being a merchant—he commanded quite a trade, and perhaps found it expedient to keep one from among their number in his employ, who shared the fate of his employer at the same hands.

The scarce less detestable creatures who apologized for the hounds in human guise on the surmise that Bierfeld was accessory to the murder of a young man a few days previous,[6] are liars inferentially we are safe to say, since no member of the Jewish race in this country, if in the world, at the present day would be accessory to a foul murder, and that, too, in a locality where he lives in peace, and prospers as a merchant. We let the aforesaid journal speak, display lines and all:

TERRIBLE MURDERS.

Two Men Killed in Franklin by a Lot of Armed Horsemen.

The *Press and Times*[7] of a late issue contains the following: At eleven or twelve o'clock on Saturday night, as great crowds of people were going to their homes after leaving Robinson's circus, a troop of horsemen dashed into town, yelling frightfully, and telling the crowd which they passed to get into their houses as quickly as possible. In a few moments every one was in doors, and a dead silence reigned around, save when heavy sounds were borne on the night from the dry-goods store of one Bierfeld, an Israelite, who carried on a little business in that line, and had a Negro man employed selling goods for him. The horsemen were breaking in his house. They dragged the Israelite out. They were about to hang him when he escaped and ran some hundred yards away from his house and took refuge in a livery stable. His enemies were upon him immediately, pistol in hand. They shot four balls into him, from the effects of which he died almost instantly. The colored man remained in the store, where they found and shot him through the body. He died yesterday morning.[8]

The cause of the intense enmity which could ripen into so fearful a crime is not definitely known. Our informants, Dr. Cliffe and N. J. Nichol, said it was thought that Bierfeld had something to do with the murder of young Ezell, some two or three weeks ago. He is the same man that was driven out of Pulaski[9] some months since by the same sort of fellows.

There is no apparent cause for the murder of the colored man. When the fiendish outrage had been committed, the squad of troopers rode furiously out of town, whooping and hallooing frightfully.

*

Since the above was in type, we have received the following statement from a gentleman from Franklin:

"On Saturday night, the 15th inst., about eleven o'clock, Mr. Bierfeld, an Israelite, who was engaged in trading, fled from his store scared by men in disguise who had entered his place of business and attempted to conceal himself in Mr. Bostick's stable, but was pursued by the said disguised parties, and violently and forcibly dragged into the streets. While pleading for his life, and begging them to spare him for his mother's sake, he was shot four times in the breast. This happened in the streets of Franklin, near Mr. Briggs' store. If any one offered to intercede for him, it is not known. The parties who say they know the reason why he was killed by the men in disguise, alledge [sic] that he was in some way connected with the killing of Ezell, and that the foul deed was done in retaliation. Six or eight witnesses will testify that Mr. Bierfeld, on the night of the killing of Ezell, slept in the house of Mr. Colby. The good citizens condemn the atrocious act, while others attempt to justify the crime by saying that it was done in retaliation. Mr. Bierfeld was an active and prominent Republican, having considerable influence with the colored people."

Our informant says that was his only crime. A clerk of Mr. Bierfeld, whose name we can not learn, was killed at the same time, and by the same parties. Mr. Bierfeld's body was brought to Nashville[10] yesterday for interment.

NOTES

1. *The Israelite*, XV, No. 8, August 28, 1868, p. 6, cols. 2–3. No mention of this incident was made in *The Jewish Messenger, The Hebrew Leader,* or *The Occident.*

2. James Welch Patton, *Unionism and Reconstruction in Tennessee, 1860–1869,* Chapel Hill, N. C., 1934, pp. 162–163, 171ff.

3. The name also appears variously as Bierstein, Bearfield, and Bierfeld, but it is given fully as S. A. Bierfield in the *New-York Daily Tribune,* August 19, 1868, p. 4, col. 6 and in the official report of the investigation made by George E. Judd, sub-assistant commissioner, stationed in Pulaski, Tenn., of the Freedmen's Bureau, to Brevet Major-General W. P. Carlin (*Senate Journal of the Extra Session of the Thirty-Fifth General Assembly of the State of Tennessee, . . .* Nashville, 1868, pp. 158–160). This report is especially valuable because it incorporates the eye-witness testimony of Henry Morton. Essentially similar accounts, with variations only in details, appeared in the *Tribune,* August 20, 1868, and in *The New-York Times,* August 19, 1868. The *Tribune,* August 28, 1868, reprinted an item from the *Memphis Post* which mentioned the murder of Bierfeld as one of many terroristic acts of southern Democrats.

4. The official report stated "that Mr. Bierfeld was an uncommon good business man . . . and was establishing an unprecedented trade." (*Loc. cit.,* 160.) His friendliness toward the Negro was undoubtedly a factor in this success. Anti-Negro southerners then and to this day resented this democratic approach. Thus Professor E. Merton Coulter says of the Jews in the Reconstruction period, "Sticking to their business and treating the freedman as an important businessman, not eschewing to call him 'Mister,' they secured . . . a great amount of the Negro's trade." (*The South During Reconstruction, 1865–1877,* Louisiana State University, 1947, p. 202.)

5. President Andrew Johnson's weak reconstruction policy, for which he barely later escaped impeachment by one vote, required nothing more of the seceded states than the ratification of the Fourteenth Amendment and the taking of the oath of allegiance to the Union. Tennessee, however, under Radical Republican leadership, had gone further and enfranchised the Negroes. It should be noted that after Union forces occupied most of Tennessee in 1862, eight Negro regiments of soldiers had been raised in that state. (W. E. Burghardt Du Bois, *Black Reconstruction,* New York, 1935, pp. 572, 575; James S. Allen, *Reconstruction, The Battle for Democracy, 1865–1876,* New York, 1937, pp. 40–42.)

6. Late in August, a young man named Ezell had taken part in the kidnaping of a Negro from a Franklin jail and in lynching him, presumably on the charge of "rape." A few days later, Negroes had shot

Ezell. Bierfield, it was claimed, had encouraged the Negroes and even sold them ammunition. (*New-York Daily Tribune,* August 20, 1868.) But the official report by Judd found that a letter published in a Nashville newspaper that was the basis of the allegation had been forged (*loc. cit.,* 159).

7. The *Nashville Daily Press and Times* was a Republican newspaper.

8. The official report states that Bierfield, after shouting that he surrendered, made a break for the stable as soon as he was confronted with the mob; he was then caught, "tortured," and shot with the pistol so close that his clothes and skin were burned. Bowman, the Negro clerk, told the doctor before he died that he had been shot in the street. The investigator complains that the civic authorities made no attempt to get further details from Bowman before he became unconscious. (*Ibid.*)

9. Pulaski, Tenn., fifty miles south of Franklin, was the city in which the Ku Klux Klan had first been organized.

10. Nashville, less than twenty miles from Franklin, was the nearest city that had a Jewish congregation (formed the same year by the merger of two congregations, one Orthodox, the other Reform).

# "For Him the 'Schwartzers' Couldn't Do Enough"

## A Jewish Peddler and His Black Customers Look at Each Other

It was an early Russian spring day in 1884 when William Pearlman returned to his home in Baisagola from a business trip to Seduva.[1] Normally, he arrived with a face full of smiles and pockets brimming with candy. This day, however, there was neither radiance on his face nor jovial tone in his voice nor bulging coat pockets. Instead, he brought the chill of the outside into the house with him as he greeted his family with an unnatural quiet. "Uncle Dave exactly remembered," vividly recalled a niece, "how his father seemed to have aged and acted as if he really didn't want to come into the house. 'From momma's face, you'd think a dybbuk (demon) was with him,' he'd used to say."[2]

Later that evening, when all the children were in bed, Gena Pearlman sat down with her husband to find out what was bothering him. Neither of them knew that David, their eldest son, had gotten out of bed and was listening quietly to the conversation from behind the curtain that acted as a door to his room. What he heard and saw was imprinted indelibly in his memory for decades to come.

After a few weak attempts at evasion, William confirmed Gena's worst fears. With a note of urgency, he told her that while he was in Seduva a sympathetic official had informed him that David could not be protected from military conscription as he had earlier promised. With fear tightening and distorting her youthful face, Gena whispered, "When?" William replied that the authorities would probably come for their sixteen year old son within the next six months. Twenty and thirty years later, Dave Pearlman could still describe in graphic detail the image of his mother giving out a little squeal of horror that she muted as she quickly raised her hands and covered her mouth; of his father sitting at the table, hunched over, defeated, with one arm leaning on the table as his head silently nodded confirmation of his words; and of Gena's hands moving from her mouth to cup her tear-laden eyes as she moved back and forth to a rhythm of sobbing and mournful groans.

With his voice cracking under the emotional strain, William told his wife that the time had arrived for them to make a decision. "What is there to decide? What can we do? It is now in God's hands," she replied. William was not listening. Slowly he put on his glasses and smoothed over some pieces of crumbled paper with his palms. William explained to his curious wife that on the table was lying a letter by Samuel Morris to her brother, Jacob Lazarus, from a "province" in America called Georgia. He went on to explain that while he was in Seduva he had spoken to her brother about David, and that

In 1983, Louis Schmier was professor of American history at Valdosta State College, Georgia.
Originally published in *American Jewish History* 73, no. 1 (1983): 39–55. Copyright © 1983, Johns Hopkins University Press. Reprinted with permission of the Johns Hopkins University Press.

Jacob had given him the letter in the belief that it contained the solution to the situation. Gena interrupted, "Who is this Samuel Morris that we should listen to him?" William calmly told her that Samuel Morris was her cousin, Shmuel Modguilowitz who had gone to America a little over a year earlier. "Samuel Morris!" Gena exclaimed. "Shmuel Modguilowitz is not good enough for him? He is a schlimiel (fool)! Because he goes to some far away place called America and changes his name he should become a messiah for our David?" With a firm "shah" (quiet), William read the letter. It was filled with glowing descriptions of a land overflowing with opportunity, success—and safety. And because, as Samuel had written, he was so prosperous, he urged his parents to send his younger brother, Charles, to him as an "apprentice shopkeeper."

Gena listened and then asked her husband what the letter had to do with their son. William explained that the religious Modguilowitzes were not going to send Charles to a land they had heard was a godless place. Maybe, as Jacob had suggested, if opportunities were that good and Samuel needed a helper badly enough, David could go in his place. At first, Gena was horrified. She refused to accept her husband's proposition. Baisagola was David's ancestral home, she protested, "How can we exile him to this America?" William calmed down his wife. Referring to the new wave of attacks on the Jews that were supported by the government of the new Czar, William responded, "It is good that he should go. There is no place any more for him here in these troubled times. What future is there for the young ones. We are too set in our ways to start all over in a strange land, but David . . ."

"How can we believe Shmuel that America is a land of Canaan," Gena desperately asked. "We must believe," William consolingly parried, "We have no other choice."

After a moment of silence, Gena reluctantly nodded her agreement. With a sullen sigh she said, "Here, there, what's the difference. A goy (Gentile) is a goy no matter where he is. But, at least, if our David is going to be persecuted, he will be better dressed for the occasion."

Dave Pearlman always laughed as he recalled these particular words. Whatever humor he might have found in this scene in later decades, he never could eliminate the sense of tragedy. There was no joy or enthusiasm in his parents' decision. Only a sense of hopelessness permeated their feelings and thoughts as they retired for the night. To these simple village Jews, neither America nor Georgia was a place. Each was a word raised to the heights of a vision out of a sudden desperation. In their own minds, their motives were simple. They were not consciously discussing the complex issues of political freedom, religious rights or the attainment of a higher quality of life. William and Gena wanted only physical safety for their son, even at the cost of tearing their family permanently apart. In their ignorance each had created compensating rationalizations that offered muted relief. "The name of Americus had an especially good sound for my zeyda (grandfather)," explained Fannie Lazarus. "He used to tell me that from the very beginning he believed that Morris fella and believed that there was no safer place for his children in America than in a town like Americus that was named after it. I guess he thought he was getting two for the price of one. And my bubba (grandmother), she didn't know any better either. So, she convinced herself and told others from the very beginning that Georgia had been set up by a bunch of Jews from Georgia Gubernia (province). 'Why else would they use the same name?' she'd always say."[3]

The following morning, William left the house to make the "proper arrangements" for his son's departure. Upon his return, William carefully told Dave of his coming journey. A gnawing sense of fear suddenly gripped the young boy and would not begin to wane until he was in his cousin's embrace on the docks of New York. Dave realized that the previous night's events were not a dream. His parents were exiling him to Americus, Georgia! Dave begged. He protested. He presented his father with schemes for evading the authorities that he had concocted that night. His pleading was of no avail. It was Friday. That was the last Sabbath the Pearlman family celebrated together. "Uncle Dave said that Shabbos they did everything a little more with a little more feeling," explained Louis Lazarus.

Two days later, as Dave stuffed his few belongings into a cloth suitcase, his father put on his ritual robe. In a touching and heart-rending scene, William lifted both his hands above the bowed head of his son and gave his blessing as Isaac had done to Jacob. With tears running down their faces, they hugged knowing they would not see each other again. William pushed his son at arms' distance and, holding his shoulders tightly, said, "Never forget us. Never forget who you are." They sadly nodded to each other; and with a kiss on his mother's forehead and a mournful embrace, Dave was out the door. Waiting for him were his brothers and sisters, his aunts and uncles, his cousins, and his family's friends. The depressing scene was a confusion of lifeless hugs, joyless kisses, whispered benedictions—and tears. Everyone knew, though no one said it, that "their David" was not embarking on an adventurous journey to some paradise about which everyone should be happy. Rather, he was escaping from the pungent odor of terror that was beginning to pollute the air they were all breathing.[4]

As David left the village, he walked backward at a slow and reluctant pace, looking through his swollen eyes at the people huddled around his home, straining to imprint in his mind every detail of what he saw. Then, with a quick kick at the dirt road and a deep inhale, he turned, picked up his pace and headed for Seduva. After a restless night's stay at his uncle's house, Dave was on his way to Memel riding on the back of a merchant's wagon hoping that his father's bribes were large enough that the Russian official would turn his head as he passed by and that the merchant would not turn him into the authorities in Memel. In Memel, more fear enveloped the isolated boy who had never been more than ten miles from Baisagola. Would the arranged bribes be sufficient to secure for him a hiding place aboard a ship bound for Hamburg. In Hamburg, still more fear plagued him about being cheated and robbed before he secured passage to America. In fact, fear was his constant companion. It took a variety of forms: depression, anxiety, uncertainty. It generated a desolate sense of far-reaching displacement and abandonment from which none of his fellow-passengers or friendly crewmen could distract him. Every night as he crossed the Atlantic, he huddled in a dark corner of his bed of wooden boards, succumbing to his overwhelming sense of loneliness, and cried as he tried to understand why his parents had sent him away. " 'America, Georgia, Americus, they all meant the same to me then—Siberia!' That's what Uncle Dave used to tell us," explained his niece. "He never could forget his mother's words about being exiled to here." Only after he had landed in New York and had embraced his cousin did he allow himself to experience any feelings of relief. "On those docks up there, he once told me," explained Sam Kalin, "that leavin' that boat was like Jonah being spitted up on shore after livin' in the fish's innards."[5] A few days later, in Americus, Dave's six thousand mile journey, that had covered the vast expanse of a continent and an ocean, ended. Within hours, however, he quickly was to discover that he also had crossed equally vast chasms of language, culture and religion.

Dave's cousin did not give him a chance to rest. At dawn of the day following their arrival in Americus, Sam awakened the exhausted boy, placed a heavy peddler's backpack filled with notions, fabrics and clothing samples at the foot of his bed, ordered the boy to dress quickly, and said, "Today we sell. If you want to eat, you must learn the business. You didn't come here to sleep."

It did not take long before Dave, laboring under more than a hundred pounds of merchandise, began experiencing pain in his legs, back and shoulders. "Uncle Dave used to kid me," chuckled Sam Kalin, "that at first he would be so hunched over you'd think he was peddling on his hands and knees."[6] Ahead of him, oblivious to Dave's aches, walked Sam—without a pack—throwing bits of advice in Yiddish back over his shoulder to his "apprentice:" Always be honest . . . Show the *goyim* (Gentiles) they can trust you . . . Don't be afraid of them . . . The *goyim* are different here. . . . Let them teach you. . . ." Perhaps the one piece of advice that was most surprising was, "Don't hide being Jewish. It makes them feel good." Why, then, Dave curiously asked Sam did he have to take off his prayer shawl, skull cap and leave them in Americus along with his phylacteries? "Because," Sam answered, "we can't be too Jewish and too different." Sam quickly changed the subject by having Dave repeat after him the English words for the various goods he was carrying and the price for each. At the same time, Sam instructed the boy to take notice of the passing landmarks since he soon would be going on the trail alone.

Dave interrupted his mentor asking innocently if they were walking to his store. "My store is on your back!" Sam boasted, "This is what in America is called a successful business?" Dave disappointingly asked. "Anything that is not near the Czar is a success," Sam philosophized. Continuing with his annoying line of questioning, Dave asked why Sam was not carrying a pack. To this inquiry, Sam abruptly replied, "It is also hard work to teach an ungrateful *mavin* (know-it-all) like you and to make sure we don't get lost." The next grunt from Dave's mouth was not uttered out of pain.

At the first house to which the two peddlers came, Sam stood aside and let Dave go ahead to make his first sale. "Let's see what you have so far learned," Sam said with an impish smile. The boy quietly opened the fence gate tip-toed onto the front porch, looked back at Sam for assurance, tapped lightly on the door half-hoping that no one inside would hear either the knock or his near-whispered and near-unintelligible, "Meestaah Poodeluh." To his dismay, he heard a commotion coming from inside the shack. The door suddenly flew open, yelling children poured out and danced around him yelling, "It's him. It's him," and he unexpectedly found himself looking into the eyes of a large, smiling black woman. The startled boy, never having seen a black person before and momentarily unable to distinguish between her skin and darkened background of the shack's interior, thought he was confronting two bodiless eyes and an empty, floating dress. He stepped back in fright; screamed, "A dybbuk;" and landed flat on his back pinned by the weight of his pack. "And that's how," laughed Louis Lazarus, "he always joked about how he got started, from the ground, up."

Sam looked down at his young apprentice, laughed, and helped him to his feet after unstrapping the pack. By this time, the blacks from the other shacks which Dave had not seen from the road were congregating around the two peddlers. Dave did not know what to make of the scene. The first imagery that made sense of what he saw was that of a demon dance he had heard the superstitious women of Baisagola describe. Terrified, he spit in the air all around him, uttered a *kayn-ahora* to ward off the Evil Eye, and started to turn to run only to be stopped by a smiling Sam who had Dave's arm in a vise-like grip.

As he cautiously followed Sam's instructions and spread the goods in the pack out on the ground, constantly glancing over his shoulder in order not to be surprised by these "dark strange looking" people, occasionally spitting in their direction for good measure, he was equally stunned by what next took place. The blacks said to his cousin in disunion: "Please, Mr. Sam take it out . . . Let us hear them words. . . . Say somethin' holy. . . . Read to us . . ." Sam then took out his prayer book and began praying in Hebrew accompanied by a discordant chorus of "amens" and "hallelulahs." Later, when again on the trail, Sam explained to the puzzled boy, "*Maschugenah goyim* (crazy Gentiles), they buy more if they think you are a personal friend of the prophets." This scene proved to be the rule rather than the exception. "Uncle Dave used to slap his knee and laugh," winked Louis Lazarus, "when he told us about that first trip. 'I was so scared,' he'd say, 'I saw a dybbuk everywhere and came back to Americus drymouthed, spitted out, and without a *kayn-ahora* left in me.' Hell, he once went into a yokel's outhouse and spit down the hole in all that mess thinking that he was being tricked by that fella and was going to be pulled down through the seat."

As the days and weeks passed, however, Dave's reliance on his saliva for protection diminished. The countryside was yielding so many surprises to the bewildered teenager that amazement, not fear, became his companion. He did not expect to find that the farmers, white and black, were a congenial lot. Sam explained that his relationship to them was the result of a trading of services. They were good customers while he was a convenient door-to-door walking general store, a messenger boy, a mailman, a newspaper boy, an area town crier, etc. The gratitude displayed by the farmers in the forms of hospitality and a respect for Jewish ways kept Dave in a state of perpetual shock. He never expected a Gentile to offer a Jew a chair at the dinner table. "His ears popped once," explained Fannie Lazarus, "when one of the farmers asked Sam to say the prayers over the food in Jewish. I remember uncle Dave tellin' us of one farmer who said to his family, 'Now you all listen closely to the real words used by God coming sure enough from one of his chosen people.' There wasn't a dry eye in that place as Sam spoke." This disbelief was only equalled when the farmers would offer the two peddlers a bed in which to sleep overnight and the extent to which the children would fight to decide whose bed would be used.

Nevertheless, however congenial the Gentile farmers seemed to be with Sam, when it came time for Dave to go out on his own, he was so nervous he could not eat or sleep the night before. Rejecting every excuse Dave could offer for not peddling alone, Sam affirmed, "You watched. Now you will earn your keep." Armed with only a sketched out map, Dave reluctantly left Americus. As he walked the dusty road he felt that same sense of exile and isolation he had during his trip to America. Only the experiences of the previous weeks kept his imagination from running wild. To his relief, he found the farmers, especially the black ones, were no less friendly to him than they had been to Sam. The only real difficulty Dave faced was the language. After less than a month in Georgia, Dave's real vocabulary was still limited to the salty language the sailors had taught him in their efforts to pull him out from his doldrums aboard ship; and in spite of a three week "cram course" from Sam, he was still confusing a seaman's profanity with a peddler's mercantile vocabulary. But, it did not matter. The blacks, who constituted the majority of his customers, since Sam kept the "better" white farmers for himself, patiently helped him. Dave would use sign language. The blacks would say the equivalent English word. Dave would shake his head in understanding and repeat the word. When someone wanted to buy an item, he would take out a price list on which Sam had written in Yiddish characters the phoenetical form of the price next to the Yiddish word for that particular item. "More than once," explained his nephew, "those people would have him repeat the price once they got past his accent and have him say the word the right way."

At the end of Dave's first day, a black farmer asked him to stay overnight in his shack and share his family's meager meal. Not realizing he was breaking a regional taboo, Dave accepted. As he went to wash up and say his evening prayers, he wondered about the surprised look on the man's face which had quickly turned into a beaming smile. He did not understand, at the time, the reason for the man's reaction.

Dave never ceased to be amazed at how these impoverished people went out of their way to respect the dietary laws of his faith, at how their respect of him seemed to be proportional to the extent of his religious devotion, and at how willing they were to help him in whatever way they could. Always the dinner table was the classroom. Taking turns, each member of the family would teach Dave the words for the items on the table or would point to items around the shack and have him repeat the English words. At times, they would help him form simple sentences using the words he had memorized. "Uncle Dave used to kid us," smiled Fannie Lazarus, "that after each peddlin' trip he'd come home speakin' like a '*yiddische schwartzer*' (Jewish black)." In return, Dave would teach them simple Hebrew or Yiddish. "He told us," exclaimed Louis Lazarus, "that they used to greet each other in Jewish saying '*shalom*' one to the other. They all got some kick out of it."

Dave returned from that first peddling trip filled with a sense of triumph until Sam's dejected look at the $15.00 which Dave had taken from his coat pocket to show for a week on the trail told the boy he still had a long way before he would master his new trade. "Uncle Dave got a big chuckle," giggled Fannie Lazarus, "when he'd recall how he'd be so excited that them negro people treated him like kin that he'd forget sometimes to sell to them. I guess just not bein' afraid of bein' hurt by a *goy* was enough for him to forget why he was there."

Sam was not as understanding as Dave explained why he had returned with empty pockets and a full pack. "You sell," he reprimanded his apprentice, "not talk." But, Dave was too excited with the fact that he had actually survived a week alone on the trail to have his spirits dampened. As he recounted every moment of his travels, he mentioned in passing that he had stayed overnight in the houses of his black customers. Sam's face suddenly turned ashen white. When Dave innocently asked what was troubling him, Sam excitedly explained that the invitation to spend the night in the home was "their" way of saying "thank you." Nobody, Sam emphasized, expected him to accept. As Sam spoke, Dave began to understand the reason for the black farmer's surprised look as the young boy had entered the shack. "It is forbidden," Sam continued in a loud voice. "You can't associate with them in that way. Sell to them—yes. Take their money—yes. Say 'Good morning'—yes. Shake their hand if you want, but do it all outside." Sam's face began to redden as he yelled at Dave. Did he not notice they had never in three trips entered a black's house? Why did the boy think they had spread their merchandise out on the ground in front of the blacks' shacks while going into the homes of the white farmers to display their wares on the dinner tables? Did he ever see him accepting a sip of water from their wells? Did he not think it a coincidence that there was always an excuse for not staying in a black's shack and that each day's peddling should have ended at the house of a white family?

Dave was confused. If it was acceptable to take their money, he asked Sam, why could they not accept their acts of gratitude? Sam slowly and deliberately explained in a way that would not be misunderstood: "The *schwartzers* here are like we are in Russia. Do you understand? They are the *goyim*'s Jews—outcasts, nothing, dirt!" After regaining his composure, Sam told Dave not to worry any further about the matter. He calmly assured Dave that he had not broken any local convention deliberately. Sam was even willing to accept some of the blame since he had not specifically warned Dave about such matters. At least, he sighed, as long as Dave does not tell anyone else about the trip and stops treating the blacks like "long-lost *mishpoche* (relatives)" nothing will happen. Dave was still bewildered. What could happen, he asked. "We can get beaten up—or worse. There are *goyische* cossacks around here who don't like people doing things like what you done," Sam shot back in a whisper. But, Dave continued, none of the white farmers with whom he had stayed had said anything nasty to him when he had explained to them that the few English words he knew he had learned from the black farmers while staying with them. "You told the *goyim* already what you done?" Sam cried out as he pressed both cheeks of his face together with his hands. Dave always got a kick out of describing how Sam, his face again white with terror, collapsed in a chair, shook his head in frightened disbelief and said tearfully as he peered at the ceiling in a call for help. "How could he be so stupid? I agreed to help him because he was a relative and was in trouble; and for this he returns my charity by ruining my business. Everyone will know. No one will buy. Maybe I should go back to Russia where it is safer."

In desperation, Sam pleaded with Dave to heed his advice. "Maybe it is not too late. We have to do what the *goyim* like. There are so many of them here; and we are alone. There is no one to hide us. There are no potato cellars. There is no one else to sell to. It is worse than in Russia. There, at least we could sell to each other. But here, if they don't like us, they will not buy from us, and then we will starve." Then, changing his tactics, Sam asked, "Is it so bad that they should hate someone else for a change? Let them. It keeps them too busy to bother with us."

"And what makes us better than the *goyim* if we do only watch?" Dave asked quietly. "Is that why I had to leave my family and to come to America—to be a cossack? We did not like that treatment in Russia, why should we like it here if it is used on someone else? If we did not like the *goyim* for what they did to us, why should the *schwartzers* like what is done to them? We should understand them because in this way they are like us. Is it so terrible to want to help those people and be kind to them and treat them like *menschen* (human beings)?"

To this series of bedeviling questions, Sam replied, "I don't want to be better than the *goyim,* only the same—alive and well. If you want to be friendly, be friendly. If you want to be charitable, be charitable. You want to treat them like a *mensch,* treat them like a *mensch.* Do anything that makes you happy and me money. But, do it quietly. I am laying down the law as if your poppa was here. There will be no more of this. You will do as I say or out in the cold you go."

To Sam's consternation, Dave did not refrain from treating his black and white customers equally. As the uniqueness of Dave's actions wore off, however, the blacks responded with a mixture of surprise, fear and caution. "They really didn't know what to make of him. That other fella hadn't treated them no differently than any other yokel," attested Louis Lazarus. "They probably thought at first that it was just another way a white made up to take advantage of them and cheat them." At first, Dave was confused by the reluctance of the blacks to respond to his kindness with open arms. When Dave asked Sam for some advice, Sam jumped on him. "I told you they won't appreciate it. David, the *goyim* say the *schwartzers* are like little children. Kindness is not always the right way to deal with them. Listen to the *goyim.* They belong here. They know more about these people. Let the *goyim* tell you how to handle these people."

Dave rejected Sam's analysis with a huff, "It is easy for you to forget how to feel and what it is like to be hurt and stepped on when you think of yourself as white today and ignore what it was like being a Jew yesterday." With each peddling trip, however, Dave began to realize that the blacks, like him, were living in physical exile, that each of their shacks was a pale of its own. As he improved his English he learned that the blacks were experiencing the same kind of ostracism, exploitation, persecution and fear that had forced him to leave Baisagola. But, they were not the "*goyim*'s Jews." Unlike him, the blacks had no place to go for escape. Their exile was a permanent one, for not only were they living in physical isolation, but they were living in an emotional pale in which they could not find the psychological resources upon which to draw for enduring their humbling way of life. "He never stopped sayin'," reported Louis Lazarus, "'They don't have a Moses or David or Esther or Maccabee to dream about to stop the hurt and to give them strength. They can't believe in themselves like us no matter what the *goyim* say or do. So, they find it hard to believe in others.' "

Dave persisted. At times, he would try to console his black customers with stories of his exodus from Russia and with explanations that the Jews in Russia were treated like them. "Those people would be agog hearin' that whites did to other whites worse than what was done to them, especially to 'holy people' like us. It sure did make them feel better knowing they weren't the only ones treated that way," explained another of Dave's cousins.[7] Eventually, Dave succeeded in overcoming the suspicion and caution of the blacks. Nevertheless, Dave was increasingly frustrated that he could not repay the blacks for their help with little more than kindness. He would become particularly depressed whenever a black family could not afford to purchase an item it needed. Whether the black families could afford to buy from Dave or not, they were grateful for his attitude. "Once they knew he was sincere in his feelings, for him the *schwartzers* couldn't do enough," reported Dave's daughter. "In fact, they couldn't do enough for each other."[8]

Once, in an effort to help his black customers, Dave suggested to Sam that if he would reduce the prices for the black families or allow them to buy on credit the volume of sales would increase. Sam screamed in reaction, "I told you that you could be charitable; so you were charitable. You kept on going into their houses. You kept on eating at their tables. You kept on washing in their tubs and using their outhouses. You even let them try on the samples. But, that is not good enough. Now you want to give away my goods. This time I put my foot down. If they want, they pay!"

One night in early 1885, Dave suddenly found himself in a position to repay his debt of gratitude to his black friends. During a dinner conversation in a large landowner's house, Dave mentioned his empathy for his black customers and how he wished he could help them as they had helped him. Shortly after dinner, the landowner asked Dave if he would be willing to sell to the black hired hands and tenant farmers working his land on credit. Without waiting for Dave to reply, the landowner put his arm around the boy and assured him that he was not being asked to take any financial risks. The landowner promised that every three months he would pay off any outstanding accounts. That way, he continued, Dave would not lose any money and the blacks on his land could purchase what they needed. When Dave meekly pointed out that some of the families would not be able to pay off the debt, the landowner replied that he was in a financial position that he could absorb any losses. Dave then asked the landowner why he had a sudden change of heart about his black laborers. "I figure if you like them," replied the landowner, "they can't be none too bad and that I ought to give them a push."

When Dave presented the scheme to Sam, Sam warned that the idea was a trick. "No one will pay once they have what they want." Even after Dave offered to put up his share of the profits as collateral Sam still hesitated to accept the idea. "Why should a *goy* want to help us and the *schwartzers?*" he asked. Dave had a rebuttal. "They want to help us because it makes them feel good to help one of the 'chosen people.' They want to help the *schwartzers* because maybe you are wrong about the *goyim*." Dave reminded Sam that no one either bothered them or refused to buy from then when he continued to treat his white and black customers equally. Sam threw up his hands in surrender, "You are goin' to get us killed and ruin my business."

Trusting Dave, the black families bought with abandoned delight. In fact, the volume of sales increased—and so did Sam's worries. When the accounts fell due, to Dave's delight and Sam's surprise, the landowner paid off all outstanding debts incurred by his workers and tenants. During the next six months both Dave and Sam made similar arrangements with other large farmers and mill operators. "You see," Dave once lectured Sam, "how wrong you were. The *goyim* here are different. We sell to the *schwartzers* and help them using *goyische gelt* (Gentile's money). The *schwartzers* are happy because they can get what they need. The *goyim* are happy because everyone is happy; and we are happy because we have more business!"

Sam had to admit Dave was right. All signs pointed to continued prosperity. At Dave's suggestion, Sam expanded his business by covering more territory with the purchase of a pack mule. It was soon replaced by a one-horse-and-wagon which, in turn, was replaced by a larger two-horse-and-wagon. Finally, in mid-1886, Sam moved his merchandise from his rented rooms to a store and fulfilled his modest dream of becoming a merchant. That same year, he reluctantly made Dave a partner.

It was not until sometime in the late 1890's that Dave discovered the cost at which he had attained prosperity. One day a local mill operator entered Dave's store and made an abusive comment about a black customer. "Dave," he bellowed, "how come you lettin' this here nigger tryin' on clothes fittin' only for white folks? Better throw them out when he's finished. Can't tell what's on them now." Dave quickly turned toward the mill operator whom he had known ever since his arrival in Americus and reprimanded him. The discussion that followed left a burning impression on Dave no less than his parents' conversation in Baisagola. "Now hold on Dave," the mill operator called out as his hands pushed out in front of him as if to fend off Dave's assaulting words, "Don't you be insultin' me that away in front of this here nigger. And don't you be so high and mighty yourself. Let me tell you somethin' I been wantin' for years . . ." The mill operator proceeded to tell Dave that all his success was achieved at the expense of his black customers. He explained that all the credit Dave had extended to them had made them so debt-ridden that they had become virtual slaves bound by their debts to the mill operators and landowners who had paid off their accounts to Dave. Dave could not believe his ears. "You told me you wanted to help them," he gasped. The mill operator continued. "Them people was gettin' uppity; and some of us was tryin' to figure out how to come down on them without hurtin' them and put them back in their place. Then, you came along and the niggers trusted you. We didn't have none of them company stores like them yankees, so we used you." Then the mill operator laughed, "Sure out-jewed you on that one."[9]

Failing to see any humor in the story, Dave angrily accused the mill operator of tricking him into becoming an unwitting accomplice in a devious scheme to hurt the people he wanted to help. "Come on, Dave. Don't feel none too bad," consoled the mill operator with a smile as he placed his hand on Dave's shoulder. "Sam knew what was goin' on and didn't mind, and so did you. Besides, all you Jews are interested in is gettin' money in any way you can. You people don't care none if you have to hurt gettin' it. All that sympathy and good talk was just show for them so they would buy more. But, we know better, don't we."

Dave straightened up and with fire in his eyes he took the mill operator's hand slowly off his shoulder, quickly pointed towards the door and snapped, "To you and *your* friends, it is now *Mr.* Pearlman! Take your business somewhere else!" As the mill operator turned to leave, Dave shouted after him, "Mumzer (bastard)!"

As soon as the mill operator was gone, Dave's defiant mood turned sullen. Reluctantly, he turned to face the black customer who had been one of those tenant farmers he thought he had helped. Before Dave could say anything, the farmer said, "Mr. Dave, now don't you pay him no mind. You didn't hurt any of us none. You tried to do right by me and the others when not even Mr. Sam would. We all took kindly to what you thought you were doin' was right." When Dave sputtered that no one, not even Sam, had told him what was happening, the black farmer smiled and answered nonchalantly, "Heck, we wasn't going no place no how. And like your momma done said, we is sure 'nough better dressed anyhow."

No amount of consolation, however, could hide the simple truth for Dave that in return for the beneficence of the black farmers he had betrayed them. No explanation could ignore the reality that the improved outward appearance of his black customers had been paid for with their dignity, respectability and liberty. No rationalization could dismiss the fact that Dave's black friends were worse off for having placed their trust in him, that because of his stupidity he had hurt the people he so dearly had wanted to help. Nothing and no one could rid Dave of his nagging guilt that plagued him to his dying day in 1916.

Realizing he could not make full restitution for having misplaced his trust in the white landowners and mill operators, he, nevertheless, attempted to make amends as best he could. Almost immediately Dave, using the then current price barter system, reduced the price of anything in the store his black customers wished to purchase—and raised them for those white customers whom he felt had lied to him. When the landowners and mill operators came into the store to pay off their workers' and tenants' accounts, Dave refused to accept their money. From now on, he told them he would take care of the matter. "Them niggers will get you broke," one landowner warned, "They'll take the shirt off your back if you give them half a chance." Without hesitation, Dave firmly replied, "They will not cheat me. You are too blind with hatred to see that they are good people, honest people. They will pay me when they can and with what they can. And if they don't, so, my creditors will yell a little louder." During particularly bad times which might have been brought on by a sickness, severe weather, or a bad harvest he would not only lower the already lower-than-usual rents paid by the black tenant farmers on his land, but he could be seen traveling through the countryside as if he were again a peddler bringing free food, clothing and firewood to his black friends. Once when his wife suggested that no one could hold him responsible for their plight, he answered, "I hold myself responsible. That is enough, and all what I do is not enough."[10]

The burden of obligation weighed heavier on Dave because he knew he owed not only his personal survival and prosperity to his black customers, but that of his family as well. At every weekend family gathering, Dave was reminded that the financial success for which his black customers were responsible had enabled him to bring his relatives and friends away from the persecutions in Russia to safety in Georgia during the decades that followed.[11] At these bi-weekly Sunday gatherings of an extended family which was by 1910 spread throughout south Georgia, Dave, acting as patriarch, would never fail to remind his brothers and sisters, his nieces and nephews, his cousins and friends, that "you are here not just because of me. You are here because of them (the blacks). What you have now is because of them."[12] In the course of telling and retelling the stories of his early experiences in Georgia, Dave tried to instill a social conscience in the members of his clan. "He would never fail to tell while peckin' the air with his big finger," recalled Louis Lazarus, "somethin' like it ain't enough just to live, but how we help others less lucky than us to live. He sure enough meant them *schwartzers*." And if anyone resisted with the question, "what will the *goyim* think," he would firmly reprimand them with the rejoinder that not everything in Southern culture was worth copying and adopting. Then, he would say, as he would stand up and turn around as if modeling a suit, he had never been assaulted for treating the blacks as he wished all Jews had been treated in Russia. "He never let us forget," testified Annie Lee Garr to Dave's success, "what we had to do. Not just because we were beholden to them, but because it was the Jewish thing to be charitable to the less fortunate. Now we didn't go out shouting and shake things up. We were quiet-like in going about treating them in all ways like the human beings they were. I remember once when one of our neighbors said something about our maid sitting at the kitchen table with momma, drinking some tea, and talking about personal stuff. Momma turned around and said, 'when the children go out and play some get so dirty they look like *schwartzers*. Underneath they are the same as the clean ones. When you scrub them, they are all alike again. Should I treat the *schwartzers* like a *dybbuk* just because their skin is always dirty?' "[13]

NOTES

1. The village of Baisagola was located in the Lithuanian province of Kovno which at that time was part of the Russian Empire. The village itself was situated one hundred miles north of the provincial capital of Kovno—the provinces took their names from that of their capitals. Twelve miles farther north, on the well-traveled Memel Road, mid-way between the towns of Panevzys and Siaulai, was the slightly larger village of Seduva.

2. A major portion of this article is based on extraordinary interviews with Fannie Lazarus of Jacksonville, Florida, which were done on April 16 & 17, 1976; with Louis Lazarus of Valdosta, Georgia, which were done on February 20 & 21, 1976; and with Sam Kalin of Hendersonville, North Carolina, which were done on November 24 & 25, 1976. All of them were relatives of Dave Pearlman. Fannie Lazarus was a niece. Both Louis Lazarus and Sam Kalin were second cousins. All three of them were present at the traditional bi-weekly family Sunday gatherings in Valdosta between 1905 and 1916. After dinner, at these gatherings and just before everyone was about to depart for their homes in the surrounding towns, Dave Pearlman, the families' patriarch, would invariably relate the story of his departure from Russia and of his early experiences in Georgia. So seldom did he change a word in his story which was tradition at these gatherings, that eventually the women would nod their heads anticipating what he was going to say and acknowledging the accuracy of their memories. The children, who always sat in front of the group as Dave reclined in his rocking chair, had memorized the story to the extent they would move their lips and silently tell the story along with Dave. Sixty to seventy years later, Fannie Lazarus (born in Baisagola in

1882), Louis Lazarus (born in Rochelle, Georgia, in 1897) and Sam Kalin (born in Baisagola in 1894) could still recall verbatim large segments of that story. I accept the validity of those sections of their accounts that I have included in this article for a number of reasons. First is the vividness of their memory and the unhesitating manner in which they told their story. Second, is their willingness to acknowledge when their memory is vague or failing. Third is their ability to corroborate each other by telling many of the same stories verbatim in separate interviews. Fourth, none of the three knew the contents of the interview of the others. Fifth, the purpose of the interviews was not to talk about Dave Pearlman. Consequently, their responses were spontaneous. And finally, none had reason to fabricate their responses to my questions. It seems that Dave Pearlman consciously wanted to start an oral tradition that would be passed down through the generations. Unfortunately, those present at these meetings rarely told them to their future children and knowledge of the stories died with the generation that listened to him. In fact, the three I interviewed were the last survivors of those gatherings, two of whom have since died. The only portions of his tale that survive are those that I have been able to secure in the course of my interviews. On a technical note, for the sake of brevity all quotes that are not footnoted are taken from the interviews with the above mentioned individuals.

3. Fannie Lazarus was the daughter of Dave's brother, Charles. After Charles died and his wife Rosa left for New York with an infant son, leaving Fannie and another brother in Baisagola, Fannie moved in to live with William and Gena for almost fifteen years until Dave brought her to Georgia. While she lived with her grandparents, she heard them speak constantly of Dave, read his letters aloud and told the stories of his departure. The stories were especially told as Dave began bringing members of the family and friends from Baisagola and Seduva to Georgia.

4. Telephone conversation with Sam Kalin, December 4, 1976.

5. *Ibid.*

6. *Ibid.*

7. Interview with Annie Lee Garr of Raleigh, North Carolina, who was a second cousin to Dave, August 8, 1978.

8. Telephone conversation with Mrs. Joe Gottlieb of Birmingham, Alabama, December 12, 1976. Mrs. Gottlieb's statements are supported by her brother, Buddy Pearlman of Columbus, Georgia, although his memory was less precise than that of his older sister. Telephone conversation with Buddy Pearlman, January 8, 1977.

9. According to Sam Kalin, in the south Georgia region during the first fifteen years of the 20th century, many of the Jewish peddlers would congregate at the local turpentine and lumber mills on pay day and collectively sell to the black workers on credit with the understanding that the owners would guarantee to pay off all outstanding accounts after an agreed period of time had passed. Some of the peddlers did not care about the consequences of indebting the black workers to their bosses. Others, however, felt somewhat guilty about this practice, but rationalized that if they did not do it someone else would. Still others were convinced they were in some way helping the blacks. This explanation is supported by Sam Myers of Tallahassee, Florida, whose father was one of those peddlers. Interview with Sam Kalin, November 2, 1976; interview with Sam Myers, June 9, 1976.

10. Telephone conversation with Mrs. Joe Gottlieb, December 12, 1976.

11. Dave's younger brother, Ben, was the first relative he brought to Americus. Ben was followed by another brother and three sisters. They, in turn, were joined by a myriad of nieces, nephews, cousins, uncles, aunts, and friends. Mrs. Gottlieb mentioned that her father's house was so filled with relatives and friends from the Old Country that her mother used to joke that when she came in from hanging up the wash she would not know whom she would find sitting at her table and sleeping in her bed. Telephone conversation with Mrs. Joe Gottlieb, December 12, 1976; Fannie Lazarus, April 16, 1976; Sam Kalin, November 2, 1976.

12. Those who came under Dave's influence demonstrated their compassion for their black customers in a number of ways. Many of them who peddled the countryside followed Dave's example by staying with their black customers overnight. Some established their own credit accounts for their black customers, a practice which was carried on after these peddlers opened stores. The black customers were

allowed to try on samples of clothing that would be pulled randomly from the clothes racks. As house-maids they were treated as members of the family who often sat with family at dinner after serving. The black customers were loaned money to purchase land or an implement when no one else would. And once a young black boy was saved from being lynched by a mob due to the intercession of the Jews. These are only a few examples. See interviews with Jack Lazarus of Valdosta, Georgia, April 14, 1979; Henry Taylor of Quitman, Georgia, July 5, 1978; Bessie Goldstein of Thomasville, Georgia, May 17, 1979; Francis Simon of Jacksonville, Florida, February 7, 1979; Mrs. Abe Pincus of Quitman, Georgia, February 27, 1979; Annie Zelkind of Valdosta, Georgia, February 4, 1976; Sam Lazarus of Brewton, Alabama, April 16, 1978; Mrs. Abe Tannenbaum of Atlanta, Georgia, January 10, 1977; Frank Stein of Americus, Georgia, December 10, 1980.

13. Annie Lee Garr, August 8, 1978.

# Black-Jewish Relations in the Opening Years of the Twentieth Century

Recent years have seen a plethora of material on black-Jewish relations, and the spectre of black anti-Semitism has haunted essayists and novelists as well as scholars. Unfortunately, most recent works exist in an historical vacuum. None of the authors concern themselves with a systematic exploration of black-Jewish relations before the 1950's.[1] In concluding a review of one recent work (*Bittersweet Encounter: The Afro-American and the American Jew* by Robert G. Weisbord and Arthur Stein), Allan Spear called for "the detailed historical study of the black-Jewish encounter that the subject clearly merits."[2]

What follows cannot be the comprehensive historical study for which Spear rightly called. I believe, however, that it is an essential part of that study, for the opening years of the twentieth century provided the first well-focused incidents of national importance in which blacks and Jews came into conflict.

The numerous references to Jews in black writings and speeches throughout the nineteenth century have been largely ignored, and it would require a separate paper merely to point out their themes and significance. In general, however, we may note that they tended to point to the similarity between the Negro and Jewish experience in this country.[3] While disparaging remarks about white immigrants ran through the speeches and writings of black Americans throughout the century, blacks were usually careful to exclude Jews from these attacks. Black Americans—conservatives, moderates and radicals—were often indignant because of the essential acceptance accorded white immigrant groups over the years while Negroes, as native Americans, remained excluded.[4] Jews alone among whites in America, whether native-born or immigrants, were viewed as sharing with black people the status of second-class citizenship. Thus in the 1860 appeal of New York Negroes for Equal Suffrage Rights, the point is made that "with the exception of Jews, under the whole heavens there is not to be found a people pursued with a more relentless prejudice and persecution, than are the free colored people of the United States."[5] In April, 1867, *The Christian Recorder,* official organ of the African Methodist Episcopal Church, noted that while Jews were white, they were forced to endure humiliations which were reserved usually for blacks. "How cruel, how unjust the spirit that mocks this unfortunate people," it commented, and called upon white America to put an end to this "narrow-minded prejudice against an honorable people, a people of your own color."[6] Twenty years later, the New York *Freeman,* a leading black

In 1975, Philip S. Foner was the Independence Foundation Professor of History at Lincoln University in Pennsylvania.
Originally published in *Phylon* 36, no. 4 (1975): 359–67. Reprinted with permission of Clark Atlanta University Press.

weekly, observed that increasingly Jews were being excluded from summer resort hotels. Since "the colored people are discriminated against not only at Summer resorts but everywhere else, we are in position to sympathize with our Hebrew fellow-citizens in this matter."[7] Still later, the same paper, now renamed the New York *Age,* in an article entitled "The Jew and the Negro," said flatly: "There is a similarity between the Jew and the Negro. One is despised almost as much as the other."[8]

Throughout the Dreyfus Affair of the late 1890's, black newspapers condemned the French government. "The cowardly persecution of Captain Dreyfus," declared the Washington *Bee* in an editorial comment typical of the black press, "will go down to posterity as the most outrageous persecution of an innocent man known to modern times."[9] The trial of Dreyfus was compared with those experienced by blacks in the United States, and much was made of the fact that like Negroes Jews were always compelled to face persecution.[10]

Apart from pointing to the problems Jews faced because of the "cant and snobbery" of American society, the black press frequently cited Jews as models for black economic and social behavior. "Let Us Learn From the Jews," was the title of an editorial which appeared frequently in the black press.[11] Rather than wallowing in despair and brooding about prejudice, the Jews allegedly reclaimed their "self-respect" through group solidarity and the creation of a sound economic foundation. "Where everything else had been denied him—political rights, social standing, even the privilege of owning real estate—the Jew yet conquered," the *A.M.E. Church Review* exclaimed admiringly in 1892. "Two things he could and did get—money and education." As a result, Jews were "among the foremost in every department of human industry and brain achievement." What the Jews had accomplished, "though as illy treated as the Negro," blacks could also, but only if they recognized that wealth was the basis of power and respect.[12] "Get money, like the Jew," Booker T. Washington advised his people in 1899, noting that while the Jew was "once in about the same position as the Negro is to-day, he now has recognition because he has entwined himself about America in a business and industrial way."[13] Said *The Colored American,* a pro-Washington paper: "The Israelite gives us our finest object lesson in the possibilities growing out of thrift and economy. Examine the names upon our trade and financial emporiums and you will find the bulk of them suggestive of Jewish origin. The Jew has learned that money is taken by the world as a measure of worth. Can we not learn the same?"[14]

In the opening years of the twentieth century the image of Jews in black writings and speeches began to change. This was a period of increasing persecution of black Americans, especially in the South, and one marked by almost total indifference of whites in the North to these developments.[15] Black Americans became increasingly disappointed and resentful that Jews, who themselves knew the meaning of persecution, of segregation and of the deprivation of elementary human rights, appeared to be indifferent to the mounting persecution of blacks.

In a letter to *The Colored American* of April, 1899, Rabbi Abram L. Isaacs, editor of the *Jewish Messenger,* published in New York City, expressed gratitude for support of Dreyfus by Negroes, and wrote that Jews could best express this feeling by supporting blacks in the battle against disenfranchisement, segregation, and lynch law. Rabbi Isaacs recalled that although there had been Jews, both North and South, who had defended slavery and discrimination before the Civil War, "the best of our people, the most idealistic and humanity-loving were to be found in the anti-slavery ranks." He assured *The Colored American* that their descendants would be no less active in behalf of the rights of black Americans.[16]

*The Colored American* was overjoyed. It featured Rabbi Isaac's letter on its first page, and declared editorially that from such statements, "the Negro may well take hope." It concluded: "In the name of the Negro race, *The Colored American* thanks Rabbi Isaacs for his sympathetic utterances. He and his kind can be a tower of strength to us in the herculean struggle before us. To the Jews we look for aid when our own resources have been tested to the utmost."[17]

Unfortunately, little aid came from the Jewish community or press, including even the *Jewish Messenger,*[18] as blacks continued to be legally disenfranchised, pushed more deeply into a segregated society, and met by an orgy of lynchings and anti-Negro riots in the South (and sometimes even in the North) when they protested. It was the lynchings, increasing in number and brutality each year, which particularly triggered the change in relationship between Negroes and Jews. Blacks had been becoming increasingly bitter because the federal government not only refused to lift a finger to protect the rights of Negroes guaranteed in the Fourteenth and Fifteenth Amendments, but remained silent in the face of the increasing number of lynchings. They were especially embittered because that same government sent diplomatic protests to Romania and Russia over the treatment of Jews in these countries.[19] Black newspapers made it clear that they condemned the pogroms against Jews, but they asked why the government could act swiftly in behalf of citizens of foreign countries while it dragged its feet over the persecution of its black citizens. On November 1, 1902, *The Voice of the People,* published by Henry M. Turner, Bishop of the African Methodist Episcopal Church in Atlanta, declared: "Surely the United States Government cannot be more sensitive over the wrongs inflicted on the Semitic people in Roumania than over the ignominious disgraces heaped upon the Afro-Americans, its citizens, by its white citizens. And the same as it can issue a note to the powers on behalf of the Hebrews, it can issue an order, a comment to the various states for a better treatment of its colored citizens."[20]

The issue reached a climax the following year as a result of pogroms incited by Tsarist minister Plehve at Kishineff, during which scores of Jews were killed, several hundred wounded, and hundreds of Jewish homes wrecked and plundered. When President Theodore Roosevelt transmitted to the Tsar, in June, 1903 the petition presented to him by the B'nai Brith denouncing the massacre, the American press, North and South, with few exceptions applauded his action.[21] But the black press did not join in. On the contrary, a number of black newspapers pointed out that the very same people who had signed the petition to the Tsar, and the same newspapers which supported it, "are dumb, when they do not approve, the savage outrages against Negroes at home."[22] Since the signers of the petition included Senators from Mississippi, who had publicly justified lynchings of Negroes as necessary to maintain "law and order," it is not difficult to understand black indignation.[23] Moreover, the petition, included the names of the Mayor and City Council members of Evansville, Indiana, where in July, 1903, a riot against Negroes drove over a thousand blacks from their homes and forced them to seek shelter in the woods. "Negroes are fleeing from the American Kishineff, Evansville, Indiana," bitterly cried *The Freeman,* a black weekly published in Indianapolis. "Shall the Negroes look to the Tsar of Russia for protection, since neither the President of the United States nor the Mayor of Evansville seem interested in protecting them?"[24] Indeed, the Russian government, in rejecting the protest from the United States, cited the lynchings of blacks and anti-Negro riots in this country, and advised President Roosevelt to concern himself with persecution of minorities in his own country before he criticized Russia. It noted, too, that while "in Russia the members of the mob, to the number of 500, have been imprisoned and punished, in America even the leaders of the lynching mob have been permitted to go free."[25]

Blacks were further antagonized by Jewish reaction to the analogy between Kishineff and anti-Negro persecution in the United States. When *The Public,* a liberal weekly published in Chicago, urged Jews to realize that the same type of persecution operating against their kinsmen in Russia was characteristic of the black experience in this country, it brought down upon itself a barrage of criticism from Jewish spokesmen.[26] Dr. Solomon Cohen, a leader of B'nai Brith in Philadelphia, summed up the nature of the criticism in a lengthy letter to *The Public,* which was endorsed by the Philadelphia organization. There was, he charged, absolutely no relationship between the treatment of Jews in Russia and that accorded Negroes in the United States, for it was simply ridiculous "to contrast the advanced stage of intellectual and moral development of the Jews in general with the limited progress that the masses of Negroes in America have made." Furthermore, the acts against Negroes in the United States, such as lynchings, "with rare exceptions, originate in crimes committed by individual Negroes." They were "directed at least primarily, and ostensibly, against the criminal, and are always theoretically, and often practically, resisted by the officers of the law." On the other hand, the massacre of Jews in Russia was of innocent people, and carried out with the connivance of the authorities. Finally, any attempt to equate the status of Jews in Russia with that of Negroes in the United States and to draw an analogy between "Russian official murder" and lynchings in the South, "is simply part of the attempt to break the force of world-wide public opinion against Russia."[27]

Such statements, widely reprinted in the black press,[28] coming after little support from the Jewish community for the struggles of blacks, had the effect of embittering relations between Jews and Negroes. The Chicago *Broad-Axe* summed up the opinion of blacks when it commented: "Of all the morally wretched defenders of this American crime of lynching, the American Jew who defends Negro lynchers while denouncing Russian massacres—and some do—is most contemptible."[29] Blacks were further angered when the position taken by Dr. Cohen gained the endorsement of the notorious Southern racist, Thomas Dixon, Jr., author of the racist novels, *The Clansman* and *The Leopard's Spot.* Writing in the *Saturday Evening Post,* Dixon challenged the idea that there was any relationship between persecution of Jews in Russia and the treatment of blacks in this country; denounced the idea that Jews and Negroes had anything in common, and criticized Booker T. Washington for denigrating the Jews by even suggesting that Negroes could ever aspire to be like the Jews, a white people which had "achieved a noble civilization," had "poets, prophets, priests, and kings." Such a people could easily be assimilated into American life because they belonged to "our race," while Negroes could never rise out of their degraded position.[30] Black newspapers took pains to record the fact that there was no evidence of Jewish repudiation of Dixon's stand.[31]

Just when the Kishineff issue was ceasing to exacerbate Jewish-Negro relations, an event occurred in Maryland which further intensified the emerging antagonism. This concerned the movement for the limitation of the franchise, admittedly aimed at the Negro voters. In the years 1903–1909, disenfranchisement of Negroes became the dominant issue, and since Maryland was the most northern state to attempt to bar blacks from the polls, the campaign attracted national attention. Thus the fact that two of the most vocal champions of the disenfranchisement were also the leaders of Baltimore's Jewish community was highlighted in the press the country over. These two men were Isador Rayner and Isaac L. Strauss, both leading Democrats in Maryland. Rayner and Strauss delivered a series of widely reported speeches in which they stressed that white society must be protected from "depraved negroes," and to accomplish this, blacks had to be entirely disenfranchised. "The race issue is not a political one," said Rayner, "but in this state is one of self-preservation. The white race must prevail over barbarism, and this can best be achieved by reducing the Negro vote to the utmost minimum in Maryland."[32]

This continued for several years, and it was with considerable fury that the Baltimore *Afro-American Ledger* reported: "Messrs Isaac Lobe Strauss and Isador Rayner scarcely ever speak at a meeting that they do not have a word to say against the despised Negro. They out Herod Herod in stirring up race prejudice against the Negro." It proceeded to remind the Jews of their own experience in Baltimore:

> It would be supposed that one who had felt the sting of prejudice because of his race or other reasons would be at least a little charitable to others in like condition. The time has not passed from the memory of people now living when the great mass of Jews in this city were largely confined to Harrison street and streets in that vicinity. It used to be a custom in those days for white boys and young men to go through those streets and rail on the detested Jews.
>
> During floods, and they happened often in that locality in those days, Harrison street was frequently flooded, and after the rain was over the streets would be crowded with street gamins jeering the Jews who were bailing out their houses. They had but little protection from the police department, and had to bear as best they could the burden of prejudice cast against them.
>
> But the Jews have forgotten those days and are busy heaping prejudice upon the head of the Negro as if nothing of the kind had ever been their lot.[33]

The *Afro-American Ledger* called Strauss "The Prosecuting Attorney of the Colored Race in Maryland,"[34] and observed:

> "Mr. Strauss ought to be ashamed of himself. The Hebrew people are not as mean, unsympathetic and cold-blooded as we would be apt to judge from the personality of Mr. Strauss. The Hebrew people have had a history, in many respects, like our own.

They have been persecuted, ostracized and oppressed, and surely they possess sufficient of the milk of human kindness to extend a helping hand or sympathy for their black brother, rather than a thrust and a kick."[35]

Throughout the disenfranchisement campaign in Maryland attention was paid to whether or not the position of men like Rayner and Strauss was repudiated by the Jewish community. The Springfield (Mass.) *Republican* indicated that on this response hinged the future of relations between the Jewish and Negro people, and should there not be a repudiation, "the future of Jewish-Negro relations may very well be a bitter one."[36]

Unfortunately, the warning was ignored. Fortunately, however, the move to disfranchise Negroes in Maryland failed—largely because foreign-born whites feared that they too would be deprived of the suffrage.[37]

It is not without significance that when W.E.B. DuBois's *Souls of Black Folks* was published in 1903, it contained a number of references to Jews as being people concerned with their own problems but indifferent to those of others.[38] (These references, incidentally, were deleted by DuBois when he consented to the reprinting of the classic book for the fiftieth anniversary edition in 1953.[39]) Perhaps another reason for the references in the original edition was indicated in DuBois's article, "The Opening of the Library," published in *The Independent* of April, 1902. Here he described the opening of the Carnegie Library in Atlanta, and noted that Negroes were not allowed to use its facilities. He told how a committee, headed by himself, went to the trustees of the library to demand the right for Negroes to use its facilities. When DuBois, who spoke for the committee, had concluded, the chairman of the board asked: "Do you think that allowing whites and Negroes to use this library would be fatal to its usefulness?" DuBois relates how, as he heard these words, he thought of the same thing being said to Jews in past centuries when they tried to gain access to facilities from which they had been excluded, and he notes in parenthesis ("for strange omen! a Jew sat here before me among the group of trustees"). The Board voted unanimously that "Negroes would not be permitted to use the Carnegie Library in Atlanta."[40]

In an interesting article published in *Phylon* last year, Eugene Levy of Carnegie-Mellon University dates the change in black-Jewish relations from the Frank case of 1915.[41] "Apart from the Frank case," he writes, "there seems to have been little hostility towards Jews among black leaders of the early twentieth century."[42] We may conclude that over a decade before the Frank case, black-Jewish relations had deteriorated from the high point achieved at the close of the nineteenth century. Black Americans reading the nation's press and particularly their own press, in the opening years of the twentieth century, must have concluded that the view they had long entertained that the Jewish experience had made Jews less anti-black than other Americans was in need of a major revision. This does not mean that praise for and sympathy with Jews, so common in black writings and speeches during the nineteenth century, was replaced by black anti-Semitism. In fact, pleas for cooperation between blacks and Jews and the view that the Jewish experience offered a viable model for blacks, continued to be voiced in the black press and by black leaders.[43] But along with these sentiments there was heard, and often in bitter tones, the viewpoint that blacks ought not to waste tears sympathizing with Jews when they experienced prejudice and discrimination, that instead they should reserve their sympathies totally for black victims of mob violence. A reading of the black press in the early years of the twentieth century leads to the conclusion that many blacks believed that the Jews had been tested and had failed to live up to the principles of Moses and the prophets.

NOTES

1. See the following collections of essays and articles: Shlomo Katz, ed., *Negro and Jew* (New York, 1967); *Negro-Jewish Relations in the United States* (New York, 1966); William H. Becker, "Black and Jew: Ambivalence and Affinities," *Soundings,* LIII (December, 1970), 413–39.

2. *Journal of American History,* LVIII (September, 1967), 504.

3. Howard Brotz, *Negro Social and Political Thought, 1850–1920* (New York, 1966), pp. 38, 41, 185–86, 241–42; Frank A. Rollins, *Life and Public Services of Martin R. Delany* (Boston, 1883), pp. 33, 45–46, 334; Hollis Lynch, *Edward Wilmot Blyden: Pan-Negro Patriot, 1832–1912* (London, 1967), pp. 63–64; *Minutes of the State Convention of the Coloured Citizens of Pennsylvania convened at Harrisburg December 13th and 14th, 1848* (Philadelphia, 1849), pp. 18–19.

4. Letter of Bishop Richard Allen in *Freedom's Journal,* November 2, 1827; James Forten to William Lloyd Garrison, February 23, 1831, William Lloyd Garrison Papers, Boston Public Library; James McCune Smith, "The German Invasion," *Anglo-African Magazine,* I (February, 1859), 50; Philip S. Foner, *Life and Writings of Frederick Douglass,* III (New York, 1952), p. 421.

5. *The Principia,* I (October 20, 1860), 385–86.

6. *The Christian Recorder,* April 13, 1867.

7. "Prejudice Against Jews," New York *Freeman,* July 23, 1887.

8. New York *Age,* May 18, 1889.

9. Washington *Bee,* August 18, 1899.

10. *Ibid.,* September 9, 1899; *The Christian Recorder,* September 8, 1899.

11. See *The Christian Recorder,* September 1, 1899; Washington *Bee,* August 11, 1899; New York *Age,* February 8, 1899.

12. *A.M.E. Church Review,* IX (1892–1893), 8.

13. Booker T. Washington, *The Future of the American Negro* (New York, 1899), p. 66.

14. *The Colored American,* April 22, 1899.

15. For an excellent discussion of the deteriorating status of Negroes during these years and the indifference of Northern opinion, see Rayford W. Logan, *The Negro in American Life and Thought, the Nadir 1877–1901* (New York, 1954).

16. Rabbi Isaacs had read about the work *The Colored American* was conducting in testing the constitutionality of the Louisiana Constitution adopted in 1898 which introduced the Grandfather Clause as a device to disfranchise black citizens in that state.

For the role of Jews in the struggle over slavery, see Max J. Kohler, "Jews and the American Anti-Slavery Movement," *Publications of the American Jewish Historical Society,* V (New York, 1897), 137–55 and IX (1901), 45–56; Philip S. Foner, *Jews in American History, 1619–1865* (New York, 1945), 51–62; Morris U. Schappes, ed., *A Documentary History of the Jews in the United States* (New York, 1952), pp. 294, 398–420, 444–88; Bertram W. Korn, *American Jewry in the Civil War* (Philadelphia, 1951), pp. 15–31; Louis Ruchames, "The Abolitionists and the Jews." *Publications of the American Jewish Historical Society,* XLII (December, 1952), 131–55, and the introductory essay by Maxwell Whiteman in *The Kidnapped and the Ransomed: the Narrative of Peter and Vina Still After Forty Years of Slavery* (Philadelphia, 1970).

17. *The Colored American,* April 29, 1899.

18. Apart from a non-committal article on the murder of black postmaster Baker and his family in South Carolina in the issue of April 7, 1899, the *Jewish Messenger* carried no news about problems facing Negroes during the next few years. An examination of the files of other Jewish papers, both English-

language and Yiddish, during the opening years of the twentieth century, reveals little attention to the Negro question.

19. There is no study devoted to United States–Romanian relations during this period, but there are two doctoral dissertations on United States–Russian relations: Edward J. Carroll, "The Foreign Relations of the United States with Tsarist Russia, 1867–1900" (Georgetown University, 1953), and George S. Queen, "The United States and Material Advance in Russia, 1887–1906" (University of Illinois, 1941).

20. See also *The Colored American,* November 4, 1902.

21. *The Literary Digest,* July 4, 18, 1903.

22. *The Colored American,* July 20, 1903. See also New York *Age,* July 16, 1903.

23. Springfield (Mass.) *Republican,* July 18, 1903.

24. *The Freeman,* July 25, 1903.

25. Springfield *Republican,* June 28, 1903; Queen, *op. cit.,* pp. 118–21.

26. *The Public,* August 8, 1903; *Jewish Messenger,* August 14, 1903.

27. *The Public,* August 22, 1903.

28. See, for example, New York *Age,* August 29, 1903; Baltimore *Afro-American,* August 27, 1903; *The Freeman,* August 28, 1903.

29. Chicago *Broad-Axe,* August 28, 1903.

30. *Saturday Evening Post,* August 19, 1903.

31. Richmond *Planet,* September 12, 1903; New York *Age,* September 14, 1903.

32. Baltimore *Sun,* October 18, 22, 1903.

33. Baltimore *Afro-American Ledger,* November 2, 1907.

34. *Ibid.,* December 7, 1907.

35. *Ibid.*

36. Margaret Law Callcott, *The Negro in Maryland Politics 1870–1912* (Baltimore, 1969), pp. 124–25.

37. Baltimore *Afro-American,* November 8, 1903.

38. W.E.B. DuBois, *The Souls of Black Folk* (Chicago, 1903), pp. 127, 132, 169, 204.

39. Herbert Aptheker, "The Souls of Black Folk: A Comparison of the 1903 and 1952 Editions," *Negro History Bulletin,* XXXIV (January, 1971), 15–17.

40. W.E.B. DuBois, "The Opening of the Library," *The Independent,* LIV (April 3, 1902), 809–10.

41. " 'Is the Jew a White Man?': Press Reaction to the Leo Frank Case, 1913–1915," *Phylon,* XXXV (June, 1974), 212–22. In July, 1913, Leo Frank, a Jew, came to trial in Atlanta, Georgia, charged with the murder of Mary Phagan, a fourteen year old white girl employed in the pencil factory managed by Frank. On August 25 the jury found Frank guilty of murder, and the following day the judge sentenced him to death. On June 21, 1915, the day before Frank was scheduled to be executed, Georgia's Governor John Slaton commuted his sentence to life imprisonment. Two days later, on August 17, 1915, a mob of white men broke into the prison where Frank was being held, took him some miles, and lynched him. (For the full details of the case, see Leonard Dinnerstein, *The Leo Frank Case* (New York, 1968).

42. *Ibid.,* p. 215.

43. See, for example, W.E.B. DuBois in *The Crisis,* IX (March, 1915), 234, and James Weldon Johnson in New York *Age,* January 28, February 25, 1915.

# Jews and Blacks

The economic mobility, assimilation, and social status of Atlanta's Jews were strongly affected by the city's large black population. Jews, in turn, provided Negroes with useful services and what appeared to be a viable model for group advancement. Relations between the two communities were highly ambivalent and influenced by circumstances beyond their control. While cordiality was the norm, resentments, frustrations, and attitudinal changes weakened what was, on the whole, a mutually advantageous arrangement. This interaction was probably quite typical in the South during the fifty years after Appomattox, yet little of the voluminous literature on Jewish-black relations deals with the phenomenon.[1]

The first sustained contacts between Jews and blacks in Atlanta were between masters and slaves. Slavery probably had a deterrent effect on antebellum Jewish immigration to the South. Between 1830 and 1860, Europeans and Northerners came increasingly to regard Negro slavery as an anachronistic and reprehensible institution, and Jewish immigrants were undoubtedly influenced by this attitude. Moreover, the growth of abolitionist and free soil thought intensified sectional strife and transformed southern fear of abolitionists into distrust of all outsiders. Slavery was the pillar of southern civilization, and the region was more likely to attract immigrants who had no strong objections to the "peculiar institution" and were willing to adapt themselves to the prevailing orthodoxy. This was more a matter of unconscious accommodation than mere protective coloration. As members of a success-oriented but economically vulnerable and isolated minority, Jews were likely to adopt the attitudes and practices of their gentile neighbors and customers. Blacks also acted as a lightning rod in deflecting prejudices which might otherwise have been manifested against Jews, and by parenthetically ordaining the equality of all whites, slavery conferred indirect benefits even on poor Jewish newcomers.

While opposition to slavery was reputedly one of the reasons why David Steinheimer resisted conscription into the Confederate Army in 1862, on the whole there was no discernible difference between local Jewish and gentile attitudes. Those Jews who had the desire and means to purchase Negro servants generally did so. Four of the six Jewish

Steven Hertzberg's interest in the Jews of Atlanta began with a research paper for John Hope Franklin's New South seminar and led to a doctoral dissertation, "The Jews of Atlanta, 1865–1915" (University of Chicago, 1975).
Originally published in Steven Hertzberg, *Strangers within the Gate City: The Jews of Atlanta, 1845–1915* (Philadelphia: The Jewish Publication Society of America, 1978), 181–201. Used by permission of the Jewish Publication Society of America.

households in 1850 contained slaves, and this figure corresponded favorably to the 75 percent of Jewish households in Charleston, Richmond, and Savannah which had slaves three decades earlier. Local Jews also participated in the slave trade: the auction and commission house of Mayer and Jacobi dealt in slaves as in other commodities; Levi Cohen purchased slaves in several Georgia counties during the war; and Solomon Cohen offered "75 LIKELY NEGROES" for sale in 1862.[2]

Jews continued to employ Negro servants after the abolition of slavery. Indeed, the low cost and abundance of free black labor placed the employment of servants within reach of the lower middle-class. Fifty percent of Atlanta's Jews in 1870 and 42 percent in 1880 resided in households which also included black domestics. Presumably, many other Jewish households employed nonresident blacks, since the trend during the post-war period was for domestics to live outside their places of employment. Most of the blacks in Jewish homes were girls or young women, sometimes with children, who worked as maids, cooks, and nurses. A few, like Mollie Alexander and her children, bore the surname of their Jewish employer. Only rarely did adult black males live on the premises. The average Jewish household contained only one live-in servant, but some had as many as four, and there was a clear association between Jewish economic status and the employment of domestic labor: 52 percent of the Jewish heads of household in 1880 with assets of at least $1,100 employed live-in help, compared with only 29 percent of those worth under that amount.

Commerce provided additional interracial contacts. Jewish peddlers and petty traders who filtered south after the war eagerly courted the patronage of blacks, willingly bargained over prices, "showed infinite patience in dealing with simple people in small business affairs," and treated their customers with a civility that the latter rarely received from white Southerners. This commercial intercourse was rooted in the marginality of both vendor and purchaser. The Jew had little capital, spoke broken English, was unfamiliar with regional mores, and in some cases was perceived as an intruder by native whites. Similarly, the freedman was disdained and feared by ex-Confederates. Perhaps more importantly, prior to going South, few of the newcomers had encountered blacks, and this made them "more willing to respond out of actual experience with the Negro than out of a twisted history of slavery, guilt and pathological hate." "When the Negro smiled at the Jew," notes Eli Evans, "the Jew smiled back."[3]

Many of the Central European Jews who settled in Atlanta during the sixties and seventies previously had extensive experience selling to blacks in the countryside. Some, like Gustave Saloshin, who had a secondhand clothing business on Decatur Street, and Alex Dittler, whose grocery and home were located in the Negro neighborhood of Summer Hill, continued to service a predominantly black clientele. Other German Jewish merchants were patronized by both races to the extent that the price of their goods and location of their stores allowed. As late as 1913, the city's three leading Jewish-owned emporiums and numerous lesser enterprises advertised regularly in the local black press. Jewish businessmen also employed a substantial number of black porters and draymen, and at least one owned houses which he rented to Negroes.[4]

As the Germans acquired the capital and skills required to tap the more lucrative white market, their former dependence on the Negro trade was inherited by newly arrived immigrants from Eastern Europe. Peddling, either in the country or the outlying sections of the city, was commonly the initial occupation of the Russians, 13 percent of whom in 1896 earned their livelihood in this way. *Landsmen* (countrymen), the Jewish relief societies, and wholesalers willingly advanced the goods and funds which they hoped would transform the destitute refugee into a nascent merchant.

Country peddlers, who carried their assortment of dry goods and notions in a sack or valise, generally spent a week at a stretch in the rural townships of Georgia and Alabama. For many immigrants like Charles Greenberg, this experience provided their initial contact with blacks and an introduction to southern racial mores. "I got off at the first station and walked a few miles until I saw black men working in the fields, carrying the same kind of bags white people in Russia would carry," Greenberg recalled.

> I walked over and greeted them as I had been instructed. So, they all stopped working and looked at me, not because I was carrying a pack, but, as I found out later, [because] I, a white person, had greeted them. It was my good luck that no white person had seen me, because no white person [in the South] greets a black one.

As dusk began to fall, the young peddler looked for a place to spend the night. "Having been advised that I should not lodge with blacks, for a white person must not lodge in a black home, I kept walking after nightfall till I reached the home of a white." Before retiring for the evening, he mused that he was no longer a "greenhorn." Not only had he made his first sale, but also learned a fundamental lesson about deportment in the South.[5]

Aside from being a seasonal activity confined largely to the autumn months when farmers had money to spend, country peddling entailed problems of finding shelter, avoiding unfriendly dogs, and keeping kosher. More convenient but less profitable was the routine of the urban basket peddler. The basket peddler learned the English names of his wares, memorized the words "Look in the basket," took one of the streetcar lines to the last stop, got off, and knocked on doors. Once again, blacks were his main customers, and after a while he might accumulate savings sufficient to advance them credit, would inscribe their names in a small book, and return after a specified time to collect. "On the Monday of the following week I went out like a businessman, now without a pack, only to collect," recalled a former practitioner of the trade. Like his colleagues, he discovered that it was easier to make sales than make collections, not only because the blacks were poor, but also since "till one gets to know them, they all seemed to have the same face."[6]

Since the peddler had little overhead and the mark-up on his goods was between fifty and one hundred percent, his peripatetic livelihood often provided the capital required to open a retail grocery or enter the dry goods or clothing business. Blacks remained his primary customers. The ownership of saloons and pawnshops—two other enterprises heavily patronized by blacks and frequently owned by Jews—required greater capital than most recent immigrants could muster, and their proprietors constituted a large share of the Russian community's economic elite.[7]

Several factors accounted for the Jews' extensive economic involvement with blacks. The destitute Russian newcomers possessed all the prerequisites essential to entrepreneurial success save capital and familiarity with American ways. Having arrived in

Atlanta substantially poorer than had their now prosperous German coreligionists, they were able to enter the overcrowded retail market only at the lowest and most stigmatized level. By necessity, the Russians were compelled to court the patronage of those whose business was scorned by more established merchants. Long accustomed to providing goods and services for a brutalized peasantry, they had few if any temperamental objections to dealing with blacks and, unlike their white gentile counterparts, had no deep-seated compulsion to manifest anti-Negro prejudice. Indeed, Jews aggressively sought the blacks' trade and treated their customers with unaccustomed courtesy.

Central to the popularity of the Jewish merchant was his willingness to extend credit—even at a personal sacrifice—to often impecunious blacks; and his ability to do so reflected, in turn, the availability of credit from benevolent societies, friendly wholesalers, and banks. In contrast, the prospective black businessmen found credit and capital more difficult to obtain and generally lacked commercial experience. The black's consequent reluctance to advance credit limited his customers to those who could pay in cash. In addition, while many blacks preferred to patronize merchants of their own race, many others suspected that merchandise sold by a Negro was bound to be inferior. The willingness of blacks to "walk three blocks or more to trade with a white man, when there is a Negro store at their door" engendered the resentment and envy of Atlanta's nascent black business class. "We have aided the Jew from the time he came into our neighborhood with his store on his back," complained one of their spokesmen in 1899,

> until now he has a large brick building, a number of clerks, and he and his family ride in a fine carriage . . . driven by a Negro. Why can we not help our brother who is struggling with all the odds against him . . . ? I am sure that what we might buy from the Negro could be no more inferior than some of the things we have bought from the Jew, and I suspect his recommendation of the article would be as truthful as that of the Jew.[8]

Finally, the commercial bond between Jew and Negro was reinforced by a vague sense of empathy between the two persecuted peoples. The New York Yiddish press, to which many of Atlanta's Jews subscribed, was very sympathetic toward the plight of blacks and frequently compared their suffering with that of the Jews in Europe—an analogy made even more often by Negro journalists. Yiddish poet I. J. Schwartz caught the flavor of this feeling.

> And it was noteworthy: how soon
> The people without a tongue understood—
> Or more clearly stated—smelled, felt,
> The naked nature of the strange Negro—
>
> .   .   .   .   .   .   .   .   .   .   .   .
>
> And it was natural, that the Negro
> On his part, also immediately sensed that these
> Were somehow people closer to him,
> Belonging, indeed, to the white race,
> But a white race of another kind.[9]

Native-born white Gentiles looked with disdain upon Jewish dealings with blacks, which they suspected entailed breaches of southern etiquette. Alan Rogers, a local feature writer, drew upon a mixed bag of stereotypes in describing Decatur Street's Jewish businessmen in 1906.

> Hugging the very curbstones for a football, this same indomitable race of nationless wayfarers withstand the crush and crowding of the black denizens quite long and strong enough to ply their natural gifts for trade, and prey upon African weaknesses and prejudices for profits in percentages sufficiently large enough to [reprieve?] the very city of Jerusalem itself.

Pawnbrokers were suspected of receiving stolen property and, much worse, selling weapons to blacks. The hero of one of Rogers's stories is a pawnbroker named Levi Eichenstein, who is initially seen anxiously awaiting the birth of his first child. Suddenly, the bell rings in his shop below, and "the natural inclination and heritage of a thousand generations . . . asserted themselves." His customer is a Negro who wishes to purchase a revolver. Eichenstein instinctively begins to praise his stock of firearms, but then hears his baby's birthcry, realizes the possibly tragic consequences of the sale, and sends the Negro from the store.[10]

The arrest in 1896 of a Decatur Street furniture dealer and a Negro employee on the charge of burglary engendered speculation that criminally inclined Jews and blacks were in collusion; both men were subsequently acquitted. Jewish-owned saloons, some of which advertised in the Negro press, were deemed even graver threats to public order. After the 1906 race riot, several saloon licenses held by Jews were revoked, and a journalist suggested that those "who catered to negro trade and negro vice" were on an even lower social level than their customers.[11]

Unlike Harlem's Jewish merchants of a later period, Jewish Atlantans who catered to a predominantly black clientele lived in close proximity to their customers. In 1896 blacks were concentrated in four sections of the city: Mechanicsville, west of the Western and Atlantic tracks in the low area near the railroad shops; the neighborhoods farther west and south near Atlanta University and Spelman Seminary; Summer Hill, southeast of the business district between Martin and Hill streets; and Shermantown, which encompassed the bottom lands in the vicinity of Houston, Wheat, and Butler streets in the northeast quadrant of the city. Smaller pockets of blacks were to be found in the alleys of otherwise white neighborhoods and bore such descriptive appellations as Hell's Half Acre and Niggertown.

Atlanta's Jews in 1896 resided in two distinct areas: the Germans, along the streets just south of the business district, and the Russians, in the vicinity of Decatur Street where most of them worked. Except for a few blocks of Orange and Crumley streets and Woodward Avenue, few Negroes lived among the prosperous southside Germans. Conditions were quite different in the Decatur Street area, where small numbers of blacks had settled prior to the arrival of the Russians. College Street and Edgewood Avenue formed the boundary between the ghetto and Shermantown, and blacks lived along Gilmer, Courtland, Butler, and Pratt streets. Negro and Jewish proprietors shared occupancy of several two-story buildings on Decatur Street, and twenty "negro tenements" (one room shacks) clustered in the alleys behind the Jewish homes on the block bordered by Decatur, Piedmont, Gilmer, and Butler streets.

Between 1896 and 1911, Atlanta's Negro neighborhoods all expanded under the influence of immigration from the rural sections of the state, and the advance of the business district pushed the Germans even further south. The Decatur Street ghetto's Jewish and black populations also increased. The consequent congestion, closer proximity to blacks, expansion of the business district, and growth of prostitution were responsible for the migration of Russian Atlantans to the streets just across the Georgia Railroad tracks. There, on the fringe of Summer Hill, they remained until further intrusions of blacks sent them into the German neighborhood to the west. Russian Jewish grocers were an exception to this tendency to cluster near but not within Negro neighborhoods. They generally lived above their small stores located inside black districts, in some cases miles from the nearest concentration of Jews.

While relations between Jews and blacks were usually amicable, this was not always the case. One major cause of friction was the high prices often charged for inferior goods, the blame for which may be attributed to the high cost of credit and the cupidity of dishonest proprietors.[12] The ensuing resentment was sometimes exacerbated by high pressure salesmanship. Such was the case with Sam Clark, who was fined $5.75 in 1900 for cursing a Decatur Street used-clothing dealer. The young Negro maintained that his language was justified by the merchant's overly aggressive attempt to induce his patronage:

> Meester Aldyman, yer hain't 'quainted lak Judge Briles widde way folks does on Decatey Street, fer ef yer wus yer nebber would be axin' me erbout cussin' de dago what tried ter drag me inter his ole shop. Des dagos habs er way ob takin' hol' ob de niggers and jest er draggin' em inter de shop and makin' em buy dey ole close. . . . I mout er sed perflamed language, but de sitterwashun was de proper time for mos' enny gemmen ter cus er leetle.[13]

Residential proximity and commercial intercourse also produced situations in which Jews were victimized by black criminals. Joe Poolinski was stabbed in his Decatur Street used-clothing store in 1898, and four years later, Peters Street clothier Morris Greenblatt fatally shot a black man whom he allegedly caught stealing for a second time.[14] Saloonkeeper A. Smullyan and several of his customers were threatened by a knife-wielding Negro in 1903, and in 1907 two Jewish women were stabbed outside Grady Hospital. The following year, Jacob Hirsowitz, one of the leading members of the Russian community, was murdered by several Negroes who attempted to steal a revolver from his pawnshop.[15] Perhaps the most tragic incident was the 1912 murder of Aaron Morris, a recently arrived barber, who had come to the aid of his landlady who was being assaulted in her Gilmer Street home.[16] Crimes of a less serious variety were even more common.[17]

Although such incidents were exceptional, they doubtlessly affected the manner in which Jews viewed their black neighbors and vice versa. Moreover, given the superficial level upon which they interacted and the Jews' ignorance of Negro history and culture, there seemed to be little that was ennobling about the black man's attributes. To Jews who respected piety, moderation, intellectual accomplishment, and material achievement, the Negro's seemingly loose sexual behavior, physicality, lawlessness, and improvidence made him the consummate Other. But if the Russian Jew was not predisposed to respect the Negro, his own recent experience with persecution enabled him to sympathize with the black man's plight. Young David Yampolsky, shocked by the Negroes' "terrible, slavish, oppressed condition"—worse than that of his brethren in Russia—described the 1906 race riot as a "pogrom on the blacks." Inclined toward socialism, Yampolsky regretted that his poor English prevented him from expressing solidarity with his black fellow proletarians.[18]

In general, the degree of sympathy which Jews had for blacks was inversely related to the amount of time the former had spent in the South. The process of americanization entailed adopting the normative traits of the white gentile majority, and these included negative attitudes toward blacks. Negrophobia made slower headway among the Russians, whose own recent experience with oppression militated against manifesting the more vicious forms of racism. Moreover, many were dependent upon black patronage and were relatively unconcerned with appearing "right" on the race question. However, Russian children who attended the city's segregated public schools were less immune to the corrosive influence of racial prejudice. When twelve-year-old Horace Mann Bond passed by a Jewish grocery in his neighborhood in 1916, the grocer's son chanted through the picket fence: "Nigger, Nigger, Nigger, Nigger." Rock-throwing fights between Negro and Jewish children also broke out occasionally, and a native of Poland recollects that he "heard the term 'nigger' used by Jewish sons of immigrant parents with the same venom and contempt as the term 'Zhid' was used in the old country."[19]

Members of the established Jewish community responded even less sympathetically to the condition of their black fellow citizens. By the turn of the century, nearly all of the former had either been born in the South or lived there for many years; even those who had been born abroad had neither experienced the kind of persecution nor been exposed to the radical ideologies which affected the refugees from Russia. The Germans tended to share the racial views of their gentile socioeconomic counterparts, and while this was primarily a consequence of assimilation, it was also related to the Germans' insecure status and desire for acceptance by their gentile peers.

At one extreme among the Germans was editor Frank Cohen of the *Jewish Sentiment*. A distinctly personal journalist not adverse to defying popular opinion, Cohen's pronouncements on the race question differed little from those of the *Atlanta Constitution* and did not necessarily reflect the views of his readers. When racial violence flared in North Carolina at the end of 1898, Cohen observed that "the laws of nature cannot be reversed by 'an act of Congress' and the white man is not only superior to the black man, but will assert his supremicy [*sic*] at the proper time and in the proper manner. . . ." Two weeks later he wrote:

North Carolina has recently done herself proud while several other states have had dignified hanging bees—provoked by the usual cause. . . . Those negroes who conduct themselves properly, are respected and protected, but the lawless brute who violates the sanctity of the white man's home deserves death and usually receives it with electrical swiftness.

And again:

The primary needs of the negro race is [*sic*] obedience to the law and recognition of the rights of others. . . . If law abiding and worthy, every opportunity will be accorded him short of social equality and this no self-respecting white man can endure. If the unmentionable crime against women is persisted in[,] mobs in the future will deal with him as they have in the past.

On two occasions the *Jewish Sentiment* condemned anti-Negro violence, but the exceptions confirm the rule. When "a negro desperado" allegedly murdered several New Orleans policemen and reprisals were made against innocent blacks, Cohen remarked that the murders "did not in the most remote manner licence whites to reck [*sic*] revenge upon the entire race." Similarly, the lynching of nine Negroes in a Georgia town was labeled a crime "without parallel or palliation" by the editor, who insisted that "there is but one provocation for lynch law." However, when such provocation presented itself in Columbus, Cohen congratulated the citizens of Columbus and Georgia "upon being forever rid of two such scoundrels as those negroes who were hung," and suggested that the governor had been too prompt in offering a reward for the capture of the mob's leaders.[20]

At the other end of the spectrum, probably more representative of popular Jewish opinion, were moderates whose support for white supremacy was tempered by a sense of paternalism and desire for racial harmony. Mrs. Victor Kriegshaber urged Atlantans to "take up the white man's burden" and establish boys clubs and summer camps for Negro youths, while Oscar Pappenheimer, wishing to distinguish between industrious and vagrant Negroes, suggested that all blacks be compelled to carry documents which would indicate their appearance, employment, abode, and prior conduct. In the wake of the 1906 race riot, David Marx was appointed a member of the Civic League, which endeavored to prevent a recurrence of the catastrophe. Two decades later, he became a leader in the Georgia Commission on Interracial Cooperation.[21]

On at least two occasions, other leaders of the Jewish community endorsed racial discrimination. Just prior to the construction of their new temple, the trustees of the Hebrew Benevolent Congregation decided in 1901 that their outmoded house of worship on Garnett and Forsyth streets should not be sold or rented to a black congregation. And the following year, the Jewish member of the Carnegie Library Board of Trustees voted to reject the petition of W. E. B. Du Bois and others that the library admit Negroes.[22]

While the Jew looked upon the Negro primarily as a customer and had almost no contact with blacks prior to settling in the South, blacks perceived Jews to be far more than mere purveyors of goods and services and were indirectly acquainted with them long before actual contact was made. Even the most unlettered knew of Moses, Joshua, David, Daniel, and Job, whose exploits provided the inspiration for innumerable spirituals and folk songs. The Negro identified strongly with the longing, suffering, and striving of the Old Testament Hebrews. Their bondage in Egypt, trek through the wilderness, conquest of the Promised Land, and punishment when they whored after false gods were highly relevant symbolic images for a people newly freed from slavery and struggling for equality. But however durable the analogy, it had its limits; when a local Negro informed members of his church that the Lord had appeared to him in a vision and revealed that Negroes were really Jews and therefore God's chosen people, he was run out of town.[23]

If the Old Testament predisposed the Negro to look upon the Jew with reverence, the New reminded him—as it did white Christians—that Jews were rebels against God's purpose. Recalling his childhood in Mississippi and Arkansas, novelist Richard Wright remarked that all of his neighbors hated Jews, not because Jewish merchants exploited them but because they had been taught at home and in Sunday School that Jews were Christ-killers. "To hold an attitude of antagonism or distrust toward Jews was bred in us from childhood" and manifested in folk ditties such as

> Bloody Christ killers
> Never trust a Jew
> Bloody Christ killers
> What won't a Jew do?

Similarly, an Atlanta reporter in 1875 heard an old woman sing,

> I hear a rumblin' in de skies,
> Jews, screws, de fi dum?
> I hear a rumblin' in de skies,
> Jews, screws, de fi dum.

When asked the meaning of the reference to Jews the woman replied: "Jews crucified him." Four decades later, young Horace Mann Bond, stung by the epithet of "Nigger," instantaneously retorted: "You Christ-killer!" As late as 1965, Bond suspected that the phrase had "hung imminent in the Atlanta air," a legacy of the Leo Frank case that had entered his subconscious and remained, waiting only for an opportune moment for release. "But of course the thought that Christ had been killed, and by the Jews, and that this little boy was such a one, may have had a more ancient basis in my-twelve-year-old mind than I can now bring myself to admit." Just as the Jews' acquisition of race prejudice was a by-product of the assimilative process, anti-Jewish prejudice was normative in a Christian society and provided blacks with a means of manifesting something they had in common with other Gentiles.[24]

Blacks could identify not only with the biblical Hebrews, but also with the Jews of the Diaspora. In an era of lynching and disfranchisement, local and national black spokesmen came to the defense of Alfred Dreyfus and expressed sympathy for the victims of Russian pogroms. These declarations of concern were motivated not only by genuine humanitarianism but also as a means of winning the support of Jews and other whites for their own cause by demonstrating the similarity between conditions in Russia and America. The failure of most whites to perceive any similarity led to black accusations of gross hypocrisy.[25] When, in the aftermath of the Bialystok pogrom, the U.S. Senate passed a resolution expressing the horror and sympathy of the American people, the editors of the local *Voice of the Negro* remarked: "With the Jews all lovers of justice are bound to sympathize.... But what right has the United States Senate to be horrified?... We are having here in America Kishinevs and Bialystoks every day." Similarly, when representatives of the Episcopal and Methodist churches declared their solidarity with oppressed Russian Jewry, Benjamin Jefferson Davis, editor of the *Atlanta Independent,* wrote: "We have but little patience in the statesmanship or religion that is so solicitous about saving the Jews of Russia, while the Negroes in their back yards ... are dying and perishing for [want of] Christian help."[26]

The superior claim that the foreign-born seemed to exert on the American conscience reinforced an existing nativist strain in Negro thought. In his widely hailed 1895 Atlanta Exposition speech, Booker T. Washington urged the white South to "cast down your bucket where you are.... among the eight millions of Negroes whose habits you know," rather than look to whites of alien ways and dubious loyalties to bring prosperity to the region. Black nativism resulted principally from the apprehension that foreign laborers would take jobs away from native blacks. To combat this threat, Negro spokesmen endeavored to tap the wellspring of white xenophobia and readily distorted the characteristics of the New Immigrants. In "The Crocodile Tears of Inconsistency," a cartoonist for the *Voice of the Negro* depicted a teary-eyed Uncle Sam kneeling on top of a prostrate Negro (labeled "American born citizen") and reaching out to embrace highly stereotyped figures labeled "Nihilist," "Socialist," "Anarchist," and "Jew" who are being expelled from Germany, Italy, and Russia. "Why not offer the Negro at your door some of the plausible opportunities you are now painting for the foreigner," queried the *Atlanta Independent,* which went on to prophesy that immigration would have a harmful effect on racial and industrial tranquility.

> These foreigners will put the devil in the Negroes' heads and another menace will be added to our labor and race problem.... The white man will [then] be perfectly willing to exchange his overpaid anarchist laborer for his old, under-paid and half-fed Negro service [*sic*].

Even more outspoken was the *Voice of the Negro,* which ridiculed the notion of replacing the "sunniest-dispositioned, most patient, most law-abiding, the meekest and the best working people in the world" with "the scum of Europe."

> The men who are plotting this immigration scheme do not stop to think how, in filling the South with cheap labor from Europe, they would thrust wages down lower and lower; how the immigrants would come here with their anarchist ideas; how the Negroes and low laborers of Europe would clash at every point, and how the very integrity of the pure white South would be threatened by intermingling with this semi-white class of people. These immigrants would be a serious factor in any national crisis. Aliens always are.[27]

While the foregoing characterization of a "semi-white class of people" was a reference to Italians, the local Negro press frequently distinguished between the Jew and the white man. This resulted from a number of factors. The new Jewish immigrant had little conception of himself as a white man; his primary self-identification was as a Jew, and he probably found cause to make this clear to his Negro customers. Second, the Jew dealt with blacks in a more civil fashion than did native-born white Gentiles and was, in turn, perceived as an outsider by the dominant group. Finally, the Negro's habit of distinguishing between the Jew and the white man paralleled the Jew's tendency of differentiating between the *shvartze* (black) and the *goy* (Gentile).[28]

However real the cultural differences separating the immigrants from their native-born white neighbors, Jews were undeniably graced with the color of privilege, and in a society preoccupied with maintaining the subordinate status of blacks, differences between kinds of whites could usually be submerged. But not always. Italian tenant farmers were often ranked with nonwhite laboring groups, and one southern writer insisted that Jews were of Negro descent. There is no indication that the Caucasian standing of southern Jews was ever seriously challenged. However, when Booker T. Washington published an article characterizing Jews as nonwhite, it was perhaps with such an eventuality in mind that Isaac Mayer Wise sternly suggested "the Rev. Prof." needed "a lesson in primary ethnology."[29]

Despite the Jew's sometimes unethical business dealings, implication in deicide, status as an alien, and ambivalent racial standing, many articulate blacks saw in him a model for their own upward mobility. This sense of identification was not only rooted in the relevance of scriptural allegories and a shared experience of exile and rejection, but also in the initial low status of both groups in America. The fact that Jews seemed to overcome the disabilities of poverty and prejudice while blacks had not, suggested that prosperity and equality could be achieved by adopting certain "Jewish qualities." However, there remained considerable disagreement over the specific characteristics and strategies responsible for Jewish success.

Booker T. Washington, who between 1895 and his death in 1915 was the most influential Negro spokesman in America, aimed to improve the economic and moral condition of the Negro through a program of racial solidarity, industrial education, and economic nationalism. Though he looked forward to a day when blacks would eventually attain their constitutional rights, he couched his program in conciliatory terms, depreciated politics, denied interest in social equality, and stressed racial harmony. Washington believed that the black man would never achieve any great success in America until he learned to follow the Jew's example of unity, pride, and economic assertiveness. "The Jew that was once in about the same position as the Negro," observed the Alabama educator, "now has complete recognition because he has intertwined himself about America in a business and industrial sense." T. Thomas Fortune, a prominent northern proponent of Washington's philosophy of "uplift," stressed a similar need for the black man to emulate the Jew in "beating down opposition gradually by high character, great abilities in all directions, the accumulation of wealth and by sticking together."[30]

Washington's most articulate Atlanta supporter was Davis of the *Atlanta Independent,* a keen admirer of Jewish self-esteem, respect for law, and skill in business— qualities in which he believed blacks were woefully deficient. "The Jew is proud that he is a Jew," Davis observed, "and he teaches his children to love the Jews and have more pride in a Jew's achievement, and points to Jewish history as the highest possibility of the human family." Other nationalities do this too, though to a lesser degree, while "the Negro is the only race that has an element in it that is ashamed of itself." As a spokesman for Atlanta's nascent Negro middle-class, Davis was embarrassed and dismayed by the depredations of less orderly blacks, and pointed to the conduct of Jews as worthy of emulation.

> The Jew is known the world over as a good and law abiding citizen. . . . The Independent holds them up to all other citizens as a model. . . . It is so rare for a Jew to commit a crime and be brought into the courts for heinous ones, that when he does commit one, every reasonable doubt is in his favor. The Independent regrets that this is not true of the Negro folks. We are all too prone to commit crimes. . . .

Moreover, unlike the indolent Negro, Jews strove "to lift themselves above the conditions that invite the white man's prejudice" by founding and patronizing their own businesses. But while Davis was a staunch advocate of "race enterprises" and urged his readers to support Negro-owned establishments, his dependence upon Jewish advertising revenue restrained him from calling for a boycott against Jewish merchants.[31]

While most articulate blacks prior to 1915 endorsed Washington's essentially accommodationist program, others—notably W. E. B. Du Bois and Kelly Miller—vigorously dissented. They too recognized the value of racial pride and group solidarity in economic matters, but also came to the defense of liberal education and believed that without political rights blacks could not secure or maintain economic prosperity. Like Washington, they saw relevant parallels in the Jewish experience. Du Bois, who taught sociology at Atlanta University between 1897 and 1910, was an ardent admirer of Jewish philanthropy, political influence, and organizational vitality. Through their vast organizational network, the Jews have made themselves a "tremendous force for good and for uplift," remarked Du Bois. "Let black men look at them with admiration and emulate them."[32]

Midway between Washington's Tuskegee Machine and Du Bois's Niagara Movement was Atlanta's monthly *Voice of the Negro,* edited by J. W. E. Bowen and J. Max Barber. Unlike the Bookerite *Atlanta Independent,* the *Voice of the Negro* was open to divergent viewpoints and even published an article by Daniel Murray who insisted, in true Bookerite fashion, that "prejudice cannot stand against self-interest. . . ."

> We have a lesson in the experience of our Jewish neighbors. I venture to say that the Negro is not more the object of dislike and prejudice than the Jew, and yet by shrewdly seeking to control all handicrafts and manufacturing processes, the Jew has forced prejudice to be silent in this country. . . .

But Bowen and Barber rejected the assumption that economic power alone would render blacks immune from bigotry. "It is [the Jews'] wealth and beautiful women that made them the object of cruel race prejudice," the editors declared. "In other words, wealth is valuable in its place, but it is not going to solve the race problem." Like

Washington, they too admired Jewish industry, orderliness, thrift, passion for liberty, and ("barring financial transactions") morality, but what they esteemed most was the Jews' ability to become socially acceptable to white people without forfeiting their "racial integrity." This, they contended, disproved the Anglo-Saxon's belief that "every other race is fairly crazy to marry into his race."[33]

Black analogies with the Jewish experience were understandable, but also simplistic. Both Washington and his critics underestimated the depth of anti-Jewish prejudice and the reasons why Jews enjoyed greater success than blacks in America. Washington was furthest off the mark. Self-help and ethnic solidarity *had* improved the Jews' economic position and widened their influence, but at the expense of increased hostility from Gentiles. Du Bois and his followers recognized the insufficiency of economic power as a solution to the race problem. However, their adulation of Jewish zeal for education, institutional strength, and political influence contrasted with gentile white fears of these same Jewish predispositions. Though more muted than Negrophobia, anti-Semitism reached a peak in the United States during the first decade and a half of the twentieth century; to an increasing pattern of social discrimination were added restrictive policies in employment, housing, and college admission, and a belief that there existed a subversive international Jewish conspiracy. The Jews' adaptable cultural tradition was certainly responsible for much of the success that they achieved, but blacks would require more than mere will in order to undo the destructive effects of slavery on their history and culture. Moreover, in the South more than elsewhere, the fact that the Jews shared the color of privilege affected their performance. Even the most versatile leopard could not change its spots.

Analogies aside, black leaders still felt betrayed by the unwillingness of Jews to speak out against racism. When Isador Rayner, the Jewish U.S. Senator from Maryland, died in 1912, Benjamin Davis commented, "Though of a race itself beaten by stripes, he invoked upon his colored neighbor the terrors of Kishinev." Nor is there evidence to suggest that any of Atlanta's Jews desired a greater amelioration in the condition of blacks than would have been acceptable to the more enlightened upholders of white supremacy. This is not surprising, for aside from a small conservative elite whose interests generally coincided with those of the business community, Atlanta's Jews kept a low political profile. Only in the case of the prohibition, free silver, and Leo Frank controversies did Jews take the unpopular side of an emotionally charged question. In each instance, their interests were directly affected, and they found themselves singled out for criticism. Even as honorary white men, sharing the color of privilege, Jews were not free to speak their minds. More than anything else, support for white supremacy was the test of a true Southerner. It was perilous enough for a southern-born white Christian to challenge the prevailing system of race relations. For a Jew to have done so would have jeopardized the position of the entire Jewish community, especially at a time when the group's status was being undermined on other fronts.[34]

There was one occasion, however, when a Jew did ally himself with the interests of Atlanta's blacks only to meet with opposition from Benjamin Davis. In 1912 a northern Jew named Rhodes visited the Gate City to popularize a new secret order called the

Knights of Moses and ostensibly dedicated to the political, industrial, and social advancement of the Negro race. Davis was not only suspicious of Rhodes's sincerity but also hostile to the very idea of a secret political order, something which might weaken the Georgia Republican Party and the Negro Odd Fellows—in both of which the editor played a leading role. "They may be honest," cautioned Davis, "but it is a little out of place for a Jew to spend his money and time, without some hope of financial return."[35]

On the whole, Atlanta's blacks enjoyed better relations with Jews than with native white Gentiles. Whatever hostilities were engendered by the cupidity of Jewish merchants, the depredations of black criminals, unfavorable stereotypes, and the effect of residential proximity were mitigated by mutual economic dependence, the Jews' sensitivity to the Negroes' condition, and the symbolic role which the Jew played in black eyes. But in 1913 a respected Jewish businessman was convicted of murder, largely on the testimony of a Negro, severely straining the relationship and forcing the Jews to question the immunitive properties of their white skin.

NOTES

1. Notable exceptions to this neglect are Bertram W. Korn, "Jews and Negro Slavery in the Old South, 1789–1865," *Publication of the American Jewish Historical Society* 50 (March 1961): 151–201 (hereafter cited as *PAJHS*); Philip S. Foner, "Jewish-Black Relations in the Opening Years of the Twentieth Century," *Phylon* 36 (December 1975): 359–67; Hasia R. Diner, *In the Almost Promised Land: Jewish Leaders and Blacks, 1915–1935* (Westport, Conn.: Greenwood Press, 1977); and Arnold Shankman, "Friend or Foe: Southern Afro-Americans View the Jew, 1880–1935" (paper delivered at Conference on the History of Southern Jewry, Richmond, Va., October 25, 1976).

2. David Marx, "History of the Jews of Atlanta" *Reform Advocate,* November 4, 1911 (Special Edition), p. 17; U.S. Census Slave Schedules, De Kalb County, Georgia, 1850; Ira Rosenwailke, "The Jewish Population of the United States as Estimated from the Census of 1820," *American Jewish Historical Quarterly* 53 (December 1963): 147 (hereafter cited as *AJHQ*); Levi Cohen's receipts for slaves dated February 29, 1862, August 1, 1863, and October 3, 1864, American Jewish Archives; *Atlanta Daily Intelligencer,* September 28, 1862, p. 2; November 12, 1862, p. 4.

3. Thomas D. Clark, "The Post-Civil War Economy in the South," *AJHQ* 55 (June 1966): 430; E. Merton Coulter, *A History of the South, The South During Reconstruction, 1865–1877,* vol. 8, (Baton Rouge: Louisiana State University Press, 1947), p. 202; Eli N. Evans, *The Provincials: A Personal History of Jews in the South* (New York: Atheneum, 1973), p. 312.

4. *Atlanta Independent,* October 22, 1910, p. 3; November 1, 1913, p. 8; *Atlanta Constitution,* May 4, 1898.

5. Charles Greenberg, Unpublished Autobiography, [1942], pp. 38–41, in possession of Mrs. David Eisenberg, Atlanta.

6. David Davis [Yampolsky], *The Passing Years: Memories of Two Worlds* (Tel Aviv, Israel: New Life Press, 1974), pp. 32–38, 84; Greenberg, Autobiography, pp. 43–45; Harry Golden, *Forgotten Pioneer* (Cleveland: World Publishing Co., 1963), pp. 68–73.

7. Greenberg, Autobiography, pp. 51–53. Jewish grocers were common in Negro neighborhoods throughout the South. See Howard N. Rabinowitz, "The Search for Social Control: Race Relations in the Urban South, 1865–1890" (Ph.D. dissertation, University of Chicago, 1973), pp. 69, 95–97.

8. W. O. Murphy, "The Negro Grocer"; and Hattie G. Escridge, "The Need for Negro Merchants," both in W. E. Burghardt DuBois, ed., *The Negro in Business,* Atlanta University Publications No. 4 (Atlanta: Atlanta University Press, 1899), pp. 61, 64–65.

9. Dubrovsky, "I. J. Schwartz's *Kentucky,*" pp. 249–50.

10. *Atlanta Constitution,* January 22, 1906, p. 4.

11. Ibid., September 9, 1896, p. 7; November 5, 1897, p. 5; October 4, 1906, p. 3; November 4, 1906, p. 1; *Atlanta Independent,* November 12, 1904, p. 5; Thomas Gibson, "The Anti-Negro Riots in Atlanta," *Harper's Weekly* 50 (October 13, 1906): p. 1457–58.

12. Interviews in Atlanta with Solomon J. Gold, December 19, 1971; David Davis, August 9, 1973; H. Taratoot, March 11, 1973; H. C. Hamilton, March 21, 1973; Mrs. Homer Nash, March 20, 1973; and Mrs. Josephine D. Murphy, March 23, 1973.

13. *Atlanta Constitution,* July 31, 1900, p. 12.

14. Ibid., April 4, 1898, p. 10; July 26, 1902, p. 9. Greenblatt was acquitted of the charge of murder.

15. Ibid., October 18, 1903, p. 5; July 29, 1907, p. 3; March 1, 1908, p. 1; March 24, 1908, p. 9. The Jewish community offered a $300 reward for the apprehension of Hirsowitz's killers, at least one of whom was later caught.

16. Ibid., March 23, 1912, pp. 1, 12; March 30, 1912, p. 1; The *Constitution* initiated a campaign which netted over $2000 (mostly from other Jews) for Morris's family.

17. Ibid., January 17, 1900, p. 10; February 15, 1912, p. 11; January 3, 1915, p. 1.

18. Interviews with Davis, Gold, and Taratoot; Greenberg, Autobiography, pp. 47, 53–60; Davis, *The Passing Years,* pp. 45–47, 57; Milton Himmelfarb, "Negroes, Jews and Muzhiks," *Commentary* 42 (October 1966): 83–86.

19. Horace Mann Bond, "Negro Attitudes Toward Jews," *Jewish Social Studies* 27 (January 1965): 3–4; Interview in Atlanta with Samuel Eplan, December 8, 1971; Charles Rubin, *The Log of Rubin The Sailor* (New York: International Publishers, 1973), p. 15.

20. *Jewish Sentiment* (Atlanta), June 5, 1896, p. 7; October 28, 1898, p. 3; November 18, 1898, p. 3; August 11, 1899, p. 3; March 26, 1899, p. 4; August 3, 1900, p. 3.

21. *Atlanta Constitution,* June 19, 1910, p. 3; October 10, 1906, p. 8; Janice O. Rothschild, *As But a Day: The First Hundred Years, 1867–1967* (Atlanta: The Hebrew Benevolent Congregation), p. 50.

22. Hebrew Benevolent Congregation Minutes, October 14, 1901 (hereafter cited as HBC); W. E. B. Du Bois, "The Opening of the Library," *Atlanta* 54 (April 3, 1902): 809–10.

23. Thomas Tally, *Negro Folk Rhymes* (New York: Macmillan, 1922), pp. 314–15; Harold Courlander, *Negro Folk Music USA* (New York: Columbia University Press, 1963), pp. 41–58; E[dward] A. McIlhenny, comp. *Befo' de War Spirituals* (Boston: Christopher Publishing House, 1933), pp. 44, 59, 77–78, 236; *Atlanta Constitution,* November 22, 1903, p. 8.

24. McIlhenny, *Befo' de War Spirituals,* pp. 38–39, 126; Richard Wright, *Black Boy: A Record of Childhood and Youth* (New York: Harper and Bros., 1945), pp. 53–54; *Atlanta Constitution,* March 23, 1875, p. 4; Bond, "Negro Attitudes Toward Jews," pp. 3–4.

25. Arnold Shankman, "Brothers Across the Sea: Afro-Americans and the Persecution of Russian Jews, 1881–1917," *Jewish Social Studies* 37 (1975): 114–21.

26. *Voice of the Negro* (Atlanta) 2 (October 1905): 675; 3 (July 1906): 546–47; *Atlanta Independent,* December 10, 1910, p. 4.

27. Louis R. Harlan, ed., *The Papers of Booker T. Washington,* vol. 3 (Urbana, Ill.: University of Illinois Press, 1974), pp. 584–85; *Voice of the Negro* 2 (September 1905): 594–96; *Atlanta Independent,* March 23, 1907, p. 4; June 19, 1909, p. 4.

28. *Atlanta Independent,* February 7, 1914, p. 4; July 12, 1913, p. 4; June 6, 1912, p. 4; *Voice of the Negro* 3 (January 1906): 20.

29. Robert L. Brafton, "The End of Immigration to the Cotton Fields," *Mississippi Valley Historical Quarterly* 50 (March 1964): 610; Arthur T. Abernethy, *The Jew A Negro: Being a Study of Jewish Ancestry from an Impartial Standpoint* (Moravia Falls, N.C.: Dixie Publishing Co., 1910); Harlan, *Washington Papers,* 3:408–12.

30. August Meier, *Negro Thought in America, 1880–1915* (Ann Arbor: University of Michigan Press, 1963), pp. 56–57, 100–118; Booker T. Washington, *The Future of the American Negro* (Boston: Small, Maynard and Co., 1902), pp. 182–83; idem, *Putting the Most into Life* (New York: Thomas Y. Crowell Co., 1906), p. 33; Harlan, *Washington Papers,* 3:408–409; Robert Factor, *The Black Response to America: Men,*

*Ideals and Organization from Frederick Douglass to the NAACP* (Reading, Mass.: Addison-Wesley Publishing Co., 1970), p. 190; *New York Age,* July 2, 1914, p. 4; May 18, 1905, p. 2.

31. *Atlanta Independent,* February 7, 1914, p. 4; April 16, 1910, p. 4; June 12, 1915, p. 4; July 12, 1913, p. 4; September 20, 1913, p. 4; January 3, 1914, p. 4.

32. Meier, *Negro Thought,* pp. 190–206; *Crisis* 9 (October 1915): 235.

33. *Voice of the Negro* 1 (October 1904): 551–52; 3 (September 1906): 623–25; 3 (January 1906): 20.

34. *Atlanta Independent,* December 7, 1912, p. 4; Alfred O. Hero, *The Southerner and World Affairs* (Baton Rouge: Louisiana State University Press, 1965), p. 499.

35. *Atlanta Independent,* June 6, 1912, p. 4.

# "Is the Jew a White Man?"

## Press Reaction to the Leo Frank Case, 1913–1915

Recent years have seen a plethora of material on black-Jewish relations; there have been numerous essays, several autobiographical accounts, and a few speculative efforts at laying down guidelines for understanding the two groups.[1] Almost all of these writings, however, exist in an historical limbo, for few have concerned themselves with explorations of black-Jewish contacts before the 1950's. In lamenting this situation, Allan Spear has called for "the detailed historical study of the black-Jewish encounter that the subject clearly merits."[2] What follows is a study of one detail of that encounter as revealed in the reaction of black, Jewish, and general circulation newspapers to the Leo Frank case. The trial, conviction, and eventual lynching of Frank has been generally treated as a flagrant example of the rise of anti-semitism in the United States. The press reaction to Frank's ordeal, however, reveals yet another aspect of American society, for the case provides the first well-focused incident of national interest in which the needs of blacks and of Jews seemed to have been in direct conflict.

The outline of the Frank case is clear enough. In July, 1913 Leo Frank, a Jew, came to trial in Atlanta, Georgia, charged with the murder of Mary Phagan, a fourteen year old white girl employed in the pencil factory managed by Frank. On August 25 the jury found Frank guilty of murder, and the following day the judge sentenced him to death. Over the course of the next two years legal appeal followed legal appeal, each one putting back the date of his execution until, in April, 1915, the United States Supreme Court took its last action in the case by denying a writ of error requested by Frank's attorneys. On June 21, the day before Frank was scheduled to be executed, Georgia's Governor John Slaton commuted his sentence to life imprisonment. It was a short reprieve, for on August 17, 1915 a mob of white men broke into the prison where Frank was being held, took him some miles, and lynched him.[3]

The Frank case generated both legal and public controversy for nearly two years, though the trial itself lasted hardly a month. During those years it became a *cause célèbre,* nearly matching in public interest the Sacco-Vanzetti case of the 1920's and the ordeal of the Scottsboro boys in the 1930's. In 1913–1915 the controversies revolved around whether the jury convicted Frank because of the evidence or because it was intimidated by the mob atmosphere which demanded the blood of a Jew. Though the prosecution produced considerable circumstantial evidence, it focused its case on the single piece of testimony explicitly connecting Frank to the murder of Mary Phagan.

In 1974, Eugene Levy was associate professor of history at Carnegie Mellon University in Pittsburgh. Originally published in *Phylon* 35, no. 2 (June 1974): 212–22. Reprinted with permission of Clark Atlanta University Press.

The central witness against Frank was James Conley, a janitor in the pencil factory. Conley, a black man, admitted to being an accessory after the fact of murder, claiming his part in the crime occurred when Frank coerced him into removing Mary Phagan's body from the spot where Frank had murdered her. In a pre-trial confession, and in four days of testimony, Conley offered a vivid description of Frank's central part in the crime. Both in the trial, and during the many months of public controversy which followed it, Frank's defenders sought to demonstrate that Conley was not to be believed; that he was in fact the most likely perpetrator of the crime which Frank stood in danger of dying for. Across the nation concerned individuals compared Conley and Frank. Who was to be believed: Leo Frank, the Jew, or James Conley, the black man? Did Frank, a Jew, kill a Christian girl, or did Conley, a black man, kill a white girl? When such questions were raised in one fashion or another in 1914 and 1915 they were likely to mean one thing to Jews, another thing to blacks, and yet something else to other Americans.

Though there had been random comments on the Frank case in papers outside the South in 1913, Frank's conviction did not become a national issue until the spring of 1914. In January, Louis Marshall (a prominent attorney, head of the American Jewish Committee, and by then one of Frank's attorneys) called the case to the attention of Adolph Ochs, publisher of the *New York Times,* and Ochs rose to Frank's defense.[4] In February, Frank lost the first of his appeals when a Georgia Supreme Court judge sustained the death sentence. The subsequent setting of a new date of execution generated editorial comments throughout the nation. Open hostility to Frank was largely limited to Populist-turned-arch anti-semite Tom Watson and his magazine, and to newspapers in the smaller towns of the South. Over the months Frank had the explicit support of almost all of America's major newspapers, including such solidly WASP papers as the *Chicago Tribune, Washington Post* and *Baltimore Sun.* Even in the South most big-city dailies either cautiously supported Frank's appeal for a new trial or remained discreetly silent.

Not surprisingly, efforts were made during the trial and afterwards to discredit James Conley's character. It was pointed out that he had served a number of jail terms for petty thievery and had been fined numerous times for disorderly conduct. He was drunk, it was claimed, on the morning the crime occurred.[5] Luther Rosser, one of Frank's lawyers, in his final plea to the jury back in August, 1913, projected an image of Conley which one would frequently see in the months to follow. "Who is Conley?" Rosser asked rhetorically. He quickly answered his own question: "He was a dirty, filthy, black, drunken, lying nigger."[6] Frank himself gave support to the "bad nigger" image of Conley when he made a widely circulated statement wondering how "the testimony of Southern white women of unimpeachable character," who spoke on his behalf, could be called lies, and "the perjured vaporizings of a black brute alone accepted as the whole truth. . . ."[7]

The theme of the "black monster," as the *New York Times* characterized Conley, appeared in many forms.[8] The *Baltimore Sun,* for example, puzzled as to why the jurors "took the word of a vicious, lying degenerate negro as against that of a white man. . . ." The crime, the *Washington Post* noted early in the public controversy, seemed "characteristic of a drunken ignorant negro," while it was evident to the editorial writer that "no intelligent white man would do such a thing. . . ."[9]

By 1915 the scene was well set. George Dougherty of Pinkerton's, in looking at the case, made clear that in his view the style of murder indicated "a negro's job."[10] In like fashion former Congressman William M. Howard, in appealing to Governor Slaton to commute Frank's sentence, pointed out that murder was "the natural thought of a negro to save his life . . . ," implying that Conley had murdered the girl to keep her from revealing his sexual advances. "The trouble with the case," Howard went on, "is that too many people have fooled with it who don't know the negro."[11] After the commutation of Frank's sentence to life imprisonment, one editor praised it as just, for Frank "was convicted solely on the testimony of a negro. . . ."[12]

It remained to be explained why a jury of twelve white Southerners would believe "the testimony of a negro." The question was put most simply by the Reverend Julian Rogers, an Atlanta clergyman who believed that Frank had not received a fair trial, when he noted that he "wouldn't hang a yellow dog on James Conley's testimony, much less a white man. . . ."[13] In Chicago the *Tribune* bluntly editorialized that "the life of a white man at the disposal of a disreputable negro reveals a complete revolution in ordinarily prevailing sentiments," and even the extremely cautious *New Orleans Times Picayune*, in expressing its pleasure at the commutation of Frank's sentence, commented that the jury had based its verdict on "testimony of a kind not very highly regarded by Southern juries under normal conditions."[14]

The basic explanation offered by Frank's supporters was that the prosecution, led by County Solicitor Hugh Dorsey, had thoroughly coached Conley in his story so as to make it believable.[15] There were several more complicated explanations as to why the jury, and much of the South, took a black man's word, believable or not. Burton Rascoe, in the *Chicago Tribune*, argued that the white South had had its fill of black blood and now was in search of a fresh victim. Adding a new twist to an old theme, Rascoe felt that in the "South they do not hate the negroes. They don't respect them, they deny rights [in order to] disfranchise, lynch and pity them; but they do not hate them. To hate them would mean some acknowledgement of the equality of white and blackamoor which no true Southerner will admit." The Jew, Rascoe went on, is "thoroughly hated, from economic jealousy as well as from religious prejudice, the one intensifying the other."[16] Another writer similarly felt that Atlantans were not especially anti-semitic; they simply hated all foreigners, largely because they did not "make fine distinctions between the negro and the white man which is the tradition in old Atlanta to demand."[17]

The Frank case obviously stimulated America's editorial writers. Behind the speculation as to why a Southern white jury would bother to believe "the negro Conley," however, lay a tacit willingness, if not an explicit desire, to see the "normal" course of Southern justice come into operation. Edward Marshall summed up this sentiment when he angrily wrote, "That Leo Frank, the highly educated, well connected and hitherto respected managing expert in lead pencil manufacturing should be doomed to die, is not more astonishing than that this black human animal, confessedly a participant in the horror, should be alive to tell his dreadful tale."[18]

Black Americans, in reading the nation's press in these years, quickly came to feel that whites were again looking for a black scapegoat. This did not appear to stem from so-called black anti-semitism. Apart from the Frank case there seems to have been little hostility towards Jews among black leaders of the early twentieth century. None claimed Jews were less anti-black than other Americans, but a number felt that the Jewish experience offered a viable model for blacks. Booker T. Washington fitted them into his scheme when he wrote that "the Jew that was once in about the same position as the Negro has now complete recognition because he has entwined himself about America in a business and industrial sense."[19] W. E. B. DuBois saw a different aspect when he praised the ability of Jews to work together for a common cause. "Let the black man look at them and emulate them," he wrote bluntly in 1915, at the height of the Frank controversy.[20] James Weldon Johnson, soon to become executive secretary of the National Association for the Advancement of Colored People, agreed with both Washington and DuBois, and went a step further, suggesting a close alliance between the groups, for the Jew "in fighting for his own rights, in some degree fights for ours also."[21]

Negative comments, however, soon flourished in black newspapers, given the continual characterization of Conley as a "black monster" and the widespread effort to shift the burden of guilt from white to black. From early stages of the case *The Crisis*, the NAACP journal, like black newspapers, felt a black man was the preferred victim. "Atlanta tried to lynch a Negro for the alleged murder of a young white girl," *The Crisis* charged, "and the police inquisition nearly killed the man. A white degenerate has now been indicted for the crime, which he committed under the most revolting circumstances."[22] Out of this sense of victimization eventually emerged a kind of half-submerged anger that such large amounts of money and effort were being spent to save the life of one accused Jew when blacks were continuing to be lynched for crimes far less serious than murder, and long before they ever reached trial. "Frank, the Jew, threatened, hounded and lynched," editorialized the *Baltimore Afro-American* in August of 1915, "presents to outraged America an entirely different spectacle from the fifty other lynchings of the year, not in the brute defiance of the law or the revolting detail of the burning, but chiefly because the dastardly crime 'customarily is reserved for those of a race other than that of Leo Frank.'" The editor of the *Chicago Broad-Ax* put it succinctly when he used a cliche: "It seems that after all, it all depends upon whose ox is gored."[23]

The *Chicago Defender* took the lead in attacking Frank's supporters by labeling the charges against Conley "ridiculous" and deliberately generated by "Frank's race hating friends." A few months later the *Defender* flatly stated that "there seems to be absolutely no question of his [Frank's] guilt," a sentiment echoed by a number of other black papers.[24] Yet blacks recognized that the fact the prosecution's chief witness was black, in the climate of contemporary America, was of great use to Frank and his supporters. "The one thing in [Frank's] favor," bitterly noted the *Philadelphia Tribune*, "is that the main witness against him is a colored man and it is against the law of the land for a white man to be convicted of a crime on the evidence of a colored man."[25]

Conley was not turned into a hero by the black press, but most felt he told the truth. He was simply displaying the slave's typical mentality, the *Savannah Tribune* claimed, in helping his white boss remove the body of Mary Phagan.[26] Perhaps James Weldon

Johnson expressed the general sentiment of most black papers when he wrote that while he had no desire to see Frank hang, nor to see a miscarriage of justice, yet to see such reputable papers as the *New York Times* and the *Chicago Tribune* attempt to pin the crime on a black man, largely because he was black, seemed equally reprehensible.[27]

Like whites, blacks also wondered why a Southern jury believed Conley. The general consensus seemed to be that if there was "a scintilla of evidence" against Conley, he would have long since been dead.[28] Only Benjamin Davis, editor of the *Atlanta Independent*, felt one "could not reach the conclusion that Frank is guilty beyond the reasonable doubt on the evidence of Jim Conley." Conley, Davis observed, was "a discreditable Negro," whose "evidence is not sufficient to take the life of an individual." Davis, however, had previously been attacked by the editor of the *Baltimore Afro-American* for overemphasizing the "low moral condition" and ignorance "of the great mass of black people," for being, in fact, more of a class man than a race man.[29]

It was the *Chicago Defender* which most bluntly confronted the question of black and Jew as it arose out of the Frank case. "Conley May Not Hang in Atlanta for Thirty Pieces of Silver," headlined the *Defender*. Again in bold type the paper announced that "Jews Raise Millions to Free Frank and Put Blame on Innocent Man." Behind these headlines lay a strong feeling that Frank and his supporters were deliberately manipulating the anti-black feelings of the American public. Frank deserved to be condemned, the paper angrily noted, when he conveniently forgot the treatment of "HIS PEOPLE" in Russia and tried to evoke race hatred in labeling Conley a "BLACK BRUTE."[30]

Yet in his anger Robert Abbott, editor of the *Defender*, saw the broader implications of the Frank case. It was here that Abbott posed the question "Is the Jew a white man?" "Shall the Jews and Afro-Americans," Abbott went on, "join hands as allies?" He invited Jews to make common cause with black Americans, for he felt that "this case proves beyond the question of a doubt that an Afro-American's word is nearly as good as a Jew's when the third party is a white man." For Abbott the Frank case seemed to be the beginning of a rapidly escalating racial confrontation in America. This confrontation would involve as distinct groups blacks, whites and Jews. The Frank case was but the first of many that will follow, Abbott prophesied. "The Jews are fighting to the last ditch to save their race and will continue to fight forever. The Christian white man is fighting to keep him back and the Afro-Americans are fighting among themselves. Somebody pray for us," Abbott concluded dolefully.[31]

The *Defender* was more vociferous than other black papers, and in its anger it most clearly reflected the tensions black men felt towards the case. After Frank's lynching neither the *Defender* nor any other black paper took overt pleasure in the incident, but several editors pointed out that it did serve the purpose of publicizing the existence of lynching.[32] Most black editors, however, bitterly commented on what they saw as the largely misplaced emotions of whites. "And while we as a race sympathize with Mrs. Frank and other relatives," the *Philadelphia Tribune* wrote soon after the lynching, "we also feel that they are now in a better position to extend sympathies to the relatives of the hundreds of families of the many colored victims of mob violence in Georgia."[33] In damning the *Chicago Tribune*'s "eleventh hour Uriah Heap pecksniffian" condemnation of the South after Frank's lynching, the *Defender* was characteristically forthright and flamboyant. "Do you, or did you," W. Allison Sweeney asked the *Tribune,* "reckon the life of one white man, this single 'murdered' Hebrew, with the millions for defense behind him, of more importance, as wielding a greater influence over the future of 'American complacency' than those of the thousands of murdered black men?"[34] The *Tribune* did not respond to the *Defender*'s question.

There was, of course, another minority group vitally interested in Leo Frank. By late 1913 many prominent Jews, led by the American Jewish Committee's Louis Marshall, were devoting a great deal of time, money, and talent to right what they felt to be a grave injustice being perpetrated against a fellow Jew.[35]

The bulk of discussion in Jewish papers revolved around the extent and significance of anti-semitism during the trial and its aftermath; Conley's character and race were of less concern to editors of Jewish papers than their counterparts on the city dailies or on black newspapers. Nevertheless, to defend Frank one generally had to counter the evidence against him, and this usually led to an attack upon James Conley.

One of the first to confront the issue was Jonah Wise, editor of Cincinnati's *American Israelite.* Wise, scion of America's best-known reform Jewish family, had spent some twenty-five years in the South, or on its fringes, and claimed to know the region thoroughly. Given this, he found it hard to believe Frank innocent for he doubted if a "well chosen jury of Southern men" would have based their guilty verdict solely on the "unsupported testimony of a low type of negro."[36] Within the year, however, Wise had shifted his view and now ascribed the eagerness of Southerners to believe "a negro ex-convict," largely to the fact that Frank was a Jew in a Jew-hating city.[37] Upon Frank's lynching Wise completely reversed his original opinion. He now damned men like Hugh Dorsey and Tom Watson for deliberately contriving Frank's "murder," so as to "protect themselves against the truth that must have come out at some time of their guilty knowledge, and to render powerless the vicious and criminal negro, the real murderer of Mary Phagan, whom they have been shielding."[38]

Wise's invective, however, was extreme; perhaps more thoroughly "Americanized" than most, his angry rhetoric put his editorials considerably closer to those in the major metropolitan dailies than to those in other Jewish papers. More common among the latter were such phrases as "the testimony of a negro with a long police record," "the testimony of a negro who has confessed that he was an accomplice," or the description of Conley and Dorsey "as black a black man and as black a white man" as any accused has had to face.[39] In like fashion, a positive view of blacks occasionally appeared. After Frank's lynching, one Jewish paper claimed that blacks were "the only defender of [Georgia's] good name," in that a black man was the only one to come forward to supply his wagon to carry away Frank's body, thus preventing its mutilation and burning.[40]

There was another aspect, however, to the treatment of the case in the Jewish press. While the editors themselves generally refrained from extreme anti-black statements, they frequently reprinted vitriolic anti-Conley editorials from the daily papers in which appear such inflammatory phrases as "black human animal," "depraved negro," "treacherous negro," and "negro dope fiend."[41] Jewish editors displayed a fundamental ambivalence in using such tactics. They seemed reluctant to engage in the kind of "nigger-baiting," and thus racism, common in the daily press, while at the same time they keenly wanted to use all means available, including anti-black statements, to aid Frank's cause.

One way to resolve this difficulty would have been to have blacks agree that Conley was not to be believed. Perhaps it was such a wish which led several Jewish papers to publish in December, 1913 what appears to have been a spurious editorial, supposedly from the Atlanta "Colored Independent," acknowledging Frank's innocence and Conley's guilt.[42] The supposed editorial began with fulsome praise: "We Negroes are of the opinion that the Jews are the best people on earth, particularly to us Negroes they are really very good." It then went on to claim that "had we been sitting on the jury, we should have convicted Conley instead of Frank . . . Conley is a disgrace to our race, and we do not wish to know aught of such negroes." As we have seen, Benjamin Davis, editor of the *Atlanta Independent*, did write in the spring of 1914 that he felt Conley's character rendered his testimony unfit to condemn a man to death, a statement he qualified a short time later with a claim that he spoke "not in the interest of Frank, but in the interest of fair play."[43] There is no evidence, however, that Davis ever made the extreme and simplistic statements attributed to him in the supposed editorial. It would seem that in this case the wish was father of the thought, and someone manufactured the anti-Conley editorial out of the Atlanta editor's known hostility to "low type" blacks.

Amidst the anger and fear generated by the Frank case, at least one writer, Allan Davis of the *Pittsburgh Jewish Criterion,* paralleled the role of prophet taken on by Robert Abbott of the *Chicago Defender.* In protesting against Southern "Bigotry," "Prejudice," and "Lawlessness," Davis predicted that "it must follow as the night the day that as yesterday a negro was lynched, what is to prevent a white from being lynched tomorrow? And if one white man, why not another?" Frank's ordeal, Davis added in an attempt to put it into some historical perspective, was "but a single incident in the endless struggle between right and wrong." The "principles of Moses and Isaiah and Hillel" left no doubt in Davis' mind on which side of the struggle the "Jewish race" must be arrayed.[44]

Davis' views found few echoes at the time, but it was perhaps some such feeling of common fate which led Louis Marshall, Frank's principal appeals lawyer, in 1923 to join the board of directors and the legal defense committee of the NAACP. "If by accepting the honor I am making amends for my apparent neglect," Marshall wrote the Association's president, "I shall be very glad to consent to serve."[45] It was not entirely by chance that Marshall decided to make up for his "apparent neglect," and place his considerable talents at the services of the Association. A few months earlier the Association's lawyers had convinced the Supreme Court to reverse the death sentences of twelve Arkansas blacks, on the grounds that a mob atmosphere prevailed during their original trial. Eight years earlier Louis Marshall had tried, and failed, to convince the Court that essentially the same grounds justifies a reversal of Leo Frank's conviction.

In looking back over the reaction to the case, the centrality of the "American" view, as mediated through the major metropolitan dailies, stands out. The newspapers of the two minorities had little direct access to the events, and they, as well as almost everyone else, largely responded to the factual reporting and editorial views of the majority press.

Reflecting the interests and prejudices of the majority society, the general circulation newspapers first condemned what they saw as overt, crude anti-semitism, and then went on to treat James Conley in a typically overt, crude, but thoroughly "American," manner.

The uniqueness of their reactions to the views of the American press made clear that blacks and Jews, each in their own way, were responding out of their experience as subjugated groups in caste societies. For blacks, subjugation in America had a hard, physical reality to it. By 1915 that system of segregation by law we know as *jim crow* was firmly entrenched, and it appeared to be digging in still deeper with a number of cities enacting residential segregation ordinances. Even the federal government, now controlled by Woodrow Wilson and the Southern Democrats, appeared to be going the way of jim crow. In this situation, the efforts to substitute a "black brute" for Leo Frank seemed but another example of blacks being victimized by whites.

While Jews experienced considerable prejudice and discrimination in America, their situation in 1915 was far from that of a subject people in a caste society. Yet millions of "American" Jews had only recently left an Eastern European Pale where they were indeed inferior members of a rigid, increasingly brutal, largely segregated society. The pogroms, the Dreyfus Affair, the Beiliss "ritual murder" case, though all took place in Europe, nevertheless combined to produce in the minds of many American Jews, even some of the most "emancipated," a deep sense of uncertainty, a sense which endured amidst New World optimism.[46] Did Frank's ordeal signify that anti-Jewish feelings were on the verge of displacing anti-black feelings? Would "jew-baiting," on the European model, become an American practice? Was the vaunted American "Melting Pot" a piece of fiction?[47] Reflecting these fears, Jewish editors chose not to emphasize that the American elite, at least as reflected by the major newspapers, overwhelmingly supported Frank. Instead they dwelt on the apparent rise of anti-semitism, so familiar from the European model. "It is little wonder," one of them wrote cynically, "that [Russia and France] smile with diabolical joy at the stellar performance of the Model Nation of the World."[48]

The caste mentality of both blacks and Jews generated, as we have seen, a few pleas for cooperation. However, under stress such as produced by the Frank case, blacks and Jews, each viewing themselves as at the mercy of the majority society, usually sought to protect their own. For some Jews that meant substituting the "black brute" for Leo Frank. For some blacks it meant saving Conley and allowing that "Hebrew with millions for defense behind him," to go to his death. Each group sensed its own weakness, and instinctively sought to offer up the other by emulating the prejudices of the majority.

Leo Frank clearly had the better of the struggle in terms of national sentiment, for editorials followed close upon one another in treating "the Jew" as a white man unjustly convicted of a crime "typically" committed by blacks. Yet such national, essentially elitist, sentiment counted for little among Southern white "plain folk," and in the end Frank died, lynched in a manner reminiscent of so many murdered blacks. Conley lived to disappear into obscurity, but the nation's papers were filled with the worst sort of anti-black stereotypes, stereotypes which only buttressed oppression. Neither blacks nor Jews sounded any note of triumph over the outcome—only a combination of anger and despair which a sense of weakness so often generates.

Later events would cause blacks and Jews to forget their conflict in the Frank case. The rise of a black-Jew-Catholic-hating Ku Klux Klan in the late teens, the triumph of Nazism in the 1930's, and the struggles which made up the civil rights movement of the post-World War II era, produced a sometimes intense sense of common cause, if not common fate, between blacks and Jews. Cooperation, however, modified but did not dissipate the feeling the two groups were competing for position within a hostile majority society.[49] The urban conflicts of the 1960's soon generated fears among Jews that in some way they were to become scapegoats for increasingly assertive blacks, and the concomitant fear among blacks that in the final instance Jews would assert their "whiteness" to maintain their influence and power.[50] Such mutual fears brought again to the surface that combination of anger and despair which had first emerged clearly during the debate surrounding Leo Frank's fate a half century earlier.

NOTES

1. See the following collections of essays and articles: Shlomo Katz, ed., *Negro and Jew* (New York, 1967); Conference on Jewish Studies, *Negro-Jewish Relations in the United States* (New York, 1966); and James Baldwin and Nat Hentoff, eds., *Black Anti-Semitism and Jewish Racism* (New York, 1970). Two speculative efforts are William H. Becker, "Black and Jew: Ambivalence and Affinities," *Soundings*, LIII (Winter, 1970), 413–39, and Ben Halpern, *Jews and Blacks* (New York, 1971).

2. Spear's comment concludes a review of Robert Weisbord and Arthur Stein, *Bittersweet Encounter: The Afro-American and the American Jew, Journal of American History,* LVIII (September, 1971), 504. The Weisbord and Stein study is the best account of the recent history of black-Jewish relations.

3. I have relied on Leonard Dinnerstein, *The Leo Frank Case* (New York, 1968) for details of the case.

4. *Ibid.*, p. 91.

5. *Ibid.*, pp. 21–22.

6. Harry Golden, *A Little Girl is Dead* (Cleveland, 1965), pp. 182–83.

7. *St. Louis Post-Dispatch*, December 9, 1914; *Baltimore Sun, Cincinnati Enquirer, Raleigh News and Observer* (Jacksonville) *Florida Times-Union*, all December 10, 1914.

8. *Times*, March 15, 1914.

9. *Sun*, November 23, 1914; *Post*, March 15, 1914.

10. *New York Times*, January 10, 1915.

11. *Baltimore Sun, Houston Post, Raleigh News and Observer*, all June 15, 1915.

12. *Philadelphia Enquirer*, June 27, 1915.

13. *Louisville Courier-Journal*, March 16, 1914. For similar statements by another Atlanta minister see *Washington Post*, (Jacksonville) *Florida Times-Union*, both March 16, 1914.

14. *Tribune*, June 25, 1915; *Times-Picayune*, June 22, 1915.

15. Dinnerstein, *op. cit.*, pp. 40, 47–48.

16. *Tribune*, December 27, 1914.

17. Edward Marshall, "Leo M. Frank, An Innocent Man, May Suffer a Disgraceful Death for Another's Crime," *New York Times*, March 15, 1914, Section IV, p. 6. This Marshall is not to be confused with Louis Marshall, Frank's attorney.

18. *Ibid.*

19. Booker T. Washington, *Character Building* (New York, 1902), p. 191, quoted in Robert Factor, *The Black Response to America* (Reading, Massachusetts, 1970), p. 190.

20. *The Crisis*, IX (March, 1915), 234.

21. *New York Age*, February 2, 1918. See also Johnson's articles in the *Age* on January 28, 1915, February 25, 1915, and February 3, 1916. Professor Philip Foner has pointed out to me that a decade earlier a number of black leaders had displayed considerable anger when Jewish American leaders refused to condemn the treatment of black Americans, while at the same time demanding that the United States government officially protest against the harsh treatment of Jews in Russia.

22. *The Crisis*, VI (September, 1913), 221.

23. *Afro-American*, August 21, 1915. For similar sentiments see the *Washington Bee*, May 1, 1915. *Chicago Broad Ax*, August 21, 1915.

24. *Defender*, February 28, 1914 and April 25, 1914. See also *Indianapolis Freeman*, August 21, 1915 and *Cleveland Gazette*, August 21, 1915.

25. *Philadelphia Tribune*, February 13, 1915.

26. *Savannah Tribune*, August 30, 1913.

27. *New York Age*, June 3, 1915 and June 24, 1915.

28. *Gazette*, December 26, 1914. See also *New York Age*, April 22, 1915 and the *Chicago Defender*, May 1, 1915.

29. *Atlanta Independent*, March 21, 1914; *Baltimore Afro-American*, December 20, 1913.

30. *Defender*, May 9, 1914 and December 12, 1914.

31. *Ibid.*, January 2, 1915.

32. *Cleveland Gazette, Richmond Planet, Chicago Defender*, all August 21, 1915. See also *The Crisis*, X (October, 1915), 276–78.

33. *Philadelphia Tribune*, August 21, 1915.

34. *Defender*, August 21, 1915.

35. Leonard Dinnerstein, "Leo M. Frank and the American Jewish Community," *The American Jewish Archives*, XX (November, 1968), 114–15.

36. *American Israelite*, November 20, 1913.

37. *Ibid.*, April 30, 1914, November 19, 1914, December 10, 1914.

38. *Ibid.*, August 19, 1915.

39. *St. Louis Jewish Voice*, November 7, 1913; *Philadelphia Jewish Exponent*, March 13, 1914; *Chicago Sentinel*, June 11, 1915.

40. *Chicago Sentinel*, August 20, 1915.

41. *Boston Jewish Advocate*, December 12, 1913; *Pittsburgh Jewish Criterion*, February 26, 1915, May 21, 1915; (Cleveland) *The Jewish World*, March 1, 1915; *St. Louis Jewish Voice*, August 27, 1915; *Cincinnati American Israelite*, March 19, 1914, September 24, 1914, August 26, 1915.

42. *St. Louis Jewish Voice*, December 5, 1913; *Boston Jewish Advocate*, December 19, 1913.

43. *Atlanta Independent*, March 21, 1914, April 4, 1914.

44. *Pittsburgh Jewish Criterion*, August 20, 1915.

45. Marshall to Moorfield Storey, November 30, 1923 in Charles Reznikoff, ed., *Louis Marshall, Champion of Liberty* (Philadelphia, 1957), I, 426.

46. Dinnerstein, *op. cit.*, pp. 72–74.

47. *Boston Jewish Advocate*, August 27, 1915; *Baltimore Jewish Comment*, October 23, 1914; *Pittsburgh Jewish Criterion*, July 2, 1915, August 20, 1915.

48. *Pittsburgh Jewish Criterion*, August 20, 1915.

49. See for example, David H. Pierce, "Is the Jew a Friend of the Negro," *The Crisis*, XXX (August, 1925), 184–86; Kelly Miller, "Negro and Jew, Partners in Distress," (Norfolk, Va.) *Journal and Guide*, November 5, 1938; and Kenneth Clark, "Candor on Negro-Jewish Relations, *Commentary*, I (February, 1946), 8–14.

50. For a vivid case study of these fears in the 1960's see Robert Weisbord and Arthur Stein, *Bittersweet Encounter: The Afro-American and the American Jew* (Westport, Conn., 1970), pp. 161–205.

# Leo M. Frank and the American Jewish Community

"The most horrible persecution of a Jew since the death of Christ,"[1] is what Reuben Arnold, the defense attorney, called the indictment and trial of his client, Leo M. Frank. A factory superintendent and part owner of the National Pencil Factory in Atlanta, Frank had been convicted of murdering one of his employees, a thirteen-year-old girl named Mary Phagan, in April, 1913. Although he denied his culpability, and the prosecution's key witness was a Negro—a rare occurrence in a Southern city at the beginning of the twentieth century—an all white jury found the superintendent guilty. The judge sentenced the defendant to hang.[2]

Within a few weeks after Frank's conviction, the most influential American Jews were alerted to the fact that prejudicial circumstances had surrounded the trial. After learning the details, Louis Marshall, president of the American Jewish Committee, described the case as "almost a second Dreyfus affair."[3] And because other prominent Jews shared this opinion, many devoted themselves to rectifying the injustice.

There were manifold reasons for Jewish involvement and concern with Leo Frank. To begin with, Jewish tradition dictated that brethren in distress had to be aided. As Louis D. Brandeis later said: "When men and women of Jewish blood suffer—because of that fact—and even if they suffer from quite different causes—our sympathy and our help goes out to them instinctively in whatever country they may live. . . ."[4] Then, too, every Jew who familiarized himself with the details of the case seems to have become convinced of Frank's innocence and to have recognized the importance of correcting a miscarriage of justice. An additional spur was the fact that anti-Semitic attacks had been growing both in Europe and in the United States since the end of the nineteenth century; the Dreyfus and Beilis affairs, in France and Russia, respectively, were perhaps the most dramatic examples of a significant, and an apparently growing, world-wide attitude. Where America was concerned, this represented a departure from past norms. The Jews—largely German and Sephardic—who had come to the United States before the 1880's had, for the most part, prospered and assimilated into the social, economic, and political life of the nation. Most of them had met with no organized persecution and were able to overcome the inconvenience of petty slights. But the influx of the East European Jews which began toward the end of the nineteenth century generated vir-

In 1968, Leonard Dinnerstein was assistant professor of American history at Fairleigh Dickinson University.
Originally published in *American Jewish Archives* 20 no. 2 (1968): 107–26. Copyright © 1968, American Jewish Archives. Reprinted with permission of American Jewish Archives, Cincinnati Campus, Hebrew Union College, Jewish Institute of Religion.

ulent anti-Semitic outbursts in the United States and threatened the Americanized Jews. To ignore Frank might suggest to other American communities that Jews could be attacked with impunity.

## CRACK THE JEW'S NECK!

The raw facts in the case were these. A girl had been found dead, and allegedly raped, in the basement of Atlanta's National Pencil Factory on April 27, 1913. Leo Frank, the factory superintendent, was by his own admission the last person to have seen her alive. Within a few days, hair identified as belonging to the dead girl, as well as bloodstains, was allegedly found in a workroom opposite Frank's office. When questioned by the police, the superintendent appeared unusually nervous. On the basis of this "evidence," the authorities arrested Frank two days after the girl's body had been discovered.[5]

Frank was incriminated further by tales of alleged indiscretions on his part. Former employees from his pencil plant accused the prisoner of having acted improperly with women. A policeman reported that he had seen Frank, a married man, caressing a young girl in the woods a year earlier, and a notorious Atlanta madam claimed that on the day of the murder Frank had phoned her repeatedly, imploring her to provide a room for him and a companion.[6] When presented with the facts gathered, the grand jury returned an indictment.[7]

Shortly thereafter the police released a series of startling affidavits, sworn to by Jim Conley, a Negro sweeper who had been employed at the pencil factory. The Negro, arrested a few days after the murder because he had been seen washing blood from a shirt, implicated Leo Frank in his statements. Conley claimed to have helped the superintendent carry the girl's body to the factory basement after Frank had committed the murder.[8]

During the trial, Conley, elaborating upon his accusations, unfolded a gruesome story. Frank, he said, had used him on many occasions to guard the front door of the factory while the superintendent entertained women in his office. The sweeper claimed that he had seen Frank in certain unnatural positions—which he did not describe—and that on the day of the murder the superintendent had practically confessed to the crime. According to Conley, Frank had told him that the girl had refused his advances and that he had subsequently struck her. The sweeper alleged then that he and Frank had together removed the corpse to the basement and that, after returning to the superintendent's office, he had obligingly written the following notes while Frank dictated their contents:

> Mam that negro hire down here did this i went to make water and he push me down that hole a long tall negro black that hoo it wase long sleam tall negro i wright while play with me

> he said he wood love me land down play like the night witch did it but that long tall black negro did buy his slef[9]

Leo Frank denied the allegation, branded his accuser an infamous liar, and attempted to account for his time on the day of the murder. Other witnesses supported his statements. *The Atlanta Constitution* observed that a "chain of testimony forged with a number of links has established a seemingly unbreakable corroboration of Frank's accounts of his whereabouts. . . ."[10]

Beyond the main testimony, the jurors had little more on which to base their decision than hearsay, rumors, and unsubstantiated accusations. Yet most members of the public were thoroughly convinced of the defendant's guilt and made their voices heard. The intense summer heat necessitated that the courtroom windows be left open, and remarks from the crowds could be heard easily by those inside. "Crack the Jew's neck!"— "Lynch him!"—were some of the epithets emerging from the more boisterous. Threats were also made "against the jury that they would be lynched if they did not hang that 'damned sheeny.' " The editors of Atlanta's three major newspapers prevailed upon the judge to hold the trial over until a Monday, rather than let it conclude on a Saturday, so that there would be fewer people milling around when the courtroom proceedings ended. Judge Leonard Roan agreed, and also requested that Frank and his attorneys, for their own safety, remain away from court when the jury rendered its verdict. Roan had allegedly confided to a friend, "If Christ and his angels came down here and showed this jury that Frank was innocent, it would bring him in guilty." Few were surprised, therefore, when the jury found the defendant guilty. Outside the courthouse the news sent thousands of persons into a jubilant revelry.[11]

### A MATTER OF JUSTICE

Shortly after the trial, Atlanta's leading rabbi, David Marx, went to New York to consult Louis Marshall. The American Jewish Committee, over which Marshall presided, had been established in 1906 by some of the most prominent Jews in the United States—men like Jacob H. Schiff, Oscar S. Straus, and Cyrus Adler—primarily to aid Jews "in all countries where their civil or religious rights were endangered or denied."[12] Marx, as well as other Atlanta Jews, believed that Frank's conviction had resulted from an anti-Semitic outburst. Under the circumstances, the assistance of the more powerful American Jews was sought.

After reviewing the case, Marshall agreed that it was "one of the most horrible judicial tragedies" that had ever come to his attention.[13] A keen judge of human behavior, he cautioned against any so-called Jewish intervention and advised Cyrus Sulzberger that "there is nothing that the [newspaper] American Hebrew should do in connection with the Frank matter. It would be most unfortunate if we made a Jewish question of the case. It is a matter which must be handled with the utmost delicacy, lest we arouse the very forces which we are seeking to destroy."[14] He repeated this sentiment to other Jews whose confidence he held. On Simon Wolf, a prominent Jewish lawyer in Washington, D.C., who did not always see eye-to-eye with the president of the American Jewish Committee, Marshall urged, "Whatever is done must be done as a matter of justice, and any action that is taken should emanate from non-Jewish sources."[15]

Yet anyone familiar with the divisions in the American Jewish community—the very term is, in fact, a misnomer because there never was any monolithic group of Jews in this country with an identical outlook—at the beginning of the twentieth century knows that no self-appointed authority could impose his views upon those whose opinions differed from his own. By the time Wolf received Marshall's advice, he had already sent out a circular letter in which he counseled members of the Union of American Hebrew Congregations to agitate in Frank's behalf. Wolf stressed the theme that racial prejudice had caused Frank's conviction, and he urged the recipients to encourage their newspapers to demand a new trial. Coincidentally, the week following Wolf's epistle, editorials appeared in Alabama, North Carolina, Minnesota, and Ohio newspapers deploring the fact that Frank's religion precluded "a fair trial and a square deal." Cincinnati's *American Israelite*—a Jewish weekly—opined, "the man was convicted at the dictates of a mob, the jury and the judge fearing for their lives, having received threatening letters, and the men who served on the jury have stated before the trial that they wanted to get on the jury to convict the Jew."[16]

The publication of these editorials enraged Marshall. To Adolph Kraus, president of the B'nai B'rith, he wrote: "I . . . regret greatly such articles as that which appeared on the editorial page of the Israelite today. They can do no good. They can only accentuate the mischief."[17] Marshall thought that his course of action, using influential people to get Southern newspapers to change public opinion, would eventually win Frank his freedom. In that way, the anti-Semitic prejudice which had been aroused in Atlanta "may not only subside, but may be absolutely counteracted and destroyed."[18]

On November 8, 1913, the executive committee of the American Jewish Committee discussed the Frank case for the first time.[19] It resolved to take no official action, although a number of the members indicated that they might personally help Frank. Louis Marshall summarized the Committee's position a year later. "It would be most unfortunate," he wrote, "if our organization were to be considered as championing the causes of Jews who are convicted of crime."[20]

### BOUGHT BY JEW MONEY

Although Marshall had advised caution and circumspection, he did not think that unpublicized assistance would do any harm. Hence, giving generously of his time to Frank's attorneys, he advised them about public relations and helped them prepare a brief for the judicial appeal. With over 100 specific allegations enumerated, the petition claimed in essence that prejudice and perjury had dominated the courtroom and that justice demanded a new hearing. The judge who had originally sentenced Frank refused the request, but acknowledged that he was not convinced of the defendant's guilt. In a second appeal, the Georgia Supreme Court disregarded the trial judge's personal opinion, and upheld his legal judgment by sustaining the courtroom verdict.[21]

The defense attorneys had been prepared for a denial of their petitions. Anticipating the result, they had begun seeking new evidence to free their client. They also hired William J. Burns, the internationally famous detective, to conduct his own inquiry. Other investigators had already obtained a number of affidavits from prosecution witnesses who claimed to have perjured themselves during the trial. Released to the newspapers over a period of weeks, these statements attested to police chicanery and fraud. Some of those who had testified for the prosecution claimed that the authorities had forced them to swear falsely in court. No sooner were these statements published, however, than the police arrested the affiants, reinterviewed them, and obtained new affidavits in which all claimed that their original stories had been correct, but that Frank's investigators had bribed them to retract.[22]

The charge that Frank's defense had used lavish amounts of money to influence persons associated with the trial traveled throughout the state of Georgia. Such rumors had been circulating, in fact, from the time of his arrest. It was said that the Atlanta newspapers gave Frank unusually kind treatment because they had been bought with "Jew money"; that Nathan Straus, a native Georgian and one of the owners of R. H. Macy's department store in New York, had brought $40,000 into the state to "buy up" the Georgia Supreme Court; that "Big Money" had purchased newspaper coverage and editorials throughout the country; that wealthy Jews had spent half a million dollars on Frank's defense; and, later on, that the figure had passed $1,000,000. That most Atlantans were convinced of the veracity of these accusations cannot be doubted. A Northern reporter discovered that "anyone who raises his voice in favor of Frank is accused of being bought by 'Jew money.'"[23]

Certainly it was true that considerable sums of money, as well as personal influence, had been used by Frank's Jewish friends. That they were used improperly, however, has never been proved. Financial contributions had been made to the defense by men like Julius Rosenwald, head of Sears, Roebuck and Co., and Jacob H. Schiff, head of Kuhn, Loeb, and by others as well, but this was so, primarily, because these men were convinced that a fellow-Jew had been unjustly convicted of murder. To be sure, they recognized the national repercussions which might result from any open assistance, and they were probably afraid also that anti-Semitic eruptions might mushroom if Frank were left to fend for himself. But the Jewish tradition of helping brethren in distress must also be considered as a motivating force. As Louis D. Brandeis later said:

> A single though inconspicuous instance of dishonorable conduct on the part of a Jew in any trade or profession has far-reaching evil effects extending to the many innocent members of the race. Large as this country is, no Jew can behave badly without injuring each of us in the end. . . . Since the act of each becomes thus the concern of all, we are perforce our brothers' keepers.[24]

The amount of assistance given Frank by influential Jews cannot be overestimated. Aside from Marshall, perhaps the most energetic worker for Frank's cause was Albert D. Lasker, the advertising wizard from Chicago. Personally informed of Frank's plight by relatives, he conducted his own investigation in Atlanta. Interviews with Frank and his lawyers convinced Lasker that a monstrous mistake had been made and that the terrible injustice had to be eradicated. Taking a year's leave from his business, Lasker marshalled nationally prominent people to the defendant's aid, directed lawyers and investigators in search of new evidence, secured funds from diverse acquaintances, and personally contributed more than $100,000 of his own money to help secure justice.[25]

Lasker and Marshall, among others, believed that Frank's chance to obtain his freedom would be strengthened if his plight were publicized nationally, thereby stimulating throughout the country a "spontaneous" demand for a new trial. Although they alerted newspapers to Frank's predicament, the two hoped that their own activities and the work of other Jews helping the prisoner would receive no mention in print. Typical of the way in which the president of the American Jewish Committee stimulated the dissemination of news was the answer that he sent to a friend who had asked what he could do for the cause. "The greatest aid that you and your friends in Baltimore can give to this cause," Marshall replied, "would be to induce some of the leading newspapers in Baltimore, Richmond, Savannah, and other Southern points which you reach, to write editorials similar to that which recently appeared in the Atlanta Journal, and to reproduce the articles which have appeared from day to day in the New York Times and the Washington Post."[26]

### GEORGIA AT BAR

In response to the initiative of those working to exonerate Leo Frank, sympathetic responses and assistance came from many non-Jews who were motivated, perhaps, by the nature of the injustice, or who felt obliged for some reason to publicize a case about which Lasker, Marshall, and others felt so strongly. The newspapers were the most vocal. In Atlanta, the *Journal* vividly recalled the temper surrounding the trial:

> The very atmosphere of the courtroom was charged with an electric current of indignation which flashed and scintillated before the very eyes of the jury. The courtroom and streets were filled with an angry, determined crowd, ready to seize the defendant if the jury had found him not guilty. Cheers for the prosecuting counsel were irrepressible in the courtroom throughout the trial and on the streets unseemly demonstrations in condemnation of Frank were heard by the judge and jury. The judge was powerless to prevent these outbursts in the courtroom and the police were unable to control the crowd outside. . . . it was known that a verdict of acquittal would cause a riot such as would shock the country and cause Atlanta's streets to run with innocent blood.[27]

New York's Yiddish-language *Forward* devoted endless reams to the case, and its editor, Abraham Cahan, made a personal investigation in March, 1914.[28] A North Dakota paper wrote: "We say without hesitation that we would have sat on that jury until this great globe hangs motionless in space and the rotting dead arise in the cerements, before we would condemn any man to death on the evidence which convicted Frank." And *The Mobile Tribune* pronounced Frank "a rank and palpable victim of prejudgment and political 'frame-up.'" *Collier's* succinctly summarized the view of those working in behalf of the Atlanta Jew: "Trial by hysteria is not trial by jury." By the end of 1914, Albert Lasker could write:

> Outside of the State of Georgia, the press of the United States, including the leading papers of every city in the South, save Georgia, are editorially not only commenting on the case, and agitating a public sentiment for the unfortunate Frank, but daily hundreds of papers, including the leading Southern papers, are editorially crying that Frank's execution would amount to judicial murder, and that in this case, the State of Georgia is more at bar than Frank. I do not exaggerate when I state that hundreds of such editorials are appearing daily.[29]

Assistance rendered, however, went far beyond alerting newspapers to the injustice. The new investigators, led by William J. Burns, made intensive efforts to unearth new evidence, and they succeeded in their tasks. The methods that Burns employed, however, irritated hypersensitive Georgians and made them reluctant to accept his findings, if not completely opposed to acknowledging them.

Mr. Burns talked too much. After his arrival in Atlanta, he announced his confidence in solving a case that the local citizenry already considered closed. For three months the famous detective exuded confidence and made public statements which he could not justify in terms of his discoveries. "I am utterly confident of success," he repeated to newspaper reporters time after time. "The trail is very plain," he revealed, but declined to elaborate.[30] His conceited assertions led Northerners to assume that he would "produce a confession from the real murderer, or at least direct evidence. Failing to do that," Albert Lasker wrote to Herbert Haas, "the people up here will be very disappointed. . . ."[31]

Burns did obtain letters from a Negro woman in Atlanta—although how he did so was never made clear—which Frank's accuser, Conley, had written to her from prison. The construction of the phrases, the handwriting, and the analogies were almost identical to those that had appeared in the so-called "murder notes" discovered near the corpse in April, 1913. The authorities, however, arrested the recipient of the letters, reinterviewed her, and then produced an affidavit stating that Conley had written only two or three letters, and that none of them were lewd. Since Frank's attorneys had about ten letters in their possession, and since graphologists had identified them as Jim Conley's, the new affidavit released by the police could not have been the truth. Yet those who doubted Burns accepted the version of the police. Among the doubters was the judge, to whom another appeal had been made.[32]

Burns's association with the Frank case proved disastrous for the defendant. "It is the belief of nearly all of our friends," one of the Atlanta attorneys wrote to Lasker, "that Burns' connection with the case has done us irretrievable damage."[33] Marshall, who had vigorously opposed employing the noted sleuth, explained his position: "I have been disgusted at the farcical methods to which Burns has resorted. Every one of his acts has been a burlesque upon modern detective ideas. It is deplorable that a case so meritorious as that of Frank should have been brought to the point of distraction by such ridiculous methods."[34]

## MOB LAW AND DUE PROCESS

Although national newspaper agitation and flamboyant investigators aggravated Georgian feeling against Frank, an inadequate legal staff must also bear some responsibility for his predicament. This opinion seems to have been universally acknowledged by those familiar with the intimate details. Louis Wiley, for example, wrote to Marshall: "While I can understand the clamor and mob feeling which led to the unjust verdict in the Frank case, I am strongly inclined to believe that the prisoner was not adequately defended. If he had been, it seems to me the dreadful situation now before us might have been prevented."[35] Others who echoed this sentiment included Abraham Cahan, editor of the *Forward*, and DeWitt Roberts, who investigated the Frank case for Atlanta's Anti-Defamation League in the 1950's. Cahan lamented that "when one reads the long stenographic report of this cross examination [of Jim Conley], one cannot help think-ing that in New York or Chicago, you could find dozens of lawyers who would have done a much better job."[36] And Roberts, a more recent chronicler, opined that "the defense of Leo Frank was one of the most ill-conducted in the history of Georgia jurisprudence."[37]

Louis Marshall was continually annoyed with the Atlanta attorneys. "One of the misfortunes of this case," he testily observed in a letter to one of them, "lies in the fact that there have been too many counsel and that they do not work in unison."[38] Marshall had prepared a number of briefs and legal arguments for the Atlanta attorneys to use, and they frequently ignored his advice. Impatient with Frank's other lawyers, he ex-pressed his wrath forcefully:

> After the motion for a new trial had been decided adversely by the Supreme Court of Georgia, and my attention was called to the circumstances attending the reception of the verdict, I insisted that a new proceeding should be instituted, for the purpose of raising the constitutional question. I took great pains in fully laying down the plan of campaign, the manner in which the questions were to be raised, and practically prepared a brief laying stress on the violation of the Federal Constitution. To my utter chagrin, the line of argument on which I proceeded, and which was the only theory on which there was the slightest hope of success, was flouted and disregarded, and it was only after plain talk that I induced you to file a supplemental brief, to some extent covering the line of argument which I had previously indicated. I prepared the assignments of error, and without rhyme or reason some of them were, without con-sultation with me, transformed into an argument, a practice which is utterly bad.[39]

The briefs prepared by the Atlanta attorneys did not lead to the desired results. The Georgia courts rejected all the arguments presented—and so, too, did the United States Supreme Court in the first appeal it received. One of the main reasons for this was, as Marshall pointed out, that "the federal constitutional question could only be discovered in it by the aid of a high-power magnifying glass. It was necessary for you to point out to me," he added in a letter to one of the Atlanta attorneys, "that there was even one line in which the Fourteenth Amendment was referred to."[40] A few days later Marshall added, "several very excellent lawyers were of the opinion that some of the concessions which you made [in the first brief to the United States Supreme Court] went further than the case warranted, and which indeed was my own view."[41]

The second appeal to the United States Supreme Court was prepared by Marshall and delivered by him also. He argued that Frank had not been present at all stages of the trial, hence he had been deprived of his constitutional rights because the due process clause of the fourteenth amendment dictated that the defendant appear in court when the jury rendered its verdict. Therefore, the State of Georgia held Frank in custody illegally.[42] The United States Supreme Court had never ruled on this particular issue before and agreed to hear arguments. Marshall devoted himself tirelessly to the presen-tation, but confided to one of the Atlanta associates an obstacle that had to be hurdled:

If the judges were confronted with the proposition, that the adoption of our views would mean the unconditional discharge of Frank whether guilty or innocent, they would struggle very hard against such a conclusion. On the other hand, if they are satisfied that Frank did not have a fair trial and that by adopting our jurisdictional theories they can accord to him a new trial, that would be in conformity with the modern tendencies in the administration of the criminal law, and would go far toward preparing the way for a favorable reception of our theories.[43]

By a vote of 7 to 2, a majority of the United States Supreme Court rejected Marshall's plea on the grounds that it was incorrect for a federal court to overrule a state court in procedural matters, that the Georgia Supreme Court had considered Frank's trial a fair one, and that no federal rights had been jeopardized. Justices Oliver Wendell Holmes and Charles Evans Hughes dissented from their brethren: "Mob law," they concluded, "does not become due process of law by securing the assent of a terrorized jury."[44]

### I WOULD BE A MURDERER

Disheartened, somewhat despondent, but nevertheless determined to save Frank's life, Marshall and other Jews inaugurated a massive campaign to obtain a gubernatorial pardon. In a series of letters written to every member of the American Jewish Committee, Marshall enunciated the plan of action:

What our people . . . should do is, to enlist in Frank's behalf the interest of United States Senators, Members of Congress, leading newspaper men and prominent church people, non-Jewish and non-Catholic, and to ask them to write at once to the Board of Prison Commissioners and to Governor John M. Slaton, urging executive clemency. The line of argument should be that doubt existed about Frank's guilt, that every tribunal which considered the case divided in its judgment, and that justice, therefore, required a commutation.[45]

The recipients of Marshall's communications heeded his advice. Letters went forth to the most influential people in the country, starting with President Woodrow Wilson and former President William Howard Taft, both of whom declined to intervene.[46]

From the amount of mail that poured into Georgia, however, it appears that almost everyone else with whom Marshall communicated responded in the desired fashion. Eight governors, a score of congressmen and senators, and prominent Americans, including the president of the University of Chicago and Jane Addams, wrote letters. Millions more signed petitions that were printed in newspapers like the Detroit *Times* and the Omaha *Bee* or simply circulated in well-traveled places.[47] In May and June, 1915, Leo Frank's application for clemency received more newspaper attention in this country than almost any other issue.[48]

John M. Slaton, governor of Georgia, worked in a goldfish bowl. The fight to save Frank catapulted both prisoner and governor to national notice, and Slaton received more than 100,000 communications.[49] (Some of the mail he received demanded that the sentence of the court be carried out.) In addition to the national hysteria, Slaton had to wrestle with the several court decisions, as well as with the recommendation of the Georgia Prison Commission which had voted 2 to 1 to uphold the verdict.[50]

The governor deliberated for more than a week. On the day before the hanging was to take place, he commuted Frank's sentence to life imprisonment.[51] In a lengthy explanation which accompanied his decision, he showed that the inconsistencies in the evidence, as well as certain glaring contradictions, prevented him from being certain of the prisoner's guilt. At the time that he released his statement, Slaton added, "I would be a murderer if I allowed that man to hang."[52]

Frank remained in prison for only two months. On August 16, 1915, a band of masked Georgians invaded the penal institution, kidnapped its most famous inmate, and drove with him all night to a grove outside of Marietta, Georgia, Mary Phagan's home town. The men tied a rope around Frank's neck, slung it over a large oak, and then let his body sway in the wind. By the time the townsfolk came to gaze, the lifeless figure was hanging limply from the tree.[53]

That a great many Jews had come to Frank's aid during his two-year ordeal was generally known. The intercession on the Atlantan's behalf was not intended to thwart justice, but to obtain it. Nevertheless, Georgia's patrician historian, Lucian Lamar Knight, wrote afterwards that "the entire Hebrew population of America was believed to be an organized unit directing and financing a systematic campaign to mold public sentiment and to snatch Frank from the clutches of the law."[54]

It was, of course, easy to criticize the nation's Jews for their participation; but what alternatives were there, and what would have been the consequence to Frank if his pleas had been ignored? In this country, unfortunately, minority groups frequently have to be defensive and have to protect their civil rights and civil liberties aggressively. Rabbi Stephen S. Wise had enunciated the problem a month before Governor Slaton commuted Frank's sentence:

> It is occasion for real regret to me that it is necessary for a Jew to speak touching the case of Leo Frank. It would have been infinitely better if non-Jews had arisen throughout the land, as they ought to have done, to plead on behalf of this man. True, there have been those non-Jews within and without this city [New York] who have lifted their voices on behalf of justice for Frank. But the burden of seeking justice has fallen upon the fellow-Jews of Frank. . . .[55]

NOTES

1. *Atlanta Constitution* [AC], October 26, 1913, p. 1.

2. *Ibid.*, August 27, 1913, p. 1.

3. Louis Marshall to Irving Lehman, September 9, 1913. Louis Marshall Papers (American Jewish Archives, Cincinnati [AJAr]). Unless otherwise specified, all letters to and from Louis Marshall are in this collection; therefore, the expression "Marshall Papers" will not be repeated. Louis Marshall will be cited hereafter as LM.

4. Jacob De Haas, *Louis D. Brandeis* (New York, 1929), p. 72.

5. *AC*, April 28, 1913, pp. 1–2; *Atlanta Georgian* [AG], April 28, 1913, p. 1; April 30, 1913, p. 1; *Atlanta Journal* [AJ], April 29, 1913, p. 1; *Frank v. State, Brief of the Evidence*, pp. 15, 43.

6. *AC*, May 8, 1913, p. 2; May 11, 1913, p. 1; May 23, 1913, pp. 1–2; *AG*, May 9, 1913, pp. 1–2.

7. *AJ*, May 24, 1913, p. 1.

8. *AJ*, May 24, 1913, p. 1; May 29, 1913, p. 1; May 30, 1913, p. 1; *AG*, May 24, 1913, p. 1; May 25, 1913, p. 1; May 28, 1913, p. 1; May 29, 1913, p. 1; *AC*, May 25, 1913, p. 1; May 30, 1913, p. 1.

9. *Frank v. State, Brief of the Evidence*, pp. 54–57; Henry A. Alexander, *Some Facts About the Murder Notes in the Phagan Case* (privately published, 1914), pp. 5, 7.

10. *AC*, August 17, 1913, p. 2A.

11. "Frank's Prophesy of Vindication Comes True to Years After Georgia Mob Hangs Him As Slayer," *Jewish Advocate* (Boston), XLII (October 18, 1923), 20; Minutes of the Executive Committee of the American Jewish Committee, November 8, 1913 (American Jewish Committee Archives, New York City) (cited hereafter simply as Minutes); *AC*, August 26, 1913, p. 1; October 24, 1913, p. 7. Judge Roan's remark is quoted in Elmer R. Murphy, "A Visit with Leo M. Frank in the Death Cell at Atlanta," *Rhodes' Colossus*, March, 1915, p. 10.

12. Minutes, November 11, 1906.

13. LM to Dr. Judah L. Magnes, September 15, 1913.

14. LM to Cyrus Sulzberger, October 3, 1913.

15. LM to Simon Wolf, October 3, 1913; to David Marx, September 9, 1913; to Irving Lehman, September 9, 1913; to William Rosenau, December 14, 1914. In many of the early letters to David Marx, the rabbi's surname is spelled as "Marks."

16. LM to Simon Wolf, September 27, 1913; clippings from *Montgomery* (Alabama) *Times*, September 25, 1913; *Tribune-Herald* (Chisholm, Minn.), September 26, 1913); *Southern Republican* (Charlotte, N.C.), September 27, 1913; all located among the Leo Frank Papers, AJAr. Since all newspaper references to the Frank papers are clippings, the word will not be repeated.

17. LM to Adolph Kraus, September 27, 1913.

18. *Ibid.*

19. Minutes, November 8, 1913.

20. LM to William Rosenau, December 14, 1914.

21. *Frank v. State,* 141 *Georgia* 246.

22. *AC*, February 24, 1914, p. 7; March 13, 1914, p. 1; March 15, 1914, p. 2A; March 28, 1914, p. 1; May 2, 1914, p. 2; May 4, 1914, p. 1; May 5, 1914, p. 10; May 6, 1914, p. 1; *AJ*, March 5, 1914, pp. 1–2; May 3, 1914, p. 1; May 5, 1914, p. 2.

23. Wytt E. Thompson, *A Short Review of the Frank Case* (Atlanta, 1914), p. 30; C. P. Connolly, *The Truth About the Frank Case* (New York, 1915), p. 14; "The Leo Frank Case," *Watson's Magazine*, XX (January, 1915), 139–40, 160; *Ledger* (Jackson, Miss.), June 22, 1915, clipping in the scrapbook of John M. Slaton (Georgia State Archives, Atlanta, Georgia); *News* (Brunswick, Ga.), November 29, 1914, Frank Papers; A. B. MacDonald, "Has Georgia Condemned an Innocent Man To Die?", *Kansas City* (Mo.) *Star*, January 17, 1915, p. 3C.

24. De Haas, *op. cit.*, pp. 197–98.

25. John Gunther, *Taken At the Flood* (New York, 1961), pp. 82–83; Julian W. Mack to LM, March 16 and 23, 1914; LM to Louis Wiley, May 5, 1914.

26. LM to Siegmund B. Sonneborn, March 13, 1914.

27. *AJ*, March 10, 1914, p. 8.

28. Theodore Marvin Polloch, "The Solitary Clarinetist: A Critical Biography of Abraham Cahan, 1860–1917" (unpublished Ph.D. dissertation, Columbia University, 1959), p. 366.

29. *American Israelite*, May 21, 1914, p. 1; *Mobile Tribune*, March 21, 1914; *Arkansas Democrat*, April 15, 1914; *Trenton* (N.J.) *Times*, March 26, 1914; *Collier's*, April 28, 1914, Frank Papers; Albert D. Lasker to Jacob Billikopf, December 28, 1914, Julius Rosenwald Papers (University of Chicago).

30. *AJ*, February 19, 1914, p. 1; March 16, 1914, p. 1; March 18, 1914, p. 1; *AC*, March 20, 1914, p. 2; April 5, 1914, p. 1.

31. Albert D. Lasker to Herbert Haas, April 20, 1914, Jacob Schiff Papers (AJAr).

32. *New York Times*, April 25, 1914, p. 8; May 6, 1914, p. 3; *AJ*, May 5, 1914, p. 2; *AC,* May 6, 1914, p. 5.

33. Herbert Haas to Albert D. Lasker, May 2, 1914, Rosenwald Papers.

34. LM to Louis Wiley, May 5, 1914, Schiff Papers.

35. Louis Wiley to LM, April 3, 1914.

36. Abraham Cahan, *Bletter fun Mein Leben* (5 volumes; New York, 1931), V, 416. The section on Leo Frank was translated for me from Yiddish by my father, Abraham Dinnerstein.

37. DeWitt Roberts, "Anti-Semitism and the Leo M. Frank Case" (unpublished essay, n.d., *ca.* 1953, located in the Leo Frank Folder of the Anti-Defamation League archives, New York City), p. 15.

38. LM to Henry Alexander, December 1, 1914.

39. *Ibid.*

40. *Ibid.*

41. LM to Henry Alexander, December 4, 1914.

42. *New York Times,* December 18, 1914, p. 6; February 21, 1915, II, 1.

43. LM to Henry Alexander, February 19, 1915.

44. *Frank v. Mangum,* 237 *U.S.* 347, 349.

45. LM to Herbert Friedenwald, May 10, 1915, and May 15, 1915; to Hollins N. Randolph, May 7, 1915. A number of other Jews also made substantial efforts to save Frank. Whether or not they acted in response to Marshall's directive is impossible to say. Herman Binder, a friend of Frank's, reported the case to B'nai B'rith's Supreme Lodge Convention

> which met in San Francisco in May, 1915. Under the leadership of the Supreme Lodge (without making a national issue of it publicly) delegates were urged to bring it before their respective lodges and Grand Lodges and work from the local level with their non-Jewish community leaders. Binder himself traveled across the country, speaking at various lodges in the Middle West, then on to the Rocky Mountain regions and the Pacific Coast states. The result of these efforts was that several state legislatures urged, through resolutions, the commutation of the death sentence of Leo Frank. Others urged a new trial, etc.

(Memo to Alex Miller from Richard E. Gutstadt, September 28, 1953, located in the Leo Frank folder of the Anti-Defamation League files, New York City).

46. Simon Wolf to Woodrow Wilson, June 10, 1915, Woodrow Wilson Papers (Library of Congress), Series VI, File #3658; Herman Bernstein to Woodrow Wilson, June 16, 1915, *loc. cit.;* William Howard Taft to Julius Rosenwald, May 17, 1915, Rosenwald Papers; LM to Herbert Haas, May 21, 1915.

47. Julius Rosenwald to Senator Lawrence Y. Sherman, May 18, 1915; Senator L. Y. Sherman to Julius Rosenwald, May 21, 1915, Rosenwald Papers; Harvey Judson, president of the University of Chicago, to the Georgia Prison Commission, May 9, 1915, Prison Commission Records (Georgia State Archives); LM to Herbert Haas, May 28, 1915; Elmer Murphy to Leo Frank, May 1, 1915, Slaton Papers (Brandeis University); *AC,* May 16, 1915, p. 1; May 24, 1915, p. 5; May 28, 1915, p. 7; May 29, 1915, p. 1; May 30, 1915, p. 5; May 31, 1915, p. 5; June 1, 1915, p. 4; *AJ,* May 29, 1915, p. 2; *New York Times,* May 18, 1915, p. 6; May 25, 1915, p. 6; May 29, 1915, p. 12; May 30, 1915, II, 14; C. Vann Woodward, *Tom Watson: Agrarian Rebel* (New York, 1963), p. 436.

48. In his biography of Watson, Woodward noted: "The Frank case for a time rivaled the European war as a subject of national attention" (p. 436).

49. Lucian Lamar Knight, *A Standard History of Georgia and Georgians* (6 volumes: Chicago, 1917), II, 1168.

50. *AC,* June 10, 1915, pp. 1–2.

51. *Ibid.,* June 21, 1915, extra, p. 1.

52. *Ibid.*

53. *Ibid.,* August 17, 1915, p. 1; August 18, 1915, pp. 1–2.

54. Knight, *op. cit.,* II, 1165–66.

55. Stephen S. Wise, "The Case of Leo Frank: A Last Appeal," *Free Synagogue Pulpit,* III (May, 1915), 80.

# From "*The Souls of Black Folks:*
# A Comparison of the 1903 and 1952 Editions"

In all likelihood it is not premature to affirm that *The Souls of Black Folk* by W. E. B. Du Bois is a classic. It was first published, of course, in 1903; thereafter it was reprinted from the original plates twenty-four times, by its first publisher, A. C. McClurg & Co. of Chicago. The last of those reprints was issued in 1940.

With the Cold War and the McCarthyism of the post-1946 era, and with Du Bois' radicalism and active opposition to both, his name and his work were consigned to oblivion by dominant governmental, educational, and communications establishments. When, therefore, the fiftieth anniversary of the publication of *Souls* approached, the Doctor moved to the issuance of a new edition through one of the publishing houses just then established—largely through the efforts of Howard Fast, at that time another prominent victim of McCarthyism and the Cold War. This was the Blue Heron Press of New York City and in 1953 it did publish a limited, autographed edition in one thousand copies.

This edition differed from the first in that it contained a three-page note by the Doctor entitled "Fifty Years After," and a three-page contribution from the author, Shirley Graham—the Doctor's wife—entitled "Comments." The body of the book was re-set with pagination identical to that of the 1903 edition.

While in his "Fifty Years After" note, Du Bois offered several ideas of great interest, in this paper attention will be focussed only upon two paragraphs in it. They read as follows:

> Several times I planned to revise the book and bring it abreast of my own thought and to answer criticism. But I hesitated and finally decided to leave the book as first printed, as a monument to what I thought and felt in 1903. I hoped in other books to set down changes of fact and reaction.
>
> In the present Jubilee Edition I have clung to this decision, and my thoughts of fifty years ago appear again as then written. Only in a few cases have I made less than a half-dozen alterations in word or phrase and then not to change my thought as previously set down but to avoid any possible misunderstanding today of what I meant to say yesterday.

What were the "alterations" that the Doctor made in the 1953 edition? The answer

In 1971, Herbert Aptheker was professor of history at Hostos Community College of the City University of New York and a member of the history department staff at Bryn Mawr College.

Originally published in *Negro History Bulletin* 34, no. 1 (1971): 15–17. Copyright © 1971 by the Association for the Study of Negro Life and History, Inc. Reprinted with permission of the Associated Publishers, Inc.

requires a line-by-line reading of the two editions; after such an effort it is possible to report that there are seven substantive changes in the McClurg text of *Souls* as issued by the Blue Heron Press in 1953. Four of them occur in the seventh chapter entitled, "Of The Black Belt"; two in the ninth chapter, "Of The Sons Of Master And Man"; one in the tenth chapter, "Of The Faith Of The Fathers." Their substance is similar; they aim at eliminating possible anti-Semitic connotations though, as to this, some ambiguity attaches to two of the alterations. The texts of the changes are as follows: in each case a reading of the 1903 edition is followed by a reading of that of 1953.

### I (P. 126—PAGINATION SAME IN BOTH EDITIONS):

*1903:*

"The Jew is the heir of the slave-baron in Dougherty [County, Georgia]; and as we ride westward, by wide stretching corn-fields and stubby orchards of peach and pear, we see on all sides within the circle of dark forest a land of Canaan. Here and there are tales of projects for money-getting, born in the swift days of Reconstruction,— 'improvement' companies, wine companies, mills and factories; nearly all failed, and the Jew fell heir."

*1953:*

Identical except: "Immigrants are heirs. . . .; most failed, and foreigners fell heir."

### II (P. 127):

*1903:*

"This plantation, owned now by a Russian Jew, was part of the famous Bolton estate."

*1953:*

"This plantation, owned now by a foreigner. . . .".

### III (P. 127):

*1903:*

"Then they took the convicts from the plantations, but not until one of the fairest regions of the 'Oakey Woods' had been ruined and ravished into a red waste, out of which only a Yankee or his like could squeeze more blood from debt-cursed tenants."

*1953:*

Identical, except for the ending which reads ". . . out of which only a Yankee or an immigrant could squeeze . . .".

Here, though anti-Semitism does not seem to be a possible reading, Du Bois did not feel impelled, apparently, to alter his attribution to Yankees! (See also V, below)

## IV (P. 132):

*1903:*

"Most of this land was poor, and beneath the notice of the slave-baron, before the war. Since then his nephews and the poor whites and the Jews have seized it."

*1953:*

Identical, except, "Since then his poor relations and foreign immigrants have seized it."

## V (P. 169):

*1903:*

"The rod of empire that passed from the hands of Southern gentlemen in 1865, partly by force, partly by their own petulance, has never returned to them. Rather it has passed to those men who have come to take charge of the industrial exploitation of the New South,—the sons of poor whites fired with a new thirst for wealth and power, thrifty and avaricious yankees, shrewd and unscrupulous foreigners."

*1953:*

Identical, except that the final word reads "immigrants" rather than "foreigners."

## VI (P. 170):

*1903:*

"I have seen, in the Black Belt of Georgia, an ignorant, honest Negro buy and pay for a farm in installments three separate times, and then in the face of law and decency the enterprising Russian Jew who sold it to him pocketed the money and deed and left the black man landless, to labor on his own farm at thirty cents a day."

*1953:*

Identical, except "the enterprising Russian Jew" is replaced with "the enterprising American".

## VII (P. 204):

*1903:*

"Political defence [for the Southern Black] is becoming less and less available, and economic defence is still only partially effective. But there is a patent defence at hand,—the defence of deception and flattery, of cajoling and lying. It is the same defence which the Jews of the Middle Age used and which left its stamp on their character for centuries."

*1953:*

>   Identical, except the words "the Jews of the Middle Age" read "peasants of the Middle Age . . .".

Among the Papers of Du Bois there is a typed manuscript of about 650 or 700 words, dated May 1953 and entitled "Fifty Years After". In pencil, in the Doctor's handwriting, there is a notation on this manuscript reading "(Souls)"; the same paper bears another notation in pencil reading "*not used.*" It is clear that this was meant to appear in the Blue Heron edition but that the Doctor decided it was not suitable and substituted for it the introduction which is in print and from which two paragraphs were quoted earlier in this paper.

In this unpublished effort, the Doctor was much more explicit than in that which saw print; in it, also he indicated that his decision—at that point—was to let the above passages remain "with some regret" as published in 1903. He added that Jacob Schiff had pointed out to him that certain passages in *Souls* were offensive but that he had resented this at the time, being firmly convinced that no race prejudice "could possibly enter my thinking." Somewhat later, however, Rabbi Stephen Wise raised similar objections and in this case Dr. Du Bois promised to reexamine this question and indeed to make changes in future editions, "if they seemed in error." Still later, Morris U. Schappes, the editor and historian, also wrote to the Doctor concerning these aspects of the book.

The Doctor added, in this unpublished note, that he was confident the record of his life would absolve him from any "intentional unfairness"; if it did not, he went on, this but illustrated "how easy it is, especially in race relations, inadvertently to give a totally wrong impression."

As has been stated, this preface was not used; the decision indicated in it was reversed and the 1953 Jubilee Edition did contain the text changes described.

It may be added that at the time the original edition of *Souls* appeared, blatant anti-Semitism in the United States in conduct and language was intense, especially in the South. In this connection it is noteworthy that so far as the present writer knows, no reviewer of the book alluded to this feature of it. Of course, in his own conduct, the Doctor was quite incapable of anything so gross as anti-Semitic behavior; on the contrary, he often denounced it in print and when an effort was made to reject Joel E. Spingarn as Storey's successor as president of the NAACP because he was Jewish, Du Bois reacted with anger and helped assure the election. It is to Spingarn that Du Bois dedicated his *Dusk of Dawn* (1940) with these words (Spingarn having died in 1939): "To keep the Memory of Joel Spingarn Scholar and Knight."*

*See also, the denunciation of anti-Semitism and the relating of the Jewish and the African and Afro-American experiences in Du Bois' "The Negro Mind Reaches Out," in Alain Locke, ed., *The New Negro* (N.Y., 1925, Boni), p. 411 (originally published in *Foreign Affairs* III, 423–444, April, 1925). Note also that, writing of Spingarn, Du Bois stated: "He was one of those vivid, enthusiastic but clear-thinking Idealists which from age to age the Jewish race has given the world"—*Dusk of Dawn* (N.Y., 1940, Harcourt, Brace), p. 255.

# Booker T. Washington's Discovery of Jews

Booker T. Washington in his struggle up from slavery learned many things the hard way, through experience. His discovery of and understanding with American Jewry was no exception. It began with a faux pas. In an early article in a black church magazine, Washington told the success story of a Jew, only a few months from Europe, who had passed through the town of Tuskegee, Alabama, four years earlier with all of his earthly possessions on his back. Settling at a crossroads hamlet, the Jew had hired himself out as a laborer, soon rented land to sublet to others, opened a store, and bought land; "and there is not a man, woman nor child within five miles who does not pay tribute to this Jew." What Washington assumed to be the unexceptionable moral of this story was that "the blackest Negro in the United States" had the same opportunity to succeed in business, pure and simple, as "a Jew or a white man." He added, "Of course the black man, like the Jew or white man, should be careful as to the kind of business he selects." Washington's article, entitled "Taking Advantage of Our Disadvantages," suggested that blacks should enter the occupations that white prejudice had left to them.[1]

Washington's expression "a Jew or a white man" aroused the wrath of Rabbi Isaac Mayer Wise of Cincinnati, editor of the *American Israelite* and one of the founders of Reform Judaism. Wise was particularly sensitive on this point, for he had been an apologist for Southern slaveholders and a Copperhead during the Civil War. What Washington needed was "a lesson in primary ethnology," wrote Wise. Assuming that Washington was a clergyman because his article appeared in a church periodical, Wise added, "All Jewish Americans are Caucasians and when the Rev. Prof. uses such an expression as 'a Jew or a white man' he commits a scientific blunder." Wise then committed his own racist blunder: "Possibly, however, the Rev. Prof. is only exhibiting the secret malice that invariably marks a servile nature seeking to assume a feeling of equality with something higher, which it does not possess."[2]

Fortunately, this contretemps with Rabbi Wise following Washington's first known reference to a Jew was only the prelude to his gradually unfolding knowledge and his fruitful collaboration not with Wise himself but with many other American Jews. Washington was not unique in bridging the cultural gap between these ethnically diverse peoples who shared a common experience of defamation, discrimination, and segregation. Many other black spokesmen, for example, suggested the Jewish model for

In 1982, Louis R. Harlan was professor of history at the University of Maryland, College Park.
Reprinted from *Region, Race, and Reconstruction: Essays in Honor of C. Vann Woodward*, ed. J. Morgan Kousser and James M. McPherson (New York: Oxford University Press, 1982), pp. 267–79. Copyright © 1982.

the rising black businessman,[3] the Jewish demonstration of the value of group solidarity,[4] and the common black and Jewish experience of proscription, suffering, and achievement. The National Association for the Advancement of Colored People also represented a collaboration of Jews with blacks and other Gentiles. Washington's experience, therefore, is significant chiefly because it was representative, because it was an early example of collaboration between the two groups, and because Washington's Tuskegee Institute was unique among black educational institutions of his time in seeking and securing substantial aid from Jewish philanthropy.[5] As we shall see, Washington also encouraged Jewish millionaires to contribute to black public schools and smaller industrial institutes founded by Tuskegee graduates.

Washington's growing involvement with Jews was also a voyage of discovery. What began in the embarrassment of his exchange with Isaac Wise became a pragmatic alliance for the endowment of his school with the Jewish millionaires, mostly of German origin, and gradually grew into a sympathetic identity with the poor Jewish immigrants of the Lower East Side and the victims of the violent pogroms of Eastern Europe in the late nineteenth and early twentieth centuries. The richness of detail in Washington's voluminous private papers affords the reader a glimpse of the beginnings of a collaboration between Negro and Jew that later flowered in the civil-rights movement of the 1960s.

In addition to his confusion about the racial identity of Jews, Washington shared with other rural and small-town Americans of his day a rhetorical anti-Semitism that identified Jews with the crossroads storekeepers who exacted high prices for goods bought on credit and charged usurious interest for crop mortgages. The Populist movement that dominated farm politics in the South and West in the 1890s also in some degree partook of anti-Semitism.[6] Unfavorable references to Jews apparently colored some of Washington's early speeches, but in his effort to secure donations to his school in the Northern cities, it was in his interest to drop his prejudice. "I would leave out the Jew as distinct from others in cheating the people," his close white adviser, the Reverend Robert C. Bedford, wrote him as he planned a fund-raising effort in Chicago. "He [the Jew] may have started it but others were quick and eager learners. I have always admired your addresses because of their freedom from any personal or race attack. This little tradition about the Jew I notice once in a while creeps in."[7]

Washington had no particular love for the immigrants who poured into the United States during his lifetime, regarding them as labor competitors of the Negro, and also perhaps unconsciously as threats to the stability of a society dominated by the rich donors to Tuskegee. He made an exception of Jews, however, particularly of Jews with money. Since these wealthier Jews were usually the settled and culturally assimilated German Jews rather than the newly arrived, more "Jewish" Jews from Eastern Europe, it was easier for Washington to see them as potential benefactors of his school than as potential competitors of his race. Despite their foreign tongue, religion, and habits, Jews symbolized to Washington a shrewd attendance to business instead of politics and abstract rights. When Simon Marx, a Tuskegee merchant, ran for county sheriff, Washington and other Tuskegee Institute faculty members voted for him and rejoiced in his election.[8] "The Jew that was once in about the same position that the Negro is to-day has now complete recognition," Washington observed, "because he has entwined himself about America in a business or industrial sense. Say or think what we will, it is the tangible or visible element that is going to tell largely during the next twenty years in the solution of the race problem."[9]

Blacks had a more compelling reason, however, to emulate the Jews in their group solidarity and pride. In *The Future of the American Negro* (1899), which was the closest he ever came to expounding a coherent racial philosophy, Washington wrote, "We have a very bright and striking example in the history of the Jews in this and other countries. There is, perhaps, no race that has suffered so much, not so much in America as in some of the countries in Europe. But these people have clung together. They have had a certain amount of unity, pride, and love of race; and, as the years go on, they will be more and more influential in this country—a country where they were once despised, and looked upon with scorn and derision. It is largely because the Jewish race has had faith in itself. Unless the Negro learns more and more to imitate the Jew in these matters, to have faith in himself, he cannot expect to have any high degree of success."[10]

As news of the Russian pogroms filled the newspapers, Washington sympathized with Jews as victims of persecution. "Not only as a citizen of the American Republic, but as a member of a race which has, itself, been the victim of much wrong and oppression," he said in a statement for the Kishineff Relief League of Chicago in 1904, "my heart goes out to our Hebrew fellow-sufferers across the sea."[11] Washington could always find a cheerful aspect of any situation, however. Speaking to a mixed audience in Little Rock in 1905, he noted, "In Russia there are one-half as many Jews as there are Negroes in this country, and yet I feel sure that within a month more Jews have been persecuted and killed than the whole number of our people who have been lynched during the past forty years, but this, of course, is no excuse for lynching."[12]

Jews frequently reminded Washington of their common bond of victimization. Rabbi Alfred G. Moses of Mobile, who was spellbound by one of Washington's speeches, sent him works on Jewish history to give him "a new conception of the Jews."[13] The rabbi's brother in New York invited Washington to dinner at the East Side settlement house where he lived and worked at problems similar to those Washington was meeting in the South. "We have people here whose faults and peculiarities are the result of persecution, as is the case with the Negro," wrote J. Garfield Moses. "So surely as the Negro is persecuted and dealt unfairly with, so surely will the status and the security of the Jews be the next object of attack."[14]

Louis Edelman, a Jewish physician in Huntsville, Alabama, befriended Washington and Tuskegee Institute in a variety of ways. Spending two days on the campus in 1903, he worked with the school physician to treat, free of charge, all students with eye, ear, or nose troubles, his specialty. He gave a lecture to an audience of a thousand in the chapel on "The Jew: His Persecutions and Achievements."[15] Edelman also defended the school against its Southern detractors in letters to the editor of Southern newspapers, but in conservative terms that suggested that a Southern attack on Tuskegee would lead to Northern interference. When Washington sent a copy of one of Edelman's letters to the chairman of the Tuskegee trustees as an example of Southern white support, the trustee replied, "Glad to see the courage of the man, and of the paper to print it. Is he an American, or Hebrew?"[16]

Tuskegee Institute attracted many Jewish supporters, partly because of Washington's aggressive canvass for funds among them and his persuasiveness as an intergroup diplomat. The nondenominational character of the institution also, no doubt, appealed to Jews of goodwill who would hesitate to aid black schools affiliated with Protestant denominations. With Jews as with Unitarians, Washington never allowed his own nominal affiliation with the Baptist faith to inhibit his active cultivation of millionaires. For whatever reasons, Jewish commitment to Tuskegee grew, both among Southern Jewish neighbors and those in the Northern cities. By Washington's own account, in 1911 "the majority of white people who come here for commencement are composed of Jews."[17] Two Jewish merchants of nearby Montgomery who did business with the school, Selig Gassenheimer and Charles F. Moritz, donated small prizes to be awarded to students at commencement, and Gassenheimer also gave money for the erection of a small building on the campus.[18] In 1905 a rabbi for the first time delivered the commencement sermon.[19]

Tuskegee originally modeled itself after Hampton Institute, where Washington had received his own education, and appealed to the old Protestant wealth and the Sunday-school collections of New England for its support. Around the turn of the twentieth century, however, Washington shifted his Northern fund-raising headquarters from Boston to New York and came into closer contact with the new wealth of industry and finance. In the same period Jewish bankers and merchants began to figure more prominently among the donors. In 1904 the idea occurred to Washington of "inviting Mr. [Paul M.] Warburg or some Hebrew of his standing" to join the board of trustees. "I feel that we need to put new life into the Board," he wrote the board chairman. He thought of two New Englanders, one a small businessman and the other a retired clergyman, who "in some way ought to be gotten rid of," as "Neither of these are of very much value to us."[20] Washington persuaded the two New Englanders to resign from the good of the school and proposed Paul M. Warburg, the New York investment banker. He was unanimously elected, and took his seat on the board.[21]

At about the same time as Warburg's election, other wealthy Jews began or increased their support of Tuskegee. Jacob and Mortimer Schiff, James Loeb, and Felix Warburg, all members of Kuhn, Loeb and Company, Paul Warburg's banking firm, gave donations. So did the Seligmans, the Lehmans, Joseph Pulitzer, Jacob Billikopf, and Julian Mack. Even Joel E. Spingarn, a founder and officer of the NAACP, made a small annual contribution to Washington's school while opposing Washington's race leadership.[22] The immensely wealthy Jacob H. Schiff, another early supporter of the NAACP, had such confidence in Washington that in 1909 he made him his almoner for other black schools. Schiff wrote to Washington that he felt "entirely at a loss to know where to contribute properly and justly," and put $3,000 at Washington's disposal, one-third to go to Tuskegee, smaller amounts to four other schools, and the remainder to schools of which Washington approved.[23] He annually sent Washington a list of the schools he had aided the preceding year on Washington's advice and asked him to make any changes he desired. The contributions, most of $100 or less, went principally to industrial schools on the Tuskegee model.[24] Schiff continued this practice until Washington's death in 1915, when his total contributions had increased threefold. He said of Washington soon after the latter's death: "I feel that America has lost one of its great men, whose life has been full of usefulness—not only to his own race, but to the white people of the United States."[25]

Though Paul Warburg resigned from the Tuskegee board of trustees in 1909, two years later Julius Rosenwald, president of Sears, Roebuck and Company, was profoundly moved by reading Washington's autobiography. He visited Tuskegee and a few months later agreed to become a trustee.[26] Rosenwald promoted the school with the same enthusiasm that he simultaneously showed in conditional grants for constructing black YMCA buildings in several major cities. He interested members of his family, friends, and other Chicago capitalists in Tuskegee, brought several parties of distinguished and wealthy visitors to the school in his private railroad car, and annually sent to Washington lists of wealthy men, many of them Jews, whom he should approach for contributions. The most imaginative of Tuskegee's philanthropists, Rosenwald gave bonuses to the Tuskegee faculty, and even sent surplus and defective Sears shoes and hats to be sold at low rates to students.[27]

Rosenwald's enthusiasm spread to some of Washington's other interests. In celebration of his fiftieth birthday in 1912 he gave $25,000 to be distributed by Washington on a matching basis to schools that had grown out of Tuskegee or were doing similar work.[28] At Washington's urging he aided the all-Negro town of Mound Bayou, Mississippi, by investing in its most ambitious enterprise, a cotton-oil mill, and lending money to its bank, both of which failed in the hard times of 1914.[29] Rosenwald's most ambitious philanthropic enterprise, however, involved a plan Washington had presented to him for aid to country public schools for blacks. Washington suggested that Rosenwald offer a small amount of money if patrons of a school would match it in money, materials, or labor for the construction of a small schoolhouse.[30] Under this program, which was institutionalized under the Rosenwald Foundation after Washington's death, hundreds of Rosenwald schools sprang up in places where white school authorities had refused to provide school facilities for blacks, and ever since freedom the black rural schools had met on weekdays in the single rooms of black country churches. Washington's close personal partnership in philanthropy with Rosenwald was the high point of his efforts to enlist the support of wealthy Jews.

Washington was always the realist. Despite his growing regard for individual Jews, both Northern millionaires and the Southern middle class, he told Tuskegee's business agent to buy supplies for the school whenever possible from Gentiles. "In looking over our bills from Montgomery," he wrote, "I very much fear that we are getting our trade too much centered in the hands of a few Jews. Wherever we can get equally fair treatment in prices and quality of goods from persons other than Jews, I prefer to have our trade scattered among them. In creating public sentiment in favor of the institution the Jews cannot be of much service. . . ." That this was a realistic business judgment rather than anti-Semitism, however, is suggested by an exception he made. He told the business agent, "Where all things are equal with our giving trade to Jews, I hope you will bear in mind Mr. J. Loeb. Quite a number of years ago when other wholesale merchants refused absolutely to deal with us and were threatened by boycott by the town merchants in case they did deal with us, Loeb paid no attention to our want of money and threatened boycott in town and stood by us and sold us goods at wholesale prices. Of course, after he was brave enough to stem the tide for several months, others fell in line, but we owe him a great deal for helping us out in this way in our earlier days."[31]

Washington found parallels in the historical experiences of blacks and Jews that bound the two peoples together more deeply than did either Jewish philanthropy or the Jewish example of self-help. In his early childhood Washington's favorite part of the Bible was the story of Moses leading the children of Israel out of the house of bondage, through the wilderness, and into the promised land. He had first heard that story from his mother when they were both slaves. "I learned in slavery to compare the condition of the Negro with that of the Jews in bondage in Egypt," he wrote in 1911, "so I have frequently, since freedom, been compelled to compare the prejudice, even persecution which the Jewish people have had to face and overcome in different parts of the world, with the disadvantages of the Negro in the United States and elsewhere." He had seen the poor Jews of New York and London, but it was not until his tour of the Continent in 1910 that he learned how life in the ghetto really was. He had thought he knew Jews on the sidewalks of New York, but after seeing those in Poland he decided that the Jews he had known were already halfway toward being Americanized. Polish Jews had lived for a thousand years, Washington observed, "as exiles and, more or less, like prisoners. Instead of trying to become like the other people among whom they lived, they seemed to be making every effort to preserve and emphasize the ways in which they were different from those about them."[32]

Washington was puzzled by the changing character of anti-Semitic prejudice from place to place and by its often religious rather than racial nature.[33] In a book about his European tour, *The Man Farthest Down,* he took the rather complacent view that, compared with the other downtrodden peoples of the earth, the Negro in the United States and especially in the South was better off.[34] On the other hand the Jews, who in America and Western Europe were often wealthy, were in Russia and parts of Austria-Hungary among the poorest of civilized people. The Jews showed superiority not in wealth but in education. Not only in America did Jews rival the recently freed blacks in their "yearning for learning," but even in Russia, where they were burdened with educational restrictions, they outdid the rest of the population in literacy.[35]

Near the end of his life, when asked by the New York *Times* to name his favorite Shakespearean passage, Washington chose Shylock's speech in *The Merchant of Venice* that begins "I am a Jew."[36] Washington had begun his career full of misunderstandings about Jews, as illustrated by his controversy with Isaac M. Wise of the *American Israelite.* By the end of his life he had come to understand and appreciate Jews not only as exemplars of self-help and mutual help but as companions in travail and striving. "Hath not a Jew eyes? Hath not a Jew hands, organs, dimensions, senses, affections, passions? Fed with the same food, hurt with the same weapons, subject to the same diseases . . . ?" This passage from Shylock's speech was a parallel to the black man's plea to be treated as "a man and brother."

Through Washington's ceaseless journeys across the color line, many Jews learned to appreciate a black man's personal qualities. Rabbi Stephen S. Wise of the Free Synagogue in New York City, where Washington had spoken several times, wrote to Washington's widow on news of his death, "He was not only the guide and friend of one race but the servant and benefactor of two races."[37] In an obituary address at his synagogue, Wise said of the Black Moses: "He was more concerned about the Negro doing justice to himself than securing justice from the white race." Wise urged whites, however, to deal more justly with blacks than they had done, concluding with a statement that went to the heart of the race problem in America: "The inward memorial to Booker Washington lies in a new and heretofore untried justness of attitude toward the Negro in remembering that he is not a problem but a man, that the Negro is not a racial question but a fellow human to be accepted and honored in the spirit of that justness which is faith."[38]

Like Columbus, who discovered a new world but never reached the mainland and died thinking it was Asia he had reached, Washington died unaware that he and Rabbi Stephen Wise were present at the birth of brotherhood week. In his pursuit of the rich Jew, Washington also never fully understood the masses of the new immigrant Jews. He showed no awareness of Zionism, of the sectarian rivalries within Judaism, of the tension between Jewish assimilationism and nationalism, of the hold of unionism and socialism on the Jewish working class, or even of the lynching of Leo Frank, a Southern Jew.[39]

If Washington never reached the promised land, however, he did move the blacks and the children of Israel far down the road to the full partnership of the civil-rights movement. Even while he was still alive, Jewish donors to Tuskegee found no inconsistency in also being the angels of the early NAACP. As Washington groped, through contacts with Jews, toward an understanding of both their differentness and their common humanity, so many key figures in American Jewry in the early twentieth century found in Booker T. Washington a bridge to understanding of America's deepest social problem. Paradoxically, it was because of Washington's ordinariness—his conventional attitudes, his intellectual mediocrity, his penchant for cliché—that he could explain each group to the other in terms each could understand.

NOTES

1. Booker T. Washington (hereafter cited as BTW), "Taking Advantage of Our Disadvantages," *A.M.E. Church Review,* 10 (1894), 478–83, reprinted in Louis R. Harlan and Raymond W. Smock, eds., *The BTW Papers* (Urbana, Ill., 1972–), III, 408–12.

2. *American Israelite,* 41 (July 26, 1894), 4. A sympathetic review of Wise's views on slavery, abolitionism, and the Civil War is in James G. Heller, *Isaac M. Wise: His Life, Work, and Thought* (New York, 1965), pp. 331–49.

3. This theme is developed in detail by Arnold Shankman, "Friend or Foe? Southern Blacks View the Jew 1880–1935," in Nathan M. Kaganoff and Melvin I. Urofsky, eds., *Turn to the South: Essays on Southern Jewry* (Charlottesville, 1979), pp. 109–14.

4. Ibid., pp. 115–16; "A Fellow Feeling Makes Us Wondrous Kind," editorial in Washington *Colored American,* May 6, 1899, p. 4; "A Few Lessons from Jews," Indianapolis *Freeman,* September 5, 1891, p. 1.

5. Lenora E. Berson, in *The Negroes and the Jews* (New York, 1971), pp. 63–79, noted that BTW made "the earliest recorded attempt" at active partnership with an American Jew, Julius Rosenwald. A more successful treatment of Jewish attitudes toward blacks, however, is Hasia R. Diner, *In the Almost Promised*

*Land: American Jews and Blacks, 1915–1935* (Westport, Conn., 1977), which despite the dates of its title has much information on BTW's era. See also Robert G. Weisbord and Arthur Stein, *Bittersweet Encounter: The Afro-American and the American Jew* (Westport, Conn., 1970); Leonard Dinnerstein and Mary Dale Palsson, eds., *Jews in the South* (Baton Rouge, 1973).

6. On the historiographical controversy over the extent of Populist anti-Semitism, see particularly Oscar Handlin, "American Views of the Jew at the Opening of the Twentieth Century," *Publications of the American Jewish Historical Society,* 40 (1951); C. Vann Woodward, "The Populist Heritage and the Intellectuals," *American Scholar,* 29 (winter 1959–60), 55–72; Norman Pollack, "The Myth of Populist Anti-Semitism," *American Historical Review,* 68 (1962), 76–80; Norman Pollack, "Handlin on Anti-Semitism: A Critique of 'American Views of the Jew,'" *Journal of American History,* 51 (1964), 391–403; and Walter T. K. Nugent, *The Tolerant Populists: Kansas Populism and Nativism* (Chicago, 1963).

7. R. C. Bedford to BTW, January 14, 1896, Container 114, BTW Papers, Library of Congress. Documents from this collection will be referred to hereafter only by the container number, in parentheses.

8. William Jenkins to BTW, August 7, 1896, G. W. A. Johnston to BTW, August 13, 1896 (118).

9. BTW, "Industrial Training for the Negro," *Independent,* 50 (February 3, 1898), 146, in Harlan and Smock, eds., *BTW Papers,* IV, 373.

10. Reprinted in Harlan and Smock, eds., *BTW Papers,* V, 369–70. The Cleveland lawyer John P. Green expressed in 1895 a common black attitude in "The Jew and the Negro," Indianapolis *Freeman,* December 21, 1895, p. 3. He wrote, "We feel and think our lot in this so-called 'white man's country,' is a hard one; and in very truth it is . . . but when we scan the blood stained recitals of what the Jews have passed through since the destruction of Jerusalem, during the first century of our Christian era, and then note how conspicuous they are in all civilized communities for their real attainments along the lines of science, art, literature and finance, we may well cheer up and persevere along the same lines until victory crowns our efforts."

11. BTW to Mrs. A. F. D. Grey, ca. June 5, 1903, in Harlan and Smock, eds., *BTW Papers,* VII, 169. See also Arnold Shankman, "Brothers Across the Sea: Afro-Americans on the Persecution of Russian Jews, 1881–1917," *Jewish Social Studies,* 37 (1975), 114–21.

12. Excerpt of address in Boston *Transcript,* December 4, 1905, clipping (27).

13. Alfred G. Moses to BTW, January 2 and 8, 1906 (328).

14. J. Garfield Moses to BTW, January 14, 1906 (809).

15. *Tuskegee Student,* 15 (May 9, 1903), 2; typescript of lecture, May 5, 1903 (257).

16. Birmingham *News,* September 5, 1903 (clipping), BTW to W. H. Baldwin, Jr., September 11, 1903, and Baldwin's marginal note (257).

17. BTW to Robert H. Terrell, April 4, 1911 (443).

18. A. R. Stewart to BTW, June 14, 1909, BTW to Selig Gassenheimer, June 16, 1909 (734).

19. A. J. Messing of Montgomery, Ala., in *Tuskegee Student,* 17 (June 17, 1905), 1.

20. BTW to W. H. Baldwin, Jr., May 20, 1904 (18). See also BTW to Baldwin, June 2, 1904 (18).

21. Marcus M. Marks to BTW, May 24, 1904, in Harlan and Smock, eds., *BTW Papers,* VII, 512; minutes of adjourned meeting of the Tuskegee Institute board of trustees, June 23, 1904 (18).

22. Spingarn to BTW, December 24, 1909 (736).

23. Schiff to BTW, June 16 and July 7, 1909 (47).

24. BTW to Schiff, March 6, 10, 16, and 17, 1910 (51).

25. Schiff to W. H. Holtzclaw, in Cyrus Adler manuscript, microfilm reel 677, Jacob H. Schiff Papers, American Jewish Archives, Hebrew Union College.

26. BTW to Ruth S. Baldwin, January 25, 1912 (916).

27. Julius Rosenwald to BTW, May 31, 1912 (56): William C. Graves to BTW, December 30, 1912 (66); BTW to Rosenwald, February 8, April 2, and September 19, 1913 (66); Morris S. Rosenwald to BTW, April 2, 1912 (755); BTW to Julius Rosenwald, undated draft, ca. May 1915 (78). For a survey of Jewish philanthropy and Tuskegee, see Diner, *In the Almost Promised Land,* pp. 166–72.

28. Rosenwald to BTW, August 5, 1912 (56).

29. A detailed account is August Meier, "Booker T. Washington and the Town of Mound Bayou,"

*Phylon*, 15 (1954), 396–401, reprinted in Meier and Elliott Rudwick, *Along the Color Line* (Urbana, Ill., 1976), pp. 217–23.

30. BTW outlined his plan in letters to Rosenwald, June 21 and September 12, 1912 (62).

31. BTW to Lloyd G. Wheeler, October 17, 1904 (551). BTW also urged a liberal order of stationery from one of the school's Jewish benefactors, Selig Gassenheimer. BTW to E. T. Attwell, April 4, 1911 (610).

32. BTW, "Race Prejudice in Europe," typescript, December 5, 1911 (957).

33. Actually, racial anti-Semitism, as represented by the writings of Houston Stewart Chamberlain, was on the increase in Europe and the United States in the late nineteenth and early twentieth centuries.

34. (New York, 1912), with Robert E. Park.

35. See Meyer Weinberg, "A Yearning for Learning: Blacks and Jews through History," *Integrated Education*, 7 (1969), 20–29.

36. Later he changed his favorite quotation to the passage in *Julius Caesar* that begins "There is a tide in the affairs of men." BTW to the editor of the New York *Times*, April 15, 18, 1914 (525).

37. Stephen S. Wise to Margaret M. Washington, November 15, 1915 (952).

38. Stephen S. Wise, "Booker Washington: American," *Southern Workman*, 45 (1916), 382–83, an abstract of his address.

39. Washington's silence may be explained by the fact that a black janitor testified he had helped Leo Frank to remove the body. If the Jew was found innocent, the black man was the logical suspect. Jonah Wise, who succeeded his father, Isaac M. Wise, as editor of the *American Israelite*, at first thought Frank guilty because he doubted that a Southern white jury would convict on the "unsupported testimony of a low type of negro," but after Frank was lynched he concluded that the real murderer was "the vicious and criminal negro." Wise's only consistency was his racism. Quoted in Eugene Levy, " 'Is the Jew a White Man?': Press Reaction to the Leo Frank Case, 1913–1915," *Phylon*, 35 (1974), 218–19.

## Among the Children of the East Side Jews (1905)

A Black Teacher Describes Her Jewish Pupils

Jessie Fortune Bowser, author of the article reprinted below, was the daughter of the famed Black journalist, Timothy Thomas Fortune[1] (1856–1928). Before considering her remarkable essay, one might mention a few things about her father and his attitudes towards Jews. Fortune, who was born a slave in Marianna, Jackson County, Fla., learned as a child that his maternal grandfather had been Jewish. This white ancestor was represented as a selfish and insensitive man, for he had been "guilty of selling his daughter by a black woman into slavery in the same village where he was a judge."[2]

But Fortune soon learned that not all Jews were alike. As a youth he worked as a store boy for Samuel Fleishman, a hardware merchant and general agent for the Altman and Brother Company. In 1869, the Ku Klux Klan ordered Fleishman out of town because he monopolized the Negro trade. Moreover, he had allegedly told Blacks that whenever white terrorists murdered one of their race, they should retaliate and kill three Klansmen. What happened to Fleishman, who had lived in Florida for over twenty years, is related in Stanley Horn's book on the KKK:

"Fleishman was summoned one day in Oct., 1869, to appear before an assemblage of more than 20 of the citizens of Marianna in J. P. Coker's store, where he was told that it had been decided that it would be safest for him and for the town for him to leave there without delay. He protested, but they told him that they would give him until sundown to get ready to leave; that if he stayed there he would certainly be killed, and if he were killed there would be an outbreak of trouble which would result in others being killed also. At sundown a committee of citizens called for him at his store and, in spite of all his protests, escorted him out of town to the Georgia[3] state line, warning him that if he ever returned to Marianna it would be at the risk of his life. Fleishman went straight to Tallahassee, where he asked for protection; but he was not given much encouragement by the state officials upon whom he called. Nothing daunted, he set out for Marianna alone, protesting that he would be ruined if forced to

Jessie Fortune was a teacher in an all-white elementary school in Manhattan in 1905. Arnold Shankman was an assistant professor of history at Emory University in 1975.

Originally published as "Among the Children of the East Side Jews," *New York Age*, January 5, 1905; reprinted with an introduction by Arnold Shankman from *Jewish Currents* 29, no. 2 (Feb. 1975): 4–7. Copyright © *Jewish Currents*.

abandon his business there. On the way to Marianna he met a white man on horseback who knew him and who advised him to turn back, telling him that he would be killed if he showed himself in Marianna; but Fleishman went resolutely ahead. The next morning his body was found in the road on the outskirts of Marianna. His assassins were never apprehended, but the Radicals all said, 'Ku Klux.' "[4]

Fortune never forgot the incident, and throughout his lifetime he displayed considerable sympathy for the Jews. He strongly condemned anti-Semitism and urged Blacks to imitate the thrift, sobriety and patience of the Jews. True, he sometimes thought that they were too preoccupied with the making of money—as did his daughter—but this may be a result of what he had been told about his grandfather. Doubtless Fortune told his children about their great-grandfather and about the fate of his Jewish employer in Marianna.

Fortune made no secret of the fact that his favorite child was his daughter Jessie. Before her marriage to Aubrey Bowser, Jessie taught at an all white elementary school in Manhattan. Virtually all of her pupils were Jewish, and in 1905 she wrote about her students for her father's newspaper, the New York *Age*, Jan. 5, 1905.

Ms. Fortune's article is eloquent. One might note, however, that at the time it was written she was only 21.

Arnold Shankman

The last bell indicating the beginning of the morning session had just been rung and lessons were about to begin when the door opened quickly and a little girl of about eight years old entered. All her haste seemed to depart as the door closed. She slowly approached the desk, apologetically raising her hand, while her eyes were upturned to me in tearful pleading, "Please to 'scuse me. I had to put mineself on. Mine mother she must stay by the dock all night, mine baby is so sick." The rising inflection on the last word and the downward quivering of the mouth in a brave effort not to cry were quite pathetic.

And yet this sad story was only one of many, and this neglected looking little girl before me was only one of a vast number of Jewish children who lived on the East Side of New York and who, through care and responsibility, are often more like little men and women than children of seven years of age. Often the doctors suggest to the mothers of very sick babies that they remain most of the night out in the fresh air, on the docks, especially during the warm weather, and the little girl at home must take the tired mother's place in the morning, prepare the smaller ones for school, "put her own self on" and prepare breakfast.

The pleasantest thing in their lives is the school. The homes are often so cramped, poorly ventilated and unsightly that the schools put up within the past few years, with the newest improvements, clean and bright with pictures and other adornments, seem like fairy halls to their little minds. On the teacher is lavished a wealth of that affection which seems to form such a large part of their natures. It seems wonderful, how a trait of character in a race will outlive centuries and changes of conditions and abodes, for that respect and implicit obedience which the Hebrew of the time of Moses accorded the patriarchs of elders of the families seem to be inherent qualities in their little descendants on the East Side, in New York. Discipline in a Jewish school is generally not nearly so hard a matter as in other schools.

A glimpse into the homes of these children reveals the surprising fact that few of them are really destitute. Jews will make money and the insignificant vendor by the curbstone or under the new bridge selling all sorts of things from cloth by the yard to household furnishings, makes a good living. His children come to school during the winter clad in good woolen dresses and fine heavy coats (so common among them) that reach to their ankles. Of course there are some exceptions, but these result not so much from lack of money as from inability to spend the money judiciously.

A greater boon to the East Side than financial help or the distribution of food, as some one suggests is the education of its girls in the way to spend money in the things necessary to comfort, and in the best methods of keeping house. The many public school[s]—there is about one to every three blocks—and mission houses are doing this in a large degree. Their desire to learn is most gratifying and anything which adds to their culture is seized upon and remembered with eagerness. On being taught to say "Excuse me," I have known children to excuse themselves when passing behind a chair or when going past a teacher in the hall; such is their desire to be refined.

Most of the families live in two or three rooms. These are seldom opened up for air, and as a result the atmosphere is redolent of stale and musty smells. Unlike the best Hollander the Jew does not seem to take naturally to cleansing or scrubbing; his sole aim seems to be earning money, and all household duties are subservient to this purpose, so that as often as not, the dining room, parlor and sitting room serve as a tailor shop or work shop as the case may be.

As I said before there is on average one school to every three or four blocks, and as every school holds from two to three thousand children, one gets an idea of how closely the people live in these tenement houses. But although their manner of living is often very unhealthy, there is one item that does much toward counteracting the progress of disease. Most of the children receive daily several pennies, and always one each day. These they spend most often for fruit. It is amazing to see the large quantities consumed by the children. Just as naturally as most children think of buying candy these children desire to get fruit. Lunch generally consists of one or two apples and a piece of bread. As a result good fruit is very cheap on the East Side, and the children are trained to regard it as a necessary portion of their diet.

Their use of English is often most amusing and peculiar, but the little foreigners pick up our language with astonishing rapidity. Sometimes the manner in which they paraphrase English idioms and phrases render them almost unrecognizable for a moment, such as—"I had to put mineself on," "she gave me a hack on the arm," "she kickled me" (tickled me). The saying "it is to laugh" probably originated on the East Side, where one often hears the remark, "she made me to laugh." A peculiar form of juvenile denunciation is quite in vogue among them. Children come to me with tears in their eyes saying "She cursed me. She told me [?] to the dead, buried in the grave with my mother and father." An excuse which one often receives for lateness is couched in this language "'Scuse, please, I was last night by a weddink, so I was this mornink such a long time sleepink." This was also given as an excuse for lateness. "Such a thief was by mine house this mornink, all thinks from the drawer he snatched" always with that quaint rising inflection on the last word.

On the whole, they are interesting, bright little children to know. Some of them are very beautiful, physically and temperamentally, and some are quite the reverse, but in either case, one grows to have an interest in their development which one would never imagine feeling when one first views the swarms of them playing around the streets.

As I said before they are very lovable and comparatively speaking they are free from prejudice. An amusing little incident which I recall will serve to show this.

School was over and two little girls had stayed to help me, when one of them approached me shyly and said, "Annie has a shame to ask you something." I understood, and encouragingly asked what it was she wanted to say. "I did want to know, Miss Fortune, was you a Jew?" I was very surprised at the question and amused at her timidity. On my replying "No" she seemed very surprised also and remarked, "I did swear you was a Jew." I thought I would test her, so I asked if she knew what a colored person was, and on her replying in the affirmative, I told her that I was colored. Then I asked her if she thought any the less of me for not being a Jew, and she replied with touching prettiness, as she laid her hand on my skirt, "Miss Fortune, I do like you just the same, no matter what you are."

NOTES

1. See Emma Lou Thornbrough's skillfully-written *Thomas Fortune: Militant Journalist*, Univ. of Chicago Press, 1972.

2. T. Thomas Fortune, "After War Times," Philadelphia *Tribune*, July 14, 1927, p. 9. Ms. Thornbrough's biography notes that the maternal grandfather of Fortune was white but does not indicate that he was Jewish.

3. There is some confusion as to whether Fleishman was escorted to the Alabama or Georgia state line. Accounts of contemporaries differ, and since Marianna was less than 20 miles from either border, it is hard to tell which is correct. See *Testimony Taken by The Joint Select Committee to Inquire into the Condition of Affairs in The Late Insurrectionary States*, XIII (Washington, Gov. Printing Office, 1872), pages 78, 145.

4. Stanley Horn, *Invisible Empire* (Cos Cob, Conn., John Edwards Publishing Co., 1969), pages 268–69. See also *Testimony*, XIII, pages 78–83, 145, 189–91, 217, and Fortune's hazy and somewhat inaccurate recollections in the New York *Age*, August 21, 1913, p. 4. It might be noted that elsewhere Horn mistakenly calls Fleishman a "carpetbagger." Since the merchant had lived in Florida from the 1840s, such a title is quite misleading.

# Black Images of Jews
## From Reconstruction to Depression

In his autobiography, *Black boy,* Richard Wright remembered the deep hostility southern blacks had for Jews in the period after the first world war. Everybody in his neighborhood, Wright recalled, hated Jews; the antagonism was bred in Negroes from childhood: ". . . it was not merely racial prejudice, it was part of our cultural heritage." As "Christ killers" among insecure black Christians, Jews were subject to all kinds of ridicule. "Folk ditties, some mean, others filthy, all of them cruel" existed for almost every situation to express contempt for the not-so-innocent Jew.[1] Other blacks had similar recollections from their childhoods.[2]

In the late 1960's such observations acquired special significance. Black strategies to counter institutional racism alarmed many whites, both Jews and gentiles. Jews were especially disturbed that criticism of whites often singled them out. Many who thought of themselves as liberals felt undeserving of these attacks and in return accused their critics of anti-Semitism. One consequence of the tension was a re-examination of black-Jewish relations. Were blacks anti-Semitic or merely anti-white? How guilty were Jews of abetting racism in white America? Questions were also raised about the historical background of black-Jewish relations.[3] In an attempt to answer such questions this essay will examine the role of Jews in black thought in the late nineteenth and early twentieth centuries.

Blacks have never been ignorant of, nor indifferent to, Jews. Indeed, Jews have been more important to them than any other ethnic group. This is true even though traditionally most blacks as rural southerners have had little contact with them. In song and folklore slaves repeated the story of a people abused and in bondage for centuries who had patiently awaited deliverance. Through all, Jews had kept faith in themselves and their God. From these accounts Negroes learned the need to persevere until such a day when a black Moses would appear to lead them out of servitude. Thus to the slave the Jew became a symbol of hope and an example of the capacity of oppressed people to overcome their subjugation.[4] It was in this way that Jews were most important to black people after emancipation.

In the post-civil war era blacks were keenly aware of the similarities between their experiences and those of Jews. Physical distinctions, bondage and persecution, the absence of a government of their own, and a refusal to be crushed were the more obvious parallels.[5] Both groups, Booker T. Washington noted, were "a peculiar people."

David J. Hellwig is a professor of history at St. Cloud State University, St. Cloud, Minnesota.
Originally published in *Societas—A Review of Social History* 8, no. 3 (1978): 205–23. Reprinted with permission of David J. Hellwig.

But distinctiveness did not prohibit Jews from enriching civilization. Indeed, it was through "their peculiar religious bent" that they had contributed to Christianity, "the finest flower of Jewry." As the Jew had left a mark on history, so could the Negro. No handicap was insurmountable. Both groups, Washington advised, should pursue what they could best do even if it were only of minor importance at the time.[6]

Above all, Jews proved the value of patience and the importance of adhering to one's faith. The most prestigious black religious journal, the *AME Church Review,* counseled:

> What power of endurance these Jews have! What power to simply wait! Sure evidence of strength this. Were they faint of heart, long since would they have been lost in the floods of generations through which they have passed. *But eminently satisfied with themselves,* they have been content to do the duty of the day, and wait the coming of the hour when the "Lord would again visit Zion." Nor have they been disappointed, though the coming has not been after their wish.

Jewish success was the best indication that blacks, too, would eventually be accepted as equals.[7] Another religious publication, the *Southern Christian Recorder,* listed seven practices by which Jews had raised themselves from a position as lowly as that of the Afro-American. "Here is encouragement for the Negro", it declared. "If the Jew has changed his condition by these rules, the Negro can change his."[8] The middle-class *Colored American Magazine* observed that Jews had earned the greatest moral victory in America simply by arming themselves with "the sword of persistence, the handle of which was Prudence." From enforced segregation they had built an "invulnerable fortress."[9] The ways in which the story was related were almost endless, but the moral remained constant: blacks could learn much, if only they would, from the struggles of the Jews. It was as a fountain of inspiration, then, that the Jewish example occupied a prominent place in black thought.

In no area were Jews more exemplary than in transforming adversity into material success. More so than others they had used economic opportunities to alter their status in both the Old and New Worlds. Wealth provided a basis to turn education, hard work, and numbers into group advancement. If blacks were also to achieve a better life, they had to do the same. So persistent was this theme in black thought that it enhanced the traditional stereotype of the Jew as an aggressive, unprincipled, opportunistic materialist who abused the power which wealth brought. But unlike anti-Semites who constantly depicted the Jew in the most scurrilous of terms, black leaders employed the image of the aggressive Jew to encourage Negroes to pattern their lives along the same lines.[10] With little attention to the perils of over-statement or over-simplification they drew a valuable lesson from the economic advancement of the Jew in America and elsewhere, and prominent people of widely differing viewpoints and vocations praised Jews for showing others the way out of misery and degradation.

If only black Americans had the same spirit and enthusiasm for enterprise as Jews had, they too would be granted the recognition denied them. If they wanted to be heard, they would have to emulate Jews who had overcome gentile reluctance to accept them. As prejudice could not stand in the way of self-interest, blacks needed power to silence their enemies. "We cannot expect the people who have something, or everything, to take kindly to persons who have nothing and who do not seem any way affected by it, but seemingly continue in the same old rut year in and year out", a black woman warned in 1889. The race had to acquire the initiative and ambition of the Jew or be content with its lowly status.[11] T. McCants Stewart, a prominent lawyer, agreed that it was "condition and not primarily color that creates the distinctions against us." If blacks were to be accepted, he continued, they had to become like the "despised Jew, the representative of business and money." Only after ownership of land, houses, and businesses became as widely dispersed among blacks as it had among Jews could Negroes enjoy civil and political equality in America.[12]

Booker T. Washington did not overlook the relevance of the Jewish experience to his work; their lives, he believed, testified to the soundness of his message. Instead of complaining, Jews had earned recognition by contributing their talents to the national good. They advanced by becoming entwined about America commercially and industrially.[13] As was his habit, Washington put the lesson in concrete and simple form:

> Four years ago a Jew, only a few months from Europe, passed through the town of Tuskegee, Alabama, on foot, with all his earthly possessions in a cheap and much-worn satchel. . . . This Jew, by accident, stopped over night. . . . Looking about the next morning with an eye to business, this Jew soon decided to remain awhile in this community, and he soon found some one to hire him for a few dollars a month. Soon he began renting land to sub-let to others: then followed the opening of a store, and the development and accumulation have gone on to the extent that today this Jew does a business of $50,000 a year. He owns hundreds of acres of land; contracts the cotton from all the plantations in that neighborhood; and there is not a man, woman nor child within five miles who do not pay tribute to this Jew. His note or check is honored at any bank, and his credit with the wholesale merchants is almost without limit.
>
> What this Jew has done, the blackest Negro in the United States can do in Alabama.[14]

True, acquisition of wealth did not necessarily destroy prejudice and many blacks were well aware of this. James Weldon Johnson noted in an editorial in the *New York Age*, "a Jew-baiter hates a rich Jew, perhaps worse than he does a poor one." But money blocked translation of ill-will into discrimination. "Prejudice against the Jews", another editorialist had earlier remarked, "is almost as general and persistent as it is against the Afro-American people; but it is displayed less, because the Jews are among the wealthy people of the country and know how to advance themselves by properly directing their wealth against those who offended them."[15]

The black press frequently noted how Jews used economic power against their enemies. The most widely publicized episode was their reaction to being denied accommodations at the fashionable resort of Saratoga, New York. Instead of meekly submitting, Jews had bought hotels in Saratoga and were thus able to enjoy local amenities despite gentile hostility. Such enterprise on the part of blacks was almost unheard of.[16] Moreover, hotel owners everywhere often yielded to the temptation to serve Jews able and willing to pay more than other whites. No hotel could deny the Jew, wrote the retired Washington, D.C., physician, Charles B. Purvis, in 1921, because "as money is the American God and as the Jew has it, he is received."[17] The white gentile press also rebuked those who excluded Jews. Why? Because Jews owned banks and stores and engaged in the practice of "You scratch my back, and I'll scratch yours." Newspapers had to condemn anti-Semitism in order to secure Jewish patronage. Like it or not, black people had to recognize the sources of power and be prepared to utilize them.[18]

While most black commentators felt Jews should be emulated, they disagreed regarding the specific characteristics and strategies responsible for Jewish success. During the quarter century following the civil war Afro-Americans relied heavily on political activity to alter their condition. With the onset of Jim Crow, however, emphasis shifted to creating an economic base for full acceptance into the larger society. The debate over which course to pursue continued well into the twentieth century. To some blacks the advancement of Jews rested primarily on their avoiding politics; others stressed the political astuteness of Jews.

Those who placed economics before politics made the greatest use of the Jewish experience. In general blacks became more secular-minded in the late nineteenth century and many came to look upon wealth as *the* symbol of success. Among many blacks, therefore, the image of Jews as patient sufferers awaiting divine intervention was gradually replaced by that of Jews as the foremost exemplars of the gospel of wealth and Social Darwinism. Some blacks heartily agreed with the views of the journalist John E. Bruce that Jews advanced by eschewing politics and devoting all their energies to pursuit of the dollar. "Nobody", Bruce observed, "had ever seen a poor and struggling Jewish merchant in the South wasting his time, energy, and cash fooling with politics." If a Jew did so, his involvement was strictly secondary: "With him, 'peezness is peezness, unt politics—vy dot is anoder stdory.' "[19] More common, however, was the assertion that Jews best exemplified the flow of political power to those with influence. True, they put business before public affairs, but after achieving a position of strength in finance and commerce they entered politics—again with great success. Jews had acquired recognition in law and were securing responsible political offices because no political party could deny them representation. All this was possible because they had, through business, become a power in civic affairs.

But the fiery editor of the *Boston Guardian,* William Monroe Trotter, vehemently rejected the notion that Jews had advanced primarily through acquisition of wealth. Booker T. Washington and his supporters, he argued, distorted history to promote the faulty claim that blacks could advance faster by abandoning politics and protest and concentrating on the "get-wealth remedy." The trouble with arguments of "anti-agitationists" was that the denial or abridgment of rights stemmed from race prejudice, not poverty. Their whole case rested on the assumption that progress in morals, intelligence, and wealth in and of themselves would erase deep-seated prejudices. But they could not substantiate the position, Trotter asserted. "Their favorite example—that of the Jews—disproves their claim." Not only had morals, wisdom, and money failed to destroy anti-Semitism, but in fact Jewish success intensified hatred against them. Furthermore, no group in America which found its rights in jeopardy refrained from public agitation. The one exception, the Chinese, had been denied both citizenship and admission. Jews got attention through the use of the ballot, and if they needed the vote as a safeguard, so did the Negro. No people could entrust their well-being to others and expect to be protected.[20]

Trotter's views received some support in the press. The *Cleveland Gazette* observed that while Jews fought every slight directed at them, some Negroes actually supported Jim Crow measures. The *St. Paul Appeal* hastened to dispel the rumor circulating in the black press that Jews never protested because of a preoccupation with "annexing the Almighty Dollar." That was "bunk, just bunk"; the situation was quite the opposite. Jews constantly directed their power and that of public opinion against their enemies. While advising readers to accumulate all the wealth possible, the *Appeal* stressed the need to continue the fight against prejudice. If it did not go on, blacks would never be able to achieve their aims.[21]

Even those who objected to the emphasis given to Jewish economic success clearly found much there that was worthy of emulation. In particular, they joined supporters of Booker T. Washington in admiring the unity, cooperation, and pride of the Jewish community. Unlike Jews, these blacks pointed out to their brethren that Negroes lacked confidence in themselves. They refused to patronize businesses run by members of their own race. They accepted the white supremacists' doctrine that everything associated with whites was superior. In rejecting their blackness they compounded existing obstacles. Jews, despite their dispersal throughout the world, never forsook each other. Even love of money did not lead them to abandon their religion or one another.[22]

Unity and organization enabled Jews to prosper despite extraordinarily adverse conditions. Their organization in America was "little less than marvelous", W.E.B. DuBois observed as he urged blacks to "look at them with admiration and emulate them." The record of three million Jews showed ten million blacks what they had to learn.[23] The black population in America was nearly as large as the entire Jewish population of the world; united Negroes could become a mighty power. Without unity, they could forget the dream of success and prosperity.[24]

Blacks also saw the aid Jews extended to the less fortunate among them as a source of their strength. "A Jewish beggar is almost an unheard of thing", the *Chicago Defender* pointed out. If a Jew was able to work, a job was secured for him; if not, "institutions royally supported by their own" assisted those in need. No one was ignored, told to go to a public agency, or left to beg. If money to start a business was short, funds were provided. Whenever there was a campaign to raise money for Jews, it was a success. Not so with blacks: "when we are interested in drives in which we are to benefit we sit back, twiddle our thumbs and wait for white people to come to our rescue", the *Defender* complained.[25]

Black admirers of Jews recognized, of course, that their emphasis on Jewish business acumen, group identity, and self-confidence could be misinterpreted. Unity and pride exposed a group to the criticism that it was incapable or unwilling to work for the good of all—that it was somehow un-American. Material success bred resentment among the less well-off. Consequently, many blacks who saw their destiny intertwined with the Jew worked to correct this impression. Jews were good citizens, they noted. They had fought valiantly in the nation's wars. Liberty was a passion for them. Furthermore, they felt at home in America, few having any desire to leave. Beyond doubt they were among the most industrious and law-abiding of all people.[26] One black physician, John R. Francis, thought it pertinent to mention the superior health of American Jews. The cause, he believed, could be summed up in the phrase, "soberness of life." Jews drank less than Christians, ate better, married earlier, and took excellent care of their children and their aged.[27]

A broader image of Jews did not detract from their importance for blacks. Jewish respect for education and cultural achievement, for example, were cited as not only worthy in themselves but as specially relevant for Negroes. Jews had demonstrated that regard for higher education and industry were not incompatible.[28] Another source of their strength was the practice of endogamy. Jews, the *Voice of the Negro* observed, helped to calm white fears that all other "races" were pre-occupied with intermarriage by marrying within their own group.[29]

While the intent of most references to Jews was to promote black advancement, some were also aimed at countering Negro criticism of the Jew. Blacks acknowledged that anti-Semitism could hurt them too. Jews, many black leaders reminded their followers, were in essentially the same position as they were themselves. As racism and religious bigotry were different sides of the same coin, a mutuality of interests united the two minorities. Blacks, of all people should be free of prejudice and should recognize that Jewish pride, cohesiveness, and distinctiveness were assets, not liabilities. It was foolish to resent Jewish success; rather, blacks should applaud their courage and persistence, join their struggles, and learn from them.[30]

On at least one occasion, however, a black publication claimed that the race gained from the general hatred of Jews. Such was the response of the iconoclastic *Messenger* to admission quotas of the 1920's for Jews and blacks at Harvard:

> Fortunately, however, crimes and evils, first visited upon one people, eventually spread to others. It is like disease: the Negro has it today, the white man tomorrow. It knows no race or color line. We have no prejudice against the Jews, but we are glad to see them being excluded along with the Negro. Hitting the Jew is helping the Negro. Why? Negroes have large numbers and small money: Jews have small numbers and large money. Together, the two have large numbers and large money. Not only that— the Jews control the powerful media for the dissemination of opinion,—namely, the press, the screen and the stage. The Negro has benefited before from fights made in interest of Jews.[31]

Significantly, neither the *Messenger* nor other journals suggested that anti-Semitism be encouraged as a means of promoting the cause of blacks.[32]

Though most blacks deplored anti-Semitism, they often inadvertently contributed to the continuation of the negative stereotype of the Jew prevalent in western civilization. Much of the praise given Jews reinforced the Shylock image. Recognition of their merits as citizens and scholars did not offset the picture of Jews as money-hungry, aggressive, and unprincipled, loyal only to wealth and each other.

One way of tainting the Jewish image was by asserting that they often over-did things. Meritorious behavior thus was transformed into a defect. For example, John R. Francis wrote that Jews were careful to prepare for the future and that they held tenaciously to all they got. While advising the Negro to emulate them he felt compelled to remark that they carried their virtues too far.[33] The *Voice of the Negro* qualified its praise by noting that "barring financial transactions", the moral life of the Jew was superior to that of the Anglo-Saxon.[34] Sometimes, as in the comment of the Brooklyn inventor, Samuel Scrotten, the ambivalence lacked subtlety:

> He [the Jew] confines himself to avenues of livelihood that the other party doesn't take to. He peddles shoe laces, blacking, pins, needles, toys, tinware, crockery, matches . . . but he never digs nor does anything that requires muscular force. He is timid, too, and beats a hasty retreat before the wild and threatening look and uplifted club of the man in brass buttons; he runs to cover and saves his skin.[35]

Some blacks were alarmed at these stereotypes and went out of their way to challenge them. The southern educator and clergyman, Morgan L. Latta, observed from the extensive dealings he had had with Jews that they were "just as good a people as other nationalities if you understand them." Latta found them a "submissive people, easy to be controlled", law-abiding, and good at business. It was true that they differed from others in some respects, but they were entitled to their opinions. In short, they were worthy citizens and undeserving of prejudice on the grounds of their Jewishness. David Fulton, a New York City essayist and pullman porter, also claimed to know the Jew. He deplored the tendency of his co-workers to accept the "common trend of feeling" in dealing with Jewish travellers. Admittedly, the Jew did not hesitate to complain; he was a "kicker." But he never did so needlessly or maliciously. Nor was he a sneak or troublemaker. Moreover any experienced hand on the trains would testify that a Jew tipped as liberally as a Christian.[36] While the statements by Latta and Fulton could have been made without reference to black preconceptions of Jews, their deliberate, even strained tone suggests they were directed to the black community.

Frequent pronouncements by middle-class blacks that Jews were among the best friends of the Negro were also aimed at incipient anti-Semitism in black America. The black masses were told that Jews were unusually sensitive to their misery. As the most liberal-minded of whites, Jews should be recognized and treated as friends.[37] Some insisted Jews were the only friends blacks had—the sole group willing to aid them.[38] They cited, for example, the record of Jewish philanthropists, most notably Julius Rosenwald of Chicago, in providing education and social services for former slaves.[39] Some recalled acts of friendship or generosity by individual Jews.[40] So enthusiastic was one black newspaper about Jewish achievements and goodwill that it was almost convinced the mistreatment of blacks would disappear if Jews were to gain control of the nation's political and economic affairs.[41]

Ironically, assertions of Jewish friendship toward blacks, as with those stressing their business success, could backfire. By accenting the relative tolerance of Jews toward them, blacks produced a double standard. Jews were supposed to be different.[42] Blacks, therefore, anticipated better treatment from them than from gentiles. When Jews did not live up to expectations, blacks were disappointed and began to censure them not as whites, but as Jews.

They argued that Jews should know better than to discriminate. An anonymous writer stated in the *New Orleans Louisianian* in 1879 that it was strange for a people whose history had been written in "tears and blood" to be among the leaders in "heaping obloquy and opprobrium" upon a race whose misfortunes paralleled theirs. It was a "melancholy fact" that Jews had to be classified with the Negro hater as a result of their efforts to win acceptance among Christian whites. Consequently, he found it most difficult to feel any sorrow over mistreatment of the Jew: "the bitter cup which he had so industriously assisted in putting to the lips of another race, has in turn been applied to his own." While not as harsh, the editor of the *Christian Recorder* shared the same sense of indignation. As fellow sufferers, Jews deserved the "sincerest sympathy" of black people and should be welcomed in America. But they had followed the Irish and almost instinctively had taken to "democracy and the spirit of negro-phobia." Jews had been among the meanest of slave-owners and the staunchest defenders of slaveocracy and, he added, emancipation had not altered their attitudes.[43] Jewish politicians were especially vulnerable to criticism. A favorite early twentieth century target was Senator Isidor Rayner of Maryland, who was attacked for supporting disenfranchisement and segregation of blacks in his state.[44] In effect, black Americans were saying that Jews should treat others, including the Negro, as they themselves hoped to be treated. Jewish prejudice was as deplorable as anti-Semitism. To the extent Jews deviated from the principle of equal opportunity for the Negro, others would be justified in withholding the same from them.

Some blacks recognized that oppressed peoples might not sympathize with each other. Indeed, the situation could easily be the reverse; one group could seek to lessen its burdens by shifting them to another weaker and more visible group. Awareness of this possibility made some blacks highly suspicious of Jews. Was not their apparent interest in the Negro only an attempt to disguise their own insecure status? Could they be motivated by a desire to use the black man as a shield or lightning rod rather than by a genuine impulse to assist him?[45]

Even Julius Rosenwald's motives were questioned. While most applauded his financial support for the construction of Negro Y.M.C.A. buildings, some suspected his motives. Rosenwald and others, they argued, revealed their true position on the racial question by aiding the establishment of separate public facilities. "Some rich Jews", the *St. Paul Appeal* warned, "alleging philanthropy, have given millions to aid in the lowering of the social status of the colored people because it pleased Caucasian American Christians and brought profits to their bulging pockets." This was "queer work" for a people oppressed for thousands of years. Not all Jews were enemies of the Negro, the paper continued, but those with power and money delighted in "gathering in the coin" while taking swipes at blacks.[46]

The *Cleveland Gazette* was especially wary of Jews. In 1911 it accused men such as Rayner and Rosenwald of conspiring to divert attention from Jews to blacks. And in 1928 it criticized a local rabbi for advising Negroes to develop distinct psychological and racial traits as their contribution to American culture while at the same time urging Jews to assimilate with white gentiles. It charged the rabbi with catering to American prejudices by discouraging black assimilation and with seeking to reduce anti-Semitism by directing gentile hatred at the Negro. If that was his purpose, the paper declared, the rabbi was mistaken. The Negro, as a citizen "to the manor born", was less incompatible with white gentiles than the Jew. The rabbi could not so easily get away with his scheme to deflect ill-will from his own people. He would be wise to devote his energies toward denouncing all prejudices, the *Gazette* counseled.[47]

Such interpretations of Jewish motives may have been erroneous. Nevertheless, the criticisms indicate that at least some blacks were sensitive to the precarious position of Jews in America. It was conceivable that they would try to reduce their own anxiety by shifting hostility to blacks and by establishing racial bonds with other whites.[48] Such fears led Richard Wright, as an adolescent, to suspect a Jewish co-worker:

> There was Don, a Jew; but I distrusted him. His position was not much better than mine and I knew that he was uneasy and insecure; he had always treated me in an off-hand, bantering way that barely concealed his contempt. I was afraid to ask him to help me get books; his frantic desire to demonstrate a racial solidarity with the whites against Negroes might make him betray me.[49]

Overt discrimination by some Jews reinforced Negro suspicions. Even blacks who admitted that Jews were less prejudiced and more friendly than other whites could distrust them. Indeed, the liberalism and goodwill of Jews as a group were all the more cause for being alert to individual signs of betrayal.

The prime source of black hostility, however, did not stem from their worry that Jews would betray them or from their disappointment in the failure of some Jews to sympathize with their cause. What angered them most was the apparent tendency of Jews to use their economic power to degrade blacks further. In the quest for security through wealth some Jews used the helpless as stepping-stones, and thus kept them at the bottom of the socio-economic scale.

Blacks were especially sensitive to this situation in the years after World War I, largely as a result of their growing numbers in northern urban centers. Previously, they had very little contact with Jews: Negroes were overwhelmingly rural and southern; Jews, urban and northern. During the war two streams of migrants, one from Europe and the other from the American south, converged. Housing pressures generated by the influx of black newcomers led to the expansion of the black ghetto into Jewish neighborhoods. Jews, like their predecessors, resented the invasion and ultimately moved away. They left behind, however, a residue of ill-will.

Black displeasure was caused in part by Jewish acceptance of racist housing patterns. More important, Jewish departure was seldom complete. In addition to the elderly who were unable or unwilling to flee. Jews maintained a presence in the black ghetto through ownership of stores and apartment buildings. Few blacks had the resources or experience to compete with Jewish businessmen, but while the latter were no more guilty of exploiting blacks than other whites, they were more easily identified, either by name or manner of dress. Afro-Americans came to think of all white landlords and shopkeepers as Jews. Discriminatory hiring practices by Jews and white gentiles added to this resentment.

As black frustrations mounted in the post-war period and as Jews gained greater power, tensions multiplied. Jews increasingly became targets for black frustration and anger. To blacks it appeared that they were making it more difficult for them to reach the Promised Land.[50] Expanding contacts between the two groups in metropolitan areas accentuated anti-Jewish sentiments among blacks but they did not initiate them. Black resentment of Jewish economic power and black vulnerability to exploitation by Jewish merchants existed well before the war and the Great Migration. In 1895, for example, Augustus M. Hodges of Brooklyn concluded "without any fear of contradiction" that Jews were by far the most objectionable of all the people in the country. From their place of power in the money market they had gained respect and the rights of citizenship. But wealth blinded them to the misery of others; they had lost the ability and desire to see beneath the surface of American life.[51]

By the eve of World War I the image of the Jew as a money-hungry demon who took advantage of naive and powerless blacks was being voiced with greater frequency. Headlines such as that of the *Chicago Defender* in 1913 left little room for misinterpretation: "Abraham Bass (Jewish) Fined $50 and Costs for Cheating in Weight at 2816 State Mrs. Hattie Brown". Such practices had been going on for years in the Chicago black belt, the paper noted. "Jews have grown rich by stealing the hard-earned money of the poor laboring class of colored people. . . . It is reported that the Jews have a system all over the city to 'skin' their brothers in black." Similar charges were made in New York City. In a viciously anti-Semitic editorial in 1912, the *New York Age* characterized Jews as "tribalistic", "parasitical and predatory." They were "as subtle as serpents and as harmless as doves, to themselves." They lived solely to accumulate money and would stop at nothing in this quest. Moreover, Jews were rapidly moving into new professions where their ability to harm blacks would be even greater. "The Jew is becoming a leader if not a dictator", the editor warned. In 1915 the separatist, Cyril B. Briggs, accused Jews of robbing blacks of jobs in Harlem that would be theirs "could we but play the Jew for only a few weeks, insisting . . . on spending our money with our own enterprises and only those white stores that give the race something in return."[52]

The northern black community did not suffer alone. Although Jews were but a tiny minority in the South, they left their mark on the whole population in general and on blacks in particular. In 1883 Timothy Thomas Fortune observed that from his experiences in the South the Jew was responsible for much of the "southern problem." As controllers of the money market, Fortune said, they kept white planters in constant "hot water." Consequently, the planter had little choice but to overwork black laborers. W.E.B. DuBois was also unhappy with the role of Jews in the emerging New South. "Shrewd and unscrupulous Jews" along with Yankees and the sons of poor whites, all of whom thirsted for wealth and power, were replacing the old, ante-bellum aristocracy, he observed. One victim was an "ignorant, honest Negro" of Georgia who had been cheated of his land by an "enterprising Russian Jew" who fled the scene, leaving the black man to work land rightfully his for thirty cents a day.[53]

Another criticism of southern Jews was the way they exploited gullible black farmers by feigning friendship. Jews deliberately established businesses in heavily black areas. They warmly welcomed their neighbors, employing all sorts of devices to suggest that they were the black man's friend. At the same time they avoided politics for fear of antagonizing powerful whites. Should a lynching occur, Jews extricated themselves from a difficult position by claiming an inadequate command of English. Once they had filled their pockets and in the process forced Negro competitors out of business, they sold their businesses to other poor ambitious Jews and moved to where they did not have to depend on the freedmen's trade.[54]

During and after World War I blacks said little about the southern Jew but continued to find fault with his northern brother for abusing them. Anti-Jewish themes based on their reputed sleazy economic practices were incorporated in a variety of formats. For example, in September 1917, McAdoo Baker devoted his column, "Business and Finance", which appeared in the strongly middle-class *Half-Century Magazine* to a fictionalized account of a young black man, George, who was opening a grocery store. George decided to seek advice from Moses Isaacstein, a competitor. But "Shrewd Moses" deliberately misled the youth, while overtly encouraging him. Worse, Isaacstein hired a black delivery boy to please his black customers and then encouraged Goldberg, his brother-in-law, to trick George into selling a useless washing fluid. Predictably, George did so and thus became another victim of the wily Jew.[55]

The traditional image of the money-making materialist who enriched himself at black expense often appeared in Negro humor. In one popular anecdote, included in an anthology compiled by William Pickens of the NAACP in 1926, representatives of various races at Creation were given whatever they desired. The Anglo-Saxon asked for political power, the Chinese for peace and isolation, the American Indian for a happy hunting ground, and the Negro for a million dollars. When the Jew, who had heard the Negro's request, was asked his, he replied, "Joost giff me dot Negro's *address!*"[56]

Distrust and resentment of the Jew was exploited by black nationalists who sought to free their people from white control. In the twentieth century, black attacks on Jews have been closely related to nationalistic movements, especially economic nationalism, as advocated by Marcus Garvey in the 1920's, the "don't buy where you can't work" crusades of the 1930's, and by Malcolm X and others in the 1950's and 1960's. While Garvey himself never launched an anti-Jewish campaign, on occasion he singled out Jews for criticism. An observer at his mail-fraud trial in 1923 reported that he "indulged in several outbursts of anti-Semitism" and shouted "Damn the Jews!" upon hearing the jury's verdict.[57] Jews had been involved in Garvey's acquisition of a vastly over-priced ship for the steamship line he had founded in order to promote black business and migration to Africa. Furthermore, the judge and prosecuting attorney in his trial were Jews. For the downhearted Garvey, therefore, Jews served as handy scapegoats. He accused them of combining with his enemies to ruin his reputation and that of the Universal Negro Improvement Association by portraying him as an ally of the Ku Klux Klan. Prominent Jews, Garvey warned, were "disarming, dis-visioning, dis-ambitioning and fooling the Negro to death" with talk of "the dream of equality that shall never materialize, as they well know, and never intended; . . ."[58] Perhaps it was not by coincidence that in the year of his trial, Garvey's wife denounced the control white immigrants exercised in Harlem. The business practices of Jake, the butcher, "a beardless Shylock", exemplified to her the unethical, if not illegal, means aliens employed to exploit the district.[59]

Complimentary references surpassed anti-Semitic comments throughout the 1920's, but a gradual intensification of resentment toward Jews was already discernible in the century's first decades. The continued involvement of Jews in the NAACP and philanthropy did not erase black suspicions. The persistent, often strained, efforts of influential Negroes to counter charges against Jews with fine-sounding praise could not dissolve the frustrations of every-day life for blacks. Moreover, the tendency of liberal black leaders to assert that Jews were, on the whole, much better than white gentiles backfired because it raised Negro expectations of help from them beyond any reasonable limits. Blacks may have become aware of Jewish contributions to their cause, but at the same time they became more alert to evidence of Jewish discrimination and ill-will.

While educated, middle-class blacks continued to affirm that genuine friendship should and did exist between Negroes and Jews, the impact of their message on the black masses was questionable. Intellectuals such as the sociologist E. Franklin Frazier may have found comfort in the recognition that Jewish dominance in the ghettos of urban America, while deplorable, stemmed from "cultural influences" rather than "certain instincts of the Jew."[60] Most Afro-Americans, however, cared little for theories; as far as they were concerned whites whom they identified as Jews directly contributed to the maintenance of the color line.

In 1930 the majority of black Americans still lived in the South. A focus on the northern, urban black community in the decade after the first world war reveals but a segment of the overall role of the Jew in black thought from reconstruction to the depression. For most of them during that period Jews were not a symbol of oppression or exploitation but a model of hope. They showed what a people with a long history of servitude and degradation could accomplish through unity, pride, cooperation, and wealth. Just as black slaves had sustained their dreams for a better future by singing of Moses and the Jews, so did their legally free descendants in succeeding generations look to the Jew for relief. These hopes, thwarted after decades of poverty, generated a need for scapegoats, and they were readily available. Jewish diligence and economic efficiency in southern towns and northern ghettos bred resentment among poor blacks who could not compete with them. Thus slowly but surely the Jew became the target for black frustration.

Black criticism, however, did not necessarily imply anti-Semitism. In the years from 1865 to 1930 black Americans were not primarily interested in the Jew *qua* Jew.[61] They censured Jews for behaving like other whites and not because they were worse than others. When Jews discriminated against them they were singled out because blacks expected more of a group who themselves had been victims of bigotry. Jews did not live up to the double standard black Americans applied to them and to gentiles.

The place of the Jew in black social thought was reflected in the narrow perspective blacks had of him. Only exceptional Jews were of interest; the great majority were ignored. As newly arrived immigrants subject to severe restrictions by gentile America, the lot of the mass of Jews was hard. They labored for others, struggled with underfinanced enterprises, and lived under conditions only slightly superior to those of native blacks. But blacks ignored such Jews for they were of little interest. They neither inspired hope nor offered an explanation for the Negro's plight.

The story of black-Jewish relations has been an ironic one. The image of the Jew which initially fostered confidence among blacks ultimately contributed to tension and conflict between the two groups. But to stress the latter at the expense of the former in a search for the origins of black anti-Semitism is to distort reality. Blacks were a uniquely introspective element in the American population, deeply concerned with survival in a hostile society. They could ill afford involvement in crusades against other minorities; nor were they able to defend the persecuted.

Little will be gained by seeking to determine whether blacks historically have been pro- or anti-Jewish. They may have been neither—or both.[62] Unquestionably, they were an insecure group looking for inspiration, while critical of those who seemingly added to their misery. Their view of Jews reflected this insecurity.[63] Because Jews symbolized both hope and oppression, the black reaction to them can best be described as one of ambivalence.

NOTES

1. Richard Wright, *Black boy: a record of childhood and youth* (New York, 1966), pp. 70–71, 268.

2. See statements by Horace Mann Bond in *The New York Times,* May 4, 1964, p. 20, and in "Negro attitudes toward Jews", *Jewish Social Studies,* XXVII (January 1965), 3–9; James Baldwin, *Notes of a native son* (New York, 1963), p. 61.

3. For discussions of the surge in interest in black-Jewish relations in the 1960's, see Lenore E. Benson, *The Negroes and the Jews* (New York, 1971); Ben Halpern, *Jews and blacks: the classic American minorities* (New York, 1971); Nat Hentoff (ed.), *Black anti-Semitism and Jewish racism* (New York, 1969); Shlome Katz (ed.), *Negro and Jew: an encounter in America* (New York, 1967); Robert G. Weisbord and Arthur Stein, *Bittersweet encounter: the Afro-American and the American Jew* (Westport, Conn., 1970).

4. An insight into the role of the Jew in the lives of slaves is provided in Charles H. Nichols. *Many thousands gone: the ex-slaves' account of their bondage and freedom* (Bloomington, 1969), pp. 96–102, and in Gayrand S. Wilmore, *Black religion and black radicalism* (Garden City, N.Y., 1972), pp. 52–53; Lawrance W. Levine, *Black culture and black consciousness: Afro-American folk thought from slavery to freedom* (New York, 1977), pp. 23, 50–51.

5. James Weldon Johnson, "The Negro and the Jew", *New York Age,* February 2, 1918; *Southern Christian Recorder* (Nashville, Tenn.), March 27, 1890.

6. Booker T. Washington, *Putting the most into life* (New York, 1906), pp. 30–32.

7. *AME Church Review,* II (1885–86), 201. Emphasis in original.

8. *Southern Christian Recorder,* March 27, 1890. The success of Jews, according to the paper, derived from the Bible, education, dedication to business, frugality, group unity, avoidance of lawsuits, and mutual support.

9. *Colored American Magazine,* X (January 1906), 9–10.

10. This interpretation, developed below, was suggested in Seth Scheiner, *Negro Mecca: a history of the Negro in New York City, 1865–1920* (New York, 1965), p. 132.

11. *New York Age,* March 16, 1889.

12. *Ibid.,* March 1, 1890. For similar statements, see *Colored American* (Washington, D.C.), July 5, 1902; *Baltimore Ledger,* January 14, 1899; *Colored American Magazine,* V (October 1920), 445; *Norfolk Journal and Guide,* March 5, 1921; May 22, 1926; *Voice of the Negro,* I (November 1904), 551; *Chicago Defender,* April 14, 1928; and D. Augustus Straker, *The New South investigated* (Detroit, 1888), pp. 49–50.

13. Washington, *Putting the most into life,* pp. 31–32; *The future of the American Negro* (Boston, 1907), pp. 65–66.

14. Washington, "Taking advantage of our disadvantages", *AME Church Review,* X (April 1894), 478.

15. *New York Age,* February 3, 1915; July 20, 1905. Also, see *Chicago Defender,* February 6, 1915.

16. *Pittsburgh Courier,* June 12, 1926.

17. Charles B. Purvis to Francis J. Grimke, November 25, 1920; January 14, 1921, in Carter G. Woodson

(ed.), *The works of Francis J. Grimke* (4 vols.; Washington, D.C., 1942), IV, 291, 294.

18. *New York Globe*, September 1, 1883. Also, *Voice of the Negro*, I (November 1904), 551; J. A. Rogers, *From "superman" to man* (4th ed.; New York, 1924), p. 117. The retreat of Henry Ford from his anti-Semitic campaign in the 1920's was also hailed by the black press as a Jewish victory. *Pittsburgh Courier*, July 30, 1927; *Broad Ax* (Chicago), April 16, 1921; Steven Bloom, "Interactions between blacks and Jews in New York City, 1900–1930, as reflected in the black press" (unpublished Ph.D. dissertation, New York University, 1973), pp. 62–74.

19. *Broad Ax*, September 11, 1897.

20. *Boston Guardian*, June 30, 1903; William Monroe Trotter, "Agitation as a means to protect equal public rights", *AME Church Review*, XXXI (January 1915), 40.

21. *Cleveland Gazette*, February 18, 1911; *St. Paul Appeal*, October 17, 1914. See also, *Broad Ax*, April 16, 1921.

22. William Wells Brown, *My southern home; or, the south and its people* (Boston, 1880), pp. 236–237; *New York Age*, April 4, 1912. The *Messenger* later disagreed with the implications of this interpretation. Jews, it noted, were probably the shrewdest business people in the world, but they never advocated "Patronize your own" as did some blacks. They knew their numbers were too few to succeed on a segregated basis—and blacks had to realize that as well. *Messenger*, VI (September 1924), 280–281.

23. *Crisis*, IX (March 1915), 235.

24. *Half-Century Magazine*, II (January 1917), 18; IV (April 1918), 3; *Chicago Defender*, September 22, 1923.

25. *Chicago Defender*, March 21, 1914; December 5, 1925. See also, *Half-Century Magazine*, IX (August–September 1920), 3; *Pittsburgh Courier*, November 7, 1925.

26. *AME Church Review*, XVII (April 1901), 358–359; *Voice of the Negro*, III (January 1906), 20.

27. John R. Francis, "What are the causes of the great mortality among the Negroes . . .?" in D. W. Culp (ed.), *Twentieth century Negro literature* (Naperville, Ill., 1902), p. 209.

28. *Ibid.*; *New York Age*, January 5, November 30, 1905; *Chicago Defender*, November 4, 1922.

29. *Voice of the Negro*, III (January 1906), 20.

30. *New York Freeman*, July 23, 1887; *Cleveland Gazette*, October 16, 1909; *Savannah Tribune*, January 28, 1899; November 15, 1913; *AME Church Review*, XXXIX (July 1922), 52; Samuel Barrett, *A plea for unity among American Negroes and the Negroes of the world* (3rd ed.; Waterloo, Iowa, 1926), pp. 38–39; Mary Church Terrell, *A colored woman in a white world* (Washington, D.C., 1940), p. 89.

31. *Messenger*, IV (August 1922), 459. The *Messenger* actually was sympathetic to Jews and defended them from attacks; *ibid.*, I (March 1919), 3; III (December 1921), 298–299.

32. Langston Hughes recalled a situation in which blacks even gained from the presence of Jews. In his Cleveland high school at the beginning of World War I he and other blacks were elected to numerous student body offices because of the division between Jews and gentiles. Hughes, *The big sea, an autobiography* (New York, 1963), p. 31. It is conceivable that the improved status of Jews in the twentieth century might have lessened black goodwill toward them. As Jews escaped persecution, they could be expected to have less sympathy for the plight of the Negro and perhaps even benefit from his subjugation.

33. Francis, "What are the causes of the great mortality among the Negroes . . .?", 209.

34. *Voice of the Negro*, III (January 1906), 20.

35. *New York Age*, August 10, 1905.

36. Morgan L. Latta, *The history of my life and work* (Raleigh, 1903), p. 321; David B. Fulton, *Eagle clippings* (Brooklyn, 1907), p. 94.

37. *Chicago Defender*, August 10, 1912; *Savannah Tribune*, November 15, 1913; *Messenger*, II (July 1919), 5–6.

38. *New York Amsterdam News*, February 14, 1923. See also, *Washington Bee*, January 8, 1921; *Messenger*, I (March 1919), 3.

39. Bloom, "Interaction between blacks and Jews in New York City", pp. 241–245.

40. For an example, see Hughes, *The big sea*, pp. 30–31.

41. *Baltimore Afro-American*, June 25, 1910.

42. [Mary Church Terrell], "What it means to be colored in the capital of the United States", *Independent*, LXII (January 24, 1907), 183; Richard Wright, *Eight men* (Cleveland, 1940), p. 239; George S. Schuyler, "Our white folks", *American Mercury*, XII (December 1927), p. 387. The tendency of blacks to have higher expectations for Jews than for other whites, and to be frequently disappointed, has been noted by several commentators on black-Jewish relations. Weisbord and Stein, *Bittersweet encounter*, pp. 216–217; Roi Ottley, *New world a-coming: inside black America* (Boston, 1943), p. 130; Lawrence D. Reddick, "Anti-Semitism among Negroes", *Negro Quarterly*, I (Summer 1942), 116; Baldwin, *Notes of a native son*, p. 62.

43. Letter from Washington, D.C., *New Orleans Louisianian*, October 4, 1879; *Christian Recorder* (Philadelphia), June 1, 1882.

44. *St. Paul Appeal*, October 9, 1909; September 11, 1915; *Cleveland Gazette*, January 7, 1911; *Atlanta Independent*, December 7, 1912.

45. This point has been made by Kenneth B. Clark: "A part of the complexity of the feelings of the Negro about the Jew is his awareness that Jews have seemed, in general, less negative toward him than have other whites. More Jews have shown active concern about racial problems and more Jews have been willing to hire Negroes for various types of jobs. The Negro's interpretation of this has not, however, been altogether favorable. There is sometimes the lurking suspicion that all this is motivated by a desire on the part of the Jew to use him as a shield and reflects a not too well disguised concern about his own status." Clark, "Candor about Negro-Jewish relations: a social scientist charts a complex social problem", *Commentary*, I (February 1946), 13.

46. *St. Paul Appeal*, September 11, 1915; October 9, 1920.

47. *Cleveland Gazette*, January 7, 1911; March 10, 1928.

48. The difficulties inherent in a black-Jewish alliance were illustrated in the Leo Frank case in 1914. Eugene Levy, " 'Is the Jew a white man?' Press reaction to the Leo Frank case, 1913–1915", *Phylon*, XXXV (June 1974), 216–217.

49. Wright, *Black boy*, p. 268. James Baldwin has commented on the inherent difficulty Jews and blacks face in establishing trust and co-operation: "The structure of the American commonwealth has trapped both these minorities into attitudes of perpetual hostility. They do not dare trust each other—the Jew because he feels he must climb higher on the American social ladder and has, so far as he is concerned, nothing to gain from identification with any minority even more unloved than he; while the Negro is in the even less tenable position of not really daring to trust anyone." Baldwin, *Notes of a native son*, pp. 62–63.

50. Descriptions of relations between blacks and Jews in northern urban areas in the post-World War I era are found in Weisbord and Stein, *Bittersweet encounter*, pp. 19, 40–44, 206; Ottley, *New world a-coming*, pp. 123–128; B. Z. Sobel and May L. Sobel, "Negroes and Jews: American minority groups in conflict", *Judaism*, XV (Winter 1966), 4. Black business people irritated by the lack of black patronage often held the Jew at least partially responsible. St. Clair Drake, *Black metropolis: a study of Negro life in a northern city* (New York, 1962), pp. 439–441, 448, 452.

51. *Indianapolis Freeman*, December 21, 1895. See also Alexander H. Newton's recollection of his clash with a Jewish clothing merchant in Hartford, Connecticut, at the close of the civil war. Newton, *Out of the briars* (Philadelphia, 1910), p. 89.

52. *Chicago Defender*, September 27, 1913; *New York Age*, February 8, 1912; *Colored American Review* (New York), October 1, 1915, quoted in Weisbord and Stein, *Bittersweet encounter*, p. 38. See also the accusation that "young Hebrews" secured fair-skinned, educated black women recently from the South for "diversion." Mrs. V. E. Matthews, "Some of the dangers confronting southern girls in the North", *Hampton Negro Conference Reports*, No. 2 (July 1898), 67.

53. *New York Globe*, February 17, 1883; W. E. Burghardt DuBois, "The relation of the Negroes to the whites in the South", *Annals of the American Academy of Political and Social Science*, XVIII (1901), 126–127.

54. *New York Age*, September 21, 1905. The image of the southern Jew was mixed and statements contrary to these exist. For example, the *Age* on August 21, 1913, saw hope in the arrival of Jews and other aliens in the region. Outside politics, they were replacing old leaders. The Jew, it observed, "has been from

the first, and still are, very helpful to the colored people, especially in the farming districts, and have helped and are helping thousands of colored farmers to 'get by' from crop to crop." The interaction of Jews and blacks in a southern city is skillfully traced in Steven Hertzberg, "The Jews of Atlanta, 1865–1915" (unpublished Ph.D. dissertation, University of Chicago, 1975), pp. 281–309.

55. *Half-Century Magazine*, III (September 1917), 11, 17. As in many other cases, this highly anti-Jewish article ran next to a laudatory description of the Jew. *Ibid.*, 18.

56. William Pickens, *American Aesop: Negro and other humor* (Boston, 1926), pp. 111–116. For an excellent discussion of black humor concerning Jews and other ethnic groups, see Levine, *Black culture and black consciousness*, pp. 301–307.

57. J. A. Rogers, *World's great men of color* (2 vols.; New York, 1972), II, 425–426.

58. Amy Jacques-Garvey (ed.), *The philosophy and opinions of Marcus Garvey* (2 vols.; New York, 1923, 1925), II, 70–71, 181, 184, 199, 217–218, 259. Edmund David Cronin, *Black Moses: the story of Marcus Garvey and the Universal Negro Improvement Association* (Madison, 1962), p. 200, maintained that Garvey "entertained strong prejudices against Jews in general", although he did not develop the point. Ottley, *New world a-coming*, p. 122, argued that "Marcus Garvey was the first Negro leader to raise the 'Jewish question' in Negro life. He disclaimed being anti-Semitic, but he spoke of 'Jewish control' of the Negro's economic life." See also, Elton C. Fax, *Garvey: the story of a pioneer black nationalist* (New York, 1972), pp. 198–199. Garveyism and Jews in New York City is discussed at length in Bloom, "Interactions between blacks and Jews in New York City," pp. 104–162, and Isabel B. Price, "Black responses to anti-Semitism: Negroes and Jews in New York, 1880 to World War II" (unpublished Ph.D. dissertation, University of New Mexico, 1973), pp. 119–137.

59. *Negro World* (New York), April 28, 1923.

60. *Opportunity*, II (October 1924), 295–296.

61. Two prominent blacks have made this point regarding the present era. See the Foreward by C. Eric Lincoln to Weisbord and Stein, *Bittersweet encounter*, xv, and James Baldwin, "Negroes are anti-Semitic because they are anti-white", *The New York Times Magazine*, April 9, 1967, pp. 26–27.

62. John Higham has noted that it was quite common for Americans in the period from 1870 to 1900 to be both pro- and anti-Jewish at the same time. Higham, "Anti-Semitism in the Gilded Age: a reinterpretation", *Mississippi Valley Historical Review*, XLIII (March 1957), 564.

63. This point is made by Scheiner, *Negro Mecca*, p. 133: "The Negro's view of Jewish business success— whether scornful or laudatory—reflected his sense of insecurity, his marginal place in American society rather than employment or business competition."

# The Dixie Volunteers

By EDGAR LESLIE
and HARRY RUBY

VOICE

742

**CHORUS**

Let's all give three cheers,___ For the Dix - ie Vol - un - teers;___ See those great big

South - ern lad-dies, Just like their dear old dad-dies; They are proud to go,___ And they want the world to

know;___ They're com-ing! they're com-ing! From the land of Old Black Joe;___ Peace-ful sons have

shoul-dered guns, And now they're go-ing to be,___ Fight-ing men like Stone-wall Jack- son

and like Rob-ert E. Lee;___ When they hit that line;___ And they cross the Riv - er

Rhine;___ You'll wish you came from Dix - ie, With the Dix - ie Vol-un - teers.___ teers.

The Dixie Volunteers - 2

F.J.LAWSON CO.N.Y.

# SILVER SWANEE
## SONG

Lyric by
EDDIE CANTOR

Music by
JEAN SCHWARTZ

I see a shad-ow stand-ing by the Swan-ee Shore once more
I hear a ban-jo strum-ming old fam-i-liar tunes sweet tunes

I see the lights a-gleam-ing as in days of yore once more
The hon-ey-bees are hum-ming 'neath the hon-ey-moon those tunes

I see the cot-ton blos-soms shin-ing bright Or is it Mam-my's hair so
I see a pick-a-nin-ny roll his eyes While Mam-my Gin-nie's bak-ing

snow-y white  Swan-ee breeze  I hear you sigh-ing  I feel blue  Just for you
pump-kin pies  Swan-ee babe  Say you are lone-ly  Do you miss  Mam-my's kiss

CHORUS

Way down up-on__ the Sil-ver Swan-ee some-one's call-ing Way

down up-on__ the Sil-ver Swan-ee Tears are fall-ing Swan-ee don't__ you cry

Swan-ee dry your eye I'm__ com-ing home Soon I'll rock-a-bye To your lul-la-bye

Silver Swanee - 4

In my Dix - ie cra - dle Way down up - on— my knee each night a -

-lone I'm pray-ing And in my dreams I see a cab-in door I

hear your gen - tle voice a - call - ing Come home come home to your

Sil - ver - y Swan - ee once more more

Silver Swanee - 4

PATTER Ad lib.

Swan-ee shore  Sy-ca-more  Dog and cat  Wel-come mat  Daf-fy-dill

Whip-poor-will  Mam-my bake  Buck-wheat cake

Serve them hot  Reach the spot  Blos-soms fall  Crick-ets call

Those were the days that I loved best of all

Give me my grip  Here is your tip—  Don't wake me up— I am on-ly dream-ing

Silver Swanee - 4

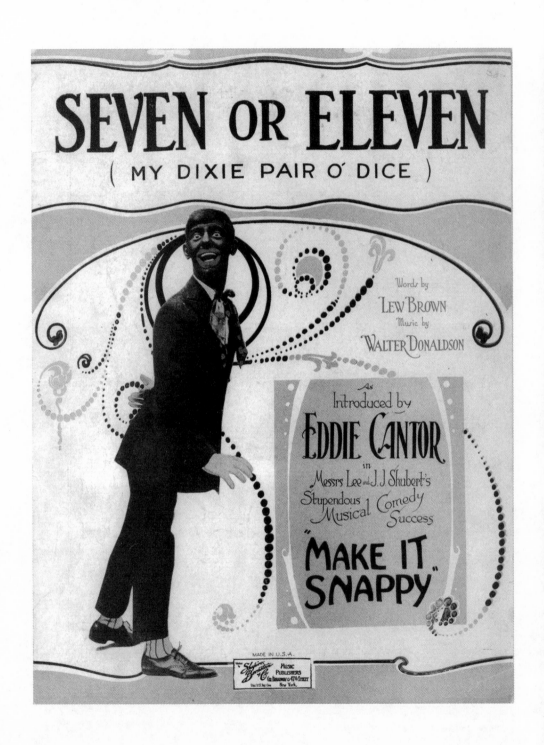

Copyright © 1923 by Shapiro, Bernstein and Co., New York.

# Seven or Eleven
## (My Dixie Pair O' Dice)

Words by
LEW BROWN

Music by
WALTER DONALDSON

Moderato

Till ready

At the rail-road sta - tion Al - most ev - 'ry day
Ev - 'ry time they break him Ru - fus goes a - way

Hang-in' round the por-ters there Try - in' hard to win his fare
Gets a brand new bank roll, then Comes to roll those bones a - gain

You'll see Ru - fus John - son Gam - blin' his dough a - way
Ne - ver seems to wor - ry While he's got dough to play

Down on his knees with the dot-ted i - vo - ries You can hear old Ru-fus say:
Wear-in' a smile and just sing-in' all the while "This may be my luck-y day:

**REFRAIN** *(Not too fast)*

Sev-en __ or E - le - ven __ means ev-'ry-thing to me Means I'm gonna see my

Mam-my, Down in sun-ny Al-a - bam-my Sev-en __ or E - le-ven, That's what it's got to be __

__ It means the scenes I'm long-in' for __ The Swa-nee and the 'Sip-py and the

Seven or Eleven - 3

Seven or Eleven - 3

1932, Joe Davis Inc., Music Publishers, New York.

# From *World of Our Fathers*

Even as this generation of performers was unmistakably Jewish and defined itself at least in part through the cultural symbols and references of Yiddish, much of its early success was gained from acts done in blackface. A considerable tradition of blackface entertainment preceded the rise of the Jewish performers, but by about 1910 they had taken it over almost entirely, making it one of their specialties and endowing it with a flavor of their own. Irving Berlin scored his first success as a songwriter with a blackface tune, "Alexander's Ragtime Band"; Al Jolson made blackface recital the foundation of a spectacular career, mostly on stage and then in the movies; Sophie Tucker was billed as the "World-Renowned Coon Shouter" or, in a more refined version, "Manipulator of Coon Melodies"; Eddie Cantor "played Salome (still in blackface)," combining racial impersonation with a veiled transvestite burlesque; George Burns "had seen Jolson and I figured if he was a hit with a big wide mouth, I'd be a riot with a bigger one"; George Jessel toured for a long time, sometimes together with Cantor, in a blackface routine. Later, when Al Jolson made *The Jazz Singer,* the first American talking picture, he brought together—for him, a quite natural thing to do—Yiddish shmaltz and blackface sentiment in a story about a successful American singer, son of a cantor, who returns to the East Side to chant the Kol Nidre while his father lies dying.

Perhaps it was no more than shrewd opportunism, an eagerness to give audiences exactly what they seemed to want, which led so many Jewish entertainers to work in blackface; but it is hard to resist the impression that some deeper affinity was also at work. Ronald Sanders, in a fine study, has suggested that blackface provided "a kind of Jewish musical fulfillment" through a strain of "ethnic pastiche." When they took over the conventions of ethnic mimicry, the Jewish performers transformed it into something emotionally richer and more humane. Black became a mask for Jewish expressiveness, with one woe speaking through the voice of another. Irving Berlin inserted Yiddishisms into songs deriving from "coon song" conventions; Sophie Tucker "started interpolating Jewish words in some of my songs, just to give the audience a kick"; George Gershwin, more subtly, blended Yiddish folk tunes and black melodies into a blue union. (Gershwin's biographer, Isaac Goldberg, found a musical kinship between the "Negro blue note" and the "blue note" of Hasidic chant. Put Yiddish and black

In 1980 Irving Howe was Distinguished Professor of English at the Graduate Center of City University of New York and Hunter College.
Excerpt from "Journeys Outward" from Irving Howe, *World of Our Fathers* (New York: Harcourt Brace Jovanovich, 1976), 562–63. Copyright © 1976 by Irving Howe. Reprinted by permission of Harcourt Brace & Company and Routledge.

together, he wrote, "and they spell Al Jolson.") "The great American tradition of ethnic pastiche," continues Sanders, "had by now [c. 1910] become a Jewish specialty. . . . Pastiche is a gift of peoples who live in culturally ambivalent situations."

Blacking their faces seems to have enabled the Jewish performers to reach a spontaneity and assertiveness in the declaration of their Jewish selves. ("Was this the only way Al Jolson could have gotten his intense Jewish shmaltz across to general audiences?") The blackface persona, bringing a freedom of the anonymous and forbidden, could become so powerful a force that sometimes the entertainer felt a need to make it clear that it was only a persona. After one of her stomping exhibitions in blackface, Sophie Tucker would peel off a glove and wave to the crowd "to show I was a white girl." A surprised gasp would rise from the audience, then a howl of laughter, as if in tribute to all that impersonation could dredge up.

# Parallels and Divergences
## Assimilationist Strategies of Afro-American and Jewish Elites from 1910 to the Early 1930s

If, as most behavioral scientists maintain, the dynamics of minority group acculturation and assimilation are crucially influenced by the assimilationist aversions of majority groups, the fact remains that historically most Afro-Americans and Jews in the United States have themselves insisted that acculturation must not lead to assimilation. Indeed, both Jews and Afro-Americans have tended to cling to reinforcing ideologies to conceal or to deny the assimilative process whenever it begins to operate with great efficacy. As a fact of social life, acculturation invariably *tends* to lead to assimilation, but it is not *inevitable* that the former process end in the latter—in self-denial and the disappearance of ethnic group identity through dispersion and intermarriage.[1] Most Afro-Americans and Jews have not wanted to disappear; this article is concerned with those who did.

The argument, simply stated, is that there was a time when a small number of socially powerful and politically privileged Jews and Afro-Americans embraced an ideology of extreme cultural assimilationism; that, although this ideology was emphatically not without paradox and illogic, its ultimate consequence entailed the abandonment of identity; and that these two elites—one, wealthy and of primarily German-Jewish descent; the other, largely northern, college-trained Afro-American—reacting to threats to their hegemony both from within and from outside their ethnic universes, decided to concert many of their undertakings in the belief that group assimilation could be accelerated through strategies of overt and covert mutual assistance. Influential Jews and "Talented Tenth" Afro-Americans feared that within a short span of time they would be powerless to promote their social and political programs because of recrudescent nativism and racism set off among old-stock Americans by uncontrolled migration from eastern Europe and the Deep South, triggering in turn divisive and strident cultural and political nationalisms among the unabsorbed, increasingly despised newcomers. The passage of their people—certainly the celerity of that passage—into the mainstream was believed to be at risk.[2]

One of the nation's most brilliant jurists and its outstanding anthropologist, both Jews, and two of the leading civil rights advocates, both Afro-Americans, publicly and privately expressed extreme assimilationist views that were, if controversial and increasingly unrepresentative of some younger leadership opinion, typical of established Jewish and Afro-American leadership until well into the 1930s. "Habits of living or of thought which tend to keep alive difference of origin or classify men according to their

In 1984, David Levering Lewis was professor of history at the University of California, San Diego.
Originally published in the *Journal of American History* 71, no. 3 (1984): 543–64. Copyright © 1984, Organization of American Historians. Reprinted with permission of the *Journal of American History*.

beliefs," Louis D. Brandeis admonished in a 1910 interview, "are inconsistent with the American ideal of brotherhood, and are disloyal." "It would seem," Franz Boas wrote in 1921, "that man being what he is, the negro problem will not disappear in America until the negro blood has been so much diluted that it will no longer be recognized just as anti-Semitism will not disappear until the last vestige of the Jew as a Jew has disappeared." Four years later Walter F. White of the National Association for the Advancement of Colored People [NAACP], expressed the view that the "greatest handicap [the Negro] experiences is that he is not permitted to forget that he is a Negro. . . . The economic and social strictures do not play, in my opinion, so large a part." In 1928 James Weldon Johnson, dean of Afro-American letters and executive secretary of the NAACP, foresaw the promised land of racial invisibility when he wrote that the " 'race problem' is fast reaching the stage of being more a question of national mental attitudes toward the Negro than a question of his actual condition." Think of us as being just like you, he was urging, and there would be no more American dilemma. In the same year he described the alleged marital preferences of Afro-American professional men for light-skinned women as a positive example of racial natural selection.[3]

Not everyone spoke so candidly or saw solutions so clearly. Indeed, the same spokespersons could and, frequently enough, did endorse opposite convictions. Abruptly, in 1914, Brandeis became the country's leading Zionist. James Weldon Johnson startled a 1917 socialist conference at Belleport, New York, with the declaration that the "only things artistic in America that have sprung from American soil, permeated American life, and been universally acknowledged as distinctively American" were the creations of the Afro-American. Psychological and situational marginality led to ambiguity and ambivalence among many of the upper-crust Jews and Afro-Americans. Many, in their personal lives and public utterances, held to acculturationist ideals, only subconsciously aware of their acts of omission and commission, small and large, that served the cause of assimilation. Jacob H. Schiff would never have considered personal religious conversion, and W. E. B. Du Bois never ceased to extol African cultural attributes in contradistinction to those of mainstream America. Ethnic pride, both men believed, could be sublimated in the dogma of unexceptionable public conformity to the best ideals and behavior of white Anglo-Saxon Protestant [WASP] America—the better to guarantee private space for retention of what was most precious in minority culture.[4] Yet the desire for retention of minority culture was clearly eroded by complex feelings about the prospects for ultimate Americanization. The suspicion that many of those men and women were prepared to see a higher price paid for full acceptance than they admitted for the record does not seem at all unwarranted.

Despite their objectively similar historical situations and, perhaps, a certain psychological affinity, the two elites were fairly slow to discover mutual interests.[5] Before 1915 there was little to distinguish Jewish "friends of the Negro" from their WASP counterparts. A quickening of Jewish interest had occurred in the wake of the Springfield, Illinois, riot of August 1908. Appalled by racial violence against Afro-Americans in the urban North, the well-born socialist William English Walling and his Russian-Jewish wife, Anna Strunsky, assisted by pedigreed New England socialists and neoabolitionists (namely, Oswald Garrison Villard, Moorfield Storey, Mary White Ovington, and

Charles Edward Russell), founded the NAACP. Most of the first whites prominent in the NAACP were gentiles, but at its organizing conference in 1910, the so-called Russian Revolution (condemning Czarist expulsion of Kievan Jews) reflected the planning-committee labors of Rabbi Stephen S. Wise, Columbia University economics professor Edwin R. A. Seligman, and social worker Henry Moskowitz. In 1911 a similar rescue operation for the Afro-American—this one also comprised mainly of white Protestants (slightly more moderate than those of the NAACP), led to the incorporation of the National Urban League (NUL). Again, Seligman's chairmanship and the presence on the board of Felix Adler, founder of the Ethical Culture Society, Lillian Wald, Fabian Socialist founder of the Henry Street Settlement on the Lower East Side of New York City, Abraham Lefkowitz, educator, and, shortly thereafter, Julius Rosenwald of Sears, Roebuck forecast significant Jewish contributions to the NUL. During the first years of both civil rights organizations, however, not only did WASP influence prevail, but also there was no discernible Jewish inclination to play a larger role.[6]

The early motives of Jewish philanthropists and social workers were varied. There were Talmudic prescriptions of charity, reinforced, for many, by the status-enhancing affiliations with Carnegie and Rockefeller interests that philanthropy among Afro-Americans afforded. There was abstract affinity for another race torn from its home-land and long persecuted. "I belong to an ancient race which has had even longer experience of oppression than you have," the outstanding jurist Louis Marshall told the 1926 annual convention of the NAACP. "We were subjected to indignities in comparison with which to sit in a 'Jim Crow' car is to occupy a palace." There were individual personality factors ranging, undoubtedly, from the noble to the clinical. Affecting all of these motives, of course, was the steady erosion of the professional and social gains of the small Sephardic and the larger Ashkenazic American Jewish communities as anti-Semitism spread throughout much of the nation. In 1898 the financial leader Schiff made his famous public protest against stated policies and the "tacit understanding" barring Jews from "trustee rooms of Columbia College, of the public museums, the public library, and many similar institutions." "The wealthy Jewish businessman and the successful members of established professions were brought face to face with a high social barrier," the standard history of Jewish leadership records. Eight years later Schiff, Julius Rosenwald, Louis Marshall, and Oscar Straus, the department-store owner, helped to establish the American Jewish Committee (AJC) and, in 1908, the New York Kehillah to mobilize influential Jews in quiet work within and outside their communities in order to counteract anti-Semitism.[7]

What the familiar details of the beginnings of American anti-Semitism do not adequately explain is why Jewish involvement with Afro-Americans greatly intensified after 1915, taking on the urgency of a special mission; why Jews of influence and wealth rapidly moved from a racial altruism barely distinguishable from that of neoabolitionist and parlor socialist WASPs to virtual management of Afro-American civil rights organizations. The predisposing factors of a vaguely kindred past and a similarly persecuted present lack the force of inevitability. They suggest, in fact, a more compelling rationale for avoidance by Jews of a special relationship with Afro-Americans. Old-stock American Jews might well have concluded that bad matters could only worsen if they were perceived as special friends of the nation's most visible pariah population. The available literature is silent about pre-1915 debate on this issue, but it is a safe presumption that the pro's and con's were explored. Nor does it seem wildly speculative to suppose that a majority of Jewish leaders, given their conservatism and caginess, would have favored continuing the policy of aloof philanthropy complementing that of liberal WASP donors to Afro-American causes.

What debate there was, was abruptly resolved by the August 17, 1915, lynching of Leo Frank in Marietta, Georgia. Frank, a Cornell University graduate whose grandfather had been a decorated Confederate officer, was a leading Atlanta businessman, his match factory a cynosure of Henry W. Grady's New South philosophy. Accused of the murder-rape of a white female employee, he was the first white in the postbellum South to be convicted of a capital offense on the testimony of an Afro-American. The incendiary speeches of Tom Watson, the nearly demented Georgia Populist leader, and the barbarism of the Marietta mob made it clear that the victim's punishment had been determined by race and class rather than by regard for evidence. The Frank case also briefly threatened Afro-American-Jewish goodwill when the Jewish-owned *New York Times* demanded that Georgia authorities try the Afro-American janitor, sole witness to the crime, as the guilty party. The case, one historian has observed, "escalated Jewish involvement in civil rights."[8]

What made the Frank case so alarming to the Jewish leaders was that even in the South, where Jews were numerically insignificant, an established Jewish merchant could be more vulnerable than a black janitor. Rather than mount a sustained, frontal attack on racial and religious injustices, which they believed would only aggravate matters, German-Jewish leaders in the United States preferred to concentrate on the victims of intolerance. Nurtured in the flexibility of Reform Judaism, possessing wealth and, many of them, great culture, the descendants of Bavarian, Baden, and Württemburg Jews had placed their bets on assimilation. The long German migration, beginning about 1830, was over by 1880, and families such as the Schiffs, Rosenwalds, Adlers, Flexners, Lehmans, Gruenings, and Spingarns had become decade by decade less distinguishable from other white Americans. "Their main concern," Yonathan Shapiro states, "was to facilitate the assimilation of their brethren. They were, to use a distinction made by Gunnar Myrdal in connection with the Negro community, leaders of accommodation rather than of protest." Israel Zangwill's *The Melting Pot* informed their credo, but the newer migrants were not "melting." The wealthy Uptown Jews of New York City were "ashamed of the appearance, the language, and the manners of the Russian Jews," Lucy Dawidowicz reports, "aghast at their political ideologies, and terrified lest the world crumble by the mad act of a Jewish radical." Too many—1.5 million between 1900 and 1914—and too different, the new immigrants were playing havoc with the assimilationist vision and timetable.[9]

Afro-American leadership in the North found itself in a similar predicament in 1915, with D. W. Griffith's *The Birth of a Nation*. The enormous passion and effort expended by the NAACP to suppress the film was the first attempt by the rising new Afro-American leadership to mobilize interracial support from coast to coast for a specific issue.[10]

During the ascendancy of Booker T. Washington, militant Afro-American spokes-persons in the North had commanded little of the loyalty of the masses of their own people nor the attention of most of white philanthropy—to say nothing of the heed of politicians. The death of the Great Accommodator in November 1915 opened a crisis in race leadership. It had already become apparent that the Bookerite philosophy of Afro-American development through subordinate agriculture and trades was far more suited to the rural South. By 1917 perhaps as many as 250,000 southern Afro-Americans were resettling in the urban North and East, and Bookerites had a few answers to the socioeconomic crises raised by the Great Migration. Consequently, many of the great industrial philanthropists turned from Tuskegee Institute and Hampton Institute political cadres to the urban, mostly northern men and women who had never forsworn faith in full civil and social equality and for whom the NAACP's Du Bois, Boston's William Monroe Trotter, Washington's Francis J. Grimké and Kelly Miller, and Chicago's Ida B. Wells-Barnett were heroes.[11] Those were the racially radical men and women with whom the socially conservative Jewish elite would form an alliance.

Many of those Talented Tenth Afro-Americans were stamped in what E. Franklin Frazier describes as the "genteel tradition of the small group of mulattoes who assimi-lated the morals and manners of the slaveholding aristocracy." But the nucleus was free black, descended from tiny colonial populations concentrated in Boston, Brooklyn, Philadelphia, and Providence, Rhode Island, gradually augmented by Underground Railroad fugitives and, after the Civil War, by southerners with some or all of the endowments of pedigree, professional distinction, good morals, and acceptable racial admixture (that is, derived from antebellum liaisons). A few names—Forten, Herndon, Purvis, Syphax, Trotter, Whipper, Downey—represented moderate fortunes from real estate, insurance, publishing, medicine, hosteling, and construction, but most had depended for generations on solid, middle-class incomes from service occupations historically monopolized by free blacks: barbering, catering, draying, carpentry, tailor-ing, and preaching.[12] The Talented Tenth typology was exemplified in the NUL leader-ship of the early 1920s: executive co-secretaries Eugene Kinckle Jones and George Ed-mund Haynes; *Opportunity* editor Charles S. Johnson; Chicago Urban League director T. Arnold Hill—all of whom were sons of professional fathers, second-generation col-lege products (graduates—with the exception of Fisk University man Haynes—of Vir-ginia Union University), polished by advanced studies at prestigious northern univer-sities, at ease in the world of white power, and usually registered Republicans. The NAACP Afro-Americans were superlative: Du Bois (intellectual and formulator of the Talented Tenth concept); James Weldon Johnson (ultracosmopolite); White ("volun-tary Negro"); and Jessie R. Fauset (one of the first female graduates of Cornell Univer-sity and of the University of Pennsylvania). Notwithstanding debates over tactics, those NUL and NAACP leaders fully shared the same cultural values.[13]

Just as established Jewish leaders were separated from the post-1880s migrants by geographic provenance, religion, culture, and wealth, so, too, were the northern Afro-American leaders of a radically different mold from the folk of the Great Migration. The members of the Talented Tenth also believed themselves (despite episodic race riots) well along toward full citizenship through circumspect politics and ostentatious patriotism, by good manners, education, and industry, and by quiet cultivation of influential WASPs. Public transportation had been accessible to them without discrimination; department stores had politely encouraged their patronage; most public schools had accepted their children; and a handful had even been elected municipal and state officials in Massachusetts and Illinois. But the relatively privileged status of the northern Afro-Americans began to deteriorate during the first years of the twentieth century. The combined migrations from Europe and from the Deep South created economic competition and residential confrontation that had already positioned race relations in the North well before the 1916 commencement of the Great Migration. In the first truly modern novella by an Afro-American, *The Sport of the Gods,* Paul Laurence Dunbar poses the dilemma starkly: " 'Oh, is there no way to keep these people from rushing away from the small villages and country districts of the South up to the cities, where they cannot battle with the terrible force of a strange and unusual environment?' " The leading Afro-American historian, Carter G. Woodson, would later predict that "the maltreatment of the Negroes will be nationalized by this exodus. The poor whites of both sections will strike at this race."[14]

Without exception, studies of northern urban Afro-America report the nostalgia for the supposedly golden days before the Great Migration. "There was no discrimination in Chicago during my early childhood days," a matron told St. Clair Drake and Horace R. Cayton, typically, "but as the Negroes began coming . . . in numbers it seems they brought discrimination with them." An Afro-American student of premigration Philadelphia reported that, with the arrival of a "group of generally uneducated and untrained persons," opportunities that had been enjoyed by cultured Afro-Americans in Philadelphia "were withdrawn." Furthermore, when Philadelphia pastors risked welcoming the migrant, "many of the congregation made him know that he was not wanted. In some cases the church split over the matter, the migrants and their sympathizers withdrawing and forming a church for themselves." A woman long resident in Harlem lamented the physical deterioration wrought by the migration and could but wonder, "Are we responsible for at least some of the race prejudice which has developed since the entry of Negroes in Harlem?" And even the young Frazier characterized the migrants as "ignorant and unsophisticated peasant people without experience [in] urban living."[15]

Like New York City's Uptown Jews who lived in terror of the Hester Street anarchist's mad act, Talented Tenth leaders complained, "We all suffer for what one fool will do." Churches and benevolent orders temporarily housed and fed the migrants; the NUL located jobs for them and studied their condition; the NAACP watched over their uncertain civil rights and collected membership dues—all amid a chorus of grief about "ignorant and rough-mannered" newcomers, "inefficient, groping seekers for something better." Like Schiff and his associates who had backed the 1906 Galveston plan for dispersal and resettlement in the Southwest of the East European Jews, Jones entreated "right-thinking Negroes . . . to discourage the wholesale migration of shiftless people." By early 1919 the Chicago Urban League was deeply divided over a recommendation by some of its members that the organization take an official stand against further migration from the South. Opposition to such a policy on the part of the organization's industrialist contributors (many of whom used the migrants as strikebreakers) led to a temporary adjournment of the debate. The race riots in late summer of that year caused the Chicago Urban League and the NUL officially to endorse continued migration; the NUL would have lost credibility with rank-and-file Afro-Americans had it not done so, although its business supporters were now increasingly wary of the dangers of all imported labor.[16]

Just as Schiff had pleaded with Lower East Side leaders to urge immigrant parents not to speak Yiddish to their children, NUL workers delivered lectures on proper English, boisterousness, proper dress, and soap and toothbrushes. NUL officials spoke of "civilizing" and "Americanizing" the migrant with the same patronizing authority as Irving Howe cites from the *Jewish Messenger:* "[Jewish migrants] must be Americanized in spite of themselves, in the mode prescribed by their friends and benefactors." The *Chicago Defender* editorialized about "habits of life little better than [those of] hottentots," and Thomas Lee Philpott's study of Chicago neighborhoods details heroic efforts to maintain standards and to transform migrants: "As migrants fresh from the cottonfields down South crowded into their neighborhoods, [old settlers] imposed their standards on the newcomers"—for a time. Leaders such as James Weldon Johnson and Haynes believed that southern migrants, because of their greater familiarity with the language and culture, would move into mainstream America more quickly than their European counterparts. With a little help and proper guidance, Haynes explained, the peasant would readily "embrace American advantages." He conceded that the migrant was "lacking in the regularity demanded by the routine of industry day by day" but counted on character improvements to come from membership in the "Dress Well Club" and from "lectures on food and dress . . . supplied by the churches." Like most NUL officials, Haynes was committed to what James Weldon Johnson's biographer calls the social-psychological, rather than the political or economic, solution to racial discrimination—a mental-states formula. In his classic study of Detroit, Haynes remonstrated that "every individual Negro needs to have it brought home to him by constant reminder that all the Negro workmen are on trial in the face of unusual industrial opportunities and that individually they must make good for the sake of all their fellow workmen." Membership in a labor union was not recommended. "Get a job," the brochure issued by the St. Louis Urban League enjoined, "get there on time, be regular, master it, dignify it, do better than the other man; this breaks down prejudice."[17]

By the early 1920s assimilationist Jews and Afro-Americans needed each other more than ever. The Palmer raids and the Red Scare of 1919 were source and symptom of exacerbated anti-Semitism, while the riots and lynchings of the Red Summer of 1919 announced the halt and, in many cases, reversal of wartime socioeconomic gains by Afro-Americans. The Anglo-Saxon leagues, various eugenics groups, and the reconstituted Ku Klux Klan gave priority to the so-called Jewish threat, as did Henry Ford's wacky *Dearborn Independent.* Harvard University and Columbia imposed admissions quotas on Jews and residential segregation on Afro-Americans. Restrictive immigration bills (opposed by Jewish organizations but, secretly, not utterly repugnant to some), which over the years had failed to become law by narrowing congressional margins, were now enacted. It was to be expected that the foreign-born, many of them Jews, would play prominent roles in the deep and widespread labor unrest of the postwar years. The Uptown Jews also knew that the spread of "radical" ideas among black workers would be blamed on their people. In reality Marxism's appeal for Afro-Americans was negligible, but the *Dearborn Independent,* intentionally mistaking the racial egalitarian radicalism of the Talented Tenth for Marxism, was a reminder of Jewish vulnerability to farfetched charges. "Let the man of color distrust those false friends who mingle with him to get his money, who seek an alliance with him on the alleged common ground of 'oppression,'" Henry Ford's paper warned in late 1923, "and who expose their whole hand when they urge him to that kind of Bolshevism found only in Moscow and on the East Side of New York." The prognosis for the virus of American anti-Semitism in the early 1920s was far from encouraging.[18]

Meanwhile, no matter to what lengths the "better classes" of northern Afro-Americans went to prove to whites that they were "capable of living in 'respectable' communities without depreciating property," the reality was one of slums and high rents. Residential covenants fell with about equal severity on both races, a factor of considerable weight in rallying Jews to support the NAACP's successful 1917 effort before the United States Supreme Court in *Buchanan v. Warley* to outlaw municipally enforced residential apartheid.[19] By 1920 the NAACP relied heavily on its Jewish connection, both for fund raising and for administration. The brothers Joel E. Spingarn and Arthur B. Spingarn served as board chairman and *pro bono* legal counsel, respectively. Herbert Lehman served on the executive committee. Arthur Sachs succeeded Wald on the board. Herbert J. Seligmann directed public relations; assertive Martha Gruening was his assistant. A Du Bois interview of the period in the *Jewish Daily Forward* is fittingly captioned, "The Negro Race Looks to Jews for Sympathy and Understanding." It is hardly surprising, then, that a newly arrived, bewildered Marcus Garvey had stormed out of the NAACP's headquarters in 1917 "dumbfounded" by the apparent domination there of whites.[20]

As the melting pot turned into a skillet for the two races, controversial new theories and ideologies of Jewish and Afro-American cultures arose to challenge the social meliorism of upper-class leaders. The Jewish pluralists Isaac B. Berkson, Julius Drachsler, and Judah L. Magnes had called at the turn of the century for educational and social programs that would maintain and enrich the traditions of Jewish life. The philosopher Horace M. Kallen rejected assimilationism and proposed instead that Jews retain their "racial" uniqueness, the better to enrich American society. By the early 1910s, in addition to Kallen, intellectuals such as Du Bois (Pan-Africanism), Randolph Bourne (transnationalism), the brothers Norman Hapgood and Hutchins Hapgood (variety), and Robert E. Park (racial temperaments) were modifying or abjuring the once sacrosanct paradigm of "Anglo-conformity"—the Wilsonian dogma that a "hyphenated" American was an impossibility. That the United States ought to reflect and to preserve the variegated traditions of its peoples was a novel enough intellectual proposition in the early twentieth century, far from broadly subscribed to and seemingly of little political moment. Yet even as an intellectual proposition, cultural pluralism was a source of malaise among elite Jews because of its potential to raise the dual loyalty charge. "To be good Americans," Brandeis declared in 1915, "we must be better Jews, and to be better Jews we must become Zionists."[21] The Kallen and Brandeis heterodoxies distressed old-stock Jews somewhat more than similar ideas worried the Talented Tenth, but neither leadership group was equipped to deal with the new, dynamic, mass-based ideologies of white and black Zionism.

The great majority of the Jews closely associated with the NAACP and the NUL—Louis Marshall, Jacob Billikopf, a lawyer and Louis Marshall's son-in-law, Boas, Melville J. Herskovits, and the Altmans, Lehmans, Rosenwalds, and Spingarns—opposed Zionism, in both its secular and its cultural manifestations, and had fully endorsed the opposition of the *New York Times* to the Balfour Declaration. Although Magnes, leader of the New York Kehillah and Louis Marshall's brother-in-law, Julian W. Mack, prominent Chicago jurist and Rosenwald intimate, and Felix Frankfurter, Brandeis's protégé, were significant Zionist exceptions among the civil rights forces, theirs was a very German-Jewish Zionism—politically cautious and emotionally cool. Brandeisian Zionism was characterized by the slogan "Silence in America; service in Palestine." For the great majority, nonetheless, there could be no such thing as circumspect Zionism. During the fierce internal debate in early 1916 over the wisdom of founding the American Jewish Congress, Schiff complained to a friend about the noisy militancy of East European backers of the congress: "Thanks to the preaching and machinations of Jewish nationalists we are gradually being forced into a class by ourselves and if this continues, it will not be many years before we shall be looked upon by our fellow citizens as an entirely separate class, whose interests are different than those of the grass [roots] of American people."[22] Zionism was not the solution to a problem, the German Jews asserted, but a deadly manifestation of the problem itself—a failure to assimilate. According to them, the correct approach—more urgent than ever, they felt—was to defuse American racism and extreme nativism by reassuring the gentile majority that it was mistaken in believing that Jews in America were different.

Such an approach would be most effective, the Jewish elite believed, if it were pursued with minimum visibility and vulnerability. When Julius Rosenwald told a friend that he was not "in the least anxious to see many Jews in politics or even on the bench," he spoke for most of his class, for whom high public profile as *Jews* was anathema. Support of and participation in the Afro-American civil rights movement was seen, after 1915, as a stratagem exactly meeting Jewish needs. Where barely ten years earlier they had supported those Afro-American forces—the Bookerites—equally averse to agitation and publicity in race relations, upper-class Jews in the aftermath of the Frank case increasingly encouraged the new Afro-American leadership—the Talented Tenth—which employed agitation and publicity as principal weapons to force the glacial pace of civil rights. By establishing a presence at the center of the civil rights movement with intelligence, money, and influence, elite Jews and their delegates could fight against anti-Semitism by remote control. "By helping the colored people in this country," the *American Hebrew* editorialized, "Mr. Rosenwald doubtless also serves Judaism." The Jewish civil rights role also relieved du Ponts, Fords, Mellons, Rockefellers, and other gentile capitalists of the burden of more than infrequent, ceremonial contact with Afro-American leaders and organizations, which in turn somewhat vaguely obligated those capitalists to closer ties with Jewish financiers and philanthropists. "I have never appealed to them for aid for the Negro . . . and been rebuffed," Villard averred, speaking for his gentile associates.[23]

Julius Rosenwald became a trustee of the Rockfeller Foundation in 1922, after disbursing more than $4,000,000 more or less out of pocket to build schools for southern blacks. Six years later the reorganized Rosenwald Fund, patterned on the Rockefeller Foundation, was launched to upgrade higher education in the South, particularly for Afro-Americans. Between 1928 and 1948 the Rosenwald Fund allocated monies toward endowment and construction to the major private Afro-American institutions of higher learning: $1,037,000 to Dillard University; $668,175 to Fisk; $542,258 to the Atlanta University Center, most of these granted in the early years of the Rosenwald Fund's existence. Fellowships to artists, educators, and scholars advanced the careers of Afro-America's most gifted or enterprising: future college presidents such as Charles S. Johnson of Fisk, Mordecai Johnson of Howard University, Horace Mann Bond of Lincoln University, Dwight O. W. Holmes of Morgan State College; humanists and social scientists such as Adelaide Cromwell Hill, Frazier, Kenneth Clark, Allison Davis, Drake, Ira De A. Reid, Abram L. Harris, and Lorenzo Turner; and artists and writers such as James Weldon Johnson (the first grantee), Sterling Brown, Langston Hughes, Claude McKay, and Arna Bontemps, Richmond Barthé, Selma Burke, Augusta Savage, Hale Woodruff, and Jacob Lawrence.[24]

Significantly, Jewish educational philanthropy accelerated shortly after Fisk, Howard, Hampton, and several other Afro-American institutions of higher learning had sustained vigorous protests in the mid-1920s against policies and curricula that a new generation of students considered racially demeaning. A crucial, if not always apparent, difference between Jewish and WASP benefaction to Afro-American higher education was the insistence of the former (notwithstanding the insuperable fact of segregation) on education of competitive quality. The erstwhile similar commitment of WASP philanthropy had become increasingly compromised after the turn of the century because of southern white pressures to supplant liberal arts and white-collar professional training with vocational instruction, reinforced by an ethic of subservient separateness.

Ever mindful of what they believed were the perils of marked cultural distinctions and anchored in a tradition in which learning was revered, the Jewish elite wished to see Afro-American college graduates able to make their way in the larger society, even able to compel that society gradually to recognize their varied competences. Billikopf, chairman of the trustee executive committee of Howard, and Abraham Flexner, president of the board of trustees of Howard, pushed for excellence unrelated to race. "There is no such thing as a university especially created for any race or denomination," Flexner told his fellow trustees in 1933. "The university is devoted to teaching competent young men and women."[25] Constructive charity, profound influence, and contribution to the formation of a kindred elite flowed quietly from the policies of Jewish leadership. An additional benefit deriving from Afro-American philanthropy, or so Alfred Stern, Julius Rosenwald's son-in-law, hoped, was the undermining of the stereotype of Jews as predatory merchants and exploiters of real estate. Rosenwald millions went to build the model Michigan Boulevard Garden Apartments ("The Rosenwald") and a medical facility in Chicago and would have underwritten a medical center in New York had not middle-class opposition in Harlem to a segregated facility defeated the proposal.[26]

For the Talented Tenth, heightened Jewish collaboration was extremely beneficial, for it, too, was caught unprepared by what the novelist and poet Claude McKay called the "African Zionism" of Garvey's Universal Negro Improvement Association (UNIA). The Garvey movement's leadership was largely West Indian, as was the majority of its true believers, but its growing appeal among Afro-Americans extended from coast to coast and deep into the South.[27] Charisma and pageantry, exotic titles and emoluments, phalanxes of uniformed cadres, the daunting cry of "Africa for the Africans!" and a strident doctrine of unique, racially purified destiny in renascent Mother Africa exploded upon the American scene after 1917. With its stress on separate development, entrepreneurship, and self-help, UNIA ideology appealed to thousands who felt the void created by Booker T. Washington's death; and Garvey, of course, professed to be a modernizing, internationalizing disciple of Washington. Although there were several significant defections to Garveyism, the overwhelming majority of Talented Tenth leadership was stunned, defensive, and resentful. Even Du Bois, who could claim to be the originator of Pan-Africanism in the United States, recoiled from Garveyism after a brief period of probing uncertainty. "Why then does he sneer at the work of the powerful group of his race in the United States where he finds asylum and sympathy?" the *Crisis* editor wondered. Du Boisian Pan-Africanism was strikingly similar to the intellectual Zionism of Brandeis, and Brandeisian Zionism was already in temporary retreat before the onslaught of militant cultural and political Jewish nationalists. Du Bois foresaw the same threat unleashed by the forces of Garveyism.[28]

From the perspective of the Talented Tenth, then, the more Garvey succeeded, the greater the dangers of racial polarization and, finally, of repression. "American Negro leaders are not jealous of Garvey," the *Crisis* protested (not entirely truthfully), "they are not envious of his success; they are simply afraid of his failure, for his failure would be theirs." But, despite Du Bois's disclaimer, the Talented Tenth was envious and afraid of having to share, and perhaps even to yield, its pretensions to leadership of the Afro-American masses. Garvey was only partly blustering when he charged that "the Negro who has had the benefit of an education of forty, thirty and twenty years ago, is the greatest fraud and stumbling block to the real progress of the race." Nor was he guilty, as some pretended to believe, of applying an inappropriate West Indian color-status theorem to Afro-American leadership in the United States. If it was vicious to call attention publicly to the light complexions of the Talented Tenth (the perennial Afro-American taboo), it was also extremely effective against Du Bois, Jesse Moorland of the Young Men's Christian Association, White, and their kind. The charge drew from Du Bois the immediate warning: "American Negroes recognize no color line in or out of the race, and they will in the end punish the man who attempts to establish it." Just as Uptown Jews tried to outflank the Zionists by combining with Lower East Side socialists, uppercrust Afro-Americans readily joined with the Harlem socialists led by the African Blood Brotherhood's Cyril Briggs to defeat the Garveyites.[29] With Garvey's imprisonment for mail fraud in 1925, black Zionism rapidly lost momentum.

The deflation of Garveyism presented the Talented Tenth leaders with an acute credibility crisis, however, for now they had to prove that Garvey's extreme pessimism about the future of the race in the United States was unjustified and that, by helping to scuttle the fervent mass movement, they had not consigned eleven million Afro-Americans to perpetual economic and social misery. But the evidence and trends supported the Garveyite predictions. Louise Venable Kennedy found that the proportion of northern Afro-Americans in manufacturing had steadily declined during the 1920s, and that "numbers of them have gone back into . . . domestic and personal service, while many of the Negro women who had given up outside employment have been forced to return to work." Talented Tenth anxieties about that dilemma permeated the writings of Alain L. Locke. Cannily observing the analogous embarrassment of older Jewish leadership, Afro-America's first Rhodes Scholar knew what a close call Garveyism had represented: "We have for the present, in spite of Mr. Garvey's hectic efforts, no Zionistic hope or intention." But what *Opportunity* called the "dark, dumb masses" were urgently in need of a new opiate, for, as Locke well understood, Garveyism had shown how much "more ready and ripe for action than the minds of the leaders and the educated few" the masses were.[30]

In his introductory essays in the special 1925 issue of *Survey,* devoted to the "New Negro," Locke spelled out the problem and the solution. "The migrant masses" were stirring, he wrote. "The only safeguard for mass relations in the future must be provided in the carefully maintained contacts of the enlightened minorities of both race groups." But time was running out, Locke warned. "There is an increasing group who affiliate with radical and liberal movements. . . . Harlem's quixotic radicalisms call for their ounce of democracy today lest tomorrow they be beyond cure." Hence, the race's leaders must be clearly seen to have influence among the movers and shakers in the white world, a role-legitimating requirement that, despite Garvey's example, Myrdal found to be a fundamental race feature. Interracial undertakings as dazzlingly mounted and as publicized as those of the UNIA were called for; promotion and celebration of symbolic racial breakthroughs were indispensable. Given the near total political and economic postwar impasse, however, Talented Tenth options were limited. Two strategies were adopted: The first and most obvious was that of redoubled advocacy of elemental civil rights before the courts and in Congress. The second, a surprisingly novel strategy, was that of harnessing art and literature for civil rights.[31]

Court victories afforded Talented Tenth leadership maximal publicity with minimal potential to overturn the real world of race relations (which would have frightened away numbers of white philanthropists). Given the shabby record of evasion and nonenforcement of court decisions on the state and local levels, civil rights advocates could claim important victories, and civil rights opponents could ignore them. A personnel problem had to be solved before going to court, however: There were no more than eleven hundred Afro-American lawyers in the entire country in 1920, few of them really well trained. The vacuum was filled by Arthur B. Spingarn and his partner, Charles Studin; Louis Marshall and his son, James Marshall; Nathan Margold, the first salaried NAACP counsel; and Frankfurter as a valuable advisor. Protestants Moorfield Storey and Clarence Darrow handled a limited number of appellate cases. Jewish support, legal and financial, afforded a string of significant court challenges and several victories.

Storey, a former American Bar Association president, presented the winning 1923 Supreme Court argument, in *Moore v. Dempsey,* that "mob spirit" had denied militant Arkansas sharecroppers a fair trial, a decision that drew Louis Marshall into NAACP work, as Louis Marshall had unsuccessfully used the same argument before the Supreme Court in the Frank appeal.[32]

James Weldon Johnson, himself a lawyer, exploited every opportunity to draw parallels between Jewish and Afro-American disabilities and to urge Louis Marshall in the unsuccessful 1926 restrictive covenant case, *Corrigan v. Buckley,* "that you might be willing to make a statement on the case calling its importance to the attention of Jewish people." Jewish assistance was also valuable in the NAACP's lobbying for the unsuccessful Dyer and Costigan-Wagner federal antilynching bills. Important Jewish support also went to A. Philip Randolph's Brotherhood of Sleeping Car Porters battle with the Pullman Company for union recognition and with the American Federation of Labor for full admission. There is less exaggeration than truth in an American Jewish Congress lawyer's assertion that legal briefs, local ordinances, and federal laws beneficial to Afro-Americans "were actually written in the offices of Jewish agencies, by Jewish staff people, introduced by Jewish legislators and pressured into being by Jewish voters."[33]

By the end of the 1920s, the Talented Tenth spoke warmly of the "special relationship" with Jews. James Weldon Johnson and White routinely scrutinized obituary columns for Jewish legacies that the NAACP might tap and listed prospective contributors, a disproportionate number of whom were Jews. "The clue to Pierre duPont [is] that his wife is a Jewess," White wrote crudely, and mistakenly, of that potential donor (du Pont's mother was Jewish). Faith in Jewish largesse was generally rewarded. During the depression William Rosenwald made a three-year grant to the NAACP, on condition of being matched by three others. Lehman, Mary Fels, and Felix Warburg—and, also, Edsel Ford—matched the grant. The second largest NUL funding source from 1924 to 1931 was the Altman Foundation. That Jews were extremely careful not to abuse the influence flowing from their contributions is evident from the one notable instance in which circumspection was abandoned. James Weldon Johnson's correspondence confirms the contemporary impression that Stern was arrogant and impolitic. After Julius Rosenwald's death in 1932, Stern interfered directly in NUL administrative matters in Chicago, expressed his dislike of Jones, the national secretary, and even notified the NUL and the NAACP that Rosenwald funds would be drastically reduced unless both organizations agreed to his plans for a merger, a scheme civil rights officials managed to bury, though not without reduction in Rosenwald revenues.[34]

The Talented Tenth's primary answer to black Zionism was the literary and artistic industry that manufactured the so-called Harlem Renaissance. The half-dozen or so Afro-American orchestrators of the Harlem Renaissance—Charles S. Johnson, James Weldon Johnson, White, Fauset, Locke, West Indian bibliophile Arthur A. Schomburg, and West Indian numbers king Casper Holstein—conceived of it as serious racial politics—art for politics' sake, or civil rights by copyright. Students of American culture have seen the Harlem Renaissance as another predictable, creative bubble in the melting pot, a savory ingredient in a New England, Knickerbocker, Hoosier, and Yiddish concoction. "The Negro writers were caught up [in] the spirit of the artistic yearnings of the time," S. P. Fullinwider argues.[35] That was true of the writers Langston Hughes and Jean Toomer, but it was not typical of most of the other artists and writers. Nothing could have seemed to most educated Afro-Americans more impractical as a means of improving racial standing in the 1920s than writing poetry and novels or painting. Art and literature were artificially created through glamorous ceremony (NAACP- and NUL-sponsored banquets and galas), prizes and fellowships (Guggenheim and Rosenwald grants, Spingarn medals, *Opportunity* literary prizes funded by Holstein), traveling art shows and well-advertised fiction and poetry (published by the Harmon Foundation, Boni and Liveright, Alfred A. Knopf), and national recruitment of talent by Fauset and Charles S. Johnson.[36]

Charles S. Johnson's staff at *Opportunity* culled the Afro-American press, kept files on promising artists and poets in remote towns, and arranged for temporary billeting and employment for them once they had accepted Charles S. Johnson's risky invitation to relocate in Harlem from, say, Topeka, Kansas. Fauset discovered Toomer and Hughes for the *Crisis*. White boasted that he had persuaded Paul Robeson to foresake law for the concert stage, as he also had encouraged the singing career of Julius Bledsoe, a Columbia medical student, and the writing career of Rudolf Fisher, a Harlem physician. Upwardly mobile Afro-Americans were at least a generation away from the special cultural alienation—the insider-as-outsider syndrome—of which the contemporary "Lost Generation" was the well-publicized example. But with the decisive infusion of white philanthropy (much of it Jewish), the entrepreneurs of the Harlem Renaissance were able to mount a generation-skipping movement, diverting to its ranks men and women who, in the natural course of events, would have devoted their exclusive energies to teaching, lawyering, doctoring, fixing teeth, and burying. The degree to which the use of arts and letters for broad political purposes was premeditated and programmatic is cogently expressed in White's voluminous correspondence. An indefatigable dispatcher of notes, letters, and telegrams about the arts movement, White's enthusiasm led him to plan for an arts institute to support black drama, dance, and music; and in Europe, a bureau for disseminating scholarly and literary attacks on racism in America.[37]

By the early 1930s the influence of White in Algonquin Hotel circles, of Locke at the Harmon Foundation, of James Weldon Johnson as trustee of the Garland and the Rosenwald funds, and of Charles S. Johnson as all-purpose advisor to foundations had made the Harlem Renaissance a well-oiled machine turning out a total of twenty-six novels, ten volumes of poetry, five Broadway plays, innumerable essays and short stories, two or three performed ballets and concerti, and a large amount of painting and sculpture. "We must admit our debt to these foster agencies," Locke wrote in acknowledgment of the *Crisis, Opportunity,* and the *Messenger.* "The three journals which have been vehicles of most of our artistic expression have been the avowed organs of social movements and organized social programs." The southern white literary critic Robert T. Kerlin evaluated the social impact of the arts and letters program more bluntly: "Here, unsegregated, the Negro poet appears on his merit by the side of the white poet, competitor with him for the same honors. The fact is immensely significant. It is hostile to lynching, and to jimcrowing." James Weldon Johnson enthusiastically concurred, writing in 1928 that it was not "too much to say that through artistic achievement the Negro has found a means of getting at the very core of the prejudice against him, by challenging the Nordic superiority complex."[38]

Not everyone agreed. Although his own magazine had helped promote the movement, Du Bois came to disapprove of a racial program offering poetry in the place of politics and Broadway musicals in the place of jobs. In time, a few of the more gifted lights of the Harlem Renaissance came to resist the mixture of art and propaganda and applauded Wallace Thurman's Pollyannaish burlesque of Locke in *Infants of the Spring:* " 'Because of your concerted storming up Parnassus, new vistas will be spread open to the entire race. The Negro in the South will no more know peonage, Jim Crowism, or the loss of the ballot, and the Negro everywhere in America will know complete freedom and equality.' " Reviewing the civil rights policies of those times for his work on the Carnegie-Myrdal project, Ralph J. Bunche concluded that "the truth of the matter is that in the thinking of the Negro elite there is a tremendous gap between it and the black mass."[39]

Although it does not appear that the Jewish leaders were the first to encourage the civil-rights-through-art program, they were not unsympathetic to it, as the special influence of Joel E. Spingarn at Harcourt, Brace and the special relationship with Alfred A. Knopf's indicate. Moreover, Jewish success in Tin Pan Alley and in Hollywood, in publishing and on Broadway was exemplary proof of the power of art and entertainment to alter ethnic images. The fact that so many successful Jewish talents used modified Afro-American materials—Al Jolsen, George Gershwin, Jimmy Durante, Benny Goodman, Artie Shaw, Sophie Tucker—was not lost on Harlem Renaissance enthusiasts.[40] But Afro-American leadership was far more influenced by analogies of history and intellect and prone to describe itself, in the manner of Jews, as an ancient, special people, achieving superiority through suffering. "The Jew has been made international by persecution and forced dispersion," Locke declared, "and so, potentially, have we." When Kelly Miller, the highly respected dean of Howard, appealed to Afro-America's most distinguished and powerful figures to meet in Chicago in early 1924 to plan for the race's future, he called his well-publicized but unsuccessful convocation the "Negro Sanhedrin." Fauset's novels depict her class as superior to privileged whites by virtue of culture and attainments that have been infinitely harder to acquire because of racism. James Weldon Johnson called on his race to emulate the Jews in measuring up "brain for brain" with mainstream Americans. When wealthy or influential Jewish leaders such as Louis Marshall or Julius Rosenwald told Afro-American audiences that, by comparison with the historic suffering of Jews, the black diaspora had been less destructive, the Talented Tenth was greatly encouraged by the prospect of analogous overcoming of prejudice and attainment of affluence and influence.[41]

Unlike their Jewish models, however, the Afro-American leaders tended to minimize or to ignore the grimy aspects of migrant Jewish business success as a basic condition for the perpetuation of collective achievement. Hence, the Harlem Renaissance literally took place in rented space—in a Harlem they did not own. Racial aristocrats steeped in liberal arts educations, they missed the significance of the butcher and tailor shops, the sweatshop, the pawn shops, and the liquor stores—and, despite some mid-1930s rhetoric, the paramount importance of organized labor. On the latter institution, Miller's pronouncement continued to elicit approval: "Logic aligns the Negro with labor, but good sense arrays him with capital." The leaders overstressed the psychosocial and juridical at the expense of economic and political approaches. In 1928 Charles S. Johnson was elated to record that "the University of North Carolina has entertained at least three Negro lecturers. The conference at Vassar, and the admission this year of a Negro girl at Bryn Mawr, are flashes of the new spirit of youth in race relations."[42]

It is not surprising, then, that on those few occasions in the early 1930s when the Talented Tenth mobilized the masses to protest economic discrimination, its specific demands were usually for middle-class advancement. "Perhaps there is nothing more significant in the social history of the United States," McKay wrote, "than the spectacle of the common black folk in overalls and sweaters agitating and parading for jobs for apathetic white-collar Negroes." Not until the controversial 1933 Amenia Conference (virtually forced on them by Du Bois and such Young Turks as Bunche, the poet Sterling Brown, and the economist Abram L. Harris) did Talented Tenth leaders begin to appreciate some of the limitations of litigation and literature and the potential of alliances with the liberal wing of the Democratic party and of the more racially progressive labor unions.[43]

It seems evident that what Jewish and Afro-American elites principally shared was not a similar history but an identical adversary—a species of white gentile. Theirs was a politically determined kinship, a defensive alliance, cemented more from the outside than from within. Believing themselves at the threshold of full acceptance by mainstream America, then knocked off balance by an unwelcome population infusion, becoming frightened and dismayed by the eruption from below of nationalisms, the privileged Ashkenazim reached for the Afro-American leadership and even helped to create it, hoping, as Louis Marshall remarked in 1924, that the success of Afro-American civil rights organizations "may incidentally benefit Jews."[44] Determined to find themselves one day also at the same threshhold of acceptance, embarrassed and alarmed by a similar explosion from below, the Talented Tenth welcomed the Jewish embrace and made Jewish success, as it was understood, a paradigm for its own. At least in the short term, the collaboration was beneficial for the Afro-Americans. Their leadership position was secured and would remain so for another forty years. The Harlem Renaissance bubble would soon go flat, but the basic assimilationist values and goals of the Talented Tenth would be perpetuated in civil rights strategies in which the emphasis remained on court cases, contracts, contacts, and culture. For the Jews, the collaboration was extremely beneficial. By assisting in the crusade to prove that Afro-Americans could be decent, conformist, cultured human beings, the civil rights Jews were, in a sense, spared some of the necessity of directly rebutting anti-Semitic stereotypes; for if blacks could make good citizens, clearly, most white Americans believed, all other groups could make better ones.

NOTES

1. Melford E. Spiro, "The Acculturation of American Ethnic Groups," *American Anthropologist*, 57 (Dec. 1955), 1244; John Higham, "American Anti-Semitism Historically Reconsidered," in Charles Her-

bert Stember et al., *Jews in the Mind of America* (New York, 1966), 243–53; Deborah Dash Moore, "Defining American Jewish Ethnicity," *Prospects*, 6 (1981), 387–409; Marshall Sklare, *America's Jews* (New York, 1971), 4–5; W. E. B. Du Bois, "The Conservation of Races," in *The Seventh Son: The Thought and Writings of W. E. B. Du Bois*, ed. Julius Lester (2 vols., New York, 1971), I, 182–83; S. P. Fullinwider, *The Mind and Mood of Black America: 20th Century Thought* (Homewood, Ill., 1969), 55; Milton M. Gordon, *Assimilation in American Life: The Role of Race, Religion, and National Origins* (New York, 1964), esp. 81–101; W. Lloyd Warner, Buford H. Junker, and Walter A. Davis, *Color and Human Nature: Negro Personality Development in a Northern City* (Washington, 1941), esp. 15.

2. Yonathan Shapiro, *Leadership of the American Zionist Organization, 1897–1930* (Urbana, 1971), esp. 12–15; Irving Howe, *World of Our Fathers* (New York, 1976), esp. 229–30; Ronald Steel, *Walter Lippman and the American Century* (Boston, 1980), 6–11; Lucy S. Dawidowicz, *The Jewish Presence: Essays on Identity and History* (New York, 1977), esp. 127; *Harvard Encyclopedia of American Ethnic Groups*, s.v. "Jews"; James Weldon Johnson, *Negro Americans, What Now!* (New York, 1938), esp. 12–15; E. Franklin Frazier, *Black Bourgeoisie* (Glencoe, Ill., 1957), 112–29.

3. Shapiro, *Leadership of the American Zionist Organization*, 61–62; Franz Boas, "The Problem of the American Negro," *Yale Review*, 10 (Jan. 1921), 395; Walter F. White to L. M. Hussey, Jan. 19, 1925, box 92, Walter F. White Collection (Library of Congress); James Weldon Johnson, "Race Prejudice and the Negro Artist," *Harper's*, 157 (Nov. 1928), 775; James Weldon Johnson, "A Negro Looks at Race Prejudice," *American Mercury*, 14 (May 1928), 52; G. Franklin Edwards, *The Negro Professional Class* (Glencoe, Ill., 1959), esp. 17–75.

4. James Weldon Johnson, *Along This Way: The Autobiography of James Weldon Johnson* (New York, 1954), 326–27; Edwin R. Embree and Julia Waxman, *Investment in People: The Story of the Julius Rosenwald Fund* (New York, 1949), 11. On W. E. B. Du Bois's complex racial chauvinisms, see W. E. Burghardt Du Bois, *The Gift of Black Folk: The Negroes in the Making of America* (Boston, 1924), esp. 287–340; W. E. Burghardt Du Bois, *Darkwater: Voices from within the Veil* (New York, 1920), 9; and Fullinwider, *Mind and Mood of Black America*, 47–71.

5. On early contacts between Jewish and Afro-American leaders, see Louis R. Harlan, *Booker T. Washington: The Wizard of Tuskegee, 1901–1915* (New York, 1983), 140–41; August Meier, *Negro Thought in America, 1880–1915: Racial Ideologies in the Age of Booker T. Washington* (Ann Arbor, 1966), 105; Hasia R. Diner, *In the Almost Promised Land: American Jews and Blacks, 1915–1935* (Westport, Conn., 1977), 171; and Lenora E. Berson, *The Negroes and the Jews* (New York, 1971), 70–71.

6. Charles Flint Kellogg, *NAACP: A History of the National Association for the Advancement of Colored People, 1909–1920* (Baltimore, 1967), 9–30; B. Joyce Ross, *J. E. Spingarn and the Rise of the NAACP, 1911–1939* (New York, 1972), esp. 116–17; Guichard Parris and Lester Brooks, *Blacks in the City: A History of the National Urban League* (Boston, 1971), 32–65; Nancy J. Weiss, *The National Urban League, 1910–1940* (New York, 1974), esp. 53–54.

7. Diner, *In the Almost Promised Land*, 151–52; *Harvard Encyclopedia of American Ethnic Groups*, s.v. "Jews"; John Higham, *Strangers in the Land: Patterns of American Nativism, 1860–1925* (New Brunswick, N.J., 1955), 92–94, 160–61; Herbert L. Feingold, *Zion in America: The Jewish Experience from Colonial Times to the Present* (New York, 1974), 142–50; Robert K. Murray, *Red Scare: A Study of National Hysteria, 1919–1920* (New York, 1964); Howard M. Sachar, *The Course of Modern Jewish History* (Cleveland, 1958), 311–13; E. Digby Baltzell, *The Protestant Establishment: Aristocracy and Caste in America* (New York, 1964), esp. 60–120; Michael N. Dobkowski, *The Tarnished Dream: The Basis of American Anti-Semitism* (Westport, Conn., 1979), esp. 123.

8. Berson, *Negroes and the Jews*, 44; Leonard Dinnerstein, *The Leo Frank Case* (New York, 1968); Steven Bloom, "Interaction between Blacks and Jews in New York City, 1900–1930, as Reflected in the Black Press" (Ph.D. diss., New York University, 1973), 20, 30, 32–33; Eugene Levy, *James Weldon Johnson: Black Leader, Black Voice* (Chicago, 1973), 158–59; Ronald Sanders, *The Downtown Jews: Portraits of an Immigrant Generation* (New York, 1969), 427–28. On the probable guilt of the black janitor, Jim Conley, see Berson, *Negroes and the Jews*, 38, 43–44.

9. Shapiro, *Leadership of the American Zionist Organization*, 60; Israel Zangwill, *The Melting Pot* (New

York, 1909); Moses Rischin, *The Promised City: New York's Jews, 1870–1914* (Cambridge, Mass., 1962), 97–98; Dawidowicz, *Jewish Presence*, 127; Howe, *World of Our Fathers*, 229; *Harvard Encyclopedia of American Ethnic Groups*, s.v. "Jews."

10. Thomas Cripps, *Slow Fade to Black: The Negro in American Film, 1900–1942* (New York, 1977), esp. 41–61; Kellogg, *NAACP*, 142–45.

11. On the "New Negro" personalities and their affiliations, see W. E. B. Du Bois, *The Autobiography of W. E. B. Du Bois: A Soliloquy on Viewing My Life from the Last Decade of Its First Century* (New York, 1968), 236–76; Elliott M. Rudwick, *W. E. B. Du Bois: Propagandist of the Negro Protest* (Philadelphia, 1968), 94–149; Stephen R. Fox, *The Guardian of Boston: William Monroe Trotter* (New York, 1970), 31–80; Alfreda M. Duster, ed., *Crusade for Justice: The Autobiography of Ida B. Wells* (Chicago, 1970), 323–28; Harlan, *Booker T. Washington*, 359–78; Kellogg, *NAACP*, 67–115; Meier, *Negro Thought in America*, 207–78; and Weiss, *National Urban League*, 47–70.

12. Frazier, *Black Bourgeoisie*, 113; E. Franklin Frazier, *The Free Negro Family: A Study of Family Origins before the Civil War* (Nashville, 1932); Lorenzo Johnston Greene, *The Negro in Colonial New England, 1620–1776* (New York, 1942), 72–99, 290–315; Edgar J. McManus, *Black Bondage in the North* (Syracuse, 1973), 160–98; David A. Gerber, *Black Ohio and the Color Line, 1860–1915* (Urbana, 1976), 60–92; Leon F. Litwack, *North of Slavery: The Negro in the Free States, 1790–1860* (Chicago, 1961), 178, 180.

13. Edwin R. Embree, *13 against the Odds* (New York, 1944), 47–70, 71–96, 153–74, 175–96; Mary White Ovington, *The Walls Came Tumbling Down* (New York, 1947), 78–91, 104–17; Patrick J. Gilpin, "Charles S. Johnson: Entrepreneur of the Harlem Renaissance," in *The Harlem Renaissance Remembered*, ed. Arna Bontemps (New York, 1972), 215–46; David Levering Lewis, "Dr. Johnson's Friends: Civil Rights by Copyright during Harlem's Mid-Twenties," *Massachusetts Review*, 20 (Autumn 1979), 501–19; David Levering Lewis, *When Harlem Was in Vogue* (New York, 1981), 119–55; Mary White Ovington, *Portraits in Color* (New York, 1927), 78–91, 104–17; Kellogg, *NAACP*, 47–65; Rudwick, *W. E. B. Du Bois*, 120–50; Weiss, *National Urban League*, 47–70; Levy, *James Weldon Johnson*, 49–74; Thomas C. Holt, "The Lonely Warrior: Ida B. Wells-Barnett and the Struggle for Black Leadership," in *Black Leaders of the Twentieth Century*, ed. John Hope Franklin and August Meier (Urbana, 1982), 39–61; Walter White, *A Man Called White: The Autobiography of Walter White* (New York, 1948), 39–80; Edward E. Waldron, *Walter White and the Harlem Renaissance* (Port Washington, N.Y., 1978), 3–22.

14. Paul Laurence Dunbar, *The Sport of the Gods* (New York, 1902), 212; Carter G. Woodson, *A Century of Negro Migration* (Washington, 1918), 180.

15. St. Clair Drake and Horace R. Cayton, *Black Metropolis: A Study of Negro Life in a Northern City* (2 vols., New York, 1970), I, 73; Sadie Tanner Mossell, "The Standard of Living among One Hundred Negro Migrant Families in Philadelphia" (Ph.D. diss., University of Pennsylvania, 1921), 9; Gilbert Osofsky, *Harlem: The Making of a Ghetto: Negro New York, 1890–1930* (New York, 1966), 139–40; Thomas Lee Philpott, *The Slum and the Ghetto: Neighborhood Deterioration and Middle-Class Reform, Chicago, 1800–1930* (New York, 1978), esp. 148–65, 169; Allan H. Spear, *Black Chicago: The Making of a Negro Ghetto, 1890–1920* (Chicago, 1967), esp. 51–56; George Edmund Haynes, *Negro New-Comers in Detroit, Michigan: A Challenge to Christian Statesmanship: A Preliminary Survey* (New York, 1918); Kenneth L. Kusmer, *A Ghetto Takes Shape: Black Cleveland, 1870–1930* (Urbana, 1976), esp. 35–76.

16. Drake and Cayton, *Black Metropolis*, I, 74; Weiss, *National Urban League*, 109–11, 121; Arvarh E. Strickland, *History of the Chicago Urban League* (Urbana, 1966), 56–72; Feingold, *Zion in America*, 155.

17. Howe, *World of Our Fathers*, 230; Philpott, *Slum and the Ghetto*, 165; James Weldon Johnson, "Harlem: The Culture Capital," in *The New Negro: An Interpretation*, ed. Alain Locke (New York, 1925), 309–10; Weiss, *National Urban League*, 123; Haynes, *Negro New-Comers in Detroit*, 18, 20. Raymond Wolters observes that, among students, "most blacks felt that their problem was more manageable than that of the Jews." Raymond Wolters, *The New Negro on Campus: Black College Rebellions of the 1920s* (Princeton, 1975), 326.

18. Albert Lee, *Henry Ford and the Jews* (New York, 1980), 1–47; Higham, "American Anti-Semitism Historically Reconsidered," 237–58; Arthur Liebman, "The Ties That Bind: The Jewish Support for the Left in the United States," *American Jewish Historical Quarterly*, 66 (Dec. 1976), 301–02; August Meier and

Elliott Rudwick, *Black Detroit and the Rise of the UAW* (New York, 1979), 14. On Communism and the Afro-American, see Harold Cruse, *The Crisis of the Negro Intellectual* (New York, 1967), 115–80; Theodore Draper, *American Communism and Soviet Russia: The Formative Period* (New York, 1960), 315–56; Nathan Glazer, *The Social Basis of American Communism* (New York, 1961), 169–84; and Mark Naison, *Communists in Harlem during the Depression* (Urbana, 1983), esp. 3–30.

19. Philpott, *Slum and the Ghetto*, 164–65; Osofsky, *Harlem*, 139–40; Diner, *In the Almost Promised Land*, 129–31; Richard Kluger, *Simple Justice: The History of* Brown v. Board of Education *and Black America's Struggle for Equality* (New York, 1976), 105–25; John Hope Franklin, *From Slavery to Freedom: A History of Negro Americans* (New York, 1980), 350; White, *Man Called White*, 73–79; Ira De A. Reid, *The Negro Immigrant: His Background, Characteristics and Social Adjustment, 1899–1937* (New York, 1939), esp. 25–29; Louise Venable Kennedy, *The Negro Peasant Turns Cityward: Effects of Recent Migrations to Northern Centers* (New York, 1930), 143–69; Levy, *James Weldon Johnson*, 282–83.

20. Kellogg, *NAACP*, 47–65; Weiss, *National Urban League*, 29–70; Diner, *In the Almost Promised Land*, 151, 164–91; Berson, *Negroes and the Jews*, 81–82; Amy Jacques Garvey, comp., *Philosophy and Opinions of Marcus Garvey,* or *Africa for the Africans* (London, 1967), 57; Tony Martin, *Race First: The Ideological and Organizational Struggles of Marcus Garvey and the Universal Negro Improvement Association* (Westport, Conn., 1976), 300.

21. Horace M. Kallen, *Culture and Democracy in the United States* (New York, 1924); Horace M. Kallen, "Democracy versus the Melting Pot: A Study of American Nationality," *Nation*, Feb. 18, 1915, pp. 190–94; *ibid.*, Feb. 25, 1915, pp. 217–20; *Harvard Encyclopedia of American Ethnic Groups*, s.v. "Jews"; Gordon, *Assimilation in American Life*, 140–50; Melvin I. Urofsky, *American Zionism from Herzl to the Holocaust* (Garden City, N.Y., 1975), 129; Shapiro, *Leadership of the American Zionist Organization*, 67–68.

22. Feingold, *Zion in America*, 219; Shapiro, *Leadership of the American Zionist Organization*, 82, 114, 167; Urofsky, *American Zionism*, 179, 318.

23. Diner, *In the Almost Promised Land*, 189, 190; Oswald Garrison Villard, *Fighting Years: Memoirs of a Liberal Editor* (New York, 1939), 529.

24. Embree and Waxman, *Investment in People*, 28–32, 101, 135–37, 143.

25. Diner, *In the Almost Promised Land*, 173. On Julius Rosenwald and the Rosenwald Fund, see Embree and Waxman, *Investment in People*, 31–33, 101–37. On white philanthropy and Afro-American education in general, see Horace Mann Bond, *The Education of the Negro in the American Social Order* (New York, 1934), 127–50; Henry Allen Bullock, *A History of Negro Education in the South: From 1619 to the Present* (Cambridge, Mass., 1967), 117–46; Louis R. Harlan, *Separate and Unequal: Public School Campaigns and Racism in the Southern Seaboard States, 1901–1915* (Chapel Hill, 1958); Kenneth R. Manning, *Black Apollo of Science: The Life of Ernest Everett Just* (New York, 1983), 115–63; David W. Southern, *The Malignant Heritage: Yankee Progressives and the Negro Question, 1901–1914* (Chicago, 1968); and John H. Stanfield, "Dollars for the Silent South: Southern White Liberalism and the Julius Rosenwald Fund, 1928–1948," *Perspectives on the American South*, 2 (1984), 117–38.

26. Myrtle Evangeline Pollard, "Harlem As Is: Sociological Notes on Harlem Social Life" (2 vols., B.B.A. thesis, City College of New York, 1936), II, 55–56; Lewis, *When Harlem Was in Vogue*, 256; Philpott, *Slum and the Ghetto*, 263–69.

27. Claude McKay, *Harlem: Negro Metropolis* (New York, 1940), 143–80; Martin, *Race First*, 343; E. David Cronon, *Black Moses: The Story of Marcus Garvey and the Universal Negro Improvement Association* (Madison, 1969), 42; Lawrence W. Levine, "Marcus Garvey and the Politics of Revitalization," in *Black Leaders of the Twentieth Century*, ed. Franklin and Meier, 105–38; Robert A. Hill, "General Introduction," in *The Marcus Garvey and Universal Negro Improvement Association Papers*, ed. Robert A. Hill (2 vols., Berkeley, 1983–), I, xxxv–xc.

28. Robert A. Hill, "The First England Years and After, 1912–1916," in *Marcus Garvey and the Vision of Africa*, ed. John Henrik Clarke and Amy Jacques Garvey (New York, 1974), 52, 65–67; W. E. B. Du Bois, "Marcus Garvey," in *ibid.*, 207; Cronon, *Black Moses*, 16–18, 19; Shapiro, *Leadership of the American Zionist Organization*, 83, 136–47; Urofsky, *American Zionism*, 250–58. For illuminating analyses of Du Boisian Pan-Africanism, see Wilson Jeremiah Moses, *The Golden Age of Black Nationalism, 1850–1925* (Hamden,

Conn., 1978), 141–43; and Theodore Draper, *The Rediscovery of Black Nationalism* (New York, 1970), 48–56.

29. Du Bois, "Marcus Garvey," 207, 209; Cronon, *Black Moses*, 99–100, 106–09, 110–11; Tony Martin, "Some Aspects of the Political Ideas of Marcus Garvey," in *Marcus Garvey and the Vision of Africa*, ed. Clarke and Garvey, 434–35; Weiss, *National Urban League*, 152; Jervis Anderson, *A. Philip Randolph: A Biographical Portrait* (New York, 1973), 132–34; Martin, *Race First*, 103, 316.; Theodore Kornweibel, Jr., *No Crystal Stair: Black Life and the Messenger, 1917–1928* (Westport, Conn., 1975), 137–42.

30. Kennedy, *Negro Peasant Turns Cityward*, 49–50, 131; Harvard Sitkoff, *A New Deal for Blacks: The Emergence of Civil Rights as a National Issue: The Depression Decade* (New York, 1978), 3–33; Strickland, *History of the Chicago Urban League*, 64; Alain Locke, "Apropos of Africa," *Opportunity*, 2 (Feb. 1924), 38, 40; "The Passing of Garvey," *ibid.*, 3 (March 1925), 66.

31. Alain Locke, "Enter the New Negro," *Survey*, 53 (March 1, 1925), 631, 632, 633. Gunnar Myrdal observed that "*leadership conferred upon a Negro by whites raises his class status in the Negro community.*" Of Afro-Americans' experience with Marcus Garvey, Ralph J. Bunche wrote: "When the curtain dropped on the Garvey theatricals, the black man of America was exactly where Garvey had found him, though a little bit sadder, perhaps a bit poorer—if not wiser." It is a statement not to be taken unqualifiedly but one that is suggestive. Gunnar Myrdal, *An American Dilemma: The Negro Problem and Modern Democracy* (2 vols., New York, 1944), II, 727, 748.

32. August Meier and Elliott Rudwick, "Attorneys Black and White: A Case Study of Race Relations within the NAACP," in August Meier and Elliott Rudwick, *Along the Color Line: Explorations in the Black Experience* (Urbana, 1976), 130; Kluger, *Simple Justice*, 113–14, 125.

33. Diner, *In the Almost Promised Land*, 131; Berson, *Negroes and the Jews*, 97.

34. Diner, *In the Almost Promised Land*, 128; Parris and Brooks, *Blacks in the City*, 39, 201–203; Weiss, *National Urban League*, 156–57. A typical Alfred Stern letter instructed James Weldon Johnson to "set aside Saturday evening, February 28, for a reading to a group of our friends. Mrs. Stern and I should be delighted to have both you and Mrs. Johnson at our home for dinner that evening." Alfred Stern to James Weldon Johnson, Jan. 14, 1931, folio 413, series 1, James Weldon Johnson Memorial Collection (Beinecke Rare Book and Manuscript Library, Yale University, New Haven, Conn.).

35. Lewis, *When Harlem Was in Vogue*, 119–97; Lewis, "Dr. Johnson's Friends"; David Levering Lewis, "The Politics of Art: The New Negro, 1920–1935," *Prospects*, 3 (1977), 237–61; Fullinwider, *Mind and Mood of Black America*, 119; Van Wyck Brooks, *The Confident Years: 1855–1915* (New York, 1952), 544–51; Arthur Frank Wertheim, *The New York Little Renaissance: Iconoclasm, Modernism, and Nationalism in American Culture, 1908–1917* (New York, 1976), 3–17.

36. Charles S. Johnson, "An Opportunity for Negro Writers," *Opportunity*, 2 (Sept. 1924), 258; Gilpin, "Charles S. Johnson," 238; Langston Hughes, *The Big Sea: An Autobiography* (New York, 1975), 218; Carolyn W. Sylvander, "Jessie Redmon Fauset: Black American Writer: Her Relationships, Biographical and Literary, with Black and White Writers, 1910–1935" (Ph.D. diss., University of Wisconsin, 1976), 71–73; Hiroko Sato, "Under the Harlem Shadow: A Study of Jessie Fauset and Nella Larsen," in *Harlem Renaissance Remembered*, ed. Bontemps, 108; Zora Neale Hurston, *Dust Tracks on a Road: An Autobiography* (Philadelphia, 1971), 168; "Arna Bontemps Talks about the Harlem Renaissance," in "The Harlem Renaissance Generation: An Anthology," comp. and ed. L. M. Collins, typescript, 1972, 2 vols., I 216 (Fisk University Library, Nashville, Tenn.); "Aaron Douglas Chats about the Harlem Renaissance," in *ibid.*, 181–82, 184; Ethel Ray Nance interview by Ann A. Schockley, transcript, p. 43, Fisk University Oral History Program (Fisk University Library); Lewis, *When Harlem Was in Vogue*, 119–97; Lewis, "Politics of Art," 237–61; Elinor Des Verney Sinnette, "Arthur Alfonso Schomburg, Black Bibliophile and Curator: His Contribution to the Collection and Dissemination of Materials about Africans and Peoples of African Descent" (D.L.S. diss., Columbia University, 1977), 111; Charles F. Cooney, "Forgotten Philanthropy: The Amy Spingarn Prizes," typescript, pp. 1–25 (in Lewis's possession); Darwin T. Turner, *In a Minor Chord: Three Afro-American Writers and Their Search for Identity* (Carbondale, Ill., 1971).

37. Lewis, *When Harlem Was in Vogue*, 138–40; Waldron, *Walter White and the Harlem Renaissance*, 113–66.

38. Alain Locke, "Art or Propaganda," *Harlem*, 1 (Nov. 1928), 12; Robert T. Kerlin, "Conquest by Poetry," *Southern Workman*, 56 (June 1927), 283; Johnson, "Race Prejudice and the Negro Artist," 776.

38. W. E. Burghardt Du Bois, "Criteria of Negro Art," *Crisis*, 32 (Oct. 1926), 294; Wallace Thurman, *Infants of the Spring* (New York, 1932), 234; Ralph J. Bunche, "Extended Memorandum on the Programs, Ideologies, Tactics and Achievements of Negro Betterment Interracial Organizations: A Research Memorandum," June 7, 1940, p. 144, Carnegie-Myrdal Study: The Negro in America, Special Collections (Schomburg Center for Research in Black Culture, New York Public Library, New York City).

40. Lewis, *When Harlem Was in Vogue*, 102–03; Willie the Lion Smith and George Hoefer, *Music on My Mind: The Memoirs of an American Pianist* (Garden City, N.Y., 1964), 131–79; Rudolph Fisher, "The Caucasian Storms Harlem," *American Mercury*, 11 (Aug. 1927), 393–98; Artie Shaw, *The Trouble with Cinderella: An Outline of Identity* (New York, 1952), 223–24; Samuel B. Charters and Leonard Kunstadt, *Jazz: A History of the New York Scene* (Garden City, N.Y., 1962), 82–238; Eileen Southern, *The Music of Black Americans: A History* (New York, 1971), 374–446; Doris E. Abramson, *Negro Playwrights in the American Theatre, 1925–1959* (New York, 1969), 22–88.

41. Locke, "Apropos of Africa," 40; Kelly Miller, "Before the Negro Becomes One with the Rest of the American People, He Must Become One with Himself," in *Black Nationalism in America*, ed. John H. Bracey, Jr., August Meier, and Elliott Rudwick (Indianapolis, 1970), 349–65; Levy, *James Weldon Johnson*, 115–16; Diner, *In the Almost Promised Land*, 153. A *Messenger* editorial declared: "Hitting the Jew is helping the Negro. Why? Negroes have large numbers and small money; Jews have small numbers and large money." Bloom, "Interaction between Blacks and Jews," 82.

42. Sitkoff, *New Deal for Blacks*, 170; Charles S. Johnson, "The Balance Sheet: Debits and Credits in Negro-White Relations," *World Tomorrow*, 11 (Jan. 1928), 15.

43. McKay, *Harlem*, 184; Bunche, "Extended Memorandum on the Programs," 145–48; Ross, *J. E. Spingarn*, 182–85; Sitkoff, *New Deal for Blacks* 250–51; John B. Kirby, *Black Americans in the Roosevelt Era: Liberalism and Race* (Knoxville, 1980), 177–78.

44. Diner, *In the Almost Promised Land*, 153.

# Part 5 **The Era of the Depression and World War II**

A number of pieces in this section describe the increasingly troubled and hostile interactions of blacks and Jews in urban areas. These include the description by St. Clair Drake and Horace R. Cayton of intense economic competition between small businesses in Chicago; the dramatic firsthand accounts reported by Ella Baker and Marvel Cooke of the unfair domestic employment situation known as "the Bronx Slave Market"; a letter from David Edwards of the Norfolk (Virginia) NAACP protesting a Jewish merchant's murder of a black child he had hired; and further NAACP correspondence expressing annoyance that allegations of Jewish discrimination against blacks were dismissed as anti-Semitic, and disappointment at the refusal of Jewish department-store owners to provide adequate facilities for their black customers.

Hostilities between some blacks and some Jews were exacerbated by the continued effects of the Depression and the rise of fervent nationalism in Europe and the Far East. The most extreme expression of these antagonisms occurred in the race riots in Harlem in 1935, referred to by Marie Syrkin, and in Detroit in 1943, analyzed here by Dominic J. Capeci.

There were, however, significant efforts made by most black and Jewish organizations to coordinate their opposition to the racism endemic in Fascism, and this cooperation served as a harbinger of an even closer partnership in the postwar period. One example of this alliance can be seen in two letters from the president of the Chicago chapter of the NAACP.

But forging a true coalition was no easy matter. In "Negro Perceptions of Jews between the World Wars," Robert G. Weisbord and Arthur Stein review the complex factors involved in black perceptions of Jews. In this same spirit, Lunabelle Wedlock offers a thoughtful, evenhanded examination of the way different black publications present anti-Semitism abroad and compare it to racism at home. Louis Harap and L. D. Reddick address the antagonism expressed by Jews against blacks and by blacks against Jews.

This section closes with an essay by Thomas Cripps that provides a perceptive discussion of the controversial relations between blacks and Jews in Hollywood.

### FURTHER REFERENCES

Black-Jewish relations during the Depression and between the two world wars are discussed in Lenora E. Berson, *The Negroes and the Jews* (1971); Hasia R. Diner, *In the Almost Promised Land: American Jews and Blacks, 1915–1935* (1977); William M. Phillips Jr., "The Nadir of Injustice and Inequality: 1890–1919," in *An Unillustrious Alliance: The African American and Jewish American Communities* (1991); and Jack Salzman and Cornel West, eds., *Struggles in the Promised Land: Toward a History of Black-Jewish*

*Relations in the United States* (1997). In *The Reaction of Negro Publications and Organiza-tions to German Anti-Semitism* (1942), a selection from which is reprinted here, Luna-belle Wedlock discusses in great detail this response (Ralph Bunche edited and wrote the introduction to this volume). See also Gabrielle S. Edgcomb, *From Swastika to Jim Crow: Refugee Scholars at Black Colleges* (1993).

As an extension of the discussion in the Drake and Cayton excerpt in this section, see Harold L. Sheppard, "The Negro Merchant: A Study of Negro Anti-Semitism" (1947), and Joe W. Trotter Jr., "African Americans, Jews, and the City: Perspectives from the Industrial Era, 1900–1950" (1998). For follow-ups to the essays in this section by Syrkin on Harlem and Capeci on wartime Detroit, see Winston C. McDowell, "Keeping Them 'In the Same Boat Together'? Sufi Abdul Hamid, African Americans, Jews, and the Harlem Jobs Boycott" (1998), and Marshall F. Stevenson Jr., "African Americans and Jews in Organized Labor: A Case Study of Detroit, 1920–1950" (1998).

The early black-Jewish cooperation on civil rights is presented in Murray Friedman, "Civil Rights," in Jack Fischel and Sanford Pinsker, eds., *Jewish-American History and Culture: An Encyclopedia,* and Stuart Svonkin, *Jews against Prejudice: American Jews and the Fight for Civil Liberties* (1997). This history is taken up in more detail in the following section.

For an extensive recent treatment of blacks and Jews in Hollywood, see Michael Rogin, *Blackface, White Noise: Jewish Immigrants in the Hollywood Melting Pot* (1996) and "Black Sacrifice, Jewish Redemption: From Al Jolson's *Jazz Singer* to John Garfield's *Body and Soul.*" Two earlier studies of the role of Jews in Hollywood are those by Neal Gabler, *An Empire of Their Own: How the Jews Invented Hollywood* (1988), and Norman Zierold, *The Moguls: Hollywood's Merchants of Myth* (1969).

# From *Black Metropolis: A Study of Negro Life in a Northern City*

## THE GROWTH OF A "NEGRO MARKET"

Chicago's first colored businessmen did not serve an exclusively Negro market.\* Most of the earliest colored businessmen were engaged in service enterprises catering to a white clientele. Reference has already been made to John Jones, the tailor, in the Seventies. There were also barbers, hairdressers, wigmakers, masseurs, and caterers. A few Negroes ran livery stables and served as draymen. One Isom Artis made his living in the Seventies by drawing water from Lake Michigan and selling it to the residents for eight cents a barrel. In the late Seventies, another Negro opened a large lumber yard from which he later made a small fortune. While most of these had a predominantly white clientele, there were also less lucrative restaurants, barber shops, and small stores in the small Negro area.

Between the close of the Civil War and the publication of the first *Colored Men's Professional and Business Directory of Chicago* in 1885, the participation of the Negro in the business life of the city developed to the extent of some 200 enterprises in 27 different fields. Most numerous were barber shops. Restaurants competed with "sample rooms" (combination liquor stores and saloons) for second place. Even as late as the turn of the century, however, the Negro market was relatively unimportant.

On the eve of the Great Migration, there were about 500 Negro businessmen concentrated either in the service occupations or in those enterprises calling for small amounts of capital and but little experience. Barber shops (now serving a Negro clientele) predominated, but it is significant that colored moving and storagemen (successors to the early draymen) serving both whites and Negroes were still numerous, for automobiles had not yet arrived in sufficient numbers to drive horses from the streets.

The Great Migration created the "Negro market." Both white and Negro merchants, as well as the Negro consumer, became increasingly conscious of the purchasing power of several hundred thousand people solidly massed in one compact community. The rapid growth of the Negro community between 1915 and 1929 was accompanied by expansion in all types of Negro-owned businesses, not the least lucrative of which was speculation in real estate.

In 1945 St. Clair Drake and Horace R. Cayton were both engaged in graduate study at the University of Chicago.

Originally published in St. Clair Drake and Horace R. Cayton, *Black Metropolis: A Study in Negro Life in a Northern City* (New York: Harcourt Brace and Company, 1945). Excerpts taken from chapter 16, "Negro Business: Myth and Fact." Copyright © 1945 by St. Clair Drake and Horace R. Cayton and renewed 1973 by St. Clair Drake and Susan Woodson. Reprinted by permission of Harcourt Brace and Company and Routledge.

The curve of Negro enterprise rose throughout the Twenties. Two colored banks and three or four insurance companies began to amass capital from within the Negro community and to lend money for the purchase of homes. As the population moved southward from the Loop, the business center moved with it. But there was little tendency among long-established white businesses (especially those on the main thoroughfares) to move away from these areas newly occupied by Negroes.

The Depression of 1929 liquidated the two colored banks and wiped out many of the larger enterprises. Paradoxically, however, it stimulated an increase in the number of smaller businesses, as many people with some savings saw in the opening of a small store one means of insuring themselves against starvation. The impact of the Depression combined with the fierce competition for good locations, for credit and capital, also resulted in an accentuation of racial antagonisms, including anti-Semitic manifestations.

The Depression also revivified the dream of organizing the purchasing power of the Negro—not only for the salvation of Negro businessmen threatened with extinction, but also as a possible method of creating jobs for the thousands of persons who were going on relief and for the impecunious and unemployed white-collar class. Attempts to organize the economic power of the Negro have followed two main lines: (1) forcing white merchants to employ Negroes through the use of the boycott, and (2) urging Negroes to trade with Negroes. The latter has, of course, been the preferred objective of Negro businessmen.

That Negroes have not become fully integrated into the commercial life of the city and do not have a larger measure of economic control even within their own communities is due primarily to the fact that their normal participation in the economic life of Midwest Metropolis is curtailed by traditional attitudes toward colored persons and by the vested economic interests of white occupational groups. These factors are reinforced by the subtle, but none the less powerful, tendencies toward dispersal of effort which result from the conditions of life in the Black Ghetto.

For Negro businesses to compete with white businesses in Negro communities, they must be able to "meet the price" and give equivalent service. Negro businessmen insist that they face five main competitive difficulties: (1) difficulty in procuring capital and credit, (2) difficulty in getting adequate training, (3) inability to secure choice locations on the main business streets, (4) lack of sufficient patronage to allow them to amass capital and to make improvements, (5) inability to organize for co-operative effort.

These circumstances have resulted in a situation in which Negroes have found it extremely difficult to compete with white businessmen in the same field as to prices and service. This, in turn, tends to reinforce the stereotype that Negroes are not good businessmen. In order to meet the competition, Negro businessmen and community leaders stress the dogmas of racial solidarity in an effort to amass capital and patronage. This results in a pattern of behavior in which both Negro customers and merchants are always on the defensive *vis-à-vis* one another, and often take refuge in mutual derogation. Despite these difficulties, some Negroes *have* been able to compete with whites for the Negro market, and some have even been able to develop businesses competing in the general city market. . . .

Negro grocers and general retailers, matching wits and prices with the small white merchants and with the chain stores in Bronzeville and the Loop, appeal loudly to "race pride" and fulminate bitterly against white storekeepers in Negro neighborhoods. These Negro businessmen, quite naturally, dream of organizing the Negro market to corral the errant dollars. When they do not succeed in doing this, they are peeved with both competitors and potential customers. Out of this anger flow both bitter invective and a sigh of resignation. "No community can hope to thrive," insists one newspaper editor, "where people come from other communities and operate businesses in this community, and at the close of day you see the money taken out of the neighborhood never to return, except in the form of some more second- or third-grade goods to take the rest of the Negro's money." Awareness of the potentialities of the Negro market has evoked many protests such as that of the Baptist minister who commented bitterly:

"The Negro in Chicago spends billions on merchandise. All of that money goes into the white man's pocket and then out of our neighborhoods. It is used to buy white men cars and homes, and their wives mink coats and servants. Our money is being used by the white man to pay us for being his cook, his valet, and his washwoman."

In its most extreme form, the dream of controlling the Negro market visualizes a completely separate Negro economy: "The idea is to be able to support ourselves instead of being wholly dependent on the white race." Despite this dream, nine-tenths of Bronzeville's money is spent with whites, and this is why the Negro businessman complains that his own people do not support him.

## BUSINESSMAN'S COMPLAINT

Bronzeville businessmen are convinced that one of the main problems facing them is the power of "the white man's psychology." "Negroes," they feel, "have never learned to patronize their own." Merchants are continually making such statements as the following (usually associated with one or two other complaints):

"I think that colored people will have to be educated to trade with each other. I notice that even now what you would call the most substantial people on this street pass my store on their way to 31st Street to trade with some Jew merchant. *Of course, the chain stores offer a deal of competition to any independent merchant,* but having come in close contact with Jews, as I did, I know they feel they can 'jive' a Negro along and get his money."

The proprietress of a beauty shop, who does not herself have white competition but who has had difficulty in securing a favorable location for her shop, was very bitter, using an epithet which Negroes would resent if applied by a white person:

"I think it is a shame that these old, dumb 'darkies' will trade in those places. They [white people] only pocket the money and leave the community. They will hire a few colored girls so they can get the business, but they aren't bothered about you after they get rich. It will never be stopped because some of our people refuse to trade with a Negro."

St. Clair Drake & Horace R. Cayton    357

Even a huckster, peddling vegetables in the alley, has similar views:

"The colored seem to prefer the whites. There was a white fellow that came through the alley and the colored used to bring their pans down to him. They would holler for me to come up to them, and then instead of really buying from me would wait for him."

Sometimes the rural, southern origin of the Negro is blamed for this alleged slavery to "the white man's psychology." Thus, a fairly successful grocer who felt that his customers patronized him only because they thought he "fronted for a Jew," was sure that "these people are used to living on the farm and trading with the white man. They don't know any better."

An unsuccessful cleaner and presser has this same view:

"Ninety per cent of Negroes in Chicago are from the South, and with that in mind they feel as if they must buy from a white man or that a white man's commodities are better than those of a Negro."

One woman offered an interesting variation on this southern theme:

"They want to appear important, and many of them go to a white man's place just to make him wait on them. It is like getting revenge for not having had the opportunity of going into some white places in the South. The one sad thing is the Negro does not realize that he is hurting himself in doing this, for his group needs his trade to stay in business."

Occasionally, a person reverses this argument, insisting that southern Negroes are more likely to trade with Negroes. Here is one grocery-store proprietor's opinion:

"One thing the average person does not realize is that a business in the South is entirely different from one in the North. There the southern white man does not want a Negro's trade and will tell him so. That makes the Negro patronize his own people. . . . Then, too, it teaches the Negroes to trade with each other. . . . I have often heard people say that Negroes do not patronize each other here. I have made a study of this and find that people from the South do." . . .

A fairly well-educated and somewhat analytical merchant summed the matter up as follows:

"Some Negroes do patronize Negro business. They are usually the laboring class, though—people who work in factories and do laboring work. The professionals and the so-called 'big Negroes' spend nearly all of their earnings with the whites. The reason for this is simple: the professional group like the school teachers, doctors, and lawyers, earn large salaries and get better fees. They have greater earning power and hence they open charge accounts and do most of their buying in the Loop. They buy not only clothes and furniture there, but also food-stuffs. They contribute very little to the success of the Negro merchants on the South Side."

Preachers are sometimes excoriated for their failure to support Negro business aggressively. One editor of a Bronzeville paper engaged in a long discussion with an interviewer about "what these no-good preachers ought to do." He insisted that they should buy all their clothing from Negroes—"every last handkerchief and necktie"— wear this clothing to church on Sunday morning, and tell their congregations to "do as they had done." "They'll get up there with Marshall Field labels all over them and tell Negroes to trade with the race," he observed scornfully. One merchant accused a very prominent pastor of "buying his daily needs from the Jew" and having the packages delivered to his home so that he wouldn't be seen coming out of the store.

One Negro merchant was so irritated by the alleged failure of Negroes to support business that he said: "Other businesses ought to force the colored man to patronize his own color by refusing to wait on him!"

With so general a feeling on the part of colored merchants that they do not receive the support of the Negro community, it might be instructive to turn to "the public" for its side of the case.

## THE NEGRO CUSTOMER'S DEFENSE

*Race Pride vs. Prices:* Over and over, Negroes in Bronzeville reveal a conflict between the economic imperative of "making ends meet" and the social demands of "race pride." They insist that Negro merchants cannot give equivalent goods and services for the same price:

"I'd like to do all my shopping—what little I do—with colored, but I can get things cheaper at the chain stores. I buy there for that reason."

"I buy at the A & P where I can get food cheapest. I try to patronize my race, but I can't on my husband's salary [$55 per month, WPA]."

"I do all of my buying at white stores. They always seem to be a penny or two cheaper."

"My real friend is a dollar. I try to patronize my people, but when it comes to saving a penny, especially at this time, I do so, even if I have to buy from whites."

*Race Pride vs. Credit:* Poor people need credit. Negro merchants on the whole are unable to grant it. This forces the Negro housewife to avoid the colored grocer as well as the chain store. One woman who formerly shopped at the A & P, and who says she now goes to "the Jew," makes the following somewhat apologetic statement:

"You see, I can get credit from him and I can't from the A & P or a colored store. I like to trade at the A & P because you can pick up quite a bit of fresh vegetables and stuff, but I tried to get credit there and couldn't."

A grocer corroborates the testimony that the credit problem is a real one:

"We have the trade of young people—penny trade. People come in here begging as soon as they want charity, but they trade regular with the Jews. People we never saw before come in and ask for credit. They've been customers of the Jew all the time. They go to

State Street and come back here with big bundles they bought from the Jew. Then they stop in here and buy a pound of sugar or two pickles. Five days after that they ask for credit. Our people would just rather trade with the Jew."

*Race Pride vs. Quality:* Colored housewives often combine with these criticisms of price and credit the charge that the quality and variety of stock in Negro stores are poor.

"I try to spend as much as I can with Negro stores, but most of them don't have what you want, or they are too high. That may be our fault for not trading with them more, but we are too poor and have to count pennies."

"There are colored businesses in the neighborhood, but they never have a good supply. The colored lady who had a store across the street is a penny or two higher than Tony."

*Race Pride vs. "Service":* Colored storekeepers are also accused of general inefficiency and ineptitude: "The Negro does not know how to wait on customers"; "The clerk forgets his work and tries to sweetheart with you"; "Our people are too slothful; they are behind the white man."

One of the most general criticisms of Negro merchants is the charge that "they are stuck up," or "hincty." As one customer complained: "The average Negro in business will frown and become very haughty at the least thing." One woman contrasted the Negro merchant with "the Jew" in this respect:

"Some of these colored people make you hate them when you try to trade with them. When you go into a store and try to be choicy they get mad. But a Jew tries to fool you and make you think he is pleasing you. . . . I trade at Jew stores *where Negroes work* most of the time because they appreciate what you buy from them."

One colored businessman shared this belief that "the average colored man who gets a few dollars takes an extra head-size and you can't touch him," but also blamed the customers for their lack of patience with the merchant: "Negroes rate their businessmen as the scum of the earth. They are ready to censure them for the least little mistake that they make."

A housewife summed up what many Negroes no doubt feel about the whole matter of supporting colored merchants:

"The Negro must learn to be independent and have the same type of goods the white man has for the same price. The Negro should not be expected to trade with another Negro because he is a black man. People of any race should have some respect for their people, but any people naturally want to get things where they can get the best bargains."

## THE MERCHANT'S REBUTTAL

*Negroes Expect Too Much:* Many Negro merchants have faced these criticisms frankly, and have studied the behavior of their customers. There is a general tendency to feel that Negroes "expect more" from a colored merchant than from a white, that they are "touchy" and constantly make comparisons with the type of service offered by whites. The woman owner of a successful hosiery shop insisted that "Negroes support our business. If they didn't, we would have closed shortly after we opened." She was just as certain, however, that "one of the biggest problems we have is trying to please the customers. The women customers will get runs in their stockings and bring them back to me with a complaint and want adjustment. The Loop stores don't have this sort of thing to contend with." A florist, too, insisted that she had "to give more service and all the trimmings to induce Negroes to buy." One merchant said: "The public expects more out of a colored man than it does out of a white man. It expects a better grade and prices, and more courtesy." He felt that Negroes should try to meet the competitive disadvantage, however, and accused most colored businessmen of "lack of courtesy." "The trouble with the Negro businessman," he observed, "is laziness, lack of energy, lack of stock, and ignorance of his public." Such a blanket indictment does not give sufficient weight to other factors, however.

*White Competition Is Keen:* The more reflective colored businessman is likely to add that Negro businesses, on the whole, lack sufficient capital and experience to compete with the average white merchant. Thus they are often unable to provide the range of goods and services which a customer has a right to expect. As one very successful merchant phrased it:

"There is one thing that gives the white merchant the jump on the Negro. The average Negro goes into business simply because he cannot find work, and the place he opens is started with very small capital and his stock is limited. A customer does not like to go to more than one place when shopping. The people who have the money and could open large, well-stocked stores do not do so because they cannot get the locations they want."

The owner of one small sandwich shop states that he plans "to make this little place one of the best-looking stores on 47th Street" because "Negroes *do* patronize each other and they would do so to a greater extent, only we do not fix up our places to encourage them." A delicatessen owner is sure that "the Negro will patronize you if you have the money to put into your store what he wants. There are lots who would rather trade with their own people if they had what they want." From her analysis of the situation, lack of capital is "the greatest handicap of the Negro merchant."

Some merchants feel that any accumulation of adequate capital is primarily dependent upon sustained support and that Negroes should "give their merchants a break." Thus, one woman who runs what she calls a "very high-class" beauty parlor and "has no serious problem" of her own, states this view at some length:

"I think Negro business in Chicago is quite progressive, especially considering the experience our people have had in business and the small amount of money they invest in it. Negro business suffers, though, from lack of co-operation from the public."

The pooling of purchasing power is frequently mentioned as a possible competitive technique, as in the following case:

"The Negro, on the whole, will try to patronize his own merchants, but the fact that they ask higher prices and often give poor merchandise causes him to stay away from them. The reason for this is that each merchant, no matter how small his place, buys independently of other merchants. This buying in small quantities makes him pay more for his commodities wholesale than the white customer asks of his customers retail.

"We, as a group, are much more lenient with other groups than with our own. If we go into a Jewish store and ask for something and the Jew doesn't have it, we either buy something else in its place or go on without a murmur. Our own people could stock everything we want, but we fuss and carry on and say: 'You see, that's the reason we can't patronize our own people; they never have anything we want.' If they'd just buy from us, we'd stock all the things they want."

Two small merchants have the same theory:

"When we opened up, we had just as good stock as any of them whites. But then, the colored did not come in and buy so we went backward. Some of our people will always trade with the Jew. They have not been educated to trade with the colored people."

"Maybe our prices are a little higher than those of the white merchant, but that's because we buy in such small quantities. If the people would spend more with us, we could give them better prices, because we could buy at a better cost." . . .

Some merchants also accused ward politicians of putting the squeeze on them. One man told the following story:

"I've had trouble here. Yesterday I was refused a license. The city says that a basement store is too unsanitary. I have been called to court several times. Through the Ward Committeeman the case has been thrown out. It's the Republicans that's doing it, and the Jews. The man that owns the building is colored. He had some political trouble. They refused me a license two years ago until I convinced them that I was not connected with him."

One owner of a small store said:

"The Jews are trying to get colored out of this basement. They have friends in the city council. They can go any place and stick. They have harassed me ever since I've been here. On Michigan Avenue a colored man had the place and had trouble. Now a Jew has the place and has no trouble."

Another store-proprietor had a similar story:

"We started here in May, 1937. We had to pay $100 for a license. We had to pay a $50 electric-light deposit. The zoning law hindered us. It was the Jew across the street. That's all. We had to get petitions to open up. I belong to the NAACP, but that didn't help.

"The Jew across the street was around here first. He's been here four or five years. He's cut prices since he has been here. He extends credit more than we do because he is able to. He has offered credit to our customers. Credit is one of my major problems."

The most frequently voiced charge is the contention that Negroes cannot lease choice business spots. All of Bronzeville believes what a grocer states:

"If we could get better locations our businesses would be better. The location I have is only fair—it is too far from the corner; but two white merchants keep the best places leased in order to prevent any Negro business from getting them. I find good locations are hard to get. I tried several months before I got this location. Several others that I tried to get rented too high."

As these typical quotations suggest, all complaints tend to assume an anti-Semitic tinge. It is hard to convince most merchants in Bronzeville that they are not victims of a "Jewish conspiracy." . . .

*Beating Whites at the Game:* But even with the odds against the Negro merchant, many manage to survive. The ones who do are usually proud of it, as in the case of a merchant who recited his experiences:

"There were nine Jewish merchants in this block when I opened. They predicted I would remain in business only one month. They sought to discourage me in many ways. When one of my customers would carry a package of merchandise purchased from me into their stores, they would open the package, criticize the merchandise, and try to get the customer to come to me for a refund. They were often seen peeping into my show windows to determine the quality and prices of my merchandise. Well, I bought as cheaply as they did and I sold at a reasonable margin of profit. So it was impossible for them to undersell me.

"I have been led many times into the discussion as to why Negroes don't patronize each other. Well, if they hadn't patronized me I would have closed many years ago, whereas I have been in this one spot thirteen years and at this time have no competitors. These favorable results have been obtained by a strict adherence to fundamental business principles. My customers are frequently advised not to buy from me merely because I am a Negro, but my merchandise and service are not excelled by any one of my competitors. Ninety-five per cent of the business I have gotten has always been from my people." . . .

### THE WHITE MERCHANT'S VERDICT

White merchants in competition with Negroes will sometimes comment on the failure of Negroes to compete successfully with them. A few hold to stereotypes such as those of the real-estate agent who said: "The happy, carefree nature of the Negroes in seeking lines of least resistance in the conduct of their business is largely responsible for the high credit risk tabulated against them." Another white merchant thinks that "as long as Negroes have enough money to spend on booze and policy, they are happy," but concedes the point that "they haven't got the dough to invest in business." He is also sure that "they don't have the brains either" and "it takes brains to make a good business-man." A Jewish furniture dealer with years of experience in Negro neighborhoods thinks that "most of the colored people you find in business are failures," and observes: "I don't know what causes this, whether they don't grasp the principles of the business or whether they want to start right out on top as big shots. I'll bet that about all their failures are due to this fault. I really think they've got too much ego. That's the way they impress me."

Other merchants tried to take into consideration the basic factors which place Negro businessmen at a competitive disadvantage, as did the owner of a very large department store in Bronzeville's main business area, who analyzed the situation as follows: "There is no possibility of the Negro merchant ever predominating in this area because of his inadequate working capital, insufficient credit extension, and lack of experience in business." . . .

A Negro preacher, however, thinks he has an answer to the weakness of Negro business enterprises:

"These dagoes and Jews come over here and start out with a peanut stand. They'll eat stale bread and live in the back of a ol' store. They'll starve themselves and get your pennies. And then one mornin' they'll move out in front with a nice fruit stand or a restaurant. While they doin' this, the lazy Negro is jitterbuggin', an' the college Negro is either lookin' for a soft job down South or else is carryin' bags down in some railroad station."

A more objective analysis, however, would take account of the fact that the average college-trained Negro, if he is not a professional man, is more likely to go into insurance or real estate, publishing or printing, than into the hurly-burly of retail merchandising, or he prefers a civil service job where he can immediately attain the standard of living to which he has been trained.

The highly individualistic motivations for entering business are of course at variance with the much touted doctrine of doing business for racial advancement. This is partly responsible, on one hand, for the lack of enthusiasm with which the Negro public responds to the "race pride" dogmas, and on the other hand, for the extreme difficulty which Race Leaders and business promoters have in organizing trade associations and buying pools.

### ODDS TO THE NEGRO

Though the odds are against the Negro in the general merchandising field, Bronzeville's undertakers, barbers, and beauticians operate within a closed market, competing only among themselves.

*Burying the Dead:* Between 300 and 400 Negroes die in Chicago every month. They must be "put away right," whether in a pine box with a $75 funeral or at a $20,000 ceremony complete with couch casket and Lincoln limousines. Negro undertakers have a virtual monopoly on burying the colored dead, most of the white undertakers taking the position of the one who said: "I've been here for over fifty years and have seen this area change from all white to all black. However, I've never catered to the Negro business and at no time conducted a Negro funeral." One colored undertaker explained this present competitive situation as follows:

"Twenty-five years ago we had competition from the white undertakers. They bury very few Negroes now. When they do, competition comes mostly from Jewish and Irish undertakers. There are some few families that will not have a Negro undertaker today. I am unable to give the reason except to say that many of these Negroes work for white families." . . .

Since an undertaker's success is based upon popularity as well as upon service and efficiency, "morticians" are very careful to maintain wide connections with lodges, churches, and civic and social clubs. Many of them arrange with a few ministers to have funerals thrown their way. Some pastors advertise a special undertaker for their church and use various forms of subtle pressure to force their members to use him. In fact, the undertaker's name appears on many church bulletin boards beside that of the pastor. Various forms of advertisement are used to dramatize the "mortician" as a social benefactor, and the largest and most consistent advertisers in the Negro press are the undertakers. (The Undertakers' Wives' Charity Club also assists in perpetuating this myth.) The opening of a new funeral parlor is usually "news," and sometimes includes "a bevy of charming ladies . . . on hand to serve all in attendance to a sumptuous tea and refreshments." . . .

The undertakers, working as they do in a closed market, have little personal reason to react violently against white businessmen. As Negroes, however, they do share the general ideologies of race pride. One rather successful undertaker with an annual turnover of about $70,000 and a profit of 17–20 per cent on his investment is proud of the fact that he buys "fluids and quite a number of caskets from Negroes," but regrets that he is "compelled to buy from whites when better qualities are selected." He does not approve of a racial business monopoly, however, insisting that he "should have the right to operate a business anywhere in Chicago and not be confined to the Black Belt." He states that he has no objection to whites' entering business in Bronzeville. Negroes who bury the dead definitely have the odds in their favor.

*Beautifying the Living:* If colored undertakers have a virtual monopoly in burying the Negro dead, the colored barber and beautician have an even more exclusive monopoly in beautifying the living. In 1938, there was not a white beauty parlor or barber shop in the Negro community, a circumstance which impelled one colored beautician to comment that "they *would* have them if they knew how to work on Negroes' hair." The fact of the matter is that few white persons have had experience with the cutting of Negro hair, or with the exceedingly complicated preparations and processes used in "straightening" the hair of colored women (and some men) who have not been favored with "good hair." Negroes often jest at themselves for trying to straighten their hair while white people are curling theirs, or for using "bleaching creams" while whites are risking sunburn to get a tan. Yet the advertisements in the colored papers continue to call attention to such products as X SKIN WHITENER which promises "the thrill of lighter, fairer, brighter, younger-looking skin," or Y HAIR POMADE—"Know the Joy of Straighter, Glossier Hair—Good-bye, Hair Kinks."

The fairly large proportion of Negro women in Chicago who are listed in the Census as proprietors is due primarily to the prevalence of "beauticians," many of whom use their homes or vacant store fronts when they cannot afford a "salon." Training in beauty culture is rather easy to get, either in the public schools or in any of several "beauty colleges." In each of the latter an exclusive "system" is taught, usually involving the use of a particular brand of cosmetics. Many operators who have apprentices complain that "they are hard to keep" because they usually want shops of their own.

Despite the intense competition in the field, some of the most successful business associations in Bronzeville are those of the beauticians. Composed of beauty-shop owners, operators, and apprentices, and beauty-school owners, these organizations have as their aims the standardizing of prices and the enforcing of state health regulations. They also function as pressure groups for "racial advancement." . . .

### HIGH FINANCE

*Insurance:* The Negro businesses that have been most successful in direct competition with whites during the last twenty years are insurance companies. In significant contrast to entrepreneurs in the field of general merchandising, these companies have been able to amass capital, secure a trained personnel, and weather the Depression. In 1940 there were four such companies with home offices in Chicago. They were valued at over 10,000,000 and employed over 2,000 persons. . . .

The mushrooming of insurance companies between 1919 and 1927 was due to a number of factors, not the least important of these being the fact that Negroes were familiar with lodges and successful colored insurance companies in the South, and there was thus no initial skepticism to overcome, as was often the case in other types of business. The companies were also able to exploit the fact that the white companies charged Negroes a higher premium than they did whites.

The secretary of one of the four companies surviving the Depression said that he entered the business in 1926, after selling all of his real estate in the South, because

"we considered it a good business. We had no charitable reasons, I assure you. We were out to make money and we felt that there was a splendid opening in Chicago. . . . A large number of the persons who were coming to Chicago were accustomed to carrying insurance policies with Negro companies. Our worst competitors are the white insurance companies. A lot of Negroes have been carrying policies with the Metropolitan ever since they were babies. Then, too, we have large white companies selling industrial insurance. There's money in it, though. All you've got to do is get it out. We've learned that you can make money if you run it right. When I came here all the colored insurance men were successful. It seemed the ideal business to enter. A great many Negroes were going into business in those days. Many of them brought money with them when they came, the way I did, and were able to start up business."

During the late Twenties, the colored insurance companies, faced with the competition of burial associations and white insurance companies, began to throw their weight behind a boycott campaign ostensibly designed to make white companies employ Negro agents. This campaign began when a militant Negro newspaper directed a letter to the Metropolitan Company complaining that the company did not employ Negro agents, that white agents were discourteous, and that they refused to collect at night when it was most convenient for Negroes to pay. The company's tactless and discourteous reply was made public in the Negro community; hundreds of Negroes were angered, and a boycott resulted.

The Negro insurance companies exploited the boycott proposal to the utmost, using large billboard posters to point out that support for colored companies would "make jobs for our boys and girls." An official of one of these companies thus appraised the effect of the campaign:

"I have no statistics on the matter, but it has probably put most prospective policy-holders in a favorable mood for an unanswerable argument that the money they put in colored companies, besides providing insurance of the best class, also provides employment for colored people and an opportunity for Negroes to acquire capital through our loans to them. This kind of sales talk, when properly handled, usually works." . . .

These insurance companies are frequently cited as proof that Negroes can successfully conduct business, run office machines, handle big money, and give employment to The Race. Such companies proudly publish the pictures of their offices and stress their function as "racial" enterprises. One company, in its twentieth-anniversary pamphlet, attributed "much of its success" to the fact that "its officials and employees never permit themselves to forget that the primary reason for being is to provide a unique service to the Negro people. . . . On its twentieth birthday, it rededicates itself to the cause of Negro progress and betterment."

The boards of directors of the largest of these companies include, in addition to businessmen, a few prominent preachers and civic leaders. Even Joe Louis is now on one insurance company board.

*Banking:* The largest measure of control and the greatest prestige in the American economy are associated with banking. It is therefore natural that the successful operation of a bank would have high symbolic significance for Bronzeville. In the Fat Years, Bronzeville had two colored banks, which held over one-third of all the combined deposits in Negro banks in the United States. The Depression wiped out both of them, as it wiped out the four white banks in the Black Belt and sixty-six banks in other parts of the city.

NOTE
*In 1938, about three-fourths of the merchants in Bronzeville were Jewish. During that year an organized anti-Semitic drive arose in Bronzeville. A small newspaper, *Dynamite,* scurrilously attacked all

Jews. Jewish philanthropists were accused of trying to dominate Negro institutions; Jewish merchants were dubbed exploiters. Suggestions were made that all Jews should be expelled from Bronzeville. Finally, after conferences between Negro and Jewish leaders as well as representatives of various labor unions, the editor of the paper was dissuaded from publishing further attacks. Because many of the interviews we quote were made when the campaign was at its height, the repeated references to Jews may represent an abnormal situation; in other years such references might be less frequent. Yet, as the most highly visible and most immediately available white persons in the community, Jewish merchants tend to become the symbol of the Negroes' verbal attack on all white businessmen, and anti-Semitic waves sometimes sweep through Bronzeville. In New Orleans, where Italian merchants predominate in Negro areas, "Dagoes" are the target of attack. In Bronzeville it is the Jew who is the scapegoat.

# The Bronx Slave Market

The Bronx Slave Market! What is it? Who are its dealers? Who are its victims? What are its causes? How far does its stench spread? What forces are at work to counteract it?

Any corner in the congested sections of New York City's Bronx is fertile soil for mushroom "slave marts." The two where the traffic is heaviest and the bidding is highest are located at 167th street and Jerome avenue and at Simpson and Westchester avenues.

Symbolic of the more humane slave block is the Jerome avenue "market." There, on benches surrounding a green square, the victims wait, grateful, at least, for some place to sit. In direct contrast is the Simpson avenue "mart," where they pose wearily against buildings and lamp posts, or scuttle about in an attempt to retrieve discarded boxes upon which to rest.

Again, the Simpson avenue block exudes the stench of the slave market at its worst. Not only is human labor bartered and sold for slave wage, but human love also is a marketable commodity. But whether it is labor or love that is sold, economic necessity compels the sale. As early as 8 a.m. they come; as late as 1 p.m. they remain.

Rain or shine, cold or hot, you will find them there—Negro women, old and young— sometimes bedraggled, sometimes neatly dressed—but with the invariable paper bundle, waiting expectantly for Bronx housewives to buy their strength and energy for an hour, two hours, or even for a day at the munificent rate of fifteen, twenty, twenty-five, or, if luck be with them, thirty cents an hour. If not the wives themselves, maybe their husbands, their sons, or their brothers, under the subterfuge of work, offer worldly-wise girls higher bids for their time.

Who are these women? What brings them here? Why do they stay? In the boom days before the onslaught of the depression in 1929, many of these women who are now forced to bargain for day's work on street corners, were employed in grand homes in the rich Eighties, or in wealthier homes in Long Island and Westchester, at more than adequate wages. Some are former marginal industrial workers, forced by the slack in industry to seek other means of sustenance. In many instances there had been no necessity for work at all. But whatever their standing prior to the depression, none sought employment where they now seek it. They come to the Bronx, not because of what it promises, but largely in desperation.

Ella Baker was active in labor movements in Harlem and Marvel Cooke was a member of the staff of the *New York Amsterdam News.*

Originally published in *The Crisis* 42, no. 11 (1935): 330–31, 342. Copyright © 1935, The Crisis Publishing Co., Inc. The editors wish to thank The Crisis Publishing Co., Inc., the magazine of the National Association for the Advancement of Colored People, for authorizing the use of this work.

Paradoxically, the crash of 1929 brought to the domestic labor market a new employer class. The lower middle-class housewife, who, having dreamed of the luxury of a maid, found opportunity staring her in the face in the form of Negro women pressed to the wall by poverty, starvation and discrimination.

Where once color was the "gilt edged" security for obtaining domestic and personal service jobs, here, even, Negro women found themselves being displaced by whites. Hours of futile waiting in employment agencies, the fee that must be paid despite the lack of income, fraudulent agencies that sprung up during the depression, all forced the day worker to fend for herself or try the dubious and circuitous road to public relief.

As inadequate as emergency relief has been, it has proved somewhat of a boon to many of these women, for with its advent, actual starvation is no longer their ever-present slave driver and they have been able to demand twenty-five and even thirty cents an hour as against the old fifteen and twenty cent rate. In an effort to supplement the inadequate relief received, many seek this open market.

And what a market! She who is fortunate (?) enough to please Mrs. Simon Legree's scrutinizing eye is led away to perform hours of multifarious household drudgeries. Under a rigid watch, she is permitted to scrub floors on her bended knees, to hang precariously from window sills, cleaning window after window, or to strain and sweat over steaming tubs of heavy blankets, spreads and furniture covers.

Fortunate, indeed, is she who gets the full hourly rate promised. Often, her day's slavery is rewarded with a single dollar bill or whatever her unscrupulous employer pleases to pay. More often, the clock is set back for an hour or more. Too often she is sent away without any pay at all.

### HOW IT WORKS

We invaded the "market" early on the morning of September 14. Disreputable bags under arm and conscientiously forlorn, we trailed the work entourage on the West side "slave train," disembarking with it at Simpson and Westchester avenues. Taking up our stand outside the corner flower shop whose show window offered gardenias, roses and the season's first chrysanthemums at moderate prices, we waited patiently to be "bought."

We got results in almost nothing flat. A squatty Jewish housewife, patently lower middle class, approached us, carefully taking stock of our "wares."

"You girls want work?"

"Yes." We were expectantly noncommittal.

"How much you work for?"

We begged the question, noting that she was already convinced that we were not the "right sort." "How much do you pay?"

She was walking away from us. "I can't pay your price," she said and immediately started bargaining with a strong, seasoned girl leaning against the corner lamp post. After a few moments of animated conversation, she led the girl off with her. Curious, we followed them two short blocks to a dingy apartment house on a side street.

We returned to our post. We didn't seem to be very popular with the other "slaves". They eyed us suspiciously. But, one by one, as they became convinced that we were one with them, they warmed up to friendly sallies and answered our discreet questions about the possibilities of employment in the neighborhood.

Suddenly it began to rain, and we, with a dozen or so others, scurried to shelter under the five-and-ten doorway midway the block. Enforced close communion brought about further sympathy and conversation from the others. We asked the brawny, neatly dressed girl pressed close to us about the extent of trade in the "oldest profession" among women.

"Well," she said, "there is quite a bit of it up here. Most of 'those' girls congregate at the other corner." She indicated the location with a jerk of her head.

"Do they get much work?" we queried.

"Oh, quite a bit," she answered with a finality which was probably designed to close the conversation. But we were curious and asked her how the other girls felt about it. She looked at us a moment doubtfully, probably wondering if we weren't seeking advice to go into the "trade" ourselves.

"Well, that's their own business. If they can do it and get away with it, it's all right with the others." Or probably she would welcome some "work" of that kind herself.

"Sh-h-h." The wizened West Indian woman whom we had noticed, prior to the rain, patroling the street quite belligerently as if she were daring someone not to hire her, was cautioning us. She explained that if we kept up such a racket the store's manager would kick all of us out in the rain. And so we continued our conversation in whispered undertone.

"Gosh. I don't like this sort of thing at all." The slender brown girl whom we had seen turn down two jobs earlier in the morning, seemed anxious to talk. "This is my first time up here—and believe me, it is going to be my last. I don't like New York nohow. If I don't get a good job soon, I'm going back home to Kansas City." So she had enough money to travel, did she?

## CUT RATE COMPETITION

The rain stopped quite as suddenly as it started. We had decided to make a careful survey of the district to see whether or not there were any employment agencies in the section. Up one block and down another we tramped, but not one such institution did we encounter. Somehow the man who gave us a sly "Hello, babies" as he passed was strangely familiar. We realized two things about him—that he had been trailing us for some time and that he was manifestly, plain clothes notwithstanding, one of "New York's finest."

Trying to catch us to run us in for soliciting, was he? From that moment on, it was a three-cornered game. When we separated he was at sea. When we were together, he grinned and winked at us quite boldly. . . .

We sidled up to a friendly soul seated comfortably on an upturned soap-box. Soon an old couple approached her and offered a day's work with their daughter way up on Jerome avenue. They were not in agreement as to how much the daughter would pay— the old man said twenty-five cents an hour—the old lady scowled and said twenty. The car fare, they agreed, would be paid after she reached her destination. The friendly soul refused the job. She could afford independence, for she had already successfully bargained for a job for the following day. She said to us, after the couple started negotiations with another woman, that she wouldn't go way up on Jerome avenue on a wild goose chase for Mrs. Roosevelt, herself. We noted, with satisfaction, that the old couple had no luck with any of the five or six they contacted.

It struck us as singularly strange, since it was already 10:30, that the women still lingered, seemingly unabashed that they had not yet found employment for a day. We were debating whether or not we should leave the "mart" and try again another day, probably during the approaching Jewish holidays at which time business is particularly flourishing, when, suddenly, things looked up again. A new batch of "slaves" flowed down the elevated steps and took up their stands at advantageous points.

The friendly soul turned to us, a sneer marring the smooth roundness of her features. "Them's the girls who makes it bad for us. They get more jobs than us because they will work for anything. We runned them off the corner last week." One of the newcomers was quite near us and we couldn't help but overhear the following conversation with a neighborhood housewife.

"You looking for work?"

"Yes ma'am."

"How much you charge?"

"I'll take what you will give me." . . . What was this? Could the girl have needed work that badly? Probably. She did look run down at the heels. . . .

"All right. Come on. I'll give you a dollar." Cupidity drove beauty from the arrogant features. The woman literally dragged her "spoil" to her den. . . . But what of the girl? Could she possibly have known what she was letting herself in for? Did she know how long she would have to work for that dollar or what she would have to do? Did she know whether or not she would get lunch or car fare? Not any more than we did. Yet, there she was, trailing down the street behind her "mistress."

"You see," philosophized the friendly soul. "That's what makes it bad for the rest of us. We got to do something about those girls. Organize them or something." The friendly soul remained complacent on her up-turned box. Our guess was that if the girls were organized, the incentive would come from some place else.

Business in the "market" took on new life. Eight or ten girls made satisfactory contacts. Several women—and men approached us, but our price was too high or we refused to wash windows or scrub floors. We were beginning to have a rollicking good time when rain again dampened our heads and ardor. We again sought the friendly five-and-ten doorway.

### "FOR FIVE BUCKS A WEEK"

We became particularly friendly with a girl whose intelligent replies to our queries intrigued us. When we were finally convinced that there would be no more "slave" barter that day, we invited her to lunch with us at a near-by restaurant. After a little persuasion, there we were, Millie Jones between us, refreshing our spirits and appetites with hamburgers, fragrant with onions, and coffee. We found Millie an articulate person. It seems that, until recently, she had had a regular job in the neighborhood. But let her tell you about it.

"Did I have to work? And how! For five bucks and car fare a week. Mrs. Eisenstein had a six-room apartment lighted by fifteen windows. Each and every week, believe it or not, I had to wash every one of those windows. If that old hag found as much as the teeniest speck on any one of 'em, she'd make me do it over. I guess I would do anything rather than wash windows. On Mondays I washed and did as much of the ironing as I could. The rest waited over for Tuesday. There were two grown sons in the family and her husband. That meant that I would have at least twenty-one shirts to do every week. Yeah, and ten sheets and at least two blankets, besides. They all had to be done just so, too. Gosh, she was a particular woman.

"There wasn't a week, either, that I didn't have to wash up every floor in the place and wax it on my hands and knees. And two or three times a week I'd have to beat the mattresses and take all the furniture covers off and shake 'em out. Why, when I finally went home nights, I could hardly move. One of the sons had "hand trouble" too, and I was just as tired fighting him off, I guess, as I was with the work.

"Say, did you ever wash dishes for an Orthodox Jewish family?" Millie took a long, sibilant breath. "Well, you've never really washed dishes, then. You know, they use a different dishcloth for everything they cook. For instance, they have one for 'milk' pots in which dairy dishes are cooked, another for glasses, another for vegetable pots, another for meat pots, and so on. My memory wasn't very good and I was always getting the darn things mixed up. I used to make Mrs. Eisenstein just as mad. But I was the one who suffered. She would get other cloths and make me do the dishes all over again.

"How did I happen to leave her? Well, after I had been working about five weeks, I asked for a Sunday off. My boy friend from Washington was coming up on an excursion to spend the day with me. She told me if I didn't come in on Sunday, I needn't come back at all. Well, I didn't go back. Ever since then I have been trying to find a job. The employment agencies are no good. All the white girls get the good jobs.

"My cousin told me about up here. The other day I didn't have a cent in my pocket and I just had to find work in order to get back home and so I took the first thing that turned up. I went to work about 11 o'clock and I stayed until 5:00—washing windows, scrubbing floors and washing out stinking baby things. I was surprised when she gave me lunch. You know, some of 'em don't even do that. What I got through, she gave me thirty-five cents. Said she took a quarter out for lunch. Figure it out for yourself. Ten cents an hour!

### MINIATURE ECONOMIC BATTLEFRONT

The real significance of the Bronx Slave Market lies not in a factual, presentation of its activities; but in focusing attention upon its involved implications. The "mart" is but a miniature mirror of our economic battle front.

To many, the women who sell their labor thus cheaply have but themselves to blame. A head of a leading employment agency bemoans the fact that these women have not "chosen the decent course" and declares: "The well-meaning employment agencies endeavoring to obtain respectable salaries and suitable working conditions for deserving domestics are finding it increasingly difficult due to the menace and obstacles presented by the slavish performances of the lower types of domestics themselves, who, unlike the original slaves who recoiled from meeting their masters, rush to meet their mistresses."

The exploiters, judged from the districts where this abominable traffic flourishes, are the wives and mothers of artisans and tradesmen who militantly battle against being exploited themselves, but who apparently have no scruples against exploiting others.

The general public, though aroused by stories of these domestics, too often think of the problems of these women as something separate and apart and readily dismisses them with a sigh and a shrug of the shoulders.

The women, themselves present a study in contradictions. Largely unaware of their organized power, yet ready to band together for some immediate and personal gain either consciously or unconsciously, they still cling to that American illusion that any one who is determined and persistent can get ahead.

The roots, then of the Bronx Slave Market spring from: (1) the general ignorance of and apathy towards organized labor action; (2) the artificial barriers that separate the interest of the relief administrators and investigators from that of their "case loads," the white collar and professional worker from the laborer and the domestic; and (3) organized labor's limited concept of exploitation, which permits it to fight vigorously to secure itself against evil, yet passively or actively aids and abets the ruthless destruction of Negroes.

To abolish the market once and for all, these roots must be torn away from their sustaining soil. Certain palliative and corrective measures are not without benefit. Already the seeds of discontent are being sown.

The Women's Day Workers and Industrial League, organized sixteen years ago by Fannie Austin, has been, and still is, a force to abolish the existing evils in day labor. Legitimate employment agencies have banded together to curb the activities of the racketeer agencies and are demanding fixed minimum and maximum wages for all workers sent out. Articles and editorials recently carried by the New York Negro press have focused attention on the existing evils in the "slave market."

An embryonic labor union now exists in the Simpson avenue "mart." Girls who persist in working for less than thirty cents an hour have been literally run off the corner. For the recent Jewish holiday, habitues of the "mart" actually demanded and refused to work for less than thirty-five cents an hour.

# David H. Edwards to James Weldon Johnson, January 13, 1926 (excerpts)

Dear Sir:

The Norfolk Branch has launched a drive to raise a local defense fund of $500.00 which said fund is to be used in an effort to secure our political and civil rights in this community. A meeting was held Sunday January 10th, at the Second Calvary Baptist Church this City, at which meeting we were fortunate enough to collect $106.00 in cash and about $100.00 in pledges. . . .

In holding these mass meetings we have endeavored to grasp opportunity by the forelock. About ten days ago Leroy Strother, a child 11 years old was wantonly murdered by one Banks, a Hebrew merchant who conducts a grocery store in a colored community. Evidence has been adduced which shows that Leroy had been employed by Banks to put away a load of wood; having completed his job the child asked for his pay, Banks offered him $0.05 and Leroy retorted that "this is not what you promised," and it was then that Banks reached under the counter for his gun and fired a bullet in Leroy's head which scattered his brains on the floor. Leroy's mother is a poor woman without sufficient means to protect her interest.

This is not the first time that colored men and boys have been shot down in this City without just cause and to my knowledge this is the third child under 13 years of age that has been killed by jews within the last ten months. Now the colored citizens of Norfolk are up in arms over this unlawful practice on the part of the people of the other race who have heretofore been committing these acts without paying the penalty therefor.

We are endeavoring to raise this legal defense fund for three purposes at least.

First, we want to aid in the prosecution of this case to see that the machinery of law is properly used in all of it's ramifications and that this Hebrew if guilty pay the penalty for the commission of this crime, and if he is innocent he must prove it; But we are looking forward into the future in using this money in that we intend using it in the prosecution of this case to show to the people of the white race that they cannot take the life of a negro without just cause and get by with it without militant opposition.

Secondly, we are making plans to fight the segregation law that has been enacted by the City Council here, the said segregation law being almost identical to the Louisville ordinance which was declared unconstitutional by the Supreme Court of the United States.

In 1926 David H. Edwards was an attorney in Norfolk, Virginia. James Weldon Johnson was secretary of the NAACP.
NAACP Papers, Box I G 208, Manuscript Division, Library of Congress, Washington, D.C.

Last but not least, we hope through this campaign to acquaint the masses with the principles and purposes of this our great organization. . . .

Yours for success,
Norfolk Branch N. A. A. C. P.
By David H. Edwards
President

# Walter White to Charles H. Houston, December 5, 1938 (excerpt)

Dear Charlie:

... I, frankly, confess that I am getting a little sick of some Jews yelling anti-Semitism when Negroes make protest against discrimination by Jews against Negroes. But we have got to remain true to our principles of opposing discrimination on the basis of race, creed or color.

Ever sincerely,
Walter
Secretary

In 1938 Walter White was secretary of the NAACP.
Charles H. Houston was special counsel to the NAACP.
NAACP Papers, Box I C 208, Manuscript Division, Library of Congress, Washington, D.C.

# J. L. LeFlore to Berney L. Strauss, October 12, 1938

Dear Sir:

We are keenly disappointed in your recent expressions regarding the providing of rest room and comfort facilities for colored women and children who shop in your store, as reported by our committee which conferred with you during the past week.

The attitude which the Hammel management now shows is obviously contrary to the spirit of your letter of July 19 to us, and a letter upon the same subject to Rev. J. Pulford (white) under date of August 29. The phraseology of the letters and your remarks to our Mr. Napoleon Rivers several weeks ago clearly indicated your sincerity in desiring to provide the facilities to which your many colored customers are entitled. It was, therefore, shocking to learn from our committee that you bluntly stated it was not a custom of department stores in the South to have comfort facilities for colored shoppers. Even if such were true in many instances it certainly cannot justify an identical attitude by the L. Hammel store. Two wrongs cannot make right. Further, the L. Hammel store enjoys a more lucrative colored patronage than the average department store. And to view the matter strictly from a business angle, it is logical to conclude that hundreds of additional colored customers would be attracted to your store if comfort facilities were provided.

Anti-Semitic waves of oppression are spreading extensively in other parts of the world. We have been sympathetic toward the Jewish people in their struggles to combat such intolerance and bigotry. Thousands of thoughtful colored people throughout the United States have contributed to efforts aimed to alleviate the plight of Jewry.

We are bewildered that a member of one oppressed group, because of favorable geographical and other conditions, would be unsympathetic and recalcitrant in regard to the rights of another persecuted minority.

In view of the fact that the colored people of the community requested by resolution and petition the necessary comfort facilities which we sought to have you provide, we are bound by principle to advise them of your decision in the matter. Therefore, beginning next Sunday, October 16, we shall issue circular letters and leaflets, and send committees to the various public gatherings, including church and fraternal, to let the people know of the attitude of the Hammel management toward a just plea made in behalf of hundreds of colored women shoppers and their children.

We shall not attempt to predict the reaction of other colored people to the facts, when

In 1938, J. L. LeFlore was secretary of the Mobile, Alabama, branch of the NAACP. Berney L. Strauss was president of L. Hammel Dry Goods Company, Mobile.

NAACP Papers, Box I G 5, Manuscript Division, Library of Congress, Washington, D.C.

they become generally known. However, I can personally state frankly and without hesitation that members of my household shall make no further purchases in the Hammel store under existing deplorable conditions denying comfort facilities to colored women and little children.

Very truly yours,
J. L. LeFlore
Secretary

# Anti-Semitic Drive in Harlem

On October 16, three Negroes were sentenced to the work-house by Magistrate Thomas Aurelio for stirring up racial hatred in Harlem. The arrest of these three Negroes marks the climax of an intensive anti-Semitic campaign which has been going full blast in Harlem for the past few months. The huge, compact colored community of Harlem, consisting of over a million souls, is a happy hunting-ground for cultists and agitators of all kinds, and it was inevitable that Nazi propagandists should get to work behind Negro "Front" organizations. One gets a slight notion of the fascist eagerness to incite the Negro population of the United States from the fact that Ezra Pound, broadcasting from Italy on September 23, found it worth while to direct himself specifically to American Negroes, urging them not to obey that "white man Jew Roosevelt." It is safe to assume that by the time the Axis is indulging in trans-Atlantic appeals, it is obviously doing some substantial spade-work nearer home to its objectives. Consequently, it is no coincidence that there have arisen in Harlem groups like the African Patriotic League, The Ethiopian Pacifist League, the Christian Peace Committee, an affiliate of the Christian Front, and similar organizations under whose auspices speakers hand out the familiar Nazi line about the "Jews' war" and the Jews.

Numerous street-corner meetings have been held this fall along Seventh Avenue, at which Negro rabbler-rousers have declaimed against the "greasy Jews who take the bread out of our mouths" and who want "our boys" to get killed for "them." It is superfluous to point out with what exactness the Nazi propaganda pattern is being followed in this campaign. Progressive Negro organizations are making valiant efforts to expose the true affiliations of these dupes or stooges who on occasion have gone so far as to announce that Hitler offered a satisfactory solution of the Negro problem. However, despite its patent absurdity, it would be idle to minimize the potential menace of fascist agitation among the colored population of the United States. The twelve million American Negroes represent a large stake for any element anxious to exploit them as a disruptive or dissident factor in a time of stress. If their votes, and sympathies, can be captured by pro-fascist, appeasement groups, they represent a considerable haul. Unfortunately, no matter how ludicrous this may appear on the surface, the fascist demagogue has a formidable array of talking-points when he invades Harlem. He has deep wrongs and honest grievances on which to harp. These are his opportunity.

Marie Syrkin was editor of the *Jewish Frontier*.
Originally published in *Congress Weekly* 8, no. 35 (1941): 6–8. Copyright © 1941 American Jewish Congress. Reprinted with permission from *Congress Weekly*.

Though no intelligent Negro has any illusions as to what a Nazi victory would mean to any non-Aryan, it is all too easy to make out a case for "peace" and "isolation" on a Harlem street-corner. Till their most recent change of heart, the Communists had ploughed the ground consistently for two years. And even if the Communists had proven remiss, no Negro requires outside intervention to discover that in a large part of the United States he is disenfranchised and maltreated; and that at best, in the North, he is the object of fierce economic and social discrimination. The line of reasoning becomes fallaciously simple: why fight for democracy abroad when there is so little of the genuine article at home? Why get excited about Nazi persecutions when Negroes get lynched in the South? These inescapable questions—rich material for the propagandist—are bound to strike a responsive chord.

The outbreak of the war found a wholly intelligible apathy among many Negroes. The white men were slaughtering each other but did a Hitler triumph in Europe really matter much to the Negro race? Did it make a real difference to the Negro if he were oppressed by the Belgians in the Congo, the French in the Sudan and Senegal, the British in Africa or the West Indies, or the Nazis? So widespread was this spirit that *Crisis,* a leading Negro journal, found it advisable to editorialize on this subject, and point out what faced the Negro people in the event of a Nazi conquest. However, despite the attempts of liberal Negro organizations and journals to emphasize the peril of the isolationist position to the black as well as to the white American, the course of recent events did not make this task easy. The stories about the maltreatment of Negro draftees in Southern camps; the discrimination against Negro workers in some defense industries; the bars against Negro aviators—all these factors militated against a wholehearted zeal for the cause of the democracies. The Administration is well aware of these grievances and has been taking steps to remedy these injustices, but the rancor engendered cannot vanish overnight.

Since the Communists have abandoned their "peace" platform, room has been made for the fascist "peace" enthusiast. For this reason the last few months have seen a well-organized fascist-inspired, appeasement campaign in Harlem. That anti-Semitism should be the foremost device of this campaign goes without saying.

One would like to believe that a persecuted people, itself the victim of the maddest racial bigotry, would be immune to appeals to race-hatred which single out another minority group for victimization. But that's not the way it works. Misery likes company. Besides, who could blame a Negro if he were not averse to the notion of relinquishing his pariah status to another group. Let somebody else be the underdog for a change! Such sentiments may be neither general or conscious, but they would be all too understandable if they existed. Furthermore, there is a perfectly legitimate resentment among Negroes at the horror which anti-Jewish persecution arouses among circles which accept Jim Crowism as a matter of fact. For instance, during the recent investigation of race prejudice in Lincoln Hospital, Negroes asked why the City Council of New York had not seen fit to probe into the exclusion of Negro physicians from city hospital staffs. Besides, one does not have to delve into the complexities of the human psyche to discover why anti-Semitism should be able to make headway in Harlem just as it does in other sections of the country. There are purely objective factors in this congested, impoverished community which explain why the hate-monger can ply his trade with profit.

To begin with, a large number of the shops and stores in Harlem are owned by Jews. The small shopkeeper may be struggling to keep body and soul together, but he is the symbol of "property" to his poverty-stricken customer who generally buys on credit. The extensive installment business in Harlem contains a good many Jews. That means that the sorry labor of collecting a few dollars a month for an article of clothing or furniture falls to Jewish hands. Though the wretched, over-crowded houses are owned for the most part by Gentile real estate corporations, the renting agents are frequently Jews. Again that means that it is a Jew who duns the poor tenant for his excessive rent. One can hardly expect the tenant to make delicate distinctions between agent and owner. He reserves his resentment for the man who appears monthly at the door demanding cash or threatening dispossessal.

Another sore point has been the existence of the notorious "slave-markets" of the Bronx, where housewives would engage domestic workers on street corners or park benches. Frequently the pay offered was shamefully low, and the Negro woman who worked for twenty cents an hour during the depression bore her employer no subsequent good will. LaGuardia's establishment of employment stations, as well as the rise in employment opportunities, has remedied this evil. But the resentment at exploitation by some Jewish women has had unfortunate after-effects. The fact that the great majority of Jewish women are as fair and considerate as any other group of employers has not prevented the formulation of unjust generalizations.

The attempt to link up Harlem economic grievances with anti-Semitic activities is not new. As far back as 1934 there was considerable agitation led by Sufi Abdul Hamid, dubbed the "black Hitler." He organized the picketing of Harlem stores in protest against the exclusive employment of white help in stores patronized by Negroes. "Don't buy where you can't work!" was his rallying cry. Though he and his followers denied the charge of anti-Semitism, claiming that they made no distinction between one white exploiter and another, the concensus of the evidence indicates that the Sufi's campaign stressed Jewish ownership quite as much as white.

The race riots which took place in Harlem in March, 1935, and which culminated in the wholesale raiding and looting of stores, were supposed to have had an anti-Semitic tinge. However, the Mayor's Committee which investigated these disturbances stated in its official report that "it was at one time alleged that most of the stores which were raided were owned by Jews. We are glad to report that there seems to be no foundation for the statement." The Committee apparently found grounds for optimism in the fact that stores were looted indiscriminately, and that the preponderance of Jewish shops gave the raiding an anti-Semitic aspect. In this connection, it is interesting to note that a survey of white grocery stores in Harlem showed 241 to be owned by Jews and 151 by Greeks, but the Greeks are taken for Jews by the Negroes (according to Claude McKay) so that all these grocery stores are viewed as Jewish by the Harlem public.

In view of the poverty of the community, anyone who has the economic role of "middle-man," who appears as owner or creditor, no matter how insignificant his own income may be, is bound to arouse antagonism. It is, therefore, easy enough to understand how reactionary elements of every description seek to make capital out of the Negro's underprivileged position and try to deflect his resentment into channels politically profitable to themselves. In the past, anti-labor forces consistently sought to exploit the Negro worker's sense of injury at the discriminatory practices of white unions by using him as scab labor. Everybody knows how Ford made a policy of employing Negro workers as a means of combating the unionization drive in his plants. In the same way, at the present time, when it is to the interest of pro-fascist elements to sow dissension and to strengthen the isolationist bloc by every device, the large Negro sector of the American people is not being overlooked. The classic technique of making the Jew the scape-goat for the Negroes' economic ills as well as "the Jews' war," in which the Negro is asked to shed his blood, is being utilized to the full.

The problem is by no means purely a Jewish one. This anti-Semitic agitation differs from previous outbursts in that it has powerful hidden backing for a purpose of national scope. It is therefore of concern to everyone anxious about the infiltration of the fascist poison into any part of the American organism. Such measures as the arrest of anti-Semitic agitators are essential curbs. Some of the more inflammatory and openly seditious spell-binders will be muzzled by the fear of police intervention. But it must be remembered that arrests can be made only when there has been a flagrant violation of the law. Much vicious and dangerous propaganda will not fall under the provisions of the ordinance forbidding the incitement of racial hatred. Most important of all, even though the presence of police may succeed in modifying the character of some of the utterances, the problem of anti-Semitic, fascist agitation in Harlem cannot be met in this way alone. Ways must be found to solve the more fundamental grievances.

One step in the right direction was taken when the Greater New York Coordinating Committee together with Harlem Chamber of Commerce formulated a trade pact according to which one third of the white collar jobs in Harlem were to go to Negroes. Though the working out of the pact has aroused criticism for failures in the actual implementation of the terms, it is nevertheless an indication of what may be achieved. The whole complex question must be faced squarely by the Harlem Merchants' Association and other groups involved in the economic structure of Harlem.

In a large sense, the situation calls for an educational campaign which should enlist every liberal group, Negro and white, that understands the significance of fascism's traditional entering wedge. The corollaries of street-corner meetings in Harlem will be reflected in attitudes taken towards every major issue facing the United States today. Harlem has known the revolutionary slogan of "Peace, it's an imperialist war" of the Communists. It still listens to the amiable hosannahs of "Peace, it's wonderful" of Father Divine. It now hears the tomtoms of "Peace, it's a Jews' war" of the fascists. The dark beat must be met with light.

# Black-Jewish Relations in Wartime Detroit
## The Marsh, Loving, Wolf Surveys and the Race Riot of 1943

While much has been written about the Detroit, Michigan race riot of 1943, scholars and contemporaries have disagreed over black-Jewish relations during the worst hostile outburst of the Second World War.[1] Most of them have recognized the disorder as an important shift from earlier white-initiated pogroms against blacks to more recent black assaults against symbols of white authority, thereby identifying two "more or less independent" phases of upheaval: interracial combat on Belle Isle and along Woodward Avenue; black looting on Hastings Street in Paradise Valley.[2] Some have explained each phase in narrow racial terms, while others have seen more than black-white antagonisms, particularly among supposedly antisemitic looters.[3] Only Donald C. Marsh, however, associate professor of sociology at Wayne University, based his interpretation on surveys of black-Jewish attitudes in the Hastings Street area. His pre- and post-riot studies provided insight into the disorder's looting phase and the larger issue of black-Jewish relations. Little used after the disturbance and little known today, Marsh's work set a precedent and posited expositions of lasting influence. Both his inquiries and the riot deserve reexamination.

Clearly, wholesale destruction and looting of predominantly Jewish-owned stores grew out of intergroup conflicts. Indeed, the history of blacks and Jews in Detroit intersected often.[4] Ten years before the Civil War both minorities were small, yet sizable enough to support their most important institutions, their houses of worship. By 1860, 1,402 blacks and 400 Jews, mostly German, had settled in the city of 45,619 inhabitants. They supported the Union cause enthusiastically, only to be victimized by riots and, in the case of Jewish Detroiters, charges of disloyalty. After the war, racism and antisemitism diminished, enabling elite blacks and Jews maneuverability within specified economic and political arenas as their increasingly numerous brethren solidified near eastside neighborhoods.

By the turn of the century, 4,111 blacks and 10,300 Jews lived in Detroit, respectively accounting for 1.4 and 3.6 per cent of the total population.[5] While few southern blacks were among these numbers, however, Russian Jews already outnumbered their German counterparts.[6] Unlike most ethnic groups who expanded toward "previously undeveloped areas of the city," they remained in clusters near downtown: Russian Jews concentrated along industrial and commercial streets like Gratiot and Hastings; blacks resided

In 1979, Dominic J. Capeci Jr. was associate professor of history at Southwest Missouri State University, Springfield.
Originally published in *Jewish Social Studies* 47, nos. 3–4 (1985): 221–42. Copyright © 1985 by the editors of *Jewish Social Studies*. Reprinted with the permission of Indiana University Press.

among them and other nationalities. Many of both races rented dilapidated quarters from absentee landlords, yet some Jewish occupants lived in "small, newly built tenement houses." Hence Russian Jews came closest of all eastsiders "to living in ghetto conditions," albeit conditions tempered significantly by recent housing investments and single family housing patterns. Religious orthodoxy among Russian Jews and racial antagonism against blacks—particularly as black numbers grew—promoted ghetto living and the highest ratio of endogamy of all Detroiters.

Between 1900 and 1920, demographic changes affected both groups, their interaction and their relations with larger society. Largely because of the influx of Russian Jews and, especially after 1915, southern blacks, the aggregate Jewish and black populations in 1920 respectively registered 51,400 and 40,838 persons or 5.2 and 4.1 per cent of all Detroit inhabitants. Migrants, however, differed in significant ways from their already established brethren. Initially, German Jews and longstanding black residents, themselves more educated, more prosperous, more secular and more urbanized than the newcomers, sympathized with their plights yet feared their behavior.[7] Specifically, they sought societal acceptance by keeping low profiles and playing down the very ethnocentrism, poverty and, in the base of blacks, peasantry that characterized recent arrivals. Moreover, Germans of Reformed Judaism and black urbanites, particularly among the middle class who advocated equal opportunity and inclusion disagreed with inward-looking, identity-conscious Orthodox Russian Jews and southern black sharecroppers. Eventually most members of each minority accommodated class and cultural differences, established community newspapers and self-help organizations—such as the *Jewish American* (1901) and the Detroit Urban League (1916)—and closed ranks in the face of escalating antisemitism and racism.

Blacks lagged behind Jews in this process, their exodus from the South beginning in earnest during the Great War. Although both groups had established eastside ports of entry in the previous century, increasingly affluent German Jews moved north toward Grand Boulevard while their incoming Russian counterparts lined Hastings Street between Elizabeth and Brewster.[8] Here, in "Little Jerusalem," hundreds of shops and stalls emerged, as poor immigrants served themselves and preserved their orthodoxy. While black newcomers entered the eastside in crushing numbers, expanding and consolidating their ghetto, Russian Jews had already begun to follow their German brethren across Grand Boulevard into the Oakland District (which became an area of first settlement for many); upwardly mobile Jews, most notably among the Germans, also moved west across Woodward into the Dexter-Twelfth Street area. Before these population shifts had been completed in the early 1920s, blacks and Jews shared the heart of the eastside, specifically the three square miles bounded by Hastings, Adelaide, Rivard and Livingston.[9]

Also during the 1920s some prosperous blacks left the eastside, creating westside and Eight Mile Road communities. In the former area—from Grand River to Dearborn, between Warren and Tireman—they came in contact with Jewish merchants along West Warren. Both minorities grew during the Great Depression, blacks numbering 149,119 or 9.2 per cent of the population in 1940, Jews comprising 81,400 or 5.0 per cent. Besides having lost numerical ground to blacks sometime in the 1920s, the Jewish population had begun leveling off—even dipping somewhat during the next decade—doubtlessly owing to political and economic upheavals at home and abroad. On the eve of the Second World War, then, both groups had created more or less homogeneous communities despite internal class and cultural distinctions, while other ethnics segmented along socioeconomic lines; both groups, though blacks much more than Jews, had endured more xenophobia than did other newcomers.[10] Indeed, between the world wars they endured constant repression: Red Scare fears of Russian Jewish communists; "loosely organized" anti-black terrorism; prospects of a Ku Klux Klan mayoralty; and Charles F. Coughlin's, Henry Ford's and Gerald L. K. Smith's antisemitic, race-baiting propaganda.

Despite similar sagas, black and Jewish experiences differed in important ways and fostered bittersweet relations. Antebellum rural slavery, southern segregation and northern racism hindered the urbanization of black newcomers, the greatest majority of whom came from Dixie. Beginning in 1915, they arrived in multitudes, established extended families, took in boarders, suffered low birth rates and rented inadequate, congested lodgings.[11] Their extended families—those very important survival mechanisms in bondage and freedom—enabled large numbers of kin to support one another, share meager resources and subsist but not prosper in harsh environments. Their boarders contributed to the payment of exhorbitant rents but left little if anything for other expenses or savings. Their unsanitary, overcrowded quarters and low wages fostered poor health and sterility-causing tuberculosis, insufficient medical care, and high infant mortality rates. Southern immigrants facing these difficulties found buying a home nearly impossible and turned inward and developed their own institutions, instead of reaching outward as did earlier black and later ethnic elites. Small wonder some of them—most probably before 1920—chose alley life as "a transitional point in the journey from the plantation to the massive ghetto" and numerous others, having been largely denied the right to acquire property in the past, stressed jobs over housing.[12]

Although persecuted, Russian Jews came from an urban tradition which eased their industrial transition. They nurtured nuclear families, housed few relatives or strangers, enjoyed high fertility rates and bought homes (though not on the scale of Italian and Polish agriculturalists, who associated status with landowning).[13] Their nuclear families and higher birthrates provided greater potential for additional income (from working children) which, in turn, promoted homeownership. Before 1920, Russian Jews accommodated boarders and experienced high population density, but never as great as that of black Detroit. No doubt, their religious orthodoxy and urban background contributed to building viable institutions and formal organizations that further facilitated their adjustment to big city life.

Ultimately, black-Jewish conflict grew out of these socioenvironmental differences and, perhaps more pointedly, the economic distinctions associated with them. Partly because of their rural experience but largely owing to racism, blacks held disproportionately large numbers of unskilled service jobs and disproportionately few white-collar positions, the reverse of Jewish Detroiters.[14] They also depended on whites for work, as more and more Jews enjoyed self-employment.[15] Essentially, Old World antisemitism relegated Jews to crafts and commerce, while Judaic observations of "the

Sabbath, daily prayers, and dietary laws" encouraged independent livelihoods. Small commercial ventures and, primarily, religious orthodoxy advanced education and a rigorous intellectual heritage among Jews, thereby reinforcing their entrepreneurship, self-employment and, by extension, white-collar vocations. In contrast, slavery denied and racism prevented high levels of literacy, formal education and scholarship among most black newcomers, who appeared culturally, economically and educationally impoverished to some Russian Jews. Both minorities entered a hostile Detroit, but black newcomers came less well equipped for an urban society.

As blacks followed and supplanted Jews in the eastside and encountered some of them in the westside, they never controlled the living quarters and shops of those communities which remained in the hands of Jewish landlords and merchants. Moreover, blacks suffered economic hardship, while Jews enjoyed economic success. In the Depression, for example, blacks comprised overwhelming percentages of the unemployed, while Jews recorded less unemployment than the average for all workers.[16] Most working blacks toiled for meager wages as domestics and unskilled laborers at a time when most Jews made as much or more than other Detroit workers, as professionals, proprietors and clerks. Such resulted from historical legacies which channeled blacks and Jews into disparate economic directions: ultimately most blacks endured an American nightmare; many Jews experienced the American Dream. Had Jews been relegated to economic marginality, had they competed en masse with larger society for industrial jobs, they, too, would have confronted more serious opposition. Certainly, elder Jews remembered being refused work in automobile factories before World War I and younger Jews, who entered the industry in greater numbers than their forebears, experienced antisemitic incidents.[17]

Hence black-Jewish views of one another emanated from their ghetto interaction and minority status, which promoted mixed reactions. By 1943, blacks viewed Jews ambivalently, seeing some as oppressors and others as philanthropists.[18] Many blacks came into economic contact with Jewish landlords, merchants and employers, symbols of white society, superior status and, in some cases, blatant exploitation.[19] Subordinate-dominant relationships would have generated tension irrespective of the groups involved or their perceptions of fairness, but blacks aware of one or two well-known Jewish proprietors who overcharged for cheap goods or slum dwellings exacerbated the conflict. Shopkeepers, their employees and, occasionally, Jobs-for-Negroes advocates who haggled over wages, working conditions and union affiliation also increased tension. Unwittingly, however, so did the Booker T. Washington Trade Association, the Renters Protective Association and some black clerics who "pushed self-help" late in the 1930s.[20] Antisemitic, anti-democratic propaganda entered the black community via black nationalists, Nazi sympathizers and Klan members during the same period, a time when antisemitism rose nationally. Small wonder that black-Jewish conflict flared between 1938 and 1941, especially along Hastings Street where youths assaulted merchants and their stores.

Nevertheless, many blacks also perceived Jews as their allies. Prominent Jewish Detroiters had supported the Urban League, genuinely but paternalistically concerned more with improving the welfare of blacks than raising their status.[21] In response to the

Hastings Street altercation, however, shopkeepers formed the East Side Merchants Association. Following the lead of the executive secretary, Samuel J. Lieberman, they became involved in community affairs, providing Christmas baskets for the needy, sponsoring brotherhood dinners at the Lucy Thurman YWCA, and donating money to several civic causes.[22] Doubtlessly most impressive to blacks was their cooperation with eastside organizations such as the NAACP, the Ys and, especially, the Sojourner Truth Citizens Committee. Created in early 1942 by several community leaders for the purpose of securing the occupancy of 200 federally-built units for black defense workers, the committee drew local and national attention before successfully placing families in the Sojourner Truth Homes.[23] Throughout the four-month struggle against Polish home owners, selfish realty interests and vacillating government officials, Lieberman and fellow merchants helped underwrite—in a considerable way—the committee's numerous expenses. Their steadfast support for delegations to Washington, D.C., publication of the *Sojourner Truth Daily News*, and court costs of blacks arrested in the controversy-related disorder drew the praise of black leaders.

Perhaps because these efforts could neither eradicate years of convention nor alter unequal customer-merchant relationships, black-Jewish antagonisms continued to surface. Within two months of the Sojourner Truth Homes victory, police reserves entered Hastings Street to quell altercations between patrons and shopkeepers.[24] These and later disturbances no doubt reflected the impact of war on the lives of ghetto residents, who experienced rising and—in comparison to white areas—higher prices, increased immigration and overcrowding, and discrimination in defense employment; they might have also sensed the national upswing in antisemitism.[25] Experiencing "personal dissatisfaction and unpleasant contact" with proprietors and landlords, their traditional and war-induced frustrations focused on the most obvious white presence among them: Jewish businessmen.[26] Black antisemitism in this context exhibited as much anti-white as anti-Jewish feeling.

Thus when eastside blacks heard of the interracial fighting at Belle Isle on 20 June 1943, they demolished Hastings Street. Rioters twisted gates and smashed windows, turning whole blocks of stores into open-air markets.[27] Still, they left intact "colored and friendly white business places." Looting occurred later, as an afterthought, reflecting greed, resentment and vengeance for past grievances—real or imagined. Taverns, pawn shops, drug, clothing, grocery and liquor stores were looted, as multitudes absconded with everything from guns to sides of beef to Reserve Port Wine; some looters acted beserk, destroying property wholesale, while others "leisurely chose their supplies." Both rioters and looters operated openly, sometimes in "crudely organized gangs" and, in some cases, with police connivance.

In the wake of this wanton destruction, several observers noted its allegedly antisemitic nature. Black reporter, John R. Williams, said rioters attacked only Jewish stores in Paradise Valley's three-mile corridor, while rival journalist, John Wood, contended they did so systematically and with "a passion seldom witnessed" even in southern riots against blacks.[28] White newsman Philip A. Adler, concurred, adding that Gerald L. K. Smith and others had played on antisemitism in earlier efforts to recruit blacks to the

America First Committee.[29] Smith himself, along with some federal investigators, considered the looting of Hasting Street an anti-Jewish act.[30]

It might have been, but these observers disagreed over the character of Jewish merchants and the conspiratorial dimension of looters. Their positions on these points revealed as much about personal prejudices as about the dynamics of riot. Jews were not in sympathy with white mobsters and blacks knew this, said John Wood. In fact, elaborated another eye witness, Jewish merchants treated ghetto customers well.[31] Gerald L. K. Smith countered that shopkeepers were perceived by eastsiders as gougers, while a special assistant to the attorney general reported that those operating pawn shops and liquor stores systematically fleeced patrons.[32] Smith went further, stating that the riot simply accelerated black plans to loot Jewish stores "on the night of the first surprise blackout." Since rioters spared black property, his theory of subversion drew investigation by the Federal Bureau of Investigation. Certainly "Colored" signs filled the windows of numerous shops, but the Bureau determined that they occurred after the riot began spontaneously.[33]

In the face of conflicting evidence and heated emotions, controversy remained. Even Gerald L. K. Smith admitted that, in the case of black perceptions of Jewish business practices, only "a thorough survey" would reveal the truth. Little did he know that one such study had been done prior to the upheaval and another was underway shortly after its end. Issac Franck of the Jewish Community Center and Dr. James J. McClendon of the Detroit NAACP "gave birth" to these investigations during the fall of 1942 and the summer of 1943.[34] Concerned over black-Jewish conflict, they provided the Graduate School of Wayne University with grants to measure customer-merchant attitudes in the black community.

Responsibility for the surveys fell to Donald C. Marsh. Born on a farm forty miles north of Chicago, Illinois, he attended a one-room school house for seven years.[35] Later he graduated from Orrington Public School in Evanston where he felt "very much an out-grouper" among much wealthier classmates and speculated that such might have sparked his interest in sociology. Continuing his education, he earned a bachelor's degree and a master's degree at Northwestern University. Marsh then began doctoral studies at the University of Michigan under Charles Horton Cooley, best known for challenging the genetic interpretation of social phenomena.

Marsh was very much influenced by his mentor, who also came from the rural midwest.[36] Both embraced Jefferson's democratic faith, James's pragmatism and their own generation's response to the ills of industrialization; both rejected Spencer's survival of the fittest theory and similar "particularistic panaceas." Essentially Cooley interpreted society as organic, capable of progressing from a closed caste to an open class system: one of democracy, opportunity and reform. He believed individualism and communication would break down caste, promote consciousness and lessen conflict.

While Marsh shared Cooley's sociological viewpoint, he was more sympathetic to minorities, more active in reform and more predisposed to statistical methodology. Unlike Cooley, who derived his thesis from clues in classical literature rather than scientific inquiry, Marsh adopted an anthropological-participatory approach grounded in quantification.[37] He combined his mentor's sociopsychological perspective with advancements in measurement, drawing together Cooley's concepts of personal and spatial knowledge.[38]

Both sociological lessons came together during the summer of 1926, when Marsh served as assistant survey director for the Mayor's Committee on Race Relations in Detroit. Created in response to the Ossien Sweet housing incident, the committee brought Marsh under the direction of social worker, Forrester B. Washington.[39] Their efforts, underwritten for $10,000 by the Detroit Community Fund, dispelled the notion that black migration lowered property values; their socioeconomic findings, recorded in ten mimeographed volumes as *The Negro in Detroit*, gathered dust. Yet the experience was not lost on Marsh. It reinforced the best of Cooley's lessons, while improving his own survey techniques and exposing him to the plight of black Detroiters. It also prompted him to introduce a course on race relations—one of the first in the nation—at the University of Kansas, where he taught for the next five years.

In 1931, Marsh returned to Michigan to work on his dissertation. Meanwhile Cooley had died, so Marsh began the study of Detroit's central business district under Roderick McKenzie's direction and accepted a position at the City College of Detroit (which became Wayne College and, much later, Wayne State University). McKenzie, himself, soon passed away, leaving Marsh without an advisor. Thereafter, Marsh concentrated on teaching courses in urban, race and ethnic relations. When approached in 1942 to supervise the black-Jewish survey, he knew well the theories and techniques for such an undertaking.

Marsh relied on graduate students for the study, providing Eleanor Paperno Wolf and Alvin D. Loving with fellowships of $250.[40] Wolf, presently professor emeritus of sociology at Wayne State University, established contacts in the Jewish community and did "the tough sociological work"; Loving, now a retired administrator for the University of Michigan, made contact among black Detroiters, as well as "valuable suggestions" for the survey.[41] In addition, Marsh also found it necessary to spend all of his free time on the studies, interviewing community leaders, developing questionnaires, selecting canvassers, computing data and writing conclusions.

Of course, the scholarly worth of the enormous effort depended on Marsh's methodology. Focusing on the cultural and socioeconomic conditions influencing group attitudes, he disregarded earlier biological determinism and contemporary psychological concepts grounded in personality structures.[42] He sought to pinpoint situations that affected black-Jewish views of each other, always cognizant of historical, personal and environmental occurrences: "bitter memories of the depression years"; "a single pleasant or unpleasant experience"; "the commissary tradition of the southern plantation."[43] Initially, Marsh planned a comprehensive study covering commercial, domestic, landlord and social relationships, but limited time and resources and, particularly, the "seemingly crucial nature of the conflict" necessitated confining it to the area of greatest antagonisms: merchant-customer relations along Hastings Street.[44] He decided to compare these with those found in the other predominantly black-Jewish business districts of Oakland and Warren Avenues.[45]

In order to measure the conflict, Marsh and his associates designed and supervised six surveys during the winter of 1942–1943.[46] They concentrated on commercial relationships, prices and interracial attitudes. Thirty members of Marsh's Urban Sociology class interviewed 151 businessmen on thirty-five points regarding their stores and customers, while "a large number" from Edward McFarland's Economics of Consumption course priced eleven items in 180 grocery stores. Similarly, a handful of Wayne College undergraduates in a class on Races and Nationalities, questioned 191 Jews and 80 white gentiles who frequented community centers near the black residences. They asked respondents fifteen questions designed to measure their tolerance toward blacks. They also circulated questionnaires among 225 black youths from the Hastings Street area and 150 black parents, relatives and adult friends of Miller High School students, seeking their attitudes toward Jews and the social genesis of these attitudes. Some of these surveys were carried out over several days, while others were completed in one day; for example, students checked the prices of all stores on a given date and before the Office of Price Administration set regulations for Detroit.

Owing to the 1943 upheaval, Marsh, Wolf and Loving followed similar procedures in a seventh study. It was conducted in the fall of 1944 by some of the original canvassers, who contacted 106 of the 151 shopkeepers questioned during the initial poll of commercial establishments.[47] It sought to determine "the effect of the riots on Negro-Jewish relations." Together the seven surveys measured pre- and post-disorder attitudes of residents and merchants in the looted area.

Marsh and his researchers took several precautions to insure the validity of their data. Doubtlessly because of prior experience and sociological training, Marsh knew well the need for black-Jewish perspectives at every stage of the surveys. He chose Loving for his contacts in the black neighborhoods, Wolf for her sociological ability, and both for their suggestions as members of the minority groups under study; the three of them "thought and talked for days and days and days."[48] From this multiple perspective, which was further bolstered by conversations with leaders of each community and interviews in the field, Marsh and Wolf—his best student ever—formulated questions that both signaled certain attitudes and checked their accuracy. In the Jewish-white gentile survey, for example, they asked questions that exposed a respondent's racial beliefs and rationale for them: answering affirmatively to "Is a black skin a sign of inferiority?" implied belief in genetic inferiority, while replying negatively to it but positively to "Are Negroes more likely to steal than white men?" suggested knowledge of environmentally-influenced behavior.[49] Similarly, Marsh and Wolf included these and similar queries to test "the acceptance of certain stereotyped prejudices" and "the degree of contact the individual would be willing to tolerate." They also asked Jews about their obligations toward relationships with and fears of blacks, comparing their responses with those given in the commercial relationships survey. Besides cross-checking questions and surveys, they established controls and comparisons: three business districts in the commercial relationships survey, white gentile stores in the price survey, white gentile responses in the attitudinal survey. For the most part, their questionnaires measured feelings themselves rather than incidental factors.[50]

Similarly, Marsh and Wolf carefully selected and trained the canvassers.[51] They assigned black students to black respondents, Jewish students to Jewish respondents and white gentile students to white gentile respondents, arming all interviewers with credentials issued by the NAACP, Jewish Community Council or similar community organizations. Perhaps they realized that canvassing produced "more complete results and a wider variety of relevant data" than other methods; certainly they knew that respondents "would talk more freely with members of their own groups," and these techniques became standard procedures for later researchers.[52]

Despite these precautions, Marsh, Wolf and Loving recognized problems that other generations of pollsters—armed with computers and greater experience—would identify, though not always resolve. For example, some of their questions were vague or loaded.[53] When rating the "honesty" of black customers, merchants interpreted the term differently, and racially-conscious black shopkeepers deliberately refrained from branding customers as dishonest.[54] Similarly, some proprietors probably fudged when asked about contributing to neighborhood causes, and several black respondents could not distinguish between Jewish and white gentile owners. Then as now, respondents were called upon "to ignore ambiguity and complexity in favor of making broad generalizations."[55] Marsh's team understood this perennial problem, which was compounded by that of transtolerance: whereby respondents say what society considers proper rather than what they really feel.[56] Possibly blacks and Jews facing increased hostility during a war for democracy brought some of their replies in line with the charges they themselves made against fascists; possibly they also projected the traditional ambivalence associated with bigotry and tolerance in an egalitarian society.

Funding difficulties required Marsh to stretch both his resources and imagination. Hence he engaged undergraduates as canvassers, restricted the study largely to commercial relationships, speculated on other areas of black-Jewish economics and, sometimes, administered the survey according to available community assistance. He knew that inexperienced canvassers and unwilling respondents occasionally produced fragmentary and unusable questionnaires.[57] He later realized that the study was "too much limited to grocery stores."[58] Unable to undertake complete studies of domestic employment, he simply asked Jews to describe their relationships with black servants as "pleasant" or "unpleasant."[59] Ninety-three per cent of the respondents registered "pleasant" relationships, which prompted incredulity from some quarters. That such a high percentage "of any people would report pleasant relations with domestic servants of any kind" surprised many, including Marsh, who attributed some of the results to the personal nature of domestic relations.[60] More probably, his canvassers recorded transtolerant replies rather than true opinions, which more systematic surveys might have disclosed. Also because of scanty funds and administrative cooperation, Marsh surveyed black students at Miller High School.

Perhaps the most serious limitations of the Marsh, Wolf, Loving study reflect the technological limitations and democratic ideal of the age. Apparently no survey sample was based on scientifically-determined random numbers. The 190 persons filling out the attitude questionnaire at the Jewish Community Center on the one evening designated for the survey might or might not have been representative of other Jews.[61] Even more questionable, the eighty respondents of the Franklin Street Settlement and Lutheran House came from predominantely Italian and native-born American families, respectively, thereby reflecting much more diversity than implied by the monolithic label "white gentile." Moreover the Franklin youths had opportunities for face-to-face contact with blacks, while the Lutheran youngsters knew none. Although Marsh and his associates failed to benefit from later, more precise measurement techniques, and seemed to embrace the melting-pot theory for white immigrants, they did break down the results according to sex and, in the case of black respondents, age, and they did consider the questionnaire "a rough and imperfect instrument for discovering attitudes."

Yet, for all the problems inherent in their study, Marsh, Wolf and Loving realized that its consistent responses suggested viable degrees of representation and validity. They noted that limited resources made "a more individualized method" of testing Jewish and white gentile attitudes impossible, but added that the "striking" results verified their procedure.[62] They also pointed out that enough interviews, sometimes with lengthy notes supplementing the quantified replies, were completed to tabulate significant results. Their use of supporting comments again predated the approach of later pollsters.

In striking opposition to those who interpreted disorder along Hastings Street as "essentially a Negro-Jewish conflict," Marsh and his co-workers considered it a black and white altercation that might have occurred in any densely populated area of Detroit.[63] They based their conclusion on numerous survey findings, twenty-two of which were circulated in pamphlet form. Their commercial relationships questionnaires revealed that Jewish merchants did not monopolize business on Hastings; that they operated shops there because Jews had formerly resided in the neighborhood, not because black customers were considered "easy marks"; that they lived outside the area, as did seventy-five per cent of all black proprietors; that they and black entrepreneurs showed similar dissatisfaction with patrons; that they charged lower prices than did their counterparts, black or white gentile; that they ran largely cash-and-carry transactions, very few operating on credit or mostly credit. Conflict, according to Marsh, Wolf and Loving, correlated with customers' transiency rather than either racially-mixed patrons and employees or black-Jewish business competition. In other words, they associated merchant-customer antagonisms to low socioeconomic conditions and played down "the factor of racial ownership."

Their attitude surveys reinforced this quasi-class interpretation, which presented Jewish proprietors as anything but callous Shylocks. More Jews than white gentiles rejected stereotypes of black inferiority, revealed greater tolerance for interracial contacts and recorded more pleasant experiences with domestics, customers, and neighbors; indeed, these findings verified their obligation "to treat Negroes well since they too have known persecution." This positive image was borne out by black respondents, sizable majorities of whom registered fair treatment by landlords and pleasant relations with domestic employers. Even fifty per cent of the black youths believed that Jews treated the race better than did white gentiles, while over forty per cent of the black adult customers indicated trading with one Jewish store for a long period of time. To Marsh, Wolf and Loving, these responses signified much less conflict and much more tolerance between Jewish merchants and black residents than "popularly rumored."

The post-riot survey of commercial establishments undertaken by Marsh and his researchers in the fall of 1944 supported these conclusions.[64] "Specially selected students" revisited over one hundred proprietors and found that intergroup contacts and minority-group empathy increased tolerance; that black-Jewish competition between businesses on "nearly equal footing" improved merchant interrelationships, while that between smaller, personal service, black stores and larger, non-service, Jewish establishments fostered conflict; that blacks believed themselves exploited by all storekeepers, a symptom of their subordinate caste position and general exploitation because of it. Hence interviewers confirmed that existing black antagonisms stemmed from socioeconomic factors rather than antisemitism per se. Indeed they noted that the greatest destruction occurred on Hastings Street, the area of abject poverty and most recent immigration, while Jewish and white gentile stores along Warren Avenue remained open and unscathed during the riot. They also attributed the vast damage on Hastings Street to "strangers" delivering "a symbolic attack on the white caste" and looting the most accessible targets, stores which happened to be owned by Jews; they speculated that this aggression mirrored larger society's antisemitism, thus becoming "permissive conduct."[65] Moreover, the security of numbers and the absence of structure reinforced the rioters.[66] This "sociology of the stranger" interpretation dovetailed with statements by Jewish merchants, who recalled that black customers and neighbors sought to protect them during the hostile outburst.

Small wonder that Marsh, Wolf and Loving deduced further that the riot both increased the number of black entrepreneurs and improved black-Jewish relations in the three business districts. Perhaps their deductions were interrelated, for new black shopkeepers replaced those Jewish and white gentile merchants who left the area owing to disorder-related damage or fear. As significantly, the researchers noted that most recent black proprietors opened larger, non-service establishments which were more compatible with the Jewish stores. Although black-Jewish conflict continued along Hastings Street when competing shopkeepers offered the same merchandise, and resentment occurred on Oakland Avenue because black rivals "invaded" the domain of small Jewish retailers, they stressed the stabilizing effect of the upheaval on intergroup relationships: Jews knew that blacks—who hid or telephoned them, who patrolled their stores or wrote "Negro" on their windows during the disorder—were much more than customers; blacks realized that Jewish merchants provided daily groceries and, most paramount, were as insecure as themselves. As a result, Marsh, Wolf and Loving sensed that Jewish businessmen exhibited greater respect for, and desire to please, their black friends, who themselves became less critical and suspicious of those they identified with as threatened minorities. Marsh and company contended that their findings "fairly well exploded" the Shylock image of Jews and the error of making them scapegoats, while demonstrating that improved socioeconomic conditions for blacks lay in "group organization and political activity." Marsh himself believed that additional surveys were needed to determine the full extent of the changes wrought by riot and the oncoming problems of postwar intergroup adjustments.[67]

While he worked toward that end, black and Jewish leaders promoted the initial Marsh, Wolf, Loving survey. "Delighted and somewhat amazed" by its results, they invited Marsh to present his research before their organizations and in their journals.[68]

He complied, addressing the Association for the Study of Negro Life and History, the Booker T. Washington Trade Association and the Jewish War Veterans of Detroit.[69] He found preparing the findings for publication in the *Journal of Negro History* and *Yivo Bleter* much more difficult, largely because of his intention to broaden the study, his lack of enthusiasm for completing manuscripts and, in mid-1944, his appointment as chairperson of the Popular Education Committee (an arm of the City of Detroit Interracial Committee).[70] Nonetheless, he distributed portions of the surveys to fifty black and Jewish organizations and leading individuals; and he prepared "Negro-Jewish Relationships," pamphlet No. 1 of Wayne University Studies in Inter-Group Conflicts in Detroit, of which 13,000 copies were distributed locally and nationally.[71] The local NAACP and Jewish Community Council underwrote his expenses and, no doubt, passed his summary on to numerous newspapers in Detroit.[72] Marsh's study also received recognition in the Philadelphia and New York presses.[73]

Meanwhile Marsh sent detailed results of the survey to the NAACP and Jewish Community Council executives, suggesting that they sponsor a post-riot study.[74] He received their cooperation, unquestionably because his conclusions demolished the assertions of several Detroit officials who blamed the upheaval on Jewish exploitation (thereby absolving themselves of malfeasance). Indirectly, however, his findings also supported those Jewish merchants seeking compensation from the municipality for disorder-related damages and black leaders wrongly accused by government spokesmen of having fomented the outburst.[75] They also resulted in his selection as head of the Popular Education Committee and Wolf's election as board member of the Jewish Community Council.[76]

As Marsh laid plans for the $400 post-riot grant, he considered seriously the possibility of expanding the survey to other cities. His interest seemed to have been sparked by Sanford Griffith of Market Analysts, Incorporated of New York City, who suggested grandiose plans for joint ventures in Chicago, New York and, possibly, Pittsburgh.[77] Marsh envisioned employing his proven method and worthy staff on a somewhat larger and more comparative scale. By the end of 1943, he sent Wolf to join Griffith in Chicago to prepare a study, and he spoke of moving into New York some time later. Early the next year, he corresponded with Cleveland Jewish leaders about the possibility of investigating the situation there.[78] While Marsh provided the expertise and experienced personnel, requesting nominal reimbursement for himself and his coworkers, Griffith failed to secure the necessary funding from philanthropic or other sources. Engaged in other, apparently more lucrative projects, he gave those of Marsh short shrift and, by late 1944, admitted that even "the Cleveland job would have to be warmed up all over again."[79]

By then Marsh realized Griffith's limitations but hoped to salvage the Cleveland survey, which held the interest of Mayor Frank J. Laushe and Western Reserve University sociologists.[80] He also envisioned an investigation of black-Polish relations to check the original Marsh, Wolf, Loving findings for Detroit and another "fuller study" to determine "just what changes have been brought about by the riots." He received no assistance from Griffith, who was planning "a large scale racial attitude testing program" for which he desired Marsh's collaboration![81] (Marsh later learned that Griffith probably represented federal concern over the war effort, which would have accounted for his disinterest in the black-Jewish studies and desire for the broader survey.)[82]

Although not utilized fully, the Marsh, Wolf, Loving surveys nonetheless challenged politically and ideologically self-serving riot interpretations, applied the closed caste-open class model of Cooley and anticipated the analysis of later upheavals by another generation of scholars. Marsh contended, for example, that Detroit was "a frontier" and—like all frontiers—it promoted concepts of self-worth and social mobility, which all laborers believed; that blacks, denied access to this supposed meritorious, "open class system," protested against caste exclusions; that riot represented "a disadvantaged group's desire for a wider participation in the life of the community."[83] Indeed, he argued, the disturbance signified "the democratic spirit" and demonstrated the "inadequacy of institutional functioning." In other words, he said the rising expectations of blacks were blocked by the resistance of whites; real or imagined black challenges to the racial status quo sparked interracial combat on Belle Isle and symbolic attacks on white property along Hastings Street. Here he argued with his peers, most notably Alfred M. Lee and Norman D. Humphrey, and foreshadowed the theories of Allen D. Grimshaw, Robert M. Fogelson and others, while falling short of interpreting the system as illegitimate and, consequently, the outburst as revolt.[84] In essence he emphasized majority-minority caste conflict and socioeconomic conditions rather than black-Jewish antagonisms per se; he defined the outbreak in racial terms—black and white—but he did not consider it a race riot. His contention that no "highly particularistic" interpretation such as antisemitism explained upheaval gained currency among later scholars, though some of them considered race as more than "a badge" or symbol.[85] Nevertheless, through the process of elaborate investigation he had verified the position of many impressionistic observers and, most significantly, proved the worth of sociological inquiry.

In particular, Marsh's conclusions about rioters and their victims endured changing times and locales. Independent and government studies interpreted the many disorders of the 1960s just as he and his researchers had done in Detroit nearly one quarter of a century earlier. Whether Lenora E. Berson's survey of the Philadelphia disturbance of 1964 or the American Jewish Committee's investigation of thirteen major cities exploding in 1968, the later conclusions echoed Marsh: Jewish proprietors bore the brunt of black attacks "as whites and as merchants . . . rather than as Jews per se."[86] Similarly the National Advisory Commission on Civil Disorders, which examined fifteen municipalities—some riot-torn, others riot-free—labeled the 1967 outbursts as protest and the unfair commercial practices affecting black customers as relatively insignificant reasons for triggering violence.[87] Significantly the commission paralleled Marsh's commercial and attitudinal surveys, though surprisingly without focusing on Jewish entrepreneurs or antisemitism.[88]

Yet many of their conclusions were similar, signifying anew Marsh's contribution and his vision for comparative studies. Although the commission benefited from advanced survey techniques, better trained personnel, more adequate funding and greater societal concern, while also experiencing time limitations as had Marsh, both investigations demonstrated that most ghetto merchants were Jewish, absentee owners of long-standing who served mostly black customers and employed some black residents.[89]

They also showed that large numbers of proprietors, especially during the war, were first generation immigrants with little formal education.[90] Marsh discovered that most entrepreneurs, particularly among the Jews, however, possessed previous experience "directly related to their work."[91] Also, while both polls found storekeepers befriending some customers, Marsh identified contributors to neighborhood causes whereas the commission detected loners shying away from civil rights organizations.[92]

These slight variations aside, Marsh's and the commission's surveys also agreed on many of the merchants' business practices, racial attitudes and riot experiences.[93] Both challenged the popular notion that proprietors operated credit businesses, which fostered conflict, while substantiating the equally popular belief that ghetto entrepreneurs charged higher prices than did their counterparts elsewhere. Marsh's inquiry only hinted at consumer-shopkeeper bargaining without judging it unethical, whereas commission researchers said over ten per cent of all merchants practiced this "most ethically questionable policy." Both studies measured retailers' attitudes toward black patrons and, when compared, reveal the deterioration of their relationship over time. Marsh's canvassers found overwhelming evidence that Detroit proprietors considered blacks honest or mostly honest, while those of the commission discovered that more than half of their respondents said "Negroes must be watched carefully." Ironically and ominously, Marsh's pollsters also noted that over one-fourth of those merchants in ghetto districts reported personal assaults, abusive language and malicious vandalism. Nevertheless most retailers disassociated the attacks on their stores in 1943 and 1967 from "the quality of customer relations," instead blaming strangers or criminal elements.[94] Perhaps for reasons of self-image and self-protection, they explained the destruction and looting in terms of location, symbolism and outsiders. Marsh's summary suggested, however tangentially, what the commission's spelled out: shopkeepers "who felt safe connected the riot to their own behavior, while those who felt threatened attached no significance to their actions. . . ."

Beyond these interpretations, Marsh pioneered the way for later studies of black-Jewish relationships and, once again, anticipated their findings. His survey, albeit less scientific, less comprehensive and largely unknown, appears uncanny for its era, particularly when compared with the University of California-B'nai B'rith Five Year Study of Anti-Semitism in the United States and other sophisticated undertakings of the 1960s.[95] Like them, he sought the keys to black-Jewish conflict in cultural, economic, historical and sociopsychological dimensions. Like them, too, he evaluated the alienation and the bonding that occurred between the two minorities before finally settling on an economic explanation of their bittersweet saga.

Clearly Marsh and subsequent scholars identified cultural differences as a causal conflict factor, though a relatively unimportant one serving merely "to heighten or intensify feelings of hostility which already exist."[96] In arriving at similar conclusions, however, they focused on different dimensions of culture. Modern researchers examined the religious issue. Black Christians and European Jews, they found, embraced "pejorative images" of one another as Christ-killers and as inferiors.[97] Blacks also identified themselves with Old Testament Israelites, and members of both minorities empathized with each other's oppression, thereby promoting intergroup tolerance.[98]

Marsh discovered more antagonism when dissimilar heritages clashed in an economic context. He noted that black customers appeared rural, unsophisticated and accustomed to inferior status, while Jewish merchants were urban and "strongly European" in their gestures, language and familial relations. Hence patrons mimicked the strange-sounding Yiddish and hand expressions of shopkeepers who, in turn, considered the relatively disorganized families and night life of the Hastings Street area proof of moral inferiority. These perceptions accentuated the strife that surfaced when blacks, who, as cowed sharecroppers rarely haggled over merchandise, believed that the Jews' first high price—their "opening gambit in an ancient bargaining ritual"—indicated they would settle for nothing less. Out of this cultural misunderstanding came hard feelings and, no doubt, images of violent-prone blacks and cold-hearted Shylocks. At a time when the great majority of Jewish entrepreneurs were foreign-born and many of the blacks immigrants, Marsh—unlike later pollsters—refrained from labeling such bargaining unethical.[99] Instead, he concluded that Jewish traditions of arbitration, conciliation and peacemaking enabled shopkeepers and consumers to live together even under "the most unfavorable conditions."

In this way Marsh connected the survival traits of one culture with the history of both minorities. Too, it was their history that constituted another causal factor for conflict. Unlike Jewish-white gentile relations in the United States, Jewish-black relations "fit" the historical role of Jews as merchants—antisemites said usurers—just as they had been in Medieval Europe.[100] Marsh and latter-day investigators knew of the history behind Jewish entrepreneurship on both continents and of the visibility, real and imagined, that it gave Jews in the ghettos. Whereas Marsh associated greater conflict with "highly disorganized areas," meaning neighborhoods with transient populations, his successors related perceived mistreatment by Jewish merchants to the harboring of antisemitic belief by black customers.[101] If, historically, Jews were economically powerful and blacks relatively powerless, everyone agreed that the key to wartime conflict and modern antisemitism lay more in the minorities' impersonal contacts than in their historical backgrounds; researchers of both eras correlated greater conflict and antisemitism with the black lower-classes.[102]

Hence for Marsh and more recent academicians, culture and history influenced black-Jewish relations, though not as significantly as economic contact. In fact, they verified statistically what less comprehensive studies of Chicago and New York, as well as black publications nationally, suggested during the war.[103] Pollsters and observers alike noted how the ghetto's structure fostered dominant-subordinate economic roles for Jews and blacks, a symbiotic relationship generating competition and stereotypes. Blacks, like whites during and since the war, considered Jews too powerful economically, singularly capable of giving or withholding from ghetto residents the necessities of life.[104] That nearly twenty-five per cent of the black youth believed all Jewish merchants rich, and fully thirty per cent of the black adults supposed they could deprive black competitors of their property alarmed Marsh.[105] Beliefs like these reinforced stereotypes of Jews as money-grabbing and shrewd, permitting wartime black respondents to perceive Jewish shopkeepers as less honest than their black and white counterparts; perhaps, as was the case among another generation of blacks, those most apt to report unfair treatment by Jewish entrepreneurs were antisemitic.[106] Marsh and his successors, then, realized that historical factors accounted for Jewish dominance, and cultural differences accentuated black stereotypes of Jews; these factors converged with economic developments to foster antagonism between the minorities.[107]

Sociopsychological aspects, they discovered, also influenced black-Jewish economics. Marsh pinpointed a correlation between intergroup conflict and transient blacks, while later sociologists identified a similar connection between antisemitism and poorly educated blacks.[108] Like blacks and whites reporting less antisemitic belief in the later period, black Detroiters from the middle and upper middle class neighborhoods of Warren and Oakland Avenues registered less discord toward Jewish merchants than their transitory, lower class Hastings Street brethren.[109] As significantly, Jewish and white gentile merchants in the Warren-Oakland areas—themselves more acculturated and better educated than the Jews of Hastings Street—tended to be "more moderate and less emotional regarding Negroes" than the retailers along that thoroughfare.[110] These class-related findings anticipated those of the postwar studies that connected higher levels of black (and white) education with lower levels of antisemitism; that identified ghetto retailers, Jewish and non-Jewish alike, as having the least sympathy for the plight of slum-locked blacks.[111] Together the surveys charted change over time, indicating that Hastings Street (rather than Warren or Oakland Avenues) emerged as the socioeconomic prototype of later inner cities and that greater black-Jewish, consumer-merchant antagonisms lay ahead.

Despite the negative impact of culture, history and socioeconomics on black-Jewish relations, Marsh and more recent investigators discovered the positive influence of these same factors. Blacks and Jews who empathized religiously as God's suffering servants and secularly as oppressed minorities exhibited significant tolerance toward one another. Marsh found that over seventy per cent of the Jewish merchants believed themselves obligated to treat blacks better than did white gentiles because they knew what it was "to be persecuted," while a later survey discovered that "Negroes expressed greater opposition to occupational and social club discrimination against Jews than did whites."[112] Moreover, Marsh noted that black youths expected better treatment from Jews for the same reason, and he and latter-day pollsters challenged the theory that blacks were more antisemitic than whites or more prone to make Jews scapegoats for their own discontent.[113] They also related the latter point to socioeconomic factors, cognizant that black stereotypes of Jews began to disappear in the absence of commercial relationships and, when prevalent, they hinged on economic-related images.[114] Even though slightly more than fifty per cent of the Jewish shopkeepers fulfilled their self-stated obligations to treat blacks better, and even though blacks believed that Jews treated them the same as white gentiles, Marsh and more contemporary sociologists challenged those, like psychologist Kenneth Clark, who doubted that black antisemitism was rooted directly in economic competition.[115]

For all of this prescience, the Marsh, Wolf, Loving surveys were limited in some ways. They focused directly on economic conflict, not antisemitism per se or antisemitism broadly defined. In doing this, they hit on the single most important factor separating black from white antisemitism and they gave support to the existing contemporary interpretations of Horace R. Cayton, St. Clair Drake, Roi Ottley, Lawrence D. Reddick and Lunabelle Wedlock, among others; but they played down—as did later sociologists—the psychological function of antisemitism that was derived from insecurity, status and other ego-related factors.[116] Largely because they concentrated on economics in Detroit, they were unable to compare their findings regionally and conclude broadly, as did later investigators, that black antisemitism flourished more in northern, urban areas than in southern, rural ones.[117] Also, they were not capable of determining, as did the more recent investigations, that young blacks reported greater antisemitism than their elders: the reverse age characteristic of white antisemites, indicating the rise of black nationalism in the 1960s.[118]

Of course, Marsh, Wolf and Loving working in the 1940s cannot be criticized for areas they never chose to examine or for failing to foresee future developments. Rather they should be commended for setting right the interpretation of critical aspects of Detroit's riot, statistically verifying earlier theories of black-Jewish relationships, suggesting the need for more comprehensive, comparative studies of those and other minority group interaction and, most notably, demonstrating the very best way that academe can serve society in its effort to resolve conflict. Breaking new ground, Marsh and his associates undertook the Detroit study and considered conducting a much larger one, exactly what their counterparts did in the 1960s. For example, Gerhard Lenski, who made a somewhat more broadly conceived study of the religious factor in Detroit, contended that his findings could be generalized and applied "to other major metropolitan centers throughout the country," while Harold Y. Quinley and Charles Y. Glock considered their survey of antisemitism among blacks living in northern metropolitan areas and in four major cities as "the first of its kind" in size and sampling.[119] Marsh, Wolf and Loving's conclusions, much more than Lenski's, have been confirmed by Quinley, Glock and others, who appear unaware of their existence.[120] Never one to overstate his or his work's importance, Marsh made no grandiose claims of its worth. Yet contemporaries knowledgeable in the field knew that the Marsh, Wolf, Loving studies of "Negro-Jewish Relationships" represented "a definite contribution toward the clarification of this important question."[121] Indeed, any study of these minority groups in Detroit must begin with the scholarship of Donald C. Marsh and his associates, who embodied the characteristics of Cooley's transitive man: "an apostle, a propagandist, an incarnation of the hypothesis that the onward process of life is worthwhile."[122]

NOTES

The author thanks Donald C. Marsh and Eleanor P. Wolf for granting interviews and the use of their personal papers. Several attempts to contact Alvin D. Loving were unsuccessful.

1. Alfred McClung Lee and Norman D. Humphrey, *Race Riot* (1943; New York, 1968); Robert Shogan and Tom Craig, *The Detroit Race Riot: A Study in Violence* (1964; New York, 1976); Harvard Sitkoff, "The Detroit Race Riot of 1943," *Michigan History*, 53 (Fall 1969), 183–206; and George W. Beatty, "The Background and Causes of the 1943 Detroit Race Riot" (Senior thesis, Princeton University, 1954) for scholarly studies. See John Wood, "I Cover the Town," Michigan *Chronicle*, 3 July 1943, p. 7 (hereafter cited as *Chronicle*) for a representative example of the contemporary accounts.

2. Lowell S. Selling, "A Study of One Hundred Offenders Who Were Apprehended during the Disturbances of June 20th and 21st, 1943, in Detroit, Michigan," 30, Box 9, Mayor's Papers (1943), Burton

Historical Collection, Detroit Public Library, Detroit, Michigan (hereafter cited as BHC) for the quotation; Allen D. Grimshaw, "A Study in Social Violence: Urban Race Riots in the United States" (Ph.D. dissertation, University of Pennsylvania, 1959), pp. 321–55; August Meier and Elliot Rudwick, "Black Violence in the 20th Century," II, 307–16, and Morris Janowitz, "Patterns of Collective Racial Violence," II, 317–39, in *Violence in America: Historical and Comparative Perspectives,* ed. Hugh D. Graham and Ted Gurr (Washington, D. C., 1969); Richard Maxwell Brown, *Strain of Violence: Historical Studies of American Violence and Vigilantism* (New York, 1975), pp. 205–35.

3. Lee and Humphrey, *Race Riot,* p. 34; Shogan and Craig, *Detroit Race Riot,* p. 49; Sitkoff, "The Detroit Race Riot of 1943," p. 319; Beatty, "The Background and Causes of the 1943 Detroit Race Riot," pp. 108–10. Many federal investigators oversimplified the destruction of white-owned stores as "Negro hoodlumism": Memorandum for the Attorney General (from Victor W. Rotnem), 9 August 1943, Box 9, OF 4245-G, Franklin D. Roosevelt Papers, Roosevelt Library, Hyde Park, New York (hereafter cited as FDRL); Richard Deverall to Clarence Glick, 28 June 1943, Box 9, OF 4245-G, FDRL; W. Roderick Brown to George Baehr, 28 July 1943, Box 11, OF 4245-G, FDRL.

4. David Katzman, *Before the Ghetto: Black Detroit in the Nineteenth Century* (Urbana, Ill., 1973), pp. 18, 45–47, 62, 135–206; Robert A. Rockaway, "Anti-Semitism in an American City: Detroit, 1850–1914," *American Jewish Historical Quarterly,* 64 (Sept. 1974/June 1975), 42, 44, 45. See also Henry J. Meyer, "The Structure of the Jewish Community in the City of Detroit (Ph.D. diss., University of Michigan, 1939), pp. 29–42, 78–121, 240–51 for an overview of Jews in Detroit from their arrival through the Great Depression.

5. Henry J. Meyer, "A Study of Detroit Jewry, 1935," p. 114, in *Jewish Population Studies,* ed. Sophia M. Robison (New York, 1943); see Melvin G. Holli, ed., *Detroit* (New York, 1976), p. 271, for all population statistics unless cited otherwise.

6. Olivier Zunz, *The Changing Face of Inequality: Urbanization, Industrial Development, and Immigrants in Detroit, 1880–1920* (Chicago, Ill., 1982), pp. 39, 130–31, 158, 161, and 247 for information in this paragraph.

7. Rockaway, "Anti-Semitism in an American City," p. 53, and "Ethnic Conflict in an Urban Environment: The German and Russian Jew, 1881–1914," *American Jewish Historical Quarterly,* 60 (Dec. 1970), 133–50; Nathan Glazer, *American Judaism* (2nd ed.; Chicago, 1972), pp. 45–46, 81–83; David Allen Levine, *Internal Combustion: The Races in Detroit, 1915–1926* (Westport, Ct., 1976), pp. 49–61; Dominic J. Capeci, Jr., *Race Relations in Wartime Detroit: The Sojourner Truth Housing Controversy of 1942* (Philadelphia, 1984), pp. 5–12, for information in this and the next paragraph.

8. Katzman, *Before the Ghetto,* pp. 58–59; Rockaway, "Anti-Semitism in an American City," p. 46.

9. Donald C. Marsh, Alvin D. Loving and Eleanor Paperno Wolf, "Some Aspects of Negro-Jewish Relationships in Detroit, Michigan: Introduction," p. 11, n.d., unprocessed material, Donald C. Marsh Collection, University Archives, Walter P. Reuther Library, Detroit, Michigan (hereafter cited as UA).

10. Zunz, *The Changing Face of Inequality,* pp. 373, 398, 324; Rockaway, "Anti-Semitism in an American City," p. 50; Kenneth T. Jackson, *The Ku Klux Klan in the City, 1915–1930* (New York, 1967), pp. 127, 143.

11. Zunz, *The Changing Face of Inequality,* p. 393, for information in this paragraph unless cited otherwise.

12. James Borchert, *Alley Life in Washington: Family, Community, Religion, and Folklife in the City, 1850–1970* (Urbana, Ill., 1980), p. 237 for the model of what undoubtedly occurred in Detroit; John Bodnar, Roger Simon, and Michael P. Weber, *Lives of Their Own: Blacks, Italians, and Poles in Pittsburgh, 1900–1960* (Urbana, Ill., 1982), p. 154, for the theory of blacks and property acquisition.

13. Zunz, *The Changing Face of Inequality,* pp. 256, 392–93; Bodnar, et al., *Lives of Their Own,* p. 154. By the 1950s Jewish Detroiters lagged behind both Catholics and Protestants in homeowning; David Goldberg and Harry Sharp, "Some Characteristics of Detroit Area Jewish and Non-Jewish Adults," p. 115, in *The Jews: Social Patterns of an American Group,* ed. Marshall Sklare (Glencoe, Ill., 1958).

14. Zunz, *The Changing Face of Inequality,* p. 339; Capeci, *Race Relations in Wartime Detroit,* pp. 3–8, 28–33.

15. By the 1950s nearly one-half of Jewish family heads were self-employed as compared with ten per

cent or fewer of their non-Jewish counterparts in Detroit: Goldberg and Sharp, "Some Characteristics of Detroit Area Jewish and Non-Jewish Adults," p. 114, for this statistic and the following quotation. Also see Meyer, "The Structure of the Jewish Community in the City of Detroit," pp. 185–88. S. Joseph Fauman, "The Jews in the Waste Industries in Detroit, *Jewish Social Studies*, 3 (1941), 41–56, and "Occupational Selection among Detroit Jews," in Sklare, *The Jews*, pp. 119–37 for the following information on Detroit Jews.

16. Sidney Fine, *Frank Murphy: The Detroit Years* (Ann Arbor, Mich., 1975), pp. 250; Meyer, "A Study of Detroit Jewry, 1935," pp. 120, 124, 125, 127.

17. Rockaway, "Anti-Semitism in an American City," p. 52; Meyer, "A Study of Detroit Jewry, 1935," p. 123; Bureau of Agricultural Economics (USDA), "The Ethnic Axis: Jews," p. 2, c. 1943, Box 9, Renis Likert Collection, Michigan Historical Collections, Bentley Historical Library, Ann Arbor, Michigan (hereafter cited as MHC).

18. Bureau of Agricultural Economics (USDA), "The Ethnic Axis: Negroes," pp. 21–22, *ibid.*

19. Lunabelle Wedlock, *The Reaction of Negro Publications and Organizations to German Anti-Semitism* (Washington, D.C., 1942), pp. 177–82.

20. Marsh, Loving and Wolf, "Some Aspects of Negro-Jewish Relationships in Detroit," pp. 12–17; Bureau of Agricultural Economics, "The Ethnic Axis: Jews," p. 1, for information in this and the next sentence.

21. Eugene I. Bender, "Reflections on Negro-Jewish Relationships: The Historical Dimension," *Phylon*, 30 (Spring 1969), pp. 56–65, for the general interpretation; Levine, *Internal Combustion*, pp. 28, 75, 77, 80, 83, 124, 193, 201, 205 and 206 for the example of Fred Butzel.

22. Detroit *Tribune*, 4 Jan. 1941, p. 11; 14 Mar. 1942, p. 1; and 17 Oct. 1942, p. 3, for information in this and the next sentence (hereafter cited as *Tribune*).

23. Capeci, *Race Relations in Wartime Detroit*, pp. 84–85, 132.

24. *Tribune*, 20 June 1942, p. 3.

25. *Chronicle*, 30 May 1942, p. 8; *Tribune*, 6 June 1942, p. 16; Walter White, "What Caused the Detroit Riots?" Box 2574, Fiorello H. LaGuardia Papers, Municipal Archives and Record Center, New York, New York (hereafter cited as FHLP); Charles H. Stember, "Reactions to Anti-Semitic Appeal before and during the War" in his, et al., *Jews in the Mind of America* (New York, 1966), pp. 110–11.

26. Office of War Information (OWI), "Attitudes toward Jews in the United States: Summary," 27 Oct. 1942, Box 9, MHC.

27. Shogan and Craig, *The Detroit Race Riot*, p. 49; Harold M. Kingsley, "Memorandum on Detroit Race Disturbances," 23 July 1943, Reel 10, Detroit Urban League Papers, Microfilm Edition (hereafter cited as DULP); White, "What Caused the Detroit Riots?" pp. 13–14; Selling, "A Study of One Hundred Offenders," p. 31; Complaint: The People of the State of Michigan v. John Davis and Willie Davis, 28 June 1943, Recorder's Court File No. A-34875, BHC; Lee and Humphrey, *Race Riot*, p. 34; Sitkoff, "The Detroit Race Riot of 1943," p. 319, for this composite.

28. Francis J. Haas, "Notebook," 1 July 1943 entry, Francis J. Haas Papers, Mullen Library, Washington, D. C. (hereafter cited as FJHP); John Wood, "I Cover the Town," *Chronicle*, 3 July 1943, p. 7.

29. Philip A. Adler, "Anti-Semitism Cited as a Prelude to Riot," *Detroit News*, 29 June 1943, p. 7.

30. Gerald L. K. Smith, "Race Riots! An Interpretation," *The Cross and the Flag*, July 1943, II, 232–34; Memorandum for the Attorney General (from C. E. Rhetts), 12 July 1943, p. 4n. 2, Box 213, Harold L. Ickes Papers, Manuscript Division, Library of Congress, Washington, D. C. (hereafter cited as HIP).

31. L. Gordon to R. J. Thomas, 7 Aug. 1943, Box 75, Harry F. Kelley Papers, Michigan State Archives, Lansing, Michigan.

32. See N. 30 above.

33. Federal Bureau of Investigation, "Survey of Racial Conditions in the United States," 1944, pp. 4, 27, Box 44, OF 10-B, FDRL.

34. Marsh, Loving and Wolf, "Some Aspects of Negro-Jewish Relationship in Detroit," p. 1.

35. Donald C. Marsh to Dominic J. Capeci, Jr., 22 Feb. 1979, for the information in this and the next three paragraphs unless cited otherwise.

36. Charles Hunt Page, *Class and American Sociology: From Ward to Ross* (New York, 1940), pp. 183–209, 188 and 203 for the quotation; Edward C. Jandy, *Charles Horton Cooley: His Life and His Social Theory* (New York, 1942); Richard Dewey, "Charles Horton Cooley: Pioneer in Psychosociology," in *An Introduction to the History of Sociology*, ed. Harry Elmer Barnes (Chicago, Ill., 1948), pp. 833–52; Robert Cooley Angell, "Introduction," in *Cooley and Sociological Analysis*, ed. Albert J. Reiss, Jr. (Ann Arbor, Mich., 1968), pp. 1–12; Stanford M. Lyman, *The Black American in Sociological Thought: A Failure of Perspective* (New York, 1973), pp. 21–22.

37. Page, *Class and American Sociology*, p. 185; Dewey, "Charles Horton Cooley," pp. 834–35; Leo F. Schnore, "Cooley as a Territorial Demographer," p. 31, for the following quotation, in *Cooley and Sociological Analysis*, ed. Reiss. Ironically, Cooley had worked as an engineer and a demographer, had taught statistics and, in his notable "The Theory of Transportation," had contributed to "the quest for knowledge by means of mathematical and statistical method."

38. Schnore, "Cooley as a Territorial Demographer," p. 30; Charles Horton Cooley, *Sociological Theory and Social Research* (New York, 1930), pp. 313–22, for his view of the statistical method.

39. Levine, *Internal Combustion*, p. 206; Mayor's Committee on Race Relations, "The Negro in Detroit" (mimeographed copy, 1926), BHC.

40. Donald C. Marsh, "Negro-Jewish Relations in Detroit," n.d., author's possession, for information in this paragraph unless cited otherwise.

41. Donald C. Marsh to Dominic J. Capeci, Jr., 22 Feb. 1979; Marsh to Sanford Griffith, 11 Nov. 1943, unprocessed material, Marsh Collection, UA; John C. Dancy, *Sand against the Wind: The Memories of John C. Dancy* (Detroit, Mich., 1966), p. 211.

42. Morton Keller, "Jews and the Character of American Life Since 1930" in Stember, et al., *Jews in the Mind of America*, p. 259.

43. Donald C. Marsh, Alvin D. Loving and Eleanor Paperno Wolf, "Negro-Jewish Attitude Analysis," p. 90, n.d., unprocessed material, Marsh Collection, UA; Donald C. Marsh, Alvin D. Loving and Eleanor Paperno Wolf, "Some Aspects of Negro-Jewish Relationships in Detroit, Michigan," n.d. pp. 40–41, in author's possession (hereafter cited as "Final Report: Pre-riot Survey").

44. Marsh, Loving and Wolf, "Some Aspects of Negro-Jewish Relationships in Detroit," pp. 4–5.

45. Marsh, Loving and Wolf, "Final Report: Pre-riot Survey," p. 4.

46. Marsh, Loving and Wolf, "Some Aspects of Negro-Jewish Relationships in Detroit," pp. 4–7 and "Final Report: Pre-riot Survey," pp. 56–63, for information in this paragraph.

47. Marsh, Loving and Wolf, "Some Aspects of Negro-Jewish Relationships in Detroit," p. 6, and "Negro-Jewish Relationships in Detroit: Post-riot," n.d., unprocessed material, Marsh Collection, UA.

48. Interview with Donald C. Marsh, Detroit, Mich., 6 June and 13 June 1978; interview with Eleanor P. Wolf, Detroit, 12 June 1978; Donald C. Marsh to Dominic J. Capeci, Jr., 20 Apr. 1982.

49. Marsh, Loving and Wolf, "Final Report: Pre-riot Survey," pp. 37–42.

50. Charles H. Stember, "Summary and Conclusions" in his, et al., *Jews in the Mind of America*, p. 214.

51. Marsh, Loving and Wolf, "Final Report: Pre-riot Survey," pp. 1, 4.

52. Robison, "Conclusion" in her *Jewish Population Studies*, p. 186; Marsh, Loving and Wolf, "Some Aspects of Negro-Jewish Relationships in Detroit," p. 5; Gary T. Marx, *Protest and Prejudice: A Study of Belief in the Black Community* (New York, 1967), p. 128 n. 4.

53. Stember, "Reactions to Anti-Semitic Appeal before and during the War," and Thomas F. Pettigrew, "Parallel and Distinctive Changes in Anti-Semitic and Anti-Negro Attitudes," in Stember, et al., *Jews in the Mind of America*, pp. 125, 383, respectively.

54. Marsh, Loving and Wolf, "Final Report: Pre-riot Survey," pp. 18, 32, 48.

55. Marx, *Protest and Prejudice*, p. 164.

56. Peter Vierck, "The Revolt against the Elite" in Daniel Bell, ed., *The Radical Right* (1963; Freeport, N.Y., 1971), pp. 140–41; Marshall Sklare and Charles H. Stember, "Introduction" in Stember, et al., *Jews in the Mind of America*, p. 21.

57. Marsh, Loving and Wolf, "Final Report: Pre-riot Survey," p. 4. Efforts to collect data on the income and expenditures of black families failed, for example, because the number of responses were so few and

the amounts recorded so high that Marsh questioned their reliability in *ibid.,* p. 49; interview with Donald C. Marsh, Detroit, Mich., 13 June 1978.

58. Donald C. Marsh to Dominic J. Capeci, Jr., 23 Feb. 1978.

59. Marsh, Loving and Wolf, "Some Aspects of Negro-Jewish Relationships in Detroit," p. 6; Marsh, Loving and Wolf, "Final Report: Pre-riot Survey," pp. 54, 46. Eighty per cent of 150 black adults living in the Hastings Street area also reported their relationships with Jewish households as "pleasant."

60. Mildred Biddick to Fritz Redl, 18 Oct. 1944, Box 3, Marsh Collection, UA; interview with Donald C. Marsh, Detroit, Mich., 6 June 1978.

61. Marsh, Loving and Wolf, "Final Report: Pre-riot Survey," pp. 37, 41n.1, for information in this paragraph.

62. *Ibid.,* p. 37; Rebecca Koretz, "Interviewing of Jewish Merchants on Oakland," n.d., in author's possession; Marx, *Protest and Prejudice,* p. 164, for information in this paragraph.

63. Donald C. Marsh, Alvin D. Loving and Eleanor Paperno Wolf, *Negro-Jewish Relationships,* Wayne University Studies in Inter-Group Conflicts in Detroit, no. 1 (Detroit, 1944), pp. 1–7, for information in this and the next paragraph.

64. Marsh, Loving and Wolf, "Some Aspects of Negro-Jewish Relationships in Detroit," p. 6, and "Negro-Jewish Relationships in Detroit: Post-riot," pp. 1–5, 120–23, for information in this and the next paragraph unless cited otherwise.

65. Donald C. Marsh to Isaque Graeber, 17 Jan. 1944, unprocessed material, Marsh Collection, UA.

66. Interview with Donald C. Marsh, Detroit, Mich., 6 June 1978; interview with Eleanor P. Wolf, Detroit, 12 June 1978.

67. Donald C. Marsh to Sanford Griffith, 5 Dec. 1944, unprocessed material, Marsh Collection, UA; Marsh, Loving and Wolf, "Negro-Jewish Relationships in Detroit: Post-riot," p. 23.

68. Gloster B. Current to Donald C. Marsh, 20 Dec. 1943, unprocessed material, Marsh Collection, UA, for quotation.

69. Donald C. Marsh to David D. Henry, 8 Dec. 1943, unprocessed material, Marsh Collection, UA.

70. C. G. Woodson to Donald C. Marsh, 18 Oct. 1943; *ibid.;* Marsh to Dominic J. Capeci, Jr., 20 Apr. 1982; Marsh to Sanford Griffith, 5 Dec. 1944, unprocessed material, Marsh Collection, UA. *Yivo Bleter* was the official journal of the Yiddish Scientific Institute.

71. Donald C. Marsh to William Pyle, 16 Mar. 1944, unprocessed material, Marsh Collection, UA; Marsh, "Negro-Jewish Relations in Detroit."

72. Isaac Franck to David D. Henry, 19 Oct. 1944, unprocessed material, Marsh Collection, UA; *Tribune,* 14 Oct. 1944, p. 1, and *Chronicle,* 29 Oct. 1944, p. 3, for examples.

73. Donald C. Marsh to William Pyle, 16 Mar. 1944, unprocessed material, Marsh Collection, UA. During 1945, he forwarded the pamphlet to several academicians, libraries, organizations and synagogues throughout the United States.

74. Donald C. Marsh to James J. McClendon, 30 Nov. 1943; Marsh to David D. Henry, 8 Dec. 1943; Gloster B. Current to William H. Pyle, 31 Mar. 1944, and Isaac Franck to Pyle, 20 Mar. 1944; *ibid.,* for information in this and the next sentence.

75. *Detroit News,* 4 July 1943, p. 8; Herbert J. Rushton, William E. Dowling, Oscar Olander and John H. Witherspoon, "Factual Report of the Governor's Committee to Investigate the Riot Occurring in Detroit on 21 June 1943," 11 Aug. 1943, BHC. While Marsh and Wolf acknowledge police prejudice, neither gave credence to the allegation by John Wood and others that patrolmen conspired against both Jews and blacks: interview with Donald C. Marsh, Detroit, Mich., 6 June 1978; interview with Eleanor P. Wolf, Detroit, 12 June 1978.

76. Marsh, "Negro-Jewish Relations in Detroit"; Donald C. Marsh to William Pyle, 16 Mar. 1944, unprocessed material, Marsh Collection, UA.

77. Sanford Griffith to Donald C. Marsh, 13 Oct. 1943; Marsh to Griffith, 11 Nov. 1943; and Marsh to David H. Henry; unprocessed material, Marsh Collection, UA, for information in this paragraph unless cited otherwise.

78. Gordon H. Simpson to Lucille Colley, 23 Mar. 1944, Box 3, and Harry I. Barron to Donald C. Marsh, 26 Apr. 1944, unprocessed material, Marsh Collection, UA.

79. Sanford Griffith to Donald C. Marsh, 2 Oct. 1944, *ibid.*

80. Donald C. Marsh to Sanford Griffith, 5 Dec. 1944, *ibid.*

81. Sanford Griffith to Donald C. Marsh, 26 Jan. 1945, *ibid.*

82. Interview with Donald C. Marsh, Detroit, Mich., 13 June 1978.

83. Donald C. Marsh, "Intercultural Conference Address," 31 Mar. 1944, Box 4, Marsh Collection, UA; interview with Donald C. Marsh, Detroit; Mich., 6 and 13 June 1978, for information in this paragraph unless cited otherwise.

84. Lee and Humphrey, *Race Riot;* Grimshaw, "A Study in Social Violence," pp. 321–55; Robert M. Fogelson, *Violence as Protest: A Study of Riots and Ghettos* (Garden City, N.Y., 1971); Charles V. Hamilton, "Riots, Revolts and Relevant Response" in William M. Chace and Peter Collier, eds., *Justice Denied: The Black Man in America* (New York, 1970), pp. 511–18; Joe R. Feagin and Harlan Hahn, *Ghetto Revolts: The Politics of Violence in American Cities* (New York, 1973), for examples.

85. William Julius Wilson, *The Declining Significance of Race: Blacks and Changing American Institutions* (Chicago, Ill., 1978) for an example that extends beyond violence.

86. Lenora E. Berson, *Case Study of a Riot: The Philadelphia Story* (New York, 1966), p. 46; Bertram H. Gold, *Jews and the Urban Crisis* (New York, 1968), p. 15.

87. Angus Campbell and Howard Schuman, "Racial Attitudes in Fifteen American Cities," in National Commission on Civil Disorders, *Supplemental Studies for the National Advisory Commission on Civil Disorders* (New York, 1968), p. 62; *National Advisory Commission on Civil Disorders* (New York, 1968), pp. 145, 196n. 222.

88. Marsh focused on blacks, Jews and white gentiles; the National Advisory Commission on Civil Disorders distinguished between Catholics, Protestants and Jews.

89. Marsh, Loving and Wolf, "Final Report: Pre-riot Survey," pp. 4, 5, 8, 13, 26, regarding Hastings Street, i.e. ghetto merchants; Peter H. Rossi, et al., "Between White and Black: The Faces of American Institutions in the Ghetto" in National Advisory Commission on Civil Disorder, *Supplemental Studies,* pp. 125–31.

90. In 1943 "the great majority" of Jewish merchants were foreign-born, while in 1967 only fifteen per cent of all ghetto shopkeepers—Jewish and non-Jewish—were immigrants. See Marsh, Loving and Wolf, "Negro-Jewish Attitude Analysis," p. 73; Rossi, et al., "Between White and Black," p. 126.

91. Marsh, Loving and Wolf, "Final Report: Pre-riot Survey," p. 11.

92. Marsh, Loving and Wolf, "Negro-Jewish Relationships in Detroit: Post-riot," p. 5, and "Final Report: Pre-riot Survey," pp. 31–32, which asked, perhaps too directly, "Do you contribute to neighborhood causes?" Rossi, et al., "Between White and Black," p. 126.

93. Marsh, Loving and Wolf, "Final Report: Pre-riot Survey," pp. 17, 18, 23; Campbell and Schuman, "Racial Attitudes in Fifteen American Cities," pp. 43–45; Rossi, et al., "Between White and Black," pp. 127, 129 for information in this paragraph unless cited otherwise.

94. Marsh, Loving and Wolf, "Negro-Jewish Relationships in Detroit: Post-riot," pp. 2, 122; Rossi, et al., "Between White and Black," pp. 130 and 131, for this and the following quotation.

95. The Five Year Study produced by Charles Y. Glock and Rodney Stark, *Christian Beliefs and Anti-Semitism* (New York, 1966); Glock, Gertrude J. Selznick and Joe L. Spaeth, *The Apathetic Majority: A Study Based on Public Responses to the Eichmann Trial* (New York, 1966); Marx, *Protest and Prejudice;* Selznick and Stephen Steinberg, *The Tenacity of Prejudice: Anti-Semitism in Contemporary America* (New York, 1969); Glock and Harold Quinley, *Wayward Shepherds: Prejudice and the Protestant Clergy* (New York, 1971); Glock, Robert Wuthnow, Jane Allyn Piliavin and Metta Spencer, *Adolescent Prejudice* (New York, 1975). It also provided the impetus for Quinley and Glock, *Anti-Semitism in America* (New York, 1979).

96. Marsh, Loving and Wolf, "Negro-Jewish Attitude Analysis," pp. 73–76, 77, for this quotation and p. 74, for the reference to "ancient bargaining" below.

97. Robert G. Weisbord and Arthur Stein, *Bittersweet Encounter: The Afro-American and the American Jew* (Westport, Ct., 1970), p. 67; Kenneth B. Clark, "Candor about Negro-Jewish Relations," *Commentary* (Feb. 1946), 10–11.

98. Marx, *Protest and Prejudice*, pp. 149–50.

99. Rossi, et al., "Between White and Black," p. 129, for example.

100. Sklare and Solotaroff, "Introduction," pp. 15–16.

101. Marsh, Loving and Wolf, "Negro-Jewish Attitude Analysis," p. 78; Marx, *Protest and Prejudice*, p. 160.

102. Marsh found the greatest conflict in the lower-class Hastings Street area; Marx discovered it among those of very low income: Marsh, Loving and Wolf, "Final Report: Pre-riot Survey," p. 24; Marx, *Protest and Prejudice*, p. 158.

103. St. Clair Drake and Horace R. Cayton, *Black Metropolis: A Study of Negro Life in a Northern City* (rev. and enlarged ed.; New York, 1970), II, 430–69; Roi Ottley *'New World A-Coming': Inside Black America* (New York, 1943), pp. 122–36; Wedlock, *The Reaction of Negro Publications and Organizations to German Anti-Semitism.*

104. Stember, "Reactions to Anti-Semitic Appeals before and during the War," p. 124; Marsh, Loving and Wolf, "Negro-Jewish Attitude Analysis," p. 102, for Samuel J. Lieberman's view.

105. Marsh, Loving and Wolf, "Final Report: Pre-riot Survey," pp. 44, 55.

106. *Ibid.*, 53; Marx, *Protest and Prejudice*, pp. 160–61.

107. *Detroit News,* 12 Apr. 1983, p. 4A, and Mary Sengstock, *Chaldean-Americans: Changing Conceptions of Ethnic Identity* (New York, 1982), for the conflict between black customers and Chaldean merchants in contemporary Detroit which reinforces Marsh's interpretation of cultural, historical and economic factors that affected black-Jewish relations.

108. Marsh, Loving and Wolf, *Negro-Jewish Relationships*, p. 5; Marx, *Protest and Prejudice*, pp. 146–47.

109. Capeci, *Race Relations in Wartime Detroit,* p. 44, for educational levels among black eastsiders and westsiders.

110. Marsh, Loving and Wolf, "Final Report: Pre-riot Survey," p. 84.

111. Quinley and Glock, *Anti-Semitism in America,* p. 58; Rossi, et al., "Between White and Black," p. 131.

112. Marsh, Loving and Wolf, "Final Report: Pre-riot Survey," p. 40; Marx, *Protest and Prejudice*, p. 147.

113. Marsh, Loving and Wolf, "Final Report: Pre-riot Survey," p. 43; Marx, *Protest and Prejudice*, p. 148ns. 22 and 23; Quinley and Glock, *Anti-Semitism in America,* p. 68. Marsh, Loving and Wolf implied these conclusions, which all latter-day researchers save one measured; for the exception, which found black images of Jews similar to those held by white Catholics and Protestants, see Gerhard Lenski, *The Religious Factor: A Sociologist's Inquiry* (New York, 1961), p. 68.

114. Marsh, Loving and Wolf, "Negro-Jewish Attitude Analysis," p. 87; Marx, *Protest and Prejudice*, p. 165.

115. Clark, "Candor about Negro-Jewish Relations," p. 13; Marsh, Loving and Wolf, "Final Report: Pre-riot Survey," pp. 40, 43; Marx, *Protest and Prejudice*, p. 159; Selznick and Steinberg, *The Tenacity of Prejudice*, p. 119; Quinley and Glock, *Anti-Semitism in America,* p. 71.

116. See N. 103 above; Lawrence D. Reddick, "Anti-Semitism among Negroes," *Negro Quarterly,* 1 (Summer 1942), 112–22; Clark "Candor about Negro-Jewish Relations," pp. 8–14, for an early psychological explanation.

117. Marx, *Protest and Prejudice*, pp. 133–34; Quinley and Glock, *Anti-Semitism in America,* p. 61.

118. Quinley and Glock, *ibid.*, pp. 58, 70–71.

119. Lenski, *The Religious Factor,* p. 33 notes "the possible exception of the South"; Quinley and Glock, *Anti-Semitism in America,* p. 59 covers Atlanta, Birmingham, Chicago and New York.

120. Marx, *Protest and Prejudice*, pp. 140–41 cites seven previous studies, the oldest having been done in 1947.

121. Edward L. Bernays to Donald C. Marsh, 4 Mar. 1946, unprocessed material, Marsh Collection, UA.

122. Quoted in Angell, "Introduction," p. 9.

# A. C. MacNeal to Walter White with Enclosure for the Organized Jewry of America in Chicago, March 23, 1933

My dear Mr. White:

Enclosed you will find copy of letter from the Chicago Branch, addressed to Jewish organizations in Chicago, offering such aid as they may direct to swell the protest against the present treatment of Jews in Germany.

The Branch feels that the acts committed against Jews in Germany, some of whom were American citizens, was a manifestation of race prejudice, and should have the condemnation of any organization interested in fair play, justice, and the stamping out of the evils of racial antagonism.

This action is recommended to the national office for its consideration.

Yours very truly,

CHICAGO BRANCH, N.A.A.C.P.

3458 S. State St.

A. C. MacNeal

President

[Enclosure]

Gentlemen:

The Chicago Branch of the National Association for the Advancement of Colored People wishes to extend to the Jewry of America any possible assistance it is capable of rendering to your protest against the violation of the fundamental human rights of Jews in Germany and elsewhere. It is the unanimous sentiment of the Chicago Branch that the elimination of prejudice and proscription on account of race, creed or color, should be the fight of every clear thinking nation if any semblance of the common humanities is to be preserved.

Our national office has been requested to take up the matter of cooperating in your protest from a national standpoint, to the end that 14 million colored people in America may add their voice to yours in this fight for human justice. If you will be kind enough to instruct us in what fashion we may cooperate, you may rest assured that we will act with a vigor and sincerity that is born of a sympathetic understanding of your cause.

In 1933 A. C. MacNeal was president of the Chicago branch of the NAACP. Walter White was secretary of the NAACP.

NAACP Papers, Box I G 51, Manuscript Division, Library of Congress, Washington, D.C.

Trusting that you will advise us to what end we may serve you, and expressing sincere hope that a successful issue will obtain in this fight, we are

Sincerely and cooperatively yours,
CHICAGO BRANCH, N.A.A.C.P.
3458 S. State St.
A. C. MacNeal,
    President.

ROBERT G. WEISBORD & ARTHUR STEIN

# Negro Perceptions of Jews between the World Wars

Before the First World War contacts between Jews and Negroes were relatively few. Black Americans prior to the Civil War were principally slaves in the rural South. Insofar as Jews did relate to blacks, they manifested the same general attitudes as other white Americans. Jews were both pro-slavery and anti-slavery. There were Jewish slaveholders and Jewish abolitionists. There were Negrophobes and Negrophiles. All told in 1860 there were approximately 150,000 Jews in America, three times as many as there were a decade earlier. Most lived in an urban environment. Hence, by dint of geography and sheer numbers, direct encounters between Jews and African-derived peoples were limited.

The period from the end of Reconstruction to Versailles was a veritable nightmare for Afro-Americans. They were disfranchised, Jim-Crowed and lynched on an incredible scale. Quite understandably, Southern Negroes who hungered for justice and thirsted for economic opportunity saw the urban North as the promised land. This prompted wholesale migration which reached its zenith during World War I. The forty years before Versailles had been tragic for European Jews also. After the assassination of the Czar in 1881 pogroms occured with unprecedented fury and frequency. As a result swarms of immigrants sought and found asylum in many of the same cities that served as havens for the Southern Negro. History had set the stage for more sustained and extensive contact between the two peoples.

Many of the encounters between Afro-Americans and Jewish Americans in Northern urban centers were scarcely the kind that promoted good will and inter-group understanding. They were instead unequal-status, friction-generating contacts, between merchants and consumers, between landlords and tenants, between housewives and domestics. In just about every instance, the black was in a subordinate position, essentially the position he had hoped to finally escape from in his flight to the North.

Underhanded business practices by white entrepreneurs in the black enclaves have long been a source of racial friction. There was often ample justification for allegations of overcharging and shortweighting and these were but two of the malpractices which frequently occurred between the two World Wars. Of course, for the poor eking out a marginal living even fair prices may seem outrageously high. Installment buying also

In 1969, Robert G. Weisbord was associate professor of history at the University of Rhode Island. In 1969, Arthur Stein was associate professor of political science at the University of Rhode Island, Kingston. Originally published in *Judaism* 18, no. 4 (Fall 1969): 428–47. Copyright © 1969, American Jewish Congress. Reprinted with permission from *Judaism*.

caused irritation. Penurious Negroes in the collapsed Depression economy became embittered when pressed to make regular payments which they could ill afford.

That retailers of many faiths and national backgrounds were guilty of unethical business habits is incontrovertible. Jews as a group were probably no more nor less culpable than Gentiles. However, significantly, they were identified more easily, either by name or manner of dress. A popular misconception in some urban ghettos where rent gouging was a constant irritant was that *all* white landlords and shopkeepers were Jews. In certain cities, Jews constituted a majority in those categories. Undoubtedly they were present out of proportion to their numbers in the overall population. This was particularly the case in cities where the black ghettos were previously Jewish neighborhoods. Boston's Roxbury, sections of Philadelphia, South Providence and Harlem, among others, fit this description.

Just before the turn of the century the face of Harlem was drastically altered by a boom in real estate. Almost overnight houses were erected. Many were occupied by East European Jews, shortly before denizens of the Lower East Side. Moving uptown earned them considerable prestige in the eyes of their co-religionists and bespoke their growing affluence. So dense was the Jewish population of lower Harlem that the district was dubbed "Little Russia" by the press of the day. Synagogues, Hebrew schools, and a whole host of social and fraternal institutions were founded or transplanted. Harlem's newest residents were not universally welcome. Gilbert Osofsky, in his fascinating *Harlem: The Making of a Ghetto*, cites a to-let sign which read in German, "No Jews, No Dogs."[1]

Afro-Americans, at first those with some resources, began to filter into the area after the real estate bubble burst in 1904–1905. Many segments of Harlem's white population tried to stem the tide of non-white Southern migrants. Their efforts were doomed to fail. By the time of the Great Depression the metamorphosis of Harlem from an elegant, expensive section to a segregated Negro slum was complete. Virtually en masse its Italian inhabitants trekked elsewhere. Jews did likewise. Many relocated further north in the Washington Heights area or in the Bronx. Shopkeepers and landlords did not necessarily dispose of their property. But regardless of the actual proportion of Jewish landlords in Harlem, their number was often exaggerated. Abetting this process of selective perception was the fact that not infrequently in the 1920's, 30's, and 40's, Christian firms used Jews to manage apartment houses and to collect rents. The percentage of Jewish-owned shops in that era is not known, but some of the very large department stores on 125th Street symbolized Jewish commercial domination of Harlem. Also, pawnbrokers who customarily deal with people in dire straits, were predominantly Jewish.

A comparable situation existed in Philadelphia. On specific streets in the Negro districts of North and South Philadelphia Jewish ownership was conspicuous. When black Americans and Jews met in the City of Brotherly Love the encounters were not likely to result in feelings of brotherly affection. Typically they involved Jewish retailers and landlords on one hand and Negro consumers and tenants on the other. Stereotypes, more likely than not disparaging ones, emerged and were disseminated by word of mouth and by the printed word. A writer in *The Philadelphia Tribune* in 1934 painted the Jews as "dollar crazy" people who were always prepared to invade black communities.[2] In 1942 Philadelphia was bluntly described by a Negro as a "hotbed of Negro anti-Semitism."[3]

Competition between nascent colored entrepreneurs and established Jewish businessmen also bred ill-will in the inner cities during the inter-war years. On the basis of their research in Chicago, St. Clair Drake and Horace R. Cayton concluded that most black storekeepers sincerely believed that there was a functioning Jewish conspiracy designed to victimize them.[4] A not uncommon complaint with a great deal of validity was that Jews, having gotten in on the ground floor, so to speak, had a distinct advantage over black competitors. The former enjoyed the best locations. In addition, because they had capital, they could cut prices and extend credit. An editorial in a weekly magazine charged that ". . . an organization of Jewish businessmen arbitrarily holds down competition. No colored merchant is permitted to operate a competing establishment in a good location except under conditions which make bankruptcy inevitable."[5] Following the formation of a Biracial Business Association with a membership eighty per cent Caucasian, the same editor was quoted as saying that a goodly number of the members lived in "Master Race" communities and were signers of restrictive covenants.[6]

There was also a feeling among black Chicagoans that people of African descent had more confidence in Jewish storekeepers than in their black counterparts. Drake and Cayton quoted a shoemaker to the effect that "the Negro has no faith in colored business. He thinks I can't fix his good pair of shoes. He don't know that the Jew down the street brings his work for me to do."[7]

Jews, who were once held up as examples for Negro entrepreneurs, increasingly became the target of their rancor. Jews who had "milked" the ghettos of millions of dollars didn't deserve Negro patronage. To offset the advantage of their more experienced Jewish rivals, black businessmen appealed for racial solidarity.

Black chauvinism in the dog-eat-dog business world can only be appreciated if it is recognized that the expanding commercial initiative among Negroes was a tremendous development. After all, the bulk of them were only a few generations removed from slavery. Black enterprises in predominantly black areas were a vehicle by which black Americans could advance in material terms without relying on "whitey." One might say that it was an embryonic form of "black power."[8]

Outside the ghettos, department stores in some cities flatly refused to serve Negro customers. That was the state of affairs in Baltimore, for example, in the late 1930's. It was not just a question of ice cream sodas and other refreshments. Wearing apparel, furniture and a myriad of other basic items could not be purchased by Americans of African descent. According to a *Crisis* editorial in 1938, the majority of the stores which so humiliated the black population were Jewish-owned or managed by Jews.[9] Rabbi Edward L. Israel, in the same publication, had previously written that only a few Jewish department store owners refused to sell to black people. Several had a completely different customer policy. Moreover, Rabbi Israel commented, Negroes were universally barred from Gentile department stores in Baltimore.[10] Negroes were infuriated and quite properly so. Such a situation was almost certain to adversely affect Negro views of Jews if they were associated rightly or wrongly with that exclusion.

Discriminatory hiring practices were another sore point exacerbating Jewish-Negro relations. E. Franklin Frazier, the noted Negro sociologist, observed that New York employers in the 1920's were of two kinds, those who adamantly refused to employ black people at all and those who hired them only in low-paying, menial capacities.[11] Gimbels belonged in the first category and Macy's in the second. Companies owned by Christians pursued essentially the same personnel policies as did these large Jewish-owned department stores. In 1930 the Metropolitan Life Insurance Company rationalized its total exclusion of Negroes by predicting strong objections on the part of white employees to a nondiscriminatory policy.[12]

On the eve of the Great Depression Negro workers in the urban North were already severely depressed. The "promised land" envisioned by migrants from the South had failed to materialize. If Pullman porters, janitors, elevator operators or waiters were needed black men could apply. If servants, charwomen or waitresses were required, black women would be taken on. Unskilled manual labor was one thing, but higher paying "clean work" was another. Attempts by skilled or semiskilled Negroes to obtain clerical, managerial, or professional jobs were ordinarily futile. As Drake and Cayton indicated in their classic *Black Metropolis,* just prior to the onset of the Depression fifty-six per cent of all black females employed and more than twenty-five per cent of all black males who held jobs were servants of one type or another. Taking into consideration their percentage of the total population, this was more than four times the Negro's proportionate share of such work.[13] They were also grossly over-represented in the ranks of the unemployed. In short they were the last to be added to the work force and almost invariably for "Negro jobs." Needless to say, they were the first to be fired.

If prejudice in employment degraded and belittled the Negro in downtown shopping areas, then the discrimination in recruitment and promotion which was rife in the ghetto itself, was unbearably galling. Some of the very same merchants who earned their livings in the black neighborhoods refused to employ Negroes except in lowly positions. Roi Ottley, writing in 1943, offered as a prime exhibit Blumstein's, a sizeable department store which is still doing business today on 125th St. in Harlem. Although willing to retain black people to run his elevators and to do cleaning work, the owner, William Blumstein, refused to hire Negroes to sell or to perform clerical work.[14]

Claude McKay, the distinguished Jamaican novelist and poet, told of a white Southerner who managed a large five-and-dime store in Harlem. When asked to hire a fixed quota of black clerks, he retorted that where he had been born in the South Negroes could not be customers in the better stores, much less employees. As long as he was in charge "not a damned 'nigger' would work behind his counters even if [his] customers were 'niggers.'"[15]

So deplorable was this state of affairs that jobs-for-Negroes direct action campaigns were launched in a number of cities—St. Louis, Baltimore, Chicago, and, of course, New York. Indignant blacks brought considerable economic pressure to bear by picketing and boycotting the guilty storekeepers. On the whole, the campaigns in the 1930's met with only moderate success. They did bring to the fore a covey of flamboyant national-ists whose rhetoric was rabidly anti-Semitic.

Especially bizarre was one Sufi Abdul Hamid. A gargantuan, booted, bearded figure, he customarily sported a turban, a robe and sometimes a cape. On occasion he was attired in a Nazi-like uniform. His stage was a stepladder or soapbox, his theatre, the streets of Harlem. His Negro Industrial Clerical Alliance appealed mainly to the wretched casualties of America's most serious Depression. The jobless Sufists included a small number of high school and college graduates. To this dispirited, impoverished audience Sufi preached the virtues of Islam. C. Eric Lincoln credits some of this coun-try's first converts to that faith to his proselytizing zeal.[16]

He fulminated against white shopkeepers who bilked Harlem but who were unwill-ing to employ Negroes. Jewish merchants received the brunt of his invective. Among his slogans were "share the jobs" and "down with the Jews." No wonder, given the melan-choly events unfolding in Germany, Sufi was labelled a "Harlem Hitler" and a "Black Hitler" by Jewish critics.[17] Apparently, he felt complimented by these characterizations. His career as a Jew-baiter ended abruptly after he was hauled into court for incitement of racial hatred. For the next few years, before his death in an air crash, Sufi resumed his earlier career as an Oriental cultist.[18]

Racial discrimination in employment also aroused the ire of Arthur L. Reid who, along with Ira Kemp and others, founded the Harlem Labor Union, Inc. Reid, a former lieutenant of Marcus Garvey's, urged his followers not to buy where they couldn't work. Instead, he advised them to buy black, to patronize Negro-owned businesses rather than those of alien merchants.[19] In enunciating his fervent advocacy of black economic power, Reid trotted out an assortment of anti-Jewish indictments. He levelled his charges against Jewish union leaders, against exploiting ghetto merchants, and against Bronx Jewish housewives who took advantage of Negro domestics.

High on the list of the most accessible, if undesirable "negro jobs" were those in domestic service. Cooks, maids and black cleaning women were commonplace in white homes. In Chicago, at the beginning of World War II, Drake and Cayton estimated that Negroes constituted almost fifty per cent of all women engaged in domestic labor.[20] Nationwide, fifty-eight per cent of the women working in private households were non-white.[21] Working conditions and wages were especially poor for those who did day work; i.e. household labor negotiated ordinarily on a day-to-day basis with a variety of employers.

Even the circumstances under which housewives hired these scrub women were frequently shocking. The scandalous situation in New York City was popularly referred to as the "Bronx Slave Market." There the labor of Negro women were bought and sold in a fashion all too reminiscent of slavery in ante-bellum Dixie. After hearing countless grievances two black women journalists, Ella Baker and Marvel Cooke, exposed the circumstances of this lively trade. Simpson Avenue in the East Bronx illustrated the slave market at its worst.

Rain or shine, cold or hot, you will find them there—Negro women, old and young—sometimes bedraggled, sometimes neatly dressed—but with the invariable paper bundle, waiting expectantly for Bronx housewives to buy their strength and energy for an hour, two hours, or even for a day at the munificent rate of fifteen, twenty, twenty-five, or, if luck be with them, thirty cents an hour. If not the wives themselves, maybe their husbands, their sons or their brothers, under the subterfuge of work, offer worldly wise girls higher bids for their time.[22]

Pressed to the proverbial wall by economic necessity, the black women were scarcely in a position to negotiate effectively. All too often the housewives were unfeeling and unscrupulous, said Miss Baker and Miss Cooke, who accumulated their data first-hand by "selling" themselves on the market. They vividly described the fate of the typical "slave" hired by "Mrs. Simon Legree" to do manifold household drudgeries.

Under a rigid watch, she is permitted to scrub floors on her bended knees, to hang precariously from window sills, cleaning window after window, or to strain and sweat over steaming tubs of heavy blankets, spreads and furniture covers.

Fortunate, indeed, is she who gets the full hourly rate promised. Often, her day's slavery is rewarded with a single dollar bill or whatever her unscrupulous employer pleases to pay. More often, the clock is set back for an hour or more. Too often she is sent away without any pay at all.[23]

For the authors of this exposé, the real significance of the Bronx slave market was that it was the "economic battle front" in microcosm. It underscored the Negroes' lack of awareness of the potential benefits of collective action and it demonstrated the apathy of white-dominated labor unions where the well-being of black people was involved.

Just how many of the callous housewives trading in the "mart" were Jewish was not made clear. But Jews were the only ethnic group explicitly named in the piece and the Bronx was characterized as a northern borough in New York City "known for its heavy Jewish population." The implication, a rather strong one, was that, by and large, the culprits were Jewish.

The Bronx was not unique. Unfavorable views of Jews were symptomatic of domestics in Chicago. Yet Drake and Cayton concluded that many of the servants in their study found Jewish employers less bigoted although more tightfisted than their white Gentile counterparts. Of one hundred and fifty interviewed no less than two-thirds thought Jews more disposed to treat Negroes as equals but less inclined to pay on a level with other employers.[24] Not atypical was the complaint of a black "washwoman," a class earning on the average $2.50 *per diem* towards the end of the Depression:

The Jewish woman that I work for tries to get a colored woman to do all of her work for as little as $2.00 a day and pay her own carfare.

She is expected to do all the washing, including the linen and towels as well as the clothes for the five members of the family. She is supposed to finish the work—that is iron the entire wash—and then clean the house thoroughly—all for $2.00 Because there are some women who will do all of the work for that amount, this Jewish woman feels that a colored woman who demands more is silly to think that she can get it. She says that she doesn't understand why, if some colored people can get along on that amount, all can't do the same.[25]

Even in retrospect such insensitivity and crass exploitation can make one's blood boil. That it spawned anti-white and frequently anti-Semitic sentiments is scarcely surprising.

In May 1941 New York's inimitable Mayor LaGuardia initiated action to end the sidewalk hiring of houseworkers and the concomitant haggling and chiseling. With funds provided by the Social Security Board to the New York State Employment Service, the Simpson Street Day Work Office was ceremoniously opened. Informal indoor negotiations were to replace the outdoor flesh exchanges.[26] Whether working conditions and wages improved as a result is questionable. Lawrence D. Reddick, writing in *The Negro Quarterly* a year later, reported that the Bronx slave market still remained as a source of anti-Semitism among Negroes.[27]

Tensions generated by this kind of unequal status contact have been reduced appreciably since World War II. Regrettably, they have not vanished altogether.[28] What has made the difference however has been expanding job opportunities for black females. No longer are black high-school graduates virtually restricted to the "whiskbroom, mop, and serving tray." They can and do become secretaries, clerks, saleswomen, etc. Others go on to higher education. Fair-employment practices and minimum-wage legislation have also been remedial factors. For the unskilled, market conditions have sometimes helped; wages have been hiked by the dwindling supply of domestics and the constantly rising demand for their labor.

Despite these changes, now as then, there are housewives, Jew and Gentile, who are slow to accept the full humanity and "adulthood" of their "girls." Frequently, the "girls" are many years older than their insensitive employers.

Contemporaneous with the Depression and its corrosive effect on Negroes was the emergence of Hitler's Third Reich. Nazi anti-Semitism was, of course, not restricted to Europe. In Detroit, relevant literature was distributed free in black sections by the notorious Jew-baiter, Father Coughlin.[29] Because of Hitler's much-vaunted theories of Nordic supremacy his career was bound to be scrutinized by the Negro press in this country. It reacted not only to the racist implications of Nazism but also to the meaning for black people of Hitler's persecution of the Jews.

A popular theme sounded in the Negro press was that oppression was no stranger to the Afro-American. Sympathy was extended to the Jew and efforts to assist him in his hour of need were applauded. But what about the suffering of America's black population? Whence would come their relief? A *Crisis* editorial, aptly titled "Charity Begins At Home," in commenting on the indignities visited upon Jews in Central Europe and our Negro citizens, found them amazingly alike. The Jews were disfranchised: so were Negroes in the South. Both were discriminated against in education and employment. Jews were either excluded from beaches, playgrounds and parks or were restricted to recreational facilities specifically designated for them. Jim-Crowism humiliated Negroes in a similar fashion. Propaganda of the vilest variety calculated to incite hatred for Jews characterized the German educational system from kindergarten to university. In white America the school system buttressed society's pejorative image of the Negro. Lastly, both Jews and Negroes were treated with great cruelty. But, whereas the plight of the former pricked the consciences of many Americans, those same Americans including the President and the Senate were unmoved by the horrible oppression of black people on American soil.[30] Seen in retrospect, official concern for the lot of German Jews was probably overrated by the *Crisis* editorial; nonetheless, the hypocrisy of America's governing elite's hand wringing (if not acting) on the Jewish question while turning a blind eye to the ongoing privations of black citizens is all too plain.

Other Negro publications made the same telling point. Shortly after Hitler came to power, *The Philadelphia Tribune* recognized that it was hell to be a Jew in Germany. But, it opined, it was twice as terrible to be a black man in the United States.[31] A 1934 editorial entitled "Germany vs. America," published in the *Tribune*, succinctly observed: "The persecution of the Jews in Germany by the Nazi Government is deplorable, stupid and outrageous. The persecution of colored Americans by Americans is cruel, relentless, and spirit breaking."[32]

Baltimore's *Afro-American*, in an editorial called "The Nazis and Dixie," compared the old slave codes with the Nuremberg Laws and other anti-Semitic measures. After enumerating some of the harsh disabilities imposed on German Jews, the editor remarked that such legislation was "designed to crush the spirit of the Jewish people and bring them down to the position our own people occupy in so many parts of the South." America below the Mason-Dixon line and Hitler's Germany were "mental brothers." The difference was that in this country the Constitution, in effect, compelled the South to resort to force and terrorism by proscribing Nuremberg-type laws.[33]

The same newspaper also scored the Fuehrer for a speech in which he immodestly lauded German civilization. Tyrannizing Jews and using insulting invective in referring to Negroes was hardly evidence of an advanced culture said the *Afro-American*. On the question of comparative cultural achievement it asserted:

> Three thousand years ago when Africans were building pyramids and Jews temples, Germans were roaming the forest armed with clubs and drinking the blood of human sacrifices.
>
> Civilization is not much over one thousand years old in Germany and it is plainly evident that what gentility it once had has departed, leaving the savage Hun in place of the well-meaning Herr.[34]

Hitler's talk reminded the *Afro-American* of a Klansman, and the force which for three and a half centuries had enslaved, lynched and hounded persons of African descent was called American Nazism.[35] Negrophobia in that troubled period in history was oftentimes called Hitlerism and the predicament in which blacks found themselves was proof of Nazism.[36] Kelly Miller, writing in *The Washington Tribune* referred to the Fuehrer as "the master Ku Kluxer of Germany."[37]

Miller, long associated with Howard University, was an esteemed essayist and one of America's leading black intellectuals for more than forty years until his death in 1939. Miller assigned Hitler the dubious distinction of being the "greatest demagogue of modern times." In an article in *Opportunity*, a monthly published by the National Urban League, Miller saw a striking analogy between the legal manifestations of race prejudice against the Negro in America and the Jew in Germany. "Between Hitler's treatment of the Jews and America's treatment of the Negro, you may pay your money and take your choice."[38] His editorial in a Norfolk Negro newspaper on "The Sad Plight of the Jews—Can It Happen Here?," took America to task for being smugly oblivious of her dismal record in relating to Indians and Negroes while it denounced Hitler. Of all peoples, Miller reflected, it was most incumbent upon the black man to lament the quandary the Jew was in "lest it forbode the day when he, too, will be battered with the shocks of doom."[39]

The tragedy of Hitlerism evoked many of the same thoughts from W.E.B. DuBois. Few figures in black history enjoy more respect among Afro-Americans today than DuBois who died in Ghana in 1963. This is true of militants and moderates alike. Born in Massachusetts in 1868, DuBois was outstanding both as a scholar and as an articulate proponent of full citizenship rights for black Americans. He was a founder of the N.A.A.C.P. in 1910, an organization then regarded as dangerously radical. For more than twenty years DuBois edited its journal, *The Crisis.*

With perhaps one exception, the opinions about Jews which DuBois expressed were virtually all sympathetic.[40] His initial exposure to anti-Semitism occurred during his student days in Berlin and his travels in Poland, years before Hitler's ascent to power. But it was the Hitlerian persecution which elicited the most poignant comments from DuBois' prolific pen.

Predictably he found Nazi racism loathsome. He thought that if Hitler were to lecture at white Southern colleges "his race nonsense would fit beautifully."[41] What Germany was doing to the Jew, America had done to the Negro. No exact parallel existed between the two minorities. Whereas the Jews were not wanted in Germany, cheap Negro labor was lucrative and hence desirable in the South. Still, he speculated, in an autobiography published in 1940, that "We may be expelled from the United States as the Jew is being expelled from Germany."[42] Only the year before the notorious Senator Bilbo of Mississippi had introduced legislation to resettle American Negroes in Africa.

The publicity accorded the plight of German Jewry contrasted sharply with the widespread complacency of white America on the Negro problem. DuBois' anger about this was made sarcastically evident in his column, "As the Crow Flies," contained in *The Crisis* of September, 1933. He "confessed" to being filled with "unholy glee" by Hitler and the Nordics. "When the only 'inferior' peoples were 'niggers' it was hard to get the attention of the *New York Times* for little matters of race lynching and mobs. But now that the damned included the owner of the *Times,* moral indignation is perking up."[43] DuBois was saying that Jews, in particular, should cry out against the oppression of Negroes. Crimes against one people were crimes against all humanity. During World War II he conjectured about a special destiny for the Chosen People.

> Suppose the Jews, instead of considering themselves a hopeless minority in the face of white Europe, should conceive themselves as part of the disinherited majority of men whom they would help to lead to power and self-realization; and at the same time imbue them with cultural tolerance and faith in humanity?[44]

Given the Jewish contributions to German civilization, the disturbing lesson of Nazi racism for the Negro was abundantly clear. Shortly after Hitler assumed the Chancellorship, in March 1933, DuBois wrote: ". . . after all, race prejudice has nothing to do with accomplishment or descent, with genius or ability. It is an ugly, dirty thing. It feeds on envy and hate."[45]

Speaking in 1952 on "The Negro and the Warsaw Ghetto," DuBois commented that his three visits to Poland, and particularly the one in 1949 to the demolished Jewish ghetto in Warsaw, had deepened his own understanding of the black man's dilemma. Specifically, his conception of the battle against religious bigotry, racial segregation and oppression by wealth had been enlarged. He had learned that the race problem "cut across lines of color and physique and belief and status and was a matter of cultural patterns, perverted teaching and human hate and prejudice, which reached all sorts of people and caused endless evil to all men."[46]

Somewhat less sympathetic to the Jews during the Hitler years was Marcus Mosiah Garvey, then in exile from the United States. Future historians may well view Garvey as the central figure in twentieth-century black history. He is already regarded as the patron saint of black nationalism and the progenitor of black power. He is honored in Africa, in London's Ladbroke Grove, in his native Jamaica and in Harlem.

Like so many other black men of lesser stature, Garvey entertained ambivalent feelings about Jews. At one and the same time he was mistrustful of them and held them up as a model to oppressed blacks. In the pages of the *Black Man*, a monthly magazine published by Garvey in London in the twilight of his checkered career, the paradox is obvious. Garvey felt that Hitler was making a fool of himself by persecuting Jews and attacking Judaism. Why? Because "Jewish finance is a powerful world factor. It can destroy organisations and nations."[47]

More caustic was Garvey's observation that most of the Jews' trouble in the world, but particularly in Germany, "has been brought on by themselves in that their particular method of living is inconsistent with the broader principles that go to make all people homogeneous. The Jews like money. They have always been after money. They want nothing else but money."[48]

Garvey minced no words when Jewish interests appeared to conflict with those of Negroes anywhere in the world. That was the case in June, 1939, when he heard that Neville Chamberlain, then British Prime Minister, was prepared to arrange for the settlement of Jewish refugees in British Guiana. No historical relationship existed between the wandering Jew and that colony. His planned introduction into Guiana, Garvey wrote, was "nothing else than an attempt to submerge and destroy the black population." While disclaiming any antipathy toward Jews as Jews, Garvey described them as a successful and cunning group. A Jew is always a Jew. His history has been one of selfishness. His greed has clouded his judgment.[49] Always the nationalist, Garvey's solution to the Jewish problem was to have the Jew establish and build a nation, but not in Guiana or the West Indies.

There were times when Garvey expressed sympathy for the Jews as he said he would for any persecuted people, and there were times when he saw them as brothers in adversity to the black man.[50] Many self-styled Garveyites have ignored this and have been more scornful of Jews than their mentor, for whom Jewish-Negro relations were of minor importance. The activities of Ira Reid have already been touched on. Another case in point is Carlos Cook, a native of the Dominican Republic who, until his death in 1966, headed the neo-Garveyite African Nationalist Pioneer Movement with headquarters in New York. In 1942, Cook, while addressing a Harlem crowd, ostensibly about housing grievances, was heard to say about Hitler: "What he's trying to do, we're trying to do."[51]

It should be understood there is nothing inherently anti-Jewish about Garveyism or black nationalism and most nationalists are not anti-Semitic. If many of the highly publicized statements in recent years criticizing Jews have originated in those circles, it is probably because nationalism's greatest appeal is precisely to those black people whose contacts with Jews are of the unequal status, friction-generating variety.

In the 1930's and 1940's, proponents of black nationalism were not the only ones whose perceptions of events in Germany were greatly influenced by the nature of Negro-Jewish encounters in America's urban North. There is a substantial corpus of journalistic impressions of the role of the Jew in the Third Reich and in this country. Many evinced unconcealed delight that the Jew was finally getting his comeuppance. Exemplifying this reaction was a column in *The Afro-American* in June, 1933:

> The Hebrews who get it in the neck are entitled to sympathy, but they, themselves, are not basically opposed to the Hitler principle. They, too, believe in hanging together and letting the devil take the hindmost. If you doubt it, try to get a job as clerk in one of those Pennsylvania Avenue department stores . . . there you will find Hitlerism in its most blatant form exercised by those who are being Hitlerized in Germany.[52]

In the same vein a *St. Louis Argus* editorial in July, 1938 maintained that despite the fact that Jews were discriminated against here and abroad, "they, themselves are not free from using the same tactics and methods to persecute and discriminate against Negroes. . . ."[53]

J. A. Rogers, a lecturer, traveler, foreign correspondent, columnist, and historian of the Negro past, tended to put the onus for the Nazi nightmare on the Jews themselves. Rogers, whose literary works were required reading for Garveyites, explained his position in *The Philadelphia Tribune,* a major black newspaper of the day:

> The Jew is accused of being an exploiter,—a charge which is, alas, but too true of a certain business element . . . the German opposition to the Jew is due largely to the fact that the Jew is powerful as a thinker, as a leader in advanced thought and as an exploiter of his fellowman.[54]

It was his opinion that conditions were decidedly worse in the South for black men than for the Jews in Germany. Jews, Rogers contended, were capitalistic exploiters and leading Communists. On both scores they were odious.

George Schuyler, another Negro author who in the 1960's has been closely identified with numerous conservative causes, was hesitant about extending sympathy to German Jewry in 1938.

I would be able to wail a lot louder and deeper if American Jews would give more concrete evidence of being touched by the plight of Negroes . . . Jewish-owned business is no more ready to hire Negroes in other than menial capacities than are Gentile-owned businesses. Jewish-owned and managed hotels and restaurants are quick to say "We don't want to serve your people" as are those owned by Catholics and Protestants.

He alluded to the deplorable Baltimore situation as symptomatic of the Pontius-Pilate outlook of Jews. "If my Hebrew friends were only as quick to employ capable Negroes as they are other people and did not get so excited when a decent family moves in their districts," Schuyler wrote, "I could pray even harder for Hitler to let up on them."[55]

Hitler's undisguised anti-Negro feelings notwithstanding, there were a few black Americans who openly admired him. *Dynamite,* a short-lived Chicago tabloid that began publication in July, 1936, voiced their thinking. Its owner and editor was one H. George Davenport, who combined careers as a sign painter and columnist. His aim was to disseminate facts "Negro Newspapers Are Afraid to Print." At first distributed free, *Dynamite* yearned for a *Fuehrer,* a man of vision. "What America needs is a Hitler and what the Chicago Black Belt needs is a purge of the exploiting Jew."[56] Hitler had restored a tottering Germany to its place as a European power. Negroes also required someone to point the way.

No organ was more vicious in its Jew-baiting than *Dynamite.* "Scurrilous" was the epithet most commonly used by its contemporary critics, black and white. In its pages Jewish philanthropists were reviled and Jewish entrepreneurs derided. Local blacks who lacked the anti-Semitic crusading zeal of *Dynamite* were taunted about their exploitation. Referring to a citizens committee which had been formed to find work for jobless Negroes, *Dynamite* said:

Now all you nice little Negroes, who are so much in love with your Jewish merchants can readily see that the very merchant you are always supporting does not want to see you prepare your son and daughter for jobs that call for better salaries, they wanted this committee to be a failure unless Jews control it.[57]

*Dynamite* further charged Jewish businessmen with making it impossible for black men to rent stores and thereby compete with them in Chicago. In addition, Negro consumers couldn't buy fish wholesale because Jews had cornered the market. Indeed, it was alleged, those same sharp business practices were used wherever Jews were involved. "It must be their religion," *Dynamite* pontificated, for such devious ways were peculiar to people of the Jewish faith.[58] Only by ceasing to trade with Jewish dealers could their chicanery be overcome. The ultimate solution would be their expulsion from the black community.[59]

So vituperative were the repeated onslaughts against the Jews that the newspaper and its publisher were investigated by the House Un-American Activities Committee, or the Dies Committee as it was known in 1938. A Negro scholar, Lawrence Reddick, tried to probe the psyche of Hitler's black fans. Given the *Fuehrer*'s utter contempt for Negroes, he concluded that his ghetto admirers were totally devoid of their rational faculties.[60]

By no means was antipathy toward Jews restricted to the unbalanced.[61] It was common, wrote Chandler Owen in 1941, to hear Negroes say, "Well, Hitler did one good thing: he put these Jews in their place."[62] By the early '40s black writers, while articulating widely divergent opinions about Jews, were virtually all agreed that Negro anti-Semitism was definitely on the increase. Those who believed that Negro-Jewish frictions are novel in the late 1960's would be well advised to note the words of Ralph Bunche penned more than a quarter of a century ago: "It is common knowledge that many members of the Negro and Jewish communities of the country share mutual dislike, scorn, and mistrust."[63] James Q. Wilson, in his study of *Negro Politics,* originally published in 1960, wrote that "Negro anti-Semitism, which at one time was so prevalent that it formed one of the major themes of the Negro press, seems to have diminished, particularly among the better educated and more cosmopolitan Negroes."[64] Yet, the overt anti-Semitism in 1968 and 1969, hardly representative of the black community, caused hysteria as well as legitimate concern. *Time* magazine thought it deserving of a cover story.[65] Jews old enough to know better regarded it as a new phenomenon, or at least, one which had reached new heights. Earlier cases of black hostility to Jews had been overlooked for a few good reasons. One was that in the '30s and '40s little notice was given to the Negro press by whites. A second was that Negroes were virtually without power to do anything in America and Jews in that era had more formidable anti-Semites to contend with in the white community.

It must not be forgotten that many Negro voices were raised in protest against the "rising tide" of Jew-baiting. Among the loudest and clearest in Harlem was that of Adam Clayton Powell, Jr. Powell, who succeeded his father as pastor of the mammoth Abyssinian Baptist Church in 1939—it had some eight thousand members—was the first black Congressman to be elected by Harlem. Lately, his difficulties with the Internal Revenue Service, his playboy escapades, and personal peccadilloes have captured the headlines and obscured his earlier substantial accomplishments. Those accomplishments actually antedate his first election to the House of Representatives in 1944. Kenneth Clark has written in his *Dark Ghetto,* that in the 1930's "Powell became the symbol of the struggle for minimal Negro rights, his name a household word."[66] When Woolworth's on 125th Street declined to hire black girls as clerks, Powell took to the picket lines. He joined in the mass picketing of Blumstein's also. Between Powell and Sufi Abdul Hamid little love was lost, although ostensibly the two were agitating for the same "don't buy where you can't work" cause. When Powell chided Sufi, the latter assailed Adam as an alcoholic fool.[67] "A professional anti-Semite" and a "black Hitler" were the terms Powell chose retrospectively to describe Sufi in his *Marching Blacks* published in 1945.[68]

In the dark days of the Depression, when anti-Semitism was on the increase, Powell was instrumental in establishing a biracial committee which made a concerted effort to open up to Negroes theretofore unobtainable jobs. Using his column, the "Soap Box," in the *Amsterdam News,* he spoke out forthrightly on Negro-Jewish relations. No battle predicated on hatred could be won, he asserted on one occasion. Enmity could not be countered with enmity. Bigotry could not be destroyed with more bigotry.

Let us stop blaming the Jew for the wrongs perpetrated and blame those who are really at fault. Wherever the blame falls, let us not follow it up with hate. The fact is the Jew doesn't wrong us any more and probably much less than any other group. Maybe the corner grocer will short weigh you a couple of ounces, but so will Joe the vegetable man and Sam the ice man. Cheating is not confined to any one race. Whereas one group might cut the change a little bit or pad the bill, it is the so-called white Christian that is giving us the most hell right now.[69]

In *Marching Blacks* he described anti-Semitism as "a deadly virus of the American bloodstream," even deadlier than anti-Negroism in some regions.[70]

Powell also took up the cudgels in defense of European Jewry. He inveighed against Hitler, Mussolini and their minions and called international Fascism civilization's greatest danger. Nazi hatred of Jews, he felt, was unwarranted. Hitler was using German Jewry as a scapegoat. "By lampooning the Jew, he could make the lowest moron and the biggest degenerate in all Germany feel that, after all, he wasn't the lowest down, there were always the Jews."[71] Exactly the same psychology underlay prejudice toward Negroes in the American South, Powell opined: "He [the white Southerner] wants the tobacco juice-stained moron of Tobacco Road to feel that there is always someone beneath him and so, he is taught that the Negro down the road is not his equal."[72]

Negroes, he argued, could not stand aloof. Neutrality and apathy were self-defeating. Prejudice in Germany, China, Spain, Haiti or wherever imperiled America's "so-called free Negroes." In Powell's view the dilemma of Harlem's unemployed and the plight of the remaining Scottsboro victims on one hand, and Hitler's persecution of German Jewry on the other were inextricably intertwined.[73]

A. Philip Randolph, head of the Brotherhood of Sleeping Car Porters, made essentially the same point in June, 1942, while addressing a Madison Square Garden audience: ". . . no Negro is secure from intolerance and race prejudice so long as one Jew is a victim of anti-Semitism or a Catholic is victimized as Governor Alfred E. Smith was by religious bigotry during the Presidential campaign against Herbert Hoover, or a trade unionist is harassed by a tory open-shopper."[74]

Ralph Bunche, in 1942 chairman of the Department of Political Science at Howard University, held both anti-Semitism among American blacks and Negrophobia on the part of Jews to be nonsensical examples of the pot calling the kettle black. For Afro-Americans anti-Jewish feeling was not just an unfortunate social phenomenon but a dangerous luxury. Bunche expressed a hope that Jewish and Negro leaders and organizations would labor to improve the strained relations between the two ethnic minorities. "In large measure," he maintained, "their problems—their grievances and their fears are cut to a common pattern."[75]

Chandler Owen, who served as a consultant on Negro relations for the Office of War Information, also wrote candidly in the face of growing anti-Semitism in the black ghettos. Owen ascribed that phenomenon to the mischief of Axis agents whose talk of Jewish control of commerce and industry was "echoed by stooges and light thinkers." Owen went so far as to say that Jewish capital invested in the ghetto had had a salutary effect there. Jews had a record of cooperation with Negroes superior to that of any other white group. In an article in the *Chicago Defender*[76] Owen surveyed Jewish contributions to the welfare of the Negro. He enumerated the inter-racial work done by Jewish foundations, Jewish activities in civil rights and Jewish benevolence in the field of entertainment. Owen found the receptivity to Negroes of Jewish labor unions, the International Ladies Garment Workers Union and the Amalgamated Clothing Workers of America, the fur workers, and cap-makers, especially praiseworthy. After looking at the record, Owen's conclusion was that the facts "should generate a measure of gratitude, . . . and stimulate reasonable appreciation among Negroes as to their Jewish brethren." Owen's statement provided a much needed balance to some of the aforementioned derogatory views, although he perhaps overdrew the basic points he was making. In this light one can conclude that the record of Jewish labor leaders and members of the entertainment media was probably somewhat better than the record of white non-Jews in terms of their relationships with blacks. Yet the Jews as a group did not warrant as much praise as that accorded by Owen. Just as black people didn't want to be judged by their worst, Owen also told his readers, they should refrain from generalizing about Jews based on their worst representatives.

Taken as a whole the data about Negro-Jewish relations between the wars leads to the following broad conclusions: One, that the confrontations between first and second generation American Jews and multitudes of transplanted Southern Negroes in Northern cities gave rise to the expression of more criticism of Jews by blacks than that heard at any time before or since, including the late '60s. Two, that the Great Depression severely worsened the already miserable position of the Negro and exacerbated tensions between Jews and Negroes who ordinarily met in a superior-subordinate relationship. Third, Hitler's rise to power accompanied by raucous anti-Semitism provided a point of departure for discussions of the Negro and the Jew in America by the Negro press. A tiny minority peddled raw anti-Semitism. Some emphasized the plight of the Jews in Germany to call attention to the way in which whites, including Jews, in America treated blacks. Others saw obvious parallels between Jewish suffering under Nazism and the predicament of black Americans. They deplored anti-Semitism. In sum, Negroes during that troubled era spoke not with one voice, but with many.

NOTES

1. Gilbert Osofsky, *Harlem: The Making of a Ghetto* (New York: Harper and Row, Publishers, 1968), p. 89.

2. Lunabelle Wedlock, *The Reaction of Negro Publications and Organizations to German Anti-Semitism* (Washington, D. C.: The Graduate School-Howard University, 1942), p. 126, quoting from *The Philadelphia Tribune,* July 26, 1934.

3. *Ibid.,* pp. 136–137.

4. St. Clair Drake and Horace R. Cayton, *Black Metropolis: A Study of Negro Life in a Northern City* (New York and Evanston: Harper and Row, Publishers, 1962), II, 448.

5. Harold L. Sheppard, "The Negro Merchant: A Study of Negro Anti-Semitism," *American Journal of Sociology,* LIII, No. 2 (September 1947), p. 98.

6. *Ibid.,* p. 99.

7. Drake and Cayton, II, 441.

8. Sheppard, 96–97; although Roi Ottley credited Jewish doctors with making it possible for black doctors to associate themselves with some of the nation's largest hospitals, there was competition among Jewish and Negro physicians. Jewish-Negro relations suffered as a consequence.

9. *The Crisis,* 45, No. 4 (April 1938), p. 177.

10. Edward L. Israel, "Jew Hatred Among Negroes," *The Crisis,* 43, No. 2 (February, 1936), pp. 39, 50.

11. Osofsky, p. 136.

12. *Ibid.,* 136–137.

13. Drake and Cayton, I, 220.

14. Roi Ottley, *New World A-Coming: Inside Black America* (Boston: Houghton Mifflin Co., 1943), p. 115.

15. Claude McKay, *Harlem: Black Metropolis* (New York: E. P. Dutton, 1940), p. 191.

16. C. Eric Lincoln, *The Black Muslims in America* (Boston: Beacon Press, 1961), p. 169. Sufi claimed that he had been born in the Sudan. In actuality he was born in the American South.

17. Ottley, p. 118; Wedlock, pp. 72–73, 132; A sympathetic account of Sufi's activities are found in McKay in his chapter entitled "Sufi Abdul Hamid and Organized Labor." McKay did not believe Sufi to be an anti-Semite.

18. Ottley, pp. 118–119.

19. See Reid's obituary in *African Opinion,* May–June 1967, p. 13.

20. Drake and Cayton, I, p. 242.

21. Department of Commerce, Bureau of Census, *Current Population Reports,* p. 57.

22. Ella Baker and Marvel Cooke, "The Bronx Slave Market," *The Crisis,* 42, No. 11 (November 1935), p. 330.

23. *Ibid.*

24. Drake and Cayton, I, 244.

25. *Ibid.,* 249.

26. *New York Times,* May 2, 1941.

27. Lawrence D. Reddick, "Anti-Semitism Among Negroes," *The Negro Quarterly* (Summer 1942), p. 113.

28. An article in the black nationalist monthly, *Liberator,* in 1967 contended that, "Domestic service, today just as much as yesterday, is nothing but a euphemism for slave labor." Louise R. Moore "Maid in Westchester," *Liberator,* 7, No. 1 (January 1967), pp. 18–19. Philip Roth's treatment of the Jewish house-wife's relations with the Negro domestic is stereotyped but nonetheless rings true: "I'm the only one who's good to her. I'm the only one who gives her a whole can of tuna for lunch, and I'm not talking *dreck* either. I'm talking Chicken of the Sea, Alex. . . . Maybe I'm too good, she whispers to me, meanwhile running scalding water over the dish from which the cleaning lady has just eaten her lunch, alone like a leper." *Portnoy's Complaint* (N.Y.: Random House, 1967), p. 13. Portnoy's "rebellion" included sitting down and eating left over pot roast (not tuna) with the *shwartze* cleaning lady. (p. 75).

29. Wedlock, p. 182.

30. *The Crisis,* 45, No. 4 (April 1968), p. 113.

31. See Wedlock, p. 92 quoting from *The Philadelphia Tribune,* October 12, 1933.

32. *Ibid.,* p. 33, quoting from *The Philadelphia Tribune,* July 5, 1934.

33. *The Afro-American,* February 22, 1936.

34. *Ibid.,* April 11, 1936.

35. See Wedlock, p. 109, quoting from *The Afro-American,* August 24, 1935.

36. *Ibid.,* p. 108.

37. *Ibid.,* pp. 104–105, quoting from *The Washington Tribune,* June 23, 1933.

38. Kelly Miller, "Race Prejudice in Germany and America," *Opportunity* XIV, No. 4 (April 1936), p. 105.

39. See Wedlock, pp. 51–52 quoting from *Norfolk Journal and Guide,* January 21, 1939.

40. A notable exception was contained in the youthful DuBois' diary of his Atlantic crossing (1895).

On that trip he met the Jewish aristocrats and the "low mean cheating Pöbel [mob]." He hadn't seen much of "the ordinary good hearted good intentioned man." Two Jews on the voyage he found congenial. As for the others, "There is in them all that slyness that lack of straight-forward openheartedness which goes straight against me." See Francis L. Broderick, *W. E. B. DuBois—Negro Leader in a Time of Crisis* (Stanford: Stanford University Press, 1959), pp. 26–27.

41. *The Crisis*, 40, No. 10 (October 1933), p. 221.

42. W. E. B. DuBois, *Dusk of Dawn, An Essay Toward An Autobiography of a Race Concept* (New York: Schocken Books, 1968), p. 306.

43. *The Crisis*, 40, No. 9 (September 1933), p. 197.

44. See Book Department, *Annals of American Academy of Political and Social Sciences*, 223 (September 1942), p. 200.

45. *The Crisis*, 40, No. 5 (May 1933), p. 117.

46. DuBois, "The Negro and the Warsaw Ghetto," *Jewish Life*, VI, No. 7 (May 1952), pp. 14–15.

47. *The Black Man*, I, No. 8 (July 1935), p. 9.

48. *Ibid.*, II, No. 2 (July–August 1936), p. 3.

49. *Ibid.*, IV, No. 1 (June 1939), p. 5.

50. *Ibid.*, I, No. 8 (July 1935), p. 9 and IV, No. 1 (June 1939), p. 3.

51. Ottley, pp. 129, 334. Both Cook and another erstwhile Garveyite, Harry Fredericks, were especially indebted to Hitler for turning whites against other whites.

52. See Wedlock, pp. 195–196, quoting from *The Afro-American*, June 17, 1933.

53. *Ibid.*, p. 78, quoting from the *St. Louis Argus*, July 15, 1938.

54. *Ibid.*, p. 149, quoting from *The Philadelphia Tribune*, September 21, 1933.

55. *Pittsburgh Courier*, November 26, 1938 and December 3, 1938.

56. Wedlock, p. 77.

57. *Ibid.*, pp. 171–172, quoting from *Dynamite*, May 28, 1938.

58. *Ibid.*, p. 173, quoting from *Dynamite*, June 25, 1938.

59. Drake and Cayton, II, p. 432.

60. Lawrence Reddick, "What Hitler Says about the Negro," *Opportunity* XVII, No. 4 (April 1939), pp. 108–110.

61. One study of racial stereotyping among black university students was reported to a professional association of psychologists in 1940. Working with a small sample (100) drawn from Negro colleges, mainly in the South, the author compared his results with a similar study done with an equal number of white Princetonians. A stereotype of the Jew was common to both groups. Choosing from some 85 adjectives both characterized the Jews as "shrewd," "grasping," "sly," "mercenary," "aggressive," "persistent," "intelligent," "ambitious," and "progressive." While blacks added "deceitful," whites listed "talkative." See James A. Bayton, "The Racial Stereotypes of Negro College Students," *The Journal of Abnormal and Social Psychology*, 36, No. 1 (January 1941), pp. 97–102.

62. Chandler Owen, "Should The Negro Hate The Jew," *Chicago Defender*, November 8, 1941. In association with A. Philip Randolph, Owen published the *Messenger* and organized the National Association for the Promotion of Labor Unionism among Negroes.

63. See his Foreword to Wedlock, p. 7. Claude McKay was one black writer who was inclined to minimize the anti-Semitism among Negroes. There seems to be general agreement that white anti-Semitism was more evident in the thirties.

64. James Q. Wilson, *Negro Politics—The Search For Leadership* (New York: The Free Press, 1960), p. 155.

65. *Time*, January 31, 1969.

66. Kenneth Clark, *Dark Ghetto—Dilemmas of Social Power* (New York and Evanston: Harper and Row, Publishers 1967), p. 164.

67. McKay, p. 190.

68. Adam Clayton Powell, Jr., *Marching Blacks—An Interpretive History of the Rise of the Black Common Man* (New York: Dial Press, 1945), pp. 75, 81.

69. *Amsterdam News,* April 16, 1938.

70. Powell, p. 66.

71. *Amsterdam News,* April 16, 1938.

72. *Ibid.*

73. *Ibid.,* February 19, 1938.

74. Gunnar Myrdal, *An American Dilemma* (New York: McGraw-Hill Book Co., 1964), II, p. 852.

75. Foreword to Wedlock, pp. 8, 10.

76. *Chicago Defender,* November 8, 1941; Many of the same points were made in Chandler Owen, "Negro Anti-Semitism: Cause and Cure," *The National Jewish Monthly,* September, 1942, pp. 14–15. In this piece Owen blames, in part, American Fascist agencies, Axis agents and Nazi propagandists for Negro anti-Semitism.

# Comparisons by Negro Publications of the Plight of the Jews in Germany with that of the Negro in America

Most of the articles in Negro publications on German anti-Semitism attempt to compare or to contrast the situation of the Jew in Germany with that of the Negro in America. It is characteristic of minority groups to interpret every event in terms of the conditions under which they themselves live. The discrimination which is effected against them forces them to become extremely chauvinistic; and often, to their detriment, they fail to consider their own conditions in the light of social forces on an international scale. They restrict their thoughts within very narrow limits, and other situations which have no direct relationship to themselves or which cannot be utilized to bring their situation into the foreground of the consciousness of their exploiters, are generally ignored. For this reason, every aspect of the German-Jewish situation has been utilized by Negroes as a means of drawing comparisons with Negro conditions in America. The validity of the comparisons is often questionable, but the principal purpose, that of making the world, and particularly the American world, realize that Negroes are persecuted in America, has been accomplished.

Comparisons in Negro publications have been divided into ten classifications, which will be discussed in this connection.

I. Within this section are, first of all, comparisons of the two situations according to similar overt methods of discrimination. In this vein an editorial in the *Afro-American* during 1933 was entitled, "Jim Crow For Jews Now." This article points out that Jews are now segregated in Germany, for example in the theatres, just as Negroes are jim-crowed in America.[1]

An editorial typical of this group is entitled, "Jews in Germany vs. Negroes in America."[2] The opening sentence which states that

> "To be a Jew in Germany is hell. For one to be a Negro in America is twice as bad,"

is indicative of the item for item comparison which follows. The writer considers: difficulty in finding work; holding of public office; attendance in public schools; beatings and disfranchisement; jim-crow in hospitals, eating places and bars, trains and theatres. This article puts it in this manner:

Lunabelle Wedlock was a student of Ralph Bunche.

Originally published as "The Reaction of Negro Publications and Organizations to German Anti-Semitism," *Howard University Studies in the Social Sciences* 3, no. 2 (1942): 91–115. Copyright © 1942, by Howard University. Reprinted with permission of the Moorland-Springarn Research Center, Howard University Archives.

"Jews are beaten and disfranchised in Germany under the mad regime of Hitler. In the 'home of the brave,' colored Americans are not permitted to vote and their bullet-ridden bodies hang from trees against the background of Southern scenery.

"Laborers, professional men, civil servants, students, bookkeepers or hired girls alike need not apply for jobs, if they cannot convincingly prove their grandparents were Aryans. That is in Germany. In America, where Hitler is branded as a despotic idiot for such tactics against Jews, colored citizens are being starved to death for lack of jobs. Aside from this, they are subjected to insults and bitter humiliation. Thousands of Negroes have died because hospitals refused to treat colored citizens. . . ."[3]

Another editorial is aptly labelled, "The German Cracker," for it concludes that the two situations are practically identical except that Negroes have now become accustomed to discrimination against them. This article states that:

"Bachrach Brothers, one of the leading department stores in Magdeburg, Germany, was closed, last week, by police who found six Jewish employees married to white German girls.

"The cops said the populace was so excited that law and order were menaced.

"All over Germany one excuse or another is used in order to close up Jewish stores and compel them to sell out to Germans.

"We are accustomed to such tricks in the South wherever white neighbors covet the stores or the farms of colored persons. Down South we don't say 'the populace was excited.' Our common expression is that 'feeling runs high'."[4]

Another article begins as follows:

"The persecution of the Jews in Germany by the Nazi Government is deplorable, stupid and outrageous.

"The persecution of colored Americans by Americans is cruel, relentless and spirit breaking."[5]

An interesting article bears the title, "Nazis, Negroes, Jews and Catholics."[6] This editorial pursues the following line of reasoning: "Of course Negroes sympathize with Jews, because they have been exposed not only to the same types of discrimination," which are enumerated, "but to even worse treatment."

A direct comparison is drawn in an editorial which opens with the sentence:

"Laws comparable with the slave codes have been put into effect in Germany against Jews."[7]

After listing some of the German regulations, the writer states that:

"These are harsh measures designed to crush the spirit of the Jewish people and bring them down to the position our own people occupy in so many parts of the South."[8]

The case of a Negro who was beaten after reporting for jury service in Texas is cited in the light of analogous conditions for Jews in Germany. The editorial suggests that:

"It may be well to consider what is happening to Negroes in some quarters in the United States in the light of what is happening to the Jews in Germany and Italy. Racially the situation may not be analogous; politically and economically it is, in effect."[9]

A front-page article in the *Philadelphia Tribune* is concerned with the jim-crow for Jews in Germany. It states that:

"After a close study of jim-crow methods practiced in the United States against Negro citizens, jim-crow cars for the segregation of traveling Jews were demanded, Tuesday, by Das Schwarze Korps, organ of Hitler's Elite Guard. The publication pointed to the example of southern sections of the United States where Negroes and whites are thus separated."[10]

Another editorial on the jim-crow in Germany is entitled, "Germans Adopt U. S. Jim Crow."[11]

The *Crisis* contained, during 1938, a detailed comparison of the two situations which began as follows:

"Hitler has disfranchised the Jews. Negroes are disfranchised in practically all of the southern states."[12]

The writer then points to discrimination against Jews in Germany and Negroes in America in schools, employment, public places, sports and in many other respects. A simple comparison is drawn in a cartoon which is captioned, "Oppressed People at Home and Abroad."[13] This cartoon shows Uncle Sam stepping on a Negro in the United States, and Hitler stepping on a man in Austria.

The *Chicago Defender* graphically portrays this type of comparison in a cartoon captioned, "Bed (Bad?) Fellows,"[14] which shows Hitler and Martin Dies in bed together. Both have evil faces, but Dies is holding a mask with a sweet expression marked "Americanism" before his. The bed is labelled, "Persecution of Minorities," and "Hypocrisy."

*Opportunity* carried an editorial entitled, "On Racial Prejudice at Home and Abroad,"[15] which stated that Germany is modelling its program of Jewish persecution after American persecution of Negroes.

II. The second type of comparison is that which states that it is all right to protest about Jewish conditions in Germany but that the Negro situation in America deserves more consideration. Typical of this is an article taken from the *Philadelphia Tribune* which states that:

"The lynchings of Negroes, disfranchisement and economic oppression have caused only a few Americans to shed any tears over the plight of the Negroes. It is easy for America to condemn Hitler for his atrocities against the Jew, but American atrocities against colored citizens remain unchallenged."[16]

A cartoon in the same paper is significantly captioned, "Clean Your Home First." It shows Uncle Sam protesting against Japan's policy in China and Hitler's Jewish persecutions, while behind him a lynched Negro is hanging.[17] The *Crisis* illustrated the same idea in a cartoon which pictures Uncle Sam and Hitler both with bloody hands. The hands of Uncle Sam are marked "The Scottsboro Mess," and "3,745 Lynchings 1889–1932," while Hitler's say, "Persecution of the Jews." Yet the former is telling Hitler that his hands are bloody.[18]

The *Afro-American* has an editorial which concludes with the statement that:

> "We rejoice that our newspapers condemn German Nazi atrocities. It's a good sign that they may yet discover the Nazism which is outside their own doors."[19]

Another editorial begins its last paragraph as follows:

> "We Negroes have been too long the victims of cruelty not to wish succor to be extended to any people anywhere who are persecuted as we are. But we think our government, raising its hands in horror over persecution on the other side of the world, might take a moment to glance at its own back yard."[20]

The same idea is expressed editorially in an article which asks:

> ". . . isn't it safer for Uncle Sam in the long run? Isn't it cheaper? Isn't it easier on his blood pressure for him to deal justly with the oppressed people at home than to shed tears in public, tear his hair and beat his breast over the way Hitler is oppressing the people of Germany and Austria?
> "We think Hitler is a tyrant and a brute, a ruffian and a cur. We detest him for the way in which he is crushing the Jew.
> ". . . But we can't forget there is a man right here at home who has his heel on our neck."[21]

One finds this isolationist policy again expressed in an editorial in the *Crisis* which states:

> "Let those whose hearts bleed so for the men and women across the sea turn their glances within their own borders. They will see Hitlerism on every side directed against citizens who happen not to be white."[22]

During 1939, the *Afro-American* published a cartoon which had for its theme President Roosevelt's appointment of a Catholic and a Jew to important governmental positions. The three are defending American democracy from Nazism, Communism, Unemployment, and Racial and Religious Hatred. The news item at the bottom states: "The President, to show his disdain of racial and religious intolerance, named a Catholic and a Jew to the highest offices in the country. The caption is, "Don't Forget The Colored People, Mr. President."[23]

III. In the third type of comparison, the editorial writers attack various Americans who have protested against the German-Jewish atrocities, but have either taken part in discrimination against Negroes here, or at least have been indifferent toward it.

The *Philadelphia Tribune,* in one of its first editorials, centered its attack upon Judge Kun, who, it stated, although protesting against German atrocities, has "never complained when America discriminates against Negroes."[24] Later, an editorialist spoke of the indifference of the *Philadelphia Record* (a white Philadelphia paper) toward Negro affairs, and the discrimination by the Home Loan Organization, in the Board of Education building and by school officials of Berwyn, Pennsylvania.[25]

Another editorial lists several American colleges which exclude Negroes from attending, whose presidents, nevertheless, have appealed to Germany to stop its Jewish persecutions. The article states that:

"Each of the above named universities is in the South. Each protesting against the atrocities in Germany against Jews, commits daily the same atrocities against Negroes.

"Each of them is lily-white despite the fact that it is supported in whole or in part by public tax funds.

"Each virtually is a party to the crime by means of which tax funds due Negro children are stolen and spent only on white children."[26]

Nothing is said about the commendable action of the presidents in appealing to stop persecution of the unfortunate Jewish minority in Germany. The incident is merely utilized to illustrate the "hypocrisy" of the southern college presidents. One Philadelphia editorialist chose as his targets John A. Phillips, president of the Pennsylvania State Federation of Labor, Attorney-General Francis Biddle, and former Mayor W. Freeland Kendrick. Phillips is attacked because the A. F. of L. "makes it impossible for thousands of skilled Negro mechanics to work at their trades." The article states that:

". . . Until labor unions let down the racial bars labor leaders should keep quiet concerning human rights."[27]

Biddle, the editorial reproaches because, although he "understands that colored teachers are barred from teaching in anything except Jim-Crow schools" and "knows that in the ten million dollar building in which the Board meets Negroes may not even run an elevator or scrub the floors which their money helps to maintain" he "has never said a word about those conditions." "Yet," it states, "he can condemn Germany." The third target, former Mayor Kendrick, it is stated, did absolutely nothing to relieve the bitter persecution of Negroes in the city of which he was the chief executive. The editorial adds that:

". . . Colored Americans may not eat or drink or sleep except in restricted areas and the silver toned voice of the ex-Mayor who is so exercised about conditions in far away Germany is never sounded in rebuke."[28]

In 1935, a Virginia editorialist centered his attack on Senator William King of Utah, who, although denouncing Nazi persecution of Jews, voted against the passage of the anti-lynch bill.[29] During the same year, the *Philadelphia Tribune* berated Governor Earle of Pennsylvania, who, although signing the Civil Rights Bill, did not protest against Negro treatment in Pennsylvania, but protests against Hitler's Jewish persecutions.[30] The article states that:

"It is a fine thing for the Governor to be alarmed on account of Germany's attitude towards certain classes of its citizens; but Governor Earle, and the state of

Pennsylvania must about-face before they can justly spank Hitler and the German Government."[31]

Earlier in that year, the *Tribune,* after stating that President Roosevelt was being urged to protest to Germany, asked rhetorically how the President can afford to protest.[32]

The *Pittsburgh Courier* takes a rap at the State Department of the United States which has attempted to aid Jewish refugees to get into Mexico. This editorial makes the following accusation:

"What strikes us forcibly in this case is the alacrity with which the U. S. State Department used all its facilities and influence to aid these aliens.

"It did more for them than it has ever done for colored American citizens who have always experienced great difficulty in getting into Mexico. It usually shrugs its shoulders when colored tourists complain of the restrictions placed upon them by Mexican immigration officials, and so far as we know it has never registered a complaint with the Mexican government against this discrimination."[33]

The least that can be said of such an article is that it tends to spread anti-Semitic ideas among the readers. In the *Crisis,* a reference is made to discrimination by the American Athletic Union against Negroes in southern states and to the lack of protest against such discrimination on the part of General Hugh Johnson, President Roosevelt and the Senate, who have nevertheless condemned Germany for its Jewish atrocities.[34]

Bishop Edwin Holt Hughes is also the object of an attack because he "told a gathering of Methodist clergymen in Philadelphia that it would be an injustice to America to say that lynching is tolerated here." The gathering refused to endorse a federal anti-lynching bill. The bishop then assisted with the passage of a resolution condemning Germany's treatment of the Jews. The editorial adds:

"But it would serve no purpose to pretend that Negroes have given their sympathy and joined in protests without clear and often bitter insight into their own position as American citizens. They look around at the Americans who can be moved to protests against brutality in another land, but who can not recognize and protest against the same conditions within their own borders."[35]

The *Amsterdam News* adds a new note when it points out that President Roosevelt did not intervene to help the Ethiopians, the West Indians, or the anti-lynch bill. After stating that,

"We wonder, however, how far Mr. Roosevelt will go with his humanitarian movement. Will he include all oppressed people and races in it—or is his plan for Whites only? Above all, will the President of the United States now personally come to the aid of oppressed American Negroes, who are compelled to endure lynchings, disfranchisement, economic and civil discrimination and many more kinds of oppression at the hands of American tyrants?"[36]

The writer adds that Negroes are "in full accord" with President Roosevelt's move, but as a result they demand a "better deal" of the government. Ralph Matthews, on the other hand, states that "we have our Hitlers here" and lists several Negroes, for example, Marcus Garvey, J. Finley Wilson, fraternal leaders, bishops, "baptist hog callers" and Father Divine.[37]

IV. In the fourth type of comparative article, the statement is made that Germans have a right to ask Americans why they protest against the Jewish situation when they practice the same discriminations against colored people here.

Typical of this type of article is the closing paragraph of an editorial in the *Afro-American* which states that:

"Uncle Sam protested unofficially to Germany about the Jewish atrocities and brown-shirted Adolf asked if Germany didn't have as much right to impose upon Jews as the United States has to exclude Chinese and Japanese."[38]

Kelly Miller also pointed out that:

"The climax of inconsistency has been reached. Georgia upbraids Germany for manifestation of race prejudice. Hitler has a ready-made answer for the reproach . . ."[39]

An editorialist while discussing the Tydings Resolution states that if something is not done for Negroes in America, "Hitler will send it back and say put your own house in order first."[40] Hitler's answer to the protests is given in this paragraph of another editorial:

"When humanitarian impulse of America impelled her to rebuke Hitler for his barbarity and inhumanity against the Jews, Adolph Hitler made but one adroit, devastating rejoinder, 'My ruthlessness against the Jew is not more harsh and inhuman than yours against the Negroes' . . . This accusative retort remains unanswered for the simple reason that it is unanswerable."[41]

The *Washington Tribune* has an editorial which states that:

"Hitler and Mussolini surely must have had a big laugh when they heard of this country's magnanimous gesture to aid Jews of Austria, Germany and other European countries who have been deprived of citizenship, and others who stand to be driven from their homes.

"The two dictators must have stood aghast when America extended a haven to the stricken people."[42]

Then the writer takes the opportunity to attack President Roosevelt for not interfering in the anti-lynch bill filibuster by stating that:

"Despite the mistreatment of the Negroes in America and the recent disgraceful scene in Congress when a bill to give some measure of protection to Negroes was introduced and filibustered to death without a word from the President who now extends a hand to Jews in Europe, this same Chief Executive has the effrontery to reach his hand across the Atlantic in the face of conditions and make this grand gesture.

"The American Negro has nothing but the deepest sympathy for Jews in Europe, but Hitler and Mussolini certainly must be tickled."[43]

*Opportunity* has an editorial which contains a rabid attack on white Americans, taking as its basis the situation of the Jews in Germany. It is put in this manner:

"The fascist governments of the world view American indignation over racial oppression with wonder and bewilderment. They can not understand why America should be so concerned with racial persecution in Europe and yet defend it with such vigor within its own borders . . .

"It is a long story—perhaps no good will come from the telling. But this much is certain: the voice of America would carry far greater authority when it speaks against racial oppression in Europe if it could be heard against racial oppression at home."[44]

George Schuyler goes even so far as to pen a reply which Hitler might make to American protestors and points out evidences of discrimination against Negroes in America. He then concludes:

"Yes, I think if the Nazi spokesman wanted to make a devastating reply to their critics in America they could say a mouthful."

The Oklahoma *Black Dispatch* reversed the usual procedure and produced an editorial which made the following statement:

"Hitler retaliates to our accusation of the inhuman treatment of the Jews in a sort of cast-the-beam-out-of-your-own-eye tone, of the similar treatment America accords its Negro population. . . .

". . . and der Feurher's Germany continues its anti-Jewish policies belittling their brutalities by condemning America.

"Isn't that just like a dictator?

"He can do no wrong and neither can those of his own nationality."[45]

Kelly Miller expressed the same idea when he stated:

"But granting counter charges of Hitler and his cohorts, how would that justify their barbarities against the Jews which shock the conscience of the world . . . Citing cruelties and outrages against Negroes in Georgia is a poor justification for atrocities against Jews in Germany. Comparisons are odious."[46]

The two articles just cited stand practically alone. Most writers have seized upon the Nazis' answers to American protests in order to attack white Americans. It is unfortunate that more of them could not see this particular problem in the same light as the *Black Dispatch* and Kelly Miller viewed it.

V. The fifth category of comparisons contains articles which either call Hitler a Ku Klux Klansman or compare him with one. Such an article is one which is metaphorically labelled, "Adolf Hitler, K. K. K." This editorial is concluded with the following statement:

> "Dr. Lewis K. McMillan, just home from four years spent in the Reich hell, says that to understand what Hitler is doing in Germany, you have only to imagine an 'Imperial Wizard' of the Ku Klux as dictator in the United States."[47]

A cartoon also graphically compares the two. Hitler is shown with a whip and a swastika; the caption is "Another Klansman."[48]

An editorial was entitled, "Hitler—The German Ku Klux" by Kelly Miller.[49] He discussed the neo-Klanism in America and the Hitler regime in Germany and concluded that they are "strikingly similar," differing only in local application. The deep-seated intolerance of the Nordic spirit, he stated, underlies them both. In the following week's issue of the same paper, there was a cartoon which shows Hitler, but his shadow, which is reflected on the wall, is the outline of a Ku Kluxer. The caption is "Another Klansman."[50]

Kelly Miller again used this type of comparison when, after pointing out what Germany and Georgia have done to the Jew and the Negro respectively, he concluded that:

> "He," (meaning Hitler) "is the master Ku Kluxer of Germany."[51]

References are made to Hitler as a Ku Klux Klansman in the *Afro-American,* which states in one place:

> "From the way Hitler talks, one would think he is a member of the Ku Klux Klan and a native of Alabama."[52]

and in another:

> "Germany is persecuting Jews, Catholics and Negroes. Hitler is a European Ku Kluxer—Hitler's Ku Kluxism is storing up for Germany mountains of hate that will deluge the Teutons for centuries."[53]

VI. Another type of comparison is to be found in articles about Jewish and Negro reactions to their respective situations. William Pickens observed in this connection that many German Jews aided Hitler and that they are now asking that subversive propaganda against the Hitler regime be suppressed. His final statement is that Negroes in America react in the same way.[54]

In the *Afro-American* an editorial entitled "Every Race Has Its Traitor" treats the same theme. It points out that:

> "We sometimes think of all minority groups as united against their enemies except ourselves. The recent persecution of Jews in Germany shows that isn't so."[55]

The editorialist, after pointing out different reactions and statements by some of the leading German Jews, concludes:

"Jewish oppression is almost as bad in Germany as Negro oppression in the United States, and German Jews are reacting just about as we do here."[56]

VII. Negro publications have utilized whenever possible statements and articles by persons and newspapers outside the realm of the Negro world, in which comparisons are made between the German-Jewish situation and American-Negro conditions. An example of this is an article which is headlined, "Paris Paper Compares Hitlerism With Race Hatred in the United States."[57] Another article reports a speech by Rev. John La Farge, editor of *America,* and leader of the Catholic Interracial Movement. The headline reads, "Says U. S. Swastikas Woven Into Jim-Crow Institutions."[58]

The *Norfolk Journal and Guide* quotes from a letter written by an American woman living in Switzerland to President Roosevelt asking him to do something to stop lynching. The headline reads, "American Practice of Lynching Forms Basis for Defense of Nazi Persecutions."[59] A speech by the Nazi, Julius Streicher, is reported with editorial comment in an article headlined, "German Scores Treatment of Negro in U. S.," "Says America Must Clean Its Own House First."[60] Many Negro newspapers referred to an editorial by Westbrook Pegler in the *Washington Post* (white), in which he stated that discriminations against Negroes in the United States and against Jews in Germany are similar.[61]

VIII. There is a similarity between the claims of some Negroes that a prominent white man has Negro blood or that a Negro is descended from a prominent white family and articles which say that Hitler may have Jewish blood. The latter assertion is found in the eighth type of comparative articles.

An example of this is an editorial entitled, "Hitler's Grandmother a Jewess,"[62] which was allegedly taken from a Vienna newspaper. This article provoked editorial comment by William Pickens who urged Jews not to claim Hitler if he is a Jew. He added:

"He will be more ruthless than ever if he is passing for Aryan."[63]

An editorial in the *Afro-American,* which is entitled, "Jewish Hitler,"[64] states that it may be true that Hitler has Jewish blood.

Negro publications were not alone in circulating the rumor that Hitler himself has Jewish blood because his grandmother was a Jewess. The false basis of the assumption, however, is pointed out by Konrad Heiden in his biography of Hitler. In discussing Hitler's family, Heiden states that although Hitler's grandmother had a name which is common among Jews in a certain area, there is no proof that she was a Jewess.[65] The assumption was utilized a great deal, however, to illustrate the ridiculous position of Hitler in perpetrating his racial theory.

IX. The ninth type of comparison is that in which Americans who discriminate against Negroes are called "Nazis," and the situations, "evidences of Nazism" and "Hitlerism." An editorial of this type is entitled, "Hitlerism Spiked in North Carolina."[66] It discusses the resignation of the dean of the medical school at the University of North Carolina because his refusal to admit more than ten per cent Jews to the school was opposed by the liberal president. In another article the following statement is made:

"They will see Hitlerism on every side, directed against citizens who happen not to be white."[67]

This convenient terminology is again utilized in an editorial which states that:

"It's a good sign that they may yet discover the Nazism which is outside their own doors."[68]

This article used the word "Nazi" metaphorically throughout. It states in one place:

"For example, United States 'Nazis' in Pennsylvania are raising a howl in the newspapers because the equal rights bill goes into effect."[69]

and in another:

"Then, as another evidence of American Nazism, we have a letter supposedly written by one George M. Quick . . . As a final picture of U. S. Nazism, the Afro points to Maryland University's acting president, Curly Byrd . . ."[70]

and finally:

"That's American Nazism which for 350 years has persecuted and lynched, hounded and enslaved, starved and burned colored people beyond anything Germans have yet imagined."[71]

An editorial entitled, "Nazis at Williams,"[72] attacks the Massachusetts college for no longer admitting Negroes. The attack is introduced by a statement to the effect that Jewish children were ordered out of German public schools. The writer concludes that:

"As between the Nazism of Hitler and Dennet there is little to choose, except that Hitler beats around the bush less."[73]

Negroes are warned by the *Afro-American* that their

". . . biggest job at the moment is to watch the Hitlers right here in our own country."

in an article which borrows a German idiom for its title, "The Nazis zu Hause."[74] Two weeks later it was reported that "Nazi Virginians" separated a husband and wife who were "guilty of" racial intermarriage.[75] Two other articles in this connection are headlined: "Nazi Spirit at Glenn Dale,"[76] which spoke of discrimination against Negroes in a District of Columbia tuberculosis sanitorium; and "Nazism in Baseball,"[77] which struck at the exclusion of Negroes from professional teams.

When the Daughters of the American Revolution and the District of Columbia Board of Education refused to allow Marian Anderson, noted Negro contralto, to sing in their buildings, Negro publications lashed out with accusations of Nazism. For example, Reverend Robert W. Bagnall titled an editorial on the subject, "Nazism in America."[78] In the *Washington Tribune,* an article is labelled, "D.A.R. Body Smells of Hitlerism."[79] M. Beaunorus Tolson, a columnist for the same paper, uses the phrase, "Fascism Strikes at Marian Anderson."[80]

Gordon B. Hancock writes in the *Norfolk Journal and Guide* that:

"The persecution of the Jews and the barring of Marian Anderson from the Constitution Hall in Washington are parts of the same phenomenon. The prejudice in Berlin is complementary to the prejudice in Washington. Neither is blacker or more hellish than the other. Both carry portents of the social and economic damnation of minority groups."[81]

In other words, Hancock leaves no room for differentiation or contrast between the two situations. The *Afro-American* adds:

"Let Jews, Catholics, and other minority groups beware the Nazi tactics of Daughter Robert which sooner or later will be used to exclude them."[82]

Another editorial which took the Marian Anderson incident for its cue was headlined, "Nazism in Washington, D. C."[83] This article states:

"Just how we can charge and snort about Fascism abroad and practice it here and still claim to be the leading democratic nation on earth can not be reconciled. The trouble is America is long on extending altruism to foreign groups, but short on extending it to home groups."[84]

The *Savannah Journal* also attacked the D. A. R., but its editorial is slightly different from the others because it stated that:

"Hitler and Mussolini accepted Miss Anderson when she visited them. They are two strides ahead of the D. A. R. They can point out to their American critics that whereas the D. A. R. was given the right to exist by the first bloodshed for the cause of democracy, that of Crispus Attucks, a Negro, it now scorns a daughter of Attucks. They can say that their countries worship their heroes and wish for one of the caliber of Attucks. The soul-stirring words of Miss Anderson ring out over their mountains and valleys."[85]

X. The last type of comparative articles to be considered is that in which the writers attempt to point out differences between the situation of the Jews in Germany and conditions under which Negroes live in America.

Most of the writers discuss the legality or illegality of persecution. For example, one article states that:

"Berlin, recently, advised Jewish citizens that they would be arrested and prosecuted if they went to the polls and voted in the coming national elections.

"The difference between Germany and Dixie is that Nazis disfranchise Jews by national law and the South keeps us from the polls by state laws or by intimidation. The result is the same."[86]

Another editorial states that:

"Our Constitution keeps the South from passing many of the laws Hitler has invoked against the Jews, but by indirection, by force and terrorism, the South and Nazi Germany are mental brothers.

"After all, this proves there is nothing new in tyranny, slavery and oppression. It has different names, and it operates among different peoples, but the manner of persecution remains the same."[87]

The *Norfolk Journal and Guide* also points out that in the case of the Jews in Germany, the situation is legal, while discrimination against Negroes is illegal, but is effective through connivance of legal authorities.[88] Again the distinction is drawn between legal and illegal persecution, when an editorialist states that the German government is the instigator, while "in America, the government forbids it by law and winks at it in practice."[89]

Other editorialists ironically criticize that differentiation. For example, one writer entitles his article, "A Rose By Any Name."[90] He states that:

> "It must be comforting to an unfortunate Negro dangling from a tree in the deep South to realize that his brutal death does not represent the 'legalized policy' of the state."[91]

The *Crisis* also belittles that distinction when it states that:

> "No one of them has explained to date just what the difference is—to a murdered man—between the government *sanctioning* his murder by decree, or *permitting* his murder, the while muttering pious technical asides."[92]

The same writer differentiates himself, however, when he points out that:

> "There is, of course, an important difference, as thoughtful Jews themselves have explained. Negroes in this country still have—in most sections—the right to protest and work to improve their lot. In Germany the Jew has no such privilege. There is no hope."[93]

Another type of differentiation was first given by Kelly Miller in his statement that:

> "Georgia fears the Negro will lower the level of Anglo-Saxon civilization; Hitler fears the Jews raise it too high."[94]

This commentator further pointed out the high visibility of the Negro in contrast with the low visibility of the Jew in Germany. He also stated that Hitler wants the Jew to get out of Germany entirely. His final contrast is given in the following paragraph:

> "The brutal frankness of the Teuton is in glaring contrast to the hypocrisy and guile of his Anglo-Saxon cousin. The German justifies his devilment in the name of practical necessity; the Anglo-Saxon casts his sins on the Lord."[95]

The *Afro-American* agrees with this when it states in one article that:

> "Nordic prejudice in the U. S. A. is said to be based on the backwardness of the colored people. In Germany it is based upon the advanced progress of the Jew."[96]

A third differentiation is presented in the following paragraph:

> "All of these oppressive measures are time worn in America, but can not succeed for long in Germany for the good reason that Jewish blood has been so mixed up with all races for centuries that none can tell who is Jewish and who is not."[97]

Other writers also seem unaware of the centuries of persecution of Jews in Germany. This unawareness is illustrated in the following statement:

"The difference is due largely to the sudden impact of the German pogroms against the Jews. In the United States, the social, political and economic proscriptions affecting Negroes have been spread over a period of seventy years."[98]

The article continues that:

"The fate visited upon the Jews in Germany is different from the experience of Negroes in the United States only in the processes of application."[99]

Another editorialist states the same "difference," when it points out that:

"The only difference between the oppression of the unfortunate Jews in Naziland and the colored citizens here is that oppression in Germany is comparatively new, while the Negro has always been victimized in a thousand and one ways here ..."[100]

The *Philadelphia Tribune* states that the Jew and the Negro have much in common, but that the persecution of the Negro in America is "more violent and cruel" than that of the Jew in Germany, probably because of the visibility of the Negro, and the better economic conditions of the Jew.[101] Even a difference in expressions used is given in an editorial which puts it in this manner:

"Down South we don't say 'the populace was excited.' Our common expression is that 'feeling runs high'."[102]

Another editorialist, after attempting to show that the Jew in Germany is much better off than the Negro in America, states that:

"Your average Southerner when it comes to the treatment of the Negro is a half-baked savage while the Germans at home are, on the whole, a very kind and cultured people even where the Negro is concerned."[103]

## CONCLUSION

It is very evident that the classifications into which the comparative articles have been placed are purely arbitrary. They have been thus divided merely to facilitate reading and to point out in broad outline the various aspects of the two situations which have been used for comparison in Negro publications. Technically, each article can be classified differently, but in many cases, the difference is but a matter of wording.

As can easily be seen, practically every item of the two situations has been utilized to illustrate similarities. The articles are of all types, and range from those which state that Negro conditions are much worse than German-Jewish conditions, through those which maintain that they are the same, to those which say that the Jew-baiting of Nazi Germany is so atrocious that it has no direct parallel in present-day America. Such articles are considering, however, only the most overt manifestations of prejudice without attempting to strike at its basis.

NOTES
1. *The Afro-American*, October 14, 1933, p. 16, editorial 11, "Jim Crow For Jews Now."

2. *The Philadelphia Tribune,* October 12, 1933, p. 4, editorial 2, "Jews in Germany vs. Negroes in America." Copied in the *Washington Tribune,* December 28, 1933, p. 4, editorial 3.

3. *Ibid.,* October 12, 1933, p. 16.

4. *The Afro-American,* December 21, 1935, p. 4, editorial 3, "The German Cracker."

5. *The Philadelphia Tribune,* July 5, 1934, p. 4, Column 2, "Germany vs. America."

6. *The Crisis,* September, 1935, p. 273, editorial 4, "Nazis, Negroes, Jews and Catholics."

7. *The Afro-American,* February 22, 1936, p. 4, col. 2, editorial 5, "The Nazis and Dixie."

8. *Ibid.,* February 22, 1936, p. 4.

9. *The Norfolk Journal and Globe,* October 8, 1938, p. 8, editorial 1, "Minorities in Texas."

10. *The Philadelphia Tribune,* December 29, 1938, p. 1, col. 5, "Hitler Learns Jim-Crow Art from America."

11. *The Amsterdam News,* December 31, 1938, p. 1, "Germans Adopt U. S. Jim Crow."

12. *The Crisis,* April, 1938, p. 113, editorial 2, "Charity Begins at Home."

13. *The Afro-American,* April 9, 1938, p. 4, cartoon captioned, "Oppressed People at Home and Abroad."

14. *The Chicago Defender,* December 16, 1939, p. 14, cartoon captioned, "Bed (Bad?) Fellows."

15. *Opportunity,* January, 1939, p. 2, The Editor Says, col. 1, "On Racial Prejudice At Home and Abroad."

16. *The Philadelphia Tribune,* April 6, 1933, p. 16, col. 1, "Hitler and the Jews."

17. *Ibid.,* May 10, 1934, p. 4, Section II, cartoon by Chase captioned, "Clean Your Home First."

18. *The Crisis,* February, 1935, p. 53, cartoon.

19. *The Afro-American,* August 24, 1935, p. 6, editorial 1, "American Nazis Quite as Bestial as Their German Brothers."

20. *The Crisis,* April, 1938, p. 113, editorial 1, "Refugees and Citizens."

21. *The Afro-American,* April 9, 1938, p. 4, col. 1, editorial 1, "Heil Hitler!"

22. *The Crisis,* September, 1938, p. 301, editorial 1, "Refugees and Citizens."

23. *The Afro-American,* January 21, 1939, p. 4, cartoon captioned, "Don't Forget The Colored People, Mr. President."

24. *The Philadelphia Tribune,* April 6, 1933, p. 16, col. 1, editorial 1, "Hitler And The Jews."

25. *Ibid.,* October 19, 1933, Section II, p. 4, editorial 2, "Hitlerism vs. Americanism."

26. *The Afro-American,* July 15, 1933, p. 10, col. 1, editorial 1, "Appeal for Negroes and Appeal for Jews."

27. *The Philadelphia Tribune,* July 5, 1934, Section II, p. 4, col. 2, editorial 2, "Germany vs. America."

28. *Ibid.,* July 5, 1934, Section II, p. 4.

29. *The Norfolk Journal and Guide,* August 10, 1935, Section II, p. 9, Sifting News from Day to Day by Lem Graves, Jr., "Kills Lynch Legislation, Denounces Nazis."

30. *The Philadelphia Tribune,* September 12, 1935, p. 4, editorial 1.

31. *Ibid.,* September 12, 1935, p. 4, editorial 1.

32. *Ibid.,* August 1, 1935, p. 4, editorial 2.

33. *The Pittsburgh Courier,* November 12, 1938, p. 22, editorial 1, "They Never Did This For Us."

34. *The Crisis,* April, 1938, p. 113, editorial 1, "Charity Begins at Home."

35. *Ibid.,* December, 1938, p. 393, editorial 1, "Negroes, Nazis and Jews."

36. *The Amsterdam News,* April 2, 1938, p. 12, editorial 1, "A Christian Act."

37. *The Afro-American,* June 17, 1933, p. 10, col. 2, Watching the Big Parade by Ralph Matthews, "Hitlerism."

38. *Ibid.,* April 15, 1933, p. 10, editorial 3, "Hitler Embarrasses Uncle Sam."

39. *The Washington Tribune,* June 23, 1933, p. 4, col. 3, Kelly Miller Says, "Race Prejudice in Georgia and in Germany Based on Cross Pretenses."

40. *The Afro-American,* February 3, 1934, p. 10, editorial 3, "Plea For Jews."

41. *The Norfolk Journal and Guide,* April 9, 1938, Section II, p. 9, "Is America The Asylum For The Oppressed?" by Kelly Miller.

42. *The Washington Tribune,* April 4, 1938, p. 4, col. 1, editorial 1, "Hitler and Mussolini Give United States Laugh."

43. *Ibid.,* April 9, 1938, p. 4.

44. *Opportunity,* January, 1939, p. 2, col. 1, article 1, The Editor Says, "On Racial Prejudice At Home And Abroad."

45. *The Black Dispatch,* July 23, 1938, p. 4, col. 3, Thinkin' Through by Freddye Harper Williams, "Queer Isn't It?"

46. *The Norfolk Journal and Guide,* December 17, 1938, p. 8, "Americans Set Pace Nazis Answer" by Kelly Miller.

47. *The Afro-American,* September 1, 1933, p. 16, editorial 1, "Adolf Hitler, K.K.K."

48. *The Philadelphia Tribune,* April 6, 1933, p. 3, cartoon "Another Klansman."

49. *The Norfolk Journal and Guide,* April 1, 1933, Section II, p. 6, cols. 4–5, "Hitler—The German Ku Klux" by Kelly Miller.

50. *Ibid.,* April 8, 1933, Section II, p. 6, cartoon captioned "Another Klansman."

51. *The Washington Tribune,* June 23, 1933, p. 4, col. 3, Kelly Miller Says, "Race Prejudice in Georgia and in Germany Based on Cross Pretenses."

52. *The Afro-American,* April 11, 1936, p. 4, col. 1, editorial 3, " 'Miss' Hitler Talks."

53. *Ibid.,* January 16, 1937, p. 4, col. 1, editorial 6, "The German Hate."

54. *The Washington Tribune,* October 13, 1934, p. 4, col. 4, William Picken's Observations, " 'Nazi' Jews."

55. *The Afro-American,* July 8, 1933, p. 8, editorial 1, "Every Race Has Its Traitor."

56. *Ibid.,* July 8, 1933.

57. *The Afro-American,* September 23, 1933, "Paris Paper Compares Hitlerism With Race Hatred in the United States."

58. *The Washington Tribune,* June 10, 1939, p. 5, cols. 3–4–5, "Says U. S. Swastikas Woven Into Jim Crow Institutions."

59. *The Norfolk Journal and Guide,* February 2, 1935, Section II, p. 9, cols. 5–6, "American Practice of Lynching Forms Basis For Defense of Nazi Persecutions."

60. *Ibid.,* August 24, 1935, p. 3, col. 3, "German Scores Treatment of Negro In U. S."; also, the *Philadelphia Tribune,* August 22, 1935, p. 5, col. 1, "Nazi Prime Minister of Hate Attacks U. S. on Negro Treatment."

61. Cf. for example, *The Amsterdam News,* January 14, 1939, p. 7.

62. *The Washington Tribune,* July 20, 1933, p. 4, col. 2, editorial 3, "Hitler's Grandmother a Jewess."

63. *Ibid.,* July 27, 1933, p. 7, col. 2, "Hitler a Jew" by William Pickens.

64. *The Afro-American,* October 14, 1933, p. 16, editorial 4, "Jewish Hitler."

65. Heiden, Konrad: *Hitler,* Chap. I.

66. *The Norfolk Journal and Guide,* October 7, 1933, Section II, p. 6, editorial 3, "Hitlerism Spiked in North Carolina."

67. *The Crisis,* September, 1938, p. 301, editorial 1, "Refugees and Citizens."

68. *The Afro-American,* August 24, 1935, p. 6, editorial 1, "American Nazis Quite as Bestial as Their German Brothers."

69. *Ibid.,* August 24, 1935, p. 6.

70. *Ibid.,* August 24, 1935, p. 6.

71. *Ibid.,* August 24, 1935, p. 6.

72. *Ibid.,* October 5, 1935, p. 6, col. 2, editorial 5, "Nazis at Williams."

73. *Ibid.,* June 4, 1938, p. 1.

74. *Ibid.,* June 4, 1938, col. 1, p. 1, editorial 6, "The Hitlers zu Hause."

75. *Ibid.,* June 18, 1938, pp. 1–2, "Nazi Virginians Separate Husband From Wife by Court Order."

76. *The Washington Tribune,* July 15, 1939, p. 1, "Nazi Spirit at Glenn Dale."

77. *The Amsterdam News,* April 15, 1939, p. 10, editorial 3, "Nazism in Baseball."

78. *The Philadelphia Tribune*, March 23, 1939, Taken in Stride by Rev. Robert W. Bagnall, p. 4, col. 2, "Nazism in America."

79. *The Washington Tribune*, January 21, 1939, p. 4, col. 1, editorial 1, "D. A. R. Body Smells of Hitlerism."

80. *Ibid.*, July 1, 1939, Caviar and Cabbage by Tolson, "Fascism Strikes At Marian Anderson."

81. *The Norfolk Journal and Guide*, April 8, 1939, p. 8, "Prejudice in Washington and Berlin" by Gordon B. Hancock.

82. *The Afro-American*, April 22, 1939, p. 14, editorial 3, "D. A. R. Defends the Indefensible."

83. *The Amsterdam News*, April 8, 1939, p. 10, editorial 3, "Nazism in Washington, D. C."

84. *Ibid.*, April 8, 1939, p. 10.

85. *The Savannah Journal*, April, 1939.

86. *The Afro-American*, May 2, 1936, p. 4, col. 1, editorial 8, "Germany and Dixie."

87. *Ibid.*, February 22, 1936, p. 4, col. 1, editorial 5, "The Nazis and Dixie."

88. *The Norfolk Journal and Guide*, October 8, 1938, p. 8, "Minorities in Texas."

89. *The Afro-American*, November 19, 1938, p. 24, col. 1, "It Sounds Familiar."

90. *The Philadelphia Tribune*, August 22, 1935, p. 4, editorial 2, "A Rose By Any Name."

91. *Ibid.*, August 22, 1935, p. 4.

92. *The Crisis*, February, 1939, p. 49, col. 2, editorial 3, "Lily White Democracy."

93. *Ibid.*, February, 1939, p. 49.

94. *The Washington Tribune*, June 23, 1933, col. 3, Kelly Miller Says, "Race Prejudice in Georgia and in Germany Based on Cross Pretenses."

95. *Ibid.*, June 23, 1933, p. 4.

96. *The Afro-American*, March 2, 1935, p. 8, col. 1, editorial 4, "Hammering Jews."

97. *Ibid.*, April 22, 1933, p. 10, editorial 1, "Strong Jewish Blood."

98. *The Norfolk Journal and Guide*, November 26, 1938, p. 8, "Oppression of Racial Minorities is World-wide."

99. *Ibid.*, November 26, 1938, p. 8.

100. *The Amsterdam News*, February 11, 1939, p. 10.

101. *The Philadelphia Tribune*, June 1, 1933, p. 4, col. 2, editorial "The Jew and the Negro."

102. *The Afro-American*, December 21, 1935, p. 4, editorial 3, "The German Cracker."

103. *The Philadelphia Tribune*, September 21, 1933, p. 17, cols. 1–2, "Negroes Suffer More in United States Than Jews in Germany" by J. A. Rogers.

# Anti-Negroism among Jews

While Nazi bombers were crumbling the historic landmarks of England, a remarkable process of social levelling began. Driven into the air-raid shelters by Nazi bombs, rich and poor were thrown together and social barriers began to give under the shattering blows of the common danger. Similarly, in America Jews and Negroes today find themselves thrown together as a consequence of direct peril from the fascists, native as well as foreign. Discrimination in industry has hit them both and thus a condition with a long history in both social groups was brought to a head. As the President's Committee on Fair Employment Practices held hearings on discrimination in city after city, Jews and Negroes appeared together, the chief victims of anti-democratic hiring policies. Side by side they made their indictments of a practice that was hindering the war effort and contrary to the principles for which our country is fighting. This circumstance has brought home to Negroes and Jews more forcibly than any recent event the essential similarity of their status as oppressed minority groups. They are beginning to realize with increasing clarity that their fate is inextricably intertwined. Nazi racism and its American anti-Negro, anti-Semitic counterpart are of one pattern. For in Germany, too, Negroes are regarded as an inferior race. A German farmer whose great-great-great-grandmother had been a mulatto was deprived of his estate because, as the Nazi court ruled, "the establishment of the existence of colored blood must necessarily lead to inability to become a peasant on German land. The requirements of blood purity are of such preponderant importance that there can be no release from them." The crisis of democracy endangers all minority groups and in times of social stress the drive against them becomes strongest; anti-Semitism becomes accentuated, and the same is true of anti-Negroism and minority persecution generally.

Unfortunately, however, the full and active realization on the part of Jews of their common destiny with Negroes has come very slowly. And because this realization is incomplete there is as yet no unity of organized Jewish and Negro action toward those common objectives for which the whole American people is engaged in the greatest war in its history. Beginnings of a conscious rapproachment between the two groups have auspiciously been made, as we shall see, but organized cooperation is still in a rudimentary stage.

On the other hand, friction has occurred between the two groups and historic circumstances have brought them into close relationship in a way that has hindered

In 1941–42, Louis Harap was managing editor of *Jewish Survey*. In 1943, he was in the U.S. Army.

Originally published in *Negro Quarterly* 1, no. 2 (1942): 105–11. Copyright © 1942, The Negro Publication Society of America, Inc.

mutual understanding. In Harlem, for instance, it happens that many of the store-keepers are Jewish. Negro resentment at high prices has been directed against them as Jews. To a certain extent such Jewish merchants have also followed the Jim Crow policy in employment—hardly a peculiarly "Jewish" practice. Jews are also employers of Negroes as domestic workers at low wages. The so-called "slave market" was the source of great antagonism. In the Bronx, most of whose inhabitants are Jewish, Negro girls and women used to stand around at certain street corners where they would be hired for temporary domestic work at very low rates, and this practice aroused hostility toward the employers, who largely were Jewish. Although New York City provided regular employment agencies that did away with this practice in May, 1941, the period of the "slave market" was responsible for a good deal of anti-Jewish feeling that was unscrupulously exploited by extreme Negro nationalists and axis agents. Another source of anti-Jewish feeling was conflict between Jewish and Negro doctors at Harlem Hospital. Unjustified blame for high rents in Harlem was placed on Jewish rent-collectors, who were only agents of the landlords.

Because of these conditions many Negroes have made an unfortunate identification of the whole Jewish people in America with this small percentage with whom they came in direct contact. For it is not true that the whole Jewish people adopted the Jim Crow attitude of their non-Jewish fellow-whites. Yet a sufficient number of Jews, themselves in an insecure position in American society owing to increasing prevalence of anti-Semitism, assumed a discriminatory attitude that fed the anti-Jewish propaganda picked up and furthered by reactionary and pro-axis Negroes.

One might well ask why many Jews were so slow to realize that their fate was linked with that of the Negro. This, despite his subjection to social, political, economic and every other form of anti-Semitism can largely be attributed to the Jews' higher economic status.

For there are great differences in the degree of oppression suffered by these two groups in American life. Where the Negro is on the whole barred from any but the most menial services in American society, the Jew has far greater freedom and can attain high positions in professional or public life. For instance, while discrimination against hiring of Jews in the colleges exists, they nevertheless are admitted to teaching positions in limited numbers. The Negro, on the other hand, is excluded from teaching at nearly all higher institutions except those of his own people. New York's City Councilman Clayton Powell has recently conducted a campaign to have Negro teachers hired on the staffs of the city colleges, pointing out that not a single Negro holds a regular teaching post. In every respect the Negro in the U. S. is immeasurably a more depressed social group than the Jew—in economic level, in opportunity for education, in access to a career, in treatment before the law, and in maintenance of equality in social relations outside of his own group. All this is too patent in American life to require further elaboration.

This different intensity of oppression has fostered in many Jews the illusion that their position is different from that of the Negro. Nor have organized Jews in the past presented a solid front with Negroes against the failure of American society to grant equal rights to the Negro. Indeed, as a presumed measure of protection against anti-

Jewish potentialities many Jews tended to identify themselves with non-Jewish whites in cleaving to the color line. Before anti-Semitism became a major American problem—a condition which revealed clearly and indefeasibly that the Jew shared a minority status with the Negro—many Jews continued to act upon the false presumption of white superiority. This has been particularly true in the South. The Jewish population in that region is relatively small so that provocation for oppressive anti-Semitism in quiet times was not great.

While Jews have never as an organized group been enemies of the Negro people, they might be said to have erred by omission rather than by commission. Partially responsible for this is the fact that for long years in American history the Jews had no inclusive organizations which could take a stand for all the Jews. Nevertheless, there are plenty of examples of Jews who have been in the front lines of the battle for Negro rights.

During the Civil War many Jews in the army of Lincoln fought with great distinction. And there were a number of Jewish participants in the dangerous, heroic abolitionist movement of the 1850's.

Three young Jewish immigrants were members of John Brown's band of abolitionists in Kansas in 1855. One of the bravest of the Jewish abolitionists was Dr. David Einhorn, Baltimore rabbi, who preached abolitionism in the pro-slavery Baltimore community and made his journal *Sinai* an organ for the movement. In 1860 this rabbi was persuaded with great difficulty to leave Baltimore to avoid mob violence; and he finally lost *Sinai* because of his espousal of this unpopular cause. In Philadelphia the rabbi Dr. Sabato Morais spoke up against slavery. Another memorable Jewish figure in the abolitionist movement was Moritz Pinner, who in 1859 founded and edited an anti-slavery paper in Missouri, a slave state. In 1853 a fugitive slave was liberated from Federal authorities in Chicago by a crowd led by Morris Greenbaum. And in Alabama, Solomon Heydenfelt, later Supreme Court Justice in California, published a pamphlet in 1849 advocating prohibition of slave immigration into Alabama.[1]

These examples suffice to show that Jews played an honorable part in the anti-slavery movement. The attitude of many Jews toward slavery is vividly portrayed in the instance of Isaac and Joseph Friedman, Southern Jews, recounted in Kate E. R. Pickard's presentation of the memoirs of Peter Still, a freed Negro.[2]

Peter Still longed to buy his own freedom but dared not entrust this hope to his white masters for fear of being defrauded. However, he came to know the brothers Isaac and Joseph Friedman, Jewish storekeepers, and of all the whites in his town he was inspired to enlist their aid. "Whenever he (Peter Still) was in their presence, although no word respecting himself was uttered, he felt that he was regarded as a man," writes Mrs. Pickard. Peter Still's faith in the Friedmans proved well-placed, for they finally did help him to gain his freedom.

Our century has also known many Jews who have fought for Negro rights. Jewish organizations, however, until recently, have pursued a "hush-hush" policy on the Negro question, as well as on the Jewish question itself. When a wave of anti-Semitism engineered by the Ku Klux Klan and Henry Ford broke out after World War I, the Jews did not meet it with effective united action with the Negroes. The Jews did not sufficiently realize that the anti-Negro and anti-labor agitation which accompanied anti-Semitism indicated that the evil authors of this agitation could be most effectively fought by joint, unified resistance by all groups attacked.

But times are changing. Hitler has flung the Jews to a sub-human level over a great part of the earth and has thereby demonstrated to the Jews that the demand for equality by the Negroes and every oppressed minority, the defense of rights of laboring people, the preservation of democracy itself constitute the single, all-embracing issue of our time. Individual Jews have through the years comprehended that the Negro and Jewish problems are parts of the same whole. Adolphe Crémieux, who though he helped destroy the Commune, had been eminent in French political life, spoke in 1840 before the General Anti-Slavery Convention in London. "All liberties are united," he cried, "and all persecutions are associated. Persecute, and you will make slaves; proclaim the equality of all, and you will create citizens. . . . I am a descendant of those Hebrews who were first to proclaim the abolition of slavery; and I this day only repeat what the Jews have always admitted in principle . . . Yes, all persecutions are akin to one another, and this was well understood by that venerable Bishop Gregoire, who, while he raised his voice in favor of the emancipation of the blacks, at the same time demanded the emancipation of the Jews."

"Yes, persecutions are akin"—of Negroes in America, of Jews by anti-Semites like Hitler and his imitators here, of trade unions and of all minorities under Hitler's heel. We are fighting a life and death war to stave off enslavement of every element in American life. The Jews are realizing that this presents them with a positive and negative task: on the positive side to unite against the discrimination that strikes at both Jews and Negro in varying measure; and on the negative to unite for the most efficient and telling prosecution of this war of liberation. There are signs of an awakening to the need of this unity. The Committee of Justice and Peace of the Central Conference of American Rabbis issued a statement in February on Race Relations Week in which "Justice for the Negroes" was demanded. This statement pointed out the indefensible conditions under which Negroes live in America. It pointed out that this is a violation of the Jewish way of life. "It is we, their (the Negro's) fellowmen, who have acquiesced in or been apathetic about their maltreatment, who have suffered spiritual hurt, for no soul that tolerates oppression remains unspoiled or unsullied," the statement warned. The statement was widely reprinted in the Anglo-Jewish press.

Negroes and Jews are giving mutual recognition to their common problem and their common stake in the war. *The Jewish Survey,* a monthly recently founded, has opened its columns to discussion of mutual problems by both Negroes and Jews. The recent hearings of the President's Committee on Fair Employment Practices have evoked editorial demands for cooperation by the press of both peoples. Said the *Jewish Review* (New York) on February 26: "The Negro has made a fine bold stand in this connection (discrimination in defense industry). It would serve the cause of Jewry well to back up the Negro in this fight—and one of the first steps would be to eliminate anti-Negro prejudice among the Jews!" In that same week (on February 28) the *Amsterdam Star-News* affirmed editorially: "This pattern of racial persecutions (by Hitler) so poignant to every Hebrew should compel him to seek an immediate alliance with colored Americans in this republic. Every Black man must realize that, though he is now the first and saddest victim of racial bigotry in America, his natural ally is the race who will inevitably be the next victim in line for cruel proscription. . . . Without reservation and camouflage Colored and Jewish Americans must unite. The wolves of intolerance are yapping savagely at the heels of both."

Awareness of the common danger is becoming more articulate among Jews. As an instance of many similar statements, we may cite *The National Jewish Monthly,* organ of B'nai B'rith, the largest Jewish fraternal order in the country. In its April, 1942 issue this journal stated that "Jews should be foremost in the practice of justice in dealing with the Negro and always vocal in protest whenever the Negro's rights are abridged." However, these sentiments should be translated further into organized co-operation. An extensive educational program undertaken by Jewish organizations on this question would advance this co-operation. In the interests of that democracy in which their mutual interests lie, Jew and Negro should act together.

NOTES

1. On the Jew's role in the abolitionist movement see Max J. Kohler, "Jews and the American Anti-Slavery Movement," Publications of the American Jewish Historical Society, vol. 5, 137–155.

2. *The Kidnapped and the Ransomed,* first published in Syracuse, N.Y. in 1856, was this year reprinted by the Negro Publication Society.

# Anti-Semitism among Negroes

To a man from Mars it must seem strange and tragically ironic that the Jewish and Negro peoples on planet Earth are not allies. The Martian observer sees the Jews kicked about in Germany and the Negroes kicked about in Georgia; and yet both Jew and Negro continue to insist upon the privilege of facing their doom separately, whereas together they could stand and fight.

The more the question is examined, the more amazing the revelation becomes—the revelation of the social blindness here. On this point, the lessons of history have been demonstrated in every corner of the globe: that no "minority" which fights alone can save itself and that the world will "little note nor long remember" any minority which howls about its own persecutions and at the same time stands indifferent when the same persecutions are inflicted upon another disadvantaged group.

The literature of discussion on the "Jewish problem" may contain a few scattered references to the Negro but where is there to be found any *direct, frontal* and *consistent* consideration based upon the premise that essentially the "Jewish struggle" and the "Negro struggle" are one? Surely not in the current Jewish publications.[1] Even on an issue as obvious and basic as anti-Negroism among Jews, the available literature, aside from this issue of *The Negro Quarterly,* does not yield so much as a single magazine article.

In Negro life and letters the situation is just as bad. From time to time anti-Semitism is discussed, allusions to the positive efforts of the Jewish people are made, but nowhere has a serious attention been given to the possibilities of joint action.

Worst of all, we must admit that there is anti-Negroism among Jews and anti-Semitism among Negroes. This truth is awful and we may hate to confess it, but nothing at all can be done to stamp out these growths, if we ostrich-like bury our heads in the sands of silence. There are those sincere souls who fear that a frank discussion of prejudice and antipathy between Jew and Negro will give ammunition to the enemy. They say that the enemy will then be able to quote us against ourselves. Perhaps. But the kind of enemy that we have will manufacture quotations of any sort whenever and wherever he needs them. Thus, we gain nothing by avoiding the issue. At the same time, we lose the chance to see the social evil for what it is and, after that, to move forward on the solid ground of understanding and mutual confidence.

The first question which comes up in this connection is how broad and deep is anti-

In 1943, L. D. Reddick was curator of the Schomberg Collection of the New York Public Library.
Originally published in *Negro Quarterly* 1, no. 2 (1942): 112–22. Copyright © 1943, The Negro Publication Society of America, Inc.

Semitism among Negroes. Is it nationwide; does it have deep historical and social-psychological roots, or is it, after all, little more than local ephemera—a passing fashion?

In answer it should be pointed out that anti-Semitism among Negroes in the United States is principally an urban phenomena. As an active element, it is virtually unknown in the rural regions, which still claim more than half of the thirteen million Negroes of this country. And in the cities, even, of the South, anti-Jewish sentiment among the colored population is slight. The line down there is generally "white" and "colored"; there is little functional differentiation in the thought of the Negro community between Anglo-Saxon, Jew or Irish. "They're white and we're colored" is the usual view.

There is, to be sure, a small body of rhymes in the folklore, which stem from the anti-Jewish elements in the Christian tradition. But aside from their utility as carriers of verbalizations which later maybe translated into active opinions, these folk-sayings have a limited significance.

It appears, therefore, that after all the exceptions have been noted, the conclusion is valid that anti-Semitism among Negroes in the United States is, in large measure, urban, Northern and historically recent. There are no organized movements. Scurrilous sheets like *Dynamite*, which was published in Chicago years ago and the completely misnamed *Negro Youth*, published in New York more recently, have been shortlived. Aside from a series of sensational articles by an unattached writer in *The Amsterdam News* last fall, the unfavorable comment in the Negro press has been sporadic.

What, then, is the nature of anti-Jewish feeling among Negroes? It should be remembered, at the outset, that Negroes are, also, Americans and as such have been subjected to the waves of anti-Semitism which have swept over Europe and the Western Hemisphere since the first World War. The rise of Hitler and his campaigns of propaganda and violence have been reflected in a sharp increase in feeling against the Jews in the United States (as elsewhere). After 1933, native fascists, some of whom were functioning here prior to Hitler's ascent to power in Germany, increased the boldness of their attacks upon the Jewish people. In the light of the influence of these activities upon the American mind, it is not very surprising that questionnaires submitted to students show that Negroes possess a similar, though not quite as unfavorable, a set of attitudes toward the Jewish people as do other Americans. In the same manner, Jews show approximately the same bias toward Negroes as do the others. As a matter of fact, such tests make it clear that all American groups, at a given economic and social level, betray quite similar conceptions of all other "racial" groups with the exception of the particular group being tested. As to be expected, the group taking the test gives itself a higher rating than is given by all other groups.

The more overt and intense forms of anti-Jewish sentiment among Negroes are to be found clustered about certain rather definite areas of competition and conflict. These arise, in the main, from the face to face contacts with the landlord, the merchant, the employer of domestic labor and to a lesser degree, the professional man.

In the congested areas of the Northern cities where Negroes have been jammed since their great trek from the South during World War I, the housing problem has been and still is acute. Residential restrictive covenants and "lily-white" agreements among property owners keep the black folk crammed into a ghetto. The pressure of the steady stream of migrants demands expansion of the "Negro neighborhood." Like rats trapped in a cellar, the mass of black humanity is thrown back upon itself again and again as it seeks to escape and ease the crowding. In New York City, for example, the population density of Harlem is over 600 persons per acre in some sections, while for Manhattan generally the population density is little more than 200 per acre. "One block in Harlem, from West 140th Street to West 141st Street, between 7th and 8th Avenues, is reputed to be the most crowded dwelling area in the world," according to the figures of the New York Housing Authority. As the Mayor's and Governor's commissions of New York report, rents take a 10–58% jump whenever Negro tenants succeed white tenants into a given block. There soon develops what is known as the "landlord monopoly." Moreover, upon the arrival of Negro renters, attention to needed repairs and other services expected of the landlord becomes indifferent. The people, naturally, are incensed at the unfairness of it all.

It is difficult to ascertain the proportion of all these landlords who are Jews or to establish statistically whether the Jewish landlord exacts higher rents than others. Probably not. A landlord is a landlord be he Negro, Greek or Turk. Nevertheless, the belief is widespread in the Negro community that a large share of the exploiting landlords are Jewish. Add to this the "high visibility" (often a distinguishing appearance) of the Jewish apartment owner or agent and the widely circulated myths about Jews and you have the stereotype of the "gouging Jewish landlord."

Many fair-minded persons have raised the question as to whether the Jewish landlord does not have the same "right" as other landlords to make his profits wherever he can. "Dollar-chasing" Negro landlords have also raised the same question in their own behalf. The Negro people (and others, of course) reject the "right" of *any* landlord to exploit an unfortunate situation. With particular contempt they look down upon the Negro landlord who would exploit his own people. They also expect more from the Jewish landlord than from landlords in general, for the Jewish people, like the Negro people, have suffered. As one street-corner orator put it, "the way they [Jews] have been cursed and beaten and robbed in Europe, you'd think that they would be considerate of us [Negroes] over here, where we are on the bottom. Instead, they rob us just like everybody else does."

The merchant-consumer situation is similar to that of the landlord-tenant. It is very well known that the retail stores in the Negro neighborhoods fleece the housewife in innumerable ways. Daily newspapers like *PM* have joined with the Negro press in exposing the outrageous fact that the groceries which one dollar will buy in other parts of New York City cost one dollar and fifteen cents in Harlem. Add to high prices, inferior quality of merchandise—stale bread, tainted meats, storage eggs, defective furniture, second class dress prints, over-ripe fruit—under weights, penny short change and you have a community of irate housewives.

Again, the statistics do not exist as to the number of Jewish merchants guilty of such dealings; still their share, in popular belief, is large. One *woman* speaking to a crowd at one of the open-air meetings quoted a passage from the Old Testament to show the

Hebraic religious sanction for the charges she was laying at the doorstep of the Jewish merchant:

> Ye shall not eat of anything that dieth of itself: thou shall give it unto the stranger that is in thy gates that *he* may eat it; or thou mayest *sell it unto an alien;* for thou art an holy people unto the Lord thy God. (Deuteronomy 14–21)

Her listeners seemed to have been impressed.

For nine years the "Bronx slave market" has been a stench in the nostrils of New York and the Nation. It is a symbol of the tension in the field of domestic labor—a third sore spot of Negro-Jewish relations. The majority of the inhabitants of the Bronx borough of New York are Jewish. In certain spots in this area the Negro domestic workers gather each morning to be hired for daily work at rates which are sometimes as low as fifteen cents per hour. These girls, bunched about the corners in all kinds of weather, are a sorry sight. With the inevitable bundle under arm, they wait their turn to "sell" themselves to the housewives who often haggle and bid for the cheapest price. The analogy to the old chattel slave marts is not inept. The public scandal of it all has called forth condemnation in the press by civic and social groups. Recently some improvement, though not enough, has been made. The Mayor and other municipal and state agencies have established "employment stations" which in the words of *PM* do little more than put a roof over the "mart." Happily, the worst abuses in terms of wages below thirty-five cents per hour have been eliminated.

But the "slave mart" in itself is not all. The tales the domestic laborers tell follow a similar pattern: they are worked to the maximum under rigid supervision. "You just can't please them," said one maid-of-all work. "I do believe that the old hussy sets the clock back," said another. "For lunch she offered me one beef sandwich—one thin slice of beef between two thin slices of bread. And after all that heavy work in the basement." These and other stories, of course, represent the point of view of the employees; the employers have their story, too. All of which emphasizes the strain at this point.

Competition and conflict on the professional level are not widespread. However, there are some. The hospitals of Harlem are a case in point. As is well known, or at least should be well known, the Negro medical student is barred or almost barred from many of the great university centers of the country. After graduation the going is tougher when it comes to finding hospitals which will permit him to serve his internship or join their staffs. The Negro physician and surgeon are almost completely excluded from all hospitals save those which serve a predominantly Negro clientele. Accordingly, the black M.D. is frustrated almost to the point of distraction when he encounters difficulty in securing a place on the staffs of these "Negro hospitals." According to the testimony of any number of Negro medical men, which again is a point of view, the white doctors— especially the Jewish doctors—work together in a clique and effectively limit the Negro staff members almost to the point of exclusion, even in jim-crow institutions like Harlem Hospital. The nurses complain, though less frequently, that they, too, suffer from such tactics.

The objective observer is thus able to understand something of the nature of anti-

Jewish feeling among Negroes in the United States. To start with, there are the general, over-all, latent stereotypes which have been lodged in the minds of Negroes by foreign and homegrown anti-Semitic propaganda. But these more or less inarticulated views would not have the excellent opportunity of coming to the surface and expressing themselves in abuse and occasional violence, out for the experience of contact, competition and conflict with landlord, merchant, employer, and medical doctor. Renters, consumers, cooks, maids and medical men moving about within the Negro community, telling and retelling their experiences are decisive in crystallizing sentiment. Extreme racialists exploit these antagonisms for their own purposes.

The large question which now suggests itself is what can be done to root out these discords between Jew and Negro? Nobody expects an overnight miracle, but there are certain definite moves which should be made immediately.

In the first place, both anti-Semitism and anti-Negroism when discussed should be discussed *at the same time* as in this issue of *The Negro Quarterly*. They should be recognized as opposite sides of the same shield. It does no good for Negroes to charge Jews with anti-Negroism and deny anti-Semitism among Negroes. Conversely, it is wrong for Jews to demand that Negroes wipe out anti-Semitism and do nothing themselves to wipe out anti-Negroism. Any approach to merit support must be a double-flank movement.

The direct attack upon the twin evils will carry with it a campaign of counter-propaganda. Negro leaders will have to assume the responsibility of pointing out to the Negro people until the issue can be no longer shrouded in confusion that a money-grabbing landlord or merchant, who happens to be a Jew, is not a representative of the Jewish people. Rather, this exploiter is a representative of a system which has nothing to do with nationality, religion or skin color. He should be fought not as "a dirty Jew" but as a callous landlord or dishonest merchant.

At the same time that these operations are conducted to deepen the understanding of this problem within the Negro community, leaders within the Jewish community will need to bring down the full pressure of their followers on the exploiters of the Negro people who happen to be Jews. This is a tender spot and involves a responsibility which some Jewish leaders have been loath to assume. Nevertheless, the fact remains that anti-Semitism will never disappear as long as the areas of conflict described above continue to exist. These furnish the only basis—nonetheless a real basis—for the anti-Jewish feeling.

A similar two-flank approach to anti-Negroism will go far toward stamping it out among the Jews.

Above all, we need to recognize that anti-Semitism and anti-Negroism are only segments of the whole question of Negro-Jewish relations. Here the central problem is how can the Jewish and Negro peoples establish in the shortest possible time an "all out" alliance? Considered in the light of what's going on in the world today, this is surely one of the important questions of our time. At this critical moment in history, the Jewish people, even in America, are fighting to maintain their rights whereas the Negro people are fighting to win theirs. On the world scene, fascism is pulverizing cultures and

L. D. Reddick    453

actually exterminating minorities and "inferior" peoples. As suggested above, in the face of common foes abroad and at home the most elemental self-interest would dictate that Jews and Negroes "close ranks" immediately.

On the positive side, Negroes and Jews have much to offer each other. The Negroes have numbers. In addition to being the largest minority in the United States, there are some 250,000,000 black folk scattered over the world. Their social consciousness is steadily rising. They would constitute a strong ally for the 17,000,000 Jews. The Jewish people, on the other side, have evolved certain survival techniques in their long history of suffering and struggle which the Negro people might well consciously examine and in certain instances boldly adopt. Moreover, in this country as elsewhere, Jews have a strategic position in the economic and social order which should prove most helpful in joint struggle. Both peoples have a rich cultural tradition with different dominant tones which would seem to complement each other.

But the question is how, concretely, may these two groups be brought together? The first essential seems to be *the need for the Jewish and the Negro peoples to identify their struggles as one.* If this is done, almost all else will follow as a natural consequence; if this is not done, all other proposals are foredoomed to failure.

It is understandable in times past as to just how and why the Jews and Negroes have had separate and distinct identifications. The middle class in both groups have had their eyes fixed on the illusion of individual success within the ranks of the dominant majority. These classes by precept and example also affixed the eyes of their respective masses to this chimerical dream which never had a chance to come true.

Many Jews, aware of noteworthy advances of individual Jews to the Supreme Court bench and to the Governor's Mansion, felt that by assuming the characteristics of the members of the dominant majority that they would achieve complete absorption into American life. Some Jews were willing to change their names, their religion, residences and to make other adjustments including the assumption of certain prejudices toward the Negro, which identified them with *white* America. In fact, some middle class Jews were only spiritually hurt and annoyed, seldom activized, when they heard about the misfortunes of the *Jewish* masses. What frustrated these Jews most was an occasional humiliation, despite all their efforts at "assimilation," in which they were treated "like Jews" or worse still, as they sometimes put it, "like we were niggers."

In similar fashion the Negro middle class, where it was buttressed by sufficient education and comparative "low visibility" (that is, its members were light-skinned enough to "pass" for white), harbored similar illusions. They denied their own people and when they were thrown back in their attempts to establish themselves securely in the dominant group, they set up bourgeois organizations of a liberal tendency whose real purpose was to assist them in obtaining their illusory objectives. Naturally, they "by passed" the Jew just as the dominant *Gentile* majority did. Thus, when these middle class groups looked away from the true interests of the masses of their own people, it could be hardly expected that they would give any real thought to alliances with other despised minorities.

But thanks to the objective conditions of world history, these phantom dreams of the middle class Jewish and Negro leadership have crumbled in the face of harsh reality. Now both the Jewish and Negro communities, each within itself, are much more closely knit than ever before. This is demonstrated not only *structurally* in the number of powerful civic and social organizations among both groups but *functionally* by victories that have been won. For example, within the past twelve months three of the most prominent anti-Jewish "baiters" in American life have been silenced. The great *Saturday Evening Post* had to apologize, though left-handedly, for its Milton Mayer article of last March.

In like manner, the Negro people were largely responsible for President Roosevelt's executive order, 8802, which provides for "the full and equitable participation of all workers in defense industries without discrimination because of race, creed, color or national origin." The United States Navy has been forced to make another step toward democracy by opening the doors of its recruiting stations to Negro volunteers. The Sojourner Truth houses for Negroes in Detroit, despite the KKK, are still Sojourner Truth houses for Negroes.

The logical step to be taken now as a natural extension of these internal developments as well as the result of outside pressures will be the joint marshalling of Negro and Jewish resources on every level. Specifically, all organizations of Jewish rights ought to incorporate the valid objectives of the Negro people in their programs. Likewise, all equivalent Negro organizations should incorporate all valid objectives of the Jewish people in their programs. Obviously, this will give a broader base and more power to every struggle. It will also provide a welcome relief from the particularism of each group yelling for its own rights—and with little regard for the threatened rights of others.

It goes without saying that this alliance will carry with it programs of education in terms of each others history and culture. There are instructive parallels in the experience of the Jewish and Negro peoples. Too, all of us need to be reminded of those occasions in times past when Jew and Negro have aided each other.

What is more, the Negro and Jewish people, after forming this union, will further widen its sweep, and thus join with all other minority, working class and progressive units who are interested in a positive struggle *against* human slavery and oppression and *for* freedom, equality and security.

Such a broadly-gauged approach raises the limited and frequently obscure contest for minority rights to the level of the universals. On its American front it would battle for equal economic, political, social and cultural rights—irrespective of creed, color or class. On its world front, the objectives would include the Four Freedoms for all men—death to fascism and specifically the liberation of Africa, Palestine, India, China and the other subject millions as well as those wretched nations who have been enslaved by "the Nazi tyranny."

These common goals of the common man everywhere would surely call forth the will-to-fight of the world masses. They would transform indifference and half-hearted support into a mighty crusade for a people's victory. Who will say that we have that now?

These, then, are the possibilities which even in this late hour have not been appreciated—if desired—by powerful leaders of warring governments. It is up to the Negro and Jew to take the lead and point the way. In doing this, they not only perform a service for mankind but incidentally they solve their own problems of anti-Semitism among Negroes and anti-Negroism among Jews in the only way that they can be solved *permanently:* that is, by banishing these and all other racisms from the earth.

NOTE

1. *The Jewish Survey* and *The Journal of Negro Education* have made splendid beginnings in this direction. See year book *Journal of Negro Education,* July 1941 and *Jewish Survey,* June 1942, which pictures three American heroes, Colin Kelly, Irish; Meyer Levin, Jew; Doris Miller, Negro.

# African Americans and Jews in Hollywood
## Antagonistic Allies

Few ethnic groups in America have enjoyed such a close association in the popular mind as have African Americans and Jews. And yet their shared affinities have often been clouded by ambiguities. From the earliest days of the alliance—such as in the heavily Jewish founding of the NAACP in 1909 or in the origins of Black-oriented Jewish foundations such as the Rosenwald Fund—lack of mutual trust has often blurred the shared goals of their common cause: the struggle to end racial and ethnic discrimination. Among Blacks in particular the alliance has been strained by a lingering sense that however philanthropic Jews had been, they also possessed the power to push buttons that allowed them to dictate the terms of the alliance. In such cases, stereotypes regain their ability to define diverse groups as one dimensional demons—Jewish conspirators or moneygrubbers as against Black wastrels and criminals.

I propose to take up this theme of the ambivalent allies as it applies to African Americans and Jews in Hollywood, particularly with respect to their intergroup relations during times of social crisis such as the Great Depression and World War II.

In the history of moviemaking, the Black and Jewish alliance often suffered schisms that fractured its sense of common cause. But the central issue here is one of perception by African Americans of their shifting place in American life rather than a matter of actual Jewish social behavior. Indeed, Jews behaved politically like the generality of Americans, save for a generalized Jewish leftward slant that Michael Lerner, editor of the Jewish journal, *Tikkun,* spoke of thus: "Jews earn like Episcopalians but vote like Puerto Ricans."[2]

Nonetheless, when it came to moviemaking most observers saw that Jews enjoyed a special seat of power that clearly reinforced the notion of a Jewish cabal that pulled the wires behind almost every scene. As early as 1918, for example, Julius Rosenwald, the first Jewish president of the mailorder firm of Sears Roebuck, enjoyed both a reputation as a "friend of the Negro" and as a man willing to place demands upon those to whom he donated money. "I really feel ashamed to have so much money," he once said of a career during which he gave away $63 million to causes that included Blacks. "I belong to a race that has suffered," he told a colored YMCA that he had underwritten. But he also snappishly told white patrons of the YMCA that "I won't give a cent unless you will include in it the building of a Colored Men's YMCA," and then admonished a Black

Thomas Cripps is a historian living and working in Baltimore.
Originally published in *Struggles in the Promised Land: Toward a History of Black-Jewish Relations in the United States,* ed. by Jack Salzman and Cornel West (New York: Oxford University Press, 1997). Copyright © 1997 by Oxford University Press. Reprinted with permission of Oxford University Press, Inc.

audience to take a hand on their own behalf. "You are going to run it," he said, "what a chance for you to make good!"[3]

The Hollywood version of this sort of having one's way helped shape a mold from which the moguls in all their arrogance were cast. Harry Cohn of Columbia was the bossy "White Fang" who *gave* ulcers to others rather than acquired them; journalists spoke of the moguls' "fiefdoms"; and actors routinely described their bosses as "a bunch of Jewish gangsters." As Frank Whitbeck, a publicist at Metro, recalled his first encounter with Jewish power he had only just muttered something about "a fat Jewish s.o.b." when a friend warned him that in Hollywood "there is no such thing as a *Jewish* sonofabitch!"[4]

But it was their power, not their Jewishness, that rankled the less powerful. Rosenwald's charity, for example, had its limits. When a coalition of Black and white allies joined to make *The Birth of a Race* (1918) as an antidote to the calculated racism of D. W. Griffith's epic of post–Civil War Reconstruction, *The Birth of a Nation* (1915), Rosenwald had offered his encouragement. But he quickly moved to a distance when one of the group let drop a hint that the philanthropist had agreed to guarantee the project against all losses.[5] It was this sense that a Jewish foot always rested on the braking pedal that stirred resentment among the beholden.

Across this gulf that divided rich from poor, stereotypes readily defined the respective groups to each other. Jews seemed to acquire money by means of some cabalistic formula—"never buy retail," or other incantation—while Blacks seemed fecklessly improvident; Jews saved, while Blacks sought immediate gratification. In mutually hard times, Jews and Blacks embraced the legend that both were victims of the same sort of oppression and thus were meant for each other as allies; in prosperous times when, however, Black fortunes lagged, Blacks found the legend wanting. Harold Cruse, for example, carped at "the myth that the Negroes' best friend is the Jew," and demanded that the African American "seriously reassess his relationship with American Jews." Thus when the Black director, Spike Lee, addressed a conference on the place of African Americans in movies, he drew upon a history of Black group-suspicions when he told his audience that he asked Warner Bros. to drop "gracefully" the celebrated director, Norman Jewison, from directing its often delayed bio-pic of Malcolm X.[6]

Stereotypes aside, the legend of a fruitful symbiosis of Jewish and Black political ambitions served Blacks well. But in their actual histories in America, the two groups only superficially shared a common heritage, whatever surface similarities drew them together. Blacks had been the victims of a Southern rural culture rooted first in slavery and then in its residual forms such as peonage, sharecropping, and political proscription. Jews, on the other hand, had come to this country in full flight from the pogroms of Czarist Russia and Wilhelmine Germany, but in possession of their own urban culture that embraced both skills and ideologies that anticipated eventual success in cities: trade unionism, socialism, cultural cohesion in the form of rabbinical devotion to scholarship, and crafts such as tailoring, all of which provided a cultural seasoning against the rigors of immigrant life. Thus Blacks fled to Northern cities as refugees while Jews fled to them as to familiar havens.

Therefore, Jews came to American cities with an edge—an inventory of skills and experiences that enabled them to enter raffish, marginal businesses apart from the staid enterprises that excluded them. Popular culture provided one of these accessible avenues. Particularly vaudeville, the popular, cheap traveling shows "creat[ed] a community of city dweller, by establishing norms of taste and behavior," as Albert McLean wrote in *American Vaudeville*.[7]

As a result of the drift of a Jewish entrepreneurial elite toward the marginal ventures of popular theatre, Jews stood poised to enter the business of moviemaking through the doorway provided by exhibiting and distributing movies rather than making them. Lacking not only these prospects but also the pool of urban skills with which to succeed at them, Blacks soon came to accept the division of labor that followed: Jewish management, exhibition, distribution, and booking, as against Black performing. Thus, whatever the merits of, say, "race movies" made by Jews for Black audiences, African Americans stood at a distance from the industry. Typically, Robert Levy's Reol firm made race movies, sometimes from original Black material such as the work of Paul Laurence Dunbar, distributed their work through Alfred Sack's bookers, and showed the films in theatres such as Frank Schiffman's *Apollo* in Harlem. Meanwhile even such an independently minded Black filmmaker as Oscar Micheaux (who often filmed his own novels) borrowed from white "angels" such as Schiffman or contracted out their lab work to Guffante and other labs willing to accept negatives as collateral against unpaid bills.

The drift of the times took a similar course in the production of the mainstream narrative movies that eventually grew into "classical" Hollywood fare. Movies at first had been produced by an old-stock, Anglo-Saxon and Irish elite that had included enterprising inventors such as Thomas Edison and W. K. L. Dickson, pioneering moviemakers such as the English J. Stuart Blackton and Albert E. Smith, and Thomas Ince. At their worst, they simply dealt in old stereotypes inherited from minstrelsy, melodrama, and vaudeville, while at their best they sometimes portrayed ethnic characters in a sweetly sentimental light. Such was the case in D. W. Griffith's *His Trust Fulfilled* (1910), in which a former slave's character is measured only by his fealty to his former mistress, and in his *The Romance of a Jewess* (1908), in which a "mixed" marriage is seen as morally advanced over the grumpy particularism of Jewish and Irish parents.

Gradually, beginning at the onset of the Great War, as Jews began to penetrate the oligopoly of old-stock patentholders (who had formed a patents "trust"), the Black image on the screen changed only in various marginal ways. Early on, Jews and Blacks alike had been hazed with unseemly ardor in the two-reel movies that were popular on the eve of Hollywood's birth. In *The Fights of Nations* (1907), for example, Blacks in "Sunny Africa, Eighth Avenue" fought with razors and danced preternaturally well, while the Jews vied with each other in fevered bouts of verbal duelling that broke off only when a gentile—an Irish cop, for example—drew the Jews together in cunning conspiracy.[8] As to moviemaking itself, William Selig's *A Night in the Jungle* (1915), like almost any jungle yarn of its day, placed its Blacks on the edge of the action with scant investment in the outcome of the plot. And, like Sam Lubin's *How Rastus Got His Pork Chops* (1910), many movies drew upon the hoariest of Southern racial lore, none of which could be traced back to Jewish cultural sources.

But with the onset of World War I, many liberal Jews stood against Griffith's *The

*Birth of a Nation* (1915) either by joining Rabbi Stephen Wise and the NAACP in the raucous demonstrations in the office of the Mayor of New York, or by joining with Rosenwald in backing some sort of cinematic challenge to Griffith such as *The Birth of a Race.*

Seemingly mere randomness rather than Jewishness set the racial agendas of moviemakers. In this connection the career of William Selig is instructive. Early on, like many figures in show business, he had managed "a genuine fast Black show" that played the Southern theatrical circuits. Later, he carried the experience into moviemaking in the form of such two-reelers as *Interrupted Crap Game* in which "darkies" break off from their gambling in order to pursue a plump chicken. Yet, paradoxically, Selig's Polyscope firm joined Rosenwald in the quest to make *The Birth of a Race,* a project also taken up in first-draft form by the German Jewish financier, Jacob Schiff, and one of the first studios to move westward to Hollywood, Carl Laemmle's IMP firm, which eventually formed the core of a real estate venture and movie company called Universal Pictures.[9] Clearly, as in all situational politics, the setting and the stakes, rather than ethnicity, set the agenda and the ideology.[10]

If the Jewish presence in this pre-Hollywood era seemed ambivalent, it must be seen that African Americans were shrewd enough to respond to both its aspects. On the one hand, Jews seemed magisterial in their knowledge of business practice; on the other, Blacks feared Jewish entrepreneurs would swamp struggling Black infant industries. "I have always been leery of the man with the thing [film cans] under his arm [as shoestring Black bookers were obliged to do]," wrote the Black critic, Tony Langston, to George P. Johnson, a cofounder of the Black Lincoln Motion Picture Company. "I learned this along with the Jews, and you know they are the last word in smartness when this game is concerned." Yet Johnson's perception of the entry of Jews into race moviemaking scared him as much as it tutored him. "The Jews are making ready for an attack upon the Negro field in the Movies," he warned the Black publisher, Robert L. Vann, only months after the Great War had ended.[11]

Meanwhile, the war had set in motion forces that transformed moviemaking in ways that defined a classical Hollywood style, opened up the entire war-weary world to the resulting products, and brought into national consciousness the image of the omnipotent Jewish mogul. Much worse news for the few Black moviemaking firms was a nationwide influenza epidemic that wiped out marginal companies while it left stronger survivors in position to form the oligopoly that became the Hollywood system of script-to-screen dominance of the marketplace. Moreover, the survivors enjoyed unaccustomed access to funds as a result of their new hegemony, with the result that the Jewish Wall Street brokers Kuhn and Loeb, Goldman and Sachs, and others, as well as the San Francisco immigrant banker, A. P. Giannini, routinely lent capital.

Still other factors joined with fiscal matters to diminish Black access to the process of moviemaking. Almost every one of the emerging "majors" took on as advisors on regional and racial matters nativeborn white Southerners—Steve Lynch and Y. Frank Freeman at Paramount, Lamar Trotti and Nunnally Johnson at Fox, Francis Harmon in the Motion Picture Association of America (MPAA) itself, among others. This meant that whenever Black material sailed "over the transom" into producers' hands it went immediately to some white man such as King Vidor whose *Hallelujah!* (1929) derived from "his own observations . . . on the everyday life of the Negro," or to Marc Connelly who directed his own *Green Pastures* (1935) which he had drawn from his reading of Roark Bradford's book of Southern Black fables, *Old Man Adam and His Chillun*.[12]

Reinforcing these conservative trends was the Production Code Administration of the MPAA, eventually a creature of Catholicism rather than of Jews in that its "don'ts and be carefuls" that segregated Black characters from white in order to assuage white fears of miscegenation were drafted by the Jesuit, Fr. Daniel Lord of the St. Louis Province; the Catholic layman and tradepaper publisher, Martin Quigley; and Joseph Breen who succeeded to the office of "czar" of the MPAA following the retirement of its first ruler, the Presbyterian Republican, Will Hays.[13] Together with the Hollywood Blacks who played the only roles that emerged from this politically conservative system, the MPAA provided the most structured ideological control over the Black image on the screen—without the intrusion of a single Jewish hand.

To take only one instance of this system in process, we could do no better than to turn to the old Fox lot in 1929 (before it became "the goy studio" in 1935 as a result of a merger with Darryl F. Zanuck's 20th Century studio). Winfield Sheehan, a veteran manager of the studio founded by William Fox and led by Joseph Schenck, drove onto the lot where he brushed against Clarence Muse, a veteran of Black theatre and race movies who had been lingering at the gate hopping for a gig. The studio, in fact, had been looking for a capable Black actor to star in *Hearts in Dixie*, a pet project that Sheehan had promoted with the result that it had grown from a sentimental two-reeler into a feature-length celebration of Dixie. In it Muse became Nappus, an exceptionally wise man whose ponderously resonant voice dominated his scenes. Moreover, the movie, along with Metro's *Hallelujah!* created a brief vogue for all-Black material and may have served as teaser to the movie version of Marc Connelly's Pulitzer-prize musical drama, *Green Pastures* (1935).

Thereafter, Muse not only became famous as Nappus but also redefined at least one sort of social role for Blacks in Hollywood. Clearly, despite an unctuous manner that made young Black activists wince, Muse advanced the cause of Blacks in Hollywood. His quiet dignity, his advice to young Black performers, his reputed study of the law, his solid training on the stage, his complex mix of Black cultural nationalism and assimilationism, and his resistance to wartime NAACP activism that seemed to run counter to Muse's hope of "build[ing] ourselves into" Hollywood all conspired to give Muse an authority among Blacks precisely because in Sheehan he possessed a "friend at court" on the white movie lots.[14] Later, he acquired yet another friend at court, the young Frank Capra, for whom he appeared in *Dirigible, Broadway Bill,* and other movies.

Why should Sheehan's Jewish bosses have taken counsel from Muse? Perhaps because they were as assimilationist as Muse seemed. A look at the movies on the screens at the onset of the Great Crash reveals a rage for a comic assimilationism that almost every studio played to: *Kosher Kitty Kelly, Clancy's Kosher Wedding,* the *Cohens and the Kellys* series, and others of the decade that saw Anne Nichols's play, *Abie's Irish Rose* run on Broadway for years. The apogee of the era came in the form of *The Jazz Singer* (1927), Samson Raphaelson's own assimilationist account of a cantor's son who becomes a jazz singer. Far from a fluke of faddishness, the ideology of universalism extended into almost every immigrant-themed movie thereafter, often embracing African Americans in the resulting lovefeast as in the 1946 remake of *Abie's Irish Rose* (following its success as an ongoing radio series) when at the wedding that forms the climax of the movie the Black servant intones her own "Mazeltov." Even in their own lives, the moguls reflected their immigrants' wish to belong by voting Republican, modulating, even muting, their Jewishness, and marrying *goyishe* women. To find in these drives the source of Jewish conspiracy is as absurd as to find a Jewish predominance in another field, that of furriers, a plot against foxes and ermines.[15]

But what of African Americans? Did they take Jewish Hollywood as conspiracy or merely as a ruling class with whom they could deal? Certainly both in the trades and in the Black press the relationship between the two groups of outsiders was celebrated as sanguine. As early as 1922, Jewish-edited *Variety* praised *Love is an Awful Thing* for its "Bert Williams touches . . . that are most welcome" while complaining of "needless" quivering Negro servants. Whenever some odd racist tract appeared, *Variety* predicted: "There is no chance for this picture to get a nickel anywhere . . . the Sunday night audience laughed it practically out of the theatre." Or the Jewish editors reported on trends such as the "clumsy housemaids [who] seem to have gone out of style." Meanwhile, the Black press played both nag and cheerleader. Every review seemed to weigh movies against Hollywood's history. The *Amsterdam News,* for example, praised Cecil B. DeMille's proposed *Porgy* which "will portray the human everyday life of the American colored man" only months after the *Afro-American* complained of a "lack of pictures with Negro characters teaching Negro ideals." "Never before has the Southern Negro had the good fortune to be selected to take part in a clean cut motion picture" such as *Uncle Tom's Cabin,* said another review.[16]

More than any other movie, *The Jazz Singer* enjoyed a special place at the intersection of African American and Jewish cultures. In its way, Raphaelson and Paul Sloane's movie brought Blacks and Jews together on the screen in an urban setting that seemed to follow from the bold Black movies of 1927 through 1929: *Uncle Tom's Cabin* (1927) with the restoration of its abolitionist core; *Hearts in Dixie* (1929), with its tragic treatment of Black Southern rural life; *Hallelujah!* (1929), King Vidor's and Wanda Tuchock's contrasting of Black pastoral life with that of the poor Black city; and *Show Boat* (1929) with its racial moral worn on its sleeve in the form of the bittersweet miscegenation subplot and Oscar Hammerstein and Jerome Kern's powerfully defining ballad, "Old Man River."

The title role of *The Jazz Singer* seemed to feed not only a general white need to cultivate a parody of Black musical and performing style, but also a specifically Jewish response to their immigration to America. Much as Eric Lott has argued of Blackface minstrelsy—that the "theft" of African American performance culture by having white people parody it while masked by burnt cork helped give identity to the white working class by portraying what white men were *not*—so too Michael Rogin has carried the argument onto the movie screen. To him, it seemed that as "Blackface made white Americans out of Irish immigrants," so movies did for the Jews of the twentieth century who "occupied an insecure position between whites and people of color."[17]

But meaning need not stop here. Both Blacks and Jews, if they in fact did not draw inferences similar to those made by Lott and Rogin, nonetheless appreciated the link between their two ethnic cultures. While it is true that the Black *Pittsburgh Courier* in 1923 reported that Jolson "seriously doubted his ability to register [Blackface] as well upon the screen as upon the stage," the doubt focused on lame and stale racial comedy in a failed script, *His Darker Self,* that both D. W. Griffith and Jolson abandoned, rather than in Jolson's performance. Later, following the success of *The Jazz Singer* in 1930, the *Amsterdam News* claimed of Jolson's rendering of Blackness: "every colored performer is proud of him."[18]

Certainly Jewish producers shared some sort of appreciation of Black culture and its place in their lives. In a year's time spanning 1929 and 1930, for example, Jewish producers of short films integrated Black musical performance into the new medium of soundfilm in a rich cycle of Black musical performance so prolific that *Variety* gave it a headline—"Colored People in Many Short Talkers." Murray Roth's *Yamacraw* (1930) was typical in its stylized, sentimental treatment of the Black squalor of the "New South" that drives a young Black man (Jimmy Mordecai) northward to an urban life that tested his character in other ways—the ways of the street and the saloon. As it often did, Jewish *Variety* praised these shorts, finding *Yamacraw* "a jazz symphony of Negro life that is arresting in movement as well as dramatic in idea."[19]

Moreover, as though the onset of the Great Depression had thrust them together in common cause against still more burdensome economic forces, Blacks and Jews in Hollywood seemed to march in step. Perhaps they followed a course that various social critics have noticed. That is, from their inventory of cultural options they selected mutually satisfying tactics arising from a loose alliance of like-minded "conscience-liberals." As disparate observers as the Italian Marxist, Antonio Gramsci, through the liberal capitalist critics, John Kenneth Galbraith and James K. Feibleman, have found that times of crisis provide moments in which the oppressed and their allies may rebargain the terms of their social status.[20]

Certainly this alliance seemed emergent during the Great Depression. Not only did the decade begin with the cycle of Black performance shorts, including Duke Ellington's *Black and Tan Fantasy* (1929) with its wry treatment of a down-and-out composer and the dancer who hoofed so that he might live to compose, but it carried onward to 1935 when Ellington's *Symphony in Black* (1935) boldly evoked African American history in four movements: the "middle passage," oppressive toil, religious epiphany, and the urbane jazz age.

Moreover, Blacks participated. Briefly, until his early death, the Black writer Wallace Thurman enjoyed a contract with a Hollywood studio. In 1933, John Krimsky, one of the producers of the film of Eugene O'Neill's *The Emperor Jones,* insisted on diluting the playwright's primitivism by asking James Weldon Johnson of the NAACP and his brother, Rosamond, to contribute a prologue. In it, Jones (Paul Robeson), the Pullman porter whose *hubris* led him to a Caribbean crown (and a tragic death), is given a pastoral Black past rather than a tomtom beating in his breast as the psychologically plausible motive for his rise and fall.[21]

Such gestures earned Black attention, contending with Black concerns such as that of the Black movie pioneer, Bill Foster, who fairly shouted at James Weldon Johnson that "If the Negro wants Big Pictures of Negro life today they [sic] will have to produce them himself [or risk others'] . . . controlling the Equipment [and] then the door will be closed." Muse, on the other hand, thought "Hollywood's not prejudiced; they'll buy anything that's successful," to which Johnson added a corollary that whites so far had handled Black material adequately because of a *Black* "reluctance . . . to see what they consider lower phases of Negro life." Indeed, after the Black congressman, Oscar De-Priest, saw *Hallelujah!* he insisted that African America stood "on the threshold of civic and cultural emancipation." And by the middle of the Depression, the Negrophile writer, Carl Van Vechten, summed up, among other news items, the arrival of Bill Robinson and Paul Robeson in Hollywood, and the release of unsentimental movies such as *Slave Ship,* by predicting to Johnson "I think this is likely to be a NEGRO WINTER."[22]

By the end of the decade, the sort of gestures that evoked such fulsome praise had become calculated and firmly linked to an endemic anti-fascism that had been rising in the wake of the assumption to power of Mussolini, Hitler, Franco, and Tojo in total-itarian states. Indeed, in the transformation of the regional novel, *Gone with the Wind* into a national movie epic, David O. Selznick specifically linked the need for a modern-ized portrayal of Blacks to the international war against fascism. "In our picture I think we have to be awfully careful that the Negroes come out on the right side of the ledger," rather than, as he told his writer, risk their movie becoming "an advertisement for intolerant societies in these fascist-ridden times." Later, many Black activists, in spite of themselves, joined the house organ of the NAACP in finding in *Gone with the Wind* "no reason for Negroes to feel indignant." Later still, when Sol Lesser attempted a sort of B-movie version of the regionalisms of *Gone with the Wind* in his *Way Down South,* he, like Selznick, wished for fairly drawn Black imagery. But unlike Selznick, he went right to the source by engaging Clarence Muse and the poet, Langston Hughes, to write as Black a movie as they could. Never mind that draft-by-draft the movie compromised and embraced many Hollywood conventions; it had begun as a product of a Jewish-Black alliance. "Messrs. Muse and Hughes are to be given the utmost liberty in develop-ing the Second Draft Screenplay," he wrote to his production unit, "so that it will contain every element of their conception of the story."[23]

Clearly, the mood of "conscience-liberalism" established by the onset of World War II placed African Americans in an enhanced bargaining position in Hollywood. Indeed, Sime Silverman's *Variety* gave such politics a banner headline: "Better Breaks for Negroes in H'wood." And Jews saw the changes—particularly those that seemed results of lobbying by Walter White of the NAACP—as especially sanguine. One of White's Jewish correspondents saw in the casting of a Black doctor in a Metro B-movie, *Dr. Kildaire's New Assistant,* an event "as stirring and as promising as any of the principles set forth in the Atlantic Charter [the pact that had defined the earliest of Allied war aims]." Routinely thereafter, critics celebrated war movies such as *Sahara* (1943) as "an outstanding contribution toward the objective stated by Mr. White."[24]

Such movies came from a cadre of Jewish "moguls" who even in prewar days had formed a Hollywood Anti-Nazi League to stand against Hitler's anti-Semitism even before the government did. They almost relished the role of propaganda warriors. In one instance of a polyethnic movie about a lost platoon, *Bataan* (1943), the cast featured obligatory soldiers that included the Jewish Sergeant Feinberg and a Black Corporal, Wesley Epps, a preacher and an artful demolition man. But when White learned during production that the Black role had been written out, he wired the MGM producer, Howard Dietz, and successfully pressed to have the role restored. Thus both the movie and its making symbolized the compelling wartime powers of the ethnic alliance. By war's end, the ethnic angle had begun to embrace Jews still more widely as in the case of Dore Schary's *Till the End of Time* (1946), in which a wounded veteran spits in the eye of a recruiter for a racist veterans' group, a gesture he offers in memory of "Maxie Klein," a dead buddy left on the beach on Guadalcanal.[25]

For their part, African Americans zealously took up White's agenda and made it their own. William G. Nunn, the publisher of the *Pittsburgh Courier*, for example, called for a "Double V" for victory simultaneously over foreign (and anti-Semitic) fascism and domestic racism. Such activism signaled the formation of a broadly based coalition that embraced Black publicists, White's lobbying in Hollywood, a link to the 20th Century-Fox boardroom through its chairman, the defeated presidential candidate, Wendell Willkie, who served as special counsel to the NAACP, and the Jewish studio chiefs themselves. As the screenwriter, Sidney Buchman, put it: "Hollywood as a whole has recently been made aware of the Negro's true position in America and our responsibility toward the subject." And speaking of his own contribution, the script for *Talk of the Town* (1942), in which he had written a Black role of substance, his motive was the "fundamental thing in this war we are fighting."[26]

Outside of Hollywood, in the circles of documentary and propaganda filmmakers the story was the same. At every turn, Jews pressed both studios and their government for opportunities to portray on film Black images that reflected the liberalizing propaganda aims of the Western Alliance. The "race movie" distributor, Ted Toddy, proposed to the War Department a saga of the Black 99th Pursuit Squadron with Paul Robeson as its star; Alfred Sack picked up *Marching On*, an espionage yarn directed by Spencer Williams, director of the evocative *The Blood of Jesus* (1940); the historian, Saul Padover, proposed to his wartime boss in Agriculture a film that would extend racial propaganda into peacetime by means of a documentary portraying the African American as "an average human being"; Gene Weltfish transformed *Race: Science and Politics*, a book by the anthropologist, Ruth Benedict, into an anti-racism comicbook and thence into the UPA movie, *The Brotherhood of Man*; and both Paramount and Warner, among other majors, pressed on with short theatrical movies on racism long after the impending end of the war rendered them both militarily obsolescent and profitless.[27]

The resulting agenda that had been set both by NAACP lobbying in Hollywood and by each new movie that pressed against former constraints on Black movie portrayals led to a Black and Jewish frame of mind that prodded the studios against inertia or backsliding. Upon the completion of the Pentagon's own *The Negro Soldier*, the studio bosses concurred in Harry Cohn's hyperbolic praise of it as "the greatest War Department movie ever made," while Edwin R. Embree, director of the Black-oriented Rosenwald Fund, urged "many of us . . . to enlist in the cause . . . to help spread the news to commercial theatres." Roy Wilkins of the NAACP extended the sentiment into the postwar era when he predicted that the Pentagon's considerably bolder sequel, *Teamwork*, "would do much to promote racial unity *now and for the future.*"[28]

So taken were these Black and Jewish activists with the prospects for a postwar liberalized national conscience that they sought to head off the release of *We've Come a Long, Long Way*, a rival to *The Negro Soldier*, that had been compiled by an independently active team of the "race movie" maker Jack Goldberg and the Black evangelist, Elder Solomon Lightfoot Michaux. At stake was their fear that a prolonged rivalry between *The Negro Soldier* and the privately made Goldberg/Michaux movie would create an unseemly "Jewish vs. Negro situation" that might undo the bicultural alliance war had helped revive.[29]

Of course, in any alliance the principals should have expected to compromise goals and even to dilute some of their ethnicity in the interest of promoting their common cause. The historian Kenneth M. Stampp spoke for the age in which unity against foreign enemies obliged propagandists to emphasize ethnic "tolerance" and even "brotherhood" when he asserted that ". . . innately Negroes *are*, after all, only white men with Black skins."[30] Unavoidably, the war became a touchstone of these sentiments borne by every liberal conscience. As a Jewish soldier says in the war movie, *The Pride of the Marines* (1946): "Don't tell me we can't make it work in peace like we did in war." One such movie, *The House I Live In* (1946), an Oscar-winning two-reeler written by the eventually politically blacklisted writer, Albert Maltz, directed by Mervyn LeRoy, underwritten by Dore Schary's RKO studio, and starring Frank Sinatra, featured a theme that sang of "all races and religions . . . that's America to me."[31]

The alliance even withstood postwar conservative countermeasures, particularly in the form of the congressional Un-American Activities Committee that masked its assault behind a campaign to root out "communists" in Hollywood. Under such pressure it seemed to Jews and Blacks alike that wartime ideals had to be kept alive in the form of both polemics and movies. And yet Jews, as usual, despite a leftward leaning, could be found on both sides of the issue. Mayer remained a Republican stalwart; Roy Cohn served as counsel to Senator McCarthy's investigators; and Dore Schary, the otherwise doctrinaire liberal, both composed and signed the "Waldorf agreement," a deceptively phrased response to proscription of political expression that ended by agreeing to fire communists because their scripts would be unsalable to good Americans.

Nonetheless, Hollywood Jews also stood in their accustomed place on the left as well. Samuel Goldwyn, for example, wrote a piece for the Urban League's *Opportunity*, entitled "How I Became Interested in Social Justice" (by reading of Allied war aims in The Atlantic Charter!). Norman Granz, already famous for his "Jazz at the Philharmonic" concerts, produced the Oscar-winning short, *Jammin' the Blues*, that seemed so authentically Black that the columnist, Walter Winchell, thought it had been shot from a hidden camera. Abraham Polonsky, eventually blacklisted for his politics, wrote *Body and Soul* (1947), in which he used the boxing ring as a trope for unrestrained capitalism by centering on "a Black man [Canada Lee] . . . to defy the conventions around us," a sequence the *New York Times* reviewer praised as "one of the finer things of the film." John Garfield (Julius Garfinkle), the actor, successfully pressed for a remake of Ernest

Hemingway's *To Have and Have Not* (1944), this time including an elided Black role. The result was *The Breaking Point* (1951) in which Juano Hernandez restored the role of the Black deckhand for which the critic, Seymour Peck, offered an "especially grateful" review. By then every major studio, including the "goy" studio, 20th Century-Fox, had produced its own "message movie" that harked back to the racial ideals of wartime propaganda and worked them into various peacetime angles—among them Schary's *Intruder in the Dust* for Mayer's studio, Zanuck's *Pinky* and Joseph Mankiewicz's *No Way Out* for Fox, and Stanley Kramer's *Home of the Brave* for Columbia.[32]

Here it must be said that Hollywood Jews were not playing the role of a sort of ideological Lady Bountiful spreading goodness to the benighted. Rather, African Americans, driven partly by the example of Walter White during the war, took an uncommonly direct hand in their collective fate. Critics such as Bob Ellis in the Black *California Eagle*, embracing the universalist ideology of the day, urged their readers to see the message movies because they seemed to assert that "Negroes are like everyone else," or, like George Norford in *Opportunity*, marked each new success as "another step for Hollywood." Within the ranks of moviemakers themselves Blacks tried to affect films at their source. Walter White's daughter, for example, worked closely with Philip Dunne, the cowriter of *Pinky*, while Henry Lee Moon of the NAACP read Ben Maddow's script for *Intruder in the Dust* and pronounced it "the kind of film we can endorse" and told White to "give Hollywood the 'Go' sign." And at the point of release, Dore Schary exhorted Metro's salesmen: "don't be afraid of" controversial movies of advocacy.[33]

Thereafter, through the era of the civil rights movement Black fortunes in Hollywood were linked directly to a cadre of Jewish leftists. Their work, at first, took two parallel courses: the one taken by Harry Belafonte as a picaresque Black hero as in Max Youngstein and Abraham Polonsky's *Odds Against Tomorrow* (1959), the other taken by Sidney Poitier in a series of squarer, more circumspect roles as doctor, African national, Anglican priest, angry rebel who sees the light, shrewd cop—always in the good hands of the Jewish keepers of his image: Lew Schreiber, Martin Baum, Sydney Pollack, Aaron Rosenberg, David Susskind, Pandro S. Berman, Stanley Kramer, and Joel Glickman.

And yet, if Jews invested in such movies for the dual purposes of serving a progressive cause and turning a profit, they also ran into the self-imposed barrier of their own universalism—a barrier inherited from their own assimilationist lives as well as from the ethnically phrased nationalism of the war years. Such sentiments allowed scant room for the expression of the racial nationalism that African Americans often turned to when their collective lot improved enough to seem to threaten their identity as a people. In moments like these they sometimes embraced the African Zionism of Marcus Garvey or the vibrant raffishness of the urban streetscape that always seemed most impervious to assimilation into the centers of American life—much in the way that the journalist, Murray Kempton, had formulated: "in bad times men cherish the elegant and in good ones they exalt the raffish."[34]

Almost predictably, Black urban youth rebelled against Poitier's increasingly stuffy image and turned to, as *Variety* called them, "blaxploitation movies." Here again, the trend toward making movies that focused upon or pleased African Americans derived not so much from Jewishness as from the generality of Americans who wished to get on with some reform that would confront endemic racism, which was not abating even in the face of evermore deeply moving television demonstrations of Black fortitude and Southern white intransigence. Indeed, by the decade of the 1960s, with the civil rights movement at its most accessible on daily television news broadcasts, one producer spoke of the medium as "the chosen instrument of the civil rights movement."[35]

The ensuing Civil Rights Acts that marked the era gave moviemen a means of diversifying the racial makeup of both their crews and their movies—all in a painless form defined by law rather than by the actions of a few bold pioneers. A mandated Office of Economic Opportunity obliged studios to keep records of hiring practices and their results. Soon, all of the studio guilds created apprenticeships and jobs for minorities, particularly in television programs that by then constituted a greater portion of output than did movies. The agency files soon swelled, either with apologies for this or that show that had not met its racial goals because "the nature of the programming did not call for negro talent," or with boasts, as Sheldon Leonard of Bill Cosby's series, *I Spy,* reported, that a "majority of the actors in this series will be from minority groups." The NAACP through its Labor Secretary, Herbert Hill, pressed the guilds for greater voluntary efforts by threatening them with challenges to their legitimacy before the National Labor Relations Board. A committee of studio bosses led by Joel Freeman, Schary, Morrie Weiner, Joseph Schenck, and Maurice Benjamin met and heard proposals directed at "cementing the bonds of friendship" across racial lines.[36] Finally, as work rules and membership roles changed under these pressures, the development of "Cinemobiles" by the firm of Fouad Said gave moviemakers a capacity to move whole units of crews out of Hollywood itself and into locations where relaxed work rules (and lower wages) opened up still more opportunities for African American journeymen.[37]

The resulting blaxploitation movies—that is, movies made with a view to their consumption by a narrowly defined Black audience—came to the nation's screens in a dizzying variety that defies any generalization that a specifically Jewish consciousness had imposed on them a conspiratorial uniformity that "messed with" young Black minds. If anything, Blacks of the time felt they had taken a hand in shaping Hollywood's future. The genre of "action" movies, wrote the Black journalist, Walter Burrell, in the Black pop-magazine, *Soul,* "has more profoundly, financially and sociologically altered the motion picture medium than anything since the . . . turn of the century."[38]

Unquestionably, Hollywood remained in mainly Jewish hands both through the studio bosses and many of their bankers. But Federal law, conscience-liberalism of moviemakers and their audiences, Black pressure not only from national Black activists and polemicists but from the local Hollywood/Beverly Hills branch of the NAACP, and increasingly bold Blacks on the sets—Gordon Parks, Ivan Dixon, and others—broke the monopoly of creativity that had kept Black roles in a narrow compass.

The result was an emerging image of Blacks as angry, urbane rebels who joined other images of a white "counterculture" that had also broken with Hollywood convention. Black audiences suddenly stood revealed. They filled the cavernously empty downtown picture palaces, almost certainly saved Mayer's old MGM lot from closure, and filled the trade papers with fables of success. A "complete metamorphosis," said *Variety* of the transformation of midtown Buffalo; a "cultural revolution," wrote the Black journalist, Chuck Stone; and only an occasional Black voice complained of the "warping" of Black minds by focusing on urban violence. Some of them merely aimed for a detective mode "like it was with Bogart," only Black; others actively sought Black writers; veteran Hollywood writers learned to write from a hip angle about "a woman with much girl in her and a man with no boy in him"; they quickly learned to insert an "elder" in place of a "witchdoctor"; and in order to reach the targeted market "fastest," they reminded each other to "hire a Black man or woman" and to buy space in the house organ of the Congress on Racial Equality (CORE).[39]

Of course it could not last. But more than any social phenomenon since World War II, the cycle had responded to a rising tide of popular Black nationalism, and introduced Black moviemakers into a formerly white monopoly (during the ensuing years the Black members of the Directors Guild of America rose from less than a dozen to more than six hundred, many of them women).[40] Rather than a Jewish cabal behind the walls of the movielots, it was many other forces which conspired to apply a brake to the trend: for in order to make a profit, a movie needed a share of the world market, which included Black investors such as the sorority, Delta Sigma Theta, occasional crossover audiences that would bring in white money, eventual television sales, bankable stars, and plausible motives other than revenge and guerrilla warfare. Often, the "quick-and-dirty" footage, the inexperienced crews, the scatological language, the gratuitous sex and violence, the transitory and often professionally limited actors, and the often apolitical mode of blaxploitation movies precluded the creation of a genre that pleased Blacks while reaching the necessarily broader marketplace.

As in earlier times, when shared goals seemed so elusive as to be unattainable and yet already attained goals seemed to threaten the roots of ethnicity itself, African Americans and Jews withdrew into their respective ghettoes of the mind where culture identities might be cultivated in a sealed-off nutrient broth. The entry of Blacks and Jews into a cultural mainstream—in this case Hollywood—threatened to end in a featureless homogeneity. As the Black bourgeoisie blanched at the prospect of separation both from "the brother on the block" and from "Mother Africa," so Jews feared the loss of Jewishness as the incidence of intermarriage across lines of faith increased. But the two groups remained linked by forces of history and circumstance that the rise and fall of cycles of moviemaking and of ethnic antipathies could not diminish.

NOTES

1. In more elaborate form, this notion was taken up by Glazer in a morning seminar on the occasion of the inaugural of President Rudenstein in Harvard University in the fall of 1991.

2. Lerner interviewed by James Bock, *Sun* (Baltimore), Feb. 17, 1994.

3. Nina Mjagkij, "A Peculiar Alliance: Julius Rosenwald, the YMCA, and African Americans, 1910–1933," *American Jewish Archives*, 14 (Fall/Winter 1992), 598.

4. Melvyn Douglas, himself Jewish, quoted in *Sun* (Baltimore), Aug. 9, 1981; Whitbeck quoted in Beth Day, *This Was Hollywood: An Affectionate History of Filmland's Golden Years* (London, 1960), 45.

5. Thomas Cripps, *Slow Fade to Black: The Negro in American Film, 1900–1940* (New York, 1977), Chap. 3.

6. Cruse quoted in an anonymous "book notice" in *American Jewish Archives,* 14 (Fall/Winter 1992), 657; Spike Lee quoted in *New York Times,* March 28, 1994, as he appeared at a conference on Blacks in film at the New York University Tisch School of the Arts.

7. Albert F. McLean, Jr., *American Vaudeville as Ritual* (Lexington, 1965), 7–8.

8. *The Fights of Nations* (1907), print in Library of Congress.

9. Laemmle's removal to Southern California was itself a step toward Jewish hegemony in moviemaking in that it was meant to break the hold of the "motion picture patents trust," a creature of the old-stock moviemen of the East Coast.

10. See Selig's catalogue, *Special List of Films Made Expressly for Selig* (Chicago, 1900), 8–9; review of *How Rastus Got His Pork Chops* cited in footnote 30, Chap. 1, Cripps, *Slow Fade to Black;* Selig's "fast Black show" cited in Terry Ramsaye, *A Million and One Nights* (New York, 1926), 303.

11. Tony Langston to George P. Johnson, Nov. 24, 1916, in George P. Johnson Collection, Special Collections Library, UCLA; Johnson to Robert L. Vann, *Pittsburgh Courier* publisher, March 27, 1920, ibid.

12. *Variety,* Aug. 22, 1928, 7, on Vidor; on Connelly, see Thomas Cripps, "Introduction" to Marc Connelly, *The Green Pastures* (Madison, WI, 1979), passim.

13. See Leonard J. Leff and Jerrold L. Simmons, *The Dame in the Kimono: Hollywood, Censorship, & the Production Code from the 1920s to the 1960s* (New York, 1990), 3–54, for a brief institutional history.

14. Cripps, *Slow Fade to Black,* 108; and interviews with Muse.

15. Neal Gabler, *An Empire of Their Own: How the Jews Invented Hollywood* (New York, 1988), Chaps. 6, 7.

16. Cripps, *Slow Fade to Black,* 139, on *Love is an Awful Thing; Variety,* April 22, 1925, 44, on *The Toll of Justice,* April 27, 1927, 20, on "housemaids"; *Amsterdam News,* April 2, 1936, on *Porgy; Afro-American,* Aug. 29, 1925; and *Amsterdam News,* Sept. 15, 1926.

17. See Eric Lott, *Love and Theft: Blackface Minstrelsy and the American Working Class* (New York, 1993), 4, for his goal: "I am after some sense of how precariously nineteenth-century white working people lived their whiteness." Michael Rogin, "Making America Home: Racial Masquerade and Ethnic Assimilation in the Transition to Talking Pictures," *Journal of American History,* 79, 3 (Dec. 1992), 1052, quoted. See also his "Blackface, White Noise: The Jewish Jazz Singer Finds His Voice," *Critical Inquiry,* 18, 3 (Spring 1992), 417–53.

18. *Pittsburgh Courier,* Dec. 29, 1923 and *Amsterdam News,* July 9, 1930.

19. *Variety,* May 8, 1929, 23.

20. On Antonio Gramsci, see Stuart Hall, "Gramsci's Relevance for the Study of Race and Ethnicity," *Journal of Communication Inquiry,* 10 (Summer 1986), 5–27; on Galbraith's notion of "countervailing powers" as a force for change, see his *American Capitalism: The Concept of Countervailing Power* (Boston, 1972), passim; and on Feibleman's idea that crises such as wars draw antagonists together in common cause, see his *The Theory of Culture* (New York, 1946, 1968), 7, 43, 96; and on my own notion of "conscience-liberalism," see my *Making Movies Black: The Hollywood Message Movie from World War II to the Civil Rights Era* (New York, 1993), x–xi.

21. Interview between John Krimsky and the author, New Brunswick, NJ, spring 1976.

22. Foster to Johnson, n.d.; Johnson to Mary Ruta, May 7, 1932; Van Vechten to Johnson, Sept. 27, 1935, all in James Weldon Johnson collection, Beineke Library, Yale University, all cited in Cripps, *Slow Fade to Black.*

23. Selznick to Sidney Howard, Jan. 6, 1937, in Rudy Behlmer, ed., *Memoir from David O. Selznick* (New York, 1972), 151; *Crisis,* 48 (Jan. 1940), 17; Sol Lesser quoted from Cripps, *Making Movies Black,* 22.

24. Lola Kovner to Walter White, Nov. 28, 1942 in NAACP Records, Library of Congress.

25. Cripps, *Making Movies Black,* 72–77, 89–92.

26. Cripps, *Making Movies Black,* 104–105; Sidney Buchman to Booker Brown, in *Courier,* Oct. 31, 1942 and Sept. 19, 1942; "Rogue's Regiment," *Ebony,* Sept. 1948, 31–33, cited in Cripps, *Making Movies Black,* 65, 67.

27. Cripps, *Making Movies Black,* 163, 167; Padover quoted, 157.

28. Cohn quoted in Truman Gibson to Anatole Litvak, April 14, 1944; Edwin R. Embree to Philleo Nash, June 29, 1944; Roy Wilkins to Gen. A. D. Surles, Aug. 22, 1945, all cited in Cripps, *Making Movies Black,* Chap. 4.

29. Walter White to Thurgood Marshall, May 4, 1944, cited in Cripps, *Making Movies Black,* Chap. 3.

30. Kenneth M. Stampp, *The Peculiar Institution: Slavery in the Ante-Bellum South* (New York, 1956, 1964), vii. Such a sentiment speaks not so much to Stampp's own enduring convictions but to the ideology of an age in which racial caste dominated and thus ideals of universalism colored the rhetoric of conscience-liberals.

31. *The House I Live In* quoted in Cripps, *Making Movies Black,* 200. As political rhetoric, Jews often eschewed special pleading for themselves, preferring, for example, to condemn Nazism for its treatment of "all civilian populations" rather than a "particular tragedy visited upon Jews." See Lowell Mellett to American Jewish Council, Feb. 1945, in *Making Movies Black,* 217.

32. *Opportunity,* Summer 1948, 100–101; interview between Polonsky and the author, July 1977; Garfield and Canada Lee, "Our Part in Body and Soul," *Opportunity,* Winter 1948, 20–21; on Peck, see Cripps, *Making Movies Black,* 258, and on "message movies," Chap. 8.

33. *California Eagle,* Aug. 18, 1949; George Norford, "The Future in Films," *Opportunity,* Summer 1948, 108–109; Moon to White, Dec. 28, 1948, in NAACP Records; and on message movies, Cripps, *Making Movies Black,* Chap. 8.

34. Kempton quoted in Liz Smith's column, *Sun* (Baltimore), May 5, 1982.

35. Quoted in Cripps, "The Noble Black Savage: A Problem in the Politics of Television Art," *Journal of Popular Culture,* 8 (Spring 1975), 690.

36. Cosby reported in *Los Angeles Sentinel,* Oct. 1, 1969; Committee for Use of Negro Roles, minutes, April 19, 1962, Screen Actors Guild records, Hollywood, CA. See also Ronald Jacobs to Charles Boren, MPAA records.

37. On Cinemobile, interview between Jon Triesault and the author, June 1977; and on MPAA efforts to introduce Blacks into television drama: Phil Benjamin to Roy Metzler, May 12, 1965; Ralph Winters to Tony Frederick, May 21, 1965; Ed Perlstein to Charles Boren, April 27, 1965, in MPAA records.

38. Walter Burrell, "Black Films," *Soul,* Dec. 18, 1972, 2–3.

39. *Newsweek,* Dec. 7, 1970, 62–74, on "counterculture"; *Variety,* Aug. 4, 1965, 22, quoted; *Philadelphia Daily News,* June 1, 1972, on Stone; *Newsweek,* Aug. 8, 1972, 88, on "warping"; on scripts, see Sterling Silliphant draft of *Shaft;* Silliphant to Daniel Melnick, MGM, Nov. 27, 1972, Silliphant mss, UCLA; Roger Lewis to Mort Segal, MGM, Sept. 3, 1971, MGM Legal File.

40. Directors Guild of America, *Directory of Members* [1991] (Los Angeles, 1991), 481–92.

# Part 6 **World War II through 1967**

The optimism that followed the defeat of fascism abroad brought with it hopes of eliminating racism and anti-Semitism at home and resulted in a period of cooperation that has been called the "golden age" of black-Jewish relations. Cheryl Greenberg notes the strengths and tensions of these alliances during this period. Her chapter offers a detailed review of the complex interactions of black and Jewish organizations as they worked together to pass legislation that affected their mutually perceived common interests, especially in the areas of employment and housing. Her article acts as an overview and an introduction to many of the issues discussed in the chapters that follow. Though prominent Jewish political figures such as Jacob Javits and Herbert Lehmann took the lead in fighting for civil rights legislation at the congressional level and received the overwhelming support of their black constituencies, mutual cooperation and understanding were by no means universal.

Disagreements about interracial integration were not only manifested between Jewish and black organizations; they occurred *within* Jewish communities as well. A number of pieces in this section discuss the different perspectives of northern and southern Jews, but even in the North, Jewish builders opposed the racial integration of their developments and were opposed in turn by Jewish proponents of integration. The account by Bruce Lambert gives details of William Levitt's initially successful efforts to limit his Levittowns to whites only.

Karen Brodkin Sacks reviews the restrictive covenants that maintained racial segregation as well as the discriminatory policies that effectively denied the GI Bill of Rights and Federal Housing Administration loans to black veterans of World War II. She argues that discrimination against black GI's, coupled with economic opportunities for various white Americans—including Jews—helped to solidify blacks' perceptions of Jews as one white group among others, all of whom shared privileges they were denied.

In the aftermath of *Brown vs. Board of Education* (1954), southern Jewish religious and secular communities were forced to decide where they stood on desegregation and other civil rights issues, and whether to take a public stance. Many southern Jews came in direct conflict with northern Jews and with national Jewish organizations, which were actively engaged in civil rights efforts. The articles by Esther Levine, Murray Friedman, and P. Allen Krause describe the intense and sometimes bitter nature of these debates. Harry Golden, as editor of the influential *Carolina Israelite,* stood out in the courageous way he mocked the racial beliefs and practices of white Southerners. Several of his pieces are included here.

The chapter by Claybourne Carson chronicles the beginning of the breakup of the postwar coalition. Bayard Rustin, a participant in that coalition, makes a moving case for continued Jewish support for black causes.

Herbert Hill details the depth of the conflict between blacks and Jews within the trade union movement, with special emphasis on how the changes in union membership were not reflected in union benefits. Seth Forman's chapter ends this section with an account of the division between northern and southern Jews that examines different views of Jewish self-interest.

Throughout this section, we have included short extracts from papers of the NAACP. Taken together, these original documents—letters, news reports, press releases, and notes from speeches—give evidence of the ongoing efforts of blacks and Jews to explain their positions and define their goals, in the interest of continuing to work together. For instance, we offer a speech by Ralph Helstein, president of the United Packinghouse Workers of America, in which he affirmed the need for the labor movement's backing of black civil rights in the difficult area of job opportunity.

Nineteen sixty-seven is recognized as a major turning point in black-Jewish relations. Black Power emerged, SNCC articulated its pro-Palestinian position, and following the Six-Day War, Jews came to identify more strongly with Israel. A bitter fight over community control of schools in Ocean Hill-Brownsville pitted black parents and children, against (essentially Jewish) teachers and unions. Although we touch on these issues in this section, we cover them more fully in part 7.

**FURTHER REFERENCES**

Many of the major studies on black-Jewish relations look carefully at this period for an explanation of the post-1967 "breakup." See Murray Friedman, *What Went Wrong? The Creation and Collapse of the Black-Jewish Alliance* (1995), and Jonathan Kaufman, *Broken Alliance: The Turbulent Times Between Blacks and Jews in America* (1988). Nathan Glazer's "Jews and Blacks: What Happened to the Grand Alliance?" appears in Joseph R. Washington Jr., *Jews in Black Perspectives: A Dialogue* (1984). In the 1963 Rosh Hashana issue of *American Judaism,* Albert Vorspan published "The Negro Victory and the Jewish Failure," an impassioned plea for the Jewish community to take risks for civil rights. See also the chapters on civil rights and Black Power in William M. Phillips Jr., *An Unillustrious Alliance* (1991). The "Papers and Proceedings of a Conference on Negro-Jewish Relations in the United States," edited by Salo Baron and Abraham Duker, with Horace Mann Bond, Bayard Rustin, Morris U. Shappes, and others as participants, appeared in *Jewish Social Studies* in 1965.

There is substantial literature on the role of blacks and Jews in the labor movement, and the work of Herbert Hill and James E. Jones Jr., in *Race in America: The Struggle for Equality* (1993), and of Herbert Hill in *Black Labor and the American Legal System* (1985) is an indispensable starting point. For an extensive discussion of issues raised by Herbert Hill, see Robert Laurentz's dissertation, "Racial/Ethnic Conflict in the New York City Garment Industry, 1933–1980" (1980). See also Julius Jacobson, *The Negro and the American Labor Movement* (1968); Hasia Diner's chapter, " 'Our Exploited Negro Brothers': Jewish Labor and the Organization of Black Workers," in her *In the Almost Promised Land: American Jews and Blacks, 1915–1935* (1977); and Tom Brooks, "Negro Militants,

Jewish Liberals, and the Unions" (1961). For more on Ralph Helstein and the United Packinghouse Workers, see Rick Halpern, *Down on the Killing Floor: Black and White Workers in Chicago's Packinghouses, 1904–1954* (1997), and Roger Horowitz, "*Negro and White, Unite and Fight*": *A Social History of Industrial Unionism in Meatpacking, 1930–90* (1997).

Although this collection has no chapters dealing with the experiences of black athletes and their Jewish employers, this subject is covered in David Wolf, "Tomming for Abe," in *Foul! The Connie Hawkins Story* (1972). Another account of the Harlem Globetrotters is in Wilt Chamberlain and David Shaw, *Wilt: Just Like Any Other 7-Foot Black Millionaire Who Lives Next Door* (1973). In Bill Russell and Taylor Branch, *Second Wind: The Memoirs of an Opinionated Man* (1979), the Globetrotters are described as a "combined dance and skit, conveying the consistent message that blacks are funny, happy-go-lucky clowns" (117). See also Peter Levine, *Ellis Island to Ebbets Field: Sport and the American Jewish Experience* (1992).

Several works focus on the attacks on southern Jews during the civil rights period, namely Melissa Fay Greene, *The Temple Bombing* (1996), Jack Nelson, *Terror in the Night: The Klan's Campaign against the Jews* (1993), and Cheryl Greenberg, "The Southern Jewish Community and the Struggle for Civil Rights" (1998). For a collection of significant writings on the role of southern Jews and the question of black equality in the twentieth century (which also has several studies on the late nineteenth century), see Mark K. Bauman and Berkley Kalin, *The Quiet Voices: Southern Rabbis and Black Civil Rights, 1880s to 1990s* (1997).

Karen Brodkin has recently published an extended study from the material in the chapter included here: *How Jews Became White Folks and What That Says about Race in America* (1998). Seth Forman, *Blacks in the Jewish Mind: A Crisis of Liberalism* (1998), also covers this period. The story of efforts to integrate the Levittowns is covered by Herbert Gans, *The Levittowners* (1967) and in "Changing a Racial Policy, Levittown, N.J.," available in the U.S. Housing and Home Finance Agency's document *Equal Opportunity in Housing* (1964). Another account of attempts at racial integration appears in Marc Lee Raphael, "Jewish Responses to the Integration of a Suburb: Cleveland Heights, Ohio, 1960–1980" (1992).

# Negotiating Coalition
## Black and Jewish Civil Rights Agencies in the Twentieth Century

African American and Jewish American communities have long sought to organize for their own advancement through a variety of institutions, from mass to elite, from nationalist to integrationist, from conservative to radical. During the middle-twentieth century agencies advocating liberalism, coalition building, and integration into the political, economic, and social mainstream have been the most prominent. Examining the relationships between these organizations in the Black and Jewish communities, therefore, offers a profitable approach to Black-Jewish relations during the period of the modern civil rights movement. Such a study avoids the dangers of generalizing from the actions of a few (the "but Goodman and Schwerner were Jewish" argument) and has the added advantage of allowing us to trace developments over time, as organizational decisions and tactics changed. Budgets and staff allocation reveal the priorities of these groups, and are thus invaluable in understanding the extent to which Black-Jewish collaboration went beyond rhetoric or good intentions. Furthermore, these agencies may in fact be the clearest representation of their communities that can be identified. Organizations that were economically supported by their community and claimed to speak for it constantly monitored their community's feelings because moving too far ahead or behind group sentiment spelled financial and political disaster. Tracing the positions and priorities of successful ethnic organizations not only reveals the level of commitment the organized community felt toward civil rights questions, but almost as reliably also uncovers broader community views.

Most prominent among the African American organizations in the early twentieth century were the National Association for the Advancement of Colored People (NAACP), National Urban League (NUL), and National Association of Colored Women (NACW). Within two decades these were joined by the National Council of Negro Women (NCNW). Pressing them from the left were the National Negro Congress and A. Philip Randolph's Brotherhood of Sleeping Car Porters, along with several prominent African American Communists, while the Garvey movement and its Universal Negro Improvement Association embodied widespread nationalist sentiment that liberal organizations ignored at their peril. Local and religious organizations also competed for the allegiance of the community. Among Jews, the American Jewish Committee (AJC), American Jewish Congress (AJCongress), National Council of Jewish

Cheryl Greenberg is associate professor of history at Trinity College.
Reprinted from *Struggles in the Promised Land: Toward a History of Black-Jewish Relations in the United States*, ed. Jack Salzman and Cornel West (New York: Oxford University Press, 1997), 153–76. Copyright © 1997 by Cheryl Greenberg. Used by permission of Oxford University Press, Inc.

Women (NCJW), Anti-Defamation League of B'nai Brith (ADL), and later the Jewish Labor Committee (JLC) navigated a path within boundaries marked by Zionist nationalists, religious conservatives, and radical anti-religious, socialist, and communist groups. These Black and Jewish organizations, very different from one another but all dedicated to liberalism, pluralism, and integrationism, emerged as leaders in their communities by the 1940s, and were supported by a wider segment of their communities than groups of any other political position. It was these groups that made the deliberate choice to cooperate with agencies outside their own communities in order to further their goals. Although these cooperative networks became extensive, embracing a variety of ethnic, racial, religious, and political groups, for a variety of reasons the collaboration between organizations of Blacks and Jews moved ahead most swiftly and with most dramatic effect. Yet this relationship, often called an alliance because of the sustained and close nature of the contacts, was not without its tensions. These tensions were in many ways rooted in American society and culture, and they contributed to the dramatic decline in cooperation between the two communities by the late 1960s. Both the positive strengths of the Black-Jewish political relationship and its significant tensions are the subject of this chapter.

Although both Blacks and Jews had been in the United States from the earliest days of colonization, relations between them had never stood out in sharper distinction than with other groups. Religious parochialism and bigotry had strained relations between Jews and both white and Black Christians, while slavery and racism defined relations between all African Americans and whites of every religion. Thus Black-Jewish tensions existed only insofar as most Jews were white, and most African Americans were Christian. The low number of Jews living in the south, and the resulting infrequency of contact, also lessened the likelihood of a distinct relationship between them. Had Jews played a prominent part in either pro-slavery or anti-slavery activity, the case might have been different, but although individual Jews and local Jewish groups took positions on both sides of the debate and the Civil War, the organized Jewish community was too small (and often, too fearful of anti-Semitism) to be of much consequence.

All this changed with the Black migration north and the Eastern European Jewish migration to American urban centers. By the early twentieth century, a sizable northern and urban Black community, freer from constraints than their compatriots in the south, had begun the long struggle for the jobs, services, and opportunities so long denied them. They formed organizations to help in that struggle and to help acculturate the new migrants, and came increasingly in contact with immigrants, among them, Jews. Meanwhile anti-Semitism rose with the immigration of these Eastern European Jews: economic, educational, and social restrictions actually increased during this period. To cope with this threat, and to help the immigrants assimilate more quickly, the established Jewish community created its own defense organizations. The immigrants quickly responded by establishing groups of their own.

Although Black and Jewish civil rights organizations had similar agendas, they rarely worked together on a sustained basis in these early years, although individuals from the two communities certainly cooperated, and agencies did work together on specific occasions where the issues overlapped directly. For example, several prominent Jews joined the Call to found the NAACP. The ADL, formed after the persecution of Leo Frank, a Jew who was later lynched, involved itself in anti-lynching activities from the start. Nevertheless, there was virtually no sustained or structured contact or collaboration.

In part, the communities' mandates were different. Despite their shared concern with the consequences of bigotry, racism was far more virulent than anti-Semitism. Discrimination against Jews, while real and severe, was virtually never as physically dangerous, ubiquitous, or economically destructive as that routinely practiced against African Americans. Thus at the forefront for Black agencies were issues such as physical violence, exclusion from skilled and white-collar work, denial of political rights, and segregation. Jewish groups focused more on social discrimination, restrictions on employment and in higher education, and immigration quotas. In part, too, neither community enjoyed much wealth or power, and thus their organizations remained small and weak for several decades. It was barely possible to meet the most pressing needs of one's own community, much less to look beyond them and tackle broader and less immediate issues.

The two communities also enjoyed a different relationship with the dominant culture. Most Jews were white people, and although anti-Semitism was real, race was the deeper rift in American society. White ethnic groups have shifted from ethnic to white over time since most rewards and opportunities in America were apportioned not by ethnicity or religion but by race, and Jews were no exception to this pattern. Jews were no more eager to embrace the cause of a pariah people than any other white community. Further, most immigrant Jews had come from urban areas, and often had job skills unavailable to most Black rural agricultural workers. The combination of better skills and lesser discrimination brought most Jews more quickly out of the ranks of the poorest urbanites, and increased class differences between the two groups.

Nevertheless, a relationship did emerge between them. More Jews than virtually any other white immigrant group could be found among the left, and Jewish tradition had long stressed the obligation to help all the oppressed "because you were strangers in the land of Egypt." Slave Christianity relied far more on the Old Testament than traditional white Christianity had, and many Black Christians identified with the trials of the children of Israel because they viewed their own plight in similar terms. Both communities viewed themselves as victims of persecution, which helped foster a bond (often cultivated or promoted by their leadership) based on a sense of a shared oppression. Hasia Diner has documented a Jewish interest in and concern with the problems of African Americans from the earliest years of the twentieth century, and even nationalist Blacks like Marcus Garvey commented positively (on at least some occasions) on the example of community and commitment set by similarly persecuted Jews. Indeed, while anti-Semitism has always been present in the Black community, and Jews have held racist beliefs, every contemporary study has documented that Jews were less racist than other whites, and Blacks less anti-Semitic than other Christians.[1] Thus at least on the rhetorical level, a certain affinity between Blacks and Jews mitigated some of the violent tensions that marked relations between Blacks and many other white ethnic groups, or between Jews and some white Christians.

It also brought Blacks and Jews into closer proximity, which both improved relations and exacerbated tensions. Jews were less likely than their white Gentile neighbors to flee neighborhoods into which African Americans moved, and even after leaving, continued to maintain their stores and other services there. This expanded the possibilities for social interaction, but led as well to economic competition and Black complaints of Jewish exploitation. Many Jews entered social service fields and became social workers and teachers in Black areas, again the source of both mutual education and the resentments inherent in hierarchical power structures. Generally more leftist in their politics, and less tainted by American racist notions, Jewish-organized or dominated trade unions were more likely to recruit or accept African American members. Nevertheless, because of seniority, more Jews than Blacks could be found in these unions' leadership ranks, as Herbert Hill and others have documented.[2] Thus while Jews enjoyed the reputation of being less racist, they also entered more often into hierarchical economic relations with African Americans, sowing the seeds for resentment based on class.

Beyond rhetorical interest, or interest born in a sense of common suffering, however, most Blacks and Jews gave little thought to the plight of the other, reflected in the lack of contact or cooperation between their representative organizations. This began to change with the rise of German Fascism, and the impact of that political movement on the concerns of both communities. For Jews, of course, the dangers were obvious. Nazi ideology espoused anti-Semitism (and racism) and posed an immediate threat to the Jews of Germany and later of all Europe. Violence against Jews, economic, educational, and travel restrictions, and segregation followed in quick succession, with little sustained protest from other European nations or the U.S. Jewish organizations turned to the plight of their European coreligionists, and also began to pay close attention to the possible spread of Nazi or Fascist thought in the United States. To that end, they contracted every possible ally, including African American organizations, to help.

But African American agencies had their own reasons to become involved in the struggle against Fascism, beyond sympathy with the plight of another persecuted minority. Nazism revealed the vicious and dangerous implications of all forms of racism, and Black groups moved to exploit white America's expressed outrage against Nazi atrocities by drawing explicit parallels with race relations at home. While sincerely opposing anti-Jewish violence and Fascism generally, Black organizations quite overtly used the political situation to raise their own issues more dramatically in the public eye. After the U.S. State Department publicly invited 29 nations to provide havens for German refugees in March of 1938, Roy Wilkins of the NAACP urged Walter White "most strongly that the Association take note publicly in some fashion that will attract attention. . . . I feel that this opening is a made-to-order one for us. . . . The obvious thing to do is to dispatch a telegram to the State Department and the President, calling attention to the plight of the Negro in this country." That day, White cabled Secretary of State Cordell Hull.

AMERICAN NEGROES APPLAUD ACTION OF UNITED STATES GOVERNMENT . . . IN OFFERING HAVEN TO JEWISH POLITICAL REFUGEES . . . BUT WE WOULD BE EVEN

MORE ENTHUSIASTIC IF OUR GOVERNMENT COULD BE EQUALLY INDIGNANT AT THE LYNCHING, BURNING ALIVE AND TORTURE . . . OF AMERICAN CITIZENS BY AMERICAN MOBS . . . WHICH HAVE SHAMED AMERICA . . . FOR A MUCH LONGER TIME THAN PERSECUTION UNDER ADOLF HITLER.[3]

They used domestic issues similarly. When Walter White wrote President Roosevelt that he was "very much disturbed, as I know you are, at the spread of anti-Semitism in certain quarters in Washington," he explained that "My reason for writing you about this is that this ties in with an attempt by certain persons . . . to tie in anti-Semitism with prejudice against Dr. Robert C. Weaver [U.S. Housing Authority]" to block appropriations for public housing serving African Americans. "Frankly, I don't know what the complete answer is to this tendency to express anti-Semitism and anti-Negro feeling with housing the victim except that I would urge that more Administrative support of housing instead of less would be the best answer."[4] For both Jews and Blacks, then, this earliest collaboration emerged primarily out of clear and explicit self-interest, albeit a self-interest that coincided with a broader moral stance.

Jews more than other whites recognized the danger of racism that Nazism raised. Even while spending most of their organized efforts on the immediate dangers of Nazism at home and abroad, Jewish organizations did begin to pay attention to the problems facing African Americans by the late 1930s. The NCJW added an anti-lynching plank to its platform in 1935, for example, and four years later the AJC joined the NAACP in meetings with Black and Jewish newspaper editors to explore tensions between the two communities, generally over employment and customer relations. The ADL lent strong support to the effort to integrate the armed forces, at least on a voluntary basis. Nevertheless, such cooperation was halting and at least some Jewish leaders were extremely reluctant to move toward closer ties with Black organizations. The AJC meetings, for example, came only after a great deal of pressure from Charles Houston and Walter White of the NAACP. Responding to complaints about allegedly anti-Semitic remarks made by a Chicago NAACP representative, Houston wrote to A. Ovrum Tapper, the ACLU's Chicago attorney,

> You can depend on my doing everything in my power to have my people see that anti-Semitism is Negro suicide.
>
> But I wish on your side you would try to show some of the wealthy Jews the fundamental identity between race persecution of minorities, regardless who. Walter White has been trying for some time to get an unpublicized conference of Jewish leaders and representative Negroes to discuss the whole question of Negro-Jewish relations, but he has been unable to get anywhere.[5]

Jewish organizations focused on African Americans as much to scrutinize them for changes in the level of anti-Semitism as to challenge American racism. Jewish groups were far more reluctant to take on questions of Black civil rights directly, partly out of fear that their already tenuous position in America might be further jeopardized by any perceived alliance with an even more reviled group. As Philip Frankel of the ADL put it in 1943, "The difficulties facing the Jews, as a minority group, are sad enough without tying ourselves up with another minority group of less influence, and by so doing, probably taking on some of their troubles—a group whose difficulties, in my estimation, are even more deplorable than our own."[6]

Not only were Blacks similarly outcast in American political life, Black organizations occasionally embraced more confrontational tactics to further their goals. While Jews sought access to officials in power to convince them to intervene in the European conflict, and therefore took the most conciliatory and politic stance possible, Black groups recognized that their similarly conciliatory tactics during World War I had resulted in no benefits for them. Therefore when A. Philip Randolph proposed a mass March on Washington to insist on equitable opportunities for Black soldiers and workers during wartime, Black organizations signed on, while many Jewish groups read it as a sign of possibly subversive activity. Responding to a query about the possibility of working with Randolph, Paul Richman of the ADL warned Director Leonard Finder, "I wonder if you are aware that the Department of Justice is watching him closely for subversive activities in connection with his 'March on Washington' movement. He has been causing the President . . . a great deal of anxiety with statements involving threat, bordering on sedition." Richard Gutstadt concurred. "The danger of our working with a man like Philip Randolph is that he is considered extremely left-wing. . . . The violence of his recommendations . . . might conceivably affect our relations with some government bureaus because Randolph does not hesitate to whip the Negroes up to the adoption of methods calculated seriously to embarrass Washington."[7] Indeed, many Jewish organizations feared any aggressive tactics might slow the war effort. A 1942 ADL report warned of

> the dangers attendant on the current demands of the Negro leaders for an immediate solution of the social aspects of the Negro problems.
> . . . It is courting disaster for Jewish organizations and interests to be tied in intimately with Negro causes and leadership under present conditions. It is certain that the[se] demands of the Negro leadership will lead to violent resistance in the southern and border states, and that extreme bitterness will be engendered in both races. The disloyal attitudes of the Negro leadership and a large percentage of their followers might break into a national scandal at any moment. It is important that Jewish leadership . . . not allow sentimental considerations to prevent them from protecting the Jews of this country from an unnecessary and terrible stigma.[8]

Nevertheless, wartime brought ample opportunities for Blacks and Jews to continue collaborating on issues of mutual self-interest. One—ironically, given initial Jewish opposition—was the product of the threatened March on Washington: the signing of a Fair Employment Practices Act which prohibited discrimination in war industries on the basis of race or religion. Enforcing the Act, expanding it to all industries, and making it permanent brought Jewish and Black groups into frequent and productive contact. Although the dream of a permanent FEPC was never realized, the leaders of the Committee for a Permanent FEPC were an African American and a Jew, and both communities worked together to pass state and local Fair Employment laws.[9]

The race riots which spread throughout the country during the war years also brought Black and Jewish agencies together. In response to the violence or threat of violence, cities and states established "unity committees" and similar ad hoc structures to examine the state of race relations and ameliorate the worst of the problems. Jewish groups, concerned with racial violence, also saw the opportunity to promote a broader message of tolerance and anti-bigotry that would challenge anti-Semitism as it would racism, and participated along with African American and other groups in these unity committees all across the country. Some committees were pure window dressing, with only the power of rhetoric behind them, but others had quite a bit of power and made effective policy recommendations or legal changes.[10] In each instance, not only did Black and Jewish leaders have the opportunity to meet one another and work together, they also each educated themselves about the other community. They identified shared problems to be fought together, and came to appreciate a bit better each group's separate burdens. When mutual action proved effective, it encouraged further cooperation.

At the same time, because of wartime successes in organizing, general post-war prosperity, and broad repugnance toward fascism, these liberal, integrationist, pro-tolerance organizations grew in size and prestige, which in turn gave them more resources with which to pursue broader agendas. Thus the benefits of cooperation and the means to cooperate more fully coincided in the post-war years and a Black and Jewish political partnership, often called an "alliance," was born. This alliance was never seamless, and full collaboration was never achieved—nor sought. Nevertheless, the number of programs and goals now shared by defense agencies in the two communities had multiplied, and the initial experience of cooperation had set the stage for continued and expanded collaboration.

These mutual efforts were still based in self-interest. What had changed was the broader definition in both communities of what self-interest entailed, and the recognition of the power of joint action. Nazi hatred of Jews and Gypsies had resulted in genocide, and the internment of west-coast Japanese in this country, including American citizens, demonstrated that Americans could not be relied upon to resist making similar racial generalizations (which of course lynching and Jim Crow had already shown). The backlash against such bigotry, and a recognition of its potential perils, brought a new shift in social thinking to an embrace of pluralism. Ill-defined as it was in the public mind, pluralism called for the recognition of the contributions of racial, ethnic, and religious groups, and both a celebration of cultural differences and a deeper presumed unanimity of values and beliefs.[11] Often expressed as "tolerance" or "brotherhood," public commitment to pluralism was certainly more rhetorical than real, but it nevertheless brought the questions of anti-Semitism and racism to the fore, and cast them both in a new light. Now they were symptoms of the same broader evil, and the most effective way to oppose discrimination against one group was to couch it in arguments against all discrimination based on heritage. Every anti-racist tract and every piece of anti-discrimination legislation demanded toleration and equality for the holy trinity of "race, religion, and national origin." Thus for African American groups to cooperate in the struggle against anti-Semitism, for Jewish groups to support Black civil rights, or for both to fight bigotry against Asian or Mexican Americans (whose causes were increasingly joined in this period as well) was in fact to challenge restrictions on their own group.

The fight against restrictive housing covenants clearly demonstrates this identity of interest. Both African Americans and Jewish Americans (as well as Asians and occasionally other white ethnics) were routinely barred from renting or buying real estate in certain neighborhoods whose residents had signed a "restrictive covenant." Although the NAACP brought the cases to the Supreme Court (*Shelley v. Kraemer, Hodge v. Hurd,* and *Sipes v. McGhee*) that declared such covenants unenforceable, it came armed with advice and briefs from the ADL, AJC, Jewish War Veterans, AJCongress, and JLC, all of whom had fought restrictive housing covenants against Jews, and all of whom recognized the decision's direct benefit for their own constituency.[12] As Rabbi Berman of the AJCongress remarked, "I think the [AJ] Congress has made a great gain . . . in that we are helping the Jews . . . to understand that this is a common struggle and not something we are doing out of the graciousness of our hearts for Negroes."[13]

Similarly, lifting immigration and citizenship barriers was a joint effort for mutual benefit. Using a broad-brush opposition to discrimination enabled Jews to argue that existing laws unfairly excluded European Jewish refugees, Japanese to argue against Asian exclusion clauses, and African Americans to promote immigration from the Caribbean and Africa. The Leadership Conference on Civil Rights, Civil Liberties Clearing House, and other coalitions of progressive organizations within which Jewish and Black groups were well represented testified before Congressional committees on hundreds of bills protecting civil rights and civil liberties of all minorities, as did every major Black and Jewish organization. In fact, the chairman of the Leadership Conference, Walter White, was Black, and its secretary, Arnold Aronson, was Jewish. The AJCongress and NAACP jointly produced *Civil Rights in the United States: A Balance Sheet of Group Relations,* annual book-length assessments of civil rights advances and setbacks from 1948 to 1952, which focused primarily on racial and religious discrimination.[14]

Black and Jewish agencies cooperated on local and state issues as well. Again, broad anti-discrimination language ensured that both communities would benefit. Jewish groups, often joined by the local chapters of the NAACP, labored to convince employers to stop requesting applicants' race or religion on applications, and newspapers to stop accepting advertisements for jobs or resorts that mentioned racial or religious restrictions. They spearheaded the drive to end quotas and restrictions in New York colleges and professional schools, supported by Black groups that saw clear benefits for their own community. Black organizations obtained the aid of Jewish ones to open housing and employment opportunities, and to persuade newspapers to cease identifying Black criminals by race, and Catholic or Jewish ones by religion. All over the south both Black and Jewish groups fought for restrictions against the racist, anti-Semitic Ku Klux Klan, including anti-mask legislation, and monitored their activities.[15]

Violence also brought cooperation. In Peekskill a Paul Robeson concert provoked attacks against both Blacks and Jews by anti-Communist rioters, and the NAACP, NUL, ADL, AJC, NCJW and others joined in demands for investigation and action. Similarly, dynamite attacks in 1951 and '52 against Blacks and Jews in Miami and the desecration of synagogues and Black churches there, culminating in the bombing death of NAACP chapter president Henry Moore and his wife, brought both communities' organizations together in mutual defense. A housing riot on Peoria Street in Chicago protesting the arrival of Black tenants turned anti-Semitic as well because it was a Jewish family that had rented to them. The ADL, AJCongress, and the NAACP wrote investigative reports of this and similar disturbances, and collaborated on their responses.[16] Meier Steinbrink, President of the ADL, recognized the power of such cooperation in a 1949 fundraising letter for the NAACP to be sent to potential Jewish donors.

> I want to cite three of the many achievements of the NAACP which make all Americans and particularly members of the Anti-Defamation League indebted to the NAACP.
> It was the NAACP which started the fight . . . against restrictive covenants which culminated in the Supreme Court victory in 1948. Our Anti-Defamation League filed a brief amicus curiae. . . .
> And it was the NAACP which caused the United States Supreme Court to reverse its unfortunate decision in the Leo Frank case . . . in Moore vs. Dempsey. . . .
> It was the Association which called the meeting on August 6, 1946 of 41 organizations of which the ADL was one out of which came the President's Committee on Civil Rights.[17]

Still, while this was mutual effort in the name of self-interest, most programs jointly undertaken in fact had a greater impact on one community or the other. Thus, for example, Jewish groups joined or spearheaded efforts to desegregate restaurants and beaches, from which they were rarely excluded, as well as country clubs and resorts which generally excluded both populations. African American organizations added their voices to efforts to resettle refugees, the bulk of whom were Jewish, and joined the battle against quotas in higher education which, though raised against both Blacks and Jews, affected Jews more since they constituted a larger proportion of the applicant pool. This represented a further development in the Black-Jewish political relationship; increasingly by the end of the 1940s, Black and Jewish groups joined in efforts primarily or exclusively benefiting the other. The definition of self-interest, which had expanded during wartime to include mutually overlapping concerns of discrimination, had expanded again. Taking their own words seriously, defense agencies argued that protecting the rights of one minority group protected the rights of all. As Isaac Toubin, Associate Director of the AJCongress, wrote in 1953:

> We must be concerned with safeguarding the democratic process as the best way to preserve our integrity and our identity as Jews. But democracy frequently ceases . . . at the boundaries of race, color and creed. It is not always the same race, color or creed that is subjected to abuse, but this abuse, no matter what its target, always poses the identical threat. . . . The only really significant way to guarantee or protect or extend Jewish rights is to round out democracy wherever it is imperfect. . . . It involves fighting on dozens of fronts to establish and safeguard the rights of all groups in America wherever those rights are curtailed.[18]

African Americans spent a good amount of time and effort in support of Jewish causes such as immigration reform and, most important for Jewish organizations, support for the state of Israel. Walter White spent months convincing the Haitian and Liberian delegations to the UN to support the 1947 partition plan, to the delight of Jewish groups. "Please accept my personal thanks and those of the AJCongress for the magnificent job you did on the partition proposal," Will Maslow wrote to White. "It was indeed heartening to see how effectively you work. I am sure that Haiti's shift was the direct result of your efforts."[19]

Jewish organizations also spent much of their time furthering the cause of Black civil rights even when Jewish interests were not at stake. Sometimes new, temporary coalitions would form around particular issues, such as the Committee for Civil Rights in East Manhattan which sought to integrate restaurants near the new United Nations building. Other times, a national Jewish organization or its local affiliate would spearhead the campaign, in consultation with African American agencies. The AJCongress spent a decade in litigation against Stuyvesant Town in New York City which refused to accept Black tenants despite municipal aid and state and city anti-discrimination laws. For years the ADL fought the American Bowling Congress on the question of permitting the participation of Black bowlers. The major Jewish organizations filed supporting briefs in every significant civil rights case before the Supreme Court and most state courts, including *Brown v. Board of Education* and the Thompson restaurant case in Washington, D.C. brought by Mary Church Terrell and the Coordinating Committee for the Enforcement of D.C. Anti-Discrimination Laws.[20]

These examples of collaboration went far beyond direct or even indirect self-interest, as both communities moved toward a sense of the indissoluble nature of equality. Far more public on each other's issues than was any other ethnic, racial, or religious community as a whole, Black-Jewish cooperation brought tremendous power to the civil rights struggle.

Nevertheless, priorities certainly differed between the communities, and even between agencies within the same community, and not every cause of discrimination was taken up as avidly by one group as by another. Jews remained more fearful of direct confrontation, for example, and therefore almost unanimously opposed CORE's 1947 Journey of Reconciliation to integrate southern interstate transport. (The NAACP and NUL also kept their distance.) Most African American groups tempered their criticism of anti-Semitism with reminders of instances in which Jews exploited Blacks.[21]

Separate considerations often led to differences in approach as well. Faced with urgent needs and gross inequality, African American agencies focused on civil rights almost exclusively, and responded so slowly to requests for help on Jewish issues that the AJCongress, the most liberal and perhaps the staunchest Jewish advocate of Black civil rights, lamented in 1960:

> our organizational structure is completely committed to the elimination of all forms of prejudice. . . . We adhere to this position even though corresponding Negro support of Jewish objectives . . . has not been extensive. Faced with problems far more severe than those of the Jewish community, Negro defense activities have been

shaped far more by their own immediate and pressing problems than by general principles. . . . If one views the situation in terms of striking a balance, there is a large Negro deficit.[22]

For their part, Jews, eager to be accepted among their white gentile neighbors, often hesitated to act in ways that might alienate them. Thus the AJC tempered its call to action against the Miami dynamiting spree with, "At the same time, there is a relationship of Jews to white Christians that needs to be maintained on friendly terms."[23] Deciding that its top priority, the promotion of tolerance as a broad virtue, could be disregarded in certain circumstances, the Institute for American Democracy, funded primarily by the ADL, produced two sets of "brotherhood" comics for children. In one, a scene of children included a Black boy. The other, for use in the south, depicted an entirely white crowd. As Walter White noted in a letter of protest, "It seems to me that if members of the ADL living in the south cannot stand up for the brotherhood of all human beings, including Negroes, there is little point spending money to print 'brotherhood' literature at all." In his reply, ADL's Ben Epstein admitted being

> as shocked as you were. . . . The IAD, largely subsidized by the ADL, nevertheless operates somewhat independently and in this specific instance we are vigorously opposed to what was done. . . . This does not at all detract from the fact that some materials will be more acceptable in the South than others.

ADL's Alex Miller noted that Black leaders expected that "Jews, as fellow objects of persecution, should be the first to rush to the aid of the Negroes." Unfortunately, he lamented, "This is . . . completely at variance with the behavior pattern of the Southern Jewish community which has clothed itself quite completely in the mores of the area."[24]

Great bitterness on both sides was reflected in the often strained relations between Black and Jewish leaders. Jews were, after all, white people, and on occasion responded to problems as whites rather than as Jews. This was particularly true when the issue was one of class, since race had a hand in helping Jews achieve middle-class status. When confronted with exploitative behavior by Jewish merchants, the ADL responded, "if it [discrimination] be common practice . . . then however regrettable the practice may be, it is hardly fair to pick only upon the Jew[s]." After all, another argued, if only Jews altered their policies, "it would affect their business." As the president of Morgan State University declared (referring to Baltimore), "I would say that . . . the Jews are white people with all the white people's psychology and prejudices when it comes to dealing with Negroes."[25]

While such differences of position could be found all over the country, they were most pronounced in the south, where Jews proclaimed their commitment to racial equality but also demanded that their representative organizations cease public efforts for integration. Rabbi Berman described white Jewish flight from Chicago neighborhoods in the late 1940s as Black families moved in, while a Brooklyn delegate to the 1956 AJCongress convention complained that "unfortunately, and it grieves me to say it, the Jews have failed to cooperate with us [AJCongress] on very basic issues of democracy."[26] Speaking of northern cities, the AJCongress warned in 1960 that contact between Negroes and Jews occurs most frequently along a front peculiarly productive of friction [with Jews in positions of economic power in Black areas. There is also] . . . the clash between new Negro members of the middle class and their Jewish competitors. . . . A [further] factor . . . is the practice of discrimination against Negroes by Jews. . . . Genuine social acceptance [of Blacks] by Jews is at a minimum and generally we find the usual fear, panic and flight to the suburbs. In such situations Jews act, in the main, like other whites.

As Walter White warned Will Maslow, "We have got a lot to do within our own ranks, Will, and the time is quite short to do it."[27]

Other tensions ran still deeper. The differential success Jews enjoyed in achieving middle-class status left them more accepting of compromise, and less conscious of the limits of liberalism than many in the Black community. As the AJCongress presciently noted in 1960,

Negroes are re-evaluating their alliances. . . . One of its results has been a mistrust of "liberals" in the struggle for civil rights. And we must recognize, for good or ill, that the Jews, more than any other group, are generally so identified. . . . The willingness of Jewish and other groups to accept, on occasion, a partial victory (because of the danger that demanding too much will result in getting nothing) has caused resentment in Negro ranks. They often feel that this compromises their position and demonstrates a lack of understanding on our part.[28]

Furthermore, anti-Semitism had declined far more quickly than had racism, and what remained was primarily social and non-governmental. Racism, on the other hand, remained firmly rooted in the law and in economic practice. Thus Jewish groups concerned about continued bigotry did not look to the legal or court system for change, but rather spent increasing amounts of effort in public relations or propaganda work: encouraging materials that highlighted tolerance and diversity.[29] Although Jewish groups argued that these materials benefited African Americans as well, since the message was broadly construed, racism was in fact far less responsive to such techniques, and in any case the central problems of racism lay in the deep structures of society rather than solely in the minds of individuals. Institutional racism had to be tackled in very different ways. So long as these methods included court and legislative work, Jewish groups continued to support civil rights efforts, even though they had little impact on anti-Semitism. When tactics turned to more direct action, most Jewish groups balked. Street demonstrations and mass marches reminded many Jews of the demagogy and appeal to the mob of fascists like Hitler. Although Jews themselves had employed boycotts against German products during World War II, even boycotts now seemed dangerously anti-democratic.[30] The more radical of these civil rights efforts challenged the very notions of liberalism that had allowed Jews to achieve so much in America, and this also proved threatening.

Already suspicious of mass action, Jewish groups grew increasingly uneasy as the 1960s progressed, with SNCC's emerging criticism of the liberalism of Kennedy, the Democratic Party, and the establishment more generally; Martin Luther King, Jr.'s opposition to the Vietnam War and its implied criticism of the wisdom of the power structure; the general move toward nationalism in a Black community dispirited by white recalcitrance and liberal inaction; and a rising sense of anti-colonial sentiment that moved many Black groups to embrace the Palestinian cause. While Jewish youths were well represented in the ranks of activist civil rights organizations like SNCC, their parents in the AJC, ADL, or NCJW remained far more suspicious. When the civil rights movement moved north, into the neighborhoods of these liberal Jews, the question of integration took on a different tone. With concerns now couched in class rather than racial terms, Jews fled to suburbs almost as quickly as white Christians to avoid what they perceived as the deterioration of their schools and neighborhoods. They pointed to riots as evidence of civil rights agendas run amok.

Suddenly, it became clear, the most basic visions of the two communities conflicted. African Americans recognized that earlier trust in the courts, the legislature, or the goodwill of well-meaning whites was misplaced, or at best naive. Just laws could still be administered unjustly. One could not rely on white administrators and employers to suddenly see the error of their ways and accept Black people equally. Only concerted pressure compelled the changes wrought by the civil rights movement, and only continued pressure would move the process further. It was not enough to press white people into hiring Black workers: Black entrepreneurial activity and economic nationalism would provide an independent base from which to rise. Affirmative action, and numerical quotas to demonstrate its successful implementation, replaced attempts to convince employers or colleges to accept qualified candidates without regard to race, because that strategy had allowed racists to argue that only white candidates were qualified.

Jews, on the other hand, held tenaciously to the ideal of a race-blind society, and viewed nationalism and race-based solutions to the problem of inequality as a dangerous undermining of that ideal. Although economic nationalism had always played a part in Jewish life, Jews nonetheless saw their success as rooted in liberal notions of merit and fair play—exactly those categories under attack. Their pluralist vision had worked for them; despite the arguments of Black nationalists few Jews could see its underlying coercive assimilationism.

These fundamental disagreements came to a head in the first open break between Black and Jewish civil rights agencies, in the court cases over affirmative action. In *De Funis v. Odegaard* (1974) and *Regents of University of California v. Bakke* (1978), Jewish and Black groups lined up on opposite sides.[31] This conflict, shocking for its visibility and apparent suddenness, was actually the logical culmination of years of slow divergence of interest, vision, and priority. And much to the dismay of Jews on the left, these divisions grew rather than lessened over the next two decades. As more time passed, more Jews attained middle-class and even upper-class status, and as anti-Semitism retreated into fewer strongholds more on the periphery of society, Jews as a group began moving rightward politically, and their organizations followed. Aided by the embrace of Israel by the right, and of Palestinians by the left, Jews in the 1980s continued to vote more liberally than their pocketbook interests might dictate, but less liberally than in the past. Jewish agencies turned their focus inward, toward support of Israel and Soviet

Jews, and to challenge the growing rate of intermarriage which seemed to threaten Jewish continuity in the United States. Now living primarily in suburbs, Jews and their agencies paid less attention to the problems of poverty and urban life than before.

Meanwhile, the gap between Black and white incomes and life chances, which had begun to shrink in the 1960s, widened again. The backlash against civil rights resulted in a weakening of civil rights laws, greater educational segregation than ever, and a new racist rhetoric of "us" and "them" which cast African Americans outside the boundary of American society. Black organizations now faced very different problems than did their Jewish counterparts. A disgust with white society and liberalism's betrayals (embodied ironically by Jews since they represented such a large proportion of the liberals perceived as betraying them) and a growing interest in nationalism and internal unity have marked African American communities, both rich and poor, and have been reflected in the changing attitudes of Black defense organizations. At the same time, some nationalist rhetoric has been overtly anti-white and anti-Semitic, which has infuriated and pained Jews. Although most liberal Black leaders have repudiated such sentiments, they also insist on the importance of working with everyone in the Black community to tackle such intractable political and economic problems. It is hardly surprising, then, that as Jewish and Black interests and concerns diverged, their level of collaboration declined.

Nevertheless, cooperation did not cease. While Jewish groups moved rightward from where they had been, they remained on the liberal side of the political spectrum, particularly in regard to domestic policies and social issues. Thus large areas of overlapping interest remained. Black and Jewish groups worked together on aid to public education, anti-poverty, hunger and homelessness programs, abortion rights, and similar causes. Further, like Black organizations, Jewish groups continued to monitor all cases of bigotry and continued their tolerance work. The ADL, for example, long in the business of producing diversity programs, launched "A World of Difference" in 1985 to help schools, workplaces, and civic groups appreciate ethnic, racial, and religious diversity and work more effectively with those different from themselves. Like the NAACP, it also keeps watch on hate groups like skinheads, the Klan, and neo-Nazis. Collaboration on hate crimes brought passage of bias or hate-crime legislation in numerous states and cities across the country.

Compared to the earlier period, then, two things have changed. One is the makeup of the coalition on progressive issues. Once dominated by Jews and Blacks it is now far broader. Asian Americans, Latinos, gays and lesbians, a growing number of activist liberal church groups, some unions, and others perceiving themselves on the margins of society routinely join efforts to challenge inequality and poverty. Second, because of class and politics, organized Jewish interest in issues of central importance to this coalition is no longer as uniform or unambivalent. Thus while African American groups remain firmly within this coalition, Jewish agencies sometimes join and sometimes stand outside, and the Black-Jewish political relationship can no longer be characterized in any sense as an alliance.

Nevertheless, some sense of linkage remains, a remnant of earlier, productive collaboration and the shared sense of vulnerability and oppression that fostered that collaboration in the first place. That is why "Black-Jewish relations" still have far more resonance than do "Black-Italian relations" or "Jewish-Latino relations," and why the tensions and anger seem so bitter. On some level, both Blacks and Jews expect more from each other, and so feel betrayed by the apparently fundamental recent rifts. On the other hand, that sense of linkage suggests that the rift need not be permanent. If Jews and African Americans find a renewed mutuality of purpose, they already have a model for a productive relationship in their past collaboration, conducted despite overwhelming tensions and differences. And they may find that shared purpose. As our cities continue to deteriorate, their problems spill increasingly over into suburban areas. Expanding divisions between rich and poor threaten both productivity and security. If hatred and bigotry continue to express themselves not only in limited opportunities but in violence, one can only hope for a return to the recognition that the problems of one group are indeed the problems of us all.

NOTES

1. Biblical injunctions: see, for example, Exodus 22:20 ("A stranger shall you not wrong; neither shall you oppress him, for you were strangers in the land of Egypt"), or Deuteronomy 10:19 ("Love you therefore the stranger for you were strangers in the land of Egypt"). Hasia Diner: *In the Almost Promised Land: American Jews and Blacks 1915–1935* (Westport, CT, 1977). Garvey: Garvey modeled his struggle on Zionism and the Irish struggle for a free and independent Ireland. He even called his followers Zionists, according to E. David Cronon, *Black Moses: the Story of Marcus Garvey* (Madison, 1969), p. 199. References to Jews and Zionism (many of them negative) are scattered through his writing and his speeches. The best collections are Amy Jacques-Garvey, ed., *The Philosophy and Opinions of Marcus Garvey,* 2 vols (1923, 1925; repr. New York, 1968); Robert Hill et al., eds., *The Marcus Garvey and Universal Negro Improvement Association Papers,* 7 vols, (Berkeley, 1983–90). Also see Judith Stein, *The World of Marcus Garvey: Race and Class in Modern Society* (Baton Rouge, 1986). Opinion polls: see, for example, Eleanor Wolf, Alvin Loving, Donald Marsh, "Negro-Jewish Relationships," Pamphlet, Wayne State Studies in Intergroup Conflicts in Detroit #1, 1944, p. 7, American Jewish Committee (AJC) Inactive Vertical File: "Negro Jewish Relations" (hereafter VF:NJR), AJC Library, New York, NY; Wolf, Loving, Marsh, "Some Aspects of Negro-Jewish Relationships in Detroit, Michigan," Part I, 1943 (funded by the Jewish Community Council and NAACP), Anti-Defamation League (ADL) microfilm: "Yellows 1944: Negro Race Problems" (hereafter Y 1944 nrp), ADL Library, New York, NY; L.D. Reddick, "Anti-Semitism Among Negroes," *Negro Quarterly* (Summer 1942): 113–17; James Robinson, "Some Apprehension, Much Hope," *ADL Bulletin* (December 1957): 4, 6; Harry Lyons, "Jewish-Negro Relationships in the Post War Period," pp. 4–5, 9–10, Report, ADL microfilm: Y 1944 nrp; Elmo Roper, "The Fortune Survey," *Fortune* (November 1942 and October 1947); H.L. Lurie, "Introductory Report on the Study Project of Negro-Jewish Relationships," 9 December 1943 in AJC Vertical File: "NJR: AJC 1938–1969" and in ADL microfilm: Y 1943 nrp: "Anti-Semitism among Negroes, in the opinion of the American Jewish Committee, has not been sufficiently extensive or menacing to receive a sustained and concentrated program," p. 1.

2. See, for example, Herbert Hill, "Black-Jewish Conflict in the Labor Context: Race, Jobs and Institutional Power," paper presented at the "Conference on Blacks and Jews: An Historical Perspective," Washington University, St. Louis, Mo., December 2–5, 1993.

3. Roy Wilkins to Walter White, Memorandum, 25 March 1938; White to Cordell Hull, Telegram, 25 March 1938; NAACP papers, box I C 208; Library of Congress Manuscript Division, Washington, D.C. When the *New York Times* printed only the first sentence of the telegram, "thus giving the impression that the Association endorsed the action of the State Department, without reservation, the National Office protested to the Times." Walter White, "Report of the Secretary to the April Meeting of the Board," 7 April 1938, p. 3, NAACP I A 18. See also George Schuyler, "Abuses of Colored Citizens in U.S.," *World-Telegram,*

21 November 1938; NAACP Press Release, "NAACP Secretary Denounces Nazi Pogroms; Says All Must Unite to Protect Minority Rights Here and Save Democracy," and "Senator King, Sorry for Jews, Urged to Support Federal Anti-Lynch Bill," 18 November [1938?]; White to Chester Ames, 18 November 1938, all NAACP I C 208; Inter-Racial Committee of the District of Columbia, Resolution, 1938, NAACP I C 208 which ["recorded] its deep abhorrence" of the treatment of Jews under Nazi occupation, adding "At the same time, we cannot forbear to point out that in many particulars, the sufferings of this innocent minority . . . are strikingly like the sufferings of a similar minority in our own country."

4. Walter White to Franklin Roosevelt, 14 September 1940, NAACP II A 325.

5. Charles Houston to A. Ovrum Tapper, 5 December 1938. Also see Tapper to Houston, 2 December 1938; White to Houston, 5 and 7 December 1938, all NAACP I C 208. Several meetings were indeed held. NY meetings: White to William Hastie, 26 July 1939; White to [Thurgood] Marshall and [George] Murphy, Memorandum, 21 September 1939; White to Ted Poston, 15 September 1939; Hubert Delany to White, 20 September 1939; Lester Granger to White, 19 September 1939; White and Walter Mendelsohn to Marshall, 27 September 1939; George Murphy, Jr. to White, Memorandum, "For the Committee Studying Anti-Semitism in Harlem," 30 September 1939; White to [Roy] Wilkins, Marshall, Murphy, Memorandum, 9 October 1939; White to Marshall and to Elmer Carter, 4 December 1939; NAACP Press Release, "Yiddish Papers Tell Jews Their Problem is Same as Negro's," 8 December 1939, all NAACP I C 277; White, "Report of the Secretary to the October Meeting of the Board," 5 October 1939, p. 4, NAACP I A 18; AJC, "The Jewish Press and the Jewish-Negro Problem," Report, 6 November 1939, AJC VF: NJR; ADL, Untitled report of articles on Black-Jewish relations in the *Jewish Daily Forward,* October 1939, ADL microfilm, "Dittoes 1939: Negroes," ADL library; Arthur Alberts to Norton Belth, Memorandum re "Harlem: Negro grievances against Jews," 17 October 1939, AJC inactive VF. NCJW: NCJW and NCJW Juniors, National Committee on Legislation, "Social Betterment Through Legislation" [lists NCJW endorsements and dates, including anti-lynching position in 1935], NCJW papers, box 142, Library of Congress Manuscript Division.

6. Philip Frankel to Richard Gutstadt, 2 September 1943. His colleague, Louis Novins, made a similar assessment: "Although we have always been concerned about the Negro situation, we have never deemed it practicable to form a united front. It would be a dangerous policy . . . because we would not only have our own enemies, but would inherit the Negroes' enemies." Novins to Richard Beisler [?illegible] 2 June 1943, both ADL microfilm Y 1943 nrp.

7. Paul Richman to Leonard Finder, Memorandum re "Philip Randolph—Railway Porters' Brotherhood Union," 3 September 1942; Richard Gutstadt to Finder, 14 September 1942. See also Finder to Richman, 4 September 1942; Stanley Jacobs [ADL] to Finder, 10 September 1942, "I could have told you that Philip Randolph is persona non grata with responsible officialdom in Washington, and his proposed March on Washington, which was stymied, would have had serious repercussions and proved most harmful to the war effort." Also Abe Rosenfeld to Finder, 22 July 1942 regarding Adam Clayton Powell, all ADL Y 1942 nrp.

8. Unidentified fragment of report or memorandum, ADL, n.d. [1942], ADL Y 1942 nrp.

9. Many of the papers of the Committee for a Permanent FEPC, the Leadership Conference for Civil Rights, and Civil Rights Mobilization can be found in NAACP files, especially boxes II A 351, 353, 186, some in NCJW Washington Bureau papers, box 18. Roy Wilkins followed A. Philip Randolph as chairman of the Committee; Arnold Aronson of NJCRAC served as secretary. See also, for example, Minutes of the NAACP Board of Directors, 11 October 1943, p. 5; 11 February 1946, pp. 3–4; 14 October 1946, pp. 2–3; 14 February 1949, p. 4, all NAACP I A 134–35; Arnold Aronson, NJCRAC (and National Council for a Permanent FEPC) to NJCRAC Committee on Employment Discrimination and Civil Rights, 17 January 1949; Isaiah Minkoff, "Report of the Executive Director to 6th Plenary Session, NJCRAC," April 1948, pp. 5–6; NJCRAC, Minutes of "informal dinner meeting" of "intergroup relations" agencies, 27 December 1951; all NAACP II A 386–87; ADL National Committee Meeting Minutes, ADL warehouse box 176, and "nrp" files in ADL micro 1945–1958; NCJW, Civil Rights Council materials and "Planks Recommended for Inclusion in 1948 National Party Platforms," 16 June 1948, NCJW box 73; "FEPC: Its Develop-

ment and Trends," n.d.; "Legislative Highlights," May 1943, pp. 2–4, NCJW box 142; AJCong Commission on Law and Social Action (CLSA) papers, AJCong library, New York, NY.

10. See, for example, ADL, "City and State Inter-racial and Good Will Commissions," June 1944, pp. 2–5, ADL Y 1944 nrp; Charles Collier, Jr., Citywide Citizens' Committee on Harlem, to Leonard Finder, 2 September 1943, ADL Y 1943 nrp; AJCong CLSA, "Report of Activities July–September, 1947," p. 2, NAACP II A 360.

11. Pluralism, first coined by Jewish sociologist Horace Kallen in 1924, has had a long and convoluted history, due in large measure to the fuzziness of the concept in the public mind. At first including only white ethnics in its description of the American cultural scene, separatist in its prognosis, and essentialist in its definitions ("Men may change their clothes, their politics, . . . their philosophies to a greater or lesser extent; they cannot change their grandfathers," Kallen argued in a famous passage in *Culture and Democracy in the United States* [New York, 1924], p. 122), it later became more assimilationist in its tone, abandoned essentialism for cultural identities voluntarily chosen, and by the 1940s included non-white groups as well. Alain Locke, the Black philosopher, was the first to apply cultural pluralism to African Americans; see, for example, Leonard Harris, ed., *The Philosophy of Alain Locke* (Philadelphia, 1989). Kallen himself later repented of his early essentialism. For an excellent history of the many meanings of pluralism see Philip Gleason, *Speaking of Diversity* (Baltimore, 1992).

12. See, for example, Meier Steinbrink, ADL, to Mr. ———[sic], fundraising letter on behalf of the NAACP, 18 May 1949, NAACP II A 363; " 'Covenants' Hit by Jewish Groups in Court Brief," *ADL Bulletin* 4 (December 1947): 1; AJCong, CLSA, "Monthly Report," July 1946, NAACP II A 360. *Shelley v. Kraemer* 334 U.S.1 (1948), *Sipes v. McGhee* 334 U.S.1 (1948), *Hurd v. Hodge* 334 U.S.24 (1948).

13. Rabbi Berman, AJCongress Executive Committee Meeting, Minutes, 11 December 1949, p. 107, AJCong papers, box "admin and exec cmttee mins 46–50."

14. Testimony can be found in the papers of the NCJW, NCNW, ADL, AJC, AJCong, NAACP, NUL, JLC, and similar organizations, as well as in the papers of each coalition. *The Balance Sheet* pamphlets were jointly published by the AJCong and NAACP.

15. There are many such examples, found throughout the records of these agencies, on both the local and national level, including a Black and Jewish effort to challenge degrading stereotypes in Hollywood, the production of tolerance literature for schools, churches and civic groups, meetings with local newspaper editors over coverage, editorial policy, or advertising guidelines, or challenging racial and religious quotas in private professional and graduate schools. To take just one, the AJCong challenged the Commercial Travelers Mutual Accident Association regarding their policy of restricting membership to "white male persons." H.E. Trevett, CTMAA to Mr. ——— [sic], 18 February 1942, NAACP II A 360. Anti-mask legislation prohibited the wearing of masks in public and was obviously directed at the Klan. Oftentimes Jewish organizations worked for Black civil rights in the south against the wishes of the local Jewish community; this was the source of a great deal of intra-community strife. For a fuller discussion of this topic see Cheryl Greenberg, "The Southern Jewish Community and the Struggle for Civil Rights," in Nancy Grant and V.P. Franklin, eds., "Blacks and Jews in American History." (forthcoming).

16. Peekskill: see, for example, ACLU, Americans for Democratic Action, AJCong, American Veterans Committee, Council Against Intolerance, NAACP, "Statement on Grand Jury Inquiry into Peekskill Riots," 22 September 1949, NAACP II A467 (which contains a folder on the riot); NJCRAC, "Suggestions for the Guidance of Jewish Organizations In Connection with the Paul Robeson Concert Tour," 19 October 1949, ADL micro "Chicago reel 12"; AJC Domestic Affairs Committee, Minutes, 4 October 1949, p. 5, bound volume in AJC library; Gloster Current, NAACP, to NY Branches, 2 and 8 September 1949, NAACP II A 369; AJC VF "Riots, Peekskill New York." Miami and anti-Klan efforts: AJC Community files; ADL National Commission Meeting, 24–25 October 1952, p. 303, ADL warehouse box 176; NUL Board of Trustees meetings, NUL papers, Library of Congress Manuscript Division; ADL "chisub: civil rights" reels; NAACP II A 362, 369; AJCong, CLSA, "Reports of Activities," in AJCong library; Alex Miller, ADL to Nelson Jackson, NUL, 21 February 1951, NUL SRO box A 124. Peoria St.: See, for example, AJCong Executive Committee minutes, 11 December 1949.

17. Steinbrink, from fundraising letter for ADL members, n.d. It appears Walter White actually wrote

the letter, and Judge Steinbrink signed it. Cover memorandum, White to Mr. Wilkins and Mr. Moon, 18 May [?] 1949, NAACP II A 363. In *Moore v. Dempsey* 261 U.S. 86 (1923) the Supreme Court ruled that the Black defendants, denied adequate counsel and tried in a court whose atmosphere resembled a lynch mob, had been denied due process.

18. Isaac Toubin to Hyman Fliegel, *B'nai Zion Voice*, 13 July 1953, contained in Will Maslow to CRC Group Relations Agencies, Memorandum, 22 October 1953, NAACP II A 362.

19. Maslow to White, 1 December 1947, NAACP II A 360. Testimony, organizing, and programming efforts by Black groups on behalf of immigration reform and other issues can be found in NAACP, NCNW, and NUL files, and occasionally in AJCong CLSA, AJC, and ADL files as well.

20. D.C.: Isaac Franck, Jewish Community Council for Greater Washington to Arnold Forster et al., 28 May 1951; Frances Levenson and Sol Rabkin, Memorandum re "Washington D.C. Civil Rights Statutes," 13 June 1951, both ADL Y 1949–52 nrp. CCREM: its papers can be found in the Columbia University Rare Book and Manuscript Division, New York, NY. Also see NAACP II A 370. Brown: The AJCong, AJC, ADL, NCJW, JLC, Central Conference of American Rabbis, and several other Jewish groups filed amicus briefs, and the Julius Rosenwald Fund and AJC funded Kenneth Clark's famous doll study. See, for example, Shad Polier, "Law and Social Action," *Congress Weekly* 17 (27 November 1950): 3; Arnold Forster, Interview, 13 August 1991, New York, NY; John Slawson, AJC Oral History Memoirs, pp. 34–6, New York Public Library; Kenneth and Mamie Clark, "Detailed Statement of Plan of Work," for Julius Rosenwald Fund, n.d. [1940?], provided by Ben Keppel. Testimony regarding anti-discrimination, anti-segregation, and immigration bills can be found by year in the papers of the NCJW (especially the Washington, D.C. branch), JLC, NCNW, NUL, NUL Southern Regional Office, AJCong CLSA (including Stuyvesant Town litigation) and AJC NJR and Community files, and ADL nrp (ABC materials can be found in 1949–52) and "chisub civ rts" microfilm records and its "Civil Rights Committee Meetings" files. The NAACP papers contain not only its own testimony on numerous issues, but copies of Jewish groups' testimony, organized by subject, date, and agency. There are literally thousands of examples of Black and Jewish groups taking up issues of primary or exclusive importance to the other, including struggles against racist store owners or employers, aiding the settling of refugees in resentful neighborhoods, or protesting segregation.

21. CORE: Samuel Markle to William Sachs, 28 December 1946, ADL Y 1946 nrp. All these organizations changed their minds after the fact and praised CORE's effort. Black temporizing: for example, a 1944 NAACP resolution "urge[s] the Board of Directors of the NAACP to adopt a program of action . . . for the purpose of eliminating anti-Semitism among Negroes, and . . . discovering and eliminating anti-Negro prejudice and practices . . . which foster anti-Semitism among Negroes." Resolutions Adopted at the War-Time Conference, National Association for the Advancement of Colored People, Chicago, 12–16 July 1944, p. 12, NAACP II A 28. "The Urban League has stated publicly its opposition to any campaign that is in the nature of an attack against a whole race of people but at the same time has expressed its recognition of the fact that there might be certain unfair and over-reaching practices carried on by Jewish merchants . . . which give rise to criticism and indignation." Earl Dickerson to White, 5 July 1938, NAACP I C 208. See also Cheryl Greenberg, "Class Tensions and the Black-Jewish 'Alliance,'" OAH Annual Meeting, Atlanta, Georgia, April 1994.

22. Nathan Edelstein, "Jewish Relationship With the Emerging Negro Community in the North," Address to NJCRAC, 23 June 1960, pp. 8–9, AJC VF NJR: AJCong. He concluded that the imbalance should not deter Jews from embracing the civil rights struggle. "Jews are dedicated to the cause of justice and equality because it is best for all Americans."

23. Particularly since local Jews owning property in Miami's Black areas "share the feelings of other southern whites." S. Andhil Fineberg to John Slawson, AJC, Memorandum re "The Situation in Miami," 21 January 1951, p. 3, AJC VF Community files.

24. White to Ben Epstein, 2 June 1949; Epstein to White, 9 June 1949, NAACP II A 363. See also White's eulogy at Stephen Wise's memorial service, 25 May 1949, pp. 11–13, NAACP II A 362. Miller: Alex Miller to Lou Novins, Memorandum re "Negro-Jewish Relations," 16 August 1945, ADL Y 1945 nrp.

25. ADL: Richard Gutstadt to Paul Richman, 19 [10?] August 1941; Berland to Leonard Finder,

12 September 1941, Memorandum re "Article by Roy Wilkins (NY Amst Star)," ADL Y 1941 nrp. Baltimore: quoted in Stanley Jacobs to ADL Staff, Regional offices, CRCs, "Negro Press—Memo #2," 17 April 1942, p. 5, ADL Y 1942 nrp.

26. Berman: Minutes, AJCong Executive Committee, 11 December 1949, pp. 105–6. Brooklyn (Stanley Henderson): AJCong National Convention, 1956, Panel: "Integration," 13 April 1956, p. 73, AJCong box "Nat'l Conventions 54–58."

27. Edelstein, pp. 4–5; White to Maslow, 10 December 1947, NAACP II A 360.

28. Edelstein, p. 6.

29. See, for example, Maslow, "The Advancement of Community Relations Objectives Through Law and Legislation," 25 October 1954, NAACP II A 386, and Edelstein.

30. See, for example, AEB [Abel Berland] to BG [?], Memorandum re "Meeting of the Civic Service Committee," 6 August 1947, ADL Y 1947 nrp (regarding a CORE-led boycott in Chicago). This fear of mass mobilizations was shared by many white liberals in the late 1940s and 1950s. See, for example, Walter Jackson, "From Moderation to Engagement: White Liberal Intellectuals and Civil Rights 1954–59," Southern Historical Association meeting, 7 November 1992; Steven Gillon, *Politics and Vision* (New York, 1987).

31. *De Funis v. Odegaard* 416 U.S. 312 (1974), *Regents of University of California v. Bakke* 438 U.S.265 (1978). Actually the Union of American Hebrew Congregations (the Reform movement) and the NCJW filed briefs on the side of the defendants, along with Black organizations.

# At 50, Levittown Contends with Legacy of Racial Bias

LEVITTOWN, N.Y., Dec. 23—The yearlong 50th-birthday party for this pioneering suburb on Long Island is winding down. The parade drew 5,000 marchers. Crowds came for candlelight church services, an antique-car show, exhibits, seminars and tours of the fabled Levitt houses that started it all.

There were even Potato Day festivities honoring the flat farmland here where Levitt & Sons began mass-producing single-family tract homes in 1947, heralding the wave of migration from cities that lasted for decades.

But not everyone touched by the Levittown experience has been celebrating.

"The anniversary leaves me cold," said Eugene Burnett, who was among thousands of military veterans who lined up for their green patch of the American dream here after World War II. But he was turned away because he is black. "It's symbolic of segregation in America," he said. "That's the legacy of Levittown."

"When I hear 'Levittown,' what rings in my mind is when the salesman said: 'It's not me, you see, but the owners of this development have not as yet decided whether they're going to sell these homes to Negroes,'" Mr. Burnett, now a retired Suffolk County police sergeant, recalled. He said he still stings from "the feeling of rejection on that long ride back to Harlem."

The salesman was not honest with him. Minorities had no chance of getting in, because Levitt had decided from the start to admit only whites. Delano Stewart, editor of *The Point of View*, a Long Island biweekly on black affairs, said: "It's something we'd like to forget rather than celebrate. It's a black mark on the Island, or maybe I should say a white mark."

The whites-only policy was not some unspoken gentlemen's agreement. It was cast in bold capital letters in clause 25 of the standard lease for the first Levitt houses, which included an option to buy, stating that the home could not "be used or occupied by any person other than members of the Caucasian race."

That clause was dropped in 1948 after the United States Supreme Court, ruling on another case, declared such restrictions to be "unenforceable as law and contrary to public policy." Ignoring the law of the land, however, Levitt continued adhering to its racial bar. Levittown quickly filled up with young white families. Minority residents trickled in during the 1950's, but the pattern was set.

Today Levittown has changed, but only a little. While the community has more

Bruce Lambert is a writer for the *New York Times*.

Originally published in the *New York Times*, December 28, 1997, 23–24. Copyright © 1997 by The New York Times Co. Reprinted by permission.

## LEVITTOWN, N.Y.

For the last four decades, blacks have represented
less than 1 percent of Levittown's population.

|                  | 1960   | 1970   | 1980   | 1990   |
|------------------|--------|--------|--------|--------|
| TOTAL POPULATION | 65,276 | 65,440 | 57,045 | 53,286 |
| WHITE            | 65,056 | 65,128 | 56,354 | 51,883 |
| BLACK            | 57     | 44     | 45     | 137    |
| OTHER            | 163    | 268    | 646    | 1,266  |

*Source: Queens College Sociology Department*

minority residents than ever, it remains overwhelmingly white—97.37 percent in the
1990 census.

"It's certainly not a melting pot, but it is a community in transition," said James A.
Edmondson, the chief executive of the Yours, Ours, Mine Community Center in Levittown, who is black. "Ethnically it's changing every day, and in 25 years it won't look like
it does today."

Although blacks account for 8 percent of Long Island's population, they are scarce
here. Of Levittown's 53,286 residents in 1990, there were 51,883 whites, 2,184 Hispanic
people, 950 Asians and Pacific Islanders, 137 blacks (0.26 percent), 31 American Indians
and Aleuts and 285 "other."

Most blacks intent on moving to Long Island ended up in the few "open housing"
communities, which became predominantly minority pockets. "We didn't have many
other choices," said Mr. Burnett, who lives in Wyandanch, in Suffolk County.

As a result, "Nassau County is the most segregated suburban county in the United
States," said Dr. Andrew A. Beveridge, a sociology professor at Queens College, basing
that view on a study of national census data.

### LIVING BY RULES THEY DID NOT MAKE

Whenever historians, planners and sociologists plumb the lessons of Levittown, race
always looms. The debate is not simple or comfortable, especially for people here. Early
Levittowners moved here under rules favoring them that they did not make. Later
arrivals inherited a history that they did not create.

"There is a sensitivity to it, because the community has for many years tried to
overcome that image," said Louise Cassano, a co-chairwoman of the Levittown 50th-
Anniversary Committee and a resident since 1951. "There was that lingering prejudice,"
she said, "but I think we've come a long way."

At the outset, some whites here fought racism, forming the Committee to End
Discrimination in Levittown. There were protests and a leaflet against "Jim Crowism,"
Mrs. Cassano said, "Some people moved in very unaware of the Caucasian clause and
were disturbed when they found out."

In the second Levittown, near Philadelphia, angry white mobs threw rocks in 1957 to
protest the prospect of blacks moving in. In the response back here, the Levittown

Democratic Club, Jewish War Veterans and a Protestant minister all spoke up for open housing.

But this Levittown has had its share of bigots. The Levittown Historical Society's president, Polly Dwyer, recalled one incident: "An Asian family moved in, and some people moved out because of them. It's so silly. They were good, quiet, decent people."

A Hofstra University political science professor, Dr. Herbert D. Rosenbaum, who lived here from 1953 to 1965, said: "In those years, even liberal people like ourselves tended to take residential segregation for granted, without approving it."

Levittown's history seems especially jarring, experts say, because the community was founded as segregation was beginning to crumble. While the first Levitt houses were being built, Jackie Robinson was breaking the color barrier in baseball. A year later, President Harry S. Truman integrated the military.

### HOPES DISSIPATED FOR BLACK AMERICANS

Another paradox was that although Levittown was built for World War II veterans, who had fought tyranny and racism, its doors were opened to at least one former German U-boat sailor, while black American soldiers were turned away.

"Because Levittown promised affordable housing, with no down payment, it offered hope to the African-American working class when no other community did—but that hope was quashed," said Dr. Barbara M. Kelly, Hofstra University's director of Long Island Studies. "After the war, blacks thought things had changed, but they hadn't, and Levittown became a microcosm of that frustration."

The role of the developer, the late William J. Levitt, is sharply debated. He often defended his actions as following the real estate and social customs of the era.

"The Negroes in America are trying to do in 400 years what the Jews in the world have not wholly accomplished in 600 years," he once wrote. "As a Jew, I have no room in my mind or heart for racial prejudice. But I have come to know that if we sell one house to a Negro family, then 90 or 95 percent of our white customers will not buy into the community. This is their attitude, not ours. As a company, our position is simply this: We can solve a housing problem, or we can try to solve a racial problem, but we cannot combine the two."

Indeed, the official Federal Housing Administration policy then called for "suitable restrictive covenants" to avoid "inharmonious racial or nationality groups" in housing.

"To paint Levitt as a villain would be unfair: the whole system was villainous," said Dr. Herbert Gans, a Columbia University sociology professor who lived in Levittown, N.J., and wrote "The Levittowners."

Dr. Kelly said, "To single Levittown out on racial covenants, as if it weren't going on everywhere else, is unfair."

But critics say Mr. Levitt was no passive bystander. His company branded integrationists as Communist rabble-rousers and barred them from meeting on Levittown property. It also evicted two residents who had invited black children from a neighboring community to their homes. Building the third Levittown in New Jersey, the company defied that state's antibias laws and opposed a lawsuit from two blacks seeking to buy homes. Levitt capitulated to integration there in 1960, after much of the development was sold out.

As late as the mid-1960's, Mr. Levitt was still defending segregated housing, at that time in Maryland. And blacks were not the only targets. Although he was the grandson of a rabbi, Mr. Levitt also built housing on Long Island that excluded Jews.

### THE BASIC IDEA WAS INNOVATIVE

No one disputes William Levitt's visionary talent in applying assembly-line methods on a grand scale. Called the Henry Ford of housing, he spurned unions to organize an army of 15,000 workers into dozens of specialized crews, including one to apply red paint and another, white. His company made its own nails and bought forests to supply lumber.

At its peak, Levitt built 36 houses a day, each on a 60-foot-by-100-foot plot. The original Cape Cods had two bedrooms and an unfinished attic. Some models had a 12-inch Admiral television set built into the staircase. Drawn by prices of about $7,000, or monthly payments of around $60, hundreds of buyers flocked here. When the last nail was driven in 1951, Levitt had created a community of 17,447 homes.

But critics say that Levittown could also have been integrated, endowing suburbia and the nation with a social vision just as innovative.

"Levittown was an opportunity tragically lost," said Dr. Kenneth T. Jackson, a history professor at Columbia. "There was such a demand for houses—they had people waiting on lines—that even if they had said there will be some blacks living there, white people would still have moved in."

Whatever the past concerns or prejudices, there is scant evidence of problems involving the minority residents who finally trickled in.

"First there's fear, then there's somebody who makes friends with the new family and says they're very human, they keep nice houses," said John A. Juliano, a real estate agent here for 32 years.

He chuckled about finding a rental for a black woman whose absent landlord did not learn her race till three years later. When the landlord found out, Mr. Juliano recalled: "He said, 'John, she's black.' I said, 'Yeah?' He said, 'She's a terrific tenant.' If I had mentioned it at first, there might have been a problem."

Few blacks in Levittown are eager to talk publicly. A couple who lived here for 20 years agreed to comment if their names were not printed. "We had a problem getting in," said the husband. But his wife added, "After we moved in, we didn't actually have any trouble. I never felt excluded." They retired and left the state, but visit friends here every year.

George Nager, a lawyer and longtime local activist, welcomes the growing mix of black, Hispanic and Asian Americans. "These are mostly upward-bound, entrepreneurial people," he said. "They're absolutely great neighbors. There are no rednecks here and never any cross burnings, I can tell you that, and I go back almost to the Year One here."

The Levittown Tribune's new editor, David Mock, is black. He said that although race may lurk as an issue, he has been accepted. "They opened up to me," he said. "I don't have any problem at all; it's been an absolute pleasure."

Mr. Edmondson, the black community center official, stood out when he started working here 28 years ago. "I can't tell you the bad words that were scrawled on the walls," he recalled, and the police sometimes stopped him to ask why he was in the neighborhood. Although he never moved to Levittown, living instead in Hempstead, he became a respected community leader here.

"The black families I know here have not had a bad experience," he said. "The thing is, I've watched the children. They really get along in a most fantastic way."

# How Did Jews Become White Folks?

The American nation was founded and developed by the Nordic race, but if a few more million members of the Alpine, Mediterranean and Semitic races are poured among us, the result must inevitably be a hybrid race of people as worthless and futile as the good-for-nothing mongrels of Central America and Southeastern Europe. (Kenneth Roberts, qtd. in Carlson and Colburn 1972:312)

It is clear that Kenneth Roberts did not think of my ancestors as white like him. The late nineteenth and early decades of the twentieth centuries saw a steady stream of warnings by scientists, policymakers, and the popular press that "mongrelization" of the Nordic or Anglo-Saxon race—the real Americans—by inferior European races (as well as inferior non-European ones) was destroying the fabric of the nation. I continue to be surprised to read that America did not always regard its immigrant European workers as white, that they thought people from different nations were biologically different. My parents, who are first-generation U.S.-born Eastern European Jews, are not surprised. They expect anti-Semitism to be part of the fabric of daily life, much as I expect racism to be part of it. They came of age in a Jewish world in the 1920s and 1930s at the peak of anti-Semitism in the United States (Gerber 1986a). They are proud of their upward mobility and think of themselves as pulling themselves up by their own bootstraps. I grew up during the 1950s in the Euroethnic New York suburb of Valley Stream where Jews were simply one kind of white folks and where ethnicity meant little more to my generation than food and family heritage. Part of my familized ethnic heritage was the belief that Jews were smart and that our success was the result of our own efforts and abilities, reinforced by a culture that valued sticking together, hard work, education, and deferred gratification. Today, this belief in a Jewish version of Horatio Alger has become an entry point for racism by some mainstream Jewish organizations against African Americans especially, and for their opposition to affirmative action for people of color (Gordon 1964; Sowell 1983; Steinberg 1989: chap. 3).

It is certainly true that the United States has a history of anti-Semitism and of beliefs that Jews were members of an inferior race. But Jews were hardly alone. American anti-Semitism was part of a broader pattern of late-nineteenth-century racism against all southern and eastern European immigrants, as well as against Asian immigrants. These

Karen Brodkin teaches in the Department of Anthropology at the University of California, Los Angeles. Originally published in *Race,* ed. Steven Gregory and Roger Sanjek (New Brunswick, N.J.: Rutgers University Press, 1994), 78–102. Copyright © 1994, Karen Brodkin Sacks. Reprinted by permission of the author, Karen Brodkin.

views justified all sorts of discriminatory treatment including closing the doors to immigration from Europe and Asia in the 1920s.[1] This picture changed radically after World War II. Suddenly the same folks who promoted nativism and xenophobia were eager to believe that the Euro-origin people whom they had deported, reviled as members of inferior races, and prevented from immigrating only a few years earlier were now model middle-class white suburban citizens.

It was not an educational epiphany that made those in power change their hearts, their minds, and our race. Instead, it was the biggest and best affirmative action program in the history of our nation, and it was for Euromales. There are similarities and differences in the ways each of the European immigrant groups became "whitened." I want to tell the story in a way that links anti-Semitism to other varieties of anti-European racism, because this foregrounds what Jews shared with other Euroimmigrants and shows changing notions of whiteness to be part of America's larger system of institutional racism.

### EURORACES

The U.S. "discovery" that Europe had inferior and superior races came in response to the great waves of immigration from southern and eastern Europe in the late nineteenth century. Before that time, European immigrants—including Jews—had been largely assimilated into the white population. The twenty-three million European immigrants who came to work in U.S. cities after 1880 were too many and too concentrated to disperse and blend. Instead, they piled up in the country's most dilapidated urban areas, where they built new kinds of working-class ethnic communities. Since immigrants and their children made up more than 70 percent of the population of most of the country's largest cities, urban America came to take on a distinctly immigrant flavor. The golden age of industrialization in the United States was also the golden age of class struggle between the captains of the new industrial empires and the masses of manual workers whose labor made them rich. As the majority of mining and manufacturing workers, immigrants were visibly major players in these struggles (Higham 1955:226; Steinberg 1989:36).[2]

The Red Scare of 1919 clearly linked anti-immigrant to anti-working-class sentiment—to the extent that the Seattle general strike of native-born workers was blamed on foreign agitators. The Red Scare was fueled by economic depression, a massive postwar strike wave, the Russian revolution, and a new wave of postwar immigration. Strikers in steel, and the garment and textile workers in New York and New England, were mainly new immigrants. "As part of a fierce counteroffensive, employers inflamed the historic identification of class conflict with immigrant radicalism." Anticommunism and anti-immigrant sentiment came together in the Palmer raids and deportation of immigrant working-class activists. There was real fear of revolution. One of President Wilson's aides feared it was "the first appearance of the soviet in this country" (Higham 1955:226).

Not surprisingly, the belief in European races took root most deeply among the wealthy U.S.-born Protestant elite, who feared a hostile and seemingly unassimilable working class. By the end of the nineteenth century, Senator Henry Cabot Lodge pressed Congress to cut off immigration to the United States; Teddy Roosevelt raised the alarm of "race suicide" and took Anglo-Saxon women to task for allowing "native" stock to be outbred by inferior immigrants. In the twentieth century, these fears gained a great deal of social legitimacy thanks to the efforts of an influential network of aristocrats and scientists who developed theories of eugenics—breeding for a "better" humanity—and scientific racism. Key to these efforts was Madison Grant's influential *Passing of the Great Race,* in which he shared his discovery that there were three or four major European races ranging from the superior Nordics of northwestern Europe to the inferior southern and eastern races of Alpines, Mediterraneans, and, worst of all, Jews, who seemed to be everywhere in his native New York City. Grant's nightmare was race mixing among Europeans. For him, "the cross between any of the three European races and a Jew is a Jew" (qtd. in Higham 1955:156). He didn't have good things to say about Alpine or Mediterranean "races" either. For Grant, race and class were interwoven: the upper class was racially pure Nordic, and the lower classes came from the lower races.

Far from being on the fringe, Grant's views resonated with those of the non-immigrant middle class. A *New York Times* reporter wrote of his visit to the Lower East Side:

> This neighborhood, peopled almost entirely by the people who claim to have been driven from Poland and Russia, is the eyesore of New York and perhaps the filthiest place on the western continent. It is impossible for a Christian to live there because he will be driven out, either by blows or the dirt and stench. Cleanliness is an unknown quantity to these people. They cannot be lifted up to a higher plane because they do not want to be. If the cholera should ever get among these people, they would scatter its germs as a sower does grain. (qtd. in Schoener 1967:58)[3]

Such views were well within the mainstream of the early-twentieth-century scientific community. Grant and eugenicist Charles B. Davenport organized the Galton Society in 1918 in order to foster research and to otherwise promote eugenics and immigration restriction.[4] Lewis Terman, Henry Goddard, and Robert Yerkes, developers of the so-called intelligence test, believed firmly that southeastern European immigrants, African Americans, American Indians, and Mexicans were "feebleminded." And indeed, more than 80 percent of the immigrants whom Goddard tested at Ellis Island in 1912 turned out to be just that. Racism fused with eugenics in scientific circles, and the eugenics circles overlapped with the nativism of WASP aristocrats. During World War I, racism shaped the army's development of a mass intelligence test. Psychologist Robert Yerkes, who developed the test, became an even stronger advocate of eugenics after the war. Writing in the *Atlantic Monthly* in 1923, he noted:

> If we may safely judge by the army measurements of intelligence, races are quite as significantly different as individuals. . . . [and] almost as great as the intellectual difference between negro and white in the army are the differences between white racial groups. . . .
>
> For the past ten years or so the intellectual status of immigrants has been disquiet-

ingly low. Perhaps this is because of the dominance of the Mediterranean races, as contrasted with the Nordic and Alpine. (qtd. in Carlson and Colburn 1972:333–334)

By the 1920s, scientific racism sanctified the notion that real Americans were white and real whites came from northwest Europe. Racism animated laws excluding and expelling Chinese in 1882, and then closing the door to immigration by virtually all Asians and most Europeans in 1924 (Saxton 1971, 1990). Northwestern European ancestry as a requisite for whiteness was set in legal concrete when the Supreme Court denied Bhagat Singh Thind the right to become a naturalized citizen under a 1790 federal law that allowed whites the right to become naturalized citizens. Thind argued that Asian Indians were the real Aryans and Caucasians, and therefore white. The Court countered that the United States only wanted blond Aryans and Caucasians, "that the blond Scandinavian and the brown Hindu have a common ancestor in the dim reaches of antiquity, but the average man knows perfectly well that there are unmistakable and profound differences between them today" (Takaki 1989:298–299). A narrowly defined white, Christian race was also built into the 1705 Virginia "Act concerning servants and slaves." This statute stated "that no negroes, mulattos and Indians or other infidels or jews, Moors, Mahometans or other infidels shall, at any time, purchase any christian servant, nor any other except of their own complexion" (Martyn 1979:111).[5]

The 1930 census added its voice, distinguishing not only immigrant from "native" whites, but also native whites of native white parentage, and native whites of immigrant (or mixed) parentage. In distinguishing immigrant (southern and eastern Europeans) from "native" (northwestern Europeans), the census reflected the racial distinctions of the eugenicist-inspired intelligence tests.[6]

Racism and anti-immigrant sentiment in general and anti-Semitism in particular flourished in higher education. Jews were the first of the Euroimmigrant groups to enter colleges in significant numbers, so it wasn't surprising that they faced the brunt of discrimination there.[7] The Protestant elite complained that Jews were unwashed, uncouth, unrefined, loud, and pushy. Harvard University President A. Lawrence Lowell, who was also a vice president of the Immigration Restriction League, was openly opposed to Jews at Harvard. The Seven Sisters schools had a reputation for "flagrant discrimination." M. Carey Thomas, Bryn Mawr president, may have been a feminist of a kind, but she also was an admirer of scientific racism and an advocate of immigration restriction. She "blocked both the admission of black students and the promotion of Jewish instructors" (Synott 1986:233, 238–239, 249–250).

Anti-Semitic patterns set by these elite schools influenced standards of other schools, made anti-Semitism acceptable, and "made the aura of exclusivity a desirable commodity for the college-seeking clientele" (Synott 1986:250; and see Karabel 1984; Silberman 1985; Steinberg 1989: chaps. 5, 9). Fear that colleges "might soon be overrun by Jews" were publicly expressed at a 1918 meeting of the Association of New England Deans. In 1919 Columbia University took steps to decrease the number of entering Jews by a set of practices that soon came to be widely adopted. The school developed a psychological test based on the World War I army intelligence tests to measure "innate ability—and middle-class home environment" and redesigned the admission application to ask for religion, father's name and birthplace, a photo, and a personal interview (Synott 1986:239–240). Other techniques for excluding Jews, like a fixed class size, a chapel requirement, and preference for children of alumni were less obvious. Sociologist Jerome Karabel (1984) has argued that these exclusionary efforts provided the basis for contemporary criteria for college admission that mix grades and test scores with criteria for well-roundedness and character, as well as affirmative action for athletes and children of alumni, which allowed schools to select more affluent Protestants. Their proliferation in the 1920s caused the intended drop in the number of Jewish students in law, dental, and medical schools and also saw the imposition of quotas in engineering, pharmacy, and veterinary schools.[8]

Columbia's quota against Jews was well known in my parents' community. My father is very proud of having beaten it and of being admitted to Columbia Dental School on the basis of his sculpting skill. In addition to demonstrating academic qualifications, he was asked to carve a soap ball, which he did so well and fast that his Protestant interviewer was willing to accept him. Although he became a teacher instead because the dental school tuition was too high, he took me to the dentist every week of my childhood and prolonged the agony by discussing the finer points of tooth filling and dental care. My father also almost failed the speech test required for his teaching license because he didn't speak "standard"—that is, nonimmigrant, nonaccented—English. For my parents and most of their friends, English was a second language learned when they went to school, since their home language was Yiddish. They saw the speech test as designed to keep all ethnics, not just Jews, out of teaching. There is an ironic twist to this story. My mother was always urging me to speak well and correctly, like her friend Ruth Saronson, who was a speech teacher. Ruth remained my model for perfect diction until I went away to college. When I talked to her on one of my visits home, I heard just how New York—accented my version of "standard" English was now that I had met the Boston academic version.

My parents' conclusion is that Jewish success, like their own, was the result of hard work and of placing a high value on education. They went to Brooklyn College during the depression. My mother worked days and started school at night, and my father went during the day. Both their families encouraged them. More accurately, their families expected this effort from them. Everyone they knew was in the same boat, and their world was made up of Jews who advanced as they did. The picture of New York—where most Jews lived—seems to back them up. In 1920, Jews made up 80 percent of the students at New York's City College, 90 percent of Hunter College, and before World War I, 40 percent of private Columbia University. By 1934, Jews made up almost 24 percent of all law students nationally, and 56 percent of those in New York City. Still, more Jews became public school teachers, like my parents and their friends, than doctors or lawyers (Steinberg 1989:137, 227). Steinberg has debunked the myth that Jews advanced because of the cultural value placed on education. This is not to say that Jews did not advance. They did. "Jewish success in America was a matter of historical timing. . . . [T]here was a fortuitous match between the experience and skills of Jewish immigrants, on the one hand, and the manpower needs and opportunity structures, on the other" (1989:103). Jews were the only ones among the southern and eastern European immigrants who came from urban, commercial, craft, and manufacturing backgrounds, not least of which was garment manufacturing. They entered the United States in New York, center of the nation's booming garment industry, soon came to dominate its skilled (male) and "unskilled" (female) jobs, and found it an industry amenable to low-capital entrepreneurship. As a result, Jews were the first of the new European immigrants to create a middle class of small businesspersons early in the twentieth century. Jewish educational advances followed this business success and depended upon it, rather than creating it (see also Bodnar 1985 for a similar argument about mobility).

In the early twentieth century, Jewish college students entered a contested terrain in which the elite social mission was under challenge by a newer professional training mission. Pressure for change had begun to transform the curriculum and reorient college from a gentleman's bastion to a training ground for the middle-class professionals needed by an industrial economy. "The curriculum was overhauled to prepare students for careers in business, engineering, scientific farming, and the arts, and a variety of new professions such as accounting and pharmacy that were making their appearance in American colleges for the first time" (Steinberg 1989:229). Occupational training was precisely what drew Jews to college. In a setting where disparagement of intellectual pursuits and the gentleman's C were badges of distinction, it was not hard for Jews to excel.

How we interpret Jewish social mobility in this milieu depends on whom we compare Jews to. Compared with other immigrants, Jews were upwardly mobile. But compared with that of nonimmigrant whites, their mobility was very limited and circumscribed. Anti-immigrant racist and anti-Semitic barriers kept the Jewish middle class confined to a small number of occupations. Jews were excluded from mainstream corporate management and corporately employed professions, except in the garment and movie industries, which they built. Jews were almost totally excluded from university faculties (and the few that made it had powerful patrons). Jews were concentrated in small businesses, and in professions where they served a largely Jewish clientele (Davis 1990:146 n.25; Silberman 1985:88–117; Sklare 1971:63–67).

We shouldn't forget Jews' success in organized crime in the 1920s and 1930s as an aspect of upward mobility. Arnold Rothstein "transformed crime from a haphazard, small-scale activity into a well-organized and well-financed business operation." There was also Detroit's Purple Gang, Murder Incorporated in New York, and a host of other big-city Jewish gangs in organized crime, and of course Meyer Lansky (Silberman 1985:127–130).

Although Jews were the Euroethnic vanguard in college and became well established in public school teaching, as well as being visible in law, medicine, pharmacy, and librarianship before the postwar boom, these professions should be understood in the context of their times (Gerber 1986a:26). In the 1930s they lacked the corporate context they have today, and Jews in these professions were certainly not corporation based. Most lawyers, doctors, dentists, and pharmacists were solo practitioners and were considerably less affluent than their postwar counterparts.

Compared to Jewish progress after the war, Jews' prewar mobility was also very limited. It was the children of Jewish businessmen, not those of Jewish workers, who flocked to college. Indeed, in 1905 New York, the children of Jewish workers had as little schooling as children of other immigrant workers.[9] My family was quite modal in this respect. My grandparents did not go to college, but they did have a modicum of small-business success. My father's family owned a pharmacy. Although my mother's father was a skilled garment worker, her mother's family was large and always had one or another grocery or deli in which my grandmother participated. It was the relatively privileged children of upwardly mobile Jewish immigrants like my grandparents who began to push on the doors to higher education even before my parents were born. Especially in New York City—which had almost 1.25 million Jews by 1910 and remained the biggest concentration of the nation's 4 million Jews in 1924 (Steinberg 1989:225)—Jews built a small-business-based middle class and began to develop a second-generation professional class in the interwar years.[10] Still, despite the high percentages of Jews in eastern colleges, most Jews were not middle class, and fewer than 3 percent were professionals, compared to somewhere between 20 and 32 percent in the 1960s (Sklare 1971:63).

My parents' generation believed that Jews overcame anti-Semitic barriers because Jews are special. My belief is that the Jews who were upwardly mobile were special among Jews (and were also well placed to write the story). My generation might well counter our parents' story of pulling themselves up by their own bootstraps with, "But think what you might have been without the racism and with some affirmative action!" And that is precisely what the postwar boom, the decline of systematic, public anti-immigrant racism and anti-Semitism, and governmental affirmative action extended to white males.

### EUROETHNICS INTO WHITES

By the time I was an adolescent, Jews were just as white as the next white person. Until I was eight, I was a Jew in a world of Jews. Everyone on Avenue Z in Sheepshead Bay was Jewish. I spent my days playing and going to school on three blocks of Avenue Z, and visiting my grandparents in the nearby Jewish neighborhoods of Brighton Beach and Coney Island. There were plenty of Italians in my neighborhood, but they lived around the corner. They were a kind of Jew, but on the margins of my social horizons. Portugese were even more distant, at the end of the bus ride, at Sheepshead Bay. The schul, or temple, was on Avenue Z, and I begged my father to take me like all the other fathers took their kids, but religion wasn't part of my family's Judaism. Just how Jewish my neighborhood was hit me in first grade when I was one of two kids in my class to go to school on Rosh Hashanah. My teacher was shocked—she was Jewish too—and I was embarrassed to tears when she sent me home. I was never again sent to school on Jewish holidays. We left that world in 1949 when we moved to Valley Stream, Long Island, which was Protestant, Republican, and even had farms until Irish, Italian, and Jewish exurbanites like us gave it a more suburban and Democratic flavor. Neither religion nor ethnicity separated us at school or in the neighborhood. Except temporarily. In elementary school years, I remember a fair number of dirt-bomb (a good suburban weapon) wars on the block. Periodically one of the Catholic boys would accuse me or my brothers of killing his God, to which we would reply, "Did not" and start lobbing dirt-bombs. Sometimes he would get his friends from Catholic school, and I would get mine from public school kids on the block, some of whom were Catholic. Hostilities lasted no more than a couple of hours and punctuated an otherwise friendly relationship. They ended by junior high years, when other things became more important. Jews, Catholics, and Protestants, Italians, Irish, Poles, and "English" (I don't remember hearing WASP as a kid) were mixed up on the block and in school. We thought of ourselves as middle class and very enlightened because our ethnic backgrounds seemed so irrelevant to high school culture. We didn't see race (we thought), and racism was not part of our peer consciousness, nor were the immigrant or working-class histories of our families.

Like most chicken and egg problems, it's hard to know which came first. Did Jews and other Euroethnics become white because they became middle class? That is, did money whiten? Or did being incorporated in an expanded version of whiteness open up the economic doors to a middle-class status? Clearly, both tendencies were at work. Some of the changes set in motion during the war against fascism led to a more inclusive version of whiteness. Anti-Semitism and anti-European racism lost respectability. The 1940 census no longer distinguished native whites of native parentage from those, like my parents, of immigrant parentage, so that Euroimmigrants and their children were more securely white by submersion in an expanded notion of whiteness. (This census also changed the race of Mexicans to white [U.S. Bureau of the Census, 1940: 4].) Theories of nurture and culture replaced theories of nature and biology. Instead of dirty and dangerous races who would destroy U.S. democracy, immigrants became ethnic groups whose children had successfully assimilated into the mainstream and risen to the middle class. In this new myth, Euroethnic suburbs like mine became the measure of U.S. democracy's victory over racism. Jewish mobility became a new Horatio Alger story. In time and with hard work, every ethnic group would get a piece of the pie, and the United States would be a nation with equal opportunity for all its people to become part of a prosperous middle-class majority. And it seemed that Euroethnic immigrants and their children were delighted to join middle America.[11]

This is not to say that anti-Semitism disappeared after World War II, only that it fell from fashion and was driven underground. Micah Sifry's (1993) revelations of Richard Nixon's and George Bush's personal anti-Semitism and its prevalence in both their administrations indicate its persistence in the Protestant elite. There has also been an alarming rise of anti-Semitic and anti-African American hate groups and hate crimes in recent years. While elites do not have a monopoly on anti-Semitism, they do have the ability to restrict Jews' access to the top echelons of corporate America. Since the war, the remaining glass ceilings on Jewish mobility have gotten fewer and higher. Although they may still keep down the number of Jews and other Euroethnics in the upper class, it has been a long time since they could keep them out of the middle class. However, a 1987 Supreme Court ruling that Jews and Arabs could use civil rights laws to gain redress for discrimination against them did so on the grounds that they are not racial whites. As historian Barbara Jeanne Fields (1990:97) notes, "[T]he court knew no better way to rectify injustice at the end of the twentieth century than to re-enthrone the superstitious racial dogma of the nineteenth century."[12]

Although changing views on who was white made it easier for Euroethnics to become middle class, it was also the case that economic prosperity played a very powerful role in the whitening process. Economic mobility of Jews and other Euroethnics rested ultimately on U.S. post war economic prosperity with its enormously expanded need for professional, technical, and managerial labor, and on government assistance in providing it. The United States emerged from the war with the strongest economy in the world. Real wages rose between 1946 and 1960, increasing buying power a hefty 22 percent and giving most Americans some discretionary income (Nash et al. 1986:885–886). U.S. manufacturing, banking, and business services became increasingly dominated by large corporations, and these grew into multinational corporations. Their organizational centers lay in big, new urban headquarters that demanded growing numbers of technical and managerial workers. The postwar period was a historic moment for real class mobility and for the affluence we have erroneously come to believe was the U.S. norm. It was a time when the old white and the newly white masses became middle class.

The GI Bill of Rights, as the 1944 Serviceman's Readjustment Act was known, was arguably the most massive affirmative action program in U.S. history. It was created to develop needed labor force skills, and to provide those who had them with a life-style that reflected their value to the economy. The GI benefits ultimately extended to sixteen million GIs (veterans of the Korean War as well) included priority in jobs—that is, preferential hiring, but no one objected to it then—financial support during the job search; small loans for starting up businesses; and, most important, low-interest home loans and educational benefits, which included tuition and living expenses (Brown 1946; Hurd 1946; Mosch 1975; *Postwar Jobs for Veterans* 1945; Willenz 1983). This legislation was rightly regarded as one of the most revolutionary postwar programs. I call it affirmative action because it was aimed at and disproportionately helped male, Euro-origin GIs.

GI benefits, like the New Deal affirmative action programs before them and the 1960s affirmative action programs after them, were responses to protest. Business executives and the general public believed that the war economy had only temporarily halted the Great Depression. Many feared its return and a return to the labor strife and radicalism of the 1930s (Eichler 1982:4; Nash et al. 1986:885). "[M]emories of the Depression remained vivid and many people suffered from what Davis Ross has aptly called 'depression psychosis'—the fear that the war would inevitably be followed by layoffs and mass unemployment" (Wynn 1976:15).

It was a reasonable fear. The eleven million military personnel who were demobilized in the 1940s represented a quarter of the U.S. labor force (Mosch 1975:1, 20). In addition, ending war production brought a huge number of layoffs, growing unemployment, and a high rate of inflation. To recoup wartime losses in real wages caused by inflation as well as by the unions' no-strike pledge in support of the war effort, workers staged a massive wave of strikes in 1946. More workers went out on strike that year than ever before, and there were strikes in all the heavy industries: railroads, coal mining, auto, steel, and electrical. For a brief moment, it looked like class struggle all over again. But government and business leaders had learned from the experience of bitter labor struggles after World War I just how important it was to assist demobilized soldiers. The GI Bill resulted from their determination to avoid those mistakes this time. The biggest benefits of this legislation were for college and technical school education, and for very cheap home mortgages.

## EDUCATION AND OCCUPATION

It is important to remember that prior to the war, a college degree was still very much a "mark of the upper class" (Willenz 1983:165). Colleges were largely finishing schools for Protestant elites. Before the postwar boom, schools could not begin to accommodate the American masses. Even in New York City before the 1930s, neither the public schools nor City College had room for more than a tiny fraction of potential immigrant students.

Not so after the war. The almost eight million GIs who took advantage of their educational benefits under the GI bill caused "the greatest wave of college building in American history" (Nash et al. 1986:885). White male GIs were able to take advantage of their educational benefits for college and technical training, so they were particularly well positioned to seize the opportunities provided by the new demands for professional, managerial, and technical labor. "It has been well documented that the GI educational benefits transformed American higher education and raised the educational level of that generation and generations to come. With many provisions for assistance in upgrading their educational attainments veterans pulled ahead of nonveterans in earning capacity. In the long run it was the nonveterans who had fewer opportunities" (Willenz 1983:165).[13]

Just how valuable a college education was for white men's occupational mobility can be seen in John Keller's study of who benefited from the metamorphosis of California's Santa Clara Valley into Silicon Valley. Formerly an agricultural region, in the 1950s the are became the scene of explosive growth in the semiconductor electronics industry. This industry epitomized the postwar economy and occupational structure. It owned its existence directly to the military and to the National Aeronautics and Space Administration (NASA), who were its major funders and its major markets. It had an increasingly white-collar work force. White men, who were the initial production workers in the 1950s, quickly transformed themselves into a technical and professional work force thanks largely to GI benefits and the new junior college training programs designed to meet the industry's growing work-force needs. Keller notes that "62 percent of enrollees at San Jose Junior College (later renamed San Jose City College) came from blue-collar families, and 55 percent of all job placements were as electronics technicians in the industrial and service sectors of the county economy" (1983:363). As white men left assembly work and the industry expanded between 1950 and 1960, they were replaced initially by Latinas and African-American women, who were joined after 1970 by new immigrant women. Immigrating men tended to work in the better-paid unionized industries that grew up in the area (Keller 1983:346–373).

Postwar expansion made college accessible to the mass of Euromales in general and to Jews in particular. My generation's "Think what you could have been!" answer to our parents became our reality as quotas and old occupational barriers fell and new fields opened up to Jews. The most striking result was a sharp decline in Jewish small businesses and a skyrocketing of Jewish professionals. For example, as quotas in medical schools fell the numbers of Jewish doctors mushroomed. If Boston is an indication, just over 1 percent of all Jewish men before the war were doctors compared to 16 percent of the postwar generation (Silberman 1985:124, and see 118–126). A similar Jewish mass movement took place into college and university faculties, especially in "new and expanding fields in the social and natural sciences" (Steinberg 1989:137).[14] Although these Jewish college professors tended to be sons of businesspersons and professionals, the postwar boom saw the first large-scale class mobility among Jewish men. Sons of working-class Jews now went to college and became professionals themselves, according to the Boston survey, almost two-thirds of them. This compared favorably with three-quarters of the sons of professional fathers (Silberman 1985: 121–122).[15]

Even more significantly, the postwar boom transformed the U.S. class structure—or at least its status structure—so that the middle class expanded to encompass most of the population. Before the war, most Jews, like most other Americans, were working class. Already upwardly mobile before the war relative to other immigrants, Jews floated high on this rising economic tide, and most of them entered the middle class. Still, even the high tide missed some Jews. As late as 1973, some 15 percent of New York's Jews were poor or near-poor, and in the 1960s, almost 25 percent of employed Jewish men remained manual workers (Steinberg 1989:89–90).

Educational and occupational GI benefits really constituted affirmative action programs for white males because they were decidedly not extended to African Americans or to women of any race. White male privilege was shaped against the backdrop of wartime racism and postwar sexism. During and after the war, there was an upsurge in white racist violence against black servicemen in public schools, and in the KKK, which spread to California and New York (Dalfiume 1969:133–134). The number of lynchings rose during the war, and in 1943 there were antiblack race riots in several large northern cities. Although there was a wartime labor shortage, black people were discriminated against in access to well-paid defense industry jobs and in housing. In 1946 there were white riots against African Americans across the South, and in Chicago and Philadelphia as well. Gains made as a result of the wartime Civil Rights movement, especially employment in defense-related industries, were lost with peacetime conversion as black workers were the first fired, often in violation of seniority (Wynn 1976: 114, 116). White women were also laid off, ostensibly to make jobs for demobilized servicemen, and in the long run women lost most of the gains they had made in wartime (Kessler-Harris 1982). We now know that women did not leave the labor force in any significant numbers but instead were forced to find inferior jobs, largely nonunion, parttime, and clerical.

Theoretically available to all veterans, in practice women and black veterans did not get anywhere near their share of GI benefits. Because women's units were not treated as part of the military, women in them were not considered veterans and were ineligible for Veterans' Administration (VA) benefits (Willenz 1983:168). The barriers that almost completely shut African-American GIs out of their benefits were more complex. In

Wynn's portrait (1976:115), black GIs anticipated starting new lives, just like their white counterparts. Over 43 percent hoped to return to school and most expected to relocate, to find better jobs in new lines of work. The exodus from the South toward the North and far West was particularly large. So it wasn't a question of any lack of ambition on the part of African-American GIs.

Rather, the military, the Veterans' Administration, the U.S. Employment Service, and the Federal Housing Administration (FHA) effectively denied African-American GIs access to their benefits and to the new educational, occupational, and residential opportunities. Black GIs who served in the thoroughly segregated armed forces during World War II served under white officers, usually southerners (Binkin and Eitelberg 1982; Dalfiume 1969; Foner 1974; Johnson 1967; Nalty and MacGregor 1981). African-American soldiers were disproportionately given dishonorable discharges, which denied them veterans' rights under the GI Bill. Thus between August and November 1946, 21 percent of white soldiers and 39 percent of black soldiers were dishonorably discharged. Those who did get an honorable discharge then faced the Veterans' Administration and the U.S. Employment Service. The latter, which was responsible for job placements, employed very few African Americans, especially in the South. This meant that black veterans did not receive much employment information, and that the offers they did receive were for low-paid and menial jobs. "In one survey of 50 cities, the movement of blacks into peacetime employment was found to be lagging far behind that of white veterans: in Arkansas 95 percent of the placements made by the USES for Afro-Americans were in service or unskilled jobs" (Nalty and MacGregor 1981:218, and see 60–61). African Americans were also less likely than whites, regardless of GI status, to gain new jobs commensurate with their wartime jobs, and they suffered more heavily. For example, in San Francisco by 1948, Black Americans "had dropped back halfway to their pre-war employment status" (Wynn 1976:114, 116).[16]

Black GIs faced discrimination in the educational system as well. Despite the end of restrictions on Jews and other Euroethnics, African Americans were not welcome in white colleges. Black colleges were overcrowded, and the combination of segregation and prejudice made for few alternatives. About twenty thousand black veterans attended college by 1947, most in black colleges, but almost as many, fifteen thousand could not gain entry. Predictably, the disproportionately few African Americans who did gain access to their educational benefits were able, like their white counterparts, to become doctors and engineers, and to enter the black middle class (Walker 1970).

### SUBURBANIZATION

In 1949, ensconced at Valley Stream, I watched potato farms turn into Levittown and into Idlewild (later Kennedy) Airport. This was a major spectator sport in our first years on suburban Long Island. A typical weekend would bring various aunts, uncles, and cousins out from the city. After a huge meal we would pile in the car—itself a novelty— to look at the bulldozed acres and comment on the matchbox construction. During the week, my mother and I would look at the houses going up within walking distance.

Bill Levitt built a basic 900–1,000-square-foot, somewhat expandable house for a lower-middle-class and working-class market on Long Island, and later in Pennsylvania and New Jersey (Gans 1967). Levittown started out as two thousand units of rental housing at sixty dollars a month, designed to meet the low-income housing needs of returning war vets, many of whom, like my Aunt Evie and Uncle Julie, were living in quonset huts. By May 1947, Levitt and Sons had acquired enough land in Hempstead Township on Long Island to build four thousand houses, and by the next February, he'd built six thousand units and named the development after himself. After 1948, federal financing for the construction of rental housing tightened, and Levitt switched to building houses for sale. By 1951 Levittown was a development of some fifteen thousand families.

Hartman (1975:141–142) cities massive abuses in the 1940s and 1950s by builders under Section 608, a program in which "the FHA granted extraordinarily liberal concessions to lackadaisically supervised private developers to induce them to produce rental housing rapidly in the postwar period." Eichler (1982) indicates that things were not that different in the subsequent FHA-funded home-building industry.

At the beginning of World War II, about 33 percent of all U.S. families owned their houses. That percentage doubled in twenty years. Most Levittowners looked just like my family. They came from New York City or Long Island; about 17 percent were military, from nearby Mitchell Field; Levittown was their first house; and almost everyone was married. The 1947 inhabitants were over 75 percent white collar, but by 1950 more blue-collar families moved in, so that by 1951, "barely half" of the new residents were white collar, and by 1960 their occupational profile was somewhat more working class than for Nassau County as a whole. By this time too, almost one-third of Levittown's people were either foreign-born or, like my parents, first-generation U.S. born (Dobriner 1963:91, 100).

The FHA was key to buyers and builders alike. Thanks to it, suburbia was open to more than GIs. People like us would never have been in the market for houses without FHA and VA low-down-payment, low-interest, long-term loans to young buyers.[17] Most suburbs were built by "merchant builders," large-scale entrepreneurs like Levitt, who obtained their own direct FHA and VA loans (Jackson 1985:215). In the view of one major builder, "Without FHA and VA loans merchant building would not have happened" (Eichler 1982:9). A great deal was at stake. The FHA and VA had to approve subdivision plans and make the appraisals upon which house buyers' loans were calculated. FHA appraisals effectively set the price a house could sell for, since the FHA established the amount of the mortgage it would insure. The VA was created after the war, and it followed FHA policies. Most of the benefits in both programs went to suburbs, and half of all suburban housing in the 1950s and 1960s was financed by FHA/VA loans. Federal highway funding was also important to suburbanization. The National Defense Highway Act of 1941 put the government in the business of funding 90 percent of a national highway system (the other 10 percent came from states), which developed a network of freeways between and around the nation's metropolitan areas, making suburbs and automobile commuting a way of life. State zoning laws and services were also key. "A significant and often crucial portion of the required infrastructure—typically water, sewer, roads, parks, schools—was provided by the existing community, which was in effect subsidizing the builder and indirectly the new buyer or renter" (Eichler 1982:13).[18]

In residential life as in jobs and education, federal programs and GI benefits were crucial for mass entry into a middle-class homeowning suburban life-style. Indeed, they raised the U.S. standard of living to a middle-class one.

It was here that the federal government's racism reached its high point. Begun in 1934, the FHA was a New Deal program whose original intent was to stimulate the construction industry by insuring private loans to buy or build houses. Even before the war, it had stimulated a building boom. The FHA was "largely run by representatives of the real estate and banking industries" (Jackson 1985:203–205; Weiss 1987:146). It is fair to say that the "FHA exhorted segregation and enshrined it as public policy" (Jackson 1985:213). As early as 1955, Charles Abrams blasted it:

A government offering such bounty to builders and lenders could have required compliance with a nondiscrimination policy. Or the agency could at least have pursued a course of evasion, or hidden behind the screen of local autonomy. Instead, FHA adopted a racial policy that could well have been culled from the Nuremberg laws. From its inception FHA set itself up as the protector of the all white neighborhood. It sent its agents into the field to keep Negroes and other minorities from buying houses in white neighborhood. (1955:229; see also Gelfand 1975; Lief and Goering 1987)

The FHA believed in racial segregation. Throughout its history, it publicly and actively promoted restrictive covenants. Before the war, these forbade sale to Jews and Catholics as well as to African Americans. The deed to my house in Detroit had such a covenant, which theoretically prevented it from being sold to Jews or African Americans. Even after the Supreme Court ended legal enforcement of restrictive covenants in 1948, the FHA continued to encourage builders to write them against African Americans. FHA underwriting manuals openly insisted on racially homogeneous neighborhoods, and their loans were made only in white neighborhoods. I bought my Detroit house in 1972 from Jews who were leaving a largely African-American neighborhood. By that time, after the 1968 Fair Housing Act, restrictive covenants were a dead letter (although blockbusting by realtors was rapidly replacing it).

With the federal government behind them, virtually all developers refused to sell to African Americans. Palo Alto and Levittown, like most suburbs as late as 1960, were virtually all white. Out of 15,741 houses and 65,276 people, averaging 4.2 people per house, only 220 Levittowners, or 52 households, were "nonwhite." In 1958 Levitt announced publicly at a press conference to open his New Jersey development that he would not sell to black buyers. This caused a furor, since the state of New Jersey (but not the U.S. government) prohibited discrimination in federally subsidized housing. Levitt was sued and fought it, although he was ultimately persuaded by township ministers to integrate. There had been a white riot in his Pennsylvania development when a black family moved in a few years earlier. West Coast builder Joe Eichler had a policy of selling to any African Americans who could afford to buy. But his son pointed out that his father's clientele in more affluent Palo Alto was less likely to feel threatened. Eichler's clients tended to think of themselves as liberal, which was relatively easy to do because there were few African Americans in the Bay area, and fewer still could afford homes in Palo Alto (Eichler 1982; see also Center for the Study of Democratic Institutions 1964).

The result of these policies was that African Americans were totally shut out of the suburban boom. An article in *Harper's* described the housing available to black GIs. "On his way to the base each morning, Sergeant Smith passes an attractive air-conditioned, FHA-financed housing project. It was built for service families. Its rents are little more than the Smiths pay for their shack. And there are half-a-dozen vacancies, but none for Negroes" (qtd. in Foner 1974:195).

Where my family felt the seductive pull of suburbia, Marshall Berman's experienced the brutal push of urban renewal. In the Bronx in the 1950s, Robert Moses's Cross-Bronx Expressway erased "a dozen solid, settled, densely populated neighborhoods like our own; . . . something like 60,000 working- and lower-middle-class people, mostly Jews, but with many Italians, Irish and Blacks thrown in, would be thrown out of their homes. . . . For ten years, through the late 1950s and early 1960s, the center of the Bronx was pounded and blasted and smashed" (1982:292).

Urban renewal made postwar cities into bad places to live. At a physical level, urban renewal reshaped them, and federal programs brought private developers and public officials together to create downtown central business districts where there had formerly been a mix of manufacturing, commerce, and working-class neighborhoods. Manufacturing was scattered to the peripheries of the city, which were ringed and bisected by a national system of highways. Some working-class neighborhoods were bulldozed, but others remained (Greer 1965; Hartman 1975; Squires 1989). In Los Angeles, as in New York's Bronx, the postwar period saw massive freeway construction right through the heart of old working-class neighborhoods. In East Los Angeles and Santa Monica, Chicano and African-American communities were divided in half or blasted to smithereens by the highways bringing Angelenos to the new white suburbs, or to make way for civic monuments like Dodger Stadium (Pardo 1990; Social and Public Arts Resource Center 1990:80, 1983:12–13).

Urban renewal was the other side of the process by which Jewish and other working-class Euroimmigrants became middle class. It was the push to suburbia's seductive pull. The fortunate white survivors of urban renewal headed disproportionately for suburbia, where they could partake of prosperity and the good life. There was a reason for its attraction. It was often cheaper to buy in the suburbs than to rent in the city (Jackson 1985:206). Even Euroethnics and families who would be considered working class based on their occupations were able to buy into the emerging white suburban life style. And as Levittown indicates, they did so in increasing numbers, so that by 1966 50 percent of all workers and 75 percent of those under age forty nationwide lived in suburbs (Brody 1980:192). They too were considered middle class.

If the federal stick of urban renewal joined the FHA carrot of cheap mortgages to send masses of Euros to the suburbs, the FHA had a different kind of one-two punch for African-Americans. Segregation kept them out of the suburbs, and redlining made sure they could not buy or repair their homes in the neighborhoods where they were allowed to live. The FHA practiced systematic redlining. This was a system developed by its predecessor, the Home Owners Loan Corporation (HOLC), which in the 1930s developed an elaborate neighborhood rating system that placed the highest (green) value on all-white, middle-class neighborhoods, and the lowest (red) on racially nonwhite or mixed and working-class neighborhoods. High ratings meant high property values. The idea was that low property values in redlined neighborhoods made them bad investments. The FHA was, after all, created by and for banks and the housing industry. Redlining warned banks not to lend there, and the FHA would not insure mortgages in such neighborhoods. Redlining created a self-fulfilling prophecy. "With the assistance of local realtors and banks, it assigned one of the four ratings to every block in every city. The resulting information was then translated into the appropriate color [green, blue, yellow, and red] and duly recorded on secret 'Residential Security Maps' in local HOLC offices. The maps themselves were placed in elaborate 'City Survey Files,' which consisted of reports, questionnaires, and workpapers relating to current and future values of real estate" (Jackson 1985:199).[19]

FHA's and VA's refusal to guarantee loans in redlined neighborhoods made it virtually impossible for African Americans to borrow money for home improvement or purchase. Because these maps and surveys were quite secret, it took the 1960s Civil Rights movement to make these practices and their devastating consequences public. As a result, those who fought urban renewal or who sought to make a home in the urban ruins found themselves locked out of the middle class. They also faced an ideological assault that labeled their neighborhoods slums and called those who lived in them slum dwellers (Gans 1962).

The record is very clear that instead of seizing the opportunity to end institutionalized racism, the federal government did its best to shut and double seal the postwar window of opportunity in African Americans' faces. It consistently refused to combat segregation in the social institutions that were key for upward mobility: education, housing, and employment. Moreover, federal programs that were themselves designed to assist demobilized GIs and young families systematically discriminated against African Americans. Such programs reinforced white/nonwhite racial distinctions even as intrawhite racialization was falling out of fashion. This other side of the coin, that white men of northwestern and southeastern European ancestry were treated equally in theory and in practice with regard to the benefits they received, was part of the larger postwar whitening of Jews and other eastern and southern Europeans.

The myth that Jews pulled themselves up by their own bootstraps ignores the fact that it took federal programs to create the conditions whereby the abilities of Jews and other European immigrants could be recognized and rewarded rather than denigrated and denied. The GI Bill and FHA and VA mortgages were forms of affirmative action that allowed male Jews and other Euro-American men to become suburban homeowners and to get the training that allowed them—but not women vets or war workers—to become professionals, technicians, salesmen, and managers in a growing economy. Jews' and other white ethnics' upward mobility was the result of programs that allowed us to float on a rising economic tide. To African Americans, the government offered the cement boots of segregation, redlining, urban renewal, and discrimination.

Karen Brodkin Sacks    515

Those racially skewed gains have been passed across the generations, so that racial inequality seems to maintain itself "naturally," even after legal segregation ended. Today, in a shrinking economy where downward mobility is the norm, the children and grandchildren of the postwar beneficiaries of the economic boom have some precious advantages. For example, having parents who own their own homes or who have decent retirement benefits can make a real difference in young people's ability to take on huge college loans or to come up with a down payment for a house. Even this simple inheritance helps perpetuate the gap between whites and nonwhites. Sure Jews needed ability, but ability was not enough to make it. The same applies even more in today's long recession.

NOTES

This is a revised and expanded version of a paper published in *Jewish Currents* in June 1992 and delivered at the 1992 meetings of the American Anthropological Association in the session *Blacks and Jews, 1992: Reaching across the Cultural Boundaries* organized by Angela Gilliam. I would like to thank Emily Abel, Katya Gibel Azoulay, Edna Bonacich, Angela Gilliam, Isabelle Gunning, Valerie Matsumoto, Regina Morantz-Sanchez, Roger Sanjek, Rabbi Chaim Seidler-Feller, Janet Silverstein, and Eloise Klein Healy's writing group for uncovering wonderful sources and for critical readings along the way.

1. Indeed, Boasian and Du Boisian anthropology developed in active political opposition to this nativism; on Du Bois, see Harrison and Nonini 1992.

2. On immigrants as part of the industrial work force, see Steinberg 1989:36.

3. I thank Roger Sanjek for providing me with this source.

4. It was intended, as Davenport wrote to the president of the American Museum of Natural History, Henry Fairfield Osborne, as "an anthropological society . . . with a central governing body, self-elected and self-perpetuating, and very limited in members, and also confined to native Americans who are anthropologically, socially and politically sound, no Bolsheviki need apply" (Barkan 1991:67–68).

5. I thank Valerie Matsumoto for telling me about the Third case and Katya Gibel Azoulay for providing this information to me on the Virginia statute.

6. "The distinction between white and colored" has been "the only racial classification which has been carried through all the 15 censuses." "Colored" consisted of "Negroes" and "other races": Mexican, Indian, Chinese, Japanese, Filipino, Hindu, Korean, Hawaiian, Malay, Siamese, and Samoan. (U.S. Bureau of the Census, 1930:25, 26).

7. For why Jews entered colleges earlier than other immigrants, and for a challenge to views that attribute it to Jewish culture, see Steinberg 1989.

8. Although quotas on Jews persisted into the 1950s in some of the elite schools, they were much attenuated, as the postwar college-building boom gave the coup-de-grace to the gentleman's finishing school.

9. Steinberg (1989: chap. 5), challenging the belief that education was the source of Jewish mobility, cites Gutman's comparison of a working-class Jewish neighborhood on Cherry Street and a business and professional one on East Broadway in 1905, showing that children of Jewish workers did not go to college.

10. Between 1900 and 1930 New York City's population grew from 3.4 million to 6.9 million, and at both times immigrants and the children of immigrants were 80 percent of all white household heads (Moore 1992:270, n. 28).

11. Indeed, Jewish social scientists were prominent in creating this ideology of the United States as a meritocracy. Most prominent of course was Nathan Glazer, but among them also were Charles Silberman and Marshall Sklare.

12. I am indebted to Katya Gibel Azoulay for bringing this to my attention.

13. The belief was widespread that "the GI Bill . . . helped millions of families move into the middle class" (Nash et. al. 1986:885). A study that compares mobility among veterans and nonveterans provides a

kind of confirmation. In an unnamed small city in Illinois, Havighurst and his colleagues (1951) found no significant difference between veterans and nonveterans, but this was because apparently very few veterans used any of their GI benefits.

14. Interestingly, Steinberg (1989:149) shows that Jewish professionals tended to be children of small-business owners, but their Catholic counterparts tended to be children of workers.

15. None of the Jewish surveys seem to have asked what women were doing. Silberman (1985) claims that Jewish women stayed out of the labor force prior to the 1970s, but if my parents' circle is any indication, there were plenty of working professional women.

16. African Americans and Japanese Americans were the main target of war-time racism (see Murray 1992). By contrast, there were virtually no anti-German American or anti-Italian American policies in World War II (see Takaki 1989:357–406).

17. See Eichler 1982:5 for homeowning percentages; Jackson (1985:205) found an increase in families living in owner-occupied buildings, rising from 44 percent in 1934 to 63 percent in 1972; see Monkkonen 1988 on scarcity of mortgages; and Gelfand 1975, esp. chap. 6, on federal programs.

18. In the location of highway interchanges, as in the appraisal and inspection process, Eichler (1982) claims that large-scale builders often bribed and otherwise influenced the outcomes in their favor.

19. These ideas from the real estate industry were "codified and legitimated in 1930s work by University of Chicago sociologist Robert Park and real estate professor Homer Hoyt" (Jackson 1985:198–199).

## REFERENCES

Abrams, Charles. 1955. *Forbidden Neighbors: A Study of Prejudice in Housing.* New York: Harper.

Barkan, Elazar. 1991. *The Retreat of Scientific Racism: Changing Concepts of Race in Britain and the United States between the World Wars.* Cambridge: Cambridge University Press.

Berman, Marshall. 1982. *All That Is Solid Melts into Air: The Experience of Modernity.* New York: Simon and Schuster.

Binkin, Martin, and Mark J. Eitelberg. 1982. *Blacks and the Military.* Washington, D.C.: Brookings.

Bodnar, John. 1985. *The Transplanted: A History of Immigrants in Urban America.* Bloomington: Indiana University Press.

Brody, David. 1980. *Workers in Industrial America: Essays of the Twentieth Century Struggle.* New York: Oxford University Press.

Brown, Francis J. 1946. *Educational Opportunities for Veterans.* Washington, D.C.: Public Affairs Press, American Council on Public Affairs.

Carlson, Lewis H., and George A. Colburn. 1972. *In Their Place: White America Defines Her Minorities, 1850–1950.* New York: Wiley.

Center for the Study of Democratic Institutions. *Race and Housing: An Interview with Edward P. Eichler, President, Eichler Homes, Inc.* 1964. Santa Barbara: Center for the Study of Democratic Institutions.

Dalfiume, Richard M. 1969. *Desegregation of the U.S. Armed Forces: Fighting on Two Fronts, 1939–1953.* Columbia: University of Missouri Press.

Davis, Mike. 1990. *City of Quartz.* London: Verso.

Dobriner, William M. 1963. *Class in Suburbia.* Englewood Cliffs, N.J.: Prentice-Hall.

Eichler, Ned. 1982. *The Merchant Builders.* Cambridge, Mass.: MIT Press.

Fields, Barbara Jeanne. 1990. Slavery, Race, and Ideology in the United States of America. *New Left Review* 181:95–118.

Foner, Jack. 1974. *Blacks and the Military in American History: A New Perspective.* New York: Praeger.

Gans, Herbert. 1962. *The Urban Villagers.* New York: Free Press.

———. 1967. *The Levittowners.* New York: Pantheon.

Gelfand, Mark. 1975. *A Nation of Cities: The Federal Government and Urban America, 1933–1965.* New York: Oxford University Press.

Gerber, David. 1986a. Introduction. In *Anti-Semitism in American History*, ed. Gerber, 3–56.

———, ed. 1986b. *Anti-Semitism in American History.* Urbana: University of Illinois Press.

Glazer, Nathan, and Patrick Moynihan. 1963. *Beyond the Melting Pot: The Negroes, Puerto Ricans, Jews, Italians, and Irish of New York City.* Cambridge, Mass.: MIT Press.

Gordon, Milton. 1964. *Assimilation in American Life.* New York: Oxford University Press.

Greer, Scott. 1965. *Urban Renewal and American Cities.* Indianapolis: Bobbs-Merrill.

Harrison, Faye V., and Donald Nonini, eds. 1992 *Critique of Anthropology* (special issue on W.E.B. Du Bois and anthropology) 12(3).

Hartman, Chester. 1975. *Housing and Social Policy.* Englewood Cliffs, N.J.: Prentice-Hall.

Havighurst, Robert J., John W. Baughman, Walter H. Eaton, and Ernest W. Burgess. 1951. *The American Veteran Back Home: A Study of Veteran Readjustment.* New York: Longmans, Green.

Higham, John. 1955. *Strangers in the Land.* New Brunswick: Rutgers University Press.

Hurd, Charles. 1946. *The Veterans' Program: A Complete Guide to Its Benefits, Rights, and Options.* New York: McGraw-Hill.

Jackson, Kenneth T. 1985. *Crabgrass Frontier: The Suburbanization of the United States.* New York: Oxford University Press.

Johnson, Jesse J. 1967. *Ebony Brass: An Autobiography of Negro Frustration amid Aspiration.* New York: Frederick.

Karabel, Jerome. 1984. Status-Group Struggle, Organizational Interests, and the Limits of Institutional Autonomy. *Theory and Society* 13:1–40.

Kessler-Harris, Alice. 1982. *Out to Work: A History of Wage-Earning Women in the United States.* New York: Oxford University Press.

Lief, Beth J., and Susan Goering. 1987. The Implementation of the Federal Mandate for Fair Housing. In *Divided Neighborhoods,* ed. Gary A. Tobin, 227–267.

Martyn, Byron Curti. 1979. Racism in the U.S.: A History of Anti-Miscegenation Legislation and Litigation. Ph.D. diss., University of Southern California.

Monkkonen, Eric H. 1988. *American Becomes Urban.* Berkeley and Los Angeles: University of California Press.

Moore, Deborah Dash. 1992. On the Fringes of the City: Jewish Neighborhoods in Three Boroughs. In *The Landscape of Modernity: Essays on New York City, 1900–1940,* ed. David Ward and Oliver Zunz, 252–272. New York: Russell Sage.

Mosch, Theodore R. 1975. *The GI Bill: A Breakthrough in Educational and Social Policy in the United States.* Hicksville, N.Y.: Exposition.

Murray, Alice Yang. 1992. Japanese Americans, Redress, and Reparations: A Study of Community, Family, and Gender, 1940–1990. Ph.D. diss., Stanford University.

Nalty, Bernard C., and Morris J. MacGregor, eds. 1981. *Blacks in the Military: Essential Documents.* Wilmington, Del.: Scholarly Resources.

Nash, Gary B., Julie Roy Jeffrey, John R. Howe, Allen F. Davis, Peter J. Frederick, and Allen M. Winkler. 1986. *The American People: Creating a Nation and a Society.* New York: Harper and Row.

Pardo, Mary. 1990. Mexican-American Women Grassroots Community Activists: "Mothers of East Los Angeles." *Frontiers* 11:1–7.

*Postwar Jobs for Veterans.* 1945. Annals of the American Academy of Political and Social Science 238 (March).

Saxton, Alexander. 1971. *The Indispensible Enemy.* Berkeley and Los Angeles: University of California Press.

———. 1990. *The Rise and Fall of the White Republic.* London: Verso.

Schoener, Allon. 1967. *Portal to America: The Lower East Side, 1870–1925.* New York: Holt, Rinehart and Winston.

Sifry, Micah. 1993. Anti-Semitism in America. *Nation,* January 25, 92–99.

Silberman, Charles. 1985. *A Certain People: American Jews and Their Lives Today.* New York: Summit.

Sklare, Marshall. 1971. *America's Jews.* New York: Random House.

Social and Public Arts Resource Center. 1990. *Signs from the Heart: California Chicano Murals.* Venice, Calif.: Social and Public Art Resource Center.

——. 1983. *Walking Tour and Guide to the Great Wall of Los Angeles.* Venice, Calif.: Social and Public Arts Resource Center.

Sowell, Thomas. 1981. *Ethnic America: A History.* New York: Basic.

Squires, Gregory D., ed. 1989. *Unequal Partnerships: The Political Economy of Urban Redevelopment in Postwar America.* New Brunswick: Rutgers University Press.

Steinberg, Stephen. 1989. *The Ethnic Myth: Race, Ethnicity, and Class in America.* 2d ed. Boston: Beacon.

Synott, Marcia Graham. 1986. Anti-Semitism and American Universities: Did Quotas Follow the Jews? In *Anti-Semitism in American History,* ed. David A. Gerber, 233–274.

Takaki, Ronald. 1989. *Strangers from a Different Shore.* Boston: Little, Brown.

Tobin, Gary A., ed. 1987. *Divided Neighborhoods: Changing Patterns of Racial Segregation.* Beverly Hills: Sage.

U.S. Bureau of the Census. 1930. *Fifteenth Census of the United States.* Vol. 2. Washington, D.C.: U.S. Government Printing Office.

——. 1940. *Sixteenth Census of the United States,* vol. 2. Washington, D.C.: U.S. Government Printing Office.

Walker, Olive. 1970. The Windsor Hills School Story. *Integrated Education: Race and Schools* 8(3): 4–9.

Weiss, Marc A. 1987. *The Rise of the Community Builders: The American Real Estate Industry and Urban Land Planning.* New York: Columbia University Press.

Willenz, June A. 1983. *Women Veterans: America's Forgotten Heroines.* New York: Continuum.

Wynn, Neil A. 1976. *The Afro-American and the Second World War.* London: Elek.

# Large Jewish Organization in Controversy
B'nai B'rith Members Disagree on Negro Issue

WASHINGTON—ANP—The nation's leading Jewish organization B'nai B'rith—has been shaken by a splitting fight over the Negro question. Southern delegates to the triennial national convention hinted at bolting the organization it was revealed last week.

The Dixie position can be summed up as follows: B'nai B'rith should stick solely to Jewish problems and leave the Negro civil rights issue to other groups. The Negro question in the South is "embarrassing" and is making some Dixie Jews the target of white supremacy pressure. In fact the civil rights issue should be soft peddled nationally.

This group is a minority within the national organization but it is highly vocal and is supported by several northern leaders.

Number one target of the Dixie conservative bloc is the Anti-Defamation league which is sponsored by the national organization. The league has done a Herculean job in exposing and fighting the enemies of the Negro people in the south. It drew international praise by exposing the race-hate Columbians in Atlanta several years ago.

At the same time advocates of a strong civil rights program have leveled serious charges against the southern-conservative wing of the organization for "embarrassing" Jews throughout the world.

One example is the invitation to Gov. Herman Talmadge of Georgia to be honored guest at a recent meeting of Southwest Georgia B'nai B'rith lodges.

Another target of liberal fire is Rabbi Arthur Lelyyeld of New York, national director of Hillel foundations—a B'nai B'rith college student organization. He is charged with attempting to discourage Jewish students from fighting the exclusion of Negroes from George Washington university in Washington. The university and its president, Floyd H. Marvin, have been under pressure for the past several years because of the university's lily-white policy.

The B'nai B'rith campus organization joined Negro and other groups in fighting this policy, and consequently was threatened with extinction by President Marvin. This action was labelled an anti-Semitic move in the true sense of the word, since he took no such drastic action against other protesting groups. Rep. Arthur Klein of New York, blasted the President for his "Herr Dr. Goebbels" conduct. A move is underway in Congress to withdraw federal funds from the institution.

In spite of all this Rabbi Lelyyeld pulled an "Uncle Tom" act by praising President Marvin as a fair-minded administrator.

At Norman Okla. some members of B'nai B'rith say they have been embarrassed by

Originally printed in *The Call* (Kansas City, Missouri), March 31, 1950. NAACP Papers, Library of Congress, Manuscript Division, Washington, D.C.

the actions of the Hillel student movement at the University of Oklahoma. Jewish students there are some of the most consistent fighters against segregation in education. A Ku Klux Klan fiery cross was burned recently on the lawn in front of Hillel house.

Joining the southerners are northern and western Jews "who would like to hide the fact that they are Jews", is the way one Jewish youth put it. Some take the position "I'm doing all right in the south as things stand, but too much talk about equal rights for Negroes will put me on the spot", he explained.

However, this issue has not been resolved in B'nai B'rith and some Jewish liberals are taking the position that the Dixie Northern conservative bloc should be permitted to take a walk for the good of the national organization.

# Herbert L. Wright to Youth Leaders

Dear Youth Leader:

Several weeks ago a group of national youth leaders got together in New York City to discuss ways and means by which youth and youth serving organizations could initiate and direct a coordinated attack on the infamous McCarran-Walter Immigration Bill which as you will recall is biased against Jewish and Negro migrants.

The response which we have received from youth and youth serving organizations in attendance at these preliminary meetings has been exceedingly good; however, we are desirous of securing as large and as representative a body of youth leaders as possible to insure the success of our action.

We are therefore extending an invitation to you to attend the next meeting of the Young Citizens Council on the McCarran-Walter Act which will be held on Thursday, December 18th at 8:00 PM at the Wendell Willkie Memorial Building (Freedom House), 20 West 40th Street, New York City. This meeting will be open only to persons receiving this special invitation. If you are unable to attend please call me at LOngacre 3-6890.

No action will be taken (at this meeting) which shall be binding on the organizations or individuals in attendance at said meeting.

Sincerely yours,
Herbert L. Wright
Youth Secretary NAACP

### A REPORT ON THE INITIAL MEETINGS

The idea of creating some kind of a national structure which would stimulate and coordinate young adult activity on the McCarran-Walter Immigration Act was developed during a series of informal chats (mostly on the telephone) between various people in young adult organizations. These people felt that there was a vital need to inform American youth and all the American people on what the McCarran-Walter Immigration Act really is and why many of the basic parts of the Act are inconsistent with democratic principles. There was a deep feeling that young adults, through their organizations and individually, had an obligation to initiate widespread discussion on the Act and to create united action for the realization of the fruits of this discussion.

An informal meeting was called for November 26 in order to sample the opinions of members of religious, educational and political groups. Because the people at this

In 1952 Herbert L. Wright was youth secretary of the NAACP.
This letter and report were sent to black, Jewish, Christian and other youth groups, December 9, 1952.
NAACP Papers, Box II E 61, Library of Congress, Manuscript Division, Washington, D.C.

meeting felt that a larger meeting would be worthwhile, a second preliminary meeting was held on December 4th. At either or both of these gatherings there were members from CCUN, NAACP, NSA, YMCA, YWCA, Newman Clubs, Young Democrats, Young Adult Council, SDA and NJYC (all came in an unofficial capacity except in the case of some of the political organizations).

At these two preliminary meetings a discussion took place on the possibilities of joint action on the McCarran-Walter Act. From the outset there seemed to be agreement that a definite need existed for united activity and at the conclusion of the second session everyone agreed that it would be worthwhile to call a larger and more formal meeting of all young adult leaders who could make a New York City meeting. Herb Wright of NAACP was elected provisional chairman, with the responsibility of arranging the next meeting. The second session concluded with a feeling of enthusiasm and with a feeling of determination that young adults could not afford to remain either silent or disorganized on a matter which affects so greatly the fundamental principles upon which democratic life must be built.

# Southern Jewish Views on Segregation

## REPORT OF A DISCUSSION ON APPROACHES
## TOWARD MEETING THE PROBLEM

*Miami Beach*

There are stirrings among Southern Jews on the segregation issue. A consideration of the role and responsibility in implementation of the Supreme Court desegregation decision was the subject of a stimulating symposium at the Workmen's Circle Lyceum in Miami Beach on June 3. About 125 people, young and old, Yiddish and English speaking, gathered to listen and take part in the symposium.

Mr. Emanuel Muravchik of New York, national field director for the Jewish Labor Committee, led off the discussion by stressing the importance of the desegregation decision to America's prestige as a democratic nation. He traced the organizational connection between the White Citizens Councils and anti-Semitic groups and emphasized the need for Jewish groups to support the Supreme Court decision. He pointed to the significance of the decision to the Jewish people both as a matter of self-interest and moral principle based on the Bible as well as on the U.S. Constitution. He criticized three types of response by Southern Jews: 1) "Join 'em"—and in this connection he stated that the vice president of the White Citizens Council of Georgia is a Jew. Such conduct he condemned. 2) "Speak out"—this he criticized as ineffective and self-defeating. 3) "Hide"—this, the most prevalent attitude, he said, is as useless as "walking down the street wearing blinders."

The solution he offered was "to do sometimes publicly, always privately, that which will advance desegregation." Don't be first, don't act alone, but join with other groups moving in the desired direction. Mr. Muravchik, however, singled out the special responsibility of the City of Miami Beach, which he called "the most Jewish city in the U.S.," to set an example in the South with reference to desegregation on local bus lines, in residence, etc.

While all speakers were in complete agreement as to the Jewish people's moral responsibility to help put the Supreme Court decisions into practice, there was sharp disagreement as to approach and tactics. Rabbi Rosenberg, a member of the American Jewish Congress, made a straightforward and eloquent demand that there be no double-talk, that Jewish leaders and organizations speak up with courage and state publicly what they are now saying behind closed doors. He called on them to stop acting

Esther Levine was a contributor to *Jewish Life*.

Originally published in *Jewish Life: A Progressive Monthly* 10, no. 118 (August 1956): 20–23, 34.

like *"golus Yidden"* (alien Jews) but as first class citizens of the South and of the U.S. Jews, he said, should not hang back one step behind other groups advancing on this issue, such as the Catholics and a number of Protestant churches.

### Southern American Jewish Committee and B'nai B'rith View

A totally different approach was taken by Mr. Seymour Samet of the American Jewish Committee and Mr. Seidman of the B'nai B'rith. Apparently both men have lived in the South much longer and their organizations have been established in the South for many years. While taking note of the fact that the mob hatred directed against Negroes has strong anti-Semitic overtones, they nevertheless emphasized the tremendous economic and other pressures being exerted against the Jewish minority, especially in deep Southern communities where some Jewish businessmen were coerced into joining the WCC under threat of economic boycott.

Mr. Seidman pointed out that in many Southern cities the WCC's are composed of some of the most highly respected public officials and community leaders. He said that many Southern Jews are Americans and Southerners first and share their neighbors' white supremacist views. He defended the B'nai B'rith record on desegregation, pointing out that it had been party to the court case which helped bring about the Supreme Court decision. "While we are in favor of the Supreme Court decision," he said, "we do not believe the Jews of the South are expendable." He explained that there are quiet, behind-the-scenes ways in which Jews could exert their influence without placing the Southern Jewish people in danger of harm and destruction.

His major solution was *education.* In that connection he mentioned the 25 brotherhood meetings held in the Greater Miami area last February, with participation of Negro groups and leaders, which attracted white audiences of both Jews and non- Jews. He claimed that this type of educational activity was responsible for the absence of violence in Dade County since the Supreme Court decision. He also warned against the Miami Jewish community running too far ahead of the rest of the state and thus nullifying its influence. He cited this example: when Congressman Dante Fascell of Miami, the only Florida congressman to refuse to sign the Southern Manifesto, was sent a telegram of greeting and support by the Florida Anti-Defamation League, the Jacksonville branch of the League asked to be disassociated from that message.

The brief comments from the audience on the whole expressed support for a more vigorous and speedy enforcement of the Supreme Court decision. Included among the speakers from the floor were two officials of the local ILGWU. They spoke of labor's stake in resisting the WCC, some of whose leaders are among the most outspoken labor-baiters and supporters of the state right-to-work laws. One trade unionist referred to the struggle now going on in connection with the seating of a Negro delegate to the Dade County Central Labor Union [see JEWISH LIFE, July issue, p. 6]. He thought there would have been no problem if the leaders of the local involved had not made a big splash in the press about it before taking it up at the CLU. The trade unionists deplored the fact that some misguided members of the labor movement have been misled into support of the WCC.

## Heroism or Education Is Not Enough

The symposium provided much food for thought. It left this writer more deeply convinced that there must be a special approach to Southern Jewry to help it find its rightful place in the struggle for equality and justice in the South. The forthright stand of Rabbi Rosenberg, for all its sincerity and earnestness, will not begin to reach the majority of Jews in the deep South. They will regard it as unrealistic because it does not take into account the special conditions in the South. Heroism alone is not enough. Even those who are ready to make sacrifices will want to know what results their sacrifices may achieve.

But neither will the solution be found in the super-cautious, super-gradual approach of "education" proposed by the American Jewish Committee and the Anti-Defamation League of the B'nai B'rith.

Why? First of all, their concept of education is very narrow. If 25 brotherhood meetings once a year is their idea of education, it is a very slender reed for a great big problem like desegregation to lean upon. How many lynchings and brutalities will be perpetrated, how many classes of Negro children will be denied full schooling opportunities, how many classes of white children will go through school without the faintest understanding of genuine democracy while this thin, slow process of education is going on?

Education is good and is needed in all adult white community organizations 52 weeks a year. There should be education on the proud history of the Negro people in the U.S., especially the South; education on the contributions of white Southerners, including Jews, to the abolitionist movement; education on the first Georgia Constitution under Oglethorpe, which outlawed slavery back in 1775. Let the ADL of Jacksonville know that their public school system first got its start owing to the tireless efforts of one Jonathan Gibbs, a Negro superintendant of schools for the State of Florida in 1872–1874. And teach the Jews of the South that Judah P. Benjamin, treasurer of the Confederacy, was not the only prominent Jew in the South. The ADL has a splendid research organization which can help seek out and publicize all that is liberal in the history of Southern Jewry.

Education should also include the lessons of current history through which the present generation has lived. There is hardly a family in the United States, including the South, that didn't have a brother or a son in the armies that fought Hitler and Hitlerism. To the Jewish families, shocked by the mass murder of six million of their people, this fight had a special meaning. Shouldn't the ADL's educational effort include a comparison between fascism in Germany and its counterpart, Eastlandism, in the South? Surely the Jewish collaborators of Hitler are despised by the masses of Southern Jews. Every one knows that silence and appeasement of Hitlerism only brought destruction to the appeasers and to those who thought they could save themselves by silence and non-resistance. These lessons written in blood cannot be overlooked in any course for the enlightenment of Southern Jewry in its struggle against Eastland's brand of fascism.

## National Jewish Action Is Needed

Furthermore, education means little if it doesn't lead to action. It is hard to understand this phrase: "We do not believe the Jews of the South are expendable." Should we then, for the sake of a false security, condone a Jew's surrendering to the white supremacists? Should we consider the threat of boycott a valid reason for knuckling under? Is there no remedy other than a weak dose of education? Does this phrase mean that all efforts at resistance are wasteful? That any struggle against the white supremacists must inevitably end in failure and destruction?

But this kind of reasoning contradicts both the lessons of the heroic history of the Jews in all past ages and the lessons current history is teaching us today. How is it that the Negro people of Mississippi, who are much poorer, were able to organize to withstand a boycott? *Cannot the national organizations of the Jewish people, whose resources have been contributed generously to many worthy causes, plan and organize to resist white supremacist pressure?* To engage in principled struggle, with mass support and wise and courageous leadership, is not being "expendable." In the long run, it's the only defense, the only guarantee of success.

This brings to mind another puzzling question about the approach and method of the ADL and AJ Committee: Why this constant stress on doing things quietly and behind the scenes? There are thousands of Jews throughout the South who are not only concerned but eager to do what they can to win equality for all. They constitute a powerful reserve which remains passive for lack of leadership. The quiet methods used involve a few top leaders who, with all their brilliance and sincere efforts, cannot possibly have a monopoly on the energy and talent that lies dormant among the people. What is more, the Jewish population, without public guidance, is bound to be overwhelmed by the seeming strength of the white supremacists because the hate-mongers seize the headlines and use them for their scare purposes while the Jewish leaders keep silent.

The leadership of the Jewish organizations in the South could make a tremendous contribution to enforce the Supreme Court decision if it were to guide the Jewish people to join hands with other liberal, religious, civic, labor and Negro groups, basing themselves on the best, rather than on the most backward traditions of the South, taking the lead wherever possible, never hesitating to exercise their full constitutional rights.

Furthermore, areas that have special reasons and opportunities to move ahead more quickly toward desegregation—like Miami Beach and Miami—should make special efforts not only to set an example but to extend aid and cooperation, both moral, organizational and material, to the Jewish communities in other parts of the South, in order to develop united resistance against the white supremacist scourge.

# One Episode in Southern Jewry's Response to Desegregation
An Historical Memoir

In July 1954, I was sent to Richmond to take over the Virginia–North Carolina office of the Anti-Defamation League (ADL) of B'nai B'rith. The office was one of the smaller operations of the national organizations, which had its headquarters in New York. It was a good place to send an inexperienced young professional to get his seasoning. In coming South, I was entering a society that was very distant from my own background. An American-born product of the Eastern European immigration tide early in the century, I had grown up and passed most of my life in the Orthodox Jewish world of Williamsburg, Brooklyn, where Jews were, in fact, a majority group. I had attended Brooklyn College, a free municipal college, and took part in the liberal-left politics that characterized the student body of that period. I was part of the generation so aptly characterized by novelist Michael Gold as "Jews Without Money," idealistic and not a little unworldly. It was following brief stints working with a housing association and with the B'nai B'rith public relations department in Washington, D.C., and on the recommendation of a Williamsburg friend and neighbor on the staff of ADL, that I was offered the post.

## RICHMOND JEWRY: SHABBAT IN SHOCKOE

In coming to the former capital of the Confederacy, I found myself plunged into an old Jewish community of eight thousand whose roots went back to the Revolutionary War. Even more perplexing for a person with my background, I was, in effect, the public relations arm of that community and of small-town Jewry in two states. I was the only full-time Jewish community relations, or "defense," official. ADL, in fact, maintained the only professionally staffed operation in this field in the South. Much of the important leadership of the Jewish community and of ADL at this time centered around Reform Congregation Beth Ahabah, which had loyally supported the Confederate cause during the Civil War by sending many of its sons into the army.[1] Current Jewish leaders—men like Irving May, chairman of the board of Thalhimer's, a department store; William Thalhimer; W. Harry Schwarzchild, Jr., president of the Central National Bank; and Samuel Binswanger, the head of Binswanger Glass Co.—were closely associated with the civic as well as business life of the community. According to the historian of Richmond Jewry, the city was free of the kind of anti-Semitism that had erupted in many Northern cities prior to World War II, but nonetheless its Jews, like their brethren

In 1981, Murray Friedman was Middle Atlantic States director of the American Jewish Committee. Originally published in *American Jewish Archives* 33, no. 2 (1981): 170–83. Copyright © 1981, American Jewish Archives. Reprinted with permission of the American Jewish Archives, Cincinnati, Ohio.

in most small communities, were deeply, almost acutely conscious of their relations with their neighbors and worried about anti-Semitism.[2] There were a small number of areas like Windsor Farms and College Hills where Jews could not buy property, the elite country club was restricted, and a number of the resorts in Virginia Beach, including the Cavalier Club, were barred to them. Many Richmond Jewish leaders served on the advisory board of, or were close to, the Virginia Anti-Defamation League—their "insurance policy," as Binswanger, its chairman for many years, was fond of saying. He and other important Richmond Jews were members also of the American Council for Judaism, which was opposed to Jews being closely identified with the State of Israel as fostering an image of "dual loyalty" in the minds of other Americans. If the "melting pot," or cultural assimilation, was the basic philosophical model of post–World War II Jewry, Southern Jews were its most prototypical exponents.

The Richmond ADL office was part of a national organization which had broadened the scope of its activities beyond dealing with prejudice and discrimination against Jews since its founding in 1913 and had become concerned about minority rights generally. It had filed an amicus curiae brief before the Supreme Court calling for an end to racial segregation in the famous Schools cases. Although at this time there were no public opinion polls measuring Jewish attitudes in Richmond, one observer who studied the feelings of Southern Jews in the early sixties reports that they "were significantly more liberal, equalitarian and desegregationist in respect to blacks" than their neighbors.[3] I found few outright Jewish segregationists in Virginia, although there were more in the Deep South. Part of the price Jews paid for the high degree of acceptance and the success they had achieved was that they had to conform to the region's racial patterns.

The major thrust of a Southern ADL operation governed by a local advisory board was to deal with incidents of anti-Semitism and discrimination. Just prior to my arrival, the Richmond office had been successful in obtaining passage through the state legislature of a law, aimed primarily at resorts in Virginia Beach, banning discriminatory religious advertising. This was one of the first modern civil rights laws in the South. The office also distributed films, film-strips, pamphlets, comic books, car-cards, blotters, bookmarks, and other items to church, civic, and labor groups throughout the region. These provided information on Jews and Jewish holidays, as well as scientific findings on religion and race, and made appeals to the essential oneness of the human family.

The Richmond office sponsored each summer, with the local office of the National Conference of Christians and Jews, an all-day Youth Seminar on Human Relations which brought together black and white high school seniors selected by their principals to discuss how groups could learn to live together. In an almost totally segregated society, this was one of the few places where the races could come together to discuss common problems. The seminar, however, had the backing of important business and civic leaders who probably saw it as their modest effort to prepare for the racial changes they knew were coming. My office carefully monitored, also, acts of violence directed against Jews and blacks. I had a cordial relationship with Virginius Dabney, the editor of the *Richmond Times Dispatch*, which was built, largely, on this issue. While the newspaper supported segregation, Dabney, who earlier in his career had won a Pulitzer Prize for fighting the Klan, would respond vigorously with editorials condemning racial violence when Binswanger or I brought to his attention such incidents as a cross burning on the lawn of a segregation critic or the growth of Klan activities near the Virginia-North Carolina border.

It is worth noting in this respect that much of the historical discussion of the role of Southern Jews in civil rights struggles at this time has focused on individual rabbis, including such courageous figures as Emmett Frank of Arlington, Virginia, Perry Nussbaum of Jackson, Mississippi, and Charles Mantinband of Alabama, Mississippi, and Texas.[4] Prior to the Freedom Rides and marches of the 1960's, however, some of the major work was done by Southern ADL offices and their lay advisory boards. An example is the work of the Atlanta office under Alexander F. Miller, who helped to develop and lobby through state legislatures, with other ADL offices, laws requiring unmasking of the Klan. Reducing the Klan's anonymity struck an important blow at its ability to terrorize whites and blacks. There was, however, no direct ADL involvement in school desegregation cases following the 1954 Supreme Court decision. These were developed by local NAACP attorneys in cooperation with the Legal Defense Fund of the NAACP nationally. As local opposition to court decisions mounted, most Southern Jews hoped to ride out the storm and the social adjustments they believed inevitable.

## MASSIVE RESISTANCE

By the summer of 1958, however, it was becoming difficult to do so. Since 1954, a major massive resistance effort had gotten underway to overturn or at least minimize the effect of the Supreme Court decision. Virginia was one of the first states where this effort reached a climax. Nine public schools in Warren County, Charlottesville, and Norfolk were about to lock their doors to thirteen thousand white children in the fall under state legislation which required such school closings and the cutting off of funds when black children were enrolled. Faced with this, Governor J. Lindsay Almond was shortly to announce to the Virginia Education Association a no-quarter policy. "I shall never willingly witness or become a party to the destruction of education by the mixing of the races in the classrooms," he declared.[5]

Massive resistance, as this policy was called, had become associated with a series of bombings and attempted bombings of synagogues throughout the South by the Ku Klux Klan and local citizens councils. Increasingly, anti-Semitic as well as anti-black agitators were coming into Virginia or distributing pamphlets and other literature attacking Jews generally and charging that they were the real force behind integration. One such magazine, the newly established *Virginian,* published in Newport News, was circulated throughout the state. A local version of the citizens council movement, the Defenders of State Sovereignty and Individual Liberties, had come into existence, and while it was, in the gentlemanly Virginia tradition, more moderate in tone and activities than its neighbors to the south, the group nevertheless made it clear that it viewed with strong disfavor any deviation from the pattern of resistance to desegregation.[6] An increasing part of ADL's work in the South, therefore, was now being given over to dealing with the anti-Semitic spillover from the desegregation fight.

Finally, as the white-black confrontation deepened, a series of legislative investigations and harassment efforts directed against "race-mixing" groups like the Urban

League, human relations councils, and labor unions were initiated, culminating in the enactment in Virginia and other states of a series of "anti-NAACP" bills. These barred efforts to "influence, encourage, or promote litigation relating to racial activities."[7] Jewish groups feared that they would be included in the sweep of this legislation. The *Virginian* had, in fact, launched a series of sharp attacks on ADL and on me personally for what it alleged was "a mongrelization pitch" contained in ADL materials and activities.[8]

In the massive resistance movement underway, the *Richmond News Leader* and its then little-known editor, James J. Kilpatrick, played a critical role. The Commonwealth at first reacted with mildness to the 1954 decision. However, in subsequent months, led by United States Senator Harry Byrd and the powerful Byrd machine, Virginia had resolved, in the words of the influential Senator, to halt the expansion of federal power and reverse the trend toward "totalitarian government." On November 21, 1955, basing himself on a pamphlet written by a Virginia county attorney, Kilpatrick launched a major editorial campaign calling for legal resistance through a doctrine called "interposition." In the *News Leader* of that date and in subsequent issues, Kilpatrick and his associates examined the nature of the federal union. They argued that the United States was, in fact, a compact of states which had not surrendered their powers when they formed a national government. The powers delegated to the latter "are painstakingly enumerated," the *News Leader* declared, and all other powers belong to the sovereign states. Since the Supreme Court had exceeded its authority, a state could interpose its authority between its citizens and the national government, Kilpatrick argued. In a style for which he would later become well known as a nationally syndicated conservative columnist and television personality, Kilpatrick built his editorials on references to the ideas of Jefferson, Madison, and John C. Calhoun and reprinted alongside them states' rights documents beginning with the Kentucky and Virginia Resolutions of 1778 and a series of public letters written for a Richmond newspaper in 1833.

This campaign was what one historian of massive resistance, Numan V. Bartley, later called "constitutional mumbo jumbo," since at the very least, the Civil War had put an end to these ideas. However, Kilpatrick's arguments satisfied a deep need of many white Southerners. By mid-1957, the *News Leader*'s editorials and historical documents, which had been reproduced in pamphlets and other forms, were widely circulated, and eight Southern state legislatures had approved resolutions of interposition. In addition, Texas endorsed the doctrine and North Carolina and Tennessee officially protested against the high court's decision.[9] Kilpatrick had become by 1958 the intellectual leader and, in some respects, the architect of the massive resistance movement in the South.

### ANTI-SEMITISM WITHOUT ANTI-SEMITES?

On July 7, 1958, the *News Leader* published an editorial entitled, "Anti-Semitism in the South." Noting that Southern Jews were "dismayed at manifestations of anti-Semitism in recent months," it suggested that they ask themselves what was prompting this deplorable violence in an area that had "no tradition of anti-Semitism" and urged them to consider the possibility that the Anti-Defamation League was responsible. "By deliberately involving itself in the controversy over school segregation, this branch of B'nai B'rith is identifying all Jewry with the advocacy of compulsory integration," the editorial declared. It pointed out that the previous week the Richmond regional office had sent "some pro-integration literature" to an NAACP workshop in Charlottesville, one of the cities preparing to close its schools. This would obviously stir up anti-Semitism, whereupon the "ADL can lustily combat it by declaring, 'Look how much anti-Semitism there is.'" The *News Leader* conceded ADL's right "to interest itself in any phase of bigotry," but such militancy as the regional office had manifested in sending the materials to the Charlottesville workshop invited "retaliation," the editorial warned. It concluded by asking "some of the South's many esteemed and influential Jews" what possible service they could find "in a Jewish organization that foments hostility to Jews."

As with Kilpatrick's massive resistance efforts, this editorial touched a vital nerve in Richmond and in the South. Many whites sincerely felt they knew blacks and were unable to understand how people whose political skills and intelligence they tended to minimize could be seeking to overturn the racial system that had existed for so many years. After all, their maids and employees had assured them that they had nothing to do with the NAACP. Whites were largely unaware of the new mood among poor as well as middle-class blacks who had become increasingly restless with the discrimination and disadvantage they faced. They knew little of the new class of black lawyers and young people graduated by Howard University and other black institutions who were intellectually and philosophically prepared to challenge the system that prescribed for them a role as permanent second-class citizens.[10] Since blacks could not be responsible for the agitation for change, there must be others who were behind these efforts, many whites felt. Though Kilpatrick had limited his attack to the Richmond ADL office, he provided a plausible answer to the problem that had been bothering so many Southern whites. "Jewish agitators" and organizations like ADL were the force behind the demand for integration.

A strict constitutionalist and libertarian philosophically, Kilpatrick was deeply angered by what he felt to be the usurpation of authority by the high court.[11] In mounting a massive resistance campaign he sought to rally all Southerners in opposition. He had skillfully helped to build a movement that was sweeping across the South, but there are indications that he did not want it to get out of hand. Two months before his attack upon ADL, the *News Leader* carried an editorial, "Conservatism and the Lunatic Fringe," in which he warned about the dangers.[12] To his credit, Kilpatrick had editorially opposed the "anti-NAACP" bills as a violation of freedom of expression. The editorial attack on ADL, however, was taken by many Jews as a not-so-subtle warning to Southern Jews generally: if they involved themselves in the desegregation fight, they would be visited with anti-Semitism and even violence.

The editorial was soon being widely circulated and became a subject of discussion throughout the South. The director of the ADL in Atlanta, on July 23, sent a copy to the national office; it had been forwarded to him from Nashville, he reported, and seemed to be "an offset job indicating heavy distribution." He noted that copies were circulating in Atlanta and felt they would soon be "springing up like mushrooms in the rainy weather we have been having."[13] The theme of Kilpatrick's piece was picked up by segregation supporters. When Rabbi Emmet A. Frank, in a Yom Kippur sermon from his pulpit in Arlington, Virginia, criticized the Byrd machine and massive resistance, the

Arlington chapter of the Defenders demanded that the Jewish community of northern Virginia condemn his slanderous statements and innuendos, warning that they "will cause irreparable damage to the hitherto friendly relations between Jews and Christians. . . ." Shortly thereafter, the Unitarian church in Arlington had to be emptied as a result of a bomb threat just before Rabbi Frank was to occupy the pulpit.[14]

The editorial struck with enormous force in the tiny Jewish community of Richmond. The Virginia ADL Board had sought carefully to negotiate the treacherous shoals of the desegregation controversy since 1954. Six months after the Supreme Court handed down its historic decision, the board adopted a resolution calling upon the national organization in New York to "take no position which would interfere with the right of a state advisory board and local ADL units to deal with this problem according to conditions in the area of local jurisdiction." It accepted the high court's decision as "the law of the land" and urged creation of fact-finding groups on how to implement that decision in cooperation with other organizations of an "inter-faith character." In November 1957, as the segregation battle heated up, the Virginia Board adopted another resolution narrowing its focus somewhat. This held that "in accordance with the religious principles of Judaism, the Anti-Defamation League of B'nai B'rith in the Commonwealth of Virginia affirms that its basic policies are to combat anti-Semitism and improve interfaith relations."[15]

The Virginia Board, through its chairman, Sam Binswanger, had regularly protested against certain national ADL policies and tactics—an instance being the latter's role in the Levittown, Pa. racial collisions. Binswanger argued that ADL should confine its role to combating anti-Semitism and to positive programming in the field of interfaith understanding. While he recognized that it would be difficult to accomplish this, since racial and religious animosities were often intertwined, he believed that every effort should be made. Several months before the *News Leader* editorial, the Virginia ADL Executive Committee had called for a meeting of Southern and national ADL leadership. Held in Atlanta in May, the discussions revolved mainly around bombings and attempted bombings of synagogues in the South. The Virginia group came away from these sessions, as a local report later noted, "with the definite feeling . . . that ADL leadership was sympathetic to the position of the Southern Jew in this crisis situation. . . ." One result of the Atlanta meetings was that in June a number of ADL staff from other parts of the country were deployed briefly to Southern offices, including Richmond, on an emergency basis.

The day after the *News Leader* editorial, Binswanger convened a meeting of the key Richmond Jewish leaders to examine the materials discussed in the editorial and the advisability of continuing to distribute those relating to race. Phone conversations were held by Binswanger and Harry Schwarzschild the following day with Benjamin R. Epstein, national director of ADL in New York, the latter urging a local response to the editorial. Both men demurred, emphasizing "the political nature of the current situation in Richmond" and "rising tensions."[16]

On July 9, a full meeting of the Virginia ADL Executive Committee was held, attended by Lester Waldman as representative of the national ADL office. Waldman brought with him the draft of a letter of response, and after a long, inconclusive discussion it was agreed to hold another meeting the following day. That evening the Richmond Jewish Community Council, the central planning and fund-raising body of Richmond Jewry, held an emergency meeting and adopted a resolution that no response be made to the editorial. On July 10, the ADL Executive Committee met again with other leaders of the Jewish community present. It was agreed that a committee would call upon the editor and publisher of the *News Leader* "to protest the attack upon the ADL and to indicate that the entire Jewish community viewed the appearance of the editorial with alarm since it served to foster religious tensions and might even invite further violence." Waldman told the group that the ADL headquarters in New York preferred a letter of record but would abide by the judgment of the local community.[17]

Apparently, this "protest" was toned down considerably when Binswanger, Schwarzschild, and Irving May met on July 14 with Kilpatrick and a representative of the publisher, who was in Europe. In a report later to the local ADL group, Binswanger said that the committee had expressed concern about the editorial but sought to assure Kilpatrick that they were not integrationists. While ADL, along with other national Jewish religious groups, had taken advanced positions on the race issue, these were not necessarily endorsed by Virginia ADL, the committee told Kilpatrick. They added that the local ADL leadership wanted to promote interfaith understanding and the position of the Jew in America. Finally, they told Kilpatrick that they realized he was not anti-Semitic. Kilpatrick responded that he was pleased that he was not seen as hostile to Jews and endorsed the concept of interfaith understanding. He noted, however, that since the materials sent to the Charlottesville NAACP workshop were not along these lines, the Richmond office was intruding directly into the race issue. He showed them a listing of ADL materials sent there to indicate that many of the items dealt directly with race.[18] The committee was assured that there would be no additional editorials on the subject and that the issue would not be prolonged by publishing letters to the editor.

Kilpatrick told the committee that he was annoyed with me personally not only because I had intruded in racial matters but because I had interfered, he said, with his freedom of expression. He said that he and another columnist had to watch every word they wrote to insure that their statements would not be considered anti-Semitic. He was referring in his own case, I believe, to several conversations I had held with him in which I pointed out that anti-Jewish elements were attempting to use the *News Leader.* His writings were being liberally quoted in the *Virginian,* which was also advertising in the newspaper. The latter had published a letter by an alleged "Israel Cohen" attacking the role of Jews in the integration controversy; the letter was later found to be a hoax. When the *Washington Star,* which had similarly run the fake letter, learned there was no Israel Cohen, it wrote an exposé to show how bigots used letters-to-the-editor columns to gain attention for their views. In calling these matters to Kilpatrick's attention, I felt he was indifferent to, and apparently resented, my interventions.[19]

Kilpatrick's own account of the meeting confirms Binswanger's report. In a letter to a North Carolina Jewish businessman, he described the discussion as "congenial." Far "from expressing 'distress' at an 'attack' on the ADL they expressed almost exactly the opposite point of view," he wrote. "While they were sorry that we had felt it necessary to publish the editorial, they felt it would do a great deal of good. . . ." The Richmond editor noted that the committee wanted "to assure us that they intended to use their influence with the ADL toward the end that the ADL's involvement in the school segregation controversy could be minimized." Kilpatrick conceded that "The editorial stirred up a small rash of lunatic fringe letters," but concluded, "I filed all of those in the nearest wastebasket, and so far as I know the matter is now closed."[20]

## ADL: CAUGHT IN THE LINE OF FIRE

But the matter was far from closed. Kilpatrick's effort to drive ADL and Jews out of the desegregation struggle was being considered now with great seriousness by Jews in the South. ADL was sharply divided. The national organization, with its Northern liberal orientation, was anxious to protect what it believed to be its fundamental role of battling for human rights for all. Moreover, in areas of northern Virginia and to a lesser degree in the state's other major city, Norfolk, where the *Virginian Pilot* stood in opposition to the Byrd machine, there was less disposition among Jews to go along with massive resistance and school closings. For many Jews in Richmond and farther to the south, however, the episode underlined their belief that ADL had gone beyond its primary purpose of combating anti-Semitism and had plunged Jewish communities into unnecessary confrontations with their neighbors.

Ceasar Cone, the North Carolina Jewish businessman who corresponded with Kilpatrick, wrote Epstein on July 30 that he thought ADL was operating on the same basis as the NAACP: the staff sought to create incidents to perpetuate itself and enlarge its numbers and salaries. Charles J. Block, a Jewish attorney in Macon, Georgia—writer of a book supporting segregation on legal grounds—wrote Kilpatrick that he agreed with him. He hoped the Richmond editor would publish another editorial along the same lines and this time include in his attack groups like the American Jewish Committee and the American Jewish Congress. If the activities of these organizations did not cease, he added, a Southern Jewish Committee should be formed.[21] Kilpatrick promptly passed the letter along to Binswanger.

There is some indication, also, that the *News Leader* episode had become embroiled in broader Jewish political wars. Apparently, the anti-Israel American Council for Judaism had sent copies of the *News Leader* editorial to Cone and other important Southern Jewish leaders, presumably to demonstrate that ADL was jeopardizing their interests in the same manner as their support for Israel did. National ADL leaders believed that these Southern Jews were being encouraged to write Kilpatrick supporting his attack on the organization. Confronted with this charge, the lay head of the American Council for Judaism, Clarence Coleman, indicated that he had no knowledge of any such effort but acknowledged that he knew of the *News Leader* editorial and approved of it.[22] Stimulated or not, there is little doubt that the critical letters ADL was receiving from some Southern Jews represented the real feelings of many Jews in the South.

Virginia ADL leaders, however, were more moderate than the position articulated by Block. While unhappy with the editorial, they did not want war with the national organization. Working with the latter, Binswanger sought to calm Block. At the July 10 meeting of the Virginia ADL Executive Committee, Schwarzschild expressed his personal thanks that Waldman had been sent down from New York to help with the problem, and a unanimous resolution of appreciation was adopted. While there was some discussion about recommending to national ADL that the Richmond office be closed, the idea was apparently not seriously considered. Nor was it ever recommended that I be removed from my job. The sense of the local ADL leaders was that I had not received sufficient guidance by them on the nature and scope of my activities, which would now be more clearly defined.

At the July 10 meeting, it was agreed to appoint a subcommittee "to survey the regional office's program and use of materials." An Evaluation Committee was organized to prepare a report and recommend to the ADL National Commission such modifications of regional office procedures as might be necessary. All activities of the Richmond office "which impinged on the desegregation issue would proceed only after consultation with the Board chairman." I did not object to this. I wrote to the national office, "I consider my role to be that of holding the group together and preventing a final rupture with National ADL. Oddly enough, this relationship is still a friendly one." There would be some modification in the local program, I reported, but when the "crisis in Virginia eases up, we could then return to our full program."[23]

The focus now shifted to the work of the Evaluation Committee. At the suggestion of Philip Klutznick, then head of B'nai B'rith and later Secretary of Commerce under President Carter, Joseph Cohen of Kansas City, chairman of ADL's community service operations, was sent to Richmond to meet with the committee.[24] An effort had been made, in constructing this group, to provide balance between "conservatives" and "liberals." "By conservative," I wrote Cohen on August 4, "I mean that [the use of] any materials or programs that impinge on race, however remotely, get voted down." The six meetings held by the group were long-drawn-out sessions that often went well into the early hours of the morning. ADL and B'nai B'rith leaders from northern Virginia and Norfolk regularly traveled to Richmond to take part in them and returned home afterwards. I wrote Cohen that I was not too worried about the curtailment of some of our educational activities but was most "disturbed by the disposition of the conservatives to halt our program for the maintenance of law and order."

Early in its deliberations, the committee adopted a formula that "the regional office will temporarily withhold from use literature, films and activities that can reasonably be interpreted to deal with the integration-segregation question." This formula was to be in effect until December 1, when it would be reviewed. In its final report, the committee agreed to halt distribution of a number of items that touched on race. It canceled the agency's sponsorship of the Youth Seminar, an action which I strongly opposed. Binswanger had been particularly fond of this program despite his opposition to ADL involvement in racial matters, but by this time he was ill and did not take part a great deal in the work of the Evaluation Committee. The committee approved, however, "participating with other groups in a program to maintain law and order" and a proposed news release describing a new ADL publication, *The South Speaks Out for Law and Order*. In such efforts, the committee agreed, the Richmond office could be used on an interracial basis. This was an oblique reference to the fact that the Richmond branch of the newly formed Virginia Committee to Preserve the Public Schools held its early meetings in the ADL office. The report concluded that the importance and usefulness of the agency's work was at its height as a result of "the crisis in human relations in the area." It declared it "vitally important" that "Virginia Jewry continue to be serviced with an alert and vigorous ADL in the difficult months ahead."[25]

The Virginia ADL report was a major item for consideration at the ADL National Commission meetings in New York on September 20 and 21. These were attended by representatives of Virginia ADL led by its current head, David Arenstein of Richmond, a moderate. In his remarks, Arenstein pledged full support to the established program and policy of ADL. He added that Virginians were convinced that integration was morally and legally wrong and this climate in the state made normal ADL operations difficult. He urged that "the Virginia Board be permitted to implement . . . [national] policy according to its best judgment." He was backed by the few "liberals" and "conservatives" from the Virginia Board. Ceasar Cone of Greensboro argued that ADL "should at this point concern itself exclusively with problems of anti-Semitism and not become involved in the rights of other minorities." Gerald Graze, a member of the Evaluation Committee from northern Virginia, pleaded, however, that "a rule of reason be applied but it should not be one of submission to the fears of intimidation of segregationists." Joseph Cohen, who had visited Richmond on behalf of the national organization, argued that the League "must not retreat from its basic policy."

Following adjournment on the evening of September 20, the discussion continued the following day. The chairman of the commission, Henry E. Schultz, pointed out that ADL must adhere to its established policy but there was room for the Virginia group to implement it according to its best judgment. Klutznick emphasized that the "proper mechanics on both a staff and lay level be established in order to handle the emergencies as they arise. . . ." At the conclusion of the discussion, it was agreed unanimously that the agency would reaffirm its October 27, 1957, resolution that any action taken by ADL affecting a regional constituency be undertaken only after consultation with that constituency. A special committee of national ADL leaders was to be created to interpret policy with respect to problems of the South, presumably on an ad hoc basis.

### "A STARTLING ABOUT-FACE"

In effect, the national organization had gone along with the Virginia group's recommendations. Without shifting away from the organization's pro-integration stance, it was prepared to move in a cautious manner in the super-heated atmosphere of Virginia.[26] To do otherwise would cause a permanent break with its Southern constituency, which had to face the consequences that Kilpatrick had so sharply pointed to. This was a setback, to be sure; nevertheless it was felt that time was running out on massive resistance and the full ADL program would inevitably be resumed. This was my feeling then, and in retrospect I believe the decision was tactically necessary. There were a few in the national ADL headquarters, however, who felt that Virginia ADL and I had gone too far in capitulating to local pressures.

Elated by the reaction they had received in New York, the Virginians returned home to continue their review of ADL materials. It was clear, however, that their hearts were not in it. After a few desultory visits to the office to screen films and look at pamphlets, the effort trailed off. By this time, too, the broader massive resistance drama being played out in Virginia was drawing to a close. The state's growing middle-class and business leadership found themselves increasingly restless with the prospects of school closings and social instability. In a startling about-face, Kilpatrick told the Richmond Rotary Club on November 11 that the courts would probably rule against the state's massive resistance laws. He called for "new tactics and new weapons to preserve segregation," admitting by implication that in some areas there might be integration.[27]

On January 29, following court rulings that Virginia's laws closing schools and withholding funds were violations of the state's constitution, Governor Almond told a special session of the Virginia General Assembly, "It is not enough for gentlemen to cry, 'Don't give up the ship!' . . . No fair minded person would be so unreasonable as to seek to hold me responsible for failure to exercise powers which the state is powerless to bestow." The following Monday, twenty-one black children walked quietly into heretofore-white public schools in Norfolk and Arlington under the protection of state and local police. With the first desegregation in Virginia, the issue was now moving to a peaceful resolution, and the pressures felt by the Jewish community declined. Even before this, in October, the Richmond office joined with B'nai B'rith Women and a number of women's church groups in Norfolk in a major conference on human relations. The operations of the Virginia office under a new director—by this time I had accepted an invitation to join the American Jewish Committee in Philadelphia—had returned to normal. School desegregation struggles now shifted to other communities, including Jewish communities farther to the south.

NOTES

This article is based on my personal recollections and files I kept on this episode now deposited with the American Jewish Archives. I would like to express appreciation to Stanley F. Chyet, director, Magnin School of Graduate Studies of Hebrew Union College—Jewish Institute of Religion in Los Angeles, for his advice in preparing this analysis.

1. Myron Berman, *Richmond's Jewry: Shabbat in Shockoe, 1769–1976* (Charlottesville: University Press of Virginia, 1979), pp. 181–182, 188–190.

2. Ibid., p. 189.

3. Alfred O. Hero, Jr., "Southern Jews and Public Policy," in Nathan M. Kaganoff and Melvin I. Urofsky, *Turn to the South* (Waltham, Mass.: American Jewish Historical Society, and Charlottesville: University Press of Virginia, 1979), p. 144.

4. For further discussion of the role of rabbis, see P. Allen Krause, "Rabbis and Negro Rights in the South, 1954–1967," *American Jewish Archives* 21, no. 1 (April, 1969); Leonard Dinnerstein, "Southern Jewry and the Desegregation Crisis, 1954–1970," *American Jewish Historical Quarterly* 62 (1972–73): 231–241.

5. Murray Friedman, "Virginia Jewry in the School Crisis: Anti-Semitism and Desegregation," *Commentary*, January 1959, p. 17.

6. The February–March 1958 issue of the Defenders' *News and Views* carried a photograph of Thurgood Marshall, NAACP special counsel, receiving a plaque from Kivie Kaplan, described as co-chairman of the NAACP's Life Membership Committee, and Arthur Spingarn, NAACP President. The caption noted, "The NAACP Is Not a Negro Organization and Never Has Been." Later, it advertised a publication, *Our Nordic Race*, which charged that "agitator Jews . . . in close cooperation with a group of Nordic Race Traitors are almost wholly responsible for the destructive 'one race, one color' Marxist campaign that has brought strife and disunity to our country and to the rest of Western civilization." Friedman, "Virginia Jewry in the School Crisis," p. 20.

7. Numan V. Bartley, *The Rise of Massive Resistance: Race and Politics in the South during the 1950's*

(Baton Rouge: Louisiana State University Press, 1969), pp. 222–224.

8. See William Stephenson and Phyllis Kyle, "ADL Attempts Sneaky Invasion of Virginia's Public Schools," December 1956, p. 1. Author's file.

9. Bartley, *Rise of Massive Resistance*, p. 129.

10. For a good discussion of the new black mood, see Richard Kluger, *Simple Justice: The History of Brown v. Board of Education and Black America's Struggle for Equality* (New York: Alfred A. Knopf, 1975).

11. For Kilpatrick's views on states' rights, see his book, *The Sovereign States* (Chicago: Henry Regnery Co., 1957).

12. I wrote to him on May 8, 1958, to compliment him on the editorial.

13. Arthur J. Levin to Alex Miller. Author's file.

14. Friedman, "Virginia Jewry in the School Crisis," p. 21.

15. Report of Evaluation Committee of the Virginia ADL Advisory Board, September 7, 1958. Author's file.

16. Benjamin R. Epstein to ADL National Commission, July 16, 1958. Author's file.

17. Ibid.

18. A memorandum I wrote at the time listed the materials. They included Parts 1 and 2 of the film *Songs of Friendship*, a "Dolls for Democracy" kit, the comic book *About People*, the pamphlets *Shall Children Be Free, Little Songs on Big Subjects, The St. Louis Story, Prejudice—How Do People Get That Way?, Your Neighbor Reads*, and *Your Neighbor Worships*, and a set of "Bible on Brotherhood" posters. Most of these materials contained information about or broad appeals for group understanding or information about Jews. The *St. Louis Story* was a description on how this city went about desegregating its schools. Murray Friedman to Alex Miller, July 7, 1958. Author's file.

19. Binswanger's account of the meeting with Kilpatrick was given at a meeting of the Evaluation Committee of the Virginia ADL Advisory Board on July 16 and was reported in a memorandum I wrote to Benjamin R. Epstein on July 21, 1958. Author's file.

20. James J. Kilpatrick to Ceasar Cone, July 23, 1958. Cone passed this letter on to ADL. Author's file.

21. July 14, 1958. Author's file. Block's book was called *We Need Not Integrate to Educate*.

22. Benjamin R. Epstein to Bernard Nath, July 30, 1958. Bernard Nath to Arnold Forster, August 12, 1958. Author's file.

23. Murray Friedman to Benjamin R. Epstein, July 21, 1958. Author's file.

24. Alexander F. Miller to Murray Friedman, August 11, 1958. Author's file.

25. Report of Evaluation Committee of the Virginia ADL Advisory Board, September 7, 1958. Author's file.

26. Minutes of the ADL National Commission meeting, September 20–21, 1958. Author's file.

27. Bartley, *Rise of Massive Resistance*, p. 321; Murray Friedman, "Virginia Desegregates—The Breakdown of Massive Resistance" (unpublished manuscript, 1959). Author's file.

# Rabbis and Negro Rights in the South, 1954–1967

For many years the American vocabulary has included the phrase "Solid South," but the phrase is more romantic than realistic, especially if from "solid" one infers "uniform." Where Negro rights are concerned, there are within the Southern region—within, that is, Alabama, Arkansas, the Carolinas, Northern Florida, Georgia, Louisiana, Mississippi, Tennessee, Northeastern Texas, and Virginia—many degrees of what James Silver calls "the closed society." Atlanta and New Orleans are worlds apart from, say, Cleveland, Mississippi, or Macon, Georgia. A continual awareness of this diversity in the make-up of Dixie is important, for, when we discuss, as we propose to do here, what the Reform rabbis[1] of the South have or have not done in the realm of civil rights since 1954, it is necessary for us to pose the question: which South? Once this is understood, a generalization about the mood of the South as a whole might prove helpful as a point of departure.

Our generalization is simply this: the reaction of the South toward the so-called civil rights movement has been one of, at the least, antipathy, if not indeed sullen defiance. Surely it is no exaggeration to say that not a single city or town in the South welcomed the Supreme Court decision of 1954. And if this applies to critics like Atlanta, New Orleans, and Nashville, how much the more so does it apply to the four "hard-core" Southern states—to South Carolina, Georgia, Alabama, and Mississippi? As John B. Martin has put it, "Segregation is not a principle upheld only by louts and bullies. It is viewed as inherently right by virtually every white person in the four-state South of which we speak."[2]

### "THEY ARE NOT WITH IT"

The South, aside from occasional Catholic enclaves, is essentially "Protestant country," and the Protestant churches of the region have been basically supportive of the typical Southern views on segregation. A survey reported in *Time* magazine on October 27, 1958, placed nearly 50 percent of Southern ministers in the segregationist camp, while the remaining 50 percent gave few outward signs of nonapproval. Especially during the 1950's, then, it was no easy task to find Protestant clergymen aligned with the

In 1973, P. Allen Krause was a Leon Watters Fellow of the Hebrew Union College-Jewish Institute of Religion, on the faculty of the University of Santa Clara, and rabbi of Temple Beth Torah, Fremont, California.

Originally published in *American Jewish Archives* 21, no. 1 (1969): 20–47. Copyright © 1969, American Jewish Archives. Reprinted with permission of the American Jewish Archives, Cincinnati, Ohio.

forces seeking social change in the South. Little difference between pulpit and pew has been evident in this matter.

Defiance, violent opposition, go-slow tactics, at best a grudging acceptance of the inevitable—such has been the mood of the South during the last two decades. There is in the South a local or regional patriotism which dies hard, if it dies at all. As much as any other incident, one related by Robert Penn Warren offers insight into this atmosphere and underscores the problem which a "Liberal" faces in Dixie Land:

> I remember sitting with a group of college students and one of them, a law student it develops, short but strong looking, dark haired and slick headed, dark, bulging eyes in a slick, rather handsome, arrogant—no bumptious—face, breaks in: "I just want to ask one question before anything starts. I just want to ask where you are from?"[3]

There are approximately 200,000 Jews in the South, as this study defines the region—that is, less than 1 percent of the total population.[4] Socioeconomically, they are to be found mainly in the middle and the upper-middle class. Most are businessmen, many are professionals, others are engaged in various other white-collar occupations, a few are planters. Their attitude toward segregation is not so easily established. One rabbi of a Louisiana congregation told a Northern audience that the "vast majority of Southern Jewry" is neither voiceless nor supine, but that in Southern cities, both large and small, Jews have taken "the courageous (though frequently unpopular) stand." Sociologist Theodore Lowi, however, in his analysis of pseudonymous Iron City, characterized probably all the Jews there as "publicly conservative," but, and this is of key importance, "easily a majority are privately conservative as well . . . the manifest values of Jews . . . are homogenized under the pressure of Southern consensus on the most important political and social issue of all."[5] The Rev. Fred Shuttlesworth, one of Dr. Martin Luther King's right-hand men, prefers an in-between position: "The response of Southern Jews to the [civil rights] movement certainly compares favorably with that of numerous other white groups."[6] But Mississippian Aaron Henry shows little sympathy with Shuttlesworth's words: "You asked about the Jews in the South and rabbis particularly. Sorry, they are not with it."[7]

Where, then, does Southern Jewry stand on the issue of segregation? Are they fighting friends, frightened friends, or foes of the Negro activists? They are, in the writer's opinion, something of all three—with emphasis on the middle epithet. Without a doubt, Southern Jews do include vocal and active desegregationists—but their number is small. They would usually be members of the group which Lowi called "new Jews" (oversimplified, that means first-generation Southerners)—people like Harry Golden.[8] In addition, they are to be found almost invariably in other than Deep-South communities. There are also vocal, card-carrying Jewish segregationists—who are so not out of fear, but out of conviction. More often than not, they will be (again using Lowi's terminology) "old Jews," but they, too, are a definite minority—amounting most likely to a percentage about equal to their liberal coreligionists. The vast majority of Southern Jews—some 75 percent of them—are in the middle; somewhat ambivalent about the whole issue, but tending toward *thoughts* sympathetic to the Negro. Fear of repercussions keeps their sympathies unspoken and makes them very difficult to live with, if one happens to be on either "extreme." They would no sooner join the White Citizens Council than the NAACP—unless abnormal pressure were applied. Absolutely essential, if they are to be understood, is their minority status. As Morris Schappes pointed out:

> Jews who live in the North and West . . . need to keep in mind . . . [that the] Jews of the South constitute seven-tenths of one percent of the total population of the South! . . . We who think of ourselves as a minority when we are approximately one quarter of the population of New York, need perhaps to shift gears a bit when we think of the minority status of Jews in the Southern States.[9]

It is to these people that the rabbi of the South preaches, it is with them that he lives, and it is before them that he is called to account for his words and deeds.

### "THE QUESTION HAS NOT BEEN DISCUSSED"

Many rabbis and Reform congregations in the South have reacted to the trials and heart-rending conflicts of the struggle for human equality in their area with courage and with fortitude. They have spoken bravely their convictions and ours, and they have put into actions their preachments and ours. Their words and deeds are precious to us. . . . In the face of threats and violence they have continued to adhere to the teachings of Judaism in word and deed. May God grant them vigor and continued courage![10]

> . . . you asked about Jews in the South and rabbis particularly. Sorry, they are not with it.[11]

If the reader is somewhat confused, he need not apologize. The first statement above, a resolution passed by the Board of the Union of American Hebrew Congregations in 1958, and the second, Aaron Henry's comment, stand in sharp contrast to each other. Have the Southern rabbis been activists, or have they "not been with it?"

A majority of Southern rabbis would fall into the category of men holding pulpits in what are usually small, deeply "Southern" cities and towns. Their participation in civil rights activity has differed on the whole from rabbinical efforts in cities whose liberal element is larger and more vocal. Though there have been one or two notable exceptions—especially Rabbi Charles Mantinband, of whom we shall have more to say—these rabbis have a record of being less noticeably involved in local desegregationist activity. *But* this is a far cry from saying that they have not been involved at all. In order to determine just how active they have been, one must look at their "civil rights" activity within their community.

When it comes to espousing civil rights causes from their own pulpits, most—the vast majority of—Southern rabbis have let it be known to their congregants that they favor change in the South's social system. Of course, there are exceptions, one of them a rabbi who has served two communities during his nearly twenty years in the South. This man informed the writer:

I don't preach to my congregation what to do with regard to this. I have my own ideas on civil rights which I don't foist upon my . . . congregation. They know—in private groups we discuss these matters. From the pulpit, I very rarely discuss it, because I don't want to harm the Jewish community in any way, shape, or form.

Another rabbi, asked to estimate how many of his congregants held prosegregationist feelings, responded: "I wouldn't know, because the question has not been discussed." Though ultimately this rabbi chose to deliver occasional remarks on civil rights matters from the pulpit, the limitations he placed on such sermons appear to have all but negated their purpose:

The question's always been how you think, whether you deliver an agitating speech or discuss . . . problems. If you discuss problems, you can discuss any problem. But, *if you are going to take sides* and agitate, you accomplish nothing except the hostility of the people. So I have always, in my discussions with individuals and within groups, just plainly discussed the problems and how to solve them. [Italics added.]

Other rabbis, too, have been unwilling "to take sides." In March, 1957, one of them, since deceased, addressed a letter to Dr. Jacob R. Marcus, Director of the American Jewish Archives:

In answer to your inquiry on the subject of desegregation, I wish to say I have made no public pronouncements on this subject either from my pulpit or in the columns of our daily press. Since you, yourself, say you appreciate the problems involved, I know you will understand why I have felt it impossible to discuss this very pressing problem.[12]

One other rabbi should be considered here. He is unique among his colleagues in that his utterances have been used by prosegregationists in support of their position. "With a few clergymen in modest rebellion against the status quo," wrote James Silver in *Mississippi, the Closed Society*, "the Citizens Council eagerly grasped to its bosom a strange new reinforcement in the person of Rabbi B . . . S . . .," who soon after his arrival in Mississippi "laid down the principles which could save America":

. . . if Mississippi had prevailed, pro-Communists would be off American college faculties . . . "red-baiter" would not be a dirty word. Traditional patriotism would sweep the land to . . . insure victory in the international crisis. As it is, America is losing, mostly because of decay among its own intellectuals.[13]

This rabbi finds little support for his views among his Southern colleagues. Though some men do not speak on civil rights or, on occasion, in the privacy of the Jewish community, speak against certain aspects of the civil rights movement, no other man seems ever to have been even peripherally associated with the segregationist position in the eyes of his community, congregants, or colleagues.

## "FATHER, FORGIVE THEM"
More common among the rabbis of the Deep South are those who advocate desegregationist goals, when they speak within the walls of their congregation. But here again

caution must be exercised in an evaluation of the "fervor" of their involvement, since many a rabbi prefers mild, carefully worded and carefully "non-inflammatory" rhetoric to a more "activist" advocacy. Thus, in November, 1955, when one man in a large, Deep-South city sermonized against the White Citizens Councils and in favor of school integration, he employed arguments similar to those reflected in this excerpt:

> There are other and better courses open. As no good comes from calling names or using measures of force, much good can come from the realization that most of us on both sides are decent people, and that, if we sat down together in good will, we could work out a course of action that might be acceptable to all. . . . I believe that such a procedure would produce this situation: that the overwhelming majority of *colored children, at least 90 or 95 percent, would remain right where they are. From previous experience, it seems that they definitely prefer it this way.* [Italics added.]

The sources available to this writer would indicate that such statements—hesitantly in favor of desegregation, but apologetic, fearful, lacking specific demands and hence easily overlooked—have been very much in evidence in Deep-South Jewish congregations. It is this fact which caused many a nonrabbinic informant to judge the rabbinate as strong in thought, but weak in word and deed, when it came to involvement in civil rights activity.

Still, there are some men whose pulpit preachments have been forcibly and directly to the issue. Some have advanced one further step and have joined word to deed. In the Deep South, Perry E. Nussbaum, Charles Mantinband, Alfred L. Goodman, and Ira E. Sanders might be cited as examples of such rabbis. One Southern rabbi in a Deep-South city has for years welcomed Negro servicemen to the synagogue, has been a member of both the regional and state branches of the antisegregationist Southern Regional Council, has played a role in the somewhat successful desegregation of the city's schools, playgrounds, libraries, and theatres, and has, in addition, become a spokesman for desegregation in the general community. Another, in an even more "closed" community, convinced his congregants to give hospitality to Jewish Freedom Riders and has used his pulpit to denounce the White Citizens Councils and all they stand for. This rabbi was also the first in his state to become intimately involved in aiding Jewish and non-Jewish Freedom Riders incarcerated in his region.

The point has been made that in Deep-South "closed" communities, men like these appear very much in the minority. It is true that the majority of the Southern rabbinate in such communities have been hesitant to speak out boldly and in specific terms within their own congregations; it follows that an even greater number have failed to do so in the community at large.

One interviewee, when asked if he had ever felt the need to become involved in the civil rights struggle outside the confines of the synagogue, responded:

> Yes, but it would have been limited to twenty-four hours. Twenty-four hours later I wouldn't be there in the state anymore. . . . The majority of the people of the city have been vehemently opposed to integration . . . including a great number of the Jewish

community. . . . The Jewish community could not exist . . . if they had been in any way involved in the civil rights movement.

This rabbi did occasionally speak to civic groups with sporadic references to "general community problems," and he noted that "there was no hostile response as long as there was no active participation," or as long as the rabbi "did not 'agitate.' "

Lest the reader be tempted to stand too quickly in judgment, let it be remembered that this man lives in the heart of the Deep South. Alfred O. Hero, Jr., discusses another rabbi's response to life in such an "Antebellum Town":

> . . . he had tended to voice disagreement with views expressed in face-to-face conversations when he first returned there. However . . . he had given up trying to change people's thinking. When someone next to him at a . . . meeting expressed irresponsible . . . views, by 1961 he either let him "rave" or changed the subject.[14]

This response has not been uncommon among the Deep South rabbinate, yet it has not been the only response evident.

A rabbi, invited to speak to a local church on "any subject except the 'Niggers,' " responded to the invitation: "While I had not intended to speak on 'The Negro,' now the issue is such that I will speak only on 'The Negro'. . . ." A rapid retraction of the invitation followed.

Ira E. Sanders, of Little Rock, appeared in 1957 before an open hearing of the Arkansas Senate to testify in opposition to four prosegregationist bills. He began by recounting his long connection with Arkansas and his love for the state. He then continued:

> Above my love for Arkansas comes my devotion to America. . . . I regard the [United States] Supreme Court as the final democratic authority of the land. . . . Once they pass on the constitutionality of the law, it should become operative as the law of the land. Higher than the legal law, however, stands the moral law. . . . When Jesus died on the cross, he repeated these immortal words: "Father, forgive them for they know not what they do!" Legislators! May future generations reading the statute books of laws not be compelled to say these words of you . . . defeat, I pray you, in toto, these four measures.

Rabbi Sanders' voice was one of the few moderate utterances to be heard in Arkansas during the black year of 1957, and it took no little courage to stand up and be counted in so open a manner.

Two years earlier another man had become involved in a situation which unexpectedly forced him to make a civil rights stand in his community. This rabbi was asked by the Jewish Chautauqua Society to take part in a Religious Emphasis Program at the University of Mississippi. Along with the Jewish clergyman, an Episcopal minister, a Catholic priest, three additional Protestant ministers, and a layman were invited to participate. About two weeks before the program a crisis developed. The Episcopal minister hit the public eye when, on the then popular *$64,000 Question* television show, he won a large sum of money. When asked what he planned to do with his winnings, the minister responded—on a coast-to-coast hookup—that he was going to donate a percentage of them to the NAACP. The dam broke in the Mississippi legislature. Epithet followed epithet, telephones rang incessantly, and the University's chancellor was ordered to cancel the invitation that had been extended to the Episcopal minister. The rabbi then began to have misgivings about participating in the University program. He placed a call to Albert Vorspan, Director of the Commission on Social Action of Reform Judaism, and through him he got in touch with the national office of Chautauqua, whom he told that he could no longer accept the invitation. He then placed calls to the six other participants and asked them to join him in rejecting the University's request that they take part in the Religious Emphasis program. All except the layman agreed. After much backstage maneuvering, it eventually turned out that the rabbi sent his friend, the chancellor, an individual telegram cancelling out his participation. The next day the local newspaper headlines proclaimed: "Rabbi refuses to speak at University." In the months that followed, telephone harassment and threats made it necessary for the F.B.I. and the local police to provide constant surveillance for the rabbi and his family. In the whole incident, this clergyman played the central public role in opposing an act demanded by "the Southern way of life."

There are a few other Reform rabbis who have played some role in opposing segregation and its manifestations in the public school systems of the Deep South. One man serving an Alabama pulpit was instrumental in forming an informal *ad hoc* committee which greatly facilitated the relatively smooth integration of the University of Alabama. One of his colleagues, in 1963, joined with a few of his fellow-citizens to form ABLE (Alabamians Behind Local Education), a group which helped prepare his community for integration of the public schools. Still another rabbi attended commission hearings and conferences with the local school board and the superintendent of schools, in order to implement similar desegregationist goals. For all this, however, the available sources do not permit the assertion that most or even many rabbis in these very difficult communities played a significant part in abetting or hastening implementation of the 1954 Supreme Court decision.

### THREE SERMONS

We turn now to the rabbis in the "less closed" societies of the South. In general, this category includes most cities and towns in Kentucky, Tennessee, Virginia, Florida, Texas, and western and southern Louisiana. Added to this list must be the city of Atlanta, Georgia, which stands out as an enclave of "Northern" ideas and influence in the land of Civil War Dixie.

In the congregations of these communities, there has been no dearth of sermons, especially since 1954, dealing with the civil rights movement. Many of these pulpit texts are presently on file in the American Jewish Archives, and they speak quite forcefully on their own behalf. Though some are vague and are content with skirting the important issues of their time and place, several come directly to the point and evidence strong desegregationist feelings. A recurrent theme is the necessity of abiding by the law of the land, and the need for the Jewish community to show the way in such acquiescence. Brief quotes from three will provide the reader with a "taste" of these pulpit messages. The first was delivered on Yom Kippur eve in 1954; the second, on November 18, 1955; and the third, on Yom Kippur eve in 1958. Each was given in a different pulpit:

> We have reached that time in American history when certain changes are to be made in our culture which will radically modify some of our customs and mores, especially in certain sections of our land. Our society is governed by . . . laws, and . . . it is the responsibility of every good citizen to abide by the laws as they are interpreted. . . . Since certain significant decisions were rendered by the highest tribunal of our judiciary last Spring, certain hate groups have been organized to resist the decisions that have been handed down. . . . Let the name of no Jew be found on the roster of these hate organizations. If there are those among us who cannot be in the vanguard striving for a better humanity, then at the very least, let us not be among those who would stifle the moral progress of mankind.

> To the newspaper reporters and visitors to the Congregation this evening I want to bid a warm and most cordial welcome. Then I want to hasten to add that whatever is written or spoken about my remarks this evening must make clear that I am speaking only for myself . . . as a rabbi of the Reform Jewish faith who has been trained in a faith founded upon the Prophetic message of the Bible. . . . This is a sermon I must preach for myself and for the sake of my soul if for no one else. . . . Anyone of intelligence who lives here and understands and loves the South knows full well the race problem is going to take time and intelligence, patience and good will on both sides, before it will be solved. But it will not be solved by unyielding, unmoving, unthinking resort to prejudice and Shintoist slogans that scream about keeping the Southern Way of Life. Greater than the Southern or Eastern or Western way of life is the *American Way of Life,* and greater still is the Judeo-Christian Way of Life.

The sermon went on then to attack any society which would condone an Emmet Till case without making some drastic changes in its "Way of Life." The third sermon, delivered from a Virginia pulpit, alluded to the segregationist views of Senator Harry F. Byrd:

> I speak as a rabbi on this issue to a Jewish congregation on our holiest evening. The significance of my remarks is heightened this evening in that I have chosen one of our holiest days to devote it to root out the evil in our midst in the form of bigots and hate peddlers who, for a headline, a misplaced vote, would attack minority after minority. When those who are not afraid to speak . . . sound like a voice crying in the wilderness—it is our moral obligation as Jews not to desist from being a light unto the nation. . . . I am afraid of silence . . . I will not be silenced! . . . The Jew cannot remain silent to injustice. . . . Let the segregationists froth and foam at their mouth. There is only one word to describe their madness—Godlessness, or to coin a new synonym—Byrdliness. Byrdliness has done more harm to the stability of our country than McCarthyism. . . .I am an American, and, yes, I am a Virginian; but not of the

vintage of Byrd and his invertebrate crew that follow him like subdued puppies, but I am a Virginian of the vintage of Jefferson, who said: "I have sworn upon the altar of God eternal hostility against every form of tyranny over the mind of man."

These are but three excerpts from numerous sermons preached by a large number of non-Deep-South rabbis. Though some of their colleagues have never devoted an entire sermon to a civil rights issue, it is no exaggeration to say that nearly all Reform rabbis in these cities and towns have touched on the subject at least occasionally. Of this large majority, a lesser number (but still a majority) have spoken several times a year, often on the High Holidays and in specifics, as sermon texts on file in the American Jewish Archives document. But the sermon has been far from the only tool employed within the congregation by rabbis who serve these communities.

### "THE TICKLISHNESS OF THE SITUATION"
Very important has been the use of integrated worship services—even before the United States Supreme Court decision of 1954. One rabbi, on Washington's Birthday in 1951, "despite some serious qualms on the part of my board," organized an interracial service complete with an integrated choir and a sermon by the president of a local Negro divinity school. Another man invited a Negro to occupy his pulpit in 1955, as a dramatic gesture in order to "indicate at a time of tension, the support of Reform Judaism not only for the decision of the Supreme Court, but to take a stand in behalf of the Negro." Not all rabbis have been as firm, when it comes to encouraging integrated worship services within their synagogues. One told of the evening when just prior to services:

> a well groomed Negro came to my office. . . . He asked for the privilege of attending Temple that night. In answer to my query what led to this request, he said that he was indeed a Jew who had been converted by a colleague in Arkansas. I immediately telephoned this man . . . and he verified the fact of the man's sincere conversion. I then suggested to the gentleman that, because of the ticklishness of the situation, I ought to discuss his request with those who had already begun to arrive. . . . Their answer was: that if anyone objected to this Jewish Negro worshipping that night, they themselves would leave in protest rather than have him embarrassed. I was proud of them as I was some years later, when a Negro sergeant from a nearby Army base asked to worship with us—for again their answer was the same.

The question which comes to mind, of course, is what the rabbi would have done if his congregation had refused the man permission. The data at hand lead one to believe that at least some of the rabbis would have made peace with the decision and done without Negro worshippers.

Along with sermons and integrated services, rabbis have used bulletin messages, study groups, personal contacts, and creative "social action" projects in order to influence their members to support local efforts at desegregation. Mention must be made, if only in passing, of a major project implemented in Nashville, Tennessee, by Rabbi Randall M. Falk. His Social Justice Committee, during October and November, 1963, initiated a series of parlor meetings which eventually involved a sizeable percentage of the Nashville Temple's membership. These meetings resulted in the adoption by the congregation of a highly liberal, responsible, and "progressive Decalogue on Race Relations."

Directing our gaze to the outside community, we find many examples of rabbis in non-Deep-South communities playing at least some role in local desegregationist activities. In most cases, much of this work has been done in conjunction with liberal ministerial groups, which have blossomed during the last two decades. Such was the circumstance which, for example, brought Rabbi Marvin M. Reznikoff, of Baton Rouge, Louisiana, to national attention in 1961, when his telephone conversations with other ministers were monitored by segregationists aiming at undermining the clergy's liberal intentions.

In the school desegregation crises which shook the South following 1954, at least a few Reform rabbis played significant roles. One, the rabbi of a community with slightly under 10,000 Jewish inhabitants, decried his state's defiance of the Supreme Court decision. Speaking in 1957 to a Methodist congregation, he warned: "If we don't rise above our partisan feelings of segregation versus integration, we'll have disintegration in our public schools." Within a few weeks' time, largely through the efforts of this man, a Committee for Public Schools was formed and played a major role in influencing the community's business forces to apply sufficient pressure for the schools to be reopened before the children should lose the entire school year of 1957–1958. Although differing in details, the role of two of this man's colleagues, one in a border state, the other in a cosmopolitan port city, was basically the same. In these latter two cases, the rabbis involved were clearly recognized by the community as leaders in the push for integration, and many recriminations and harassing acts followed. On the whole, however, rabbinical involvement of this sort appears to be quite exceptional. More common, it would seem, were rabbis who occasionally lent their moral support to the struggle toward implementation of the 1954 decision, but who took little part in the actual behind-the-scene and public fighting.

## "YOU CAN'T LEGISLATE SOCIOLOGY"

At this point, it might prove helpful to look a little more closely at three "case-studies," men who have long served Southern pulpits and have responded in their own way to the pressures and problems of being a rabbi in the South.

Rabbi "A" is the spiritual leader of a semi-Deep-South community which he has served for the past eight years. Prior to this, he spent a number of years in an even more "closed" city, to the east of his present home. Both of these communities have Jewish enclaves of about 500 souls, and both can trace their Jewish settlement back to pre-Civil War times. The rabbi's present city is more amenable, though certainly not friendly, to civil rights activity than his former city was. Nevertheless, his participation in such activity has been quite minimal. Asked about the response to civil rights on the part of the ministers in his community, he replied that "most of [them] . . . wouldn't touch it with a ten-foot pole." Yet, in 1965, the Ministerial Association in his present city voted to integrate, while the rabbi played no major role in this development.

Rabbi "A" 's congregants in both cities have been and are mainly merchants, with the majority of the non-merchants being professional people. In his first pulpit, he felt the greatest percentage of them to be fully acculturated to the "Southern Way of Life," including their views on Negro rights. Thus, the rabbi refrained from any activity which would "create ill will" or potentially "harm the Jewish community in any way, shape, or form." When discussing his present pulpit, he informed the writer that he had served on the local Board of Economic Opportunity and had participated in a small group which worked to prepare the community for school desegregation. Other than these two involvements, he could recall no additional ways in which he had been connected with anything which could be even nominally considered a "civil rights activity." Where speaking in his congregation and community was concerned, he refused to be "argumentative about the situation" or to "foist his own ideas upon his people." It might be instructive to note exactly what some of his ideas are. Asked whether or not Freedom Riders had ever entered his community, he replied:

No, thank goodness . . . I don't think it accomplishes much. . . . I've lived in the South for twenty years now. . . . I feel that the people here are going to have to solve their own problem, and they're solving it, even if they had to be prodded through legislation . . . they're still doing it, nonetheless, and to add salt to the wounds is not helping the situation one bit.

The writer then inquired as to what specifically his goals were for the entire civil rights movement.

I don't know, I've never really thought about the question, to tell you the truth. I would like to see, of course, the Negro to have fair treatment, in all respects, but I think . . . he's going to have to earn it to a certain degree himself. We're going to help him. . . . This is not going to happen overnight, even with legislation, because you can't legislate sociology . . . and the background of the Negro is such that he is going to have to prove himself—through education, through his own morals (which he will do, but it's going to take time)—and I think that rushing these things through with Freedom Marches and all kinds of picketing and strikes—this is not going to do it— it's only going to create ill will.

### THE BOMBING CREATED A REACTION

Rabbi Jacob M. Rothschild came to Atlanta, Georgia, in 1946. Even at that early date the city already had the makings of what was to become the atmosphere most "open" to racial liberalism in the South. Rothschild has proved eminently suited to take advantage of the opportunities which such a milieu can provide the religious leader. From the very beginning, he expressed himself as a racial "liberal" and had every intention of guiding his congregants along the same path. In a Yom Kippur sermon delivered on October 3, 1948, during the early years of his Atlanta ministry, he expressed a sense of shame at "the growing race hatred that threatens the South" and called for his people to "be among those who are willing to *do* something" to reverse the tide.

Rothschild himself has not neglected the deed. In 1957, he joined with seventy-nine other Atlanta clergymen in order to issue the now famous "Atlanta Manifesto"—one of the earliest and most influential clerical statements proclaimed throughout the South. In his congregation, to supplement his frequent antisegregationist sermons, he began seminars to help prepare his people for the entrance of desegregation. In 1958, chiding his fellow-members of Rotary, he advised them that the Negro had every right to be impatient with a white community unreceptive to racial progress.[15] At the mayor's request, Rothschild gave the key speech to a meeting of hotel and restaurant owners during a time when the public accommodations issue was especially urgent. In 1961, he was one of the founders of, and speakers for, a group created to prepare the community for school integration; it was called HOPE (Help Our Public Education). In short, Rabbi Rothschild was involved in practically every civil rights issue in Atlanta.

This multilevel involvement with the Negro's struggle for equality has, of course, brought the rabbi into touch with many members of the Negro community. He has often graced their pulpits, and they his. One striking example of an activity which Rothschild carried on in contact with the Negro community was the 1965 testimonial dinner for Dr. Martin Luther King. The idea was Rothschild's, and, though some elements of the Negro power structure tried to turn it into a money-raising function, the rabbi persisted in his desire to keep it nothing more than a community's way of expressing its pride in its first Nobel Prize winner. Mainly due to Rothschild's labors, the evening proved an enormous success—1,600 people were in attendance, and many more had to be turned away for lack of room. At the dinner's close, all of these people, Negro and white alike, stood up and sang the civil rights anthem, *We Shall Overcome*. It was, in Rothschild's words, "the most significant meeting that Atlanta ever had—everybody said so."

But the events of 1965 take us too far ahead of our story. On October 12, 1958, Atlanta had become the fifth Southern city within eight months to look upon the crumbled walls of a Jewish community building. Only hours after it rang with children's voices, Rabbi Rothschild's synagogue echoed with the boom of a dynamite blast which caused well over $200,000 in damages. Why his synagogue? According to the rabbi:

I suppose that part of it, at least, was because I was so obviously identified with the civil rights movement. . . . What happened was . . . a small group of so-called Nazis . . . took advantage of the atmosphere of violence. . . . They used the atmosphere to bomb a synagogue, because they were specifically anti-Semitic . . . [But] they misread the attitudes of the community. . . . The bombing . . . created a reaction . . . of such outrage that it backfired, and as a *result* of the bombing of the Temple, it now, for perhaps the first time in Atlanta, became possible to speak out. I'm firmly convinced that it was *this* episode that prevented Atlanta from becoming the same kind of closed society that Birmingham became, or Mississippi became. . . .

In his congregation, in his community, in the South as a whole (Rabbi Rothschild has been a member of the Southern Regional Council), Rothschild has been a constantly outspoken opponent of the system of segregation. Protestant civil rights workers, Negro activists, writers on the contemporary South—if they had heard of any "activist" rabbis—offered or recognized the name of Jacob M. Rothschild more often than any other name—except one other, the name of Rabbi Charles Mantinband.

### "TOO SMART FOR YOUR PANTS"

Since 1946, Charles Mantinband, a native of Norfolk, Virginia, has served three Southern communities. His pulpit from 1946 to 1951 was in Florence, Alabama. In 1951, he left for Hattiesburg, Mississippi, remained there until 1962, and then departed for his present home in Longview, Texas.

Hattiesburg, Mississippi, not unlike Florence, Alabama, is about as closed as the closed society gets. It is a small community, numbering less than 50,000—with a Jewish population of about 175. The mood of Hattiesburg, when Rabbi Mantinband first arrived, and even more so after 1954, was sullen and defiant. It is Klan country, and not a place to look for liberals. All this notwithstanding, Charles Mantinband had made certain vows to himself at the beginning of his years in the rabbinate, and he intended to live by them in Hattiesburg. As he told the writer:

> From the very beginning, I had to make up my mind to two things as to what I would do. . . . The first thing was that the pigmentation of a person's skin would make no difference to me in my relationship to him. . . . I would judge a man, if I would judge him at all . . . in terms of his merit, his worth. That means that Negroes came to my home, through the front door, sat at my table, all the time, and that was my private affair. That was not too difficult. . . . The second thing was much harder. I vowed that I would never sit in the presence of bigotry and hear it uttered . . . that I would not [fail to] voice a contrary opinion, and make my opposition felt. . . . I wouldn't be histrionic about it . . . I wouldn't try to make a speech. I just would register . . . what my religion compels me to think, and feel, and be, and how it makes me behave. And when they would say to me, "God is a segregationist, because the Bible is full of it," I always ripped out a Bible, and I would open it to where the opposite is stated and say, "Do you mean here? Or do you mean there? Or do you mean the other place?" And then they would say, "You're too smart for your pants."

Rabbi Mantinband's open association with Negroes on an at-home social basis, his refusal to keep to himself his ideas about the evil of segregation, his very active participation in the Southern Regional Council, and the numerous speeches he made at nearby Negro colleges—all this precipitated many a crisis between him and his congregation and community. One of his board members claimed that the rabbi's home was Temple property and attempted—unsuccessfully—to pressure the rabbi into closing the door of his home to Negroes. The response was: "Yes, it is your house, but it is my home. If you want your house back, I'll give it to you . . . but you can't tell me how to live my personal private life."

Equally unsuccessful was an act of intimidation by one of Hattiesburg's ex-mayors, who was at the time, in 1958, the president of the local White Citizens Council. Following the bombing of the Atlanta synagogue, Mantinband happened to meet this man on the street. In the ensuing conversation, the ex-mayor informed the rabbi that, at the last meeting of the White Citizens Council, he had advised the membership that bombing a synagogue was silly, for, if they wanted to get to the bottom of the trouble in their own city, it was not a building but a person. "His name," he related, "is Rabbi Mantinband. I know his personal habits, I know where he lives, I can tell you how to get at him if you decide that's what you really want to do." Thinking quickly, Mantinband pulled out a pen and pad, recorded what had been said, and told the ex-mayor that he was going to have it "signed by the first five representative white Christians I meet," and that he would then send it on to the F.B.I. As Rabbi Mantinband told the writer: "That fellow and I lived in that town—he never looked me in the face again because I had called his hand."

How could a man so decidedly at odds with the closed society make it through eleven years as rabbi in Hattiesburg, Mississippi, and be given the key to the city when he finally decided to leave? Harry Golden has one answer which he has related to Rabbi Mantinband. Respect for religion is so great in the South, he suggested, that people there will not molest a man of the cloth, even if he is attacking the "Southern Way of Life." Of course, this explanation fails to take into account a fact which Golden himself has noted—scores of Protestant ministers have been driven from their pulpits by these very same people.[16] Much closer to the truth, in the present writer's opinion, is a statement made in *The New South*, the official publication of the Southern Regional Council.

> . . . it is possible in the South for a man to be what he is, speak what he believes and stand up to segregationist hatred, as our Rabbi, Charles Mantinband, has stoutly demonstrated for 15 or 16 years in darkest Alabama and Mississippi. . . . I think Rabbi Mantinband . . . survives his environs so handsomely, despite his freely and frequently expressed view that all men are equal, because he sees no man as his enemy. . . . The first time I saw him . . . I figured that if you're good enough you can say and do what you believe anywhere.[17]

Viewed in the light of this perspective, Rabbi Mantinband has indeed been good enough.

### A FORCE IN READINESS

In a nearby town a Negro said, "I'm in a bad position. I make four thousand dollars a year as a school principal, and I'm also a preacher and I make five thousand dollars a year out of that. If I say I don't believe in integration they'd run me out of the church, and if I do they'll run me out of the school."[18]

A few of the facts have been presented. The moment has come for conclusions—judgments, if one will. And also for a few suggestions. What have the Southern rabbis done, and what more could they do? If the writer has learned nothing else from his preparation of this study, he has learned that to generalize about the Southern rabbinate is to fall prey to all the misconceptions which usually accompany generalizations. There have been many different levels of involvement among the Southern rabbis, from the few fully engaged in the civil rights struggle, battering at the walls of the old system, to the one who is a keeper of the gates. There are men who speak and act, men who speak, but rarely act, and men who rarely speak. Examples have been given, and one hopes this point has been made. Still, though faulty instruments, generalizations have their use, especially if the reader is forewarned to accept them only as the view of the forest which cannot fully do justice to its individual trees.

Our first generalization, then, is that the Orthodox and Conservative rabbinate in the South has been conspicuous by its absence from the fray. According to the writer's informants and also to the written sources at his disposal, these representatives of the more traditional branches of Judaism "haven't participated to any great extent." Of the two groups, the writer was able to trace civil rights activity to but two Conservative rabbis, Seymour Atlas, of Montgomery, and Arie Becker, of Memphis. Though there probably have been others, no Jewish or Christian informant could recall their names or activities. The highest praise accorded to some of their number was that they signed petitions prepared by other clergymen, or that they discussed the subject within their congregations. The A.D.L. informant, himself a member of a Conservative synagogue, was asked if he detected a difference between the involvement of Southern Reform, Conservative, and Orthodox rabbis in the civil rights struggle. His reply was:

> I guess I would have to say yes. In the first place there were more Reform rabbis in the Southern region. . . . Also the Reform rabbis . . . by philosophy and background felt that they had a greater involvement publicly in community affairs than either the Conservative or Orthodox did. Matter of fact, the Orthodox rabbinate, where it existed, was not at all involved.

Though the Conservative and Orthodox rabbis in the South did little or nothing, their Reform colleagues, on the whole, played a respectable, if not overly important role. They were, as Shuttlesworth described them, "a force in readiness . . . giving some support . . . some tacit, some active." Much of what they did was unpublicized and behind-the-scenes. Many among them spoke in their congregations and in the outside community; a few involved themselves in civil rights groups and activities. There is probably not a single community where the Reform rabbi has played *the* key role in battling segregation (although Hattiesburg, Mississippi, might be an exception), but there are a number of communities in which Reform rabbis played valuable secondary or supportive roles. Such has been the case especially with regard to the battles for school integration. And the fact that this is so—that the rabbis have not led the parade— is not necessarily a derogatory evaluation. At least Harold Fleming, the Southern Regional Council director, was hesitant to condemn the Southern rabbinate because of this:

> I'm not sure that the more defeatist rabbis were not right, in practical terms, that there were very stringent limits on how much direct or unilateral action by rabbis could have changed the situation in those days. . . . I wasn't one of those who felt that if every rabbi would get "gung ho" on this issue that it would change it substantially. I think a whole predominantly WASP . . . region had to be moved on this.

The rabbis have played a respectable role. The question is, have they played as great a role as they could have played? The answer must be "no."

## A ROLE TO PLAY

It is easy for those who sit in Northern cities to condemn the Southern rabbi as a disgrace to prophetic Judaism. Many have done so. Many have made weekend trips down South to teach their colleagues some Judaism. This writer, however, feels obliged to question the reasonableness of their words and deeds. If we must condemn those who minister to Southern Jewry, it should not be because they have not been outspoken liberals, leading the picket lines in their Deep-South communities. It should be because they have not done what it was within their power to do.

What can almost any Southern rabbi do to advance the cause of Negro equality? The absolutely essential thing which he must do is work to win his congregation over to the struggle. A rabbi who is silent within his congregation is worthy of an unfavorable judgment. What might his procedure be? First, at hiring time, he must clearly convey to the congregation what he stands for. "Liberalism" should not spring forth, newborn and unexpected, one afternoon or evening, days or weeks or months after the "marriage" between rabbi and synagogue has taken place. The "marriage" should be a totally honest one.

Next, the rabbi must begin an intensive educational job upon his own people. He should employ every means at his disposal—the pulpit, the study group, interpersonal relationships—to sensitize his people to the ethical demands Judaism must make on them, if it is to be of any importance to them. There is no surety that his efforts will succeed; it might be a lifelong battle. But if the rabbi fails to make it *his* battle, he has defaulted in his role as spiritual leader.

Then, while the job is being pursued within his congregation, the rabbi should turn to the outside community. This need not be done with fanfare or speech making, especially if the community is a difficult one in which to operate. But he should make it his duty to know, and to be known by, the various members of the power structure—the mayor, the police chief, the school superintendent, important businessmen. The relationship should not be one-way—if the rabbi is always criticizing or seeking favors, he will not have strengthened his possibilities of influencing people toward moderation when important crises develop. Here, the service groups might prove helpful. Also a certain degree of friendliness on the rabbi's part. How he does it is less important than that he does it—the Southern rabbi will be immeasurably more important in his community if he is able to approach the community's leaders on a first-name basis.

At the same time, the rabbi should be reaching out in other directions. It should not take him long to discover the liberal elements, few though they might be, in his city. He should quietly "cast in his lot" with them. He will undoubtedly be strengthened by them, and they by his presence. If all that it is possible to do is talk, then he must talk. When the hour is propitious for more dramatic and meaningful action, there will at least be a core group ready to act. And the rabbi should be among them.

Finding kindred souls among the clergy in the community is of utmost importance. In most communities there will be at least a handful. Religion still is a "respected force" in the South—interfaith activities in which the rabbi has participated can only strengthen the cause. The rabbi should know, and be known to, the liberals and moderates among the priests and ministers.

Finally, the rabbi should quietly extend a hand of friendship to the Negroes in the community—certainly the ministers and professors among them. Again, he need not be dramatic, although some rabbis have been quite obvious about this in the Deep South and have managed to retain their pulpits and their effectiveness. But the Negro community should know at the very least that this man is sympathetic to their cause. The time will come, if the rabbi has been at all diligent and blessed with an average amount of luck, when he will be able to bring Negroes into his home and Temple. This, too, should be a goal not easily deferred by a Southern rabbi.

This is, at best, a minimal program. But some communities might necessitate such a program—at least for the early years of the rabbi's ministry. We have said nothing about sending sermons to the local press, participating in prayer vigils, loudly doing battle with the city's Klan and White Citizens Council. A man who can do these things, and more, has found a more fortunate community, or is a "mighty man of valor," or possibly both. But a man who has not attempted to do the minimal has not done justice to his calling.

The simple fact is that the Negro, at least to date, has been unable to do the job alone. He needs votes, jobs, political pressure, education, good will—things which can be provided only by the whites among whom he lives. And the whites must be convinced to provide the votes, education, jobs, and so forth. It is for the leaders of the Southern communities, the molders of public opinion, to respond to their task. And the rabbis— though seemingly insignificant—are among the leaders. The leaders must choose their tactics well—the battle will not be won by bravado alone. Melvin Tumin reported in *Desegregation: Resistance and Readiness:*

> The principal advocacy of social change . . . comes from those who have the widest perspective on themselves and their communities. The development of this sense of perspective leads one to be deliberate rather than impulsive; to be reflective rather than hasty; to be willing to bargain delayed gratification of several desires against immediate impulsive gratification of only one; to be concerned for the obligations of one's membership in the larger society along with the obligations of membership in one's local province; and, finally, to take into account, in deciding upon a course of action, some notion of responsibility to one's community and its organized patterns of life, as well as listening to the clamor of the inner voice. . . .[19]

President John F. Kennedy, during a White House conference of Southern clergymen, advised his audience that "they were a most fortunate group—that it was not often that people have had such a role to play in history." So far, the clergy of the South have played their role halfheartedly, even badly. Rabbis, though small in number, must be considered among those men of all generations to whom Edmund Burke's dictum was addressed: "The only thing necessary for the triumph of evil is for good men to do nothing."

Rabbi Jacob M. Rothschild, in 1954, compared the struggle with a slowly building logjam:

> At the present moment, the two races are separated by a rushing torrent. No one can safely cross to the other side. But one day a log will lodge itself between the opposite

shores and balance precariously there. Some more courageous—and perhaps you will want to say—more foolhardy than the rest will take a chance and dart across it. A few more may take the risk. But soon another log will rest against the first, creating now a more secure footing. Others will find the courage to brave the torrent. Then still a third . . . will add itself to the other two. . . . At long last, a bridge will be built, firm and safe, upon which even the most timid will walk without fear. This, I believe, is the way it will be.

The rabbis of the South must carry some of those logs and cross the bridge, if they are to do justice to their calling. Some have already shown the way. The battle, though very far from being over, has made a few incursions into enemy territory. One old Negro slave preacher once said: "We ain't what we ought to be, and we ain't what we want to be, and we ain't what we're going to be. But, thank God, we ain't what we was."

There will be no progress in the South without those who are working constantly, day in and day out, to bring it about. No man who claims the role and title of a religious leader can afford the luxury of inaction, silence, waiting. The rabbi must join himself to the struggle, and must do his part. There is only so much passivity which can be excused by the atmosphere of the community in which he lives. The man who sees his hands utterly tied, his mouth completely muted, is rightfully open to criticism—his master is as much within as without. The Southern Reform rabbi has done a good deal, but he could do so much more.

NOTES

For his research, Rabbi Krause relied largely on a questionnaire which he sent to some seventy rabbis in the South (about twenty-five responded); on taped interviews which he conducted with a number of Southern rabbis, Negro activists, teachers, and officials of The Union of American Hebrew Congregations Religious Action Center in Washington, D.C., the Anti-Defamation League of B'nai B'rith, the American Jewish Committee, and the Southern Regional Council; and on correspondence with Southern Regional Council and Mississippi N.A.A.C.P. representatives. The statements in this present epitome of his thesis are carefully and extensively documented in the original work, which, together with the questionnaires, tapes, and correspondence involved, is on file at the American Jewish Archives.

1. This investigation is limited to the Reform rabbi, first, because adequate data on the Southern Conservative and Orthodox rabbinate have not been available to the writer, despite his efforts to get in touch with such rabbis, in sufficient quantity to merit inclusion; then, because the writer's information about non-Reform rabbis has come, in the great majority of cases, from their Reform colleagues, and this might, rightly or wrongly, be open to charges of excessive subjectivity; and, finally, because there are simply not many non-Reform rabbis in the South. In the entire state of Mississippi, for example, there is only one Orthodox minyan served by a rabbi: see Charles Mantinband, "Mississippi, the Magnolia State" (1961), Nearprint File, American Jewish Archives [AJAr].

2. John B. Martin, *The Deep South Says Never* (New York, 1957), p. 9.

3. Robert Penn Warren, *Segregation, the Inner Conflict in the South* (New York, 1956), pp. 24–25.

4. *American Jewish Year Book*, LXVI (1966), 83 ff.

5. Theodore Lowi, "Southern Jews: The Two Communities," *Jewish Journal of Sociology*, VI (July, 1964), 111.

6. Taped interview with the Rev. Fred Shuttlesworth, July 15, 1966 (AJAr).

7. Excerpt from a letter from Aaron Henry to P. Allen Krause, July 22, 1966 (AJAr).

8. See note 5, *supra*.

9. "Jewish Young Freedom Fighters and the Role of the Jewish Community: An Evaluation," *Jewish Currents*, XIX (July–August, 1965), 22.

10. Emmet A. Frank file, AJAr.

11. See note 7, *supra*.

12. Segregation file, AJAr.

13. James Silver, *Mississippi, the Closed Society* (New York, 1964), p. 131.

14. Alfred O. Hero, Jr., *The Southerner and World Affairs* (Baton Rouge, 1965), p. 499.

15. Jacob M. Rothschild Microfilm, AJAr.

16. Harry Golden, *Mr. Kennedy and the Negroes* (Cleveland, 1964), pp. 191 ff.

17. Margaret Long, editorial, *The New South*, XVII (October, 1962), 2, 17.

18. Melvin Tumin, *Desegregation: Resistance and Readiness* (Princeton, 1958), p. 66.

19. *Ibid.*, pp. 199–200.

# Press release from Robert Gary, May 22, 1956

## AMERICAN JEWISH CONGRESS LEADER DEPLORES FAILURE OF TWO NATIONAL JEWISH AGENCIES TO TAKE STAND ON SEGREGATION

NEW HAVEN—Recalling the "unconscionable guilt" of the world Christian community during the Nazi persecution of the Jewish people, Isaac Toubin, acting director of the American Jewish Congress tonight (Monday, May 21) deplored the failure of two major Jewish agencies to announce any public position on the problem of segregation.

In an address at the second annual dinner meeting of the community relations committee of the New Haven Jewish Community Relations Council, Mr. Toubin noted that the two organizations have been "significantly silent" on the issue. "The White Citizens Councils of the South apparently have not only blackmailed their southern Jewish neighbors, but have effectively silenced two national Jewish organizations which pride themselves on their defense of the civil rights of all," he declared. "How can we achieve a moral society if we ourselves are guilty of immoral behavior?"

"Is it not immoral to pose as a defender of civil rights when one applies for an allocation from a Jewish welfare fund in the North and then to have another set of answers when one applies for an allocation from a Jewish welfare fund in the South? It is not enough to claim that the Jewish community of the South is being held hostage in the civil rights struggle. Even if that were true, which it is not, the Jews of America should be the very last to consider the desertion of their Negro brothers in this struggle for human equality."

Mr. Toubin emphasized that "no crisis is more critical for the welfare of America than the just and full correction of the evil treatment accorded the Negro. It is a pernicious national sin; it has dangerous international implications; the white man should dread the retribution he has accrued, and there is a great moral and religious decision at stake for all of us."

The position of the Jewish community on "this moral and social crisis should be as unequivocal as it is inevitable," he said. "Our religious teachings, our historic experience, our human instinct, our concern for America's welfare should compel us to seek for the Negro the same justice which, on so many bitter occasions, has been denied to us. No one should minimize the dilemma that confronts the Jewish communities in the South, but their plight, real or imagined, cannot relieve us of making clear where we stand."

In 1956 Robert Gary was director of the Department of Public Relations of the American Jewish Congress. American Jewish Congress, May 22, 1956. Library of Congress, Manuscript Division, Washington, D.C.

## Resolution adopted by the Biennial Convention of the American Jewish Congress, May 14–18, 1958

### CIVIL RIGHTS AND FEDERAL RESPONSIBILITY

Our country faces the grave danger that a number of Southern states may succeed in their effort to nullify the Constitutional guarantee of equal protection of the laws and that they will be allowed to maintain racial segregation in their public schools and other tax-supported institutions in defiance of the decisions of the United States Supreme Court issued four years ago. The progress toward school integration made during the first few years following the Supreme Court's decisions has now come almost completely to a halt. It is a shocking fact that in seven states no steps whatever have been taken to end segregation in a single public school. In a number of others, no more than a token beginning has been made.

Eleven Southern state governments have also launched a program of "massive resistance" to the desegregation decisions of the Supreme Court, by various measures such as attempting to block access to the courts, by outlawing the NAACP, and intimidating law-abiding elements in the South from expressing their support of desegregation. A tragic consequence of this resistance is a contempt for law that has encouraged the KKK and other secret gangs to resort to dynamiting and other acts of violence. This campaign of terror is likely to continue unless the impetus to anarchy engendered by state governments is removed.

In addition, our conspicuous failure to fulfill the promise of equality to all our citizens has a grave adverse impact on America's leadership of the Free World. Continuing failure to solve promptly and peacefully what has aptly been called the "American dilemma" can only jeopardize that leadership and the preservation and extension of freedom throughout the world.

The effort to end the shame of racial segregation has suffered from a lack of leadership on the part of the national Administration, which has tended to treat racial segregation as an abstract issue with equal degrees of right on each side and has counselled unending "patience" to those whose rights are being denied. At a time when the defenders of White Supremacy are moving close to success in their effort to nullify the Constitution in a large part of the country, we cannot afford any "breathing spells." We must not indulge the vain hope that this problem will settle itself in a manner

In 1958 Will Maslow was director of the Department of Public Affairs, American Jewish Congress. Henry Lee Moon was in the leadership of the NAACP and author of *Balance of Power: The Negro Vote.*

These resolutions were enclosed in a letter from Will Maslow to Henry Lee Moon, May 21, 1958. NAACP Papers, Box III A 196, Library of Congress, Manuscript Division, Washington, D.C.

consistent with our ideals. We need vigorous action by the Federal government designed to end state-imposed segregation as rapidly as possible.

Enactment of a civil rights act by the United States Congress during 1957, the first such law in more than 80 years, has given proof of the strength of the American people's desire that the democratic promise of equality should be more nearly realized. Yet the substantive provisions of that law deal only with the narrow area of voting rights. There is much more that the United States Congress can and must do to enforce constitutional guarantees that are known to be widely ignored. It can enact statutory provisions, similar to those stricken from the 1957 Civil Rights Act, to improve enforcement procedures for a wide range of Federal rights.

Enactment of the 1957 Civil Rights Act was accomplished despite the rules of the United States Senate that permit a minority of its members to defeat legislation by filibustering. Those rules remain as obstacles to the enactment of further necessary civil rights bills. Every effort must be made to change those rules so as to restore majority rule to our national legislature.

This Convention of the AJCongress therefore urges that:

(1) The United States Congress should empower the Attorney General to bring civil proceedings to enjoin violation by state officials, of any Federal Constitutional or statutory right, including the right to attend a desegregated school.

(2) The United States Congress should enact legislation forbidding the grant of financial or other assistance by the Federal government to educational, housing and other programs which discriminate or segregate on racial or religious grounds.

(3) The Department of Justice should take more vigorous steps to exercise the powers conferred on it by the Civil Right Act of 1957 to protect the right to vote from discrimination or denial based on race.

(4) The rules of the United States Senate should be revised to end the filibuster and so protect majority rule in the Senate.

(5) The Eisenhower Administration should abandon the neutral attitude between those who favor and those who oppose compliance with the constitutional guarantee of equality. It should:

    (a) Use the vast influences of the President's office to develop a climate of acceptance of the national policy of desegregation.

    (b) Call a White House Conference of religious, educational, and other civic leaders to devise measures to secure acceptance of and speed up compliance with the Supreme Court desegregation decision.

    (c) Prosecute criminally in the Federal Courts all hoodlums, KKK, and other lawless elements that interfere with the enforcement of any Federal court order directing desegregation.

The American Jewish Congress will work with other organizations and with all those willing to join in a resolute effort to end the contradiction between our inspiring principle of equality and the offensive practices of segregation and discrimination that still oppose millions of Americans and warp the lives of us all.

## SOUTHERN BOMBINGS

In recent months, six bombings and attempted bombings of Jewish places of worship and community centers have occurred in Southern cities: Charlotte and Gastonia, North Carolina; Nashville, Tennessee; Birmingham, Alabama, and Miami and Jacksonville, Florida. Evidence has accumulated that these incidents are the work of an organized group calling itself the "Confederate Underground" and that this group is also responsible for a number of similar attacks upon Negro institutions.

The mayors and police chiefs of the cities affected have shown their concern with these developments by meeting in Jacksonville with the mayors and police chiefs of other Southern cities to plan joint action to discover and punish the persons responsible for these acts of violence. Federal law enforcement officials, however, have taken no action in this matter. They have insisted that there is no ground for believing that Federal laws may have been violated and that consequently the FBI has no authority to intervene. They have even declined an invitation to send a representative to the Jacksonville meeting of mayors. The FBI refuses even to begin an investigation to determine whether Federal law has been violated.

In the past the FBI has not raised such technical objections to its investigative powers. In 1947, one-hundred FBI agents for months investigated a race riot in Monroe, Georgia. In 1952, the FBI investigated the bombing in Florida that killed an NAACP leader.

Nor has the Administration urged any legislation, like the Lindbergh anti-kidnapping law, that would remove any question of jurisdiction and clearly empower the FBI to investigate acts of violence where criminals have crossed state lines.

This Convention of the American Jewish Congress therefore urges that:

(1) The Attorney General of the United States direct an immediate FBI investigation of such violence;

(2) Although we are satisfied that the FBI already has the legal authority to initiate such an investigation, in order to free the question from any doubt the United States Congress should enact legislation making it a Federal crime to transport any explosive across state lines with the intention of using such material in violation of the criminal law of any state.

## THE SOUTHERN JEWISH COMMUNITY

This Convention of the American Jewish Congress, meeting in Miami Beach, Florida, extends warm greetings to the Jewish communities of the South. Mindful of the tensions and pressures to which they are subject, we express our encouragement to them in dealing with the efforts now being made by White Citizens Councils, Ku Klux Klan and other racist elements to prevent compliance with the constitutional prohibition of State imposed racial segregation. It is a source of pride to Jews everywhere that despite these extreme pressures the overwhelming majority of our faith have followed their ethical heritage and rejected the evil doctrine of "white supremacy."

The American Jewish Congress and virtually all other national Jewish organizations concerned with combatting anti-Semitism have long acted on the principle that racial and religious discrimination, in all its forms, is a single evil that must be combatted wherever it appears. We are opposed to racial segregation both because of its inherent immorality and because anti-Semitism will not be ended as long as racial segregation endures.

Believing that security for Jews lies in eliminating all forms of prejudice and discrimination, the American Jewish Congress pledges unremitting efforts to end the system of racial segregation wherever it exists. We are confident that, in this work, we will have the cooperation of the Southern Jewish community.

## INTEGRATION IN THE NORTH

Segregation of Negroes in the public schools of the North is altogether too widespread. Northern segregation, however, comes about not because of state statutes or governmental policy establishing all-Negro or all-white schools but in large measure as the inevitable result of segregated housing patterns. These segregated neighborhoods in turn result from un-official but nevertheless potent forces: certain real estate and banking interests fortified by local community sentiment.

The evil consequences of segregated schools are the same, however, whether they result from law or segregated housing. Segregated schools mean "problem" schools, inferior teaching and lower levels of pupil achievement. In brief, inferior education.

Similar evils flow from segregated housing in the North: exhorbitant rents, dreadful overcrowding, dirty and unsafe streets, in short, blighted areas and slums. These slums in turn produce a disproportionate amount of crime, disease, juvenile delinquency and heightened racial tensions.

These problems are thus as complex in the North as similar problems in the South. The vital difference, however, is that in the South, the whole panoply of state power commands such segregation; in the North, state power is simply indifferent to it. This vital difference, however, points toward a solution, however slow and tortuous.

The Jewish community in the North cannot be indifferent to these problems. It has lived too long in religious ghettoes to be indifferent to racial ghettoes. It has suffered too long from religious prejudice to be indifferent to racial prejudice.

The American Jewish Congress therefore calls upon the Jews of the North and upon all men of good will to resist the forces that bring about segregation. It pledges all-out support for anti-discrimination laws and programs and for educational campaigns to awaken the mind and conscience of the North to these evils.

# Correspondence between Isaac Toubin and Roy Wilkins

Dear Roy:

Last Sunday night at a plenary session of the NCRAC [National Community Relations Advisory Committee], I became involved in a somewhat strenuous debate with two of my southern colleagues. One of them, from Norfolk, quoted you as having said something to this effect: "Not only does the activity of the Jewish community not help the Negro in the South, but it is actually harmful in the fight against segregation." I impulsively challenged the statement from the floor. After the speaker had concluded and there was an interruption for refreshments, I apologized for my impulsiveness and asked the speaker for the source of this quote. He said that the national executive of another national Jewish agency had reported this to him. From another person, I learned that the regional director of this national Jewish agency had quoted you to this effect.

When the meeting resumed, I proceeded to set forth what I thought to be the position of the Jewish community on the subject of integration and denied that you had ever made such a statement. Once before, Negro leaders had been quoted in a similar vein and I must say that the use of such a quote is devastating in the course of any debate.

I know that in our conversations on this subject you have denied saying or believing such a thing. I have no doubt that there are times and peculiar circumstances that require a strategy in which the Jewish minority should not play a conspicuous role in this struggle, but our southern friends are apparently quoting you effectively as a proponent of a thesis that the efforts of Jews are harmful. It would be helpful, therefore, to have a succinct denial in writing to which we can refer in the event this argument is used in the course of debate once again.

With every good wish to you for a pleasant summer, I am—

Sincerely yours,
Isaac Toubin

Dear Isaac:

I am astonished (and disturbed) to have your letter of June 18 with its alleged quotation from me as follows: "Not only does the activity of the Jewish community not help the Negro in the South, but it is actually harmful in the fight against segregation."

In 1958 Isaac Toubin was the executive director of the American Jewish Congress. Roy Wilkins was the executive secretary of the NAACP.

This exchange took place on June 18 and 26, 1958. NAACP Papers, Box III A 198 Library of Congress Manuscript Division, Washington, D.C.

Neither this statement nor anything faintly approximating it was ever made by me on any occasion, in Norfolk, Virginia, or elsewhere.

I fully understand the feelings of some members of Southern Jewish communities on the integration struggle. They would prefer not being identified with it in any way. They regret the pronouncements and activities of their national Jewish agencies on the topic. I am informed of the heated debates that have taken place in meetings held in the North and in the South, in which Southern Jewish leaders have been vigorous in advancing the position that national Jewish agencies should not "embarrass" them by stating forthright views in support of desegregation. I think I can understand their position even if I cannot agree with it.

But for them to go the the extreme of attributing to me a statement which they feel validates their stand is carrying matters pretty far.

We have rejoiced in the aid and understanding we have received in this monumental struggle from courageous members of the American Jewish community, North and South. It is discouraging, indeed, that in their anxiety to remain above the conflict the dissidents should resort to hearing what was never said and disseminating what was never even a thought, much less a word.

With all good wishes,

Very sincerely yours,
Roy Wilkins,
Executive Secretary

# Correspondence between C. L. Dellums and Roy Wilkins

Dear Roy:

I have read the articles about Harold L. Keith in the Courier and have been wondering if this bird is interested in anything other than circulation. It is still difficult for me to understand how a so-call newspaperman could write such articles without clearing with and most certainly interviewing the leadership on both sides. I was tempted to write Keith and tell him that he is nuts and that there most certainly is no difficulty between the Negro and Jewish Leadership on the West Coast, but he has been answered most thoroughly and far more competently than I could have done. . . .

I wouldn't attempt to speak for the East because I don't know nearly that much about it, but I think in my position I am certainly qualified to say what does go on out here. The Jewish Labor Committee, Negro Trade Union Leadership and the N.A.A.C.P. work together hand in glove. As a matter of fact, the Jewish Labor Committee rendered greater service to the cause of establishing F.E.P. in California than any other single agency. They allowed their paid staff personnel in both San Francisco and Los Angeles to devote as much time as needed to F.E.P.C. during the last two sessions of the California Legislature. I cannot praise the Jewish Labor Committee too highly for the part they played in our campaign for an F.E.P. law in California during the last 5 or 6 years. I just wanted you to know that at least on the Pacific Coast the articles this guy wrote just doesn't apply in any respect. And as a matter of fact it couldn't exist in the Labor Movement nationally without my knowledge. . . .

Very sincerely yours,
C. L. Dellums

Dear C.L.:

Thank you for your letter on the Pittsburgh Courier article on alleged Negro-Jewish conflict in the labor movement over civil rights.

Keith blundered on this, using a petty racial-religious approach to what you certainly know is a very complex problem.

Very sincerely yours,
Roy Wilkins,
Executive Secretary

In 1960 C. L. Dellums was third international vice-president of the Brotherhood of Sleeping Car Porters, based in Oakland, California. Roy Wilkins was executive secretary of the NAACP.
This exchange took place on January 13 and 26, 1960. NAACP Papers, Box III A 179, Library of Congress, Manuscript Division, Washington, D.C.

# From *The Best of Harry Golden*

## THE VERTICAL NEGRO PLAN

Those who love North Carolina will jump at the chance to share in the great responsibility confronting our Governor and the State Legislature. A special session of the Legislature (July 25–28, 1956) passed a series of amendments to the State Constitution. These proposals submitted by the Governor and his Advisory Education Committee included the following:

(A) The elimination of the compulsory attendance law, "to prevent any child from being forced to attend a school with a child of another race."

(B) The establishment of "Education Expense Grants" for education in a private school, "in the case of a child assigned to a public school attended by a child of another race."

(C) A "uniform system of local option" whereby a majority of the folks in a school district may suspend or close a school if the situation becomes "intolerable."

But suppose a Negro child applies for this "Education Expense Grant" and says he wants to go to a private school too? There are fourteen Supreme Court decisions involving the use of public funds; there are only two "decisions" involving the elimination of racial discrimination in the public schools.

The Governor has said that critics of these proposals have not offered any constructive advice or alternatives. Permit me, therefore, to offer an idea for the consideration of the members of the regular sessions. A careful study of my plan, I believe, will show that it will save millions of dollars in tax funds and eliminate forever the danger to our public education system. Before I outline my plan, I would like to give you a little background.

One of the factors involved in our tremendous industrial growth and economic prosperity is the fact that the South, voluntarily, has all but eliminated VERTICAL SEGREGATION. The tremendous buying power of the twelve million Negroes in the South has been based wholly on the absence of racial segregation. The white and Negro stand at the same grocery and supermarket counters; deposit money at the same bank teller's window; pay phone and light bills to the same clerk; walk through the same dime and department stores, and stand at the same drugstore counters.

It is only when the Negro "sets" that the fur begins to fly.

Harry Golden was the editor of the *Carolina Israelite*.
Reprinted from Harry Golden, *The Best of Harry Golden* (Cleveland: World Publishing, 1967). Copyright © 1967. Reprinted by permission of HarperCollins Publishers.

Now, since we are not even thinking about restoring VERTICAL SEGREGATION, I think my plan would not only comply with the Supreme Court decisions, but would maintain "sitting-down" segregation. Now here is the GOLDEN VERTICAL NEGRO PLAN. Instead of all those complicated proposals, all the next session needs to do is pass one small amendment which would provide only desks in all the public schools of our state—no seats.

The desks should be those standing-up jobs, like the old-fashioned bookkeeping desk. Since no one in the South pays the slightest attention to a VERTICAL NEGRO, this will completely solve our problem. And it is not such a terrible inconvenience for young people to stand up during their classroom studies. In fact, this may be a blessing in disguise. They are not learning to read sitting down, anyway; maybe standing up will help. This will save more millions of dollars in the cost of our remedial English course when the kids enter college. In whatever direction you look with the GOLDEN VERTICAL NEGRO PLAN, you save millions of dollars, to say nothing of eliminating forever any danger to our public education system upon which rests the destiny, hopes, and happiness of this society.

My WHITE BABY PLAN offers another possible solution to the segregation problem— this time in a field other than education.

Here is an actual case history of the "White Baby Plan to End Racial Segregation":

Some months ago there was a revival of the Laurence Olivier movie, *Hamlet*, and several Negro schoolteachers were eager to see it. One Saturday afternoon they asked some white friends to lend them two of their little children, a three-year-old girl and a six-year-old boy, and, holding these white children by the hands, they obtained tickets from the movie-house cashier without a moment's hesitation. They were in like Flynn.

This would also solve the baby-sitting problem for thousands and thousands of white working mothers. There can be a mutual exchange of references, then the people can sort of pool their children at a central point in each neighborhood, and every time a Negro wants to go to the movies all she need to do is pick up a white child—and go.

Eventually the Negro community can set up a factory and manufacture white babies made of plastic, and when they want to go to the opera or to a concert, all they need do is carry that plastic doll in their arms. The dolls, of course, should all have blond curls and blue eyes, which would go even further; it would give the Negro woman and her husband priority over the whites for the very best seats in the house.

While I still have faith in the WHITE BABY PLAN, my final proposal may prove to be the most practical of all.

Only after a successful test was I ready to announce formally the GOLDEN "OUT-OF-ORDER" PLAN.

I tried my plan in a city of North Carolina, where the Negroes represent 39 per cent of the population.

I prevailed upon the manager of a department store to shut the water off in his "white" water fountain and put up a sign, "Out-of-Order." For the first day or two the whites were hesitant, but little by little they began to drink out of the water fountain belonging to the "coloreds"—and by the end of the third week everybody was drinking the "segregated" water; with not a single solitary complaint to date.

I believe the test is of such sociological significance that the Governor should appoint a special committee of two members of the House and two Senators to investigate the GOLDEN "OUT-OF-ORDER" PLAN. We kept daily reports on the use of the unsegregated water fountain which should be of great value to this committee. This may be the answer to the necessary uplifting of the white morale. It is possible that the whites may accept desegregation if they are assured that the facilities are still "separate," albeit "Out-of-Order."

As I see it now, the key to my Plan is to keep the "Out-of-Order" sign up for at least two years. We must do this thing gradually.

## NEGRO ANTI-SEMITES

I have heard a disturbing question in recent months.

"How come you speak so strongly for Negro integration, Mr. Golden? Don't you know there are Negro anti-Semites?"

This is a puzzling attitude, one that dismays me. Assuming the truth of some Negro anti-Semitism, it is minimal compared to the other forms of this virulent prejudice. Why do the folks think democracy is a matter of you-scratch-my-back-and-I'll-scratch-yours?

The Negroes are people, not paragons. As people they have the same faults, vices, fears and are as badly informed as anybody else. Negroes have their share of greed, avarice, hatred, and ignorance. But they have the same virtues, or potential virtues, as humanity everywhere.

I do not doubt there are Negro anti-Semites. Negroes so afflicted are like children who don't get the point of the joke but who laugh because the adults are laughing. They are like the Copts in the Middle East who imitated the walk of the French officers.

Neither Negro anti-Semitism nor any Negro vices bear on the important subject of civil rights for all.

My own experience tells me a Negro anti-Semite is about as convincing as a Jewish white supremacist (and indeed we do have Jewish white supremacists): both think they can become French officers by merely imitating the walk.

# From *Negro and Jew: An Encounter in America*

During the question and answer period after a lecture at the Concord Hotel in the Catskills a lady rose to ask: "Mr. Golden, why do you always talk about civil rights? What have the Negroes ever done for us? Don't you know that most of them are anti-Semites?" To which I replied, "As soon as the Negroes have a Concord Hotel I'll stop talking about civil rights. Furthermore, I assure you, a Negro anti-Semite is about as convincing as a Jewish white supremacist."

After all, why should we segregate anti-Semites? Is there really a difference between a colored anti-Semite and a white anti-Semite? Are there different ways of dealing with anti-Semites? And why should we be surprised that there are Negro anti-Semites?

I am convinced, along with Horace Kallen and Maurice Samuel, that anti-Semitism is a *constant* of western culture. Thus as the Negro enters the middle class he will reflect some of the attitudes of his former masters; indeed, as many Jews in the South reflect the attitudes and even the prejudices of the surrounding white Protestant society.

Long before there was any talk of Negro anti-Semitism, Jewish laymen in the South were demanding that their rabbi "stick to religion and leave civil rights alone," precisely the same instructions the Methodist, Presbyterian and Baptist laymen gave their clergy.

I spent a morning interviewing several members of New York's PAT (Parents and Taxpayers). These women were picketing against the bussing of their children to school in other neighborhoods to facilitate integration in the city. After talking to several of these indignant mothers, I finally asked, "Are there any Gentile PAT's?" This was in 1964. In 1966, it is easier to see that the anger of the Jewish PAT is the same anger and fear the Poles of southside Chicago express when they hurl rocks at Negro demonstrators. The only difference is the Poles fly Confederate flags in their forays against the black man.

More, of course, is involved than the fear of property depreciation, sloppy neighbor-hoods, or interracial marriages. The antipathy to the Negro social revolution involves more, much more: this antipathy is a manifestation of the dilemma of the American middle and near-middle class. Gaining wealth and/or middle-class status is no longer the goal in itself. Instead, these classes are afflicted by the fear of displacement.

At dozens of Jewish fund-raising dinners around the country, I hear whispers on every dais about Negro anti-Semitism. But all I interpret in those whispers is the voice of a man who wants *out* on a commitment.

Harry Golden was the editor of the *Carolina Israelite*.
Reprinted from *Negro and Jew: An Encounter in America: A Symposium Compiled by* Midstream Magazine, ed. Shlomo Katz (New York: Macmillan, 1967). Copyright © 1967 by the Theodor Herzl Foundation. Reprinted with permission of Simon and Schuster.

Negro anti-Semitism takes into consideration, too, the Negro's own resentment. No one who has ever succeeded likes his "first friend." It is much easier to believe one has pulled oneself up by one's own bootstraps.

And the Jew was indeed the Negroes' "first friend" almost from the day the Negro was allowed a friend. The Jew was the first white man to grant the newly liberated Negro some degree of humanity. In the most rigid days of segregation, following the Reconstruction period, Jewish peddlers and merchants began to sell to the Negroes on credit, and a Jew was the first white man to sell the Negro an insurance policy. When most of the uptown stores warned Negroes: "Don't touch unless you buy," the Jewish merchant allowed the Negro to try on the dress or suit or the hat. Elderly Negro women have told me that when the "Jew collector-man" came around they insisted the children see the book with their name written on the account sheet: "Mr. and Mrs. Isaac Jones." Those were the days, in the Southern Christian society, when even the Negro's purchase of a plug of tobacco had to be put on the account sheet of the farmer or landlord for whom he worked.

After the Emancipation, the white native-born Americans kept the Negro securely locked out of the open society. And no other immigrant group paid him the slightest attention: not the Germans, nor the Irish, nor the Poles, nor the Italians, nor the Hungarians, nor the Slovaks; only the Jew established a line of communication, albeit a line of communication in trade and credit merchandising. True, the Jew had an advantage. To him the American Negro was no different from the Gentile peasants among whom he lived and with whom he dealt in the towns and villages of Russia, Galicia, Hungary and Poland.

The Negroes burned the Jewish stores in Watts in 1965 and Jewish stores in Detroit twenty years earlier, because, in the main, Jewish stores were the only stores to burn. *The Jew was often the only white man in a Negro ghetto.* He was there because he was willing to take a chance he could make a modest living out of the poverty-stricken slum.

(It was not until the Negro began to receive a regular government check during the New Deal that the white Christian merchants began to beckon to him for the first time.)

There were times when only the Jewish storekeeper would advance the money a Negro mother needed to bail her son out of the police station. In countless instances, the Jewish store was the place to which the Negro came when in trouble, when a Negro parent needed a lawyer, or advice on other important matters.

I do not mean that there was no exploitation of the slum Negro. Indeed there was. The poor always pay more for less and the Negro is no exception. Dick Gregory, the Negro comedian, told me his mother was a pious, decent woman, who thought nothing of asking, "Go down to the store and get a few bananas." Though she gave him no money, he came back with the bananas. If the Jewish merchant overcharged his customers penny after penny, the Negro children of the slum helped even the score. The whole process of racial segregation and discrimination is a dehumanizing process, corrupting both the buyer and the seller, the tenant and the landlord.

There is no doubt there are Negro anti-Semites; and I know that as Negroes escape the margins of society, there will probably be many more Negro anti-Semites. And as Negroes enter the open society, they may find the Jews a terrible burden. As his "first friend," the Jew must remain forever linked to the Negro's original status of racial inferiority. Fellowship with the Jew will prove no bargain for the Negro. The Jew knew him "when." Negro writers refer to the "white liberals" as "phonies." We know whom these writers have in mind and it is neither Bishop Pike nor Lillian Smith. It was hardly a Freudian slip for novelist James Baldwin to have said, "Georgia has its Negro and Harlem its Jew."

Indeed at its last NAACP convention I observed the growing resentment against Kivie Kaplan. Mr. Kaplan, an Orthodox Jew, is the organization's President. Ten years ago he liquidated a highly profitable business saying: "I feel that I must march with the Negroes." But for James Baldwin and thousands like him yet to come, fellowship with a Kivie Kaplan will add nothing to self-esteem. James Baldwin will know he has arrived, for example, not when a Kivie Kaplan buys his books and invites him to his home, but when a Senator Herman Talmadge buys his books and offers fellowship. This is still a long, long way off, but without it, I am afraid the Baldwins will never consider their victory complete, no more than middle-class Jews, even into the third generation, who aspire so desperately to be welcomed by a Fair Haven Golf Club or even by the Palm Springs Regatta.

But what has really surprised me is that there are so many Jews who still do not understand the mysteries of anti-Semitism. I've heard arguments recently, from responsible sources, that Jews are disproportionately represented in low-cost housing and retail establishments in the Negro ghetto. Ah, if only our fathers shaved their beards we'd become Americans immediately, is what we youngsters heard sixty years ago; or ah, if only more of the Jews were farmers. . . . There are people who still refuse to believe, *es vet gornisht helffen,* that if there were no Jewish "slumlords" or Jewish stores in the ghetto, anti-Semitism would hardly miss a beat.

But I also wonder at Negro writers who have had so much to say about the "Jewish" slumlord. I think of the thousands of Southern Protestants who have built vast fortunes on Negro slum housing. In every city and town the richest man, next to the mill-owner and the Coca Cola distributor, is the man with what are called, "nigger houses." Fortunes have been made and multiplied. The dwellings, which even today cost about $2500 with rare repair and paint bills, usually house four Negro families who pay their rent weekly and return to the owner every year more than his original investment. The Southern ladies call this property, more delicately, "nigs." An elderly grande dame of the United Daughters of the Confederacy, says, "My father was smart—didn't bother with cotton, or get into the jungle of the mill business; he was smart, left us about two hundred 'nigs.'" These "nigs" are one of the reasons the Southerners fight against (a) slum clearance, and (b) including laundry workers and domestics in the one-dollar-minimum-wage legislation of the several states.

I make no apology for Jewish slumlords of Harlem. I do condemn a society that has tolerated for so long the "nigger houses" of Harlem, Dallas, Watts, Charlotte, and of a thousand other cities and towns of America, owned by Protestants, Catholics, Jews, Negroes, and anonymous insurance companies.

Basically, however, Negro anti-Semitism is peripheral to the whole subject, the main issue. Whether some Negroes are or are not anti-Semites bears not at all on whether all

Negroes enjoy first class citizenship and move about as free men, and their children are unimpeded and uninhibited by segregation and discrimination.

The struggle for civil rights, insofar as some whites have participated, is not a struggle solely for the Negro. In the late 1940's it was already clear that the Negro civil rights movement was for all America, perhaps for the Jews most of all. The Negro has indeed given the Jew a free ride. The Negro lawyers who have walked in and out of the American court rooms during these past twenty years have made the Constitution of the United States a living document. Their struggle has convinced Americans, and continues to convince them every day, that the Constitution means just what it says. Thus we Jews have achieved a great victory, without even being exposed to the firing line.

# Blacks and Jews in the Civil Rights Movement

I don't know whether any further discussions of Afro-American–Jewish relations would be productive. To merely describe the mutually supportive relations that have existed and continue to exist between some Afro-Americans and some Jews would probably not reduce the mutually hostile relations that have existed and continue to exist between other blacks and other Jews. Thus, despite the fact that no major civil rights group—and certainly not the NAACP—has ever taken an official position that was hostile toward Jews or toward Israel, considerable attention has been directed toward black individuals and non–civil rights groups that have taken such positions. One might suggest that Afro-Americans and Jews who wish to cooperate should do so, but, for reasons rooted in history, many of those who wish to cooperate are often unable to avoid focusing their attention on those who do not.

This is clearly evident, for example, in the ever-growing body of writings by Afro-Americans about black anti-Semitism. During the past forty years, a highly stylized ritual has developed that involves Afro-American writers explaining to a largely Jewish readership why anti-Jewish sentiments exist in Afro-American communities. The avowed purpose of these writers is to reassure Jews, but the fact that reassurance is not lasting and that the process is repetitive suggests that other motives might be involved. James Baldwin's article, "Negroes Are Anti-Semitic Because They're Anti-White," published in 1967, added little of substance that had not already been stated in Lawrence Reddick's article, "Anti-Semitism among Negroes," published in 1942, or Kenneth Clark's "Candor in Negro-Jewish Relations," published in 1946.[1] One suggests that Baldwin, Reddick, and Clark each realized that their Jewish friends would not be completely reassured by their rejection of anti-Semitism and their simultaneous inciteful explorations of the sources of anti-Jewish sentiments in the life experiences of millions of Afro-Americans.[2]

Can we move beyond ritualistic disavowals of anti-Semitism and equally ritualistic efforts to locate anti-Jewish attitudes within the logic of Afro-American history and Afro-American culture? Can a black person comment on the problem of Afro-American-Jewish conflict without becoming part of the problem? I am not sure about the answers to these questions, but I believe that the questions at least lead us beyond

Claybourne Carson Jr. is professor of history at Stanford University and editor and director of the Martin Luther King, Jr., Papers Project.

Originally published in *Jews in Black Perspectives: A Dialogue,* ed. Joseph R. Washington Jr. (Rutherford, N.J.: Fairleigh Dickinson University Press, 1984), 113–31. Copyright © 1984, Associated University Presses, Inc. Reprinted with permission of Associated University Presses, Inc.

the confines of the existing literature on Afro-American-Jewish relations. The questions lead us away from efforts to express and explain intergroup attitudes toward an attempt to understand the historical settings that sometimes alters these attitudes and affects their social salience. I am not sure whether we can ever conclusively decide whether black anti-Semitism or Jewish racism are becoming more or less significant or whether Afro-American and Jewish concerns are diverging or converging. Perhaps, however, we can leave behind sterile intergroup arguments about such matters and look instead at the multitude of historical factors that affect the perception each group has of the other and that periodically produce conflicts between the two groups. I would argue that previous writings on Afro-American-Jewish relations have succeeded more in expressing the hopes and fears of the writers than in altering the attitudes each group holds toward the other.

My hope nonetheless is that historical perspective will enable us to view anew a few incidents during a recent period of Afro-American-Jewish conflict by placing the incidents in the web of individual lives and of history. I will argue that many of the Afro-American-Jewish conflicts of the period after 1966 were manifestations of internal conflicts and ambivalences within the Afro-American community, and that these conflicts among Afro-Americans had significant parallels among Jews.

Ambivalence and complexity certainly characterize the attitudes and actions of blacks associated with the Student Nonviolent Coordinating Committee (SNCC), a group that became enmeshed in the Afro-American-Jewish conflicts of the period after 1966. Most SNCC workers did not seek to become involved in these conflicts, but the history and character of the organization insured that it would play a singular role in them. Because SNCC was unique among civil rights organizations, its history of interactions with Jews was also unique. Unlike the NAACP and CORE, which had had significant Jewish involvement since their inceptions, SNCC only gradually attracted Jews in noticeable numbers. Moreover, Jews who associated themselves with SNCC did so on terms established by the black student militants who dominated the organization. SNCC's relations with Jews, and with other whites, cannot be compared to the high-level alliance that existed among leaders of other civil rights and Jewish organizations, because SNCC offered no quid pro quo in return for Jewish support. As political scientist Michael Walzer noted during the early stages of the black student sit-ins, black students did not "ask, or even hint, that whites should join their picket lines. It will be better for them, and for us, I was told, if *they* came unasked."[3] Jewish SNCC supporters gave their support without asking for SNCC support of Jewish causes; indeed, Jews did not call attention to their religious background. From SNCC's perspective, they entered the Movement simply as whites, although some would leave as Jews.

Founded by Southern black students who had led the lunch counter sit-ins of 1960, SNCC developed into a cadre of full-time activists and organizers, most of whom were Southern blacks. Whites who joined SNCC's staff were primarily Southern whites, and even the handful of Northern whites were, during the early 1960s, more often Christians than Jews. Publicist Dotty Miller, a graduate of Queens College, and adviser Howard Zinn, then a professor at Spelman College, were, in the early 1960s, among a small number of Jews directly involved in SNCC's work. Even after an influx of Jewish volunteers during the Mississippi Summer Project of 1964, Jews working full time with SNCC were considerably outnumbered by white Protestants and even more by blacks, Northern and Southern.

SNCC's reliance on ad hoc fund-raising efforts outside the South led to the development of extensive ties between SNCC and Northern Jews. This indirect involvement contained seeds of future conflict, however, since it led SNCC leaders to ignore the increasingly evident divergences between the prevailing Jewish conception of the civil rights movement as an effort to gain new legal protections against discrimination and the increasingly accepted view among blacks that it was an effort to gain direct government intervention on behalf of blacks to overcome past racial inequities. Although it is impossible to determine precisely what proportion of SNCC's financial support came from Jews, there are many indications that it was considerable. During SNCC's early years, crucial support came from radical lawyer, Victor Rabinowitz. Subsequently, Rabinowitz and other Jewish lawyers associated with the National Lawyers Guild made it possible for SNCC to avoid becoming dependent upon the more restrictive legal assistance provided by Jack Greenberg's NAACP Legal Defense Fund.

From 1963 through 1966, SNCC's New York office, headed by Elizabeth Sutherland, concentrated its efforts on attracting Jewish support and succeeded in raising far more contributions than any other SNCC office. At least one-fourth and sometimes more than half of the monthly contributions SNCC received during this period came from the New York area.[4] Prominent Jewish supporters such as Theodore Bikel also aided SNCC by participating in fund-raising concerts or cocktail parties. A symbiotic relationship developed between SNCC, which needed financial support yet refused to compromise its militancy in return for that support, and a radical minority of Northern Jews, who were attracted by SNCC's uncompromising militancy and by its singular willingness to have help from sources that would have been viewed with suspicion by more moderate civil rights groups.

SNCC's decision to concentrate its fund-raising efforts in the Jewish community and the positive response of that community, even as SNCC became more radical, was an outgrowth of a shared Afro-American–Jewish radical culture. This culture was the product of a long history of cultural and historical interactions, concentrated particularly in the Communist party during the years after World War I and especially evident in New York City. Although SNCC's early leaders, often training for the Christian ministry, initially directed their appeals toward the Northern Christian student movement, SNCC's radicalization and the redirection of its fund-raising efforts each resulted from the entry into the group of blacks who were products of this radical culture centered in New York.

Thus the often-noted parallels between the Biblical stories of Jewish oppression and the travails of Afro-Americans were less significant in accounting for SNCC-Jewish ties than were the common experiences of a small minority of Afro-Americans and Jews: those whose attitudes were shaped by awareness of secular radicalism and political dissent, from labor organizing in the 1930s to more isolated protest activity during the 1940s and 1950s. To refer to the outgrowths of these common experiences as a culture may stretch the term somewhat, but I would argue that a number of blacks and Jews became similarly alienated from prevailing white cultural values to the point that they became more like each other than like the most culturally distinctive members of their own group.

One does not have to accept Harold Cruse's conclusions about the damaging consequences of Afro-American–Jewish interactions within the Communist party to recognize the validity of his view that Afro-American–Jewish radicalism never encompassed Jewish culture, for that was known to be the preserve of Jews alone.[5] Because Cruse was so determined to condemn black radical intellectuals for separating themselves from black nationalist culture, he was reluctant to admit the understandable appeal, particularly during the period from Garvey's fall to Malcolm's emergence, of a dynamic, activist-oriented, intellectually vibrant, Afro-American–Jewish radicalism over a moribund, accommodationist, intellectually stagnant black nationalism.

Jewish radicals rejected the staid, thoroughly WASPish, approaches of the Socialist party and actively sought black support even after the Communist party lost its effectiveness as a vehicle for radical activism. Especially in New York, an Afro-American–Jewish radical community survived occasional internal conflicts during the 1930s, 1940s, and 1950s to become a seedbed for civil rights activism during the 1960s. It was in this Afro-American–Jewish radical community that blacks gained awareness of protest and propaganda techniques and a faith that these techniques, despite the fact that they were used by small numbers of radicals, might someday change American society. No comparable faith existed among black nationalists of the period after Garvey.

Although he was by the 1950s a staunch anti-Communist, Bayard Rustin was a crucial link between this Afro-American–Jewish radical culture and the most radical of the civil rights groups of the 1960s: SNCC. Because his political life bridged the years from the radicalism of the 1930s to the rebirth of black militancy in the 1950s, Rustin was a central fixture in the Afro-American-Jewish civil rights coalition that developed in New York after World War II. He also influenced several of the activists who would later steer SNCC toward a radical course. In the early 1960s, when Rustin was organizing New York support for Martin Luther King, Jr., he noticed the dedication of a young black teacher at Horace Mann School, Bob Moses, who patiently worked stuffing envelopes and doing other mundane chores.

It was Rustin who sent Moses to Atlanta to work with Martin Luther King's Southern Christian Leadership Conference. After Moses spent the summer of 1960 working alongside student activists in the SCLC office in Atlanta, he returned the following summer to begin SNCC's Mississippi Summer Project. Rustin also influenced several of the Howard University students who would later play crucial roles in SNCC's transformation through his meetings with members of the Nonviolent Action Group at Howard University. Influential NAG members included Tom Kahn, a Jewish socialist who had worked closely with Rustin in New York, and Stokely Carmichael, who was himself a product of the New York Afro-American–Jewish culture of radicalism.

That Carmichael could be both a product of this culture and also a central figure in the Afro-American-Jewish conflicts after 1966 may require some explanation but also should not be surprising. The Afro-American-Jewish radical culture is an urban culture, but in urban centers it coexists with a resilient black separatist culture (and also, for that matter, with an irrepressible Jewish separatist culture). Although Carmichael moved toward a black nationalist philosophy, his ideological development was initially more strongly influenced by Jewish radicalism. In this respect, he followed a pattern similar to that of West Coast black nationalist Ron Karenga, who also developed his initial political awareness as a result of extensive contacts with Jewish socialists in Los Angeles.[6] Like Moses, Carmichael's political development was influenced by the Jews he met after winning admittance into one of New York's selective secondary schools—in Carmichael's case, Bronx High School of Science.

He envied the greater intellectual awareness of his white classmates. "All the other kids I went to school with, their fathers were professors, doctors; they were the smartest kids in the world," he later told Howard Zinn.[7] One of his best friends was Gene Dennis, the son of a New York Communist party leader and a resident of Harlem—unlike Carmichael, whose family lived in an otherwise all-white neighborhood in the Bronx. Carmichael associated with various socialist and communist youth groups while in high school. His first demonstration was on behalf of Israel. He later recalled: "Someone at the U.N. had said something anti-Semitic; I can't exactly remember who, but [the Young Peoples Socialist League] drew up a big picket-line at the U.N."[8]

Ironically, it was through Carmichael's contacts with Jews, especially Dennis, that he became acquainted with Benjamin Davis and other black radicals who were themselves products of the Afro-American–Jewish political culture that developed inside the Community party. By the end of Carmichael's high school years, his world view had clearly been shaped by his contacts with Jews. His ambition was to go to Brandeis University and become a teacher. Only the attraction of being near the sit-in protests led Carmichael to give in to his parents wishes that he attend a black school. After arriving at Howard in the fall of 1960, Carmichael, like other Northern blacks, was attracted to those aspects of SNCC that corresponded to the values of the urban radical culture.

More than other civil rights groups, SNCC increasingly rejected bourgeois culture; it demanded a moralistic commitment to sacrifice one's welfare on behalf of oppressed people; it stressed the value of rigorous discourse as a component of political action. It distrusted the prevailing white-Anglo-Saxon-Protestant liberalism that made civility and respectability preconditions for effective political action, and, most importantly, it saw the black struggle as a necessary component of fundamental social change.

Carmichael's election as SNCC's chairman in May 1966 marked the culmination of the displacement of Southern black activists, such as former chairman John Lewis, by Northern blacks who saw Lewis as too moderate and as lacking the kind of political sophistication they saw in themselves. Many of SNCC's new leaders were directly or indirectly influenced by the Northern tradition of Afro-American–Jewish radicalism, although by 1966 they also reflected the influence of Northern black nationalism.

The newly elected head of SNCC's International Affairs office, James Forman, had become involved in civil rights activities while living in Chicago, but, as SNCC's executive secretary, he had guided the development of the group's Northern fund-raising network. His move to New York during 1966 was part of a general drift of SNCC personnel from the rural South to the urban North and part of a gradual shift of

SNCC's emphasis from civil rights goals to broader economic and political objectives. Although this shift would ultimately result in conflict between SNCC and Jewish leftists, SNCC failed to recognize quickly the implications of the conflict between its objectives and its financial base. It remained permeated by the complex mixture of socialistic and nationalistic ideas advocated by Carmichael, Moses, Forman, Courtland Cox, Ivanhoe Donaldson, and many other Northern black activists.

Although these black activists were moving toward black nationalist ideas, which they hoped would allow them to express the sentiments of the urban black masses, they had initially stressed the need for socialistic economic reforms. By 1966, Carmichael and Cox had broken with Rustin and Kahn, but they were still part of a group of blacks, including Forman but no longer Bob Moses, who believed that interracial alliances were possible, if not probable, and still served as SNCC's primary links with Northern Jewish supporters.

After Carmichael's election as chairman and his subsequent highly publicized use of the "Black Power" slogan on the Mississippi march of June 1966, Carmichael was portrayed as a proponent of black nationalism, but he is more accurately seen as a man who stood uneasily between an urban black nationalist tradition with which he had had little personal contact and the radical culture that continued to shape his rhetoric. In his "Black Power" speeches he often pointed to parallels in Afro-American and Jewish experiences, sometimes misreading the historical evidence but always seeking to place blacks in the historical continuum of militant ethnic politics. He often mentioned Jews as a group that Afro-Americans should emulate while seeking to build a basis for social power.

Carmichael reflected earlier currents of Afro-American-Jewish radicalism in his verbal attacks on the hypocrisy of conventional liberalism and middle-class values. At the same time, he departed from that tradition by bringing to the fore issues of racial and ethnic identity that had always been a problematical, though still significant, part of the Afro-American-Jewish radical tradition. Significantly, Carmichael did not refer to the Jewish model in his discussion of the need for black cultural autonomy, perhaps recognizing that to do so would be to suggest that black separatism might become as conservative as were some forms of American Jewish Zionism.

Carmichael's expressed goals at the time did not extend much beyond the pluralism best articulated by Jewish liberals. Having abandoned Jewish socialism, Carmichael's views unwittingly converged with those of sociologist Nathan Glazer, who in 1964 had revealed the divisions among Jews regarding civil rights reforms by pointing to the conflicting interests of Afro-Americans and Jews, because, he argued, Afro-Americans sought equality of economic results while Jews sought equality of opportunity. Carmichael also foreshadowed the black consciousness theme by suggesting that blacks should not continue to break down the legitimate barriers imposed by surrounding ethnic groups while failing to preserve what was valuable to their own group.[9]

Despite his public reputation, within SNCC Carmichael was a firm advocate of maintaining contacts with those whites who were sufficiently alienated from the white majority to support SNCC on terms set by blacks. He remained on close terms with individual white activists and supported the use of SNCC funds to help white organizers found the Southern Students Organizing Committee and resisted efforts to expel whites from SNCC.

Carmichael's efforts to translate the new black militancy into terms SNCC's former white supporters could understand took the form of articles in the *New York Review of Books* and the *New Republic,* certainly not forums designed to reach the black urban masses. It also took the form of numerous appearances at predominantly white colleges and on radio and television shows, including extended interviews on "Face the Nation" and on the David Susskind show.

Many Jews, like other former SNCC supporters, were not willing to accept the new militancy, but Carmichael's background helps account for the successes he had in making black power a topic worthy of serious discussion within the Jewish Left. For some Jews, continued support for SNCC brought them into conflict with more conservative Jews who were only too willing to use SNCC as an example of the terrible consequences of Jewish radicalism. Despite their growing vulnerability to attack from other Jews, many Jewish SNCC supporters remained optimistic that SNCC would continue to be worthy of support.

*Jewish Currents* was among the Jewish journals to defend SNCC, arguing in 1966 that it was "particularly important for Jews, who are so alert to the dangers of racism as it affects them, to avoid misjudging an idealistic, heroic movement like SNCC, which is dedicated consciously to abolishing racism."[10] Journalist I. F. Stone saw the cry for black power as "psychological therapy" rather than "practical politics," but nonetheless he applauded SNCC's opposition to the Vietnam War and expressed hope that black militancy would prod the nation into eliminating ghetto poverty.[11]

Although some Jews cut off their support to SNCC during 1966, most did so because they, like many former non-Jewish supporters, disagreed with SNCC's antiwar stance and with Carmichael's inflammatory rhetoric. I located only one letter in SNCC's files that suggested that Jewish supporters saw anti-Semitic overtones in the black power rhetoric. SNCC responded to his note from a New York attorney in a polite letter claiming that nothing in its policies or programs suggested anti-Semitism, adding that the organization was "very aware of the support it has received, both 'physical' and financial, from American Jews and appreciates it."[12] In contrast to this one negative letter were those like the one from a sixty-six-year-old Los Angeles Jew who wrote Carmichael to object to what he considered to be the effort by Susskind to inject the issue of anti-Semitism into Carmichael's discussion of black power.[13]

SNCC files also contain a revealing letter from the executive secretary of a Chicago temple, who gently chided Carmichael after the SNCC chairman had quoted Hillel and incorrectly referred to him as a German. Carmichael's apologetic reply insisted that he had quickly recognized his own mistake and that it did not betray a general lack of understanding of Jewish history.[14] It is likely that continued Jewish support of SNCC, even after it began promoting black power, was the result of the extensive history of personal contacts between SNCC workers and Jewish supporters. Thus, the support SNCC received from Rabbi Irving Ganz in California was at least partially the result of the fact that Ganz's son, Marshall, had worked with SNCC in Mississippi. Rabbi Harold

Saperstein of Temple Emanu-El of Lynbrook, New York, who had worked for a brief time with Carmichael in Lowndes County, was one of those who did not agree with the black power theme but still understood SNCC workers' frustrations and continued to support the organization.[15]

Carmichael, Forman, and other blacks who remained close to the white Left during 1966 faced enormous pressures from SNCC's black separatists, however, and these pressures resulted in bitter internal conflicts that would have profound impact on SNCC's relations with an outside world that included Jews. At a staff meeting held in upstate New York during December 1966, SNCC's veteran leaders came under strong attack from separatists in SNCC's recently established Atlanta Project. Several of the Atlanta separatists were themselves from Northern backgrounds, but their ideological orientation was more strongly influenced by the black nationalist tradition than were the veterans. In place of an economic emphasis, they argued for great recognition of the importance of racial identity; rather than to Marx, they looked to Franz Fanon or Malcolm X for ideological guidance. Rejecting the previously dominant view that struggle itself was SNCC's reason for being, they insisted that ideological conversion was a necessary precondition for future struggles.

In their effort to purify SNCC of all white influences, the Atlanta separatists used as weapons the charge that SNCC's leaders had not cut themselves off from white people. Interestingly, just as SNCC's ties with the white New Left were based on common positions on foreign policy issues, the tenuous threads that held together SNCC's factions were more often support for Third World alliances than common positions about strategies for achieving black power. Although SNCC's officers hoped that the few remaining whites on the staff would not become an issue dividing black staff members, the Atlanta separatists were willing to disrupt the New York staff meeting until they had achieved their goal. Carmichael argued at the start of the meeting that SNCC needed white financial support and a "buffer zone" of white liberals to forestall repression, but the separatists repeatedly insisted "whites had to go."

After days of seemingly endless discussion, a vote was finally taken. Nineteen staff members voted for expulsion, eighteen against, and twenty-four, including most officers and all whites, abstained. Despite the expulsion, however, SNCC remained divided as the separatists continued to deny the racial loyalty of SNCC's leaders and sought to undermine their authority. During the winter of 1967, after repeated acts of insubordination, Carmichael fired or suspended all members of the Atlanta project. This firing was upheld at the March Central Committee meeting, but when the entire staff met in June a member of the Atlanta staff came to lambast those who had betrayed the cause of "blackness." His outburst established an atmosphere of hostility that permeated the rest of the meeting. It was in this tense atmosphere that the issue of SNCC's position in the Arab-Israeli conflict was raised.

Staff members elected H. Rap Brown as chairman, believing that he could remove SNCC from public controversy. They also voted to declare that SNCC would henceforth be a "Human Rights Organization" that would "encourage and support the liberation struggles against colonization, racism, and economic exploitation" around the world. In addition, they proclaimed a position of "positive non-alignment" in world

affairs, indicating their willingness to meet with Third World governments and liberation groups and authorizing an application for Non-Government Organization status
on the United Nations Economic and Security Council. To coordinate these activities,
SNCC established an International Affairs Commission headed by Jim Forman. These
actions to establish international ties were taken despite the almost total collapse of
SNCC projects in Afro-American communities; indeed the redirection of SNCC's
interests into those of the Third World served as a cohesive theme for a divided group,
still torn between its roots in an interracial culture of dissent and its search for the
illusive ideas that would unify Afro-Americans.

Reacting to the separatist demand that SNCC break its umbilical cord to white
supporters, most of the seventy-six remaining staff members agreed that SNCC support
for the Third World should extend to the Palestinians. They did not agree, however,
about whether the group should allow the Palestinian issue to further separate SNCC
from its declining body of white financial supporters.

Shortly before leaving on a trip to Africa, Forman cautioned Stanley Wise, who had
replaced him as SNCC's Executive Secretary, about the dangers of taking an anti-Israel
stand. Forman noted that such a stand would result in "a certain isolation from the
press." Forman warned against adopting "a reactionary position that even the Syrians
and the Egyptians do not articulate: namely a hatred for the people of Israel." He
suggested that SNCC must begin to build bases of financial support in Afro-American
communities to replace Jewish support if SNCC were to take a position against Israel.
Forman also expressed sympathy for leaders of CORE, who had refused to take a stand
on the issue for fear of dividing their organization. He stressed the need for staff
members to educate themselves regarding the dispute and asked that SNCC be placed
on the mailing lists of all the Arab nations. He argued that a public stand should not be
taken until the staff became more knowledgeable and a special meeting was held to
discuss the issue.[16]

Forman's cautionary admonitions were stated even more strongly in the first published statement by a staff member on the Arab-Israeli conflict. Veteran SNCC worker
Fred Meely wrote an article for a SNCC newsletter called *Aframerican News for You,* in
which he suggested that black leaders should not take a stand on the crisis, for they were
"already under enough pressure" as a result of the black power controversy. "We black
people neither need [nor] deserve the wrath of Arab or Jew, for we are even denied
access to this debate that may well affect the future of all mankind."[17]

Soon after Forman wrote to Wise, SNCC's Central Committee meeting in the midst
of Israel's six-day victory over Arab forces in June 1967, requested that SNCC's search
and communications staff investigate the background of the conflict. Ethel Minor,
editor of SNCC's newsletter, volunteered for this task. She recalled that the committee
wanted an "objective critique of the facts." Minor was not impartial on the issue,
however, for she had been close friends with Palestinian students during her college
years and was acquainted with the urban black nationalist tradition through her involvement with the Nation of Islam. Minor never wrote a position paper, nor did SNCC
ever conduct an extended discussion of the Middle Eastern dispute.

Nonetheless, SNCC suddenly found itself at the center of a bitter conflict with former allies when Minor published a piece that she claimed would provide staff members with information not available in the "white press." In the *SNCC Newsletter*, she listed thirty-two "documented facts" regarding "the Palestine Problem," including assertions that the Arab-Israeli war was an effort to regain Palestinian land and that during the 1948 war, "Zionists conquered the Arab homes and land through terror, force, and massacres." By itself, the *Newsletter* article would have provoked controversy, but accompanying photographs and drawings by SNCC artist Kofi Bailey heightened its emotional impact through clearly anti-Semitic drawings. The caption on one of the photographs, which portrayed Zionists shooting Arab victims who were lined up against a wall, noted "This is the Gaza Strip, Palestine, not Dachau, Germany."[18]

Although Minor later claimed that those who prepared the article intended it for internal education rather than as a policy stand, other SNCC workers, particularly in the New York fund-raising office, realized immediately that the article would bring swift condemnations from Jewish leaders. Johnny Wilson, most recently installed as head of the office and unaware that the article would be published, called a press conference to announce that the article did not present SNCC's official position. Wilson's disclaimer went unnoticed in the subsequent press reports, however, because Minor and other workers at SNCC headquarters quickly called their own press conference to reiterate the anti-Israel position. Program Director Ralph Featherstone explained to reporters in Atlanta that the article did not indicate that SNCC was anti-Semitic, but he inflamed the emotions of Jews by criticizing Jewish store owners in Afro-American ghettoes. Forman, still out of the country when the newsletter was published, privately expressed his dismay that his counsel of caution had been ignored, but publicly backed the stand against Israel. He decided that SNCC should support the Arabs on the Palestinian question "regardless of how ragged the formulation of our position" and concluded that "no formulations of our position would have satisfied the Zionists and many Jews."[19]

Whether Forman was correct is disputable, but the strength of the negative response to the Minor article suggests that it symbolized more than it said. Actual incidents of publicly expressed black anti-Semitism were few in number, and none involved persons who still identified themselves as civil rights leaders. Most such incidents would not have gained much notice if they had not been brought to public attention by Jews who saw them as indications of a trend, despite the fact that no civil rights group ever took an official anti-Israeli or anti-Jewish stand.

For blacks in SNCC, the anti-Israel stand was a test of their willingness to demonstrate SNCC's break from its civil rights past and a reconfirmation that ties with whites were inconsistent with their desire to express racial aspirations and frustrations without restraint. Veteran staff member Cleveland Sellers later acknowledged that afterward many donations "from white sources just stopped coming in," but he added: "Rather than breaking our will, this made us more convinced than ever that we were correct when we accused the majority of America's whites of being racists."[20]

Forman might have succeeded for a time in convincing SNCC's Jewish supporters to ignore or downplay the existence of private anti-Israel sentiments in SNCC, except that Jews who had long been hostile to SNCC quickly directed national attention to the Minor article. The executive director of the American Jewish Congress labeled the article "shocking and vicious anti-Semitism." Similar criticisms came from the heads of other Jewish groups and from black leaders Whitney Young, A. Philip Randolph, and Bayard Rustin. Theodore Bikel and author Harry Golden added to the furor by announcing publicly that they were resigning from SNCC, an organization to which they did not belong. Bikel mentioned the sacrifice of Mickey Schwerner and Andrew Goodman, who had been lynched in Mississippi during the summer of 1964, saying that SNCC had no right to "spit on their tomb."[21] More restrained was the response of Rabbi Saperstein, who privately informed SNCC leaders that he could not continue to support a group that "so readily allowed itself to become a mouthpiece for malicious Arab propaganda."[22]

Although the highly publicized controversy over the *Newsletter* article was described in the press as a split in the civil rights movement, it was actually a more complex event. For some time, SNCC's goals had extended beyond civil rights, a fact confirmed by its self-definition as a human rights organization seeking ties with the Third World. Many SNCC workers had once shared a wide range of values with SNCC's Jewish supporters, but they had gradually and self-consciously separated themselves from that culture, because its values were not shared by the black masses whose support they sought. In retrospect, it is easy to see that the Pan-Africanism toward which SNCC workers were moving would not automatically guarantee widespread Afro-American support, but that was not evident in the heady political climate of 1967. SNCC workers were surprised at how rapidly and completely they had destroyed the bridges to their ideological past, but historical continuity was evident in their firmly held belief that it was their destiny, even as a small minority, to bring into being a better world.

Having destroyed their bridges, SNCC workers tried to build new ones in the less-known cultural territory of the Third World. Reacting to the criticisms of the earlier article, a *SNCC Newsletter* article in the fall of 1967 stated that SNCC had

> placed itself squarely on the side of oppressed peoples and liberation movements. . . . Perhaps we have taken the liberal Jewish community or certain segments of it as far as it can go. If so, this is tragic, not for us but for the liberal Jewish community. For the world is in a revolutionary ferment. . . . Our message to conscious people everywhere is "Don't get caught on the wrong side of the revolution."[23]

Even after SNCC workers had burned their bridges, however, they continued to insist that they were not anti-Semitic. Their defense of themselves rested on the semantic issue of whether attacks against Israel or against the role of Jewish businessmen in black communities necessarily constituted anti-Semitism. On occasion SNCC workers used the facile argument that Arabs were also Semitic peoples. Such arguments did little to bridge the gulf between SNCC and Jews, and SNCC workers were undoubtedly far more interested in establishing new ties to angry urban blacks than in reestablishing old ties with angered Jews. Whether SNCC could have found a way of expressing its opposition to Israeli policies without making itself vulnerable to the charge of anti-Semitism is an interesting question, but there is little evidence that SNCC workers expended much effort searching for such a way or that Jews expended much effort aiding in the search. For many Jews, there was no proper way for blacks to condemn Israel.

During the summer of 1967, Forman and SNCC's new chairman, H. Rap Brown, led a successful black effort at the National Convention for New Politics to gain adoption of an anti-Israeli policy stand. The fact that the resolution contained a statement that the condemnation of Zionist expansion did "not imply anti-Semitism" was not nearly as significant for Jews as the fact that it was introduced by the Black Caucus at the convention. An issue that, at the beginning of the summer of 1967, had unexpectedly cost SNCC needed financial support became by the end of the summer the central issue by which SNCC militants demonstrated their own militancy and tested the loyalty of their erstwhile white allies in the New Left.

Thus it happened that a few dozen black activists became the first, and for some time the only, major black organization to take a stand against Israel in the Middle-East dispute. SNCC itself rapidly disintegrated after the summer. Deprived of former sources of financial support and weakened by internal conflicts and external repression, it lost black support and access to power even as it made black power its central focus. The small SNCC staff had lost the ability to serve as a catalyst for massive mobilizations of black people, but they retained the ability to serve as a catalyst for a major disruption of the Afro-American–Jewish reform alliance of the post–World War II period. As ideological consistency gained priority over the goal of political effectiveness, they eagerly sought opportunities to display their independence from the constraints of alliances.

Many SNCC workers refused even to accept the constraints of working within their own organization and left it rather than compromise their militancy. Carmichael rejected SNCC's efforts to control his actions while touring the Third World in 1967, and after his return moved gradually away from SNCC until making a final break in July 1968. Forman was forced to resign a year later. There was a considerable degree of irony in Earl Raab's suggestion in the late 1960s that the black movement was "developing an anti-Semitic ideology,"[24] for it was only while the Afro-American–Jewish civil rights alliance lived that it was possible to speak of a black movement coherent and unified enough to possess a single ideology.

The hostility that developed as a result of SNCC's anti-Israel stand survived longer than did SNCC, however, because the hostility had many sources in the web of Afro-American–Jewish interactions. Once Jewish supporters of the civil rights movement had discovered evidence of what they deemed black anti-Semitism in SNCC, a group spawned by the Afro-American–Jewish civil rights coalition, it became much easier to find evidences of anti-Semitism in the more alien black world outside of SNCC, where its expression was less likely to be inhibited than in SNCC.

The publicity focused on SNCC during the summer of 1967 was redirected toward other isolated anti-Jewish statements, and the publicity itself probably stimulated the anti-Semitism that it sought to denounce. There is little evidence that anti-Jewish sentiments among blacks increased substantially during the late 1960s, but it is apparent that anti-Israeli or anti-Jewish statements symbolized a new willingness among that minority of Afro-Americans who had been part of the interracial civil rights movement to break with their past.

Former SNCC worker Julius Lester provides a final illustration of the complex motives that shaped black responses to issues of concern to Jews during the late 1960s. Lester was by no means a typical SNCC worker, if such a construct can ever exist, but his multifaceted experiences in the movement reflect many aspects of the dynamics of Afro-American–Jewish relations during the late 1960s. That he found himself a central figure in Afro-American–Jewish conflicts was both an accident of history and a consequence of historical trends that made such accidents inevitable. Lester was not exposed to the New York culture of radicalism until the early 1960s, when as a young folksinger and writer he came to New York with his new wife, a white socialist studying at the New School.

Despite growing up in the South and attending Fisk University, Lester had resisted joining the Southern civil rights movement until 1964 when he discovered that he and SNCC were each moving toward a new sense of racial identity. Unlike the Northern-born blacks who joined SNCC, Lester did not adopt Marxian ideas, and perhaps for this reason he did not feel compelled to supplant Marx with the "black" ideology of Fanon or Nkrumah or Malcolm X. In the spring of 1966, he left his wife to join the SNCC staff on a full-time basis as head of the photography department. Although he kept his feelings to himself during that spring, he was privately critical of the tendency of Moses and other SNCC activists to stress Afro American ties with Africa rather than identify with the unique racial consciousness that already existed among Afro-Americans who had not been exposed to such large doses of white culture as had SNCC's college-educated black nationalists. He later attributed this tendency to the Northern backgrounds of much of SNCC's leadership. Referring to his own upbringing, he was instructive:

> Those of us from the South had lived outside the perimeter of white culture; northern blacks were infected with it. Their black militancy was so strident that I regarded them as recent converts to the race, and their rage at whites, misdirected self-hatred.[25]

Lester did not express his reservations at the time, however, and instead became one of the chief propagandists for the black power theme. Among the large number of his writings were "The Angry Children of Malcolm X," a classic essay of the 1960s and the popular tract, *Look Out, Whitey! Black Power's Gon' Get Your Mama.* Both these uncompromising statements of black militancy demonstrated the extent to which he became caught up in the angry mood of the time. They also demonstrated how completely he suppressed any feelings of doubt. Much later he would comment, "I was so determined to be a revolutionary that I refused to look at anything within me which might contradict who I wanted to be."[26]

After leaving SNCC in 1967, Lester returned to New York, where he observed the eruption of Afro-American–Jewish conflicts during the dispute over the firing of nine white teachers from the black-controlled Ocean-Hill–Brownsville school district. The teachers' union president, Albert Shanker, accused the local school board of anti-Semitism, a charge that led to bitter exchanges between striking Jewish teachers and black parents and students.

Lester invited a black teacher, Les Campbell, to appear on his weekly radio show, and when Campbell showed Lester an anti-Semitic poem that had been written by a black student, Lester encouraged the teacher to read it on the air to indicate how the strike was affecting the attitudes of black youths. For two weeks after the broadcast, Lester heard no protests—probably a result of the limited nature of his audience—but early in 1969 the United Federation of Teachers announced that they were asking that the license of Lester's station be revoked because of the airing of the poem. As had been the case for SNCC in 1967, the controversy around the program intensified as Lester found that his refusal to condemn the poem encouraged some blacks to view the controversy as an opportunity to demonstrate to other blacks how completely they ignored Jewish and white sensibilities.

Soon afterward, a black high school student appeared on the show and offhandedly remarked, "Hitler didn't make enough lampshades out of them." Lester wrote that he "found the remark obscene and personally offensive, but [said he] lacked the maturity to know how to dissociate myself from it while upholding the student's First Amendment right to make it."[27] The student's remark prompted demonstrations at the station by the Jewish Defense League and further poisoned an already volatile atmosphere. When Lester replied to his critics on the air, his comments echoed those of Baldwin, Reddick, and Clark, for they superficially appealed for Jewish understanding while simultaneously providing a rationale for anti-Jewish sentiments among Afro-Americans. He announced that the "old relationship" that had existed between Afro-Americans and Jews had "been destroyed and the stage [was] set now for a real relationship where our feelings, *our* views of America and how to operate has to be given serious consideration."[28]

Despite Lester's announcement of a new relationship, the continuities of history were displayed in interesting subtle ways. The board of the Pacific Foundation, which operated Lester's stations, stood firmly behind him throughout the controversy and no one remained more firm than board member Bob Goodman, a Jew and the father of Andrew Goodman, who had been lynched in Mississippi in 1964.

Even as the Lester controversy continued, Nathan Glazer provided an indication of the extent to which Afro-American-Jewish conflict reflected intra-Jewish as well as intrablack conflicts. As in his earlier article mentioned above, Glazer continued to oppose black militancy (although his definition of it had changed since 1964) and Jews who supported such militancy. In *Commentary,* he combined an attack on Afro-American leaders, who he said were guilty of "justifying and legitimizing" black anti-Semitism, with an even stronger attack against Jewish radicals, who "abetted and assisted and advised" black intellectuals.[29]

Glazer may have exaggerated the degree of consensus among black militants about issues of concern to Jews, but his twofold attack on black militants and white radicals clearly demonstrated the close connection between the issue of Afro-American–Jewish conflict and the broader political currents that brought the issue public attention during the late 1960s.

The lack of communication between black militants and Jewish critics of black militancy during this period is revealed in the contrasting conclusions drawn by Glazer and Lester. For Glazer, black militancy was infected with anti-Semitism and could be supported only by Jews who had a nihilistic view of American society and its political system. "All they can do is give the blacks guns, and allow themselves to become the first victims,"[30] he wrote. Lester followed a different route to arrive at a similar state of cynicism. While Glazer was defining his conditions for continued Jewish support of black civil rights efforts, Lester and other blacks were insisting that conditional white support was no longer acceptable. "Black anti-Semitism is not the problem," he answered his critics.

> Jews have never suffered at the hands of black people. Individuals, yes. But en masse, no. The issue is not black anti-Semitism. This issue is what it has always been: racism. . . . If this fact cannot be faced, then there is little else to be said. It is this which black people understand. I guess it just comes down to questions of who's going to be on what side. If there are Jews and other white people out there who understand, never was there a more opportune time for them to let their voices be heard. All I hear is silence, and if that's all there's going to be, then so be it.[31]

NOTES

1. James Baldwin, "Negroes are Anti-Semitic Because They're Anti-White," *New York Times Magazine,* 9 April 1967, pp. 26, 27ff.; L. D. Reddick, "Anti-Semitism among Negroes," *Negro Quarterly* I (Summer 1942): 112–22; Kenneth Clark, "Candor in the Negro-Jewish Relations," *Commentary,* February 1946, pp. 8–14. See also bibliography in *Negro-Jewish Relations in the United States,* Papers and Proceedings of a conference convened by the Conference on Jewish Social Studies, New York City, (New York: Citadel Press, 1966), pp. 67–71.

2. Earl Rabb probably spoke for many Jews when he suggested that Afro-American writers were in danger of crossing the fine line between explanation and rationalization. He charged that

> Negroes trying to reassure Jewish audience repeatedly and unwitting make the very point they are trying to refute. "This is not anti-Semitism," [black writers] say. "The hostility is toward the whites." When [blacks] say "Jew," they mean "white." But that is an exact and acute description of political anti-Semitism: "The enemy" becomes the Jew, "the man" becomes the Jew, the villain is not so much the actual Jewish merchant on the corner as the corporate Jew who stands symbolically for generic evil.

See Earl Rabb, "The Black Revolution & the Jewish Question," *Commentary,* January 1969, p. 29.

3. Quoted in Clayborne Carson, *In Struggle: SNCC and the Black Awakening of the 1960s* (Cambridge: Harvard University Press, 1981), p. 17.

4. Available financial statistics are incomplete, but the following table is representative:

| | |
|---|---|
| May 1965: | New York provided $50,000 of the $82,292 SNCC received. |
| June 1965: | $12,000 of $37,997 |
| July 1965: | $8,000 of $29,300 |
| April 1966: | $12,000 of $30,753.45 |
| May 1966: | $20,000 of $29,910.37 |

See SNCC Papers, Subgroup B, New York Office, Series III (Microfilm edition by Microfilming Corporation of America); and Civil Rights Movement in the United States Collection, Box 8, University of California, Los Angeles.

5. Cf. Harold Cruse, *The Crisis of the Negro Intellectual: From Its Origins to the Present* (New York: William Morrow, 1967).

6. Karenga's political development is revealed in my extended interview with him, conducted on 4 October 1977.

7. Interview conducted in Mississippi during the summer of 1963.

8. Ibid.

9. See Nathan Glazer, "Negroes & Jews: The New Challenge to Pluralism," *Commentary,* December 1964, pp. 29–34.

10. "Is SNCC Racist or Radical" (editorial), *Jewish Currents,* July–August 1966.

11. I. F. Stone, "Why They Cry Black Power," *I. F. Stone's Weekly,* 19 September 1966.

12. Myron Cohen to Stokely Carmichael, 9 November 1966; unsigned letter to Cohen, 11 November 1966. SNCC Papers, Series I, Chairman's Files, New York.

13. Fred Buch to Stokely Carmichael, 9 November 1966, SNCC Papers, Series I, Chairman's Files.

14. Mrs. Joseph Walzer to Stokely Carmichael, 17 January 1967, SNCC Papers, Series I, Chairman's Files.

15. See Rabbi Harold I. Saperstein to H. Rap Brown, 5 January 196[8], SNCC Papers I, Chairman's Files.

16. See letters in James Forman, *The Making of Black Revolutionaries* (New York: Macmillan, 1972), pp. 492–96.

17. Fred Meely, "The Chicken or the Egg of the Middle East," *Aframerican News for You,* July 1967.

18. "Third World Round Up; The Palestine Problem: Test Your Knowledge," *SNCC Newsletter,* June–July 1967, pp. 4–5.

19. Forman, *Black Revolutionaries,* p. 496; Jean Wiley interview with author, 11 May 1978, in Washington, D.C. See also "S. N. C. C. Charges Israel Atrocities," *New York Times,* 15 August 1967; "Zionism Assailed in Newsletter of SNCC," *Los Angeles Times,* 15 August 1967; "SNCC and the Jews," *Newsweek,* 29 August 1967.

20. Cleveland Sellers, with Robert Terrell, *The River of No Return: The Autobiography of a Black Militant and the Life and Death of SNCC* (New York: William Morrow, 1973), p. 203.

21. "Bikel Scores Attack on Jews by S.N.C.C. and Quits the Group," *New York Times* 17 July 1967; "Golden Criticizes S.N.C.C. and Quits," *New York Times,* 22 August 1967.

22. Saperstein to Brown, 5 January 196[8].

23. "The Mid-East and the Liberal Reaction," *SNCC Newsletter* September–October 1967, p. 5.

24. Raab, "Black Revolution," p. 29.

25. Julius Lester, *All Is Well* (New York: William Morrow 1976), p. 130.

26. Lester, *All Is Well,* p. 131.

27. Lester, *All Is Well,* p. 153.

28. See text in Lester, *All Is Well,* p. 158.

29. Nathan Glazer, "Blacks, Jews & the Intellectuals," *Commentary,* April 1969, pp. 33–39.

30. Ibid., p. 39.

31. Lester, "A Response," in *Black Anti-Semitism and Jewish Racism* (New York: Richard W. Baron, 1969), p. 237.

# The Civil Rights Struggle

A great number of problems both in the Negro and in the Jewish community militate at this period against a great deal of affection between both communities at a grass roots level. We ought to face these problems very clearly and very honestly, if it is our real intention to make progress.

The first of these is the lack of empathy for the current Negro struggle on the part of a great number of Jewish people. Fundamentally, this lack springs from a tendency in the United States to oversimplify social issues. Let me illustrate. I have spoken with Jews recently who, without thought or understanding, immediately ask the following: "Why are Negroes raising so much sand? Why don't Negroes look to their problems internally as we did?" The chairman of the Parents and Taxpayers on the East Side in Yorkville told me at a meeting where we were having a debate, "Well you know, Mr. Rustin, the problem is I was born in a ghetto; I got out of it, I now own a Cadillac, I have my three children in college." Jews must first of all understand that no matter what problems they faced in this country, they faced them with a 5000-year history of a culture and a civilization behind them, with a history of family development which defied most family developments in the United States. Negroes, on the other hand, are burdened with a heritage of slavery, disruption of the family, and denial of rights. Also, the Jewish struggle against antisemitism and for American citizenship was fought simultaneously with the fight for trade unionism. But more significant is the fact that the Jewish development toward acceptance took place at a time of an expanding economy. But the Negro struggle takes place in a time of automation and cybernation. It takes place when, instead of economic expansion, which would make it possible for the Negroes, as some Jews say, "to lift themselves by their bootstraps," we have a reduction of jobs and economic opportunities. They cannot pull themselves up by their bootstraps. I reject even the Malcolm X claim that he is transforming prostitutes and dope addicts from being prostitutes and dope addicts into functioning citizens. This is not to say that he may not change one or two. But it is the closed ghetto which produces monstrosities— and I use these words advisedly—and for every prostitute or dope addict that Malcolm X thinks he has cured, the closed ghetto will make ten. Now here is something that Jews must understand, namely, that they never faced a closed ghetto such as the Negro faces. First of all, they could change their name—and they could escape. The Negro has

Bayard Rustin was a lifelong civil rights activist and director of the A. Philip Randolph Institute.
Originally published in *Jewish Social Studies* 27, no. 1 (1965): 33–36. Copyright © 1965 by Indiana University Press. Reprinted with permission of Indiana University Press.

never had such avenues of escape. Hence for Jews to compare the closed ghetto with the ghetto they faced is a distorting oversimplification.

The second point is that the Negro people at this period have neither the economic nor the political power to solve their problems. There is ultimately no way to get jobs, housing and quality education with integration for Negroes unless many segments of this society which are not now in movement, join in movement. When we were dealing with public accommodations, it was possible for us to make considerable progress without anybody's help, because we were dealing only with segregation and discrimination. The tragedy of the Negro community at this moment is that it is formed to move when few others are in movement, especially the Jewish people, especially the trade union movement. Backed to the wall, in a situation of utter desperation, the Negroes are now forced not only to fight segregation and discrimination, but to fight the basic economic institutions of this country, if they are to have work. For to find work for Negroes in the time of automation means that Negroes and whites shall end up fighting in the streets over the few jobs, as the plumbers are doing. *Therefore the way out is not the civil rights revolution but the creation of an American revolution.* When the private sector of the economy cannot put men back to work, it is the responsibility of government to do so. We need planning in this economy, so that we may know what men can be trained for. President Johnson's effort at training men in a vacuum without planning is not only a lie, it is a hoax. We must have a 30 to 50 billion dollar works programs which will put men back to work. That is a program on which Negroes and whites can and must combine. Ten years after the Supreme Court decision, more Negroes are in segregated schools, in segregated housing, and without jobs than in 1954. This is a desperate situation.

Let me tell you about the incident near the Brooklyn Yeshiva. I will not excuse what happened. In a situation of this kind, in desperation, where no other segment of this society is prepared to move, Negroes will be desperate with everybody. And they will adopt as a slogan, "give everybody hell regardless of color or race or creed." When Jews think they are being singled out, that every little incident that occurs must be interpreted as some rise of Hitlerism, they understand neither the nature nor the complexity of the problem. For the people who believe that they must "give them hell regardless of race, color and creed" do not mean Jews first. They mean Roy Wilkins first and Jim Farmer first. They are tired, desperate, and fed up. In such a situation of desperation, not knowing what to do, they see people who look very queer and strange and who play no role which is understandable to them. These they will attack violently. They will also attack Negroes with whom they do not feel they have empathy. If you want to get to the bottom of what happened in Brooklyn, you need to remember that this is the way men behave when they are desperate. I, a pacifist who was opposed to all war and violence, have often publicly stated that I have nothing but complete respect for Jews who in the Warsaw ghetto rose up in arms. Why? Because in spite of my pacifism I have empathy enough to understand that men who have been forced into desperation must behave desperately. I do not mean to suggest that the Negro youth in Brooklyn had anything other than this in common with the fight in the Warsaw ghetto.

To my mind the greatest speech made at the March on Washington, historically, philosophically, was not Dr. King's, but Rabbi Prinz's, because Rabbi Prinz said something which makes a connection between the pecking system and double jeopardy. He said, "It is not the men who are evil and who behave in an evil manner. It is those who are silent." Now that combined two problems. If it is true that the Negroes engage in pecking, then it is also true that Jews in the South are involved in avoiding the problem out of the principle of double jeopardy. Which is worse? Both are evil. For I am here to tell you that the Jews in the South are playing no creative role in the struggle. When you think of what happens in Brooklyn or of antisemitism on the streets of Harlem, to which I am unalterably opposed and which I have fought and will fight, then you have to compare the sides, under the fear of double jeopardy, and cross it off with the pecking system which takes place here. Anybody in his right mind knows that as long as the Negro faces the frustration which he does, he will peck on somebody. This is a law of human behavior. The answer to both the double jeopardy and pecking lies in what Rabbi Prinz called "the courage to be open, the courage to fight."

Another great problem that is not a Jewish but an American problem, not a Negro, but an American problem, is that just as the N.A.A.C.P. lacks fundamental roots in the Negro community, so the Jewish organizations had better face the fact that they lack fundamental roots in their community. If that were not so, there would not be so many Jews in P.A.T. The problem here is that there is so broad a breach between (and I'm not only talking about Jews, now, I'm talking about NAACP and CORE, too), is that there is such a terrible breach between leadership and followership that we end up letting these people wallow because we do not give them real leadership. There is only one way to give them real leadership, and that is not by press releases, not by meetings, not by resolutions, but by joining the American struggle where it is taking place, in the streets. Let us get rabbis and ministers going out into the streets, not only for Negro rights. I, my friends, who was one of the first in the streets years ago, now know that, while we must stay in the streets for demonstrations, we have to stay in the streets simultaneously for a political program which will solve the problem. For no matter how many people lie in the streets to get jobs, lying in the streets is merely pointing out that jobs are needed. To produce jobs, one needs a political program in which the Negroes need allies. They need all religious groups, the best segments of labor, everyone, going into the streets, calling for ways of putting American workers back to work.

Finally, Jews are in a delicate and dangerous situation, as are all who stand for the right thing as a result of their history and out of their announced program. If you think the young fellows in CORE jump on Roy Wilkins and Jim Farmer and Martin King first because they dislike them, you are mistaken. In times of desperation, socially, you act like a child having a tantrum, a child saying, "watch me mother, I'm going to do something naughty, because I want you to come and show me a better way." After following Jim Farmer and Roy Wilkins and Rev. King, and all of the leaders, it is most likely that they will next jump on Jews who historically have been friendly to them. He who does not understand this, does not understand the psychology of people in motion.

# Remarks at an NAACP Labor Dinner

I am personally, as is our Union, highly honored at the invitation to be with you tonight. By participating at this occasion we are part of the most dramatic, vital and democratic movement we have experienced within our Nation for better than two decades. The struggle for justice and democracy is never-ending, for those who profit by denying equality, who prey on the fears and prejudices of the unknowing, the uninformed, do not yield their privileges easily. Each age must fight its battle to advance the cause of the rights of man, and in each age there is no more rewarding, inspiring or ennobling effort than to be identified with these historic causes. No man can really fulfill his destiny without being part of such a struggle.

We in the labor movement have special reason to be sensitive to the struggle for the recognition of the rights of all men regardless of such irrelevant considerations as race, creed or color. The labor movement was born from such gestation. It took its vitality from the rising of the downtrodden and the exploited against their oppressors. It was committed for its very existence to the cause of eliminating economic injustice. It recognized that "necessitous men could not be free men."

In the decade of the thirties the most urgent and insistent issue before the nation was the right of workers to organize and bargain collectively through representatives of their own choosing.

In this struggle was enlisted all the progressive and liberal forces of the nation. They found allies in all walks of life as they fought to make men free from economic servitude. This was a battle for the rights of man. The right of the worker to a fair share of the goods he helped produce. The right to act collectively. The right to a voice in fixing the conditions under which he worked. The right, above all, to self-respect, to walk with his head high, and with dignity. In America the assertion of these rights was revolutionary in the 30's. The guardians of the past were not adverse to using all the weapons in the arsenal of privilege to put down this effrontery. Violence, Jail, Injunctions, Police, the National Guard (except only, I believe, in this state of Minnesota) were only some of the weapons employed against the claim of workers that their humanity be recognized, that their right to a voice in their destiny be accepted as part of the reality of the age. The files of LaFollette Committee are full of reactions and attempts to deny justice to millions. The struggle was won. The dust of the battle settled and there was revealed a new social order. A society that recognized as a matter of law the right of workers to

In 1960 Ralph Helstein was president of the United Packinghouse Workers of America, AFL-CIO.
These remarks were given on June 24, 1960, at Hotel St. Paul, St. Paul, Minnesota. NAACP Papers, Box III A 117, Library of Congress, Manuscript Division, Washington D.C.

organize, to bargain collectively for minimum wages, social security, guarantees of bank deposits, utility regulations were written into the Federal law. Franklin D. Roosevelt announced that the "money changers were chased out of the Temple of Government. The air was fresh, spirit was high. There was a new morality among men. The morality of a living democracy." Even the faint hearted got courage. Great deeds were done by the poor, the dispossessed. Man was his brother's keeper. This was the decade of the 30's. This was the age in which the modern labor movement came to maturity.

Today, two decades later, at this the beginning of the 6th decade of the 20th Century we in the labor movement, taking time for honest introspection must say Democracy is threatened, our institutions are not equal to their tasks. The bright promise of the 30's has become tarnished. The vital organs of democracy are not working. Collective action is failing because of a lack of collective responsibility. The forms of democracy and its symbols are there but its morality has been missing and without morality democracy is not man's hope.

For today the single most important domestic issue facing America—the issue which more than any other domestic issue will determine the character of our future is the question of civil rights. The recognition of the Negro community as a vital, important and integral part of America. Our society can no longer indulge itself with having any part of our people as second class citizens. All American citizens have a right to vote— we must see to it that they are permitted to exercise that right. All Americans have a right to the full and free use of all public accommodations—hotels, restaurants, stores, transportation, barber and beauty shops, swimming pools, bathing beaches and others—we must see to it that they are permitted to use that right. Above all the right to go to any school of one's choice is a right now clearly stated in the law—we must see to it that all Americans are permitted to use this right. Token integration is not enough. There must be full citizenship—1st class citizenship for all means full integration. It is a maxim of political philosophy that rights without the power to use them are worse than no rights at all. It is sheer hypocrisy. Just as liberal and progressive forces came to the support of the labor movement in its struggle for life in the 30's so must these same forces with the labor movement in the vanguard came to the support of the fight for civil rights in the 60's. The time is now—a hundred years is a long time to wait for promises to be fulfilled and democracy cannot tolerate a further delay. On this question the labor movement cannot equivocate—it cannot procrastinate. The time for action is here—it is now. The spirit of a victorious struggle is in the air. It is all around us. From it the faint hearted can take courage. The future awaits us but it will not wait long and American labor must in my judgment, marshall the full force of its numbers, the power of its prestige, influence and resources which are not inconsiderable and throw them wholeheartedly and without reservation into this battle. To do this, however, it must throw off the shackles and inhibitions of its own failures. It must drive out discrimination from its own ranks. There are none, I believe who are informed who will deny that American labor on the whole has done more in this respect than has any other group in American society but this is not enough. It is not enough to do more when so many do nothing at all.

The issue is not only one of economics. It is not just a question of organizational solidarity. It is above all, as it was in the 30's an issue of morality. It is immoral to deny promotions because of color. It is immoral to have any semblance of Jim Crow at any level in the labor movement and the labor movement cannot survive except as an institution dedicated to man's welfare. When rank and file Negro members raise such grievances as equal pay, work loads, seniority, or any other questions, these issues must be dealt with on the merits even in the face of opposition from some of the membership who generally have profited by the discrimination. These are questions that the leadership cannot, and I would hope that increasingly they will not want, to duck.

# Black-Jewish Conflict in the Labor Context
## Race, Jobs, and Institutional Power

Largely forgotten in the many discussions of black-Jewish relations is the fact that the current conflict between the two groups was preceded by an older continuing discord within the labor movement. Indeed, it may be argued that the antagonism that developed in the labor union arena is emblematic of the larger black-Jewish conflict, one which has its roots in the profoundly different condition of Jews and blacks in American society.

Close scrutiny of the racial labor issues that developed soon after the merger in 1955 between the American Federation of Labor and the Congress of Industrial Organizations reveals much about the characteristics of the subsequently strained relations between blacks and Jews and the tensions between them. The years immediately following the merger were marked by widespread disappointment among black workers as the AFL-CIO failed to implement the civil rights policy adopted with much fanfare at the time of the labor Federation's formation. These were also the years of a great black awakening, of the emergence of new militant black protest movements in the North as well as in the South.

Soon after the merger black workers protested against the continuing pattern of discriminatory practices by many AFL-CIO affiliated unions, both industrial and craft. The National Association for the Advancement of Colored People repeatedly documented practices such as provisions in union contracts that limited black workers to segregated job classifications, the widespread exclusion of blacks from craft unions, the existence of segregated locals, the refusal to admit nonwhite workers into union-controlled apprenticeship training programs, and other forms of labor union discrimination.

### JEWISH LABOR COMMITTEE

In April 1957, James B. Carey, president of the International Union of Electrical Workers, a former CIO affiliate, and a member of the Federation's executive council resigned as chairman of the AFL-CIO Civil Rights Committee because of its ineffective-

Herbert Hill is Evjue-Bascom Professor of African American Studies and Professor of Industrial Relations at University of Wisconsin, Madison. He is the former national labor secretary of the NAACP, author of *Black Labor and the American Legal System* and other books, and frequently appears as expert witness in federal court litigation involving employment discrimination.

This is an expanded and revised version of a paper given at the Conference on Blacks and Jews: An American Historical Perspective, Washington University, St. Louis, Missouri, December 2–5, 1993. A shorter, earlier version of this essay appeared in *Race Traitor*, ed. Noel Ignatiev and John Garvey (New York and London: Routledge, 1996), and material from it is used here with permission. Copyright © 1998 Herbert Hill. Printed with permission of the author.

ness, and he publicly criticized the Federation. According to the *New York Times,* Carey believed that "the committee had not been given enough power or freedom to do an effective job of stamping out racial bias in unions," and felt that "he was being hamstrung in his anti-bias assignment."[1] Carey was replaced as chairman by Charles S. Zimmerman, vice president of the International Ladies Garment Workers Union (ILGWU) and a prominent leader of the Jewish Labor Committee (JLC). At the time of his appointment he was chairman of the National Trade Union Council of the JLC and later became president of the organization.[2]

The JLC was founded in 1934 in response to the rise of Nazism in Germany and provided assistance to European Jewish labor leaders. It performed valuable service in rescuing endangered anti-fascists and arranged for their resettlement in the United States and elsewhere.[3] With the end of World War II, the JLC had completed its task and, given its original purpose, no longer had a function to perform. In an effort to justify its continued existence, the JLC tried to become a civil rights organization within the labor movement.

By the late 1940s, with financial support mainly from the International Ladies Garment Workers Union, the JLC was revived and began referring to itself as "the civil rights arm of the labor movement." But although it presumed to represent the interests of minorities within organized labor, the Committee had no contact with the great mass of black workers in the industrial unions where they were concentrated, or with black community institutions. The JLC was in a very dubious position as it presumed to speak on behalf of those who had not authorized it to do so, since it had no membership and no constituency beyond a small group of Jewish labor leaders from the needle trades unions mainly in New York City. Typical of its leadership was David Dubinsky, president of the ILGWU, who was a founder of the Jewish Labor Committee and served as its treasurer for many years.[4]

When Charles S. Zimmerman became chairman of the AFL-CIO Civil Rights Committee he remained a major figure in the leadership of the JLC, which intensified its efforts to expand its influence within organized labor. But Zimmerman's term in office was a stormy one and as black demands for effective action against labor union racist practices intensified, Zimmerman's impotence as a leader and his repeated attempts to defend or rationalize labor union discrimination increasingly placed him in direct conflict with black workers and civil rights organizations.

A typical example—one of many—is the case of *Ross* v. *Ebert,* involving Local 8 of the Bricklayers Union in Milwaukee.[5] This case began in 1946 when James Harris, who had settled in Milwaukee after serving three years in the South Pacific with the U.S. Air Force, was dismissed from his job at the insistence of the union because he was not a member, although subsequently the union refused his repeated requests for membership.[6] Harris had learned the trade while working with his uncles who belonged to an all-black local of the Bricklayers Union in his hometown of Opalaca, Alabama, and in 1953 he and Randolph Ross, another skilled black worker, applied for membership and were again rejected.[7] All efforts to obtain support from the international union and the AFL-CIO for Harris and other black workers seeking membership in Local 8 were to no avail,[8] as the international union defended its local affiliate,[9] and George Meany, president of the AFL-CIO, urged the state government to refrain from legal enforcement of Wisconsin's anti-discrimination law.[10] This conflict, which came before the Supreme Court of Wisconsin, received national attention and resulted in the legislature amending the state's Fair Employment Practices Law.

In 1955 the Wisconsin Fair Employment Practices Division, after long delay, found the union, whose membership had always been limited to white persons, guilty of racial discrimination in violation of state law and ordered the admission of two fully qualified black men, but the union refused to comply and challenged the authority of the state agency.[11] On September 24, 1957, James Harris, Randolph Ross, and two other black workers were finally admitted into the union, but only after the state legislature enacted a new judicially enforceable anti-discrimination law. After eleven years of efforts by public and private agencies, three rounds of litigation, and finally action by the legislature, Zimmerman defended the racist labor organization and stated in defiance of all the facts that "the denial of membership to them was not based on their race but was due to their failure to submit satisfactory evidence of their trade qualifications."[12] The extensive litigation record in this case directly contradicted Zimmerman's statement, including the fact that former employers gave testimony verifying that both Harris and Ross were fully competent skilled masons.[13] Zimmerman repeatedly defended discriminatory labor unions in many other contexts, acting on behalf of a white labor bureaucracy committed to perpetuating the prevailing pattern.

The intransigence of the Milwaukee Bricklayers Union in refusing to admit African Americans was a characteristic of many craft unions in the building trades. In New York City there were forty years of litigation involving the discriminatory racial practices of Local 28 of the Sheetmetal Workers Union;[14] in Philadelphia, many years of litigation against Local 542 of the Operating Engineers Union;[15] and in Chicago, extensive litigation against Local 597 of the Pipefitters Union,[16] to take but three examples.

At the 1959 annual conference of the NAACP, A. Philip Randolph, president of the Brotherhood of Sleeping Car Porters, called for the formation of the Negro American Labor Council (NALC) and at its founding convention he stressed that black workers must speak for themselves within organized labor. He said that "We ourselves must seek the cure" and that the establishment of the NALC would "make it possible for Negro workers to take a position completely independent of white unionists. . . . History has placed upon the Negro and the Negro alone this basic responsibility."[17] With the emergence of the Negro American Labor Council and the increasing involvement of the NAACP in the issue of labor union discrimination, the Jewish Labor Committee found itself in conflict with black unionists and with black civil rights groups. On December 12, 1959, there appeared the first of a series of articles on antagonism between blacks and Jews within organized labor in the *Pittsburgh Courier,* a respected and widely circulated black newspaper with editions in Chicago, Detroit, and New York. Under a front-page headline "Will Negro, Jewish Labor Leaders Split Over Civil Rights?" an article by managing editor Harold F. Keith began, "Negro and Jewish labor leaders are on the 'brink' of outright war between themselves with the civil rights issue spread out before them as a prospective field of battle." In that issue and in those following, Keith reviewed the history of the conflicts between the AFL-CIO Civil Rights Committee and black trade unionists. The *Courier* criticized the Jewish Labor Committee and Zimmerman for presuming to speak for blacks and reported that Jewish labor leaders had adopted a "paternalistic and missionary" attitude toward Negroes. The article in the *Courier* also reported that the AFL-CIO was "ignoring the mounting bitterness in Negro communities" over "scandalous racial discrimination" by both craft and industrial unions. According to Keith, the Jewish Labor Committee exerted "more influence upon the AFL-CIO than any non-union group" and had "more say-so than the NAACP or the National Urban League."[18] Keith also charged that pressure from the Jewish Labor Committee was a factor in the failure of the Federation to act against the racist practices of many affiliated unions.

Randolph and Roy Wilkins, executive secretary of the NAACP, argued that the fundamental problem was discrimination and denied that the conflict with the AFL-CIO was an issue between blacks and Jews. Zimmerman, who was trying to expand the role of the Jewish Labor Committee within the AFL-CIO as well as advance his own career, was eventually forced to resign. However, the Jewish Labor Committee, by defending discriminatory labor organizations and by functioning as an apologist for racist unions, succeeded in transforming a black-white conflict into a black-Jewish conflict. Sadly enough, this was not the last time Jewish trade unionists would engage in such behavior.

In 1961 the NAACP issued a report documenting the continuing discriminatory racial practices of many AFL-CIO unions.[19] The Negro American Labor Council (NALC) endorsed the NAACP's report, and Randolph in his address to the NAACP's annual convention stated:

> We in the Negro American Labor Council consider the report timely, necessary, and valuable. . . . Moreover, the Negro American Labor Council can, without reservation, assert that the basic statements of the report are true and sound, and that delegates of the Brotherhood of Sleeping Car Porters have presented these facts to convention after convention of the American Federation of Labor for a quarter of a century.[20]

George Meany, at a conference of the Jewish Labor Committee held at Unity House, the summer resort of the ILGWU, attacked the NAACP, the NALC, and the black press because of their criticism of the racial practices of organized labor.[21] That Meany chose a meeting of the Jewish Labor Committee for his widely reported denunciation was not lost on black workers and civil rights groups.

### INTERNATIONAL LADIES GARMENT WORKERS UNION

Events in the early 1960s, involving the International Ladies Garment Workers Union in New York City, were to have a major impact on black-Jewish relations and also upon the liberal coalition for years to come. On November 21, 1962, Roy Wilkins sent to all members of the Leadership Conference on Civil Rights and to other organizations a memorandum which read:

Because of the current widespread discussion of the relationship between the NAACP, and organized labor, with particular but not exclusive reference to the International Ladies Garment Workers Union, and because a resolution of the Jewish Labor Committee on this subject has been distributed widely to labor groups and to persons in the intergroup relations field, we attach for your information, our letter of October 31, 1962.[22]

Wilkins was responding not only to recent attacks by the AFL-CIO against the NAACP but also to a resolution adopted by the Jewish Labor Committee, widely distributed and reported in the press, which denounced the Association and accused it of anti-Semitism. In his letter to Emanuel Muravchik, executive secretary of the Jewish Labor Committee, Wilkins stated:

When you declare in 1962 that the NAACP's continued attack upon discrimination against Negro workers by trade union bodies and leaders places "in jeopardy" continued progress towards civil rights goals or rends the "unity" among civil rights forces, or renders a "disservice" to the Negro worker or raises the question "whether it is any longer possible to work with the NAACP" you are, in fact, seeking by threats to force us to conform to what the Jewish Labor Committee is pleased to classify as proper behavior in the circumstances. Needless to say, we cannot bow to this threat. We reject the proposition that any segment of the labor movement is sacrosanct in the matter of practices and/or policies which restrict employment opportunities on racial or religious or nationality grounds. We reject the contention that bringing such charges constitutes a move to destroy "unity" among civil rights groups unless it be admitted that this unity is a precarious thing, perched upon unilateral definition of discrimination by each member group. In such a situation, the "unity" is of no basic value and its destruction may be regarded as not a calamity, but a blessed clearing of the air.[23]

In reply to the charge of anti-Semitism Wilkins went on to say:

This is a grave charge to make. . . . We do not deign to defend ourselves against such a baseless allegation. Its inclusion in the resolution, as well as in the statements to the press by Mr. Zimmerman is unworthy of an organization like the Jewish Labor Committee which in the very nature of things, must be conversant with the seriousness of such a charge and with the evidence required to give it substance. . . . Similarly, we do not feel that the general denials and outraged protests which have been the response of the ILGWU to our charges of discriminatory practices are in any way an adequate answer to those charges.[24]

In taking its stand, the NAACP demonstrated that black institutions would no longer be junior partners in coalitions dominated by liberal whites whose institutional interests and priorities were often in conflict with those of the black community.[25]

A scholarly study published in 1953 of racial and ethnic conflict in the ILGWU reported: "The strains and tensions in the shops are not without their echo in the union, where they become problems of ideology, power, and administration." Access to leadership was identified as "the most serious union problem in which the relation of ethnic groups enters. . . . The leadership of the union is overwhelmingly in the hands of the old-timers. . . ." The study concluded that "the crisis of leadership" in the ILGWU was a consequence "of the cleavage between two membership generations, differing very considerably in composition, background and outlook."[26]

Although their numbers had greatly increased within the ILGWU by the 1960s, black workers were limited to the lowest paying, unskilled job classifications in New York's garment manufacturing industry, as they were largely excluded from the craft locals where much higher wages prevailed. In the 1960s, blacks in New York as elsewhere were overcoming the passivity of the past, and increasingly they struggled against the forces that were responsible for their subordinate and depressed condition. This was the period in which rising black expectations challenged the shoddy compromises of the past, in labor unions no less than in other institutions.

The ILGWU, founded by European socialist immigrants in 1900, was not immune to these developments, especially since its membership base had become increasingly black and Latino. Through a series of restrictive procedures (of doubtful legality under the Labor-Management Reporting and Disclosure Act of 1959), the ILGWU excluded nonwhite workers from the leadership of the union. Not a single black or Latino was an officer of the international union or served as a member of the general executive board, or functioned as the manager of a local union.[27] The social psychologist Kenneth B. Clark, in his study of the consequences of ghetto life stated: "A significant example of the powerlessness of the Negro worker in a major trade union with a 'liberal' reputation is found in the status of Negroes in the International Ladies Garment Workers Union in New York City."[28] Clark recalled the discrimination his mother experienced as a member of the ILGWU. In a memoir he later wrote, "I was very pleased years later when the NAACP exposed the discriminatory pattern in New York's garment industry and attacked the racial practices of the ILGWU."[29]

The general suppression of membership rights within the ILGWU in conjunction with the extreme exploitation of nonwhite workers in the garment industry resulted in an increasingly restive labor force. During this period the majority of black and Puerto Rican garment workers in New York received less than $1.50 an hour in wages under ILGWU contracts. In 1960, according to the U.S. Bureau of Labor Statistics, only 11 percent of unionized garment workers in New York earned enough to maintain a "modest but adequate standard of living."[30] The union was rigidly controlled by a self-perpetuating bureaucracy of white males whose Jewish working-class base no longer existed and who were now increasingly in conflict with their nonwhite, largely female membership.

The transformation of the ethnic and racial composition of the garment industry labor force that began in the 1930s caused serious problems for the ILGWU since its traditional Jewish leadership was unwilling to accept blacks and Puerto Ricans as equal partners in an interracial union, to share control of the organization with nonwhites, and to permit them to share in the power that derived from such institutional authority. Instead of honestly confronting and resolving these issues, the union leadership, increasingly isolated from its membership, attempted to maintain the racist and sexist status quo by bureaucratic means. In response, rank-and-file workers protested in a variety of ways including demonstrating at union headquarters and filing petitions with the National Labor Relations Board seeking the decertification of the ILGWU. Typical of this development was the action of Puerto Rican workers at the Q-T Knitwear Company in Brooklyn in 1958 who charged the union with negotiating a "sweetheart contract" with their employer. They marched around the factory with picket signs that read "We're Tired of Industrial Peace. We Want Industrial Justice." After interviewing the workers, a reporter noted that the wildcat strike was a protest against their boss and "most important, against the workers' own union."[31] Conflict between the ILGWU and its nonwhite membership intensified when black and Puerto Rican organizations campaigned for a new $1.50-an-hour city minimum wage law, only to be opposed by the union.[32]

The increasing discontent of black and Latino workers employed in the New York garment industry provided the context for actions that occurred in the 1960s on these issues. On April 4, 1961, Ernest Holmes, a black worker who was a member of the NAACP, filed a complaint with the New York State Commission for Human Rights against Local 10, a craft unit of the ILGWU,[33] charging the union with discriminatory practices, including the refusal to admit him to membership on the basis of race, in violation of state law.[34] The New York Herald-Tribune, in a front-page report headlined "ILGWU Condemned for Racial Barriers" summarized the findings of the state commission with the comment that "the New York Cutters local of the International Ladies Garment Workers Union was judged guilty of racial discrimination in a report released yesterday by the State Commission for Human Rights." The newspaper noted that the cutters are "the most highly skilled and highly paid workers" and that wages for members of Local 10 "are roughly double that for other workers in the industry."[35] According to the New York Times, the State Commission for Human Rights found Local 10, the cutter's local of the ILGWU, responsible for discriminatory acts, and "the union was told that the commission would maintain a continuing interest in its training and admission practices and that these would be reviewed periodically to assure that the terms of the decision would be fully and conscientiously carried out."[36]

The ILGWU initially failed to comply, but after additional hearings and protracted negotiations, on May 17, 1963, twenty-five months after the original complaint was filed in Holmes v. Falikman, the union entered into a stipulation agreement to comply with the law without admitting guilt.[37] The Holmes case received much public attention as it symbolized widespread black and Latino discontent with the ILGWU and it led to a congressional investigation of the ILGWU's racial practices.

The ILGWU was greatly embarrassed by the revelations of the investigation and often distorted the history of the congressional proceedings. Gus Tyler, assistant president of the union, wrote for example, that Adam Clayton Powell, chairman of the House Committee on Education and Labor, was "riding a little wave of anti-Semitism" and that the union was exonerated. According to Tyler, "There was no case. There was nothing. . . . We won the round. We won the war."[38] The official record directly contradicts Tyler's claim, for the union was not exonerated.[39] Documentation in congressional files, together with extensive interviewing of congressional staff members by the author, revealed that the ILGWU used its considerable political influence at the highest levels of government to stop the hearings. An announcement was made at the last session, on September 21, that the hearings were "recessed, to reconvene subject to call." But they were never reconvened. After the union succeeded in making certain political arrangements, the congressional committee quietly abandoned the hearings, which were never formally concluded, and there was no final report.[40]

Florence Rice, a black woman who was a member of ILGWU Local 155 in New York, had been warned by a union official that if she gave testimony before the congressional committee she would never work again in the garment industry. She told the committee in a sworn statement that "workers have been intimidated by union officials with threats of losing their jobs if they so much as appear at the hearing."[41] Soon after her appearance before the committee in open hearings, she was dismissed from her job and was not able to obtain employment thereafter as a garment worker.[42] (Rice later became a leading community activist and director of the Harlem Consumer Education Council.)

After the *Holmes* case, ILGWU officers, in an attempt to ward off further criticism, added a black woman and a Puerto Rican man to the union's general executive board, moved some black and Latino workers into better paying, more skilled jobs in the industry, and employed several in previously all-white positions within the union. Furthermore, anticipating exposure, the union found it necessary to cancel its financial support for the ILGWU wing of the Workmen's Circle Home in the Bronx, a home for retired workers built with union funds and annually subsidized by the union, but which did not admit black and Puerto Rican members.[43]

Conflict between the ILGWU leadership and its minority group members continued as black, Asian and Latino garment workers filed a lawsuit against the East River Houses, known as the ILGWU Co-Operative Village, which refused to rent apartments to nonwhites. Federal Judge Robert L. Carter found that there was indeed a pattern of unlawful racial exclusion.[44] Documentation introduced into the court record revealed that the ILGWU had contributed more than $20 million of union funds to subsidize a housing project for middle-class whites who were not ILGWU members, adjacent to a vast area of substandard housing inhabited mainly by members of racial minorities.

This became a major issue among nonwhite ILGWU members in the New York area. Several thousand workers signed petitions demanding an end to the racist pattern in the East River Houses, and union members mounted a protest demonstration at the head-quarters of the ILGWU.[45] One union member, Margarita Lopez, was quoted in a newspaper report of the demonstration as saying:

How could this happen? How could this happen in a union that is supposed to be so liberal? The blacks, Hispanics, the Chinese are the workers. The dues come from these people, but the housing is all white and middle class. These were union pension funds. They give union funds but union workers who are black and Hispanic and Chinese cannot live in those houses.[46]

Protests from nonwhite workers against the racial practices of the ILGWU continued as black, Latino and Asian American workers began to organize dissident groups within various local unions. This activity led to the filing of complaints with federal agencies and the initiation of litigation on a variety of issues relating to race and violations of internal union democracy. Among these was the intervention in 1971 by the U.S. Department of Labor in the election proceedings within the 15,000 member Knitgoods Local 155 of the ILGWU, in response to a formal complaint filed by a black and Latino caucus known as the Rank and File Committee.[47]

The caucus charged that the union, in violation of federal law, had engaged in illegal practices to prevent the election of black and Latino workers to leadership positions within the local. After investigation, the Department of Labor ordered a rerun of the election. At a press conference, the Rank and File Committee charged that ILGWU officials signed contracts that forced them to work "under sweatshop conditions" and noted that black and Spanish-speaking workers constituted 75 percent of the membership of Local 155, but were denied any voice in determining union policies.

In its press release, the Rank and File Committee protested racist characterizations of its members that had appeared in the *Jewish Daily Forward*, the leading Yiddish-language newspaper in New York. The Committee cited articles in the *Forward* reporting on the conflict within Local 155, which contained "racist insults and slanderous lies . . . such as calling black and Spanish-speaking members of the Rank And File Committee a 'gang,' 'marijuana smokers,' 'drug addicts and pushers,' and 'bewildered children.' " According to the Rank and File Committee, such "slanders" were "a vicious and obvious attempt to whip up race hatred between the younger workers and our older, mostly Jewish co-workers in the shops. We are not anti-Semites. . . . We struggle with all workers, black, white and Spanish-speaking, of all religions, for a strong local."[48]

The *Jewish Daily Forward*, in a story headlined "Knitgoods Local 155 And the Elections" by Y. Fogel, reported that the "Communist Rank and File" are involved in a "Communist web of intrigues" and identified the black and Latino caucus as the work of "Communist agents." The article concluded with the explanation that "the communists only really want to take over the locals and the Union and offer them up on a Red tray to the Stalin inheritors who, together with El-Fatah, want to eliminate Israel."[49]

To the great dismay of the union's leadership, after the effective date of Title VII, the employment section of the 1964 Civil Rights Act, union members filed complaints against the ILGWU with the U.S. Equal Employment Opportunity Commission (EEOC). In many of these cases the EEOC sustained charges of race and sex discrimination against both the international union and its locals. In the *Putterman* case, a federal court in New York found "willful and intentional" violations of the legal prohibitions against discrimination by both the local and the international union.[50] Among the many EEOC charges filed against the ILGWU were cases in Chicago, Philadelphia, Cleveland, Atlanta, and New York.[51]

To divert attention from the central issue of racial discrimination, the ILGWU conducted an intensive campaign characterized by prevarication and distortion in an effort to make anti-Semitism the issue. The ILGWU repeatedly claimed that criticism of its racial practices was a malicious anti-Semitic attack upon the Jewish leadership of the union; many local and national Jewish organizations including the American Jewish

Committee, the American Jewish Congress, the Anti-Defamation League of B'nai B'rith, and the Jewish Labor Committee became actively involved and each group distributed a torrent of resolutions, correspondence, newsletters, bulletins, press releases, and brochures defending the ILGWU.[52]

The reaction of the union leadership demonstrates how white immigrant groups, once they achieve integration in American society, defend their own privileges and power when confronted with demands from blacks. The criticisms of the ILGWU raised in the course of the *Holmes* v. *Falikman* case and in its aftermath charged the union with perpetuating a pattern that limited nonwhites to the least desirable jobs and that violated the basic requirements of internal union democracy. To put it simply, an institution controlled by an established stratum of Jewish leaders who were anxious to preserve the privileges of their group within the industry and who by then had more in common with employers than with their nonwhite members, rejected the demands for advancement of a growing black and Latino working class. With the rise of the labor bureaucracy and the racial conflicts within the ILGWU, the tradition of the Jewish left in organized labor came to an end.

## THE RESPONSE TO BLACK DEMANDS FOR
## ECONOMIC ADVANCEMENT: A CASE HISTORY

From the 1890s, the garment industry in New York City absorbed successive waves of European immigrants. Many became skilled workers within an industry that offered stable employment and increased earnings; some eventually became small entrepreneurs employing immigrant workers themselves, while others moved out of the industry entirely to more desirable jobs in other sectors of the economy. As early as 1900, there were blacks working in the New York garment industry.[53] The census for 1930 reported that 35,400 blacks were employed in the needle trades,[54] and in that same year 20,000 blacks were working in the garment industry in New York,[55] but for them such employment did not provide the means to escape from poverty and share in the economic and social progress enjoyed by white immigrant workers and their children. For them, the ILGWU was to become part of the problem.

Herman D. Bloch, in his study of black workers in New York, concluded that in the 1930s:

both the International Ladies Garment Workers Union (ILGWU) and the Amalgamated Clothing Workers of America had Negro Americans in their New York locals; it was disputable as to whether these unions practiced "egalitarianism." Both unions accepted the colored American primarily as a means of controlling the trade, but they restricted him to the least skilled trades (finishers, cleaners, and pressers). Control over these workers was essential to carry on effective collective bargaining in the industries. Secondly, the ILGWU accepted the bulk of its Negro American membership during organizing drives, taking the Negro American into the union in order to make a union shop. . . .

Unionization of the colored Americans neglected a crucial issue: What occupations were open to these black Americans? What chance of upward economic mobility was available through a seniority system? The cutters' locals of both unions had no Negro American behind a pair of shears.[56]

Thirty years later the same pattern prevailed in workshops organized by the ILGWU, the largest labor union in New York City.

The experience of black workers was fundamentally different from that of European immigrants. For all their other problems, Jewish workers were white, and, together with other whites, they benefited from racial exclusionary practices and from the limitations on job advancement imposed on black workers because of their race. The theory that attempts to explain the problems of blacks in New York City as a consequence of their being the latest in a series of "newcomers" ignores history, ignores the fact that blacks were not recent immigrants, that they had been in the New York area for many generations before the European immigration of the late nineteenth century, and ignores the factor of race that was decisive in determining their occupational status.[57]

Black organizations understood that what nonwhite workers were doing in attacking the union's practices was precisely what Jews and other immigrant groups had done in the past. Indeed, the history of immigrants in America is a continuum of efforts in which ethnic groups, as they rose, fought as a bloc within institutions to advance their interests, using the availability of particular occupations as a lever for their goals. But in the 1960s, when the ILGWU was the focus of criticism, Jewish organizations viewed this tactic as an assault on the Jewish community. Thus they reacted as a community in defense of the ILGWU leadership and denounced as anti-Semites advocates of black advancement.

The response of Jewish institutions to the effort of blacks to advance economically in New York's garment industry demonstrated the profound changes that had occurred in the status of Jews in American society. With the rising affluence of the Jewish population and its assimilation into American society, the foundations of Jewish radicalism disintegrated. Many descendants of Jewish socialist immigrants now were upwardly mobile professionals or corporate managers with a stake in the perpetuation of existing social institutions. The intellectual skepticism cultivated by previous generations of radicalized Jews gave way to an acceptance of the legitimacy and indeed the virtue of existing values and institutions, including those relating to racial dominance and subordination. By the 1960s, Jews in America had become "white," that is they had become assimilated and affluent enough in a society sharply divided by race to enjoy the privileges of "whiteness"; furthermore, they regarded themselves as "white" and by and large they were accepted as such by the majority of the population.

The unprecedented transformation of Jewish life in the United States and its implications required analysis and explanations, especially within the Jewish community, and this was the purpose of Nathan Glazer's writing in *Commentary,* a publication of the American Jewish Committee, as well as in other journals. In "Negroes and Jews: The New Challenge to Pluralism," which appeared in the December 1964 issue of *Commentary,* Glazer asserted that the crisis in the early 1960s between blacks and Jews occurred because these groups had "different capacities to take advantage of the opportunities that are truly in large measure open to all."[58] The environment, Glazer said, is not prejudicial to one group or the other. Jews, he asserts, are able to take advantage of the "democracy of merit" which he believes characterizes contemporary American society. According to Glazer, patterns of Negro personality and behavior are responsible for the Negro's incapacity to realize the opportunities available to all.

In his version of cultural pluralism, Glazer argues that Jewish resistance to new Negro militancy is based "on a growing awareness of the depths of Negro antagonism to the world that Jewish liberalism considers desirable." Jews, he wrote, lived a different kind of life in American society, with their own businesses, neighborhoods, schools, and unions. Jews never attacked social discrimination per se, Glazer asserted, they never challenged "the right of a group to maintain distinctive institutions," but now Negro demands "pose a serious threat to the ability of other groups to maintain *their* communities." Negroes, Glazer complained, had no distinctive institutions of their own and wanted, therefore, to become integrated into all of American life. Glazer reprimanded the Negro for wanting to enter on an "equal footing" into "Jewish business . . . the Jewish union . . . or the Jewish (or largely Jewish) neighborhood and school." The "force of present-day Negro demands," said Glazer, "is that the sub-community, because it either protects privileges, or creates inequality, has no right to exist." The separatism which "other groups see as a value," Glazer wrote, "Negroes see as a strategy in the fight for equal rights." He also noted, "The resistance of Jewish organizations and individual Jews to such demands as preferential union membership and preferential hiring. . . ."

Glazer's comment about "Jewish unions" and the irresponsibility of blacks trying to enter them is an example of the application of his theory. What union did Glazer have in mind? The only union regarded as a "Jewish union" that came under attack from blacks at the time because of discriminatory racial practices was the ILGWU. In what ways could the ILGWU be classified as "Jewish"? Jewish immigrants founded the ILGWU, constituted a majority of its membership until the late 1930s, and Jews remained in control of the organization long thereafter.

Two decades before Glazer wrote his article, the Jewish membership in the union had fallen to 30 percent and continued to decline steadily.[59] The blacks accused of forcing themselves upon this "Jewish union" constituted—together with Latinos—a far greater proportion of the union membership than did Jews. In the central ILGWU membership base of New York City, where the garment industry and the union was concentrated, blacks and Latinos constituted a majority of the membership. In this context, the "privileges" of the ethnic "sub-community" described by Glazer are in fact derived from the institutionalization of racial discrimination and the exploitation of subordinate groups. When the nonwhite victims of that arrangement attempt to advance themselves by doing what other groups, including Jews, have succeeded in doing, they are, according to Glazer, "challenging the very system under which Jews have done so well."[60] The result that blacks desired, according to Glazer, was structural integration as a group into American society, something Jews already had but that blacks could not have because of their well-known defects, hence Glazer advised blacks to forego that aim.

Nathan Glazer argued for an interpretation of the black condition based on the alleged inability of blacks to take advantage of the "democracy of merit." He formulated a theory corresponding to the needs of an affluent Jewish population that while highly assimilated also sought to maintain an unusual degree of group distinctiveness. These divergent goals raise certain problems however, notably an anxiety about the status of assimilated groups whose roots are in an immigrant past. Demands for substantive change in the racial status quo are understood to threaten established institutional arrangements that are conducive to Jewish advancement, but not to the advancement of blacks.

### OCEAN HILL–BROWNSVILLE

If the conflicts between blacks and Jews regarding the racial practices of the ILGWU raised doubts about the future of a black-Jewish alliance, the bitter conflict that developed in 1968 between blacks and Jews in the Ocean Hill–Brownsville school controversy involving the United Federation of Teachers in New York City shattered whatever limited consensus may have still existed. According to Steven R. Weisman of the *New York Times*, "The 55-day teachers strike, an event so corrosive that, a generation later, people say it determined many of their views about race . . . [was] a war that lacerated the city and left wounds that have never fully healed."[61] The president of that union, Albert Shanker, who came from a Jewish socialist background, used the issue of anti-Semitism as a response to black demands for decentralization and community control of public schools. Shanker widely circulated an anti-Semitic leaflet allegedly published by a black community group which, upon investigation, was found not to exist.[62] His purpose was to provoke black-Jewish conflict thereby stimulating support from the Jewish membership of the union and Jewish organizations during a strike initiated by the teachers union. According to Dwight Macdonald, the United Federation of Teachers was actively seeking "to increase fear and hatred driving Negro against Jew in this city."[63] Ira Glasser, head of the New York Civil Liberties Union, reflecting on these events years later, stated "I have always blamed Shanker for whipping up the anti-Semitism issue. I think the union manufactured much of it. It caused a rupture between blacks and Jews that hasn't healed and I think it's unforgivable."[64]

At the conclusion of the Ocean Hill–Brownsville teachers' strike, which Richard Parrish, a national vice-president of the American Federation of Teachers described as "a strike against black parents and teachers," the liberal coalition lay in ruins. The Ocean Hill–Brownsville confrontation symbolized the end of the liberal consensus on race in New York and throughout the North. Since Jews were such a significant part of that consensus, this development had of necessity much significance as a Jewish issue.

Buttressed by the emergence of a new body of constitutional law on race and the adoption of the 1964 Civil Rights Act, blacks demanded not merely an abstraction called "equal opportunity," which usually resulted in little change, but rather substantive equality as a fact. Black institutions sought affirmative measures to narrow the great gap between the condition of blacks and whites in every aspect of the society. Such an approach demanded the recognition of racism, in the past and in the present, as a basic and pervasive fact of American life and, confronted by this challenge, the traditional appeals of liberalism fell before the imperative of race. It is in the context of affirmative action that the consequences of this development were most sharply demonstrated.

An examination of briefs amicus curiae filed in Supreme Court cases involving affirmative action reveals the very active role of Jewish organizations in attacking affirmative action. In 1974 in the *De Funis* case,[65] where the issue was access to higher education for minorities, briefs to the Supreme Court opposing affirmative action came from the Anti-Defamation League of B'nai B'rith, the American Jewish Committee, the American Jewish Congress, and the Jewish Rights Council. The National Organization of Jewish Women, however, filed a brief in support of affirmative action which was endorsed by the Commission on Social Action of the Union of American Hebrew Congregations. In 1978 in *Bakke*,[66] also an education case, among the groups which filed amici briefs against affirmative action were the American Jewish Committee, American Jewish Congress, Anti-Defamation League, Jewish Labor Committee, and the National Jewish Commission on Law and Public Affairs. The two Jewish groups that had supported affirmative action in the *De Funis* case did not file in *Bakke*.

In *Weber*,[67] a 1979 case involving employment discrimination, the Anti-Defamation League of B'nai B'rith and the National Jewish Commission on Law and Public Affairs urged the Supreme Court to decide against affirmative action. In 1980 in *Fullilove*,[68] a challenge to an Act of Congress providing a contractual set-aside for minorities in federally subsidized construction, the Anti-Defamation League joined with employer groups and the reactionary Pacific League Foundation to argue against affirmative action. The Anti-Defamation League also filed briefs in opposition to affirmative action in several lower court cases and has been among the most active of all groups in attacking affirmative action in the courts. For example, in 1983 the ADL filed a brief against minority interests in *Boston Firefighters Union, Local 718* v. *Boston Branch, NAACP*;[69] and it did so again in 1984 in the Memphis case known as *Firefighters Local Union No. 1784* v. *Stotts*.[70] This pattern of opposition to affirmative action was to continue. In addition to filing briefs amicus, ADL has also initiated its own litigation against affirmative action.[71] For more than two decades, Jewish organizations have led the attack against affirmative action and prominent Jewish leaders, institutions, and publications have engaged in a campaign against affirmative action characterized by misrepresentation and the exploitation of racial fears.[72] They have succeeded in making the term "quota," like "bussing," a code word for resistance to demands for the elimination of prevailing patterns of discrimination.

The pages of *Commentary* have been repeatedly filled with shrill denunciations of affirmative action. Jewish neoconservatives such as Irving Kristol, Nathan Glazer, Norman Podhoretz, Elliot Abrams, and Carl Gershman, among others, have provided the ideological basis for the civil rights retreat of the Reagan and Bush administrations, the most reactionary administrations on civil rights in the twentieth century.

In defense of their attacks upon affirmative action, Jewish leaders often cite the past experience of Jews as victims of discriminatory quota systems. But no justification can be found for the continuing attack on affirmative action by invoking the memory of discrimination against Jews in the Czarist empire or by elite educational institutions in the United States. The issue is current racial discrimination and the purpose of affirmative action is to include those groups that have long been excluded on the basis of race.

Affirmative action developed as the most effective means of eliminating the present consequences of past discrimination and of correcting the wrongs of many generations. Affirmative action is not directed against Jews; it is directed against white racism.

One must also note the disingenuous argument of those Jewish spokesmen who state that they are not against affirmative action but only against "quotas." Affirmative action without numbers, whether in the form of quotas, goals, or timetables, is meaningless; there must be some benchmark, some tangible measure of change. Statistical evidence to measure performance is essential; there cannot be effective affirmative action without numbers.

By now it should be very clear that the opposition to affirmative action is based on narrowly perceived group self-interest rather than on abstract philosophical differences about "quotas," "reverse discrimination," "preferential treatment," and all the other catch-phrases commonly raised in public debate. After all the pious rhetoric equating affirmative action with "reverse discrimination" is stripped away, it is evident that the opposition to affirmative action is rooted in the effort to perpetuate the privileged position of whites in American society.

Race has been and remains the great division in American society, and as the civil rights gains of the 1960s are eroded the nation becomes even more mean-spirited and self-deceiving on the issue of race. That Jews have played an all too prominent role in this retreat reveals much about the status of Jews in American society and about how the descendants of Jewish immigrants are playing out their role in the continuing anguish of American racism.

### FROM HISTORY TO MYTHOLOGY

The current conflict between blacks and Jews has stimulated racism among some Jews and anti-Semitism among some blacks and these destructive forces feed upon and reinforce each other. In such volatile circumstances, it is often a quick jump from history to mythology, hence the myth of the "grand old alliance" of blacks and Jews or the counter myth of their innate antagonism accompanied by a growing mutual demonization. John Bracey and August Meier have pointed out, "There has been much speculation about the nature and extent of Jewish support for black causes, and involvement in black advancement organizations, but precious little careful empirical research exists. . . . of an alliance which has been romanticized and considerably exaggerated."[73]

Sherman Labovitz, in his study *Attitudes towards Blacks among Jews: Historical Antecedents and Current Concerns,* concludes that there is "a general tendency to romanticize the relationships and overemphasize the extent to which Jews and Blacks have worked harmoniously."[74] Cornel West, for example, celebrates an imagined past of interracial cooperation when he calls the decades between 1910 and 1967 "the period of genuine empathy and principled alliances between Jews and blacks [that] constitutes a major pillar of American progressive politics in this century."[75] But Kenneth Clark, writing in *Commentary* in 1946, argued against the view that blacks and Jews perceived their struggles against white racism and anti-Semitism as similar. According to Clark, such beliefs ignored "the very wide difference between Jewish and Negro social, political, and economic status." While Jews who survived the horrors of World War II rejected racism, many were not sensitive to the differences between their own experience and that of blacks in America: "Many Negroes, rightly or wrongly, see the struggle of Jews in American society as primarily a conservative one, to consolidate gains already made; and secondarily to expand those gains to a higher level of economic, political, educational and social integration with the dominant group." Clark observed that for their part "many Negroes are disinclined to view [American Jews'] struggles as fundamental or as critical as their own—the struggle of the Jew is after all not one of life and death, to wring from society the bare necessities of life."[76]

Based upon my own experience of four decades in the civil rights movement, I am forced to question the much exaggerated assumptions of a black-Jewish alliance. What did emerge in the 1940s was the participation of some Jewish organizations in the legal and legislative civil rights efforts of that period, activities limited to leadership elites and professional staffs, but there was no mass involvement of the Jewish people with African Americans in a joint struggle for racial justice. The National Council for a Permanent Fair Employment Practices Committee formed in 1943 was a typical example of this pattern, where relations between the respective organizations were entirely bureaucratic in nature and did not in any way address the profound class and racial differences between the participating groups.[77] Since that time two distortions have emerged regarding the history of the civil rights movement during the late 1950s and 1960s: that Jews and other whites dominated and diverted the struggle into safe, irrelevant, integrationist channels against the true interests of blacks, and that the Jewish community, having deeply involved itself in the battle for racial justice, was displaced by ungrateful, racist blacks and is therefore understandably resentful and hostile to black demands. Both of these falsifications ignore the crucial fact that the leadership of the civil rights struggle was African American. No one could be involved in the movement during those years without recognizing that black people were taking their destiny into their own hands and leading their own struggles. This was, of course, the most important characteristic of that history. The southern civil rights movement, wrote George M. Fredrickson "was in many ways an expression of black autonomy and self-determination. Led by blacks, premised on black solidarity, and drawing on the distinctive traditions of the black church, it was in its own way a manifestation of African-American ethnic identity and assertiveness."[78]

The always small group of civil rights workers and volunteers involved in direct action and mass protest during the 1960s has mythically grown into an army. But there were only about three hundred Freedom Riders in all, and the Mississippi voter registration campaign of 1964 brought no more than about one thousand volunteers to the South for a few weeks and often less than that. Clayborne Carson reported that "even after an influx of Jewish volunteers during the Mississippi Summer Project of 1964, Jews working full time with SNCC were considerably outnumbered by white Protestants and even more by blacks, northern and southern."[79]

The civil rights movement of the 1960s was based upon the mass involvement of local black communities,[80] whereas the number of organizational staff and volunteers was very small, and accordingly involved an even smaller number of Jews. Although Jewish students were represented disproportionately in the voter registration campaigns, in not a single one of the movement groups—Southern Christian Leadership Conference (SCLC), Congress of Racial Equality (CORE), Student Non-Violent Coordinating Committee (SNCC), National Association for the Advancement of Colored People (NAACP), and the Council of Federated Organizations (COFO), which was important in the Mississippi struggle—did Jews or other whites play a decisive policy role, certainly not in the field, hardly ever in headquarters staff. A very small number of Jews functioned as second-level staff at the national offices of CORE and the NAACP and a few others sat on the largely honorific boards of directors of some organizations. (The NAACP Legal Defense and Educational Fund, Inc. was not part of the National Association for the Advancement of Colored People and did not engage in mass protest activities. Since 1957 it had been a separate organization of lawyers engaged solely in litigation.)[81]

Jews and other whites who joined in civil rights activity out of a private passion for racial justice correctly perceived the historic significance of the movement as the struggle of African Americans for their own liberation. Involved Jews undoubtedly believed that social justice was not only the concern of the oppressed, but they were few in number and at no time were black and Jewish communities joined together in an alliance.

With the adoption of the Civil Rights Act of 1964, the attention of black interest groups was drawn increasingly to the urgent problems of African Americans trapped in the decaying ghettoes of the urban North. In large measure, emerging black-Jewish conflict was a consequence of the shift of civil rights activity to the North. After substantive civil rights enforcement began, there was intense opposition by northern whites to compliance with the law, in regard to affirmative action, school desegregation, housing, and job seniority. These and other issues now clearly affected the lives of urban whites including Jews. Earlier civil rights struggles were concentrated largely in the South and advances required no change in the daily lives of white people living in the North. But after 1964, the civil rights movement directly affected the lives of northern whites, who sought to maintain their traditional race-connected privileges.

I have argued above that the charges of anti-Semitism made by the leadership of the International Ladies Garment Workers Union in 1962 not only had no justification but were a dishonest attempt to divert attention from the union's own discriminatory practices. Thirty-five years later self-declared black messiahs are resorting to anti-Semitism in their effort to control and manipulate black anger, and there is a danger that in some instances the struggle against white racism may take the degraded form of anti-Semitism.

The epic legacy of the historic black struggle for freedom must not be tarnished, must not be compromised by anti-Semitism, which is not part of the black heritage in America or in Africa. On the contrary, there is an old strain of folk philo-Semitism in African American life that continues to be expressed within the church community.[82] Anti-Semitism belongs to the history and culture of the white Christian world. It belongs to those who are responsible for the creation and perpetuation of a culture of racism based upon white supremacy.

While both black and Jewish leaders have a mutual responsibility to break the cycle of charge and countercharge, it may be argued that Jews have a special, a unique obligation to initiate action on behalf of justice and reconciliation. Steven Schwarzschild, professor of philosophy and Judaic studies at Washington University and a dear friend until his death in 1989 explained why. According to Professor Schwarzschild:

> Jews are defined by neither doctrine nor credo. We are defined by *task*. That task is to redeem the world through *justice*. To accomplish that task, the Jewish people needs to stay alive, but survival is not an end in itself but rather a means to enable us to pursue our task. Indeed to make survival into an end in itself, to seek it for its own sake, is to belie the values of the Jewish tradition, of Jewish law. If the notion of "chosenness" means anything supportable, it is that our portion, our task, is unlike that of other peoples, being in fact the duty to refine, exemplify and apply human and social justice.[83]

NOTES

1. *New York Times,* April 12, 1957, 52.

2. "Jewish Labor Body Elects Zimmerman," *AFL-CIO News,* Washington, D.C., May 11, 1968, 11.

3. For documentation on the activities of the Jewish Labor Committee during its early years, see *The Papers of the Jewish Labor Committee: Robert F. Wagner Labor Archive,* New York University, ed. Arieh Liebowitz and Gail Malmgren, vol. 14, "Archive of the Holocaust" (New York: Garland Publishing, 1993).

4. Supra, note 2.

5. *Ross* v. *Ebert,* 275 Wis. 223 (1957).

6. "Personal Record of James Harris," memorandum by Virginia Huebner, Administrative Assistant, September 25, 1946 (Fair Employment Practices Division, Industrial Commission of Wisconsin, Case Files 1945–1974, Series 1744, Box 4, Folder 16, Archives Division, State Historical Society of Wisconsin, Madison).

7. Huebner memorandum, February 16, 1953; Huebner notes of meeting with Charles Ebert, March 13, 1953; and letter to Ebert from Huebner, December 12, 1953 (Fair Employment Practices Division, Industrial Commission of Wisconsin, Case Files 1945–1974, series 1744, Box 6, Folder 16, Archives Division, State Historical Society of Wisconsin, Madison).

8. Memorandum from Herbert Hill, Labor Secretary, NAACP, to Boris Shishkin, Director, Civil Rights Department, AFL-CIO, Re *Ross* v. *Ebert,* January 21, 1957 (AFL-CIO Department of Civil Rights, Discrimination Case Files [#36] Box 3, Folder 21, George Meany Memorial Archives, Silver Spring, Md.).

9. Letter from William R. Conners, 5th Vice President, Bricklayers, Masons and Plasterers International Union, to Reuben G. Knutson, Industrial Commissioner, State of Wisconsin, January 25, 1954 (Fair Employment Practices Division, Industrial Commission of Wisconsin, Case Files 1945–1974, Series 1744, Box 4, Folder 16, Manuscript Division, State Historical Society of Wisconsin, Madison).

10. Letter from George Meany, to Huebner, April 26, 1957 (Fair Employment Practices Division, Industrial Commission of Wisconsin, Case Files 1945–1974, Series 1744, Box 4, Folder 16, Manuscript Division, State Historical Society of Wisconsin, Madison).

11. Transcripts of Hearing conducted by the Industrial Commission of Wisconsin, *Randolph Ross and James Harris* v. *Bricklayers, Masons and Plasterers International Union of America–Local 8,* January 19, 1955 (Fair Employment Practices Division, Industrial Commission of Wisconsin, Case Files 1945–1974, Series 1744, Box 4, Folder 14 and Box 6, Folder 12, Archives Division, State Historical Society of Wisconsin, Madison); also letter from Virginia Huebner, Administrative Assistant, Fair Employment Practices Division, Industrial Commission of Wisconsin, to Boris Shishkin, Director, Civil Rights Department AFL-CIO April 15, 1957 (AFL-CIO Department of Civil Rights, Discrimination Case Files [#35] Box 3, Folder 21, George Meany Memorial Archives, Silver Spring, Md.).

12. Charles S. Zimmerman, "Our Drive for Civil Rights," *American Federationist,* December 1957, 18.

13. Letter from Jack Reynolds, Assistant Manager, Wisconsin State Fair Park, to Virginia Huebner, Octo-

ber 21, 1946, and Huebner, notes of discussion with R. E. Oberst, October 15, 1946. See also letter to Huebner from T. J. Novak, Builder, August 27, 1953; also "Report on Conference with Andrew Harenda, General Contractor," September 2, 1953, by Huebner, and letter from Andrew G. Harenda, to Huebner, September 2, 1953 (Fair Employment Practices Division, Industrial Commission of Wisconsin, Case Files 1945–1974, Series 1744, Box 4, Folder 16, Archives Division, State Historical Society of Wisconsin, Madison).

14. *Local 28, Sheet Metal Workers International Association* v. *EEOC,* 478 U.S. 421 (1986). This union has been a defendant before a variety of administrative and judicial bodies since 1948. See *Lefkowitz* v. *Farrell,* C-9289-63, New York State Commission for Human Rights, 1948. For a discussion of the racial practices of other building trades unions in New York City, see Herbert Hill, "The New York City Terminal Market Controversy: A Case Study of Race, Labor and Power," *Humanities in Society* 6, (Fall 1984): 351–91. For information on the racial practices of construction unions nationally, see Herbert Hill, "The AFL-CIO and the Black Worker: Twenty-Five Years after the Merger," *Journal of Intergroup Relations* 10, no. 1 (Spring 1982).

15. *Commonwealth of Pennsylvania and Williams* v. *Local 542, International Union of Operating Engineers,* C.A. No. 71-2698, November 8, 1971. U.S. District Court, Eastern District of Pennsylvania, 18 FEP Cases 1560. In addition, on August 14, 1969, the Equal Employment Opportunity Commission initiated a commissioner's charge against the union. See EEOC, *In the Matter of Local 542, International Union of Operating Engineers,* Philadelphia, Pennsylvania, Case No. YCL 9-207.

16. *Daniels* v. *Pipefitters Local Union No. 597,* 53 FEP 1669 (N. D. ILL, 1990), aff'd., 945 F. 2d 906 (7th Cir. 1991), *cert. denied,* 503 U.S. 951 (1992), affirming on other grounds, 983 F. 2d 800, 60 FEP 942 (7th Cir. 1993). Injunctive relief and consent decree issued.

17. A. Philip Randolph, "The Civil Rights Revolution and Labor," address to the NAACP Annual Conference, New York, N.Y., July 15, 1959.

18. Harold F. Keith, "Will Negro, Jewish Labor Leaders Split Over Civil Rights," *Pittsburgh Courier,* December 12, 19, and 26, 1959, and January 3 and 10, 1960.

19. Herbert Hill, "Racism within Organized Labor: A Report of Five Years of the AFL-CIO, 1955–1960," NAACP, New York, 1961, reprinted in *Journal of Negro Education* (Spring, 1961): 109–18.

20. Address by A. Phillip Randolph to the Fifty-first Annual Convention of the NAACP, St. Paul, Minnesota, June 24, 1961. Copy in author's files.

21. Joel Seldin, "Meany Hits Negro Groups for Attacking Union Bias," *New York Herald-Tribune,* May 28, 1961, 1.

22. Memorandum from Roy Wilkins, executive secretary, NAACP, to members of the Leadership Conference on Civil Rights, November 21, 1962 (Reuther Collection, Box 504, Folder 1, Archives of Labor History and Urban Affairs, Wayne State University, Detroit).

23. Letter from Roy Wilkins, executive secretary, NAACP to Emanuel Muravchik, executive secretary, Jewish Labor Committee, October 31, 1962 (Reuther Collection, Box 504, Folder 1, Archives of Labor History and Urban Affairs, Wayne State University, Detroit).

24. Ibid.

25. For a detailed account of conflicts within the civil rights lobbying coalition during the 1960s, see Herbert Hill, "Black Workers, Organized Labor, and Title VII of the 1964 Civil Rights Act: Legislative History and Litigation Record," in *Race In America, The Struggle for Equality,* ed. Herbert Hill and James E. Jones Jr. (Madison: University of Wisconsin Press, 1993), 263–341.

26. Will Herberg, "The Old-timers and the Newcomers: Ethnic Group Relations in a Needle Trades Union," *Journal of Social Issues* 9, no. 1 (1953): 12–19.

27. For a description of the restrictions on political activity within the ILGWU and the eligibility rules for union office during the period under discussion, see Herbert Hill, "The ILGWU Today: The Decay of a Labor Union," and "The ILGWU: Fact and Fiction," in *Autocracy and Insurgency in Organized Labor,* ed. Burton H. Hall (New Brunswick, N.J.: Transaction Books, 1972), 47–160; 173–200.

28. Kenneth B. Clark, *Dark Ghetto, Dilemmas of Social Power* (New York, Harper & Row, 1965), 43.

29. Kenneth B. Clark, "Racial Progress and Retreat: A Personal Memoir," in Hill and Jones, *Race in America,* 7.

30. The wage rates of unskilled and semiskilled union garment workers in New York, most of whom were nonwhite, were below subsistence levels as indicated by the 1960 Interim City Workers Family Budget for New York City ($5,048), established by the Bureau of Labor Statistics. ("Employment, Earnings and Wages in New York City, 1950–1960," Bureau of Labor Statistics, New York, Middle Atlantic Office, June 1962.) The contract between Local 98 of the ILGWU and the Manufacturers Association in effect until August 14, 1963, was typical and provided the following minimum wages, page 7, Article 4(A):

| | |
|---|---|
| Floor Girls | $1.15 per hour |
| Operators | $1.20 per hour |
| Shipping Clerk | $1.20 per hour |
| Cutters | $1.20 per hour |

Describing the collective bargaining agreement in force in 1971 between Knitgoods Workers Local 155 of the ILGWU and the employers in New York City, New Jersey, and Long Island, the labor lawyer Burton H. Hall wrote that take-home pay is "between $57 and $59 for a full week. Sweatshops have not disappeared; they are hiding behind an ILGWU union label." Burton H. Hall, "The ILGWU and the Labor Department," in Hall, *Autocracy and Insurgency in Organized Labor,* 295.

31. Peter Braestrup, "Life among the Garment Workers, Puerto Ricans Rebel against Boss and Union" *New York Herald-Tribune,* October 8, 1958, 15. See also Braestrup, "Life among the Garment Workers" *New York Herald-Tribune,* October 6, 1958, 19, and October 10, 1958, 20. For the background to these developments see *Spanish Speaking Workers and the Labor Movement* (New York: Association of Catholic Trade Unionists, 1957). See also the Association's monthly publication, *Labor Leader,* which provided frequent reports of minority labor insurgency. A further source of information has been the author's interviews with Daniel J. Schulder, president of the Association of Catholic Trade Unionists, New York, November 18, 24, and December 2, 1958, together with examination of data in the Association's files.

32. Murray Kempton, "The Wage Fight," *New York Post,* August 21, 1962, 17; Arnold Witte, *New York World Telegram and Sun,* October 5, 1962, 15; and Michael Myerson, "The ILGWU: Fighting for Lower Wages," *Ramparts,* October, 1969, 51–55. See also Herbert Hill, "The Racial Practices of Organized Labor: The Contemporary Record," in *The Negro and the American Labor Movement,* ed. Julius Jacobson (Garden City, N.Y.: Anchor Books, 1968), 326–30.

33. *Holmes* v. *Falikman,* C-7580-61, New York State Commission for Human Rights (1963).

34. The union's response was to engage in repeated evasion and distortion, as when Moe Falikman, manager of Local 10, told the *New York Times* (May 18, 1961) that there were "more than 500 Negroes and Puerto Ricans" (27) in the cutters local. Later the ILGWU said there were 400 nonwhite members in this craft local, but subsequently reduced the figure to 300 and then to 200. The state commission challenged the ILGWU to produce names and addresses and places of employment of these alleged members, and the NAACP said it would withdraw the complaint if the union would comply, but such identification was never produced. The NAACP asked the American Jewish Committee to provide such identification since it was circulating the union's claim under its own name. The Committee also failed to respond (Herbert Hill, Labor Secretary, NAACP, to Harry Fleishman, Director, National Labor Service, American Jewish Committee, October 23, 1962. NAACP Papers, Group III, Box A 190, Manuscript Division, Library of Congress, Washington, D.C.). Gus Tyler, assistant president of the ILGWU, wrote, "In Local 10, there are 199 known Negro and Spanish-speaking members" ("The Truth About the ILGWU," *New Politics* [Fall 1962]: 7). Tyler explained that his figure included "Cubans, Panamanians, Colombians, Dominicans, Salvadorans, Mexicans, etc., as well as Puerto Ricans" (ibid.). But later he stated, "We had 275 black members in that local" (Gus Tyler, "The Intellectuals and the ILGWU," in *Creators and Disturbers: Reminiscences by Jewish Intellectuals of New York,* ed. Bernard Rosenberg and Ernest Goldstein [New York: Columbia University Press, 1982], p. 173). According to a tract published by the American Jewish Committee and distributed by the ILGWU, there were "250 Negro and Spanish-speaking cutters in Local 10" (Harry Fleishman, "Is the ILGWU Biased?" [National Labor Service of the American Jewish Committee, New York, November 1962]). The evident disparity in these numbers and their obviously arbitrary nature require no further comment.

35. Joel Selden, "ILGWU Condemned for Racial Barriers," *New York Herald-Tribune*, July 2, 1962, 1; See also Fred Feretti, "Crusading Negro Finds Road is Rough," *New York Herald-Tribune*, July 2, 1962, 8.

36. "Union Told to Get Job for Negro," *New York Times*, July 2, 1962, 22.

37. *Stipulation and Order on the Complaint of Ernest Holmes* v. *Moe Falikman et. al.*, Case No. C-7590-61, May 17, 1963 (*Holmes* v. *Falikman*, File 1963, New York State Commission For Human Rights). Copy in author's files.

38. Gus Tyler, "The Intellectuals and the ILGWU," 155–75.

39. See *Hearings before the Ad Hoc Subcommittee on Investigation of the Garment Industry, Committee on Education and Labor, United States House of Representatives,* 87th Congress, 2d Session, August 17, 18, 23, 24, and September 21, 1962.

40. For the author's testimony before the hearings, see *Congressional Record-House*, January 31, 1963, 1496–99.

41. Testimony of Florence Rice, *Hearings before the Ad Hoc Subcommittee on Investigation of the Garment Industry,* 167.

42. Interviews with Florence Rice by author, November 17, 1962, May 17, 1966, and April 9, 1972.

43. In 1959, the union had begun construction of the ILGWU wing, at a cost of $1,300,000, and after it was dedicated on June 11, 1961, continued to make substantial annual financial contributions to its operation, though fully aware of protests by Latino and black members against the use of union funds to build and maintain a facility closed to them. In 1965, after the *Holmes* case, the ILGWU canceled its agreement with the Workmen's Circle Home. See *Report of the General Executive Board,* 32nd Convention, International Ladies Garment Workers Union, 1965, pp. 57–58; also June 1961 issue of *Justice*, with page 1 headline reading "ILGWU Wing of Circle Home Opening June 11."

44. *Huertas, et. al.* v. *East River Housing Corp, et. al.*, U.S. District Court (S.D.N.Y., 1977), 77 C. 4494 (RLC) 1977.

45. Interview by author with Frederic Seiden and Francis Golden of the Lower East Side Joint Planning Council, New York, March 24 and 25, 1983. Sources that document the ILGWU's role in sponsoring and financing the $20 million ILGWU Co-Operative Village are Max D. Danish, *The World of David Dubinsky* (Cleveland: World Publishing, 1957), 305–7; David Dubinsky with A. H. Raskin, *David Dubinsky: A Life With Labor* (New York: Simon and Schuster, 1977), 216–18; and *Justice*, May 1, 1952, 1. See also *Report of the General Executive Board,* 32nd Convention, International Ladies Garment Workers Union, 1965, 8.

46. Quoted in Earl Caldwell, "When a House Can't Be Your Home," *New York Daily News,* June 1, 1983, 4.

47. *In the Matter of Edward J. Tucker, James Malloy and Raymond Tucker, Against Local 155, Knitgoods Workers' Union, International Ladies' Garment Workers' Union, AFL-CIO.* This was a complaint to the U.S. Department of Labor requesting the department's intervention to prevent continuing violations of the legal rights of union members pursuant to Section 482 of Title 29 of the United States Code (Landrum-Griffin Act).

48. Press Release, Rank And File Committee of Local 155, ILGWU, February 24, 1971. Copy in author's files.

49. Y. Fogel, "Knitgoods Local 155 and the Elections," *Jewish Daily Forward*, February 17, 1971, 1. English translation made by Abraham Friend. Copy in author's files.

50. *Violetta Putterman* v. *Knitgoods Workers Union Local 155 of ILGWU, International Ladies Garment Workers Union, Sol Greene and Sol C. Chaikin,* U.S. District Court, S.D.N.Y., Memorandum Opinion and Order, 78 Civ. 6000 (MJL), August 20, 1983.

51. A sample of the charges against the ILGWU filed with the EEOC includes the following in New York: TNY9-0648; TNH1-1413, 9-0059, and 1754. In charge YNK3-063, the International Union itself was a respondent. The charges filed against the ILGWU outside New York included those in Chicago (TCH8-0277); Kansas City, MO (TKC1-1101); Memphis (TME1-1091); San Francisco (TSF-0853); Baltimore (TBA3-0084); Philadelphia (TPA2-0651); Cleveland (TCT2-0468, 2-0043, 1-0002, 1-0004, 1-0006, 1-0010); and Birmingham (TB10-0954, 1-0357, 1-0195, 1-0873, 9-0098, 2-0975).

52. The following is a small selection. The American Jewish Committee gave wide distribution to an eight-page tract, "Is the ILGWU Biased?" written by Harry Fleishman, a member of its staff, and through

its newsletter, *Let's Be Human,* repeatedly praised the ILGWU and denounced its critics. A letter dated November 13, 1962, from John A. Morsell, assistant to the executive secretary of the NAACP, to Harry Fleishman provides a thoughtful response to Fleishman's assertions, which contain many errors of fact. (NAACP Papers, Group III, Box A190, Manuscript Division, Library of Congress, Washington, D.C.). Data in ILGWU files indicate that Fleishman was actively involved in the union's campaign (International Ladies Garment Workers Union Archives, Zimmerman Collection, Box 26, Folder 8, Labor Management Documentation Center, Cornell University, Ithaca, N.Y.). Later, Fleishman tried to intervene with the State Commission for Human Rights on behalf of the ILGWU. See letter to George H. Fowler, Chairman, SCHR from Harry Fleishman, Director National Labor Service, American Jewish Committee, December 19, 1962 (NAACP Papers, Group III. Box A184, Manuscript Division, Library of Congress). The American Jewish Congress, on December 6, 1962, sent a statement signed by Shad Polier, chairman of the organization's governing council, to all its members, defending the union and repeating Fleishman's distortions. The Anti-Defamation League of B'nai B'rith, the largest Jewish fraternal order in the United States, also came to the union's defense. Oscar Cohen, national program director of the league, reported its efforts on behalf of the union to Zimmerman in a letter dated December 3, 1962. He closed by promising Zimmerman to "do as much as [he] can." The Jewish Labor Committee was extremely active on behalf of the union, as the ILGWU provided major financial support to the organization and many of its leaders were officials of the union. Among the many mailings sent by the JLC to individuals and groups throughout the country in defense of the ILGWU was that by Emanuel Muravchik to various organizations, September 5, 1962, and Muravchik's memorandum with enclosures, October 17, 1962, as well as many press releases and assorted statements and resolutions. Archival sources for documentation of this history are the NAACP Papers in the Library of Congress; Jewish Labor Committee Files, Robert F. Wagner Labor Archives, New York University, New York; Library of Jewish Information of the American Jewish Committee, New York, as well as the ILGWU archives cited above, and the author's files.

53. See Sterling D. Spero and Abram L. Harris, *The Black Worker* (New York: Columbia University Press, 1931), 337. For information on black workers in New York in the early 1900s, see Mary White Ovington, *Half a Man: The Status of the Negro in New York* (New York: Longmans, 1911); Ovington, "The Negro in the Trade Unions of New York," *Annals of the American Academy of Political and Social Science,* May 1906, 64–75; George Edmund Haynes, "Effects of War Conditions on Negro Labor," *Proceedings of the Academy of Political Science,* February 1919, 299–312; Haynes, *The Negro at Work in New York City: A Study in Economic Progress* (New York: Columbia University Press, 1912); Charles L. Franklin, *The Negro Labor Unionist of New York: Problems and Conditions Among Negroes in the Labor Unions in Manhattan with Special Reference to the N.R.A. and Post N.R.A. Situations* (New York: Columbia University Press, 1936); Seth M. Scheiner, *Negro Mecca: A History of the Negro in New York City, 1865–1920* (New York: New York University Press, 1965), chap. 2, 45–64; and Herman D. Bloch, *The Circle of Discrimination* (New York: New York University Press, 1969).

54. United States Bureau of the Census, Census of Population, 1930.

55. Lazare Teper, *The Women's Garment Industry* (New York: Education Department, International Ladies' Garment Workers' Union, 1937), 7.

56. Bloch, *The Circle of Discrimination,* 107.

57. Among several studies see Scheiner, *Negro Mecca,* 1–12, and Bloch, *Circle of Discrimination,* 1–34. See also James Weldon Johnson, *Black Manhattan* (New York: Knopf, 1930); Gilbert Osofsky, *Harlem: The Making of a Ghetto* (New York: Harper and Row, 1966); and R. Ottley and N. Weatherby, eds., *The Negro in New York, 1626–1940* (New York: Praeger, 1967).

58. Nathan Glazer, "Negroes and Jews: The New Challenge to Pluralism," *Commentary,* December, 1964, 29–35. Reprinted in Nathan Glazer, *Ethnic Dilemmas* (Cambridge: Harvard University Press, 1983), chap. 5.

59. The percentage of Jewish membership in the ILGWU had been declining since the late 1930s and continued to fall thereafter. By 1960, blacks together with Latinos constituted a majority of the union membership in New York City. See Ben Seligman, *Contemporary Jewish Record,* December 1944, 606–7; Will Herberg, "The Old-Timers and the Newcomers: Ethnic Group Relations in a Needle Trades Union," *Journal of Social Issues* 9, no. 1 (1953): 12–19; *Jewish Labor in the United States* (New York: American Jewish

Committee, 1954); and Roy B. Helfgott, "Trade Unionism among the Jewish Garment Workers of Britain and the United States," *Labor History* (Spring 1961): 209; also Irving R. Stuart, "Study of Factors Associated with Inter-Group Conflict in the Ladies Garment Industry in New York" (doctoral diss., School of Education of New York University, 1951); and Robert Laurentz, "Racial/Ethnic Conflict in the New York City Garment Industry, 1930–1980" (doctoral diss., Department of Sociology, State University of New York at Binghamton, 1980). In 1995, as a result of dwindling membership and declining resources, the ILGWU merged with the Amalgamated Clothing and Textile Workers Union to form the Union of Needle Trades, Industrial and Textile Employees (UNITE).

60. Supra, note 56, p. 32.

61. Steven R. Weisman, "A City at War: The Painful Legacy of a Teachers' Strike," *New York Times*, March 1, 1997, 18.

62. Earl Lewis, in an authoritative study, wrote "Curiously, the patently anti-Semitic flyer attributed to Blacks identified a community group that did not exist. Certainly members of the Black community were capable of producing such statements. Nonetheless, in light of the scope of CONINTELPRO activities by the FBI and other law enforcement groups, one might also suspect agent provocateurs" (Earl Lewis, "The Need to Remember: Three Phases in Black and Jewish Educational Relations," in *Struggles In the Promised Land*, ed. Jack Salzman and Cornell West (New York: Oxford University Press, 1997), 254–55. For information on Shanker's political history, see Taylor Branch, *Pillar of Fire: America in the King Years, 1963–1965* (New York: Simon and Schuster, 1996), 292.

63. Dwight MacDonald, "An Open Letter to Michael Harrington," *New York Review of Books*, December 5, 1968, 48. For a discussion of these issues see exchange between Albert Shanker and Herbert Hill, "Black Protest, Union Democracy and the UFT," in Hall, *Autocracy and Insurgency in Organized Labor*, 218–35.

64. Quoted in John Kifner, "Ocean Hill-Brownsville, '68, Echoes of a New York Waterloo," *New York Times*, December 22, 1996, E5. The literature on this history is extensive, see especially *Confrontation at Ocean Hill-Brownsville: The New York School Strikes of 1968*, ed. Maurice Berube and Marilyn Gittell (New York: Praeger, 1969) which contains some of the most important documents of these conflicts. See also Naomi Levine, *Schools in Crisis* (New York: Popular Library, 1969); Mario Fantini, Marilyn Gittell, and Richard Magat, *Community Control and the Urban School* (New York: Praeger, 1970); Henry Levin, ed., *Community Control of the Schools* (Washington, D.C.: Brookings Institution, 1970); Diane Ravitch, *The Great School Wars: New York City 1805–1973* (New York: Basic Books, 1974), esp. 251–404; David Rogers, *110 Livingston Street Revisited: Decentralization in Action* (New York: Random House, 1983); and Jerald E. Podair, " 'White' Values, 'Black' Values: The Ocean Hill-Brownsville Controversy and New York City Culture, 1965–1975," *Radical History Review* (Spring 1994): 36–59.

65. *De Funis* v. *Odegaard*, 416 U.S. 312 (1974).

66. *Regents of the University of California* v. *Bakke*, 438 U.S. 265 (1978).

67. *United Steelworkers of America* v. *Weber*, 443 U.S. 193 (1979).

68. *Fullilove* v. *Klutznick*, 448 U.S. 448 (1980).

69. *Boston Firefighters Union, Local 718* v. *Boston Chapter NAACP*, U.S. Supreme Court 1983, remanded as moot, 31 FEP Cases 1167.

70. *Firefighters Local Union No. 1794* v. *Stotts*, 467 U.S. 561 (1984).

71. See for example, Press Release, Anti-Defamation League of B'nai B'rith, New York, January 14, 1975.

72. Two exceptions in later cases should be noted; *Local 28, Sheet Metal Workers International Association* v. *EEOC*, 478 U.S. 421 (1986), and *United States* v. *Paradise*, 480 U.S. 149 (1987), where the American Jewish Committee, American Jewish Congress, Union of American Hebrew Congregations, and the Central Conference of American Rabbis joined in an amicus brief in support of affirmative action. These cases involved a challenge to court ordered affirmative action plans for admitting blacks to a construction labor union in New York and to jobs in a public agency in Alabama. There were extensive judicial findings of prior discrimination in both cases and the Supreme Court sustained affirmative action plans.

73. John Bracey and August Meier, "Towards a Research Agenda on Blacks and Jews in United States History," *Journal of American Ethnic History* 12, no. 3 (Spring 1993): 65–66.

74. Sherman Labovitz, *Attitudes toward Blacks among Jews: Historical Antecedents and Current Concerns* (Saratoga, Calif.: RPE Research Associates, 1975), 7.

75. Cornel West, *Race Matters* (Boston: Beacon Press, 1993), 73.

76. Kenneth B. Clark, "Candor about Negro-Jewish Relations," *Commentary*, February, 1946, 12–13.

77. Records of the National Council for a Permanent Fair Employment Practices Committee are to be found in the NAACP Papers, Group II, Boxes A351, 353 and 186, Manuscript Division, Library of Congress, Washington, D.C.

78. George M. Fredrickson, "America's Caste System: Will It Change?" *New York Review of Books,* October 23, 1997, 70.

79. Clayborne Carson, "Blacks and Jews in the Civil Rights Movement: The Case of SNCC," in *Bridges and Boundaries: African Americans and American Jews,* ed. Jack Salzman (New York: George Braziller, 1992), 37.

80. See John Dittmer, *Local People: The Struggle for Civil Rights in Mississippi,* (Urbana: University of Illinois Press, 1994) and Charles M. Payne, *I've Got the Light of Freedom,* (Berkeley: University of California Press, 1995). See also Aldon D. Morris, *The Origins of the Civil Rights Movement* (New York: Free Press, 1984).

81. See Jack Greenberg, *Crusaders in the Courts* (New York: Basic Books, 1994), chap. 35.

82. For a valuable account that demonstrates this tradition, see Hollis R. Lynch, "A Black Nineteenth-Century Response to Jews and Zionism: The Case of Edward Wilmot Blyden," in *Jews in Black Perspectives: A Dialogue,* ed. Joseph R. Washington Jr., (Lanham, Md: University Press of America, 1989). Blyden's essay "The Jewish Question" is his own statement on this subject. An interesting discussion regarding the cultural implications of the diaspora experience of both blacks and Jews appears in Paul Gilroy, *The Black Atlantic: Modernity and Double Consciousness* (Cambridge: Harvard University Press, 1993), 208–17.

83. Letter from Steven Schwarzschild to Herbert Hill, February 22, 1988.

# The Unbearable Whiteness of Being Jewish
## Desegregation in the South and the Crisis of Jewish Liberalism

Since the early 1970s the relationship between blacks and Jews has been the subject of a substantial amount of scholarly attention, not least because of the conflicts between the two groups which came to the surface in the 1960s.[1] During this period longstanding differences over such issues as community control of school districts, affirmative action, the role of Israel in world politics, open admissions at universities and the open anti-Semitism of some controversial black leaders began to outweigh mutually perceived common interests which for decades had worked to cement cooperation between significant segments of both groups.

But while much has now been written about blacks and Jews, not enough has been said about how the relationship bears on the primary Jewish dilemma of continuity in a free society. While prior histories by authors such as David Levering Lewis and Harold Cruse speak to what they believe has been the negative impact the relationship has had on blacks, no one has ever explored the possibility that the Jewish involvement with the black struggle for equality may, in certain instances, not have been beneficial for *Jews*.[2] Specifically, it needs to be determined whether or not the persistence of a widespread liberalism among American Jews has resulted in attitudes toward blacks and issues of racial equality that are consonant with the interests of all the various and sundry communities which constitute American Jewry.

### LIBERALISM AND JEWISH IDENTITY

Obviously, it would be a mistake to attribute a monolithic liberalism to American Jews. Highly pluralistic throughout modern history, Jews have been "Tories, Confederates, and Know-Nothings as well as Socialists, Progressives and liberal Democrats."[3] But Jews do appear to be exceptional among white ethnic groups in their historical adherence to the traditions of modern liberalism, a liberalism that includes such values as individual freedom, equality of opportunity, universal education, and government economic intervention. As two prominent sociologists recently concluded, "while Jews earn more than any ethnoreligious group for whom data exist (including Episcopalians), they are more liberal to left in their opinions than other white groups, and they vote like hispanics."[4] While the nature of Jewish liberalism may now be evolving, recent polls testify to the fact that more than any other group of comparable socioeconomic status, Jews continue to cling to the values of equality and the welfare state.[5] Essentially,

Seth Forman recently published *Blacks in the Jewish Mind: A Crisis of Liberalism.*
Originally published in *American Jewish History* 85, no. 2 (1997): 121–42. Copyright © 1997, Johns Hopkins University Press. Reprinted with permission of the Johns Hopkins University Press.

as another sociologist recently wrote, "political allegiance in the United States is affected most strongly by economic status—but Jews break the pattern."[6]

There has been considerable speculation as to the causes of the Jewish attraction to liberalism. Some have seen the wellspring of American Jewish liberalism in the values of the Torah, in which the high regard for *zedakah* ("righteousness"), learning, and non-asceticism are reflected in Jewish respect for welfare, educational spending, and government interventionism in general.[7] Others have interpreted American Jewish liberalism as the twentieth-century extension of the European Jewish response to emancipation, that originated with the left and opposed the predominantly anti-Semitic right.[8] Another interpretation has it that the liberalism of most second and third-generation American Jews stems from lingering feelings of marginality.[9] But whatever the emphasis, central to any explanation of American Jewish liberalism is the vulnerability of Jews in the Diaspora. That is, a unique history of persecution appears to have imbued Jews with a more conscious recognition that the values of individual freedom, political and religious liberty, and civic equality are matters of paramount concern, even more so perhaps than marginal economic gain.

These attitudes have been reflected nowhere more conspicuously than in Jewish behavior toward blacks. There remains little doubt that Jewish interest in black affairs was strengthened after 1915, the year a Jew named Leo Frank was lynched by a Georgia mob after being falsely convicted of raping and murdering a fourteen-year-old employee of his family's pencil factory.[10] Apparently, the Frank case sensitized Jews to the plight of American blacks, the primary victims of lynchings throughout the first two decades of the twentieth century.[11] After 1915 it appears that American Jews were alone among American ethnic groups in seeking out similarities between themselves and black Americans and, at least in elite circles, in mobilizing politically around an alliance with black Americans.[12] Jews and Jewish organizations during this period contributed heavily to organizations such as the NAACP and to dozens of other philanthropic projects designed to help blacks, including the funding of black education in the South. Major Jewish figures like Julius Rosenwald, Jacob Schiff, and Felix Warburg contributed to dozens of black elementary and vocational schools and institutions of higher and professional education, hospitals, orphanages, libraries, settlement houses, and social clubs.[13] At other levels, Jewish sympathy for blacks was demonstrated by the generally warmer attitudes of predominantly Jewish labor unions toward prospective black members and the outpouring of compassion for the plight of blacks that flowed from most large-circulation Anglo-Jewish and Yiddish newspapers.[14]

Historian Hasia Diner has shown that, especially after the Frank lynching, the minority status of Jews bound them to the ideals of equality and freedom far more intensely than even the " 'real' Americans," and thus made it possible for Jews to carve out a unique place for themselves in American life by assisting blacks in their historic fight for equal citizenship.[15] The one thing that brought Jews together with blacks in the cause of civil rights, therefore, was not religion or "Socialist-Zionism," though these factors undoubtedly influenced some. As the famed civil rights attorney Jack Greenberg explains, "That pro-civil rights sentiment spanned German and Eastern European Jews suggests the power of the shared experience of anti-Semitism and its resemblance to the black experience."[16] Liberalism and involvement in black affairs was, in large measure, an accommodation of the Jewish past to American life. It is now suitable to ask if this accommodation was an entirely appropriate one for Jews who now find themselves living in a nation defined largely by the enormity of the black experience and the racial divide. What, the unanswered question now seems to be, can the study of Jewish attitudes toward blacks, as an integral component of American Jewish liberalism, tell us about the postwar experience of American Jews as a distinct cultural group?

In answering this question it is helpful to begin with the desegregation crisis in the South of the 1940s and 1950s, an episode in post–World War II race relations that is perhaps most illustrative of how Jewish identification with the liberal fight for equality often clashed with other Jewish communal interests, including such obvious and agreed-upon ones as the physical safety of American Jews and Jewish unity. Having made important contributions to the war effort as both servicemen and civilians, many Jews felt the tension between their identity as Jews and as Americans dissipate, and it became far less obvious to many Jews how they differed from other Americans. As the late historian Lucy Dawidowicz wrote, the "experience of the war years had had a transfiguring effect on American Jews and on their ideas of themselves as Jews."[17] Specifically, the postwar decline of anti-Semitism in terms of public opinion, economic opportunity, educational opportunity, political and religious tolerance, and the vastly improved image of Jews in popular culture, together with the establishment of a Jewish state and increasing suburbanization, seriously reduced the capacity of anti-Semitism and Jewish ghettoization to define the terms of Jewish commitment.[18] If Judaism had gained equal legal status with Christianity and Jews were continuing to gain equality as individuals, then discrimination and exclusion could no longer act as the focal point for the concept of choseness which had been at Judaism's spiritual core throughout the ages and which had long blurred the line in Jewish thought separating the Jewish religion from Jewish ethnicity. The search for meaning sparked a debate in which some Jewish scholars, like Herberg and Arthur A. Cohen, called for a revitalization of Jewish life through ritual, and others, like Conservative Rabbi Robert Gordis, who urged Jews to revitalize their religious life through a commitment to social justice.[19] Nevertheless, the Holocaust, the failure of the Allies to stop it, and lingering pockets of discrimination made it likely that many Jews would continue to identify with the one aspect of being Jewish most accessible to them: the experience of anti-Semitism and the fight against it. But the incongruity between the Jewish emphasis on anti-Semitism as a central mode of group identity and the actual leveling of anti-Semitism in the United States was conspicuous, if only for the enormous effort many Jews made to be counted on the side of the persecuted. Liberal Jews rallied around new sociological research indicating that the causes of bigotry were the same no matter who the object of hatred was and that therefore, wherever prejudice against one group was found, prejudice against other minority groups was almost always just off the horizon.[20] This confirmed the belief that Jewish self-interest was at stake in the struggle for black equal rights and that Jewish involvement was, therefore, more than justified. Increasingly, many Jews found their identity in the work of national defense organizations like the American Jewish Committee, the American Jewish Congress, and the B'Nai B'Rith's Anti-Defamation League.

In these organizations, the lines between religion and ethnicity remained blurred, and, in the mission to act on behalf of Jews as an ethnic group with distinct political interests, the defense agencies simultaneously helped to define the religious dimension of Jewish life in terms of democracy, equality, civil rights, and racial brotherhood.[21] In 1945 Alexander Pekelis, the legal counsel for the American Jewish Congress, wrote "American Jews will find more reasons for taking an affirmative attitude toward being Jews . . . if they are part and parcel of a great American and human force working for a better world . . . whether or not the individual issues touch directly upon so-called Jewish interests."[22] Pekelis was typical of Jewish communal leaders in his belief that by providing a "Jewish" platform for general political action, Jewish identity would be catalyzed by reconciling the need for communal purpose with the need for faith. As historian William Toll has written of Jewish leadership in the postwar era, "the great majority of influential rabbis and laymen set about reconciling the Jewish sense of choseness with the moral mission of America as exemplar of democracy and self-determination."[23] This approach to Jewish identity found Jews at the vortex of the fast-developing postwar civil rights coalition. In 1945 the American Jewish Congress began working with the NAACP to form the central axis around which other groups—such as the American Civil Liberties Union, the Jehovah's Witnesses, the Japanese-American Citizen's League, the Anti-Defamation League, the National Lawyers Guild and the AFL-CIO—gathered to campaign for antidiscrimination statutes and fair employment practices legislation. In 1947, in response to a request from the NAACP to support an antilynching bill in Congress, the politically reserved American Jewish Committee formally made the commitment to minority causes not specifically Jewish with the statement that "it is a proper exercise of the powers of our charter that the AJC join with other groups in the protection of the civil rights of the members of all groups irrespective of race, religion, color or national origin."[24] At the 1956 Conference of the National Community Relations Advisory Council, the coordinating body of six national Jewish organizations and 35 local community relations councils, Chairman Bernard Trager pointed out that "the entire substantive program of Jewish Community Relations rests upon the thesis that Jewish equality is only as secure in a democratic society as the equality of other groups."[25] The Columbia University economist Eli Ginzburg warned in 1949 that a Jewish identity based on fighting anti-Semitism and prejudice would not provide a sufficient basis for the sustenance of the Jewish community. "Today at least among large numbers of American Jews," he wrote, "the 'defense activities' have usurped a position of priority. This was more or less inevitable since many of these Jews have lost all interest in positive Jewish values, their entire adjustment is externally oriented."[26] But Ginzburg's warning went unheeded, and "Working for a society in which economic disadvantage and intolerance would have no place became for Jews an almost religio-cultural obsession."[27]

## LIKE ALL OTHER SOUTHERNERS . . .

The years 1945 through 1965, in which the great postwar civil rights victories were achieved, have been called the Golden Years of the black/Jewish alliance.[28] But the first indication that the development of Jewish identity in terms of the fight for black equality might prove problematic for some American Jews was the battle for desegregation in the American South because it was in the South, paradoxically, that Jews had first gained their designation as somewhat privileged whites whose status and welfare were not so clearly tied to the dark-skinned victims of Southern racial prejudice. While the Southern racial system was brutal and unjust, it was perhaps the postwar venue in which Jews were most clearly distinguished from the people on the lowest rung of the racial hierarchy—blacks—making it far easier for Southern Jews to see themselves among the privileged rather than among the victimized. The liberal image of the South as a violent and savage place for Jews had not been born out over the years. As far back as the Civil War, when General Grant issued his infamous Order 11, expelling Jews from the Department of the Tennessee, public opinion so heavily favored the Jews that the order was completely ignored in certain communities.[29] Louis Galambos found that Southern farmers were far more likely to attack big business at the turn of the century than Jews, indicating that animosity of the rural Southerner over his rapidly changing environment was not completely unfocused. Historian John Higham maintains that the Ku Klux Klansmen of the late nineteenth and early twentieth centuries centered their anger on the distant Jew of the Northern urban centers and felt "guilty and ashamed at picking on the Jews whom they had known as good neighbors all their lives."[30] It has also been pointed out that even before the Civil War, and especially after it, the political climate in the South was such that Jews were able to hold a number of powerful elective and appointive political offices.[31]

The historic lack of a consistent and systematic anti-Semitism in the South can be attributed to two phenomena, the first being the dominance of Protestantism in the region and its reverence for the Old Testament. The editor of the *Carolina Israelite*, author and humorist Harry Golden, has explained that from this Anglo-Calvinist devotion to the Old Testament and the Hebrew prophets came a solid tradition of philo-Semitism.[32] But the racial divide was the most substantial reason why anti-Semitism in the South remained tempered. "Negroes acted as an escape-valve in Southern society," wrote Bertram Korn. "The Jews gained in status and security from the very presence of this large mass of defenseless victims who were compelled to absorb all of the prejudices which might otherwise have been expressed more frequently in anti-Jewish sentiment."[33]

While there were a variety of caste and class distinctions among whites in the South, the presence of blacks and the primacy of the color line fostered the acceptance of Jews in high places. As I. J. Benjamin wrote, "The white inhabitants felt themselves united with, and closer to, other whites—as opposed to the Negroes."[34] In this sense then, blacks not only acted as a "lightning rod for prejudice," but Southern fears of black advance also relieved Southern Jews of the animus caused by economic competition with other whites that many Northern Jews felt keenly.

The liberal assumption that ethnic prejudice is unified and all of the same kind is almost certainly mistaken. Scholars have long pointed out that the prejudices held by bigots vary in source and kind and have a great deal to do with the type and intensity of discrimination that is meted out.[35] Perhaps the most eloquent refutation of the liberal belief in the "unity of prejudice" comes from George McMillan, an expert on the Ku

Klux Klan. McMillan has explained that to "hate blacks is not to hate everything else equally as well. If blackness can become symbolic enough in a psychological sense, then hatred of blacks can sufficiently fill your psychological need to hate."[36]

All of this does not mean that the position of Southern Jews was not in any way precarious. Living in a region characterized largely by an overpowering caste system and fierce racial bigotry, Southern Jews treaded lightly and made their way in a place that was largely ambivalent about their presence.[37] Since the arrival in the South of the first group of Jews in 1733, Jews faced periods of significant discrimination and were subject from time to time to a number of legal proscriptions, as they were throughout most of pre-Revolutionary America. But these restrictions were very loosely applied and were aimed far more at disabling Catholics than Jews.[38] Perhaps the most significant strain of Southern anti-Semitism came in the form of the agrarian populism of the 1890s, whose obsession with money, credit, and conspiracy led populist writers like Ignatius Donnelly to identify the Jew with the usurer and the "international gold ring."[39] While populist denunciations of Jews were primarily rhetorical and rarely resulted in riots, pogroms, or even exclusionary laws, the populist rabble-rouser Thomas E. Watson was able to incite the mob that lynched Leo Frank using anti-Semitic imagery.[40] For the most part, however, these kinds of actions were mitigated by countervailing Southern ideas concerning the equality of all white men, the overriding concern with the subordination of black Americans, and the usefulness of the Jews as merchants and artisans.[41]

Spread thinly throughout the vast region, the Jews in the South tended to avoid taking public stands on controversial issues. When the issue of slavery tore the country in two during the Civil War, for example, Southern Jews largely accepted slavery and supported the South.[42] Given their propensity not to rock the political boat, Southern Jews were quite shaken by the movement toward desegregation, which came to a head in May 1954 with the Supreme Court's decision striking down the constitutionality of "separate but equal" public schools. It was immediately clear that this decision would cause a serious division among America's Jews. The Jews who lived in the Southern states most impacted by the *Brown* decision had acclimated themselves to a much different social and political milieu than Jews in the North and had long dropped any pretensions to being an ethnic group with a distinct political outlook. The Jews of the South did not share the psychological attachment to the black cause that so many Northern Jews did, and the matter of civil rights was not integral to their identity as Jews, as it had become for so many Jews in the North.

### . . . ONLY LESS SO

As during the Civil War, the Jewish community of the 1950s constituted less than one-half of one percent of the Southern population and was largely composed of merchants dependent on the goodwill of the community. For some Jews in the South the situation was more complicated because of the willingness of the Jewish merchant, beginning after the Civil War, to cater to black clients as well as white. The need to appeal to both blacks and whites necessitated that the Jewish merchant strive hard to avoid alienating either party.[43] It was a position that black Americans themselves seemed to be aware of. The black psychologist Kenneth Clark wrote that most blacks in the South believed Southern Jews were vulnerable to propaganda, subtle pressure, and threats from the more aggressive segregationist groups. After talking with several hundred black residents of the South, Clark concluded that "this sensitivity seems to dominate the general attitude and feelings of Negroes toward Jews in the South."[44]

On balance, Southern Jews remained cautious on the issue of desegregation, often pressuring national Jewish agencies through local community councils to soft pedal the issue so as not to associate Jews with the cause.[45] Nevertheless, while Jews in the South did not embrace the cause of desegregation with as much enthusiasm as Northern Jews or the national Jewish organizations did, polls and surveys from the period indicate overwhelmingly that Jews were on the whole more accepting of desegregation than other Southern whites. A 1960 survey indicated that Jews were more than twice as likely as Southern Protestant whites to feel that desegregation was both inevitable and, in general, desirable in the long run, and only about one-third as inclined as the latter to believe that blacks were constitutionally inferior to whites. Moreover, only a handful of Jews were actively racist beyond the conformity apparently required for maintaining their businesses or professional careers in strongly segregationist communities.[46] Researcher Joshua Fishman found that many Southern Jews who objected to the public statements of national Jewish organizations often privately agreed with them.[47] In another survey administered between 1959 and 1962, Alfred Hero found that Southern Jews were "distinctly less inclined than white Southern gentiles to express segregationist, and particularly racist, ideology." Hero explained that even when educational, occupational, and social differences were held constant, "significant differences [between Southern Jews and Southern gentiles] were evident in their views on race relations." The survey found that the majority of Jewish informants ranged from "mild segregationists to integrationists" and that "white gentiles of similar occupation and income were almost twice as likely as the local Jews to be relatively strong white supremacists."[48]

In his study of a Southern Jewish community, Theodore Lowi found Jews who had lived in the South longer tended to be more conservative politically than Jews who had recently moved South, but "the old Jews will make the inevitable adjustment to integration more easily and more quickly than their white Christian brethren."[49] According to a study of Jews in Roanoke, Virginia in the mid-1950s, seventy percent of Jews surveyed supported the Supreme Court's decision to integrate the public schools.[50] These survey findings were backed up by the testimony of at least one major black leader. The Reverend Fred Shuttlesworth, a close aide to Dr. Martin Luther King, Jr., claimed that "the response of Southern Jews to the [civil rights] movement certainly compares favorably with that of numerous other white groups."[51]

But the response of Southern Jews to the desegregation campaign was considered entirely inadequate by many liberal Jews in the North for whom the fight for black equality had become a particularly Jewish concern. For many Northern Jews the situation of the Jews in the South as a relatively privileged people challenged their fundamental beliefs about what it meant to be a Jew and of the sacred connection between race prejudice and anti-Semitism. Isaac Toubin, Director of the American Jewish Congress, insisted that the Southern Jew knew that "the hatemonger who today suppresses the Negro . . . tomorrow, with equal venom, may suppress the Jew."[52] In some instances, the strength with which some Jews felt this unity with blacks resulted in an alarming insensitivity to the circumstances of Jews in the South. In 1946 Carl Alpert accused the Jews of the South of being accessories to the crime of injustice against blacks: "The law makes provisions, we must remember, for accessories before and after a crime. Southern Jews, alas, go beyond passivity—they are accessories."[53] At the 1956 National Jewish Community Relations Council meeting, professor Arnold Rose compared the reluctance of Jews in the South to speak out in favor of desegregation with Nazi collaborationists: "If [Jewish leaders] do not take a long run and courageous view of the current crisis [on segregation], they are playing the same role as the collaborationist Jews played in Europe during the Nazi period."[54] Referring to the segregationist senator from Mississippi, James Eastland, another Jewish writer drew an analogy between Southern Jews and Nazi collaborationists: "Shouldn't the Anti-Defamation League's educational effort include a comparison between fascism in Germany and its counterpart, Eastlandism in the South? Surely the Jewish collaborators of Hitler are despised by the masses of Southern Jews. Everyone knows that silence and appeasement only brought destruction to the appeasers and to those who thought they could save themselves by silence and non-resistance."[55]

Nevertheless, the involvement of Jewish organizations in the *Brown* case and the vocal support of liberal Jews for desegregation in the South concerned Southern Jews, many of whom believed the behavior of their coreligionists did not take sufficient account of their safety and status.[56] Southern Jews who believed that the national Jewish agencies had succeeded in implicating them in the eyes of extremists in the cause of desegregation were bolstered in this view by the seven acts of terrorist violence against Jewish institutions in the South between June 1954 and October 1958 and by the emergence of the antiintegrationist and occasionally anti-Semitic White Citizen's Councils.[57] In 1956 Rabbi Gerald Wolpe, spiritual leader of synagogue Emmanuel in Charleston, South Carolina, recommended that "Jewish 'self-protection organizations' do not rush into print with opinions which are not based on personal investigation in the South" and that Jewish professionals "refrain from arriving armed with programs of action which were outlined in the insulated security of a New York office."[58] Rabbinic and lay organizations needed, according to Wolpe, "an understanding encouragement of the Southern Jews' moral fibre . . . more than a reckless condemnation of a Jew who stands between the Scylla of indecision and the Charybdis of an insidious bigotry."[59]

Morton Gaba, Executive Director of the Jewish Community Council of Norfolk, Virginia, believed it was of primary concern that the battle for desegregation be fought by Jews on an individual basis, as Americans, rather than as Jews: "We feel that those of us who are strongly moved by the issue should act solely as individuals and not as representatives of another minority group. I feel certain that point of view represents majority thinking."[60]

Perhaps no one expressed the desperation of some Southern Jews better than Rabbi Perry Nussbaum of Jackson, Mississippi. Nussbaum had an admirable record on speaking out on civil rights but explained that he was not apt to ask the same of his congregants. "In the Delta area of our state, where the Jewish merchant is pressured into taking sides, I would be the last to ask that he make a martyr of himself and his family and prepare to move when he is compelled to join the Citizen's Council."[61] In 1963, after the death of the black civil rights leader Medgar Evers in Mississippi, Nussbaum bitterly reported that all the clergymen in his state who had been outspoken in the cause of civil rights had been removed or forced from their pulpits—all except him.[62] Nussbaum concluded his article with this lament: "Support for civil rights? Who argues? A solution to the problem of the last survivor, who has it?"[63]

It is no accident that the bulk of the criticism of the national Jewish organizations came from Southern rabbis, who often found themselves in the most precarious of circumstances. The clergy generally held a status in the South rarely afforded them in the North, and Southern rabbis were considered the spokesmen for the Jewish community, thus helping to create a natural friction between them and the national Jewish agencies, led in many instances by secular Jewish leaders. Writing in *Conservative Judaism*, Rabbi William Malev of Houston, spiritual leader of one of the South's largest Conservative congregations, explained that in the South the Jews were seen by non-Jews as a religious and not an ethnic group, in which capacity they were not a minority but one-third of the community of the "three great faiths." The defense organizations, on the other hand, were an anomaly to the non-Jew in the South, and served to confuse outsiders as to who the Jews were properly represented by. Because the Anti-Defamation League is a secular organization like the NAACP, Malev argued, it is despised in the South and therefore is a liability to Southern Jewish communities. Malev recommended that the national defense organizations stop "their unfortunate habit of beating the drum on every possible occasion" and "let religious leaders of the Jewish communities be the spokesman for them."[64] Malev clearly articulated the Southern belief that it was Jewish leadership on the matter of desegregation that had linked Jews and blacks in the mind of the Southern racist, but that in fact this linkage was false. "It is because the demagogue and the agitator equate the Jew and the Negro, and thereby separates the Jew from the rest of the community, that much of the difficulty has come."[65]

While there were a number of outspoken integrationist rabbis in the South, including Charles Mantinband of Mississippi, Emmet Frank of Virginia, and Jacob Rothschild of Georgia, in general the Southern rabbinate varied in its approach to desegregation according to the size of the Jewish population in the general community, the openness of the community, the number of "Old South" Jews in the congregation, and the proportion of congregants who were businessmen.[66] But even Jacob Rothschild, one of the most outspoken integrationist rabbis, expressed his doubt that "the rabbi in today's South will serve any good purpose in leading crusades. Where there are forces at work in the community—human relations councils and the like—he should become a part of them by all means. But let him labor alongside others of like mind and dedicated purpose."[67]

It may be useful here to contrast the Southern Jewish fear of extremism expressed by these rabbis with the approach of one prominent Northern liberal to the attacks on Jewish institutions in the South. The desperation with which liberal Jews in the North sought to define themselves among the oppressed was revealed to an almost embarrassing degree when Albert Vorspan, Director for the Committee on Social Action of the Union of American Hebrew Congregations, the national body of the Reform movement, responded with something only slightly short of glee to the bombings of Jewish institutions in the South. "The Jew is caught up in the storm of the South whether he likes it or not," wrote Vorspan, who seemed pleased that the bombings had once again restored Jews to their proper place as certifiable victims: "The Jew has often been the barometer of the moral health of a society. The bombers have again unwittingly rendered to the Jew this tribute."[68] These comments indicate that the heart of the problem between Northern and Southern Jewry involved the question of Jewish identity. Having been isolated so long from larger Jewish communities and having assimilated the Southern love of the land, Southern Jews, particularly those longest in the South, had largely accepted the definition of Jewishness as strictly a religious designation and rejected the idea that Jews had distinct political interests.[69] By mid-century Southern Jewry had become significantly more diverse as a result of continued migration from the North, but for the most part Southern Jews showed a greater unwillingness to define themselves as a "minority" group.[70] Jewish identity, religious or otherwise, was perhaps more attenuated in the South but relied more heavily on religious forms than the ethnic/political identity of the majority of Jews in the Northern-based civil rights movement.[71] The point here is not to enter the debate concerning the ethical precepts of Judaism, as they relate to civil rights or to posit a specific Jewish tradition, but rather to demonstrate that the Southern Jewish community had been characterized at one and the same time by strong religious identification and low ethnic solidarity, and that for liberal Jews who had so fully transposed their Jewish identity toward the crusade for desegregation, the "Jewishness" of Southern Jews who appeared squeamish or apprehensive about desegregation became highly suspect.[72]

It is not surprising therefore that much of the criticism of Southern Jewry coming from the North on the desegregation issue centered around the identity of Southern Jews and the supposed willingness of Jews in the South to assimilate. A tepid approach by any Jew toward desegregation, in the mind of the liberal Jew, was the ultimate sacrilege.

One Jewish civil rights lawyer compared the anxious Jews of the South to the Marrano Jews of Spain who publicly denied their Judaism during the inquisition.[73] Writing in *The Reconstructionist*, Carl Alpert explained that the problem with the Southern Jew was not that he was more anti-Negro than his gentile neighbor: "his only crime is that he is like his neighbor. The sort of Jews who fear to be distinctively Jewish might gain some comfort from that thought, and use it to prove again and again that Jews are no different from anybody else, as if that fact itself were a virtue."[74] Joel Dobin, a rabbi from Pennsylvania, complained that the small Jewish community in the South he had visited had patterned its religious life after the Christian community to such an extent that rabbis were called "preachers" or "reverends," synagogues were often called churches, and dietary laws were almost never observed. For Dobin it was an "incorrect" Jewish orientation that was at the heart of this small Southern Jewish community's lack of enthusiasm for the desegregation campaign. While acknowledging the peculiar economic and social pressures on Southern Jews, Dobin wrote that "there is a need for constructive action. There is a need for reviving in these Jews a sense of positive Jewish identification, for instilling in them a serene pride in Jewishness, and for helping them to see that they will gain moral courage as they repose their faith in what Judaism teaches to be right and honorable."[75]

Albert Vorspan conducted one of the most vitriolic attacks on the Jewishness of Southern Jews for what he considered a lack of Jewish aggressiveness in the area of civil rights. Making reference to a young Episcopal priest who had excommunicated a congregant who objected to attending church with blacks, Vorspan asked, "can this be said of Jews?" Coming from a leader of Reform Judaism, a movement whose very existence is predicated upon Judaism's lack of a central authoritative body with powers of excommunication (*cherem*), this is startling.[76] More than the other Northern liberals, Vorspan defined Judaism in terms of radical racial protest and then questioned the Judaism of anyone who did not adhere to this criterion. In a tirade that reads like it could have been written by a member of the Orthodox leadership at the turn of the century, when Reform Judaism was in its ascendancy, Vorspan decried the excessive tolerance of American Judaism: "There are no standards for synagogue membership . . . He [the Jew] has only to pay his dues in the temple and he has as much right there as anybody else . . . Are there no lines to be drawn? No standards to be met? No demands to be made upon ourselves?"[77]

It must here be acknowledged that some national Jewish organizations and Jewish leaders moderated their desegregation activities in response to requests by local Jewish communities, indicating that they were not willing to completely ignore the concerns of Southern Jews regarding their safety and livelihood.[78] But the disparate approaches of Northern and Southern Jews to desegregation should not be minimized. The conflict between the Jews of the North and the Jews of the South over racial desegregation reflected the difference between liberal Jews for whom, on balance, the black struggle for equality came to take precedence over any perceived risks to the welfare of fellow Jews and a group of Jews who were perhaps the first in the United States to discover that their well-being and livelihood were not directly linked to the fate of black Americans. The opposition of the local Jewish community to the presence of 19 Conservative rabbis in a May 1963 protest march in Montgomery, Alabama, dramatized the differences between Southern Jews and liberal Northern Jews. Andre Ungar, perhaps the most prominent member of the rabbinical delegation, reported that the local community seemed to be saying, "Boychiks, we know you are right, but still, how could you do this to us, your brothers?" and the rabbis were saying, "Jews, dear scared little Yidden, how can you side with racism, with Hitler's heritage; and yet, you are our brothers, and we love you, we love you, forgive us, please."[79] One cannot help but notice the irony in a group of Southern Jews, most of whom had long deemphasized Jewish peoplehood, asking the rabbis for special consideration in the name of Jewish brotherhood. But this episode also demonstrates that in the battle over desegregation, the needs of Southern Jewish communities in conflict with liberal ideals were often sacrificed against the increasingly dubious need of Jewish liberals to be counted among the persecuted. One suspects that this motivation may be behind the response of liberal Jews to other related historical episodes, including the conflict over racial integration in Northern cities and the rise of Black Power in the late 1960s and early 1970s.[80] While the precise details of these episodes require further study, and while it is foolish to suggest that Jewish involvement in civil rights came always at the expense of larger Jewish concerns, it does seem that the objectives of American liberalism have diverged from important Jewish communal concerns far more often than is generally acknowledged, and that this has been perhaps nowhere more evident than in the case of race relations.

Perhaps to a degree rarely noted, Northern and Southern Jews were in fact responding the best way they knew how to similar historical pressures. Harry Golden has pointed out that in some ways the Jew in the South envied the black because, despite never having been entirely excluded from the white gentile world, the Jew still asks "What will happen to us here?" but the black "never thinks of himself in terms of actual survival."[81] In a similar way, liberal Jews in the North were also asking themselves "What will happen to us here?" but in reference to the increasingly open and democratic United States. While Southern Jews faced issues of physical safety and economic viability, the issues facing Jews outside of the South were freedom and assimilation, and their answer to the challenge of Jewish survival was reflected in the adoption of the cause of racial justice as their own. At the very moment Jews outside of the South became aware that it was possible for them to melt away as an ethnic group, they were refusing to do so, in part, through their involvement in the march toward equal rights.[82] The decision of the major Jewish organizations to pursue civil rights for all constituted a commitment to Jewish otherness through liberalism. If the Jews of the South had assimilated the attitudes of Southern whites, only less so, they believed this was the best way to ensure their survival. If the Jews in the North absorbed the postwar commitment to freedom and equality, only more so than other Americans, they believed it was one way of ensuring communal purpose and survival. Just as Golden had suggested that the Jew in the South envied the black, the involvement of the Northern Jew in the civil rights movement, and the insistence that desegregation was every bit as much a Jewish fight as it was a black fight, indicates that in the deepest recesses of their consciousness many Jews may have coveted the special status of black Americans, the weight of whose historical presence on the American scene precluded any foreboding about group survival.

As the Jewish scholar Ben Halpern once intimated, Jews and Judaism are not integral to the American way of life, as blacks are. Unlike Jewish history, which began before the advent of the United States and way beyond its borders, the travail of the black American belongs fully and tragically to American history.[83] One must consider when drawing conclusions about blacks and Jews that whatever else the black struggle for equality has meant it has never been, and is not now, a struggle principally about the continued corporate existence of black Americans. Conversely, the struggle for corporate existence appears to be one in which American Jews are now intimately engaged.[84] In light of the vast governmental efforts made in the postwar period on behalf of black equality and group recognition, as well as the priority that so many Jewish leaders made of the black struggle, even against occasionally urgent Jewish needs, the conclusion that the American Jew has been the true "invisible" man of the postwar decades is not so preposterous as it may have once seemed.

NOTES

1. For histories of black-Jewish relations before World War II see David Levering Lewis, "Parallels and Divergences: Assimilationist Strategies of Afro-American and Jewish Elites from 1910 to the Early 1930s," in *Journal of American History* 71 (December 1984): 543–64; Hasia Diner, *In the Almost Promised Land: Jews and Blacks, 1915–1935* (Westport, Conn., 1977); Philip S. Foner, "Black-Jewish Relations in the Opening Years of the Twentieth Century," *Phylon* 36, no. 4 (Winter 1975): 359–67; Oscar R. Williams, Jr., "Historical Impressions of Black-Jewish Relations Prior to World War II," *Negro History Bulletin* (July–August 1977): 728–731; David Brion Davis, "Jews in the Slave Trade," *Culturefront* I, no. 2 (Fall 1992): 42–5.

For more general scholarly surveys see Robert G. Weisbord and Arthur Stein, *Bittersweet Encounter: African Americans and American Jews* (Westport, Conn., 1970); Robert G. Weisbord and Richard Kazarian, Jr., *Israel in the Black American Perspective* (Westport, Conn., 1985); William M. Phillips, Jr., *An Unillustrious Alliance: The African American and Jewish American Communities* (New York, 1991); Joseph R. Washington, Jr., ed., *Jews in Black Perspective: A Dialogue* (Rutherford, N.J., 1984); John Bracey and August Meier, "Towards a Research Agenda on Blacks and Jews in United States History," *Journal of American Ethnic History,* 12, no. 3 (Spring 1993).

For studies of neighborhood conflict see Jonathan Reider, *Canarsie: The Jews and Italians of Brooklyn Against Liberalism* (Cambridge, Mass., 1985); Hillel Levine and Lawrence Harmon, *The Death of an American Jewish Community: A Tragedy of Good Intentions* (New York, 1992).

For an interesting, albeit ideologically compromised, analysis of Jews and blacks in Hollywood see Michael Paul Rogin, *Blackface, White Noise: Jewish Immigrants in the Hollywood Melting Pot* (Berkeley, 1996).

2. Harold Cruse, *The Crisis of the Negro Intellectual* (New York, 1967); Lewis, "Parallels and Divergences," reprinted in *Bridges and Boundaries: African-Americans and American Jews,* ed. Jack Salzman, Adina Black, and Gretchen Sullivan Sorin (New York, 1992), 17–35.

3. Lawrence Fuchs, "Introduction," *American Jewish Historical Quarterly* 66, no. 2 (December 1976): 187.

4. Seymour Martin Lipset and Earl Raab, *Jews and the New American Scene* (Cambridge, Mass., 1995), p. 148. This is a paraphrase of a statement widely attributed to the Jewish sociologist Milton Himmelfarb.

5. See Earl Raab, "Are American Jews Still Liberal?" *Commentary* 101, no. 2 (February 1996): 43–5; Charles S. Liebman and Steven M. Cohen, "Jewish Liberalism Revisited," *Commentary* 102, no. 5 (November 1996): 51–3.

Alan Fisher, "The Myth of the Rightward Turn," *Moment* 8, no. 10 (1983): 25; Steven Cohen, *1988 National Survey of American Jews* (New York, 1988), 3; William B. Helmreich, "American Jews and the 1988 Presidential Elections," *Congress Monthly,* 56 (January 1989): 3–5; Peter Steinfels, "American Jews Stand Firmly on the Left," *New York Times,* 8 January 1988, E7; "Portrait of the Electorate," *New York Times,* 5 November 1992, table 89; Raab, 43–5; Lipset and Raab, 147–8.

6. Nathan Glazer, "The Anomalous Liberalism of American Jews," in *The Americanization of the Jews,* eds. Robert M. Seltzer and Norman J. Cohen (New York, 1995), 133.

7. Lawrence H. Fuchs, *The Political Behavior of American Jews* (Glencoe, Ill., 1956); *idem,* "Jews and the Presidential Vote," in *American Ethnic Politics* (New York, 1968), 50–76.

8. Werner Cohn, "The Sources of American Jewish Liberalism," in *The Jews: Social Patterns of an American Group,* ed. Marshall Sklare (Glencoe, Ill., 1958), 120–34.

9. Charles S. Liebman, *The Ambivalent American Jew: Politics, Religion, and Family in American Jewish Life* (Philadelphia, 1973), 149–50.

10. Lenora Berson, *The Negroes and the Jews* (New York, 1971), 29–45. There are two histories of the Leo Frank case: Harry Golden, *A Girl is Dead* (New York, 1952) and Leonard Dinnerstein, *The Leo Frank Case* (New York, 1968).

11. Robert Zangrando, *The NAACP Crusade against Lynching, 1909–1950* (Philadelphia, 1980).

12. There were, to be sure, a number of instances in which certain other ethnic groups before World War II, still victimized by various levels of discrimination, saw parallels between themselves and black Americans and rejected an identity based on whiteness. But these instances of immigrant group/black solidarity were subplots against the more common theme in which both groups generally saw the other, for a variety of complicated and unfortunate reasons, as rivals for the common goal of full citizenship. See David Roediger, *Towards the Abolition of Whiteness: Essays on Race, Politics, and Working Class History* (London, 1994), 186–94; Thaddeus Radzialowski, "The Competition for Jobs and Racial Stereotypes: Poles and Blacks in Chicago," *Polish-American Studies* 33 (Autumn 1976): 16–7; Paola Giordano, "Italian Immigration to the State of Louisiana," *Italian Americana* (Fall–Winter 1977): 172; Hodding Carter, Sr., *Southern Legacy* (Baton Rouge, 1950), 105–6; Jean Scarpaci and Garry Boulard, "Blacks, Italians and the Making of New Orleans Jazz," *Journal of Ethnic Studies* 16 (Spring 1988); Donna Misner Collins, *Ethnic Identification: The Greek Americans of Houston, Texas* (New York, 1991), 210–11; James W. Loewen, *The Mississippi Chinese: Between Black and White* (Cambridge, Mass., 1971); "Irish Mornings and African Days on the Old Minstrel Stage: An Interview with Leni Sloan," *Callahan's Irish Quarterly* 2 (Spring 1982): 49–53; Douglas S. Massey and Nancy A. Denton, *American Apartheid: Segregation and the Making of the Underclass* (Cambridge, Mass., 1993), 25–60.

13. Diner, *In the Almost Promised Land*, 164–191.

14. *Ibid.*, 89–117, 128–133. On Jewish labor unions and blacks see Edith Kline, "The Garment Union Comes to the Negro Worker," *Opportunity*, April 1934, p. 108; Roger Waldinger, *Still the Promised City? African-Americans and New Immigrants in Postindustrial New York* (Cambridge, Mass., 1996), p. 144, 146.

15. *Ibid.*, 238.

16. Jack Greenberg, *Crusaders in the Courts: How a Dedicated Band of Lawyers Fought for the Civil Rights Revolution* (New York, 1994), 52–3.

17. Lucy Dawidowicz, *On Equal Terms: Jews in America, 1881–1981* (New York, 1982), 129.

18. For public opinion data see Charles Stember, ed., *Jews in the Mind of America* (New York, 1966), especially "Recent History of Public Attitudes," 127–34.

For religious acceptance see Will Herberg's landmark *Protestant, Catholic, Jew: An Essay in American Religious Sociology* (Garden City, New York, 1955), 28–59. Herberg espoused the belief that American pluralism was rapidly becoming a pluralism of the major religious faiths, each representing an equally valid expression of a common American faith. For images of Jews in films see Patricia Erens, *The Jew in American Cinema* (Bloomington, Ind., 1984), 170–3; Lester D. Friedman, *Hollywood's Images of the Jew* (New York, 1982), 125.

For the best discussion of the downward trend in anti-Semitism after the war see Edward Shapiro, *A Time for Healing: American Jewry since World War II* (Baltimore, 1992), 28–59.

19. Herberg, *Protestant, Catholic, Jew*, 20, 27, 30–1; Arthur A. Cohen, *The Natural and Supernatural Jew: A Historical and Theological Introduction* (New York, 1964), 6–7; Robert Gordis, *The Root and the Branch; Judaism and the Free Society* (Chicago, 1962), 66, 76, 158–71; William Toll, "Pluralism and Moral Force in the Black-Jewish Dialogue," *American Jewish History* 77, no. 1 (Spring 1987): 103–4.

20. See Leonard Dinnerstein, "American Jewish Organizational Efforts to Combat Antisemitism in the United States since 1945," in *Antisemitism in the Contemporary World*, ed. Michael Curtis (Boulder, Colo., 1986), 305; Murray Friedman, "Civil Rights," in *Jewish-American History and Culture: An Encyclopedia*, eds. Jack Fischel and Sanford Pinsker (New York, 1992), 89.

For an example of this outlook see Shad Polier, "Law and Social Action," *Congress Weekly* 17, no. 31 (November 27, 1950): 2.

See Jewish-sponsored studies by T. W. Adorno et al., *The Authoritarian Personality* (New York, 1950); Charles Y. Glock and Rodney Stark, *Christian Beliefs and Anti-Semitism* (New York, 1966); Gary T. Marx, *Protest and Prejudice: A Study of Belief in the Black Community* (New York, 1967); Harold F. Quinley and Charles Y. Glock, *Anti-Semitism in America* (New York, 1979).

21. For a discussion of this transformation see Nathan Glazer, *American Judaism*, 2nd ed. (Chicago, 1957), 135–6.

22. Alexander Pekelis, "Full Equality in a Free Society," in *Law and Social Action: Selected Essays of Alexander H. Pekelis*, ed. Milton Konvitz (Ithaca, 1950), 223, 242.

23. Toll, "Pluralism and Moral Force," 103–4.

24. Naomi Cohen, *Not Free to Desist: The American Jewish Committee, 1906–1966* (Philadelphia, 1972), 386.

25. Quoted in Esther Levine, "Southern Jews' Views on Segregation," *Jewish Life* 10, no. 10 (August 1956): 35.

26. Eli Ginzburg, *Agenda for American Jews* (New York, 1950), 1–90. For an interesting discussion of this paper see Arthur Hertzberg, *The Jews in America: Four Centuries of an Uneasy Encounter* (New York, 1989), 331.

27. Friedman, "Civil Rights," 89.

28. Berson, *The Negroes and the Jews*, 97.

29. James Wax, "The Attitude of the Jews in the South toward Integration," *Central Conference of American Rabbis Journal* 26 (June 1959): 16.

30. Louis Galambos, *The Public Image of Big Business in America, 1880–1940* (Baltimore, 1975), 63–4; John Higham, "Social Discrimination against Jews in America, 1830–1930," *American Jewish Historical Quarterly* 47 (September 1957): 30–1; Stephen Whitfield, "Jews and Other Southerners," in *Voices of Jacob, Hands of Esau: Jews in American Life and Thought* (Hamden, Conn., 1984), 219.

31. Whitfield, "Jews and Other Southerners," 220; Eli Evans, *The Provincials: A Personal History of Jews in the South* (New York, 1973), appendices A and B.

32. Harry Golden, "Jew and Gentile in the New South," *Commentary* 20, no. 5 (November 1955): 403.

33. Bertram Wallace Korn, "Jews and Negro Slavery in the Old South, 1789–1865," in *Jews in the South*, eds. Leonard Dinnerstein and Mary Dale Palsson (Baton Rouge, 1973), 123.

34. I. J. Benjamin, *Three Years in America* (Philadelphia, 1956), 76.

35. Norman Cohn, "The Myth of the Jewish World-Conspiracy," *Commentary* 41, no. 5 (June 1966): 40. For the varying images of black Americans and Jews in American folklore see Nathan Hurvitz, "Blacks and Jews in American Folklore," *Western Folklore* (October 1974). See also Stember, *Jews in the Mind of America*, 224–5.

36. Quoted in Evans, *The Provincials*, 212.

37. Whitfield, 224.

38. Howard Sachar, *A History of the Jews in America* (New York, 1992), 23; Leonard Dinnerstein, *Anti-Semitism in America* (New York, 1994), 5.

39. See Richard Hofstadter, *The Age of Reform; From Bryan to F.D.R.* (New York, 1955), 77–81; Daniel Bell, "The Grass Roots of American Jew Hatred," *Jewish Frontier* 6 (October 1948): 374–8; Oscar Handlin, "American Views of the Jew at the Opening of the Twentieth-Century," *Publications of the American Jewish Historical Society* no. 40 (June 1951): 323–44.

40. Hofstadter, 81.

41. Leonard Dinnerstein, "A Neglected Aspect of Southern Jewish History," in *Uneasy at Home: Anti-Semitism and the American Experience* (New York, 1987), 83–99.

42. Korn, "Jews and Negro Slavery," 123.

43. John Dollard, *Caste and Class in a Southern Town* (New York, 1937), 128–9.

44. Kenneth Clark, "A Positive Transition," *Anti-Defamation League Bulletin* (12 December 1957): 5.

45. Will Maslow, "My Brother's Keeper . . . ," *World Jewry* 1, no. 2 (April 1958): 5; Cohen, *Not Free to Desist*, 392–3.

46. Alfred Hero, "Southern Jews," in *Jews in the South*, 222.

47. Joshua A. Fishman, "Southern City," in *Jews in the South*, 323.

48. Hero, "Southern Jews," 216–17.

49. Theodore Lowi, "Southern Jews: The Two Communities," *Jewish Social Studies* 6 (June 1964): 112.

50. Fuchs, *Political Behavior*, 108.

51. Quoted in Allen Krause, "Rabbis and Negro Rights in the South, 1954–1967," in *Jews in the South*, 362.

52. Isaac Toubin, "Recklessness or Responsibility," *Southern Israelite* (27 February 1959): 14.

53. Carl Alpert, "A Jewish Problem in the South," *The Reconstructionist* 12, no. 3 (March 22, 1946): 11.

54. Levine, "Southern Jews'," 35.

55. *Ibid.*, 23.

56. The American Jewish Committee hired black psychologist Kenneth B. Clark to conduct a study in 1950 on the impact of segregation on black children. In the 1954 Brown decision, the Court cited the original Clark manuscript as well as two other investigations conducted by the American Jewish Congress in its famous footnote 11.

57. See Arnold Foster, "The South: New Field for an Old Game," *The Anti-Defamation League Bulletin* 15, no. 8 (October 1958): 1–2; David Halberstam, "The White Citizens Councils," *Commentary* 22, no. 4 (October 1956): 293–4.

58. Gerald Wolpe, "The Southern Jew and 'The Problem,'" *The Reconstructionist* 22, no. 16 (December 14, 1956): 29.

59. *Ibid.*

60. Morton J. Gaba, "Segregation and a Southern Jewish Community," *Jewish Frontier* 21, no. 10 (October 1954): 12–5.

61. Perry E. Nussbaum, "Pulpit in Mississippi Anyone?: The Southern Rabbi Faces the Problem of Desegregation," *Central Conference of American Rabbis Journal* 14 (June 1956): 2–3.

62. Perry E. Nussbaum, "And Then There Was One—In the Capital City of Mississippi," *Central Conference of American Rabbis Journal* 11, no. 3 (October 1963): 16–7.

63. *Ibid.*, 19.

64. William Malev, "The Jew of the South in the Conflict on Segregation," *Conservative Judaism* 13, no. 1 (Fall 1958): 40.

65. *Ibid.*, 50.

66. Krause, "Rabbis and Negro Rights," 379.

67. On Rothschild see Melissa Fay Greene, *The Temple Bombing* (New York, 1996). Jacob M. Rothschild, "The Rabbi Will Serve No Good Purpose in Leading Crusades," *Central Conference of American Rabbis Journal*, 14 (June, 1956): 6.

68. Albert Vorspan, "The Dilemma of the Southern Jew," *The Reconstructionist* 24, no. 18 (9 January 1959), 7–9.

69. Lowi, "Southern Jews," 112; Golden, "Jew and Gentile," 403.

70. Lowi, "Southern Jews," 106–7, 12.

71. Golden, "Jew and Gentile," 404–5.

72. Lowi, "Southern Jews," 115. On Jewish ethics and liberalism see Liebman and Cohen, 52; Steven Plaut, "Jewish Liberal PC and Ethical Posturing," *Midstream* 42, no. 6 (August/September 1996): 20–3.

73. Marvin Braiterman, "Mississippi Marrano," *Midstream* (September 1964): 32.

74. Alpert, "A Jewish Problem," 11.

75. Joel C. Dobin, "Portrait of a Southern Community," *Congress Weekly* 25 no. 9 (28 April, 1958): 8.

76. Albert Vorspan, "The Negro Victory and the Jewish Failure," *American Judaism* 13, no. 1 (Fall 1963): 50.

77. *Ibid.*, 52.

78. Murray Friedman, *What Went Wrong: The Creation and Collapse of the Black-Jewish Alliance* (New York, 1995), 288; *idem*, "One Episode in Southern Jewry's Response to Desegregation: An Historical Memoir," *American Jewish Archives* 33, no. 1 (April 1981): 178; *idem*, "Virginia Jewry in the School Crisis: Anti-Semitism and Desegregation," in *Jews in the South*, 349–50.

79. Andre Ungar, "To Birmingham, and Back," *Conservative Judaism* 18, no. 1 (Fall 1963): 11.

80. On the problems and possibilities of racial integration in American Jewish communities see Marc Lee Raphael, "Jewish Responses to the Integration of a Suburb: Cleveland Heights, Ohio: 1960–1980," *American Jewish Archives* 44, no. 2 (Fall 1992): 541–61; C. Bezalel Sherman, "In the American Jewish Community—Negro-Jewish Relations," *Jewish Frontier* (July 1964): 17; Abraham Duker, "On Negro-Jewish Relations: A Contribution to a Discussion," *Jewish Social Studies* 27, no. 1 (January 1965): 22; Lloyd Gartner, "The Racial Revolution and Jewish Communal Policy," *Conservative Judaism* 20, no. 3 (Spring 1966): 46.

For examples of Jewish responses to Black Power and black anti-Semitism see Briefs, in *The National Jewish Monthly* 84, no. 2 (October 1969): 7, 18–19; "American Jewry Divided on Strategy," *Reconstructionist* 34, no. 14 (November 22, 1968): 1; Murray Zuckoff, "Jewish Priorities in the Urban Crisis," *Israel Horizons* (April 1969): 19; Harry Halpern, "Confrontation and Anti-Semitism," *United Synagogue Review* (January 1969), 6; Harry Fleischman, "Negroes and Jews: Brotherhood or Bias?" *Pioneer Woman* (March 1967): 4.

81. Golden, "Unease in Dixie," 40.

82. Toll, "Pluralism and Moral Force," 96.

83. Ben Halpern, *Jews and Blacks: The Classic American Minorities* (New York, 1971), 65.

84. See Joshua O. Haberman, "The New Exodus out of Judaism," *Moment* 17, no. 4 (August 1992): 34–5; Barry Kosmin et al., *Highlights of the CJF National Jewish Population Survey* (New York, 1991); Jack Wertheimer, *A People Divided: Judaism in Contemporary America* (New York, 1993).

# Part 7 **1968 to the Present**

The emergence of Black Power in 1966, the Six-Day War in 1967, and the assassination of Martin Luther King Jr. in 1968 were followed by massive urban unrest and increased nationalism and concern with ethnic or religious identity in both the Jewish and black communities. The shock-wave caused by the threat to the survival of Israel in the 6-Day War produced for the Jewish community a drastic turning-in and a revitalization of traditional religious and cultural practice and identity. At the same time, the appeal of Black Power combined with grief at the death of Martin Luther King Jr., the embodiment of the nonviolent and integrationist wing of the civil rights movement, to produce similar political and cultural responses in the black community. Thus, the analyses and documents in this section reflect growing tensions based on conflicting perceptions of identity and loyalty, played out in allegations of racism and anti-Semitism. We start this section with the introduction by Shlomo Katz for his 1967 anthology, which attempted even then to head off the escalating antagonisms between the two groups. The bitterness of the accusations that Katz recounts, including the epithet "self-hating Jew," indicates the high level of emotions that came to characterize much of this phase of the debate.

Part of the complexity of the Ocean Hill–Brownsville conflict, with which a number of pieces in this section deal, lay in contradictory goals. On the one hand, in pushing for decentralization of the school system the black community hoped to achieve local control and to foster black involvement in governance of the Ocean Hill and Brownsville school systems. On the other hand, some groups in the Jewish community, despite their own fervent nationalism on behalf of Israel, perceived this move as a reflection of Black Nationalism or separatism and vehemently denounced these black aspirations as antithetical to American values of merit and individual qualifications, values identified with Jewish success. From the black perspective, Jewish insistence on these values was just another example of Jewish power and demonstrated an unwillingness to acknowledge the aspirations of other groups. These complex issues are laid out in the eyewitness account of Fred Ferretti, in the full-page advertisement taken out by the Jewish Citizens Committee for Community Control (written by Walter Karp and H. R. Shapiro), and in Nat Hentoff's interview with Julius Lester. The short personal reflections by Elise Rollock and Rayner Mann published in *Jewish Currents* suggest some of the disagreements within the black community. The study by Kitty Cohen, conducted more than a decade after the Ocean Hill–Brownsville crisis, assesses black opinion on key "Jewish issues" in both the black community and Congress.

Concerned about the growing conservatism and narrowing of group interests on the part of the American Jewish leadership, Joseph Rauh, a lawyer, a civil rights lobbyist, and a founder of Americans for Democratic Action, criticized the Jewish community in

1973 for abandoning its earlier commitment to racial equality and called upon Jews to renew their efforts on behalf of civil rights.

The dispute between Oscar Williams and Morris Schappes, included in part 1, illustrated divergent black and Jewish interpretations of their historic connections. Williams, in fact, questioned the historical basis for any "special relationship." In this section, the short Op-Ed piece by Herbert Gutman and the longer assessments by Joel Dreyfuss and Ellen Willis show the extent to which fractures between blacks and Jews reflect sharp ideological fractures within the Jewish community. The resignation of Andrew Young as U.N. ambassador, widely attributed to pressure from Jewish organizations, and described here by Dreyfuss and Adolph Reed, was another occasion for fracture.

The selections by Cohen and Reed attempt, in different ways, to sort through the rhetoric and bitterness to arrive at some rational basis for understanding the reasons for the breakdown of the black-Jewish alliance, as well as the basis for continuing mutual support. Cohen examines the views of members of the Black Congressional Caucus on a range of topics important to the Jewish community. Reed develops the theme of unequal partners by detailing instances of the paternalistic attitudes and actions of some members of the Jewish community in their political relations with blacks within the civil rights movement.

Several of these selections move beyond New York and demonstrate that these tensions are more than the consequence of the large size or special history of the New York black and Jewish populations. Taylor Branch focuses attention on the interactions of blacks and Jews in Chicago, which erupted in bitter recriminations and media frenzy over the anti-Semitic speeches of Steven Cokely. Branch notes the irony of this "present conflict [setting] the most scapegoated people in America against those who hold the record across all prior history."

**FURTHER REFERENCES**

The debate over affirmative action, which continues to this day and on which the Jewish community remains divided, is discussed in chapters by Jerome Chanes and Theodore Shaw in Jack Salzman and Cornel West's collection, *Struggles in the Promised Land* (1997). For three collections that introduce readers to the complexities of the affirmative action controversy, see George Curry, *The Affirmative Action Debate* (1996); Nicolaus Mills, *Debating Affirmative Action: Race, Gender, Ethnicity, and the Politics of Inclusion* (1994); and Harold Orlans and June O'Neill, *Affirmative Action Revisited* (1992). For a more recent study, see Gary Bryner, "Affirmative Action: Minority Rights or Reverse Discrimination?" (1998).

The trend toward neoconservatism on the race question among Jewish scholars involves issues such as the right to maintain the ethnic integrity of neighborhoods, access to schools, tracking within schools, and job opportunities. These positions are represented by or discussed in, for example, Nathan Glazer and Daniel P. Moynihan, *Beyond the Melting Pot* (1963; 1970); Nancy Haggard-Gilson, in a chapter in *African Americans and Jews in the Twentieth Century: Studies in Convergence and Conflict,* ed. V. P. Franklin et al. (1998); Jonathan Rieder, *Canarsie: The Jews and Italians of Brooklyn against Liberalism* (1985); Jim Sleeper, *The Closest of Strangers: Liberalism and the Politics of Race in New York* (1990); and James Traub, *City on a Hill: Testing the American Dream at City College* (1994). For a critique of neoconservatism, see Stephen Steinberg, *The Ethnic Myth: Race, Ethnicity and Class in America* (1981).

The Ocean Hill–Brownsville conflict over community control of schools is exhaustively covered in Lenora E. Berson, *The Negroes and the Jews* (1971); Maurice Berube and Marilyn Gittell, eds., *Confrontation at Ocean Hill–Brownsville: The New York School Strikes of 1968* (1969); Mario Fantini, Marilyn Gittell, and Richard Magat, *Community Control and the Urban School* (1970); Jerald E. Podair, "'White' Values, 'Black' Values: The Ocean Hill–Brownsville Controversy and New York City Culture, 1965–1975" (1994); Jonathan Rieder, "Reflections on Crown Heights: Interpretive Dilemmas and Black-Jewish Conflict," in *Antisemitism in America Today: Outspoken Experts Explode the Myths*, ed. Jerome A. Chanes (1995); Melvin Urofsky, ed., *Why Teachers Strike: Teachers' Rights and Community Control* (1970); and Robert G. Weisbord and Arthur Stein, *Bittersweet Encounter: The Afro-American and the American Jew* (1970). James Baldwin et al., *Black Anti-Semitism and Jewish Racism* (1969), includes Baldwin's much-anthologized "Negroes Are Anti-Semitic Because They're Anti-White" (1967) and Harold Cruse's "My Jewish Problem and Theirs" (1969), written in response to Podhoretz's "My Negro Problem—and Ours" (1963). For an insightful account of how a young Jewish boy, growing up in Irish Boston, came to identify strongly with the culture of black people, see Nat Hentoff, *Boston Boy: A Memoir* (1986). Shlomo Katz, *Negro and Jew: An Encounter in America* (1967), papers from a symposium sponsored by *Midstream Magazine*, has a number of provocative short pieces written in response to the growing conflict.

Alphonso Pinkney, "Recent Unrest between Blacks and Jews: The Claims of Anti-Semitism and Reverse Discrimination" (1978–79), examines Ocean Hill–Brownsville in the context of the Bakke case and the opportunities available to the two communities in the United States, and questions the notion that blacks and Jews were ever traditional allies, claiming that "alliances among unequal partners are impossible" (55). Reverend Herbert D. Daughtry Sr. has defended his remarks concerning the Jewish role in the Ocean Hill–Brownsville and Crown Heights conflicts in *No Monopoly on Suffering: Blacks and Jews in Crown Heights (and Elsewhere)* (1997). For an insightful and tough-minded outsider's view of black-Jewish conflicts in the context of power struggles, access to status, and competing victim status, see John Murray Cuddihy's chapter, "Jews, Blacks, and the Cold War at the Top: Malamud's *The Tenants* and the Status-Politics of Subcultures," in his *The Ordeal of Civility: Freud, Marx, Levi-Strauss, and the Jewish Struggle with Modernity* (1974). An informative focus on the issues at stake in the decentralization controversy appears in Louis Kushnick, "Race, Class and Power: The New York Decentralisation Controversy," in his *Race, Class & Struggle: Essays on Racism and Inequality in Britain, the U.S. and Western Europe* (1998).

Kitty Cohen's interviews with black state senators appear in book-length form in *Black-Jewish Relations: The View from the State Capitols* (1988). Studies of black anti-Semitism were conducted by Ronald Tsukashima in Los Angeles (*The Social and Psycho-*

*logical Correlates of Black Anti-Semitism,* 1978) and reviewed by Hubert Locke in *The Black Anti-Semitism Controversy: Protestant Views and Perspectives* (1994).

Morris Schappes's journal, *Jewish Currents,* has extensive and probing coverage of black-Jewish issues, a few notable examples being Martin Luther King Jr.'s 1968 statement, "Negroes, Jews, Israel and Anti-Semitism"; essays by Schappes, "Black Power and the Jews" and "James Baldwin and Anti-Semitism" (1967), and his report of the Socialist Scholars Conference, April 19, 1986; Jesse Jackson, "On Black-Jewish Relations" (1988); Albert Vorspan, "Black-Jewish Coalition: Troubled, but Still Alive" (1989); and William Shneyer, "Black-Jewish Relations: Yesterday and Tomorrow" (1989).

The heated controversies of the 1990s, anticipated in the piece here by Taylor Branch, are touched on (but hardly limited to) Tony Martin, *The Jewish Onslaught: Despatches from the Wellesley Battlefront* (1993); Robert Rockaway, *"The Jews Cannot Defeat Me": The Anti-Jewish Campaign of Louis Farrakhan and the Nation of Islam* (1995); Milton D. Morris and Gary E. Rubin, "The Turbulent Friendship: Black-Jewish Relations in the 1990s" (1993); and Gary E. Rubin, "How Shall We Think about Black Antisemitism?" (1995). Jennifer Golub reviews surveys of black attitude toward Jews in *What Do We Know about Black Anti-Semitism?* (1990).

# Introduction to *Negro and Jew: An Encounter in America*

The voice on the phone trembled with indignation. "Where do you live? I bet you live in a safe white neighborhood and have your office in a safe area in mid-Manhattan. Do you know what it means to fear attack every time you walk down the street? If you did, you wouldn't talk that way. . . . You're just another Jewish self-hater. . . . You don't care what happens to your own people. . . ." and the voice trailed off into incoherent hysteria.

This phone call was but the first after I had published a letter in a liberal Jewish periodical shortly after some Negro rioting during which numerous Jewish stores were sacked. The letter protested an editorial that, it seemed to me, was hectoring, and that smugly boasted how "we," Jews, that is, had all along stood "in the front ranks" of the struggle for Negro rights, and vaguely threatened that unless "responsible" Negro leadership ("if there are responsible Negro leaders") puts a stop to outbreaks of violence "we," while remaining liberal, might nevertheless be driven to some sort of agonizing reappraisal.

For nearly a week after the first call my line was busy. The anonymous callers would always begin with a reasonable appeal for understanding the plight of Jews living or conducting their businesses within or on the margins of Negro ghettos, their sense of insecurity, the violence they were subject to. Then would follow bitterly sarcastic requests for advice as to what they should do under the circumstances, and finally a deluge of vituperation, sometimes accompanied by threats. On a few occasions the callers would put their argument on a personal level: "What's the matter? Aren't you scared of Negro hoodlums and muggers?" But all attempts to answer this question with statements that I was indeed very much afraid of muggers and hoodlums, but not especially so because they were black; that I was probably more afraid of white anti-Jewish violence; and that any Jew of our generation, remembering what the white Germans, in cooperation with other European whites, did to us within our own memory, could not, must not, allow himself to fall into the trap of associating anti-Semitism and its concomitant violence with Negroes in particular were wasted effort, for the voices on the phone were genuinely urgent with fear and confusion and anger, and, above all, with surprise. Beneath the furious taunts of "nigger lover," "self-hater," "traitor," could be discerned the bewilderment of people caught unawares. How could this happen in America? How could this happen to us who are relatively recent newcomers to the

Shlomo Katz was the editor of *Midstream Magazine*.
Reprinted from *Negro and Jew: An Encounter in America: A Symposium Compiled by* Midstream Magazine, ed. Shlomo Katz (New York: Macmillan, 1967). Copyright © 1967 by the Theodor Herzl Foundation. Reprinted with permission of Simon and Schuster.

American scene and are not part of the Negro-white tragedy that has been in the making for three centuries?

In the course of our long history, and especially during the past nineteen centuries of dispersion, we Jews have come in contact, for better or for worse, with many peoples. We have been in Spain and in Poland, in Germany and in Russia, in France and in Rumania. But it was not until we came to America in substantial numbers that we encountered the black race. In the dim beginnings of our history the problem of Negro-Jewish relations had briefly cropped up in the somewhat ominous and vaguely outlined story of Moses and the Cushite wife he had taken, how his brother and sister, Aaron and Miriam, resented this alliance, and how they were punished for it. But this encounter, wrapped in the fog of mythology, had no followup. Here and there a Negro appears peripherally in ancient Jewish history, in the entourage of King David, for instance, but this contact is ephemeral. Our encounters, our loves and hates, unfolded their destinies in the European and Mediterranean world.

And then we came en masse to America. We learned English, we traversed the odyssey from sweatshop to a measure of affluence, we became active in the economic, political, and academic life of the country, but for more than a generation we remained virtually oblivious of the millions of Negroes as an important part of the American scene.

In the course of our struggle of adaptation, it seems we have made some grave errors. Granted that New York's Jewish ghetto on the Lower East Side was remote from the Negro concentrations in the South. Still, in terms of our history in the United States, this obliviousness to the Negro presence in the country and to its implications for the future is not entirely forgivable. For the Jewish masses who streamed to this country at the turn of the century were not a shapeless mob rushing blindly from persecution to a haven of safety. These were people with an ancient history and long experience in the implications of living among both majorities and other minorities in eastern Europe. And these Jewish immigrant masses had an informed, sophisticated, and articulate leadership—the same leadership that by means of communal organization and economic struggle led them within a brief period from ghetto slums to an enviable status of welfare and equality. But these same leaders who organized the big strikes in the garment industries early in the century, who set up huge fraternal organizations for education and mutual assistance, who were informed about and responsive to the needs of oppressed people a continent away remained strangely unaware of the problems of the Negroes living in the same country with them.

Another error consisted in the failure to see America in all its complexity, culturally, historically, and ethnically. At first glance the immigrant, and only too often, his leaders, saw America as a kind of deracinated social and political entity that operated mechanically on the basis of a set of noble principles enunciated in the Constitution, that, except for some ignoble and temporary exceptions that presumably only proved the rule, opportunity was really unrestricted, and, given suitable effort and an appropriate IQ, all obstacles could be overcome. For a time, this faulty vision seemed to operate. Hence much of the surprise when it broke down and when we are now made painfully aware that America is not simply a geographical aggregate of so many millions of individual citizens entitled to equal rights, which, with some effort, can be implemented in practice.

This may very well account for the confusion now surrounding the concept of integration, for instance. Seized upon as the natural banner in the struggle for Negro rights, it has quickly become problematic. In a deracinated society of millions of political entities, it might be ideal. But what if we are not merely citizens of the United States? What if we are at the same time Jews, Negroes, Mexicans, Puerto Ricans? What if some, perhaps a growing number, of the Negroes do not wish to integrate to the point of ethnic or cultural disintegration? For though the prophetic ideal of the ultimate unity of the race of man is no doubt the highest that the human mind has conceived, it cannot be expected to serve as a practical solution for problems that are contemporary and that demand other solutions.

Nor have Jews who think along Zionist lines been more sensitive to the emerging pattern of Negro evolution in this country. This is distressing because of the numerous similarities between the two groups. Not only do both share a status of minority and dispersion, but the evolution of their groups and national consciousness has in many respects followed along parallel lines. Yet when the slogan of Black Power was raised recently, with its primary aim of placing the Negro struggle for equality in Negro hands, even avowed Zionists failed to perceive that such too were the beginnings of the Jewish national liberation movement in Europe, commencing with Pinsker's *Autoemancipation* down through *kibbush avodah* and the other stages of Zionist evolution, and that these aims, like the Black Power movement, required that somewhere along the line something would have to give, someone would have to move to make room for the new aspirants with a just claim not only to equality but to their own identity.

Not last to feel discomfited by the new demands of the Negro movement were those idealistic and self-sacrificing young Jews who had abandoned the comforts that were theirs for the asking and joined the Negro struggle at its very cutting edge. Imbued with the noblest sentiments, they are now told that they are no longer wanted, not too closely anyway. And they are dismayed.

As a by-product of our recent Jewish history, and growing out of its frustrations, we have given rise to small but articulate and competent cadres of idealistic youth, who with a full knowledge of the geography of revolution and social regeneration are ever-ready to lend their talents wherever these occur. It is not pleasant, and now comes as a shock, to be told by Negro fellow-militants, "We don't need you any longer. We don't want you in our midst. We prefer to do our self-liberating ourselves, even if we don't do it as well or as fast as you." (In much the same way, Chairman Nikita Khrushchev not so many years ago told the leaders of the Polish Communist Party, "There are too many Rabinoviches among you.")

Even on the level of emotional perception, there has arisen a tragic distance of misapprehension. Nobody in his right senses will justify the violence, and some of the slogans under which it has recently been conducted, in Negro ghettos. But the depth of the anger behind it should have been understood. Yet the same people who read as Holy Scripture outbursts of anger over an ancient wrong, such as, "Pour out thy wrath upon the nations . . . for they have devoured Jacob and laid waste his dwelling place" (Psalms, 79), or, "O daughter of Babylon . . . happy shall be he that taketh and dasheth thy little ones against the stones" (Psalms, 138), fail to understand the rage next door.

Is this because we, as Jews, have lost the capacity for great anger? Is it that, because we suffer from a measure of confusion about the meaning of our own identity and recent history, the necessary element of empathy is missing?

And on the Negro side there is the temptation to isolate Jews as the target of their anger for inexcusable, even if facile, reasons. For one thing, Jews are an easy, and historically speaking, a socially acceptable target. They are also a safe and readily accessible one. That in the long run this choice is likely to be morally degrading, no less than slavery was for the white slave owners, does not alter the situation, and must be reckoned with in assessing the future relations between the two groups and what steps should be taken to avoid tragedy.

Negroes and Jews—two dispersed minorities, both harboring deep grievances against their treatment by the white Christian world—now meet in America. The Jews are overwhelmingly urban; Negroes are rapidly becoming so. They live next to each other; indeed, one follows in the footsteps of the other in the geography of the cities. They have never met in the past. There are no ancient wrongs between them to poison their attitudes toward one another. Here is one instance in which two groups can begin their mutual relations with a clean slate. Yet the horizon between them is becoming clouded with misunderstandings and resentments. A thorough examination of the situation has become an urgent necessity.

FRED FERRETTI

# New York's Black Anti-Semitism Scare

*To many Jews, the school strike and related troubles were evidence that [Mayor] Lindsay was willing to do anything to placate black militants, even those with anti-Semitic leanings, and even if it meant damaging the educational system.*
—Time, Oct. 3, 1969

*As Mayor Lindsay moved to the lectern in the auditorium of Congregational Beth Shalom . . . the Meshugeneh Brigade of the Jewish Defense League was there . . . the eyes as wild as those of any crowd on a Mississippi road.*
—New York Post (Pete Hamil) Oct. 8, 1969

It is provable that anti-white sentiment exists among black people in the United States. It is demonstrable in New York City and in other urban centers that this anti-white disposition contains a component of anti-Semitism. What is debatable is its depth.

Black anti-Semitism was an abstraction, a sometime issue—in New York City, at any rate—until last year, when the city prepared to commit itself to decentralization of its public school system and to experiment with limited community control of local school boards. Then a critical mass of volatile elements suddenly was brought together: a union of 57,000 teachers, an organization of 6,000 school principals and administrators, and a Board of Education hierarchy, all largely Jewish and all dedicated essentially to the maintenance of the status quo of the nation's largest educational system; a strong feeling in the city's liberal community that something had to be done about the schools' mediocrity; an experimental school district in the Ocean Hill-Brownsville section of Brooklyn in which virtually all of the students were either black or Puerto Rican; in which the district superintendent Rhody McCoy was black, and in which four principals were black, one was Puerto Rican, and another Chinese.

Tensions created by the decision to give blacks limited control over one aspect of their lives—the education of their children—led first to a walkout of 350 union teachers from Ocean Hill-Brownsville in Spring 1968, and subsequently to three citywide strikes by most of the United Federation of Teachers and the Council of Supervisory Associations. For two months—thirty-nine school days—between September 9 and November 18 last year, the city's 900 schools were closed and 1.1 million pupils were without teachers. During that time opponents of the educational experiment needed something to demonstrate that it couldn't work, something to obscure the educational nature of

Fred Ferretti is a journalist and author.

Reprinted from *Columbia Journalism Review* 8, no. 3 (Fall 1969): 18–29. Copyright © 1969 by Columbia Journalism Review.

the experiment. Black anti-Semitism became that "something." It was an issue fearful enough to make the liberal group which favored educational reform back away. It was, moreover, an issue which, once discovered by the UFT and its president, Albert Shanker, could be neutralized only by an alert and responsible press. As we shall see, however, the communications media in most cases repeated docilely the utterances of the sowers of hate; they merely recorded hysterical accusations usually made just prior to deadline, giving them credence beyond what they deserved; and in general they failed to hold the accusers accountable for their words and their deeds.

Albert Shanker began his campaign to discredit the experiment in education quite early. On February 6 of last year, the UFT president was quoted by the *Times* as being concerned that teachers were "becoming targets of a mounting volume of attacks by extremist groups." On February 12 in the *Times* Shanker was quoted as saying that "a sort of hoodlum element" had gained control over several schools, including several in the experimental district there, and that this was the sort of thing that could be expected under the city's decentralization proposal. By May 10, after nineteen educators had been ordered transferred out of the Ocean Hill-Brownsville district, he changed the code words to say, according to the press, that teachers in the Ocean Hill schools were being made victims of a "kind of vigilante activity." Four days later the media relayed the report that children of the district were chanting "Black Power slogans." On May 20, the *Times* quoted Shanker as saying "forty outsiders" from Harlem and other parts of the city had "come in and taken over" the Ocean Hill-Brownsville schools.

Five days later, Dr. Kenneth Clark, a sociologist and a member of the state Board of Regents, accused Shanker of lobbying with tactics that "bordered on the irresponsible" to get decentralization killed by the state legislature, and he charged further that the UFT president "promoted anti-Semitism in the Negro community." (Shanker eventually was successful in Albany; the legislature refused to enact a decentralization bill, in effect saying let's leave things as they are.) And on June 3, with the Ocean Hill-Brownsville dispute more than three weeks old, the *Times* reported Shanker as declaring, "even if the dispute were somehow resolved within the next week, the kind of hatred that's been engendered there is something that takes a cooling off period."

Through the summer the UFT remained strident, and on September 1, the union voted to strike. That day Shanker said, according to the *Times*, that allowing local boards to hire and dismiss teachers would "open up a field day for bigots and racists." When, one week later, a black UFT teacher at a delegate assembly meeting said that the strike could be interpreted as nothing else but a vote against the black community, the *Times* printed Shanker's most revealing answer: "This is a strike that will protect black teachers against white racists, and white teachers against black racists." His implication was clear, and the cheers of the assembled teachers proved they had gotten the message. Several days later Shanker added, again as reported in the *Times*, that the strike was "not a matter of black or white" because the "union would be there" to oppose white racism, too, if it should arise. And later he declared that if a white school were to oust a Negro principal or Negro teachers "then we will be back here again fighting their battle."

On September 13, the UFT ran an ad in the *Times*, signed by Shanker, which said that when the teachers in question in Ocean Hill-Brownsville tried to get back into the schools there, "an organized mob tried to prevent them from returning." The ad advertised a rally against "mob rule." Three days after the ad, Shanker, on *Searchlight*, a WNBC-TV Sunday morning public affairs show, said that he thought some element of anti-Semitism was involved in the opposition to the reinstatement of the teachers. This followed a union demand for the removal of "extremist teachers" who were reported to be inciting "bands of youths" to violence; and the Association of Assistant Superintendents' going on record as requesting a special legislative session to investigate "all aspects of the work stoppage and the unlawful actions of extremist groups occuring in the New York Schools."

The strike was page one news from the outset. It was certainly the first item—and often the entire first half—of evening TV news programs. *Time* and *Newsweek* began sending reporting teams to Ocean Hill-Brownsville. To their credit, both dealt perceptively with the educational aspects of the district as well as with the conflict and the burgeoning issue of black anti-Semitism. But Shanker continued to get the most space, throwing terms such as "extremists" and "vigilantes" at every opportunity. There was never, so far as can be determined, a sustained attempt to force him to define them. The TV and radio newscasters seemed content to label anybody in any experimental school district as "black militant." And yet there was Shanker quoted without argument, pleading, according to the *Times* of September 22, not to make the school strike "a racial conflict," and, three days later when a settlement was proposed, saying, "this means putting teachers in a room with Sonny Carson and the Panthers." (Robert "Sonny" Carson, chairman of Independent Brooklyn CORE, more than once worried teachers in Ocean Hill-Brownsville but he was not more an object of terror than were the Black Panthers, who wear machine gun bullets around their necks and are useful to scare people with.)

I recall a Shanker press conference I attended as a reporter for WNBC-TV. It was held at UFT headquarters, late in the afternoon as usual. During his customary round of charges, the UFT president alleged that city employees had abetted harassment of teachers in the experimental district. With the camera rolling, I asked Shanker for the names or name of the employees or employee to which he referred. He answered:

"You know who they are."

I said I didn't, and since he was making the charge he should be prepared to identify the alleged culprit.

"You know who they are," he repeated. "Look at your film."

I again said I didn't know, and I asked again who they were. Once again, he said, "You know who they are."

The colloquy was repeated several times over. I did not get an answer. That evening, after some prodding by me, WNBC-TV used that film clip. But there was no real media effort to make Shanker more circumspect in subsequent press conferences. Indeed, on September 26, he was quoted as asking his union to dig in on the strike because he wanted "to see if there are enough people with guts to stand up to vigilantes." That same day, Luis Fuentes, principal of one the of Ocean Hill schools and the only Puerto Rican principal in the entire school system, said that when there was talk about "prejudice, racism, hatred, Mr. Shanker, I don't have to turn around to see where the heavy boot is."

As the strike began its second month, Christian Herter, Jr., chairman of the New York Urban Coalition, pleaded for settlement "in the interest of peace and racial harmony." He added, "the harm being done to our children is immense and the damage to harmonious race relations in the city incalculable." And on October 10, the New York Civil Liberties Union issued an investigative report entitled *The Burden of Blame,* the thesis of which was that Albert Shanker, the UFT, and the Board of Education had systematically tried to "sabotage" the experimental school program. It received scant attention, except in Harlem's weekly *Amsterdam News,* which printed the full text serially. (Ironically the report was bigger news early this year when dissident members of the NYCLU protested it as political and pressed for and got an intra-NYCLU debate on whether it should have been issued.)

Early in the school confrontation Jewish organizations had preached restraint, as was their tradition. Walter Karp and H. R. Shapiro, in *The Public Life,* [Feb. 19, 1969] detail, for example, that in 1966 an American Jewish Congress spokesman had derisively coined the phrase "Jewish backlash"; had denounced tales of black anti-Semitism as "overblown"; and had instead emphasized "the strong identification Negroes have with Jews." In October, 1967, the National Community Relations Council, representing many Jewish groups, had warned Jews not to mistake black "legitimate protest" for anti-Semitism. And a month later the Union of Hebrew Congregations had urged "the exercise of moral pressure by the congregations and the rabbis upon those Jewish slumlords and ghetto profiteers." That same year, the Anti-Defamation League of B'nai B'rith reported that a five-year study of black attitudes had shown blacks to be the least anti-Semitic group in the country, and further, that the more militant a black man was, the less likely he was to be anti-Jewish. As late as October 23, 1968, the ADL was reporting that its study of anti-Jewish leaflets distributed in the school dispute had proved them to be crudely done, sporadically produced, and not the product of any organized effort.

But the pendulum had begun to swing the other way just one day earlier, on October 22. Rabbi Marc Tannenbaum, national director of interreligious affairs of the American Jewish Committee, at a WCBS *World of Religion* taping session with the Ocean Hill-Brownsville governing board chairman, the Rev. C. Herbert Oliver, was reported in the *Times* to have said that the UFT and Shanker were "using the Jewish community" in what was essentially "a labor-management problem." Chairman Oliver maintained that anti-Semitism had been made an issue in the dispute by Shanker; Rabbi Tannenbaum, in addition to his charge against the UFT, urged black leaders to "take a position against anti-Semitism unleashed from outside the community." The next day's *Times* reported that Rabbi Tannenbaum had been quoted incorrectly by the Associated Press, and instead of criticizing Shanker and the UFT the rabbi had referred to extremist elements on both sides of the dispute. Then on October 25, the *Times* reported that Rabbi Tannenbaum, based on the transcript of the radio program, had indeed charged the UFT with manipulation and had been quoted properly.

The *Long Island Press,* meanwhile, had carried a story that the Mayor had met with representatives of five Jewish organizations and requested support, saying in effect, "You Jews have made me use up all my Negro credit cards." The organizations deplored the *Press* article for what they called distortion of "a meeting held for constructive purposes [that] is being used to inflame racial and religious tensions in our city." The *Times* reported the *Press* article, along with the organizations' denials that the meeting had been called to get them to "control" Shanker and his union. The *Times* also stated that the article had been reproduced "anonymously" in handbill form. I saw it being given out by striking teachers in Queens.

This was but one of scores of leaflets, many if not all of them reproduced and distributed—in one case the UFT says as "a public service"—by the United Federation of Teachers. The leaflet which most community control opponents use as a ghastly example reprints the masthead of Cowles Communications' *Education News* [see page 23]. It includes a picture of a teacher, Leslie Campbell, a member of the African-American Teachers Association, who was accused of anti-Semitism during and after the strike. Campbell, in a lesson plan, is discussing the concept of black power. The leaflet calls it "Preaching Violence Instead of Teaching Children in Ocean Hill-Brownsville (An observation of an Actual 'Lesson' in JHS 271)," and goes on to say that "this excerpt is one example of what the Ocean Hill-Brownsville Governing Board feels is suitable curriculum for the children in that district."

The fact is that the lesson did not take place in Ocean Hill-Brownsville as the leaflet says. The date of the magazine was omitted—it was October 30, 1967, one year earlier— when Campbell was a teacher not in Ocean Hill, but at JHS 35, in quite another school district. The UFT claim that the lesson is an example of Ocean Hill curriculum is, according to the New York Civil Liberties Union, "a conclusion based on an untruthful premise." This leaflet was composed and distributed by the UFT.

The second example consists of two leaflets devised by the Council of Supervisory Associations. They concern an evening adult program to be given in JHS 271. One is signed by the CSA, the other by the supervisors of District 29 in Queens. The latter depicts a skeleton in cap and gown holding a cocked pistol. Readers are asked, "Do You Approve New Community Curriculum!" Both score an adult program with courses in revolution, staging of demonstrations, and self-defense. Both imply that racists and extremists were operating the Ocean Hill-Brownsville schools.

Yet the facts are that local school officials had nothing to do with the programs, nor did the central Board of Education, which the CSA says "approved" the program. In a court case in which the New York Civil Liberties Union represented William Buckley against Hunter College, it was ruled that the content of an extracurricular program is not a valid basis for denying an organization the right to use public facilities. The CSA, the NYCLU pointed out, is composed of people "regularly involved in arranging for the use of school facilities by outside groups" and should have been aware of the facts, but, says the NYCLU, the "leaflets have systematically slandered Ocean Hill-Brownsville in a smear campaign reminiscent of Joe McCarthy."

There were other UFT leaflets. One said, "The issue in Ocean Hill-Brownsville is the violent, disruptive activity of a group of militants, including teacher partisans, who have made a shambles of education by harassing and intimidating UFT teachers, subjecting them to degrading vilification and preventing them from teaching." Another states in large type, in THREE DAYS YOU WILL BE DEAD, and attributes this quotation to "a nonunion teacher at JHS 271." The rest of the leaflet is a series of "quotations" from "McCoy teachers . . . documented . . . by eyewitnesses." It goes on to warn, "Your School Can Be Next!!!"

The UFT never identified the teacher, nor produced eyewitnesses. The NYCLU concluded:

> It is of course difficult to know how to check such a leaflet; how do you investigate anonymous statements produced by unnamed informants? However, the frauds contained in those leaflets which do contain information that can be checked make us very skeptical about the UFT's contentions in this particular leaflet. Seen in the context of the UFT's strategy of lying and distorting in order to whip the city into a frenzy of fear of Ocean Hill-Brownsville, this leaflet emerges as yet another element of that strategy.

Finally, there is what has come to be known as the "Ralph Poynter" leaflet. Entitled *Tentative Plan—Parents Community Council, JHS 271, Ocean Hill-Brownsville,* it is actually two leaflets put together, printed, and distributed by the UFT. The top half is a demand for "absolute" black control of "our schools," and, according to a UFT note, "is a VERBATIM TEXT of a leaflet distributed by the Parents Community Council of JHS 271 and phoned in to a UFT representative." The second half of the leaflet, which according to the UFT was "placed in teachers' mailboxes at JHS 271 and PS 144," is violently anti-Semitic, speaking of "Middle East Murderers of Colored People" and "Bloodsucking Exploiters."

The fact is that there was no such organization as the Parents Community Council of JHS 271; the alleged "chairman," Ralph Poynter, was a Manhattan teacher who had no connection with Ocean Hill-Brownsville; the phone number listed was an Oregon number, in Manhattan. When it was dialed, it was found to be disconnected. At the bottom of the leaflet the UFT asserted it was distributed by the "Parents Community Council"—which did not exist. It does not say who "phoned in" the "verbatim text." The anti-Semitic second half is anonymous, and attempts to determine its authorship were unsuccessful. The UFT, concluded the NYCLU, "perpetrated a multiple fraud." That it also perpetrated hatred is borne out by the NYCLU report that among the hundreds of calls it received, most cited this leaflet as evidence that Ralph Poynter was an anti-Semitic official of Ocean Hill-Brownsville.

The UFT made much of the fact that leaflets "were placed in teachers' mailboxes." That is true—but the implication that the local board knew and approved of it is false. The fact is that they were placed anonymously, and subsequently deplored by the local school board. It said:

> The Ocean Hill-Brownsville Governing Board, as well as the entire Ocean Hill-Brownsville Demonstration School District, has never tolerated anti-Semitism in any form. Anti-Semitism has no place in our hearts or minds and indeed never in our schools. While certain anti-Semitic literature may have been distributed outside our school buildings, there is absolutely no connection between these acts and the thoughts and intents of the Ocean Hill-Brownsville Governing Board. We disclaim

any responsibility for this literature and have in every way sought to find its source and take appropriate action to stop it.

Charles Isaacs, 22, one of the young new teachers who went to Ocean Hill-Brownsville to teach mathematics, wrote in the *Times Magazine* of Sunday, November 24:

> I read in the UFT literature and in the Jewish press about "black racism," but I have never experienced it in Ocean Hill, and, to my knowledge, neither has anyone else on the faculty. While the storm rages around Ocean Hill-Brownsville, it is not *about* Ocean Hill-Brownsville. But one fact of life does stand out: This issue of anti-Semitism, true or false, preys on the fears of the one ethnic group that, united behind it, could destroy us; if this happens, I expect a real problem of black anti-Semitism, and the cycle of self-fulfilling prophecy will be complete.

Eugenia Kemble wrote this:

> One thing people seem to agree on at PS 144 in Ocean Hill-Brownsville is that black anti-Semitism is not a part of the thinking of the school's staff or its students' parents. In fact, most of the teachers, administrators, and parents of that school do not believe that the city-wide discussion being carried on over the issue by the press, city officials, and others is taking a hard or deep enough look at grass-roots black opinion on the subject.

Who is Eugenia Kemble? She is assistant editor of *The United Teacher*—the official newspaper of the UFT. Her article, entitled "Black Anti-Semitism Seen as EXAGGERATED ISSUE by Parents and Staff of Ocean Hill School," appeared long after the strike—on March 12, 1969—but nonetheless Shanker protested it. In the March 23, 1969, issue of *The United Teacher,* he wrote, "When a full page is devoted to such a piece by a UFT staff member, it inevitably leads our members and all readers to believe that the article represents official UFT policy—*which it does not.*" He went on to repeat his extravagances against the school district and to criticize Miss Kemble's news-gathering technique.

The NYCLU after its study of the hate literature was concluded, said "the UFT leadership, and in particular Albert Shanker, systematically accused the Ocean Hill-Brownsville Board and Rhody McCoy of anti-Semitism and extremism, and then 'proved' those accusations only with half-truths, innuendoes, and outright lies." It said further "that the joint UFT-CSA effort to make Ocean Hill-Brownsville appear to be a haven for terrorism was in sharp conflict with the actual facts."

In October, the NYCLU released its critique of the leaflets. The only reference to it was three paragraphs in the jump of a page one *Times* story, which concerned yet another day of fruitless negotiations. The three paragraphs were in the last part of the story and quoted NYCLU associate director Ira Glasser as charging the UFT with being the "major source of extremist leaflets" being circulated.

Interestingly, Aryeh Neier, executive director of the NYCLU, had become concerned, he said, when his eight-year-old son had come home from his school in Greenwich Village clutching one of the Poynter leaflets. The NYCLU research into the leaflets was reported to an aide to Mayor Lindsay, together with a suggestion that an investigation be undertaken. The aide suggested that Neier write a letter of request to the Mayor. He did. A Special Committee on Racial and Religious Prejudice, chaired by Bernard Botein, presiding justice of the Appellate Division of the State Supreme Court, was formed by the Mayor, with the staff of the Anti-Defamation League of B'nai B'rith, under general counsel Arnold Forster, as the committee's investigative arm.

The Botein Committee investigated for two months, and as it did, Shanker kept the pressure on. When Dr. Clark accused him of making a "flagrant appeal to backlash," Shanker ignored him. When Whitney Young, executive director of the Urban League, was quoted in the *Times* as accusing Shanker of "plunging the city into racial strife," the UFT president said merely that it was a "vile smear." When a UFT vice president, John O'Neill, asked the union to discharge Shanker because he was guilty of "the most vicious racial demagogy ever seen in this city," Shanker replied with, "It's mostly sour grapes on his part. He doesn't represent anybody." (O'Neill soon became an ex-vice president, when he was stripped of his union position and salary by the UFT in a "reorganization.")

Finally in late November the school strike ended. But the Botein Committee kept delving. And on November 22, during the first week of school after the strike, Shanker was quoted by the *Times* as saying, "large numbers of children" at JHS 271 "have been indoctrinated, they are full of hate." By December 2, according to Shanker in the *Times*, groups of "especially trained" JHS 271 students were intimidating and harassing union teachers.

In a December 3 *Times* story covering the removal by the state of Ocean Hill-Brownsville district trustee Herbert F. Johnson—an appointment of a trustee had been one of the terms of the strike settlement—it was reported that "a state observer" had said Dr. Johnson had been locked in a closet by persons who objected to his attempts to oversee JHS 271 in the district. The story quoted Shanker as having been informed that Dr. Johnson had been "physically threatened at knife point" by someone in a group when, at one stage, he had ordered the school shut down for the day. The notice of the closet and knife incidents were in paragraph twelve of a forty-four-paragraph story, at the top of the jump from page one. The next day, the following paragraph appeared in a lengthy *Times* report: "Dr. Johnson flatly denied the report of his having been locked in a closet. He said that if he had been threatened with a knife he did not know about it, and added that he had no idea how the report originated." That story, which began on page one, had sixty-one paragraphs; Dr. Johnson's denial was the last paragraph.

On January 17, 1969, the Botein Committee surfaced with a report that "an appalling amount of racial prejudice—black and white—in New York City" had arisen "in and about the school controversy." The Committee had been given a NYCLU memorandum detailing its information on the leaflets, their origin, and their distribution. What did it say of these?

> The Committee has decided against incorporating in this statement copies of or excerpts from any of the bigoted printed matter which has been distributed during the course of the school dispute—because we see no constructive purpose served in thus adding to the circulation of such material. Similarly, the Committee has decided

against naming blameworthy individuals or organizations in this statement because none of them has been asked to appear before the Committee to testify.

The Committee so decided despite a mandate from the Mayor to include in its report "a chronology of the school dispute, including the factors and actions which led to the appearance of religious or racial bigotry; available information regarding the sources and distributions of such printed matter." Then, six days later, on January 23, Arnold Forster and the Botein Committee's ADL staff issued an ADL report, and it was not restrained:

The use of anti-Semitism—raw, undisguised—has distorted the fundamental character of the controversy surrounding the public schools of New York City. The anti-Semitism has gone unchecked by public authorities for two and a half years, reaching a peak during the school strike of September-November 1968 and in the post-strike period. It is still going on.

Furthermore, the report said, anti-Semitic acts were "perpetrated largely by black extremists," and anti-Semitism's "growth has been aided by the failure of city and state public officials to condemn it swiftly and strongly enough, and to remove from positions of authority those who have utilized anti-Semitism." Specifically charged were the African-American Teachers Association; its president, Albert Vann; Leslie Campbell; and Luis Fuentes. The Board of Education and two of its past presidents, Lloyd Garrison and John Doar, were charged with passivity in the face of anti-Semitic outbursts. Cited was an editorial from the *African-American Teachers Forum,* which in effect calls Jews the exploiters of black and Puerto Rican children. Also cited was a poem read over station WBAI and dedicated to Albert Shanker. [See page 28.]

But the report failed to say why men like Vann or Campbell became prominent. Who created them? More, who created the climate in which they were allowed to grow? And should not Forster have included not only Albert Vann's anti-Semitism, but also a paragraph from the editorial which said in part: "It is time to declare that Albert Shanker and all who support his racist diatribes do a disservice to the entire Jewish community." Would it have not been more responsible to have included not just Campbell's poetry reading, but part of the radio discussion which accompanied it?

The media made the Campbell poem page one news, and the climate of the city was such that the Board of Education, the Mayor, and some editorialists were soon asking for Campbell to be banished—anywhere. There was never, so far as I can determine, any effort to show in what context the poem was read. It was certainly anti-Semitic, but then Julius Lester, who moderated the WBAI program, is not "Adolph Hitler" or a "Nazi" as certain UFT and Jewish Defense League posters claimed. And, oddly, there was never a transcript of the program on which the poem was read. Nobody requested one, according to WBAI spokesman Frank Milspaugh, until I asked for a tape and made a transcript.

In all, forty-three separate instances of what the ADL defines as anti-Semitic conduct were listed. The report was widely publicized, and since the ADL has long been the official delineator of what constitutes anti-Semitism, it was widely accepted. In view of that, two critiques are particularly instructive. One is by Leonard J. Fein, associate director and director of research for the Harvard-MIT Joint Center for Urban Studies and also chairman of the Commission on Community Interrelations of the American Jewish Congress. Fein recognizes, he says, that anti-Semitism among blacks is a painful and most sensitive issue. Accordingly, he says, it should be dealt with carefully and precisely. What is needed, he wrote to Arnold Forster on February 6 of this year, is not "a continuation of the vague but panicked rhetoric which has marked so much of the debate," and of which the ADL report "is an example . . . which exacerbates an already volatile issue." He then said this of the report:

> It fails to distinguish between gutter anti-Semitism—epithets and obscenities from the mouths of a mob . . . and the statements of public men; it equates vulgar imprecation and sophisticated if specious reasoning; it neglects entirely the counter-provocations which, though they can never justify anti-Semitism, at least help to explain it. As a result, it does not contribute to either understanding or constructive action; it merely inflames. . . . Where, for example, we are informed that "a demonstrator was heard to shout . . ." we can hardly conclude that the unnamed demonstrator was an extremist. Yet, of the forty-three instances, even if all are accepted as in fact anti-Semitic:
>
> *Four* surround the Metropolitan Museum of Art controversy, noting the names of Messrs. [Thomas] Hoving, [Francis] Plimpton, and [William] Booth and Miss [Candice] Van Elliston, none normally considered a black extremist;
>
> *Four* report the opposition of unnamed black students and parents to the cancellation of school holidays in the settlement of the strike;
>
> *Three* are the work of white extremists: Messrs. [Harold] Koppersmith, [John] Lawrence, and [James] Madole;
>
> *Five* describe anti-Semitic outbursts during the strike by unnamed pickets;
>
> *Two* describe anti-Semitic remarks by unnamed persons at district meetings on decentralization;
>
> *Five* are quotes from leaflets, authors unknown.

This, wrote Fein, adds up to twenty-three, which leaves twenty, "including a number involving the same people and a number not clearly anti-Semitic." He further accuses the ADL of "gratuitous slurs," and criticizes the UFT circulation of that "particularly scurrilous leaflet." He concludes by calling for repair of whatever rupture exists between the Jew and the black man, and for "research and investigation" which "would emphasize both causes and productive solutions."

Fein's analysis has received no public circulation.

The other criticism of the ADL report was written by Henry Schwarzchild, currently a fellow at the Metropolitan Applied Research Center; a member of the Commission on Religion and Race of the Synagogue Council of America; former executive director of the Lawyers Constitutional Defense Committee; and, from 1962 to 1964, National Publications Director of the ADL. Schwarzchild's study is entitled "An Anti-Semitic Herring." Although private, it has been circulated among Jewish organizations in recent months, and has earned him, he says, the honor of "being denied access to the ADL offices" here. He begins his critique with a quotation, uttered only a year ago, by Benjamin Epstein, national director of the ADL: ". . . the Jewish Community would be well advised . . . to drop preoccupation with Negro anti-Semitism, which only serves to divert energies from the civil rights struggle." Then he states:

> Two considerations come immediately to mind from the face of this report. One is that if the ADL's research had been able [to locate] twenty more such anti-Semitic statements or incidents, we should assuredly have had a report cataloguing sixty rather than forty items. . . . The second striking aspect is that the ADL's general counsel and fact-finding staff had just served immediately prior . . . as the research staff of the Botein Commission, in which capacity they had had submitted to them a wealth of material not only on anti-Semitic statements and incidents in the city but about anti-black, racist ones as well.

He hypothesizes that had the ADL put its staff to work cataloguing anti-black racist remarks made in New York during the "past two and a half years by whites (or by Jews)" then it could "hardly be doubted that such a recital would comprise not twenty-five pages and forty incidents . . . but literally thousands of statements and incidents, some overt and raw as the anti-Semitic ones, some disguised and half-cooked, couched in the Aesopian language in which this society talks about race."

> One needs only to remember the patently racist remarks of United Federation of Teachers President Albert Shanker . . . or teachers and supervisors screaming "nigger lover" at parents and children who crossed the UFT picket lines. . . . One might also remember that the black community of this city lives not with forty or so offensive incidents but with some 120,000 New Yorkers who voted for George Wallace. . . .

Schwarzchild asks, if the ADL did not see fit to include instances of anti-black sentiment, why has some black organization not done so? His answer:

> Negroes are not interested in a nosecounting contest with the ADL over which minority group has suffered more verbal assault, even though they could win this sad competition hands down. Negroes are now struggling to end the oppressive force over them of fundamentally racist liberal institutions of the society. It is *liberal racism* that is the enemy. And this produces puzzlement, discomfiture, and resentment among liberals, intellectuals, and in the Jewish community. . . .
>
> The ADL report should have comforted everyone who was concerned with an apparent rise in the noise level of Negro anti-Semitism. To find forty anti-Semitic incidents in two and a half years in a city of 1.2 million Negroes and almost 2 million Jews, beset with a multitude of social, racial, and class problems that make for some inevitable friction between ethnic groups, that is a surprising datum of relative tranquility. . . .
>
> Racism is rampant in this community. But those who suffer most massively from its effects are not the Jewish community but the nonwhite minority groups. . . .

Henry Schwarzchild wrote his critique on February 3. It has never been circulated. Ironically, when one looks at the *Times* just one day before that, there again is Albert Shanker, with UFT contract time coming up, talking of the "alliance" that was against him in the school dispute. This included, he said, "black separatists, the Students for a Democratic Society, the lawyers association [sic], and white liberals who are racists because they always say yes to black demands." And in April there was a principal, Abraham Lass, chairman of the committee on student unrest of the High School Principals Association, quoted as declaring that "fear and chaos are in the saddle" in the city's schools; and Albert Shanker claiming that Mayor Lindsay's handling of the strike had brought the city to a "point of racial warfare."

The pattern to these events now is evident, as is their portrayal by the media. One can point to distinguished individual performances: for example, analytical stories by Fred Hechinger in the New York *Times;* an earnest October 23, 1968, effort by *Times* reporter Bill Kovach to dissect the anti-Jewish feeling among blacks; and several of the *Times'* editorials. Nat Hentoff's writings in the *Village Voice* were passionate and relevant, as were Jason Epstein's in the *New York Review of Books.* Columnist Murray Kempton in the New York *Post* was an oasis of reason amid the general shrillness of that paper's daily coverage (the reporting of Kenneth Gross excepted). The *Daily News* saw little need to discuss issues when there was so much juicy confrontation to report on.

I. F. Stone, in his *Weekly* of November 4, 1968, did a remarkable job of delineating the fakery of black anti-Semitism. "John V. Lindsay," he wrote, "is in trouble because he suddenly finds himself Mayor of a Southern town." Sol Stern in *Ramparts* did a fine, sympathetic report on the new, young teachers who went out to work in the experimental schools. And there was a biting series of editorials entitled "A Divided City," on WCBS-TV. But except for these, efforts at analysis on radio and TV were sorry. Each day the airwaves were filled with the catch phrases—"black militants," "extremists," and "outsiders." TV's concept of objective coverage was to read the *Times*, discover the day's issue, get a UFT spokesman, then a spokesman for the beleagured schools, and have them speak to the issue. It dwelt only on confrontation. Radio reporting was the same, except for WCBS' Ed Bradley.

There was, with the predictable exception of Harlem's *Amsterdam News,* no *real* effort made to present the black man's side of the conflict. A confidential report done for the New School for Social Research's Urban Reporting Project has disclosed that community people most affected by the strike thought that media coverage was superficial; that it did not delve; that it lacked objectivity; that it distorted. Certainly there was no follow-up effort to fix responsibility in the UFT for vicious and fraudulent leaflets *circulated under its auspices.* Was any official disciplined for his acts? Were there grounds for prosecution? Is not the same UFT pamphleteering machinery intact today?

The pattern, then, is one of sobering shortcomings in media initiative and perspective, one which demonstrates the frightening ease with which clever demagogues can manipulate a sensitive issue in a vast metropolis—one, in short, which should discomfit all media in the media capital of the nation. The question now is what lessons have been learned, and which will be applied? Surely the answer cannot be "none." For the lessons are too clear to be missed—and the social cost of ignoring them is far too high.

## THE WBAI INCIDENT

Last January 15, the public relations director of the United Federation of Teachers, in one of a series of actions to draw attention to comments made to the modest-size audience of station WBAI-FM, filed a complaint with the FCC about the station's "Julius Lester" program of December 26, 1968. The portion of the program in question, an interview with controversial Leslie Campbell—one of 57,000 New York City public school teachers—follows:

*Vann:* I also brought with me some works by a young sister in Brooklyn who is fifteen years old . . . a sister by the name of Thea Behran. She has written a poem about anti-Semitism and she dedicates this poem to Albert Shanker, and the name of this is "Anti-Semitism":

> *Hey, Jew boy, with that yarmulka on your head*
> *You pale faced Jew boy—I wish you were dead*
> *I can see you Jew boy—no you can't hide*
> *I got a scoop on you—yeh, you gonna die*
> *I'm sick of your stuff*
> *Every time I turn 'round—you pushin' my head into the ground*
> *I'm sick of hearing about your suffering in Germany*
> *I'm sick about your escape from tyranny*
> *I'm sick of seeing in everything I do*
> *About the murder of 6 million Jews*
> *Hitler's reign lasted for only fifteen years*
> *For that period of time you shed crocodile tears*
> *My suffering lasted for over 400 years, Jew boy*
> *And the white man only let me play with his toys*
> *Jew boy, you took my religion and adopted it for you*
> *But you know that black people were the original Hebrews*
> *When the U.N. made Israel a free independent State*
> *Little four and five-year-old boys threw hand-grenades*
> *They hated the black Arabs with all their might*
> *And you, Jew boy, said it was all right*
> *Then you came to America, land of the free*
> *And took over the school system to perpetrate white supremacy*
> *Guess you know, Jew boy, there's only one reason you made it*
> *You had a clean white face, colorless, and faded*
> *I hated you Jew boy, because your hangup was the Torah*
> *And my only hangup was my color.*

*Lester:* I had you read that in the full knowledge, of course, that probably one half of WBAI's subscribers will immediately cancel their subscriptions to the station, and to all sorts of other things because of the sentiments expressed in that particular poem; but nonetheless, I wanted you to read it because she expresses . . . how she feels. . . .

*Campbell:* I'm glad you said that, man, because some of our listeners are going to get hung up on discussing that and they are going to say that that is anti-Semitism, etc. but I don't think that is the question. . . .

(*Campbell reads another poem, "Day and Night." He comments that "when people begin to hear the young people they will realize there is no way they can put a gag in the mouth of black people." Then the segment begins in which listeners phone in questions and observations.*)

*Listener:* That was a very ugly poem. What was it about the poem that made you feel we should have heard it? It aroused anger in me.

*Lester:* People should listen to what a young black woman is expressing. I hope that will properly cause people to do some self-examination and react as you have reacted. An ugly poem, yes, but not one half as ugly as what happened in school strikes, not one one-hundredth as bad as what some teachers said to some of those black children. I would hope that you would not have the automatic reaction, but raise a few questions inside yourself. I had it read over the air because I felt that what she said was valid for a lot of black people, and I think it's time that people stop being afraid of it and stop being hysterical about it. . . .

(*Listeners discuss other comments on the program.*)

*Listener:* With all of this discussion about racism and the difference between black and white, doesn't it make it hard for a decent person to contact or communicate with a black person?

*Lester:* All black people are saying is, if there is going to be communication between black people, our point of view and our attitudes are going to be a major consideration. In the past they have not been because we have kept quiet, and now we are saying it's a two-way street, and you have to at least come one half way on our terms. The question is not one of communication but one of justice for black people. . . .

On March 26, FCC Secretary Ben Waple communicated to the UFT the Commission's decision: that WBAI had "fulfilled its obligation imposed by the fairness doctrine to afford reasonable opportunity for the presentation of conflicting viewpoints" [*FCC Reports* 69-302]. In its review of the case, the Commission quoted these statements of Julius Lester on a January 30, 1969, program:

I'm willing to admit that anti-Semitism is a vile phenomenon. It's a phenomenon which I don't totally understand as it has existed in the world. It's a phenomenon which has caused millions upon millions of people to lose their lives. However, I think that it's a mistake to equate black anti-Semitism with the anti-Semitism which exists in Germany, in Eastern Europe, and in the Middle East. If black people had the capability of organizing and carrying out a program against the Jews, then there would be quite a bit of fear. Black people do not have that capability. Not only do blacks not have the capability, I doubt very seriously if blacks even have the desire.

Part of the personal controversy is coming about because no one has bothered to try and see that black anti-Semitism, if it can be called that, and I'm not sure it can, is a much different phenomenon. It is a different phenomenon because the power relationships which exist in this country are different. In Germany, the Jews are the minority surrounded by a majority which carried out against them rather heinous crimes. In America, it is we who are the Jews. It is we who are surrounded by a hostile majority. It is we who are constantly under attack. There is no need for black people to wear yellow Stars of David on their sleeves; that Star of David is all over us. In the city of New York a situation exists where black people, being powerless, are seeking to gain a degree of power over their lives and in the institutions which affect their lives. It so happens that in many of those institutions, the people who hold the power are Jews. Now in the attempt to gain power, if there is resistance by Jews to that, then of course blacks are going to respond. . . .

The Commission added:

Mr. Lester then made similar observations concerning the remarks by Tyrone Woods that Hitler should have made more Jews into lampshades, and stated that he feels "confident that those who have listened to this program more than once know that I have an intense reverence for life; and likewise, an intense love of people."

In another statement, the licensee invited the following organizations to engage in cooperative action over the station's facilities to combat "the dangers of bigotry, whether from blacks or whites": the Anti-Defamation League of B'nai B'rith, the American Jewish Congress, the Workmen's Circle, the Jewish Defense League, the New York Council of Rabbis, the National Jewish Committee on Law and Public Affairs, the United Federation of Teachers; the Afro-American Association, Black Student Unions, CORE, the Urban League, and the NAACP.

It also stated that it was resuming an earlier regular feature in WBAI's program schedule, the weekly commentary on Jewish affairs, a program in which spokesmen for all the Jewish organizations in the city are now being invited to participate.

Finally, WBAI's general manager stated that throughout the course of the teacher's strike, WBAI "respectfully invited the union to avail itself of our aim to respond to criticism and to publicize its position; that on some occasions, union spokesmen availed themselves of the offer, while at other times, they did not accept the offer. . . ."

# Exploding the Myth of Black Anti-Semitism

This is the story of a political lie, a New York political lie that clangs through the city like a false alarm in the night. It breeds hatred between two of the largest ethnic groups in the city—as it was meant to do. It allows the powerful to step on the powerless—as it was meant to do. It has made many men so frightened they are now willing to forego their own rights as citizens in order to prevent other citizens from enjoying the same rights. And this, most of all, it was meant to do. The lie has a name: it is "black anti-semitism."

What? people will say, how can black anti-semitism be a lie. Didn't Leslie Campbell, a black teacher from the Ocean Hill-Brownsville school district, read a student's anti-semitic verse over radio station WBAI-FM? Didn't black "militants" at public meetings cast aspersions on the motives of the "Jewish-dominated UFT" (the United Federation of Teachers) and the performance of the "Jewish-dominated school system?" And what of those ugly anti-Jewish leaflets the UFT thoughtfully flooded the city with to teach us the depth and extent of black anti-semitism? What New Yorker has not heard of these things, especially during the past three months.

*As will be seen, the above "incidents" pretty much sum up the case for black anti-semitism now being made by interested parties. But the charge of black anti-semitism does not rest on such incidents; it takes off from them and never looks back.*

We are told in January by a Special Committee on Race and Religious Prejudice, appointed by Mayor John Lindsay last November, that "an appalling amount of racial prejudice—black and white—surfaced in and about the school controversy. The anti-white prejudice has a dangerous component of anti-semitism." As matters now go in New York, this is the *fairest* comment you are likely to find, but note that while anti-black prejudice is "appalling," anti-semitic prejudice is "dangerous," which is to say, the first is morally repellent but the latter, in addition, is *politically* significant.

Other spokesmen are not quite this subtle. We are told by the Anti-Defamation League, a Jewish watchdog agency, that "raw, undisguised anti-semitism is at a crisis-level in New York City schools" and that "the use of anti-semitism—raw, undisguised—has distorted the fundamental character of the controversy surrounding the public

In 1969 Walter Karp and H. R. Shapiro founded *The Public Life,* a journal on American politics and self-government.

Originally published as "How New York's Jews Were Turned against Black Men: Exploding the Myth of Black Anti-Semitism," *The Public Life,* February 21, 1969. Reprinted here from its republication as a public service advertisement in the *New York Times,* sponsored by the Jewish Committee for Community Control. It was later reprinted as "Exploding the Myth of Black Anti-Semitism" in James Baldwin et al., *Black Anti-Semitism and Jewish Racism* (New York: Richard Baron, 1969).

schools of New York City." We are told by a member of the New York City Board of Education, Mrs. Rose Shapiro, that "there is a battle raging to destroy the city's fabric. This new wave of racism has engulfed our city." Engulfment, nothing less.

Calls now go out almost daily to find and denounce the black culprits; to denounce, dismiss and impeach any official deemed derelict in his duty to suppress these black attacks upon Jews. "We put black racists on notice," warns the American Jewish Committee, "that we are determined to use every legal means to let no one get away with any efforts to inflict pain or suffering on any Jewish person."

For failing to combat black anti-semitism with sufficient "vigor," William Booth, a black man, lost his post as head of the city's Human Rights Commission. Back in November, Mayor Lindsay could still tell a Jewish audience that "we will not tolerate false attacks of anti-semitism against all those who have favored community responsibility in our schools. Many of the attacks were vicious slander." Now, for not acting as if every slander were proven fact, Mr. Booth is found unfit for his job.

A Jewish official writing in *Commentary,* an eminent intellectual journal sponsored by the American Jewish Committee, has now drawn the political implications of this new insurgent black anti-semitism. It is no longer a question, he argues in the January issue, of Jews being "liberal" toward black aspirations. "There is, more clearly than ever before the legitimate and independent imperative for self-survival." In plain words, black anti-semitism has grown so threatening that Jews must cease to *support* black activists and start defending themselves *against* them.

This then is the significance we are asked to give to black anti-semitism. It is a force so intense and so potent (though but a few months old) that it constitutes a "crisis," "engulfs" the city, tears apart its "fabric" and threatens the safety of the city's 1.8 million Jews. For three hundred years black men in America have been as politically impotent as doormats. Suddenly, in the past three months they are being portrayed as the most potent force in a giant metropolis.

## HOW BLACK ANTI-SEMITISM ROSE TO THE "SURFACE"
## JUST IN THE NICK OF TIME

One interesting feature of black anti-semitism is its extraordinary timeliness from the viewpoint of the teachers' union and others opposing school decentralization. It "surfaced" so the story goes, during the UFT's bitter strikes last fall and has been publicized with ever increasing intensity during the past two months, just when the Mayor's decentralization plan nears the New York State legislature for approval next month.

The plan would give New York's citizens the wholly novel (for New York) opportunity to elect their own, partly independent, local school boards, but the sudden upsurge of black anti-semitism has tarnished the plan considerably. It is "proving" to many that decentralization will pave the way for vicious vendettas against the Jewish school teachers of the city, a point the head of the UFT, Albert Shanker, has made from the start. Local control of the schools, he has frequently charged, "would open up a field day for bigots." Now men of good will are coming around to his farsighted view. Mrs.

Shapiro, who as president of the Board of Education, opposed school decentralization before there was a hint of racial strife, now suavely votes against it on the grounds that "there must be a respite for the schools until the community can recover its sanity."

*How convenient the black anti-semitism charge is. Indeed, it is difficult to see what the opponents of decentralization—the UFT, the school bureaucracy, the trade union movement, the Democratic city machine—would have done without it. A recent Louis Harris poll (which stacked the deck against decentralization by terming it "community influence," a veritable pejorative) showed, nevertheless, that the majority of Jews still favors decentralization, that the large majority of black men favor decentralization, that three out of four New Yorkers think it would do some good in improving education.*

*Black anti-semitism has had a lot of work to do and now, in the nick of time, it is doing it.*

It is time, now too, to unmask the lie and in doing so a fundamental point about charges of anti-semitism must be made clear. The *extent,* the *intensity,* and the *danger* of anti-semitism in any community is a direct function of whether or not Jewish leaders and powerful political figures *choose* to minimize or maximize its significance. Some anti-semitic incidents occur in every community. The question is how will they be assessed. One example from the January 1969 Anti-Defamation League report on black anti-semitism illustrates the point. In its dossier it slates a black man for saying that his group is "demanding teacher responsibility. If they can't produce, go elsewhere. If they can't get these black kids up to grade level—teach elsewhere." This can be considered a perfectly reasonable remark, or it can be viewed as the ADL now insists it be viewed, as an example of "attempts to drive Jewish teachers and principals out of the schools." The decision is entirely a political one.

Practically speaking, two conditions are required to make anti-semitism a political issue. First, it can only be attributed to people who are politically powerless like black people, for the powerless can be portrayed as being anything those with power wish to describe them as being. Secondly, it requires the active complicity of powerful political elements, for the Jewish organizations have neither the power, nor, being for the most part liberal-minded, the desire to exaggerate charges of anti-semitism—*especially* against black people. The political decision to do so lies in other hands and in the present case the Jewish organizations were pressured to follow suit.

### JEWISH GROUPS SWING FROM MINIMIZING
### BLACK BIGOTRY TO EXAGGERATING IT

*From 1966 to the fall of 1968, it was the consistent policy of almost every major Jewish organization to minimize the significance of occasional reports of black anti-semitism.* Again and again, Jewish organizations warn their membership (source for the following is The New York Times) that such tales are "exaggerated" and misrepresented. What they feared was not black prejudice against Jews, but Jewish prejudice against black men. They warn time and again that too many Jews were using a few statements by unrepresentative "extremists" (the same unrepresentative extremists are now held to be powerful enough to tear apart New York) as an excuse for their own bigotry. On

April 28, 1966, for example, an American Jewish Congress spokesman coined the term "Jewish backlash" and denounced stories of black anti-Jewish sentiment as "overblown," emphasizing instead "the strong identification Negroes have with Jews."

On October 13, 1967, the National Community Relations Council, representing many Jewish organizations, issued a guide which warned Jews against mistaking "legitimate protest" by black men for anti-semitism and warned them further against "exaggerating the true dimensions" of any anti-Jewish sentiments that might arise in future. To black criticism of Jewish merchants and ghetto landlords the Union of Hebrew Congregations replied on November 12, 1967, not with an attack on black anti-semites, but with open criticism of certain Jews, urging "the exercise of moral pressure by the congregations and the rabbis upon those Jewish slumlords and ghetto profiteers." If a black man said those very words today in New York he would be slotted at once into an Anti-Defamation League dossier.

With few exceptions Jewish organizations followed the minimizing policy until the city-wide teachers' strike last autumn against the Ocean Hill school district, a black-led district with its own elected governing board that had been officially set up as an "experiment" in decentralization. At that point the first swing from minimizing to maximizing occurs.

*The B'nai B'rith, already on record against "exaggerating" black anti-semitism, now takes up (September, 1968) a defamatory slur against black men the UFT had been making for many months: "reverse racism."*

"Negro demands," said B'nai B'rith president William Wexler, "to replace white teachers and others in the black community—many of whom are Jews—raises the question of whether the evil of discrimination can really be cured by substituting another." In May, 1968, the Ocean Hill governing board, one of the few black-led groups with any real power to practice discrimination, had transferred from the district, 19, mainly Jewish, teachers. Although the ineffable Shanker had promptly termed this "Nazism," the B'nai B'rith had refused *at that time* to play the union leader's game. *Now, three months later when Ocean Hill was actually* hiring *scores of Jewish teachers, the B'nai B'rith begins crying up black anti-semitism. One down.*

As late as October 22, a spokesman for the American Jewish Committee could publicly accuse Shanker of "using the Jewish community" for his own purposes. Today the Committee is clamoring harshly for Jewish self-defense against the threat of black anti-semitism, which in late October it strongly suspected Shanker of whistling up.

The American Jewish Congress has been vacillating woefully for months. A liberal group staunch in its opposition to Jewish "backlash" and a supporter of school decentralization from the start, the Congress did not cave in until early this February. On the second of the month it publicly called for delaying school decentralization on the grounds that more evidence about it was needed, which is to say, the Congress was for decentralization when nothing was known about it and is now against it because too little is known. Blaming the need for delay on black anti-semites would have been far more persuasive, but the Congress still lacks the heart to credit its newly-discovered significance.

## THE ANTI-DEFAMATION LEAGUE WORKS UP A DOSSIER OF "INCIDENTS"

*Nothing, however, illustrates more graphically the abject surrender of the Jewish organizations than the record of the Anti-Defamation League, whose current stand on black anti-semitism ("crisis-level") repudiates everything it has said before and does so with every cheap trick it can muster.*

*On May 24, 1967, it is well worth recalling, the League issued the results of its five-year study of black attitudes toward Jews. Its findings make interesting reading today. The ADL's survey found that black men were the least anti-semitic Christian group in the country; that they were less likely than any white group to vote for a candidate who ran on an anti-semitic platform: that the more "militant" a black man was, the less likely he was to be anti-white and anti-Jewish.*

As late as October 23, 1968, when the teachers' strike was already in its second month, the ADL still held the line. That day it reported the results of its intensive study of anti-Jewish leaflets and found no evidence of any organized effort behind them. The leaflets were sporadic in content and issuance, a handful of ugly little productions without significant origin.

Now let us look at the dossier on black anti-semitism in the city schools this same organization has compiled for its January report. We are, to put it mildly, in another world. *From minimizing anti-semitism, the League has turned with a vengeance to the task of blowing it up to "crisis" proportions. It does even more than this. Forgetful of the fact that until the end of October it had reported no dangerous evidence of black anti-semitism, the League now tries to prove that in the two years prior to October, 1968 black anti-semitism was steadily "building up" in the schools.* The strategic significance of this is obvious: if black anti-semitism merely "surfaced" during the strike, people might attribute it to the heat of battle, a battle in which the UFT defamed black men every time it took out a full-page ad warning against "mob-rule," a racist code word if ever there was one.

In the January report, the leaflets, hitherto insignificant, take the place of honor in the dossier. Not a word of their being sporadic is said, but the ADL, in its effort to show that black anti-semitism flourished long before the strike, says too much. *It notes now that the leaflets "had early origins and distribution and were recirculated" during the strike. Now these leaflets, as the ADL had insisted in October, represented no organized effort. Since the UFT undeniably recirculated them, it is obvious that the union had saved them up over a two year period and unleashed them in a frightening barrage at the suitable moment.* The ADL's account of how one such leaflet got circulated is a model of evasiveness. "The recipients [teachers] often reproduced it and sent it to friends as an indication of the climate in some city schools and the schools were soon flooded with copies." No wonder the UFT reprinted the ADL's report in the January 22 issue of its house organ.

In addition to the leaflets, the bulk of ADL's "proof" of a dangerous effort to "drive" Jewish personnel out of the schools consists of seven remarks made in April, May, June, and September 1967, and again in September, 1968. As if that were not meager enough, it turns out that four of the remarks were made by one Robert "Sonny" Carson, and two by his sidekicks in a rump organization known as Brooklyn Independent Core. The expulsion of the Jews—surely a pivotal point in demonstrating the *danger* of black anti-semitism—turns out to be the theme song of a one-man band.

The ADL's attempt to prove that some key black *leaders* are anti-semitic is similarly a dismal failure, though this too is a crucial point, since if only "extremists" are anti-semites (as all agree) they must be the leaders of *something* to constitute a danger. The League's one effort involves David Spencer, Chairman of the I.S. 201 Complex governing board (the I.S. 201 Complex is an experimental district like Ocean Hill-Brownsville). Spencer is slated for anti-semitism because of a letter he wrote in October, 1968 which the dossier describes as follows: "After complimenting Jews who are 'working tirelessly behind the scenes for self-determination in Black and Puerto Rican communities'—Spencer said, nevertheless, it is hard to keep from reacting against everyone Jewish when the full weight of the Jewish Establishment is not only beating our Black and Puerto Rican communities, but also accusing us of being the aggressor."

Any honest man would call this the plaintive cry of an ill-used man, and it is worth stopping a moment to consider the mind-torturing nastiness of this ADL citation. *Here is a man openly and manfully complaining about organized Jewish efforts to use anti-semitism as a weapon* against *him and for that he is charged with anti-semitism. If you want to create anti-semites* that *is as good a way as any to start.*

Two-thirds of the way through the dossier we finally reach the "strike incidents" and learn that "anti-semitism has also been clearly in evidence" during *the* whole two-and-a-half month period. Aside from the ever-usable pamphlets "recirculated" by the UFT at the time, the bulk of the evidence here consists of racial slurs hurled by black men at Jewish teachers standing on picket lines. Even Martin Mayer, who defended the UFT in a 23,000 word essay in The New York Times Magazine (February 2), was willing to admit that the teachers hurled as many insults at black onlookers as the onlookers hurled at them. So much for the "strike incidents," which seem to consist chiefly of street-slanging matches between bitter political opponents in a heated emotional state.

So much, too, for the ADL report whose general drift can be judged first by noting that the following statement made by a black man appears in the dossier as evidence of anti-semitism: "The Jewish people have been in control of the public schools in this city and have done nothing to improve the education of Negro and Puerto Rican children." We are to take it that any black failure to compliment Jewish teachers is bigotry. It can be judged second by noting that the bulk of its evidence comes from statements by anonymous UFT members.

*In truth, the ADL's efforts to demonstrate the menace of black anti-semitism only proves the very opposite to be true. Consider that the black people of New York are provoked every day by vicious lies and slanders; consider that it finds itself baffled at every turn by a Jewish union chief, by Jewish organizations, by Jewish Board of Education members, by Jewish judges and Jewish legislators and then consider the paltry findings of the ADL report. Truly, as that organization once demonstrated, there is no people in America less anti-semitic than black people.*

## HOW THE TEACHERS' UNION STARTED THE "MENACE" OF
## BLACK ANTI-SEMITISM

*One agent and one agent alone initiated the campaign to concoct a fake threat of black anti-semitism. That was the United Federation of Teachers. Its intentions are transparent enough: the black anti-semitism lie was the best means at hand to break the alliance between the liberal Jewish middle class and the black people of the city and so destroy the chances of school decentralization.*

As far back as 1966, Shanker had begun sounding off about "reverse racism," a term meant to imply that if New Yorkers ever gained a voice in running their schools, white teachers would fall victims to black bigotry. The specific charge of black prejudice against Jews Shanker did not at first make public, beyond calling Ocean Hill's transfer of Jewish teachers "Nazism."

What he did instead was issue a dual set of accusations, one for the public and one for internal union consumption. In public he raised the disguised racist cry of "mob rule," in confident expectation that ordinary white prejudice against black men would be sufficient to defeat decentralization. Within the teachers' union, however, he had a different hand to play. The great majority of his members are Jewish. Whether they were anti-black or not they felt, being Jewish liberals, that they *ought* not to be. Nonetheless, under Shanker's leadership they were asked to fight militantly against black aspirations and they were hungry for justification. Shanker provided it. *Within* the union, starting around May, 1968, the now famous anti-Jewish leaflets were widely circulated to the rank-and-file by union chapter chairmen who got their sample copies at chapter chairmen meetings with the leadership.

It was not hard to convince Jewish teachers that their fight against decentralization was a fight to prevent black militants from launching pogroms against them. Most wanted to believe it anyway. *Lest the anti-semitic charge be thought too diffuse, an effort was made to link anti-semitism directly to the Ocean Hill experimental district. One widely circulated leaflet was alleged by UFT circulators to have come from Ocean Hill teachers, a fabrication the New York Civil Liberties Union exposed in late October 1968. Another was attributed to an Ocean Hill parent group which, it turned out, was not from Ocean Hill, did not issue any such leaflet and, in fact, had Jewish members.*

By the time the strikes began in early September, not only were teachers convinced of the anti-semitism menace, but in an urgent effort to justify themselves they were carrying what the ADL describes as "the virus of anti-semitism" from Jew to Jew, namely their families, relatives and friends, which itself made up a sizeable number.

As the strikes grew more bitter and the union's success in crushing Ocean Hill looked less and less assured, it took a drastic step: *the union now made black anti-semitism a public issue in order to raise Jewish people en masse against black men. The ever-useful leaflets, so carefully culled for so long, were now unleashed in Jewish neighborhoods while organized UFT hecklers invaded numerous public meetings to cry up charges of anti-semitism whenever a proponent of decentralization began addressing a Jewish audience.*

The seed once planted grew fast. To charges of anti-semitism many Jews are highly susceptible. There are Jews, especially older people, who think of nothing else when they think of public affairs at all. To such people a single racist leaflet looks like the high road to Auschwitz. All sense of reality flees. That a few nameless impotent bigots scarcely constitutes a city-wide menace is not a convincing argument to people whose first retort would likely be that Hitler was once powerless too.

## OFFICIAL JEWISH LEADERS NOW CAVE IN
## MEEKLY UNDER GROWING PRESSURE

This susceptible Jewish element, turned in on itself and its historic fears, is a minority among Jews, but its anxieties were being daily inflated by the press, by television and by friends of friends of striking teachers. Most importantly there was scarcely anybody of repute in the city who wished to bring these panicky people back to reality. The mighty "liberals" of the trade unions did not tell them that the UFT was continually slurring black people. Instead the whole union movement supported the UFT and accepted Shanker's basic premise about the dangers of "reverse discrimination." The Democratic bosses sat back contentedly, for the more Jews turned against Lindsay, the silent apostle of decentralization, the better they liked it. Nor were Democratic legislators, themselves the creatures of the city machine, about to tell any Jewish constituents to cease becoming hysterical.

*The decisive moment occurred when this tide of Jewish fears and hatred began exerting its inevitable pressure on the most illustrous Jewish organizations.* These groups may make flossy pronouncements about national policies, but for all their political pretensions they are no more nor less than Jewish protective societies, mere ethnic mouthpieces. They had no means to resist the pressure. If their members wanted their fears confirmed, the menace certified, the villains denounced, then that is what the membership would get. *One by one the Jewish organizations broke and accepted the lie of black anti-semitism. When they did they confirmed its existence for thousands upon thousands of Jews previously untouched by Shanker's propaganda.*

## WHY POWERFUL POLITICAL ELEMENTS GAVE SHANKER THEIR SUPPORT

What is more, having accepted Shanker's story, these Jewish spokesmen are permanently wed to it, for to tell the truth now would expose their complicity. The Anti-Defamation League is so completely under Shanker's thumb it is virtually his propaganda machine. And since the League is the official definer of anti-semitism, Shanker's story is now an established "truth." Thanks to the hysteria built up this January, Mayor Lindsay no longer talks of "vicious slanders" against black people. He is too busy placating Jewish audiences with promises to put the black menace under control.

*By turning his allegations into a truth, Shanker has now come in sight of his goal: the political isolation of the black people of the city and the consequent defeat of any real school decentralization plan.*

Shanker, of course, could not accomplish this feat alone. It required the active cooperation and complicity of the trade union movement, their purblind "liberal" supporters and, most of all, the Democratic city machine and its minions, men like Judge Bloustein who termed Shanker's circulation of the leaflets "extremely unwise," as if it were merely a matter of poor judgment. Nor did Shanker win their cooperation because these leaders give a damn about school teachers. There was more to the defeat of decentralization than protecting the right of New York teachers never to be accountable to the public.

*Decentralization means the establishment of locally elected school boards.* It means the coming into municipal politics of locally elected officials who just *might* represent the citizens who elected them instead of the city rulers. It means, in other words, the exposure and destruction of the Democratic machine and with it the trade union leadership's loss of power over their workers, for that power depends on their workers being politically impotent and so incapable of being citizens. *It means the seed of local democracy in New York and now we know who benefits from the lie of black anti-semitism. Not only Albert Shanker, but every other petty tyrant protecting his power to lord it over somebody else.*

## Blacks and Jews
An Interview with Julius Lester

Leslie Campbell is a teacher in Ocean Hill-Brownsville, a focal point in the struggle for community control of schools in New York City between the black community and the predominantly white United Federation of Teachers (headed by Albert Shanker). Last December, on Julius Lester's WBAI-FM program, Campbell read a poem by a fifteen-year-old student of his. Titled "Anti-Semitism," and "dedicated to albert shanker," the poem begins: "Hey, jew boy with that yamaka on your head / You pale faced Jew boy, I wish you were dead." The last two lines are: "I hated you jew boy cause your hang up was the Torah / And my only hang up was my color."

The tumultuous aftermath of the reading was the filing of a complaint to the FCC by the United Federation of Teachers and demands that the station's license be revoked or suspended by the New York Board of Rabbis, the Workmen's Circle, and the Jewish Defense League, among other groups.

QUESTION: *By now, that poem has become an issue not only in New York, but nationally as well. You said you expected some degree of reaction at the time, but was the extent and durability of the hostile response surprising to you?*

ANSWER: Yes, very surprising, because the reaction came three weeks after the poem was read on the air. I felt, at the time, that it was simply being used as a device to get at Les Campbell, who has been under attack for some months now. And then, secondly, it was interesting that Shanker's complaint to the FCC about WBAI was made the day after the courts ruled that the principals should go back into Ocean Hill-Brownsville. I felt it was a politically inspired move. Why wait three weeks? In terms of the reaction of people who heard the program—yes, they were disturbed; they were upset. They talked about it on the air, on the show, but I didn't start receiving hate mail until after *The New York Times* came out with their story.

Q: *And was there much hate mail?*

A: Oh, tons. Quite a bit. And you know, threats and this type of thing.

Q: *Getting back to the poem itself, I'm not asking you to speak for Les Campbell, but speaking for yourself, having seen the poem, if you had been her teacher, wouldn't you then have tried to communicate with the student and explore with her the stereotypical reactions manifested in her poem? It was, after all, clearly anti-Semitic and indiscriminately made* all *Jews the enemy.*

A: One thing people don't understand is that when you're working with blacks, there is a

In 1969, Nat Hentoff was a staff writer for *The New Yorker* and a columnist for the *Village Voice.*
Originally published in *Evergreen Review* 13, no. 65 (1969): 21–22, 25, 71–76.

time when people are ready to hear certain things, and that time is not now for some things. Let's put it this way: You start where the people are and try to move from there. So, OK, you involve yourself in things which you yourself disagree with. But if there's going to be any change of attitude, then it's not going to come by preaching moralistic sermons; that's just like what white people have always done. And so, when I saw the poem—yeah, there were things wrong in terms of intellectual content. However, I'm not concerned with that. I'm concerned with the basic emotion that's there, and if all the facts are wrong, it's totally irrelevant to that basic emotional content. So it's redundant and ridiculous of me to point out that Jews have suffered for more than fifteen years; the girl who wrote the poem doesn't care. And it wouldn't change what she was feeling.

Q: *And that not all Jewish teachers are the kind of teachers she's talking about?*

A: Right.

Q: *But if this kind of feeling is allowed to grow unchallenged, won't the result be that the girl will grow up rigidly prejudiced—just as most whites, if not all, have had racism embedded in them? You say that you have to move from where the people are, but do you withhold all comment of your own?*

A: I think that you have to consider the genesis of the poem. To my mind, the poem is an act of self-defense, because of the racism which was involved in the teacher's strike. The black community was attacked head-on, and specifically in Ocean Hill-Brownsville, where this girl is a student. And so, as far as I'm concerned, she is defending herself with the only weapon at her command. She is hurt, and therefore she is going to hurt back as much as she can.

I think one of the difficulties is that people are equating the poem with traditional anti-Semitism, which is rooted in God knows what—Christ-killers and what have you. That has no relationship to the black community. The black community does not fall within that. I mean, even at thirty years of age, I don't know that a person is a Jew from looking at him, or by his name, or anything like that. Now that's true of most black people, I think.

Q: *Richard Wright, in* Black Boy, *said "All of us black people who lived in the neighborhood hated Jews, not because they've exploited us, but because we have been taught at home and in Sunday School the Jews were 'Christ-killers.'" That's not analogous to your experience?*

A: No. I was twenty years old before I began to have any consciousness that there was anything other than black people and white people, that there were sub-categories of white people, and that Jews were one of them. It came about through *Exodus,* and then, from that I went to a synagogue. Yes, I was aware in terms of the Bible, and in terms of spirituals—Moses, this kind of thing. It meant nothing, except later I became conscious that Einstein was a Jew, that Jews had an intellectual tradition, and being an intellectual of sorts, I could respect that. So what feelings I had were, shall we say, kindred.

Q: *You came initially from the South, and I wonder whether you think that the hostility toward the Jew in some black urban communities comes from the fact that a preponderance of the merchants in these black areas are Jewish?*

A: Yes, but growing up in Nashville, they were *white* people. They weren't Jews. There were crackers and there were niggers. So I came to New York in '61, and I found out—well, Jesus, there are Irish, and there are Polish, Germans, and all these other things. Each one acts differently. But I was conscious of white people, and that was all.

Q: *And you don't think this identification with the Jew as merchant and then as white is as widespread as many sociologists claim?*

A: Perhaps in the North it is. In terms of Harlem, yes. I would say it is.

Q: *I asked because someone pointed out in an analysis that in some areas the Negro would frequently refer to his "Jew landlord," even though his name might be O'Reilly, Kowalski, or Santangelo. And, I suppose, again that comes out of the preponderance of Jewish merchants and landlords in those areas.*

A: Right, yes.

Q: *In another program on WBAI, and this is something you've commented on, there was a remark by a black student from N.Y.U.: "As far as I'm concerned, more power to Hitler. He didn't make enough lampshades out of them." Well, that's the kind of thing that, to a Jew listening in, even if he's totally out of the religion, out of any kind of Jewish communal feeling, immediately conjures up the very real, quite recent past. And he would ask, "How come you didn't say anything about* that *at the time?"*

A: The reason I didn't say anything about it at the time was that I recognized he was speaking symbolically, and that he was speaking from a feeling of how can I most effectively hurt these people. It should be obvious that black people don't have the capabilities to carry out any pogrom against Jews, and then, I don't even think black people have the desire to carry out any pogrom against Jews. I took his statement totally on the symbolic level.

Q: *Because he was so angry, particularly in the context of the recent teachers' strike and the various reactions after that to Les Campbell, this was the kind of thing he would say—to hurt?*

A: Yes, right. And, OK, if you want to isolate it from that, yes, like it's a horrible statement; it's a horrible thing that happened. But, once again, emotionally, black people have no connection with what happened in Germany and in Eastern Europe. We were too busy fighting for our own survival.

Q: *Some social scientists would say, "OK, it was symbolic. It was perhaps defensive." But it's out of symbolism, out of this use of rhetoric, that the climate in the past in places you've mentioned eventually led to political anti-Semitic movements and actual pogroms and concentration camps.*

A: What really gets me angry, see, is that, for crying out loud, for six months we had a George Wallace going around the country who *created* an atmosphere that *did* provoke unwarranted attacks upon black people, that *did* create a whole climate in the country of which the UFT thing is a part. And where were these so-called friends, be they either Jews or Anglo-Saxons, when this was happening? A few of them were interested, a few of them were protesting, but they were all saying, "Oh, if Wallace ever did get elected, America would never wipe out black people"—the same thing that was said in Germany. If white people started a pogrom against Jews, then OK, Jews would be in trouble, because whites have the power to carry it out. But black people have no thought of carrying out any sort of pogrom against Jews.

Q: *During the UFT strike, which closed down the schools and was, in reality, an attempt to destroy the Ocean Hill-Brownsville Experimental District and community control of the schools, there was a large amount of racist, anti-black invective on UFT picket lines, which was barely reported, and against which I don't think there was much of a record of protest by any group, certainly by none of the groups clamoring now. And after the strike, there was a teacher at Franklin K. Lane High School, who is as yet unidentified, who was quoted in the* New York Post *as saying, "Well, we're not going to live in fear. I think that if the black people don't get into line, then we'll have to either annihilate them or neutralize them. That's not as harsh as it sounds. It has happened in other societies. It may be the only way of dealing with this." So what I'd ask you, and I suppose it's in a sense a rhetorical question, how does one expect—let's say the girl in Les Campbell's class, the student at N.Y.U., to exist under this kind of state of siege, as they see it, and not react emotionally?*

A: I react emotionally to that, you know. Because that is a reality as far as I'm concerned; the teacher at Franklin K. Lane is not joking. This country *is* capable of annihilating black people.

But how else is one to react to that? I didn't see Mayor Lindsay going around to a Baptist church, putting on the choir robes to explain to the black congregation that he wasn't going to allow that in the city. You know, like I was not even interested in Ocean Hill-Brownsville, the school fight—nothing. Until one day I was looking at TV, and all of a sudden, I hear Shanker talking about mob action and extremists.

Q: *Vigilantes, Nazis.*

A: Right. *That* to me means *one thing!* He's so hung up on *niggers!* They wouldn't be accusing us of anti-Semitism if we had the finesse of George Wallace and Shanker. Like, the guy who made that statement that Hitler should have made more lamp-shades could have got on there and said the same thing in Shanker's way. But he's the cat off the block; he said it direct from the gut. And why be dishonest about it? But you say that Shanker said he is for decentralization of the schools and all that. And so people take this and they don't hear what *I'm* hearing the man say. Hell, we were talking about decentralization and education and Shanker starts yelling anti-Semi-tism. Rhody McCoy was talking politics; Shanker started talking race.

Q: *Then what is your explanation for so many Jews having reacted so emotionally and so vehemently to the poem and to the statement by the N.Y.U. student? In other words, why were you so surprised at this reaction?*

A: Well, I guess because my knowledge of the Jewish community as such is nonexistent. I know quite a few individuals who are Jews. I expected some reaction, yes. But it was just ignorance on my part as to how deep the fear is inside the Jewish community. But that's not saying I would've done differently in this situation.

I think there's another aspect to it. For the past five or ten years in this country, Jews have sort of been "in"—the Jewish novel, *How to Be a Jewish Mother.* For the first time in world history, a country exists where Jews are "in"—*Fiddler on the Roof,* and what have you. And they were feeling good with this, and all of a sudden comes this attack from the left—or from the right, depending on where you sit—which, of course, feeds back again into what I guess is an insecurity.

Then there's the whole Israel thing. I've been thinking about the progression in terms of this whole issue of black anti-Semitism. The first column I wrote for the *Guardian,* in the fall of 1967 I think, dealt with Israel and the Mideast War and the whole thing. In that column, I said it was necessary for Jews to look upon Israel politically, at what its political role was. And, of course, the reaction I got was the same that came this time—that there's another black-Jewish division here, that naturally the Jewish attitude toward Israel was going to be very personal, very emotional, and a very moral one. And because six million Jews were killed during World War II, it sort of seems that a Jew can do no wrong, that the State of Israel can do no wrong. And I think Jews in this country have that sort of attitude. Nobody mentions the ten million who died in Stalingrad alone in World War II; there were twenty million in Russia that got wiped out, which explains a lot to me about Russia's present international position. What about these people who are just forgotten? Hell, fifteen million died in the camps. It would seem to me that Jews are falsifying history to let nine million people be forgotten.

Then the other things is that the cat in the corner would say, "OK, six million Jews got it. *I* didn't do it. Don't tell me about it."

Q: *Which, to a Jew, I think, would be the attitude of the non-Jewish population at large. I think the essential thing to keep in mind is that those Jews who still have any kind of concept of themselves as Jews are aware of the fact that it's been a long, tough pull for an awfully long time. The fact that any Jew survived is quite remarkable. Israel to them is not only the last place, but the only place, where anybody can go if he's Jewish. It's also a radical change in Jews' attitude toward themselves. To use a term from the new movement, "It's one place where Jews don't play victims anymore."*

A: Right, OK. Then why is it that they can understand Israel and can't let us have Ocean Hill-Brownsville? That's the same thing; they should understand that better than *anybody* in this country. But the reason is that they have the power now, and they don't want to relinquish their power to the black people. So therefore we fight.

Q: *In an article in* Commentary, *"The Black Revolution & the Jewish Question," Earl Raab, executive director of the Jewish Community Relations Council in San Francisco, says the black movement "is developing an anti-Semitic ideology. On one coast, there's talk about how the 'Jewish establishment' is depressing the education of black students. On the other coast, a black magazine publishes a poem calling, poetically of course, for the crucifying of rabbis. 'Jew Pig' has become a common variant of the standard expressivist metaphor. On this level, there are daily signals." Do you think he is taking these "signals" out of proportion in building this case?*

A: I would think so. There's a certain expression which comes from what the press would describe as militant black intellectuals. There's another expression which I think comes from black people in the community. I think he is taking it out of proportion. In a ghetto situation, the people are not adverse to the idea of sharing power. They're not at the point of, say, where Kenya is in terms of kicking out Asians. I haven't heard of any Jewish merchants being firebombed out of the ghettos since this has happened—any sort of campaign directed against them. I think the danger is that, because of the Jewish reaction to what's been going on, the blacks will move to an absolute position, which, of course, is very dangerous because then you're pitting one power against another power, and that's a war.

Q: *You mean that the reaction is of such vehemence, like the demand that you be fired and WBAI be shut down, that that in itself will create anti-Semitism?*

A: I don't know if you can call what blacks feel anti-Semitism. It's more of an anti-racism racism, that act of self-defense, and to call it anti-Semitism is to fail to understand it.

You see, the thing which has hurt me most in this is where has the New Left been? Where has the radical movement been? OK, you know, they say we want to be relevant in the black struggle. We want to speak to the white community. Here is opportunity busting down the door. Here it is, if you're a white who understands anything about the black framework. But what happens is that so many young kids in SDS, whose background is Jewish, hate that background so much and want to get so far away from it that they refuse to relate to where they've come from.

Q: *Whereas they could have been of some help in moving around in Jewish communities, putting all this in perspective?*

A: As far as black radicals go, I'm a conservative because I have a theoretical belief in coalition, and if it's possible for me to say to a cat who don't want to hear white people, "Hey man, listen, ten thousand white folks were out there on the line yesterday doing this, that, and the other," he might change his mind. But then he looks out there and sees, like *I* do, a hostile mass, and the rest silent. Hey, well, you know, fuck it!

Q: *All during the teachers' strike, and all during this furor about the poem, about WBAI, I don't know of any attempt, organized, anyway, where white radicals, or people who call themselves white radicals, went into their home communities or into communities in which they can easily move, to try to explain what was going on.*

A: I know of no attempt. I know of only two groups which have done anything, and that was Youth Against War and Fascism, and Coalition For An Anti-Imperialist Movement. And then it was very gratifying to me that both groups came up and counter-picketed the night others were out picketing me at the station.

I did a column on the Arab-Israeli thing and one on the school strike, both saying the same thing—that I felt the Jewish community should examine itself, and re-examine a lot of the things that it had formerly thought. One of my instincts in terms of the poem, and it was very conscious at the time—like the Zen monk who used to slap the student in the face—OK, let's try it and see what happens. But that's not my role, really. It's the responsibility of young Jews who have been in the radical movement to be the Zen monks, not me. But maybe I'm wrong.

At any rate, I think all of this has caused some self-examination inside the Jewish community and some discussions by the Jewish community, but *I* cannot really speak to the Jewish community; I don't know the Jewish community.

Q: *Leonard Fein, Associate Director of the MIT-Harvard Joint Center for Urban Studies, said in* Time: *"Jews, in a perverse kind of way, need anti-Semites. Jews in this country*

*are in fairly serious trouble spiritually and ideologically, and it is very comforting to
come once again to an old and familiar problem. By confronting others, you can avoid
the much more challenging confrontation with yourself." A big problem, as people
always say at meetings of Jewish organizations, is that the young people are falling away
from Judaism, and I would add that it is doubtful that they'll come back on a program of
anti-anti-Semitism. As Rabbi Arthur Hertzberg puts it, "Negatives won't work to create
a Jewish identity for our young people. The only thing that will work is a set of affirma-
tives that forms them as a people."*

A: There seems to me to be a schizophrenia in the Jewish community. I get many letters
and take many phone calls on the air and people say, "I'm white and I'm Jewish,"
which means that, like, when it's convenient I can be white, and then, when I'm
attacked, I'm Jewish. They got to deal with that.

Q: *That's a "schizophrenia" that's almost endemic to the American Jewish experience. The
lower-class Jew, whose parents came from Eastern Europe, has always felt himself an
outsider. I can't imagine any such Jewish kid in school pledging allegiance to the flag who
really thought that it was his flag entirely. That feeling of vulnerability intensifies in time
of stress.*

A: I find it interesting that every other group, including blacks, will say they are Italian-
American, German-American, Afro-American—except Jews. I think one of the
things which is happening now, if it can be allowed to happen, is that the relationships between the Jewish community and the black community are being reordered.
It's been a very patronizing relationship; the Jews haven't realized that. OK, Shanker
marches in Selma. Be serious. I mean who cares, for crying out loud! The relationship has *not* been defined by black people. And so you go around the country, and
you talk and talk and talk, or you write and write and write—I just reread *The Fire
Next Time*—it is fantastically contemporary, just as valid now as it was in '62. Best-
seller and all that—it didn't do no good; nobody listened to it. So it takes a poem by a
fifteen-year-old girl, that kick in the stomach, that Zen slap, to finally make people
really take what you say seriously. Like Baldwin says in *The Fire Next Time*—is there
going to be any hope, will it mean that white people, and I include Jews, are going to
have to look at themselves differently, are going to have to change themselves. You
know, I didn't know that Shanker was a Jew until he accused me of being an anti-
Semite; I'm talking about me, as a black person. Then I figured that he was a Jew. All
right, when he's going to accuse me of being something which I'm not—then my only
defense is, all right, I'll go ahead and be it, god-dammit!

Q: *But in your own case, being an intellectual, isn't there a tension between intellect and
emotion at that point?*

A: Well, I think it's a question of being an intellectual who is divorced by twenty leagues
from the masses of people or being divorced by five leagues. You're never going to be
totally with them. And my reaction is just as a human being—I'm not much of an
intellectual, you know—I had this experience: I did a TV interview in Cleveland. I
*really* hated the producer and the moderator of the show. I really hated them. I hated
them as people. *They* thought I hated them as *whites*. There was no way I could let
them know that I hated them as *people,* because of who they were. And this is the

same thing! They were the kind of liberals whose basic attitude was, "Yes, you can come here and say what you want to say, but I'm not going to listen, and it's not going to change my mind. I'm going to be nice and courteous the entire time, and you're just not going to reach me." If Shanker accuses me of being an anti-Semite, then I cannot prove that I'm not anti-Semitic. It would be futile for me to stand up and say, "Oh no, but I'm not; don't accuse me of that." Then I'm fighting the battle on his territory as he defines it, and that becomes a problem. The problem is one of the relationship of power. But Jews think it's a question of morality.

Q: *But does that necessarily mean, as you said earlier, that if he's going to call you one, you're going to be one? I mean, if you're not an anti-Semite, why let him make you into one?*

A: Let's put it this way: If it's very clear that he is brutalizing me for his own ends, then I'm going to retaliate, and I will retaliate in the way that will most hurt him. I don't think I have any other choice. I don't want to be called an anti-Semite for it. And that can be better understood if you understand that black people are a colonized people. You have, you know, two groups—the colonized and the colonizers. And the Jewish community is in the position of being on the side of the colonizer.

Q: *This reminds me of your line on the radio the other night, which was not covered by the press, that "We are America's Jews, the Jews think we are the Germans."*

A: Right. And the Jews are in the position of being Germans.

Q: *Yet there is this thesis, that black people, if and when they are anti-Semitic, feel them- selves, at least in that way, to be part of the majority. And there is a corollary to that, from historian Joseph Boskin, that selecting the Jew as a scapegoat fills an important psychic need for the black. To bait the Jew is to claim superiority to the Jew and to identify with the white community that still contains considerable elements of anti-Semitism.*

A: You see, once again, he's hooking into traditional concepts of anti-Semitism. Jews are not being used as a scapegoat for the problems of black people. Jews happen to be in a position of power. Blacks want power, thus Jews and blacks are in conflict. There is no scapegoat involved; they are directly involved in the life and the control of the black community. We are not reaching outside. It's not that the schools are filled with Irish and we are looking over to Scarsdale or someplace, and it's the fault of the Jews. They are right there in the community. So no scapegoat; *they are the ones.* They are not the *only* ones. Every black person I've had on my show has pointed that out, and Les pointed it out, and the three guys from N.Y.U. pointed it out—they are not what's called "the enemy"; but if you are a colonized people, then you are not going to break down the colonizer into categories of lesser or greater magnitude of enemy. The enemy is the enemy, and you deal with him as you come to him, and right now we are dealing with him on the level of schools, and there he is.

Q: *In Ocean Hill-Brownsville, where there is at least some degree of community control, twenty-two of the Jewish teachers, led by Chuck Isaac, said at a press conference the other day they didn't feel any anti-Semitism there, and specifically not from Les Campbell.*

A: What really ticks me is the fact that I didn't know until I went out to do some interviews at Ocean Hill-Brownsville that over 50 per cent of the new teachers they had hired were Jewish. And then you find out the thing which you pointed out in your column, about passing out a leaflet to the kids explaining what Rosh Hashana was, and all of this. I've sat in Les' Black History class twice. I've been amazed that Les never *once* used the word white. He used a variety of words, slave trader, slave owner; he never *once* used the word white. Whereas, in my class, you know, I'm much harder than Les is in terms of talking about white people. I spent quite a bit of time talking to the Jewish teachers who were there, the young kids. My feeling was I wish the school had all black teachers, but there aren't enough blacks available who could do the job these white kids are doing. They are pulling really fantastic poetry out of these kids, doing what seemed to me to be good things; I had no objection to it. If the time comes when the black community can take over the school completely and do the same job, then I want blacks to do it, but in the meantime, I mean like, wow, these whites were really filling a role. And these were young kids who had been politically active, politically involved, and were very aware and were working hard. There are some beautiful kids out there.

Q: *Now there comes the inevitable question. You say, if at such time the black community can staff the schools by itself, with all black teachers—does that mean you are opting for separatism?*

A: Let me put it this way. At the present point in my own life, and at the present point in American history, I don't see any other alternative. We *are* separate, you know. Great Neck, L. I., is going to bus in some black kids to add some color. That's a Jewish community and it's separate. It would be much better to institutionalize that as much as possible and to take care of business, rather than to keep trying to deal with a bunch of people who don't understand, who won't understand.

Q: *So you would probably say that the function of the white Jewish teachers who are now in Ocean Hill-Brownsville and doing well would be to perhaps address their educational and spiritual skills to white kids if and when the time comes when black teachers will fully staff the Ocean Hill-Brownsville schools?*

A: They are the only ones who can do it, and they could do a fantastic job. That's where it needs to happen. White kids need to study black history as much as black kids do. And you know, if a white cat's running it down to white kids, white teachers who understand the black frame of reference, that black reality, that's the only way the change is going to happen. But the thing that it comes down to is that young whites don't like white people, and blacks happen to like black people, so they want to be with us. I come back to what I said before: Where has the New Left been when we needed them? Like, I'll speak to white high school students now; I will *not* speak to white college students anymore.

Q: *Why?*

A: Because you speak and you speak and you speak, you write books, they read books, and all that, and they understand, you know. Still, when you need them, they aren't there. There is a need which exists in the black community which I can fill. There is a need in the white community which *they* can fill. I mean, why hasn't SDS been able to run into a synagogue as quick as they ran into N.Y.U. to keep James Reston of *The Times* from speaking?

Q: *You've mentioned SDS going into N.Y.U. to stop Reston from speaking; they also shouted down the South Vietnamese ambassador to the U.N. It seems to me that this, in its way, is very similar to people trying to suppress you and WBAI. So that if I am, and I am, for Les Campbell having absolute freedom to say whatever he wants to say anywhere, I have to add that applying "discriminative tolerance," as Herbert Marcuse would put it, anywhere, really injures anyone's right to free speech and thereby seriously limits the possibility of bringing real social and political change.*

A: I've had very mixed reactions, you know, having been picketed and having that strange experience of being escorted through a police line by a cop.

Q: *How did that feel?*

A: It felt very normal—the people were going to kill me if they could have gotten me, but I could understand that. I felt that the cop was doing what he should be doing, helping black people. But my feeling toward the people who were picketing me was that they had a right to do that. I thought first of going to the station early, at four o'clock; they wouldn't be there until seven—and just staying inside the station. And then I said, no, they have a right. They hate me so much, they should at least have a chance to see me and really scream and yell and do whatever else. I even felt, which is my own personal whatever you want to call it, that they had a right to beat me if they could have gotten me. I wouldn't willingly have given myself to them. But I understood how they felt because if I could have gotten my hands on Dean Rusk I would have felt that I had the right to beat him. OK now, you know, there is the position that the oppressed can do no wrong. And the oppressor can do no right. On a humanistic basis, I would have to agree with you. On a revolutionary basis, I don't think that the ambassador from South Vietnam should be allowed to speak.

Q: *But this is like the cliché about being slightly pregnant. Once you start limiting that right to speak—even for what you consider the best revolutionary reasons—you start precedents that other people can use against you.*

A: Who am I to say who can speak and who can't speak? If I don't feel this cat has a right to say who can speak and who can't speak, then he feels that naturally I don't have the right to limit him. So to reach a compromise everybody speaks, and I support that. I have to support that, I really do, despite the fact that there are a lot of people I don't want to speak to and whom I would like to punch in the mouth once they start speaking. OK, let them talk. So that makes me an Uncle Tom revolutionary, I guess.

But there's another dimension here. One of my black listeners wrote me and said that freedom of speech is OK as long as it is white people's. I have really resented all the people who ask me, why I didn't say something to disclaim the remark the guy made—you know, about Hitler and the lampshades. There's the assumption that I was the Establishment's representative on the air. He made a flat statement. I was shocked by the statement. I would not have said it. However, knowing damn well that the black community does not have honest access to the air, I was not going to put him down. He had a perfect right to say that, you know. And that is my role in the media—to give the black community access to speak as they see fit. I'm not going to set the standards. But white folks and I guess Jews, too, expected me to be their representative, and that's what shook them up—that they had a black man at a microphone who was not going to be their representative.

Q: *Probably for the first time in your life you've had this kind of instant fame, if fame is the word, in which you have become a stereotyped, faceless person to all those people who are demanding all kinds of things done to you, or because of you. How does that feel?*

A: On the one hand, it makes me feel like I'm a sitting duck, because *The New York Times* can sit there and shoot at me, day after day after day, and I can't do a damn thing. I know that my listeners, however many I have, do not have the same reaction. I've been thinking a lot about Alger Hiss who is now synonymous with traitor, and will be through time immemorial—like Benedict Arnold—and Alger Hiss is probably a very beautiful cat. It doesn't matter. On the other hand, I'm glad that my listeners know me as an individual and I think they relate to me like that, not as a black individual. I'm very, very patient on the air with people, I am a person who happens to be black whom they can talk to. I won't cuss them out and all that—that's my personality, I don't cuss out people, because it takes too much energy. And also I really believe in people. I believe if you take people where they are, and don't put them down, they will move from point A to point B. It's a political decision I made a couple of years ago to be that way. So to them, my listeners, I became an individual. But I'm not. For most of my life, I was a nigger. So you write a couple of books and you're on the radio and suddenly you're an individual. I was in no danger of being under any illusion about being an individual, and this only helps remind me that when I say something white folk don't like, I'm still a nigger, you know, ain't nothing changed. They will view me as they seek to view me, not as I define myself. They won't come to me and find out. I don't want my listeners or anybody to ever forget that any differences between me and the young brother on the block with a .38 in his belt are only superficial.

Q: *Did* The New York Times *ever contact you to find out what you thought?*

A: Never, never. The story broke in the early Thursday morning edition of the *Times*. The *New York Post* called me at 3 A.M. and asked me my reaction, and they printed it. New York's Channel 2 (WCBS) has interviewed me twice, even though they only used ten or fifteen seconds once, but *The New York Times* never contacted me about any of it. They published a few sentences from the WBAI statement on it. They, more than any other news media in New York, I hold responsible for this problem, and I'm really very, very bitter about the way they have handled it. I mean, they don't realize it, not that it matters, but they have set the black community up for the most dire of consequences—given the hatred of blacks which exists and which I think Jews have been surprised to feel in themselves. What if Nixon makes any moves against the black community in toto? You see, I will never forget the *Times* editorial on the death of Malcolm X. They said he who lives by the sword shall die by the sword, and good riddance. That is exactly what they said. If anything is being created in the city, it's an anti-black hysteria which I have not even seen in the South. This is the second time it's happened since I've been here. The first time was in 1964—when the attempt was made to close the World's Fair on the first day, and was followed by the whole "Blood Brothers" myth and the Harlem Six case. I thought I was back down South. I really feel that the reaction of even sedate middle-class black people I've been in contact with has been one of "I have no choice but to go out in the streets and start shooting people." No, they don't even give us the benefit of the doubt that maybe we have a thought-out position. They hear the dog bark and so they react and they say that is what the dog is barking about.

Q: *And the Jews who are now so fearful seem unable to recognize the fear that black people feel?*

A: Yeah, right. I can sit down and be interviewed, talk on the radio, write and all this, but whites have to communicate with that fifteen-year-old kid on the block with the .38 in his belt; he ain't going to talk to them like I do. If he sees 100,000 white people on the street marching on City Hall, marching against *The New York Times,* that will communicate to him, but don't tell him about no good white folks or no good Jews, because he is not an individual. They are not going to ask him, did you major in English or did you shine your shoes this morning—they are going to shoot him.

Q: *Do you think it is going to get worse?*

A: Hey, it is election year. 1969 in New York City is going to be so bad. You know, I would not be surprised if Mayor Lindsay takes a trip to Israel before the election. And if Mayor Lindsay has totally written off the black community, he is running scared and whoever the Democrats put up—you already have hints that they are going to use the school thing, they are going to use the law and order thing, they are going to use . . .

Q: *The first candidate is James Scheuer, the Congressman from the Bronx, who has a good voting record in Congress, but is so far running in part on a law and order program.*

A: Right. And I think that this election is going to so further divide this city and exacerbate what now exists—and what now exists is thousands of tons of TNT—that, you know, I feel like we are sitting in this damn canoe going down the Colorado Rapids and there ain't nothin' nobody can do because they never believe what black people say anyway. We screamed racism for 400 years. It was not believed until the Kerner Commission comes out and says, hey, there's racism. Now all the white folks say, "Yeah, there's racism in America, that's right!" We've been saying it all along. So that once again, we're asking, where are those people who understand, why aren't they saying something?

# A Negro Speaks to Jews

To say that Negroes are anti-Semitic is to deny the humanity of both Negroes and Jews. Every human being is by nature ambivalent in his loves and hatreds. On a personal level the individual one loves most, often becomes the object of the most intense hatred. The child loves its parents but also hates them intensely when they must exercise control or deny a trifling privilege that seems important to him. The adult loves other adults who are mentally attuned to the ideals that he considers right and just, and hates others who seem to deny him his rights. To say that Negroes love or hate Jews or that Jews love or hate Negroes is to say that neither group is composed of human beings with the normal human components of virtues and weaknesses.

I, an African-American adult, respect and love many Jews with whom I work and in whom I confide personal and family problems as they confide in me. The longer our association lasts, the closer we become as we realize that our problems are the universal problems of mankind.

As a black American, living in a Negro community, I can empathize with the human problems of the poor Jewish couple eking out a miserable existence in the local candy store. I feel an emotional response to the wife when she tells me of a sick child at home in the care of an older child. She must help her husband in the store because he speaks little English and is easily frustrated by the teasing and the petty pilfering of some of the neighborhood youths.

She also bears the hostility of some prejudiced colored folk who, despite the evidence of their eyes, insist on identifying her with "the rich Jews who take bags of money out of the Negro ghetto every night to deposit their ill-gotten gains in a Chase National Bank, which thereupon uses this money to buy bonds in South Africa to keep apartheid a going concern." As a mother, I know about sick children. As a wife I know about protecting a husband from committing suicide by instinctively lashing out against his tormentors. How could I possibly hate these people who are trapped in the same vicious cycle in which I am caught?

Yet, as a black adult, I too have my "Antis." When my Jewish colleagues tell me that I must struggle for recognition in these United States as they did when they migrated here a generation or two ago, I agree. When they tell me I must be peaceful and affable while conducting the struggle and that I must disassociate myself immediately and vocally

Elise C. Rollock was an assistant principal in the New York City public school system.
Originally published in *Jewish Currents* 22, no. 2 (February 1968): 13–15. Copyright © 1968 by Jewish Currents, Inc. Reprinted with permission of *Jewish Currents*.

from those who talk militantly and those who throw rocks, my "Antis" come rushing forth. I know and I am sure they know that no struggle has ever been won by people sitting down and chanting, "We shall overcome, some day."

When a Jewish colleague of mine goes to South Africa and writes back that life is wonderful there, "no civil rights demonstrations and no riots"; when he is welcomed back among his complacent colleagues and chided gently for this *faux pas,* my "Antis" boil over again.

All life consists of a struggle to reach the ideal. The ideal for each of us is the same, the development of the best qualities of our own humanity and the recognition of these qualities in all other human beings. When any group, whether Negro or Jewish, decides that the acquisition of money and power can substitute for the human ideal of concern for one's brothers, that group is in trouble.

Anti-Semitism among Negroes arises very often from the well-meaning attitude of some Jews which says, in effect: "See where we are. You can become just as rich and just as important if you will only become educated. Stop fighting the Establishment and get into it, as we did."

Any schoolboy, black or white, in New York City, can accept that statement at face value. The Establishment he knows is largely Jewish. Most of his teachers and his school principal are likely to be Jewish. He later learns that these positions of authority were achieved at tremendous cost to generations of Jews who struggled to educate their children to fill them.

The black adult, however, realizes that he now has an additional hurdle to face. Jewish members of the Establishment, ready with good advice as to how they made it, have no intention of jeopardizing their hard-won positions by advocating the right of another group to come in. They would be more than human if they did. Therefore, if the African-American wishes to join the Establishment he faces a struggle not only with the so-called Christians but also with those Jews who keep telling him, "See how we did it."

It should be obvious to all of us that a democracy which permits the murder of a Chaney, a Schwerner, a Goodman to go unpunished [see appendix at end of chapter] has no regard for the rights of its African-American nor its Jewish citizens. Therefore, the stance of the Jewish liberal who tells us, "we have arrived. Do as we did and you too will arrive," is utterly ridiculous. The Jew who fights on the side of human rights is fighting his own battle for survival, whether he is standing beside a Negro or another Jew.

The question of anti-Semitism is irrelevant and meaningless in the context of our struggle for human rights. More important, it puts a handle to something that endangers us all. The pilfering black youth who snatches your wallet or who breaks your store window does not do it because you are Jewish. He would as soon do it to me. The Jew who refuses to rent an apartment to me in his building doesn't do it because I am black. He also refuses to rent to another Jew whose old-world customs would embarrass his middle class tenants.

Unquestionably, there is at least as much anti-Semitism among certain Jews, against the Jew whose manners and customs seem to fit an ancient stereotype, as there is anti-Negroism among certain middle class Negroes who deplore the manners and customs of the unsophisticated, loud-mouthed Negro. It is ironic for one group to ask the members of any other group to accept us and love us as a group when none of us can accept and love our own group in its entirety.

Both as individuals and as groups we are involved in the struggle to reach the full development of our own humanity and the recognition of humanity's best qualities in our fellow man. It is necessary that we cooperate with those who are fighting the same battle. It is also essential that we awaken the complacent in our own groups who think their battle is already won.

Had Andrew Goodman been slain in a foreign land with an American passport in his pocket, his murderers would have been sought out and punished immediately lest the mighty forces of the United States move in to make this an international incident. Has the "self help and mutual responsibility that Jews have practiced from 1880 to 1914" helped to avenge the death of Andrew Goodman? Has it made it safe for a Jew to travel in Mississippi, with or without a beard? Or does it mean that Jews are willing to write off their casualties in the struggle because certain Negroes are being "abrasive" in saying to smug Jews the same harsh words they are saying to other complacent whites and blacks who think they can rest on their laurels now that the battle is won.

The battle, my friends, has just begun. If you wish to pick up your toy guns and go home because I call you a harsh name, then by all means go in peace. I can only hope that you will discover, before it is too late, that this struggle for human rights is not just a Negro struggle in which you have the choice of helping us or not. It is also your struggle. You bought it with the blood of Andrew Goodman and Michael Schwerner, just as I bought it with the blood of James Chaney and all those others who have gone in the same way before and since.

You and I, my friends, are in the same leaky boat. Neither you nor I have a choice of leaving or staying. It doesn't really matter what we say to each other at this point. Perhaps we just ought to stop talking and keep rowing together, if we wish to survive.

## [APPENDIX]
### TRIAL IN MISSISSIPPI

Following a verdict Oct. 20 by a federal jury that convicted 7 of 18 white men of conspiring to deprive James Chaney, Andrew Goodman and Michael Schwerner of their civil rights, Federal Judge W. Harold Cox handed down his sentences Dec. 29. None got the maximum of 10 years plus a $5,000 fine. Two were sentenced to 10 years; two to six years, including Cecil R. Price, chief deputy sheriff of Neshoba County; three to three years. The defendants are appealing the verdict, given by an all-white jury in Meridian, Miss. Judge Cox stated that the prison terms were "indeterminate," thus the convicts are immediately eligible for parole! Since murder is not, by present law, a federal crime, the prosecution could try them only on the conspiracy charge. The state can still try them for murder . . .

# A Negro Discusses Anti-Semitism

The recent article published in *JEWISH CURRENTS* in Feb., 1968, written by Mrs. Elise C. Rollock, a Negro assistant principal in the New York schools, leads one to conclude that anti-Semitic sentiments and attitudes are simply normal behavior in human beings. Mrs. Rollock wrote: "To say that Negroes are anti-Semitic is to deny the humanity of both Negroes and Jews." In other words, to be anti-Semitic is to be human. She argues that substantiating evidence for the phenomenon may be observed in the selective and discriminating behavior in all human beings in a variety of social settings.

We do not deny the validity of the concept that all human beings seem to be highly selective and discriminating in social areas. However, we do deny that anti-Semitism is a necessary concomitant of the way human beings see reality.

There is a recent and frightening upsurge of anti-Semitic pronouncements by Negro militants, who are in the vanguard of the civil rights movement in the United States. Anti-Semitism is generalized and universalistic in nature and serves an altogether different function in society. It is not a consequence nor concomitant of man's discriminating powers. One is first anti-Semitic or prejudiced toward Negroes; the results are expressed in the forms of segregation, discrimination and in the extreme phenomenon of genocide.

Generalized attitudes and sentiments of human beings result from the socialization process by which an individual learns to live in a group. One does not make a particular choice as in particularized behavior. Quite the contrary occurs. The process of socialization precludes the opportunity for one to discover the irrationality of anti-Semitism without deliberate and conscious effort. Anti-Semitism is anti-social and is not required for the human being to survive in his environment. Anti-Semitism is a force in society for annihilation of human beings rather than for survival. When a Negro expresses and even justifies anti-Jewish sentiments, he is expressing attitudes acquired during the socialization process in a society in which anti-Semitism has been accepted and given channels of expression.

The following is a recent example of anti-Semitic sentiments pronounced by a Negro militant: The Negro has identified with the colored people of the Arab World and is responding to "Israeli acts of imperialism" against his brothers. Also the Jews in the United States have been attacked and identified as the sole exploiters in the Negro

In 1968, Rayner W. Mann was a teacher in the Los Angeles City schools.
Originally published in *Jewish Currents* 22, no. 6 (June 1968): 14–17. Copyright © 1968 by Jewish Currents, Inc. Reprinted with permission of *Jewish Currents*.

ghettos. The attackers neglect to point out that exploitation is a necessary feature of all business interests regardless of their ethnic identification.

The irrationality of such attacks may be clearly seen in the existing and historical stance of Arab leaders in regard to colonial economic exploiters of both the African and Arab masses. Neither the Arab World nor its leadership took a position against the shipment of African slaves to the United States, the enslavement of Africans in the Sudan nor the exploitation of the Arab masses. The economic reality is that Arab leaders collaborated with colonial exploiters.

Why then attack the Jews? Certainly there are other vulnerable minorities that could serve just as well the function of a scapegoat for the oppressed Negro. The explanation is that the Jews are an easy scapegoat, made so by centuries of persecution and propaganda throughout the Christian world. Economic stereotypes have replaced the old Christian notions and anti-Semitism is perpetuated in Western society. The Negro has acquired the prejudices against Jews and accepted the economic and social myths. Therefore, instead of attacking the Jews in the name of Christianity or Aryan purity, the Negro denounces the Jew as an economic exploiter in the ghetto in the name of social and economic justice.

A look at the structure of the ghetto is important in understanding the phenomenon in the present social context. A most striking feature of the ghetto is the absence of a business class among Negroes. The lack of opportunity and capital along with emerging large chain-markets are factors which militate against the Negro's ability to rise as entrepreneur.

The businesses of immigrant groups remained in the ghettos as their community moved into better living conditions, for they too are a relatively insecure group, sometimes merely subsisting from the returns of the shop. When they retire, their progeny rarely continues the business, for they have become educated for other economic pursuits. Therefore, when the large supermarket is established in the ghetto, the Negro mistakenly assumes that Jewish shopkeepers have become rich and acquired supermarkets by exploiting the Negro community.

Contrary to sociological research findings, Negro-Jew proximity and relationships have not resulted in eliminating the racial prejudice in either group. The Negro masses too are victims of the social disease that exists throughout the Western world. Blatant anti-Semitism exists in the Negro community despite the disproportionate numbers of Jewish youth who have gone into the Southern areas, lending their skills to the Negro organizations, even dying with Negro youth at the hands of white Southern extremists. The Jewish community has also been a great source of funds for the civil rights movement.

Lacking an independent frame of reference and code of ethics, the Negro has been unable critically to assess the values of the society in which he finds himself. It is not necessary here to repeat the history of Negro enslavement and dehumanization in the United States. However, a disastrous consequence of the Negro's historical experience in the United States is that he was stripped of his cultural base for evaluating the norms and values of the oppressor. This cultural condition grossly contributes to the narrow perspective observed in the literary works of Negroes in the United States. This is the disadvantage point from which the Negro begins to assess his condition in the social structure.

Negro militants who call for economic and political power and direct an attack against Jewish economic interests in the Negro ghettos are reflecting this narrow perspective when they fail to perceive the economic system in its relation to the economic oppression of their people. Fundamental to Stokely Carmichael's concept of black power is the "take over" of the economic means in the black community, and since the Negro has been conditioned to believe that the Jews control their economic destiny, it follows that the Jews must be driven from this base of economic and political power in the ghetto. Missing is the ability to see that the interests of the former master and the racist elements in the society are buttressed and served through this conflict.

It is an accepted fact that Negro political representation can be achieved only by forming meaningful alliances with other minorities; the Jews have been both manifestly and latently a dominant political ally. Even in the Black Belt of the United States, where Negroes outnumber whites, minority coalitions are fundamental to the achievement of Negro representation. Financial resources for independent political efforts simply do not exist in the Negro community. All this suggests that anti-Semitism does not serve the interests of the Negro civil rights movement.

Then why has the Jew become the target of attack of the Negro radical? Till the present generation, the Negro in the United States has unreservedly accepted the culture of his white master and thus became infected with the virus of anti-Semitism, which is endemic to the Christian world. In the act of hating Jews, the Negro joins the Christian world in using the Jew as a scapegoat. Like prejudice against Negroes, anti-Semitism is one of the symptoms in the racist syndrome.

When the Negro radical seizes upon anti-Semitism to mobilize the Negro in the ghetto around achieving economic and political goals, and to account for the economic condition of Negroes in the ghetto, he follows the illogic of the lynch mobs in the South as observed by several social scientists: "If the per-acre value of cotton in the southeastern section of the United States is low, the number of lynchings of Negroes in that area is high." Lynch mobs do not relate their actions to the cotton price. However, in both cases, the justification is the same. The scapegoat has been fashioned by the society; there is no sanction against persecuting or destroying a scapegoat.

Mrs. Rollock states that the Negro sees the system as his enemy and sees the Jews as a part of the system. We can add: so is the Negro a part of the system as expressed by his goals, aspirations and expectations. The Negro entrepreneur is also forced in the profit-making system to exploit his own people.

In the Russian pogroms in 1881, the same paradox was observed: complaints of Russian serfs had substance. Through propaganda, attacks of the dispossessed were directed away from the real enemy and toward the also victimized Jews. They were both victims of a system of economic oppression.

There is no doubt that the power structure in the United States will not accept the concept of redistribution of the economic resources in order to create a society in which all people will share in the goods of the society more equitably. It is an imperative that the Negro re-evaluates the methods of achieving his economic share.

The Negro must examine sentiments and attitudes of anti-Semitism in the present social context in terms of its meaning for perpetuating the status quo in this society. Present solutions articulated and outlined by some Negro militants can have only disastrous consequences for both minorities. Negroes and Jews must cooperate to secure necessary equitable means for accomplishing this transition. Negro leadership must take time out to explore the problems and the issue of anti-Semitism in the Negro civil rights movement. Creative means rather than old techniques of the oppressor must be devised for achieving black people's economic goals. Black power cannot be achieved by the Negro's joining the ranks of those who commit crimes against any minority in the name of social progress.

KITTY O. COHEN

# Black-Jewish Relations in 1984
## A Survey of Black U.S. Congressmen

On 6 February 1985, twenty-four Black and Jewish leaders met on Capitol Hill in a closed conference. The purpose of the meeting was to hold a frank dialogue on the state of Black-Jewish relations. This conference concluded the first stage of a joint effort made by the President of the World Jewish Congress, through the Institute of Jewish Affairs, and the Chairman of the Interreligious and the Community Relations Department of the World Zionist Organization. Within the framework of this joint effort, they commissioned this writer to conduct a survey among the members of the Congressional Black Caucus on their respective perceptions of Black-Jewish relations and on the problems and perspectives of co-operation between the two communities.

This article is a summarized version of the report based on the survey, which was submitted to the Washington Conference of Black and Jewish Leaders on 6 February. The report is an analysis of the interviews with 16 of the 21 members of the Congressional Black Caucus of the 98th Congress. These 16 Representatives make up 76.2 per cent of the Black Caucus members. They are among the highest Black elected officials in the United States. Even though the respondents are few in number, they are the voices of millions of constituents, as well as the moulders of opinion in their communities.

This survey was not intended to be a piece of definitive research with a statistically valid sample of the Black community as a whole. Additionally, it was not intended to establish facts; rather, its purpose was to assess the perceptions of the Representatives on social and political issues involving relations between the Black and Jewish communities, the impact of Jesse Jackson's presidential campaign, issues such as the Jewish bond to Israel, Israel's relations with Black Africa and Israel's relations with South Africa.

The sixteen Representatives who took part in the survey were interviewed individually and responded orally to the questionnaire, which consisted of fifteen questions. Due to the complexity of the issues and limited time frame of the interviews, the questions varied in presentation and alternated between open-ended questions which provided opportunities for amplifications and comments, and closed questions, many of which allowed for multiple responses. All interviews were conducted between 7 June and 13 November 1984.

The sixteen members of the Congressional Black Caucus[1] who participated in this survey are a diverse group. Their backgrounds, districts and political careers vary

Kitty O. Cohen is the author of *Black-Jewish Relations: The View from the State Capitols.*
Originally published in *Patterns of Prejudice* (London) 19, no. 2 (1985): 3–17. Copyright © 1985, Patterns of Prejudice. Reprinted by permission of Sage Publications Ltd.

widely. The only constant is that all are Democrats. The districts of the respondents are evenly split between those that are more than 50 per cent Black, and those that are 50 per cent Black or less. Black Caucus members chair or are high-ranking members of important committees and subcommittees. Most Congressional Black Caucus members sit on committees related to public affairs.

Congressional Black Caucus members are moving into powerful positions within the Congress. Black Congressmen are rising not only because of the seniority system but because of their hard work and political acumen. Though the Congressional Black Caucus is not monolithic, it is now a cohesive, increasingly powerful group of national Black leaders who are in the vanguard of Congressional efforts in civil rights and social welfare issues. A leading member can now say, 'These days you don't have to hold up signs to demand to get into meetings. We convene the meetings.'[2]

## DOMESTIC (US) ISSUES

*The Image of the American Jewish Community*

The initial question concerned the image of the American Jewish community in the eyes of the American Black community. The question focused on what distinguishes the Jewish community from other communities and whether the Jews are part of the ruling majority establishment in the United States.

Of the 16 respondents interviewed, 3 made the distinction between their own views and those of their community. Seven out of the 16 respondents believe the communities they represent see the Jewish community in ethnic terms, that is, defined by race, nationality and culture. Two see the Jews strictly in religious terms, and 5 see them as both ethnic and religious. The remaining 2 identify the Jewish community as primarily White.

Of those who conceive of the Jews as an ethnic minority, some see Jews as being predominantly bound by culture, others by nationality, and others by race. Some reject the religious component completely. Some respondents who reject the religious/ethnic minority question altogether see the Jews as distinguished by the economic factor. Two expressed the view that the Jew is also defined in terms of his economic contacts with the Black community. According to one, it depends on 'who chases the cheque'. Another sees them as 'rich white people'. Yet another perceives them as primarily an urban group. Some consider the Jews primarily Whites. They are friendly and understanding but the bottom line is that they are White.

Six respondents specifically referred to the political activity of the Jewish community. It seems that while Blacks perceive the Jewish community as politically active, they do not necessarily categorize all Jews as being affiliated with any one political party or ideology. One respondent attributed the increase in Jewish political prominence to their emergent economic power.

Though the Black perception is that Jews are sensitive to questions of civil rights and discrimination, Blacks also see Jews as patronizing to them. This view reflects a general resentment in segments of the Black community that believe Jews feel superior— socially, culturally and intellectually. In the perception of many Blacks, Jewish ethnocentricity precludes an adequate appreciation of other groups' accomplishments.

One respondent, perhaps projecting his own racial consciousness and the historic affinity and alliance between Blacks and Jews in the 1950s and 1960s, explicitly defined Jews as a race. Another commented on the alliance between Blacks and Jews in the civil rights movement, acknowledging the strong Jewish support which helped the Black community win the voting Rights Act of 1965.

On the question of whether Jews are considered part of the ruling establishment, 13 replied in the affirmative, and 1 did not answer the question. One respondent said some Blacks see the Jews as part of the ruling establishment and other Blacks do not, and another said Blacks see some Jews as part of the establishment.

The image of the Jewish community in the Black community is that of an ethnic minority which is economically well-off, politically organized, powerful, and part of the ruling White establishment. Although Jews are singled out as a friendly group within the White community, in the final analysis they are still part of it.

The consensus of 14 out of 16 respondents is that the relationship between Blacks and Jews has deteriorated in the last year, as 'a greater realization of divergent points of views has increased the potential for or perception of conflict'. Eleven out of 16 respondents attributed the tensions between the Black and the Jewish communities and the deterioration of the relationship between them to the Jewish reactions to Jesse Jackson and to remarks he made during his presidential campaign.

Ten of the 16 respondents felt that the Jewish reaction to Jackson was exaggerated: 'The Jews attempted to punish Jesse Jackson, they reacted to his candidacy with excessive hostility'.[3]

Two of the respondents mentioned the Jewish Defence League (JDL) by name and others referred to it indirectly as having played a role in the worsening of relations between Blacks and Jews. One respondent made the point: 'People in my community don't make the distinction between the JDL and the AJC [American Jewish Congress], just as often in the Jewish community people don't make the distinction between the Nation of Islam and the Baptist Ministers' Conference'. Blacks and Jews apparently formulated an image of each others' communities based on the more vocal and extreme elements of the community. Jews reacted primarily to Jackson's and Farrakhan's remarks while the Blacks reacted primarily to JDL statements.[4] Those respondents who expressed reservations about the Jewish criticism of Farrakhan thought the Jewish reaction to his racism was out of proportion, even if they did not support him themselves.[5]

Two of the respondents also attributed the decline in relations in part to New York's Mayor Koch and his public comments that all Blacks were basically antisemitic. Five of the respondents observed that deterioration had occurred on a national political level and not on the local district level of community relations. One said it had come up in connection with aid to Israel. Three connected the deterioration to present socioeconomic conditions. In general it appears that Black-Jewish relations were not as important an issue in the Black community during the campaign year as they were in the Jewish community. Nine respondents mentioned that unconscious anti-Jewish feelings in the Black community had come to the surface in the past year. One viewed the dispelling of myths and unrealistic perceptions in a positive light and observed that dealing with honest feelings furthers co-operation.

### Co-operation between Blacks and Jews

Another question dealt with possible co-operation between the Black and Jewish communities and the priority given to various issues on the Black agenda. Most of the Representatives believe that there is sufficient ground for co-operation between the two communities. This consensus is based on genuine concern for issues of priority in their communities and a realistic appraisal of the extent of possible co-operation with the Jewish community.

There is unanimity in the responses that education is the top priority on their agenda. Blacks see education as the primary instrument for achieving social equality. There is little doubt that affirmative action is near the top of the Black agenda. Quotas are seen by most as a means of achieving the goal of social justice. One respondent echoed the words of Vernon Jordan: 'Our differences about affirmative action are based on our different historical experiences. Many Jews see quotas as a ceiling to their aspiration; Blacks see quotas as a floor. So let us agree to disagree on this issue'.[6] Some relegated affirmative action to a lower position on their list because they believed it to be a divisive issue. They instead chose to focus on mutual Black-Jewish interests and responded in terms of 'possible fruitful co-operation'.

In spite of the differences in their districts and backgrounds, the order of priorities is similar for all respondents. The cumulative order of priorities is as follows: (1) education; (2) affirmative action and quotas; (3) youth employment; (4) Black business; (5) youth vocational and technical training; (6) women's employment; (7) medicare; (8) one-parent families; (9) infant mortality; (10) food programmes.

The respondents were also asked to assess impediments to co-operation between the Black and Jewish communities. Eight of the 16 answered that the main impediments are mutual misconceptions. This points to a lack of understanding between the two communities—a lack of contact at the grassroots level:

> Therefore, you've got two communities which are insulated and isolated and know very little about each other. The average 18 to 25 year-old Black doesn't know anything about the Jewish community. They are not cognizant of the 'civil rights alliance', they've never seen that. The same is true in the Jewish community.

Another respondent attributed the misconceptions to misunderstandings 'perpetuated by press stories'.

Three respondents said differences in priorities are the main impediment to co-operation. 'Blacks perceive the Jewish community as being overwhelmingly interested in Israel as opposed to social welfare issues at home'. Seven of the respondents asserted that differences on issues, in particular affirmative action and quotas, are the main problem. Other issues of concern which were brought up by the respondents included: militarization in foreign policy, South Africa, and Jewish fear of Jesse Jackson.

There are obviously both substantive and perceptual differences between the Black and Jewish communities. To lessen the misconceptions each community holds of the other, education and information at all levels seem necessary; different means would be required to resolve some of the substantive issues.

Another question examined to what extent common action and joint effort on social issues would benefit the Black community and Black leadership. Although the question was geared to the Black community and Black leadership alone, many of the answers referred to the possible benefits of joint efforts to the Jewish community as well. One said that 'more progress' for Blacks could be achieved through mutual effort. One noted a rise in anti-Black feelings among Jews and said that co-operation between the two communities would reduce racist feelings.

Twelve respondents discussed the advantages of Black-Jewish co-operation for the Jewish community. Eight of the 16 spoke of communication barriers and a recent increase in antisemitism and expressed the belief that co-operation could address both of these problems. Co-operation between the two communities would 'fight antisemitism' as one of them put it. Although one respondent said that there were 'barriers' on certain issues that would be difficult to overcome, another said joint efforts would help the two communities to understand each other better.

The respondents also discussed the 'down side' or disadvantages for both Blacks and Jews. For Blacks the problem has to do with the role of leadership. One said 'liberals have a tendency to want to lead'. Four respondents spoke directly about the quality of the partnership they viewed as a precondition for any joint efforts. They all stressed an intangible but important factor: the perception that one leadership has of the other. One stressed that it must be a real partnership. It also must be a true joint effort based on mutual respect. Another respondent added that co-operation can only take place if Jews become part of Jackson's 'Rainbow Coalition'; that is, if they actively support that coalition.

Certain trends appeared in the answers: Jews and Blacks must work as peers, without patronizing each other; joint efforts would help the Blacks achieve their goals and would generate more understanding in the Black community for the Jewish community and would decrease antisemitism.

The respondents were then asked whether co-operation with the Jewish community would enhance the election potential of more Black candidates on the national, state and local levels. Eleven respondents believe co-operation with other communities will help elect Black representatives. Two of the respondents focused on aspects of Jewish political activity that could benefit Blacks, such as Jewish fund-raising. Intercommunity co-operation with Jews would enhance Black political initiatives far more than co-operation with other ethnic groups, they argued.

While one respondent viewed a Jewish voting bloc for Blacks as 'desirable', he felt that financial assistance by Jews was the 'down side' for Blacks. It thus appears that the respondents who see co-operation as potentially helpful put the emphasis on the ability of the Jewish community to provide financial and organizational support. Another respondent said benefits would result if Blacks and Jews worked together on redrawing voting districts because it is at the state level that Blacks have the most difficulty.

Three respondents said co-operation would not or need not enhance the election potential of Blacks. One said that co-operation would help because 'people vote their ethnic groups; it's a practical political reality'.[7] Another said co-operation probably would not help because

> it does not necessarily follow that members of a particular community would support a candidate because he's Black and because the communities have worked together on a particular agenda. It comes down to what the candidate's positions are on the issues. People will support a candidate based on the issue, which they should, not on the colour of his skin.

A third respondent did not think that co-operation would enhance the election of Blacks because Jews have little influence in the areas in which Blacks need the most help. 'The real battleground is in the South, but the Jews exert little political power in 8 of the 9 southern states.'

The respondents were asked whether joint efforts between Blacks and Jews would help influence policy-making on the following issues: the appointment policy to the Civil Rights Commission and the revitalization of that commission; the appointment of minority justices to the Supreme Court; the appointment of minority representatives to the two major political parties; and changes in the primaries and the electoral college system.

Fourteen of the respondents believe that the coalition between Blacks and Jews may exercise a positive influence on the issues. In all cases the majority of the respondents said mutual efforts could help influence policy-making, but there were variations in the possible benefits in each area. Fourteen of the 16 said joint efforts between Blacks and Jews could have a positive effect on the appointment policy to the Civil Rights Commission and the revitalization of the Commission. Fourteen respondents saw benefits from joint efforts in helping minority justices be appointed to the Supreme Court. Two respondents specifically noted that when Jews served on the Supreme Court it passed decisions which helped minorities. Thirteen respondents said it would be possible to bring about changes in the primary and electoral college systems through the common efforts of Blacks and Jews. Regarding the Civil Rights Commission and the Supreme Court, 3 respondents noted that even joint efforts would not help during the Reagan administration. Three respondents expressed doubts about how far even joint efforts could change the primaries or the electoral college system because it is 'too deep-seated and traditional to change'.

While 15 respondents thought joint efforts would help minorities get represented in the political parties, they said it would only be possible in the Democratic Party because the Republican Party 'is a party of elites'. Another said there was not much that could be done about minority representation in the parties, because 'the Democratic Party already has 90 per cent of the Black vote. It has a large percentage of the Jewish vote too. The Democratic Party doesn't utilize the base it has when it comes down to the Black majority'.

It appears from the answers to this question that there is a positive attitude to common efforts between Blacks and Jews, and a desire to co-operate on these issues. What also emerges is the perception among the respondents of an affinity of ideals and interests between them and the Jews and a conviction that together the two communities may achieve more than each could separately.

*Social Discrimination*

Asked if there is social discrimination against Jews in the US, 14 respondents replied in the affirmative. One said that discrimination is not as explicit as before and not as bad as that against Blacks.

Regarding Jewish discrimination against Blacks, 6 respondents answered that Jewish attitudes were different from those of other Whites. Another said that Jews discriminate just as much as other Whites, but not because of the same racist reasons. Concerning executive employment, one respondent said 'Jews look out for each other and hire each other, thus Blacks are indirectly discriminated against'. With respect to integrated neighbourhoods one respondent said segregation in the Jewish community is based on economic standards and not on racial prejudice. Finally, in discussing intermarriage one respondent said, 'Jews look for other Jews. They seem to want to stick to their own'.

What emerges from these answers is a fairly even split between those seeing Jewish attitudes as different from those of other Whites, and those seeing them as the same. Two respondents expressed a firm belief that Jewish attitudes were different. In the cases of executive employment and intermarriage, two said Jewish attitudes were different in that they were worse than other Whites.

In general the Jews are perceived as being more liberal than other Whites. Many respondents explicitly said that Jews are 'more sympathetic', 'much more liberal', 'generally regarded as being more liberal', 'more sensitive, more just, more equitable', and 'more progressive, liberal, and open-minded'. Those who disagreed said, 'There is very little difference; "when you are White you're right".'

The respondents were asked about their own experience in intercommunity relations. All 16 answered that they have had interactions with Jews on various levels— private, social, business, public, or political. Thirteen said they have had private or family contacts with Jews, all said they have had social, public, and political contacts, 7 said that they have had religious contacts, and 10 said they have had business contacts with the Jewish community. There appears to be a wealth of contacts on the leadership level between the two communities. The answers indicate a good working relationship, especially on the public and political levels. It is not unreasonable to assume that Black leadership would be interested in seeing more co-operation between the two communities on the grass-roots level, if they have reason to believe such co-operation would enhance their own efforts in their communities.

*Jewish Opposition to Jesse Jackson*

In response to a question on the Black community's perception of Jewish opposition to Jesse Jackson, the Black leaders interviewed understood the political dimension of Jewish opposition to Jesse Jackson but, as one respondent noted, the real reasons for the Jewish opposition did not come out in the media. (Once Jewish opposition to Jesse Jackson was dubbed 'an issue' by the media, it received a disproportionate amount of media attention, which only increased the potential for conflict between the two communities.) This opposition was 'often articulated in stereotypical terms offensive to the Black community and leaders'. Twelve of the respondents said Jewish opposition to Jesse Jackson was not seen as opposition to a black candidate. Eight of those indicated that this perception was their own. Their constituents believed that Jewish opposition to Jackson occurred because he is Black. Four said they believed Jewish opposition was because Jackson is Black.

Three of the respondents pointed to Jackson's reference to 'Hymietown' as the reason for the Jewish opposition. One said that if he were a Jew, he 'would think Jesse Jackson's statements bordered on antisemitism'.[8] Among the specific reasons given for Jewish opposition to Jackson were Jackson's stand on political issues, especially on the Middle East and the Palestinian question, and Jackson's controversial relationship with PLO leader Yassir Arafat.

Only one respondent did not see any difference between Jewish and other White opposition to Jackson. Four of the 16 indicated that Jewish opposition is seen as worse than other White opposition, because it comes from a community that the Blacks had considered friends, outside of the rest of a White majority. Six answers dealt with the exaggerated intensity of the reaction of the Jewish community: 'Criticism of Jesse Jackson was much too intense'; 'the Jews overreacted'. Five respondents saw Jewish opposition to Jackson as different from Black opposition because 'people scoff at Black opposition as selling out their brothers. They don't take it seriously.'[9]

What emerges from the responses to this question and from comments throughout the interviews is that Jesse Jackson's campaign has had several effects. First it had a positive impact on the Black community. Jackson's campaign inspired many Blacks to enter the political process and was a dramatic campaign which challenged the system and renewed Blacks' faith in themselves. Second, it had a negative effect on Black-Jewish relations. His positions on international issues such as Israel and the Palestinians, his 'Hymietown' remark, the Farrakhan issue, and the media's use of these issues increased tensions between the two communities. Finally, Jackson's campaign redefined the problem areas between Blacks and Jews. Previously, tensions were based on economic, ethnic and religious antagonisms on the local level and were confined to specific issues such as unemployment, education, affirmative action, and South Africa. Jackson's campaign shifted the focus from the local situational tensions between Blacks and Jews to basic differences between the communities on the national level. We have come full circle. In the first question some respondents said that the Jews are not an issue for the average Black community on the local level. The issue turned up, however, in their own words, on the national level.

### FOREIGN ISSUES

*The Special Bond between Jews and Israel*

Another question addressed the effect of the special bond between the Jewish community and the State of Israel on co-operation between Blacks and Jews. Ten of the respondents answered that the bond between the Jewish community and the State of Israel does affect the co-operation between Blacks and Jews, but their replies varied as to what kind of effect the bond has.

The most commonly expressed reason for a deterioration in the co-operation between Blacks and Jews was Israel's ties with South Africa. Five respondents explicitly cited this as a source of friction.

Four respondents mentioned that an additional note of discord is the extent of American aid to Israel in comparison to American aid to African countries. One noted in general that foreign aid to Israel is a source of disagreement. Another voiced the fear that higher levels of aid to Israel would increase taxes. One respondent expressed 'concern that increased aid for Israel means a lack of funds for Africa'.

Two respondents looked at different sources of tension. One said President Reagan is unsupportive of poor Blacks, and Israel has continued to maintain a relationship with Reagan. Another respondent claimed the issue of moving the American Embassy from Tel Aviv to Jerusalem was controversial and divisive.

Four respondents said *how* the Jewish community relates to Israel has an effect on Black-Jewish relations. One respondent said Jews have not stressed their bond with Israel to the Black community at large. Three respondents said a problem arises because Jews take any Black opposition to the policies of the State of Israel as evidence of antisemitism. One respondent noted Jews have a greater concern for Israel while Blacks have a greater concern for the welfare of the US.

The respondents were also asked to compare the attitude of Jews to Israel with the attitude of Blacks to Black African countries. To this question all of the respondents answered that Jewish ties to Israel are stronger than Blacks' ties to Africa. One respondent viewed these Jewish ties negatively, the other 15 respondents saw the strength of the Jewish commitment to Israel positively.

Five respondents said it would be good for the Black community to develop similar ties to their Black African heritage. While the development of closer ties to Black Africa may benefit the Black community in the United States, such ties are difficult to achieve. Five observed that Africa is a continent of fifty-one states while Israel is just one small country. Others also stressed the effects that years of slavery have had on American Blacks' relations with Africa: 'Slavery cut all ties with Africa'. The last respondent concluded on a positive note: 'the growth of the Black relationship with Africa is moving very rapidly'.

The bond between the Jewish community and the State of Israel is seen negatively in the Black community. In the context of the increasing bond between the American Black community and Black Africa, however, the bond between Jews and Israel is seen in a positive light. It appears from the respondents' answers that the Black community views favourably a spiritual and cultural bond with Black Africa similar to that which exists between the Jews and Israel.

### Perceptions of Israel

Questioned on their perceptions of Israel, the 16 respondents said Israel is a democratic country, not a totalitarian country. Twelve respondents saw the problems of Israel as social and economic rather than racial. One thought the problems 'flow from Ashkenazi and Sefardi social and economic tensions. Tensions inside and outside Israel between Jews and Arabs also have economic grounds'.

Four respondents believed that Israel is a developing country. The other 12 said it is a developed country. To the question of whether or not Israel is theocratic, 8 expressed the opinion that 'Israel is a theocracy'.

In spite of the 8 respondents' perception of Israel as a theocracy—which reflects a negative view—the totality of the answers reflects a positive view of Israel, in light of the unanimity that Israel is a democracy and the majority (12) who do not see the problems of Israel as primarily racial.

The respondents were asked whether Israel is part of the Third World. Three answered in the affirmative, but qualified their replies. One said that Israel is perceived as being part of the Third World. Another said that Israel is part of the Third World, but 'doesn't realize it'. The third said that 'they should be, but I am not sure they consider themselves to be'. One respondent, who believed that Israel is not part of the Third World, qualified his answer by saying: 'Israel is a developing country but that doesn't necessarily mean it is part of the Third World'. Thirteen of the respondents do not perceive Israel as part of the Third World. One remarked that Israel is 'too advanced to be part of the Third World'.

These respondents who see Israel as a Western country gave several reasons. Some focused on Israel's relations with the free world. Others focused on the economic and technical aspects.

The respondents were asked whether Israel deserves American aid and if so, how much? All 16 respondents said that Israel should receive American aid. However, 3 respondents said that Israel should be given only limited aid, and 1 said Israel should be given less aid than it currently receives from America. Three respondents simply said yes, Israel should receive US aid and the remaining 9 said that Israel should receive extensive aid from America. One respondent said more balance is necessary; more consideration should be given to the needs of African countries.

The answers of the respondents can thus be divided into two categories: some judge Israel according to the country's level of technological and industrial development, while others judge it according to its ideological orientation or its political alignment. From both points of view, most answers indicate that Israel is not perceived as part of the Third World—it is too developed according to some; too pro-Western or pro-American according to others.

What emerges from the respondents' replies is an *a priori* favourable attitude to the Third World: as the political orientation of the Third World is seen positively, the fact that Israel is not perceived as part of the Third World is not to Israel's credit. Nevertheless, the respondents' answers with regard to the Third World question do not appear to influence their views when the question of aid to Israel arises: they are unanimous in their support of aid to Israel, although they differ in how much aid should be given.[10]

*South African Trade and Aid to Black Africa*
Another question examined the awareness of the respondents to the facts regarding two issues: the volume of South Africa's trade with various nations;[11] and the extent of aid to Black Africa from various nations.

Thirteen respondents said there is some trade between Black African countries and

South Africa. Thirteen answered that West European countries have trade relations with South Africa to some extent. Regarding US trade with South Africa, 14 answered in the affirmative. Fifteen respondents also answered in the affirmative with regard to Israel.

In the context of this question, 3 respondents used the word 'perception' in their answers. One of these made the following distinction between perception and reality. 'The perception is that South Africa is doing business primarily with the United States and Israel. The reality is that there is some trade with other Black African countries'. Another made the distinction between his own perception and that of his community. 'All of them trade with South Africa in my opinion. In the perception of my constituency it is mostly Israel.' Only 1 of the 16 respondents explicitly ranked Israel lower than Western Europe and the United States.

While Israeli technical training and social development programmes have continued on a steady but limited basis to several Black African countries, the Black community generally is not aware of such aid programmes, as one of the respondents observed. As with the issue of South African trade, a clear distinction between the perceptions of the leadership and those of the community is evident.

### Jews and Apartheid

The respondents were then asked to give their constituents' perceptions of the Jewish attitude toward apartheid and specifically of Jewish opposition to apartheid in the United States, in Israel, and in South Africa. Five respondents said that the Jews were not opposed to apartheid, 7 said the Jews were opposed to apartheid, although 3 of these said they were not strong enough in their opposition.[12] Three said they were unaware of any Jewish opposition to apartheid, and 1 said the Black community had no perception of Jewish opposition to apartheid. Three respondents said that the American Jewish community is opposed to apartheid, 4 said the Jews were not strong enough in opposition and 1 said: 'In theory they are against it, in practice they are not'.

Eight respondents said they were unaware of American Jewish opposition to apartheid. One respondent indicated this might be because Jews fail to relate 'the oppression of Blacks in South Africa to the oppression of Jews in the Soviet Union'.[13] Several respondents made distinctions between their own opinions and those of their constituents: 'The biggest advocates of anti-apartheid in Congress other than the Black Caucus are the Jews . . . we had the Solarz Amendment. . . . The Black community would not be aware of the Solarz Amendment.' Similarly, a majority of 11 said they were unaware of Israeli opposition to apartheid. One respondent said the Israelis do not oppose apartheid, 2 said they do, 1 said they do on an individual level but not in an organized way.[14] One said Israeli Jews are not strong enough in their opposition. Another respondent commented that 'some policies seem to indicate an evolving opposition to apartheid, as I see it. My constituents are unaware of this'.

Although Jews have been strongly represented in the White resistance in South Africa, 10 of the respondents said they were unaware of South African Jewish opposition to apartheid. Two respondents said South African Jews are not opposed to apartheid and 2 said they are. 'The masses of Black people are unaware [of South African Jewish opposition to apartheid] . . . On the leadership level there is an awareness that the most progressive elements of the Afrikaaner community are often led by Jewish South Africans'. One respondent distinguished between his opinion and that of his constituents: 'Some great liberators and statespeople in South Africa are Jews. My constituents don't know this. . . . That's the purpose of Black-Jewish dialogue'.

What emerges from these responses is that this is one of the areas in which more communication and information between the two communities is needed.

## CONCLUSION

Throughout the interviews there emerged a general consensus among the respondents that the relationship between Blacks and Jews has deteriorated in the past year. The majority of the respondents attributed the deterioration of the relationship between the communities to Jewish reactions to Jackson and to remarks he made during his presidential campaign. More than half of the respondents believe unconscious anti-Jewish feelings have come to the surface.

What happened during the 1984 presidential election campaign is in some ways new. Of course, there were strains before, but the causes were different. Whereas anti-Jewish and anti-Black feelings had centred on situational, socio-economic and—only in rare cases such as Ambassador Andrew Young's resignation from his UN post—political factors, the strains in 1984 focused more on political issues and could perhaps be attributed to a new kind of antisemitism brought to national attention. All of a sudden, thanks to front page, editorial page, and dinner-table attention to the Jesse Jackson remark, a new kind of racism of an almost socially acceptable variety was revealed. This has been detrimental to both Blacks and Jews. Ironically, Jackson's remark pulled the two communities together under the same umbrella—controversy. Perhaps, as one of the Representatives expressed it, 'This created an opportunity to deal with honest feelings and to dispel myths, to destroy unrealistic perceptions and to begin to work together; it's better that way'.

This positive attitude towards joint efforts by the Jewish and Black communities was reflected in the recommendations which emerged from the survey. All the respondents favour co-operation. However, some respondents said that the success of such co-operation would depend on the quality of the partnership between the two communities: joint efforts must be based upon honest, realistic dialogue and mutual respect.

On international issues, the respondents envisioned dialogue and communication that would afford the Black community at large a better understanding of the bond between the American Jewish community and Israel, increase factual understanding of Israeli development assistance to Black Africa, increase understanding of Israel's trade with South Africa, and increase awareness in the Black community of Jewish opposition to apartheid. On the national level, the respondents welcome Jewish organizational and financial support for selected political issues such as the appointment policies of the Civil Rights Commission, the Supreme Court, and the political parties. While their replies varied for each area, they share the perception that there is an affinity of ideals and interests between themselves and the Jews; they also share the belief that together the two communities can achieve more than they could separately. On the local community level, the respondents recommend co-operation on priority issues of the Black agenda, chiefly education. They also hope to achieve consensus—even if it is an agreement to disagree—on affirmative action and quotas.

Many comments emphasize the need to extend co-operation between the two communities beyond the Congressional and leadership level to the grass-roots of the two communities. Inter-community activities and programmes, improved contacts and co-operation between the communities at large, will work to dispel mutual misconceptions and stereotypes, thereby decreasing various forms of racism including antisemitism.

While recognizing the strains which have occurred in Black-Jewish relations during the past year, the respondents believe that a realistic appraisal of inter-community relations including the recent strains on Black-Jewish relations is a first step in strengthening co-operation between the two communities. In this spirit the interviews and the Washington conference which followed them proved to be the beginning of a candid dialogue in which each side was willing to listen to the views of the other.

Granted, some of the criticism expressed in this survey is harsh. Some of the respondents were critical of Jews who oppose quotas, of Jewish responses to Black leaders, and of Jews and Israel in their support of the South African apartheid regime. However, this criticism was not levelled at Jews as an ethnic or religious group. Rather, it conveyed a deep disappointment in the US Jewish community with whom the Blacks had worked, had marched, and finally had won their first civil rights goals. Therefore, criticism which may have sounded harsh in any other context was tempered by the knowledge of the old alliance. In the view of the Congressmen, this alliance still endures.

NOTES

1. In 1971, Congressman William Clay transformed an informal group of Black Representatives into the Congressional Black Caucus, a group which has grown more influential with each Congress.

2. Quoted by Milton Coleman, 'Black Caucus comes of age', *The Washington Post*, 7 January 1985.

3. On the question of Jewish reaction to Jesse Jackson, the Jewish community perceived itself as reacting very cautiously, as can be seen in the statement issued by the American Jewish Congress on 22 February 1984. Whether the Jewish reaction was exaggerated is not the issue. What is important is whether the Black community perceived the Jewish reaction to be exaggerated. It is not facts that are important here but the perceptions of those facts by the communities.

4. In connection with the issue of the JDL, it should be noted that this organization has always been viewed by the American Jewish community as an extreme element, an insignificant minority, and an outcast from the community.

5. Jewish criticism of Louis Farrakhan, leader of the Nation of Islam, has been directed solely against his anti-Jewish and anti-Israel remarks and not against other facets of Farrakhan's programme, such as his social work activities (see Robert A. Jordan, 'Farrakhan's challenge to America', *The Boston Globe*, 22 June 1984). Farrakhan's remarks have been criticized not only by the Jewish community but by many other Whites, Christians and Muslims, such as Black Muslim leader Warith Deen Muhammed, and Blacks such as *Washington Post* journalist Carl T. Rowan.

6. Vernon E. Jordan Jr., 'Blacks and Jews: what went wrong', *Washington Post*, 18 April 1984.

7. Proportionately more Jews voted for the Black mayors of Chicago, Los Angeles and Philadelphia than any other ethnic group.

8. The use of stereotypical language has disturbed the Jewish community as well. For example, when Jesse Jackson explained that he was anti-Zionist and not antisemitic, Jews reacted because, as a result of the UN Zionism-racism equation, anti-Zionism has become a code word for antisemitism.

9. However *The Washington Afro-American* (14 March 1984), among many other Black and White

publications, also condemned the 'Hymietown' remark: '. . . Jackson's original remarks . . . were not merely offensive, but fundamentally compromised the central premise of any Rainbow Coalition. Anti-semitism must have no place in American politics . . .'.

10. Most Black Congressmen have supported every foreign assistance bill. Recently, most of them voted for the 1985 Foreign Aid Authorization Bill which contained $2.6 billion in aid to Israel. Black Congressmen also voted against the Rahall Amendment which would have crippled Israeli development of the Lavi fighter plane. Those Black Congressmen who recently voted against aid to Israel did so partly because they oppose military aid *per se* and partly because the bill contained aid to El Salvador. The fact that the size of their Arab-American constituencies has increased may also have had some influence.

11. For information on South African trade, see *Direction of Trade Statistics, Yearbook 1984* (International Monetary Fund), 342–3.

12. Jewish opposition to apartheid, stemming from the Jewish historical experience of oppression, has been expressed throughout the years; more recently in letters to the Editor of the *New York Times* by Jewish leaders (18 December 1984), the statements of Jewish leaders, such as Congressman Howard Berman, who was arrested in demonstrations at the South African embassy in Washington, and Anthony Lewis, 'It is so simple', *The New York Times,* 10 September 1984.

13. Support for Soviet Jewry has always been concomitant with support for the anti-apartheid movement. The *Washington Jewish Week* of 20 December 1984 reported that the official co-ordinating group for supporters of Soviet Jewry, the Union of Councils for Soviet Jews, expressed its solidarity with the victims of apartheid.

14. In fact, official Israeli opposition to apartheid has been consistently expressed by the government in Israel and in international fora. See, for example, Ambassador Yehuda Blum's speech to the UN General Assembly of 17 November 1983 and Ambassador Benjamin Netanyahu's speech of 21 November 1984 in the General Assembly.

# Remarks before the Milwaukee Jewish Council Dinner

The easy speech to make tonight—especially for a liberal Democrat from The Nation's Capital—would be one ridiculing a self-styled law and order Administration that produces Watergates and cover-ups at the highest level. We could spend the evening basking in self-righteous indignation over Constitutional violations by those charged with defending and protecting the Constitution and we might even have some fun telling John Dean or Martha Mitchell jokes on the side. And certainly there has never been an Administration in our lifetime, if ever, more deserving of censure for its hypocrisy in talking law and order while practicing criminal conduct, deceit, and deception.

But I would prefer to speak tonight of a different problem—one more at home for us in this room and one we can ourselves do more about—the slow but perceptible swing of the Jewish community to the right.

I am not speaking primarily of the brigade of wealthy Jews who chose to forsake their long allegiance to the liberal Democratic Party and last Fall gave vast sums to defeat a candidate whose crime was to propose some modicum of redistribution of wealth. Nor am I speaking of those who, in the misguided view that they were helping Israel, supported the outrageous military assaults in Southeast Asia. Nor even do I speak of those who today lead the cheers for the chief Senatorial spokesman for the military-industrial complex, Henry Jackson, in the hopeful expectation he will one day be their presidential candidate.

Rather, tonight I want to express my deep and anguished concern that, for the first time in my remembrance, Jews and Jewish organizations are largely on the wrong side of the great civil rights issues of the day.

Jews who only a generation ago were barred by restrictive covenants and other discriminatory practices from desirable residential areas now seek to block housing projects which would afford blacks the opportunity to leave the ghetto and live in areas more hospitable to decent family life. Jews who once saw their children barred from schools that offered the best educational opportunities now join the taunting of black children bussed to schools for a better education. Jews who once complained about discrimination in employment—and some of whom still do—now oppose the only effective method by which blacks can be assured jobs from which they have been so long

Joseph L. Rauh Jr. was a lawyer and lobbyist for liberal causes and one of the founding members of Americans for Democratic Action.
Rauh made these remarks on June 26, 1973. Joseph Rauh Papers, Box 22, Library of Congress, Manuscript Division, Washington, D.C.

excluded—the use of goals and timetables to measure the effectiveness of government and private employers in overcoming past discriminations. And all the while the leading Jewish magazine on contemporary affairs, *Commentary,* seems intent, in the words of the NAACP's distinguished John Morsell, "upon dampening the receptivity of liberal whites to the thesis that race is as critical an issue as it ever was and that massive effort is required to produce genuine correctives."

Volumes could be spoken on current Jewish reaction to each of these three issues—housing, busing, employment. Opposition to black housing in Jewish areas flares up only too often over such low-income projects as Forest Hills; possibly saddest of all, organized Jewish pressure pushed a reluctant candidate McGovern into the code words for segregation that neighborhoods "should be protected from projects that destroy the familiarity and identity that go with the concept of home." School boycotters at Canarsie in Brooklyn taunting black children getting off the bus about their clothes from welfare disgraced the heritage of those courageous Jews who helped form the NAACP early in this century and participated in all the daring struggles of the blacks right down through the sixties. But there isn't time to speak fully of housing and busing and so-called job quotas, so I shall limit myself to the latter.

First and foremost, no one in America—at least no one I know or ever heard of—is in favor of quotas. The use of that word by those who oppose vigorous measures to insure black hiring and promotion is at best confusing and at worst deliberately misleading. I speak tonight in the context of remedying the ancient discrimination against Negroes, though much that is being said applies with equal relevance to discrimination against other minorities and women.

Many years ago President Ernest Martin Hopkins of Dartmouth College announced that there was a limit—I believe it was ten percent but maybe it was less—on the number of Jews who could enter Dartmouth. This was a real quota, a ceiling on educational opportunities for our young people. It has nothing to do with goals and timetables that measure progress by government or other employers in hiring and promoting blacks and other minorities and women.

What black organizations are pleading for today is that after 300 years of discrimination, a means be found at long last to overcome at least some part of this long heritage of discrimination. To implement this concept, they ask that goals and timetables be set so that one can measure the progress of the government and other employers in meeting their responsibilities to hire and promote blacks. As Vernon Jordan, the able head of the National Urban League, has put it:

> ". . . there has been developed a flexible system of guidelines for progress, goals to assure eventual equality of opportunity and timetables to assure progress. When we hear these reasonable mechanisms for insuring the success of affirmative action programs labeled as 'quotas' and attacked, we can only conclude that the artificial issue of 'quotas' is another wall raised to exclude black people."

There is no mystery concerning these goals and timetables about which Mr. Jordan speaks, only the confusion caused by the misuse of the word "quota." Goals and timetables are simply standards for the measurement of progress of government and other employers in overcoming past discrimination against blacks and other minorities and women. They are a means of measuring progress and, unlike quotas, they are flexible. For example, let us assume a court or an administrative agency sets a goal of so many Negroes in so many different types of jobs by such and such a time. The employer can still show, if he does not meet the goal within the set timetable, that qualified Negroes were *not* available for hiring or promotion. No action could possibly be taken against an employer who makes such a showing.

What the goals and the timetables do is to make the program for minority hiring effective; they shift the burden of proof from the back of those suffering discrimination and put that burden of proof where it belongs—on the hiring and promotion agencies. Such a shift in the burden of proof does no more than follow normal life experience that, when blacks are not represented in any fair way in the work force, there is a reasonable probability that this has resulted from discrimination against them. And by putting the burden of proof on the employer, he has an added incentive to hire and promote blacks; when he does so, he has nothing to explain.

No one is suggesting that anybody hire or promote unqualified people. But, just like the preference for veterans among qualified applicants in the civil service, so goals and timetables support a black preference *among qualified applicants* in order to remedy past discrimination. What the goals and timetables do is to make an employer either hire and promote a reasonable number of blacks to overcome past discrimination or demonstrate that he cannot find such qualified blacks to hire and promote. Once a government agency or private employer knows he has to justify his failure to meet the goals and timetables, he stops making excuses and starts looking for qualified blacks.

One has only to sit in my office to see the importance of this matter of the burden of proof. Time and again frustrated Negroes walk in with tales of losing this job or that promotion because they are black. I do not say all the cases are meritorious factually, but I do say that over and over again I have seen meritorious cases that could not be won because the burden of proof could not be met by the complaining black asserting discrimination. It is always simple enough for an agency or employer to talk about insubordination, uppityness, sloppiness, etc., and it is always extremely difficult for a single individual to prove he is the unblemished employee. But let me tell you that when there is a goal of hiring and promotion that has to be reached and the agency has to prove the insubordination, uppityness and sloppiness to defend itself against charges that it hasn't met its goal, the situation changes mighty fast.

Talk of "affirmative action" to help minority hiring and promotion, without goals and timetables to measure the effectiveness of the affirmative action, is too often window dressing. I am sick and tired of people who talk about affirmative action in recruiting programs, training programs, upgrading programs, etc. and oppose the only way to find out whether anyone is really making a serious effort to provide such programs. You can direct people to recruit and train and do this and do that until you are blue in the face, but unless you have a measure for the success of the programs and unless you put the burden of proving efforts to recruit and train on those with the responsibility of doing it, you are never going to make the programs really work.

I hope you will forgive me for the bluntness of my comments, but the gravity of the problem requires some plain speaking. We are at one of the most difficult periods in American life on the issue of race. I have already quoted the head of the Urban League "that the artificial issue of 'quotas' is another wall raised to exclude black people." I have heard Roy Wilkins, the responsible and courageous leader of the NAACP, speak repeatedly of the forthcoming end of the second Reconstruction. And possibly the saddest of all to me personally was the statement issued after the last election by Aaron Henry, my old comrade-in-arms in so many battles against Mississippi repression:

"Those of us who have advocated a policy of non-violence will have to admit that 'our way' has not produced the right answers nor attitudes within a majority of our Nation's citizens. We will therefore have little if any credentials, and will be unable to convince the masses that 'our way' is the way, and we too must yield the reign of leadership to persons who desire to proceed another way. A return to confrontation is inevitable. Our streets will again become the battleground . . . In a violent struggle, I can see the numerical disadvantage, in addition to the moral and humane negatives. But if death itself is the price that some of us must pay in our efforts to prevent more de-humanization, and violations of personal, legal and social fulfillment, in addition to the prevention of more debasement of human rights for the minorities of our Nation, then nothing could be more redemptive."

Confrontation, battleground, violence—this is not the idle talk of revolutionaries and crackpots. It comes from great men who have devoted their lives to making our democratic system work. It evidences the serious plight of American race relations and the danger to our society. If we, one of the most discriminated-against people in the history of mankind, do not heed the cries for help, who will stop the downward spiral?

Some months ago Benjamin V. Cohen, wise counsellor to the Nation, addressed himself to this general problem in thoughtful words:

"The Jewish community in the past has played a constructive role in stressing the common interest which should unite the various groups in our society, including their common interest in finding means of reconciling their differences. But I was deeply pained to read recently the suggestion from a Jewish source that the Jews were now a middle-class group and their interest could best be served by identifying their interest with that of other middle-class groups rather than with the poorer ethnic groups.

"Group interest like national interest may mean different things to different people. I suggest we ask ourselves where our heart lies. Prudence as well as virtue suggests that we try to reconcile our interests with the dictates of our heart, and not the other way around."

Our Nation is in bad trouble on the race issue—an issue which played a bigger role in the past election than at any time since the infamous anti-black deal of 1876. Responsible black leadership has done all that it can. The time has come for new white leadership towards a more integrated America in every field including housing, schools and jobs. The descendants of the Jewish ghettos of Europe, upon whom American democracy has shone so brightly and to whom it has brought so much prosperity and happiness, must not be found wanting when the rights of the less fortunate are at stake. Our self-interest in the preservation of democratic processes and our gratefulness for opportunities bestowed upon us, should motivate us to defend and support the rights of those who have too long been the victims of discrimination. Let us resolve anew that the Jewish community will once again become the spearhead of the efforts for civil rights for all.

# Black-Jewish Relationships: Healing the Wounds

The role of some Jewish organizations in the DeFunis* case has brought into the open points of serious disagreement and misunderstanding between the Jewish and black communities. Smoldering racial fires have been fanned and latent animosities brought to the foreground. Blacks wonder, "Is the Jewish community for us or against us?"

The Jewish community is not monolithic in thought and many Jewish people and organizations did take a stand in opposition to that of ADL in the Defunis case. Nevertheless, some blacks and whites attribute ADL's point of view to all Jews. This is unfortunate but understandable, because the media have given a great deal of coverage to the role of the Anti-Defamation League of B'nai B'rith and the American Jewish Committee in the Defunis case and in other cases involving affirmative action. Now, I know and you know that ADL has supported affirmative action and on occasion has accepted quotas in specific situations. However, the general public (which includes the black community) has not been aware of this positive role, because the media have said very little about it. As a result, many blacks do not have an entirely balanced view of the situation.

The area of limited disagreement between ADL and black leaders is over what constitutes affirmative action for minorities and what constitutes preferential treatment. There is no simple answer to this question, and the persisting vagueness of federal guidelines causes everyone consternation.

Let me raise several points that I feel are crucial to consider in this matter. Crippling racist practices have been impeding blacks for a long time. More than the removal of legal barriers is needed to assure their entry into the mainstream of society. Training, practice, and assistance are necessary. Blacks are still segregated in schools, particularly in the North, and they receive inferior preparatory education. Many blacks attend predominantly black colleges which suffer many handicaps. And much of the black community is enmeshed in poverty currently aggravated by runaway inflation and increasing unemployment. Affirmative action would be a transitional mechanism, if our society was providing equal opportunity to all its citizens.

Tests and other measures that have kept blacks out of many jobs and colleges have been found to be discriminatory and culturally biased. They often do not predict success or achievement. Therefore, the modification of job and college admissions

In 1974, Alvin Poussaint was associate professor of psychiatry at Harvard Medical School, Boston.
Synopsis of "Black-Jewish Relationships—Healing the Wounds" by Alvin F. Poussaint, an address delivered November 3, 1974 at the annual meeting of the Anti-Defamation League of B'nai B'rith. Printed with permission of the author.

criteria is partly an attempt to be fair and objective and is not necessarily preferential treatment. I do not like the application of the term "quota" to affirmative action programs. It implies that jobs and openings in schools will be filled without regard for qualifications. Generally, minorities have not been placed in jobs in such a haphazard fashion. Terms like "target goals" are preferable because they indicate an attempt to find qualified applicants instead of arbitrarily filling places to satisfy a quota.

At many schools admission figures for blacks are declining. The drop is a sign of backlash and disappointment in programs and practices that did not work or have lost financial support. In college and professional schools it is nearly impossible to overcome deficiencies experienced by black children in elementary and secondary school.

Affirmative action has not been a cure-all for minority group problems; yet one would think from all the clamor that scores of whites are unemployed as a result of affirmative action. Have Jews and other whites been hurt by affirmative action programs? That question cannot be answered directly. I know ADL feels that affirmative action has hurt the advancement of Jews in the New York educational system. But I suspect that the careers of very few young Jewish men and women are adversely being affected. Do we have comparable data on the number of Jews and blacks being enrolled in professional schools and colleges and being hired to work at well-paying occupations? It is important to know the facts in order to cope with what is fantasy and what is real in the minds of many whites.

We are in a period of reactionary sentiment against blacks in America. Blacks are under attack by all segments of society, including government. Does ADL want to seem supportive of racist backlash? In my opinion, the Defunis posture of ADL is at odds with a commitment to human rights.

Siding with reactionaries and bigots may harm the Jewish community. There is still a correlation between being anti-black and being anti-semitic. In addition, blacks are gaining power through elections to city, state, and federal offices, and it is crucial that good relations between the two minority groups be maintained. We can and should help each other, not fight each other.

In the past, alliances between Jews and blacks have been important to our mutual advancement in America. When principles held by one minority conflict with those of another on a particular question, the difference must not be allowed to jeopardize long-standing agreements about other things. Blacks and Jewish leaders should not let their alliance lapse because of quota arguments or because of the Israeli dispute. Most issues are simply not so one-sided as they may at first appear. We must not destroy the potential for even greater coalitions, needed now more than ever in this time of moral decay, to make America the kind of spirited democracy that we so much want her to be.

NOTE

* Marco DeFunis was a Sephardic Jew who sued the University of Washington Law School, alleging that his initial rejection was an instance of "reverse discrimination" (*Defunis v. Odegaard,* 1974). He was later admitted.—Eds.

# As for the '02 Kosher-Food Rioters

The blackout and the accompanying social disorders among many very poor black and Hispanic New Yorkers soon will become part of contemporary urban folklore. Judging by much that has been written and spoken in the last week, it is possible that too many New Yorkers may remember little more than what some have misleadingly, and unpardonably, described as "the night of the animals." Others, as reported in the press, characterized the disorderly as "vultures," "a jackel pack," "buffalo," and "predatory animals."

The use of these and similar animal metaphors is inappropriate, but, sadly, predictable. We learn why by examining similar events in United States history. After all, disorders by poor Americans, New Yorkers among them, are not new. An examination of some reactions to one such incident distances us from the night of looting and fires so that we can better comprehend what happened.

Consider the following newspaper editorial:

> "The class of people . . . who are engaged in this matter have many elements of a dangerous class. They are very ignorant. . . . They do not understand the duties or the rights of Americans. They have no inbred or acquired respect for law and order as the basis of the life of the society into which they have come. . . . Resistance to authority does not seem to them necessarily wrong, only risky, and if it ceases to be risky the restraint it can have on their passions is very small; practically it disappears. . . . The instant they take the law into their own hands, the instant they begin the destruction of property and assail peaceable citizens and the police, they should be handled in a way that they can understand and cannot forget . . . let the blow fall instantly and effectually. . . .
>
> "These rioters were plainly desperate. They meant to defy the police and were ready for severe treatment. They did not get treatment nearly severe enough, and they are therefore far more dangerous than they were before. . . ."

These words have a familiar ring. During the last week, for example, the well-known behavioral psychologist Ernest Dichter told us that "people resort to savage behavior when the brakes of civilization fail," and the futurist Herman Kahn said of the disorderly in New York City: "They have no idea of what moral standards are. This 'sup-

In 1977, Herbert G. Gutman was professor of history at the Graduate Center, City University of New York. Originally published in the *New York Times,* July 21, 1977, Op-Ed. Section. Copyright © 1977 by the New York Times Co. Reprinted with permission.

pressed rage' idea is crap. This kind of reasoning will make the same thing happen all over again."

But the editorial quoted above was not published last week. It appeared in The New York Times on May 24, 1902. And the rioters described were not poor disorderly black and Hispanic New Yorkers. They were poor disorderly immigrant Jewish women, mostly Orthodox and mostly living on the Lower East Side.

The 1902 and 1977 disorders differ in important ways. Poor Jewish women, mostly housewives, formed the Ladies Anti-Beef Trust Association to protest the rapidly rising price of kosher meat and the betrayal of a promised boycott of wholesale distributors by Jewish retail butchers. They boycotted the retail butchers, battered butcher shops that remained open, threw meat into the streets and poured kerosene on it, and prevented nonboycotters from buying meat. Dozens of women were beaten by the police, arrested, and fined. Some spent time in jail.

Their rage had clear objectives. "Eat no meat while the Trust is taking meat from the bones of your children and women," said a Yiddish circular decorated with a skull and crossbones. Some women called for a rabbi to fix the price of meat for the entire New York Jewish community, as in the East European *shtetl*, or village. Others formed a cooperative retail outlet.

The disorders started on the Lower East Side on a Thursday morning, ceased on Friday at sundown, and resumed the following evening, spreading to Williamsburg, Brownsville, East Harlem, the South Bronx, and to Newark's and Boston's poor Jewish communities. Angry Jewish women punished retail butchers by destroying their merchandise and property. Although no looting occurred, a New York World reporter compared the women to "a pack of wolves."

Using such animal metaphors to describe very poor and sometimes disorderly Americans has a long history. It began well before July 1977, even earlier than May 1902. Disorders among the Jersey City Irish seeking wages due them from the Erie Railroad in 1859 convinced the Jersey City American Standard that they were "animals . . . a mongrel mass of ignorance and crime and superstition." A generation later, The Chicago Post-Mail said the city's Bohemian poor were "depraved beasts." And the city's discontented East European residents were scorned by The Chicago Times as "Slavonic wolves" from "European dens."

The animal metaphor always serves a base function. It separates the *behavior* of the discontented poor (striking, rioting, looting, boycotting) from the *conditions* that shape their discontent. Animal behavior, it is wrongly believed, is "natural" and "lawless"— therefore inexplicable. The best that can be done is to restrain it. The most appropriate responses: the leash, the cage, and the National Guard.

Such thinking distances the successful, the comfortable, and the powerful ("us") from what is social, and therefore human, in the behavior of the very poor and powerless ("them"). That is just as true in 1977 as in 1902 and in 1859; it is just as true in the age of electric power as in the age of horse power. It prevents us from understanding what they are telling us about themselves and their condition.

Mrs. Rebecca Ablowitz, one of the Lower East Side Jewish women arrested in 1902, had a good deal to tell her contemporaries. In "The World of Our Fathers," Irving Howe reports the following exchange between her and a magistrate:

"Why do you riot?"

"Your Honor, we know our wounds. We see how thin our children are and that our husbands haven't strength to work . . ."

"But you aren't allowed to riot in the street."

"We don't riot. But if all we did was to weep at home, nobody would notice it; so we have to do something to help ourselves."

The magistrate fined her $3.

Women like Mrs. Ablowitz were condemned as "lacking an inbred and acquired respect for law and order," deserving little more than "severe treatment" and "blows," and belonging to "a pack of wolves." Now, from the distance of 75 years, we know better about the world of our mothers and grandmothers.

But do we understand enough about ourselves and the world in which the contemporary American poor live to comprehend the pained message that came to us on the deplorably misnamed "night of the animals?"

## Such Good Friends
Blacks and Jews in Conflict

Andrew Young would be out of character if he did not attempt to play down the ethnic frictions that have been exposed by his sudden resignation as the American Ambassador to the United Nations. Young was known as a conciliator during the Civil Rights era. It was this instinct that led him to the fateful meeting with the representative of the Palestinian Liberation Organization that precipitated his downfall. But Young's considerable talent will be hardpressed to soothe the troubled waters of relations between Jews and Blacks. It should be said now that the conflict is real and that its origins go far beyond the boundaries of international diplomacy.

Anyone who has followed the disintegration of the civil rights alliance in recent years knows that open conflict was inevitable. Blacks and Jews in this country have been on a collision course for more than a decade. The only surprise is Andy Young serving as unwilling catalyst for the escalation of hostilities. Any number of other events could have triggered the confrontations: the war against affirmative action waged by the major Jewish organizations; the role of Jewish-controlled institutions in perpetuating racial stereotypes; and the political relationship of Israel to southern Africa.

It is dishonest to suggest that Andy Young's color had nothing to do with the uproar he caused as U.N. Ambassador. As a black man, he articulated a view of the world shared by many Blacks and some whites in this country and elsewhere. The objections to Young's statements came from people who take a different view of world events, a view that has long been dominant in Western countries but whose credibility has come under intense pressure as the balance of power in the world has begun shift.

The resignation of Andrew Young therefore, is metaphor for a struggle between competing ethnic groups; for relations between the "have's" and "have-nots" here and elsewhere; and for differing visions of the future. The conflict between Blacks and Jews reflects the fact that these two groups have made their alliances with opposing camps in an international struggle for power.

My interest in Jewish-black relations begins with my own origins. My grandfather, Emmanuel Dreyfuss, migrated from France to Haiti in the 1880s to escape anti-Semitism and married into an old Haitian family. As the child of international civil servants growing up in the Caribbean, West Africa, and Europe, I found no contradictions between being Black and having roots that were Jewish, French African, and Latin

In 1979 Joel Dreyfuss was a journalist and writer.
Originally published in the *Village Voice*, August 27, 1979, it is reprinted here from the monthly report of the Institute of the Black World, September/October 1979. Copyright © 1979 by Joel Dreyfuss. Reprinted with permission of the author.

American. But when my family settled in New York in 1960, I learned early that I could no longer straddle my multiple origins. I was black in America, but I retained a deep personal concern about American Jews and their relationship with American Blacks.

I had grown up in a world where class was more important than color, and power more effective than morality, so I was fascinated by race relations in America. The civil rights movement seemed terribly naive, but its successes confirmed the promise of America. During my Americanization in New York public schools and at City College, I accepted without question the explanation that Blacks and Jews were allies because of their common history of oppression. Most of my white friends were Jews and we seemed to share a vision of the benefits, contradictions, and injustices of the American system. But a series of events in the 1960's began to strain that alliance—and my own personal relationships with Jewish friends.

## BLACK POWER AND THE CIVIL RIGHTS COALITION

The emergence of the Black power movement seemed logical to me. I had grown up accustomed to Blacks exercising power in Haiti and in Africa. Once the laws declaring racial equality were put in place here, I thought it natural for Blacks to want to control institutions that would meet their needs and reflect their own perceptions. Stokely Carmichael's famous 1966 declaration that whites should combat racism and leave Blacks to organize themselves hardly seemed to warrant the hostile reaction it provoked in the Jewish community. I couldn't understand why Jews were so resentful of a sense of group identity among Blacks that they themselves had always enjoyed.

From conversations with my friends I concluded that the reaction was more emotional than rational. Jews had provided much support to the civil rights movement and they felt Blacks were being ungrateful. The fact that Blacks played no prominent role in B'nai B'rith and the American Jewish Committee was not an acceptable comparison to them. I would learn much later that some Jewish intellectuals were beginning to have serious doubts about the direction of the movement and could foresee a time when Blacks would threaten their achievements. Affirmative action, then known as "preferential treatment," was considered dangerous by the editors of *Commentary* who also feared that Blacks were becoming anti-Semitic and would switch their allegiance to the Wasp establishment.

Most studies show, however, that Black anti-Semitism is concentrated among poorer Blacks whose contacts with Jews is limited to exploitive shops and stores in ghetto areas. In his essay "The Harlem Ghetto," James Baldwin explained the problem as being "in accordance with the American business tradition," to which the *Jewish Press* responded by claiming that were it not for the Jews in Harlem there would be no business at all there to provide jobs for Blacks. The fallacy of Baldwin's and the *Jewish Press*'s reasoning was exposed by Harold Cruse in the *Crisis of the Negro Intellectual,* when he says that "There was a time, not too many years ago, when these Jewish-owned businesses would not hire Negro help at all. They did not do so in fact until forced to—by the Black Nationalist Movement [and Adam Clayton Powell, Cruse should have added]."

The issue was not just political theory. There was a real conflict over roles. The coalition of Blacks and Jews, the joining of two groups with vastly unequal power and resources, was more symbiosis than alliance. Blacks had benefited from Jewish involvement in the civil rights movement and would suffer a damaging blow when that support was withdrawn. The Jews had also benefited from the civil rights era. They had been able to confront their own alienation from the American mainstream—an exclusion similar in conception but vastly different in degree from the black experience in America—by participating in the struggle for equality. The rebuff by Blacks forced Jews to reevaluate their standing in America and led them to conclude that they could no longer classify themselves among the "have nots" of this country. If they had become a powerful force in America, what was the benefit of associating with a powerless and increasingly unpopular group?

For some Blacks, the patronizing tone of some Jews and their unwillingness to cooperate on a more equal basis indicated that the racial attitudes of Jews were not so different from that of other whites. Blacks self-assertion, often exaggerated in its novelty, was as much a threat to liberal friends as it was to conservative foes. To those Blacks who had hoped that Jews would somehow be "different," the revelation provoked a disappointment that was matched by Jewish dismay at Black "separatism."

The parting of the ways came at a time when civil rights leaders were realizing the inadequacy of protest for confronting economic issues. Martin Luther King's Chicago campaign, his first movement North, had been a dismal failure. There had been fierce white resistance. Mayor Daly sidestepped the issue and King was literally stoned. This caused trepidation in the Northern liberal community. King's early opposition to the Vietnam War completed the break. This after all, was the war against Communism, and besides, Blacks as a *Time* editorial counseled at the time, should not be concerned with foreign policy matters. (Andy Young's appearance on Face the Nation recently showed how little this attitude has changed: *Washington Post* reporter Martin Schram wondered aloud if Blacks should be concerned about the Middle East issue.) King was also criticized by Roy Wilkins, then head of the NAACP, and Whitney Young of the National Urban League for his position on the war. This rift reflected their dependence on Jewish support that undermined the credibility of these organizations in the eyes of militant nationalist Blacks at the time. After King's death, the fear of Black violence chased some liberals back to the fold, but the alliance could not last because Black and Jewish interests no longer coincided.

Neither did their perceptions of the methods useful for Black liberation. In an April 30, 1954, issue of the *Jewish Press,* the Black Muslims were compared to American Nazis like Lincoln Rockwell and likened to racists and extremists. Harold Cruse suggests, however, that this was a convenient forgetting of the fact that the Irgun Zvai Leumi and the Stern Gang in pre-1948 Israel were called the same things. "Yet," says Harold Cruse, "it was these very people who truly forged Israel by forcing the British Army to vacate the territory." In fact, the Black Muslims and the movement of Malcolm X which tried to forge an international black consciousness movement was heavily attacked by Jews and other white liberals. As time goes on, the need for black institutions seems more legitimate than ever. The relative lack of black political and economic power seems the result of the lack of such institutions.

American Jews had routed anti-Semitism and opened all but the most sacred doors of the American system. Blacks were still on the outside and they would become their natural competitors in the urban middle classes.

The peculiar madness of being Black in America in the 1970's is due primarily to the chasm between our experiences and their interpretation by whites. Public opinion polls show most whites believe that racism is no longer an obstacle to black progress. Yet racism, in its more subtle forms, is an experience shared by Blacks regardless of background, education, or class.

Journalism is an area where black-white relations have never been good. American newspapers rank among the most segregated institutions in this country, undoubtedly because of the power they wield in their communities. Recently, a young black woman on the staff of an influential newspaper was congratulated by a colleague for a front-page article she had written about one of the country's most powerful families.

"Great article," gushed her white colleague, "The editors did a great job of putting in that background material."

"What background material? What editors?" asked the bewildered reporter.

"You know, all that research?"

"Wait a minute," said the black woman. "My by-line was the only one on the story, why do you assume I didn't do that research?"

Black reporters at the *New York Times* who have accused their employers of racial discrimination in a Title VII class-action suit tell the story of the editor who walked into the newsroom one evening and came upon a group of black reporters chatting after a hard day's work.

"Can we help you?" asked one of the black reporters.

"No," the editor replied. "I came to look for some writers, but I see everyone has left."

The Invisible Man has made a comeback in the 1970's. The experiences that most Blacks live never make the evening news, prime time television or the world of Woody Allen. Whites continue to deny their racism and reveal it for all to see in their fantasies. Blacks will obviously play no role in the future of "Star Wars" and "Close Encounters." They don't exist in the present of "Manhattan" and "Superman." They are written out of the past in the "Deerhunter" and "Loose Change." Blacks don't exist in the pages of best selling books or in the indexes of journals and magazines.

While Blacks are absent from the experiences of whites, they find it nearly impossible to express their own vision. Black writers cannot get published. Black actors are asked to play Blacks that exist only in the mind of white writers and white directors. This situation reflects the distribution of power in this country, but it has other ramifications.

## JEWISH POWER IN AMERICA

Jewish power in America has always been a difficult subject to address. Jewish leaders, fearing a backlash, have tried to downplay their influence on America. Their most effective tactic has been to attack any references to the power of Jews as "anti-Semitic," immediately blocking further discussion of the issue. But it is impossible to discuss the conflict between Blacks and Jews without addressing the issue of power. American Jews exert an economic, political, and intellectual influence on this country far out of proportion to their numbers. American Blacks have far less impact than their numbers could lead them to expect.

American Jews dominate the image-shaping industries of our era: film, television, journalism, and book publishing. In the past, Hollywood excused its racism on the grounds that it was only catering to the taste of the marketplace. Now, some Blacks suspect, the seriously distorted representation of Blacks in America may not be accidental but the product of hostilities that go back to the 1960's. The fact that these industries are associated with Jews does little for relations between the races.

Blacks, envious of the power that Jews wield in America, find it difficult to understand the profound insecurity of Jews about their own role in this country. This insecurity led to the reaction against black power and is reflected in the vehemence of the attacks against affirmative action. Any system which looks at numbers in the population is seen as a threat to Jewish achievement. But a sensitivity to race has been the most effective way of bringing Blacks into the mainstream. To pretend that racial attitudes do not affect evaluations, selection, and promotions is to deny hundreds of years of conditioning in America. That is the kernel of last June's Weber Supreme Court decision, an acknowledgement of historical fact strangely absent from the Bakke decision of 1978.

In briefs filed in the Bakke case, notably those of B'nai B'rith and the Neoconservative Committee for Academic Non-Discrimination and Integrity (Sidney Hook, Nathan Glazer, Bruno Bettleheim), there were attempts to equate the Jewish experience in America with that of Blacks. The CANI brief even went so far as to argue that Allan Bakke had fewer rights under affirmative action than a Black after Reconstruction.

Unsatisfied with the Bakke decision, the Anti-Defamation League of B'nai B'rith declared this summer that it would visit major professional schools to ensure that the Supreme Court ban was not violated in the procedures for admitting minority students. This is another example of Jews applying considerable power for their own interest without considering the possible repercussions.

The only indication of Jewish concern about relations with Blacks in recent years was a decision by the American Jewish Congress and the American Jewish Committee not to file briefs in the Weber Supreme Court case. They were persuaded by the argument that Jews did not have such vital interests in a case involving blue-collar jobs. However, the Anti Defamation League pressed on with its campaign to prevent any consideration of race in the redistribution of opportunities, which, to the ADL, meant that Jews, more highly represented in professional schools and the blue-collar work force than their 2 percent of the population, would lose these places to Blacks.

Jews were certainly denied opportunities in this country. But that denial was never a part of official government policy. It can never compare to the systematic cruelty and frequent savagery of efforts to enforce white supremacy in America. Jews and other white ethnics were able to work, to vote, to join unions, and form political organizations. The advantages these groups have over Blacks today can be attributed to the 100 years that followed emancipation. To suggest, as Nathan Glazer has in his famous book

*Affirmative Discrimination,* that white immigrants played no part in oppressing Blacks is not only bad history but down-right dishonest. The union movement was all white. Political patronage systems did not include Blacks. Traditionally, immigrants adopted the racial attitudes of those who were already here.

The strategy for resisting minority pressures for a share of the wealth has been to deny any responsibility for their lower status in this country; The theories of the "underclass" come dangerously close to arguments for white supremacy. I learned that a couple of years ago in conversation with an Afrikaner professor about the Bakke case. He was a member of the Verligkter, or enlightened group which wants to find a solution to South Africa's racial impasse. His description of arguments against integration made by his colleagues had an uncanny resemblance to those made here by opponents of affirmative action. The concern about "lowered standards" and "the culture of poverty" had a distinct American ring.

In the eyes of many Blacks, American Jews have cast their lot with those who would maintain the status quo. Because many Jewish intellectuals are prominent in this movement, there is a danger that Blacks will view all Jews as the enemy.

Many black people believe that as the power of Jews has increased, so has their insensitivity to different views and different cultures. While Blacks have to struggle to get the United States to pay any attention to the problems of Africa, the Middle East consumes the energies of successive American administrations. Jewish dissidents in the Soviet Union enjoy a flood of publicity, but black dissidents in South Africa are ignored until they are killed. Black complaints about racism in television fall on deaf ears, but the selection of Vanessa Redgrave to play a concentration camp victim creates an uproar. And now, the suspicion is that Andy Young was ousted to appease Jewish and Israeli anger.

### "WHAT GOES 'ROUND, COMES 'ROUND"

But there have been changes in the recent years. The roles of the "have" and "have nots" have shifted. The American defeat in Vietnam was an important symbol for the emerging nationalism of the Third World. If a tiny country could survive the rage of the world's most powerful nation, then the struggle for self-determination was not hopeless. The rout of the Portuguese (and their NATO weapons) in Angola and Mozambique reinforced this belief.

The Cold Warriors, righteous in their power, could only see red. Racism contributed to the perception of liberation movements as dupes of Soviet Communism. After all, it was difficult to believe that Blacks in this country could know what was best for them.

In 1967, Israel's bold military victory in the Six Day War captured the world's imagination. But Israel as an occupying force soon lost its image as an underdog. By the time of the 1973 war, Israel was being viewed in the Third World as a surrogate for Western interest in the Middle East. Israel and its allies had difficulty understanding this shift. In their arrogance of power, the Western nations had ignored the changes taking place around them. After several generations of military supremacy, they had come to confuse power and merit. They had forgotten that a philosophy backed by power becomes politics. The powerful often end up believing that their views are the most logical, their systems the most perfect, their actions the most just.

The value of Andrew Young was his ability to empathize with the aspirations of Third World countries. His presence gave credibility to American foreign policy toward the developing countries. He did not approach Africa with the arrogance of Henry Kissinger, who convened his Vienna summit on southern Africa in 1976 without a single Black at the conference table. Kissinger represented an archaic style of foreign diplomacy, a throwback to the days when white men could sit around a table and partition Africa amicably.

Andy Young understood why the Blacks of Zimbabwe and South Africa saw white supremacy as a greater threat than Communism. Africans, like their brethren in America, had experienced the cruelties of racism. They could not be intimidated by the invocation of the red bogey-man. They also knew that the regimes in southern Africa survived because the Western powers supported them. That part of the world became the test of America's willingness to abandon white supremacy as an ally.

But the Arab states, frustrated militarily, had discovered the power of oil. They had found a tool that would accelerate the redistribution of power and force the Western nations to reevaluate their international politics. The fall of the Shah of Iran removed the last buffer between the oil nations and their customers. As long as the Shah was still in power, Iran would not act in concert with oil producers in any boycott. After the revolution, Iran not only cut off oil to Israel but to South Africa. Therefore, it is not by accident that the Palestinian cause has suddenly become a legitimate issue. And the fact that there is so much resistance to even considering the cause of the Palestinians could even lead Blacks in this country to sympathize with them as the underdog.

As long as Andrew Young confined himself to African issues, his critics would tolerate him as Jimmy Carter's burden. But once he stepped into the sacred arena of Middle East politics, he became expendable. American Jews have always demanded unequivocal support for Israel from successive administrations and they have always regarded the Middle East as something that should not concern Blacks. But in our changing world, two major strands of American foreign policy began to intertwine.

Israel was developing a close relationship with South Africa. There was economic and military cooperation, and even hints that the two countries had shared their nuclear weapons technology. The "Muldergate" influence-buying scandal was the result of Israel's advice to South Africa to concentrate on public relations. Israeli helicopters, purchased from the United States, turned up in Rhodesia. Just as American Jews were being regarded as foes at home, Blacks were beginning to view Israel as an enemy abroad.

The Israelis and their allies could ignore black and Third World indignation as long as they could depend on American power. But the new reality of power eluded them. The frothings of Senator Moynihan and the *Commentary* crowd was little more than nostalgic—but still dangerous. Suggestions that the United States get tough or seize Arab oil fields revealed the desperateness of people bewildered by change. Andy Young's so-called diplomatic gaffes were intended to open a dialogue in areas that had to be confronted before genuine peace could be achieved. The black struggle for equality in this country provided an important perspective for liberation struggles in other countries. There are reports that President Carter will appoint another Black to replace Andy Young. But unless that ambassador can continue Young's mission, the president's appointment will be exposed as an empty gesture. If we are to live in peace, we must understand and respect one another. History is on the side of the "have nots" here and abroad. Those that have power today had better make friends among the powerless for tomorrow. There is an old African saying: "What goes 'round, comes 'round."

# The Myth of the Powerful Jew
## The Black-Jewish Conflict, Part 2

*Anti-Semitism is the socialism of fools.*
*—August Bebel, German socialist and leader of the Social Democrats in the late 19th century*

Obviously, the fury of black people at Andy Young's departure reflects a decade or more of increasing tensions between blacks and Jews. What is perhaps less obvious is how much the entire incident reflects deteriorating relations between Jews and non-Jews generally. Any useful discussion of black-Jewish conflict must begin by acknowledging two basic realities. One is that American Jews are white and predominantly middle class, and so tend to have a white middle-class perspective on racial issues. The other is that blacks are part of the gentile majority and so tend to share the misconceptions about Jews and the overt or unconscious anti-Jewish attitudes that permeate our culture. Unfortunately, neither group has been eager to accept its share of responsibility for the conflict. If Jews have often minimized their privileges and denied or rationalized their racism, blacks have regularly dismissed Jewish protest against anti-Semitism in the black community as at best oversensitivity, at worst racial paranoia. And in the end, guess who benefits from all the bitterness? Hint: the answer isn't blacks or Jews.

Blacks have repeatedly argued that black hostility toward Jews is simply the logical result of Jews' behavior, either as landlords, teachers, and other representatives of white authority in black neighborhoods, or as political opponents of black goals. As a Jew who stands considerably left of the mainstream Jewish organizations, let alone neo-conservative intellectuals—and as a feminist who supports affirmative action for women as well as minorities—I don't think it's that simple. To attack a ripoff landlord with standard anti-Semitic rhetoric about greedy, exploitative Jews is to imply that the problem is the iniquity of Jews rather than the race and class of white landlords. (When blacks protest the behavior of white cops, who are rarely Jewish, they don't feel compelled to mention the officers' ethnic backgrounds.) Black criticism of Jewish politics invites the same objection. At worst Jews have been no more hostile to black power than the rest of the white population, though most people couldn't withdraw from the civil rights movement since they hadn't been involved in it in the first place. While the resistance of Jewish organizations to affirmative action has been to some extent based on fear of maximum quotas for Jews, it has much more to do with the fact that most Jewish men share with most other white men the belief that affirmative action is illegitimate "reverse

Ellen Willis is associate professor of journalism at New York University.
Originally published in the *Village Voice*, September 3, 1979. Copyright © 1979 V.V. Publishing Corporation. Printed by permission of the *Village Voice*.

discrimination." In fighting community control, the Ocean Hill–Brownsville teachers were acting not as Jews but as white people whose livelihood was threatened. Besides, on all these issues a significant number of Jewish liberals and radicals has supported blacks and opposed the Jewish establishment. So why have blacks made such a point of singling out Jews for criticism?

As Joel Dreyfuss noted in last week's *Voice,* disillusionment is a factor; Jews have talked a better line and had a better record on race than other whites, and groups with a history of oppression are always supposed to be more sensitive to each other's aspirations, although, as James Baldwin put it, "if people did learn from history, history would be very different." The disillusionment is compounded when Jews invoke their status as an oppressed people to avoid confronting their racism (although blacks have committed the same evasion in reverse). It is also convenient and tempting to vent one's anger at a visible and relatively vulnerable minority. But the main impetus to black resentment of Jews as *Jews* seems to be that black people do not perceive Jews as vulnerable. Dreyfuss argues that the issue for blacks is Jewish power; he claims that "American Jews exert an economic, political, and intellectual influence on this country far out of proportion to their numbers" and repeats the familiar allegation that Jews dominate the media.

I would guess that this view is shared by a great many, if not most, non-Jewish whites as well as blacks. I think it is profoundly wrong. Jewish privilege is real; Jews certainly exert intellectual influence; but actual power is another matter. As business people, professionals, journalists, academics, Jews are in a position to further whatever interests they share (or think they share) with the rest of the white middle class or with the ruling elite. But the real test of power is whether Jews can protect specifically Jewish interests when they diverge from—or conflict with—the interests of non-Jews. If the United States government decides it is in America's economic and military interest to abandon Israel, do Jews have the power to prevent a change in policy? If there is a resurgence of anti-Semitism in this country, do Jews have the power to quell it and insure their survival? These questions are not hypothetical; America's Middle East policy is certainly changing, to the dismay of most Jews, and I experience more anti-Semitism (mostly from white people) than I did 10 years ago.

If Jews have power, its sources are mysterious. Jews may own newspapers and movie studios, but the truly powerful own banks, factories, and oil. Jews have been virtually excluded from America's corporate and financial elite. There are few Jews at the highest levels of government or the military. As a tiny minority—3 per cent of the population—Jews do not have the political clout of sheer numbers, except in a few heavily Jewish areas like New York. With the decline of the cities, Jewish influence has decreased; power to set national policy is now centered in the Southwest, hardly a Jewish stronghold, and the widespread anti-New York, anti-urban sentiment that has fed the conservative backlash is aimed at Jews as well as blacks.

Jews are relatively well-organized and vocal politically, but as with other well-organized minorities, their effectiveness has depended on the absence of any strong counterforce. It is ridiculous to imagine, as Dreyfuss apparently does, that the United States' Middle East policy is or ever has been dictated by Jews. Here he displays some confusion, since he also points out that Israel is "viewed in the Third World as a surrogate for Western interests" and faults Jews for once again choosing the wrong side. So which is it? Does America support Israel because of the Jews, or are Jews merely bolstering American imperialism? The reality is that until recently, Jewish pressure on behalf of Israel dovetailed neatly with the American government's political objectives. But Jews' stake in Israel and United States interests in the Middle East are by no means the same. Whatever our differences about the Israeli government, Palestinian rights, or American foreign policy, most Jews agree on the absolute need for a Jewish state. The American government encouraged the establishment of Israel for power-political reasons (and perhaps as a way of dealing with the embarrassing problem of Jewish refugees no country was willing to absorb); it has continued to support Israel as a pro-Western, anti-Soviet ally in a strategically vital region. But in the past few years, the U.S. has been reevaluating its stance, in line with changing political realities; as a result Jewish lobbying has met increasing resistance. Despite supposed Jewish control of the media, coverage of the Middle East and the climate of public opinion have evolved more or less in accordance with government policy, growing steadily less sympathetic to Israel.

In general, the major media—including Jewish-owned institutions like *The New York Times*—reflect establishment politics, whether or not they coincide with Jewish interests or opinion. Evidently, either Jews are less dominant in the media than popular wisdom insists, or Jewish publishers and Hollywood producers put their class loyalties before their Jewishness. Dreyfuss complains that "Jewish dissidents in the Soviet Union enjoy a flood of publicity, but black dissidents in South Africa are ignored until they are killed." Can he seriously believe this bias reflects Jewish influence rather than government and corporate hostility to the U.S.S.R. and sympathy with the staunchly capitalist South African regime? He contrasts indifference to racism in television with the "uproar" that followed the casting of Vanessa Redgrave as a concentration camp victim. Yet the Jewish protest elicited no serious, thoughtful response, only condescending lectures about the evils of blacklisting and the right to criticize Israel, (I keep waiting for someone to notice that these days dumping on Israel is about as daring as defending the family, but no such luck.)

The danger of getting carried away with fantasies about Jewish power is manifest in Dreyfuss's assertion that "Jews have taken control of [New York City's] political apparatus. In the process of exercising their new powers they have neglected to appease the powerless. . . ." Just a minute. Who is this "they?" It certainly isn't me, or even the American Jewish Committee; it would seem, actually, to be one lone Jew, Ed Koch. (What about poor Abe Beame? He may not have been memorable, but he did exist.) In his zeal to pin blacks' troubles on the Jews, Dreyfuss not only makes a dubious leap from the particular to the general, he totally ignores the context of Koch's administration—draconian fiscal retrenchment imposed on the city from outside. Koch's brushing aside of minority concerns is indefensible (again, his whiteness, not his Jewishness, is the relevant category), but the people who really call the shots on New York are the president, Congress, and a bunch of bankers and realtors. I fail to see what Jews as a group are getting out of this depressing situation.

It is disingenuous of Dreyfuss to argue that "Jewish power in America has always been a difficult subject to address. . . . Their most effective tactic has been to attack any references to the power of Jews as 'anti-Semitic,' immediately blocking further discussion." Talk about blocking discussion! I can only pursue this one honestly if I'm permitted to say what I think, which is that the notion of Jewish power is a classic anti-Semitic myth. There are historical parallels to Jews' present position in America. In pre-Inquisition Spain, in Weimar Germany, Jews were a privileged and seemingly powerful group, a conspicuous cultural force. But their status did not protect them; on the contrary, charges of excessive Jewish power and influence in behalf of their own nefarious ends served as a rationale for persecution. Hence American Jews' feelings of insecurity, which—according to Dreyfuss—blacks find so mystifying.

Discrimination against Jews in America has not been comparable to the systematic, relentless bigotry inflicted on blacks. But in concluding that Jewish oppression can be defined as "exclusion similar in conception but vastly different in degree from the black experience," Dreyfuss makes a common mistake. Though there are obvious parallels between white racism and anti-Semitism—particularly racial anti-Semitism of the Nazi variety—the psychology of anti-Semitism, the way it functions in society, and the nature of the threat to the Jews are in certain respects unique. Unlike racism, anti-Semitism does not necessarily involve straight-forward economic subjugation. Historically, Jews' distinctive class and cultural patterns, their visibility as representatives or symbols of authority (from the Harlem storekeeper on up the class ladder, but rarely at the very top), and their reputation as hustlers, achievers, intellectuals, and social activists have been the basis of anti-Semitic stereotypes used to justify attacks on Jews. Jews are simultaneously perceived as insiders and outsiders, capitalists and communists, upholders of high ethical and intellectual standards and shrewd purveyors of poisonous subversive ideas. The common theme of these disparate perceptions is that Jews have enormous power, whether to defend established authority or to undermine it. It is this double-edged myth of Jewish power that has made Jews such a useful all-purpose scapegoat for social discontent. The classic constituency for fascism is the conservative lower middle class, oppressed by the rich, threatened by the rebellious poor (particularly if the poor are foreign or another race); for this group Jews are a perfect target, since they represent the top and the bottom at once. Oppressed classes like the peasants in czarist Russia have traditionally directed their anger at the Jews just above them in the social hierarchy.

The advantage to ruling classes of keeping Jews around as surrogate authority figures is obvious. But anti-Semitism can't be explained simply as a political tool; it is deeply irrational. The insane obsessiveness of Hitler's determination to wipe out the Jews even at the expense of his war effort was, in my view, not an aberrational form of anti-Semitism, but its logical extreme. I think anti-Semitism is bound up with people's anger not only at class oppression but at the whole structure of patriarchal civilization—at the authoritarian family and state, at a morality that exalts the mind, denigrates the body, and represses sexuality. As Freud observed, "civilized" self-denial generates an enormous reservoir of unconscious rage. I believe it is this rage, along with misdirected anger at economic and political oppression, that erupts in the murder of Jews. In one sense Jews *have* been immensely powerful: they created a potent myth—influential in both Christian and Islamic cultures—that explains patriarchal civilization and includes an elaborate set of rules for right living in it. And Jews themselves play a special role in this myth, as God the Father's chosen people, commanded to carry out an ethical and spiritual mission in behalf of the world—to obey God's laws and by doing so bring the Messiah, who will redeem and liberate us all. As the protagonists of this paradoxical vision, Jews are at once superego figures and symbols of revolution, who evoke all the ambivalent feelings that stem from the contradictions of patriarchy.

Just as the idealization of femininity is inseparable from male resentment of women, anti-Semitism is two-faced. It includes admiration of Jewish achievements, the idea that Jews are morally superior, guilt, and identification with the Jew-as-victim. The complementary attitudes inevitably follow; envy; the conviction that Jews are too powerful; a combination of special outrage and covert gloating whenever Jews are revealed to be, alas, morally imperfect (check out the reaction to any Jew judged guilty of unsaintly behavior, from Bernard Bergman to Menachim Begin); resentment at having to feel guilty about the Jews, it was 35 years ago, after all; a mixture of self-congratulation and defensiveness at daring to criticize Jews; anger at Jews who refuse to act like victims. (In his column on the Vanessa Redgrave flap, Eliot Fremont-Smith pointed to her acceptance of the role as evidence that anti-Zionism and anti-Semitism are not synonymous. On the contrary, Redgrave exemplifies a mentality that has flourished ever since 1967, when Israel became the prime metaphor for the powerful Jew; she hates Bad Jews—Zionists—and loves Good Jews—victims, preferably dead.) But the power of Jews as emotional symbols would mean little if they were not hugely outnumbered and so, in reality, powerless. It is the combination that makes anti-Semitism so appealing: to kill a gnat, imagining it's an elephant, is to feel powerful indeed.

I think people's feelings about Jews are largely unconscious, that discrimination and outbreaks of anti-Jewish persecution are only the most obvious symptoms of a chronic social disease that exists mainly under the surface. This is why anti-Semitism flares up so readily in times of social crisis; it is why Jews feel permanently insecure; it accounts for the gap in communication between Jews who feel that gentiles are always looking for anti-Semites under the bed. Anti-Semitism involves dark impulses that most people would rather not recognize in themselves, impulses connected with our deepest guilts and anxieties. Even people who are sophisticated about the politics of race and sex tend to cling to a simplistic view of anti-Semitism as plain old discrimination, punctuated from time to time with persecution by evil lunatics—in either case, nothing to do with *them*. There is enormous resistance, even among Jews, to analyzing anti-Semitism as a serious, ongoing social force, or to recognizing the anti-Jewish subtext in superficially reasonable political arguments. A lot of Jewish alienation has to do with the subterranean character of anti-Semitism. Suppose your friends and colleagues were always having fits of selective amnesia, during which they insisted that what you clearly remembered was your imagination. Eventually you would begin to question your reality: What's going on? Am I crazy? Is she doing this to me on purpose? By means of a similar process, Jewish "paranoia" about anti-Semitism often becomes paranoia in fact.

Black people who scapegoat Jews for white racism and exaggerate Jewish power are collaborating in a familiar and scary game. That black leaders should blame Jews for

Andy Young's resignation is not surprising, but the evidence doesn't bear them out. Jews, who can add two and two like anyone else, could not fail to note that Young's meeting with Zehdi Terzi was consistent with the noises the administration has been making for some months. It is Carter's policy Jews care about, not Young—a point Jewish spokespeople have taken care to emphasize. If Carter starts talking to the PLO, Young's dismissal won't gain him any Jewish support; if he doesn't, Young's retention wouldn't have lost him any. (And what about black support? Carter's decision to get rid of Young may well have cost him reelection.) Besides, Jewish organizations are hardly unaware of Black-Jewish tensions. As subsequent events have shown, it was not in their interest for Young to resign, and most of them pointedly refrained from suggesting it. Did Carter act to appease the Israeli government? I doubt it—I think the Israelis understand that Carter is their problem, not Young—but if he did it was in behalf of American diplomacy, not the Jews.

I don't know why Carter let Young resign instead of slapping him on the wrist. Maybe it was just what it looked like—that in arranging to talk with Terzi and then lying about it, Young took his individualism a step too far and convinced the president he couldn't be trusted. Maybe not. The affair still has its loose ends, particularly the question of whether, as Murray Kempton plausibly suggested, Young is taking the rap for a meeting that actually was the State Department's idea. But there is a disturbing irony in the fact that (Jewish-dominated media notwithstanding) blacks have succeeded in defining the issue as Jewish power. Given the energy crisis and the general economic malaise, Americans may be more than normally receptive to the idea that Jews have been controlling our foreign policy. If Carter plans to move significantly closer to the PLO (and anyone who thinks such a move would reflect solicitude for the Palestinians, as opposed to solicitude for oil, is less cynical than I), it can't hurt him to have anti-Jewish sentiment floating around.

Behind the furor over Young lurks the larger issue of how relations between Jews and blacks, Jews and gentiles, blacks and whites affect or are affected by the Israeli-Palestinian conflict. Dreyfuss draws clear battle lines: Jews, white racists, and imperialists for Israel; blacks for the Palestinians, as victims of racist colonialism. But he leaves something important out of this picture—or cartoon—of reality, and that something is anti-Semitism (a semantically unfortunate terms since Arabs are also Semites). Middle East politics would be a lot less confusing and agonizing if anti-Zionism and anti-Semitism were, as so many people want to believe, entirely separate issues. Which is to say that things would be a lot simpler if the Israelis weren't Jews. But if anti-Semitism is, as I have argued, a systemic and pervasive pathology endemic to Christian and Islamic cultures (and, I would imagine, easily communicable in any patriarchy), then anti-Semitism is as much a factor in the Middle East as oil, the military importance of the region, the Palestinians' demand for a homeland, and anti-Arab racism. Anti-Semitism is an actual or potential influence on the conduct of the United States, the Soviet Union, Europe, the United Nations, the Arab countries, and the Palestinians themselves. (Overt anti-Semitism has never been as widespread or severe in the Islamic world as in the Christian West, but since World War II the Arabs have been using explicitly anti-Jewish propaganda, borrowed from Europe, as a weapon against Israel.) Fear of genocidal anti-

Semitism is a determining influence on Israeli policy, far more decisive, I believe, than expansionism, racism, or the fanaticism of religious nationalists. Without anti-Semitism, there would still be a power struggle between the West and the Third World, but the Israeli-Palestinian conflict would not exist, since there would be no political Zionism and no Jewish state.

Anti-Zionism, in the modern political sense, is the argument that a Jewish state in Palestine inherently violates the rights of the Palestinian people. It regards Zionism as a racist, imperialist movement in which the European Jewish bourgeoisie (Jewish power, again) acted in concert with the colonial powers to displace the indigenous Arabs, furthering white Western domination of the Middle East. It assumes that religious belief is the movement's ideological rationale, and so the PLO calls for the abolition of the Israeli state in favor of a "democratic, secular" Palestine. The essential problem with this argument is that it ignores or denies the reality of the Jewish condition. First of all, to get around the fact that the Jews also have historic ties to Palestine, that they are not simply aliens and interlopers, anti-Zionists tend to define Jewishness purely in terms of religion, and dismiss as mythology the idea that Jews around the world are one people. But Jews have always regarded themselves, and have been regarded by others, as an organic entity, in some sense a nation; a traditional excuse for anti-Semitism has been that Jews have divided loyalties. Nor is political Zionism basically a religious movement. Orthodox Jews who believe in the Biblical prophecies are Zionists by definition, but they did not conceive of Zion in political terms—indeed, many opposed the establishment of a Jewish state as sacrilegious. The movement for statehood came from "emancipated" Jews who believed that Jews would always be oppressed so long as they were homeless and forced into marginality in gentile societies. Zionism is a national liberation movement, and despite the rise of religious nationalism and a powerful religious establishment that (like the Catholic Church elsewhere) has imposed some religious laws on an unwilling majority, Israel is essentially a secular state.

As for the charge that Zionism is an imperialist plot, it does not simply misdefine the Jews but makes them disappear. The relationship between Zionists and the Western nations has always been tense and ambiguous; they have served each other's needs, but their needs are very different. And the Jews who settled in Palestine after World War II were neither ambitious capitalists nor Zionist ideologues; they were traumatized refugees who were unwelcome anywhere else. Some years ago I asked a woman who supported the PLO if she thought Jews had no right to national aspirations. Not at all, she assured me, so long as their nation wasn't on someone else's land. Which set me to musing about possibilities. The Sahara Desert? The Amazon jungle? Imagine what would have happened if the Zionists had accepted Britain's offer of a homeland in Uganda.

As far as I'm concerned, the only solution to the Israeli-Palestinian impasses that makes moral sense is two independent states. Whatever one's intellectual position on Zionism—that is, the idea that all Jews should settle in Israel—Israel's existence as an alternative has clearly reduced Jewish vulnerability and, I believe, is a psychological deterrent to anti-Semites. The abolition of Israel and the incorporation of a Jewish minority in an Arab-dominated Palestine would at best put all Jews back in a pre-

Holocaust situation, and for the Israelis, the reality could be far worse. It is questionable whether all Israelis would be allowed to remain as equal citizens; the PLO's charter, which defines as Palestinians only Jews who lived in Palestine before "the Zionist invasion," is not reassuring on this point. And is the mutual hatred of all these years expected to just evaporate? But practically speaking these questions are irrelevant, because the Israelis will defend their state until they are massacred or driven out. In which case the world will no doubt blame them for being stubborn.

Another difficulty with the idea that anti-Zionism has nothing to do with anti-Semitism is that the great majority of Jews perceive the two issues as inseparable. One might argue, with equal logic, "I'm not a racist, I'm just against forced integration," or "I love women, it's feminists I can't stand." Vanessa Redgrave may think that Zionism is "a brutal racist ideology" and "the opposite of Judaism," but she will find precious few Jews who agree with her. This puts her in the peculiar position of implying that except for an enlightened minority, Jews are brutal racists, and that she know what Judaism is better than we do. Which is why her ritual tributes to Jews' heroic record of struggle, and so on, are not only empty but obnoxious. As most Jews see it, the Israelis' right to national self-determination would be taken for granted if they weren't Jewish. The Palestinians have the same right, of course. What makes the Middle East situation so excruciating is the spectacle of two displaced, oppressed peoples, each of them victimized by more powerful nations, trying to kill each other. But at this point in history, absolute justice for the Palestinians would mean absolute injustice for the Jews.

My guess is that most *Voice* readers have no quarrel with this last point. Anti-Zionist thinking predominates in most of the world, but here it has been mostly confined to the sectarian left. Nearly everyone agrees, in principle, on Israel's right to exist. Yet I feel that non-Jews in America—particularly my peers, middle-class liberals and radicals, the vanguard of "enlightened" opinion—do their own milder version of making the Jews disappear. In theory, they acknowledge that Jews are oppressed. In practice, they see Israel much as Dreyfuss sees the Jews—as a powerful nation beating up on the have-nots. They assume that Israeli chauvinism, expansionism, and refusal to admit the justice of the Palestinian cause are primarily or entirely to blame for preventing a settlement. But a two-state compromise can work only if the international community supports and enforces it, and the international atmosphere is overwhelmingly hostile to Israel. Most countries endorse the PLO's claim to all of Palestine; if it weren't for the United States, Israel would be long gone. And now American support is eroding.

In this situation, the Israelis are damned if they do and damned if they don't. If they resist a Palestinian state they stand condemned as oppressors and obstructionists, and give their only major ally an excuse for withdrawing support. If they agree, the Palestinians with their own state as a base will be in an infinitely better position to pursue their claim to what they deeply believe is theirs, and the Israelis have no good reason to believe that anyone will lift a finger to defend them. Is it any wonder that they resist what has got to look like suicide by installments? Why should they trust the PLO to accept a state as more than a temporary expedient? Why should they trust the United States when no country has ever proved trustworthy in its dealing with Jews? The American ruling class is profoundly anti-Semitic; it is not going to protect Israel for humanitarian reasons, any more than it was willing to provide a haven for Jewish refugees during World War II, or "waste" a few planes to bomb Auschwitz. Under the circumstances, the self-righteous, simplistic condemnation of Israel that currently passes as a "balanced view" is, in my opinion, anti-Jewish. Many aspects of Israeli government policy, including its alliances with reactionary regimes, disturb me enough to make me wonder if in its determination to survive Israel will lose its reason for being. But at least I can recognize desperation when I see it; at least I understand—no, share— the bitterness that says, "To hell with morality and world opinion! World opinion never did a thing for the Jews!"

The Israelis are in the classic Jewish bind. To the Palestinians and the Third World, they are white oppressors, but to their fellow white oppressors they are Jews. If they are surrogates for the West, it is largely in having to pay for Western sins. For once, the West may end up paying as well; Dreyfuss is probably right. "History is on the side of the 'have-nots,' here and abroad." But no matter whose side history is on, Jews have always been expendable. And so long as we are expendable, to talk of "Jewish power" is obscene.

# Blacks and Jews in the Democratic Coalition

The logic of [Jesse] Jackson's conflict with organized Jewry is more complex than his hostility to labor because the political connection between Afro-Americans and Jews is more ambiguous. Recognition of this ambiguity is limited by a ritualistic pattern of discussion of black/Jewish relations that obscures the dynamics joining the groups. At the nucleus of this discourse are the shibboleths that affirm unity and proclaim a continuing history of common purpose. Commitment to these shibboleths forces expressions of conflict into one of two modes: (1) oblique arguments couched in terms of formal principles (for example, quotas) and abstracted from the goals of Jews and blacks as historically specific social agents; or (2) an Aesopian criticism in which disagreement over issues that are structurally remote from the groups' sphere of mutuality (for instance, the Middle East) is adduced to stand for bases of tension closer to home. The path to comprehending the structural foundations of alliance and dissension, both in general and as they were reflected through the Jackson phenomenon, requires breaking the delicately crafted ritual code and addressing squarely the practical substance of the black/Jewish dialectic in American politics.

## JEWS' DUAL STATUS IN RACIAL DIALOGUE

Certain points need to be made as a precondition for decoding. First, there is no simple "historic political relation between blacks and Jews." Instead, there have been several fields of political action in which fairly distinct congeries of Jews and blacks have mutually participated. Among these are Communist and other left-wing activity in the 1930s and 1940s, civil rights activism and its organizational elaboration into professionalized civil rights engineering, the national Democratic coalition, and its local articulations. With the exceptions of the radical Left (and to a slightly lesser extent grass-roots civil rights activity) where "Jewishness" and/or "blackness" have been less significant as overtly institutionalized, official status categories, the Jewish/Afro-American relationship has been determined through the mediation of elite-driven formal advocacy organizations such as the NAACP and National Urban League on the one side and the American Jewish Congress, American Jewish Committee, and Anti-Defamation League of B'nai B'rith on the other.

Jewish elites have had at least two advantages in this mediated interaction. Because

Adolph L. Reed Jr. was a professor of political science at the University of Illinois, Chicago.
Reprinted from Adolph L. Reed Jr., *The Jesse Jackson Phenomenon: The Crisis of Purpose in Afro-American Politics* (New Haven: Yale University Press, 1986). Copyright © 1986, Yale University Press. Reprinted with permission of Yale University Press.

the interaction has been largely governed by an ideological commitment to interracialism, Jews have been able to steer "dialogue" from each side, both as representatives of autonomous Jewish interest groups and as prominent forces within interracial civil rights organizations. The peculiarity of Jewishness as a status that is neither racial, nor national nor, for that matter, necessarily religious exonerates Jewish elites from the imperative of organizational interracialism in their own domain while demanding obeisance to it from black civil rights organizations, as in the case of the black power elaboration out of the civil rights movement.[1] The double standard of this Jewish/black dialectic is so deeply ingrained that it generally does not surface for public observation and comment. However, a recent controversy may be illustrative.

In the early 1980s trustees of New York's famed Schomburg collection of Afro-Americana hired a curator who was white and rumored to be Jewish. Outraged black nationalists marched, demonstrated, and otherwise expressed anger and dismay at what they considered a travesty. Despite its origination from a rather crude and narrow-minded parochialism, the protest incisively brought the double standard into relief. While the idea of a Jewish Schomburg curator is plausible to the public consciousness, opponents observed, appointment of a black director of the Wiesenthal Center or a similar institution devoted to Jewish cultural documentation would seem somehow counterintuitive, if not plainly ludicrous. Notwithstanding the merits of the Schomburg case, which are very much open to debate, this incident exposes clearly one of the senses in which Jewish elites are advantageously situated in the "historic relations" with blacks; Jewish representation of black interests is legitimated by prevailing cultural norms while the notion of black custodianship of Jewish interests is not.

The second advantage redounding to Jews is related to the first. Black racial advocacy organizations depend largely on private philanthropy, access to which often runs through or can be vetoed by elites of Jewish interest organizations. Obviously, Jewish advocacy is not similarly constrained to placate black concerns. As a case in point, in the spring of 1976 I attended what amounted to a public job interview of Julian Bond, who recently had expressed an interest in succeeding Roy Wilkins as executive director of the NAACP. Bond, who from his Student Nonviolent Coordinating Committee days until that year had refrained from supporting Israeli policy in the Middle East, had been invited to a "Meet the Press" forum at the Jewish Community Center in Atlanta. Although Bond finally had signed Bayard Rustin's annual Black Americans in Support of Israel Committee (BASIC) statement that year, he was apparently reluctant to attend what he suspected would be a grilling on the Middle East. According to a *Time* magazine reporter close to Bond and to the incident, Henry Lee Moon, an NAACP official, telephoned Bond and advised him very strongly of the need to attend the session if he were at all serious in his desire to replace Wilkins. He attended, and the tenor of the event approximated an inquisition or show trial, with some questioners explicitly characterizing Bond's attempt to maintain critical distance from Israel's interpretation of Middle East conflict as consequential for his NAACP aspirations. The reverse situation is unthinkable; black insistence on endorsement of affirmative action quotas or repudiation of Israel's ties to South Africa, for instance, never would be a pertinent criterion for organizational legitimation of Jewish leadership.

Insofar as the relationship follows that pattern, the association of Jewish and black leadership is acted out on a terrain defined by the former. The hypothesis of commonality of interest therefore assumes the comparatively advantageous position occupied by Jewish organizational elites. This is not to suggest that blacks are duped, coopted, or coerced to pursue "Jewish interests." A more accurate view is that black and Jewish elites pursue their independent interests on the basis of pragmatic rationality that defines objectives within a given set of options. The apparent finitude of the options expresses acceptance of or acquiescence to an arrangement of social forces that constitutes the "rules of the game."[2] The elites' sphere of mutuality derives from their respective readings of possibilities afforded. The environmental condition of greater Jewish institutional entrenchment combines with interracialism to structure a context of action in which rational, independent articulation and pursuit of pragmatic goals by black elites requires a nonreciprocal attentiveness to Jewish organizational interests.[3] The sacrosanct status of Israel in the Jewish agenda, for example, prohibits black elites' capacity to press their opposition to apartheid by criticizing the Israeli/South African axis. Despite the growth in the 1970s and 1980s of an elite-centered, Afro-American Africa lobby, organized Jewry's defensiveness concerning Israel limits public criticism among *black* leadership. Jewish Zionism, to put the matter somewhat provocatively, overrides black Zionism—even in the black organizational apparatus!

The black elite agenda is organized according to a hierarchy of priorities in which, among other considerations, objectives that might engender opposition from Jewish organizations are treated as less important than those for which Jewish support or neutrality might be expected. (Continuing black support for quotas to achieve affirmative action goals appears to be an exception to this norm.) This hierarchy reinforces the notion of a special black/Jewish unity. The apparent convergence of black and Jewish elite interests, however, reflects a rational adaptation by blacks to a context in which the material costs of potential Jewish alienation are high. What makes for inequality in this sense—in addition to material dependency—is that black elites, because they do not similarly penetrate the core of Jewish strategic activity, cannot replicate the tacit (and sometimes not so tacit) veto power that Jewish elites have held in black interest articulation processes.

Obviously, the relative cost of loss of Jewish support is a function of the significance attached to that support in black leadership's strategic calculus, which is in turn dependent on the elite's particular perception of the range of acceptable options. To that extent, this situation ultimately is a symptom of black political elites' century-long pattern of uncritical acceptance of fundamental power relations in the general society and reliance on external sources of legitimation. However, the black/Jewish epicycle may contribute on its own as well to the Afro-American elite's crisis of political direction. Jewish representation on both sides of interracial dialogue not only has meant that an injunction to account for Jewish elite interests is embedded in black leadership's agenda-forming activity. The conceptual and discursive framework thus developed influences black political activity in two additional respects, with a single effect. On the one hand, elevation of interracialism to the status of a political principle—required to justify extrinsic intervention in agenda-setting—thoroughly conflates means and ends, goals, strategies, and tactics, and affirms a criterion for political debate that has little direct connection to public policy. On the other hand, because the programmatic basis for the unity of black and Jewish elites has become increasingly fragile, commonality can be vouchsafed only by restricting the scope of black political involvement as much as possible to a narrowly construed project of race relations engineering, or in the parlance of an earlier period, "race adjustment." Potential conflict is avoided by excluding certain areas of public policy from the realm of autonomous concern for black spokespersons. This restriction, of course, is consistent with the racial protest ideology that undergirds contemporary black politics anyway. The destabilization of the "historic unity" of black and Jewish elites since the civil rights era suggests that structural differentiation of the interests of their upper status and upwardly mobile constituencies may have reached a point at which mutuality cannot be assured even around the most incremental program of race relations management.

Distilled from the absurdly reified discourse of collective "hurt," "suffering," and "healing" through which it was voiced, the controversy between Jackson and Jewish elites says much about the present state of the "historic unity." Although Jackson's slurring references and links with Louis Farrakhan created much furor, he had been viewed with considerable circumspection by Jewish elites from the beginning of his campaign.[4] Certainly, his history of association with the PLO and other Arab groups had much to do with Jewish wariness. Reaction to the "Hymie town" slurs, moreover, brought to light a series of anti-Semitic utterances made by Jackson in recent years.[5] Yet the Jackson camp's complaints that attacks on their candidate's insulting remarks were a smokescreen covering other objections, while hardly overcoming Jackson's culpability, have some basis.

Jackson's incidental remarks provoked a shrillness strikingly absent from reaction to the more programmatic and ideological anti-Semitism emanating from such quarters as the Moral Majority. In this regard, it is significant that Arthur Hertzberg, past president of the American Jewish Congress, has observed the spread of "revolt" against liberalism among middle class Jews motivated by a desire to "protect their class interest as 'haves.'" Hertzberg notes that this tendency extends even to toleration of "the emergence of a right-wing 'Christian America.'"[6]

Albert Vorspan, vice president of the Union of American Hebrew Congregations, indicated that he had rarely seen Jews so upset as they were over the Jackson controversy, and his explanation for the "deep dismay" also focused on material concerns. "For many Jews," Vorspan maintained, "this is an excuse to bolt concern for blacks, cities and the rest of it. For others, it will be an excuse to go for Ronald Reagan."[7] Although fears concerning widespread Jewish defection to Reagan were not realized, the material bases of black/Jewish tension remain intact.[8]

## STATUS DISPLACEMENT IN BLACK/JEWISH CONFLICT

Black/Jewish conflict springs from two main sources: (1) competition within the professional apparatus of social administration; and (2) black encroachment—via extension of the logic of affirmative action as an elite mobility strategy—on enclaves of relative Jewish privilege in education and elsewhere. Development of a community control orientation within black activism in the 1960s led to dramatic manifestation of the contraposition of blacks as clients of service agencies and institutions (for example, public schools) and Jews as professional service providers. This relation was overlapped by the tension between relatively entrenched Jews and upwardly mobile blacks seeking to carve out niches of their own in the public service apparatus. Of course, this class of objectives ultimately involved blacks and Jews only to the extent that they operated on that contested terrain, and the fundamental lines of cleavage were status-linked and structural rather than attitudinal.[9] However, the explosion surrounding the New York school crisis of 1967–68 set a precedent for redefining structurally generated conflict between blacks and Jews in terms purporting the rise of anti-Semitism among blacks.

The Ocean Hill–Brownsville controversy was the occasion of another instance of rare Jewish disturbance, and, as in the Jackson case, the frenzy was precipitated by charges of black anti-Semitism. The underlying substantive issue—conflict between the primarily black and Hispanic parents on one side and the primarily white teachers union over control of the recently decentralized Ocean Hill–Brownsville school district in Brooklyn[10]—was lost in the outcry. Albert Shanker, president of New York City's United Federation of Teachers, fought the impetus to community control, opposing the state's legislative provision for decentralization by describing it as "an attack on teachers" and raising the specter of "anti-Semitic conspiracy."[11] Thus the terms in which the mainly black parents had expressed a demand for participation were redefined and the nature of the debate altered.

Rabbi Jay Kaufmann, then executive director of B'nai B'rith, reduced the entire controversy to the significance of marginalia: an anti-Semitic leaflet, a child's anti-Semitic poem that had been read on the radio, and a handful of other, more vague horror stories. On this basis Kaufmann proclaimed "the prevalence and virulence of anti-Semitism presently festering in the Negro community,"[12] and contended that there was "no question that the Negro community is ripe for a neo-fascism."[13] He acknowledged, almost in passing, the objective grounds of tension in Jewish visibility in administering black dispossession through the schools, public service apparatus, housing markets, and commercial infrastructure in the black community.[14] His proposals, however, were one-sided, calling on blacks to remember the extent to which their political interests have been connected with Jews'; more to the point, he chided black power–era blacks, instructively, for being "less willing than the youngsters of previous ethnic groups to demonstrate the patience required for the laborious, step-by-step ascent up the economic ladder [and] insisting that . . . their people be allowed to leapfrog over their peers and superiors into posts others are unwilling to abandon or forgo."[15] In this light Alan W. Miller, rabbi of the Society for the Advancement of Judaism, while denouncing the smattering of anti-Semitism around Ocean Hill–Brownsville as "the moronic lucubrations of illiterate racists," suspected that "those who are making the most noise about *black* anti-Semitism have a hidden agenda, a covert ideological bias."[16] He concluded from his experience as a parent in one of the schools affected by the teachers' strike against the community school board that "anti-Semitism was being used by Jews as part of a deliberate policy to unite New York Jews against the legitimate aspirations of black and Puerto Rican parents and children in a school system which has abysmally failed them."[17]

The "hidden agenda," then as now, was material interest. Albert Vorspan, who attempted both in 1968 and again in 1984 to project a voice of reason, asked: "Why is it that we Jews, who were not panicked by Wallace, Rockwell, Gerald L. K. Smith or the Ku Klux Klan, can be panicked by anti-Semitism coming from blacks? And why is it that, when we talk about anti-Semitism today, we talk about *black* anti-Semitism almost exclusively?" His answer was the same in 1969 as in 1984; the hysteria was an excuse "to justify disengagement and withdrawal from the social scene."[18] Specifically in the school issue, the agenda was "manipulation of the Jewish community by those who sought to line it up on one side (to fight the 'black Nazis') in an economic dispute."[19] While joining in criticism of black leadership for not appearing properly aggressive in denouncing expressions of anti-Semitism among blacks, Vorspan also noted the nearly complete silence of Jewish spokespersons with regard to racist effusions from the Jewish Defense League, striking teachers, and others.[20] In so doing, he pointed to the core tension in the Jewish/Afro-American relationship, which extends beyond the issue of conflict in social service agencies—a conflict, he observed, that is to a considerable degree peculiar to New York City. The broader and more enduring problem stems from the double standard that has organized the groups' political interaction. As Vorspan said:

> The truth is that [black-Jewish relations] never were really good. We Jews did a great deal *for* black people, and that is precisely the point. We were the leaders, we called the shots, we set the timetable, we evolved the strategy, we produced the money . . . we were the superior people. This was no relationship of peer to peer, equal to equal, powerful group to powerful group.[21]

Although Jews have been more visible than other whites in support of black causes, this support has grown by no means from altruism alone. Vorspan's 1969 characterization remains persuasive:

> Jewish racial liberalism has operated in inverse relation to the distance from Jewish economic interests. Jewish organizations were strong on desegregating the South; relatively few Jews were involved, and they were safely ignored. Jews supported fair housing and fair employment in the North; it was largely the WASP establishments which were cracked open, both for Jews and for blacks. Jewish organizations supported Lindsay's referendum for a civilian review board in New York City, that was directed against Irish cops. But the school strike impinged upon large number of Jews. . . . Jews have become a successful part of the American system. . . . They will resist efforts to smash [it], to restructure it fundamentally, or to "sacrifice Jewish interests" in the process of reform.[22]

While not belittling the extent to which Jewish individuals have come together with blacks around honestly shared commitment to positions of democratic principle, it is necessary to recognize that the black/Jewish nexus has benefited Jews also by enabling them to mobilize black support for agendas that advance Jewish interests. As black elites' interests uncouple from Jews', the foundation of the general alliance becomes unsteady.

The fight against discrimination in higher education, restricted housing covenants, and the like aided Jews as much as blacks—if not more, given the Jews' relatively better position to realize the benefits of strict equality of opportunity. The demand that old-boy admissions standards at elite universities be replaced by a "meritocratic" principle based on "objective" criteria such as standardized tests has worked doubly to Jews' advantage, by eliminating the nefarious practice of maintaining quotas on Jewish admissions and by advocating the adoption of a standard of intelligence or capacity demonstrated by the test operations that Jewish applicants typically perform well. In this sense, Anglo-Saxon wealth and its cultural and stylistic attributes were the "meritocratic" criteria used by the entrenched old-boy crowd to deny access to other claimant groups, including Jews and the unwashed. Performance on "objective" Scholastic Aptitude Tests (SATs) became the compensatory affirmative action vehicle allowing Jews to overcome their "isolation" from WASP, old-boy networks.

Generalization of "objective" testable standards of capacity—for university admissions, civil service employment, professional certification, and so on—both expands and constricts access simultaneously. On the one hand, it limits access by narrowing selection to a one-dimensional criterion, the ability to perform certain mensurable operations (largely involving quick recall) in a particular kind of controlled context. This criterion undoubtedly approaches a notion of capacity that is more inclusive, more compatible with the values of intellectual subculture, and more tolerable to the democratic temper than is assignment of privilege on the basis of unmediated reference to ascriptive characteristics. After all, though SATs and Graduate Record Exams are hardly flawless predictors of performance, they nonetheless can be useful in identifying certain strengths and weaknesses that may influence academic performance. (The utility of standardized exams for mail carriers, firefighters, and social workers, of course, is more dubious.) However, since it tends to restrict definition of merit to ability to complete a specified range of abstract mental performances, that impersonalized standard discounts other attributes that might equally be valuable as indicators of capability or, for that matter, as components of a definition of the goals of education or of a given profession. Put another way, selection of one or another criterion of ability to perform in a role is premised on a prior assumption concerning the proper composition of the role; such assumptions entail specific views regarding social utility and are to that extent political choices.

In the old-boy view of elite education, for example, access is governed by a goal of socialization directed toward securing transgenerational reproduction of a cohesive upper-class culture. Therefore, correct breeding is a standard of "merit" because it is a functional requirement for participation in advanced socialization processes whose intended outcome is production of well-rounded members of an elite. The attack on this restrictiveness conducted from below in the name of equality of opportunity demands opening of access to groups incapable of satisfying requirements of pedigree and thus proposes an amendment to the functional definition of elite education. The more "objective" standard of test-brightness represents a compromise that mediates the breeding requirement—though in principle more than fact—by installing a criterion which, while protecting entrenched elites' access through the prep school network, is oriented to producing test-brightness and technically is accessible to those who have assimilated the skill by other means. At the same time, this opening—which is at any rate qualified—is accompanied by a functional redefinition of the educational project that tends to reduce it to completion of a series of discrete, finely measured performances. The goal of multifarious socialization, that is, is deemphasized by the objectivistic criterion.

The point of this excursus is simply that the practical notion of meritocratic standards that has been taken to fulfill equality of opportunity ideology is neither intrinsically more inviolable nor necessarily freer of bias than that which it replaces or any other. Recognition of its partiality in turn repoliticizes the specific programmatic basis of black/Jewish tension that has developed in the post–civil rights era. At the time of the Ocean Hill–Brownsville controversy even Miller and Vorspan opposed the developing orientation among black elites to shift from formal equality of opportunity to equality of outcome as a focus of antidiscrimination activity. (Vorspan, at least, seems subsequently to have retreated from his opposition.) Other, less sympathetic Jewish elite spokespersons laid down an unequivocal anti–affirmative action line, supported by old bromides to the effect that blacks should be content in their place in the queue of ethnic succession and follow in the footsteps of other groups—specifically Jews—while waiting their turn. There is no need to rehearse the various arguments concerning the propriety of or need for affirmative action strategies. Regardless of their efficacy or lack thereof, the important fact is that those strategies are understood by Jewish elites as infringements on norms for allocation of privilege from which they benefit and which they interpret as rights. This, then, is the substantive basis of black/Jewish conflict in the current period.

Jesse Jackson's simple-minded anti-Semitic discourse, which on one occasion at least he projected as "talking black," reflects his opportunistic appropriation of the outlook of an upwardly mobile but harried stratum in the black community, a stratum which—like Kafka's burrowing animal—is consumed by fearful visions of antagonists pressing from all sides. This outlook yields a meanness of spirit and small-mindedness that historically have opened to protofascistic articulations in Europe, Latin America, and elsewhere.

Certainly, the cathartic frenzy that Jackson cultivated, with its elimination of debate among Afro-Americans, reveals the dangerous tendencies inherent in that mind-set. As William Raspberry observed after the obious "Hymie" incident, Jackson ruined the one contribution that he might have made to national political debate during the primary season, that is, the call for a more reasonable approach to United States policy on the Middle East.[23] In one stroke Jackson sacrificed the moral authority on which he might have stood to demand a Middle Eastern policy that acknowledges the legitimacy of interests other than Israel's. However, in an environment in which the American Zionist lobby is disposed to brand any criticism of Israel as anti-Semitism, Jackson's slurs not only tainted his image; they also destroyed—albeit unfairly—the credibility of the stance with which he had aligned himself. Yet neither Jackson's offensive remarks nor his association with a critical posture toward Israel can account for the intensity of Jewish elites' reaction and the proliferation of accusations of black anti-Semitism. Similar or worse slurs by others—for example, the Southern Baptist Convention president's blunt assertion that God will not answer the prayers of a Jew, or James Watt's occasional epithets—have failed to elicit comparably strident reactions.

The source of the caterwauling over Jackson is the same "hidden agenda" that Rabbi Miller sensed in the Ocean Hill–Brownsville controversy. The anti-Jackson diatribe was expressed consistently on three levels: two emotional and hysterical, one calm and programmatic. Most overt was castigation of his anti-Semitic statements and his link to Farrakhan. Then his association with Arafat and receipt of Arab money simultaneously reinforced the image of black support of genocide against Jews *and* the notion that criticism of Israel equals anti-Semitism. Finally, and invariably, came reaffirmation of Jewish opposition to affirmative action quotas. The three were tied together neatly, and—in line with the 1968–69 experience—it was the last that was the substantive issue. At the height of the Jackson controversy, Charles Wittenstein of the Anti-Defamation League volunteered that "we don't think a racial quota is ever benign because, while conferring a benefit on one race, it imposes a disability on another."[24] Vorspan intimated that affirmative action lay at the crux of the problem when, at a forum organized to quell tension, he acknowledged that he was "deeply troubled by those who are so insensitive to . . . black needs that they turn affirmative action into a black-Jewish confrontation, which it never must be."[25]

It is in this context that the brutally adamant line taken on Jackson by Jewish elites around the Democratic convention should be perceived. It was at the same time that Jackson was pressing his anemic platform—which included endorsement of affirmative action quotas—that Jewish spokespersons insisted most strongly that Mondale repudiate him as the price for Jewish support.[26] Even after Jackson's plea for forgiveness in his convention address, spokespersons from the Anti-Defamation League (ADL), American Jewish Congress, American Jewish Committee, and Synagogue Council of America remained aloof. Nathan Perlmutter, director of the ADL, in fact escalated his requirements of Jackson on the spot to include repudiation of Castro and the Sandinistas as "echo chambers of Anti-Zionism and anti-Americanism."[27] (It was not clear, however, on what basis the ADL claimed authority to define and protect "Americanism" from other citizens.) It is difficult in this light to resist the argument that the furor about Jackson's anti-Semitism conceals a more immediately programmatic alienation. Vorspan's question of 1969 answers as much in this regard as it asks: "If special provisions are made to bring black youngsters into universities, should Jews convert the issue into one of anti-Semitism on the ground that such quotas would, in practice, lessen the opportunities of some Jewish youngsters to be judged on individual merit alone?"[28]

What all this means is that the political relationship between blacks and Jews is ambiguous, within the Democratic party and otherwise. To the extent that there is reason behind concerns expressed by Hertzberg and others that Jewish elites are poised to bolt from the party's liberal wing, that relationship becomes even less precise. Clarification is possible, but it requires fulfillment of two conditions. First, it is necessary to discard the shibboleths of special unity. That unity is an ideological fiction, a product of the circumstance that Jewish elites have dominated discussion of the black/Jewish nexus. As Rabbi Miller observed, "In the absence of a black Anti-Defamation League, anti-black remarks by Jews have rarely received the same publicity as anti-Semitic remarks by blacks."[29] In the past Jews and blacks have been joined sporadically in pursuit of common or compatible agendas; even then compatibility often has been exaggerated by the skewed character of the union. Jews do not appear to be significantly different from other white groups in their attitudes and behavior toward Afro-Americans. Cruse expresses a broader black opinion in contending that

> American Negroes have, in deference to Jewish sensibilities, tolerated Jewish ambivalence, Jewish liberalism, Jewish paternalism, Jewish exploitation, Jewish racism, Jewish radicalism, Jewish nationalism, in the same way in which they have lived with similar attributes in the white Anglo-Saxon.[30]

Once that empty ideological baggage is jettisoned, it will be possible to satisfy the second condition for clarification of the Jewish/Black political relation: comparison of Afro-American and Jewish leadership's independently articulated agendas for a programmatic consensus within American politics in general and the Democratic party in particular. Dialogue and debate over those agendas, within the party as a forum, will clarify the political directions and visions of the future of the polity with which the two groups identify and will in the process resolve the issues pertaining to their capacity for concerted action.

With respect to this project, the Jackson phenomenon is an emblem of the broader failure of the black political elite. Not only was Jackson's initiative itself bereft of vision or program; it was possible to conduct such an enterprise only because the spokesmanship stratum, of which Jackson was a part, has generated no programmatic discourse that is sensitive to the structural environment in which the Afro-American population (especially the black poor) is embedded. In a context in which, since 1980 at least, the value of the Democratic party's commitment to its liberal constituency has been increasingly assailed from within,[31] the absence of a coherent black agenda tends to forfeit leverage to Democratic neoconservatives who favor driving blacks to the coalition's periphery. Ironically, while the Jackson campaign claimed just the opposite intention, its effect was to take blacks out of the mainstream of the important debate over the party's future—all the more because the Jackson forces could find no position to press other than the right to be accounted for properly in the party hierarchy.

NOTES

1. Harold Cruse observed this irony with regard to developing Black Power nationalism (*The Crisis of the Negro Intellectual* [New York, 1967], esp. 484). Cruse did not anticipate the circumstance, noted by sociologist Oliver Cox several years later, that the articulation of Black Power ideology toward ethnic pluralism—a development which Cruse advocated—was received favorably and reinforced by Jewish elites who had their own reasons to endorse an ethnic pluralist model for American group life. See Oliver C. Cox, "Jewish Self-interest in 'Black Pluralism,'" *Sociological Quarterly* 15 (Spring 1974): 183–98. In a separate critique Cox challenges the explanatory utility of pluralism as a mode of interpretation of American group dynamics in general ("The Question of Pluralism," *Race* 12 [Fourth Quarter 1971]: 385–400).

2. This observation corresponds to the descriptions of agenda formation processes generally operative in interest-group pluralism that have been proffered by Bachrach and Baratz, Stone, and others under such rubrics as "nondecision-making" or different "faces of power." In each case the focus is on the extent to which actual agenda setting depends on a prior—and politically consequential—delimitation of courses of action that can be considered "legitimate." See Peter Bachrach and Morton S. Baratz, *Power and Poverty: Theory and Practice* (New York, 1970), esp. 39–51; John Gaventa, *Power and Powerlessness* (Champaign-Urbana, 1980), 3–33; Steven Lukes, *Power: A Radical View* (London, 1974). Within this general approach Stone is perhaps clearest in distinguishing the ways in which systemic and relational constraints function ideologically to screen possibilities by determining the "logics of success and failure for individuals and institutions" (Clarence N. Stone, "Social Stratification, Nondecision-Making, and the Study of Community Power," *American Politics Quarterly* 10 [July 1982]: 275–302, and "Systemic Power in Community Decision Making: A Restatement of Stratification Theory," *American Political Science Review* 74 [December 1980]: 978–90).

3. This interpretation centers on the interaction of black and Jewish elites within the status group structures legitimized in the Democratic coalition, where Jews and Afro-Americans function principally as such and not as proletarian activists, free-floating individuals committed to a just society or other competing identities.

4. See, for example, Ellen Hume, "Blacks and Jews Find Confrontation Rising over Jesse Jackson," *Wall Street Journal* (May 29, 1984). Irving Kristol characteristically was a principal ideologue of fissure, stating the line in "The Political Dilemma of American Jews," *Commentary* (July 1984).

5. Paul Berman lists several of these in "Jackson and the Left: The Other Side of the Rainbow," *The Nation* (April 7, 1984): 407–08.

6. Arthur Hertzberg, "Behind Jews' Political Principles," *New York Times* (November 2, 1984). Indeed, if there were a reason to fear a mobilization of blacks on behalf of anti-Semitic purposes in the present period, it would lie in the propagation of the religio-political ideology that accompanies the mythology of the political church in the black community. Enlistment of black support for school prayer, anti-abortion politics, and so forth could increase the critical mass pushing for a dangerous Christian "purification" of the polity.

7. Hume, "Blacks and Jews."

8. Jews, in fact, were the only white religious group that Reagan did not carry in 1984, and he did not even run as well among Jewish voters (32 percent) as he had in 1980 (39 percent) ("*New York Times*/CBS News Poll: Portrait of the Electorate," *New York Times* [November 8, 1984]). For an analysis of Jewish voting patterns see Arthur Hertzberg, "Reagan and the Jews," *New York Review of Books* (January 31, 1985), 11–14.

9. Frances Fox Piven and Richard Cloward observe that while professional provider groups and recipients shared a common interest in expansion of the urban public service apparatus over the 1960s, the latter—especially the poor and dependent—constituted less a constituency of the former than a subordinate clientage. The demand for community control challenged this relation. See their essays in *The Politics of Turmoil* (New York, 1974). Lipsky examines the decisional and organizational logics that pattern the priorities of direct providers of human services (public safety, education, welfare, and so on) and their attitudes and behavior toward service recipients. He notes that those "street-level bureaucrats" often have considerable interpretive latitude at the point of execution of policy and program but are constrained primarily by imperatives deriving from bureaucratic and professional norms, rather than client interests (Michael Lipsky, *Toward a Theory of Street-Level Bureaucracy* [New York, 1980]).

10. The genesis and particulars of the dispute between the community school board and teachers' union are detailed—from a viewpoint generally sympathetic to the parents—by the various contributions to Annette T. Rubinstein, ed., *Schools against Children* (New York, 1970).

11. John O'Neill, "The Rise and Fall of the UFT," in Rubenstein, *Schools against Children,* 181.

12. Rabbi Jay Kaufmann, "Thou Shalt Surely Rebuke Thy Neighbor," in James Baldwin et al., *Black Anti-Semitism and Jewish Racism* (New York, 1969), 44.

13. Ibid., 63.

14. Ibid., 52–53.

15. Ibid., 55. Compensatory affirmative action was only beginning to surface as a black demand.

16. Rabbi Alan W. Miller, "Black Anti-Semitism—Jewish Racism," in Baldwin et al., *Black Anti-Semitism*, 84.

17. Ibid., 93. In the same volume Karp and Shapiro recount the success of Shanker and other opponents of decentralization in mobilizing Jewish support—which had been mixed—on their behalf by propagating hysteria over the red herring of black anti-Semitism (Walter Karp and H. R. Shapiro, "Exploding the Myth of Black Anti-Semitism," in Baldwin et al., 129–41). Noting the flimsiness of the Anti-Defamation League's dossier alleging evidence of rampant anti-Semitism, Karp and Shapiro observe that "any black failure to compliment Jewish teachers [was presented as] bigotry" (137).

18. Albert Vorspan "Blacks and Jews," in Baldwin et al., *Black Anti-Semitism*, 220–21.

19. Ibid., 204.

20. Ibid., 200–04.

21. Ibid., 208.

22. Ibid., 216. He asks whether it is "tolerable that the flag of anti-Semitism shall be run up whenever it is Jews who are asked to give up some power?" (217).

23. William Raspberry, "The Cost of Jackson's Slur," *Washington Post* (March 2, 1984).

24. Cited in Hume, "Blacks and Jews."

25. Albert Vorspan, "Blacks, Jews and Tensions in New Rochelle: Longtime Allies 'Joined at the Hip,' " *New York Times* (September 23, 1984).

26. Joseph Berger, "Jewish Leaders Criticize Jackson: The Democrats Are Also Warned," *New York Times* (July 11, 1984).

27. William G. Blair, "Jewish Leaders Hail Jackson Unity Plea but Voice Caution," *New York Times* (July 19, 1984). Perlmutter noted that Jackson attacked South Africa but not the others. The reverse standard easily could be applied to Jewish elites who refuse to criticize Israel's support of South Africa.

28. Vorspan, "Blacks and Jews," 217.

29. Miller, "Black Anti-Semitism," 96.

30. Harold Cruse, "My Jewish Problem and Theirs," in Baldwin et al., *Black Anti-Semitism*, 184.

31. The contending positions—in the aftermath of Reagan's reelection—are exemplified in the exchange by Peter Rosenblatt and Michael Calabrese, "The Election's Lessons for the Democrats," *New York Times* (November 19, 1984).

# Blacks and Jews in the Chicago Heartland

Chicago magnifies reality. Everything seems rawer and bigger than elsewhere—the wind, the heat, the cold, the memory of great fires and bloody gangsters and vast stockyards that reeked of entrails and beef. Its concrete looks thicker, denser, more massive than New York's. Gothic glass and sculpted granite mingle with frontier classicism, hewn by giants. Political subtlety remains elusive in the city that produced archetypal riots of labor (1886), race (1919), and ideology (the 1968 Democratic convention). Chicago regulars are extraregular, like the legendary Boss Daley, and its high-octane radicals range from Jane Addams and Saul Alinsky to Minister Louis Farrakhan. The city owns the mold for machine politicians who run what amount to street gangs for grown-ups, carving up turf in ethnic rumbles called elections.

It seemed perversely fitting that the quarrel simmering for two decades between blacks and Jews should have erupted last year in Chicago. News broke last May that Steve Cokely, a minor aide to acting mayor Eugene Sawyer, had been lacing his moonlighting speeches at Farrakhan's headquarters with vulgar, anti-Semitic remarks. Although clerks and street vendors from the Nation of Islam had been peddling tapes of his speeches for seven months, the chasm between Chicago's races was so vast that the *Tribune* claimed discovery of Cokely's words as an investigative coup. The world found little news in his drumbeat use of the word *nigger* to scold prominent fellow blacks, such as sociologist William J. Wilson ("dumb nigger"), Michael Jordan ("air nigger"), Jesse Jackson ("a nigger running fourth in Iowa"), and Mayor Harold Washington ("this nigger up there placating the Jews"). But Cokely was granted no license to violate other taboos. He pictured the wholesale victimization of the black underclass by a LaRouche-style conspiracy that included a supersecret Jewish cabal, and his darting, nihilistic theories ripped across the grain of public sensitivity.

Mounting pressure pried Cokely loose from his city job within a week, by which time the controversy was spilling into other regions of the country. After years of intermittent conflicts between blacks and Jews—the 1979 forced resignation of UN ambassador Andrew Young for his unauthorized contact with the PLO, Jesse Jackson's "Hymietown" scandal in 1984, among others—the Chicago crisis brought widespread acknowledgment of a fundamental rupture in the old civil rights coalition. Al Raby, the gentle

Taylor Branch is a Baltimore writer. He is the author of *Parting the Waters* and *Pillar of Fire* in a projected trilogy entitled *America in the King Years*.
Originally published as "Blacks and Jews: The Uncivil War," *Esquire Magazine*, May 1989. Reprinted with permission of Taylor Branch.

holdover from the King years, declared in July that "the evil of bigotry threatens to poison the atmosphere of our city."

The conflict between blacks and Jews amounts to a parable of pride. Even its surface realities are deeply disturbing. Two minorities of long-standing mutual empathy have suddenly become both the victims and the perpetrators of racial hatred. In the arts, a political feud endangers a historic creative collaboration between America's foremost outsider cultures. Two sources of votes for the Democratic party, and moral guidance for both parties, appear to have split apart. More ominously, these spasms of enmity affect two of the most volatile areas in contemporary politics—the Middle East, which remains a most likely spot for the world's next major war, and the black inner cities of the United States, which already seethe with signs of social breakdown.

### WHAT THEY SHARE

Black and Jewish leaders have projected themselves as rescuers against a protracted siege, organizing peace parlays and prayer breakfasts in New York, New Orleans, Atlanta, Chicago, and elsewhere. But a layman's journey through Chicago produced countless scenes that did not fit the hostile pattern described by most organizers. The ordinary ranks of blacks and Jews, who are alleged to nurse explosive grudges based on memories from opposite sides of the pawnshop counter, were consistently oblivious to street-level conflict between them. Among Chicago's black underclass in particular, questions about the feud elicited puzzled shrugs. The fabled resentment toward ghetto entrepreneurs was aimed not at Jews but at Koreans and, ironically, at Palestinian shop owners who are seeping into the South Side. There was plenty of anger—at whites in general, at fate, cops, drug dealers, bosses, kinfolk, and the system—but Jews were an unfamiliar target. Many Chicago blacks are doubtless correct in asserting that they have never seen a Jew, as Jews evacuated their neighborhoods more than a generation ago.

The leaders masquerade as peacemakers, but the fight is almost exclusively theirs. It is confined not just to the articulate but to those whose chosen role is to speak of power, pride, and religion. Waged between two peoples who have practically no daily contact, this war continues precisely because they are peoples for whom such abstractions reach deeper than pocketbooks or parking spaces. The ancient Jews forged religious and historical ideas so powerful that they blended into a distinctive race (making the followers of Moses what Disraeli and others called Mosaic Arabs). Working in the opposite direction, some blacks have struggled to fit a religion to race. Even so, they often find themselves borrowing their symbols from Judaism. Farrakhan, for instance, appropriates the Hebrew prophets along with their concepts of Moses, Exodus, and the chosen people.

For mainstream American blacks, the vast majority of churches have Hebrew names—Ebenezer, Mount Zion, Canaan, Mount Moriah, Tabernacle, New Hebron, Mount Olive. Hebraic traditions run deep in the black church. More than any people on earth, including the Jews, American blacks have adopted the Mosaic model of social organization, with the exalted political prophet bonded to the "children of Israel" below. Blacks and Jews have in common a history of cyclical swings between cultural separatism and assimilation. Black Zionists helped establish an independent Liberia in 1847, some fifty years before the emergence of modern Jewish Zionism. Jews, who have canonized no new prophets in two millennia and who shudder at the memory of their false messiahs, look with both longing and horror upon the last generation's procession of black prophets: Malcolm X, Martin Luther King Jr., Louis Farrakhan, and Jesse Jackson. Depending on one's prediction of the outcome, blacks and Jews are either intimate enemies or quarrelsome cousins.

### A CENTURY OF EXODUS

There is little in the early record of blacks and Jews in Chicago to foreshadow a Steve Cokely. Throughout their early history, the two groups traveled on parallel tracks, and when they overlapped, they did so with surprising calm.

Chicago's first Jewish colonists were fortune seekers on the great tide of emancipation that followed the Enlightenment. By the 1840s, a minyan (religious quorum) of Bavarians established the first Jewish body of worship, *Kehillath Anshe Maariv* (Men of the West Congregation). In a revolutionary era that had churned fitfully between egalitarian nationalism and Napoleonic empires, the financial emergencies of early capitalism helped liberate the Jews of Western Europe from more than a thousand years of Christian and Muslim repression. German Jews had distinguished themselves in a prolonged campaign of assimilation, penetrating the upper reaches of sophisticated culture. Germans pioneered the nineteenth-century Reform movement within Judaism, aimed at "rationalizing" the faith in the tradition of Maimonides and Spinoza. A new class of Reform rabbis stripped Jewish observance of rules that seemed most foreign to the gentile mainstream.

By 1880 American opportunity and failed revolutions in Europe had driven some ten thousand German Jews to Chicago. As elsewhere in the United States, most of them belonged to Reform congregations. The Chicago colony and the Reform movement itself seemed to be grand-scale achievements until a great, unexpected tide overwhelmed them from the East.

A single murder in 1881 became one of the decisive turning points in Jewish history. Russian and eastern European Jews had been oppressed for centuries before the murder. Barred from most professions and deprived of the right to own or rent land, they fell into a fatally unstable position as overseers and rent collectors to the post-feudal nobility. Serfs hated Jews as the faces of oppression. Nobles—often indolent and absentee— blamed them for the decline of the old order, and the czars considered them a blot upon the embattled Christian motherland. By czarist ukase, some five million Jews were squeezed into a region of the sub-Baltic provinces known as the Pale of Settlement, and when an assassin struck down Czar Alexander II, frustrations from all quarters fell heavily upon the Jews.

Romanov officials struck from above with draconian edicts, such as the summary expulsion of ten to twenty thousand Jews from Moscow on the first day of Passover, and the May Laws, which further quarantined Jews within the Pale. They abetted an endless series of confiscations and murderous pogroms across the remaining decades of czarist rule. During the next thirty years, a sudden but continuous flood of Russian and eastern European emigrants poured forth, of whom more than two million reached the United States.

Chicago's share of the new immigrants swamped the prosperous colony of Reform German Jews. The newcomers were conspicuously destitute. They spoke Yiddish. The men wore wide-brimmed hats, beards, and long black overcoats called kapotes. The women wore heavy shawls. Nearly all of them supported Orthodox rabbis. Their only education was in the Torah, which seemed a poor qualification for employment in brawling, sprawling, Victorian Chicago, but the odd-looking Jews adapted with alacrity to the needle-trade sweatshops and other exploitative cottage industries that followed their bulging settlements southward and westward from the downtown Loop. By the turn of the twentieth century, they had re-created a giant American version of their familiar shtetl around the intersection of Maxwell and Halsted. Called Jewtown by less polite Chicagoans, the Maxwell Street ghetto was a bustling, self-contained world of open-air markets, live chickens, pawnshops, Yiddish newspapers, street musicians and magicians, *moyles* (circumcisers), *shochtem* (ritual meat slaughterers), and other specialists in Jewish custom. Poverty wore people to the edge of starvation, which moved Jane Addams to create Hull House as a community refuge in 1889, but the boundless energy of Maxwell Street also produced talents ranging from Al Capone's accountant Jake "Greasy Thumb" Guzik to swing clarinetist Benny Goodman, from "Boss" Jake Arvey to CBS tycoon William Paley and Justice Arthur Goldberg.

Chicago's elite German Jews reacted to the eastern Europeans with a mixture of solidarity and revulsion, in keeping with the cyclical class dynamics of minority ethnic groups. They donated millions for resettlement assistance—for clinics, language schools, and housing—and for some of the highly assimilated patrons, the shocking experience reawakened their Jewish spirit. On the other hand, most established German Jews saw the unwashed newcomers as a profound threat. They were "too Jewish," too foreign, and much too Orthodox. They made the German Jews feel like flushed fowl. Jacob Schiff headed a delegation that actually pleaded in vain with European authorities to divert the tide of emigrants elsewhere—anywhere but the United States.

German Jews also tended to disparage the Zionist movement that sprang up in the early years of the twentieth century as escapist, tribal, and primitive, not to mention as a ground for suspicion about professions of undivided American loyalty. But eastern Jews longed for the Promised Land of Zion as protection against the accumulated woes of their history. As they spilled outward from downtown, the Germans pushed southward while the newcomers pushed into separate neighborhoods to the west. The Slavs' great numbers—some 200,000, about twenty times the city's entire Jewish population of 1880—enabled them to petition the local government successfully for a public school named for Theodor Herzl, their beloved founder of modern Zionism. Herzl Elementary still operates seventy-five years later, now a windowless fortress against surrounding drug dealers and vandals in an all-black neighborhood.

Southern blacks invaded Chicago in a compressed march that was even more spectacular than the flight of the eastern Jews. Its catalyst was a turn-of-the-century settler named Robert Abbott, founder of the *Chicago Defender,* who decided at the beginning of World War I that the parallel surges of defense jobs in the North and the Klan in the South made it foolish for blacks to cling to farms in segregated Mississippi or Alabama. A flamboyant editor, Abbott fixed a date—May 15, 1917—for the beginning of a colossal migration that he called "The Flight Out of Egypt." He lied shamelessly about the attractions of the Chicago climate and gave banner headlines to stories of blacks who froze to death in Georgia or Louisiana. EXODUS TO START, cried the *Defender,* and within two years of Abbott's starting date, some 65,000 southern blacks had moved to Chicago. The *Tribune* warned of the national phenomenon in scare stories tinged with economic pride: HALF A MILLION DARKIES FROM DIXIE SWARM TO THE NORTH TO BETTER THEMSELVES.

Following the path of least resistance, the black immigrants pushed into South Chicago behind the less numerous German Jews. The Jews absorbed them slowly at first, then leaped to better neighborhoods along the North Shore, but non-Jewish whites adopted a pattern of warfare and evacuation. More than twenty-six bombings plagued black homeowners between 1917 and 1919, when thirty-eight people died in the terrible riot touched off by the stoning of a young black swimmer who unwittingly floated across an imaginary segregation line in Lake Michigan.

Abbott's refugees kept riding north on the Illinois Central, and the most prosperous of their kinsmen inched southward along Grand Boulevard. The black Bethesda Baptist Church bought B'nai Sholom Temple Israel, which was later bombed, reportedly by the Klan. Greater Bethel A.M.E. bought the Jewish Lakeside Club in 1922. Mount Pisgah Missionary Baptist Church bought the imposing Temple Sinai building, designed by Alfred Alschuler in the style of the Italian Renaissance. Finally, Chicago's oldest "Bavarian" synagogue, KAM, retreated south into Kenwood, leaving to Pilgrim Baptist Church its magnificent edifice at the corner of Thirty-third and Indiana. Since then, black worshipers from Pilgrim have entered through old Temple KAM's scalloped stone archway, beneath scripture carved in Hebrew and English: "Open for me the gates of righteousness, that I may enter through them, to praise the Lord."

## THE ROOTS OF TOLERANCE

By 1930 Chicago was a city of 3.5 million people, nearly three quarters of whom came from immigrant or refugee stock. White ethnics checkered the city by neighborhoods— Poles, Germans, Italians, Irish, Lithuanians, and assorted others. A few Jewish refugees soon trickled in from Hitler's Germany, but most of the city's 275,000 Jews came from the Soviet Union and Eastern Europe. Chicago held the third largest Jewish population among the world's cities, behind only New York and Warsaw. Most of the Slavic Jews had abandoned the picturesque Maxwell Street shtetl after a generation's incubation. Some 100,000 of them rolled in a dense wave into the Lawndale community to the west. Even against the grim unemployment of the Depression, Lawndale flourished as a lively middle-class settlement of Eastern Jews. All along the central artery of Douglas Boulevard, known then as the *Judenstrasse,* synagogues and yeshivas sprang up in stately rows.

During World War II, a renewed mass exodus of southern blacks streamed into Chicago. Eventually, the largest public housing project in the world went up: Robert Taylor Homes, twenty-eight gargantuan sixteen-story buildings along the South Side

Rock Island tracks. They were segregated, built to hold 100,000 people per square mile, and because 20,000 of the first 27,000 tenants were black children, city officials themselves expressed instant remorse over the giant configuration of concrete griddle stacks. "What is the role of a fourteen-year-old boy in a large project?" wondered housing director Elizabeth Wood. She saw the construction as "anti-family and inhumane," but inevitable "because land acquisition was so difficult."

Still, they were not enough, and many other large housing projects failed to stop the overflow of black newcomers, who, blocked by the hard-shell white ethnics elsewhere, had filled up the Maxwell Street ghetto and spilled westward among the Slavic Jews of Lawndale. Only small numbers had moved into Lawndale by 1950, but then a titanic double rush replaced nearly 100,000 Jews with blacks. Fifteen historic synagogues closed in the year 1953 alone, and the Jewish identity all but disappeared after the Hebrew Theological College moved in 1954. By 1960 all forty-eight synagogues had vanished from Lawndale.

Since Robert Abbott's exodus of 1917, rivers of black immigrants had overrun Chicago in the same pattern as the Jews who had gone before them. They even duplicated the status cleavage among the Jews, such that South Side blacks—and especially those whose Chicago roots went back before 1917—claimed privilege over the parvenu west-siders. Even today, it is an axiom of Chicago politics that no west-sider can be elected mayor.

Since World War I, there had occurred massive, street-level displacement of Jews by blacks—block by block, synagogue by synagogue. Yet for all the wailing of the uprooted, and the ceremonial cries of the rabbis ("Do not forsake us, O God, at our old age. . . ."), there was surprisingly little rancor. The sum of public protest over four decades came nowhere near the uproar over one Steve Cokely speech in 1988. As usual in those days, Jews seemed willing victims. They gave ground, sent their kids to public schools with black children, and relocated when tides made them feel lost or threatened. Often the Orthodox Jews of the West Side were ready to move anyway. After a generation in Lawndale, and perhaps an earlier one around Maxwell Street, their families had raised themselves from frightened, Yiddish-speaking peddlers to college-educated professionals. Sophisticated, perhaps more secular than their forebears, they sought larger homes along the North Shore or in the suburbs, where distinctions between Slavic and German Jews had blurred.

On the South Side, the forbearance of the Reform congregations sprang from their emphasis on the populist morality of the Jewish prophets. From the heart of their tradition, Reform Jews believed in, and supported, the cause of the downtrodden blacks who were crowding in upon them. In the 1930s and 1940s, Rabbi Jacob Weinstein of KAM became an eloquent advocate of civil rights and one of the foremost Reform rabbis in the country. When angry WASPs tried to silence black artists such as Paul Robeson and Langston Hughes, Weinstein repeatedly offered them a platform in his synagogue. He also welcomed union organizers, social gadflys, black preachers, crusaders for the homeless, and many others who had married the universalist stream of Reform thought to the radical politics more common to Slavic Jews.

By Weinstein's time, Hitler had chilled away most of Reform Judaism's comfortable, universalist scorn toward Zionism. Apologetic Reform spokesmen waxed strong even before the creation of Israel in 1948, laying stress on their exceptional predecessors who had supported the movement in its less fashionable days. "By the end of World War II," wrote a Reform historian, "only three anti-Zionist pulpits were to remain in Chicago." What remained distinctive was Reform's egalitarian spirit. The Jewish prophets had introduced mankind to a religion grounded in universal moral codes that applied to kings no less than commoners, to outsiders as well as fellow tribesmen. In fact, the prophets went further to extol a justice that leaned to the side of the downtrodden, glorifying their righteous humility: "What mean ye that ye beat my people to pieces, and grind the faces of the poor? saith the Lord of hosts" (Isaiah 3:15).

The founding Hebrews had inverted the pagan value system by identifying pride as the most heinous sin and by calling down the wrath of Jehovah against those who put their faith in great armies, temples, and worldly possessions. An ethos of righteous, humble awe became Judaism's lasting answer to the mysteries of creation and existence, liberating the mind for more rational exploration of the world. This ethos became a central tenet of Christianity—inserted by converted Jewish writers into the very beginning of Gospel accounts, even before the arrival of the stable-born Jesus: "He hath scattered the proud in the imagination of their hearts. He hath put down the mighty from their seats, and exalted them of low degree" (Luke 1:51–52).

Such a moral sensibility has appeared at various times in all the warring phases of Jewish identity. Karl Marx—an assimilated German Jew from the effusive period of early Reform and an atheist nominally baptized into Christianity—took a Jewish obsession with the dispossessed and set it against his own raging anti-Semitism. (He associated all capitalists with foul qualities, calling them "inwardly circumcised Jews," and predicted that "in emancipating itself from *hucksterism* and money, and thus from real and practical Judaism, our age would emancipate itself.") The Marxist result was a theoretical machine aimed toward revolution and revenge.

A century later, during the American civil rights movement, qualified Marxists and ex-Marxists of all stripes joined vague Jews who retained the gentlest instincts of the prophets. "I grew up with a very strong sense that being Jewish was being ethical," recalls Jane Ramsey, who became a cabinet officer under Chicago's first black mayor. All these disparate types felt something special for the preaching of the civil rights movement, and especially for Martin Luther King, whose "dream" speeches consistently invoked the rhapsodies of his favorite Hebrew prophets, Amos and Isaiah.

At the other pole from the various secular Jews, Conservative Rabbi Abraham Heschel also came marching with King. A lyrical philosopher, Heschel was known for his paradoxical argument that the millennium of confined Jewish suffering in eastern Europe had produced the religion's golden age. By making alliance with King, Heschel proved that even the most self-absorbed, mystical Jews responded to the sweep of the prophets' cries for justice. For a moment at least, the democratic moralism of the civil rights movement touched every corner of the Jewish heritage—from Isaiah to Marx, from Einstein to Schwerner and Goodman, from the Rosenbergs to Rabbi Heschel. In keeping with this association, it came as no surprise that Chicago's original Congregation KAM, on finally retreating from all-black Kenwood in 1971, should turn over its eight-columned structure to become national headquarters for Jesse Jackson's Operation PUSH. The shock came more recently—when Jackson and his PUSH lieutenants, engaging equal venom from Jewish critics, bridled against the Jews from the same pulpit where Rabbi Weinstein had embraced Paul Robeson.

### THE WARRIOR'S PRIDE

It was Israel's Six-Day War of 1967 that cracked the psychological bond between the blacks and Jews. Contrary to popular assumption, many American Jews had felt less than intensely involved with Israel before then. A Chicago survey from the late 1950s, cited by author Jonathan Kaufman, found that "only one in five Jews thought being a good Jew meant it was essential to support Israel. Twice as many believed it essential to support the struggle for the Negro in America." Undoubtedly, many American Jews felt uncomfortable about Israel because its very creation raised the expectation that all good Jews would make aliyah (literally "ascent") as emigrants to their natural homeland, or because they were too agnostic to accept rabbinical teachings that a reestablished Israel foretold the imminent advent of the Messiah. Or perhaps they were simply complacent about Israel as a protected ward of the Great Powers.

All this psychic distance vanished when Nasser blockaded Israel's egress from the Gulf of Aqaba and moved seven divisions of the Egyptian army across Suez. The armies of Syria, Jordan, and Iraq advanced under united command. Mass demonstrations for jihad, or holy way, broke out in Muslim nations from Saudi Arabia to Morocco. French president De Gaulle shut off military supplies to Israel, and the U.S. Congress, mired in war commitments to Vietnam, stalemated all efforts to defend Israel against enemies on three sides. Israel appeared fated to a second Holocaust.

At this moment, wrote Rabbi Arthur Hertzberg, American Jewry "supported Israel with a vehemence that astonished itself." Hertzberg saw instantly that the mood in the American Diaspora "underwent an abrupt, radical, and possibly permanent change." Pollsters found that 99 percent of all American Jews firmly backed Israel's war aims. Jews who had not visited a synagogue in years crowded into them spontaneously and stood vigil at continuous, unannounced services. Huddled together, they experienced a historic swing of emotion as the threat of extinction suddenly became a miracle of triumph. Fighting alone, Israel defeated the superior numbers of each opposing army. American Jews let loose a torrent of joy and money that has not since abated. One man sold his gas station and donated the proceeds to the Israeli war effort.

The senior black leaders of the American civil rights movement rushed to Israel's defense. Dr. King issued a statement in support of Israel's "independence, integrity, and freedom," and A. Philip Randolph, speaking to labor leaders in New York, pledged the united effort of 22 million black Americans to help protect against Arab attack. The Chicago *Daily Defender* published tributes to the stunning new valor of Jewish soldiers: ISRAELI GENERALS LIKENED TO BIBLE'S MOSES, JOSHUA. Against all this cross-racial euphoria, however, the newsletter of the Student Nonviolent Coordinating Committee (SNCC) planted a seed of ominous protest. The more radical black students denounced Zionism. They adopted Arabs, especially displaced Palestinians, as fellow Third World allies of color.

The Six-Day War had come only one year after SNCC chairman Stokely Carmichael publicly espoused his electrifying "black power" slogan. American blacks had begun a sharp shift of identity. They changed the most commonly accepted name for the race from "Negro" to "black" almost overnight. SNCC soon expelled its white members, discarded the old "We Shall Overcome" rhetoric as sappy, and fashioned an ideology blended of separatism, Pan-Africanism, Marxism, racial pride, and don't-tread-on-me-ism.

Blacks and Jews veered off on parallel courses of militant ethnic separatism, turning inward upon themselves. America's secular Jews bonded themselves to Israel with special fervor after the Six-Day War, for it was through it that many of them re-discovered their Jewishness. They stopped changing their names, stopped trying to blend in with the Gentiles. Similarly, blacks put on their dashikis and strutted their culture.

Separatism seemed alternately thrilling, grimly necessary, fearful, and ridiculous. The special burden of the black nationalism that took hold in 1967 was that its cultural satisfactions bore few fruits in politics. Against the backdrop of the Six-Day War, black nationalism was but a dreary shadow. The Israelis had a real army that had just whipped the surrounding hosts; the guns of the few U.S. black nationalists never amounted to more than media props. (Even so, the Black Panthers and other careering separatists were viciously suppressed by the authorities even before the white press grew bored of them.) In falling back to regroup, black nationalists had no ready-made psalms, no private comfort or accumulated wisdom of four thousand years. Their own heritage remained largely to be discovered, let alone evaluated and tested. Jews already had the Torah; blacks waited for Alex Haley to write *Roots*.

### PREJUDICE AND PRIDE

In Chicago as a student at the all-boys Catholic high school, De La Salle Institute, Steve Cokely bristled with the energy of the black-power movement. During the Six-Day War, he survived disputes with the priests and fights with some white boys over the propriety of Afros and power salutes, then went on to three different Illinois public colleges under open-admission/low-tuition programs that were a short-lived legacy of the civil rights movement. Having studied penology, Cokely secured a job as a federal prison guard in 1975. From that position, with his Mau-Mau street chutzpah finely tuned, he walked into the local NAACP office and accused its officials of "stealing the people's money" by running a social club disguised as an engine of racial progress. The NAACP recoiled from Cokely's effrontery but promptly awarded him a seat on its board of directors. He ran an NAACP voter-registration team but never forgot the demonstration that the black establishment could be hypersensitive and hollow.

Cokely kept his prison job until 1979, the year Andrew Young took the conflicting pride of blacks and Jews to the national headlines. Young's reckless candor had earned him a mixed record as Jimmy Carter's ambassador to the United Nations. He single-handedly raised American stock in Africa, but his trenchant comments on the racism of nearly every national grouping in the world produced more resentment than insight. Young badly miscalled the Iranian revolution—predicting a near sainthood for the Ayatollah as a vast improvement upon the Shah, and hailing the spirit of the Iranian Muslims as a positive energy for the Middle East. What finally ruined Young seemed relatively trivial by contrast: in violation of U.S. policy, he met privately in New York with a PLO representative.

Cut loose by Carter, Young went on a consolation tour that soon took him to the old Temple KAM in Chicago, where guests of Operation PUSH fumed over the short shrift given the highest-ranking black man in the United States. Having recovered his usual polish as a long-range politician, Young smoothly and perhaps truthfully assured the PUSH crowd that organized Jewish pressure had not engineered his downfall. This was too much for Jesse Jackson. He sent an aide scurrying for a newspaper listing Jewish groups that had called for Young's resignation, and at first opportunity he read the entire list with an impish, scolding look. Jackson, who had long resented Young's air of aristocratic superiority, was delighted to see him playing the unruffled schoolmaster even after he had been paddled. The crowd booed the name of every Jewish group. Young managed a weak smile. "You could have bought Andy for a dime," recalled a journalist who had slipped into the event.

A dozen years had passed since the explosions of black and Jewish pride in 1967. For American Jews, the bonds of identification with Israel had strengthened over half a generation of grim but triumphant consolidation, including the Yom Kippur War of 1973 and a decade of front-page terrorism. A new "muscular Judaism" had largely replaced the tradition of seeking refuge in Enlightenment principles. Jews had served as the vanguard inventors of neo-conservatism, which now felt menaced rather than protected by the old moralism, protected rather than menaced by the cold statecraft of Metternich. Neoconservative Jews suddenly saw danger from the political Left instead of the Right. They adapted quickly to power, and some of them fixed the source of the world's evil in Soviet communism, writing as though Lenin had introduced anti-Semitism to Russia.

For American blacks, the fizzling of black power as a sound-bite revolution had given way to a retrenchment of pride in a lower key. Their leaders became regular fixtures on the editorial pages and a familiar sight in the downtown business districts, conquering professions on their own prowess and taking over cities on the strength of racial solidarity. Like Jews, prominent blacks became more reluctant to advance moral claims, because to do so gave implicit recognition to a universal community. Outward appeals to principle receded in favor of inward cries for unity. Cross-cultural awareness became a chore, clannish grievance a ticket.

Steve Cokely lacked the experience and the pedigree for front-rank service in politics or education, but he possessed enough flair to insert himself as a tourist among Chicago's politicians at a time when blacks reached the near fringes of power. To do so, Cokely resigned from the Bureau of Prisons, cashed in his pension fund, and spent the early 1980s as a free-lance observer at city hall. He became an errand runner and an amiable fixer, capable of glad-handing both black and white aldermen. Billing himself as a "community organizer and political researcher," Cokely filled a gap between the black leaders and their increasingly desperate constituents on the South and West sides. He applied his precocious talents as a black-pride theorist to the paradox that the ghetto underclass was sinking even as the power of Chicago's black politicians was growing. There was no easy explanation for this rankling phenomenon.

By the spring of 1981, Cokely was lecturing at Chicago conferences such as a forum on government spying and white national violence. The program for the event featured a flag-draped skull of Uncle Sam on the White House lawn, holding up a mirror with bullets on its rim and Dr. King's face centered in its cross hairs. Cokely had immersed himself in the details of the 1970s investigations into the 1960s spy operations against the civil rights movement, especially the FBI's Cointelpro. From these facts, far more detached minds than his had been drawn to the theory of a government plot to assassinate King. Adopting conspiracy as pride's answer to baffling showers of pain, Cokely postulated a parent conspiracy that was at once subtler and more sinister than murder, capable of co-opting black leaders for camouflage while bleeding the underclass. Its masters were the Trilateral Commissioners. Its moneymen were bankers such as Felix Rohatyn, who were designing mortgage plans for bankrupt school systems and cities.

Cokely's most original stroke was to identify what he called the "early warning system." From Chicago's celebrated "Red Squad" lawsuit, he seized upon the disclosure that the police had maintained files on the city's "inter-group communications project." The project, modeled on the U.S. Justice Department's Community Relations Service, was designed to "monitor developing racial tensions" in order to administer timely doses of troubleshooting and dialogue. The inter-group roster included the leaders of all the major black and Jewish organizations—such as the American Jewish Committee, the NAACP, the National Council of Jewish Women, the Urban League, the Association of Reform Rabbis—plus the ACLU, various church confederations, and assorted do-gooder coalitions. Cokely marked them all as infiltrators.

Only a transfused black nationalism could stand against such an insidious combination of enemies, Cokely decided. In private sessions, he drew his allies into a circle tightly bound by wariness and race, much like the posture the Israeli government had developed toward the Palestinian Arabs. Ironically, since he was beginning to count the most progressive Jews within the hostile camp, Cokely looked to establish a black champion ever more in the mold of Moses. He landed a job on the staff of Alderman Marian Humes and began to evaluate the contenders while he developed his reputation as an innovative theorist of black nationalism. There was no scarcity of potential champions within his orbit, as all the potential black prophets—obscure and famous, national and local—hailed from the heartland of Chicago.

### FOUR IN THE ROLE OF MOSES

The least likely Moses was Ben Carter. As a young Chicago bus driver in the 1960s, he had been intrigued by rumors of a strange neighborhood on the West Side—black people who spoke a quaint language called Yiddish. The origins of the Black Hebrews remain obscure, but Ben Carter was soon captured by the neighborhood's sectarian pull, which included the dietary regimen, the special prayers, holidays, clothes, and other elements of a complete way of life. Carter, in turn, captured the Black Hebrews. To mark his growth into the group's self-trained rabbi, he changed his name to Ben-Ami Carter. In 1969 a host of black Chicagoans followed his command to give up their possessions for a journey of aliyah to their ancestral homeland in Israel.

Some three thousand black American settlers still live today in the ancient city of

Dimona. The rabbis and bureaucrats of Israel first welcomed them as Jews, then changed their minds, and for most of the succeeding twenty years the two sides have been locked in mutual vexation. The Black Hebrews demand Israeli citizenship under the Law of Return. Israeli authorities demand that they first convert to Judaism under Orthodox rabbinical supervision, but the Black Hebrews refuse on the ground that to do so would make their prior Judaism confessedly false.

The potentially embarrassing dispute has been kept mercifully quiet, from an Israeli point of view, largely because the Black Hebrews have been passed off as a kookish sect. Ben-Ami Carter is too literal a mimic of Moses. He demands a childlike obeisance from his followers and, in the style of Solomon, reportedly advocates polygamy.

Yet the Black Hebrews remain an affront to Israel. Since the days of Herzl, Zionist theorists have struggled to reconcile the idea of a Jewish homeland with the principles of the secular, enlightened nation-state. Now, in the form of a strangely charismatic former bus driver, Israeli leaders confront a man who swears on the sacrifice of three thousand Black Hebrews that Israel falls short of both its democratic *and* religious ideals, that it is reverting to the primitive tribalisms of the ancient Hebrews. Spurned by the rabbis, Carter claims to be more Jewish than they.

Whatever the prospects of Ben-Ami Carter's exodus, he is a quirkish and obscure version of the original Moses. To the majority of black Chicagoans, the thunder of modern deliverance hit their city in the far more traditional person of Mayor Harold Washington. In 1982 U.S. representative Washington was still a machine politician who had risen through the ranks of Mayor Daley's black ally, William Dawson. But recognizing his shrewdness and his humor, the city's black activists, including Cokely, persistently urged Washington to become the first serious hope for a black mayor.

The mayoral race in early 1983 became a great divide in Chicago history. In the Democratic primary, the Jewish vote split between incumbent Jane Byrne and Washington, and at first the black vote itself appeared uncertain. When some 150 black preachers gathered to endorse State's Attorney Richard Daley, son of the old Boss, the Washington campaign mustered only twenty preachers to oppose them.

In the end, however, the most consequential split was among the city's predominantly white, Catholic voters. Byrne and Daley, both underestimating Washington's appeal, campaigned against each other. Byrne and Daley each gathered nearly 400,000 votes, but Washington's 419,000 gave him the Democratic nomination under the plurality rules. His "It's Our Turn" miracle instantly transformed the pro forma general election into a titanic struggle. Bernard Epton, a Jewish businessman who until then had been the token Republican nominee, suddenly became a desperate white hope. Ironically, Jewish voters gave Washington his victory margin. He won more than 40 percent of their votes, whereas Epton drew less than one percent of the blacks'.

Epton withdrew to a short remaining life of open bitterness, consuming depression, and failing health. "I don't belong in politics," he said. "I never did. . . . I've got nothing to be happy about." Denouncing his fellow Jews, he attributed their failure to support him partly to self-hatred and to the corresponding assumption that a Jewish mayor would reactivate anti-Semitism. "All I can tell you is there was almost a Hitler mentality," he said. "The Jews were so afraid of the violence that might result if a Jew were elected." Polls soon showed Epton to be widely despised by much of the same white ethnic constituency that had supported him. Some disliked him as a Jew, or as a Republican, and many others as the politician responsible for Harold Washington's election. Other whites blamed Daley or Byrne. Happening upon Daley in McCrory's department store, a young employee of the city's Department of Streets and Sanitation attacked the losing candidate for "selling out city hall to the blacks." Daley and his assailant traded punches in the store aisles, proving to any doubters among the startled bystanders that ethnic patronage is serious business in Chicago.

American readers elsewhere might well have taken the McCrory's brawl as a symbol of modern Chicago. Much of the national press portrayed the Washington regime as a racial slugfest. To those nearer the city, however, the deeper reality was that Washington gradually expanded beyond his original base into coalition politics. He added more Jews and white ethnic reformers to his inner circle of advisers. Much of Chicago cheered his efforts to transcend the old machine government, but this very broadening made Washington a turncoat to the black nationalists who had first urged him to run. In their eyes he was leaving too many of the chosen people behind.

To Steve Cokely, it was a danger sign that Mayor Washington threw his lot in with the very white liberals Cokely had marked as infiltrators from the hidden conspiracy against the black underclass. But Cokely's early lectures on the insidious control exercised by the Trilateral Commission aroused little interest. "Our community is not into facts," he says. Working on the theory that his constituency learned most readily from public manifestations of white anger, Cokely searched for what he mischievously called "a pebble to throw in the cave and trick the beast out." He found his pebble at Louis Farrakhan's Nation of Islam headquarters, where a visiting author lectured on his theory that African explorers had reached ancient America long before Columbus.

After many excited trips to the library, Cokely produced a leaflet advertising his "First Annual Anti-Columbus, Anti-Colonialism Day" for October 1985, to compete with the traditional Columbus Day parade and rally. His factual predicate was simple: the holiday insulted American Indians by implying that they had not existed until Columbus "discovered" their land; it celebrated colonialist expansion at the expense of those who had been enslaved or wiped out in the process. Besides, Cokely argued, Christopher Columbus never set foot on American soil, did not speak Italian, and was probably not of Italian origin, being most likely a Genoan related to the Sephardic Jews who were expelled from Spain in 1492, the year of his voyage. Cokely was especially proud of the Jewish twist. He figured that while some Jewish scholars actually did lay claim to Columbus, they would shrink from a public squabble with the Italians.

Cokely's pebble drew an instant bellow of rage in the white press of Chicago. Aldermen of Italian extraction lined up to denounce him as a "loudmouth" who was "full of baloney." Even before the story broke, a furious Alderman Humes called from her Las Vegas vacation to demand an explanation from her aide. Humes, who would lose her seat in 1987 and be indicted for corruption, banished Cokely from her city hall office.

As Cokely was packing to leave, he was surprised to receive a visit and a job offer from then-alderman Eugene Sawyer. As a rather dull, conventional politician, Sawyer seemed to be among the last of the black aldermen to welcome a troublesome gadfly like Cokely, but the seasoned vote counter saw in Cokely a partial answer to a vexing problem. Black-voter turnout—especially among the marginal and the dispossessed—was diminishing across the city. These former voters from the fringes of the underclass were precisely the ones who responded most heartily to Cokely. His guerrilla theater and his jousting matches with the white establishment created excitement in the roughest areas, where the best black politicians were beginning to draw cold looks of despair.

Only the professionals noticed the threatening drop-off. Although Mayor Washington won reelection in the spring of 1987, his black support fell ominously in the city's poorest wards. By then the *Chicago Tribune* had published a devastating, book-length portrait of North Lawndale entitled *The American Millstone: An Examination of the Nation's Permanent Underclass.* The *Tribune* reporters found that the number of welfare recipients in North Lawndale had grown by 45 percent over the preceding decade. Along the former *Judenstrasse* of Douglas Boulevard, the rundown condition of converted synagogues testified to the battered persistence of the black middle class. Crime was, and is, epidemic in the streets around the old landmarks. The high school dropout rate exceeded 50 percent in most schools. At one school, nearly a quarter of the female students gave birth during a single year.

These afflictions gave new meaning to the phrase "white collar," as the inner city of Chicago seemed to be ringed by a noose of affluence. Drained of tax base, talent, and hope, the poorer black neighborhoods crumbled inexorably toward rebellion or coma. All the more galling to black nationalists, this un-American, retrograde trend gained recognition precisely in the years after blacks had finally grasped the advertised levers of deliverance. Chicago had a black mayor, police chief, school superintendent, and so on—all prospering in their second terms, markedly in contrast to the mass of their fellow blacks.

It was this wrenching divergence between the fortunes of politician and voter that Cokely sought to explain in his street-academy lectures. "We have been led into a collapsing industry," he said. Cokely struggled to refute the theory that seemed to be gaining at least tacit endorsement among whites—that the underclass was indeed permanent and baffling, caused perhaps by an inferior substrain of humanity that was best left forgotten. Such thinking foreshadowed a kind of "new segregation" policy, in which middle-class blacks and whites would constitute a separate world from the open-air prisons of the underclass.

Only hints of such resignation reached polite society. Downtown Chicago shined with the edgy prosperity of the late Reagan years, and Mayor Washington commanded advancing respect. By the fall of 1987, Cokely did make the media beast howl with a new pebble—he identified the sailing vessel on the official city seal as a "slave ship"—but the campaign had an air of a nervous comedy. That October, Cokely's third annual "Anti-Columbus Day" protest attracted Farrakhan but no members of the city government. When Cokely begged Mayor Washington himself not to march in the traditional Columbus Day Parade, he received only an exasperated look. "I got to march in the parade," Washington replied. "There's *votes* out there."

The next month, vandals struck three synagogues and six shops in the transplanted Jewish commercial district of North Chicago. All along West Devon Avenue—a neon-lighted strip with the jumble and bustle of an Eastern bazaar, featuring Gandhi Electronics near The Four Cohn's Shoe Store, the Old Style Russian Restaurant near Pakistani Videos—painted swastikas and shattered windows made for a chilling anniversary of *Kristallnacht*. Exactly forty-nine years earlier, Nazi raiding parties had simultaneously struck thousands of Jewish businesses and hundreds of synagogues, killing ninety-two Jews and hauling off some twenty thousand others to concentration camps. Jews in Chicago were relieved to learn that Mayor Washington personally called their leaders on the night of the vandalism, even before the news broke. The next day, he toured West Devon Avenue with the rabbis and the heads of Jewish organizations, assuring them that the city of Chicago would act swiftly.

These acts of immense reassurance to Jews struck Steve Cokely as more hostile infiltrations of undercover social control. Ten days after the vandalism, Cokely delivered a lecture at Farrakhan's headquarters. His announced purpose was to explain the lemminglike destruction of black children in the Chicago public school system. The speech was a cross between a Richard Pryor monologue and a Paul Goodman essay—raw and insightful on the surface, driven by humor born of pain. In the face of such an immense personal disaster, the only explanation accessible to Cokely was that the school system was *designed* to produce cretins, just as the stockyards had been built to make bacon. Practically speaking, he told a ghetto audience, school only hampered their children's prospects. "So I advocate that we leave school," he concluded. This was empty bravado, to be sure, and from a distance it was suicidally or subversively insane, but at least his remedy was proportionally desperate to the condition it addressed.

More dangerously, so was Cokely's estimate of the conspiracy supporting the status quo. The racial-crimes intelligence unit—just created in response to the vandalism on West Devon Avenue—was to Cokely an insidious tool of repression. Its purpose was to build secret files on racially motivated radicals. "In other words," he said, "we will be accused of being racists. We've been slaughtered, killed, beat up, locked down four hundred years, and we the victim, and we will be accused of being racist when we have oppressed nobody."

Cokely, lacking the slightest historical appreciation for the significance of *Kristallnacht*, could interpret the amazingly swift government response only as a sinister trick. The excitement on West Devon must be a mere pretext—"Them four little windows that was broke on them four little Jewish businesses up north by some Jew. . . ." The conspiracy made a puppet of Mayor Washington: "Made that nigger go up there. They bustin' peoples' *heads* in our community. He went up there for some *windows*. . . . When infant mortality went up, he didn't come out and pledge to help the babies. He renounced the statistics."

At the close of 1987, scattered events marched with ghostly precision: Chicago's little *Kristallnacht* on November 9; Cokely's school lecture on November 18; Mayor Washington's death of a heart attack on November 25; the outbreak of the Palestinian *intifada* on December 9 after four Palestinians were killed by an Israeli truck in Gaza. Of these, only Washington's sudden death in city hall became an instant news sensation. Thousands of mourners gathered spontaneously. In its funeral edition, even the staid *Tribune* registered shock in banner headlines: RITES OF GRIEF . . . AN EMOTIONAL OUTPOUR-

ING FOR MAN, SYMBOL. Citizens of all races spoke of the transcendent loss, the irreplaceable man. Monsignor John Egan, a civil rights activist from the 1960s, remarked that not even the assassination of President Kennedy had affected him so deeply. In death, Washington acquired the aura of a modern Moses. He had led at least the politicians and the respectable Chicago citizens into a promised land of hope. To Cokely and those he represented, however, Washington had failed as a Moses figure by putting politics over racial pride and deliverance.

Much the same would be said in Chicago of Jesse Jackson, who flew in from the Mediterranean to throw his weight behind the candidacy of South Side alderman Tim Evans for acting mayor. But the white anti-Washington aldermen engineered the compromise choice of Eugene Sawyer, Cokely's boss, as a respectable but none-too-formidable caretaker. When it was over, some black politicians criticized Jackson for trying to "anoint" Evans as mayor and, alternatively, for failing to succeed. The episode reinforced Jackson's image as one whose political wishes were not honored in his own city. It recalled the night of Washington's primary victory over Daley and Byrne nearly five years earlier, when Jackson had seized the role of cheerleader, shouting, "We want it all! We've won the playoffs! Now we want the Super Bowl!" Over and over. His performance had seemed oddly out of keeping with Washington's own thankful magnanimity, and there was an air of self-revelation to it that had plagued Jackson since, compromising both the practical and the prophetic aspects of the Moses persona. Jackson was too special, too removed to gain political power in Chicago. He could only pay homage to Harold Washington. But there was also a self-seeking side to him that ill-suited the principles he espoused. The great prophets abased themselves as well as the pride of their people. Neither Isaiah nor Martin Luther King could have pictured his mission as a Super Bowl.

On the national political scene, Jackson remained, despite his visibility in the 1984 presidential race, a hybrid figure. He was too big for any office except the one he wanted, too black or too principled for national politics. A smoother, more disciplined campaign in 1988 gained Jackson second place. Cultivating farmers and other white voters with a vengeance, he suffered no "Hymietown" scandal. Still, Jackson ran into a ceiling support of 9 percent among white voters. At the end of the campaign, a poll for the American Jewish Committee showed that 59 percent of American Jews considered Jackson an anti-Semite. In mainstream America, he remained shackled to Louis Farrakhan. Although Jackson shunned him throughout the campaign, he convinced few that he really wanted to. He sought out Jewish audiences, but convinced few that he wanted to do that, either. On both fronts, Jackson projected an evasive discomfort that served neither a politician nor a prophet.

Louis Farrakhan is the closest thing to a banned person this side of South Africa. Barred from television and many black colleges, he is a man whose inclusion makes any prospective gathering almost instantly disrespectable. Far more actively than Jackson, Farrakhan has pricked the issue between blacks and Jews. He is the source—the cause or release point of tensions. Although Jackson gathers hosannas from coast to coast, hailed as the new black Moses, it is Farrakhan who for better or worse is more closely modeled on the prophet.

Like Malcolm X, who was his mentor, Farrakhan began his career in deep obeisance to the patriarch Elijah Muhammad. Muhammad had been born Elijah Poole, after the ancient Hebrew prophet said to have ascended deathless to Yahweh. By keeping his given name, Muhammad bridged the two religions built on scripture and authoritarian regimen.

Louis X, a converted calypso singer, dutifully received the new surname Farrakhan from Elijah Muhammad in 1965. By accepting it, he severed any competing loyalty to Malcolm X, who had become a devil instead of a disciple by challenging Elijah Muhammad's black supremacist interpretation of Islam. Talented but badly damaged by the schism and subsequent assassination of Malcolm, Farrakhan preached in relative obscurity until Muhammad's death in 1975. Then came a new torment when Muhammad's sons effectively repudiated their father by taking the Muslims back into more orthodox, nonracial Islamic faith. Farrakhan obeyed for three years before leading a fresh secession into his own Nation of Islam. Isolated from a recognized world faith, Farrakhan sought alliances with the political rebels within the vast Muslim world, such as Muammar Qadaffi. At home he found himself embroiled in protracted litigation over church property. When evicted from the Muslim mosque, he landed in the run-down office building in South Chicago where Cokely would give his speeches. Farrakhan led a remnant of followers on behalf of the black dispossessed, who had no money.

Like Jesse Jackson, Farrakhan entered the 1980s essentially as a Chicago street preacher in midcareer crisis. Each of them sustained a creaky, revolution-minded institution largely by hustle, brains, and lung power. Each was mightily inspired by the election of Harold Washington in 1983. Farrakhan registered to vote for the first time in his life, sidestepping Elijah Muhammad's separatist teaching that only fools participated in white man's politics. He and Jackson began to cooperate on plans for their overlapping causes, often traveling together. Farrakhan knew Arab politicians and Muslim etiquette well enough to be of help to Jackson on their daringly successful trip to rescue Lieutenant Goodman, the black American pilot who had been shot down over Syria. Farrakhan was so little known that his role drew no public notice, but all that changed when the "Hymietown" scandal broke a month later. With hostility between Jackson and Jews crackling in the press, Farrakhan hosted one of the early Jackson-for-President rallies in Chicago. As a national politician, Jackson has never recovered from that night.

Farrakhan is mercurial, perhaps even unstable. He began what was supposed to be an upbeat introduction of the next president with a disputation on Jewish lineage. He cast doubt on the existence of the original Moses from the Bible, saying that the Exodus story does not appear in contemporary African or Arab history. Although stupefyingly out of place, he was correct so far, as most experts on Jewish history concede that the Torah is the only evidence of Moses. Then Farrakhan offered up one of his unique turns at this juncture of racial and religious genesis. He declared that black people were the "real Israel." By this he meant that the role of God's children had been offered to blacks along with the original "mixed multitude of Jews," and that after unrighteousness had successively spoiled the Jews, Christians, and Arabs, blacks carried the mantle of faith.

Never had a presidential rally begun with such a speech. From there, Farrakhan warned American Jews not to dislike Jackson too much. "We are ready to talk," he said.

"But if you harm this brother, I warn you in the name of Allah, this will be the last one you harm. We are not making any idle threats. We have no weapons. . . . If you want to defeat him, defeat him at the polls. We can stand to lose an election, but we cannot stand to lose our brother." As always, Farrakhan qualified himself in a number of safe directions, but the quotable spike of death and retaliation was there.

Shortly after this rally, the late Nathan Perlmutter of the Anti-Defamation League reportedly compared Farrakhan to Adolf Hitler. An enraged Farrakhan replied in scattershot quotations. "How in the hell am I a Hitler?" he cried. "I haven't killed nobody . . . don't compare me with your wicked killers." But he also said that Hitler had been "a great man" because he had raised up his people from the defeat of World War I, just as Farrakhan was trying to raise up his people from the ashes of slavery. The "great man" quotation stuck to Farrakhan in the press, making him a confessed admirer of Hitler.

From a business point of view, being branded a black Hitler was a great boon to Farrakhan. By 1988 he was able to buy out the disputed title to the Elijah Muhammad Mosque #2 and also Elijah Muhammad's yellow-brick residences near Hyde Park. The acute sensitivity of the American press briefly opened to him the formula that had made rich men of sectarian religious leaders such as Father Divine: any black man who can make white America leap on its chair in fright or revulsion will win the generous admiration of suffering black America for the sheer guts of the deed.

Up close, Farrakhan's performances give an effect mixed of discipline, theater, and pathos. The discipline is a legacy of Elijah Muhammad's iron laws of psychic conversion, which have made new creatures of hardened criminals since the days of Malcolm X. Stiff Muslims assume the quasi-martial pose of drug-rehab boot camp. They eat but one meal a day, glorify the family as the unit of salvation, and reject all aspirants who are too weak to purge themselves of society's major poisons, ranging from smack to cigarettes. Such fortitude earns the Muslims respect from literati and black aristocrats as well as the poor. Abdul Wali Muhammad, Farrakhan's young chief of staff, is the son of *Ebony* magazine's distinguished correspondent who covered the Freedom Rides of 1961, Simeon Booker.

By swearing off self-disgust and pessimism, the Muslim stalwarts drew large crowds of dispossessed blacks to their public events. The elaborate Fruit of Islam security searches awe or terrorize those visitors who cannot appreciate them as advertising spectacles that purposefully occupy an otherwise idle army of bow-tied young men. Then to the stage comes Farrakhan with his prophet's denunciation of America as a land morally blinded by gluttony, followed by his showtime declarations on "evil America" and the "errant Jews." Finally, however, to the eventual deflation of those who arrive hungry for jobs and survival, Farrakhan often urges the audience to buy the Muslim line of skin-care products. Holding their arms aloft to show where POWER deodorant belongs, they halfheartedly echo his chant of "Power! At last! Forever!"

Within his mosque, Farrakhan often evokes the pathos of a man laboring to create his own religion from a jumbled past. "Talk to me!" he commands, soliciting the call and response of the black Christian church. "Right!" comes the reply. "Yeah!" "Go ahead!" Farrakhan preaches from Isaiah: "The voice of one crying in the wilderness, prepare ye the way of the Lord. . . ." After a detour through the story of Jacob wrestling with the angel, he veers suddenly into a graphic description of the crucifixion: "A nail goes in. Unnnhh!"

Sometimes distracted, sometimes nearly incoherent, Farrakhan speaks intermittently of Pharaoh's army, of Simon Peter's rejection of Jesus, and of the decline of Islam after the Four Rightly Guided Caliphs. In lectures, he usually returns to the quest for righteousness on the part of the ancient Hebrews. After reverently describing the moment in the Passover seder when the door is opened for the return of Elijah, harbinger of the Messiah, he abruptly asks, "But what would you do if Elijah came and he was black?" His tone flashes between dead cold and impish humor. "Would you say 'Call 911'?"

Farrakhan works vainly to explain away his attacks upon Jews, saying that he believes all nations have dishonored their respective faiths: "Now look, Muslims have practiced dirty religion. The Koran is pure. Our actions are not. Christians have practiced dirty religion. Jesus didn't tell none of you to bring us into slavery. . . . I said that the practice of taking that land from the Palestinians, leaving them homeless and vagabonds, I call that unclean." While praising the Jews as pioneers in world civilization, Farrakhan challenges them to live by the laws of righteousness that their prophets gave to the world. "If God made a covenant with you," he asks, "did you uphold it?"

### THE NEW JEWS

At Temple KAM/Isaiah Israel, not too many miles away from Farrakhan's mosque, lay volunteers run the Friday evening services. Taken out of context, Farrakhan's question about their principles would not sound unfamiliar. The service retains an organ, a full harmony choir, and a sermon, but nearly all the other nineteenth-century reforms, except for the movement toward equality for women, have retreated in the face of a general yearning for piety and tradition. Young Jews lead the Conservative revival. They are more likely to learn Hebrew than their parents, the men more likely to wear head coverings than their fathers. Those brought up Reform are likely to try a Conservative congregation, Conservatives to flirt with Orthodoxy. Jonathan Levine, director of the American Jewish Committee's Midwest office, switched to a synagogue with more Hebrew in the service even though he understands little Hebrew—just because he found the ancient language more reassuring.

A young woman psychologist delivers a passionate sermon on Moses, whom she introduces as "the greatest human being that ever lived." Even Moses was human, she declares, summoning up the morality of the prophets. "Once we raise ourselves above any other human soul in this universe in a judgmental capacity, we have sunk lower than low. . . ." she says. "We are responsible for trying to make peace where there are those who are so twisted with pain and their own internal agonies that they strike out at everyone in their paths in pain. We are responsible for respecting each other and for the grace to forgive even where forgiveness is not asked, to understand even where insight could not be accepted."

Her message applied to Israel as well. By May 1988 the Palestinian *intifada* was in its sixth month of sustained protest, mostly by young people. In response, Israeli defense minister Yitzhak Rabin had announced a policy of "force, power, and beatings" to repress the revolt. Most international reaction condemned the "broken-bones campaign," but the Israelis made only modest adjustments between real bullets and plastic ones. Rarely did a day go by without at least one Palestinian killed. Some Israeli soldiers carried sledgehammers to break open the doors of shop owners who honored work stoppages. Others bulldozed clumps of homes belonging to Palestinian suspects and, in one especially poignant case, destroyed a small garden because it was deemed dangerous for anything Palestinian to grow too near a Jewish settlement in the occupied areas.

American Jews writhed in distress. One national leader defended Israel's predicament by saying that the Palestinians "are not people joining hands and singing 'We Shall Overcome.' They're throwing rocks and Molotov cocktails." This was partly true, but the larger point was that one of Israel's staunch American allies was identifying with Bull Connor and taking pains to distinguish the Palestinians from American blacks under segregation. Once that happened, character defects could not long impeach the Palestinian cause, any more than bad grammar had disqualified blacks from full legal citizenship.

### SHUT OUT

Just before last year's scandal erupted, *Chicago* magazine profiled Steve Cokely as a whirlwind "facilitator" and gladhander in Mayor Sawyer's office: "Like Cortés striding onto the shore of Mexico, he takes big steps." The article portrayed Cokely as a man matured by responsibility. He had reconciled with the Italian aldermen over his Anti-Columbus Day crusades. He had even cried at the sight of Sawyer dancing with a blonde at a German-American masquerade ball. They had joined hands to sing a German song. It felt like the old "We Shall Overcome" to Cokely, "only with more oompah."

There is some evidence of cooperation between anti-Sawyer politicians and the Chicago office of the Anti-Defamation League. When the tapes of his "placating the Jews" speech reached the front page of the *Tribune*, Cokely heard himself denounced and supported by politicians he barely knew. The public furor spread across the country within a matter of days as resentment of Cokely's anti-Semitism overwhelmed the layers of Chicago politics. Sawyer slowly grasped the strength of the pressure to fire Cokely, who forgot all about reconciliation and oompah. When tossed back on the street, Cokely first glowed as a new celebrity, boasting that blacks crowded around just to touch him. He tried to take his most inflammatory ruminations about Jews onto the promotional circuit, but he got no further than a few lectures and an appearance on *The Morton Downey Jr. Show*. By the end of 1988, Cokely felt shut out, like a black dropout from the public schools. "Jews suppress dissent rather than reasoning with it," he complained. "That's gonna be one of their undoings."

### THE SOUNDS OF CHICAGO

At WVON Talk Radio in South Chicago, black activist Lu Palmer had taken his shoes off and was squinting into the microphone. His studio might have passed for the back office of a gasoline station in the countryside. Off the air, Palmer scoffed at the possibility that callers might fuss at the Jews. "Let's keep rolling," he growled, and what rolled in was a chorus of disgust. A man announced that Chicago's black churches reap about $10 million *every* Sunday and wondered how to siphon off just $2 million to fight unemployment. He predicted that the Muslims would control the country by the year 2000. A breathless woman reported seeing a man buy his girlfriend $13,000 worth of leather clothes at the posh Water Tower Place. "These white people have got *beaucoup* of money," she said. To declare their intention of boycotting the next election, several callers asked for a fishing pole. A Robert X called to say, "I am not a Muslim. That 'X' is for ex-American." A woman said, "All black men are not black." A man denounced blacks for being too dependent upon the government. "You don't find the Chinese getting upset about the President and the mayor," he said. "Or the Arabs. Or the Italians."

An alderman in the studio took up the last point. "We need to teach kids how to go into business," he said.

Palmer squinted. "But Ed, how can we teach them if we don't know?" he inquired.

The alderman squinted back. "There are people who know," he replied.

After a few more Muslims, two crime reports, and several political gripes, Palmer rolled the tape of chirpy Jesse Jackson urging listeners to register. "Your vote can make a difference," he said, sounding at once Pollyannaish and impossibly brave.

## THE LADDER AND THE LEADERSHIP

An invisible ring protected Mount Sinai Hospital during the 1968 King assassination riots. Now a window was broken at the last Jewish establishment in North Lawndale. The hospital board had nearly moved out when the Chicago Medical School scooted thirty-seven miles north to the suburbs, but after the miracle survival of the riots they decided to stay on the same site where Slavic immigrants had built Maimonides Hospital in 1912. In 1988, twenty years after that decision, Mount Sinai employed 350 doctors and 1,500 staff. Nearly all the patients were blacks and Hispanics from the immediate neighborhood.

Most of the Jewish patients at Mount Sinai were fresh immigrants from the Soviet Union—almost two thousand of them new to Chicago last year. For them, the chain of assimilation still worked. Organized Jewish groups welcomed, placed, and settled them, helped teach them English, and competed by synagogue and denomination for their allegiance. Most often they still made it from language classes and taxis to the suburbs within ten years. No such ladder exists for the blacks of North Lawndale or elsewhere. Overwhelmed, they lack the social cohesion and the facility to adapt that Jews have acquired over a four-thousand-year obsession with literacy.

In 1989 blacks and Jews each face historic, largely unacknowledged, crises of leadership. For blacks, it is that the Mosaic model may not serve to raise the underclass from suffering—that a great march now may lead to a blind door rather than the land of milk and honey. The historic model of uplift by politics, in a mass march behind a great Moses figure, may have no application to the modern dispossessed. This possibility, together with the realization that American Jews themselves did not reach prosperity by such a path, presents dilemmas of nearly unbearable sensitivity.

For Jews, the crisis lies in the combination of worldly comforts and a reestablished Israel, which are both the promise and the curse of Judaism. Nearly all the religion's distinctive traditions developed in the absence of a Jewish state. Passover, Yom Kippur, the other holidays, and indeed the social and religious canons of Rabbinic Judaism itself were all born in the Diaspora. For a culture steeped in exile and outsider status, the core teachings present success as a threat to Jewish morality, and history warns that a kingdom of Israel has brought a flash of glory followed by corruption and destruction. This has occurred both times Jerusalem was a Hebrew capital, first after King David and again under the Hasmonaean kings.

American public life is accustomed to the faces and words of tormented black prophets, but none of them dares to tell their people that they may have to become more like Jews—rising from the rubble family by family, shop by shop. They summon the rest of America to help them avoid this awesome chore rather than to join it, and most of the lesser black prophets speak for those who would rather picket a business than run one. Against this surfeit of black prophets, Jews have no commanding voices. There are rabbis who tell them that unstable societies, with extremes of poverty and wealth, are a threat to Jews, but there is no preeminent leader who summons Israel to do justice by the Palestinians in the name of Amos and Isaiah. In many respects, blacks and Jews need an exchange rather than a war of leadership, but their steep paths are littered with pride.

The pain of such forebodings is worse than having no ears. The faintest sound of them usually drives leaders into fits of prideful avoidance, or into scapegoating, a practice invented by the Hebrews and other ancient peoples to project upon sacrificial animals a ritualized cleansing from mortal confusion. A recurring perversion of this primitive idea—the mass scapegoating of people by tribe—has shamed empires and spawned evils that have numbed historians and theologians alike. Ironically, the present conflict sets the most scapegoated people in America against those who hold the record across all prior history. Having regenerated interchangeable limbs for old wounds, they are wrestling over mixed pieces of a hybrid identity.

# Part 8 **Where Do We Go from Here?**

This closing section offers modest hopes for rebuilding political coalitions between blacks and Jews. Barbara Smith inventories the many historical and sociological obstacles to moving beyond the "rock" of black suspicion and disapproval and the "hard place" of Jewish antagonism. She devotes separate sections to her black and Jewish audiences in order to develop better understanding between the two communities and the possibility of coalition work. Noting that black-Jewish relationships "are the very opposite of simple," she argues that ongoing coalitions are formed not on shared or parallel histories or moral imperatives, "but on the pragmatic basis of shared commitments, politics, and beliefs."

Melvin Drimmer, who devoted his entire academic career to the study of African American history, offers several suggestions for moving toward more honest relations. Derrick Bell, who understands the fears aroused among Jews by the hostility of black spokesmen, makes a case for legitimate black resentment at Jewish attempts to intimidate black leaders who have only color in common with extremists. Jewish groups don't expect other spokespersons to condemn the anti-Semitism by members of their ethnic groups—Ted Kennedy isn't asked to explain Pat Buchanan; John Kenneth Galbraith isn't required to apologize for David Duke, although both are Scottish. Bell points out that blacks object to Jews' seeing them as the only perpetrators of anti-Semitism when it is obvious that much anti-Semitism comes from white right-wing groups. These difficulties notwithstanding, Bell, like Barbara Smith, is clear that "we will join in projects that serve our interest" and "that may be as close to an alliance as any of us can get."

Julius Lester reflects on what blacks and Jews have in common, as well as on the profound difference in their Diaspora experiences: "similarity of experience is not *sameness* of experience. . . . The Jewish experience of oppression is primarily, though not exclusively, European. The black experience is almost exclusively American." Lester reviews the history of black-Jewish relations and finds that Jews are "merely the lightning rod" for desperate conditions within urban, poor communities. Reminding us that the leveling experience of immigration does not extend to the intractability of color prejudice in American society, Lester concludes, "This is not a call for a new black-Jewish coalition, but for coalitions across the racial and ethnic spectrum, coalitions of people with a shared concern for the spiritual and moral well being for all of America, not just the particular group to which one belongs."

David Schoem and Marshall Stevenson's description of teaching black and Jewish students about each other using a dialogue approach suggests one promising way of forging the kind of intergroup understanding that has the potential of leading to future efforts at cooperation.

The measured optimism expressed in some of these essays takes us back to the essay by Julian Bond which began this volume:

> In the long run, however, the cost of achieving justice is never so great as the cost of justice denied; that cost is measured in social disruption and human decay. The coalition between blacks and Jews helped make the American promise real. Strengthened, that coalition can finish what it helped to begin, and in the process, revive the spirit that brought black and white, Jew and Gentile together in common cause.

### FURTHER REFERENCES

There is an emergent literature on black/Jewish dialogue groups. One early instance is described by Letty Cottin Pogrebin, who records some of issues at stake in "Ain't We Both Women," in her *Deborah, Golda, and Me: Being Female and Jewish in America* (1991). Letty Cottin Pogrebin and Earl Ofari Hutchinson's "A Dialogue on Black-Jewish Relations" is in *Race and Ethnic Conflict* (1994), ed. Fred L. Pincus and Howard J. Ehrlich. Black-Jewish bridge-building has been fostered by materials such as Lynne Landsberg and David Saperstein's *Common Roads to Justice: A Programming Manual for Blacks and Jews* (1991).

Another recent instance of black-Jewish collaboration is the new journal *common-Quest: The Magazine of Black/Jewish Relations,* edited by Russell Adams and Jonathan Rieder and published by the American Jewish Committee and Howard University. Three relatively recent books on black-Jewish relations are collaborative efforts, namely Jack Salzman and Cornel West, eds., *Struggles in the Promised Land: Toward a History of Black-Jewish Relations in the United States* (1997); Michael Lerner and Cornel West, eds., *Jews & Blacks: A Dialogue on Race, Religion, and Culture in America* (1995); and the volume from which the opening selection in this section is taken, Elly Bulkin, Minnie Bruce Pratt, and Barbara Smith, *Yours in Struggle: Three Feminist Perspectives on Anti-Semitism and Racism* (1984). *Jewels of the Diaspora* is a collaborative song group that performs African American and Jewish music, headed by Laura Wetzler and Janiece Thompson.

A few recent works have focused on the identity dilemmas of people with black and Jewish ancestry, as in Katya Gibel Azoulay, *Black, Jewish, and Interracial: It's Not the Color of Your Skin, but the Race of Your Kin* (1997); Naomi Zack, "On Being and Not-Being Black and Jewish" (1996); Sarah Blustain, "The New Identity Challenge: 'Are You Black or Are You Jewish?' " (1996); and Yelana Khanga, *Soul to Soul: The Story of a Black Russian American Family, 1865–1992* (1992).

# Between a Rock and a Hard Place
## Relationships between Black and Jewish Women

> *Our strategy is how we cope—how we measure and weigh what is to be said and when, what is to*
> *be done and how, and to whom and to whom and to whom, daily deciding/risking who it is we*
> *can call an ally, call a friend (whatever that person's skin, sex, or sexuality). We are women*
> *without a line. We are women who contradict each other.*[1]
> —Cherríe Moraga

I have spent the better part of a week simply trying to figure out how to begin. Every day, I've asked myself, as I sifted through files and pages of notes that were not getting me one bit closer to a start, "Why in hell am I doing this?" and when most despairing, "Why me?" Despair aside, I knew that if I could remember not just the reasons, but the feelings that first made me want to speak about the complicated connections and disconnections between Black and Jewish women, racism and anti-Semitism, I might find my way into this piece.

The emergence in the last few years of a Jewish feminist movement has of course created the context for this discussion. Jewish women have challenged non-Jewish women, including non-Jewish women of color, to recognize our anti-Semitism and in the process of building their movement Jewish women have also looked to Third World feminists for political inspiration and support. Not surprisingly, as these issues have been raised, tensions that have characterized relationships between Black and Jewish people in this country have also surfaced within the women's movement. Jewish women's perception of Black and other women of color's indifference to or active participation in anti-Semitism and Third World women's sense that major segments of the Jewish feminist movement have failed to acknowledge the weight of their white-skin privilege and capacity for racism, have inevitably escalated suspicion and anger between us.

To be a Black woman writing about racism and anti-Semitism feels like a no-win situation. It's certainly not about pleasing anybody, and I don't think it should be. I worry, however, that addressing anti-Semitism sets me up to look like a woman of color overly concerned about "white" issues. What I most fear losing, of course, is the political support and understanding of other women of color, without which I cannot survive.

This morning, for guidance, I turned to Bernice Johnson Reagon's "Coalition Politics: Turning the Century," because besides all the pain that has led me to examine these

In 1984, Barbara Smith was an artist in residence at Yaddo.

issues, there is also the positive motivation of my belief in coalitions as the only means we have to accomplish the revolution we so passionately want and need. She writes:

> I feel as if I'm gonna keel over any minute and die. That is often what it feels like if you're *really* doing coalition work. Most of the time you feel threatened to the core and if you don't you're not really doing no coalescing. . . . You don't go into coalition because you just *like* it. The only reason you would consider trying to team up with somebody who could possibly kill you, is because that's the only way you can figure you can stay alive.[2]

It helps to be reminded that the very misery that I and all of us feel when we explore the volatile links between our identities and the substance of our oppressions is only to be expected. If we weren't upset about the gulfs between us, if we weren't scared of the inherent challenge to act and change that the recognition of these gulfs requires, then we wouldn't "really [be] doing no coalescing."

What follows is one Black woman's perspective, necessarily affected by the generally complicated character of Black and Jewish relations in this country. This is not pure analysis. Far from it. I am focusing on relationships between Black and Jewish women, because in my own life these relationships have both terrorized me and also shown me that people who are not the same not only can get along, but at times can work together to make effective political change. Although this discussion may be applicable to dynamics between other women of color and Jewish women, I am looking specifically at Black-Jewish relationships because of the particular history between the two groups in the U.S. and because as an Afro-American woman this is the set of dynamics I've experienced first hand. Although the subject of Black and Jewish relationships cannot help but make reference to systematically enforced racism and anti-Semitism, I am emphasizing interactions between us because that feels more graspable to me, closer to the gut and heart of the matter.

Because of the inherent complexities of this subject, one of the things I found most overwhelming was the sense that I had to be writing for two distinct audiences at the same time. I was very aware that what I want to say to other Black women is properly part of an "in-house" discussion and it undoubtedly would be a lot more comfortable for us if somehow the act of writing did not require it to go public. With Jewish women, on the other hand, although we may have a shared bond of feminism, what I say comes from a position outside the group. It is impossible for me to forget that in speaking to Jewish women I am speaking to white women, a role complicated by a racist tradition of Black people repeatedly having to teach white people about the meaning of oppression. I decided then to write sections that would cover what I need to say to Black women and what I need to say to Jewish women, fully understanding that this essay would be read in its entirety by both Black and Jewish women, as well as by individuals from a variety of other backgrounds.

### EMBEDDED IN THE VERY SOIL

I am anti-Semitic. I am not writing this from a position of moral exemption. My hands are not clean, because like other non-Jews in this society I have swallowed anti-

Semitism simply by living here, whether I wanted to or not. At times I've said, fully believing it, that I was not taught anti-Semitism at home growing up in Cleveland in the 1950's. In comparison to the rabid anti-Semitism as well as racism that many white people convey to their children as matter-of-factly as they teach them the alphabet and how to tie their shoes, my perception of what was going on in my house is relatively accurate. But only relatively.

On rare occasions things were said about Jews by members of my family, just as comments were made about white people in general, and about Cleveland's numerous European immigrant groups in particular. My family had "emigrated" too from the rural South during the 1920's, 30's, and 40's and their major observation about Jewish and other white people was that they could come to this country with nothing and in a relatively short period "make it." Our people, on the other hand, had been here for centuries and continued to occupy a permanent position on society's bottom. When I was growing up there were Jewish people living in Shaker Heights, one of the richest suburbs in the U.S., where Blacks were not allowed to purchase property even if they had the money, which most, of course, did not. The fact that Jews were completely barred from other suburbs and perhaps restricted to certain sections of Shaker Heights was not of great import to us. I remember vividly when my aunt and uncle (my mother's sister and brother) were each trying to buy houses in the 1950's. They searched for months on end because so many neighborhoods in the inner city including working-class ones were also racially segregated.[3] I was six or seven, but I remember their exhausted night-time conversations about the problem of where they might be able to move, I felt their anger, frustration, and shame that they could not provide for their families on such a basic level. The problem was white people, segregation, and racism. Some Jews were, of course, a part of that, but I don't remember them being especially singled out. I did not hear anti-Semitic epithets or a litany of stereotypes. I do remember my uncle saying more than once that when they didn't let "the Jew" in somewhere, he went and built his own. His words were edged with both envy and admiration. I got the message that these people knew how to take care of themselves, that we could learn a lesson from them and stop begging the white man for acceptance or even legal integration.

Despite how I was raised, what I've come to realize is that even if I didn't learn anti-Semitism at home, I learned it. I know all the stereotypes and ugly words not only for Jews, but for every outcast group including my own. Such knowledge goes with the territory. Classism, racism, homophobia, anti-Semitism, and sexism float in the air, are embedded in the very soil. No matter how cool things are at home, you catch them simply by walking out of the house and by turning on the t.v. or opening up a newspaper inside the house. In the introduction to *Home Girls*, I wrote about this unsettling reality in relationship to how I sometimes view other women of color:

Like many Black women, I know very little about the lives of other Third World women. I want to know more and I also want to put myself in situations where I have to learn. It isn't easy because, for one thing, I keep discovering how deep my own prejudice goes. I feel so very American when I realize that simply by being Black I have not escaped the typical American ways of perceiving people who are different from myself.[4]

I never believe white people when they tell me they aren't racist. I have no reason to. Depending on the person's actions I might possibly believe that they are actively engaged in opposing racism, are anti-racist, at the very same time they continue to be racially ignorant and cannot help but be influenced as white people by this system's hatred of people of color. Unwittingly, anti-racist whites may collude at times in the very system they are trying to fight. In her article "Racism and Writing: Some Implications for White Lesbian Critics," Elly Bulkin incisively makes the distinction between the reality of being *actively* anti-racist and the illusion of being non-racist—that is, totally innocent.[5] She applies to racism, as I do here to anti-Semitism, the understanding that it is neither possible nor necessary to be morally exempt in order to stand in opposition to oppression. I stress this point because I want everybody reading this, and particularly Black women, to know that I am not writing from the position of having solved anything and because I have also heard other Black women, white non-Jewish women, and at times myself say, "But I'm not anti-Semitic." This kind of denial effectively stops discussion, places the burden of "proof" upon the person(s) experiencing the oppression, and makes it nearly impossible ever to get to the stage of saying: "This is an intolerable situation. What are we going to do about it?"

### A LOVE-HATE RELATIONSHIP

If somebody asked me to describe how Black and Jewish feminists, or Blacks and Jews in general, deal with each other I would say what we have going is a love-hate relationship. The dynamic between us is often characterized by contradictory and ambivalent feelings, both negative and positive, distrust simultaneously mixed with a desire for acceptance; and deep resentment and heavy expectations about the other group's behavior. This dynamic is reflected in the current dialogue about Jewish identity and anti-Semitism in the feminist movement, when Jewish women seem to have different expectations for Black and other women of color than they do for white non-Jewish women. Often more weight is placed upon the anti-Jewish statements of women of color than upon the anti-Semitism of white non-Jewish feminists, although they are the majority group in the women's movement and in the society as a whole, and have more direct links to privilege and power.

I think that both Black and Jewish people expect more from each other than they do from white people generally or from gentiles generally. Alice Walker begins a response to Letty Cottin Pogrebin's article "Anti-Semitism in the Women's Movement" by writing:

> There is a close, often unspoken bond between Jewish and black women that grows out of their awareness of oppression and injustice, an awareness many Gentile women simply do not have.[6]

Our respective "awareness of oppression" leads us to believe that each other's communities should "know better" than to be racist or anti-Semitic because we have first-hand knowledge of bigotry and discrimination. This partially explains the disproportionate anger and blame we may feel when the other group displays attitudes much like those of the larger society.

It's true that each of our groups has had a history of politically imposed suffering. These histories are by no means identical, but at times the impact of the oppression has been brutally similar—segregation, ghettoization, physical violence, and death on such a massive scale that it is genocidal. Our experiences of racism and anti-Semitism, suffered at the hands of the white Christian majority, have sometimes made us practical and ideological allies. Yet white Jewish people's racism and Black gentile people's anti-Semitism have just as surely made us view each other as enemies. Another point of divergence is the fact that the majority of Jewish people immigrated to the United States to escape oppression in Europe and found a society by no means free from anti-Semitism, but one where it was possible in most cases to breathe again. For Black people, on the other hand, brought here forcibly as slaves, this country did not provide an escape. Instead, it has been the very locus of our oppression. The mere common experience of oppression does not guarantee our being able to get along, especially when the variables of time, place, and circumstance combine with race and class privilege, or lack of them, to make our situations objectively different.

The love-hate dynamic not only manifests itself politically, when our groups have functioned as both allies and adversaries, but also characterizes the more daily realm of face-to-face interactions. I think that women of color and Jewish women sometimes find each other more "familiar" than either of our groups find Christian majority W.A.S.P.s. A Black friend tells me, when I ask her about this sense of connectedness, "We don't come from quiet cultures." There are subliminal nuances of communication, shared fixes on reality, modes of expressing oneself, and ways of moving through the world that people from different groups sometimes recognize in each other. In his collection of interviews, *Working,* Studs Terkel uses the term the "feeling tone."[7] I think that Black and Jewish people sometimes share a similar "feeling tone." Melanie Kaye/Kantrowitz corroborates this perception in her instructive article, "Some Notes on Jewish Lesbian Identity." She describes the difficulties a group of non-Jewish women had with her "style" during the process of interviewing her for a job:

> Most of the women troubled by me had been sent to expensive colleges by their fathers, they spoke with well-modulated voices, and they quaked when I raised mine. They didn't understand that to me anger is common, expressible, and not murderous. They found me "loud" (of course) and "emotional." Interestingly, I got along fine with all the women of color in the group. . . .[8]

In a different situation a woman of color might very well feel antagonism toward a Jewish woman's "style," especially if she associates that "style" with a negative interaction—for example, if she experiences racist treatment from a Jewish woman or if she has to go through a rigorously unpleasant job interview with someone Jewish.

Nevertheless, Black and Jewish women grow up knowing that in relationship to the dominant culture, we just don't fit in. And though the chances of a Jewish woman being accepted by the status quo far exceed my own, when I'm up against the status quo I may turn to her as a potential ally. For example, on my way to an all white writers' retreat in

New England, I'm relieved to find out that the female director of the retreat is Jewish. I think she might understand the isolation and alienation I inevitably face as the only one. Feelings of outsiderness cover everything from self-hatred about features and bodies that don't match a white, blue-eyed ideal, to shame about where your father works, or how your mother talks on the telephone. These feelings of shame and self-hatred affect not just Black and Jewish women, but other women of color and white ethnic and poor women. Class can be as essential a bond as ethnicity between women of color and white women, both Jewish and non-Jewish. Chicana poèt Cherríe Moraga describes her differing levels of awareness about Jewish and Black genocide in "Winter of Oppression, 1982," and also remarks on the positive link that she has felt to Jewish people:

> . . . I already understood
> that these people were killed
> for the spirit-blood
> that runs through them.
>
> They were like us in this.
> Ethnic people with long last names
> with vowels at the end or the wrong
> type of consonants
> combined    a colored kind of white people[9]

There are ways that we recognize each other, things that draw us together. But feelings of affinity in themselves are not sufficient to bridge the culture, history, and political conditions that separate us. Only a conscious, usually politically motivated desire to work out differences, at the same time acknowledging commonalities, makes for more than superficial connection.

### TO JEWISH WOMEN

I was concerned about anti-Semitism long before I called myself a feminist, indeed long before there was a feminist movement in which to work. Perhaps because I was born a year after World War II ended, that whole era seems quite vivid to me, its essence conveyed by members of my family. I got a basic sense about the war years and about what had happened to Jewish people because people around me, who had been greatly affected by those events, were still talking about them. Books, films, and history courses provided facts about Jewish oppression. Being friends with Jewish kids in school provided me with another kind of insight, the perception that comes from emotional connection.

My problems with recent explorations of Jewish identity and anti-Semitism in the women's movement do not result from doubting whether anti-Semitism exists or whether it is something that all people, including people of color, should oppose. What concerns me are the ways in which some Jewish women have raised these issues that have contributed to an atmosphere of polarization between themselves and women of color. My criticisms are not of Jewish feminism in general, but of specific political and ideological pitfalls that have led to the escalation of hostility between us, and that cannot be explained away as solely Black and other women of color's lack of sensitivity to anti-Semitism.

These polarizations have directly and painfully affected me and people close to me. One major problem (which I hope this essay does not contribute to) is that far too often these battles have been fought on paper, in published and unpublished writing. Besides the indirectness of this kind of confrontation, I want to say how sick I am of paper wars, when we are living on a globe that is literally at war, where thousands of people are dying every day, and most of the rest of the world's people still grapple for the barest human necessities of food, clothing, and shelter. In *Home Girls* I wrote the following to Black women about negative dynamics between Black and Jewish women in the movement:

> . . . I question whom it serves when we permit internal hostility to tear the movement we have built apart. Who benefits most? Undoubtedly, those outside forces that will go to any length to see us fail.[10]

I ask the same question here of Jewish women.

One of the most detrimental occurrences during this period has been the characterizing of Black and/or other women of color as being more anti-Semitic and much less concerned about combatting anti-Semitism than white non-Jewish women. Letty Cottin Pogrebin's article "Anti-Semitism in the Women's Movement" which appeared in *Ms.* magazine in June, 1982, and which was widely read, exemplifies this kind of thinking. She cites "Black-Jewish Relations" as one of ". . . the five problems basic to Jews and sisterhood," and then uses a number of quotes from Black women who are unsupportive of Jewish issues, but who also are not apparently active in the women's movement.[11] I have already referred to the social and historical circumstances that have linked our two groups and that might lead to our higher expectations for commitment and understanding of each other's situations. The desire for recognition and alliances, however, does not justify the portrayal of Black women, in particular, as being a bigger "problem" than white non-Jewish women or, more significantly, than the white male ruling class that gets to enforce anti-Semitism via the system. Black women need to know that Jewish women can make distinctions between the differing impact, for example, of a woman of color's resentment against Jews, her very real anti-Semitism, and that of the corporate giant, the government policy maker, or even the Ku Klux Klan member. Jewish women need to acknowledge the potential for racism in singling out Black and other women of color and that racism has already occurred in the guise of countering anti-Semitism. I expect Jewish women to confront Black women's anti-Semitism, but I am more than a little suspect when such criticism escalates time and again into frontal attack and blame.

I think Jewish women's desire for support and recognition has also resulted at times in attempts to portray our circumstances and the oppressions of racism and anti-Semitism as parallel or even identical. The mentality is manifested at its extreme when white Jewish women of European origin claim Third World identity by saying they are not white but Jewish, refusing to acknowledge that being visibly white in a racist society has concrete benefits and social-political repercussions. How we are oppressed does not have to be the same in order to qualify as real. One of the gifts of the feminist movement has been to examine the subtleties of what comprises various oppressions without needing to pretend that they are all alike. As a Third World Lesbian I know, for example, that although her day-to-day circumstances may look nothing like my own, a white heterosexual middle-class woman experiences sexual oppression, that she can still be raped, and that class privilege does not save her from incest.

Trying to convince others that one is legitimately oppressed by making comparisons can either result from or lead to the ranking of oppressions, which is a dangerous pitfall in and of itself. In a letter responding to the Pogrebin article, a group of Jewish women write: "We sense a competition for victim status in Pogrebin's article and elsewhere. . . ."[12] I have sensed the same thing and I know it turns off women of color quicker than anything.

In a white dominated, capitalist economy, white skin, and if you have it, class privilege, definitely count for something, even if you belong at the very same time to a group or to groups that the society despises. Black women cannot help but resent it when people who have these privileges try to tell us that "everything is everything" and that their oppression is every bit as pervasive and dangerous as our own. From our frame of reference, given how brutally racism has functioned politically and historically against people of color in the U.S., such assertions are neither experientially accurate nor emotionally felt.

The fact that we have differing amounts of access to privilege and power can't help but influence how we respond to Jewish women's assertions of their cultural and political priorities. For example, in the last section of "Some Notes on Jewish Lesbian Identity," Melanie Kaye/Kantrowitz names Jewish women who resisted inside the concentration camps and in the Warsaw Ghetto, usually at the price of their lives. She concludes her article:

> Those were Jewish women. I come from women who fought like that.
> I want a button that says *Pushy Jew Loud Pushy Jew Dyke.*[13]

Despite the fact that this is a proud affirmation, reading the last sentence makes me wince, not because I don't understand the desire to reshape the negative words and images the society uses against those of us it hates, but because my gut response is, "I don't want to be treated like that." The positive image of Jewish women, who, like many Black women, refuse to disappear, who are not afraid to speak up, and who fight like hell for freedom, comes up against my experience as a Black woman who has, at times, felt pushed around and condescended to by women who are not just Jewish, but, more significantly, white. Because I come from a people who have historically been "pushed" around by all kinds of white people, I get upset that a traditional way of behaving might in fact affect me differently than it does a white non-Jewish woman.

Black and other women of color are much more likely to take seriously any group which wants their political support when that group acknowledges its privilege, at the same time working to transform its powerlessness. Privilege and oppression can and do exist simultaneously. I know, because they function together in my own life. As a well educated, currently able-bodied individual from a working-class family, who is also Black, a woman, and a Lesbian, I am constantly aware of how complex and contradictory these intersections are. Being honest about our differences is painful and requires large doses of integrity. As I've said in discussions of racism with white women who are sometimes overwhelmed at the implications of their whiteness, no one on earth had any say whatsoever about who or what they were born to be. You can't run the tape backward and start from scratch, so the question is, what are you going to do with what you've got? How are you going to deal responsibly with the unalterable facts of who and what you are, of having or not having privilege and power? I don't think anyone's case is inherently hopeless. It depends on what you decide to *do* once you're here, where you decide to place yourself in relationship to the ongoing struggle for freedom.

Another extremely negative wedge that has been driven between women of color and Jewish women is the notion that white Jewish and non-Jewish women have been "forced" to confront racism while women of color have not been required to, or have been completely unwilling to confront anti-Semitism. This is, of course, untrue. There are Black and other women of color who have taken definite stands against anti-Semitism (and our commitment to this issue cannot be measured, as I suspect it probably has been, by what is available in print). On the other hand, obviously not all white feminists or white people have sufficiently challenged racism, because if they had, racism would be a thing of the past. The implied resentment at having been "forced" to confront racism, is racist in itself. This kind of statement belies a weighing mentality that has no legitimate place in progressive coalition politics. Our support for struggles that do not directly encompass our own situations cannot be motivated by an expectation of pay-back. Of course we're likely to choose ongoing political allies on the basis of those groups and individuals who recognize and respect our humanity and issues, but the bottom line has got to be a fundamental opposition to oppression, period, not a tit-for-tat of "I'll support 'your' issue if you'll support 'mine'." In political struggles there wouldn't be any "your" and "my" issues, if we saw each form of oppression as integrally linked to the others.

A final matter that I want to discuss that can be offensive to Black and other women of color is the idea put forth by some Jewish feminists that to be or to have been at any time a Christian is to be by definition anti-Semitic. Traditional, institutionalized Christianity has, of course, had as one of its primary missions the destruction and invalidation of other systems of religious belief, not only Judaism, but Islam, Buddhism, Hinduism, and all of the indigenous religions of people of color. Holy wars, crusades, and pogroms qualify, I suppose, as "Christian totalitarianism,"[14] but I have great problems when this term is applied to the mere practice of Christianity.

In the case of Black people, the Christian religion was imposed upon us by white colonizers in Africa and by white slaveowners in the Americas. We nevertheless re-shaped it into an entirely unique expression of Black spirituality and faith, which has been and continues to be a major source of sustenance and survival for our people. Being Christian hardly translates into "privilege" for Black people, as exemplified by the fact that most white churches do not encourage Black membership and many actually maintain tacit or official policies of racial segregation. Christian privilege becomes a reality when it is backed up by race and class privilege. It is demoralizing and infuriating to have Black and other people of color's religious practices subsumed under the catch-all of white Christianity or Christian "totalitarianism." If anything has been traditionally encouraged in Afro-American churches, it is an inspirational identification with the bondage of "the Children of Israel" as recounted in the Old Testament. This emphasis did not, of course, prevent anti-Semitism (during slavery there was virtually no contact between Black and Jewish people in this country), but there needs to be some distinction made between being raised as a Christian, being anti-Semitic, and the historical role of the institutionalized Christian church in promoting anti-Semitism when its powers and goals have been directly tied to the power and interests of the state.

### TO BLACK WOMEN

Why should anti-Semitism be of concern to Black women? If for no other reason, anti-Semitism is one aspect of an intricate system of oppression that we by definition oppose when we say we are feminist, progressive, political. The Ku Klux Klan, the Christian right wing, and the American Nazi Party all promote anti-Semitism as well as racism. Lack of opposition to anti-Semitism lines us up with our enemies. People of color need to think about who our cohorts are when we express attitudes and take stands similar to those of the most dangerous and reactionary elements in this society. I'm talking here out of political principles, which can be a useful guide for approaching complicated questions. But needless to say, principles are not what any of us operate out of one-hundred per cent of the time.

Certainly principles have only taken me so far in trying to deal with my gut responses to the ways that issues of anti-Semitism and Jewish identity have been raised in the women's movement. Like many Black feminists I could not help but notice how Jewish feminism arose just at the point that Third World feminist issues were getting minimal recognition from the movement as a whole. I saw how the feminism of women of color helped to lay the groundwork for Jewish feminists to name themselves, often without acknowledgment. I've seen how easy it has been for some Jewish women to make the shift from examining their role as racist oppressors, to focusing solely on their position as victims of oppression. I've also found the uncritical equating of the impact of anti-Semitism in the U.S. with the impact of racism absolutely galling.

If such "oversights" have made it difficult for us to get to the issue of anti-Semitism, continuing to experience racism from those women who seemingly want us to ignore their treatment of us and instead put energy into opposing an oppression which directly affects them has made commitment to the issue feel nearly impossible. The history of Black people in this country is a history of blood. It does not always dispose us to being altruistic and fair, because history has not been fair. Our blood is still being spilled. I know with what justification and fury we talk among ourselves about white people, Jews and non-Jews alike, and we will undoubtedly continue to talk about them as long as racism continues to undermine our lives.

In the case of racist Jewish people, we have something to throw back at them—anti-Semitism. Righteous as such comebacks might seem, it does not serve us, as feminists and political people, to ignore or excuse what is reactionary in ourselves. Our anti-

Semitic attitudes are just that, both in the political sense and in the sense of reacting to another group's mistreatment of us. Although it isn't always possible or even logical for us to be "fair," being narrowminded and self-serving is not part of our Black ethical tradition either. Trying as it may seem, I think we are quite capable of working through our ambivalent or negative responses to arrive at a usable Black feminist stance in opposition to anti-Semitism.

A major problem for Black women, and all people of color, when we are challenged to oppose anti-Semitism, is our profound skepticism that white people can actually be oppressed. If white people as a group are our oppressors, and history and our individual experiences only verify that in mass they are, how can we then perceive some of these same folks as being in trouble, sometimes as deep as our own? A white woman with whom I once taught a seminar on racism and sexism told me about a friend of hers, also a teacher, who used John Steinbeck's *The Grapes of Wrath* in a class that had a large number of Black students. She told me how these students were absolutely convinced that the characters in the novel were Black because their situation was so terrible. It had never occurred to them that white people could suffer like that and the instructor had quite a job to do to get them to believe otherwise. I think it was in many ways an understandable mistake on the Black students' part, given how segregated Black life still is from white life in this country; the extreme arrogance and romanticism with which white people usually portray themselves in the media; and also how lacking all North Americans are in a class analysis (economic exploitation was the major force oppressing Steinbeck's characters).

On the other hand, this incident points to a basic attitude among us that I think often operates when the issue of anti-Semitism is raised. Almost all Jews in the United States are white people of European backgrounds, and therefore benefit from white-skin privilege, which is often combined with class privilege. Our frequent attitude when this particular group of white people tells us they're oppressed is (in the words of Ma Rainey) "Prove it on me!"[15] Many Black women who I've either talked to directly or who I've heard talk about the subject of anti-Semitism simply do not believe that Jews are now or ever have been oppressed. From our perspective it doesn't add up, because in those cases where Jewish people have white skin, high levels of education, economic privilege, and political influence, they are certainly not oppressed like us. I have to admit that this is certainly the aspect of the position of Jewish people in this country that I have the most problems with and I think many other people of color do too. White skin and class privilege make assimilation possible and provide a cushion unavailable to the majority of people of color. Sometimes I actually get disgusted when I see how good other people can have it and still be oppressed. When white, economically privileged Jews admit to their privilege, as opposed to pretending that it either doesn't exist or that it has no significant impact upon the quality of their lives, then I don't feel so envious and angry.

Jewish oppression is not identical to Black oppression, but it is oppression brought to bear by the same white-male ruling class which oppresses us. An investigation of Jewish history, as well as of the current situation of Jews in countries such as Russia, reveals centuries of abuse by traditionally Christian dominated states. Anti-Semitism has taken many forms, including physical segregation, sanctions against the practice of the Jewish religion, exclusion from certain jobs and professions, violent attacks by individuals, state co-ordinated pogroms (massacres), and the Nazi-engineered Holocaust which killed one-third of the world's Jews between 1933 and 1945. Anti-Semitism has been both more violent and more widespread in Europe than in the U.S., but it is currently on the increase as the political climate grows ever more reactionary. Because it is not point-for-point identical to what we experience doesn't mean it is not happening or that it is invalid for people to whom it is happening to protest and organize against it.

Another instance of skepticism about whether white people can actually be oppressed sometimes occurs when Black people who do not identify with feminism are asked to consider that sexual politics affect all women. Their disbelief leads to at least two equally inaccurate responses. The first is that sexism is a white woman's thing and Black women are, of course, already liberated. The other is that it is not possible for a rich white woman, "Miss Ann type" to be oppressed in the first place. In neither response is sexual oppression taken seriously or seen as an independently operating system. White-skin privilege is assumed to compensate for lack of power and privilege in every other sphere. All white women are assumed to be exactly alike, a monolithic group who are wealthy, pampered, and self-indulgent. However, as Third World feminists we know that sexual oppression cuts across all racial, class, and nationality lines, at the same time we understand how race, class, ethnicity, culture and the political system under which one lives determine the specific content of that oppression. The ability to analyze complicated intersections of privilege and oppression can help us to grasp that having white skin does not negate the reality of anti-Semitism. As long as opposing anti-Semitism is narrowly viewed as defending white people's interests, we will undoubtedly be extremely reluctant to speak out about it.* We need to understand that we can oppose anti-Semitism at the very same time that we oppose white racism, including white Jewish people's racism.

In political dialogue and in private conversation, it is more than possible to attack and criticize racism and racist behavior without falling back on the stereotypes and ideology of another system of oppression. The bankruptcy of such tactics is exemplified by a front page headline in *The Black American* newspaper (notable for its reactionary stances on just about everything) which derisively referred to New York's mayor, Edward Koch, as a faggot.[16] Koch's general misrule and countless abuses against people of color in New York are a matter of public record. Homophobia aimed at him did not directly confront these abuses, however; his racism in no way justified a homophobic put-down; and finally such tactics were transparently the weapons of the weak and weak-minded. The self-righteousness with which some individuals express homophobia parallels the self-righteousness with which some of these same individuals and others express anti-Semitism. In both instances, such attacks are not even perceived as wrong, because of the pervasive, socially sanctioned contempt for the group in question. I'm not suggesting that people merely talk nice to each other for the sake of talking nice, but that as progressive women of color it is our responsibility to figure out how to confront oppression directly. If we are not interested in being called out of our names, we can assume that other people don't want to be called out of theirs either, even when the larger white society thoroughly condones such behavior.

The disastrous situation in the Middle East is used as yet another justification for unbridled anti-Semitism, which crops up in political groupings ranging from the most reactionary to the most ostensibly radical. The fact that the left, including some Third World organizations, frequently couches its disagreements with Israel's politics in anti-Semitic terms further confuses us about how to state our criticisms effectively and ethically.[17] Too often when I've brought up the problem of anti-Semitism, a woman of color responds, "But what about the Middle East?" as if opposition to Israeli actions and support for the Palestinians' right to a homeland can only be expressed by making anti-Semitic remarks to reinforce valid political perspectives. This tactic "works" all too often because so many non-Jews do not perceive verbalized anti-Semitism as unacceptable or when confronted, they act as if it has not even occurred.

Without delving into the pros and cons of the convoluted Middle East situation, I think that it is essential to be able to separate what Israel does when it functions as a white male-run imperialist state from what individual Jewish people's responsibility in relation to that situation can be. What do Jewish people who are not the people who run that state, by and large, actually want and stand for? There is a peace movement in Israel of which Israeli feminists are a significant part. In this country progressive groups like the New Jewish Agenda are defining a more complex political stance of supporting the continued existence of the state of Israel, while voicing grave criticisms of current policies and recognizing the rights of Palestinians to a homeland. Black and other Third World women must express our opposition to Israeli actions in the Middle East, if in fact we are opposed, without assuming that every Jewish person both there and here uncritically agrees with Israeli actions and colludes with those policies. Can criticisms be expressed without throwing in the "obligatory" anti-Semitic remarks and attitudes? Can Jewish women hear criticisms of Israeli actions not only from women of color but also from white non-Jewish women without assuming that their rights as Jews and as human beings to continue to survive are being questioned?

Of course, there is an emotional layer to Black and Jewish women's attitudes about the Israeli-Palestinian conflict that is directly linked to who we are. Many Jewish women view Israel as a place of refuge. They support it as the only existing Jewish state, the one place where Jews were allowed to emigrate freely following the Holocaust, and where most Jews are still granted automatic citizenship.** Often Black and other women of color feel a visceral identification with the Palestinians, because like the Vietnamese, Nicaraguans, and Black South Africans, they are a colored people struggling for the liberation of their homeland. Our two groups very often have differing responses to the Middle East situation and I am not so naive as to expect total agreement between us about the best course for rectifying what has been up to now an intractable and violent situation. I am only asserting that our anti-Semitic or Jewish people's racist attacks do not comprise legitimate "criticisms" of the other group's point of view.

How we deal as Black women with anti-Semitism and with Jewish women ultimately boils down to how we define our politics which are admittedly diverse. What I've written here are some ways to think about these vastly complicated issues, growing out of my particular political perspective. As a Black feminist I believe in our need for autonomy in determining where we stand on every issue. I also believe in the necessity for short and long term coalitions when it is viable for various groups to get together to achieve specific goals. Finally, there is my personal belief that political interactions and all other human connections cannot work without some basic level of ethics and respect. We don't oppose anti-Semitism because we owe something to Jewish people, but because we owe something very basic to ourselves.

### BETWEEN A ROCK AND A HARD PLACE

Some of the pitfalls that have characterized the growth of Jewish feminism can be traced to ideological tendencies in the women's movement as a whole. I want to outline several of these here, because of the effect they have had upon relationships between Black and Jewish women, as well as upon relationships between other women of different cultures, classes, and races. These tendencies have also led to numerous misunderstandings within feminism, generally, about the nature of oppression and how to fight it.

The concept of identity politics has been extremely useful in the development of Third World feminism. It has undoubtedly been most clarifying and catalytic when individuals do in fact have a combination of non-mainstream identities as a result of their race, class, ethnicity, sex, and sexuality; when these identities make them direct targets of oppression; and when they use their experiences of oppression as a spur for activist political work. Identity politics has been much less effective when primary emphasis has been placed upon exploring and celebrating a suppressed identity within a women's movement context, rather than upon developing practical political solutions for confronting oppression in the society itself.

A limited version of identity politics often overlaps with two other currents within the movement: Lesbian separatism and cultural feminism (which emphasizes the development of a distinct women's culture through such vehicles as music, art, and spirituality). These approaches to dealing with being social-cultural outsiders only work when the more stringent realities of class and race are either not operative (because everybody involved is white and middle-class) or when these material realities are ignored or even forcibly denied. Lesbian separatism, which might be thought of as an extreme variety of identity politics, has seldom been very useful for poor and working-class white women or for the majority of women of color, because in attributing the whole of women's oppression to one cause, the existence of men (or of patriarchy), it has left out myriad other forces that oppress women who are not economically privileged and/or white. When Jewish feminism has subscribed to or been influenced by cultural feminism, separatism, or a narrow version of identity politics, it has been limited in both analysis and strategy, since, for example, anti-Semitism does not manifest itself solely as attacks upon individuals' identities, nor does it only affect Jewish women.

Another major misunderstanding within feminism as a whole that has affected the conception of Jewish feminism is the notion that it is politically viable to work on anti-Semitism, racism, or any other system of oppression solely *within* a women's movement context. Although all the systems of oppression cannot help but manifest themselves inside the women's movement, they do not start or end there. It is fallacious and irresponsible to think that working on them internally only with other feminists is ultimately going to have a substantial, permanent effect on the power structure from which they spring. I don't live in the women's movement, I live on the streets of North America. Internal women's movement solutions are just that. They have only fractional impact on the power of the state which determines the daily content of my life.

Although I've focused on relationships between Black and Jewish women, I do not think for a moment that the whole of our respective oppressions can be reduced to how we treat each other, which is yet another mistaken notion afloat in the movement. Yes, it helps for us as feminists to respect each other's differences and to attempt to act decently, but it is ultimately much more "helpful" to do organizing that confronts oppression at its roots in the political system as a whole.

There is a last point I want to make about the political work we do and the people we are able to do it with. My intention in addressing the issues of Black and Jewish relationships, racism and anti-Semitism has been to encourage better understanding between us and to support the possibility of coalition work. It is obvious, however, that there are substantial political differences and disagreements between us and that some of these, despite efforts to alleviate them, will no doubt remain. Ongoing coalitions are formed, in truth, not on the basis of political correctness or "shoulds," but on the pragmatic basis of shared commitments, politics, and beliefs. Some Jewish women and some women of color are not likely to work together because they are very much in opposition to each other *politically*. And that's all right, because there are other Jewish women and women of color who are already working together and who will continue to do so, because they have some basic political assumptions and goals in common.

Relationships between Black and Jewish women are the very opposite of simple. Our attempts to make personal/political connections virtually guarantee our being thrust between "the rock" of our own people's suspicion and disapproval and "the hard place" of the other group's antagonism and distrust. It is a lot easier to categorize people, to push them into little nastily-labelled boxes, than time and again to deal with them directly, to make distinctions between the stereotype and the substance of who and what they are. It's little wonder that so often both Black and Jewish women first label and then dismiss each other. All of us resort to this tactic when the impact of our different histories, cultures, classes, and skins backs us up against the wall and we do not have the courage or desire to examine what, if anything, of value lies between us. Cherríe Moraga writes, "Oppression does not make for hearts as big as all outdoors. Oppression makes us big and small. Expressive and silenced. Deep and dead."[18] We are certainly damaged people. The question is, finally, do we use that damage, that first-hand knowledge of oppression, to recognize each other, to do what work we can together? Or do we use it to destroy?

NOTES

* It is also important to know that significant numbers of Jews outside the U.S. are people of color, including Jews from Ethiopia, China, India, Arab countries, and elsewhere.

** Jewish Lesbians and gay men are excluded from the Law of Return.

Portions of this essay originally appeared in a shorter version, based upon my presentation at the plenary session on "Racism and Anti-Semitism in the Women's Movement" at the 1983 National Women's Studies Association Convention. See "A Rock and a Hard Place: Relationships Between Black and Jewish Women," *Women's Studies Quarterly,* vol. XI, No. 3 (Fall, 1983), pp. 7–9.

1. Cherríe Moraga, "Preface," *This Bridge Called My Back: Writings by Radical Women of Color,* eds. Moraga and Gloria Anzaldúa (New York: Kitchen Table: Women of Color Press, 1981, 1983), pp. xviii–xix.

2. Bernice Johnson Reagon, "Coalition Politics: Turning the Century," *Home Girls: A Black Feminist Anthology,* ed. Barbara Smith (New York: Kitchen Table: Women of Color Press, 1983), pp. 356–357.

3. Lorraine Hansberry's classic play *A Raisin in the Sun* written in 1958 revolves around this very dilemma of housing discrimination and a Black family's efforts to buy a house in an all-white neighborhood. Cleveland author Jo Sinclair's novel *The Changelings,* which I first read as a teen-ager, describes the summer when a working-class Jewish and Italian neighborhood begins to change from white to Black. The story is told from the perspective of a pre-teen-age Jewish girl, Vincent, and traces with more complexity and compassion than any work I know what it is that lies between us as Black and Jewish women. Despite my efforts to interest several women's presses in republishing *The Changelings,* it continues to be out of print, but is sometimes available in libraries. Jo Sinclair (Ruth Seid), *The Changelings,* (New York: McGraw-Hill, 1955).

4. Barbara Smith, "Introduction," *Home Girls,* pp. xlii–xliii.

5. Elly Bulkin, "Racism and Writing: Some Implications for White Lesbian Critics," *Sinister Wisdom* 13 (Spring, 1980), pp. 3–22.

6. Alice Walker, "Letters Forum: Anti-Semitism," *Ms.* (February, 1983), p. 13.

7. Studs Terkel, "Introduction," *Working* (New York: Pantheon Books, 1972, 1974), p. xviii.

8. Melanie Kaye/Kantrowitz, "Some Notes on Jewish Lesbian Identity," *Nice Jewish Girls: A Lesbian Anthology,* ed. Evelyn Torton Beck (Trumansburg, New York: The Crossing Press, 1981, 1984), p. 37.

9. Cherríe Moraga, "Winter of Oppression, 1982," *Loving in the War Years: Lo Que Nunca Pasó Por Sus Labios* (Boston: South End Press, 1983), pp. 73–74.

10. Smith, p. xliv.

11. Letty Cottin Pogrebin, "Anti-Semitism in the Women's Movement," *Ms.* (June, 1983), p. 46.

12. Deborah Rosenfelt et al., "Letters Forum: Anti-Semitism," *Ms.* (February, 1983), p. 13.

13. Kaye/Kantrowitz, p. 42.

14. Gloria Greenfield, "Shedding," *Nice Jewish Girls,* p. 5.

15. Gertrude "Ma" Rainey, "Prove it on Me Blues" (performed by Teresa Trull) *Lesbian Concentrate* (Oakland, California: Olivia Records, LF915, 1977).

16. "Diana Ross: The White Lady and the Faggot," *The Black American* (New York), Vol. 22, No. 29, July 14–July 20, 1983, pp. 23 ff.

17. See for example the All African People's Revolutionary Party's Educational Brochure Number One, "Israel Commits Mass Murder of Palestinian & African Peoples: Zionism is Racism. . . . It Must Be Destroyed" (A-APRP, Box 3307, Washington, D.C. 20009).

18. Moraga, *Loving in the War Years,* p. 135.

# Blacks and Jews
## Thoughts on an Agenda for the Eighties

In dealing with the subject of Blacks and Jews, I believe it appropriate that a personal statement from the author is in order. Readers have a right to know "where I am coming from."

For a number of years I have been reading, thinking, and writing about the relationships between Blacks and Jews, a relationship which two scholars have called "Bittersweet Encounters."[1] But, in addition to the academic interest in the subject, I have considerable self-interest, and do not claim to approach the issue as a neutral observer.

As I wrote for my entry in *Who's Who in America*, "I am a product of the great Civil Rights revolution of the 1960s." For nearly 10 years I taught at Spelman College, a college for Black women in Atlanta, and in turn, was taught a great deal of history from my colleagues at Spelman and the Atlanta University Center. I had continual contact with the leaders of the Civil Rights movement and feel that I contributed something positive to that turbulent yet creative period. I participated in sit-ins, transported civil rights workers throughout Alabama and Georgia, and was jailed in Atlanta by Judge Durwood Pye for telling that honorable gentleman that justice was being unfairly meted out to civil rights workers in his court, and the Judge, I regret to say, did just that by sentencing me to 20 days in jail for contempt of court.

Out of this experience in the South came a best-selling textbook, *Black History* (Doubleday, 1968). I produced 40 one-hour television programs on the Black experience and embarked on an academic career involving the teaching, research, and writing of the Afro-American experience. In addition, I founded the American Forum for International Study which in its 14 years trained more than 2100 educators and students in African Studies through summer study programs in Africa and the Caribbean. I travelled to Africa 21 times, and was honored with an award by the government of Senegal. In 1981 I was appointed Research Associate at the W. E. B. Du Bois Institute at Harvard, and if this can be believed, my biography can be found in *Who's Who Among Black Americans*.

On the other hand, despite opinions to the contrary, and the numerous letters I

Melvin Drimmer was a professor of History at Cleveland State University, where he taught African American history for many years.

Originally published in *Blacks and Jews: A New Dialogue* (selected papers from the proceedings of the National Conference on African American/Jewish American Relations), ed. Ja A. Jahannes (Savannah: Savannah State College Press, 1983), 26–48. Reprinted in Melvin Drimmer, *Issues in Black History: Reflections and Commentaries on the Black Historical Experience* (Dubuque: Kendall-Hunt, 1987). Used with permission of Ja A. Jahannes.

received calling me a self-hating Jew after I defended Andrew Young in the "Letters Column" of the *New York Times,* I am a proud and self-conscious Jew. I am a member of Fairmount Temple (Reform) in Cleveland, and of Workmen's Circle. I identify myself as a Zionist, and am currently enrolled in a class on the history of Eastern European Jewry at the Cleveland College of Jewish Studies. I have sent my son and daughter to Israel, participated in a study seminar in Israel sponsored by the American Jewish Committee, and spent a short time on a Kibbutz. Moreover, I love my mother and father, and in fact, some of my best friends are Jews.

During a very heated debate in the history department of which I was chairman, I was called "a loud mouthed, New York, nigger-loving Jew bastard." At first I was highly offended to be described in such vivid terms, but on second thought, I found those words to be a very accurate description of me. With this in mind, I wish to share some thoughts on a Black-Jewish Agenda for the 1980s.

## I

The Reverend Jesse Jackson, head of Operation PUSH, and Rabbi Irwin Black, president of the Synagogue Council of America, concluded a meeting in Chicago in November between 50 Black and Jewish religious leaders. The purpose of the meeting was to "re-establish the working coalition that was formed during the Sixties and that collapsed over the last few years." For two days these men of goodwill aired their differences "on such thorny issues as affirmative action, busing, the status of Israel, and the moral and economic crisis in American life."

At the conclusion of the meetings, the participants issued a statement which pledged the Black and Jewish conferees to work for "a program of full employment as a matter of right," an adoption of an anti-inflation program which does not sacrifice the poor, the weak, the minorities, and the elderly who bear an unequal burden," the passage of a national health and child care program, and lastly, "an effective affirmative action program for women, Blacks, and other minorities."

This agenda reflected immediate Black concerns. What did Jews want in return? Rabbi Blank spelled out the price of Jewish support. "As long as Jews persist," he warned the Black conferees, "in seeing black people as symbols of threats to economic security, community stability, and Third World hostility to Israel, then a constructive approach to our concerns will be stifled before it can take shape."

These warnings are familiar to all concerned with the recent history of Black-Jewish relations. But I purposely omitted an important fact in my summary of that November meeting in Chicago. The meeting did not take place this past November. *The meeting took place in November, 1974.* (A full report appeared in *Reform Judaism.*)

Why was nothing done to implement this program?

From hindsight we can document a precipitous decline in the fortunes in Black-Jewish relationships. Part of the decline was brought on by forces outside the control of the Black and Jewish communities. Some of the wounds were inflicted on each other, and some, born out of frustration, were self-inflicted.

**II**

Before we move on to consider what could be done to re-kindle Black-Jewish relationships, if they can be re-kindled at all, we need to examine what happened in the 1970s, taking note of the losses and gains.

For Blacks, a partial inventory would include:

1. The Viet Nam War which hastened the end of the programs of the Great Society.

2. The urban riots which substituted "law and order" solutions for the problems of poverty and institutional racism.

3. The murders within two months of each other of Martin Luther King, Jr. and Robert Kennedy, the Black and White hopes of American reform. For both Blacks and Whites, the leadership vacuum created by their deaths has not been filled.

4. The narrow defeat of Hubert H. Humphrey and the election of Richard M. Nixon. Despite imperfections, Humphrey was a friend of Blacks and Jews, and he had supported their causes and, in turn, they were loyal to him.

5. The emergence of the neo-conservatives with their policies of "benign neglect" followed by their attacks on affirmative action, job quotas, open admissions, police review boards, community control, school integration, busing, public housing, welfare, food stamps, and various other social program instituted in the 1960s. Their attacks played on the anxieties of urban populations trying to adjust to a greater Black presence in the total structures of their communities.

6. The lackluster American economy of the 1970s became the recession economy of the 1980s. For whites it was a recession with an unemployment rate of 8.9% (March, 1983). For Blacks it had become a depression with adult unemployment rates of 20.8%. Among Black youth, the unemployment rose beyond 50%. And in the industrial centers of the north—Detroit, Cleveland, Chicago—the decline of heavy industries hit Black workers very hard.

7. The decline in Black leadership following the death of King. No one Black leader managed to develop a broad constituency. Would be inheritors of King's mantle were unable to fill his role: age, ill-health and death took Roy Wilkins; the ouster from Carter's Cabinet of Andrew Young removed him from the center of power; the near murder and subsequent resignation of the Urban League's Vernon Jordan quieted his voice as a national spokesman; illness forced Barbara Jordan to give up her political career; and erratic political behavior raised concerns about the leadership of Ralph Albernathy, Benjamin Hooks, and Jesse Jackson. In particular, Jackson's career suffered a notable eclipse after his ill-fated trip to the Middle East with his embrace of Yasir Arafat.

8. And, of course, the election of Ronald Reagan. Despite the attempts of some to look the other way, the evidence is clear that the Reagan revolution has rigorously attempted and, in part, has succeeded in braking the social, economic, and civil rights gains of the last forty years. For Blacks, it is as if American history is repeating itself, and a century after the first Reconstruction, we are witnessing a re-enactment of history.

Moreover, Reagan has not only aimed his fire at the poor. His "reforms" now directly threaten the existence of the greatly enlarged Black middle class whose jobs have been increasingly tied to servicing the educational, social welfare, and governmental sectors of the economy. No wonder that Vice President George Bush told reporters after addressing a middle class Black audience: "Well, I'll be honest with you. I don't see any evidence of black support."

### III

But if the 1970s were disappointing for Blacks, it was equally disappointing for Jews, although on a different scale. As Irving Howe reminds us, there is much difference between Jewish discomforts and Black ordeals.

The Sixties and Seventies found a dramatic change in the fortunes of Jews in America. Jewish life became distinctly middle class and suburban and, for some, even gentryfied. It was not uncommon to find Jews in the upper echelons of government, the universities, and big business. Jews, more than Blacks, were "moving on up to that new de-luxe apartment in the sky."

Yet, if one surveyed Jewish opinion as reflected in Jewish magazines or in the agendas of Jewish communal conferences, one would get the impression that they were not enjoying their newly achieved status. Perhaps, *arriviste* never do. This has been one of the problems facing Jewish neo-conservatives. Memories of youth spent in poverty followed by careers on the margins of academia and finally their late arrival into the security of the university has played an important role in the considerable status insecurities of Jewish neo-conservatives. Just as they got comfortable, Blacks knocked loudly at the door.

But there were more immediate factors which troubled the Jewish community:

1.  The heavy involvement of Jewish youth in the anti-Vietnam protests, the Chicago Seven trials, and the Kent State killings, points that did not escape President Nixon.
2.  The pronouncements of support for the Palestinian cause by the New Left, various mainstream Christian organizations, and large corporate interests tied to the Middle Eastern oil and business conglomerates.
3.  The 1973 Yom Kippur War and the constant threat to Israel's existence.
4.  The silence or acquiescence on the part of African and Asian nations to the attempts of the radical Arab nations to delegitimize Israel and brand it a racist nation at the United Nations.
5.  And continual PLO terrorism highlighted by the murders at the 1972 Munich Olympics, the 1976 highjacking at Entebbe, and the wanton and senseless murders of an endless number of Jewish men, women, and children. To these obscenities, the so-called civilized world remained indifferent.

Jewish frustration over events in the Middle East found release in blaming the Nixon, Ford, Carter, and now Reagan administrations with being too-hard on Israel and too soft on the PLO. Even a Jewish Secretary of State, a conservative, and an architect of the shuttle diplomacy which eventually led up to the Camp David accord, Henry Kissinger, had to defend himself time and again of the charges that he was anti-Israeli or anti-Semitic. "No criticism has hurt me more," Kissinger told a Jewish audience. He reminded them that "thirteen members of my family died in concentration camps."

But probably the deepest malaise affecting the Jewish community on a day to day basis came from the decay of the cities, the notable increase in street crimes, the decline of the public schools, harassments of the Jewish elderly and small shopkeepers, and the "resettlement" of the Jewish community to the suburbs. There has probably not been a Jewish family in an urban northeast or midwestern American city that on any given Sunday did not ride joylessly through the old neighborhoods lamenting "the way it was," and openly blaming Blacks for the decay. Whether the place was Roxbury in Boston, Georgia Avenue in Washington, Glenville in Cleveland, Joseph Avenue in Rochester, Flatbush in Brooklyn, Washington Heights in Manhattan, or the Grand Concourse in the Bronx, urban decay was everywhere. The word *schwartzes,* seldom heard in polite company, was now commonly and openly expressed among Jews. Race and not class was blamed for the decay and crime. Somehow, the policies of the liberals and Democrats were at the root of this urban rot.

Black-Jewish tensions reached a crescendo in the Andrew Young affair. Despite denials from the Israelis and organized Jewish organizations that Jews had nothing to do with Andrew Young's fall from power and despite attempts to shift the blame onto President Carter, these denials did not wash in the Black community.

Black leadership was bitter and angry and laid responsibility directly on the Jews. In their rage Black leadership let "everything hang out" including the anti-Semitic charges about Jewish power, dual loyalties, "Zionist racist pressure," Jewish bankers and the like. Mayor Richard Hatcher of Gary expressed the hurt of the Black community when he said "the Jewish community and Israel don't realize how large a stake Andy had with us and how important he was and is to us." The Jewish community underestimated what Young meant to Blacks. He was, said *Ebony,* "the most powerful Black politician in American history."

Young's meeting with the PLO representatives at the United Nations were well known but why the Israelis leaked the story to a *Newsweek* correspondent in Israel remains a question to be answered someday by historians. But the Black response frightened Jewish leadership, and brought Black-Jewish relations to a new all-time low. Whatever misgivings official Jewish leadership had about Black nationalists and "street niggers," great care had been taken to cultivate the middle class, mainstream, educated Black leadership. Many Black leaders had made sponsored trips to Israel, returning favorably impressed. Mainstream Black leadership supported Israel (See the full page ad which appeared in the *New York Times,* November 23, 1975). Years of hard work in cultivating Black leadership were destroyed overnight. The Jewish community expressed incredulity at the Black response and backed off very quickly. The spokesmen for Jewish organizations went to great lengths to deny they had anything to do with Young's resignation from the United Nations and the Cabinet.

Andrew Young had correctly predicted a day after his resignation that the Israeli decision to make public his meeting with the PLO would create a Palestinian constituency in the United States where none hardly existed. By Fall, 1979, a nationwide poll indicated that adult Blacks were now more supportive of the Arab states than of Israel, and 54% believed that Palestinians should be granted a homeland on the West Bank.

If the Jewish community helped inflict a wound upon Blacks, the response of the Black community was equally destructive. Two large Black delegations travelled to the Middle East in the Fall to meet with the PLO. These groups were telling Jewish America: "O.K. We'll show you. You say Young cannot meet with a PLO representative in New York. We will meet the PLO face to face in Lebanon." The Reverend Joseph Lowery's SCLC delegation met with Yasir Arafat, with both SCLC and PLO delegations singing "We Shall Overcome." And Jews were aware that for the PLO, the *Overcome,* meant them. Not to be outdone, Jesse Jackson led his Operation PUSH delegation to Lebanon, Jordan, and Israel, and came away endorsing "the just demands of the dispossessed Palestinian people." Bayard Rustin understood quite well what the Lowery and Jackson trips would mean for Black-Jewish relations. "We risk," he wrote in the *New York Times* of "becoming accomplices of an organization committed to the bloody destruction of Israel!—indeed of the Jewish people." One of the major casualties was to be Jesse Jackson whose career went into immediate eclipse. He became a nonperson to the media, and for a person whose career depended so much on press coverage, his endorsement of the PLO, put him outside the mainstream.

If there was one bright spot in the otherwise sorry litany of Black-Jewish destruction—a mutual destruction which Bernard Malamud had written about in his gripping and largely ignored novel, *The Tenants,* it was the Carter administration. Despite the overwhelming rejection of Carter by the voters—and Jews gave 40% of their votes to Reagan and helped bankroll Anderson—I believe that historians will give Carter much higher marks than did the American people. For both Blacks and Jews, the Carter administration was a highwater mark. Blacks and Jews were appointed to important high level positions in record numbers. At one time there were four Jews sitting as cabinet members, and Jews were to be found in the inner circles of the Carter White House. Carter set a record in his appointment of women, Blacks, minorities, and liberals to the Federal bench. His record on federal hiring and enforcement of affirmative action programs was better than previous administrations and certainly much better than what was to follow. The Justice Department was viewed as a friend of civil rights organizations. His administration actively opposed legislative attempts to curtail busing, voting rights, and preferential quotas in hiring. Carter's administration bailed out New York City, in which Blacks and Jews have a tremendous stake, and in which Jewish organizations were slow in seeing as a Jewish issue. Carter provided increased funds for a wide range of social welfare organizations, and the Department of Labor made sure that millions in funds were funnelled through Vernon Jordan's Urban League and Jesse Jackson's Operation PUSH.

In foreign policy Carter was instrumental in negotiating the Camp David Agreement, the most important single event in the dreary history of Arab-Jewish relations. The Carter government, for the first time, made a positive and activist tilt towards Black African aspirations. Andrew Young became American pro-consul in Africa. Carter put human rights pressure on South Africa, began negotiations for a free Namibia, and saw the resolution of a bitter Zimbabwean war.

And despite the open uneasiness, crankiness, or even hostility towards Carter by Jewish leadership, the historical record shows that on the matter of getting Jews out of the Soviet Union, a very central concern for American Jewry, Carter's record has yet to be equalled. Jewish leadership says very little about this. In 1979, 51,300 Jews were allowed to leave Russia. Yet in 1982, under a Reagan government that courted Jewish voters, less than 3,000 Soviet Jews were allowed to emigrate. In fact, more Falashas—the Black Jews of Ethiopia—came to Israel in 1982 than did Jews from the Soviet Union.

For his efforts, Carter received little thanks from Black or Jewish leaders.[2] On the other hand, Carter's accomplishments in these areas—areas which I view as positive—were probably seen in negative terms by the American community as a whole, and was one of the factors which caused Carter to be viewed as "soft" by the American electorate. If this was the case, then the least that can be said was that Carter held back the tide of reaction for four years.

## IV

What then should the agenda be for Black-Jewish relations in the 1980s or in the words of Martin Luther King, "Where Do We Go From Here?"

If I could present an agenda to the Jewish community, it would include the following points:

1) *Real dialogue in America cannot take place between Blacks and Jews.* Real dialogue should take place between Black and White America. Jews should not put themselves into the position of being brokers for White America. When is the last time White Christian America sat across the table from Black Christian America?

White Christian America controls the governments at all levels, the banks, the military, the foundations, the largest corporations, the universities, the medical and law schools, the hospitals and so forth. Since Jews make up less than 3% of the population and Blacks make up about 12%, neither holds substantial power in this country. Both groups should be talking to the other America, the real source of power and problems.

Furthermore, by acting as surrogate, the myth of Jewish "power" is perpetuated. What Jews have in America is, and only at times, "influence." The so-called all powerful Israeli-Jewish American lobby fell before Ronald Reagan when the issue was put "Reagan or Begin" on the sale of the AWACS to the Saudis. The Jewish lobby was unable to stop the confirmation of Bechtel executives, Casper Weinberger or George Shultz, or of preventing them from holding up the sale of F-16's to Israel or of proposing to sell America's newest tanks, the M-1's, to Saudi Arabia. Jews, like other Americans, can influence policies on occasion but only when there is a general consensus on the issues. All the Jewish "power" behind President Roosevelt did not move our most popular and powerful President to save European Jewry from extermination. So much for Jewish "power"! I make this point because I have seen too many Black-Jewish meetings where the Black participants see themselves as coming face to face with America's power brokers. With White America refusing to talk to Black America, Blacks often vent their justified frustrations on the only White American group that has worked and spoken with them in the past.

Jewish groups should stop responding to Black criticism with the knee-jerk reaction of "Let's sit down to talk." This was the typical reaction of Jewish leadership in the aftermath of Andrew Young's resignation. In many respects Jews and Blacks do not have much to talk about and often these talks produce the opposite results from what was intended. In 1974 I participated in one such meeting in Nashville which left deep wounds. One of the Jewish conveners was still angry five months later when he wrote me about the "kind of anti-Semitic garbage that some professors and others there spewed forth." Actions speak louder than words and talks between Jews and Blacks should be selective, used to formulate specific strategies and concrete plans of actions.

*2) A real dialogue should take place, however, between Jewish liberals and activists and Jewish neo-conservatives.*

It has been said that behind every neo-conservative is a liberal who has been mugged the previous night. Behind every neo-conservative is a middle-aged New Yorker or ex-New Yorker rightfully frightened by street crime and urban rot. It should be the duty of Jewish liberals to redirect their outrage from the Black poor, who are the principal victims of the criminal elements within their communities and are as frightened and confused as the neo-conservatives and the rest of the citizenry. Neo-conservatives should be encouraged to use their considerable journalistic talents to rally the entire community against a bureaucracy that has been unwilling or unable to administer the cities of this nation. I have read many articles by neo-conservatives attacking affirmative action, busing, Black Studies, the inefficient welfare system, the public schools, and the decline of American standards and life styles. Yet I have read little in *Commentary, The Public Interest, Midstream,* and of recent, *The New Republic* about the administrators and bureaucrats who are responsible for making the cities liveable.

In the 1970s American cities were governed by their kind of people, tough talking politicians, and often, like the mayors of Detroit, Minneapolis, Los Angeles, and Philadelphia, men with police backgrounds. "Law and Order" was the theme of their rule. Where was *Commentary* these last years when Ed Koch, one of their heroes, told us that now that he has been re-elected mayor, he will do something about the deplorable condition of New York's subways? Where have the law and order mayors been or their neo-conservative supporters while the streets were filthy, the housing inspectors on the take, and police unable to stop drug trafficking. Since the neo-conservatives can no longer blame the "Lindsays" of the Sixties, they now direct their attention to the courts and the judges.

The Jewish community should dialogue with the Jewish neo-conservatives and ask what Jews in this country gain by appearing to be the point men against affirmative action, busing, and the like? Why are Jews continually out front on these issues? Whenever there is an attack upon affirmative action, we see the names of Nathan Glazer, Irving Kristol, Normal Podhoretz, Walter Berns, Edward Koch, and Morris Abram.

Why should Morris Abram, former president of Brandeis University and former president of the American Jewish Congress, show up in Washington to testify before Orin Hatch's hearings, seeking a constitutional amendment against affirmative action? What purpose is served?

The attacks on affirmative action, in the press, the courts, and by academics has seen a drastic curtailment in minority enrollment in graduate and professional schools. In a national survey of graduate schools in December, 1980, the *New York Times* found the following:

- At Stanford University, minority enrollment in MA and Ph.D. programs dropped more than 50%.
- At the University of Michigan, Black, Hispanic, and American Indian graduate enrollment declined from 594 in 1978 to 453 in 1980.
- At the University of California at Berkeley, minority enrollment dropped from 712 to 649 between 1978 and 1980.
- At Harvard's Graduate School of Arts and Sciences, the enrollment of new Black students dropped from 22 in 1978 to 21 in 1979 to 9 in 1980.
- At the University of California at Davis, site of the Bakke case, only two Blacks enrolled in Medical School in 1981, none in 1980 and one in 1979. In the seven years prior to the 1978 decision, when the school set aside places for minority students, four to eight Black students were admitted each year.

Affirmative action has not served to keep Jewish applicants out of professional schools. Quite the contrary. *Affirmative action programs have led to record enrollments of Jewish students.* That this increase has been by Jewish women is overlooked by Jewish organizations. Even Charles Silberman, in an otherwise hostile piece in *The New Republic* (December 29, 1979) admitted that the number of Jewish students at the Columbia University Law School had increased. He reported a slight reduction in the number of Jewish males but a *substantial increase* in the number of Jewish females. Is it any wonder that the National Council of Jewish Women, having a much clearer grasp of what was at stake than their male Jewish counterparts, supported the NAACP and other civil rights groups in the Defunis, Bakke, and Webber cases?

What purpose is served the Jewish community to frighten already reluctant and timid university and medical schools with law suits and constitutional amendments from enrolling Black and other minorities? It is in the long term interest of the Jewish community in America to see that as many Blacks and minorities as possible become members of the solid middle class. Black men and women and Jewish women have been beneficiaries of the affirmative action/quota policies of the 1970s.

- *In 1970* there were 261,151 lawyers in the U.S. 245,743 or 94.1% were white males; 12,012 or 4.6% were white women; 2,872 or 1.1% were Black men; 522 or 0.2% were Black women.
- *In 1980* there were 501,800 lawyers; 84.3% were white men; 65,234 or 13% were white women—an increase of 53,222—9,534 or 1.9% were Black men, an increase of 6,662; 4,014 or 9.8% were Black women, an increase of 3,492.
- In 1970 white men made up 88.7% of all doctors. In 1980 this percentage had dropped to 83.9%. For Black men the percentage increased from 2% to 2.7%; for Black women the figure rose from 0.4% to 0.7%. For white women the percentage increased from 9.9% to 12.7%.

American society already recognizes preferential treatment for those who have suffered or were otherwise disadvantaged such as veterans who receive extra points when applying for civil service jobs. Affirmative action/quotas is seen as a temporary solution to long term discrimination.

Jews have become entrapped in their own misreading of history. Whatever quotas were used against Jews in Czarist Russia or in America in the early years of this century, Jews have broken through to where at Harvard today they make up 20–25% of the student body and a sizeable portion of the faculty. No one has suggested that Jews be held to 2.94% of the undergraduate enrollment at American colleges, and to speak and act as if this is so, while minority enrollment continues to fall, is to act against Jewish self-interest.

Another item on the agenda of this dialogue between Jewish liberals and neo-conservatives is the questions as to what good is served the American Jewish Committee in continuing to sponsor *Commentary*. Does *Commentary* under Norman Podhoretz's direction really reflect the interests of the membership of the AJC or American Jewry? If Podhoretz wishes to make *Commentary* the centerpiece of neo-conservative thought, he should be consistent and try supplyside economics, taking his magazine without subsidies into the market place. I am not being fanciful about this. For example, it is interesting to note that John Johnson, publisher of *Ebony*, folded *The Black World* when that magazine, the original cornerstone of the Johnson publishing empire, began to trumpet cultural nationalism, separatism, and Third World ideologies in contrast to Johnson's own integrationist and mainstream views.

*3) Jewish intellectuals and communal leaders should refrain from holding up Black extremists as legitimate spokesmen for the Black community.* Just as the Jewish Defense League does not represent any sizeable segment, even minority of the Jewish community, so Black nationalists and separatists such as Roy Innis, Imamu Baraka, and others do not represent mainstream Black thought. I even question to what extent Joseph Lowery or even Jesse Jackson has a solid following within the Black community. In the recent Chicago mayoralty race, Jackson was a major embarrassment to the Washington campaign, and he was advised to remain silent.

Yet, in Jewish publications, vocal extremists within the Black community are cited most often. Positive and cooperative developments among Blacks and Jews are seldom featured. Recently, a Jewish communal leader told a group that he was unable to find more than two Black leaders in New York City to appear on a Black hosted program to answer Arab charges. He cited his inability to come up with pro-Israel panelists as an example of anti-Semitism among Blacks. I suggest it reflects more his inability to get away from his fashionable office and to widen his narrow sphere of Black connections.

*4) On the other hand, there is a serious question of who speaks for Jewish interests.* There have been a number of studies trying to determine who speaks for Blacks. It is time to find out who speaks for Jews, if anyone can or should. There is considerable truth, as Blacks have long complained, that the media creates the leadership. I would venture to guess that there is not one Jewish American in a hundred who can name the head of the American Jewish Committee, the American Jewish Congress, Hadassah, the B'nai B'rith, the Union of American Hebrew Congregations, the Jewish War Veterans, etc. As much as I have tried to follow Jewish affairs, I never knew or heard of Rabbi Joseph P.

Sternstein, president of the American Zionist Federation, although he was the man who demanded the resignation of Andrew Young.

Whenever any problem in Black-Jewish relations arises, the *New York Times* immediately calls Dr. Alexander Schindler, president of the Union of American Hebrew Congregations, or Howard Squadron, president of the American Jewish Congress. There are a number of Jewish Americans who are far more representative of the thinking of Jewish Americans or are better trained and more sensitive to interracial dynamics than Rabbi "What's-His-Name" from "Who Knows Where." Why not call on Senator Howard Metzenbaum or Irving Howe, or Leonard Fein or Oscar Handlin or Arthur Miller or Saul Bellow or Isaac Singer or Arthur Goldberg or Nat Hentoff? Or for that matter Mel Brooks or Woody Allen. Certainly with all the Jews who are currently eminent in the social sciences and have written extensively about interracial and inter-ethnic relations, the media could do better than they have done to identify a representative cross-section of Jewish opinion.

Following from this, we need to admit that there has been a serious decline in the quality of Jewish leadership throughout the Jewish American community. Where are today's Louis Brandeises, Louis Marshalls, Abba Hillel Silvers, Stephen Wises, etc. who once dominated Jewish thought and organizations? It appears that in most communities throughout America Rabbis have been replaced by the wealthiest real estate or shopping center developer, corporate lawyer, or businessman. The need to raise millions for Israel has put great emphasis on moneyed people as Jewish spokesmen, and this has created an intellectual vacuum at the top. Both Jewish and the Black communities suffer from a crisis in leadership. Both communities need to bring into top leadership a more intellectual and thoughtful group to make and carry out policies.

*5) Jews need a clearer understanding of their own self-interest.* How much does it benefit the Jewish community to continue to lead the fight against affirmative action and job quotas? Shouldn't Jewish organizations use their considerable talents to work with others for holistic reforms which will benefit all Americans and the poor in particular? For example, a national health insurance plan would greatly benefit the Black and Jewish populations, and at the same time help all Americans.

Jews and Blacks have been historical and natural allies since the formation of the NAACP in 1909. Not only have both groups been loyal supporters of the Democratic party dating back to the New Deal, but they both have an important stake in that party.

Despite the tensions of the Seventies, Jews and Blacks have worked successfully together in Congress and on the state and municipal levels. Following the 1982 elections thirty congressmen and eight senators are Jewish. There are twenty-one congressmen who are Black. Together they make an almost solid block which will continue to grow. This relationship should be maintained and expanded possibly formalized with an executive director, staff, lobbyists, and publications, modeled after the Congressional Black Caucus. A "Black Jewish Congressional Caucus" might serve as a vehicle for intergroup dialogue and programs.

It need to be stated, for it is seldom brought up, that on the issue of Israel, Black congressmen have been strong and almost unanimous in support of the Jewish state.

On the 1981 AWACS vote, for example, Black congressmen voted against the sale of these weapons to the Saudis with but one exception and that person did not vote. In addition, as Leonard Fein, editor of *Moment* magazine, has called to our attention, all five Hispanic congressmen voted against the AWACS sale as well. The Black and Hispanic congressional delegations represent a growing and important ally for Jewish concerns and should not be ignored.

Jews need to recognize that in the 1980s more and more American cities will be electing Black mayors. Already Los Angeles, New Orleans, Atlanta, Birmingham, Detroit, Newark, Gary, Washington D.C., and now Chicago have Black mayors. These new mayors and their administrations will be in a position to reward their friends and punish their enemies. This is traditional American political behavior. How these Black leaders respond to Jewish businessmen, civil servants, educators, housing and land developers, health and welfare workers, lawyers, and other Jewish citizens who have important stakes in the cities may well hinge on how they perceive Jews in relationship to matters they consider high on their agenda.

*6) Jews in America need to take a more active and forceful role in bringing about peace in the Middle East, even if this means speaking openly against the present right-wing government that now governs Israel.* The fate of Israel is too important to be left exclusively to Menachem Begin.

For Jewish Americans there is an added dimension to bringing about peace in the Middle East. Israel, in seeking to break out of its isolation, has been forced to make alliances with governments and movements which historically have been anathema to the liberal bent of the Jewish American community. Jewish organizations in America have found themselves defending Israeli-South African relations, Israeli-Argentinian relations, the Moral Majority, the Reverend Jerry Falwell, Richard Nixon, and other strange friends. Recently the Anti-Defamation League of the B'Nai B'rith sponsored a high-level trip to Israel for the Reverend Bailey E. Smith, president of the Southern Baptist Convention. Smith is the same man who proclaimed that "God Almighty does not hear the prayer of a Jew."

Such alliances between Israel and this rag-tag army of right-wingers has strained the relationship, built up over many years, between Jewish Americans and its traditional American allies. Not only has Jewish relationships with Black Americans been affected but also Jewish ties with labor, liberal, left, religious, and university communities. Jews in America need to ask the questions if whether or not *any* friend of Israel automatically becomes a friend of Jews in this country.

There has been a concerted effort to move the Jewish community to the right and into the Reagan camp. But this relationship has not yet born fruit. Reagan rode roughshod over Jewish supporters and the Jewish lobby with his $8.5 billion dollar sale of AWACS to the Saudis. He was not above accusing the Israelis of interfering in American foreign policy and implied that if it were not for "parts of the American Jewish community, the AWACS sale would go through." Even Normal Podhoretz, Reagan's chief neoconservative Jewish supporter, admitted that Jewish support for the president had "been set back. It's bad for everyone," said Podhoretz, "that this issue (AWACS) has been framed as Begin versus Reagan. The President's attack on Israel for interfering was disturbing and even alarming to people," he concluded. The *New York Times* quoted a Jewish Republican as saying that after the AWACS confrontation, Reagan would be "lucky to get 15 percent of the Jewish vote."

Given the actions of the administration since the AWACS sale, that prediction might be high. Albert A. Spiegel, a longtime supporter of Reagan and his adviser on Jewish concerns, resigned his post in April after he read a story in the *Wall Street Journal* reporting that Reagan told King Hussein that he knows he is going to lose the Jewish vote in 1984 but he feels he could win reelection without those votes.

The Israeli-Reagan connection has not paid off for Jewish Americans. One also wonders where the new relationship between the Christian right wing Evangelicals and the Jews will lead. The Evangelicals are openly pro-Israel and have been welcomed in Israel by Prime Minister Begin, and have gained support from Rabbi March Tanenbaum of the American Jewish Committee. The Evangelical support of Israel along with the perception that the National Council of Churches has been sympathetic to the PLO has brought Jews into an uneasy alliance with the most fundamental, conservative, forces of the Christian right. Do Jews now support the Moral Majority in return for their support of Israel? Time will tell.

I contend that Jewish commitment to liberal causes, the traditional allies of Jews, has been severely strained by the necessity of supporting Israeli-right wing alliances. Are Jewish interests in America served by alliances, as one commentator characterized them, between "the American right and the most chauvinistic elements in Israel?" Further Jewish American support for right wing causes threatens any effective alliance in America for the extension of civil rights and the protection of civil liberties. Do Jews now support prayers in the schools and tuition tax credit for private schools as the price of support for Israel by the right?

*7) One specific way in which Jewish institutions can directly assist the Black community is through the use of Jewish community federations.* The federations may be the most important and original contribution of Jews to American social welfare. Jewish federations could teach Black organizations a great deal about effectively organizing and tapping the resources of the community. A program of internships with the newly formed United Black Fund may produce a Black version of the United Jewish Appeal. The Jewish communal model for organizing the community and for fund raising is something Jews could offer the Black community without making it appear to be a handout or patronizing.

*8) Finally, as Jews we need to remember who we are, what our traditions have been, and how fortunate we have been to have lived in America.*

And in so doing, we must be very selective in answering Blacks by invoking the memory of the Holocaust. Rabbi Ben-Zion Gold, Hillel chaplain at Harvard and a survivor of the concentration camps, reminds us that we must not use the Holocaust experience to immunize ourselves from the Black experience in this country.

When the talk turns to suffering, Jews often tend to counter the suffering of blacks with the Holocaust. Why should American Jews, the vast majority of whom were spared the agonies of the Holocaust, vie with those who are still suffering over who suffered more? Americans are highly advanced economically and educationally. Why should they wrap themselves in the mantle of suffering of European Jews vis-a-vis a people that have suffered right here in the U.S. and continue to be at the bottom of the economic and educational ladder? Nothing good can come from such strange charades.

We should also keep in mind that the enemies of Blacks never forget who we are and that despite any differences Jews and Blacks may have among themselves, in the minds of the racists and anti-Semites, we are one. Being Jewish made no difference to the lynch mob that murdered the three civil rights workers in Mississippi.

The late Harry Golden summed it up in his own unique way. When asked how he managed to survive in the South despite his strong civil rights convictions, he replied: "I got away with my ideas because no Southerner takes me—a Jew, a Yankee, a radical— seriously. They mostly think of a Jew as a substitute Negro, anyway."

**V**

If I could suggest an agenda to the Black community it would include the following points:

*1) It is imperative that Blacks establish a realistic agenda for the 1980s.* If Blacks make support of the PLO, for example, high on their list of priorities, they may as well "kiss off" the Jews as domestic allies. Whatever differences Jews have with the Israeli governments, they stand united on the question of Israel's survival. Therefore, support for the PLO will, in the words of Bayard Rustin, "Mortgage Black domestic interest and squander the moral capital of Black America." On the other hand, Blacks may decide to make support for the PLO and the Palestinians high on their agenda and hope for money and support from radical Arab groups and from Muslims.

At the NAACP meeting in Boston in June, 1982, Benjamin Hooks, NAACP Executive Director, exhorted his audience to stand up for the powerless, and he went on to list causes and peoples which the organization should support. At one point he called upon the audience to "stand up for the human rights of the Palestinians and Lebanese people." But Jews, like Blacks, know all about Code Words, and they knew precisely what he meant, and fired off telegrams and letters to the convention. Mr. Hooks said nothing of standing up for the right of Israel to be free of PLO terrorists. Listening to his speech would not have given encouragement for any Jewish group to forge an alliance with the NAACP. What did Mr. Hooks hope to accomplish? To date I have not learned of Middle Eastern oil money coming into NAACP headquarters or of foodstuffs from the Middle East to feed the thousands of Black Americans currently standing in food lines.

*2) The above should not be interpreted to mean that Blacks have no role in bringing about peace in the Middle East.* Let us remember that it was a Black American, Ralph Bunche, who brought about the first successful cease fire in the Middle East, and for which he was awarded the Nobel Prize for Peace in 1950. Let us not forget, either, that by the standards Americans use to judge who is Black—that is, color—it was a Black man, Anwar el-Sadat, who initiated the breakthrough that led to the Camp David Accord and who paid for his bravery with his life.

Although the missions of Joseph Lowery and Jesse Jackson originated solely as a reaction to Andrew Young's resignation, the idea of introducing Martin Luther King's philosophy of non-violence into the Middle East is not without merit. I would have liked to think that if Martin Luther King had lived, he would have tried to bring his presence to bear on the question of peace between Arab and Israeli, and between Christian and Muslim.

Jewish Americans should also explore with Black Americans the possibility of Blacks using their growing influence with the nations of Africa in modifying or changing their positions regarding Israel. African nations may use their own leverage with the nations of the Middle East to bring about a peace settlement. In the mid-Seventies, Leopold Senghor of Senegal led a mission of African leaders to the Middle East to try to bring about a settlement. This idea should be revived. Possibly a joint Afro-American/African mission to the Middle East might serve a useful purpose.

Black Americans might ask Jewish Americans to reciprocate by having a Jewish delegation persuade the Israelis to modify or change its relationship with South Africa.

*3) Just as some Jews have allowed their frustrations about the Middle East and America's urban rot to find a target in affirmative action, quotas, busing, etc., so Blacks have found in Israel and the Jewish neo-conservative targets for their disappointments.* What both Blacks and Jews need to remember is that they are not the problem, and they need to keep a clear vision of what must be done. Both need each other to present a strong, united front, possibly even a common agenda, before a growing conservative white America. Name calling is not a substitute for cooperation.

In developing an agenda Blacks must reach out and find groups they can work with. Jews have been one of the groups Blacks have traditionally been able to count on. This means developing a philosophy of cooperation, of integration, of alliances, of using political strength to gain concessions with other groups.

In seeking allies, the record will show that despite a Jewish voter swing to the right in 1980, Jews were the only white ethnic group in California to vote against overturning the state's fair housing laws. In New York City, Jews were the only white ethnic group to vote in favor of the civilian review board. In Philadelphia, Jews were the only white ethnic group to vote solidly (69%) against the re-election of Mayor Rizzo in 1979. And on the issue of affirmative action, while some Jewish groups filed briefs in favor of Defunis, Bakke, and Webber, other Jewish groups and groups in which Jews are heavily represented filed briefs on the other side.

Furthermore, in seeking allies, Blacks can identify unions, women's groups, the Democratic party, universities, the teaching and social welfare professions, and possibly the media. In all these groups Jews are heavily represented. This is particularly true in the communications industry—publishing, radio, television, movies, theatre, recording, advertising, public relations—industries where Jews can be found in higher numbers and in more key positions than in any other group. If Jews have "power" in any area of American business, it is in the communications fields. If Blacks are to get their message across to white America, the support of Jews will be crucial. This was dramatically illustrated in the *Roots* television series. Jews played the principal roles in producing, financing, writing, and directing one of the most widely viewed series ever seen on American television.

On the other hand, it would be safe to say that Jews will be turned off as allies by Black separatist, nationalistic, anti-Semitic, anti-Israeli rhetoric. As Blacks must decide on their agenda, so must Jews, and it is not for Jews to call for their own destruction.

*4) Just as the question arises as to who speaks for Jews, so the question must be raised for Blacks.* Throughout the Seventies, Black Americans were making names for themselves in industry, politics, education, government, law, philanthropy, journalism and the arts. Yet, the media always turned to the same old faces to speak for Black thought and opinion. Why not Black spokesmen such as Franklin Thomas, head of the Ford Foundation; Clifford Wharton, Chancellor of the State University of New York and newly elected Chairman of the Board of the Rockefeller Foundation; Clifford Alexander, formerly Secretary of the Army; John Hope Franklin, recognized as the premier authority on the Black Historical experience; Earl Graves, publisher of *Black Enterprise* magazine; Andrew Brimmer, formerly on the Board of the Federal Reserve, or William T. Coleman, Jr., notable constitutional lawyer?

Also, the newly elected Black mayors need to be heard from. Power in the Seventies has shifted from civil rights leadership to the political leaders. The civil rights movement may have been institutionalized by the political process. The transition of Andrew Young from civil rights activist to Member of Congress to Cabinet Member/Ambassador in the United Nations/American proconsul in Africa to mayor of Atlanta personifies the recent and coming trend. Marion Berry, mayor of Washington is another civil rights leader who transferred his activities to City Hall.

*5) Another need for Black leadership is to restore the Black intellectual to a place of legitimacy as centerpiece of the Black community.*

In my ten years in Atlanta, we were conscious of the role the colleges of the Atlanta University Center had in shaping the men, the issues, the events of the period. From the days of W. E. B. Du Bois, John Hope, and Benjamin Brawley through the days of Benjamin Mays, Whitney Young, Samuel Williams, C. Eric Lincoln, Samuel Dubois Cook, and others, the Black intellectuals of Atlanta were role models for their students and members in the community. This was true in other Black communities. Blacks in America have a great history of teachers, writers, artists, poets, religious leaders, and intellectuals who once were more nearly the focus of Black thought and community than they are today.

The shrill voice of the "militants" in the late Sixties drowned out these voices. Compare the older Black leadership with the likes of Eldridge Cleaver, Huey Newton, Bobby Seale, Angela Davis, Stokely Carmichael, James Forman, Roy Innis, Malcolm X, Muhammed Ali, H. Rap Brown, Ron Karenga and others now conveniently forgotten. One New York militant claimed that the true representatives of the Black community were the "welfare mothers, the students, and a lot of the young bloods." Much of their rhetoric was anti-Semitic and anti-White and their threats served as a divisive factor in the Black-Jewish-White Liberal coalition.

Dr. Kenneth Clark aptly observed that students at the colleges chose as their heroes

. . . only those blacks that shared their black racist anxieties and fears. Only those black scholars who agreed with the students' demands for separate black studies programs, separate black social facilities and cultural centers were applauded. Black scholars who dared to question the logic, the strategy and morality of black separatism were at best ignored and at times sharply challenged, cursed, and sometimes threatened.

What has happened to the Black intellectual?

An indication of the low status of Black intellectuals is provided by *Ebony*'s survey listing the 100 most influential Blacks. Of the one hundred listed, I could identify six intellectuals including Lerone Bennett, one of *Ebony*'s editors, and Alex Haley. Missing from the list was Kenneth Clark, John Hope Franklin, Martin Kilson, Nathan Huggins, Benjamin Quarles, Vincent Harding, C. Eric Lincoln, Harold Cruse, Charles Hamilton, John Blassingame, Mary Berry, Nikki Giovanni, Thomas Sowell, James Baldwin, Ralph Ellison, Toni Morrison, Alice Walker, Elliott Skinner, Alvin Poussaint, Samuel DuBois Cook, Alvin Ailey, Gwendolyn Brooks, Robert Browne—to name a very short list.

Perhaps this is one of the reasons dialogues between Blacks and Jews have not turned out well. Until Black intellectuals are recognized and returned to the center of Black life, the level of discourse between Blacks and Jews, as well as Blacks and other allies, will continue to be unsatisfactory.

*6) Another group that has been ignored within the Black community is the middle and working classes.*

Employed in teaching, the health and social services, municipal government, law enforcement, the courts, and enrolled as union members throughout organized labor, this productive and stable element has been in constant contact with Jewish co-workers. Their relationships with Jews have been productive for the most part. The Black working classes live in modest neighborhoods, keep up their property, pay taxes, join unions, and are the backbone of Black religious, fraternal, and civil rights organizations.

However, their voices are seldom heard when it comes to the issues of contemporary urban life which constantly faces Jews, Blacks, and Ethnics of the major cities.

Jewish communal leaders rarely see them or know they exist. What they hear are the "young bloods" of the streets or the newly upwardly mobile Black elite—lawyers, publicists, politicians, school administrators, managers—labelled the "Young Turks." Both the "Bloods" and the "Turks" often employ an anti-White and anti-Semitic rhetoric. Jews are seen as a group standing in their way of advancement and upward mobility. They are not interested in the past, either as it applies to the older Black leadership or to Jewish allies. Their voices are the loudest.

My reading of the situation is that the productive Black working classes are not interested in power struggles with the Jewish community or with Jews. They are concerned, however, with crime, drugs, schools, declining city services, adequate and moderate priced housing, health care, and the like. They have a commonality of interests with whites in a similar situation. For years Bayard Rustin of the A. Philip Randolph Institute was one of the few Black leaders who gave expression to the concerns of the Black middle and working classes. Rustin urged coalitions with trade unionists, political progressives, and Jews.

Recently the Urban League under the direction of its newly-elected president, John E.

Jacob, is giving priority to four of these concerns: pregnancy among Black teenagers, the plight of female-headed households, crime in Black neighborhoods, and voting registration and education.

The newly emerging Black conservatives, bankrolled to respectability by conservative foundations and the Reagan government, has argued that the concerns of the Black middle and working classes have been soft-pedaled by their traditional liberal spokesmen. They understood that the loyalties of this group are up for grabs. This was clearly indicated by the articulate Thomas Sowell on his recent appearance on *Meet the Press*. Sowell is clearly the intellectual leader of the Black conservatives. He used the television program to attack the mainstream Black organizations such as the NAACP and the Urban League for being "soft on crime." "The traditional Black organizations," he claimed, "are taking a much more liberal stand . . . as regards turning criminals loose and fighting against the death penalty—than I find in the Black community, again, either by my observations or by the polls that I've seen."

If mainstream Black organizations do not address themselves effectively to these concerns, which are real for Blacks, Whites, Hispanics, the poor and elderly and the middle and working classes, then other groups will fill the vacuum. Already the Reagan Republicans are making appeals to these groups. The Republicans and conservative forces may capture these issues and turn these groups away from their traditional liberal, Jewish, civil rights, labor and Black allies. There are indications this has happened with Cubans, the Orthodox Jewish community in New York, and among the Irish-Polish-Ethnic populations of the lower middle class suburbs of midwestern and northeastern cities. Large segments of the Jewish Orthodox religious community, particularly in New York City, have turned their anger against Blacks, and their vote has been exploited by Mayor Koch and other politicians who promise law and order first and reform, if any, later.

Black leadership has been slow in dealing with the resentments and feelings of their constituents. Police brutality may be less a concern than the brutality of criminals, and support of the death penalty is heard more and more in the Black community.

*7) In looking for role models, Blacks need to disregard Jews and look more to the Irish.* As one Jewish leader expressed it recently, "I wish the Blacks would get off our backs. Instead of trying to use us as an example they should follow the Irish."

It was the Irish who first used their votes to take political control of American cities in the late 19th century. We must understand the dimensions of the Irish accomplishment. All cities in the great industrial belt from Boston-New York through Detroit and Chicago became Catholic between 1890–1920. The Irish took over the City Halls and with political control they immediately built an economic base. Irish filled the city payrolls, contractors built the streets and harbors, and jobs and opportunities were provided for people who only a few years before faced signs of "No Irish Need Apply." For the Irish, civil service was their salvation. This is one of the reasons the Irish have been less dependent on affirmative action program. From control of city politics, the Irish built a strong middle class. Their power was built with loyalty to the Democratic party, bloc voting, memories of oppression and humiliation, and Gaelic pride. St. Patrick's Day was not simply another ethnic holiday. It was an open recognition of Irish power—Catholic, political and economic.

As Blacks are elected mayors of more cities, they will dominate city administrations and payrolls as the Irish did before them. And now the payrolls and numbers on the payrolls are many times larger. Black businessmen and contractors will get a larger share of the contracts. In Atlanta, Maynard Jackson used MARTA (Metropolitan Atlanta Regional Transportation Authority) and the construction of the city's great new airport to insure that Blacks received a piece of the action. Is it any wonder that in the late Sixties and Seventies Atlanta became the mecca for Black professionals from around the nation, or that Herman Russell's Atlanta contracting firm became the second largest Black business in America? The Black middle class will continue to flourish under Andrew Young.

In Cleveland, George Forbes, recognized to be one of the most powerful men in the city as President of the Cleveland City Council, has negotiated with Standard Oil of Ohio (SOHIO) for Black contractors to obtain twenty percent of the $200,000,000 contract to build SOHIO's new corporate headquarters. Forbes, in turn, used his considerable power, to insure that SOHIO obtained the prime downtown property it wanted, even if it meant that the city had to condemn a number of perfectly fine and fully rented buildings.

8) *The Eighties are going to find Black organizations hard pressed for cash.* Prior to the Seventies civil rights organizations received little federal funding. In the Seventies, however, Black organizations began to receive millions from the federal government, mostly for job training programs. It was these federal funds that helped pay for the organizations' overhead. Under Reagan there have been drastic cuts. The Urban League had its federal funds cut from 100 million to 54 million.

The national headquarters of the Urban League received only 12 million in 1982, down from 29 million. The NAACP membership has declined sharply in recent years. Federal funds for operation PUSH have been curtailed.

Where will the funds come from? In the Sixties, Kivie Kaplan working with the NAACP and Stanley Levison with the Southern Christian Leadership Conference were able to tap both Jewish and non-Jewish sources to these organizations. Funds from Jewish contributors were largely responsible for the growth of SNCC and CORE. Albert Shanker's United Federation of Teachers supplied most of the funds for Bayard Rustin's A. Philip Randolph Institute.

It remains to be seen in the Eighties if Jewish organizations and individuals can be tapped once more. The money is still there. Can a strategy among Black leadership be devised to renew Jewish interest in the civil rights movement?

9) *Blacks need Jewish support to revitalize the public schools across America.* This is particularly true in New York City. The alienation of the Jewish middle and working classes in New York City due to the disastrous Teachers' Strike of 1968 has not yet been resolved. In fact, if any single event has led to the Jewish flight out of the city it was that strike.

Of all urban Americans, Jews have been the principal users, beneficiaries, and believers in the public schools and public college systems. Black leadership needs to understand the deep alienation felt by Jews who believed that the system was being turned over to the militants, separatists, and nationalists. The move of Jews to the suburbs was accelerated by the seeming chaos in the schools. Even the Black middle classes began fleeing urban schools and they were only one step behind Jews.

Without Jews as allies to revitalize the public schools, who do urban Blacks have to work with? The Ford Foundation? The parochial and private school systems? Corporate America?

*10) Black leadership needs to take a hard look at just what is happening to Black Americans, and begin to work with those Jews who are still their allies to rekindle a viable coalition.* Blacks are more isolated than they have been since the early 1950s. "More than a decade of civil rights law, practice and policy at the national level is being reversed," said Representative John Conyers of Michigan. Reagan has thrown three civil rights activists off the U.S. Civil Rights Commission and replaced them with three conservative Democrats who have already voiced their opposition to affirmative action, job quotas, and busing. One of these is Morris Abram, former head of the American Jewish Congress. And the Black middle class, so dependent on the public sector for jobs, is being reduced by Reagan's cutbacks in social spending. Even the *Wall Street Journal* has recognized this (Editorial, May 28, 1983). The increasingly dire situation among Blacks was expressed by the City Manager of Miami, Howard Gary, the highest paid municipal official in the United States ($98,500 a year), and a Black. Gary told a group of health officials:

> The only difference between Mr. Reagan and the fellows that wear white sheets at night in Mississippi is that Mr. Reagan doesn't wear a white sheet and he doesn't terrorize black folks at night. Instead he wears a suit and a smile and legally terrorizes black folks day and night, in the name of the president of the United States. (quoted by Richard Reeves, *The Plain Dealer* (Cleveland), May 26, 1983).

Black leadership cannot continue to stick its head in the sand and make believe that all is fine with the civil rights organizations which did so much to lead the nation in the Sixties. SNCC is no more. CORE is a fringe nationalist/separatist organization. SCLC is only a shadow of its days under Martin Luther King. The Urban League is being restructured downward to fit the realities of the Reagan era. The NAACP is in disarray, both in its internal organization, and after its senseless fight with the NAACP Legal Defense and Education Fund. The NAACP has still not shaken the nationalist and separatist tendencies within its own organizational and chapters' ranks which is a holdover from the late Sixties and early Seventies, and is still not comfortable dealing with its old White friends and allies. Benjamin Hooks' leadership of the NAACP has not helped. Membership is way down.

But on the other hand, Jews should not write off Blacks as potentially powerful allies. Blacks contributed one of every five votes gathered by the Democrats in 1980, and there has been a dramatic resurgence of Black voting power. Jesse Jackson has resurfaced from near media oblivion after his flirtation with the PLO, and is leading a massive voter registration drive geared to the 1984 presidential election. Jackson may even enter the Democratic primaries in an attempt to bring out the Black vote.

The Black vote is something that Jewish interests should watch with great care. The Joint Center for Political Studies, a respected Black think tank, has noted that Blacks "are in a position to serve as a crucial swing vote" in the Northeastern industrial belt and in the South.

A Democratic victory in 1984 with strong Black support and with lukewarm Jewish response would serve to undermine the leverage of Jewish and Israeli interests on issues that are of primary concern to them. Jews would find themselves out in the cold along with their newly found friends of the right, the evangelicals, and neo-conservatives.

The old Black-Jewish alliance may not be able to be resurrected. The suburban and middle class status of Jews may find them moving into the camp of their Republican neighbors. The Jewish vote will no longer be automatically Democratic. Already four of the eight Senators who are Jewish identify with the Republican party.

Jews should be prepared for the Black vote, in turn, to be more independent in supporting ever Israeli request for more military and economic assistance, or to ask Jewish Americans and Israelis to reassess their position vis-a-vis South Africa.

## VI

The problems confronting Blacks and Jews in a pluralist society cannot be neatly solved, but a dialogue is needed, and I hope that we can begin. A Black-Jewish alliance is not only good for Blacks and Jews. It will be good for America.

Irving Howe, editor of *Dissent* and a middle-aged New Yorker who did not despair, exhorted a Jewish audience in 1973 that "this is not the time for parochial retreat, it is the time for compassion and commitment once again." I hope my call for compassion and commitment finds a better fate than his. Yet, we must try. Martin Luther King reminded us "that all life is interrelated" and that "all humanity is involved in a single process, and to the degree that I harm my brother, to that extent I am harming myself."

NOTES

1. Robert Weisbord and Arthur Stein, *Bittersweet Encounter: The Afro-American and the American Jew* (Westport, Conn., 1970).

2. See Dr. Kenneth Clark, *Cleveland Plain Dealer,* February 19, 1983, p. 9A.

## Great Expectations
Defining the Divide between Blacks and Jews

I have been trying to make sense of the highly-publicized controversy over the hostile statements about Jews made in the last few months by members of the Nation of Islam and a few black scholars. I find some parallels between the reaction of some Jews to the inflammatory statements made about them and my response to an incident that happened to me.

It was a few years ago, during the first year of my protest leave of absence against the lack of diversity on the Harvard Law School faculty. I had decided to remain at the school and made plans to teach one of my courses without pay to students willing to take it without credit. My action was hailed by students and much of the liberal community. Then, one late summer afternoon, I received a reality check.

A somewhat seedily dressed but quite articulate black man came to my office. He said his name was Nat T, and he was seeking the real-life model for Geneva Crenshaw, the fictitious heroine of many of my allegorical stories about race. He told me that he had learned of her in reading my book, *And We Are Not Saved*. Later, I heard that he had visited several other black Harvard faculty members in his search for Geneva. I tried to assure him that the Geneva Crenshaw character was purely fictional. He would have none of it. "She thinks like I do," he told me seriously. "I will find her and together we will lead a long-overdue racial revolution."

I am always pleased when someone likes my books, but Nat T's seriousness made me nervous. He did not seem mentally disturbed, just scarily purposeful. He told me that he had been a law student several years ago—he didn't say where—and that he had been flunked out because the faculty didn't like what he called his "black nationalist" views.

"Well, I'm sorry" I said with a touch of unintended sarcasm, "but if you talked about a revolution instead of the issues of contracts and property, your teachers probably weren't amused."

Nat T was not amused. "I was a good student," he retorted levelly. "I worked hard. They decided I was too militant. I only wanted to understand how the law was able to preach justice and still keep my people down. I wanted maybe to teach others some day. They told me I would never make a good law teacher with my attitude. It's the story of my life. I have the brains, I work hard, but I lose jobs because I do not have the right

During the 1993–94 school year, Derrick Bell was Scholar-in-Residence at the New York University Law School.
Lecture presented in Spring 1994 as part of the Robert C. Weaver Series in Higher Education, Baruch College, the City University of New York. Reprinted with permission of Derrick Bell.

'attitude,' meaning I do not walk a racial tight-rope trying to be myself and still not threaten white folks."

"Law schools grade exams anonymously to prevent bias of that character," I suggested. He just looked at me as though I was the most pathetically naive person he had ever met. I decided not to push the point.

"After I flunked out and they refused to give me another chance," he said, "my life kind of fell apart. I had always wanted to be a lawyer, a sort of legal Malcolm X. He was my hero. When I couldn't find a decent job with my under-graduate degree, my wife took our son and headed back to the west coast to stay with her folks. She hoped to find work there. On the way, she and my son were killed in an auto crash."

"That's awful," I asked cautiously, "and you connect her tragic accident with your treatment by the law school?"

"It surely was one cause, but it is the overall hostility of the society that brings us down and keeps us down. Professor, it is time we give back in kind the harm we are done because we are black."

"An eye for an eye," I responded, "is neither moral nor, for the most part, has it been how black people have responded to racist oppression."

"And look where we are as a result, or," and he looked hard at me, "most of us. Black people need to adopt a law of racial retaliation."

"Racial what?" I asked incredulously.

"Racial retaliation," he repeated. "In a society that has practiced racism actively since its inception, it's no surprise that except for some feeble, hard to enforce, anti-discrimination laws, white can discriminate against blacks for either fun or profit, and because we do not retaliate, nothing happens to them. Look at how they administer the criminal justice system, the so-called 'War on Drugs,' and particularly the death penalty."

"Well," I conceded, "I can hardly disagree with your assessment, but . . ."

"Professor, whites should know or be held to know that their acts of discrimination will have broad ramifications. They need to exercise due care in the light of this knowledge, and they should be held to full account for actions that are likely to set in motion devastating racial reactions."

"Do you really think you could get this legal system to adopt your 'Law of Racial Retaliation' I asked him?"

"The law is what the society wants it to be," Nat T responded angrily. Do you really think the law, including the U.S. Constitution, condoned slavery for all those years, because it was right and moral? Slavery was enormously profitable for some, and quite threatening to others. It was ended when its divisiveness threatened to destroy the country. When white society realizes that blacks have turned their frustration and rage from killing one another and re-directed their rage at the real causes of their desperation, the law will change."

"With all your anger," I ventured, "you have a lot more faith that this society will respond rationally to your plans than I do." Nat T ignored me and began describing in more detail than I really cared to hear how he was going to organize the black community and build an effective retaliatory force. He obviously had given the matter of revolution a great deal of thought—a fact that made his schemes seem even more insane to me.

He sensed what I was thinking. "You think I am crazy, but we have all been crazy to rely all these years on whites ever treating us decently unless they see something in it for them. Well, rather than moan about it, I am going to show them that not treating us well is going to be very, very costly."

At that point, I had heard enough. I told Nat T that I really had to get back to work. He raised several more questions about Geneva Crenshaw: In which department was she working? When had I last seen her? When did I expect to see her again? Again, I told him that she did not exist.

He shook his head. "Don't you recognize that in denying Geneva Crenshaw's existence, you are denying your existence. There is no hope for you, man. No hope."

Nat T headed for the door, then turned and told me that I would see him again, that he was coming back. "Oh?" I remarked dubiously.

"Yes," he responded with that same seriousness. "Once Geneva Crenshaw and I link up and get our revolution started, one of my first missions will be to return and blow your head off."

I was unnerved, but I tried to take it lightly and responded by questioning his priorities. "You know," I told him, "in order to reach my office, you will have to pass the offices of several of my white colleagues."

"I know that," he replied, "but the revolution will have to deal first with all you black tokens in high places. As black agents of the enemy, you are as dangerous and more damaging than the real enemy."

"So," I said, feeling my anger rise, "your racial retaliation theory will begin at home."

"It will begin with the enemy," he responded. Then, as suddenly and resolutely as he'd come, he left.

My encounter with Nat T was traumatic. And, given their vigorous response, the attacks by CUNY Professor Leonard Jeffries, the Rev. Louis Farrakhan and his former spokesperson, Khalid Muhammed, frighten some Jews as much as Nat T's threat frightened me. And, I suggest, for three quite similar reasons. First, statements filled with so much venom are distressing in themselves. Second, the individual statements remind us of group hostility in the society aimed at us. Third, by lashing out and seeking to trounce a rather vulnerable enemy, we nourish our denial of the major enemy we dare not challenge. I want to examine these responses seriatim.

First, the hostile statements are distressing in themselves. The automatic response to a verbal attack is defense and then counter-attack. In my case, after Nat T left, I called the campus police, and had them involve the Cambridge and Boston police departments. They found him at a homeless shelter and warned him to stay away from the University. I was not relieved. At that point, I felt some guilt for "turning in a brother," but insufficient sympathy for the cruel hand that fate had dealt him to simply ignore his threat on my life. To tell the truth, I rather hoped the police would arrest Nat T and put him away. Here, my good sense, or rather lack of influence, kicked in. What charges could I bring? A threat to kill me at some time in the future? Likely, Nat T's threat was an assault, but in the context of crime in today's world, who would take it seriously?

In the face of verbal abuse by Minister Louis Farrakhan, and his now deposed spokesperson, Khalid Muhammed, some Jews react in a fashion quite similar to mine against Nat T. "After all we have been through," they seem to say, "why should we have to be subjected to gratuitous insults by demagogues seeking to use hate tactics to gain power at our expense. We know the tactic and have been victimized by it over the centuries. But no more. The place to draw the 'never again' line is right here."

Of course, the Jewish response to what they deemed anti-Semitic attacks makes my call for police action seem mild in comparison, but no less futile. The Nation of Islam has been castigated in a full page ad and dozens of opinion columns. The U.S. Senate has voted a resolution condemning Muhammed's speech at Keen College. But like Br'er Rabbit after being tossed in the briar patch by Br'er Fox, the Nation of Islam spokespersons are glorying in levels of public attention and acclaim from their followers that they could not have purchased with love or money.

Some Jewish groups supported a major, though unsuccessful, effort to remove Professor Leonard Jeffries from his teaching post at CUNY. Citing first amendment and due process violations in the process, Professor Jeffries sued and obtained a judgement of $400,000, which the University is appealing.[1] An appellate court has just agreed with the trial court's finding for Jeffries, but has remanded the punitive damages for further consideration. According to Wellesley College Professor Tony Martin, college administrators and Jewish groups have tried to have him removed as a result of his use of a book deemed disparaging of Jews.[2] He has written a book, *The Jewish Onslaught: Dispatches from the Wellesley Battlefront* detailing these efforts.[3] As with my calling in the police on Nat T, these efforts to use position and influence to punish our attackers tend to encourage rather than discourage the abuse from which we seek relief.

The second reason for our actions likely prevented us from hearing, much less heeding, advice about restraint. The threatening statements remind us of a broad range of hostility in the society aimed at us. Thus, my fear of Nat T was less what he said than what he symbolized. He reminded me that he is neither alone nor entirely inaccurate in viewing successful blacks as the enemy—no matter how hard we may work for the progress of all blacks. Our success has served to separate us from the great mass of our people.

We live and work apart, our children are not in the same schools. We attend different places for shopping, recreation, and even worship. Middle-class life is not without its problems, but those problems pale beside the daily dangers and wrenching frustrations of the black poor and working class. The presence of achieving blacks provides a convenient excuse for society's failure to provide these victims of racism with the aid we offer so readily to those harmed by natural disasters. Regrettably, there are a few blacks—thankfully few—who are quite willing to grab tainted fame and fortune by giving a corrupted "racial legitimacy" to such views. Given this climate, it is a wonder that there are not more blacks who, like Nat T, believe we "black tokens" are their enemy. As economic conditions worsen for poorer blacks, the numbers of those who share Nat T's opinion will increase.

I speak of the isolation of successful blacks—and the sense of unease based on that isolation—based on experience. My reading and discussion with Jews indicates that many share my sense of isolation. As Paul Berman puts it: "The styles of Jewish New World success follow patterns that were established in the Old World ghettos, and the successes themselves are fated now and then to call up, out of the creepier depths of Christian civilization, the old paranoid accusations about conspiracies and evil."[4] Acknowledging the miracle that has taken place merely by the act of Jews fleeing from the Old World to the New, Berman says: "Even the fat-and-happiest of American Jews has to shudder at the spectacle, which is always taking place, of some eminent person, not only spokesmen of the Nation of Islam, standing up to give the ancient libels a fresh new airing."[5] For many Jews, Louis Farrakhan and the Nation of Islam evoke these fears. Unlike blacks, most Jews are successful in all the ways this society measures success. And, yet there is justifiable concern that their very success has heightened rather than reduced the hostility vented against them—simply because they are Jews.

Thus, openly expressed, racial-religious epithets revive the never far from the surface fear that, as writer-activist Letty Cottin Pogrebin puts it, "the dominant majority may suddenly turn against the Jews (as some Americans did during the energy crisis and the Gulf War), fear of possible peril to the state of Israel (every Jew's haven of last resort), and fear of the slippery slope that propelled another 'civilized society' from spewing hate to building gas chambers."[6] Pogrebin acknowledges that one cannot compare the current suffering of blacks with the fear of potential suffering, but she explains "for Jews one generation removed from the Holocaust, the fear is real and the vulnerability deeply felt."[7]

The third explanation for our response is a form of aggressive denial. We hope that by soundly squashing the relatively powerless individual whose words upset us, we are symbolically defusing the major powers in the society whom we fear to upset and refuse to challenge. These are the forces who, while less vocal than those who taunt us, are far more capable of doing us in—when the time is right. Again, my fear was less Nat T, himself, or even all the Nat T's our society has embittered. Rather, I fear the power of those who have to be aware of the policies on schooling, unemployment, poverty, welfare, crime and crime fights, that are the direct and indirect cause of so many black deaths that they render capital punishment, at least as administered in this country, both slower and a far less certain method of death.

I wonder. Do any of those who demand that black spokespersons drop everything and denounce the rantings of a few blacks, have any sense of what is happening to black people in this society? Does it mean anything that in most urban areas, 80 to 85 percent of black men will be caught up in the criminal justice system before they reach their 30th birthday—if they reach their 30th birthdays? The number of black men in prison now exceeds 800,000, the largest number of any country in the world. And what is this country doing about it? The Congress is finishing its work on a new law that the President is all too anxious to sign. It will provide billions for new prisons and create new categories of crime to fill those prisons.[8]

If the nation's policies toward blacks were revised to require weekly, random round-ups of several hundred blacks who were then taken to a secluded place and shot, that policy would be more dramatic, but hardly different in result, than the policies now in effect, which most of us feel powerless to change. Nat T knows this, and he views me as a danger precisely because I don't see or, rather, don't want to see it. How much easier it is to rail against Harvard for failing to hire a few more people of color for its faculty. Or, in the context of this lecture, I can rail against the anti-anti-Semitic excesses of the *New York Times*, A. M. Rosenthal or the Anti-Defamation League.

Like Michael Lerner, I "can't stand the hypocrisy from a white media and white establishment that does everything it can to exploit and degrade blacks, then looks on in pretended horror when pathologies start to develop in the black community."[9] And if my ranting and raving is loud enough, for a time I may block out the awful truth Professor Delores Aldridge will not let us forget, namely that "both Jews and blacks occupy a somewhat precarious position in American society and culture. Neither group has the power to determine the destiny of the other. They both warily monitor the mood of the White American mainstream." Then she adds, "Allies do not have to be good friends."

True, but even alliances are hard unless the allies agree on the identity of their common enemy, and do not lambaste each other in a futile effort to deny the truth about that common enemy that is too scary to acknowledge. The more vocal elements of the Jewish community are committed to denunciation and retaliation as the appropriate means of combatting black anti-Semitism. Black spokespersons who refuse to join in the denunciation are deemed to have sided with the anti-Semites. Few blacks will join in a response so broad-based that it includes all of us. Just as Nat T is not a unique individual, Minister Farrakhan is not alone in his view that hate, rather than love, marks the road to power. Indeed, as has happened with so many outspoken black leaders before him, Farrakhan could be removed violently from the scene tomorrow, and the danger would remain and might worsen. Farrakhan draws tremendous crowds to his three-hour speeches, but in addition to castigating whites and countless other groups, he preaches a quite conservative message of nonviolence and self-help.

In commenting on Farrakhan's recent book, *A Torchlight for America*,[10] I observed, "Unlike those conservatives, black and white, who only preach self-help to the poor as a crowd-pleasing abstraction, Farrakhan's formulas emphasize the Nation of Islam's experience in educating black children, rehabilitating black prisoners, ridding black communities of drug dealers, and rebuilding respect for self—the essential prerequisite for individuals determined to maintain the struggle against the racism that burdens our lives and, unless curbed, will destroy this country."[11]

I certainly don't expect many Jews to agree with this assessment. They despise Farrakhan, probably for all three reasons discussed above. When he attacks, their reaction is retaliation. This proactive response is likely satisfying, but as with my hope that Nat T would be jailed, it is not very rational and often seems counter-productive. Entities deemed supportive of the Nation of Islam or its spokespersons have been threatened with economic reprisals, and black leaders and groups—though they have no more in common than color with the Nation of Islam speakers—have been urged to condemn the speakers and those who refuse are interpreted as supporting the attackers.

Recently, Benjamin F. Chavis, NAACP executive director, warned his ADL counterpart, Abraham Foxman, that continued ADL attacks on Farrakhan could create precisely what Jewish leaders say they fear: black anti-Semitism. Foxman acknowledged the risk, but said he was willing to take it, warning on his part that if African American leaders do not clearly distance themselves from views such as Farrakhan's, "it will undermine the moral underpinnings of a coalition."[12]

This pattern of hard-line response to blacks and civil rights policies deemed threatening to Jews did not begin with Louis Farrakhan. While some Jews helped establish the NAACP early in this century, and provided both financial support and legal acumen to black educational programs and the civil rights movement, the Black Power movement in the late 1960s, and the widespread adoption of affirmative action policies in the 1970s, alienated many formerly supportive whites. Their number included a great many Jews, some of them later called neoconservatives, who sensing the ebb of public support for racial remedies, became highly regarded spokespersons for opponents of school busing, affirmative action, welfare, and most of the causes their former civil rights colleagues espoused.

They also supplied a most effective chorus of condemnation when former UN Ambassador, Andrew Young, was discovered to have met secretly with the Palestinians. The Jesse Jackson case is, of course, the classic example of the retaliatory response. Jackson has done everything but offer to jump off a tall building to explain his position on Israel and Palestine, and to atone for his hymietown remark, all, seemingly, to no avail. Despite his position as the leader most blacks respect most, many Jewish groups will not forgive him. As one Jewish friend who opposes such tactics put it, they are "demanding penance without hope of forgiveness."

Jews should respond vigorously to statements they deem anti-Semitic. On the other hand, it seems to me an example of "piling on" when Jewish groups ignore efforts by blacks like Jackson to apologize for their statements, and use their greater influence in the community to block political aspirations and other activity not connected with the statements or actions that offended them. In addition, there is their use of economic clout to threaten business enterprises of those deemed dangerous to Jewish interests. Thus, some Jewish groups are seeking to prevent the Nation of Islam from obtaining or holding contracts with public housing authorities to provide the projects with much-needed security. While, according to the recent *Time Magazine* story, the Nation of Islam has not always been successful in reducing crime in their security businesses, they do provide jobs and build entrepreneurial skills in communities much in need of both.[13]

Regrettably, the pressures exerted against the Nation of Islam adhere to a pattern. The writer, teacher, and publisher Haki R. Madhubuti, recalls years ago mounting a protest against John Johnson, the publisher of *Ebony, Jet,* and other black publications.[14] The protest followed Johnson's discontinuance of *Black World,* and the dismissal of the magazine's editor, Howard Fuller, a highly respected journalist. Madhubuti reports that a large group set up picket lines around Johnson's new, multi-story building on Michigan Avenue in downtown Chicago. Within the first hour of the demonstration, Mr. Johnson, himself, appeared and invited the group inside for a talk. There, Johnson told the group that he had halted the publication of *Black World* and fired Fuller for refusing to cease publishing the Palestinian side of the Middle-East struggle and the African support for that struggle. He did so, he said, "because Jewish businessmen threatened to pull their advertising out of *Ebony* and *Jet* magazines and would have convinced their white friends to do the same if the Middle-East coverage didn't stop."[15] Madhubuti confesses the reaction to an exercise of overwhelming power: "We were stunned into a weakening silence. Our responses were few because we knew it was both an economic and political decision and as an astute businessman, Mr. Johnson did what he felt was best for his company."[16]

How, one might ask, do Jewish boycotts or their threat, differ from those blacks have used since the 1930s to get jobs in white-owned and—more recently—Korean-owned businesses located in black communities? The difference may seem more lawyer-like than real, but I think there is a distinction based on the relative power of the backwaters. Blacks resorted to boycotts as a substitute for political and economic power in an effort to pressure businesses to treat blacks fairly. Jewish groups utilize their superior economic power to intimidate blacks into halting actions that Jews find offensive.

I can acknowledge the determination of Jews to do what they felt was necessary to protect the image of Israel. But it should not be a surprise that many blacks resent the use of Jewish political clout in this way. It serves, among other things, to heighten the antagonism toward Jews rather than—as I assume is the purpose—lessen it. Many blacks, including myself, have been all too reticent about expressing publicly our resentment at pressure tactics of this type. There is, to be frank, the same silencing character of economic clout that Madhubuti's group experienced. And there is also the rationalization that we have more important priorities demanding our energies. But we blacks should find the courage to speak out as Michael Lerner did in condemning "some in the Jewish world who for decades have used the Holocaust and the history of our very real oppression as an excuse to deny our own racism toward blacks or Palestinians." In the frantic effort to make it in America, Lerner writes, "we also began to buy the racist assumptions of this society and to forget our own history of oppression."

Had we blacks been more forthright in the past, there might not be the current consternation among Jews about the reluctance of some of us to step forward and publicly condemn the disparaging statements made about them. There is a frequently posed question, "whatever our differences, should we not stand shoulder to shoulder in opposing racist statements?" That question, as New York State Senator David A. Paterson explained, must be answered in the light of the tolerance of pervasive racism against blacks. With such figures as Jesse Helms in the Senate and Rush Limbaugh as a national icon, blacks are very suspicious of white efforts to focus our anti-racist efforts on any black political leader—including the appalling statements of Khalid Muhammad.[17] Paterson acknowledges the historical reluctance of blacks to engage in public criticism, adding "for generations, whites have called on black leaders to denounce other blacks' offensive or radical ideas. Many leaders have actually been denounced as a result of such pleas, leading to crippling battles among black political leaders. Betrayals and self-defeating efforts to exclude rival leaders have undermined hard-fought efforts to gain and hold political power all across the country."[18]

Blacks complain, with some justified bitterness, that spokespersons of other ethnic groups are not asked to stand and condemn anti-Semitic statements made by individuals within those groups. Thus, Senator Edward Kennedy is not required to condemn the clearly anti-Semitic rantings of Pat Buchanan at the last Republican National Convention. It would be ludicrous to insist that John Kenneth Galbraith denounce the anti-Semitism of David Duke simply because both men are of Scotch ancestry. Some Jews demand that blacks condemn hate speech and its propagator even when they have no connection beyond race. Whether or not it is a conscious action, such demands reflect recognition of blacks as society's "other," a role of social subordination that Jews have had to play as much as any other people in history. In the status of "other," there is no distinction among the group. The unsettling statements of one can be "cancelled" by the denunciation of another.

Letty Cottin Pogrebin, a long-time civil rights activist, would disagree. She says that "the need to hear reassuring words from blacks can be read as a measure of the high regard Jews have for the opinion of the African-American community," and that "the demand for a response from black voices bespeaks a greater recognition and respect than the rest of America extends to the authority and power of black leadership."[19] I am certain that Ms. Pogrebin speaks sincerely for herself and, likely, many other Jews. The chapter on Black-Jewish relations in her book, *Deborah, Golda, and Me,* is one of the most objective and thorough I have read on this subject.[20] But blacks have been down so long that they recognize demands based on dominance when they hear them.

First, the demands are unilateral. That is, blacks must condemn statements deemed by Jews to be anti-Semitic, but there is no similar willingness of those Jews to condemn any racist statements and actions by Jews. For example, Michael Lerner must not be the only Jew ready to acknowledge the hypocrisy among "Jewish neoconservatives at *Commentary* magazine and Jewish neoliberals at the *New Republic* [who] have led the assault on affirmative action (despite the fact that one of its greatest beneficiaries has been Jewish women); have blamed the persistence of racism on the victims' culture of poverty; and have delighted in the prospect of throwing black women and children off welfare as soon as possible."[21]

Second, the demands are limited to blacks. Where is the pressure that Jewish groups should be placing on right-wing groups and their leaders who are ready to match anti-Semitic words with deeds? Micah Sifry, noting that the Anti-Defamation League comes down far harder on relatively powerless blacks making anti-Semitic statements than on those whites in high positions, writes: "There is no question the A.D.L. takes its minority anti-Semitism seriously, as well it should. But what about anti-Semitism elsewhere, among the white majority and by the powerful?"[22] Sifry makes the point that as some Jewish groups have turned more conservative, they tend to excuse the anti-Semitism of those on the right while bearing down on blacks. Sifry's long article offers impressive support for his position, but it is not one likely to influence ADL leaders who sat out the David Duke races in 1990 and 1991 for senator and governor, allegedly because of its tax-exempt status, but quietly circulated a nineteen-page memo to reporters detailing Jesse Jackson's past statements regarding Jews, even before the "Hymietown" furor broke.[23] When the "Hymietown" furor broke, Sifry reports, "A.D.L. officials leapt at the opportunity to nail him as an anti-Semite. Apologies were of no use. 'He could light candles every Friday night, and grow sidecurls, and it still wouldn't matter . . . he's a whore,' Nathan Perlmutter, then the A.D.L.'s director, told CBS News reporter Bob Faw."[24]

Andrew Young suggested recently that the Jews' quite understandable determination, expressed in the phrase, "never again," is not inconsistent with a willingness to forgive. Of course, forgiveness works both ways. My determination to speak out more vigorously about Jewish statements and policies I find upsetting, should not prevent me from getting beyond those actions once I have been heard. It also means that I am simply not going to join my Afrocentric colleagues who find of great seriousness the percentage of Jews who engaged in the slave trade or who are responsible for Hollywood stereotypes of black people. There is enough to debate in the present without digging up centuries-old challenges that, even if proved, would not alter our current difference.

For a host of reasons in addition to those discussed here, the tension and enmity that has marked and marred black-Jewish relations since the mid-1960s is likely to continue. I am confident though that my relationship with Jews who make up what is likely a majority of my friends and associates will also continue. They will agree with much in this lecture and, from time to time, we will join in projects that serve our interest. No doubt, other groups of blacks and Jews will do the same. That may be as close to an alliance as any of us can get, and it may be enough to frustrate those in power who must enjoy the battling between the two groups most likely to be sacrificed "in the nation's interest" if the need arises.

In the effort to avoid the fate of all societal scapegoats, many Jews will support the statement by Albert Vorspan and David Saperstein, two leaders of the Reform movement, who write in their book, *Tough Choices: Jewish Perspectives on Social Justice*:

> We can find no safety in turning inward upon ourselves, severing our links with the general community. We can find safety only if we help America deal not only with the symptoms—hatred, rage, bigotry—but with the root problems of our society—slums, powerlessness, decay of our cities, and unemployment, which spawn the evils of bigotry and conflict. Our task as Jews must go beyond the defensive job of countering the attacks of anti-Semitism to helping bring about a just and peaceful society.[25]

Similarly, many blacks will agree with Cornel West in his view when he writes:

> My fundamental premise is that the black freedom struggle is the major buffer between the David Dukes of America and the hope for a future in which we can begin to take justice and freedom for all seriously. Black anti-Semitism—along with its concommitant xenophobias, such as patriarchal and homophobic prejudices—weakens this buffer. In the process, it plays into the hands of the old-style racists, who appeal to the worst of our fellow citizens amid the silent depression that plagues the majority of Americans. Without some redistribution of wealth and power, downward mobility and debilitating poverty will continue to drive people into desperate channels. And without principled opposition to xenophobias from above and below,

these desperate channels will produce a cold-hearted and mean-spirited America no longer worth fighting for or living in.[26]

NOTES

1. Michael Cottman, "The Campus 'Radicals': Leonard Jeffries and other Afrocentric Professors refuse to whitewash their lesson plans," V *Emerge* 26 (Feb. 1994).

2. The book, *The Secret Relationship between Blacks and Jews* was prepared by the Historical Research Department, Nation of Islam. It contains a quite controversial history of Jewish involvement in the Transatlantic slave trade and African slavery. This book was subjected to severe criticism by Professor Louis Henry Gates in a full-page, op-ed article titled "Black Demagogues and Pseudo Scholars," published in the *New York Times* on July 20, 1993. A series of responses to this article, several of them quoted in this lecture, was published in *16 Black Books Bulletin: WordsWork* (Winter 1993–1994). This Bulletin is published by the Third Century Group, P.O. Box 19730, Chicago, IL 60619.

3. Cottman, *supra* note 1 at 28.

4. Paul Berman, "The Other and the Almost the Same," *The New Yorker*, 61, 63 (Feb. 28, 1994).

5. *Id.*

6. Letty Cottin Pogrebin, "What Divides Blacks and Jews," New York *Newsday*, 48 (Mar. 2, 1994).

7. *Id.*

8. Andrew Hacker, *Two Nations: Black and White, Separate, Hostile, Unequal* (1992).

9. Michael Lerner, "The Real Crisis is Selfishness," *Time Magazine*, 31 (Feb. 28, 1994).

10. Louis Farrakhan, *A Torchlight for America* (1993).

11. *Id.* at back cover.

12. Lynne Duke, "A Continuing 'Dialogue of Disagreement,'" *Washington Post* A6 (Feb. 28, 1994).

13. William Henry, III, "Pride and Prejudice," *Time* 21, 23 (Feb. 28, 1994).

14. Haki Madhubuti, "Blacks, Jews and Henry Louis Gates, Jr." *16 Black Books Bulletin* 3 (Winter 1993–1994).

15. *Id.* at 8.

16. *Id.*

17. David Paterson, "White Outrage, Black Suspicion," *New York Times*, E. 17 (Mar. 20, 1994).

18. *Id.*

19. Pogrebin, *supra*, note 6.

20. Letty Cottin Pogrebin, "Ain't We Both Women? Blacks, Jews, and Gender," in *Deborah, Golda, and Me*, 275 (1991).

21. Lerner, *supra*, note 9.

22. Micah Sifry, "Anti-Semitism in America," *The Nation* 92, 93 (Jan. 25, 1993).

23. *Id.* at 96.

24. *Id.*

25. *Id.* at 99.

26. Cornel West, *Race Matters*, 81 (1993). See, also West, "How Do We Fight Xenophobia?" *Time*, 30–31 (Feb. 28, 1994).

# Blacks and Jews
## Where Are We? Where Are We Going?

To talk about blacks and Jews is to talk not about politics but the lives people live. It is the lives we live that influence what we call our politics. Unless those lives are respected, there is no possibility of understanding the words we say to one another.

In recent years Jews and blacks have disagreed often over each other's words. Neither has understood sufficiently that in so doing, they are disagreeing with each other's lives. Thus, blacks have hurt Jews and Jews have hurt blacks.

Lives are not philosophical premises with which one is allowed to disagree, or over which one can have an argument. Lives are sacred. They are God's attempt to create prayers of bone and flesh. All too often Jews and blacks regard each other as merely issues to be analyzed and debated. When human beings reduce each other to abstractions, enmity must follow. Who should know this better than Jews and blacks?

First, let us acknowledge that blacks and Jews have real and serious differences, differences that may not be resolved by the most well-meaning of dialogues. That is O.K. Agreement is not a prerequisite for alliance. Understanding and respect are.

A fundamental difference between blacks and Jews is how each group views the history of black-Jewish relations. Jews are convinced they have much in common with blacks, because the two groups share histories of oppression and suffering.

This Jewish version of black-Jewish histories is not shared by many blacks. To the contrary, many blacks feel they have nothing in common with Jews. An examination of the historical record indicates that both groups are right, and both are also wrong.

What do blacks and Jews have in common?

(1) The histories of both begin in slavery.

(2) Throughout Western history blacks and Jews have been subjected to stereotyping by the white majority, and, often, the same stereotypes have been applied to both peoples. Jews and blacks have been equated with the devil and considered to have horns and tails and Europeans stereotyped both groups as being sexually licentious.

(3) Both people have been physically segregated from the majority. The word, ghetto, was first used to describe the section of Venice where Jews were segregated from Gentiles in the sixteenth century. *Geto* is Italian for iron foundry, because it was next to the iron foundry the Jews of Venice were forced to live.

Julius Lester is a professor at the University of Massachusetts at Amherst and teaches in the Judaic studies, English, and history departments.
An earlier version of this essay, "The Lives People Live," appeared in *Blacks and Jews: Alliances and Arguments*, ed. Paul Berman (New York: Delacorte Press, 1994). Copyright © 1999, Julius Lester. Printed with permission of Julius Lester.

(4) Jews and blacks suffered forced separation from their homelands and were dispersed throughout the Western world. Many blacks refer to themselves as living in the Diaspora, not recognizing, perhaps, that they are using a word from the Jewish experience to describe their own.

However, there is a profound difference in the Diaspora experience of Jews and blacks. Jews not only knew that Israel was their home, they kept Israel alive within themselves as a homeland for two thousand years, a remarkable historical feat. For blacks, such a feat was not within the realm of possibility. Being brought to the so-called New World from so many different parts of Africa, blacks had no common language, no common past, no common memories. For blacks the Diaspora is permanent.

(5) Both have been politically subjugated, with laws being passed restricting their movement in society, choices of occupation and social relationships.

(6) Both groups have been subjected to heinous violence. The pogroms against Jews in eastern Europe have a parallel in this country in violent attacks by whites on black communities during the first two decades of this century.

While blacks as a group have not been targeted—as yet—for extermination as were Jews during the Third Reich, the number of Africans who perished during the centuries of the slave trade is staggering. A conservative historical estimate is 15 million.

I can think of no two peoples who have endured so many of the same experiences throughout Western history. Both Jews and blacks have been condemned by the white majority, not because of anything we may have done but because of who we are. We are condemned for being, and nothing we do can eradicate who we are. We are Jews; we are blacks; therefore we are Other. The dominant society in whatever country we have lived has imposed a negative value on who we are. Jew and black are epithets in the vocabulary of the ruling majority and we are looked upon as pariahs.

In their broad histories, then, Jews and blacks have many similarities, both in historical experiences and their responses to those experiences. So similar are some of the experiences, blacks use words from Jewish history to describe their own.

These similarities are important and neither blacks nor Jews are enough aware of them. I would like to believe that if we know and love what we share, it will be easier to talk about and accept the differences.

However, the differences are profound. The broad historical similarities I have just described are true, and it is these which Jews point to when they speak of what blacks and Jews share. However, these similarities are not, for the most part, the shared experiences of *American* Jews and *American* blacks. They describe the histories of *European* Jews and American blacks.

In other words, in the broad context of Western history, Jewish and black history have many similarities. But similarity of experience is not *sameness* of experience. This is the crucial difference of which many blacks are keenly aware and many Jews are not. Jews and blacks have parallel historical experiences in the broad context of Western civilization. They do not share experiences of oppression in the same time and the same place. The Jewish experience of oppression is primarily, though not exclusively, European. The black experience is almost exclusively American.

The first time blacks and Jews encounter each other historically is on American soil and the differences are immediate when one considers how blacks and Jews came to the North American continent. Blacks were brought to America in 1619 as indentured servants. Within forty years, their status had been reduced to slavery.

In 1654, the Jewish community in America was founded in New Amsterdam by Sephardic Jews fleeing persecution in Brazil. Blacks were brought to America in chains, enslaved and persecuted. Jews came seeking freedom and to escape persecution. Jews found in America what they had found nowhere else in the Diaspora: A place where they could live free as Jews. In America blacks found a place of enslavement.

The first and very profound difference is, therefore, that blacks and Jews have radically different experiences of this land both call America. During slavery Jews were indistinguishable from white Americans in their attitudes and treatment of blacks. Some were abolitionists; others were slave owners, slave traders and slave catchers. Southern Jewish businessmen and leaders defended slavery eloquently, and the vice-president of the Confederacy was a Jew.

Here are the seeds of black-Jewish antagonisms. Jews had a choice: They could be white and American in all things secular, and Jewish in all things religious. This option was unavailable to blacks for obvious reasons.

I do not want to leave the impression that Jews came to America and found the yellow-brick road, that Jews were not subjected to anti-Semitism in many forms, that Jews did not suffer from discrimination in industry, education, and the professions, etc. They did, and blacks are not enough aware of the ways in which Jews suffered, in addition to the many ways in which Jews organized themselves to fight back.

However, anti-Semitism in America did not organize itself into a violent and totalitarian system as did anti-black racism. Despite anti-Semitism, American Jewry was able to pursue its life because there was a group lower on the socioeconomic scale, and most important, that group was of another color. Anti-black racism was more pervasive and virulent than anti-Semitism.

The differences in the black and Jewish experiences in America can be summarized thus:

(1) Jews were not penalized for their color. They had what can be called "white skin privilege." This "white skin privilege" was also Jewry's biggest threat, because it held out the promise of assimilation, and, through intermarriage especially, many Jews have ceased to identify or be identified as Jews. Because of white skin privilege, the American Dream was accessible to American Jews and Jews could assume that by hard work, their poverty would be relieved. This is an assumption blacks cannot make, even now.

The pervasiveness and seeming intractability of color prejudice is not sufficiently recognized. But the *New York Times* of January 10, 1991, reported "Three of four whites believe black and Hispanic people are more likely than whites to prefer living on welfare . . . to be lazy, violence-prone, less intelligent and less patriotic."

This prejudice on the basis of color affects practically every aspect of life, especially for poor blacks. The chief of surgery at Harlem Hospital wrote, in 1990, that "a black man in Harlem was less like to reach 65 years of age than a man in Bangladesh." The primary reason was "high rates of disease." [*New York Times*, 12/24/90]

(2) Another difference bearing on these statistics is that Jews entered America at an

economically propitious time. In other words, economic opportunities existed for Jews which did not exist for blacks. The greatest number of Jews entered the country at a time of great need for unskilled or semi-skilled labor. Jews would be hired where blacks would not be. Blacks have been economically viable only when we were slaves.

(3) The final difference is that Jews brought an indispensable intangible to America— a highly developed religion and culture. This gave them a sense of self, a history. They were literate, with a long history of love of learning which facilitated their advancement in the professions and their acculturation.

The black process was radically different, given that slave owners deliberately did all they could to destroy black cultural cohesion. The remarkable thing is how the slaves and those who came after took the remnants of African cultures and combined them with European culture to create new forms of cultural expression in language, dance, music and fashion.

Yet, despite these differences, for a period of time some blacks and some Jews forged an alliance that spearheaded a period of significant social, cultural and legal change, change that benefitted both groups. To put it simply, blacks and Jews came together to end segregation and insure the right of blacks to vote. What has not been acknowledged sufficiently is that the black-Jewish coalition succeeded. But the golden age of the black-Jewish alliance did not last and the reasons are not mysterious.

In 1966 black America was galvanized by Black Power, Black Pride and Black Consciousness. In 1967 Israel won a decisive war in a mere six days and in the course of that war reclaimed the Old City of Jerusalem and Jews once again had access to the Western Wall. Thus, at the same historical moment, black nationalism and Jewish nationalism asserted themselves and blacks and Jews were on a collision course.

Jewish identity was reborn after the Six-Day War. The Jew, history's whipping boy, the eternal victim, had defended himself with a military brilliance that stunned the world. Jews could no longer consider themselves victims. Blacks could no longer see in Jews a people who knew what it was to suffer. Blacks did not know what it was like to be victorious, and for the first time, Jews did. The black-Jewish alliance came to an end not only because blacks and Jews no longer had the same priorities but because their vision shifted from that of an all-inclusive community to one of competing nationalisms.

Dissonant nationalisms make it difficult for one group to communicate with another, make it difficult for one group to hear another. Once blacks and Jews had assumed a commonality of interest and intent. After 1966–67 they became suspicious and mistrustful of each other. Each made assumptions about the other's motives and neither wanted to be told that its assumptions might be false. And so it continues.

Sometimes blacks assume that Jews are more "white" in their attitudes than may be the case. Sometimes Jews assume that the problems blacks face are little different than those faced by their immigrant ancestors. Jews sometimes misinterpret black anti-Semitic expression and assume all black anti-Semitism is identical to that anti-Semitism expressed throughout European history. But every black who expresses anti-Semitism is not a potential brownshirt or Hitler. Some black anti-Semitic expression stems from the volatile and unstable socioeconomic environment in America today. Although the words are anti-Semitic, the content may not be. It is understandable that many Jews find it difficult to grasp such subtle distinctions given the realities of Jewish history. But learning to make such distinctions will enable American Jewry to modify its approaches to black anti-Semitism and black-Jewish relations.

I wonder if black anti-Semitic expression is not seeking to tell us something about the health and well-being of our nation today. Let me outline briefly the wider context from which I see black anti-Semitic expression coming.

America is presently undergoing the most profound cultural changes since the Emancipation Proclamation. These changes are confronting us with the challenge of redefining what it means to be an American. Within the first two decades of the next century, demographers predict that, in the aggregate, African Americans, Hispanics and Asians will outnumber whites. For the first time in the nation's history, whites will be in a minority. This means that America will have to reconceptualize itself from the white, Anglo-Saxon Protestant image in which it was created.

On the one hand, we have a tremendous opportunity. America could become the first genuinely heterogeneous nation in the history of humanity, bringing together people from every country on the globe, and creating a new whole. There is a danger, however, that America could disintegrate into ethnic enclaves as much of eastern Europe is doing. Instead of engaging in an actual war, the American one would set groups against groups in a psychological cold war in which each group defends its psychic turf from all other groups.

Ethnic identity has become a substitute for national identity. For many American blacks, the declaration that "I am an African American" is an article of faith resonating to the very depths of the soul. This declaration gives the individual a positive collective identity which seeks to offset the negative onus being black has had in the West.

However, one should not be deceived that the aggressive articulation of a positive collective identity has done much to dispel the demons of racial self-hatred in the black psyche. There is in black America today a nihilism heretofore unknown in American history. It is not a philosophical and political nihilism. It is a nihilism born from the absence of self and the absence of hope. It is a condition without precedent in black American history because even during slavery, blacks had hope because they believed in a merciful deity and redemptive suffering. Today, many consider God to be dead and suffering the self-indulgence of fools.

The issue is not one of tensions between blacks and Jews. Jews are merely the lightning rod making visible a loss of self and a consequent violent desperation that all of us, black, white, Jew and Gentile, ignore at our peril.

Such an analysis does not exculpate those who lack the moral sensibility to know that public anti-Semitic expression is as unacceptable as anti-black racist expression. Many black supporters of the 1995 Million Man March claimed that they did not agree with Farrakhan's anti-Semitism. If that was so, the marchers should have let Farrakhan know that verbal attacks on Jews, that historical lies about Jews, were unacceptable if he wanted to represent African Americans. Jews cannot make Farrakhan mend his anti-Semitic ways. However, Farrakhan would stop his anti-Semitism if those million black men told him that talking the way he does about Jews is as unacceptable to them as it would be if a Jew talked that way about blacks. Black tolerance of anti-Semitic expression helps create an environment in which anti-black racist expression becomes even more acceptable. Thus, it is in the black self-interest to be in the forefront of those speaking out against black anti-Semitism.

It is in Jewish self-interest to understand that America is in the midst of an ethnic transformation and the American black community finds itself in the position of being economically surpassed, generation after generation, by successive waves of immigrants—the most recent ones being Indians, Pakistanis, Arabs, Koreans, Vietnamese, Cambodians.

The immigrant success story is the quintessential American paradigm, and it is a story in which black Americans have had their noses rubbed for all too long. The lesson of the story is simple: "My ancestors came here; they had nothing; they couldn't even speak English. They made it. If you people haven't made it, it's your own fault."

To cite the immigrant experience as the paradigm is to be blind to the seeming intractability of color prejudice in American society. In a 1988 study of racial attitudes conducted by the National Research Council, the conclusion was reached that the "status of blacks relative to whites has stagnated or regressed since the early 1970s," that "the ideals of equal opportunity and equal treatment for blacks were not endorsed by whites 'when they would result in close, frequent or prolonged contact.'" [*New York Times*, 8/5/89]

The U.S. Conference of Mayors issued a report in February 1998, which said that 71.3 percent of whites own their own homes, compared with 43.6 percent of blacks and 41.7 percent of Hispanics. Quoting a report of the Federal Reserve, the mayors concluded that blacks and Hispanics who apply for mortgages were "much more likely" to be rejected than whites with similar incomes.

While a color blind society is a wonderful ideal, a color conscious society remains the reality. Thus it is not only disturbing but infuriating to blacks when whites and Jews come out against affirmative action because they believe each person should be judged on his or her merit. They don't realize that the concept of meritocracy was introduced into American thought by black people who, in colonial times, were begging to be judged solely as individuals. If whites had listened to blacks 200 years ago, America would never have had a racial problem, and let me add, that the racial problem in America is not about blacks. The racial problem is about whites and their racism.

The black historical experience has been that all too many white people were and are incapable of or unwilling to judge blacks as individuals. Non-blacks, and especially white men, think it is in their self-interest to judge people not on the basis of merit but in terms of color and gender.

One need not look further than the health care system for evidence of just how color conscious American society remains. *The New York Times* of January 26, 1998, reports on a study done by the federal Centers for Disease Control and Prevention. Let me share with you some of the statistics from that study. From 1980 to 1994 the number of diabetes cases among blacks rose 33 percent, three times the increase among whites. "The gap in cases of infectious diseases has grown by the same magnitude."

Breast cancer: From 1990 to 1995 the death rate from breast cancer for white, Asian and Latino women fell from 23.1 per 100,000 to 21. The rate of 27.5 per 100,000 for black women did not change.

Infant mortality: Blacks still have two times the infant mortality rate of whites, a gap that has not changed in at least a decade.

Cancer: Since the early 60s, the death rate from cancer for black men rose 62 percent compared with 19 percent for other American men.

The *Times* reports, "Blacks often receive less, and worse, health care than whites, meaning that they are sicker than whites and typically die at about age 70, six or seven years earlier than whites."

While acknowledging that limited education, violence and addiction are certainly partly responsible, health professionals are "finding growing evidence that race, discrimination and social and cultural factors influence the care people receive, and, consequently, their health."

Sara Rosenbaum, director for the Center for Health Policy Research at George Washington University, was frank: In hospitals and clinics, blacks often receive worse care than whites. "When you take black and white Americans, and exactly the same situation like being hospitalized for a heart attack and having the same insurance, the chance that the black patient will get the advanced care is much less than it is for the white patient. The medical system appears to treat them differently." In other words, all too many white medical professionals do not put as high a value on the lives of black people as they do on whites.

One form of expression black anger has taken has been that of anti-Semitism and without question, some black anti-Semitic expression is malicious and hateful. Some black anti-Semitic expression, however, is a desperate attempt to be heard by people whose just grievances are ignored. If they hurl epithets at white people, white America doesn't listen. Say something anti-Semitic, however, and Jews will hear. Anti-Semitic expression draws attention to the speaker. It does not matter if that attention is negative. Negative attention is better than none at all. Under the glare of moral censure, one becomes visible.

Much of black anti-Semitic expression is the ugly and desperate agony of those who cannot hope because they cannot dream, because to hope and dream one must feel secure about his and her place on the earth. Without existential security one either becomes free or goes mad. I would suggest that in black America today there are pockets of collective madness.

We have reached a point in time when an emphasis on black-Jewish relations is misplaced. We can no longer afford to be nostalgic for the golden days of black-Jewish harmony and cooperation, which were not as harmonious as hindsight would have us believe. The political challenge for all of us, black, white, Jew and Gentile, is to create a coalition across the ethnic spectrum. None of us want to see anti-black racist or anti-Semitic expression coming in a generation or two from the descendants of today's Hispanic and Asian immigrants.

American Jewry can only participate in a new coalition building if it understands that it is no longer an offshoot of German or eastern European Jewry. American Jewry is its own entity now, one unlike any Jewry that has ever been. In Europe Jews had a distinct identity as Jews and were seen as a minority. In America the distinctiveness of that identity has been moderated because there is another group whose distinctiveness is more marked, namely, blacks. In America Jews became white because there existed a people called blacks. Regardless of the extent to which individuals may regard themselves as Jews, when they walk down the street, they blend in with the majority. White-skinned Jews look white in a crowd.

Because Jews partake of and share in the majority identity as whites, they have benefited economically. In Europe Jews were victims; in America Jews became a success story. Understandably, the very success makes many Jews nervous because the Jews of Weimar Germany were also a success story and we know what happened to them in less historical time than it takes to blink the eyes. There are not many Jews sanguine enough to think the same could not happen here.

From a black perspective, however, there is something jarring in hearing white-skinned Jews talk about suffering. No black denies that Jews suffered in Europe, but the Jewish experience in America has not been characterized by such suffering. The black experience has.

Many blacks feel that some Jews borrow suffering from history to give themselves an identity and status as victims and then use this vicarious suffering as the credentials to tell blacks what they should do.

Thus, what often comes out as black anti-Semitism is an attempt to express resentment toward Jews for assuming a relationship of shared suffering. As far as many young blacks are concerned, none exists. Blacks resent the Jewish assumption of shared oppression and use the language of anti-Semitism to make that resentment clear.

This absence of shared suffering can be illustrated by two chilling statistics: (1) Blacks comprise 12 percent of the population but account for 45 percent of all deaths by fire; (2) 47 percent of all black 17-year-olds are functionally illiterate.

If we are dismayed that so many blacks listen to demagogues it is because only the demagogues are speaking to the despair and hopelessness of those trapped in poverty and ignorance. Unfortunately, too often Jews unwittingly enhance the status of such black anti-Semites. One could almost say that if you are black and want to be considered a leader in certain parts of black America today, say something anti-Semitic and get attacked by Jews.

It is time Jews stopped assisting black anti-Semites in their thirst for attention. De-nunciations of black anti-Semitism are in danger of being counterproductive. Equally, so much hand-wringing and agonizing over black-Jewish relations is also in danger of being counterproductive. Focusing on black-Jewish tensions takes our attention away from the problem. If I were paranoid and believed in conspiracies, I would say that Minister Farrakhan was employed by the far Right to attack Jews and distract blacks from the fact that they do not have a place in America's economic future. But I am not paranoid and I do not believe in conspiracies but the effect of Farrakhan's nineteenth-century political ideology is to divert attention and energy away from the very serious problems faced by black America.

It is time we stopped speaking of a black problem and began talking about an

American problem because blacks are American citizens, to state an obvious fact that America has not grasped. The quality of all our lives as Americans is threatened because there are all too many other Americans who are not economically viable. Can you imagine the hatred felt by one who knows that he or she is of absolutely no use socially, economically, politically? Can you imagine the rage in one who knows that his or her existence simply does not matter?

This is the context of today's black anti-Semitism. We should not be surprised or dismayed that so many blacks hate Jews. They hate themselves far, far more.

Self-hatred and despair do not justify black anti-Semitism. Yet there are those who seek to justify it by saying such things as "Oppressed people can't be racist," or "We are not anti-Semitic because Arabs are Semites." Such statements would be laughable if they were not so obscenely immoral. All too often they seek to minimize it by saying "We don't believe in that part of what Farrakhan says. Don't take it so seriously." Yet we all know that if a Jew dared tell blacks not to take racism so seriously, blacks would be outraged—and justifiably so.

Black leaders have failed when they have not spoken out and said that anti-Semitism damages the black soul as surely as anti-black racism damages the white soul, that, in the words of James Baldwin, "It is a terrible, an inexorable, law that one cannot deny the humanity of another without diminishing one's own: in the face of one's victim, one sees oneself. . . . It is so simple a fact and one that is so hard, apparently, to grasp: *Whoever debases others is debasing himself.*"

America does not care how black people live; it does not care if black people live. This is the black reality, and to speak of black-Jewish relations without addressing the concrete despair of blacks is to indulge in nostalgia for a time that never was. Poverty does not ennoble; it embitters. It embitters until people are left with no power except that of hatred and destruction.

If there is to be any kind of new black-Jewish coalition it must first put aside sentimental notions that there is some kind of God-ordained bond shared by blacks and Jews. The notion that blacks and Jews should be friends is romanticism at its worst.

Let me close by suggesting the outline for a possible course of action:

(1) It is time to make real the vision in our national motto, "Out of Many, One." The political philosophy of Louis Farrakhan is dependent on keeping people separate. We must not permit him to succeed. But he may unless we aggressively rearticulate the liberal vision that stresses what we as Americans have in common while celebrating and respecting the cultural differences. And in age of unprecedented economic prosperity and obscene salaries and perks for corporate CEOs, we must also rearticulate what our collective responsibility is to those among us who suffer inordinately because our society has defined them and treated them as Other. This is not a call for a new black-Jewish coalition but for coalitions across the racial and ethnic spectrum, coalitions of people with a shared concern for the spiritual and moral well being for all of America, not just the particular group to which one belongs.

(2) A second step is to identify areas of common interest that can be worked on at the local level. It is in the self-interest of black, white and Jewish Americans that the cities be clean and safe. It is in the self-interest of black, white and Jewish Americans that drug

use be reduced. It is in the self-interest of black, white and Jewish Americans that all citizens be literate.

(3) It is a mistake to think that any expression of anti-Semitism is a problem for Jews to combat. The reality is quite the contrary. Anti-Semitism is a problem created and continued by Gentiles. Public anti-Semitic expression will only be curtailed when Gentiles, black and white, recognize that any kind of racist expression damages the society as a whole, not only the group denigrated. Public expressions of anti-Semitism will not cease until Gentiles say to other Gentiles, "Enough." Public expressions of anti-black racism will not cease until non-blacks say, "Enough."

What needs to be done, then, is that we save ourselves, Jew and Gentile, black and white. But sometimes, we become so focused on our hurts as blacks or Jews, or women or whatever, we forget that such particulars are not the totality of who we are. What we share and what we must acknowledge we share is a common humanity and common aspirations for life, liberty and the pursuit of happiness.

Perhaps it is time, then, that all of us, black, white, Jew and Gentile, enlarge our visions beyond our particular pains. Perhaps it is time that all of us, black, white, Jew and gentile, come together and address ourselves to the pain of our nation.

DAVID SCHOEM & MARSHALL STEVENSON

# Teaching Ethnic Identity and Intergroup Relations
## The Case of Black-Jewish Dialogue

That we live in separate worlds on our campuses is certainly not a new observation, yet with the recent attention given to incidents of racism on campus, curricular revision, and talk of the multicultural university of the twenty-first century, it is important that we begin to devote more attention to face-to-face intergroup dialogue as well as other means of teaching for the new curriculum and the multicultural university of the future. To study race relations without offering opportunity for dialogue between races, or to be a part of a diverse student body but to have no experience with groups other than one's own, certainly represents a severe limitation on students' education.

This article is a description of one class using intergroup dialogue as a means of studying blacks, Jews, and black-Jewish relations in the context of exploring broader issues of ethnic identity and intergroup relations. In the six years that Blacks and Jews: Dialogue on Ethnic Identity has been taught, nothing has been more striking than the fact that these classes have represented for almost all the students the very first opportunity to talk with individuals of another ethnic group about anything more than passing superficialities. The emphasis of this class on active learning, through discussion and dialogue, allowed for a deeper understanding of blacks, Jews, and their intergroup relations through both theory and practice, study of text and of personal experience. The description and analysis that follow are intended to offer insights both into the teaching process itself and into the substantive learning and insights, the rich personal understanding of topics, and the degree of personal empowerment that emerged from this approach to learning.

## METHODOLOGY
### RESEARCH METHODS

This study was conducted using a variety of research methods, including classroom observation, survey data, and student journals.[1] The two researchers, Schoem and Stevenson, chose to study a class that Schoem had previously taught for three years. Schoem's role was as a full participant: He led the research, organized class sessions, gave lectures, led discussions, held conferences with students, read journals and papers and commented on them, and gave grades to students. In addition, Schoem kept a separate notebook of observations and thoughts regarding the research study.

In 1990, David Schoem was assistant dean for the freshman and sophomore years at the University of Michigan, where he was also a lecturer in sociology. In 1990, Marshall Stevenson taught African-American urban and labor history at Ohio State University.
Originally published in *Teachers College Record* 91, no. 4 (Summer 1990): 579–94. Copyright © 1990 by Teachers College, Columbia University. Reprinted with permission of *Teachers College Record*.

It is important to note that Schoem is a white Jewish male. Although most students denied that this was a factor in their ability to participate fully and openly, it must be considered as a possible factor in evaluating the description of classroom activities.

A second factor that clearly influenced the nature of classroom discussion and attitudes was that students self-selected to apply for admission to the course, as had been the case in prior years. Admission to the course was by permission of the instructor, primarily on the basis of a willingness to participate honestly and fully and be open to different viewpoints. Eighteen students enrolled: eight black students, nine white Jewish students, and one black Jewish student. Fifteen students were female and three were male. About thirty to forty other students were turned away. Students were informed of the research project the first day of class. All agreed to participate and continue in the class.

A third factor that obviously influenced the nature of classroom discussion was Schoem's structuring of the course. The extent to which he encouraged participation and dialogue and controlled the levels of intensity of discussion undoubtedly had an impact on learning and on the focus and outcome of mediation.

The second researcher, Stevenson, attended all class sessions as a participant observer. Like Schoem, Stevenson's role as researcher was made clear to students on the first day of class. Stevenson took extensive notes during class, had access to student journals, and occasionally spoke with students outside of class at the students' request. Stevenson also participated in class discussions, although infrequently, and gave a lecture. Stevenson is a black non-Jewish male.

The role distinctions between Schoem and Stevenson were established for several reasons. First, the degree of intensity and involvement that the class demanded of the teacher made it valuable to have one researcher who could observe and take notes without being absorbed as a full participant in the class. Second, funding for the project was not sufficient to permit Stevenson to teach. Third, the inspiration for the research was Schoem's previous experience teaching this class as the sole teacher; it was that classroom model that was the desired research focus of this study. Certainly it would also be interesting to study, as another project, this same class with Schoem and Stevenson sharing teaching responsibilities equally. At the conclusion of the semester, the researchers together reviewed their notes and re-read the student journals.

INSTRUCTIONAL METHODS

Blacks and Jews: Dialogue on Ethnic Identity is one of a group of freshman seminar courses at the University of Michigan that stress critical thinking and writing about focused topics in small classroom settings. The class met twice weekly for fourteen weeks over a four-month period for two hours per session. Class sessions included lectures, films, group exercises, and student presentations of research. However, class time was devoted primarily to discussion and analysis of readings and of personal feelings and attitudes on personal and public issues and events.

The syllabus was divided into four equal parts. The first part was devoted to a general discussion of majority-minority relations and ethnic identity and introduced students to group processes that were facilitative of the developing dialogue. The second part focused on the black experience in America and the third part focused on the Jewish experience in America. Throughout, there was considerable opportunity and encouragement for students to question one another within each group and between the groups. Finally, the group discussed black-Jewish relations in America during the last section of class.

Students were required to read eight books and an extensive coursepack of readings. A journal (thirty to fifty pages), including personal reflections as well as formal responses to specific questions posed by the instructor, was also required. A short research paper (about ten to fifteen pages), jointly authored by two students, was the final requirement. Students were evaluated and graded in this course based on their journals, class participation, and research papers.

### HISTORICAL CONTEXT

The way in which the body of literature on black-Jewish relations has grown is significant. For the most part, it corresponds with issues and events in the history of the groups' relations. One can trace the tone and emphasis of the literature in three chronological phases. The first phase began in the early 1940s and lasted through the very early 1960s. Its focus was on the problems of blacks and Jews in urban America that originated in the 1930s.

As the so-called alliance sought to consolidate itself among black and Jewish elites involved in the work of the National Association for the Advancement of Colored People (NAACP) and other organizations, catastrophe struck. The Great Depression transformed the United States from a nation of prosperity to a nation whose citizens lived on the edge of poverty. A crucial development in most northern urban areas was increased tensions among Jewish merchants and landlords and the predominantly black clientele. The poor economic conditions and the shortage of jobs throughout the decade influenced many blacks and Jews to try to take advantage of each other. In cities like New York, Chicago, Philadelphia, Baltimore, and Detroit, black-Jewish relations deteriorated into sometimes violent and overt cases of black anti-Semitism and Jewish racism. The very early literature focused on these events.[2]

Despite the tensions, the explicit message in a number of writings toward the mid to later 1950s was that blacks and Jews were somehow "natural allies" because of the similar discrimination they had faced.[3] Yet, by the second phase of historiographic literature (1965–1975), the period that has produced most of what has been written on the subject, the tone and message again shifted to the emerging tensions. During the second phase, blacks and Jews seemed to be more in conflict than cooperation.[4]

The majority of writings emphasized specific issues and aspects of social interaction that polarized the black and Jewish communities. Most distressing was the sometimes overt but more often latent anti-Semitism of the late 1960s Black Power movement. Jews feared that black demands for a greater share of America's economic pie threatened their economic and occupational security.[5] These disagreements continued into the 1970s over the idea of affirmative action. Thus, by 1975, the so-called alliance was often nothing more than a spiteful dialogue.[6]

The third phrase of literature on black-Jewish relations began in the late 1970s and continues today. Its emphasis is on objectivity and solid historical documentation rather than the polemical opinion of certain blacks and Jews so close to the issues that they were overtly influenced by emotion and bias. The present work is an extension of the third phase, but is more sociological than historical. However, it relies heavily on past works and the general history of black-Jewish relations in the use of its methodology and conclusions.[7]

## LEARNING STAGES

The researchers observed six distinct stages of learning and process during the course of the semester. The description of class format and analysis of the class that follows is organized according to these six stages.

*Stage One:* Students entered the class guarded, saying they had no prejudices. They looked for similarities between the groups. They were ignorant of the other group's history and experience.

*Stage Two:* Students listened to each other in a supportive but guarded manner. They looked for simplistic answers to black-Jewish relations, but started to become better informed.

*Stage Three:* Students began to open up more and also to challenge one another. Disagreements occurred and some anger was expressed.

*Stage Four:* Students attempted to understand concerns of the other group from their own perspective and experience; they also became more defensive. Students began to realize how little they knew about the topic and to appreciate how much they had to learn.

*Stage Five:* Students realized the dimensions of the complexity of black-Jewish relations. They grew increasingly frustrated with the difficulty of achieving resolution of conflicts and the futility of looking for easy answers. However, they became more aware of how much they were growing and learning through this difficult process.

*Stage Six:* Students began to attempt to understand concerns of the other group from the other group's perspective, although they were not necessarily able to do this very well. They were visibly exhausted from the intensity of these emotional discussions; they looked forward to the approaching end of the term for a break, but they also expressed a desire to continue this kind of dialogue after a period of "cooling out."

## DESCRIPTION

A fuller elaboration of what went on in each of these stages is provided below.

STAGE ONE
*Classroom Format*
On the first day, students eased into discussion by talking about themselves in relation to external characteristics—hometown, focus of study, residence hall on campus— and a brief comment on why they chose the class. Later, a chapter from *Black and White Styles in Conflict*[8] provoked consideration of how students would talk to each other in this class setting. Another article, on mediation and negotiation,[9] gave students an opportunity to focus on their own communication skills in a setting with different

groups and people with different backgrounds and different perspectives. Throughout the course, the importance of listening skills, openness to new ideas, expression of honest opinions and of critical analysis, along with sensitivity to targeted individuals, were discussed as a group.

An "in-group/out-group" exercise was used to help students relate to some of the "feelings" of minorities in minority-majority relations. The exercise called for students to describe situations in which they had been part of an in-group or an out-group. Students were then asked to consider the economic, social, political, and often life-threatening implications beyond the feelings associated with ascribed minority-majority statuses in society. Subsequently, there were readings and discussions about a variety of ethnic and minority-majority conflicts beyond the black and Jewish experiences. Discussion also focused on different definitions and perceptions of what it means to be a member of a minority. Throughout the semester the class examined the varied socioeconomic successes and experiences of different ethnic groups in the United States, the widely held "myths" that have been used to explain those differences, and alternative explanations for those differences.[10]

### Analysis and Issues Arising

For most students, this class represented their first opportunity to talk with individuals of the other group, Jews or blacks, in anything more than a passing superficiality. Most students were cautious in their initial presentation of self, and while just a few actually stated "I am not prejudiced," several others felt that way in the first class discussions.

Students initially expressed disdain for the need to talk about *how* to talk to one another, presenting themselves as being sufficiently sophisticated to engage in this dialogue without discussion of process issues. One said, "We can argue and not be offended." Yet students often referred to the discussions of process in their journals and in private conferences throughout the semester as they later struggled with feelings of hurt and anger.

Although both groups considered themselves minorities, Jewish students did so on the basis of being a numerical minority and black students did so on the basis of current and historical socioeconomic oppression. Each group, in turn, attempted to understand the other as a minority in terms of its own definition. The result was that black students had difficulty accepting the Jews' self-definition as a minority and Jewish students had difficulty accepting the depth of feeling that blacks associated with their sense of themselves as a minority.

### STAGE TWO

### Classroom Format

During the third week of class students participated in a "fishbowl" discussion of black identity and Jewish identity. At the first session Jewish students were seated in a small circle surrounded by a circle of black students. The seating arrangement and process was reversed the second day. Students were asked to describe their Jewish or black identity—what it meant to them to be Jewish or black. Members of the inner group spoke one at a time with no interruptions permitted. This was followed by questions and discussion by members of the inner circle and, finally, by questions and discussions with members of both circles.

The next section of the course marked a shift in focus to an introductory examination of the black experience in America. In the first session two films were shown: *I Have a Dream: Martin Luther King* and *El Hajj Malik El Shabbaz: Malcolm X*. The next session allowed for a lecture and discussion comparing and contrasting these two leaders' philosophies. Students were required to read King's *Why We Can't Wait* and Malcolm X's *On Afro-American History*.[11]

### Analysis and Issues Arising

The fishbowl structure allowed the groups to form a bond, sitting close together and talking about personal opinions and important group issues. At the same time it made clear that within each group there were important differences in attitude and experience, and that neither group was monolithic. Each group also had a unique opportunity to "listen in" to an insider's conversation that, in most cases, they had never been privy to before (and probably would not be again after the end of the semester). Students found the rather simple opportunity to "tell one's story" in class without interruption to be very empowering.

The Jewish students talked about their strong ties to Israel and their undefined but strong sense of Jewish values. Although none of the Jewish students were religiously observant by traditional standards, a rather sharp and lengthy discussion took place over the "correctness" or "rightness" of the different Jewish denominations represented—that is, Reform and Conservative branches of organized Jewry. Black students took note of this debate with some surprise and were eager to learn more about the different denominations that seemed to be the cause of intragroup antagonism.

The black student discussion was more affirming of the group, yet no less emotional. Discussion raised some difficult issues, such as the ability to unite as a people, conflict between lighter- and darker-skinned blacks, and the comparative (to Jews) strength of their cultural heritage because of slavery. However, the focus of this discussion was on their sense and strength of identity coming from the historic struggle to overcome oppression. The Jewish students took note of what the black students said but did not seem to fully comprehend their feelings and the depth of their emotion about their history of oppression and discrimination.

During this time frame, one Jewish student was anxious to have answered the question of why Jews in America had achieved greater socioeconomic success than blacks. Despite readings, a lecture, and discussion of that question directly and comparatively, she continued to ask the question—not comprehending, not listening, or not hearing an answer that she wished to hear.

Both black and Jewish students greatly admired Martin Luther King, Jr., but Jewish students disliked and feared Malcolm X's ideas and statements. Black students identified with the forceful and direct preaching of Malcolm X, particularly his pointed description and analysis of white racist behavior toward blacks. However, in the journals of black students the praise for Malcolm X was mixed with ambivalence compared with that for King. In class, in reaction to the negative comments of Jewish students about Malcolm X, black students verbally defended and applauded Malcolm X.

Through various exercises and discussions, an initial trust was developed that allowed for issues of difference and conflict to begin to be stated. However, both groups still worked under a shield of "feeling good," allowing that while prejudice and discrimination and conflict existed, the members of this class were not a part of those problems and, in fact, this group, through their study and these discussions, would find the solutions and the way around such conflicts and problems.

The instructor made a largely unsuccessful attempt to use the experience of blacks and Jews as examples of minority-majority experience in a broader context. The immediacy of exploring their own and the other group's identity initially inhibited the students' interest and ability to look beyond the classroom for a broader comparative experience.

The decision to discuss the black experience before the Jewish experience was one attempt to balance the white Jewish instructor's influence. Although Jewish students questioned this format later in the semester, it did seem to be a useful symbolic measure: The black students saw that their concerns and experience would not be studied or considered "second" to the concerns and experiences of the Jewish students.

STAGE THREE

*Classroom Format*

The syllabus was altered to allow for discussion of a racist incident on campus that had involved two black women from the class as victims. Discussion focused on the incident itself, involving a racist flier, its meaning, and the appropriate response, if any, to be taken by black and Jewish students. This particular incident, other incidents, and the subsequent engagement of the entire university population in protests, demands, negotiations, and debates about issues of overt and institutional racism influenced the content and tone of discussions for the remainder of the term.

*Analysis and Issues Arising*

In the course of continuing discussions about minority-majority relations, black students spoke of discomfort at the experience of being one of only two or three black students in a 300-person lecture hall, and being aware of stares from the majority white students as they would walk into class to take their seats. Jewish students could not relate to this experience, and some suggested that the experience was more imagined than real. These Jewish students said that they and their white friends never took notice of the race of students in their classes and denied staring at the few blacks in their classes. A source of tension in this recurring debate came over the denial by some Jewish students of an experience reported as real by black students. This was a difficult yet important discussion, because of the broader issues involved regarding an understanding of the other party's perspective and the resultant ability to mediate differences.

The racist incident on campus mentioned earlier was an inflaming spark to what eventually became an enormous political issue on campus addressing long-standing charges of institutional racism and neglect as well as immediate overt racist harassment on campus. Many black students had begun to mobilize a rally against racism on campus. In class, discussion centered around whether the Jewish students understood how the black students felt and whether they would participate in the rally.

Copies of the flier were distributed in class to all of the students who had not seen it. The initial Jewish response was that it was "more than just a joke." All of the students, black and Jewish, felt that more vigorous action should have been taken by the student body and the administration. When the black students asked the Jewish students if they were going to participate in the rally, many felt placed on "the spot." After a brief discussion, several black students voiced the opinion that "whites were not taking enough interest in stamping out racism."

This was the first case in the class of blacks and Jews directly challenging one another and tensions were high. Most of the Jewish students seemed offended because the blacks kept pressing them for a commitment to participate in the rally. To do so would have involved missing classes. In this case, blacks openly sought out and seemingly expected the support of whites—no less Jews, as they had recently read of Jewish support for Martin Luther King, Jr., and the civil rights movement. One black student said, "Just don't disappoint us; don't say you're going to be there to show support and then not show up. That would be the worst thing to do." The Jewish students' response to the rally and to these issues was as whites, not as Jews. In their own minds, their analysis and personal reaction to these events had little or nothing to do with their being Jewish; to them, this was a black-white issue.

Although tension levels had increased in classes, most students felt good about each other on an individual basis. Blacks were clearly the leaders in these discussions, with Jews reacting to issues that blacks put forward.

STAGE FOUR

*Classroom Format*

Students played a simulation game to look at the influence of class differences apart from racial differences. This was part of the discussion and follow-up on significant reading on socioeconomic issues.[12] The class had a single "circle" discussion to talk about personal racism and to react to class discussions. The class also read and discussed Shange's *Betsey Brown* as part of the discussion of personal racism and experiences as victims of racism.[13] At the close of this section, students viewed and discussed the film *In Search of a Past*, about black high school students visiting Africa and examining issues of identity, roots, struggles for freedom, and black-American/black-African relations.

The third part of the course shifted the focus to an introductory examination of the Jewish experience in America. The first session was devoted to a film and discussion on the Holocaust, and others to Wiesel's *Night* and Timerman's *Prisoner without a Name, Cell without a Number*.[14]

*Analysis and Issues Arising*

Another class session was similarly shaped by the external events around campus. The focus of the discussion dealt with the issue of Jews allegedly having become assimilated. Black students were of the opinion that since Jews were part of the larger white majority and had risen to occupations of "power" (doctors, lawyers, etc.), they were more inclined to be apathetic on civil rights issues. The Jewish students challenged this black view that they were "on top," and drew on the Holocaust experience to demonstrate the tenuousness of the Jewish position in the social order. In that case, all Jews, regardless of occupation or social status, were marked for persecution and death. The Jewish students pointed out that regardless of the way it might appear, they viewed themselves as marginal and always on guard against anti-Semitism.

Some of the black students maintained a view that discounted Jewish apprehension and saw the issue as purely one of color. As they viewed the issue, there was no way a white person could be persecuted to the same degree that blacks have been or are. Thus both groups digressed into what might be called the "who has suffered the most" syndrome.

The discussion of *Betsey Brown* led to wider discussions of students' first contact with racism while growing up.[15] One of the most intriguing discoveries for black students was to learn that for half of the Jewish students in the class, their first experience with blacks was through their housekeepers. The Jewish students expressed nothing but positive feelings and experiences from the interactions with their black housekeepers, yet this example pointed to the wide socioeconomic disparities of the two groups and the mostly separate worlds they came from.

The Jewish students, with one exception, indicated that they had had no personal experience with anti-Semitism in their lives. Yet they spoke of their concern for anti-Semitism often and attempted to equate their own personal/group struggle against oppression with that of their black peers in the class. Nevertheless, when the specific racist incidents occurred on campus, the Jewish students had no response or connection to those incidents as Jews and even challenged that question being raised. It appeared that their definition of their Jewish self included memory of Jewish oppression and concern for Jewish survival. That memory, however, was from history and not from personal experience and the survival concern did not extend to a broader sense of struggle against oppression. As whites, the Jewish students carried a class perspective that had difficulty understanding the issues of lower and lower-middle classes and a social and racial perspective that generally "felt bad" about overt racism.

Students did considerable reading and participated extensively in discussions of socioeconomic issues. However, it was the experience of role-playing different economic positions in the simulation game that seemed to bring home the reality of the disparities between economic privilege and disadvantage and to make concrete the substance of the readings.

The ability of this course to incorporate the experience of outside events such as the racist incident, to learn from it, and to move on and go beyond it reinforces the value of the extended length of this dialogue. As one example, when a teach-in on confronting racism took place on campus, black students from this class were able to lead discussion sessions precisely because of their experience in and comfort with engaging with others in these types of discussions. The Jewish students, as well, distinguished themselves in this respect. While they were not leaders at the teach-in, their attendance and participation set them apart from their Jewish friends and from most other white students (who stayed away in large numbers).

The Jewish students were deeply moved by the readings on the Holocaust and on anti-Semitism and were anxious to discuss with black students this aspect of the Jewish experience. However, the Jewish students did not report direct or personal experience with anti-Semitism and had great difficulty articulating the depth of pain and emotion they had learned and felt about anti-Semitism and the Holocaust in particular.

It seemed that Jewish students were frustrated in their inability to satisfactorily express their feelings. At the same time, they were disappointed that blacks in class did not seem stirred by the readings and discussions, and they were angry at what they felt was a lack of interest in, close attention to, and even careful reading of books on this topic by black students. Black students responded that they did sympathize and were horrified by what they saw in the film *Let My People Go*, but they felt that their own experience was worse and more personal—it had happened to them. They acknowledged the horror of the Holocaust but also questioned whether Jews gave it too much attention. When blacks asked "Why do people hate the Jews?" or "Does it have to do with physical distinction?" the Jewish students inferred a lack of sympathy and almost a denial of the history of oppression faced by Jews.

The discussion of Jewish identity was highlighted by the resistance of Jewish students to acknowledging the importance of religion to their identity. It was black students who raised the issue of religion frequently in this discussion. They were surprised and confused to hear Jewish students describe their Jewish identity by saying "I'm not religious, but . . ." Blacks wondered aloud, "What makes you Jewish then?" and Jewish students struggled to give anything but ambiguous and unclear answers.

STAGE FIVE
*Classroom Format*
Discussion during the next few weeks focused on topics such as Jewish identity, Israel, education, and socioeconomic issues.

*Analysis and Issues Arising*
The experiences of the last two months of class were at once the most painful and the most educational. There was emotional exhaustion and, in fact, some students missed classes because they needed a break. There were tears shed and tears held back during this period.

Tension grew for several reasons. There was a reliance on comparison between the two groups to a point where it was no longer useful. The comparison had served a purpose in developing understanding at first, but as time went on, students expected the understanding to go from "understanding on the other group's terms" to "understanding on our own terms." In terms of student expectations, it was no longer sufficient, for example, for blacks to understand the Holocaust from a black perspective; now the

Jewish students expected them to understand it from a Jewish perspective. The same comments and level of concern that would have been "acceptable" and appreciated earlier were not enough now.

The brief discussion of Judaism and Israel made students realize how much they had to learn, just as they had when discussing black history a month earlier. Some suggested that students be required to take a Jewish history and an Afro-American history course as prerequisites for this course. The discussion of socioeconomic issues at this point focused on the possible roles and the lack of models for minority groups (in this case, Jews who had become socioeconomically successful) and for individuals (in this case, blacks who had "made it") from groups that Ogbu calls "caste minorities."[16]

At the same time, each group wanted a degree of understanding from the other that could not be achieved. At a certain point, each group felt enormous frustration that the other still "didn't really understand" and they blamed one another for not trying hard enough. It became clear during the calm of the circle discussion just how much each person had attempted to listen and understand the other, and yet it was also clear that each side still was not satisfied. At that point, students began to realize that neither group could ever fully appreciate the other's pain as the other experienced it. Nevertheless, what they could do and did do was to try as fully as possible to understand, and then to realize and remain aware that there was much more feeling that only the in-group could know and experience.

STAGE SIX

*Classroom Format*

At the end of the third section of the class there was again a full-circle discussion to address unanswered questions and express unspoken feelings from the previous weeks' work. The final section of the course focused on relations *between* the two groups, blacks and Jews. Two sessions were devoted to lecture and discussion of assigned readings. The remaining sessions were given over to students' presentations of research they were conducting on specific topics within black-Jewish relations.

*Analysis and Issues Arising*

The level of frayed emotions led the instructor to direct a full-circle discussion for the class. Students were again given an opportunity to "tell" so that all felt they had an adequate opportunity to speak to the other group and be heard. Each student was able to complete both of the following: (1) "What I want to say about being black/Jewish is . . ." and (2) "What I want the black/Jewish students to hear is . . . ."

By April, students were emotionally exhausted from the intensity of class discussions, which during this particular semester were exacerbated by campus events. As in previous years, students had been directed to work in black/Jewish pairs to conduct research on black-Jewish relations and to report to the class. In almost all cases, students reported problems in doing the work together. The quality of the work produced was not very good and tensions developed between some individuals.

The paired research papers had a negative effect. While the idea of some required joint effort is probably worthwhile, this was the wrong project. The enormous pressure of grades at the end of the semester and the total lack of experience in collaborative research projects made this attempt unnecessarily difficult.

At the end of the semester, students were ready for a vacation. There had been enormous learning and growing. There were now complicated feelings about black-Jewish relations, and there were both good and bad individual relationships. If the reaction of former students is any indication, all would be ready to take a second semester of the course after an extended cooling-off period.

## SUMMARY

Students selected this course out of an intellectual curiosity to learn more about blacks or Jews, about relations between the two groups, and about their own group. They also came to this class for the personal opportunity it presented to meet and talk with individual blacks and Jews, to explore firsthand relations between the two groups, and to examine their own ethnic identity. The data indicate that the class was comprised of students who arrived with virtually no information, historical or literary, about the other group. The classroom setting, therefore, with substantial reading required as a grounding basis for extensive dialogue, was considered essential.

The issues discussed in class were deeply rooted, emotional, and tied to sensitive, important, and personal life concerns. Discussion of these issues, particularly with members of other groups with whom they had had little or no contact, required a strong commitment to meet regularly and over time. The experience of this class demonstrated the necessity of ample time both for the level of discussion to reach an appropriate level of honesty and intensity and for periods of "cooling out" and reflection, so that the group could properly digest one segment and move on to the next. That this was an official credit course helped to ensure a continuing commitment to class attendance and study, and the university calendar provided an adequate length of time for meaningful dialogue and learning between the groups.

Students moved in stages from a naive and simplistic notion of black-Jewish relations to one that was better informed. They began the class expecting to find "answers" or a happy ending to the status of black-Jewish relations and came away with not necessarily a more positive view, but certainly a more realistic one. Significantly, students expressed both a need and a desire to learn more about the topic beyond the end of the semester.

Students learned about themselves as blacks and/or as Jews, and also learned about the other group. They found that they were able to participate in a mixed black-Jewish group, but some indicated at the end of the semester that they preferred separate groups. They learned that apart from examining broad theoretical approaches to intergroup relations and the experience of different groups, they were able on a personal level to like some individuals and dislike others of different groups. Finally, after just about a third of the semester, several of the students had demonstrated their leadership potential and newly learned skills in intergroup dialogue that clearly set them apart from their peers who had not taken a course like this.

Substantively, the students learned how complex were the issues they were studying and came to realize how little they had known about either group when first entering the class. They understood better that there could be no concluding lecture with simple answers to black-Jewish relations at the end of the semester and were determined to pursue further study. Still, from the extensive list of readings assigned and the face-to-face discussions, they had gained an overview of important themes in each group's history and learned about key issues facing each group. Students were now able to place the experience of each group within broader social contexts and were more aware of both commonalities and differences between the groups. The Jewish students had been challenged by black students to more closely examine their identity as Jews apart from being "just like other whites" (especially if they did not consider themselves to be religious Jews), and the black students were pushed to make distinctions among whites, to recognize that not all nonblacks were part of a single white monolith.

NOTES

We wish to acknowledge the support of the Program on Conflict Management Alternatives of the University of Michigan and thank Mark Chesler, Elizabeth Douvan, Helen Weingarten, and Edith Lewis for their helpful comments on earlier drafts of this paper.

1. These methods are discussed in Raymond Gold, "Role in Sociological Field Observations," *Social Forces* 36 (1958): 217–23.

2. See Lawrence D. Reddick, "Anti-Semitism among Negroes," *Negro Quarterly* 1, no. 2 (Fall 1942): 112–22; Chandler Owen, "Negro Anti-Semitism: Cause and Cure," *National Jewish Monthly* 57, no. 1 (September 1942): 14–15; and Kenneth Clarke, "Candor about Negro-Jewish Relations," *Commentary,* February 1946, pp. 8–14.

3. Sanford Goldner, *The Jewish People and the Fight for Negro Rights* (Los Angeles: Committee for Negro-Jewish Relations, 1953); and Louis Ruchames, "Parallels of Jewish and American History," *Negro History Bulletin* 19, no. 3 (December 1955): 63–64, 66.

4. Lenora Berson, *Negroes and Jews* (New York: Random House, 1971); Eddie Ellis, "Semitism in the Black Ghetto," *Liberator,* January–April 1966, pp. 6–7; John Hatchet, "The Phenomenon of the Anti-Black Jews and the Black Anglo-Saxon: A Study in Educational Perfidy," *Afro-American Teachers Forum* (Brooklyn: Afro-American Teachers Association, November–December 1967), pp. 1, 3–4; Nicholas Polos, ed., "Black Anti-Semitism in 20th Century America," *American Jewish Archive* 27 (1975): 8–31; and Robert Weisbord and Arthur Stein, *Bittersweet Encounter: The Afro-American and the American Jew* (Westport, Conn.: Negro Universities Press, 1970).

5. Herbert Gans, "Negro-Jewish Conflict in New York City—A Sociological Evaluation", *Midstream,* March 1969, pp. 3–15; and Peter G. Sinder, "Anti-Semitism: and the Black Power Movement," *Ethnicity* 7 (1980): 34–46.

6. Michael B. Pearlstein, "Selected Jewish Responses to Affirmative Action Admission: Toward a Conceptual Understanding" (Ph.D. diss., University of Minnesota, 1980).

7. Hasia Diner, *In the Almost Promised Land* (Westport, Conn.: Greenwood Press, 1977); David G. Singer, "An Uneasy Alliance: Jews and Blacks in the United States 1945–1953," *Contemporary Jewry* 4, no. 2 (Spring/Summer 1978): 35–50; Marshall F. Stevenson, Jr., "Points of Departure, Acts of Resolve: Black-Jewish Relations in Detroit 1937–1962" (Ph.D. diss., University of Michigan, 1988); Joseph R. Washington, ed., *Jews in Black Perspectives: A Dialogue* (Cranbury, N.J.: Associated Universities Press, 1984); and Oscar R. Williams, Jr., "Historical Impressions of Black Jewish Relations Prior to World War II," *Negro History Bulletin* 40 (1977): 728–31.

8. Thomas Kochman, *Black and White Styles in Conflict* (Chicago: University of Chicago Press, 1981), ch. 2.

9. Roger Fisher and William Ury, *Getting to Yes* (New York: Penguin Books, 1981), ch. 2.

10. Steven Steinberg, *The Ethnic Myth: Race, Ethnicity, and Class* (Boston: Beacon Press, 1981); and Stokely Carmichael and Charles Hamilton, *Black Power* (New York: Vintage, 1967).

11. Martin Luther King, Jr., *Why We Can't Wait* (New York: Harper & Row, 1964); and Malcolm X, *On Afro-American History* (New York: Pathfinder Press, 1971).

12. Reynolds Farley, *Blacks and Whites* (Cambridge: Harvard University Press, 1981).

13. Ntozake Shange, *Betsey Brown* (New York: St. Martin's Press, 1985).

14. Elie Wiesel, *Night* (New York: Avon Books, 1970); and Jacobo Timerman, *Prisoner without a Name, Cell without a Number* (New York: Vintage Books, 1982).

15. Shange, *Betsey Brown.*

16. John Ogbu, *Minority Education and Caste* (New York: Academic Press, 1978), p. 23.

# BIBLIOGRAPHY

Azoulay, Katya Gibel. *Black, Jewish, and Interracial: It's Not the Color of Your Skin, but the Race of Your Kin.* Durham, N.C.: Duke University Press, 1997.

Baldick, Julian. *Black God: The Afroasiatic Roots of the Jewish, Christian, and Muslim Religions.* Syracuse, N.Y.: Syracuse University Press, 1997.

Baldwin, James. "Negroes Are Antisemitic Because They're Anti-White." *New York Times Magazine,* April 19, 1967.

Baldwin, James, et al. *Black Anti-Semitism and Jewish Racism.* New York: Richard W. Baron, 1969.

Bauman, Mark K., and Berkeley Kalin. *The Quiet Voices: Southern Rabbis and Black Civil Rights, 1880s to 1990s.* Tuscaloosa: University of Alabama Press, 1997.

Bender, Eugene. "Reflections on Negro-Jewish Relationships: The Historical Dimension." *Phylon* 30, no. 1 (1969): 56–65.

Bennett, Lerone, Jr. *Before the Mayflower: A History of Black America,* 6th rev. ed. New York: Penguin, 1988.

Berger, Graenum. *Black Jews in America: A Documentary with Commentary.* New York: Federation of Jewish Philanthropies of New York, 1978.

———. "Black Jews in America." In *Jewish-American History and Culture: An Encyclopedia,* edited by Jack Fischel and Sanford Pinsker. New York: Garland, 1992.

Berman, Paul, ed. *Blacks and Jews: Alliances and Arguments.* New York: Delacorte, 1994.

Berson, Lenora E. *The Negroes and the Jews.* New York: Random House, 1971.

———. "Zionism and Black Nationalism." In *The Negroes and the Jews,* edited by Lenora Berson. New York: Random House, 1971.

Berube, Maurice, and Marilyn Gittell, eds. *Confrontation at Ocean Hill–Brownsville: The New York School Strikes of 1968.* New York: Praeger, 1969.

Blustain, Sarah. "The New Identity Challenge: 'Are You Black or Are You Jewish?'" *Lilith* 21, no. 3 (1996): 21–29.

Bond, Horace Mann, et al. "Papers and Proceedings of a Conference on Negro-Jewish Relations in the United States." *Jewish Social Studies* 27, no. 1 (1965).

Brackman, Harold. "The Ebb and Flow of Conflict: A History of Black-Jewish Relations through 1900." Ph.D. diss., University of California, Los Angeles, 1977.

———. *Farrakhan's Reign of Historical Error: The Truth behind "The Secret Relationship between Blacks and Jews."* Los Angeles: Simon Wiesenthal Center, 1992.

———. *Ministry of Lies: The Truth behind the Nation of Islam's "The Secret Relationship between Blacks and Jews."* New York: Four Walls Eight Windows, 1994.

Branch, Taylor. *Parting the Waters: America in the King Years, 1954–1963.* New York: Simon and Schuster, 1988.

———. *Pillar of Fire: America in the King Years, 1963–65.* New York: Simon and Schuster, 1998.

Brodkin, Karen. *How Jews Became White Folks and What That Says about Race in America.* New Brunswick, N.J.: Rutgers University Press, 1998.

Brooks, Tom. "Negro Militants, Jewish Liberals, and the Unions." *Commentary* 32, no. 3 (1961): 209–16.

Brotz, Howard. *The Black Jews of Harlem: Negro Nationalism and the Dilemmas of Negro Leadership.* New York: Macmillan, Free Press of Glencoe, 1964.

Bryner, Gary C. "Affirmative Action: Minority Rights or Reverse Discrimination?" In *Moral Controversies in American Politics: Cases in*

*Social Regulatory Policy,* edited by Raymond Tatalovitch and Byron W. Daynes. Armonk, N.Y.: M. E. Sharpe, 1998.

Budick, Emily Miller. *Blacks and Jews in Literary Conversation.* Cambridge: Cambridge University Press, 1998.

Bulkin, Elly, Minnie Bruce Pratt, and Barbara Smith. *Yours in Struggle: Three Feminist Perspectives on Anti-Semitism and Racism.* Ithaca, N.Y.: Firebrand Books, 1984.

Chamberlain, Wilt, and David Shaw. *Wilt: Just Like Any Other 7-Foot Black Millionaire Who Lives Next Door.* New York: Macmillan, 1973.

Chanes, Jerome A. "Affirmative Action: Jewish Ideals, Jewish Interests." In *Struggles in the Promised Land,* edited by Jack Salzman and Cornel West. New York: Oxford University Press, 1997.

Chanes, Jerome A., ed. *Antisemitism in America Today: Outspoken Experts Explode the Myths.* Secaucus, N.J.: Carol Publishing Group, 1995.

Cohen, Kitty O. *Black-Jewish Relations: The View from the State Capitols, a Survey Based on Interviews with Black State Senators.* New York: Cornwall Books, 1988.

*commonQuest: The Magazine of Black/Jewish Relations.* Edited by Russell Adams and Jonathan Rieder. Washington, D.C.: American Jewish Committee and Howard University, 1996–present.

Cronon, E. David. *Black Moses: The Story of Marcus Garvey and the Universal Negro Improvement Association.* Madison: University of Wisconsin Press, 1955.

Cruse, Harold. "My Jewish Problem and Theirs." In James Baldwin et al., *Black Anti-Semitism and Jewish Racism.* New York: Richard W. Baron, 1969.

Cuddihy, John Murray. "Jews, Blacks, and the Cold War at the Top: Malamud's "The Tenants" and the Status-Politics of Subcultures." In *The Ordeal of Civility: Freud, Marx, Levi-Strauss, and the Jewish Struggle with Modernity.* New York: Basic Books, 1974.

Curry, George, ed. *The Affirmative Action Debate.* Reading, Mass.: Addison-Wesley, 1996.

Daughtry, Herbert D., Sr. *No Monopoly on Suffering: Blacks and Jews in Crown Heights (and Elsewhere).* Trenton, N.J.: Africa World Press, 1997.

Davis, David Brion. "A Big Business." *New York Review of Books,* June 11, 1998, 50–53.

———. "The Slave Trade and the Jews." *New York Review of Books,* December 22, 1994.

Davis, Lenwood G. *Black-Jewish Relations in the United States, 1752–1984: A Selected Bibliography.* Westport, Conn. Greenwood Press, 1984.

Dawidowicz, Lucy S. *On Equal Terms: Jews in America, 1881–1981.* New York: Holt, Rinehart and Winston, 1982.

Diner, Hasia R. "Black-Jewish Relations." In *Jewish-American History and Culture: An Encyclopedia,* edited by Jack Fischel and Sanford Pinsker. New York: Garland Publishing, 1992.

———. "Our Exploited Negro Brothers: Jewish Labor and the Organization of Black Workers." *In the Almost Promised Land: American Jews and Blacks, 1915–1935.* Westport, Conn.: Greenwood Press, 1977.

———. *A Time for Gathering: The Second Migration, 1820–1880.* Vol. 2 of *Jewish People in America.* Baltimore, Md.: Johns Hopkins University Press, 1992.

———. *In the Almost Promised Land: American Jews and Blacks, 1915–1935.* Westport, Conn.: Greenwood Press, 1977.

Dinnerstein, Leonard. *Anti-Semitism in America.* New York: Oxford University Press, 1994.

Dinnerstein, Leonard, and Mary Dale Palsson. *Jews in the South.* Baton Rouge: Louisiana State University Press, 1977.

Drake, J. G. St. Clair. "African Diaspora and Jewish Diaspora." In *Jews in Black Perspectives: A Dialogue,* edited by J. R. Washington Jr. Rutherford, N.J.: Fairleigh Dickinson University Press, 1984.

Drescher, Seymour. "Jews and New Christians in the Atlantic Slave Trade." In *The Jews and the Expansion of Europe to the West, 1450–1825,* edited by P. Bernadini. 2 vols. Providence, R.I.: Berghahn Books. Forthcoming.

Early, Jack. "Who Is the Jew? A Question of African-American Identity." *CommonQuest* 1, no. 1 (1996): 41–45.

Edgcomb, Gabrielle Simon. *From Swastika to Jim Crow: Refugee Scholars at Black Colleges.* Malabar, Fl.: Krieger Publishing, 1993.

Faber, Eli. *Jews, Slaves, and the Slave Trade: Setting*

the Record Straight. New York: New York University Press, 1998.

——. A Time for Planting: The First Migration, 1654–1820. Vol. 1 of Jewish People in America. Baltimore, Md.: Johns Hopkins University Press, 1992.

Fantini, Mario, Marilyn Gittell, and Richard Magat. Community Control and the Urban School. New York: Praeger, 1970.

Fauset, Arthur Huff. Black Gods of the Metropolis: Negro Religious Cults of the Urban North. Philadelphia: University of Pennsylvania Press, 1944.

Feingold, Henry L. A Time for Searching: Entering the Mainstream, 1920–1945. Vol. 4 of Jewish People in America. Baltimore, Md.: Johns Hopkins University Press, 1992.

Finkelstein, Norman H. Heeding the Call: Jewish Voices in America's Civil Rights Struggle. Philadelphia: Jewish Publication Society, 1997.

Forman, Seth. Blacks in the Jewish Mind: A Crisis of Liberalism. New York: New York University Press, 1998.

Franklin, John Hope, and Alfred A. Moss Jr. From Slavery to Freedom: A History of African Americans. 7th ed. New York: Alfred A. Knopf, 1994.

Franklin, V. P., Nancy L. Grant, Harold M. Kletnich, and Genna Rae MacNeil, eds. African Americans and Jews in the Twentieth Century: Essays in Convergence and Conflict. Columbia: University of Missouri Press, 1998.

Friedman, Murray. "Civil Rights." In Jewish-American History and Culture: An Encyclopedia, edited by Jack Fischel and Sanford Pinsker. New York: Garland Publishing, 1992.

——. What Went Wrong? The Creation and Collapse of the Black-Jewish Alliance. New York: Free Press, 1995.

Friedman, Saul S. Jews and the American Slave Trade. New Brunswick, N.J.: Transaction Publishers, 1998.

Gabler, Neal. An Empire of Their Own: How the Jews Invented Hollywood. New York: Crown Publishers, 1988.

Gans, Herbert J. The Levittowners: Ways of Life and Politics in a New Suburban Community. New York: Pantheon Books, 1967.

Gerber, David, ed., Anti-Semitism in American

History. Urbana: University of Illinois Press, 1986.

Gerber, Israel J. The Heritage Seekers: American Blacks in Search of Jewish Identity. Middle Village, N.Y.: Jonathan David Publishers, 1977.

Glazer, Nathan. "Jews and Blacks: What Happened to the Grand Alliance?" In Jews in Black Perspectives: A Dialogue, edited by J. R. Washington Jr. Rutherford, N.J.: Fairleigh Dickinson University Press, 1984.

Glazer, Nathan, and Daniel P. Moynihan. Beyond the Melting Pot. 1963. Reprint, Cambridge: MIT Press, 1970.

Golub, Jennifer. What Do We Know about Black Anti-Semitism? New York: American Jewish Committee, 1990.

Greenberg, Cheryl. "The Southern Jewish Community and the Struggle for Civil Rights." In V. P. Franklin et al., African Americans and Jews in the Twentieth Century: Essays in Convergence and Conflict. Columbia: University of Missouri Press, 1998.

Greenberg, Jack. "Prologue: The Moses of the Journey." In Crusaders in the Courts: How a Dedicated Band of Lawyers Fought for the Civil Rights Revolution, edited by Jack Greenberg. New York: Basic Books, 1994.

Greene, Melissa Fay. The Temple Bombing. Reading, Mass.: Addison-Wesley, 1996.

Halpern, Rick. Down on the Killing Floor: Black and White Workers in Chicago's Packinghouses, 1904–1954. Urbana: University of Illinois Press, 1997.

Hellwig, David J. "The Afro-American and the Immigrant, 1880–1930: A Study in Black Social Thought." Ph.D. diss., Syracuse University, Syracuse, N.Y., 1973.

Henry, Charles P. Ralph Bunche: Model Negro or American Other? New York: New York University Press, 1999.

Hentoff, Nat. Boston Boy: A Memoir. New York: Alfred A. Knopf, 1986.

Hill, Herbert. Black Labor and the American Legal System. Madison: University of Wisconsin Press, 1985.

Hill, Herbert, and James E. Jones Jr., eds. Race in America: The Struggle for Equality. Madison: University of Wisconsin Press, 1993.

Hill, Robert A. "Black Zionism: Marcus Garvey and the Jewish Question." In V. P. Franklin et al., *African Americans and Jews in the Twentieth Century: Essays in Convergence and Conflict.* Columbia: University of Missouri Press, 1998.

Horowitz, Roger. *"Negro and White, Unite and Fight": A Social History of Industrial Unionism in Meatpacking, 1930–90.* Urbana: University of Illinois Press, 1997.

Jackson, Jesse. "On Black-Jewish Relations." *Jewish Currents* 42, no. 2 (1988): 4–8, 37.

Jacobson, Julius, ed. *The Negro and the American Labor Movement.* Garden City, N.Y.: Doubleday, Anchor Books, 1968.

Katz, Shlomo, ed. *Negro and Jew: An Encounter in America: A Symposium Compiled by Midstream Magazine.* New York: Macmillan Co., 1967.

Kaufman, Jonathan. *Broken Alliance: The Turbulent Times between Blacks and Jews in America.* Updated edition. New York: Simon and Schuster, 1995.

Kaye/Kantrowitz, Melanie. "Class, Feminism, and 'The Black-Jewish Question.'" In *The Issue Is Power.* San Francisco: Aunt Lute Books, 1992.

Khanga, Yelena, with Susan Jacoby. *Soul to Soul: The Story of a Black Russian American Family, 1865–1992.* New York: W. W. Norton, 1992.

King, Martin Luther, Jr. "Negroes, Jews, Israel and Anti-Semitism as Seen by a Leader of the Negro Freedom Movement." *Jewish Currents* 22, no. 1 (1968): 7–9.

Korn, Bertram Wallace. *American Jewry and the Civil War.* New York: Atheneum, 1970.

——. *Jews and Negro Slavery in the Old South, 1789–1865.* Philadelphia: Reform Congregation Keneseth Israel, 1961.

Kushnick, Louis. "Race, Class, and Power: The New York Decentralisation Controversy." In *Race, Class and Struggle: Essays on Racism and Inequality in Britain, the U.S. and Western Europe.* London: Rivers Oram Press, 1998.

Landsberg, Lynne, and David Saperstein, eds. *Common Road to Justice: A Programming Manual for Blacks and Jews.* Washington, D.C.: Religious Action Center for Reform Judaism, 1991.

Laurentz, Robert. "Racial/Ethnic Conflict in the New York City Garment Industry, 1933–1980. Ph.D. diss., State University of New York, Binghamton, 1980.

Lerner, Michael, and Cornel West. *Jews and Blacks: A Dialogue on Race, Religion, and Culture in America.* New York: G. P. Putnam's Sons, 1995.

Levine, Peter. *Ellis Island to Ebbets Field: Sport and the American Jewish Experience.* New York: Oxford University Press, 1992.

Lieberson, Stanley. *A Piece of the Pie: Blacks and White Immigrants since 1880.* Berkeley: University of California Press, 1980.

Locke, Hubert G. *The Black Anti-Semitism Controversy: Protestant Views and Perspectives.* Selinsgrove, Pa.: Susquehanna University Press, 1994.

Maclean, Nancy. "The Leo Frank Case Reconsidered: Gender and Sexual Politics in the Making of Reactionary Populism. *Journal of American History* 78, no. 3 (1991): 917–48.

Malcioln, Jose V. *The African Origin of Modern Judaism: From Hebrews to Jews.* Trenton, N.J.: Africa World Press, 1996.

Martin, Tony. *The Jewish Onslaught: Despatches from the Wellesley Battlefront.* Dover, Mass.: Majority Press, 1993.

McDowell, Winston C. "Keeping Them 'In the Same Boat Together'? Sufi Abdul Hamid, African Americans, Jews, and the Harlem Jobs Boycotts." In V. P. Franklin et al., *African Americans and Jews in the Twentieth Century: Essays in Convergence and Conflict.* Columbia: University of Missouri Press, 1998.

Meier, August, and Elliott Rudwick. *From Plantation to Ghetto.* New York: Hill and Wang, 1976.

Mills, Nicolaus, ed. *Debating Affirmative Action: Race, Gender, Ethnicity, and the Politics of Inclusion.* New York: Delta, 1994.

Morris, Milton D., and Gary E. Rubin. "The Turbulent Friendship: Black-Jewish Relations in the 1990's." *Annals of the American Academy of Political and Social Science* 530 (1993): 42–60.

NAACP Papers. Manuscript Division. Library of Congress.

Nation of Islam Historical Research Department. *The Secret Relationship between Blacks and Jews.* Volume 1. Chicago: Latimer Associates, 1991.

Nelson, Jack. *Terror in the Night: The Klan's Campaign against the Jews.* New York: Simon and Schuster, 1993.

Novick, Peter. *The Holocaust in American Life.* Boston: Houghton Mifflin Co., 1999.

Orlans, Harold, and June O'Neill, eds. *Affirmative*

*Action Revisited.* Thousand Oaks, Calif.: Sage, 1992.

Painter, Nell Irvin. *Exodusters: Black Migration to Kansas after Reconstruction.* New York: Alfred A. Knopf, 1977.

Peck, Abraham J., ed. *Blacks and Jews: The American Experience, 1654–1987.* Cincinnati, Ohio: American Jewish Archives, 1987.

Phillips, William M., Jr. "The Nadir of Injustice and Inequality: 1890–1919." In *An Unillustrious Alliance: The African American and Jewish American Communities.* Westport, Conn.: Greenwood Press, 1991.

Pinkney, Alphonso. "Recent Unrest between Blacks and Jews: The Claims of Anti-Semitism and Reverse Discrimination." *Black Sociologist* 8, nos. 1–4 (1978–79): 38–57.

Podair, Jerald E. " 'White' Values, 'Black' Values: The Ocean Hill–Brownsville Controversy and New York City Culture, 1965–1975." *Radical History Review* 59 (1994): 36–59.

Podhoretz, Norman. "My Negro Problem— and Ours." *Commentary* 35, no. 2 (1963): 93–101.

Pogrebin, Letty Cottin. "Ain't We Both Women." In *Deborah, Golda, and Me: Being Female and Jewish in America.* New York: Crown Publishers, 1991.

Pogrebin, Letty Cottin, and Earl Ofari Hutchinson. "A Dialogue on Black-Jewish Relations." In *Race and Ethnic Conflict,* edited by F. L. Pincus and H. J. Ehrlich. Boulder: Westview, 1994.

Quarles, Benjamin. *The Negro in the Making of America.* 3rd ed. New York: Simon and Schuster, 1996.

Raphael, Marc Lee. "Jewish Responses to the Integration of a Suburb: Cleveland Heights, Ohio, 1960–1980." *American Jewish Archives* 44, no. 2 (1992): 541–63.

Rieder, Jonathan. *Canarsie: The Jews and Italians of Brooklyn against Liberalism.* Cambridge: Harvard University Press, 1985.

——. "Reflections on Crown Heights: Interpretive Dilemmas and Black-Jewish Conflict." In *Antisemitism in America Today: Outspoken Experts Explode the Myths,* edited by J. A. Chanes. Secaucus, N.J.: Carol Publishing Group, 1995.

Rockaway, Robert A. *"The Jews Cannot Defeat Me": The Anti-Jewish Campaign of Louis Farrakhan and the Nation of Islam.* Tel Aviv: Tel Aviv University Faculty of Humanities, 1995.

Rogin, Michael. *Blackface, White Noise: Jewish Immigrants in the Hollywood Melting Pot.* Berkeley: University of California Press, 1996.

——. "Black Sacrifice, Jewish Redemption: From Al Jolson's *Jazz Singer* to John Garfield's *Body and Soul.*" In V. P. Franklin et al., *African Americans and Jews in the Twentieth Century: Essays in Convergence and Conflict.* Columbia: University of Missouri Press, 1998.

Rubin, Gary E. "How Shall We Think about Black Antisemitism?" In *Antisemitism in America Today: Outspoken Experts Explode the Myths,* edited by J. A. Chanes. Secaucus, N.J.: Carol Publishing Group, 1995.

Russell, Bill, and Taylor Branch. *Second Wind: The Memoirs of an Opinionated Man.* New York: Random House, 1979.

Sachar, Howard M. *A History of the Jews in America.* New York: Vintage Books, 1993.

Salzman, Jack, ed. *Bridges and Boundaries: African Americans and American Jews.* New York: George Braziller in association with the Jewish Museum, 1992.

Salzman, Jack, and Cornel West, eds. *Struggles in the Promised Land: Toward a History of Black-Jewish Relations in the United States.* New York: Oxford University Press, 1997.

Schappes, Morris U. "Black Power and the Jews." *Jewish Currents* 21, no. 1 (1967): 14–16.

——. "For Material on Black-Jewish Relations." *Jewish Currents* 39, no. 2 (1985): 20–21.

——. "James Baldwin and Anti-Semitism: Commentary on Baldwin and Rabbi Gordis Confrontation in [the New York] *Times Magazine.*" *Jewish Currents* 21, no. 6 (1967): 3–6.

——. "Our Panel at the Socialist Conference, April 19." *Jewish Currents* 40, no. 6 (1986):23.

——, ed. *A Documentary History of the Jews in the United States, 1654–1875.* 2nd ed. New York: Citadel Press, 1971.

Shankman, Arnold. *Ambivalent Friends: Afro-Americans View the Immigrant.* Westport, Conn.: Greenwood Press, 1982.

——. "Brothers across the Sea: Afro-Americans on the Persecution of Russian Jews, 1881–1917." *Jewish Social Studies* 37, no. 2 (1975): 114–21.

Shapiro, Edward S. *A Time for Healing: American Jewry since World War II.* Vol. 5 of *Jewish*

*People in America*. Baltimore, Md.: Johns Hopkins University Press, 1992.

Shaw, Theodore M. "Affirmative Action: African-American and Jewish Perspectives." In *Struggles in the Promised Land,* edited by Jack Salzman and Cornel West. New York: Oxford University Press, 1997.

Sheppard, Harold L. "The Negro Merchant: A Study of Negro Anti-Semitism." *American Journal of Sociology* 53, no. 2 (1947): 96–99.

Shneyer, William. "Black-Jewish Relations: Yesterday and Tomorrow." *Jewish Currents* 43, no. 7 (1989): 4–6, 38.

Sleeper, Jim. *The Closest of Strangers: Liberalism and the Politics of Race in New York.* New York: W. W. Norton, 1990.

Sorin, Gerald. *A Time for Building: The Third Migration, 1880–1920.* Vol. 3 of *Jewish People in America.* Baltimore, Md.: Johns Hopkins University Press, 1992.

Steinberg, Stephen. *The Ethnic Myth: Race, Ethnicity and Class in America.* Boston: Beacon Press, 1981.

Stevenson, Marshall. "African Americans and Jews in Organized Labor: A Case Study of Detroit, 1920–1950." In V. P. Franklin et al., *African Americans and Jews in the Twentieth Century: Essays in Convergence and Conflict.* Columbia: University of Missouri Press, 1998.

Svonkin, Stuart. *Jews against Prejudice: American Jews and the Fight for Civil Liberties.* New York: Columbia University Press, 1997.

Toll, William. "Pluralism and Moral Force in the Black-Jewish Dialogue." *American Jewish History* 77, no. 1 (1987): 87–105.

Traub, James. *City on a Hill: Testing the American Dream at City College.* Reading, Mass.: Addison-Wesley, 1994.

Trotter, Joe W., Jr. "African Americans, Jews, and the City: Perspectives from the Industrial Era, 1900–1950." In V. P. Franklin et al., *African Americans and Jews in the Twentieth Century: Essays in Convergence and Conflict.* Columbia: University of Missouri Press, 1998.

Tsukashima, Ronald T. *The Social and Psychological Correlates of Black Anti-Semitism.* San Francisco: R & E Research Associates, 1978.

Urofsky, Melvin I., ed. *Why Teachers Strike: Teachers' Rights and Community Control.*

Garden City, N.Y.: Doubleday, Anchor Books, 1970.

Urquhart, Brian. *Ralph Bunche: An American Life.* New York: W. W. Norton, 1993.

U.S. Housing and Home Finance Agency. *Equal Opportunity in Housing: A Series of Case Studies.* Washington, D.C.: Government Printing Office, 1964.

Vorspan, Albert. "Black-Jewish Coalition: Troubled, but Still Alive." *Jewish Currents* 43, no. 8 (1989): 7–9, 32.

——. "The Negro Victory and the Jewish Failure." *American Judaism* 13, no. 1 (1963):7, 50–54.

Washington, Joseph R., Jr., ed. *Jews in Black Perspective: A Dialogue.* Cranbury, N.J.: Associated University Presses, 1984.

Wedlock, Lunabelle. *The Reaction of Negro Publications and Organizations to German Anti-Semitism,* edited by Ralph Bunche. Howard University Studies in the Social Sciences, vol. 3, no. 2. Washington, D.C.: Graduate School of Howard University, 1942.

Weisbord, Robert G. "Israel and the Black Hebrew Israelites." *Judaism* 24, no. 1 (1975): 23–38.

Weisbord, Robert G., and Arthur Stein. *Bittersweet Encounter: The Afro-American and the American Jew.* Westport, Conn.: Negro Universities Press, 1970.

West, Cornel. "On Black-Jewish Relations." *Race Matters.* New York: Random House, 1994.

Wetzler, Laura, and Janiece Thompson. *Jewels of the Diaspora: A Celebration of African-American and Jewish Song.* Cummington, Mass.: Nervy Girl Music (concert), 1998.

Windsor, Rudolph R. *From Babylon to Timbuktu: A History of the Ancient Black Races including the Black Hebrews.* New York: Exposition Press, 1969.

Wolf, David. "Tomming for Abe." *Foul! The Connie Hawkins Story.* New York: Holt, Rinehart, Winston, 1972.

Zack, Naomi. "On Being and Not-Being Black and Jewish. In *The Multiracial Experience: Racial Borders as the New Frontier,* edited by Maria P. P. Root. Thousand Oaks, Calif.: Sage Publications, 1996.

Zierold, Norman. *The Moguls: Hollywood's Merchants of Myth.* New York: Coward-McCann, 1969.

# INDEX

Beni Israel of India, 86

Ben-Isreal, Asiel, 93, 95

Benjamin, I. J., 175, 624

Benjamin, Judah P., 142–143, 148, 169, 176, 199, 526

Benjamin, Maurice, 468

Bennett, Lerone, Jr., 797

Berkson, Isaac B., 338

Berlin, Irving, 329

Berman, Marshall, 514

Berman, Pandro S., 467

Berman, Paul, 806

Berman, Rabbi (Miami), 483, 486

Berns, Walter, 788

Berson, Lenora E., 396

Berwyn, Pennsylvania, 431

Bethesda Baptist Church (Chicago), 745

Bettleheim, Bruno, 716

Bible: Deuteronomy, 58, 59; New Testament, 253; Old Testament, 51, 55, 74, 252–253; and slavery, 190–191, 200–202, 207. *See also* Christianity; Judaism; Moses (biblical figure)

Biddle, Francis, 431

Bierfield, S. A., 46, 219–221

Bikel, Theodore, 576, 584

Billikopf, Jacob, 290, 339, 340

Binswanger, Samuel, 528, 533–534

Biracial Business Association (Chicago), 411

*Birth of a Nation, The* (film), 334, 458, 460

*Birth of a Race, The* (film), 458, 460

*Bittersweet Encounter: The Afro-American and the American Jew* (Weisbord and Stein), 237

Black, Irwin, 782

*Black American, The,* 776

Black Americans in Support of Israel Committee (BASIC), 730

*Black and Tan Fantasy* (film), 463

*Black Boy* (Wright), 300

*Black Dispatch,* 434

blackface, 329–330, 462

Black Hebrews. *See* Jews: black

*Black History* (Drimmer), 781

*Black Intellectual,* 796, 797

black-Jewish relations. *See* relations, black-Jewish

black Jews. *See* Jews: black

*Black Man,* 418

*Black Metropolis* (Drake and Cayton), 412

black nationalism. *See* nationalism: black

Black Panthers, 647

Black Power, 579, 643, 686, 713

blacks and Jews. *See* relations, black-Jewish

*Blacks and Jews at Wellesley News* (Martin), 132

Blackwell, Charles, 94

*Black World,* 790, 808

black Zionism, 91, 339, 343

"blaxploitation movies," 467, 468

Bledsoe, Julius, 344

Bloch, Herman D., 605

Block, Charles J., 535

*Blood of Jesus, The* (film), 465

Blue Heron Press, 283

Blumstein, William, 412

B'nai B'rith, 212, 239, 240, 274, 448, 520, 536, 663, 713; and anti-racism, 520; and desegregation, 525. *See also* Anti-Defamation League of B'nai B'rith (ADL)

B'nai Sholom Temple Israel, 745

Board of Delegates of American Israelites, 159–160, 206, 212

Boas, Franz, 332

*Body and Soul* (film), 466

Bond, Horace Mann, 12, 251, 253, 340

Bond, Julian, 730

Bondi, August, 44, 186

Bontemps, Arna, 340

Booker T. Washington Trade Association, 387, 395

Booth, William, 661

Boskin, Joseph, 676

Boston, 335

*Boston Firefighers Union, Local 718 v. Boston Branch (NAACP),* 609

*Boston Guardian,* 303

Botein, Bernard, 652, 653

Bouey, Harrison, 66

Bourne, Randolph, 338

Bowen, J. W. E., 256

Bowman, Lawrence, 219

Bowser, Jessie Fortune, 296

boycotts, 367, 412, 809

Bracey, John, 610

Brackman, Harold, 132–133

Bradford, Roark, 461

Brandeis, Louis D., 271, 275, 331–332, 338

Brandenburg Africa Company of 1682, 108

Brazil, 108, 110

*Breaking Point, The* (film), 467

Breen, Joseph, 461

Bricklayers Union, 597

Briggs, Cyril B., 309, 341

Briggs, Nathaniel, 117–121

Brimmer, Andrew, 796

*Broadway Bill* (film), 461

Brodkin Sacks, Karen, 500–519

Bronx, 369, 382, 414, 514

Bronx Slave Market, 37, 369–374, 413, 445, 452

Bronzeville (Chicago), 257

Brooklyn, 335

Brooklyn College, 504

Brooklyn Independent Core, 664

Brooklyn Yeshiva, 591

*Brotherhood of Man, The* (film), 465

Brotherhood of Sleeping Car Porters, 343, 422, 476, 566, 598, 599

Israel, Edward L., 411
*Israelite, The*, 207, 219

Jackson, Henry, 702
Jackson, Jesse: and anti-Semitism, 690, 732, 736,
    808, 810–811; and Chicago politics, 756, 782,
    790; and Jews, 694–695, 729; and Operation
    PUSH, 747–748, 750; and Palestinians, 786
Jackson, Kenneth T., 498
Jackson, Maynard, 799
Jackson, Mississippi, 627
Jacob, John E., 797–798
Jacobi, Abraham, 187
Jacobs, George, 210
Jacobs, Solomon, 157
*Jammin' the Blues* (film), 466
*Jazz Singer, The* (film), 329, 461, 462–463
Jeffries, Leonard, 24, 105, 106, 132, 804, 805
Jehovah's Witnesses, 623
Jessel, George, 329
*Jewish American*, 385
*Jewish Background and Influence in the
    Confederacy* (Marcus), 47
Jewish-black relations. *See* relations, black-Jewish
Jewish Chautauqua Society, 545
Jewish Commission on Law and Public Affairs,
    609
Jewish Community Center (Detroit), 389, 392, 730
Jewish Community Council (Detroit), 395
Jewish Community Council (Norfolk, Va.), 627
*Jewish Currents*, 580
*Jewish Daily Forward*, 90, 338, 604
Jewish Defense League (JDL), 587, 690, 790
*Jewish Family Journal*, 87
Jewish Labor Committee (JLC), 477, 483, 566,
    597–600; and ILGWU, 605; and segregation,
    524
Jewish Lakeside Club (Chicago), 745
*Jewish Messenger*, 192, 205, 238, 239, 337
*Jewish Press*, 713, 714
*Jewish Record*, 208–209
*Jewish Review*, 447
Jewish Rights Council, 609
*Jewish Sentiment* (Atlanta), 251–252
*Jewish Survey, The*, 447
Jewish War Veterans, 395, 483
Jewison, Norman, 458
Jews: Ashkenazic, 51, 184; black, 51, 84–101; Black
    Hebrews, 51, 92–99, 751, 752; Falashas, 51, 85–
    87; German, 246, 249, 331, 385, 416–417, 427–
    440; Marrano, 109, 629; Russian, 223–234, 239–
    241, 247, 249, 284, 319–321, 385; as seen by
    blacks, 689; Sephardic, 51, 131, 134, 184. *See also*
    immigrants, Jewish; Judaism; relations, black-
    Jewish; *specific topics*
Jews, Southern, 34, 35, 131, 147–176; and

desegregation, 624, 625–629; and integration,
    565; and Northern Jews, 630–631; and
    segregation, 541–542; and slavery, 147–176, 183–
    194, 198–212
Jim Crow, 268, 427, 429
Joden Savanne (Jewish Savanah), Surinam, 111–112
Johnson, Charles S., 335, 340, 343, 344, 346
Johnson, George P., 460
Johnson, Herbert F., 652
Johnson, Hugh, 432
Johnson, James Weldon, 302, 332, 335, 337, 343, 345,
    463, 464; and Leo Frank, 264–265; and
    Rosenwald Fellowship, 340
Johnson, John, 790, 808–809
Johnson, Lyndon, 8
Johnson, Mordecai, 340
Johnson, Nunnally, 460
Joint Center for Political Studies, 801
Jolson, Al, 329, 463
Jones, Eugene Kinckle, 335
Jones, Israel I., 159–160
Jordan, Barbara, 783
Jordan, Vernon, 691, 703, 783
*Journal of Negro History*, 395
Judaism: and abolitionism, 200; and black Jews,
    51, 89, 163; Conservative, 554, 628, 759;
    Orthodox, 192, 385, 554, 726; Reform, 184,
    188–190, 192, 194, 287, 334, 554, 629, 630, 743,
    746
Juliano, John A., 498

Kahn, Herman, 709
Kahn, Tom, 577
Kakeles, Seligman, 199
Kallen, Horace M., 338, 570
*Kansas Post*, 199
Kaplan, Kivie, 4, 572, 799
Karabel, Jerome, 504
Karenga, Ron, 578
Karp, Walter, 648
Kaufman, David S., 169
Kaufman, Sigismund, 186
Kaye/Kantrowitz, Melanie, 769, 772
Kehillath Anshe Maariv (KAM)(Chicago), 743,
    744, 745, 759
Keith, Harold, 566, 598–599
Keller, John, 509
Kelly, Barbara M., 497
Kemble, Eugenia, 651
Kemp, Ira, 413
Kempton, Murray, 467, 656
Kendrick, W. Freeland, 431
Keneseth Israel Congregation (Philadelphia), 204
Kennedy, John F., 556
Kennedy, Louise Venable, 342
Kerlin, Robert T., 344

Lubin, Sam, 459
Lutheran House (Detroit), 392
Lynbrook, New York, 581
Lynch, Steve, 460
Lynch, W. D., 72, 73
lynching, 219–222, 252, 261, 264, 265, 337;
    compared to pogroms, 239

McCabe, E. P., 79
McCarran-Walter Immigration Bill, 522
McCarthyism, 283. *See also* House Un-American
    Activities Committee
McClendon, James J., 389
McCoy, Rhody, 645, 651
Macdonald, Dwight, 608
Mack, Julian W., 290, 339
McKay, Claude, 340, 412
McKenzie, Roderick, 390
McMillan, George, 624
Maddow, Ben, 467
Madhubuti, Haki R., 808, 809
Madison Parish, Louisiana, 67, 70
Magnes, Judah L., 338
Magold, Nathan, 342
Malcolm X, 714, 757, 828
Malev, William, 628
Maltz, Albert, 466
*Man Farthest Down, The* (Washington), 292
Mankiewicz, Joseph, 467
Mantinband, Charles, 530, 542, 544, 552, 628
manumission of slaves, 138, 141, 153–154. *See also*
    emancipation of slaves
Manumission Society of New York City, 199
*Marching Blacks* (Powell, Jr.), 421
*Marching On* (film), 465
Marcus, Jacob Rader, 47, 150
Marietta, Georgia, 280
Marrano Jews, 109, 629
Marsh, Donald C., 384–400
Marshall, Edward, 263
Marshall, Frederick, 72
Marshall, Louis, 333, 339, 342, 343; and Leo
    Frank case, 262, 266, 267, 271, 273, 274, 277–
    279
Martin, John B., 540
Martin, Tony, 132, 805
Marvin, Floyd H., 520
Marx, David, 252, 273
Marx, Simon, 288
Marxism, 338, 747
Maryland, 203–204, 241
Maslow, Will, 485, 487
Masonic lodges, 90
Matthew, Wentworth Arthur, 87–91
Matthews, Ralph, 433
May, Irving, 528, 534

Mayer, Martin, 665
Meany, George, 597, 599
Mechanicsville (Atlanta), 249
media. *See* movies; press, black; press, Jewish
Meely, Fred, 582
Meier, August, 610
*Melting Pot, The* (Zangwill), 334
*Memphis Daily Appeal*, 201
Memphis Lodge of B'nai B'rith, 212
merchants. *See* economic relations, black-Jewish
meritocracy, 735
*Messenger*, 206, 305
Metropolitan Life Insurance Company, 412
Miami, Florida, 483–486, 524
Michaux, Solomon Lightfoot, 466
Micheaux, Oscar, 459
Michelbacher, J. M., 210–211
middle class. *See* class, socioeconomic
Middle East, 777
Middleton, Reverend (Vicksburg, Miss.), 70
Mielziner, Moses, 201
migration, black, 3, 28, 30, 36, 217; to Chicago,
    744–745; to Kansas, 66–83; of Southern blacks,
    335–336, 355–356, 385, 409
Miller, Alan W., 733, 737, 738
Miller, Alexander F., 486, 530
Miller, Dotty, 575
Miller, Kelly, 256, 335, 345, 416, 433, 434, 435, 439
Million Man March, 817
Milwaukee, Wisconsin, 597
Milwaukee Jewish Council, 702
Minor, Ethel, 582, 583
miscegenation, 162–168. *See also* intermarriage
Mississippi, 165, 239; and Kansas Fever Exodus, 67,
    68, 72, 75, 76, 77
*Mississippi, the Closed Society* (Silver), 543
Mississippi Summer Project of 1964, 22, 576, 577,
    611
Missouri state convention, 44, 187
Mitchell, Clarence, 4
Mizpe Ramon, Israel, 95
Mobile, Alabama, 149, 159–160, 289, 378–379
*Mobile Daily Advertiser and Chronicle*, 156
*Mobile Tribune*, 276
Mock, David, 498
Monrovia, Liberia, 93–94
Montgomery, Alabama, 630
Moon, Henry Lee, 467, 730
Moore, Henry, 484
*Moore v. Dempsey*, 343
Morais, Sabato, 188, 446
Mordecai, Alfred, 172
Mordecai, George W., 171
Mordecai, Samuel, 170
Moritz, Charles F., 290
Morris, Aaron, 250

Morris, Samuel, 223
Morsell, John, 703
Morton, Henry, 219
Moses, Alfred G., 289
Moses, Bob, 577
Moses, J. F., 199
Moses, J. Garfield, 289
Moses, Franklin, Jr., 165
Moses, Raphael J., 148, 176
Moses, Robert, 514
Moses, Samuel, 137–138
Moses (biblical figure), 53–56, 58, 61, 207, 208,
    292, 300; Charles H. Houston as, 52; Harriet
    Tubman as, 64; Booker T. Washington as,
    293. *See also* Garvey, Marcus; Washington,
    Booker T.
Moskowitz, Henry, 333
Motion Picture Association of America, 460–461
Mound Bayou, Mississippi, 291
Mount Hebron Baptist Church (Vicksburg,
    Miss.), 70
Mount Pisgah Missionary Baptist Church
    (Chicago), 745
Mount Sinai Hospital (Chicago), 761
movies, 30–31, 457–469, 716
Muhammad, Abdul Wali, 758
Muhammad, Elijah, 757
Muhammad, Khalid Abdul, 1, 24, 25, 132, 804–805,
    809
mulattos, 163–168. *See also* intermarriage
Muravchik, Emanuel, 524, 600
Murray, Daniel, 256
Murrell, William, 70
Muse, Clarence, 461, 464
music, 316–328
Muslims, black, 714. *See also* Nation of Islam
Myrdal, Gunnar, 334

NAACP. *See* National Association for the
    Advancement of Colored People
NAACP Legal Defense and Educational Fund,
    Inc., 4, 576, 612
Nager, George, 498
NALC. *See* Negro American Labor Council
Nashville, Tennessee, 548–549
*Nashville Daily Press and Times*, 220
*Nashville Republican*, 220
Nassau County, New York, 496
Natchez, Mississippi, 72
National Advisory Commission on Civil
    Disorders, 396
National Association for the Advancement of
    Colored People (NAACP), 332–335, 375, 474,
    564–566, 800; and Anti-Defamation League
    (ADL), 532; and "anti-NAACP" bills, 531;
    and anti-Semitism, 600; and black-Jewish

relations, 288, 480; Chicago branch of, 407;
    and civil rights movement, 623; Detroit branch
    of, 389; and W.E.B. Du Bois, 417; and Leo
    Frank case, 264, 267; and German treatment of
    Jews, 407; and Hollywood, 460, 464, 465, 466,
    468; Jewish involvement in, 4, 32, 338–339, 343,
    484–484, 572, 612, 799; and Jewish Labor
    Committee, 600; and labor movement, 593–
    595, 596, 598–600, 602
National Community Relations Advisory Council
    (NCRAC), 564, 623, 627, 648, 663
National Conference of Christians and Jews, 529
National Convention for New Politics, 585
National Council for a Permanent Fair
    Employment Practices Committee, 611
National Council of Jewish Women (NCJW),
    476–477, 480, 483, 488, 789
National Fast Day (January 4, 1861), 190, 199, 206
nationalism, 488, 489, 637; and anti-Semitism, 310,
    419; black, 387, 418, 577–579, 713, 749, 751, 816;
    Jewish, 339. *See also* Black Power; identity
*National Jewish Monthly*, 448
National Labor Relations Board (NLRB), 468, 602
National Lawyers Guild, 576, 623
National Negro Congress, 476
National Organization of Jewish Women, 609
National Research Council, 818
National Trade Union Council, 597
National Urban League (NUL), 333, 335, 339, 476,
    703, 714, 799; and civil rights movement, 483,
    485
Nation of Islam, 1, 24, 25, 753–758, 802, 804–805,
    808–809, 817–819, 821; and anti-Semitism, 741;
    and *Secret Relationship between Blacks and
    Jews, The*, 132–136
Nazism, 380, 417–418, 479, 480, 755; and anti-
    Semitism, 415; and black organizations, 380;
    and Jim Crow laws, 429; and racism, 437, 444;
    and sympathizers, 387. *See also* Hitler, Adolf
Nebraska, 79, 279
Negro American Labor Council (NALC), 598–599
*Negro in Detroit, The*, 390
Negro Industrial Clerical Alliance, 413
"Negro-Jewish Relationships" (Marsh), 395
*Negro Politics*, 421
*Negro Quarter*, 415
*Negro Soldier*, 465, 466
Negro Trade Union Leadership, 566
*Negro Youth*, 450
Neier, Aryeh, 651
neo-conservatism, 750, 783, 788, 790
New Amsterdam, 815
Newark, New Jersey, 87
New Christians (Conversos), 109–110, 112
New Haven, 164, 559
New Jewish Agenda, 777

peddlers, 225–234, 247. *See also* economic relations, black-Jewish

Peekskill, 483

Pegler, Westbrook, 436

Pekelis, Alexander, 623

Pennsylvania State Federation of Labor, 431

Perlmutter, Nathan, 737, 758, 811

Phagan, Mary, 271, 280

Philadelphia, 204, 240, 335, 336, 410, 598; and black Jews, 87

*Philadelphia Record*, 430

*Philadelphia Tribune*, 265, 410–411; and World War II, 416, 419, 429, 430, 431, 440

philanthropy, Jewish, 5, 33, 307–308, 333, 343, 458. *See also* Rosenwald, Julius

Phillips, John A., 431

Phillips, Philip, 16

Phillips, Wendell, 142

Philpott, Thomas Lee, 337

*Phylon*, 242

Pickard, Kate E. R., 43, 173, 446

Pickens, William, 310

Pilgrim Baptist Church (Chicago), 745

*Pinky* (film), 467

Pinneger, William, 117

Pinner, Moritz, 199, 446

Pipefitters Union, 598

*Pittsburgh Courier*, 432, 463, 465, 566, 598–599

*Pittsburgh Jewish Criterion*, 267

Platner, Hanoch, 96

Podhoretz, Norman, 609, 788, 790, 792

Pogrebin, Letty Cottin, 771, 806, 810

pogroms, 4, 239–241, 251, 289

*Point of View, The* (Long Island, N. Y.), 495

Poitier, Sidney, 467

Poland, 107, 112

political parties. *See* Democratic Party; Republican Party

politics, 7–8, 688–701; Jewish involvement in, 303. *See also* Democratic Party; relations, black-Jewish; Republican Party

Pollac, Sydney, 467

Pollard, Andrew, 72

Polonsky, Abraham, 466, 467

Poolinski, Joe, 250

Popular Education Committee, 395

populism, 288, 625

Pound, Ezra, 380

poverty, 71; black, 754. *See also* class, socioeconomic

Powell, Adam Clayton, 602

Powell, Adam Clayton, Jr., 421–422

Powell, Clayton, 445

prejudice, 303–304. *See also* anti-Semitism; discrimination; racism

President's Committee on Fair Employment Practices, 447

press, 267–268; and Leo Frank case, 276

press, black, 238–239, 261–270, 599; and anti-Semitism, 309, 310, 420, 450; and Hitler, 415; Jewish ads in, 246; and Jewish economic power, 302; and Jews in Germany, 427–440; and praise of Jews, 301. *See also specific titles*

press, Jewish, 4, 35, 248, 261–270. *See also* Ocean Hill-Brownsville; *specific titles*

Price, Cecil R., 683

*Pride of the Marines, The* (film), 466

Prinz, Joachin, 592

*Progressive*, 24

Prosser, Gabriel, 60

Protestants. *See* Christianity

*Protocols of the Elders of Zion, The* (Nation of Islam), 132

Providence, Rhode Island, 335

*Public, The*, 240

*Public Life, The*, 648

Pulitzer, Joseph, 290

Pye, Durwood, 781

Quakers, 117, 142

Quigley, Martin, 461

Quinley, Harold Y., 400

Quinn, William Paul, 61

Raab, Earl, 585, 673

rabbis: and the civil rights movement, 540–558, 628; and slavery, 198–212

Rabin, Yitzhak, 8, 759

Rabinowitz, Victor, 576

Raby, Al, 741

*Race: Science and Politics* (Benedict), 465

racism, 21, 23, 24, 79, 302, 337, 487, 501–503, 510; and anti-Semitism, 230, 305, 769; compared to anti-Semitism, 479–480; and assimilation, 251; and Federal Housing Administration, 513–515; and feminist movement, 774; and health, 818–819; in ILGWU, 601–605; and Jews, 23, 257, 307, 445–446, 449, 453; in Kansas, 79; and Ocean Hill-Brownsville, 655, 672. *See also* discrimination, prejudice

"Ralph Poynter" leaflet, 650

*Ramparts*, 656

Ramsey, Jane, 747

Randolph, A. Philip, 4, 343, 422, 481, 584, 598, 599, 748

Randolph Institute, A. Philip, 799

Rangel, Charles, 25

Rank and File Committee, 604

Raphaelson, Samson, 461

Raphall, Morris J., 190–191, 199–200, 206, 208

Rascoe, Burton, 263

Raspberry, William, 736
Rauh, Joseph L., Jr., 4
Rayner, Isador, 241–242, 257, 307
Reagan, Ronald, 783
Reagon, Bernice Johnson, 765
*Reconstructionist, The*, 629
Reddick, Lawrence D., 400, 415, 420, 574
Redgrave, Vanessa, 724
Red Scare of 1919, 337, 501
Redwood, Abraham, 117
Reform Judaism. *See* Judaism
Reid, Arthur L., 413
Reid, Ira De A., 340
relations, black-Jewish, 237–243; as allies, 265,
    454, 714; coalition, 476–494, 763, 766; and
    common experiences, 300–301, 415, 813;
    comparison of, 229, 237, 631; conflict, 732;
    cooperation, 43, 265, 455, 482, 611, 691–692,
    734, 782; and 1943 Detroit race riot, 394;
    education about, 823–826; historical
    differences of, 590; history of, 610, 825–826;
    Jews as role models, 238, 255, 300–301, 345; Jews
    patronizing blacks, 692, 714; treatment of Jews
    compared to blacks, 237, 239–240. *See also* civil
    rights movement; economic relations, black-
    Jewish; intermarriage; miscegenation; Ocean
    Hill-Brownsville; organizations, black and
    Jewish; politics; press; press, black; press,
    Jewish; *specific organizations*
*Reminiscences of Charleston* (Cardozo), 170
Renters Protective Association (Detroit), 387
Republican Party, 31, 44, 141, 192, 335, 801; in
    Georgia, 258; in New York, 143
Resnikoff, Bernard, 96
restrictive covenants, 495, 513. *See also* housing;
    Levittown
Reznikoff, Marvin M., 549
Rice, Florence, 603
Richards, Leonard L., 187–188
Richman, Paul, 481
Richmond, Virginia, 156, 210, 246, 528–538
*Richmond Daily Dispatch*, 200
*Richmond in By-Gone Days* (Mordecai), 171
Richmond Jewish Community Council, 534
*Richmond News Leader*, 531–535
*Richmond Times Dispatch*, 529
right-wing groups, 12, 810
riots, 396; and blacks, 332, 388–389, 709; in
    Chicago, 1919, 337; in Detroit, 1945, 384; in
    Harlem, 1935, 382; and Jews, 641, 709–710; in
    Kishineff, 239–241; and pogroms, 251; response
    to, 481–482. *See also* violence
Rivera, Jacob, 34
Roan, Leonard, 273
Roberts, DeWitt, 277
Roberts, Kenneth, 500

Robertson, Wyndham, 201
Robeson, Paul, 344, 463, 464, 465, 483
Robinson, Bill, 464
Rockfeller Foundation, 340
Rogers, Alan, 249
Rogers, J. A., 419
Rogers, Julian, 263
*Romance of a Jewess, The* (film), 459
Roosevelt, Franklin D., 432, 480, 594
Roosevelt, Theodore, 239, 502
Roper, George, 141
Rose, Arnold, 627
Rose, Ernestine L., 43, 193
Rosenbaum, Herbert D., 497
Rosenbaum, Sara, 819
Rosenberg, Aaron, 467
Rosenberg, Rabbi (Miami Beach), 524, 526
Rosenwald, Julius, 32, 306, 333, 339, 340, 457–458,
    621; black response to, 307; and Leo Frank case,
    275; and schools, 5; and Tuskegee Institute, 291
Rosenwald, William, 343
Rosenwald Fellowships, 5
Rosenwald Foundation, 291
Rosenwald Fund, 340, 465
Rose of Sharon Theological Seminary, 88
Ross, Randolph, 597, 598
Rosser, Luther, 262
*Ross v. Ebert*, 597
Roth, Murray, 463
Rothschild, Jacob M., 550–551, 556, 628
Rothschild, Salomon de, 175
Rothstein, Arnold, 505
Royal Order of Ethiopian Hebrews, 90. *See also*
    Jews, black
Russell, Charles Edward, 333
Russian Jews. *See* Jews: Russian
Rustin, Bayard, 99, 577, 584, 730, 786, 794, 797, 799

Sachs, Arthur, 338
Sadat, Anwar, 794
*Sahara* (film), 464
St. Louis, Missouri, 67, 68, 73–74; and black Jews,
    87
*St. Louis Argus*, 419
St. Louis Urban League, 337
*St. Paul Appeal*, 304, 307
Saloshin, Gustave, 246
Samet, Seymour, 525
Samuel, Maurice, 570
Sanders, Ira E., 544, 545
Saperstein, David, 811
Saperstein, Harold, 580–581, 584
Sartre, Jean-Paul, 47
*Saturday Evening Post*, 240, 455
Savage, Augusta, 340
Savannah, 171, 246

South Carolina, 35, 144, 148, 149, 165, 167
South Carolina College, 165
South Carolina Constitutional Convention of
    1868, 164
South Carolina State Council of Union Leagues,
    164
Southern Christian Leadership Conference
    (SCLC), 577, 612, 786, 799
*Southern Christian Recorder*, 301
Southern Regional Council, 544, 552, 553, 554
Southern Students Organizing Committee, 580
*South Speaks Out for Law and Order, The* (ADL),
    536
Sowell, Thomas, 798
Spain, 106, 108, 134
Spear, Allan, 237
Special Committee on Racial and Religious
    Prejudice, 652, 660
Spencer, David, 665
Spiegel, Albert A., 793
Spingarn, Arthur B., 4, 338, 342
Spingarn, Joel E., 4, 286, 290, 338
*Sport of the Gods, The* (Dunbar), 336
Springfield, Illinois, 332
*Springfield (Mass.) Republican*, 242
Squadron, Howard, 791
Stampp, Kenneth M., 466
State Department of the United States, 432
Stein, Arthur, 47, 237
Steinberg, Stephen, 24, 504
Steinbrink, Meier, 484
Steinheimer, David, 245
stereotypes, 2, 21, 723, 813; of blacks, 268, 363–364;
    of blacks and Jews, 458; of Jews, 45, 232, 253,
    301, 305–306, 309, 398, 670. *See also* anti-
    Semitism; racism
Stern, Sol, 656
Sternstein, Joseph P., 790–791
Steward, Maria, 60
Stewart, Delano, 495
Stewart, James Brewer, 187–188
Stewart, T. McCants, 302
Stiles, Ezra, 59
Still, Peter, 173, 446
Stone, I. F., 580, 656
store owners. *See* economic relations, black-
    Jewish
Storey, Moorfield, 332, 343
*Story of the Jew, The* (Levinger), 85
Stowe, Harriett Beecher, 161
Straus, Lazarus, 172
Straus, Nathan, 275
Straus, Oscar S., 273
Strauss, Isaac L., 241–242
Streicher, Julius, 436
Strother, Leroy, 375

Strunsky, Anna, 332
Student Nonviolent Coordinating Committee
    (SNCC), 578, 611, 612, 730, 748, 800; and anti-
    Israel position, 583; and anti-Semitism, 584,
    585; and black separatism, 581–582; Jewish
    support of, 575–576, 580; and Palestinians, 582
Studin, Charles, 342
Sudanese Jews, 86
sugar trade, 134
Sulzberger, Cyrus, 273
Summer Hill (Atlanta), 249
Supreme Court of Georgia, 262, 274, 278
Supreme Court of the United States, 29, 278, 483,
    503, 507, 513, 567, 609, 693; and desegregation,
    524
Supreme Court of Wisconsin, 598
Surinam, 111–112
Susskind, David, 467
Sutherland, Elizabeth, 576
Sweeney, W. Allison, 266
*Symphony in Black* (film), 463
Synagogue Council of America, 737, 782
synagogues: black, 84–85; bombing of, 551;
    violence agianst, 530

Taft, William Howard, 279
"Talented Tenth," 335–336, 338, 339, 341; and
    assimilation, 331; and relations with Jews, 343
*Talk of the Town* (film), 465
Talmadge, Herman, 520, 572
Tannenbaum, Marc, 648, 793
Tanner, B. T., 66
Tapper, A. Ovrum, 480
teachers, 19, 296–299, 676–677. *See also* education;
    Ocean Hill-Brownsville; schools
*Teamwork* (film), 466
television: and Ocean Hill-Brownsville, 656
Temple Emanu-El (New York City), 202
Temple KAM/Isaiah Israel (Chicago), 759
Temple Sinai (Chicago), 745
Temple Street Congregational Church (New
    Haven), 164
Terman, Lewis, 502
Terrell, Mary Church, 485
Texas, 67, 70, 77
Thalhimer, William, 528
Thind, Bhagat Singh, 503
Thirteenth Amendment, 206
Thomas, Franklin, 796
Thomas, M. Carey, 503
Thurman, Wallace, 345, 463
*Till the End of Time* (film), 465
*Time*, 645, 647
Toddy, Ted, 465
Toff, William, 623
*To Have and Have Not* (Hemingway), 467